GEOSYSTEMS

Combination of satellite *Terra* MODIS sensor image and *GOES* satellite image produces a true-colour view of North and South America from 35,000 km (22,000 mi) in space. [Courtesy of MODIS Science Team, Goddard Space Flight Center, NASA and NOAA.]

Along Hudson Bay, Manitoba, Canada, in November, these two males are play fighting, a form of exercise, with plenty of mock attacks. Dramatically, both bears stand on their hind legs and throw jabs at their sparring partner, then into a clinch and back on the ground, each taking his turn as the lead aggressor. You can see movie clips made by Robert Christopherson on the *Student Animation CD* featuring polar bears. Climate change is reducing sea-ice extent, this reduces food availability for the bears. Forecasts predict an ice-free Arctic Ocean in as little as a decade; devastating for the polar bears since they depend on the ice. [Photo by Bobbé Christopherson.]

SECOND CANADIAN EDITION

GEOSYSTEMS

An Introduction to Physical Geography

Robert Christopherson

American River College, Emeritus

Mary-Louise Byrne

Wilfrid Laurier University

PEARSON

Prentice
Hall

Toronto

Library and Archives Canada Cataloguing in Publication

Christopherson, Robert W.
 Geosystems: an introduction to physical geography/Robert W. Christopherson,
 Mary-Louise Byrne.—2nd Canadian ed.

Includes index.
ISBN 978-0-13-515456-4

1. Physical geography—Textbooks. I. Byrne, Mary-Louise, 1961– II. Title.

GB54.5.C47 2009   910'.02   C2008-901042-6

ISBN-13: 978-0-13-515456-4
ISBN-10:   0-13-515456-1

Vice President, Editorial Director, Canada: *Gary Bennett*
Development Editor: *Ginger Birkeland*
In-House Production Liaison: *Shari Toron*
Production Editors: *Cindy Miller, Suganya Karuppasamy*
Assistant Managing Editor, Science: *Gina M. Cheselka*
Production Assistant to the Author: *Bobbé Christopherson*
Director of Marketing: *Marlene Olsavsky*
Supplements Developmental Editor: *Madhu Ranadive*
Director of Operations: *Barbara Kittle*
Senior Operations Supervisor: *Alan Fischer*
Art Director: *Suzanne Behnke*
Interior Design: *Tamara Newnam*
Cover Designer: *Bobbé Christopherson, Tamara Newnam*
Media Project Manager: *Rich Barnes*
AV Production Liaison: *Connie Long*
Art Studio: *Precision Graphics*
Senior Project Manager, Precision: *JC Morgan*
Lead Artist: *Ron Kempke*

Proofreader: *Jeff Georgeson*
Image Permission Coordinator: *Elaine Soares*
Image Coordinator: *Debbie Latronica*
Composition: *GGS Book Services*
Cover Photo Credits: *Winter scene on the edge of the boreal forest west of Hudson Bay; Rainbow rises from the Bow River Valley with Mount Rundle; The Canadian Falls on the Niagara River; Temperate rain forest in Macmillan Provincial Park, central Vancouver Island—Parts I, III, and IV by Bobbé Christopherson; Part II by Robert Christopherson. Background astronaut photo from International Space Station courtesy of NASA, JSC.*

Dedication Page Quote: *Barbara Kingsolver, Small Wonder (New York: Harper Collins Publishers, 2002), p. 39*

Printed and bound in the United States of America.
2 3 4 5 12 11 10 09 08

Environmental Statement

This book is carefully crafted to minimize environmental impact. Pearson Prentice Hall is proud to report that the materials used to manufacture this book originated from sources committed to sustainable forestry practices, tree harvesting, and associated land management. The binding, cover, and paper come from facilities that minimize waste, energy usage, and the use of harmful chemicals.

Equally important, Pearson Prentice Hall closes the loop by recycling every out-of-date text returned to our warehouse. We pulp the books, and the pulp is used to produce other items such as paper coffee cups or shopping bags.

The future holds great promise for reducing our impact on Earth's environment, and Pearson Prentice Hall is proud to be leading the way in this initiative. From production of the book to putting a copy in your hands, we strive to publish the best books with the most up-to-date and accurate content, and to do so in ways that minimize our impact on Earth.

Contents

Preface xi

1 Essentials of Geography 1

The Science of Geography 2
  Geographic Analysis 3
  The Geographic Continuum 3
Earth Systems Concepts 5
  Systems Theory 5
  Earth's Four "Spheres" 13
  A Spherical Planet 15
  Measuring Earth in 247 B.C. 16
Location and Time on Earth 16
  Latitude 16
  Longitude 17
  Great Circles and Small Circles 19
  Prime Meridian and Standard Time 23
Maps, Scales, and Projections 26
  The Scale of Maps 26
  Map Projections 27
Remote Sensing and GIS 29
  Remote Sensing 31
  Geographic Information Systems (GIS) 34
Summary And Review 35
News Report 1.1: Frogs at a Tipping Point—Check the System 11
News Report 1.2: The Coordinates of the North 18
News Report 1.3: The Great White North? 20
News Report 1.4: GPS: A Personal Locator 22
News Report 1.5: Careers in GIS 35
Focus Study 1.1: The Scientific Method 8
Focus Study 1.2: The Timely Search for Longitude 21
High Latitude Connection 1.1: Meltponds as Positive Feedback 7

PART I

The Energy–Atmosphere System 38

2 Solar Energy to Earth and the Seasons 40

The Solar System, Sun, and Earth 42
  Solar System Formation and Structure 42
Solar Energy: From Sun to Earth 42
  Solar Activity and Solar Wind 44
  Electromagnetic Spectrum of Radiant Energy 46
  Incoming Energy at the Top of the Atmosphere 47
The Seasons 50
  Seasonality 50
  Reasons for Seasons 52
  Annual March of the Seasons 54
Summary And Review 59
News Report 2.1: The Nature of Order is Chaos 45
News Report 2.2: Monitoring Earth Radiation Budget 51
Applied Physical Geography: Calculating the Energy from Sunlight over a 12-Hour Period 58

3 Earth's Modern Atmosphere 62

Atmospheric Composition, Temperature, and Function 64
  Atmospheric Profile 64
  Atmospheric Composition Criterion 66
  Atmospheric Temperature Criterion 69
  Atmospheric Function Criterion 70
Variable Atmospheric Components 70
  Natural Sources 74
  Natural Factors That Affect Air Pollution 75
  Anthropogenic Pollution 78
  Benefits of the Clean Air Act 85
Summary And Review 87
News Report 3.1: Falling Through the Atmosphere—The Highest Sky Dive 67
Focus Study 3.1: Stratospheric Ozone Losses: A Worldwide Health Hazard 71
Focus Study 3.2: Acid Deposition: Damaging to Ecosystems 83
High Latitude Connection 3.1: Arctic Haze 78
Applied Physical Geography: Radiation and Temperature 86

4 Atmosphere and Surface Energy Balances 90

Energy Essentials 92
  Energy Pathways and Principles 92
Energy Balance in the Troposphere 98
  The Greenhouse Effect and Atmospheric Warming 99
  Clouds and Earth's "Greenhouse" 99
  Earth–Atmosphere Energy Balance 101

Energy Balance at Earth's Surface 102
Daily Radiation Patterns 102
Simplified Surface Energy Balance 103
The Urban Environment 109
Summary And Review 114
News Report 4.1: Earthshine Studies—Possible Energy
Budget Diagnostic 96
Focus Study 4.1: Solar Energy Collection
and Concentration 107
Applied Physical Geography: Energy Balance Model 113

5 Global Temperatures 118

Temperature Concepts and Measurement 120
Temperature Scales 120
Measuring Temperature 121
Principal Temperature Controls 122
Latitude 122
Altitude/Elevation 122
Cloud Cover 124
Land–Water Heating Differences 124
Earth's Temperature Patterns 127
January Temperature Maps 129
July Temperature Map 132
Annual Temperature Range Map 133
Record Temperatures and Greenhouse Warming 136
Summary And Review 139
Focus Study 5.1: Air Temperature and the Human Body 134
High Latitude Connection 5.1: Overview of Temperature
Trends in the Polar Regions 137
Applied Physical Geography: Humidex 139

6 Atmospheric and Oceanic
Circulations 142

Wind Essentials 145
Air Pressure and Its Measurement 145
Wind: Description and Measurement 146
Global Winds 147
Driving Forces Within the Atmosphere 148
Pressure Gradient Force 148
Coriolis Force 150
Friction Force 154
Atmospheric Patterns of Motion 154
Primary High-Pressure and Low-Pressure Areas 154
Upper Atmospheric Circulation 159
Multiyear Oscillations in Global Circulation 162
Local Winds 164
Monsoonal Winds 168
Oceanic Currents 169
Surface Currents 169
Thermohaline Circulation—The Deep Currents 170
Summary And Review 172
News Report 6.1: Coriolis, a Forceful Effect
on Drains? 153
News Report 6.2: MANTRA's Big Balloon—Blowing
in the Wind? 163
News Report 6.3: A Message in a Bottle and Rubber
Duckies 171
Focus Study 6.1: Wind Power: An Energy Resource for
the Present and Future 166

PART II

The Water, Weather, and Climate
Systems 176

7 Water and Atmospheric Moisture 178

Water on Earth 180
Worldwide Equilibrium 181
Distribution of Earth's Water Today 181
Unique Properties of Water 183
Heat Properties 184
Heat Properties of Water in Nature 186
Humidity 187
Relative Humidity 187
Expressions of Humidity 188
Atmospheric Stability 192
Adiabatic Processes 192
Stable and Unstable Atmospheric Conditions 194
Clouds and Fog 196
Cloud Formation Processes 196
Cloud Types and Identification 196
Fog 200
Summary And Review 206
News Report 7.1: Breaking Roads and Pipes and Sinking
Ships 185
News Report 7.2: Harvesting Fog 203
Applied Physical Geography: Measuring Relative
Humidity 204

8 Weather 210

Weather Essentials 212
Air Masses Affecting North America 212
Air Mass Modification 213
Atmospheric Lifting Mechanisms 214
Convergent Lifting 215
Convectional Lifting 215
Orographic Lifting 217
Frontal Lifting (Cold and Warm Fronts) 218
Midlatitude Cyclonic Systems 222
Life Cycle of a Midlatitude Cyclone 222
Analysis of Daily Weather Maps—Forecasting 224

Violent Weather 227
Ice Storms 227
Thunderstorms 227
Derechos 231
Tornadoes 233
Tropical Cyclones 235
Summary and Review 246
News Report 8.1: Mountains Set Precipitation Records 220
Focus Study 8.1: Atlantic Hurricanes and the 2005 Season 241
Applied Physical Geography: Adiabatic Warming and the Rain Shadow 245

9 Water Resources 250

The Hydrologic Cycle 252
A Hydrologic Cycle Model 253
Surface Water 253
Soil-Water-Budget Concept 254
The Soil-Water-Balance Equation 255
Drought 261
Sample Water Budgets 261
Water Budget and Water Resources 263
Groundwater Resources 266
Groundwater Profile and Movement 266
Aquifers, Wells, and Springs 267
Overuse of Groundwater 268
Pollution of Groundwater 272
Our Water Supply 274
Water Supply in Canada 276
Instream, Nonconsumptive, and Consumptive Uses 276
Desalination 276
Future Considerations 278
Summary and Review 280
News Report 9.1: Middle East Water Crisis: Running on Empty 271
News Report 9.2: Personal Water Use in Canada 275
Focus Study 9.1: High Plains Aquifer Overdraft 269
Focus Study 9.2: Walkerton, Ontario: Groundwater Contamination, Water System Mismanagement, and Tragedy 272
Applied Physical Geography: A Thornthwaite Water Balance Problem 279

10 Global Climate Systems 284

Earth's Climate System and Its Classification 286
Climate Components: Insolation, Temperature, Pressure, Air Masses, and Precipitation 287
Classification of Climatic Regions 287
Tropical Climates (equatorial and tropical latitudes) 293
Tropical Rain Forest Climates 293
Tropical Monsoon Climates 293
Tropical Savanna Climates 297
Mesothermal Climates (midlatitudes, mild winters) 298
Humid Subtropical Climates 299
Marine West Coast Climates 300
Mediterranean Dry-Summer Climates 303
Microthermal Climates (mid- and high latitudes, cold winters) 303
Humid Continental Hot-Summer Climates 305

Humid Continental Mild-Summer Climates 305
Subarctic Climates 305
Polar and Highland Climates 309
Tundra Climate 310
Ice Cap and Ice Sheet Climate 310
Polar Marine Climate 311
Arid and Semiarid Climates (permanent moisture deficits) 311
Desert Characteristics 312
Tropical, Subtropical Hot Desert Climates 312
Midlatitude Cold Desert Climates 314
Tropical, Subtropical Hot Steppe Climates 314
Midlatitude Cold Steppe Climates 315
Global Climate Change 315
Global Warming 317
Climate Models and Future Temperatures 320
Consequences of Global Warming 323
Political Action and "No Regrets" 324
Summary and Review 325
News Report 10.1: Coordinating Global Climate Change Research 317
Focus Study 10.1: The El Niño Phenomenon—Global Linkages 289

PART III

The Earth–Atmosphere Interface 328

11 The Dynamic Planet 330

The Pace of Change 332
Earth's Structure and Internal Energy 334
Earth's Core and Magnetism 334
Earth's Mantle 336
Earth's Lithosphere and Crust 337
The Geologic Cycle 339
The Rock Cycle 341
Igneous Processes 341
Sedimentary Processes 344
Metamorphic Processes 348

Plate Tectonics 349
    A Brief History 350
    Sea-Floor Spreading and Production of New Crust 350
    Subduction of the Lithosphere 351
    The Formation and Breakup of Pangaea 351
    Plate Boundaries 356
    Earthquake and Volcanic Activity 359
    Hot Spots 361
Summary and Review 366
News Report 11.1: Radioactivity: Earth's Time Clock 332
News Report 11.2: Drilling the Crust to Record Depths 337
News Report 11.3: J. Tuzo Wilson and the Theory of Plate Tectonics 359
Focus Study 11.1: Tectonic Setting of the Pacific Coast of Canada 359
Focus Study 11.2: Heat from Earth—Geothermal Energy and Power 364
High Latitude Connection 11.1: Isostatic Rebound in Alaska 338

12 Tectonics, Earthquakes, and Volcanism 368
Earth's Surface Relief Features 371
    Crustal Orders of Relief 371
    Earth's Topographic Regions 371
Crustal Formation Processes 374
    Continental Shields 374
    Building Continental Crust and Terranes 374
Crustal Deformation Processes 375
    Folding and Broad Warping 379
    Faulting 380
Orogenesis (Mountain Building) 384
    Types of Orogenies 385
    The Appalachian Mountains 386
    The Western Cordillera 387
    The Innuitian Mountains 388
    World Structural Regions 389
Earthquakes 390
    Expected Quakes and Those of Deadly Surprise 391
    Focus, Epicentre, Foreshock, and Aftershock 391
    Earthquake Intensity and Magnitude 391
    The Nature of Faulting 393
    Earthquakes and the San Andreas Fault 397
    Los Angeles Region 397
    Earthquake Forecasting and Planning 397
Volcanism 398
    Volcanic Features 399
    Location and Types of Volcanic Activity 399
    Effusive Eruptions 402
    Explosive Eruptions 404
    Canadian Volcanoes 409
    Volcano Forecasting and Planning 410
Summary and Review 411
News Report 12.1: Mount Everest at New Heights 373
News Report 12.2: Seismic Gaps, Nervous Animals, Dilitancy, and Radon Gas 398
News Report 12.3: Is the Long Valley Caldera Next? 402
Focus Study 12.1: Exotic Terranes in Western Canada 377
Focus Study 12.2: The 1980 Eruption of Mount St. Helens 406

Applied Physical Geography 12.1: Magnitude and Frequency 410

13 Weathering, Karst Landscapes, and Mass Movement 414
Landmass Denudation 416
    Dynamic Equilibrium Approach to Landforms 416
Weathering Processes 417
    Factors Influencing Weathering Processes 420
    Physical Weathering Processes 421
    Chemical Weathering Processes 423
Karst Topography and Landscapes 427
    Formation of Karst 427
    Lands Covered with Sinkholes 428
    Caves and Caverns 428
Mass-Movement Processes 431
    Mass-Movement Mechanics 431
    Classes of Mass Movements 433
    Human-Induced Mass Movements (Scarification) 439
Summary and Review 442
News Report 13.1: Amateurs Make Cave Discoveries 433
Focus Study 13.1: Frank Slide: Coal Mining and an Early Morning Disaster 436
Applied Physical Geography 13.1: The Role of Gravity in Landform Development 441

14 River Systems and Landforms 446
Fluvial Processes and Landscapes 448
    Base Level of Streams 449
    Drainage Basins 450
    Drainage Density and Patterns 453
Streamflow Characteristics 455
    Exotic Streams 456
    Stream Erosion 458
    Stream Transport 458
    Flow and Channel Characteristics 459
    Stream Gradient 460
    Stream Deposition and Landforms 465
Floods and River Management 475
    Rating Floodplain Risk 476
    Engineering Failures in New Orleans, 2005 476
    Streamflow Measurement 480
Summary and Review 482
News Report 14.1: Scouring the Grand Canyon for New Beaches and Habitats 457
News Report 14.2: Rivers Make Poor Political Boundaries 463
News Report 14.3: The 1997 Red River Flood 469
News Report 14.4: The Nile Delta Is Disappearing 472
Focus Study 14.1: Floodplain Strategies 476
Applied Physical Geography 14.1: Flood Frequency Analysis 481

15 Eolian Processes and Arid Landscapes 486
The Work of Wind 488
    Eolian Erosion 488
    Eolian Transportation 490

Eolian Depositional Landforms 491
Loess Deposits 495

Overview of Desert Landscapes 498
Desert Climates 498
Desert Fluvial Processes 500
Desert Landscapes 505
Basin and Range Province 507
Desertification 510
Climate Change and Increased Aridity in Canada 511

Summary and Review 513

Focus Study 15.1: **The Colorado River: A System Out of Balance** 501

Applied Physical Geography 15.1: **Wind Erosion** 512

16 The Oceans, Coastal Processes, and Landforms 516

Global Oceans and Seas 518
Chemical Composition of Seawater 518
Physical Structure of the Ocean 520

Coastal System Components 521
Inputs to the Coastal System 521
The Coastal Environment and Sea Level 521

Coastal System Actions 523
Tides 524
Waves 526

Coastal System Outputs 532
Erosional Coastal Processes and Landforms 532
Depositional Coastal Processes and Landforms 532
Biological Processes: Coral Formations 540

Wetlands, Salt Marshes, and Mangrove Swamps 542
Coastal Wetlands 542

Human Impact on Coastal Environments 543

Summary and Review 548

News Report 16.1: Sea Level Variations and the Present MSL Increase 522

News Report 16.2: Size Matters When It Comes to Tides 527

News Report 16.3: Quake and Tsunami Strike! 531

News Report 16.4: Elephant Rock Collapses 534

Focus Study 16.1: **An Environmental Approach to Shoreline Planning** 544

High Latitude Connection 16.1: **A Rebounding Shoreline and Coastal Features** 535

Applied Physical Geography 16.1: **Coastal Geomorphology—Sediment Budgets** 546

17 Glacial and Periglacial Processes and Landforms 550

Rivers of Ice 552
Alpine Glaciers 553
Continental Glaciers 556

Glacial Processes 558
Formation of Glacial Ice 558
Glacial Mass Balance 558
Glacial Movement 562

Glacial Landforms 564
Erosional Landforms Created by Alpine Glaciation 564
Depositional Landforms Created by Alpine Glaciation 566

Erosional and Depositional Landforms Created by Continental Glaciation 568

Periglacial Landscapes 570
Geography of Permafrost 570
Ground Ice and Frozen Ground Phenomena 573
Humans and Periglacial Landscapes 576

The Pleistocene Ice-Age Epoch 576
Changes in the Landscape 577
Glacial Great Lakes 578
Paleolakes 578
Lowered Sea Levels and Lower Temperatures 580

Deciphering Past Climates: Paleoclimatology 581
Medieval Warm Period and Little Ice Age 581
Mechanisms of Climate Fluctuation 582

Arctic and Antarctic Regions 585
Changes are Underway in the Polar Regions 586

Summary and Review 589

News Report 17.1: Western Glaciers Lose Mass 560

News Report 17.2: Increase in Meltponds Indicates Changing Surface Energy Budgets 586

Focus Study 17.1: **GRIP, GISP-2, and Dome C: Boring Ice for Exciting History** 582

High Latitude Connection 17.1: **Climate Change Impacts an Arctic Ice Shelf** 587

PART IV

Soils, Ecosystems, and the Biomes 592

18 The Geography of Soils 594

Soil Characteristics 596
Soil Profiles 596
Soil Horizons 597

Soil Properties 598
Soil Colour 598
Soil Texture 598
Soil Structure 599
Soil Consistence 599
Soil Porosity 600
Soil Moisture 600
Soil Chemistry 600
Soil Acidity and Alkalinity 601

Soil Formation Factors and Management   602
   Natural Factors   602
   The Human Factor   602
   Soil Classification   606
**The Canadian System of Soil Classification
(CSSC)**   606
   Categories of Classification in the CSSC   606
   Soil Horizons in the CSSC   606
   The Ten Soil Orders of the CSSC   608
   CSSC and Worldwide Soil Taxonomy   618
Summary and Review   623
**News Report 18.1: Soil Is Slipping Through Our
   Fingers**   604
Focus Study 18.1: Selenium Concentration in Western
   Soils   605
Applied Physical Geography 18.1: **Soil Density and
   Porosity**   622

19 Ecosystem Essentials   626
Ecosystem Components and Cycles   628
   Communities   629
   Plants: The Essential Biotic Component   631
   Photosynthesis and Respiration   633
   Abiotic Ecosystem Components   636
   Elemental Cycles   637
   Limiting Factors   642
Biotic Ecosystem Operations   644
   Producers, Consumers, and Decomposers   644
   Examples of Complex Food Webs   644
   Efficiency in a Food Web   646
   Ecological Relations   648
Ecosystems, Evolution, and Succession   648
   Biological Evolution Delivers Biodiversity   650
   Ecosystem Stability and Diversity   651
   Ecological Succession   655
   Terrestrial Succession   656
   Aquatic Succession   658
Summary and Review   666
**News Report 19.1: Earth's Magnetic Field—An Abiotic
   Factor**   639
News Report 19.2: The Dead Zone   643
**News Report 19.3: Biodiversity in Alberta
   and Saskatchewan—Cypress Hills**   652
Focus Study 19.1: **The Great Lakes**   660
Applied Physical Geography 19.1: **Species Diversity
   and Species Richness**   664

20 Terrestrial Biomes   668
Biogeographic Realms   670
   Transition Zones   671
   Terrestrial Ecosystems   671
Earth's Major Terrestrial Biomes   672
   Equatorial and Tropical Rain Forest   677
   Deforestation of the Tropics   679
   Tropical Seasonal Forest and Scrub   679
   Tropical Savanna   685
   Midlatitude Broadleaf and Mixed Forest   685
   Needleleaf Forest and Montane Forest   687
   Temperate Rain Forest   690
   Mediterranean Shrubland   690
   Midlatitude Grasslands   691
   Deserts   692
   Arctic and Alpine Tundra   693
Summary and Review   696
**News Report 20.1: Aquatic Ecosystems and Marine
   Protected Areas**   672
News Report 20.2: Alien Invaders of Exotic Species   676
News Report 20.3: ANWR Faces Threats   695
Focus Study 20.1: **Biodiversity and Biosphere
   Reserves**   681

21 Earth and the Human Denominator   698
The Human Count and The Future   702
An Oily Bird   703
The Need For Cooperation   705
Twelve Paradigms for the 21st Century   706
Who Speaks for Earth?   707
News Report 21.1: Gaia Hypothesis Triggers Debate   707

Appendix A   Maps in this Text and
                Topographic Maps   A.1

Appendix B   The 12 Soil Orders of the U.S.
                Soil Taxonomy   A.6

Appendix C   The Köppen Climate
                Classification System   A.10

Appendix D   Common Conversions   A.13

Glossary   G.1

Index   I.1

Preface

Welcome to *Geosystems, An Introduction to Physical Geography*, Second Canadian Edition! Much has happened since the previous edition of *Geosystems* (© 2006). The International Polar Year (IPY; http://www.ipy.org/) began in 2007 and concludes March 2009. The Intergovernmental Panel on Climate Change (IPCC; http:www.ipcc.ch/) completed its Fourth Assessment Report and published four supporting volumes of its consensus science regarding human-forced climate change. The high latitudes, which include much of Canada, continue to be profoundly affected by climate change with all terrestrial and aquatic ecosystems in response and transition.

In every chapter, *Geosystems* presents updated science, information, and Internet URLs to enhance your understanding of Earth systems. The currency of *Geosystems* makes it important for students and teachers alike to take advantage of the updated content by using this latest edition.

Your selection of *Geosystems* and its companion text *Elemental Geosystems* made them the leaders in Canadian physical geography through all their editions. To honour this acceptance and to serve Canadian geographic education, we produced this updated second Canadian edition of *Geosystems*. As in the first edition, we include hundreds of new Canadian examples, illustrations, photos, maps, and satellite images.

Students and teachers continue to communicate their appreciation of the up-to-date content, systems organization, scientific accuracy, clarity of the summary and review sections, and overall relevancy Armed with the spatial analysis tools of geographic science, physical geographers are well equipped to participate in a planetary understanding of environmental conditions. Welcome to physical geography!

New to the Second Canadian Edition of *Geosystems*

There is not room in this Preface to list all the changes and additions to our Canadian *Geosystems*. Begin by examining all 21 chapter-opening and 4 part-opening photos and images and read their captions—all but one are new. You see photos of the Midnight Sun in the Arctic, the Mauna Loa Climate Observatory, a blizzard across the Canadian tundra, Katrina damage photos, 1983 and 2007 comparative photos updating the decline of Lake Mead at Hoover Dam, a glacier as it calves into the sea, harvesting peat, among others. These are content-specific and begin the learning process from the start of the chapter. Throughout the text there are many new photos and satellite images to illustrate content, many used in compound figures with arts and maps.

We continue the "High Latitude Connection" feature, linking chapter material to the polar regions. The world's attention is on the high latitudes to better understand present global climate change. Robert Christopherson and his photographer wife completed nine polar and northern Canada expeditions since 2003, gathering materials and photos from the rapidly changing high latitudes for all the *Geosystems* texts. An image of the record low sea-ice extent in the Arctic Ocean, reached September 2007, appears in HLC 5.1 and Figure 21.8. In addition, the polar region temperature maps are enlarged in Figures 5.14 and 5.17.

The 2005 Atlantic tropical storm season set many records, including 27 named storms (average is 10); 15 hurricanes (average is 5); and 7 intense hurricanes, category 3 or higher (average is 2). *Geosystems* takes the approach that the 2005 storm was named Katrina but the disaster that followed was of human origins due to poorly conceived planning and flawed engineering. A new aerial photo from August 30, 2005, shows the Inner Harbor Navigation Canal levee break. A new section in Chapter 14, "Engineering Failures in New Orleans, 2005," with satellite before-and-after *Landsat* images of the city with a detailed locator map illustrates the catastrophe.

The latest climate-change science is woven throughout the book and into Chapter 10 with 10 new graphs and charts from the IPCC and results from the ice cores. All temperature data have been updated through the latest available measurements. Focus Study 17.1 has expanded coverage of Dome C, Antarctica, and the ice-core analysis that now stretches the climate record back to 800,000 years ago, confirming present levels of greenhouse gases in the atmosphere as highest in the record.

Geosystems presents many current examples for discussion as new applied topics, such as: the extinction of 67% of all harlequin frog species as an example of applied systems analysis; an updated air pressure section including the 2005 records; the unexpected hurricanes that have hit Brazil, Spain, the Persian Gulf, and mid-Pacific since 2004, and, Hurricane Juan that struck Nova Scotia in 2003; the losses of sand inventory from the Chandeleur Islands in the Gulf of Mexico in a new before-and-after Katrina photo comparison in Figure 16.17; new High Plains aquifer maps showing its status through 2002; new IPCC comparisons of several climatic scenarios for this century; a photo and description of the new Ocean Drilling Program research ship; a new Pu'u O'o crater aerial photo at Kīlauea volcano, Hawai'i, from summer 2007 placed next to an aerial photo made at roughly the same location in 1999 showing huge collapses on the west side; a new sediment-accumulation-model illustration added to the deflation-model art for desert pavement formation, representing both hypotheses; the latest information on the troubled Colorado River system and western drought, a subject present in all *Geosystems* books since the first edition in 1992; and the endangered status of polar bears and the USGS forecast of a two-thirds loss of their population by 2050.

In Chapter 11, a new Figure 11.3 features an Earth's profile overlying a map of North America from the Earth's central core placed in Anchorage, AK, across Canada, to the crust placed in Miami, FL. Chapter 13 features new headings "Salt-Crystal Growth (Salt Weathering)," and "Dissolution of Carbonates," replacing "Crystalization" and "Carbonation and Solution," respectively. Included is a redone world karst map and new weathering photo examples. Chapter 14 and the dramatic Chapter 21 opener feature new photos of Niagara Falls. Again, this is but a brief sample of what you will discover in the pages ahead.

Systems Organization Makes *Geosystems* Flow

Each section of this book is organized around the flow of energy, materials, and information. *Geosystems* presents subjects in the same sequence in which they occur in nature. In this way you and your teacher logically progress through topics that unfold according to the flow of individual systems, or in accord with time and the flow of events. See Figure 1.7 in the text for an illustration of this systems organization.

A good example of the systems organization is the eruption of Mount Pinatubo in the Philippines. The global implications of this major event (one of the largest eruptions in the twentieth century) are woven through seven chapters of the book (see Figure 1.6 and Chapter 12 for a summary) and not just in the chapter dealing with volcanoes. Another example is the updated coverage on global climate change and its related potential effects included as part of the fabric of many chapters since numerous systems are impacted, not just the temperature or climate chapters.

For flexibility, *Geosystems* is divided into four parts, each containing chapters that link content in logical groupings. The diagram on Figure 1.8, illustrates our part structure. A quick check of the table of contents and this illustration shows you the order of chapters within these four parts.

The text culminates with Chapter 21, "Earth and the Human Denominator," a unique capstone chapter that summarizes physical geography as an important discipline in understanding Earth's present status and possible future. Think of the world's population and the totality of our impact as the *human denominator*. Just as the denominator in a fraction tells how many parts a whole is divided into, so the growing human population and the increasing demand for resources and their rising planetary impact suggest how much the whole Earth system must adjust. This chapter is sure to stimulate further thought and discussion, dealing as it does with the most profound issue of our time, Earth's stewardship.

Geosystems Is a Text That Teaches

Teaching and learning begin with the front cover photographs. An astronaut provides the background photo from the International Space Station over the tropical Pacific Ocean, the shadows of cumulonimbus thunderheads are cast on the ocean. The four photos dramatically express Earth's diversity: energy, atmosphere, weather, landscapes and weathering, and the complexity of life in biogeography. Thus is the scope of our discipline of physical geography.

To assist you in becoming acquainted with physical geography, this edition of *Geosystems* features more than 550 photographs from across the globe and more than 125 remote-sensing images from a wide variety of orbital platforms. For spatial analysis and location support, 265 maps are utilized, and more than 400 illustrations locate and explain concepts.

Three heading levels are used throughout the text and precise topic sentences begin each paragraph to help you outline and review material. **Boldface** words are defined where they first appear in the text. These terms and concepts are collected alphabetically in the Glossary with chapter-number references. Our complete Glossary appears on the *Student Animations CD* that accompanies this text. *Italics* are used in the text to emphasize other words and phrases of importance. Every figure has a title that summarizes the caption. Also, in the introduction to each chapter, a feature called "In this chapter" gives you an overview.

An important continuing feature is a list of *Key Learning Concepts* that opens each chapter, stating what you should be able to do upon completing the chapter. These objectives are keyed to the main headings in the chapter. At the end of each chapter is a unique *Summary and Review* section that corresponds to the key learning concepts. Grouped under each learning concept is a narrative review that defines the boldfaced terms, along with a key terms list with page numbers and specific review questions for that concept. You can conveniently review each concept, test your understanding with review questions, and check key terms in the Glossary, then return to the chapter and the next learning concept. In this way, the chapter content is woven together using specific concepts.

Applied Physical Geography and *Critical Thinking* sections end each chapter, challenging you to take the next step with information from the chapter. The key learning concepts help you determine what you want to learn, the text guides you in developing information and more questions, the summary and review assesses what you have learned and what more you might want to know about the subject, and the critical thinking and problem-solving sections provoke action and application.

We now live on a planet served by the Internet and its World Wide Web, a resource that weaves threads of information from around the globe into a vast fabric.

The fact that we have Internet access in almost all the compartments aboard Spaceship Earth is clearly evident in *Geosystems*. Many entry points link directly from the words in a chapter to an Internet source, allowing you to be up to the minute. You will find more than 200 URLs (Internet addresses) in the body of the text (printed in blue and boldface), many for Canadian sources of information. Given the fluid nature of the Internet, URLs were rechecked at press time for accuracy. If some URLs changed since publication, you can most likely find the new location using elements of the old address. This Internet link begins with Table 1.1 presenting the URLs for major geography organizations. The Geosystems texts remain the only ones with embedded URLs for your use.

The *Geosystems* Learning/ Teaching Package

The Second Canadian Edition provides a complete physical geography program for you and your instructor.

For You, the Student:

- *Student Animations CD*, by Robert Christopherson, is included in each copy of the book. This exciting learning tool contains 67 animations with self-tests, 18 satellite loops (including 4 Notebook features), a searchable Glossary, and a World Map Reference library, including: "Living Earth/Earth at Night" morphing maps; "The Blue Marble" rotating Earth; 7 maps with grabber and zoom control; 5 High Latitude Connection video clips. Also,
- 4 new movies:

  "Niagara Falls Close Up"
  "1891–2006 Temperature Anomalies Movie"
  "27 Storms Arlene to Zeta—The 2005 Season"
  "Polar Bear Mom and Cubs on the Pack Ice"

- 4 photo galleries with narrated scripts:

  "Geographic Scenes: East Greenland"
  "High Latitude Animals"
  "Earth's Varied Landscapes, Aerial Photos"
  "Polar Bear Photo Gallery"

- *Geosystems Companion Website* (**www.pearsoned.ca/ christopherson**). This site gives you the opportunity to further explore topics presented in the book using the Internet and provides on-line resources for the chapters on the World Wide Web. You will find self-tests that are graded, review exercises, specific updates for items in the chapters, and in "Destinations" many links to interesting related pathways on the Internet. Designed as an online study guide, this web site gives you the opportunity to test your knowledge of the concepts presented in each chapter. *Career Link* essays, including several new ones, feature geographers and other scientists in a variety of professional fields practising their spatial analysis craft.

For You, the Teacher:

Geosystems is designed to give you flexibility in presenting your course. The text is comprehensive in that it is true to each scientific discipline from which it draws subject matter. Although this diversity is a strength of physical geography, it makes it difficult to cover the entire book in a school term. *Geosystems* is organized to help you customize your presentation. You should feel free to use the text based on your specialty or emphasis, rearranging parts and chapters as desired. The four-part structure of chapters, systems organization within each chapter, and Focus Study and News Report features will all assist you in sampling some chapters while covering others in greater depth. The following materials are available to assist you—have a great class!

- *Instructor's Resource CD-ROM* (*IRCD*), (ISBN: 013-504724-2). Find all your digital resources in one, well-organized, easy-to access place. Included on this CD-ROM are:

Figures—JPEGs of all illustrations and, new to this edition, all the photos from the book.

Animations—All the animations ready to use in your classroom presentations as PowerPoint slides or Flash files.

PowerPoint™ Lecture Slides—Preauthored slides outline the concepts of each chapter with embedded art for use in the classroom or to customize with other items for your own presentation needs.

TestGen—by Robert Christopherson, Charlie Thomsen, and Mary-Louise Byrne. This collaboration has produced the most extensive and fully revised test bank available in physical geography. This test bank employs **TestGen** software, a computerized test generator that lets you view and edit test bank questions, transfer questions to tests, and print customized formats.

Instructor's Resource Manual—by Robert Christopherson and Mary-Louise Byrne. The Instructor's Resource Manual, intended as a resource for both new and experienced teachers, includes lecture outlines and key terms, additional source materials, teaching tips, complete annotation of chapter review questions, and a list of overhead transparencies.

The complete Instructor's Resource Manual in Word or PDF format and the TestGen in MAC or PC format can be downloaded from the Pearson Education Canada online catalogue at **www.pearsoned/ca**.

Available *Geosystems* Seventh Edition Instructor Supplements:

- *Overhead Transparencies* (ISBN: 0-13-601185-3) including hundreds of illustrations from the text on 175 transparencies, all enlarged for excellent classroom visibility.
- *Applied Physical Geography—Geosystems in the Laboratory*, Seventh Edition (ISBN: 0-13-601181-0),

by Robert Christopherson and Charlie Thomsen. The new seventh edition is the result of a careful revision. Twenty lab exercises, divided into logical sections, allow flexibility in presentation. Each exercise comes with a list of learning concepts. We integrate **Google Earth**™ mapping service links to KMZ files into the exercises so that students can actually fly through and experience 3-D landscapes as they work problems. Our manual comes with its own complete glossary and stereolenses and stereomaps for viewing photo stereopairs in the manual. A complete **Solutions and Answers Manual**, 7/e, is available to teachers (ISBN: 0-13-601180-2).

• **Geosystems 18-month Calendar** highlights important dates relevant to physical geography and our text. Seventy content-specific photos by Bobbé Christopherson grace the pages of our first calendar, which covers January 2008–June 2009.

Acknowledgments

Robert and Mary-Louise offer thanks to the many authors and scientists who published research articles and books that enrich this work; to all the colleagues who served as specific reviewers to this edition, or those who offered helpful suggestions at our national and regional geography meetings; and, although unnamed here, to all the correspondence received from students and instructors from across the globe who shared with the authors over the Internet, e-mail, fax, and phone—a continuing appreciated dialogue. We are grateful to all of them for their generosity of ideas and sacrifice of time.

The authors and publishers thank all of the reviewers who participated in reading material at various stages during the development of both Canadian editions and previous *Geosystems* editions:

Alec Aitken, *University of Saskatchewan*
Peter Ashmore, *University of Western Ontario*
Chris Ayles, *Camosun College*
Bill Buhay, *University of Winnipeg*
Leif Burge, *Okanagan College*
Ian Campbell, *University of Alberta–Edmonton*
Norm Catto, *Memorial University*
Ben Cecil, *University of Regina*
Gail Chmura, *McGill University*
Daryl Dagesse, *Brock University*
Robin Davidson-Arnott, *University of Guelph*
Dirk H. de Boer, *University of Saskatchewan*
Joseph R. Desloges, *University of Toronto*
John Fairfield, *Malaspina University College*
William Gough, *University of Toronto*
Mryka Hall-Beyer, *University of Calgary*
Peter Herren, *University of Calgary*
J. Peter Johnson, Jr., *Carleton University*
David Jordan, *Trinity Western University*
Colin Laroque, *Mount Allison University*
Joyce Lundberg, *Carleton University*

Robert McClure, *North Island College*
Ben Moffatt, *Medicine Hat College*
Catherine Moore, *Concordia University*
Darryl Carlyle-Moses, *Thompson Rivers University*
Mungandi Nasitwitwi, *Douglas College*
Lawrence C. Nkemdirim, *University of Calgary*
Kathy E. Runnalls, *Douglas College*
Ann-Marie Ryan, *Dalhousie University*
Dave Sauchyn, *University of Regina*
Cheryl P. Schreader, *Capilano College*
Geraldine Sweet, *University of Winnipeg*
Alan Trenhaile, *University of Windsor*
Michael Tripp, *Malaspina University College*
Susan Vajoczki, *McMaster University*
James Voogt, *University of Western Ontario*
Gordon Weary, *Northwest Community College*

We extend gratitude to the editorial, production, and sales staff of Pearson Education in Canada and the U.S. Thanks to Gary Bennett, Vice President, Editorial Director, at Pearson Education for his oversight and guidance, and to Dan Kaveney, Robert's Geosciences Publisher, for his role in both *Geosystems* and *Elemental Geosystems* as we forge this *Geosystems* bridge between two countries.

We appreciate developmental editor Ginger Birkeland for her skillful work helping us meld new research and materials into this new edition. We extend thanks for the expertise of Associate Editor Amanda Brown, who oversees the ancillaries and *Applied Physical Geography* lab manual, for all the years of our friendship; and warm recognition to Charlie Thomsen for his collaboration on the lab manual and ancillaries; to Media Editor Andrew Sobel for skill and creativity on the CD and web site projects; and thanks to Project Managers Tim Flem and Shari Toron, who operate the organizational switching yard, for all their coordination effort, help, and conversation. To Marketing Manager Marlene Olsavsky and the many sales representatives who spend months in the field communicating the *Geosystems* approach, as always, thanks and safe travels to them—may the wind be at their backs!

Our thanks to our colleague Production Editor Cindy Miller of GGS Book Services for such friendship and managerial ability through several editions, and to Suganya Karuppasamy of GGS for her skills and oversight of pages, converting materials into this textbook; and to Jeff Georgeson our diligent, detailed proofreader. Thanks to the art and design team at Prentice Hall for carrying out Bobbé Christopherson's cover design, for their beautiful text design, and for letting us in on many decisions.

From Robert: I give special gratitude to all the students and colleagues over 30 years at American River College for defining the importance of Earth's future, for their questions, and their enthusiasm. I recognize my family, for they never waver in supporting *Geosystems*' goals. When I look into our grandchildren's faces and think of their lives this century, that tells me why we need to work toward a sustainable future, one for the children. We honor our children and grandchildren in the Dedication to this edition.

At the heart of *Geosystems* and of this life's work is a partner, photographer, and special editorial assistant, my wife Bobbé Christopherson. She has worked tirelessly on all the *Geosystems'* projects. You see more than 250 of her photographs in the second edition and on the cover, all carefully made to illustrate physical geography concepts. Please visit the four photo galleries on the *Student Animation CD* to see her artistry with a camera. She processes satellite imagery and all photos, cropping and sizing them for pages. She produced 70 photos for use in our new *Geosystems 18-month Calendar*. Bobbé's love for the smallest of living things and her strength guide me forward. And, she continues as my best friend, colleague, and expedition companion, by my side on our nine polar-region expeditions.

Robert W. Christopherson
P. O. Box 128
Lincoln, California 95648
E-mail: bobobbe@aol.com
Web sites: http://www.pearsoned.ca/christopherson
(Cdn) http://www.prenhall.com/christopherson (U.S.)

From Mary-Louise: The incredible journey continues and once again I need to thank so many for their help. I owe my greatest thanks to my immediate family—my husband, Alain Pinard, and our children, Madeleine and Julianne, who now use their verb "textbooking" in phone conversations with their friends. To my extended family I am indebtted to your honest comments and criticisms.

Robert and Bobbé Christopherson continue to develop an amazing textbook, and I am so pleased to join them on the journey. I thank all my colleagues in the geographic community in Canada who, by comment, communication, or review, helped shape the contents of this text. I am forever indebted to Brian McCann for teaching me to look at physical processes from many perspectives and to integrate in order to explain. He is sadly missed. And Sue Vajoczki, your comments and understanding of geographic education have informed me often when I reviewed the pages of this book.

Finally, to all the students with whom I had contact in 17 years of teaching at Wilfrid Laurier, your enthusiasm and curiosity kept me focused on the goal of explaining planet Earth. I have had the pleasure of communicating with several current students from across the country who have had positive and constructive criticism about the book. I took your comments seriously and have addressed them where appropriate. It is amazing to hear from you and I encourage you to continue. To future students, our planet is in your hands: Care for it.

Mary-Louise Byrne
Associate Professor,
Geography and Environmental Studies
Wilfrid Laurier University
Waterloo, Ontario
N2L 3C5
Email: mlbyrne@wlu.ca

And from both Robert and Mary-Louise: Physical geography teaches us a holistic view of the intricate supporting web that is Earth's environment and our place in it. Dramatic changes that demand our understanding are occurring in many human–Earth relations as we alter physical, chemical, and biological systems. Our attention to the polar regions is in recognition of the linkages between all planetary systems and the high latitudes. All things considered, this is a critical time for you to be enrolled in a physical geography course! The best to you in your studies—and *curpe diem*!

To all the students and teachers of Earth,
our home planet, and a sustainable future.

For the polar bears and all the children and grandchildren
who will enjoy them—may there be sea ice.

The land still provides our genesis,
however we might like to forget
that our food comes from dank,
muddy Earth, that the oxygen in our lungs was
recently inside a leaf, and that every newspaper or
book we may pick up is made from the hearts of
trees that died for the sake of our imagined lives.
What you hold in your hands right now,
beneath these words,
is consecrated air and time and sunlight.

–Barbara Kingsolver

The edge of the northern boreal forest west of Hudson Bay, Canada, is a region undergoing climatic change and increasing temperatures. Here the pioneer spruce trees take root as the forest moves northward into the tundra biome, young seedlings leading the way. [Photo by Bobbé Christopherson.]

1

Essentials of Geography

■ Key Learning Concepts

After reading the chapter, you should be able to:

■ *Define* geography and physical geography in particular.

■ *Describe* systems analysis, open and closed systems, and feedback information, and *relate* these concepts to Earth systems.

■ *Explain* Earth's reference grid: latitude and longitude and latitudinal geographic zones and time.

■ *Define* cartography and mapping basics: map scale and map projections.

■ *Describe* remote sensing and *explain* geographic information systems (GIS) as tools used in geographic analysis.

Welcome to the second Canadian edition of *Geosystems, An Introduction to Physical Geography*! Much has happened since the last edition of *Geosystems* in Canada. The International Polar Year (IPY, http://www.ipy.org/) began in 2007 and concludes March 2009, providing new research, data, and discoveries from the changing polar regions. The Intergovernmental Panel on Climate Change (IPCC, http://www.ipcc.ch/) completed its Fourth Assessment Report and published four supporting volumes of its consensus science regarding human-forced climate change. In every chapter, our Canadian edition of *Geosystems* presents updated science and information to enhance your understanding of Earth systems.

Imagine the challenge society as a whole and we in physical geography face to understand how Earth's systems operate and then to forecast change in these systems to determine what future environments we may expect. The scope of this challenge was outlined by scientist Jack Williams:

By the end of the 21st century, large portions of the Earth's surface may experience climates not found at present, and some 20th-century climates may disappear. . . . Novel climates are projected to develop primarily in the tropics and subtropics.*

Physical geography deals with powerful Earth systems that influence our lives and the many ways humans alter Earth's systems. Therefore, as we near the end of this first decade of the twenty-first century, a century that will see many changes to the natural environment, now is a scientifically exciting time to be enrolled in a physical geography course, studying the building blocks that form the landscapes and seascapes upon which we depend. Perhaps you will consider physical geography for a major as we move through the chapters together—we'll see.

Scientists and governments research to understand the worldwide impact of global changes. Former United Nations Secretary General and recipient of the 2001 Nobel Peace Prize, Kofi Annan, speaking to the Association of American Geographers (AAG) annual meeting in March 2001, offered this assessment:

As you know only too well the signs of severe environmental distress are all around us. Unsustainable practices are woven deeply into the fabric of modern life. Land degradation threatens food security. Forest destruction threatens biodiversity. Water pollution threatens public health, and fierce competition for freshwater may well become a source of conflict and wars in the future . . . the overwhelming majority of scientific experts have concluded that climate change is occurring, that humans are contributing, and that we cannot wait any longer to take action . . . environmental problems build up over time, and take an equally long time to remedy.

A U.N. Environment Programme (UNEP, http://www.unep.org/) report in 2005 that included data from 15 of the largest financial institutions estimated that weather-related damage losses (drought, floods, hail, tornadoes, derechos, tropical systems, monsoon intensity, storm surges, blizzard and ice storms, and wildfires) will exceed Can$1 trillion by A.D. 2040 (adjusted to current dollars)—up from $210 billion in 2005 (Hurricane Katrina alone produced $125 billion in losses). Global climate change is driving this increasing total, at a pace that is accelerating. Physical geography is the one course you will take that explains the operations of Earth systems from a spatial perspective and gives you the tools to understand what is happening.

*Jack Williams, et. al., "Projected distributions of novel and disappearing climates by A.D. 2100," *Proceedings of the National Academy of Sciences*, 3 April 2007.

Why do all of these conditions occur? How are these events different from past experience? Why does the environment vary from equator to midlatitudes, between deserts and polar regions? How does solar energy influence the distribution of trees, soils, climates, and lifestyles? What about the record level of wildfires we are experiencing? Why are earthquakes and volcanoes active in certain regions and what is the nature of the risk? What produces the patterns of wind, weather, and ocean currents? Why are global sea levels on the rise? Why did the countries of the world join in the IPY study of the polar regions? How do natural systems affect human populations, and, in turn, what impact are humans having on natural systems? In this book, we explore those questions, and more, through geography's unique perspective. Welcome to an exploration of physical geography!

We live in an extraordinary era of **Earth systems science**. This science contributes to our emerging view of Earth as a complete entity—an interacting set of physical, chemical, and biological systems that produce a whole Earth. Physical geography is at the heart of Earth systems science as we answer the *spatial* questions concerning Earth's physical systems and their interaction with living things.

In this chapter: Our study of geosystems—Earth systems—begins with a look at the science of physical geography and the geographic tools we use. Physical geography is key to studying entire Earth systems because of its integrative spatial approach.

Physical geographers analyze systems to study the environment. Therefore, we discuss systems and the feedback mechanisms that influence system operations. We then consider location, a key theme of geographic inquiry—the latitude, longitude, and time coordinates that inscribe Earth's surface and the new technologies in use to measure them. The study of longitude and a universal time system provide us with interesting insights into geography. Next, we examine maps as critical tools that geographers use to portray physical and cultural information. This chapter concludes with an overview of the technology that is adding exciting new dimensions to geography: remote sensing from space and computer-based geographic information systems (GIS).

The Science of Geography

Geography (from *geo*, "Earth," and *graphein*, "to write") is the science that studies the relationships among natural systems, geographic areas, society, cultural activities, and the interdependence of all of these *over space*. The term **spatial** refers to the nature and character of physical space, its measurement, and the distribution of things within it. For example, think of your own route to the classroom or library today and how you used your knowledge of street patterns, traffic trouble spots, parking spaces, or bike rack locations to minimize walking distance. All of these are spatial considerations.

Humans are spatial actors, both affecting and being affected by Earth. We profoundly influence vast areas because of our mobility and access to energy and technology. In turn, Earth's systems influence our activities in a most obvious way—these systems give us life, thus we study them in physical geography.

The Canadian Council for Geographic Education (CCGE) was established in 1993 to guide geographic education. CCGE is mandated to increase emphasis on geography at all levels of education by supporting geography teachers in the classroom and by facilitating national-level action to strengthen the position of geography in the school curricula. The organization also exists to improve geography teaching methods, to promote the flow of geographic knowledge, and to foster development of geographic skills. Finally, the CCGE works to promote public awareness of geography, the importance of geographic literacy, and geographic education. For a listing of some important geography organizations and their URLs, see Table 1.1.

We simplify the standards of geographic science using five important spatial themes: **location**, **region**, **human–Earth relationships**, **movement**, and **place**, which are illustrated and defined in Figure 1.1. *Geosystems* draws on each theme.

Geographic Analysis

Within these five geographic themes, geography is governed by a *method* rather than a specific body of knowledge, and the method is **spatial analysis**. Using this method, geography synthesizes (brings together) knowledge from many fields, integrating information to form a whole Earth concept. Geographers view phenomena as occurring in spaces and areas having distinctive characteristics. The language of geography reflects this spatial view: *space, territory, zone, pattern, distribution, place, location, region, sphere, province*, and *distance*. Geographers analyze the differences and similarities among places and locations.

Process, a set of actions or mechanisms that operate in some special order, governed by physical, chemical, and biological laws, is central to geographic analysis. As examples in *Geosystems*, numerous processes are involved in Earth's

vast water–atmosphere–weather system, or in continental crust movements and earthquake occurrences, or in ecosystem functions. Geographers use spatial analysis to examine how Earth's processes interact over space or area.

Therefore, **physical geography** is the *spatial analysis of all the physical elements and processes that make up the environment: energy, air, water, weather, climate, landforms, soils, animals, plants, microorganisms, and Earth itself*. We add to this the oldest theme in the geographic tradition, that of human activity. As a science, geographers employ the **scientific method**, a methodology important to physical geography. Focus Study 1.1 (pp. 8–9) explains this essential process of science.

The Geographic Continuum

Geography is eclectic, integrating a wide range of subject matter from diverse fields; virtually any subject can be examined geographically. Figure 1.2 shows a continuous distribution—a continuum—along which the content of geography is arranged. Disciplines in the physical and life sciences are at one end, and those in the human and cultural sciences are at the other. As the figure shows, various specialties within geography draw from these subject areas.

The continuum in Figure 1.2 reflects a basic duality, or split, within geography—*physical geography* versus *human/cultural geography*. Society parallels this duality. Humans sometimes think of themselves as exempt from physical Earth processes—like actors not paying attention to their stage, props, and lighting. We all depend on Earth's systems to provide oxygen, water, nutrients, energy, and materials to support life. The growing complexity of the human–Earth relation requires that we shift our study of geographic processes, and perhaps our link to Earth systems, toward the centre of the continuum in Figure 1.2 to attain a more *holistic*, or balanced, perspective—such is the thrust of *Geosystems*.

Table 1.1

A Few Geography Organizations	URL Addresses
Canadian Council for Geographic Education	http://www.ccge.org/ccge/english/default.asp
Canadian Association of Geographers	http://www.cag-acg.ca/en/
Canadian Geophysical Union	http://www.cgu-ugc.ca
Canadian Geoscience Council	http://www.geoscience.ca
Canadian Geomorphology Research Group	http://cgrg.geog.uvic.ca/index.html
Canadian Society of Soil Science	http://www.csss.ca/index.html
Royal Canadian Geographical Society	http://www.rcgs.org/
American Geographical Society	http://www.amergeog.org/
Association of American Geographers	http://www.aag.org/
National Council for Geographic Education	http://www.ncge.org/
National Geographic Society	http://www.nationalgeographic.com/
Institute of Australian Geographers	http://www.iag.org.au
Australian Geography Teachers Association	http://www.agta.asn.au/
European Geography Association	http://www.egea.eu/
Royal Geographical Society, Institute of British Geographers	http://www.rgs.org/
Complete global listing of geography organizations	http://www.geoggeol.fau.edu/Links/GeographicalSites.htm

Location

Absolute and relative location on Earth. Location answers the question *Where?*— the specific planetary address of a location. This road sign, posted along Bruce County Road 9 in Ontario, is located on the 45th parallel of latitude, halfway between the equator and the North Pole.

Region

Areas having uniform characteristics; how they form and change; their relation to other regions. A grain freighter moves through the Welland Canal in the Niagara region of southern Ontario, passing from Lake Ontario (75 m above sea level), rising to Lake Erie (174 m above sea level) in an "upstream" direction. Seven lifting locks bring vessels up 99 m in elevation, connecting the St. Lawrence Seaway and Atlantic with farms and markets in the Midwest and Prairies.

Human–Earth Relationships

Humans and the environment: resource exploitation, hazard perception, and environmental pollution and modification. A coal-fired power plant at Barentsburg on Spitsbergen Island in the Arctic Ocean adds greenhouse gases and pollution to the atmosphere.

Geographic Science

Place

Tangible and intangible living and nonliving characteristics that make each place unique. No two places on Earth are exactly alike. The coast of Cornwall in southwest England is a place of myth and legend. Here the ruins of Tintagel Castle sit starkly against the Celtic Sea. This was the site of Uther Pendragon's castle, and in myth where King Arthur was born. These coastal headlands have a rich and varied history, including the mining of slate from the bedrock beneath.

Movement

Communication, movement, circulation, migration, and diffusion across Earth's surface. Global interdependence links all regions and places. The radiating waves of energy in an Indian Ocean tsunami generated by a magnitude 9.3 earthquake off the coast of Sumatra, Indonesia, on December 26, 2004. Damage and loss of life exceeding 170,000 people resulted when waves hit distant shores.

FIGURE 1.1 Five themes of geographic science.
Definitions of five fundamental themes in geographic science with examples of each—location, region, human–Earth relationships, movement, and place. Drawing from your own experience, can you think of several more examples of each theme? [Location photo by Mary-Louise Byrne; Human–Earth Relationships, Region, and Place photos by Bobbé Christopherson; Movement *GFO-Satellite* image courtesy of NOAA, Laboratory for Satellite Altimetry.]

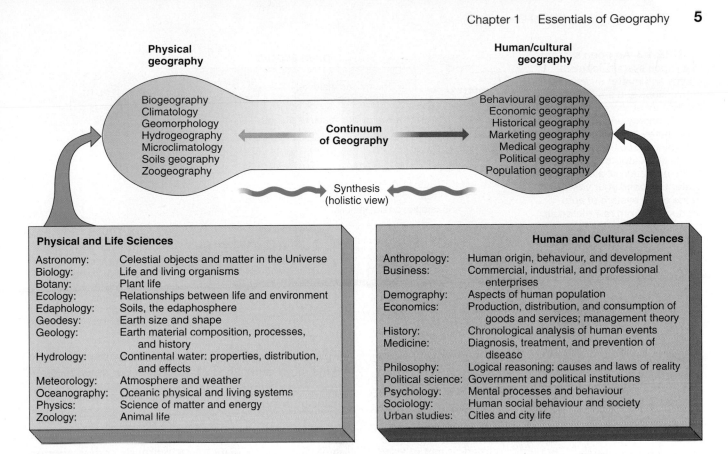

FIGURE 1.2 The content of geography.
Distribution of geographic content along a continuum (a continuous distribution). Geography derives subject matter from many different sciences. The focus of this book is physical geography, but we also integrate some human and cultural components. Synthesis of Earth topics and human topics is suggested by movement toward the middle of the continuum— a *holistic*, or balanced, view. Examine the subjects listed in the two boxes for any course you completed. Do you find any subjects you have taken? Think for a moment and recall any spatial aspects you remember studying in that course.

Earth Systems Concepts

The word *system* pervades our lives daily: "Check the car's cooling system"; "Is a broadband system available for my Internet browser?"; "How does the grading system work?"; "There is a weather system approaching." Systems of many kinds surround us. *Systems analysis* techniques began with studies of energy and temperature (thermodynamics) in the nineteenth century and were further developed in engineering during World War II. Today, geographers use systems methodology as an analytical tool. In this book's 4 parts and 21 chapters, content is organized along logical flow paths consistent with systems thinking.

Systems Theory

Simply stated, a **system** is any ordered, interrelated set of things and their attributes, linked by flows of energy and matter, as distinct from the surrounding environment outside the system. The elements within a system may be arranged in a series or interwoven with one another. A system comprises any number of subsystems. Within Earth's systems, both matter and energy are stored and retrieved and energy is transformed from one type to another. (Remember: *Matter* is mass that assumes a physical shape and occupies space; *energy* is a capacity to change the motion of, or to do work on, matter.)

Open Systems   Systems in nature are generally not self-contained: Inputs of energy and matter flow into the system, and outputs of energy and matter flow from the system. Such a system is an **open system**. Within a system, the parts function in an interrelated manner, acting together in a way that gives each system its character. Earth is an open system *in terms of energy*, because solar energy enters freely and heat energy leaves, going back into space. Most natural systems are open in terms of energy. Figure 1.3 schematically illustrates an open system and presents the inputs and outputs of an automobile as an example.

Most Earth systems are dynamic (energetic, in motion) because of the tremendous infusion of radiant energy from thermonuclear reactions deep within the Sun. This energy comes through the outermost edge of Earth's atmosphere to power terrestrial systems, being transformed along the way into various forms of energy, such as *kinetic energy* (of motion), *potential energy* (of position), or as chemical or mechanical energy. Eventually, Earth radiates this energy back to the cold vacuum of space as heat energy. Earth's interior is likewise a dynamic system, with a fluid core and physically

FIGURE 1.3 An open system. In an open system, inputs of energy and matter undergo conversions and are stored as the system operates. Outputs include energy and matter and heat energy (waste) that flow from the system. See how the various inputs and outputs are related to the operation of a car—an open system. Expand your viewpoint to the entire system of auto production, from raw materials, to assembly, to sales, to car accidents, to junkyards. Can you identify other open systems that you encounter in your daily life?

convecting mantle that influences crustal plates that are in motion as energy flows toward the surface.

Closed Systems   A system that is shut off from the surrounding environment so that it is self-contained is a **closed system**. Although such closed systems are rarely found in nature, Earth is essentially a closed system *in terms of physical matter and resources*—air, water, and material resources. The only exceptions are the slow escape of lightweight gases (such as hydrogen) from the atmosphere into space and the input of frequent but tiny meteors and cosmic and meteoric dust. Since the intial formation of

our planet, no significant quantities of new resources have entered the system. The fact that Earth is a closed material system makes recycling efforts inevitable if we want a sustainable global economy.

System Example   Figure 1.4 illustrates a simple open-flow system, using plant photosynthesis and respiration as an example. In *photosynthesis* (Figure 1.4a), plants use sunlight as an energy input and material inputs of water, nutrients, and carbon dioxide. The photosynthetic process converts these inputs to stored chemical energy in the form of plant sugars (carbohydrates). The process also

(a) Plant photosynthesis

(b) Plant respiration

FIGURE 1.4 A leaf is a natural open system.
A plant leaf provides an example of a natural open system. (a) In the process of photosynthesis, plants consume light, carbon dioxide (CO_2), nutrients, and water (H_2O), and produce outputs of oxygen (O_2) and carbohydrates (sugars) as stored chemical energy. (b) Plant respiration, illustrated here at night, approximately reverses this process and produces outputs of carbon dioxide (CO_2) and water (H_2O), using oxygen and consuming (oxidizing) carbohydrates to produce energy for cell operations.

releases an output from the plant system: the oxygen we breathe.

Reversing the process, plants derive energy for their operations from respiration. In *respiration*, the plant consumes inputs of chemical energy (carbohydrates) and oxygen and releases outputs of carbon dioxide, water, and heat energy into the environment (Figure 1.4b). Thus, a plant acts as an open system, in which both energy and materials freely flow into and out of the plant. (Photosynthesis and respiration processes are discussed further in Chapter 19.)

System Feedback   As a system operates, it generates outputs that influence its own operations. These outputs function as "information" that is returned to various points in the system via pathways called **feedback loops**. Feedback information can control (or at least guide) further system operations. In the plant's photosynthetic system (see Figure 1.4), any increase or decrease in daylength (sunlight availability), carbon dioxide, or water will produce feedback that elicits (causes) specific responses in the plant. For example, decreasing the water input will slow the growth process; increasing daylength will increase the growth process within limits.

If the feedback *information* discourages response in the system, it is **negative feedback**. *Further production in the system decreases the growth of the system.* Such negative feedback causes self-regulation in a natural system, stabilizing and maintaining the system. Think of a weight-loss diet—the human body is an open system. When you stand on the scales, the good or bad news reported about your weight both act as negative feedback to you. This, in turn, provides you with guidance (negative feedback) as to how inputs (food Calories) need to be adjusted, or how exercise and increased metabolism are needed to burn excess Calories.

If feedback *information* encourages increased response in the system, it is **positive feedback**—like good reviews affecting ticket sales for a film. *Further production in the system stimulates the growth of the system.* In finance, a compound interest-bearing account provides an example: The larger the account becomes, the more interest it earns, thus the larger the account becomes, and so on. Unchecked positive feedback in a system can create a runaway ("snowballing") condition. In natural systems, such unchecked growth will reach a critical limit, leading to instability, disruption, or death of organisms.

Think of the numerous devastating wildfires that occurred in Indonesia, Mexico, and Florida in 1998, and the western United States and Canada between 1999 and 2003, as examples of positive feedback. As the fires burned,

High Latitude Connection 1.1

Meltponds as Positive Feedback

Another example of positive feedback is the significant increase in meltponds in the polar regions—on icebergs, ice shelves, and the Greenland ice sheet. As explained in News Report 17.3, Chapter 17, meltponds are darker and reflect less sunlight (have a lower albedo) and therefore absorb more solar energy, which in turn melts more ice, which forms more meltponds, and so forth. Thus, a positive feedback system is in operation, further enhancing the effects of higher temperatures and warming trends.

Based on satellite images and aerial surveys, scientists determined a spatial increase in meltpond distribution of 400% between 2001 and 2003 across the Arctic, then slightly retreating through 2005 (Figure 1.1.1). Overall ice-mass losses from Greenland more than doubled between 1996 and 2005. The meltponds are symptomatic of climatic warming.

Note that throughout *Geosystems* you find these brief High Latitude Connection features. We continue this

FIGURE 1.1.1 High-latitude meltpond increase results from positive feedback.
Meltponds on the western region of the Greenland ice sheet in 2003. The darker water-saturated surface layer from melt and blue-coloured meltponds indicate significant increase in temperatures. [Image by MODIS sensor, *Terra* satellite, courtesy of MODIS Rapid Response Team, NASA/GSFC.]

feature in the book because the polar regions are experiencing dynamic changes in system operations that appear to be accelerating. Many people think these polar environs are

acting as our "miner's canary," that is, our early warning system. Watch for these points of applied geographic science in the chapters ahead.

The Scientific Method

The term *scientific method* may have an aura of complexity, but it shouldn't. The scientific method is simply the application of common sense in an organized and objective manner. A scientist observes, makes a general statement to summarize the observations, formulates a hypothesis, conducts experiments to test the hypothesis, and develops a theory and governing scientific laws. Sir Isaac Newton (1642–1727) developed this method of discovering the patterns of nature, although the term *scientific method* was applied later.

Scientists are curious about nature and appreciate the challenge of problem solving. Society depends on the discoveries of science to decipher mysteries, find solutions, and foster progress. *Complexity* dominates nature, making several outcomes possible as a system operates. Science serves an important function to reduce such uncertainty. Yet, the more knowledge we have, the more the uncertainty and awareness of other possible scenarios (outcomes and events) increase. This in turn demands more precise and aggressive science.

A problem for society occurs when scientific uncertainty fuels an antiscience viewpoint, whereas defining uncertainty is a by-product of discovery. As we realize scientific principles of complexity and chaos in natural and human-made systems, the need for critical thinking and the scientific method deepens in all aspects of life.

Steps in the Scientific Method

Follow the scientific method illustration in Figure 1.1.1 as you read. The scientific method begins with our perception of the real world and a determination of what we know, what we want to know, and the many unanswered questions that exist. Scientists who study the physical environment turn to nature for clues that they can observe and measure. They figure out what data are needed and begin to collect those data. Then, these observations and data are analyzed to identify coherent patterns that may

be present. This search for patterns requires *inductive reasoning*, or the process of drawing generalizations from specific facts. This step is important in modern Earth systems science, in which the goal is to understand *a whole functioning Earth*, rather than isolated, small compartments of information. Such understanding allows the scientist to construct models that simulate general operations of Earth systems.

If patterns are discovered, the researcher may formulate a *hypothesis*—a formal generalization of a principle. Examples include the planetesimal hypothesis, nuclear-winter hypothesis, and moisture-benefits-from-hurricanes hypothesis. Further observations are related to the general principles established by the hypothesis. Further data gathered may support or refute the hypothesis, or predictions made according to it may prove accurate or inaccurate. All these findings provide feedback to adjust data collection and model building and to refine the hypothesis statement. Verification of the hypothesis after exhaustive testing may lead to its elevation to the status of a *theory*.

A theory is constructed on the basis of several extensively tested hypotheses. Theories represent truly broad general principles—unifying concepts that tie together the laws that govern nature (for example, the theory of relativity, theory of evolution, atomic theory, Big Bang theory, stratospheric ozone depletion theory, or plate tectonics theory). A theory is a powerful device with which to understand both the order and chaos (disorder) in nature. Using a theory allows predictions to be made about things not yet known, the effects of which can be tested and verified or disproved through tangible evidence. The value of a theory is the continued observation, testing, understanding, and pursuit of knowledge that the theory stimulates. A general theory reinforces our perception of the real world, acting as positive feedback.

Pure science does not make value judgments. Instead, pure science provides people and their institutions with objective information on which to base their own value judgments. Social and political judgments about the applications of science are increasingly critical as Earth's natural systems respond to the impact of modern civilization. From Jane Lubchenco's 1997 AAAS Presidential Address:

> Science alone does not hold the power to achieve the goal of greater sustainability, but scientific knowledge and wisdom are needed to help inform decisions that will enable society to move toward that end.

The Method and Applied Science

The growing awareness that human activity is producing global change places increasing pressure on scientists to participate in decision making. Numerous editorials in scientific journals have called for such *applied science* involvement. F. Sherwood Rowland and Mario Molina provide an example, discussed in Chapter 3, for they first proposed a hypothesis that certain human-made chemicals caused damaging reactions in the stratosphere. They hypothesized in 1974—along with Paul Crutzen, who also contributed to these discoveries—that chlorine-containing products such as chlorofluorocarbons (CFCs), commonly used as aerosol propellants, refrigerants, foaming agents, and cleaning solvents, were depleting our protective stratospheric ozone (O_3) layer.

Subsequently, surface, atmosphere, and satellite measurements confirmed the photochemical reactions and provided data to map the real losses that were occurring and led to international treaties and agreements to ban the disruptive chemicals. In 1995, the Royal Swedish Academy of Sciences awarded these three scientists the Nobel Prize for chemistry for their pioneering research and for their direct involvement in later political change.

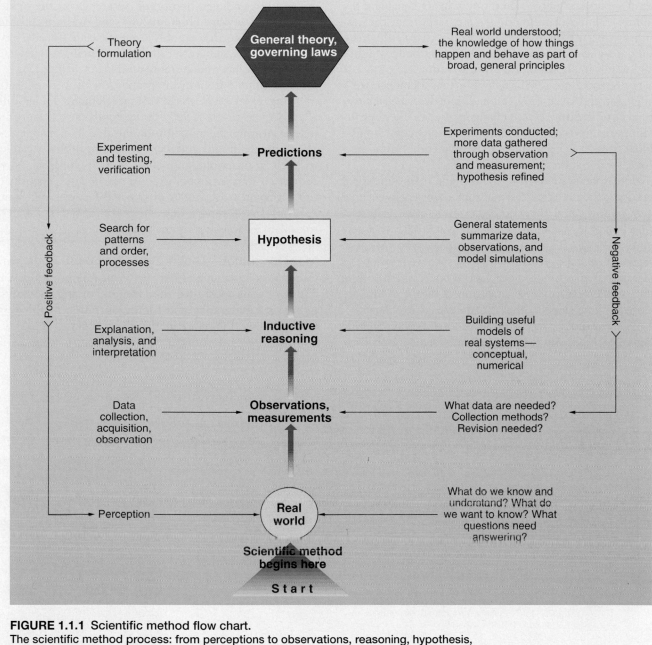

FIGURE 1.1.1 Scientific method flow chart.
The scientific method process: from perceptions to observations, reasoning, hypothesis, predictions, and possibly to general theory and natural laws.

they dried wet shrubs and green wood around the fire, thus providing more fuel for combustion. The greater the fire, the greater becomes the availability of fuel, and thus more fire is possible—a positive feedback for the fire. Control of the input of flammable fuel and oxygen is the key to extinguishing such fires. Knowing this process allows us to design strategies for controlling fuel availability, regulating excessive landscaping in vulnerable urban areas, and practicing "control burns."

Another example of positive feedback is the significant increase in meltponds on icebergs, ice shelves, and the Greenland ice sheet, as explained in our first High Latitude Connection and in Chapter 17.

Take a moment to assess negative and positive feedback in the automobile illustration in Figure 1.3. For instance, how would the inputs and outputs be affected if tailpipe exhaust emission standards are weakened or strengthened? What if the automobile is operated at high elevation? Or if the car is a sports utility vehicle (SUV) that weighs 2300 kg (5070 lb)? Or if the price of gasoline increases or decreases? Assess the effect of such changes on automobile system operations.

System Equilibrium Most systems maintain structure and character over time. An energy and material system that remains balanced over time, in which conditions are constant or recur, is in a *steady-state condition*. When the rates of inputs and outputs in the system are equal and the amounts of energy and matter in storage within the system are constant (or more realistically, as they fluctuate around a stable average, such as a person's body weight), the system is in **steady-state equilibrium**.

However, a steady-state system may demonstrate a changing trend over time, a condition described as **dynamic equilibrium**. These changing trends of either increasing or decreasing system operations may appear gradual. Figure 1.5 illustrates these two equilibrium conditions, steady-state and dynamic.

Note that systems try to maintain their functional operations; they tend to resist abrupt change. However, a system may reach a **threshold**, or *tipping point*, where it can no longer maintain its character, so it lurches to a new operational level. This abrupt change places the system in a *metastable equilibrium*. An example of such a condition is a landscape, such as a hillside or coastal bluff, which adjusts after a sudden landslide. A new equilibrium is eventually achieved among slope, materials, and energy over time.

This threshold concept raises concern in the scientific community, especially if some natural systems reach their tipping-point limits. The relatively sudden collapse of ice shelves surrounding a portion of Antarctica, or the sudden crack up of the Ward Hunt (in 2003) and Ayles (in 2005) ice shelves on the north coast of Ellesmere Island, Canada, serve as examples of systems at a threshold, changing to a new status, that of disintegration (more on this in Chapter 17).

As examples from biogeography, the bleaching (death) of living coral reefs worldwide accelerated dramatically after 1997; as much as 50% of the corals on Earth are ailing or nearing collapse (more on this in Chapter 16). Warming conditions and some pollution in the ocean led to such a threshold and coral system collapse. News Report 1.1 looks at a tipping point reached by a majority of the harlequin frog species of tropical Central and South America. In this report, note the power of systems analysis to explain what is causing these extinctions.

Mount Pinatubo—Global System Impact   A dramatic example of interactions between volcanic eruptions and Earth systems illustrates the strength of spatial analysis in physical geography and the organization of this textbook. Mount Pinatubo in the Philippines erupted violently in 1991, injecting 13-18 million metric tons (15–20

Coastal systems pass a threshold.

FIGURE 1.5 System equilibria: steady-state and dynamic.
(a) A steady-state equilibrium over time; system operations fluctuate around a stable average. Other systems are in a condition of dynamic equilibrium, with an increasing or decreasing operational trend as in (b). Rather than changing gradually, some systems may reach a *threshold* where system operations lurch (change abruptly) to a new set of relations—a "tipping point." Landslides along a coastline destroyed homes and property as a threshold was reached and the bluffs collapsed. [Inset photo by Sam Sargent/Liaison Agency Inc.]

News Report 1.1

Frogs at a Tipping Point—Check the System

Global climate change is pressing systems to their threshold. Many amphibian species are threatened by these changes. The "Declining Amphibian Population Task Force," founded in 1991 and merged with the IUCN (World Conservation Union) Amphibian Group in 2006, is a response to this growing crisis. Scientific understanding of frog population declines from habitat loss and pollution, and now rising temperatures, is emerging.

The key to unraveling what was happening to harlequin frogs (*Atelopus varius*; Figure 1.1.1) and golden toad (*Bufo periglenes*) species in the Monteverde Cloud Forest Reserve, Costa Rica, and elsewhere in Central and South America, was a consideration of climate change and how this alters optimum conditions for the transmission of diseases and pathogens. Research had to uncover complex synergistic interactions (combined actions that magnify results) in physical and biological systems. One infectious agent, the *chytrid fungus* (*Ductruchochytrium dendrobactidis*), was spreading as thermal-optimum conditions were reached in its mid-elevation range (1000 m to 2400 m; 621 mi–1491 mi) in the mountain-cloud forest. Here is how system operations and feedbacks produced this species failure.

Human-forced climate change is increasing the temperature of the ocean and atmosphere. Higher temperatures cause higher evaporation rates. However, even though humidity (water-vapour content of the air) is higher, relative humidity is lower because the air can absorb more, which affects the condensation level (see Chapter 7). As the warm, moist air moves onshore and reaches the mountains, the air mass

FIGURE 1.1.1 Harlequin frog extinction alarm.
About two-thirds of harlequin frog species went extinct over the last two decades as a result of climate change, specifically increasing temperatures. The frog is nearing extinction due to a pathogen that thrives in the climate-altered ecosystem. [Photo by Michael & Patricia Fogden/Corbis. All rights reserved.]

lifts, cools, and condensation occurs at higher elevations than before (see Chapter 8). Increasing levels of air pollution provide more condensation nuclei for cloud droplets to form (see Chapters 3 and 7).

Increased clouds affect the daily temperature range: clouds at night, acting like insulation, raise nighttime minimum temperatures, whereas clouds during the day act as reflectors, sending sunlight back into space and lowering daytime maximum temperatures (see Chapter 4). Nighttime minimum temperatures are increasing more rapidly than daytime maximums. The chytrid fungus does best when temperatures are between 17°C and 25°C, stops growing at 28°C, and dies at 30°C. The cloud cover keeps the daytime maximum below 25°C (77°F) at the leaf-litter and moss-ground cover microscale; without cloud cover the surface reaches 30°C. In these more favorable conditions the disease pathogen flourishes.

Harlequin frogs have moist, porous skin that the fungus penetrates, killing the frog. Between 1986 and 2006, approximately 67% of the 110 known species of harlequin frogs went extinct—extinction is forever. The IUCN Red List classifies the

remaining population as "Critically Endangered."

From this example can you see the power of systems analysis? Global warming intensifies the hydrologic cycle, raises air and water temperatures, and increases evaporation, all of which changes the nature of cloud formations and alters daily temperature patterns. These changes impact ecological systems by increasing the range and number of infectious disease pathogens, which attack species and ultimately end their existence. A summary of the research by J. Alan Pounds, and his team of scientists, concluded with a sobering thought:

The powerful synergy between pathogen transmission and climate change should give us cause for concern about human health in a warmer world. . . . The frogs are sending an alarm call to all concerned about the future of biodiversity and the need to protect the greatest of all open-access resources—the atmosphere.*

*A. Blaustein and A. Dobson, "A message from the frogs," summary of J. A. Ponds, et. al., "Widespread amphibian extinctions from epidemic disease driven by global warming," *Nature* 439 (January 12, 2006): p. 144.

---

million tons) of ash and sulfuric acid mist into the upper atmosphere (Figure 1.6). This was the second greatest eruption during the twentieth century; Mount Katmai in Alaska (1912) was the only one greater. The eruption materials from Mount Pinatubo affected Earth systems in several ways, which are noted on the map.

As you progress through this book, you see the story of Mount Pinatubo and its implications woven through eight chapters: Chapter 1 (systems theory), Chapter 4 (effects on energy budgets in the atmosphere), Chapter 6 (satellite images of the spread of debris by atmospheric winds), Chapter 10 (temporary effect on global atmospheric

Eruption cloud spread to 500-kilometre diameter, 35-km height.

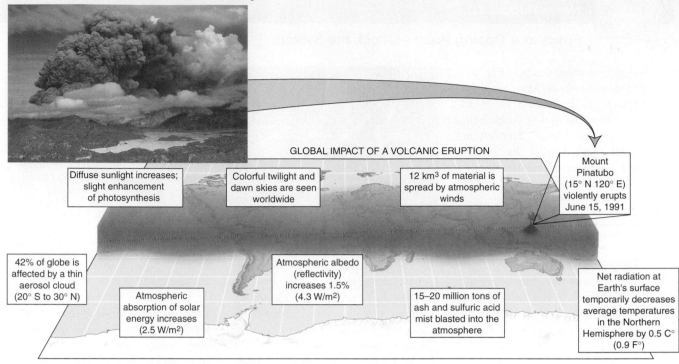

GLOBAL IMPACT OF A VOLCANIC ERUPTION

Diffuse sunlight increases; slight enhancement of photosynthesis

Colorful twilight and dawn skies are seen worldwide

12 km³ of material is spread by atmospheric winds

Mount Pinatubo (15° N 120° E) violently erupts June 15, 1991

42% of globe is affected by a thin aerosol cloud (20° S to 30° N)

Atmospheric absorption of solar energy increases (2.5 W/m²)

Atmospheric albedo (reflectivity) increases 1.5% (4.3 W/m²)

15–20 million tons of ash and sulfuric acid mist blasted into the atmosphere

Net radiation at Earth's surface temporarily decreases average temperatures in the Northern Hemisphere by 0.5 C° (0.9 F°)

FIGURE 1.6 The eruption of Mount Pinatubo.
The 1991 Mount Pinatubo eruption affected the Earth–atmosphere system on a global scale. Geographers and other scientists use the latest technology to study how such eruptions affect the atmosphere's dynamic equilibrium. For a summary of the impacts from this eruption, refer to **Chapter 12**. [Inset photo by Van Cappellen/REA/SABA.]

temperatures), Chapters 11 and 12 (volcanic processes), and Chapter 17 (past climatic effects of volcanoes).

Systems in *Geosystems*   To further illustrate the systems organization in this textbook, notice that chapters and portions of chapters are presented in simple sequences organized around the flow of energy, materials, and information (Figure 1.7). This book presents subjects in the same sequence in which they occur in nature. In this way, topics follow a logical progression that unfolds according to the energy and material flows within individual systems or with time and the flow of events.

The sequence (Figure 1.7a)—*input* (components and driving force), *actions* (movements, processes, and storage changes), *outputs* (results and consequences), and *human impacts/impact on humans* (measure of relevance)—is seen in Part I as an example. The Sun begins Chapter 2: The energy flows across space to the top of the atmosphere and through the atmosphere to the surface and surface energy budgets (Chapters 3 and 4). Then we look at the outputs of temperature (Chapter 5) and winds and ocean currents (Chapter 6). Note the same logical systems flow in the other three parts and in each chapter of this text—Part II and Chapter 16 also are shown as examples.

Models of Systems   A **model** is a simplified, idealized representation of part of the real world. Models are designed with varying degrees of generalization. In your life, you may have built or drawn a model of something that was

a simplification of the real thing—such as a model airplane or model house. Physical geographers use simple system models to demonstrate complex things in the environment.

The simplicity of a model makes a system easier to understand and to simulate in experiments (for example, the leaf model in Figure 1.4). A good example is a model of the *hydrologic system*, which models Earth's entire water system, its related energy flows, and atmosphere, surface, and subsurface environments through which water moves.

Adjusting the variables in a model produces differing conditions and allows predictions of possible system operations. A general circulation model (GCM) of the atmosphere (see Figure 10.31), operated by the Goddard Institute, accurately predicted the effect of Mount Pinatubo's ash on the atmosphere, the lowering and subsequent recovery of global air temperatures, and continues to produce accurate temperature forecasts for the future. However, predictions are only as good as the assumptions and accuracy built into the model. It is best to view a model for what it is—a simplification to help us understand complex processes.

We discuss many *system models* in this text, including the hydrologic system, water balance, surface energy budgets, earthquakes and faulting as outputs of Earth systems, river drainage basins, glacier mass budgets, soil profiles, and various ecosystems. Computer-based models are in use to study most natural systems—from the upper atmosphere, to climate change, to Earth's interior. Each of Earth's four "spheres" represents such a model of Earth's systems.

FIGURE 1.7 The systems in *Geosystems*.
(a) Chapters, sections, and topics are organized around simple flow systems, or around time and the flow of events, at various scales. (b) This systems structure as it is applied to Parts I and II. As a chapter example, turn to Chapter 16 on coastal processes and see how the chapter is organized using the systems flow.

Earth's Four "Spheres"

Earth's surface is a vast area of 500 million square kilometres (193 million square miles) where four immense open systems interact. Figure 1.8 shows a simple model of three **abiotic** (nonliving) systems overlapping to form the realm of the **biotic** (living) system. The abiotic spheres are the *atmosphere*, *hydrosphere*, and *lithosphere*. The biotic sphere is the *biosphere*. Because these four systems are not independent units in nature, their boundaries are really transition zones rather than sharp barriers.

As noted in the figure, these four spheres form the part structure in which chapters are grouped in this text. The various arrows in the figure show that content in each part and among chapters interrelates as we build our discussion of Earth's abiotic and biotic systems.

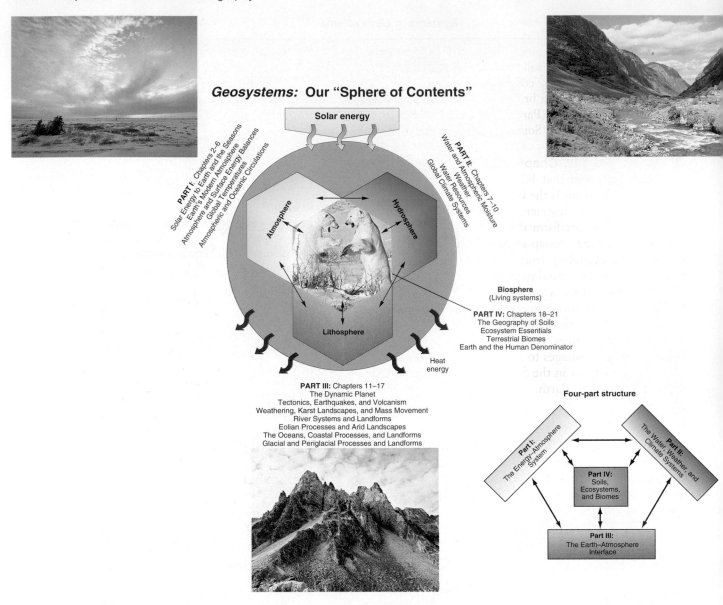

FIGURE 1.8 Earth's four spheres.
Each sphere is a model of vast Earth systems. This four-part structure is the organizational framework for *Geosystems.* [Photos by Bobbé Christopherson.]
    Part I—Atmosphere: The Energy–Atmosphere System
    Part II—Hydrosphere: The Water, Weather, and Climate Systems
    Part III—Lithosphere: The Earth–Atmosphere Interface
    Part IV—Biosphere: Soils, Ecosystems, and Biomes

Atmosphere (Part I, Chapters 2–6) The **atmosphere** is a thin, gaseous veil surrounding Earth, held to the planet by the force of gravity. Formed by gases arising from within Earth's crust and interior and the exhalations of all life over time, the lower atmosphere is unique in the Solar System. It is a combination of nitrogen, oxygen, argon, carbon dioxide, water vapour, and trace gases.

Hydrosphere (Part II, Chapters 7–10) Earth's waters exist in the atmosphere, on the surface, and in the crust near the surface. Collectively, these waters form the **hydrosphere**. That portion of the hydrosphere that is frozen is the **cryosphere**—ice sheets, ice caps and fields, glaciers, ice shelves, sea ice, and subsurface ground

ice—and topics related to it are covered in chapters in all four parts of the book. Water of the hydrosphere exists in all three states: liquid, solid (the frozen cryosphere), and gaseous (water vapour). Water occurs in two general chemical conditions, fresh and saline (salty). It exhibits important heat-storage properties. Water is an extraordinary solvent. Water is the medium of life. Among the planets in the Solar System, only Earth possesses surface water in such quantity, adding to Earth's uniqueness among the planets.

Lithosphere (Part III, Chapters 11–17) Earth's crust and a portion of the upper mantle directly below the crust form the **lithosphere**. The crust is quite brittle compared with the layers deep beneath the surface, which move slowly in response to an uneven distribution of heat energy and pressure. In a broad sense, the term *lithosphere* sometimes refers to the entire solid planet. The soil layer is the *edaphosphere* and generally covers Earth's land surfaces. In this text, soils represent a bridge between the lithosphere (Part III) and biosphere (Part IV) and are featured in the first chapter in Part IV, "Soils, Ecosystems, and Biomes."

Biosphere (Part IV, Chapters 18–20)   The intricate, interconnected web that links all organisms with their physical environment is the **biosphere**. Sometimes called the **ecosphere**, the biosphere is the area in which physical and chemical factors form the context of life. The biosphere exists in the overlap among the abiotic, or nonliving, spheres, extending from the seafloor and even the upper layers of the crustal rock to about 8 km (5 mi) into the atmosphere. Life is sustainable within these natural limits. In turn, life processes have powerfully shaped the other three spheres through various interactive processes. The biosphere evolves, reorganizes itself at times, faces extinctions, and manages to flourish. Earth's biosphere is the only one known in the Solar System; thus, life as we know it is unique to Earth.

A Spherical Planet

We all have heard that some people believed Earth to be flat. Yet Earth's *sphericity*, or roundness, is not as modern a concept as many think. For instance, more than two millennia ago, the Greek mathematician and philosopher Pythagoras (ca. 580–500 B.C.) determined through observation that Earth is spherical. We do not know what observations led Pythagoras to this conclusion. Can you guess at what he saw to deduce Earth's roundness?

He might have noticed ships sailing beyond the horizon and apparently sinking below the water's surface, only to arrive back at port with dry decks. Perhaps he noticed Earth's curved shadow cast on the lunar surface during an eclipse of the Moon. He might have deduced that the Sun and Moon are not just the flat disks they appear to be in the sky, but are spherical, and that Earth must be a sphere as well.

Earth's sphericity was generally accepted by the educated populace as early as the first century A.D. Christopher Columbus, for example, knew he was sailing around a sphere in 1492; that is one reason why he thought he had arrived in the East Indies.

Earth as a Geoid   Until 1687, the spherical-perfection model was a basic assumption of **geodesy**, the science that determines Earth's shape and size by surveys and mathematical calculations. But in that year, Sir Isaac Newton postulated that Earth, along with the other planets, could not be perfectly spherical. Newton reasoned that the more-rapid rotational speed at the equator—the equator being farthest from the central axis of the planet and therefore moving faster—would produce an equatorial bulge as centrifugal force pulls Earth's surface outward. He was convinced that Earth is slightly misshapen into what he termed an *oblate spheroid*, or more correctly, an *oblate ellipsoid* (*oblate* means "flattened"), with the oblateness occurring at the poles.

Today, Earth's equatorial bulge and its polar oblateness are universally accepted and confirmed with tremendous precision by satellite observations. The "geoidal epoch" is our modern era of Earth measurement because Earth is a **geoid**, meaning literally that "the shape of Earth is Earth-shaped." Imagine Earth's geoid as a sea-level surface that is extended uniformly worldwide, beneath the continents. Both heights on land and depths in the oceans are measured from this hypothetical surface. Think of the geoid surface as a balance among the gravitational attraction of Earth's mass, the distribution of water and ice along its surface, and the centrifugal pull caused by Earth's rotation.

Figure 1.9 gives Earth's average polar and equatorial circumferences and diameters. The Greek geographer, astronomer, and librarian Eratosthenes (ca. 276–195 B.C.) first measured Earth's polar circumference more than 2200 years ago. The ingenious reasoning by which he arrived at his calculation follows.

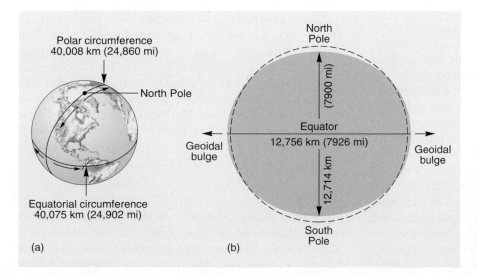

(a)   (b)

FIGURE 1.9 Earth's dimensions.
Earth's equatorial and polar circumference (a) and diameter (b). The dashed line is a perfect circle for reference to Earth's geoid.

FIGURE 1.10 Eratosthenes' calculation. Eratosthenes' work teaches the value of observing carefully and integrating all observations with previous learning. Calculating Earth's circumference required application of his knowledge of Earth–Sun relationships, geometry, and geography. (Several values can be used for the distance of a Greek stadium—the 185 m used here represents an average value.)

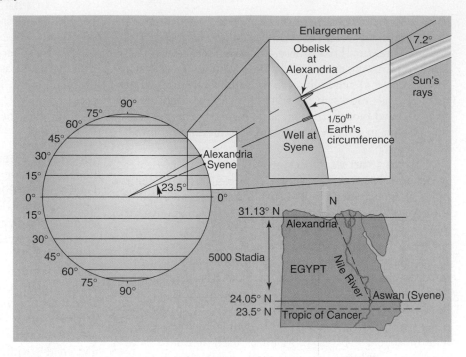

Measuring Earth in 247 B.C.

Foremost among early geographers, Eratosthenes served as the librarian of Alexandria in Egypt during the third century B.C. He was in a position of scientific leadership, for Alexandria's library was the finest in the ancient world. Among his achievements was calculating Earth's polar circumference to a high level of accuracy, quite a feat for 247 B.C. Here's how he did it. As you read, follow along on Figure 1.10.

Travelers told Eratosthenes that on June 21 they saw the Sun's rays shine directly to the bottom of a well at Syene, the location of present-day Aswan, Egypt. This meant that the Sun was directly overhead on that day. North of Syene in Alexandria, Eratosthenes knew from his own observations that the Sun's rays never were directly overhead, even at noon on June 21. This day is the longest day of the year and the day on which the noon Sun is at its northernmost position in the sky. He knew objects in Alexandria, unlike objects in Syene, always cast a noontime shadow. Using his knowledge of geometry, Eratosthenes conducted an experiment to explain the different observations.

In Alexandria at noon on June 21, he measured the angle of a shadow cast by an obelisk (a perpendicular column). Knowing the height of the obelisk and measuring the length of the Sun's shadow from its base, he solved the triangle for the angle of the Sun's noon rays, which he determined to be 7.2° off from directly overhead. However, at Syene on the same day, the angle of the Sun's rays was 0° from a perpendicular, arriving from directly overhead.

Geometric principles told Eratosthenes that the distance on the ground between Alexandria and Syene formed an arc of Earth's circumference equal to the angle of the Sun's rays at Alexandria. Since 7.2° is roughly 1/50 of the 360° (360° ÷ 7.2° = 50) in Earth's total circumference, he knew the distance between Alexandria and Syene must represent approximately of Earth's total polar circumference.

Next, Eratosthenes determined the surface distance between the two cities as 5000 stadia. A *stadium*, a Greek unit of measure, equals approximately 185 m (607 ft). He then multiplied 5000 stadia by 50 to determine that Earth's polar circumference is about 250,000 stadia. Eratosthenes' calculations convert to roughly 46,250 km (28,738 mi), which is remarkably close to the correct value of 40,008 km (24,860 mi) for Earth's polar circumference. Not bad for 247 B.C.!

Location and Time on Earth

An essential for geographic science is an internationally accepted, coordinated grid system to determine location on Earth. The terms *latitude* and *longitude* were in use on maps as early as the first century A.D., with the concepts themselves dating back to Eratosthenes and others.

The geographer, astronomer, and mathematician Ptolemy (ca. A.D. 90–168) contributed greatly to modern maps, and many of his terms and configurations are still used today. Ptolemy divided the circle into 360 degrees (360°), with each degree having 60 minutes (60′) and each minute having 60 seconds (60″) in a manner adapted from the ancient Babylonians. He located places using these degrees, minutes, and seconds. However, the precise length of a degree of latitude and a degree of longitude remained unresolved for the next 17 centuries.

Latitude

Latitude *is an angular distance north or south of the equator*, measured from the centre of Earth (Figure 1.11a). On a map or globe, the lines designating these angles of latitude run east and west, parallel to the equator (Figure 1.11b).

YOUR ACCESS TO SUCCESS

Welcome to the Companion Website for
Geosystems, Second Canadian Edition
by
Robert W. Christopherson
and Mary-Louise Byrne

Chapter 1: Essentials of Geography

Chapter 2: Solar Energy to Earth and the Seasons

Chapter 3: Earth's Modern Atmosphere

Chapter 4: Atmosphere and Surface Energy Balances

Chapter 5: Global Temperatures

Students with new copies of *Geosystems,* Second Canadian Edition **have full access to the book's** Companion Website—a 24/7 study tool with review exercises, web destinations, and other features designed to help you make the most of your study time.

Just follow the easy website registration steps listed below...

To Access Your Online Resources for the First Time
You will need to register online using a computer with an internet connection and a web browser. This process takes just a couple of minutes, and needs to be completed only once.

Registering for access

1. Go to *www.pearsoned.ca/christopherson* and select the cover or title of your book if there are several to choose from.
2. Click on **Register.**
3. Follow the onscreen instructions to redeem your access code and to create a user account (code found underneath the metallic strip, below). If you need help during the registration process, simply click **Need Help?**
4. Once your personal login name and password have been confirmed, you can begin using your online resources.

Logging into the website

1. You can log into the website at any time by returning to *www.pearsoned.ca/christopherson,* selecting your textbook if there are more than one to choose from, and logging in as a **Returning User.**
2. Enter the login name and password you created during the registration process and click **Log In.**

If your instructor gave you a Class ID...

Complete the steps below only if your instructor provides you with a Class ID (looks like cm130412) and instructs you to join the online class. When you join an online class, the results of your work will also be viewable by your instructor

1. Log into the website and click **Join a Class.**
2. Enter the Class ID and click **Next.**
3. Confirm your instructor's name and class information and click **Next.**
4. Click **Enter Class Now** from the Class Confirmation page.

If you need technical assistance with registration, or if you would like to ask a question or submit feedback, you can visit our Customer Technical Support website at http://247.pearsoned.com to submit an online support request or use the online chat service.

- Email assistance available 24 hours a day, 7 days a week
- Chat service hours are 08:00 AM to 08:00 PM EST, Monday through Friday, and 05:00 PM to 12:00 AM on Sunday

Grade Tracker supports the following operating systems: Windows XP, Windows Vista, Mac OS 10.3x and 10.4x.

Grade Tracker supports the following web browsers: Internet Explorer 6.0 (XP only), Internet Explorer 7.0, Firefox 2.0, Safari 1.3 (Mac)X 10.3x only), Safari 2.0 (Mac OS 10.4x only)

ISBN-13: 978-0-13-504631-9
ISBN-10: 0-13-504631-9

Your Access Code is:

CSWCGS-JEDDA-HAVEL-MANNA-BUSBY-HONES

FIGURE 1.11 Parallels of latitude.
(a) Latitude is measured in degrees north or south of the equator, which is 0°. Earth's poles are at 90°. Note the measurement of 49° latitude. (b) These angles of latitude determine parallels along Earth's surface. Do you know your present latitude?

Because Earth's equator divides the distance between the North Pole and the South Pole exactly in half, it is assigned the value of 0° latitude. Thus, latitude increases from the equator northward to the North Pole, at 90° north latitude, and southward to the South Pole, at 90° south latitude.

A line connecting all points along the same latitudinal angle is a **parallel**. In the figure, an angle of 49° north latitude is measured, and, by connecting all points at this latitude, we have the 49th parallel. Thus, *latitude* is the name of the angle (49° north latitude), *parallel* names the line (49th parallel), and both indicate distance north of the equator. The 49th parallel is a significant one in the Western Hemisphere, for it forms the boundary between Canada and the United States from Lake of the Woods on the Ontario–Manitoba border to the Pacific Ocean.

Latitude is readily determined by observing *fixed celestial objects* such as the Sun or the stars, a method dating to ancient times. During daylight hours, the angle of the Sun above the horizon indicates the observer's latitude, after adjustment is made for the season and for the time of day. Because Polaris (the North Star) is almost directly overhead at

the North Pole, persons anywhere in the Northern Hemisphere can determine their latitude at night simply by sighting Polaris and measuring its angle above the local horizon. The angle of elevation of Polaris above the horizon equals the latitude of the observation point.

In the Southern Hemisphere, Polaris cannot be seen, because it is below the horizon. Instead, latitude measurement south of the equator is accomplished by sighting on a constellation that points to a celestial location above the South Pole. This indicator constellation is the Southern Cross (*Crux Australis*). Tracking the location of the magnetic North Pole is the focus of News Report 1.2.

Latitudinal Geographic Zones Natural environments differ dramatically from the equator to the poles. These differences result from the amount of solar energy received, which varies by latitude and season of the year. As a convenience, geographers identify *latitudinal geographic zones* as regions with fairly consistent qualities. "Lower latitudes" are those nearer the equator, whereas "higher latitudes" are those nearer the poles.

Figure 1.12 portrays these zones, their locations, and their names: *equatorial* and *tropical, subtropical, midlatitude, subarctic* or *subantarctic*, and *arctic* or *antarctic*. These generalized latitudinal zones are useful for reference and comparison, but they do not have rigid boundaries; rather, think of them as transitioning one to another.

The *Tropic of Cancer* (about 23.5° north parallel) and the *Tropic of Capricorn* (about 23.5° south parallel) are the most extreme northern and southern parallels that experience perpendicular (directly overhead) rays of the Sun at local noon. When the Sun arrives overhead at these tropics, it marks the first day of summer in each hemisphere. (Further discussion of the tropics is in Chapter 2.) The *Arctic Circle* (about 66.5° north parallel) and the *Antarctic Circle* (about 66.5° south parallel) are the parallels farthest from the poles that still experience 24 uninterrupted hours of night, including dawn and twilight, during local winter or of day during local summer. There are many ways to define latitudinal geographic zones. News Report 1.3 outlines how Statistics Canada attempts to quantify the concept of north.

Longitude

Longitude *is an angular distance east or west of a point on Earth's surface*, measured from the centre of Earth (Figure 1.13a). On a map or globe, the lines designating these angles of longitude run north and south (Figure 1.13b). A line connecting all points along the same longitude is a **meridian**. In the figure, a longitudinal angle of 60° E is measured. These meridians run at right angles (90°) to all parallels, including the equator.

Thus, *longitude* is the name of the angle, *meridian* names the line, and both indicate distance east or west of an arbitrary **prime meridian**—a meridian designated as 0° (Figure 1.13b). Earth's prime meridian passes through the old Royal Observatory at Greenwich, England, as set by treaty—the *Greenwich prime meridian*.

News Report 1.2

The Coordinates of the North

What is North and where is it located? There are several ways to measure the most northern point of the planet. The first method is to coordinate the north geographic pole—the axial pole centred where the meridians of longitude converge. This is *true north* and does not change over time.

The second way to measure North is by use of magnetic north (the direction a compass needle points). At the *North Magnetic Pole*, Earth's magnetic field is directed vertically downward (the magnetic dip) relative to Earth's surface. This is the observed magnetic pole, located and mapped by magnetic surveys. As the magnetic field of Earth changes, the North Magnetic Pole slowly drifts across the Canadian Arctic. Scientists have traced a long history of change in the location of the North Magnetic Pole (Figure 1.2.1).

The Geological Survey of Canada (GSC) tracks the motion of the North Magnetic Pole by periodically carrying out magnetic surveys to locate the pole's location. Surveys are collaborative efforts between the GSC and the Bureau de Recherches Géologiques et Minières (BRGM), France. These surveys establish that the pole is moving northwest at approximately 40 km per year. The observed positions for 2001–2006 and estimated position for 2007 are given in Table 1.2.1.

The third method to coordinate North is through the use of the *North Geomagnetic Pole*. This is a mathematical model of Earth's magnetic field. The Canadian Geomagnetic Reference Field (CGRF) is a mathematical model of the geomagnetic field over Canada. It is produced by synthesizing numerous observations—made between 1960 and 1999—of the magnetic field on the ground, at sea, in the air, and at satellite altitudes. This model is run periodically to refine locations for the time interval 1960 to 2005. Values of magnetic declination, or any other magnetic field measurement over Canada and adjacent areas, are obtained using the Magnetic Information Retrieval Program (MIRP)

FIGURE 1.2.1 The location of the North Magnetic Pole from 1831 to 2007.
The geographic location of the North Magnetic Pole changes with variations in Earth's magnetic field. [Used by permission of the Minister of Public Works and Government Services Canada and Natural Resources Canada, Geological Survey of Canada.]

and the CGRF. Outside Canada, MIRP automatically uses the International Geomagnetic Reference Field (IGRF) to calculate magnetic field values. At present, the north geomagnetic pole position is 79.3° N 71.5° W and the south geomagnetic pole position is 79.3° S 108.5° E. These positions are used frequently to generate the geomagnetic coordinate system.

Table 1.2.1	Coordinates of the North Magnetic Pole 2001 to 2007	
Year	**Latitude (°N)**	**Longitude (°W)**
2001	81.3	110.8
2002	81.6	111.6
2003	82.0	112.4
2004	82.3	113.4
2005	82.7	114.4
2006	83.9	119.9
2007	84.4	121.7

Source: Reproduced with the permission of the Minister of Public Works and Government Services Canada; Natural Resources Canada, Geological Survey of Canada, see http://gsc.nrcan.gc.ca/geomag/nmp/northpole_e.php.

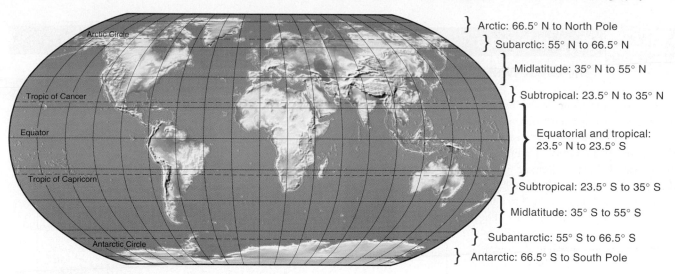

FIGURE 1.12 Latitudinal geographic zones.
Geographic zones are generalizations that characterize various regions by latitude. Think of these as transitional into one another over broad areas.

Determination of Latitude and Longitude Table 1.2 compares the length of latitude and longitude degrees. Because meridians of longitude converge toward the poles, the actual distance on the ground spanned by a degree of longitude is greatest at the equator (where meridians separate to their widest distance apart) and diminishes to zero at the poles (where meridians converge). In comparison, note the consistent distance represented by a degree of latitude from equator to poles.

We noted that latitude is determined easily by sighting the Sun or the North Star or by using the Southern Cross as a pointer. In contrast, a method of accurately determining longitude, especially at sea, remained a major difficulty in navigation until the late 1700s. The key to measuring the longitude of a place lies in accurately knowing time. The

relation between time and longitude and an exciting chapter in human discovery is the topic of Focus Study 1.2.

Today, using a handheld instrument that reads radio signals from satellites, you can accurately calibrate latitude, longitude, and elevation. This is the **Global Positioning System (GPS)** technology. News Report 1.4 discusses how GPS works and the dramatic applications of GPS.

Great Circles and Small Circles

Great circles and small circles are important concepts that help summarize latitude and longitude (Figure 1.14). A **great circle** is any circle of Earth's circumference whose centre coincides with the centre of Earth. An infinite number of great circles can be drawn on Earth. Every meridian

(text continued on page 23)

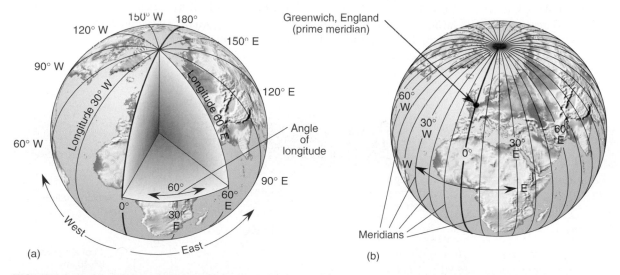

(a)

(b)

FIGURE 1.13 Meridians of longitude.
(a) Longitude is measured in degrees east or west of a 0° starting line, the prime meridian. Note the measurement of 60° E longitude. (b) Angles of longitude measured from the prime meridian determine other meridians. The prime meridian is drawn from the North Pole through the Royal Observatory in Greenwich, England, to the South Pole. North America is west of Greenwich; therefore, it is in the Western Hemisphere. Do you know your present longitude?

News Report 1.3

The Great White *North*?

In Canada, the concept of *north* is something that pervades our national identity. But, how far north is north? When are you south? Traditionally, north was defined as latitude greater than 60° N. A team of geographers at Statistics Canada collaborated to define north in a more detailed manner. They began with the concept of *nordicity*—the degree of "northerliness," a quantitative measure of place that was first calculated in the 1970s. The team proposed a new, inclusive definition of the concept of north by examining a wide range of variables, including physical characteristics of climate and biota as well as social and cultural measures.

The results of the study are summarized in a map that illustrates four zones: the north, the north transition, the south transition, and the south (Figure 1.3.1). The majority of Canadians live in the south and south transition zones—there are no large urban centres in the north or the north transition zones. Divisions between zones do not simply follow lines of latitude, but deviate to the north or south in various parts of the country.

Using this index of *northerliness*, Labrador, the northern parts of Québec, Ontario, Manitoba, Saskatchewan, Alberta, and a portion of northern British

FIGURE 1.3.1 A new definition of north.
The Statistics Canada definition of north and south indicators with boundary lines drawn to reflect average values of northerliness based on physical, biological, social, economic, and cultural measures. In which region do you live? Do your perceptions agree with Statistics Canada? [Adapted from *Delineation of Canada's North: An Examination of the North–South Relationship in Canada*, catalogue 92F0138, February 3, 2000, map 4.]

Columbia qualify as "*the north*" even though they lie south of 60° N, a traditional boundary line. The study is important because it emphasizes the idea of "the north" as a concept rather than a geographic area. There is no clearly demarcated line that separates north from south, but a transition from Canada south to Canada north that extends in a broad band across the country. The idea of the transition zones was intended to deal with comparisons of "north" and "south" that may interfere with recognition of the interesting physical, social, economic, and cultural differences within northern regions.

Table 1.2	Physical Distances Represented by Degrees of Latitude and Longitude			

| | Latitude Degree | | Longitude Degree | |
| | Length | | Length | |
Latitudinal Location	**km**	**(mi)**	**km**	**(mi)**
90° (poles)	111.70	(69.41)	0	(0)
60°	111.42	(69.23)	55.80	(34.67)
50°	111.23	(69.12)	71.70	(44.55)
40°	111.04	(69.00)	85.40	(53.07)
30°	110.86	(68.89)	96.49	(59.96)
0° (equator)	110.58	(68.71)	111.32	(69.17)

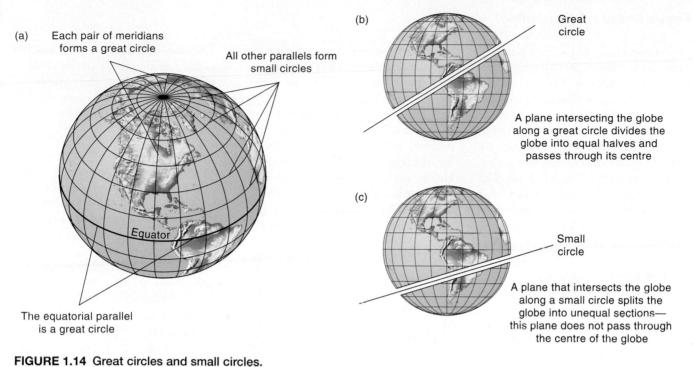

(a)   Each pair of meridians forms a great circle

All other parallels form small circles

Equator

The equatorial parallel is a great circle

(b)   Great circle

A plane intersecting the globe along a great circle divides the globe into equal halves and passes through its centre

(c)   Small circle

A plane that intersects the globe along a small circle splits the globe into unequal sections—this plane does not pass through the centre of the globe

FIGURE 1.14 Great circles and small circles.
(a) Examples of great circles and small circles on Earth. (b) Any plane that divides Earth into equal halves will intersect the globe along a great circle; this great circle is a full circumference of the globe and is the shortest distance between any two surface points. (c) Any plane that splits the globe into unequal portions will intersect the globe along a small circle.

Focus Study 1.2

The Timely Search for Longitude

Unlike latitude, longitude cannot be determined readily from fixed celestial bodies. Determining longitude is particularly critical at sea, where no landmarks are visible. The problem is Earth's rotation, which constantly changes the apparent position of the Sun and stars.

In his historical novel *Shogun*, author James Clavell expressed the frustration of the longitude problem through his pilot, Blackthorn: "Find how to fix longitude and you're the richest man in the world. . . . The Queen, God bless her, 'll give you ten thousand pound and a dukedom for the answer to the riddle. . . . Out of sight of land you're always lost, lad."*

In the early 1600s, Galileo explained that longitude could be measured by using two clocks. Any point on

*From J. Clavell, *Shogun*, Copyright © 1975 by James Clavell (New York: Delacorte Press, a division of Dell Publishing Group, Inc.), p. 10.

FIGURE 1.2.1 Clock time determines longitude.
Using two clocks on a ship to determine longitude. For example, if the shipboard clock reads local noon and the clock set for home port reads 3:00 P.M., ship time is 3 hours earlier than home time. Therefore, calculating 3 hours at 15° per hour puts the ship at 45° west longitude from home port.

Earth takes 24 hours to travel around the full 360° of one rotation (1 day). If you divide 360° by 24 hours, you find that any point on Earth travels through 15° of longitude every hour.

Thus, if there were a way to measure time accurately at sea, a comparison of two clocks could give a value for longitude.

(continued)

Focus Study 1.2 (continued)

One clock would indicate the time back at home port (Figure 1.2.1). The other clock would be reset at local noon each day, as determined by the highest Sun position in the sky (solar zenith). The time difference between the ship and home port would indicate the longitudinal difference traveled: 1 hour for each 15° of longitude. The principle was sound; all that was needed were accurate clocks. Unfortunately, the pendulum clock invented by Christian Huygens in 1656, and accurate on land, did not work on the rolling deck of a ship at sea!

In 1707, the British lost four ships and 2000 men in a sea tragedy that was blamed specifically on the longitude problem. In response, Parliament passed an act in 1714—"Publik Reward . . . to Discover the Longitude at Sea"—and authorized a prize worth more than $2 million in today's dollars

to the first successful inventor of an accurate seafaring clock. The Board of Longitude was established to judge any devices submitted.

John Harrison, a self-taught country clockmaker, began work on the problem in 1728 and finally produced his brilliant marine chronometer, known as *Number 4*, in 1760. The clock was tested on a voyage to Jamaica in 1761. When taken ashore and compared to land-based longitude, Harrison's ingenious *Number 4* was only 5 seconds slow, an error that translates to only 1.25′ or 2.3 km (1.4 mi), well within Parliament's standard. After many delays, Harrison finally received most of the prize money in his last years of life.

With his marine clocks, John Harrison tested the waters of space–time. He succeeded, against all odds, in using the fourth—

temporal—dimension to link points on the three-dimensional globe. He wrested the world's whereabouts from the stars, and locked the secret in a pocket watch.[†]

From that time it was possible to determine longitude accurately on land and sea, as long as everyone agreed upon a meridian to use as a reference for time comparisons—after more than a century that became the Royal Observatory in Greenwich, England. In this modern era of atomic clocks and satellites in mathematically precise orbits, we have far greater accuracy available for the determination of longitude on Earth's surface and a basis for precise navigation.

[†]From Dava Sobel, *Longitude, The Story of a Lone Genius Who Solved the Greatest Scientific Problem of His Time* (New York: Walker and Co., 1995), p. 175.

News Report 1.4

GPS: A Personal Locator

The Global Positioning System (GPS) comprises 24 orbiting satellites, in six orbital planes, that transmit navigational signals for Earth-bound use (backup GPS satellites are in orbital storage as replacements). Originally devised in the 1970s by the Department of Defense for military purposes, the present system is commercially available worldwide. Think of the satellites as a constellation of navigational beacons with which you interact to determine your unique location. Every possible square metre of Earth's surface has its own address relative to the latitude–longitude grid.

Small receivers, some about the size of a pocket radio or smaller, receive signals from three or more satellites at the same time, calculate latitude and longitude within 10-m (33-ft) accuracy and elevation within 15 m (49 ft), and display the results. The key is the time lag the signals take, travelling at the speed of light (Figure 1.4.1). With the

FIGURE 1.4.1 Using satellites to triangulate location through GPS.
Imagine a ranging sphere around each of three GPS satellites. These spheres intersect at two points, one easily rejected because it is some distance above Earth and the other at the true location of the GPS receiver. The three spheres can only intersect at two points. The key is gauging the distance between the satellites and the GPS receiver—signals travel at the speed of light.

shutdown in 2000 of the Pentagon Selective Availability, commercial resolution is the same as that for military

applications and its Precise Positioning Service (PPS). *Differential GPS (DGPS)* increases accuracy by comparing readings with another base station (reference receiver) for a differential correction (Figure 1.4.2).

Relative to earthquakes in southern California, the Jet Propulsion Laboratory (JPL) operates the GPS Observation Office that monitors a network of 250 seismic stations. GPS is also useful to the backpacker and sportsperson. Commercial airlines use GPS to improve accuracy of routes flown and thus increase fuel efficiency. Scientists used GPS to accurately determine the height of Mount Everest in the Himalayan Mountains—now 8850 m compared to the former 8848 m (29,035 ft; 29,028 ft) (Figure 1.4.3). In contrast, GPS measurements of Mount Kilimanjaro lowered its summit from 5895 m to 5892 m (19,340 ft; 19,330 ft).

The importance of GPS to geography is obvious because this precise technology reduces the need to maintain ground control points for location, mapping, and spatial analysis. Instead, geographers working in the field can determine their position accurately as they work. Boundaries and data points in a study area are easily determined and entered into a data base, reducing the need for traditional surveys.

For this and myriad other applications, GPS sales are exceeding $10 billion a year. Additional frequencies were added in 2003 and 2006, which increased accuracy significantly. Also, the European Union is launching its own GPS system of 30 satellites. For a GPS overview, see http://www.colorado.edu/geography/gcraft/notes/gps/gps_f.html.

FIGURE 1.4.2 GPS in action. A DGPS unit in operation, surveying the elevation changes in the dunes at Sauble Beach on Lake Huron, Ontario. [Photo by Mary-Louise Byrne.]

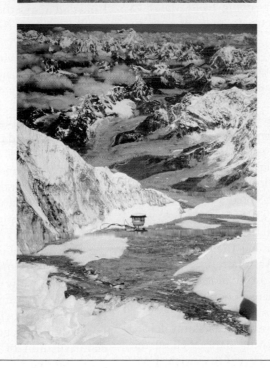

FIGURE 1.4.3 GPS used to measure Everest's summit height. Installation of a Trimble 4800 GPS unit at Earth's highest benchmark, only 18 m (60 ft) below the 8850 m (29,035 ft) summit of Mount Everest. This GPS based revised height measurement was announced in 1999. Scientists are using the GPS data collected from a regional GPS network to accurately analyze the height of the world's tallest mountain and the rate that the mountain range is moving due to tectonic forces. [Photo and GPS installation by adventurer/climber Wally Berg, May 20, 1998.]

---

is one-half of a great circle that passes through the poles. On flat maps, airline and shipping routes appear to arch their way across oceans and landmasses. These are *great circle routes*, the shortest distance between two points on Earth (discussion with Figure 1.21 is just ahead).

In contrast to meridians, only one parallel is a great circle—the *equatorial parallel*. All other parallels diminish in length toward the poles and, along with any other non-great circles that one might draw, constitute **small circles**. These circles have centres that do not coincide with Earth's centre.

Figure 1.15 combines latitude and parallels with longitude and meridians to illustrate Earth's complete coordinate grid system. Note the dot that marks our measurement of 49° N and 60° E, a location in western

Kazakstan. Next time you look at a world globe, follow the parallel and meridian that converge on your location.

Prime Meridian and Standard Time

Coordination of international trade, airline schedules, business and agricultural activities, and daily living depends on a worldwide time system. Today, we take for granted standard time zones and an agreed-upon prime meridian, but such a standard is a relatively recent development.

Setting time was not a great problem in small European countries, most of which are less than 15° wide. But in North America, which spans more than 90° of longitude (the equivalent of six 15° time zones), the problem was

FIGURE 1.15 Earth's coordinate grid system. Latitude and parallels, longitude and meridians allow all places on Earth to be precisely located. The red dot is at 49° N latitude and 60° E longitude.

serious. In 1870, railroad travelers going from Maine to San Francisco made 22 adjustments to their watches to stay consistent with local time.

In 1870, a traveller going from Halifax to Toronto had to change time at Saint John, Québec City, Montreal, Ottawa, and Toronto. When it was noon in Washington, D.C. in the United States, it was 12:54 P.M. in Halifax, 12:14 P.M. in Montreal, and 11:51 A.M. in Toronto! In 1878, Sandford Fleming, a railway surveyor and engineer who immigrated to Canada from Scotland, suggested a method for standardizing time. Despite early objections, Canada and the United States adopted his system for railway scheduling in 1883. Standard time was widely accepted after the International Prime Meridian Conference in 1884 (see http://wwp. greenwichmeantime.com/info/time-zoneshistory.htm).

Twenty-seven countries attended the 1884 International Meridian Conference in Washington, D.C. Before that year, most nations used their own national capital as a prime meridian for their land maps, whereas more than 70% of the world's merchant ships were using Greenwich as a prime meridian on marine charts. After lengthy debate at the conference, most participating nations chose the highly respected Royal Observatory at Greenwich, London, England, as the place for the prime meridian of 0° longitude for all maps. Thus, a world standard was set—**Greenwich Mean Time (GMT)**—and a consistent Universal Time was established. (See http://www. gmt2000.co.uk/meridian/place/plco0a1.htm.)

The basis of time is that Earth revolves 360° every 24 hours, or 15° per hour ($360° \div 24 = 15°$). Thus, a time zone of 1 hour is established, spanning 7.5° on either side of a *central meridian*. Assuming it is 9:00 P.M. in Greenwich, then it is 5:30 P.M. in St. John's (+3.5 hr), 5:00 P.M. in Halifax (+4 hr), 4:00 P.M. in Toronto (+5 hr), 3:00 P.M. in Winnipeg (+6 hr), 2:00 P.M in Edmonton (+7 hr), and 1:00 P.M in Vancouver (+8 hr). To the east, it is midnight in Ar Riyāḍ, Saudi Arabia (−3 hr). The designation A.M. is for *ante meridiem*, "before noon," whereas P.M. is for *post meridiem*, "after noon." A 24-hour clock avoids the use of these designations: 3 P.M. is stated 15:00 hours; 3 A.M. is 3:00 hours.

Today, only four adjustments are needed to cross Canada—standard time zones include Atlantic, Eastern, Central, Mountain, and Pacific—and three changes to cross the continental United States. Newfoundland Standard Time is one-half hour earlier than Atlantic Standard Time because the island of Newfoundland lies entirely in the eastern half of the Atlantic Time zone.

As you can see from the modern international time zones in Figure 1.16, national boundaries and political considerations distort time boundaries. For example, China spans four time zones, but its government decided to keep the entire country operating at the same time. Thus, in some parts of China clocks are several hours off from what the Sun is doing. In the United States, parts of Florida and west Texas are in the same time zone.

International Date Line An important corollary of the prime meridian is the 180° meridian on the opposite side of the planet. This meridian is the **International Date Line** and marks the place where each day officially begins (at 12:01 A.M.). From this "line" the new day sweeps westward. This *westward* movement of time is created by Earth's turning *eastward* on its axis.

At the International Date Line, the west side of the line is always one day ahead of the east side. No matter what time of day it is when the line is crossed, the calendar changes a day (Figure 1.17). Note in the illustration the departures from the IDL and the 180° meridian; this deviation is due to local administrative and political preferences.

In 1995 when Kiribati moved the IDL designation to east of their islands, placing them west of the IDL, they could claim "first dawn" on Earth. This curious political move did not apply to the ocean between their territorial waters and the 180th meridian—note the dotted lines on the map—as political control of island nations extends only 3.5 nautical miles (4 mi) offshore.

Locating the date line in the sparsely populated Pacific Ocean minimizes most local confusion. However, early explorers before the date-line concept were "lost." For example, Magellan's crew returned from the first circumnavigation of Earth in 1522, confident from their ship's log that the day of their arrival home was Wednesday, September 7. They were shocked when informed by insistent local residents that it was actually Thursday, September 8. Of course, without an International Date Line they had no idea that they must advance a day somewhere when sailing around the world in a westward direction. Imagine the confusion as the arriving crew knelt down on the dock accounting for each day in their log!

Coordinated Universal Time For decades, Greenwich Mean Time from the Royal Observatory's astronomical clocks was the world's Universal Time (UT) standard for accuracy. GMT was broadcast using radio time signals as early as 1910. Taking the initiative in 1912, the French government called a gathering of nations to better coordinate the various radio time signals from many countries.

FIGURE 1.16 Modern international standard time zones.
Numbers along the bottom of the map indicate how many hours each zone is earlier (plus sign) or later (minus sign) than Coordinated Universal Time (UTC) at the prime meridian. If it is 7 P.M. in Greenwich, determine the present time in Moscow, London, Halifax, Chicago, Winnipeg, Denver, Los Angeles, Fairbanks, Honolulu, Tokyo, and Singapore. [Adapted from Standard Time Zone Chart of the World, Defense Mapping Agency, Bethesda, Maryland. See http://aa.usno.navy.mil/faq/docs/world_tzones.html.]

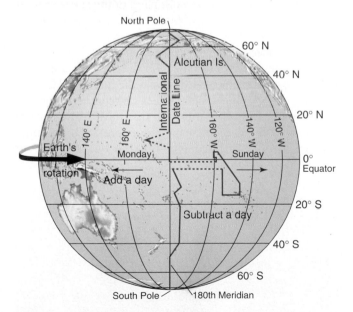

FIGURE 1.17 International Date Line.
International Date Line location, approximately along the 180th meridian. Officially you gain one day crossing the IDL from east to west.

At this conference, GMT was made standard, and a new organization was set to be the custodian of "exact" time—the International Bureau of Weights and Measures (BIPM) (see **http://www.bipm.fr/**). Progress in accurately

measuring time progressed rapidly with the invention of a quartz clock in 1939 and atomic clocks in the early 1950s.

Accurate time is not a matter of simply keeping track of Earth's rotation, since it is slowing down from the tug of tidal forces and rearrangement of water. Note that 150 million years ago a "day" was 22 hours long and 150 million years in the future a "day" will be approaching 27 hours in length.

The time signal system of **Coordinated Universal Time (UTC)*** replaced GMT universal time in 1972 and became the legal reference for official time in all countries. Although the prime meridian still runs through Greenwich, UTC is based on average time calculations collected by the BIPM near Paris and broadcast worldwide.

Regular vibrations (natural frequency) of cesium atoms in primary standard clocks measure the length of a second and UTC—accuracies now range down to 15 decimal places, or nanoseconds of time. Time and Frequency Services of the National Institute for Standards and Technology (NIST), U.S. Department of Commerce, operates several of the most advanced clocks. (For the time, call 303-499-7111 or 808-335-4363, or see **http://nist.time.gov/** for UTC.) In Canada, the Institute for Measurement

*UTC is in use because agreement was not reached on whether to use the English word order, CUT, or the French order, TUC. UTC was the compromise and is recommended for all timekeeping applications; use of the term GMT is discouraged.

Standards, National Research Council Canada, participates in determining UTC (English, 613-745-1578; French, 613-745-9426; for more see http://www.nrc.ca/).

Daylight Saving Time In 70 countries, mainly in the temperate latitudes, time is set ahead 1 hour in the spring and set back 1 hour in the fall—a practice known as **daylight saving time**. The idea to extend daylight for early evening activities (at the expense of daylight in the morning) was first proposed by Benjamin Franklin. It was not adopted until World War I and again in World War II, when Great Britain, Australia, Germany, Canada, and the United States used the practice to save energy (1 less hour of artificial lighting needed).

In 1986 and again in 2007, the United States and Canada increased daylight saving time. Time "springs forward" 1 hour on the second Sunday in March and "falls back" an hour on the first Sunday in November, except in a few places that do not use daylight saving time. In Europe, the last Sundays in March and October are used to begin and end what is called "summer-time period." (See http://webexhibits.org/daylightsaving/.)

Despite standardization efforts, local preferences persist. In Québec, the area east of 63° W does not change to daylight saving time and remains on Atlantic Standard Time year round. In Ontario, Atikokan uses Eastern Time in winter and Central Time in summer; Pickle Lake and New Osnaburgh do not change to daylight saving time, and Big Trout Lake uses Central Time even though it lies in the Eastern Time zone. Most of Saskatchewan does not change to daylight saving time, but uses Central Standard Time throughout the year. Denare Beach and Creighton use daylight saving time even though they are in Saskatchewan. Lloydminster uses Mountain Time although it lies in the Central zone. Creston, Fort St. John, and Dawson Creek, B.C., ignore daylight saving time by using Mountain Time in winter and Pacific Time in summer.

Maps, Scales, and Projections

The earliest known graphic maps date to 2300 B.C., when the Babylonians used clay tablets to record information about the region of the Tigris and Euphrates rivers (the area of modern-day Iraq). Today, the making of maps and charts is a specialized science as well as an art, blending aspects of geography, engineering, mathematics, graphics, computer science, and artistic specialties. It is similar in ways to architecture, in which aesthetics and utility combine to produce a useful product.

A **map** is a generalized view of an area, usually some portion of Earth's surface, as seen from above and greatly reduced in size. **Cartography** is that part of geography that involves mapmaking. Maps are critical tools with which geographers depict spatial information and analyze spatial relationships.

We all use maps at some time to visualize our location in relation to other places, or maybe to plan a trip, or to coordinate commercial and economic activities. Have you found yourself looking at a map, planning real and imagined adventures to far-distant places? Maps are wonderful tools! Understanding a few basics about maps is essential to our study of physical geography.

The Scale of Maps

Architects, toy designers, and mapmakers have something in common: They all create scale models. They reduce real things and places to the more convenient scale of a drawing; a model car, train, or plane; a diagram; or a map. An architect renders a blueprint of a structure to guide the building contractors, selecting a scale so that a centimetre (or inch) on the drawing represents so many metres (or feet) on the proposed building. Often, the drawing is 1/50 to 1/100 of real size.

The cartographer does the same thing in preparing a map. The ratio of the image on a map to the real world is **scale**; it relates a unit on the map to a similar unit on the ground. A 1:1 scale means that a centimetre on the map represents a centimetre on the ground (although this is an impractical map scale, for the map is as large as the area mapped!). A more appropriate scale for a local map is 1:24,000, in which 1 unit on the map represents 24,000 identical units on the ground.

Cartographers express map scale as a written scale, a representative fraction, or a graphic scale (Figure 1.18). A *written scale* simply states the ratio—for example, "one centimetre to one kilometre" or "one inch to one mile." A *representative fraction* (*RF*, or *fractional scale*) is expressed with either a colon or a slash, as in 1:125,000 or 1/125,000. No actual units of measurement are mentioned because any unit is applicable as long as both parts of the fraction are in the same unit: 1 cm to 125,000 cm, 1 in. to 125,000 in., or even 1 arm length to 125,000 arm lengths, and so on.

A *graphic scale*, or *bar scale*, is a bar graph with units to allow measurement of distances on the map. An important advantage of a graphic scale is that if the map is enlarged or reduced, the graphic scale enlarges or reduces along with the map. In contrast, written and fractional scales become incorrect with enlargement or reduction. As an example, you can shrink a map from 1:24,000 to 1:63,360, but the

FIGURE 1.18 Map scale.
Three common expressions of map scale—written scale, representative fraction, and graphic scale.

Table 1.3	Sample Representative Fractions and Written Scales for Small-, Medium-, and Large-Scale Maps		
System	Scale Size	Representative Fraction	Written Scale
Metric	Small	1:1,000,000	1 cm = 10.0 km
	Medium	1:250,000	1 cm = 2.5 km
	Large	1:10,000	1 cm = 0.10 km
Imperial Units (in the U.S.)			
	Small	1:1,000,000	1 in. = 16 mi
	Medium	1:63,360	1 in. = 1 mi
	Large	1:24,000	1 in. = 2000 ft

- Parallels and meridians always cross each other at right angles.

The problem is that all these qualities cannot be reproduced on a flat surface. Simply taking a globe apart and laying it flat on a table illustrates the challenge faced by cartographers (Figure 1.19). You can see the empty spaces that open up between the sections, or gores, of the globe. This reduction of the spherical Earth to a flat surface is a **map projection**. Thus, no flat map projection of Earth can ever have all the features of a globe. Flat maps always possess some degree of distortion—much less for large-scale maps representing a few kilometres; much more for small-scale maps covering individual countries, continents, or the entire world.

scale will still say "1 cm to 200 m," instead of the new correct scale of 1 cm to 10 km.

Scales are *small*, *medium*, and *large*, depending on the ratio described. In relative terms, a scale of 1:24,000 is a large scale, whereas a scale of 1:50,000,000 is a small scale. The greater the denominator in a fractional scale (or the number on the right in a ratio expression), the smaller the scale and the more abstract the map is in relation to what is being mapped. Examples of selected representative fractions and written scales are listed in Table 1.3 for small-, medium-, and large-scale maps.

If there is a globe or map available in your library or classroom, check to see the scale at which it was drawn. See if you can find examples of representative, graphic, and written scales on wall maps, highway maps, and in atlases. In general, do you think a world globe is a small- or a large-scale map of Earth's surface?

Map Projections

A globe is not always a helpful map representation of Earth. When you go on a trip, you need more detailed information than a globe can provide. Consequently, to provide local detail, cartographers prepare large-scale *flat maps*, which are two-dimensional representations (scale models) of our three-dimensional Earth. Unfortunately, such conversion from three dimensions to two causes distortion.

A globe is the only true representation of *distance*, *direction*, *area*, *shape*, and *proximity*. A flat map distorts these properties. Therefore, in preparing a flat map, the cartographer must decide which characteristic to preserve, which to distort, and how much distortion is acceptable. To understand this problem, consider these important properties of a *globe*:

- Parallels always are parallel to each other, always are evenly spaced along meridians, and always decrease in length toward the poles.
- Meridians converge at both poles and are evenly spaced along any individual parallel.
- The distance between meridians decreases toward the poles, with the spacing between meridians at the 60th parallel equal to one-half the equatorial spacing.

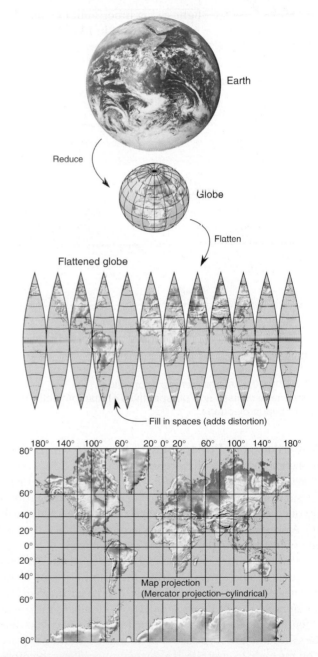

FIGURE 1.19 From globe to flat map.
Conversion of the globe to a flat map projection requires decisions about which properties to preserve and the amount of distortion that is acceptable. [NASA astronaut photo.]

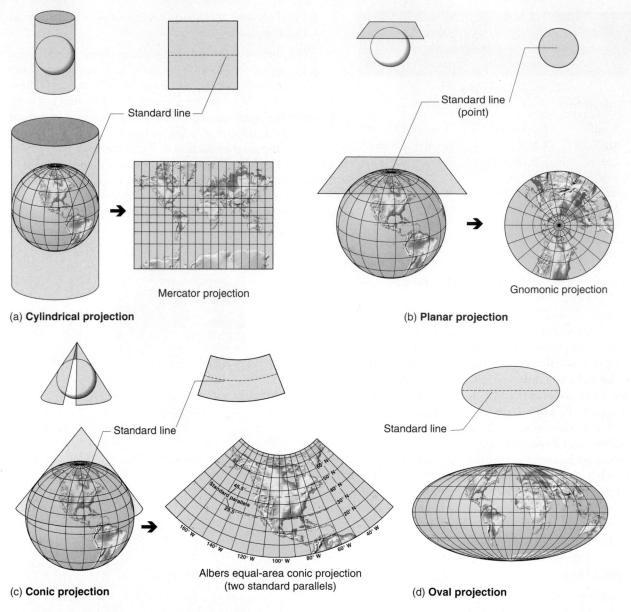

FIGURE 1.20 Classes of map projections.
Four general classes and perspectives of map projections—(a) cylindrical, (b) planar, (c) conic, and (d) oval projections.

Properties of Projections There are many map projections, four of which are shown in Figure 1.20. *The best projection is always determined by its intended use.* The major decisions in selecting a map projection involve the properties of **equal area** (equivalence) and **true shape** (conformality). A decision for one property sacrifices the other, for they cannot be shown together on the same flat map.

If a cartographer selects equal area as the desired trait—for example, for a map showing the distribution of world climates—then true shape must be sacrificed by *stretching* and *shearing*, which allows parallels and meridians to cross at other than right angles. On an equal-area map, a coin covers the same amount of surface area no matter where you place it on the map. In contrast, if a cartographer selects the property of true shape, such as for a map used for navigational purposes, then equal area must be sacrificed, and the scale will actually change from one region of the map to another.

The Nature and Classes of Projections Despite the fact that modern cartographic technology uses mathematical constructions and computer-assisted graphics, the word *projection* is still used. The term comes from times past, when geographers actually projected the shadow of a wire-skeleton globe onto a geometric surface. The wires represented parallels, meridians, and outlines of the continents. A light source then cast a shadow pattern of latitude and longitude lines from the globe onto various geometric surfaces, such as a *cylinder*, *plane*, or *cone*.

Figure 1.20 illustrates the general classes of map projections and the perspectives from which they are generated. The classes shown include the cylindrical, planar (or azimuthal), and conic. Another class of projections, which cannot be derived from this physical-perspective approach, is the nonperspective oval shape. Still other projections derive from purely mathematical calculations.

(a) **Gnomonic Projection**

(b) **Mercator Projection (conformal, true shape)**

FIGURE 1.21 Determining great circle routes.
A gnomonic projection (a) is used to determine the shortest distance—great circle route—
between San Francisco and London, because on this projection the arc of a great circle is a
straight line. This great circle route is then plotted on a Mercator projection (b), which has true
compass direction. Note that straight lines of constant direction (or bearing) on a Mercator
projection—rhumb lines—are not the shortest route in terms of distance.

With projections, the contact line or contact point between the wire globe and the projection surface—called a *standard line* or *standard point*—is *the only place where all globe properties are preserved.* Thus, a *standard parallel* or *standard meridian* is a standard line true to scale along its entire length without any distortion. Areas away from this critical tangent line or point become increasingly distorted. Consequently, this line or point of accurate spatial properties should be centred by the cartographer on the area of interest.

The commonly used **Mercator projection** (from Gerardus Mercator, A.D.1569) is a cylindrical projection (Figure 1.20a). The Mercator is a true-shape projection, with meridians appearing as equally spaced straight lines and parallels appearing as straight lines that are spaced closer together near the equator. The poles are infinitely stretched, with the 84th north parallel and 84th south parallel fixed at the same length as that of the equator. Note in Figures 1.19 and 1.20a that the Mercator projection is cut around the 80th parallel in each hemisphere because of the severe distortion at higher latitudes.

Unfortunately, Mercator classroom maps present false notions of the size (area) of midlatitude and poleward landmasses. A dramatic example on the Mercator projection is Greenland, which looks bigger than all of South America. In reality, Greenland is an island only one-eighth the size of South America and is actually 20% smaller than Argentina alone.

The advantage of the Mercator projection is that a line of constant direction, known as a **rhumb line**, is straight and thus facilitates plotting directions between two points (see Figure 1.21). Thus, the Mercator projection is useful in navigation and is the standard for nautical charts prepared by the National Ocean Service since 1910 (formerly, U.S. Coast and Geodetic Survey).

The *gnomonic*, or *planar*, *projection* in Figure 1.20b is generated by projecting a light source at the centre of a globe onto a plane that is tangent to (touching) the globe's surface. The resulting severe distortion prevents showing a full hemisphere on one projection. However, a valuable feature is derived: *All great circle routes, which are the shortest distance between two points on Earth's surface, are projected as straight lines* (Figure 1.21b). The great circle routes plotted on a gnomonic projection then can be transferred to a true-direction projection, such as the Mercator, for determination of precise compass headings (Figure 1.21b).

For more information on maps used in this text and standard map symbols, turn to Appendix A, Maps in This Text and Topographic Maps. Topographic maps are essential tools of landscape analysis. Geographers, other scientists, travelers, and anyone visiting the outdoors may use topographic maps. The National Topographic System (NTS) provides topographic maps in Canada. There is good coverage of the entire country at 1:50,000 and 1:250,000 scales (**http://maps.nrcan.gc.ca/index_e.php**).

Additionally, the *Atlas of Canada* (**http://atlas.gc.ca/ site/english/index.html**) allows you to select and view maps online. U.S. Geological Survey (USGS) topographic maps appear in several chapters of this text because they are useful in depicting the tremendously varied features of the physical landscape. Perhaps you have used a "topo" map in planning a hike.

Remote Sensing and GIS

Geographers probe, analyze, and map our home planet through remote sensing and geographic information systems (GIS). These technologies enhance our understanding of Earth. Among many subjects, geographers use remote-sensing data to study humid and arid lands, natural and economic vegetation, snow and ice, Earth energy budgets, seasonal variation of atmospheric and oceanic circulation, sea-level measurements, atmospheric chemistry, geologic features and events, changes in the timing of seasons, and the human activities that produce global change.

Space Shuttle

International Space Station

Landsat series

Orbital sensors

High-altitude aircraft

Medium altitude

Low altitude

Ground-based sensors

Band 1

Band 2

Band 3

Target area

Numerical values assigned

Composite digital image

A sample of orbital platforms

Envisat: ESA environment-monitoring satellite; 10 sensors, including a next-generation radar.

ERBS: Earth Radiation Budget Satellite.

GOES: Weather monitoring and forecasting.

JASON: Measures sea level heights.

Landsat: First in 1972 to *Landsat-7* in 1999, millions of images for Earth systems science and global change.

NOAA: First in 1978 through *NOAA-15, -16*, -17, and -18 now operating, global data, short- and long-term weather forecasts.

RADARSAT-1, -2: Synthetic Aperature Radar in near polar orbit operated by Canada Space Agency.

SciSat-1: Analyzes trace gases, thin clouds, atmospheric aerosols with Arctic focus.

SeaStar: Carries the SeaWiFS (Sea-viewing Wide Field-of-View instrument) to observe Earth's oceans and microscopic marine plants.

Terra and Aqua: Environmental change, error-free surface images, cloud properties, through five instrument packages.

TOMS-EP: Total Ozone Mapping Spectrometer, monitoring stratospheric ozone, similar instruments on *NIMBUS-7* and *Meteor-3*.

TOPEX/POSEIDON: Measures sea level heights.

TRMM: Tropical Rainfall Measuring Mission, includes lightning detection and global energy budget measurements.

UARS: Since 1991 measuring atmospheric chemistry and ozone layer changes.

For more info see:
http://www.nasa.gov/centers/goddard/mission/index.html

FIGURE 1.22 Remote-sensing technologies.
Remote-sensing technology measures and monitors Earth's systems from orbiting spacecraft, aircraft in the atmosphere, and ground-based sensors. Various wavelengths (bands) are collected from sensors. Computers process the data to produce digital images for analysis. A sample of remote-sensing platforms is in the margin. The Space Shuttle is shown in its inverted orbital flight mode. (Illustration is not to scale; e.g., the Space Shuttle is 37 m in length whereas the International Space Station is 44.5 m long by 78 m wide by 27.5 m tall.)

Remote Sensing

In this era of observations from orbit outside the atmosphere, from aircraft within it, and from remote submersibles in the oceans, scientists obtain a wide array of remotely sensed data (Figure 1.22). Remote sensing is nothing new to humans; we do it with our eyes as we scan the environment, sensing the shape, size, and colour of objects from a distance, registering energy from the visible-wavelength portion of the electromagnetic spectrum. Similarly, when a camera views the wavelengths for which its film or sensor is designed (visible light or infrared), it remotely senses energy that is reflected or emitted from a scene.

Our eyes and cameras are familiar means of obtaining **remote-sensing** information about a distant subject without having physical contact. Aerial photographs have been used for years to improve the accuracy of surface maps faster and more cheaply than can be done by on-site surveys. Deriving accurate measurements from photographs is the realm of **photogrammetry**, an important application of remote sensing.

Remote sensors on satellites, the International Space Station, and other craft sense a broader range of wavelengths than can our eyes. They can be designed to "see" wavelengths shorter than visible light (ultraviolet) and wavelengths longer than visible light (infrared and microwave radar).

Following launch, satellites can be set in several types of orbits: geostationary, polar, and Sun-synchronous, illustrated in Figure 1.23. Figure 1.23a shows a geostationary (geosynchronous) orbit, typically 35,790 km (22,239 mi) altitude, where satellites pace Earth's rotation speed and therefore remain "parked" above a specific location, usually the equator, which provides a full hemisphere and is good for recording weather; an example is *GOES*.

Figure 1.23b shows a polar-orbiting satellite typically residing between 200 km and 1,000 km (124 mi–621 mi) altitude and passing over every portion of the globe as Earth rotates beneath it, completing each orbit in 90 minutes. Such satellites are good for difficult regions such as the poles, for environmental studies, and for spy surveillance; examples include *Terra* and *Aqua*.

Figure 1.23c demonstrates a Sun-synchronous orbit, shifting its 600-km to 800-km (373-mi to 497-mi) altitude, near-polar track about 1° per day (365 days in a year, 360° in a circle), providing a surface below in constant sunlight for visible-wavelength images or in constant darkness for longwave radiation images.

Satellites do not take conventional-film photographs. Rather, they record *images* that are transmitted to Earth-based receivers in a way similar to television satellite transmissions or a digital camera. A scene is scanned and broken down into pixels (*pic*ture *el*ements), each identified by coordinates named *lines* (horizontal rows) and *samples* (vertical columns). For example, a grid of 6000 lines and 7000 samples forms 42,000,000 pixels, providing great detail. The large amount of data needed to produce a single image requires computer processing and data storage at ground stations.

(a) Geostationary Orbit 35,790 km altitude
(b) Polar Orbit 200–1,000 km altitude
(c) Sun-Synchronous Orbit 600–800 km altitude

FIGURE 1.23 Three satellite orbital paths.
(a) Geostationary (geosynchronous) orbit, typically 35,790 km altitude. (b) Polar orbiting satellites typically are between 200 and 1,000 km altitude. (c) Sun-synchronous orbits shift their near-polar track at 600 to 800 km altitude.

Digital data are processed in many ways to enhance their utility: simulated natural colour, "false" colour to highlight a particular feature, enhanced contrast, signal filtering, and different levels of sampling and resolution. Active and passive are two types of remote-sensing systems.

Active Remote Sensing Active systems direct a beam of energy at a surface and analyze the energy reflected back. An example is *radar* (*ra*dio *d*etection *a*nd *r*anging). A radar transmitter emits short bursts of energy that have relatively long wavelengths (0.3 to 10 m) toward the subject terrain, penetrating clouds and darkness. Energy reflected back to a radar receiver for analysis is known as *backscatter*. An example is the computer image of wind and sea-surface patterns over the Pacific in Figure 6.6a, developed from 150,000 radar-derived measurements made on a single day by the *Seasat* satellite.

Several radar-imaging satellites are operating. Canada operates *RADARSAT–1* and *–2* and the Japanese have *JERS-1* that image in radar wavelengths (Figure 1.24). The European Space Agency (ESA) now operates two Earth resource satellites (*ERS 1* and *2*). They work in tandem, producing a spectacular 10-cm (3.9-in.) resolution, imaging the same area at different times. Pairs of images produce a digital three-dimensional data set.

ESA's newest environment-monitoring satellite, *Envisat*, went into service in 2002. In addition to more sophisticated radar than *ERS*, *Envisat* carries nine passive sensor packages, making it a multitalented craft. It monitors ocean temperatures, sea level, and wave patterns, polar ice, forests, biological activity in the oceans and on land, cloud heights, atmospheric ozone and pollution, and carbon dioxide concentrations (see http://envisat.esa.int/).

In addition, NASA sent imaging radar systems into orbit on several Space Shuttles. The subjects of study

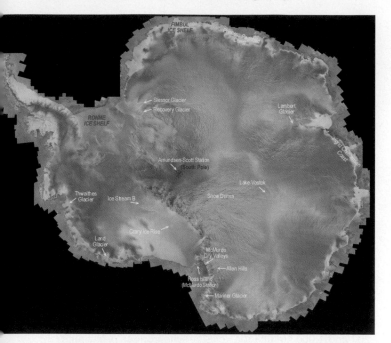

FIGURE 1.24 *RADARSAT* composite image of Antarctica. A mosaic of Antarctica produced by analysis of 18 days of *RADARSAT-1* data gives us a new view of the entire Antarctic continent. [Photo courtesy of RSI/Canadian Space Agency, 2004.]

included oceanography, landforms and geology, and biogeography. Shuttle missions in 1994 by *Endeavour* and *Atlantis* marked dramatic contributions to Earth observations using radar and other sensors to study stratospheric ozone, weather, volcanic activity, earthquakes, and water resources, among many subjects.

One Space Shuttle mission in September 1994 was appropriately loaded with radar sensors to study volcanoes. Only 8 hours after launch, the Kliuchevskoi Volcano on the Kamchatka Peninsula of Russia erupted unexpectedly. Previously this volcano had erupted in 1737 and 1945. The Shuttle radar was able to see through ash and smoke and expose lava flows and the volcanic eruption in dramatic images (Figure 1.25). Astronaut Mission Specialist Dr. Thomas Jones operated the radar and camera to make the image and photo in the figure. He is profiled in a Career Link on the Geosystems website. Chapter 12 discusses volcanic processes.

Passive Remote Sensing Passive remote-sensing systems record energy radiated from a surface, particularly visible light and infrared. Our own eyes are passive remote sensors, as was the *Apollo 17* astronaut camera that made the picture of Earth on the back cover of this book from a distance of 37,000 km (23,000 mi).

Passive remote sensors on five *Landsat* satellites, launched by the United States, provide a variety of data, as shown in images of the Appalachian Mountains and Mount St. Helens in Chapter 12, river deltas and New Orleans before and after Katrina in Chapter 14. Two *Landsats* remain operational, *Landsat–5* and *–7*. See http://landsat. gsfc.nasa.gov/ and http://geo.arc.nasa.gov/sge/landsat/ landsat.html for more information and additional links.

A NASA, National Oceanic and Atmospheric Administration (NOAA, see http://www.noaa.gov/), and U.K. joint venture, the *Polar Operational Environmental Satellites* (*POES*) complete nearly polar orbits 14 times a day and carry the *advanced very high resolution radiometer* (*AVHRR*).

Visible light   Radar

FIGURE 1.25 A volcanic eruption seen from orbit.
Photograph (passive, visible light) and image (active, radar) of the eruption of the Kliuchevskoi Volcano on the Kamchatka Peninsula of Siberia, Russia, as captured by the Space Shuttle *Endeavour*, September 1994. [Image and photo by JPL/NASA.]

These are in Sun-synchronous orbits aboard *NOAA-15* and *NOAA*-17 for morning hours, and *NOAA-16* and *NOAA-18* for afternoon hours. These sensors are sensitive to visible and infrared wavelengths. They are used for weather analysis and forecasting, sea-surface temperature measurement, ozone concentrations, and temperatures in the stratosphere, among many other functions. See http://www.oso.noaa.gov/poesstatus/

Key to NASA's Earth Observing System (EOS) is satellite *Terra*, which began beaming back data and images in 2000 (see http://terra.nasa.gov/), followed by another satellite in the series called *Aqua*. Five instrument packages observe Earth systems in detail, exploring the atmosphere, landscapes, oceans, environmental change, and climate, among other abilities. Of more than 100 remote-sensing images presented throughout this text, watch for those from the *Terra* satellite, such as the Chapter 14-opening image of the Mackenzie River delta. The image of Earth on the half-title page of this book includes a cloud snapshot from *GOES* added to *Terra* MODIS images in 2000.

The *Geostationary Operational Environmental Satellites*, known as *GOES*, became operational in 1994, providing frequent infrared and visible images—the ones you see on television weather reports. Geostationary satellites stay in semipermanent positions because they keep pace with Earth's rotational speed at their altitude of 35,400 km (22,000 mi).

GOES-9 launched in 1995 is now above 160° E in a backup orbital mode. *GOES-10*, active in 1998, was moved in December 2006 to monitor South America from above 60° W. *GOES-12* sits above 75° W longitude to monitor central and eastern North America and the western Atlantic (Figure 1.26). Think of these satellites as hovering over these meridians for continuous coverage, using visual wavelengths for daylight hours and infrared for nigthtime views. *GOES-11* operates above 135° W longitude for western North America and eastern Pacific Ocean weather. *GOES-13*, launched in May 2006, is parked in orbit to become next in line when needed. (See the Geostationary Satellite Server at http://www.goes.noaa.gov/. The *GOES* Project Science appears at http://rsd.gsfc.nasa.gov/goes/ or see http://www.ghcc.msfc.nasa.gov/GOES/.) For the future, *GOES-O* launched in July 2007, will become *GOES-14*, and *GOES-P*, after a successful 2008 launch, will be operational as *GOES-15*.

SCISAT is a Canadian satellite launched by NASA in 2003 and contains an Ace Fourier Transform Spectrometer and an instrument known as MAESTRO (Measurements of Aerosol Extinction in the Stratosphere and Troposphere Retrieved by Occultation). These instruments measure the concentration and distribution of chemicals in the ozone layer as sunlight passes through Earth's upper atmosphere. *SCISAT* orbits Earth 15 times daily to capture information for 15 sunrises and sunsets.

CLOUDSAT, launched in 2006, uses a radar hyperfrequency sensor to gather three-dimensional cloud data to improve our knowledge of clouds and weather. (See: http://www.space.gc.ca/asc/eng/satellites/default.asp for more on all Canadian satellites.)

FIGURE 1.26 *GOES-12* first image.
The first image from *GOES-12* demonstrates excellent quality from its 37,000 km (23,300 mi) orbital post. This satellite is stationed above 75° W longitude for central and eastern North American coverage. [Image courtesy of NOAA.]

Other satellites used for weather include Japan's *MTSAT-1R* (Multi-Functional Transport Satellite, 2005) and *MTSAT-2* (2006), which now serve weather and communication needs over the western Pacific (*GOES-9* serves as backup). China's *Feng Yun-2B* and *Feng Yun-1D* above 105° E cover the Far East, and *METEOSAT-7*, above 58° E, covers Europe and Africa and is operated by the European Space Agency. (See the Remote Sensing Virtual Library at http://virtual.vtt.fi/space/rsvlib/ for remote-sensing links; click on "Satellite Data" for specific coverage.)

One of two commercial systems includes the three French satellites (1, 2, and 4) called *SPOT* (Systeme Probatoire d'Observation de la Terre) that resolve objects on Earth down to 10 to 20 m (33 to 66 ft), depending on which sensors are used. Other commercial systems are operated by GeoEye, formerly Space Imaging, which was acquired by ORBIMAGE. Its satellites offer 0.41-m to 4-m resolution from *Ikonos–2*, *OrbView-2*, *-3*, *and –5*, and its new *GeoEye-1* satellite, all in Sun-synchronous orbits at 680 km (420 mi) altitude (http://www.geoeye.com/). See Figure 12.1a image for an example of an image from *Ikonos–2*.

For a sampling of global remote sensing coverage from a variety of satellite platforms go to the USGS Global Visualization Viewer, select the satellite and click on the map for a location, and then watch (http://glovis.usgs.gov/).

Geographic Information Systems (GIS)

Techniques such as remote sensing acquire large volumes of spatial data that must be stored, processed, and retrieved in useful ways. A **geographic information system (GIS)** is a computer-based, data-processing tool for gathering, manipulating, and analyzing geographic information. Today's sophisticated computer systems allow the integration of geographic information from direct surveys (on-the-ground mapping) and remote sensing in complex ways never before possible. Through a GIS, Earth and human phenomena are analyzed over time.

An example is shown in Figure 1.27. GIS is a rapidly expanding career field in many sectors of the economy. Regardless of your academic major, the ability to analyze data spatially is important. Be sure to check some of the URLs listed in News Report 1.5 for information on professional career directions in this exciting field.

The beginning component for any GIS is a coordinate system such as latitude–longitude, which establishes reference points against which to position data. The coordinate system is digitized, along with all areas, points, and lines. Remotely sensed imagery and data are then added on to the coordinate system.

A GIS is capable of analyzing patterns and relationships within a single data plane, such as the floodplain or soil layer in Figure 1.27. The GIS also can generate an overlay analysis where two or more data planes interact. When the layers are combined, the resulting synthesis—a *composite overlay*—is a valuable product, ready for use in analyzing complex problems. A research study may follow specific points or areas through the complex of overlay planes. The utility of a GIS compared with that of a fixed map is the ability to manipulate the variables for analysis and to constantly change the map—the map is alive!

Before the advent of computers, an environmental-impact analysis required someone to gather data and painstakingly hand-produce overlays of information to determine positive and negative impacts of a project or event. Today, this layered information is handled by a computer-driven GIS, which assesses the complex interconnections among different components. In this way, subtle changes in one element of a landscape may be identified as having a powerful impact elsewhere.

GIS is particularly helpful in analyzing natural hazards and society. An example is the European earthquake catalogue that records more than 20,000 earthquakes,

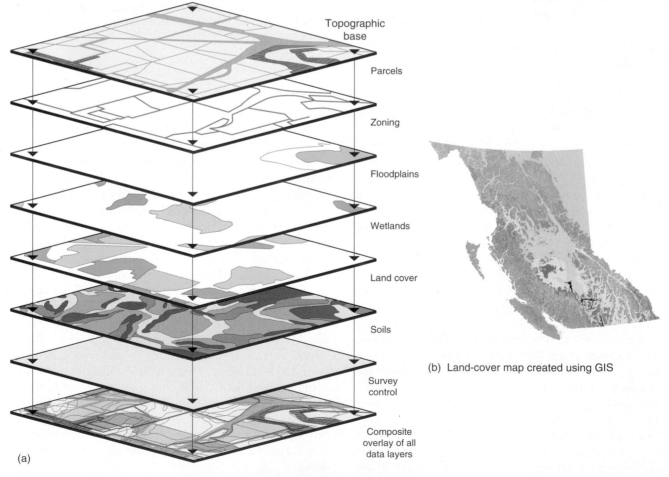

(a)

(b) Land-cover map created using GIS

FIGURE 1.27 A geographic information system (GIS) model.
(a) Layered spatial data in a geographic information system (GIS) format. (b) This biogeoclimatic map of British Columbia is a valuable tool for forestry management in the province. [(a) After USGS; (b) copyright © 2004 Province of British Columbia. All rights reserved. Reprinted with the permission of the Province of British Columbia, www.ipp.gov.bc.ca.]

News Report 1.5

Careers in GIS

Geographic information system (GIS) methodology offers great career opportunities in industry, government, business, marketing, teaching, sales, military, and other fields. Right now, geographers trained in GIS analyze ozone depletion, deforestation, soil erosion, and acid deposition. They map ecosystems and monitor the declining diversity of plant and animal species. Geographers plan, design, and survey urban developments, follow the trends of global warming, study the impact of human population, and analyze air and water pollution.

We are in the midst of a growing GIS revolution. Potent new careers are emerging in almost every academic area as GIS programs are implemented at many universities and community colleges. GIS applications are used in environmental analysis, weather forecasting, natural hazard assessment, business and marketing, industry location analysis, criminal justice, and natural resources exploration, among many examples. (For a list of current trends in GIS, simply enter this topic in your search engine; for an alphabetized GIS resources list, check out http:// www.geo.ed.ac.uk/home/giswww.html.)

GIS degree programs are available at many colleges and universities. GIS curriculum and certificate programs are now available at several community colleges. Many universities have listings of careers and jobs in GIS. Check out the University of Toronto site (http://www.geog.utoronto.ca/info/facweb/Boyes/GIS/Weblinks_General.htm) for a great summary of GIS information. Additionally, the University of British Columbia (http://www.geog.ubc.ca/gislinks/index.php) has a summary of jobs, careers, Web sites, and tools.

---

dating back to 500 B.C. Having this data base installed in a GIS permits detailed spatial analysis of these events, along with country boundaries, human settlements, rivers, lakes, seas, nuclear power plant locations, hazardous materials storage sites, and other economic considerations.

One of the most extensive and longest operating systems is the Canada Geographic Information system (CGIS). Roger Tomlinson, a Canadian geographer recognized as the father of GIS (see Royal Canadian Geographic Society award at http://www.rcgs.org/rcgs/awards/awards_

gold03.asp), was key in the development of the Canadian GIS. To create the system, environmental data about natural features, resources, and land use were taken from maps, aerial photographs, and orbital sources, reduced to map segments, and entered into the CGIS. The development of this system has progressed with the ongoing Canada land inventory project (visit the Canada Land Inventory Web page at http://geogratis.cgdi.gc.ca/CLI/frames.html). A summary timeline for development of GIS is found at http://www.casa.ucl.ac.uk/gistimelinc/welcome.htm.

Summary and Review—Essentials of Geography

To assist you, here is a review in handy summary form of the Key Learning Concepts listed on this chapter's title page. Each concept review concludes with a list of the key terms from the chapter, their page numbers, and review questions. Such summary and review sections follow each chapter in the book.

■ *Define* geography and physical geography in particular.

Geography brings together disciplines from the physical and life sciences with the cultural and human sciences to attain a holistic view of Earth—physical geography is an essential aspect of the emerging **Earth systems sciences**. **Geography** is a science of method, a special way of analyzing phenomena over space; **spatial** refers to the nature and character of physical space. Geography integrates a wide range of subject matter. Geographic education recognizes five major themes: **location**, **region**, **human–Earth relationships**, **movement**, and **place**. Geography's method is **spatial analysis**, used to study the interdependence among geographic areas, natural systems, society, and cultural activities over space or area. **Process**—that is, analyzing a set of actions or mechanisms that operate in some special order—is central to geographic synthesis.

Physical geography applies spatial analysis to all the physical elements and processes that make up the environment: energy, air, water, weather, climate, landforms, soils, animals, plants, microorganisms, and Earth itself. Understanding the complex relations among these elements is important to human survival because Earth's physical systems and human society are so intertwined. The development of hypotheses and theories about the Universe, Earth, and life involves the **scientific method**.

Earth systems science (p. 2)
geography (p. 2)
spatial (p. 2)
location (p. 3)
region (p. 3)
human–Earth relationships (p. 3)
movement (p. 3)
place (p. 3)
spatial analysis (p. 3)
process (p. 3)
physical geography (p. 3)
scientific method (p. 3)

1. What is unique about the science of geography? On the basis of information in this chapter, define physical geography and review the geographic approach.

2. In general terms, how might a physical geographer analyze water pollution in the Great Lakes?

3. Assess your geographic literacy by examining atlases and maps. What types of maps have you used—political? Physical? Topographic? Do you know what projections they employed? Do you know the names and locations of the four oceans, seven continents, and most individual countries? Can you identify the new countries that have emerged since 1990?

4. Suggest a representative example for each of the five geographic themes and use that theme in a sentence.

5. Have you made decisions today that involve geographic concepts discussed within the five themes presented? Explain briefly.

■ *Describe* systems analysis, open and closed systems, and feedback information, and *relate* these concepts to Earth systems.

A **system** is any ordered, related set of things and their attributes, as distinct from their surrounding environment. Systems analysis is an important organizational and analytical tool used by geographers. Earth is an **open system** in terms of energy, receiving energy from the Sun, but it is essentially a **closed system** in terms of matter and physical resources.

As a system operates, "information" is returned to various points in the system via pathways called **feedback loops**. If the feedback information discourages response in the system, it is called **negative feedback**. (Further production in the system decreases the growth of the system.) If feedback information encourages response in the system, it is called **positive feedback**. (Further production in the system stimulates the growth of the system.) When the rates of inputs and outputs in the system are equal and the amounts of energy and matter in storage within the system are constant (or as they fluctuate around a stable average), the system is in **steady-state equilibrium**. A system that demonstrates a steady increase or decrease in system operations—a trend over time—is in **dynamic equilibrium**. A **threshold** is the moment at which a system can no longer maintain its character, so it lurches to a new operational level, one which may not be compatible with previous conditions. Geographers often construct a simplified **model** of natural systems to better understand them.

Four immense open systems powerfully interact at Earth's surface: three nonliving **abiotic** systems (**atmosphere**, **hydrosphere** [including the **cryosphere**], and **lithosphere**) and a living **biotic** system (**biosphere**, or **ecosphere**).

✓system (p. 2)
✓open system (p. 2)
✓closed system (p. 6)
feedback loops (p. 7)
✓negative feedback (p. 7)
✓positive feedback (p. 7)
steady-state equilibrium (p. 10)
dynamic equilibrium (p. 10)
threshold (p. 10)
model (p. 12)
abiotic (p. 13)
biotic (p. 13)
atmosphere (p. 14)
hydrosphere (p. 14)
cryosphere (p. 14)
lithosphere (p. 14)
biosphere (p. 15)
ecosphere (p. 15)

6. Define systems theory as an organizational strategy. What are open systems, closed systems, and negative feedback? When is a system in a steady-state equilibrium condition? What type of system (open or closed) is the human body? A lake? A wheat plant?

7. Describe Earth as a system in terms of both energy and matter; use simple diagrams to illustrate your description.

8. What are the three abiotic spheres (nonliving) that make up Earth's environment? Relate these to the biotic (living) sphere: the biosphere.

■ *Explain* Earth's reference grid: latitude and longitude, and latitudinal geographic zones and time.

The science that studies Earth's shape and size is **geodesy**. Earth bulges slightly through the equator and is oblate (flattened) at the poles, producing a misshapen spheroid called a **geoid**. Absolute location on Earth is described with a specific reference grid of **parallels** of **latitude** (measuring distances north and south of the equator) and **meridians** of **longitude** (measuring distances east and west of a prime meridian). A historic breakthrough in navigation and timekeeping occurred with the establishment of an international **prime meridian** (0° through Greenwich, England) and the invention of precise chronometers that enabled accurate measurement of longitude. Latitude, longitude, and elevation are accurately calibrated using a handheld **global positioning system** (**GPS**) instrument that reads radio signals from satellites. A **great circle** is any circle of Earth's circumference whose centre coincides with the centre of Earth. Great circle routes are the shortest distance between two points on Earth. **Small circles** are those whose centres do not coincide with Earth's centre.

The prime meridian provided the basis for **Greenwich Mean Time** (**GMT**), the world's first universal time system. A corollary of the prime meridian is the 180° meridian, the **International Date Line**, which marks the place where each day officially begins. Today, **Coordinated Universal Time** (**UTC**) is the worldwide standard and the basis for international time zones. **Daylight saving time** is a seasonal change of clocks by 1 hour in summer months.

geodesy (p. 15)
geoid (p. 15)
latitude (p. 16)
parallel (p. 17)
longitude (p. 17)
meridian (p. 17)
prime meridian (p. 17)
Global Positioning System (GPS) (p. 19)
great circle (p. 19)
small circles (p. 23)
Greenwich Mean Time (GMT) (p. 24)
International Date Line (p. 24)
Coordinated Universal Time (UTC) (p. 25)
daylight saving time (p. 26)

9. Draw a simple sketch describing Earth's shape and size.

10. How did Eratosthenes use Sun angles to figure out that the 5000-stadia distance between Alexandria and Syene was 1/50 of Earth's circumference? Once he knew this fraction of Earth's circumference, how did he calculate the entirety of Earth's circumference?

11. What are the latitude and longitude coordinates (in degrees, minutes, and seconds) of your present location? Where can you find this information?

12. Define latitude and parallel and define longitude and meridian using a simple sketch with labels.

13. Define a great circle, great circle routes, and a small circle. In terms of these concepts, describe the equator, other parallels, and meridians.

14. Identify the various latitudinal geographic zones that roughly subdivide Earth's surface. In which zone do you live? How do the concepts of north and northerliness describe your location?

15. What does timekeeping have to do with longitude? Explain this relationship. How is Coordinated Universal Time (UTC) determined on Earth?

16. What and where is the prime meridian? How was the location originally selected? Describe the meridian that is opposite the prime meridian on Earth's surface.

17. What is GPS and how does it assist you in finding location and elevation on Earth? Give a couple of examples where it was utilized to correct heights for some famous mountains.

■ *Define* cartography and mapping basics: map scale and map projections.

A **map** is a generalized view of an area, usually some portion of Earth's surface, as seen from above, and greatly reduced in size. The science and art of mapmaking is called **cartography**. For the spatial portrayal of Earth's physical systems geographers use maps. **Scale** is the ratio of the image on a map to the real world; it relates a unit on the map to an identical unit on the ground. Cartographers create **map projections** for specific purposes, selecting the best compromise of projection for each application. Compromise is always necessary because Earth's round, three-dimensional surface cannot be exactly duplicated on a flat, two-dimensional map. **Equal area** (equivalence), **true shape** (conformality), true direction, and true distance are all considerations in selecting a projection. The **Mercator projection** is in the cylindrical class; it has true-shape qualities and straight lines that show constant direction. A **rhumb line** denotes constant direction and appears as a straight line on the Mercator.

map (p. 26)
cartography (p. 26)
scale (p. 26)
map projections (p. 27)

equal area (p. 28)
true shape (p. 28)
Mercator projection (p. 29)
rhumb line (p. 29)

18. Define cartography. Explain why it is an integrative discipline.

19. What is map scale? In what three ways may it be expressed on a map?

20. State whether the following ratios are large scale, medium scale, or small scale: 1:3,168,000; 1:24,000; 1:250,000.

21. Describe the differences between the characteristics of a globe and those that result when a flat map is prepared.

22. What type of map projection is used in Figure 1.12? In Figure 1.16? (See Appendix A.)

■ *Describe* remote sensing and *explain* geographic information systems (GIS) as tools used in geographic analysis.

Orbital and aerial **remote sensing** analyze the operation of Earth's systems. Satellites do not take photographs, but record images that are transmitted to Earth-based receivers. Satellite images are recorded in digital form for later processing, enhancement, and generation. Aerial photographs have been used for years to improve the accuracy of surface maps. This is the realm of **photogrammetry**, an important application of remote sensing.

The mountain of data collected is put to work in **geographic information system** (**GIS**) technology. Computers process geographic information from direct surveys and remote sensing in complex ways never before possible. GIS methodology is an important step in better understanding Earth's systems and is a vital career opportunity for geographers.

The science of physical geography is in a unique position to synthesize the spatial, environmental, and human aspects of our increasingly complex relationship with our home planet—Earth.

remote sensing (p. 31)
photogrammetry (p. 31)
geographic information system (GIS) (p. 34)

23. What is remote sensing? What are you viewing when you observe a weather satellite image on TV or in the newspaper? Explain.

24. Describe the *Terra*, *Landsat*, *GOES*, and *NOAA* satellites and explain them using several examples.

25. If you were in charge of planning for development of a large tract of land, how would GIS methodologies assist you? How might planning and zoning be affected if a portion of the tract in the GIS is a floodplain or prime agricultural land?

Critical Thinking

A. Select a location (for example, your campus, home, workplace, a public place, or a city) and determine the following: latitude, longitude, and elevation. Describe the resources you used to gather this geographic information. Have you ever used a GPS unit to determine these aspects of your location?

B. Let's say there is a world globe in the library or geography department that is 61 cm (24 in.) in diameter. We know that Earth has an equatorial diameter of 12,756 km (7926 mi), so the scale of the globe is the ratio of 61 cm to 12,756 km. We divide Earth's actual diameter by the globe's diameter (12,756 km ÷ 61 cm) and determine that 1 cm of the globe's diameter equals about _____ cm of Earth's actual diameter.

Thus, the representative fraction for the globe is expressed in centimetres as 1/_____. (*Hint*: 1 km = 1000 m, 1 m = 100 cm; therefore, Earth's diameter of 12,756 km represents 1,275,600,000 cm.)

C. The various geographic information technologies discussed in your text (GIS, GPS, remote sensing) promise to revolutionize many aspects of modern life. How are they used now, and what sorts of changes might we expect in the near future? Use the Net Search and Destinations sections on the Companion Website to find examples, and write a brief description of what you find. Be sure to include URLs for the sites you visit.

The Energy–Atmosphere System

CHAPTER 2   Solar Energy to Earth and the Seasons

CHAPTER 3   Earth's Modern Atmosphere

CHAPTER 4   Atmosphere and Surface Energy Balances

CHAPTER 5   Global Temperatures

CHAPTER 6   Atmospheric and Oceanic Circulations

PART I

Sunlight powers this field of wheat. Of the visible light spectrum, chlorophyll absorbs orange-red and violet blue wavelengths for photochemical operations within leaves. Wheat, along with maize (corn) and rice, provides more than 50% of the world grain supply. Canada ranks sixth among countries for wheat production.
[Photo by Bobbé Christopherson.]

SOLAR ENERGY

Atmosphere

Hydrosphere

Biosphere

Lithosphere

Our planet and our lives are powered by radiant energy from the star that is closest to Earth—the Sun. For more than 4.6 billion years, solar energy has traveled across interplanetary space to Earth, where a small portion of the solar output is intercepted. Because of Earth's curvature, the energy at the top of the atmosphere is unevenly distributed, creating imbalances from the equator to each pole—the equatorial region experiences energy surpluses; the polar regions experience energy deficits. Also, the annual pulse of seasonal change varies the distribution of energy during the year.

Earth's atmosphere acts as an efficient filter, absorbing most harmful radiation, charged particles, and space debris so that they do not reach Earth's surface. In the lower atmosphere the unevenness of daily energy receipt empowers atmospheric and surface energy budgets, giving rise to global patterns of temperature and circulation of wind and ocean currents. We see this in the part-opening photo, wheat plants almost aglow with the infusion of this radiant energy. Each of us depends on many systems that are set into motion by energy from the Sun. These systems are the subject of Part I.

The Midnight Sun seen from a research ship in the Arctic Ocean. The camera points due north, viewing the Sun's rays from across the North Pole some 885 km (550 mi) distant (see the inset illustration). This seemed so strange at the time to have natural lighting that felt like about 3 P.M. (15:00 hours), yet have my watch clearly show it to be midnight. See Figure 2.16 for a near-midnight Antarctic scene. [Photo by Bobbé Christopherson.]

2

Solar Energy to Earth and the Seasons

■ Key Learning Concepts

After reading the chapter, you should be able to:

- ■ **Distinguish** among galaxies, stars, and planets, and **locate** Earth.

- ■ **Overview** the origin, formation, and development of Earth, and **construct** Earth's annual orbit about the Sun.

- ■ **Describe** the Sun's operation, and **explain** the characteristics of the solar wind and the electromagnetic spectrum of radiant energy.

- ■ **Portray** the intercepted solar energy and its uneven distribution at the top of the atmosphere.

- ■ **Define** solar altitude, solar declination, and daylength, and **describe** the annual variability of each—Earth's seasonality.

The Universe is populated with billions of galaxies. One of these is our own Milky Way Galaxy, consisting of billions of stars. Among these stars is an average yellow star we call the Sun, although the dramatic *SOHO* satellite image in Figure 2.2 seems anything but average! Our Sun radiates energy in all directions and upon its family of orbiting planets. Of special interest to us is the solar energy that falls on the third planet, our immediate home.

In this chapter: Incoming solar energy that arrives at the top of Earth's atmosphere establishes the pattern of energy input that drives Earth's physical systems and daily influences our lives. This solar energy input to the atmosphere, plus Earth's tilt and rotation, produce daily, seasonal, and annual patterns of changing daylength and Sun angle. The Sun is the ultimate energy source for most life processes in our biosphere.

The Solar System, Sun, and Earth

Our Solar System is located on a remote, trailing edge of the **Milky Way Galaxy**, a flattened, disk-shaped mass estimated to contain nearly 400 billion stars (Figure 2.1a, b). Our Solar System is embedded more than halfway out from the galactic centre, in one of the Milky Way's spiral arms, called the Orion Arm. A supermassive black hole some 2 million solar masses in size, named *Sagittarius A**, sits in the centre (pronounced "*Sagittarius A Star*"). From our Earthbound perspective in the Milky Way, the Galaxy appears to stretch across the night sky like a narrow band of hazy light. On a clear night, the unaided eye can see only a few thousand of these billions of stars.

Solar System Formation and Structure

According to prevailing theory, our Solar System condensed from a large, slowly rotating and collapsing cloud of dust and gas called a *nebula*. **Gravity**, the mutual attracting force exerted by the mass of an object upon all other objects, was the key force in this condensing solar nebula. As the nebular cloud organized and flattened into a disk shape, the early *protosun* grew in mass at the centre, drawing more matter to it. Small accretion (accumulation) eddies swirled at varying distances from the centre of the solar nebula; these were the *protoplanets*.

The beginnings of the Sun and its Solar System are estimated to have occurred more than 4.6 billion years ago. The early protoplanets, called *planetesimals*, orbited at approximately the same distances from the Sun as the planets are today. The **planetesimal hypothesis**, or *dust-cloud hypothesis*, explains how suns condense from nebular clouds with planetesimals forming in orbits about the central mass. Astronomers study this formation process in other parts of the Galaxy, where planets are observed orbiting distant stars. By the end of 2007, astronomers had discovered more than 250 planets orbiting around other stars. Closer to home in our Solar System, some 165 moons (planetary satellites) are in orbit about the eight planets. As of 2007, the new satellite count for the four outer planets was: Jupiter, 63 moons; Saturn, 60 moons; Uranus, 27 moons; and Neptune, 13 moons.

Dimensions and Distances The **speed of light** is 300,000 kmps (kilometres per second), or 186,000 mps (miles per second)—in other words, about 9.5 trillion kilometres per year, or nearly 6 trillion miles per year. (In more precise numbers, light speed is 299,792 kmps, or 186,282 mps.) This tremendous distance that light travels in a year is known as a *light-year*, and it is used as a unit of measurement for the vast Universe.

The known Universe that is observable from Earth stretches approximately 12 billion light-years in all directions. The Milky Way Galaxy is about 100,000 light-years from edge to edge (Figure 2.1b). For spatial comparison, our entire Solar System is approximately 11 hours in diameter, as measured by light speed (Figure 2.1c). The Moon is an average distance of 384,400 km (238,866 mi) from Earth, or about 1.28 seconds from Earth in terms of light speed—for the *Apollo* astronauts this was a three-day journey. (See a Solar System simulator at **http://space.jpl.nasa.gov/**.)

Earth's Orbit Earth's orbit around the Sun is presently *elliptical*—a closed, oval path (Figure 2.1d). Earth's average distance from the Sun is approximately 150 million km (93 million mi), which means that light reaches Earth from the Sun in an average of 8 minutes and 20 seconds. Earth is at **perihelion** (its closest position to the Sun) during the Northern Hemisphere winter (January 3 at 147,255,000 km, or 91,500,000 mi). It is at **aphelion** (its farthest position from the Sun) during the Northern Hemisphere summer (July 4 at 152,083,000 km, or 94,500,000 mi). This seasonal difference in distance from the Sun causes a slight variation in the solar energy incoming to Earth but is not an immediate reason for seasonal change.

The structure of Earth's orbit is not a constant, but instead exhibits change over long periods. As shown in Chapter 17, Figure 17.32, Earth's distance from the Sun varies more than 17.7 million km (11 million mi) during a 100,000-year cycle, placing it closer or farther at different periods in the cycle. This variation is thought to be one of several factors that create Earth's long-term cyclical pattern of glacial (colder) and interglacial (warmer) periods.

Solar Energy: From Sun to Earth

Our Sun is unique to us but is a commonplace star in the Galaxy. It is only average in temperature, size, and colour when compared with other stars, yet it is the ultimate energy source for most life processes in our biosphere.

The Sun captured about 99.9% of the matter from the original solar nebula. The remaining 0.1% of the matter formed all the planets, their satellites, asteroids, comets, and debris. Consequently, the dominant object in our region of space is the Sun. In the entire Solar System, it is the only object having the enormous mass needed to sustain a nuclear reaction and produce radiant energy.

The solar mass produces tremendous pressure and high temperatures deep in its dense interior. Under these conditions, the Sun's abundant hydrogen atoms, the lightest of all the natural elements, are forced together, and pairs of hydrogen nuclei are joined in a process called **fusion**. In the fusion reaction, hydrogen nuclei form helium, the second-lightest element in nature, and enormous quantities of energy are liberated—literally, disappearing solar mass becomes energy.

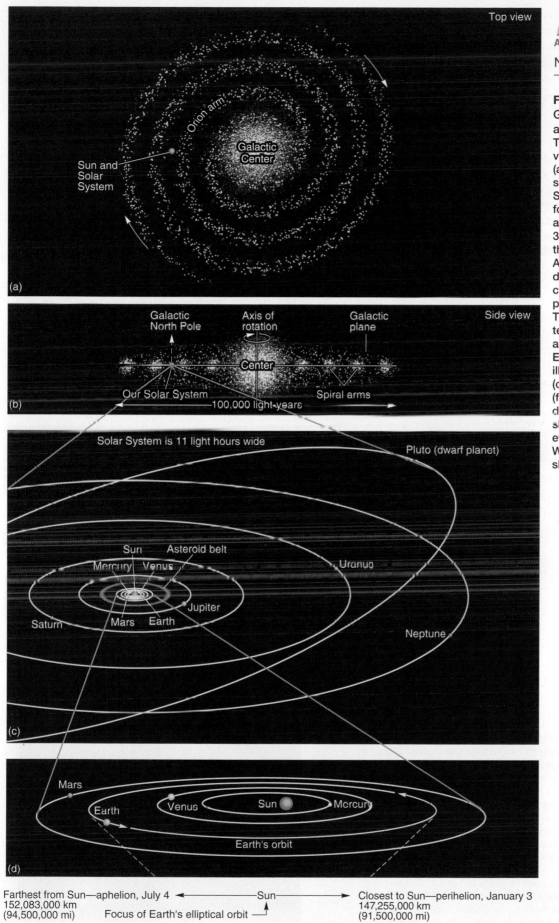

Top view

(a)

Side view

(b)

(c)

(d)

Farthest from Sun—aphelion, July 4 ◄─────────── Sun ──────────► Closest to Sun—perihelion, January 3
152,083,000 km   147,255,000 km
(94,500,000 mi)   Focus of Earth's elliptical orbit ─┘   (91,500,000 mi)

ANIMATION

Nebular Hypothesis

FIGURE 2.1 Milky Way Galaxy, Solar System, and Earth's orbit. The Milky Way Galaxy viewed from above (a) and cross-section side view (b). Our Solar System of eight planets, four dwarf planets, and asteroids is some 30,000 light-years from the centre of the Galaxy. All of the planets except dwarf Pluto have orbits closely aligned to the plane of the ecliptic (c). The four inner terrestrial planets and the structure of Earth's elliptical orbit, illustrating perihelion (closest) and aphelion (farthest) positions during the year, are shown in (d). Have you ever observed the Milky Way Galaxy in the night sky?

A sunny day can seem so peaceful, certainly unlike the violence taking place on the Sun. The Sun's principal outputs consist of the solar wind and radiant energy in portions of the electromagnetic spectrum. Let us trace each of these emissions across space to Earth.

Solar Activity and Solar Wind

The Sun constantly emits clouds of electrically charged particles (principally hydrogen nuclei and free electrons) that surge outward in all directions from the Sun's surface. This stream of energetic material travels much more slowly than light—only about 50 million km (31 million mi) a day—taking approximately 3 days to reach Earth. The term **solar wind** was first applied to this phenomenon in 1958. Solar wind extends from the Sun to a distance beyond Pluto's orbit. The *Voyager* and *Pioneer* spacecraft launched in the 1970s are now far beyond our Solar System and have yet to escape the solar wind.

The Sun's most conspicuous features are large **sunspots**, caused by magnetic storms on the Sun. Individual sunspots may range in diameter from 10,000 to 50,000 km (6200 to 31,000 mi), with some growing as large as 160,000 km (100,000 mi), more than 12 times Earth's diameter (Figure 2.2). These surface disturbances produce flares and prominences. In addition, outbursts of charged material referred to as *coronal mass ejections* contribute to the flow of material to space in the solar wind.

A regular cycle exists for sunspot occurrences, averaging 11 years from maximum to maximum; however, the cycle may vary from 7 to 17 years. In recent cycles, a solar minimum occurred in 1976 and a solar maximum took place during 1979, with more than 100 sunspots visible at maximum. Another minimum was reached in 1986, and an extremely active solar maximum followed in 1990, with more than 200 sunspots visible at some time during the year. In fact, the 1990–1991 maximum was the most intense ever observed—11 years after the previous maximum. A sunspot minimum in 1997, an intense maximum in 2001, a minimum in 2007, and a forecasted maximum in 2012 roughly maintain the average. (For more on the sunspot cycle, see **http://solarscience.msfc.nasa.gov/ SunspotCycle.shtml**.) The order and patterns we see in nature are the result of chaotic interactions of many systems, which are discussed in News Report 2.1.

Solar Wind Effects   The charged particles of the solar wind first interact with Earth's magnetic field as they approach Earth. The **magnetosphere** is a magnetic field

(a)

(b)

FIGURE 2.2 Image of the Sun and sunspots.
(a) The Sun and large sunspot group (visible dark patches) in a recent active cycle, imaged by the MDI (Michelson Doppler Imager) instrument aboard satellite *SOHO*. This group was the source of numerous flares and coronal mass ejections, including the largest flare in recent decades. The area within the sunspot group is more than 13 times the entire surface area of Earth (that is, 13 times 500 million km^2)—Earth is shown for scale. (b) A dramatic Sun captured by instruments aboard the *SOHO* satellite. A twirling prominence rises into the Sun's corona, and other prominences are also visible.
[(a) Image courtesy of *SOHO/EIT* (Solar and Heliospheric Observatory/Extreme Ultraviolet Imaging Telescope) Consortium.
(b) Image courtesy of *SOHO/MDI* Consortium—MDI is from Stanford-Lockheed/Martin Institute for Space Research. *SOHO* is an international project of cooperation between the European Space Agency and NASA. See **http://sohowww.nascom.nasa.gov/**.]

News Report 2.1

The Nature of Order Is Chaos

In 1960, Edward Lorenz, an MIT scientist, rocked the scientific world with the statement that a butterfly flapping its wings in Brazil might produce a tornado in Texas. He used this strange example to suggest that the interaction of orderly and deterministic systems may produce chaotic and unpredictable results.

For example, ice has a rigid internal structure, forced by bonding between water molecules. This structure dictates that all ice crystals are six-sided, yet no two ice crystals, despite this similarity, are identical. Beneath this chaos of design exists an order dictated by physical principles (see Figure 7.6).

A major shift in our real-world view occurred with the advent of *chaos theory*, of complexity thinking, a revolution in science that considers the nonlinear and unpredictable behaviour of operational systems. This theory suggests that the scientific method must consider the coexistence of disorder and order, randomness and pattern, and symmetry and chaos in natural systems—the science of complexity and complex systems.

Consider the weather: Mathematical models and numerical equations describe the behavior of water vapour, temperature, and pressure patterns. Yet weather systems are sensitive to very small fluctuations in any of those ingredients. Therefore, it is difficult to exactly predict how a weather system will develop, what track it will follow, or how severe it might be (see Chapter 8). Two similar chaotic weather systems might produce a similar result, although it is not possible to say exactly what the output will be. This understanding of the role of chaos is helping scientists to improve forecasting of weather phenomena. In a dynamic weather system, chaos is the rule, just as it is in chemical and biological systems.

Chaos theory is useful in studying all of Earth's physical environments. For example, a river flows in branched channels over a floodplain in a pattern to conserve energy. The channels constantly shift in a randomness that is irregular and difficult to predict. See the *Terra* satellite image of the many mouths of the Ganges River in Figure 14.26 for an example of such *fractal branching*—irregular, curving channels that may or may not repeat their pattern.

This may seem strange, but the nature of order we observe is the result of chaos and complexity and the almost infinite interaction among physical elements! Chaos theory is an exciting dimension of the scientific method and physical geography.

---

surrounding Earth, generated by dynamo-like motions within our planet. The magnetosphere deflects the solar wind toward both of Earth's poles so that only a small portion of it enters the atmosphere.

Because the solar wind does not reach Earth's surface, research on this phenomenon must be conducted in space. In 1969, the *Apollo XI* astronauts exposed a piece of foil on the lunar surface as a solar wind experiment (Figure 2.3). When examined back on Earth, the exposed foil exhibited particle impacts that confirmed the presence and character of the solar wind.

Interaction of the solar wind and the upper layers of Earth's atmosphere produces the remarkable **auroras** that occur toward both poles. These lighting effects are the *aurora borealis* (northern lights) and *aurora australis* (southern lights) in the upper atmosphere, 80–500 km (50–300 mi) above Earth's surface (Figure 2.4). During the 2001 solar maximum, auroras were visible as far south as Jamaica, Texas, and California. Also, the solar wind disrupts certain radio broadcasts and some satellite transmissions, causes overloads on Earth-based electrical systems, and may affect weather patterns.

Our understanding of the solar wind is increasing dramatically as data are collected by a variety of satellites: the *SOHO* (*Solar and Heliospheric Observatory*), *FAST* (*Fast Auroral Snapshot*), *WIND*, *Ulysses*, the *Dynamics Explorer*, and *Genesis* with solar wind collectors, among others. All satellite data are available on the Internet. (For auroral

FIGURE 2.3 Astronaut and solar wind experiment. Without a protective atmosphere, the lunar surface receives charged particles of the solar wind and all the Sun's electromagnetic radiation. An *Apollo XI* astronaut in 1969 deploys a sheet of foil in the solar wind experiment. Earth-bound scientists analyzed the foil upon the astronauts' return. **Why wouldn't this experiment work if set up on Earth's surface?** [Photo by NASA.]

(a)

(b)

FIGURE 2.4 Auroras from an orbital perspective and from the ground in Manitoba.
(a) *Polar* satellite false-colour image of auroral halo over Earth's North Pole region from April 1996—the UVI sensor is able to capture the aurora on the day and night sides of Earth. (b) View from the ground of an aurora borealis in the night sky over Churchill, Manitoba. [(a) Image from the Ultraviolet Imager (UVI) aboard *Polar* satellite courtesy of NASA. (b) Photo by Richard Petrone.]

activity, see **http://www.sel.noaa.gov/pmap/**, and for forecasts see **http://www.gi.alaska.edu**.)

Weather Effects Another effect of the solar wind in the atmosphere is its possible influence on weather and climate cycles. Why do wetter periods in some midlatitude areas tend to coincide with every other solar maximum? Why do droughts often occur near the time of every other solar minimum? For example, sunspot cycles during nearly 260 years from 1740 to 1998 coincided with periods of wetness and drought, as estimated by an analysis of tree growth rings for that period throughout the western United States and elsewhere, as well as instrumental weather records. These variations in weather tend to lag 2 or 3 years behind the solar maximum or minimum.

Electromagnetic Spectrum of Radiant Energy

The key essential solar input to life is electromagnetic energy of various wavelengths. Solar radiation occupies a portion of the **electromagnetic spectrum** of radiant energy. This radiant energy travels at the speed of light to Earth. The total spectrum of this radiant energy is made up of different wavelengths. Figure 2.5 shows that a **wavelength** is the distance between corresponding points on any two successive waves. The number of waves passing a fixed point in 1 second is the *frequency*.

The Sun emits radiant energy composed of 8% ultraviolet, X-ray, and gamma-ray wavelengths; 47% visible light wavelengths; and 45% infrared wavelengths. A portion of the electromagnetic spectrum is illustrated in Figure 2.6, with wavelengths increasing from the top of the illustration to the bottom. Note the wavelengths at which various phenomena and human applications of energy occur.

An important physical law states that all objects radiate energy in wavelengths related to their individual surface temperatures: the hotter the object, the shorter the wavelengths emitted. This law holds true for the Sun and Earth. Figure 2.7 shows that the hot Sun radiates shorter wavelength energy, concentrated around 0.5 μm (micrometre).

The Sun's surface temperature is about 6000 K (5727°C, 10,340°F), and its emission curve shown in the figure is similar to that predicted for an idealized 6000 K surface, or *blackbody radiator*. An ideal blackbody emits as much radiant energy as it absorbs—the hotter the blackbody, the more radiation it emits at all wavelengths, with shorter wavelengths dominant at higher temperatures.

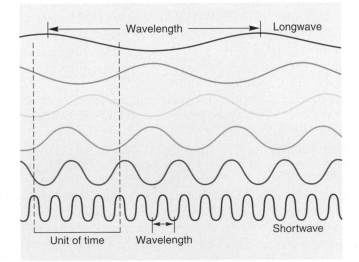

FIGURE 2.5 Wavelength and frequency.
Wavelength and frequency are two ways of describing the same phenomenon—electromagnetic wave motion. More short wavelengths pass a given point during a unit of time, so they are higher in frequency, whereas fewer long wavelengths pass a point in a unit of time, so they are lower in frequency.

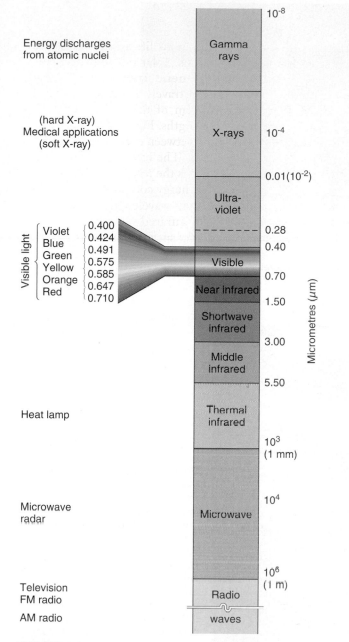

FIGURE 2.6 A portion of the electromagnetic spectrum of radiant energy.
The spectrum is oriented with shorter wavelengths toward the top and longer wavelengths toward the bottom.

Absorption by oxygen and ozone

Absorption by water vapour and carbon dioxide

Absorption by carbon dioxide, water, and other radiatively active gases

FIGURE 2.7 Solar and terrestrial energy distribution by wavelength.
The solar output peaks in shorter wavelengths of visible light in relation to its higher surface temperature, whereas Earth's emissions are concentrated in the infrared portion of the spectrum in relation to its lower surface temperature. Ideal blackbody curves for a radiating body like the Sun (hotter) and Earth (cooler) illustrate the concept. The dropouts in the plot lines of solar and terrestrial radiation represent absorption bands of water vapour, water, carbon dioxide, oxygen, ozone (O_3), and other gases. [Adapted from W.D. Sellers, *Physical Climatology* (Chicago: University of Chicago Press, 1965), p. 20. Used by permission.]

ANIMATION   Electromagnetic Spectrum and Plants

The Sun emits a much greater amount of energy per unit area of its surface than does a similar area of Earth's environment.

Earth is a cooler radiating body, so longer wavelengths are emitted. In comparison to a shorter-wavelength emitting hot body, the lower temperatures at Earth's surface produce radiation mostly in the infrared portion of the spectrum. Figure 2.7 shows that the radiation emitted by Earth occurs in longer wavelengths, centred around 10 μm and entirely within the infrared portion of the spectrum. Figure 2.8 illustrates the flows of energy into and out of Earth systems.

To summarize, the solar spectrum is *shortwave radiation* that peaks in the short visible wavelengths, whereas Earth's radiated energy is *longwave radiation* concentrated in infrared wavelengths. In Chapter 4, we see that Earth, clouds, sky, ground, and things that are terrestrial are cool-body radiators in contrast to the Sun.

Incoming Energy at the Top of the Atmosphere

The region at the top of the atmosphere, approximately 480 km (300 mi) above Earth's surface, is the **thermopause**. It is the outer boundary of Earth's energy system and provides a useful point at which to assess the arriving solar radiation before it is diminished by scattering and absorption in passage through the atmosphere.

Earth's distance from the Sun results in its interception of only one two-billionth of the Sun's total energy output. Nevertheless, this tiny fraction of energy from the Sun is an enormous amount of energy flowing into Earth's systems. Solar radiation that reaches a horizontal plane at Earth is **insolation**, derived from the words *in*coming *sol*ar radi*ation*. Insolation specifically applies to radiation arriving at Earth's atmosphere and surface. Insolation at the top of the atmosphere is expressed as the *solar constant*.

FIGURE 2.8 Earth's energy budget simplified.
Inputs of shorter wavelengths arrive at Earth from the Sun. Outputs of longer wavelengths of
infrared radiate to space from Earth. The data plotted in Figure 2.10 and the map in Figure 2.11
are derived from data gathered along the top of the atmosphere.

FIGURE 2.9 Insolation receipts
and Earth's curved surface.
Solar insolation angles determine
the concentration of energy
receipts by latitude. Lower
latitudes receive more
concentrated energy from a more
direct solar beam. Higher
latitudes receive slanting (oblique)
rays and more diffuse energy.
Note the area covered by identical
columns of solar energy arriving
at Earth's surface at higher
latitudes (more diffuse, larger area
covered) and at lower latitudes
(more concentrated, smaller area
covered).

Solar Constant Knowing the amount of insolation intercepted by Earth is important to climatologists and other scientists. The **solar constant** is the average insolation received at the thermopause when Earth is at its average distance from the Sun. That value is 1372 W/m² (watts per square metre).* The constancy of the solar constant over time is important, for small variations of even 0.5% or 1.0% could prove dramatic for Earth's energy system.

*A *watt* is equal to one joule (a unit of energy) per second and is the standard unit of power in the International System of Units (SI). (See the conversion tables in Appendix C of this text for more information on measurement conversions.) In nonmetric *calorie* heat units, the solar constant is expressed as approximately 2 calories per square centimetre per minute, or 2 *langleys* per minute (a langley being 1 cal/cm²). A calorie is the amount of energy required to raise the temperature of one gram of water (at 15°C) one degree Celsius and is equal to 4.184 joules.

As we follow insolation through the atmosphere to Earth's surface (Chapters 3 and 4), we see that the value of the solar constant is reduced by half or more through reflection, scattering, and absorption of shortwave radiation.

Uneven Distribution of Insolation Earth's curved surface presents a continually varying angle to the incoming parallel rays of insolation (Figure 2.9). Differences in the angle of solar rays at each latitude result in an uneven distribution of insolation and heating. The only point receiving insolation perpendicular to the surface (from directly overhead) is the **subsolar point**. During the year this point occurs at lower latitudes between the tropics (23.5° north and 23.5° south latitudes), where the energy received is more concentrated. All other places away from the subsolar point receive insolation at an angle less than 90° and thus experience more diffuse energy; this effect is pronounced at higher latitudes.

The thermopause above the equatorial region receives 2.5 times more insolation annually than the thermopause above the poles. Of lesser importance is the fact that the lower-angle solar rays toward the poles must pass through a greater thickness of atmosphere, resulting in greater losses of energy due to scattering, absorption, and reflection.

Figure 2.10 illustrates the daily variations throughout the year of energy at the top of the atmosphere for various latitudes in watts per square metre (W/m^2). The chart shows a decrease in insolation from the equatorial regions northward and southward toward the poles. However, in June, the North Pole receives more than 500 W/m^2 per day, which is more than is ever received at 40° N latitude or at the equator. Such high values result from long daylengths at the poles in summer: 24 hours a day, compared

with only 15 hours of daylight at 40° N latitude and 12 hours at the equator. However, at the poles the summertime Sun at noon is low in the sky, so a daylength twice that of the equator yields only about a 100 W/m^2 difference.

In December, the pattern reverses. Note that the top of the atmosphere at the South Pole receives even more insolation than the North Pole does in June (more than 500 W/m^2). This is a function of Earth's closer location to the Sun at perihelion (January 3 on Figure 2.1d).

Along the equator, two maximum periods of approximately 430 W/m^2 occur at the spring and fall equinoxes, when the subsolar point is at the equator. Find your latitude on the graph and follow across the months to determine the seasonal variation of insolation where you live. The four graphs to the right show plots of the energy received at the North Pole, along 50° N, along the equator, and at the South Pole during the year to give you energy profiles to compare.

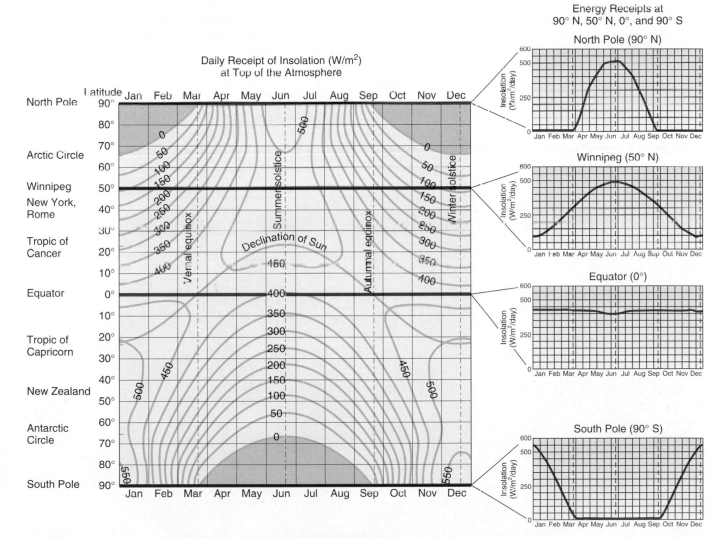

FIGURE 2.10 Daily insolation received at the top of the atmosphere.
The total daily insolation received at the top of the atmosphere is charted in watts per square metre per day by latitude and month (1 W/m^2/day = 2.064 cal/cm^2/day). A profile of annual energy receipts is graphed to the right for the North Pole, along 50° north latitude, along the equator, and for the South Pole. [Reproduced by permission of the Smithsonian Institution Press from *Smithsonian Miscellaneous Collections: Smithsonian Meteorological Tables*, vol. 114, 6th edition. Robert List, ed. (Washington, DC: Smithsonian Institution, 1984), p. 419, Table 134.]

Global Net Radiation   *Earth Radiation Budget Experiment (ERBE)* instruments aboard several satellites measured shortwave and longwave flows of energy at the top of the atmosphere. ERBE sensors collected the data used to develop the map in Figure 2.11. This map shows *net radiation*, or the balance between incoming shortwave and outgoing longwave radiation—energy inputs minus energy outputs. See News Report 2.2 for more on these experiments.

Note the latitudinal energy imbalance in net radiation on the map—positive values in lower latitudes and negative values toward the poles. In middle and high latitudes, approximately poleward of 36° north and south latitudes, net radiation is negative. This occurs in these higher latitudes because Earth's climate system loses more energy to space than it gains from the Sun, as measured at the top of the atmosphere. In the lower atmosphere, these polar energy deficits are offset by flows of energy from tropical energy surpluses (as we will see in Chapters 4 and 6). The largest net radiation values, averaging 80 W/m², are above the tropical oceans along a narrow equatorial zone. Net radiation minimums are lowest over Antarctica.

Of interest is the −20 W/m² area over the Sahara region of North Africa. Here, typically clear skies—which permit great longwave radiation losses from Earth's surface—and light-coloured reflective surfaces work together to reduce net radiation values at the thermopause. In other regions, clouds and atmospheric pollution in the lower atmosphere also affect net radiation patterns at the top of the atmosphere by reflecting more shortwave energy to space.

The atmosphere and ocean form a giant heat engine, driven by differences in energy from place to place and causing major circulations within the lower atmosphere and in the ocean. These circulations include global winds, ocean currents, and weather systems—subjects to follow in Chapters 6 and 8. As you go about your daily activities, let these dynamic natural systems remind you of the constant flow of solar energy through the environment.

Having examined the flow of solar energy to Earth and the top of the atmosphere, let us now look at how seasonal changes affect the distribution of insolation as Earth orbits the Sun during the year.

The Seasons

Earth's periodic rhythms of warmth and cold, dawn and daylight, twilight and night have fascinated humans for centuries. In fact, many ancient societies demonstrated an intense awareness of seasonal change and formally commemorated these natural energy rhythms with festivals, monuments, ground markings, and calendars (Figure 2.12). Such ancient seasonal monuments and calendar markings are found worldwide, including thousands of sites in North America.

Seasonality

Seasonality refers to both the seasonal variation of the Sun's position above the horizon and changing daylengths during the year. Seasonal variations are a response to changes in

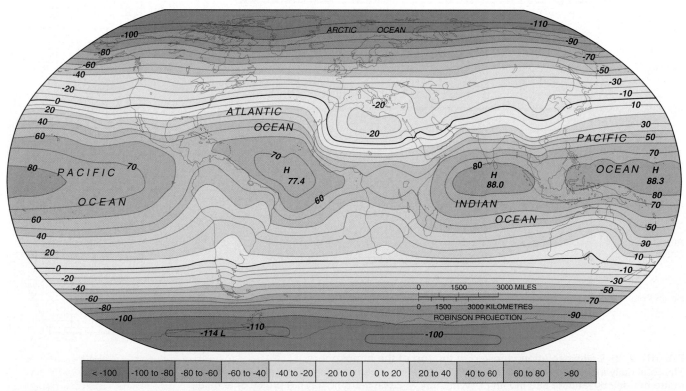

| < -100 | -100 to -80 | -80 to -60 | -60 to -40 | -40 to -20 | -20 to 0 | 0 to 20 | 20 to 40 | 40 to 60 | 60 to 80 | >80 |

FIGURE 2.11 Daily net radiation patterns at the top of the atmosphere.
Averaged daily net radiation flows for a 9-year period (1979–1987), measured at the top of the atmosphere by the Earth Radiation Budget Experiment (ERBE) aboard the *Nimbus-7* satellite. Units are W/m². [Data for map courtesy of Dr. H. Lee Kyle, Goddard Space Flight Center, NASA.]

News Report 2.2

Monitoring Earth Radiation Budget

Earth's weather and climate are a direct result of the balance between sunlight received from space and energy reflected and radiated to space. Patterns of insolation absorption and energy reradiation by Earth systems produce an energy budget. Since 1978, the Earth–atmosphere energy budget has been monitored by the Earth Radiation Budget (ERB) package on board the Nimbus-7 satellite, and originally aboard *NOAA-9* and *NOAA-10*, with later energy budget monitoring by the NOAA series of satellites, now with *NOAA–15* through *NOAA–19* active. The original program satellites collected more than a decade of data. ERB sensors mapped the complex exchanges of energy among atmosphere, ocean, and land.

Measurements include monthly energy budget and variations, seasonal shifts in energy between equator and poles, and daily energy budgets at the regional scale. The map in Figure 2.11 is a direct result of ERBE, showing regions that absorb more energy than radiated (a heat-energy source, rose colour on map in Figure 2.11) and that radiate more energy than received (a heat-energy sink, purple colour).

A new tool in understanding Earth's radiation budget is the CERES (Clouds and Earth Radiant Energy System) sensor aboard satellite *Terra*. CERES monitors shortwave (light) and longwave (heat energy) and, thus, Earth's energy balance of incoming and outgoing radiation—a pair of CERES images are in Chapter 4.

In addition, ERB measurements determined that solar irradiance, or the luminous brightness of solar radiation, is directly correlated to the sunspot cycle discussed earlier. During solar maximums the solar constant rises slightly above the 1372 W/m² average, whereas during solar minimums it shifts slightly lower, below the average. The ERBE findings help scientists better understand the systems described in Part I of this textbook (see http://asd-www.larc.nasa.gov/erbe/ASDerbe.html).

---

the Sun's **altitude**, or the angle between the horizon and the Sun. At sunrise or sunset, the Sun is at the horizon, so its altitude is 0°. If during the day, the Sun reaches halfway between the horizon and directly overhead, it is at 45° altitude. If the Sun reaches the point directly overhead, it is at 90° altitude. The Sun is directly overhead (90° altitude, or *zenith*) only at the *subsolar point*, where insolation is at a maximum. At all other surface points, the Sun is at a lower altitude angle, producing more-diffuse insolation.

The Sun's **declination** is the latitude of the subsolar point. Declination annually migrates through 47° of latitude, moving between the *Tropic of Cancer* at 23.5° N and the *Tropic of Capricorn* at 23.5° S latitude. Other than Hawai'i, which is between 19° N and 22° N, the subsolar point does not reach the continental United States or Canada; all other states and provinces are too far north.

Also, seasonality means changing **daylength**, or duration of exposure to insolation. Daylength varies during the year, depending on latitude. The equator always receives equal hours of day and night: If you live in Ecuador, Kenya, or Singapore, every day and night is 12 hours long, year-round. People living along 40° N latitude (Philadelphia, Denver, Madrid, Beijing) or 40° S latitude (Buenos Aires, Capetown, Melbourne) experience about 6 hours' difference in daylight between winter (9 hours) and summer (15 hours). At 50° N or S latitude (Winnipeg, Paris, Falkland, or Malvinas Islands) people experience almost 8 hours of annual daylength variation.

FIGURE 2.12 Stonehenge on the Salisbury Plain. Neolithic peoples beginning about 5000 years ago constructed this complex of standing rock—sarsen uprights, topped by lintel capstones. Inherent in the layout is indication of important seasonal dates and precise lunar-cycle predictions. [Photo by Bobbé Christopherson.]

At the North and South Poles, the range of daylength is extreme with a 6-month period of no insolation, beginning with weeks of twilight to darkness then on to weeks of pre-dawn. Following sunrise, daylight covers a 6-month period of continuous 24-hour insolation—literally the poles experience one long day and one long night each year! The chapter-opening photo illustrates the shock to a midlatitude person at seeing the Midnight Sun.

Reasons for Seasons

Seasons result from variations in the Sun's *altitude* above the horizon, the Sun's *declination* (latitude location of the subsolar point), and *daylength* during the year. These in turn are created by several physical factors that operate in concert: Earth's *revolution* in orbit around the Sun, its daily *rotation* on its axis, its *tilted axis*, the unchanging *orientation of its axis*, and its *sphericity* (Table 2.1). Of course, the essential ingredient is having a single source of radiant energy—the Sun. We now look at each of these factors individually. As we do, please note the distinction between revolution—Earth's travel around the Sun—and rotation—Earth's spinning on its axis (Figure 2.13).

Revolution   Earth's orbital **revolution** about the Sun is shown in Figure 2.1d and 2.13. Earth's speed in orbit averages 107,280 kmph (66,660 mph). This speed, together with Earth's distance from the Sun, determines the time required for one revolution around the Sun and, therefore, the length of the year and duration of the seasons. Earth completes its annual revolution in 365.2422 days. This number is based on a *tropical year*, measured from equinox to equinox, or the elapsed time between two crossings of the equator by the Sun.

The Earth-to-Sun distance (aphelion to perihelion) might seem a seasonal factor, but it is not significant. It varies about 3% (4.8 million km or 3 million mi) during

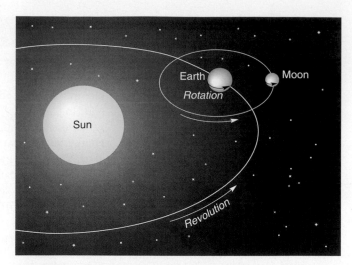

FIGURE 2.13 Earth's revolution and rotation. Earth's *revolution* about the Sun and *rotation* on its axis, viewed from above Earth's orbit. Note the Moon's rotation on its axis and revolution are counterclockwise about Earth, as well.

the year, amounting to a 50 W/m² difference between local polar summers. Remember that the Earth–Sun distance averages 150 million km (93 million mi).

Rotation   Earth's **rotation**, or turning on its axis, is a complex motion that averages slightly less than 24 hours in duration. Rotation determines daylength, creates the apparent deflection of winds and ocean currents, and produces the twice-daily rise and fall of the ocean tides in relation to the gravitational pull of the Sun and the Moon.

Earth rotates about its **axis**, an imaginary line extending through the planet from the geographic North Pole to the South Pole. When viewed from above the North Pole, Earth rotates counterclockwise around this axis. Viewed from above the equator, Earth rotates west to east, or eastward. This eastward rotation creates the Sun's *apparent* westward daily journey from sunrise in the east to sunset in the west. Of course, the Sun actually remains in a fixed position in the centre of the Solar System. (Note in Figure 2.13 that the Moon both revolves around Earth and rotates on its axis in a counterclockwise direction.)

Although every point on Earth takes the same 24 hours to complete one rotation, the linear velocity of rotation at any point on Earth's surface varies dramatically with latitude. The equator is 40,075 km (24,902 mi) long; therefore, rotational velocity at the equator must be approximately 1675 kmph (1041 mph) to cover that distance in one day. At 60° latitude, a parallel is only half the length of the equator, or 20,038 km (12,451 mi) long, so the rotational velocity there is 838 kmph (521 mph). At the poles, the velocity is 0. (This variation in rotational velocity establishes the effect of the Coriolis force, discussed in Chapter 6.) Table 2.2 lists the speed of rotation for several selected latitudes.

Earth's rotation produces the continually changing daily pattern of day and night. Half of Earth is in sunlight and half is in darkness at any moment. The dividing line

Table 2.1	Five Reasons for Seasons
Factor	**Description**
Revolution	Orbit around the Sun; requires 365.24 days to complete at 107,280 kmph (66,660 mph)
Rotation	Earth turning on its axis; takes approximately 24 hours to complete at 1675 kmph (1041 mph) at the equator
Tilt	Axis is aligned at a 23.5° angle from a perpendicular to the plane of the ecliptic (the plane of Earth's orbit)
Axial parallelism	Remains in a fixed alignment, with Polaris directly overhead at the North Pole throughout the year
Sphericity	Appears as an oblate spheroid to the Sun's parallel rays; the geoid

Table 2.2	Speed of Rotation at Selected Latitudes		
	Speed		**Cities at Approximate**
Latitude	**kmph**	**(mph)**	**Latitudes**
90°	0	(0)	North Pole
60°	838	(521)	Seward, Alaska; Oslo, Norway; Saint Petersburg, Russia
50°	1078	(670)	Chibougamau, Québec; Kyyîv (Kiev), Ukraine
40°	1284	(798)	Valdivia, Chile; Columbus, Ohio; Beijing, China
30°	1452	(902)	Pôrto Alegre, Brazil; New Orleans, Louisiana
0°	1675	(1041)	Quito, Ecuador; Pontianak, Indonesia

between day and night is called the **circle of illumination** (as illustrated in Figure 2.15). Because this day-night dividing circle of illumination intersects the equator, *daylength at the equator is always evenly divided*—12 hours of day and 12 hours of night. All other latitudes experience uneven daylength through the seasons, except for 2 days a year, on the equinoxes. (Any two great circles on a sphere bisect one another.)

A true day varies slightly from 24 hours, but by international agreement a day is defined as exactly 24 hours, or 86,400 seconds. This average, called *mean solar time*, eliminates predictable variations in rotation and revolution that cause the solar day to change slightly in length throughout the year.

The complexity of Earth's rotation is now exactly measured by satellites that are in precise mathematical orbits: GPS (global positioning system, see News Report 1.4, Chapter 1), SLR (satellite-laser ranging), and VLBI (very-long baseline interferometry). All contribute to our knowledge of Earth's rotation. The International Earth Rotation Service at **http://www.iers.org/** issues monthly and annual reports. Earth's rotation is gradually slowing, partially owing to the drag of lunar tidal forces. A "day" on Earth today is many hours longer than it was 4 billion years ago.

Tilt of Earth's Axis   To understand Earth's **axial tilt**, imagine a plane (a flat surface) that intersects Earth's elliptical orbit about the Sun, with half of the Sun and Earth above the plane and half below. Such a plane touching all points of Earth's orbit is the **plane of the ecliptic**. Earth's tilted axis remains fixed relative to this plane as Earth revolves around the Sun. The plane of the ecliptic is important to our discussion of Earth's seasons. Now, imagine a perpendicular (at a 90° angle) line passing through the plane. From this perpendicular, Earth's axis is tilted 23.5°. It forms a 66.5° angle from the plane itself (Figure 2.14).

The axis through Earth's two poles points just slightly off Polaris, which is named, appropriately, the *North Star*.

This text uses "about" with the tilt angle just described because Earth's axial tilt changes over a complex 41,000-year cycle (see Figure 17.32). The axial tilt roughly ranges between 22° and 24.5° from a perpendicular to the plane of the ecliptic. The present tilt is 23° 27′ (or 66° 33′ from the plane). In decimal numbers, 23° 27′ is approximately 23.45°. For convenience this is rounded off to a 23.5° tilt (or 66.5° from the plane) in our discussion. Scientific evidence shows that the angle of tilt is lessening in its 41,000-year cycle.

Hypothetically, if Earth were tilted on its side, with its axis parallel to the plane of the ecliptic, we would experience a maximum variation in seasons worldwide. In contrast, if Earth's axis were perpendicular to the plane of its orbit—that is, with no tilt—we would experience no seasonal changes, with something like a perpetual spring or fall season, and all latitudes would experience 12-hour days and nights.

Axial Parallelism   Throughout our annual journey around the Sun, Earth's axis *maintains the same alignment* relative to the plane of the ecliptic and to Polaris and other stars. You can see this consistent alignment in Figure 2.15. If we compared the axis in different months, it would always appear parallel to itself, a condition known as **axial parallelism**.

Sphericity   Although Earth is not a perfect sphere, as discussed in Chapter 1, we can refer to Earth's *sphericity* as a part of seasonality, for it produces the uneven receipt of insolation from pole to pole shown in Figures 2.9 and 2.10. All five reasons for seasons are summarized in Table 2.1: revolution, rotation, tilt, axial parallelism, and sphericity. Now, considering all these factors operating together, let us examine the annual march of the seasons.

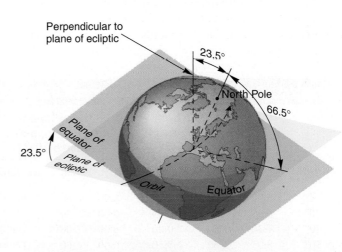

FIGURE 2.14 The plane of Earth's orbit—the ecliptic—and Earth's axial tilt.
Note on the illustration that the plane of the equator is inclined to the plane of the ecliptic at about 23.5°.

FIGURE 2.15 Annual march of the seasons.
Annual march of the seasons as Earth revolves about the Sun. Shading indicates the changing position of the circle of illumination. Note the hours of daylight for the equator and the poles. To follow the text, begin on the right side at December 21 and move counterclockwise.

ANIMATION

Earth-Sun Relations, Seasons

Annual March of the Seasons

During the annual march of the seasons on Earth, daylength is the most obvious way of sensing changes in season at latitudes away from the equator. Daylength is the interval between **sunrise**, the moment when the disk of the Sun first appears above the horizon in the east, and **sunset**, that moment when it totally disappears below the

horizon in the west. Table 2.3 lists the average times of sunrise and sunset and the daylength for various latitudes and seasons in the Northern Hemisphere. (For the Southern Hemisphere, merely switch the solstice column headings and switch the equinox column headings.)

The extremes of daylength occur in December and June. The times around December 21 and June 21 are

Table 2.3	Daylength Times (Sunrise and Sunset) at Selected Latitudes (Northern Hemisphere)											
	Winter Solstice (December Solstice) December 21–22			**Vernal Equinox (March Equinox) March 20–21**			**Summer Solstice (June Solstice) June 20–21**			**Autumnal Equinox (September Equinox) September 22–23**		
Latitude	A.M.	P.M.	Daylength	A.M.	P.M.	Daylength	A.M.	P.M.	Daylength	A.M.	P.M.	Daylength
0°	6:00	6:00	12:00	6:00	6:00	12:00	6:00	6:00	12:00	6:00	6:00	12:00
30°	6:58	5:02	10:04	6:00	6:00	12:00	5:02	6:58	13:56	6:00	6:00	12:00
40°	7:30	4:30	9:00	6:00	6:00	12:00	4:30	7:30	15:00	6:00	6:00	12:00
50°	8:05	3:55	7:50	6:00	6:00	12:00	3:55	8:05	16:10	6:00	6:00	12:00
60°	9:15	2:45	5:30	6:00	6:00	12:00	2:45	9:15	18:30	6:00	6:00	12:00
90°	No sunlight			Rising Sun			Continuous sunlight			Setting Sun		

Note: All times are standard and do not consider the local option of daylight saving time.

Table 2.4 Annual March of the Seasons		
Approximate Date	**Northern Hemisphere Name**	**Location of the Subsolar Point**
December 21–22	Winter solstice (December solstice)	23.5° S latitude (Tropic of Capricorn)
March 20–21	Vernal equinox (March equinox)	0° (equator)
June 20–21	Summer solstice (June solstice)	23.5° N latitude (Tropic of Cancer)
September 22–23	Autumnal equinox (September equinox)	0° (equator)

termed *solstices*. Strictly speaking, the solstices are specific points in time at which the Sun's declination is at its position farthest north at the **Tropic of Cancer**, 23.5° N, or south at the **Tropic of Capricorn**, 23.5° S. "Tropic" is from *tropicus*, meaning a turn or change, so a tropic latitude is where the Sun's declination appears to stand still briefly (Sun stance, or *sol stice*); then it "turns" and heads toward the other tropic.

Table 2.4 presents the key seasonal anniversary dates during which the specific time of the equinoxes or solstices occur, their names, and the subsolar point location (declination). During the year, places on Earth outside of the equatorial region experience a continuous but gradual shift in daylength, a few minutes each day, and the Sun's altitude increases or decreases a small amount. You may have noticed that these daily variations become more pronounced in spring and autumn, when the Sun's declination changes at a faster rate.

Figure 2.15 demonstrates the annual march of the seasons and illustrates Earth's relationship to the Sun during the year. Let us begin with December, on the right side of the illustration. On December 21 or 22, at the moment of the **winter solstice** ("winter Sun stance"), or **December solstice**, the circle of illumination excludes the North Pole region from sunlight but includes the South Pole region. The subsolar point is at 23.5° S latitude, the Tropic of Capricorn parallel. The Northern Hemisphere is tilted away from these more direct rays of sunlight—our northern winter—thereby creating a lower angle for the incoming solar rays and thus a more diffuse pattern of insolation.

From 66.5° N latitude to 90° N (the North Pole), the Sun remains below the horizon the entire day. This latitude (66.5° N) marks the **Arctic Circle**, the southernmost parallel (in the Northern Hemisphere) that experiences a 24-hour period of darkness. During this period, twilight and dawn provide some lighting for more than a month at the beginning and end of the Arctic night. During the following 3 months, daylength and solar angles gradually increase in the Northern Hemisphere as Earth completes one-fourth of its orbit.

The sunset photo in Figure 2.16 was made approaching the Antarctic coast, December 14, 2003, at 11:30 P.M. local time, just a week before the December solstice. We were crossing the Branfield Strait at 63° S at the time. Sunrise was only a couple of hours later, at 2 A.M. local time—making the sunless twilight/dawn period only a little over 2 hours!

FIGURE 2.16 Antarctic sunset, 11:30 P.M.!
Approaching the continent of Antarctica at 63° south latitude in December. The low Sun angle produces incredible sunset colours that persist for almost an hour; note a large iceberg and ice-covered mountains ahead. [Photo by Bobbé Christopherson.]

The moment of the **vernal equinox**, or **March equinox**, occurs on March 20 or 21. At that time, the circle of illumination passes through both poles so that all locations on Earth experience a 12-hour day and a 12-hour night. People living around 40° N latitude (New York, Denver) have gained 3 hours of daylight since the December solstice. At the North Pole, the Sun peeks above the horizon for the first time since the previous September; at the South Pole, the Sun is setting—a dramatic 3-day "moment" for the people working the Scott–Amundson Base.

From March, the seasons move on to June 20 or 21 and the moment of the **summer solstice**, or **June solstice**. The subsolar point migrates from the equator to 23.5° N latitude, the Tropic of Cancer. Because the circle of illumination now includes the North Polar region, everything north of the Arctic Circle receives 24 hours of daylight—the *Midnight Sun*. Figure 2.17 is a multiple-image photo of the midnight Sun as seen north of the Arctic Circle. In contrast, the region from the **Antarctic Circle** to the South Pole (66.5°–90° S latitude) is in darkness the entire 24 hours. Those working in Antarctica call this *Midwinter's Day*.

September 22 or 23 is the moment in time of the **autumnal equinox**, or **September equinox**, when Earth's orientation is such that the circle of illumination again passes through both poles so that all parts of the

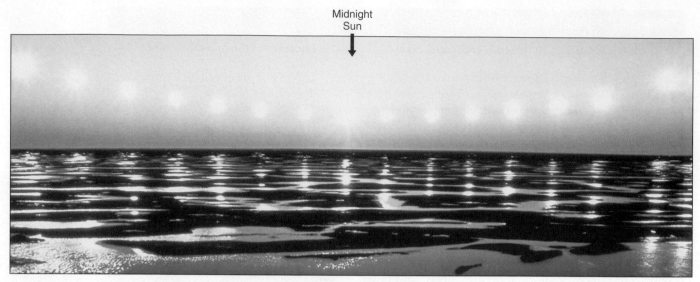

FIGURE 2.17 The Midnight Sun.
The Midnight Sun north of the Arctic Circle captured in a series of 18 exposures on the same piece of film. The camera is facing due north. Midnight is the exposure showing the Sun closest to the horizon. The photographer removed the lens cap at regular intervals to make the multiple exposures. The middle exposure is marked *Midnight Sun*. [Photo by Gary Braasch/Tony Stone Images.]

globe experience a 12-hour day and a 12-hour night. The subsolar point returns to the equator, with days growing shorter to the north and longer to the south. Researchers stationed at the South Pole see the disk of the Sun just rising, ending their 6 months of darkness. In the Northern Hemisphere, autumn arrives, a time of many colourful changes in the landscape, whereas in the Southern Hemisphere it is spring.

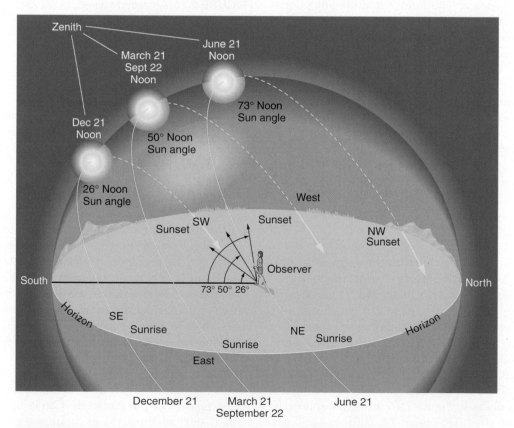

FIGURE 2.18 Seasonal observations—sunrise, noon, and sunset through the year.
Seasonal observations are at 40° N latitude for the December solstice, March equinox, June solstice, and September equinox. The Sun's altitude increases from 26° in December to 73° above the horizon in June—a difference of 47°. Note the changing position of sunrise and sunset along the horizon during the year. For a useful sunrise and sunset calculator for any location, go to http://www.srrb.noaa.gov/highlights/ sunrise/sunrise.html.

Dawn and Twilight   *Dawn* is the period of diffused light that occurs before sunrise. The corresponding evening time after sunset is *twilight*. During both periods, light is scattered by molecules of atmospheric gases and reflected by dust and moisture in the atmosphere. The duration of both is a function of latitude, because the angle of the Sun's path above the horizon determines the thickness of the atmosphere through which the Sun's rays must pass. The illumination may be enhanced by the presence of pollution aerosols and suspended particles from volcanic eruptions or forest and grassland fires.

At the equator, where the Sun's rays are almost directly above the horizon throughout the year, dawn and twilight are limited to 30–45 minutes each. These times increase to 1–2 hours each at 40° latitude, and at 60° latitude they each range upward from 2.5 hours, with little true night in summer. The poles experience about 7 weeks of dawn and 7 weeks of twilight, leaving only 2.5 months of "night" during the 6 months when the Sun is completely below the horizon. In the high latitudes, this extended period of diffused light produces beautiful colours.

Seasonal Observations   In the midlatitudes of the Northern Hemisphere, the position of sunrise on the horizon migrates from day to day, from the southeast in December to the northeast in June. Over the same period, the point of sunset migrates from the southwest to the northwest. The Sun's altitude at local noon at 40° N latitude increases from a 26° angle above the horizon at the winter (December) solstice to a 73° angle above the horizon at the summer (June) solstice—a range of 47° (Figure 2.18).

Seasonal change is quite noticeable across the landscape away from the equator. Think back over the past year. What seasonal changes have you observed in vegetation, temperatures, and weather? Figure 2.19 presents two composite images of vegetation cover in winter and late summer as recorded by the AVHRR sensors aboard polar-orbiting satellites. Recently, the timing of the seasons is changing as global climates shift in middle and high latitudes. Spring and leafing out is occurring as much as 3 weeks earlier than expected from average conditions. Likewise, the timing of fall is happening later. Ecosystems are changing in response.

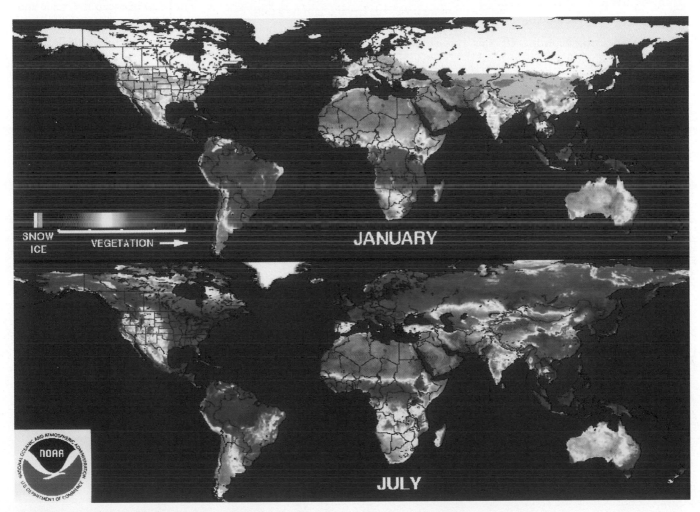

FIGURE 2.19 Seasonal change from orbit.
Seasonal change is monitored and measured by sensors aboard polar-orbiting satellites. Compare and contrast similar regions for January and July: central Canada, China, Argentina, and Europe. Orbital remote sensing is tracking an earlier spring and later fall seasons worldwide. [Images courtesy of Garik Gutman, NOAA, National Environmental Satellite, Data, and Information Service (NESDIS).]

Calculating the Energy from Sunlight over a 12-Hour Period*

How much energy does any spot on Earth receive over the span of a 12-hour day? How does this vary by season?

Recall that the solar constant, 1372 W/m² (expressed in milliwatts as 137.2 mW/cm²), is a measure of power per unit area at high noon with the Sun directly overhead (as would occur at the equator or in the tropics). The energy from the sunlight can be extracted from this number.

First, remembering that 1 watt is equal to 1 joule per second, if we take energy in mJ (millijoules), from the units alone we obtain

$$mJ = (mW/cm^2) \times (\text{Area in } cm^2) \times (\text{Time in seconds})$$

(since mW = mJ/second). If the Sun were always directly overhead, the amount of energy incident upon a 1-cm² solar collector oriented perpendicular to the sun's rays in 12 hours would be

$$(137.2 \text{ mW/cm}^2) \times (1 \text{ cm}^2) \times (12 \text{ hours})$$
$$= (137.2 \text{ mW/cm}^2) \times (1 \text{ cm}^2) \times (4.3 \times 10^4 \text{ seconds})$$
$$= 5.93 \times 10^6 \text{ mJ}$$

Because of Earth's rotation and orbit around the sun, however, the Sun appears to move East–West throughout the course of a day and North–South throughout the course of a year. This yearly variation can be accounted for. We know that the Sun moves ± 23.5° above and below the equator between the two tropics over

the course of a year. Typically, it is on the equator every March 21 and September 21. We may estimate θ, the Sun's position north of the π equator, by calculating

$$\theta = 23.5° \sin (2\{\delta T/365.25\})$$

where δT is the number of days counted from the vernal equinox (April 21). (Notice that for northern winter months, θ is negative.) We may then estimate the solar constant for any particular day by calculating

$$\sigma_D = (137.2 \text{ mW/cm}^2) \cos (L - \theta)$$

where L is latitude in degrees.

The daily variation is a little more involved. Let the Sun be at altitude A (angle above the eastern horizon) at a given time t during the day. Then at time $t + \delta T$, the altitude will have increased to $A + \delta A$. The differential time is related to the differential altitude by

$$\delta T = (12/\pi) \delta A \text{ h}$$

because the Sun travels through π radians (180°) in 12 hours.

If we again try to calculate the amount of energy incident upon a 1 cm² solar collector oriented perpendicular to the Sun's noon-time rays in 12 hours, we have to use

$$\text{Area} = (\sin A) \text{ cm}^2$$

for the equivalent collecting area as we want only the amount of area projected perpendicular to the Sun's rays at time t. The differential energy δE incident upon our solar collector in time δT is

$$\delta E = \sigma_D(\sin A) \delta T$$
$$= \sigma_D(\sin A)(12/\pi)(3600 \text{ seconds/hour}) \delta A$$
$$= \sigma_D(4.3 \times 10^4 \text{ seconds/}\pi)[(\sin A) \delta A].$$

The expression in square brackets may be integrated from A = 0 to A = π to yield

$$E = \sigma_D(4.3 \times 10^4 \text{ seconds/}\pi)$$

If, for comparison, we set $\sigma_D = 137 \text{ mW/cm}^2$ (i.e., if we were to take our collector to the tropics), we find

$$E = 3.7 \times 10^6 \text{ mJ}$$

The ratio between this value and the one derived above is $2/\pi$. At latitude 42° N, for example, the midsummer value is

$$E = 1.8 \times 10^6 \text{ mJ}$$

and the midwinter value is

$$E = 7.2 \times 10^5 \text{ mJ}$$

The ratio of the midwinter to the midsummer values is

$$(7.2 \times 10^5 \text{ mJ})/(1.8 \times 10^6 \text{ mJ}) = 0.4,$$

which means that over a 12-hour period at this latitude, the solar collector receives a mere 40% of the energy in midwinter that it would in midsummer.

*Modified from **http://www.lerc.nasa. gov/WWW/K-12/Numbers/Math/ Mathematical_Thinking/sun12.htm**, by Joe Kolecki, Glenn Learning Technologies Project/NASA.

Summary and Review—Solar Energy to Earth and the Seasons

■ *Distinguish* among galaxies, stars, and planets and *locate* Earth.

Our Solar System—the Sun and nine planets—is located on a remote, trailing edge of the **Milky Way Galaxy**, a flattened, disk-shaped mass estimated to contain up to 400 billion stars. **Gravity**, the mutual attracting force exerted by the mass of an object upon all other objects, is an organizing force in the Universe. The process of stars (like our Sun) condensing from nebular clouds with planetesimals (protoplanets) forming in orbits around their central masses is the **planetesimal hypothesis**.

> Milky Way Galaxy (p. 42)
> gravity (p. 42)
> planetesimal hypothesis (p. 42)

1. Describe the Sun's status among stars in the Milky Way Galaxy. Describe the Sun's location, size, and relationship to its planets.

2. If you have seen the Milky Way at night, briefly describe it. Use specifics from the text in your description.

3. Briefly describe Earth's origin as part of the Solar System.

4. Compare the locations of the nine planets of the Solar System.

■ *Overview* the origin, formation, and development of Earth and *construct* Earth's annual orbit about the Sun.

The Solar System, planets, and Earth began to condense from a nebular cloud of dust, gas, debris, and icy comets approximately 4.6 billion years ago. Distances in space are so vast that the **speed of light** (300,000 kmps, or 186,000 mps, which is about 9.5 trillion km, or nearly 6 trillion mi, per year) is used to express distance.

In its orbit, Earth is at **perihelion** (its closest position to the Sun) during our Northern Hemisphere winter (January 3 at 147,255,000 km, or 91,500,000 mi). It is at **aphelion** (its farthest position from the Sun) during our Northern Hemisphere summer (July 4 at 152,083,000 km, or 94,500,000 mi). Earth's average distance from the Sun is approximately 8 minutes and 20 seconds in terms of light speed.

> speed of light (p. 42)
> perihelion (p. 42)
> aphelion (p. 42)

5. How far is Earth from the Sun in terms of light speed? In terms of kilometres and miles?

6. Briefly describe the relationship among these concepts: Universe, Milky Way Galaxy, Solar System, Sun, and planet Earth.

7. Diagram in a simple sketch Earth's orbit about the Sun. How much does it vary during the course of a year?

■ *Describe* the Sun's operation and *explain* the characteristics of the solar wind and the electromagnetic spectrum of radiant energy.

The **fusion** process—hydrogen atoms forced together under tremendous temperature and pressure in the Sun's interior—generates incredible quantities of energy. Solar energy in the form of charged particles of **solar wind** travels out in all directions from magnetic disturbances on the Sun, such as from

conspicuous features of large **sunspots**. Solar wind is deflected by Earth's **magnetosphere**, producing various effects in the upper atmosphere, including spectacular **auroras**, the northern and southern lights, which surge across the skies at higher latitudes. Another effect of the solar wind in the atmosphere is its possible influence on weather.

The **electromagnetic spectrum** of radiant energy travels outward in all directions from the Sun. The total spectrum of this radiant energy is made up of different **wavelengths**—the distance between corresponding points on any two successive waves of radiant energy. Eventually, some of this radiant energy reaches Earth's surface.

> fusion (p. 42)
> solar wind (p. 44)
> sunspots (p. 44)
> magnetosphere (p. 44)
> auroras (p. 45)
> electromagnetic spectrum (p. 46)
> wavelength (p. 46)

8. How does the Sun produce such tremendous quantities of energy?

9. What is the sunspot cycle? At what stage is the cycle in the year 2008?

10. Describe Earth's magnetosphere and its effects on the solar wind and the electromagnetic spectrum.

11. Summarize the presently known effects of the solar wind relative to Earth's environment.

12. Describe the various segments of the electromagnetic spectrum, from shortest to longest wavelength. What are the main wavelengths produced by the Sun? Which are principally radiated by Earth to space?

■ *Portray* the intercepted solar energy and its uneven distribution at the top of the atmosphere.

Electromagnetic radiation from the Sun passes through Earth's magnetic field to the top of the atmosphere—the **thermopause**, at approximately 500 km (300 mi) altitude. Incoming solar radiation that reaches a horizontal plane at Earth is **insolation**, a term specifically applied to radiation arriving at Earth's surface and atmosphere. The term **solar constant** describes insolation at the top of the atmosphere: the average insolation received at the thermopause when Earth is at its average distance from the Sun. The solar constant is measured as an average of 1372 W/m² (2.0 Cal/cm²/min; 2langleys/min). The place receiving maximum insolation is the **subsolar point**, where solar rays are perpendicular to the surface (radiating from directly overhead). All other locations away from the subsolar point receive slanting rays and more diffuse energy.

> thermopause (p. 47)
> insolation (p. 47)
> solar constant (p. 48)
> subsolar point (p. 48)

13. What is the solar constant? Why is it important to know?

14. Select 40° or 50° north latitude on Figure 2.10 and plot the amount of energy in watts per square metre (w/m²) per day on a graph for each month throughout the year. Compare this with the amount at the North Pole and at the equator.

15. If Earth were flat and oriented perpendicularly to incoming solar radiation (insolation), what would be the latitudinal distribution of solar energy at the top of the atmosphere?

■ *Define* **solar altitude, solar declination, and daylength** and *describe* **the annual variability of each—Earth's seasonality.**

The angle between the Sun and the horizon is the Sun's **altitude**. The Sun's **declination** is the latitude of the subsolar point. Declination annually migrates through 47° of latitude, moving between the *Tropic of Cancer* at 23.5° N (June) and the *Tropic of Capricorn* at 23.5° S latitude (December). Seasonality means an annual change in the Sun's altitude and changing **daylength**, or duration of exposure.

Earth's distinct seasons are produced by interactions of **revolution** (annual orbit about the Sun), **rotation** (Earth's turning on its **axis**), **axial tilt** (at about 23.5° from a perpendicular to the **plane of the ecliptic**), **axial parallelism** (the parallel alignment of the axis throughout the year), and *sphericity*. Earth rotates about its axis, an imaginary line extending through the planet from the geographic North Pole to the South Pole. In the Solar System, an imaginary plane touching all points of Earth's orbit is termed the **plane of the ecliptic**. As it rotates, the traveling boundary that divides daylight and darkness is called the **circle of illumination**. Daylength is the interval between **sunrise**, the moment when the disk of the Sun first appears above the horizon in the east, and **sunset**, that moment when it totally disappears below the horizon in the west. The **Tropic of Cancer** parallel marks the farthest north the subsolar point migrates during the year: 23.5° north latitude. The **Tropic of Capricorn** parallel marks the farthest south the subsolar point migrates during the year: 23.5° south latitude.

On December 21 or 22, at the moment of the **winter solstice** ("winter Sun stance"), or **December solstice**, the circle of illumination excludes the North Pole but includes the South Pole. The Sun remains below the horizon the entire day. This latitude (66.5° N) marks the **Arctic Circle**, the southernmost parallel (in the Northern Hemisphere) that experiences a 24-hour period of darkness, or on June 21 a 24-hour period of daylight. The moment of the **vernal equinox**, or **March equinox**, occurs on March 20 or 21. At that time, the circle of illumination passes through both poles so that all locations on Earth experience a 12-hour day and a 12-hour night.

June 20 or 21 is the moment of the **summer solstice**, or **June solstice**. The subsolar point migrates from the equator to 23.5° N latitude, the Tropic of Cancer. Because the circle of illumination now includes the North Polar region, everything north of the Arctic Circle receives 24 hours of daylight—the "Midnight Sun." In contrast, the area from the **Antarctic Circle**

to the South Pole (66.5°–90° S latitude) is in darkness the entire 24 hours, or on December 21 in constant daylight. September 22 or 23 is the time of the **autumnal equinox**, or **September equinox**, when Earth's orientation is such that the circle of illumination again passes through both poles so that all parts of the globe experience a 12-hour day and a 12-hour night.

altitude (p. 51)
declination (p. 51)
daylength (p. 51)
revolution (p. 52)
rotation (p. 52)
axis (p. 52)
circle of illumination (p. 53)
axial tilt (p. 53)
plane of the ecliptic (p. 53)
axial parallelism (p. 53)
sunrise (p. 54)
sunset (p. 54)
Tropic of Cancer (p. 55)
Tropic of Capricorn (p. 55)
winter solstice, December solstice (p. 55)
Arctic Circle (p. 55)
vernal equinox, March equinox (p. 55)
summer solstice, June solstice (p. 55)
Antarctic Circle (p. 55)
autumnal equinox, September equinox (p. 55)

16. The concept of seasonality refers to what specific phenomena? How do these two aspects of seasonality change during a year at 0° latitude? At 40°? At 90°?

17. Differentiate between the Sun's altitude and its declination at Earth's surface.

18. For the latitude at which you live, how does daylength vary during the year? How does the Sun's altitude vary? Does your local newspaper publish a weather calendar containing such information?

19. List the five physical factors that operate together to produce seasons.

20. Describe Earth's revolution and rotation and differentiate between them.

21. Define Earth's present tilt relative to its orbit about the Sun.

22. Describe seasonal conditions at each of the four key seasonal anniversary dates during the year. What are the solstices and equinoxes, and what is the Sun's declination at these times?

Critical Thinking

A. Using the concepts in Figure 2.18, use a protractor and stick or ruler to measure the angle of the Sun's altitude at noon (or 1 P.M., if in daylight saving time). Do not look at the Sun; rather, with your back to the Sun, align the stick so that it casts no shadow as you measure its rays against the protractor. Place this measurement in your notebook and affix a Post-It® in the textbook to remind you to repeat the measurement near the end of the semester. Compare and analyze seasonal change using your different measurements of the Sun's altitude.

B. Also in reference to the concepts in Figure 2.18, post a reminder in your notebook to check the position of sunrise and sunset at least twice during the semester. If you have a magnetic compass, note the degrees from north for sunrise and sunset (*azimuth* is read from north in a clockwise direction—0° and 360° being the same point, north). Find some place where you can see the horizon. If new to such observations, the degree of location change over the span of months in a school term will surprise you. Be sure and ask your teacher about the magnetic declination of your location to adjust your compass readings.

C. The variability of Earth's axial tilt, orbit about the Sun, and a wobble to the axis is described in Figure 17.32. Please refer to this figure and compare these changing conditions to the information in Table 2.1 and the related figures in this chapter. Speculate on the effects of each of these changes on the annual march of the seasons.

In this chapter: We examine the modern atmosphere using criteria of composition, temperature, and function. Our look at the atmosphere also includes the spatial aspects of both natural and human-produced air pollution. We all participate in the atmosphere with each breath we take, the energy we consume, the traveling we do, and the products we buy. Human activities caused the stratospheric ozone predicament and the blight of acid deposition on ecosystems. These topics are essential to physical geography, for we are influencing the atmospheric composition for the future.

Atmospheric Composition, Temperature, and Function

The *modern* atmosphere probably is the fourth general atmosphere in Earth's history. Therefore, this modern atmosphere is a gaseous mixture of ancient origin, the sum of all the exhalations and inhalations of life on Earth throughout time. The principal substance of this atmosphere is air, the medium of life as well as a major industrial and chemical raw material. **Air** is a simple mixture of gases that is naturally odourless, colourless, tasteless, and formless, blended so thoroughly that it behaves as if it were a single gas.

In his book *The Lives of a Cell*, the late physician and self-styled "biology watcher" Lewis Thomas compared the atmosphere of Earth to an enormous cell membrane.

The membrane around a cell regulates the interactions between the cell's delicate inner workings and the potentially disruptive outer environment. Each cell membrane is selective as to what it will allow to pass through. The modern atmosphere acts as Earth's protective membrane, as Thomas described so vividly (Figure 3.1).

As a practical matter, we consider the top of our atmosphere to be around 480 km (300 mi) above Earth's surface, the same altitude we use in Chapter 2 for measuring the solar constant and insolation receipt. Beyond that altitude is the **exosphere**, which means "outer sphere," where the rarefied atmosphere is nearly a vacuum. It contains scarce lightweight hydrogen and helium atoms, weakly bound by gravity as far as 32,000 km (20,000 mi) from Earth.

Atmospheric Profile

As critical as the atmosphere is to us, it represents only the thinnest envelope, amounting to less than one-millionth of Earth's total mass. Think of Earth's modern atmosphere as a series of imperfectly shaped concentric "shells" or "spheres" that grade into one another, all bound to the planet by gravity. To study the atmosphere let's view it in layers, each with distinctive properties and purposes. Figure 3.2 charts the atmosphere in a vertical cross-section profile, or side view, and is a useful reference for the following discussion. To simplify we use three atmospheric criteria detailed in Table 3.1:

> Viewed from the distance of the Moon, the astonishing thing about Earth, catching the breath, is that it is alive. The photographs show the dry, pounded surface of the Moon in the foreground, dead as an old bone. Aloft, floating free beneath the moist, gleaming membrane of a bright blue sky, is the rising Earth, the only exuberant thing in this part of the cosmos. . . . It has the organized, self-contained look of a live creature, full of information, marvelously skilled in handling the sun. . . . When the Earth came alive it began constructing its own membrane, for the general purpose of editing the sun. . . . Taken all in all, the sky is a miraculous achievement. It works, and for what it is designed to accomplish it is as infallible as anything in nature.
>
> *Lewis Thomas*

FIGURE 3.1 Earthrise.
Earthrise over the stark and lifeless lunar surface. [Photo by NASA; quotation from "The World's Biggest Membrane" in *The Lives of a Cell* by Lewis Thomas. Copyright © 1973, Massachusetts Medical Society. Reprinted by permission of Viking Penguin, Penguin Books USA, Inc.]

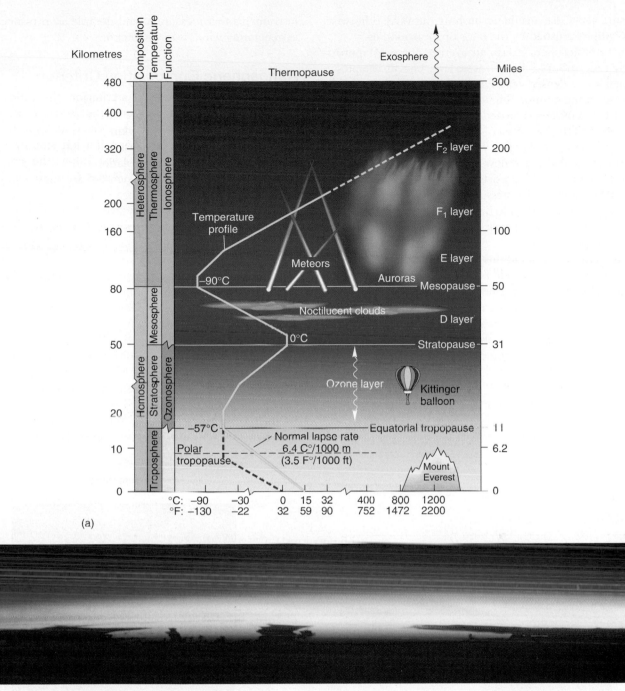

(a)

(b)

FIGURE 3.2 Profile of the modern atmosphere.
(a) The integrated chart of our modern atmosphere is from Earth's surface to the top of the atmosphere at 480 km (300 mi). The columns along the left side show the division of the atmosphere by composition, temperature, and function. The plot of temperature by altitude relates to the scale along the bottom axis. (The small balloon shows the height achieved by Kittinger, discussed in News Report 3.1.) (b) Space Shuttle astronauts captured a dramatic sunset through various atmospheric layers across the "edge" of our planet—*Earth's limb*. A silhouetted cumulonimbus thunderhead cloud is topping out at the tropopause. [Space Shuttle photo from NASA.]

composition, *temperature*, and *function*, noted along the left side of Figure 3.2a.

Earth's atmosphere exerts its weight, pressing downward under the pull of gravity. Air molecules create air pressure through their motion, size, and number. Pressure is exerted on all surfaces in contact with the air. The weight (force over a unit area) of the atmosphere, or **air pressure**, pushes in on all of us. Fortunately, that same

Table 3.1	Atmospheric Criterion	
Composition	**Temperature**	**Function**
Heterosphere	Thermosphere	Ionosphere
Homosphere	Mesosphere	
	Stratosphere	Ozonosphere
	Troposphere	

pressure also exists inside us, pushing outward; otherwise, we would be crushed by the mass of air around us.

The atmosphere exerts an average force of approximately 1kg/cm^2 (14.7 lb/in^2) at sea level. Gravity compresses air, making it denser near Earth's surface; it thins rapidly with increasing altitude (Figure 3.3a), and with reduced air pressure, less oxygen is carried in each breath a person takes.

Over half the total mass of the atmosphere is compressed below 5500 m (18,000 ft), 75% occurs below 10,700 m (35,100 ft), and 90% is below 16,000 m (52,500 ft). All but 0.1% of the atmosphere exists below an altitude of 50 km (31 mi), as shown in the pressure profile in Figure 3.3b (percentage column is farthest to the right). Few people are aware that in routine air travel they are sitting above 80% of the total atmospheric volume!

To better understand this pressure profile, imagine sky diving from a high-altitude balloon 32 km (20 mi) above Earth. What would you experience? How fast would you fall? What sounds would you hear? See News Report 3.1 to read about someone who actually did this before NASA's Mercury astronaut program.

At sea level, the atmosphere exerts a pressure of 1013.2 mb (*millibar*, or *mb*; a measure of force per square metre of surface area) or 29.92 in. of mercury (symbol, Hg), as measured by a barometer. In Canada and other countries, normal air pressure is expressed as 101.32 kPa (*kilopascal*; 1 kPa = 10 mb). More information on air pressure, the

instruments that measure it, and the role air pressure plays in generating winds is in Chapter 6.

Atmospheric Composition Criterion

Using chemical *composition* as a criterion, the atmosphere divides into two broad regions, the *heterosphere* (80 to 480 km altitude) and the *homosphere* (Earth's surface to 80 km altitude), as shown along the left side of Figure 3.2a. As you read, note that the text follows the same path that incoming solar radiation travels through the atmosphere to Earth's surface.

Heterosphere The **heterosphere** is the outer atmosphere in terms of composition. It begins at about 80 km (50 mi) altitude and extends outward to the exosphere and interplanetary space transition (see Figure 3.2). Less than 0.001% of the atmosphere's mass is in this rarefied heterosphere. The International Space Station and most Space Shuttle missions orbit in the middle to upper heterosphere.

As the prefix *hetero-* implies, this region is not uniform—its gases are *not evenly mixed*. Gases in the heterosphere occur in distinct layers sorted by gravity according to their atomic weight, with the lightest elements (hydrogen and helium) at the margins of outer space and the heavier elements (oxygen and nitrogen) dominant in the lower

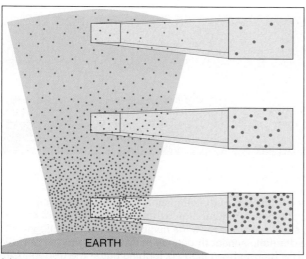

(a)

FIGURE 3.3 Density decreases with altitude.
(a) The atmosphere, denser near Earth's surface, rapidly decreases in density with altitude. The difference in density is easily measured because air exerts its weight as pressure. Have you experienced pressure changes that you could feel on your eardrums? How high above sea level were you at the time? (b) Pressure profile of the atmosphere. Note the rapid decrease in atmospheric pressure with altitude and that about 90% of the atmospheric mass resides in the troposphere (far-right column).

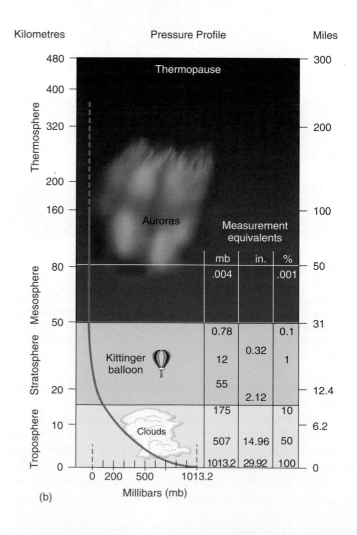

(b)

News Report 3.1

Falling Through the Atmosphere—The Highest Sky Dive

Imagine a small, unpressurized compartment large enough for only one person, floating at 31.3 km (19.5 mi) altitude, dangling from a helium-filled balloon. Even though it is daytime, the sky is almost black, because the balloon is above all but 1.0% of the atmospheric mass. The air pressure at 31,300 m (102,800 ft) is barely measurable—this altitude is the beginning of space in experimental aircraft testing. The year is 1961. (See the position of this balloon on Figures 3.2a and 3.3b.)

Captain Joseph Kittinger, Jr., an Air Force officer, stood at the opening in his capsule. He paused for the view of Earth's curved horizon, the New Mexico landscape over 31 km below, and the dark heavens above, and then leaped into the stratospheric void (Figure 3.1.1). He placed himself at tremendous personal risk for an experimental reentry into the atmosphere. What do you think he would initially hear and feel? At what speed would he fall? What would the temperature be? How long would he fall before opening his parachute?

Initially frightening to him was that he heard nothing, no rushing sound, for there was not enough air to produce any sound. The fabric of his pressure suit did not flutter, for there was not enough air to create friction against the cloth. He had no sensation of movement until he glanced back at

FIGURE 3.1.1 Stratospheric leap into history.
A remotely triggered camera captures Captain Joseph Kittinger's historic exploration of the atmosphere as he leaps from the capsule. The lanyard cord is attached to his parachute pack and snaps to set a timer that opens a small stabilization chute 16 seconds into the free fall. The clouds are more than 26,000 m (85,000 ft) below him. He carries an instrument pack on his seat, his main chute, and pure oxygen for his breathing mask. [Volkmar Wentzel/NGS Image Collection, used by permission from the National Geographic Society, *National Geographic Magazine*, Dec. 1960, p. 855. All rights reserved.]

the balloon and capsule. They retreated rapidly from his motionless perception. This lack of a sense of speed was unnerving as he fell.

His speed was remarkable. Near the ground, objects fall at "terminal velocity," reaching about 200 kmph (125 mph) in a few seconds. However, in the rarefied stratosphere the lack of air resistance permits incredible speeds. Captain Kittinger quickly accelerated to 988 kmph (614 mph), near the speed of sound at sea level.

His free fall took him through the stratosphere and its ozone layer. As he encountered denser layers of

atmospheric gases, frictional drag slowed his body. As he fell past 15,240 m (50,000 ft), he slowed to 400 kmph (250 mph). He dropped into the lower atmosphere, finally falling below airplane flying altitudes. His free fall lasted 4 minutes and 25 seconds, slowing to terminal velocity and the opening of his main chute at 5500 m (18,000 ft). He safely drifted to Earth's surface. This remarkable 13-minute 35-second voyage through 99% of the atmospheric mass remains a record to this day. To better understand the atmosphere, Kittinger placed himself in harm's way in this experiment at the early beginnings of human space exploration.

---

heterosphere. This distribution is quite different from the blended gases we breathe in the homosphere near Earth's surface.

Homosphere Below the heterosphere is the **homosphere**, extending from an altitude of 80 km (50 mi) to Earth's surface. Even though the atmosphere rapidly changes density in the homosphere—increasing pressure exerted toward Earth's surface—the blend of gases is nearly uniform throughout. The only exceptions are the concentration of ozone (O_3) in the "ozone layer," from 19 to 50 km (12 to 31 mi), and the variations in water vapour, pollutants, and some trace chemicals in the lowest portion of the atmosphere.

The stable mixture of gases comprising air in the homosphere evolved slowly. The present proportion, which includes oxygen, evolved approximately 500 million years ago. Table 3.2 lists by volume the stable ingredients that constitute dry, clean air in the homosphere.

The air of the homosphere is a vast reservoir of relatively inert *nitrogen*, originating principally from volcanic sources. Nitrogen is a key element of life, yet we exhale all the nitrogen we inhale. The explanation for this contradiction is that nitrogen integrates into our bodies not from the air we breathe, but through compounds in food. In the soil, nitrogen is bound to these compounds by nitrogen-fixing bacteria, and it returns to the atmosphere by denitrifying bacteria that remove nitrogen from

Table 3.2 Stable Components of the Modern Homosphere

Gas (Symbol)	Percentage by Volume	Parts per Million (ppm)
Nitrogen (N_2)	78.084	780,840
Oxygen (O_2)	20.946	209,460
Argon (Ar)	0.934	9,340
Carbon dioxide (CO_2)[*]	0.039	386.54
Neon (Ne)	0.001818	18
Helium (He)	0.000525	5
Methane (CH_4)	0.00014	1.4
Krypton (Kr)	0.00010	1.0
Ozone (O_3)	Variable	
Nitrous oxide (N_2O)	Trace	
Hydrogen (H)	Trace	
Xenon (Xe)	Trace	

[*]2007 average measured at Mauna Loa, Hawai'i (see: http://cdiac.esd.ornl.gov/ftp/maunaloa-co2/maunaloa.co2 and http://www.esrl.noaa.gov/gmd/ccgg/trends/co2_data_mlo.html

organic materials. A complete discussion of the nitrogen cycle is in Chapter 19.

Oxygen, a by-product of photosynthesis, also is essential for life processes. Slight spatial variations occur in the percentage of oxygen in the atmosphere because of variations in photosynthetic rates with latitude, seasonal changes, and the lag time as atmospheric circulation slowly mixes the air. Although it forms about one-fifth of the atmosphere, oxygen forms compounds that compose about half of Earth's crust. Oxygen readily reacts with many elements to form these materials. Both nitrogen and oxygen reserves in the atmosphere are so extensive that, at present, they far exceed human capabilities to disrupt or deplete them.

The gas *argon*, constituting less than 1% of the homosphere, is completely inert (an unreactive "noble" gas) and therefore is unusable in life processes. Argon is a residue from the radioactive decay of an isotope, or chemical form, of potassium called potassium-40 (symbolized ^{40}K). All the argon present in the modern atmosphere comes from slow accumulation over millions of years. Because industry has found uses for inert argon (in lightbulbs, welding, and some lasers), it is extracted or "mined" from the atmosphere, in addition to nitrogen and oxygen, for commercial and industrial uses.

Carbon dioxide is a natural by-product of life processes. It is essentially a stable atmospheric component, qualifying it for inclusion in Table 3.2. Although its present percentage in the atmosphere is small at about 0.039%, it is important in maintaining global temperatures.

Chapters 4, 5, and 10 discuss the role of carbon dioxide as an important greenhouse gas and its role in present global temperature increases. Carbon dioxide concentrations in the atmosphere since 1958 are graphed in Figure 3.4. The annual fluctuation between summer and winter is evidence of seasons and the work of plant photosynthesis. Scientists agree that the increase is human-forced.

Over the past 200 years, its percentage increased as a result of human activities, principally the burning of fossil fuels and deforestation. According to ice-core records, CO_2 is higher now than at any time in the past 800,000 years. This increase appears to be accelerating. From 1990 to 1999 CO_2 rose at an average of 1.1% per year; compare this to the average increase since 2000 of 3.1%

FIGURE 3.4 Carbon dioxide concentrations increase 1958–2007.

Fifty years of CO_2 data measured at the Mauna Loa Observatory (see chapter-opening photos). The highest and lowest average months are plotted for each year on the graph. [Data originally by Drs. David Keeling, and now his son Ralph Keeling, and Tim Whorf, of Scripps Institute of Oceanography; since 1974 along with NOAA's Earth Systems Research Laboratory, Dr. Pieter Tans.]

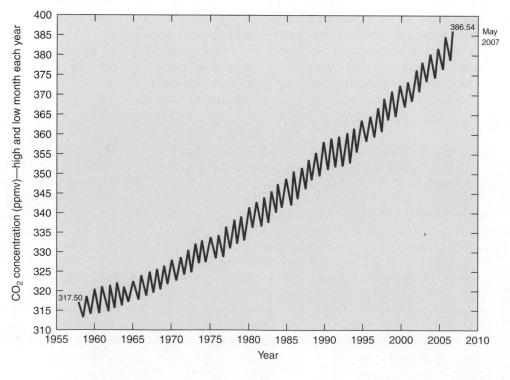

per year. If this rate continues unabated, business-as-usual, the rest of the century, then Table 3.2 could read 1390 ppm CO_2 in A.D. 2100, according to forecasts. Scientists are telling us to avoid this by reducing CO_2 emissions. Chapter 10 discusses the implications of CO_2 increases for global warming and climate change.

Atmospheric Temperature Criterion

Shifting to temperature as a criterion, the atmosphere has four distinct temperature zones—the *thermosphere, mesosphere, stratosphere,* and *troposphere* (labeled in Figure 3.2). Let's look at each of these beginning with the highest in altitude.

Thermosphere   We define the **thermosphere** ("heat sphere") as roughly corresponding to the heterosphere (80 km out to 480 km, or 50–300 mi). The upper limit of the thermosphere is the **thermopause** (the suffix -*pause* means "to change"). During periods of a less active Sun when there are fewer sunspots and coronal bursts, the thermopause may lower in altitude from the average 480 km (300 mi) to only 250 km altitude (155 mi). An active Sun causes the outer atmosphere to swell to an altitude of 550 km (340 mi), where it can create frictional drag on satellites in low orbit.

The temperature profile in Figure 3.2 (yellow curve) shows that temperatures rise sharply in the thermosphere, to 1200°C (2200°F) and higher. Despite such high temperatures, the thermosphere is not "hot" in the way you might expect. Temperature and heat are different concepts. The intense solar radiation in this portion of the atmosphere excites individual molecules (principally nitrogen and oxygen) to high levels of vibration. This **kinetic energy**, the energy of motion, is the vibrational energy that we measure as *temperature*.

However, the actual heat involved is small. The reason is that the density of molecules is so low. There is little actual **heat** produced, or the flow of kinetic energy from one body to another because of a temperature difference between them. Heating in the atmosphere near Earth's surface is different because the greater number of molecules in the denser atmosphere transmits their kinetic energy as **sensible heat**, meaning that we can measure and feel it. (Density, temperature, and heat capacity determine the sensible heat of a substance.) There is more on this topic in Chapters 4 and 5.

Mesosphere   The **mesosphere** is the area from 50 to 80 km (30 to 50 mi) above Earth and is within the homosphere. As Figure 3.2 shows, the mesosphere's outer boundary, the *mesopause*, is the coldest portion of the atmosphere, averaging −90°C (−130°F), although that temperature may vary considerably (25–30 C°, or 45–54 F°). Note in Figure 3.3b the extremely low pressures (low density of molecules) in the mesosphere.

The mesosphere sometimes receives cosmic or meteoric dust, which acts as nuclei around which fine ice crystals form. At high latitudes, an observer may see these bands of ice crystals glow in rare and unusual night **noctilucent**

clouds. For reasons not clearly understood, these unique clouds are on the increase. See, among several sites, http://lasp.colorado.edu/science/atmospheric/.

Stratosphere   The **stratosphere** extends from 18 to 50 km (11 to 31 mi) from Earth's surface. Temperatures increase with altitude throughout the stratosphere, from −57°C (−70°F) at 18 km at the tropopause, warming to 0°C (32°F) at 50 km at the stratosphere's outer boundary, the *stratopause*.

Troposphere   The **troposphere** is the final layer encountered by incoming solar radiation as it surges through the atmosphere to the surface. It is the home of the biosphere, the atmospheric layer that supports life, and the region of principal weather activity.

Approximately 90% of the total mass of the atmosphere and the bulk of all water vapour, clouds, and air pollution are within the troposphere. An average temperature of −57°C (−70°F) defines the **tropopause**, the troposphere's upper limit, but its exact altitude varies with the season, latitude, and surface temperatures and pressures. Near the equator, because of intense heating from the surface, the tropopause occurs at 18 km (11 mi); in the middle latitudes, it occurs at an average of 12 km (8 mi); and at the North and South Poles it only averages 8 km (5 mi) or less above Earth's surface.

Figure 3.5 illustrates the normal temperature profile within the troposphere during daytime. As the graph

FIGURE 3.5 The temperature profile of the troposphere. During daytime, temperature decreases with increased altitude at a rate known as the *normal lapse rate*. Scientists use a concept called the *standard atmosphere* as an accepted description of air temperature and pressure changes with altitude. Note the approximate locations of the equatorial and midlatitude tropopauses.

shows, temperatures decrease rapidly with increasing altitude at an average of 6.4 C° per kilometre (3.5 F° per 1000 ft), a rate known as the **normal lapse rate**. This temperature plot also appears in the troposphere portion of Figure 3.2.

The normal lapse rate is an average. The actual lapse rate at any particular time and place, which may deviate considerably because of local weather conditions, is the **environmental lapse rate**. This variation in temperature gradient in the lower troposphere is central to our discussion of weather processes in Chapters 7 and 8.

In the stratosphere, the marked warming with increasing altitude causes the tropopause to act like a lid, essentially preventing whatever is in the cooler (denser) air below from mixing into the warmer (less dense) stratosphere. However, the tropopause may be disrupted wherever jet streams produce vertical turbulence and an interchange between the troposphere and the stratosphere, as we see in Chapter 6. Also, hurricanes occasionally inject moisture above this temperature-inversion layer at the tropopause, and powerful volcanic eruptions may loft ash and sulfuric acid mists into the stratosphere, as did the Mount Pinatubo eruptions in 1991.

Atmospheric Function Criterion

Looking at our final atmospheric criterion of *function*, the atmosphere has two specific zones, the *ionosphere* and the *ozonosphere* (*ozone layer*), which remove most of the harmful wavelengths of incoming solar radiation and charged particles (Focus Study 3.1). Figure 3.6 depicts in a general way the absorption of radiation by the various functional layers of the atmosphere.

Ionosphere   The outer functional layer, the **ionosphere**, extends throughout the thermosphere and into the mesosphere below (Figure 3.2). The ionosphere absorbs cosmic rays, gamma rays, X-rays, and shorter wavelengths of ultraviolet radiation, changing atoms to positively charged ions and giving the ionosphere its name. The glowing auroral lights discussed in Chapter 2 occur principally within the ionosphere.

Figure 3.2 shows the average daytime altitudes of four regions within the ionosphere, known as the D, E, F_1, and F_2 layers. These are important to broadcast communications, for they reflect certain radio wavelengths, including AM radio and other shortwave broadcasts, especially at night. However, during the day the ionosphere actively absorbs arriving radio signals, preventing distant reception. Normally unaffected are FM or television broadcast wavelengths, which pass through to space, requiring the use of communication satellites.

Ozonosphere   That portion of the stratosphere that contains an increased level of ozone is the **ozonosphere**, or **ozone layer**. Ozone is a highly reactive oxygen molecule made up of three oxygen atoms (O_3) instead of the usual two atoms (O_2) that make up oxygen gas. Ozone absorbs certain wavelengths of ultraviolet (principally, all the UVC, 100–290 nm, and about 90% of UVB, 290–320 nm).* This absorbed energy subsequently reradiates at longer wavelengths as infrared radiation.

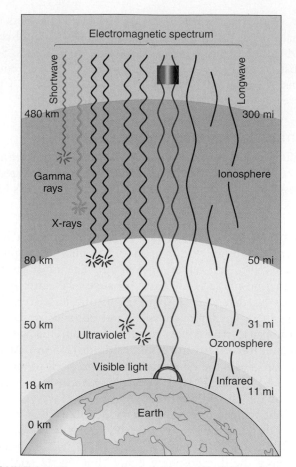

FIGURE 3.6 The atmosphere protects Earth's surface. As solar energy passes through the atmosphere, the shortest wavelengths are absorbed. Only a fraction of the ultraviolet radiation, and most of the visible light and infrared, reaches Earth's surface.

 Ozone Breakdown, Ozone Hole

This process converts most harmful ultraviolet radiation, effectively "filtering" it and safeguarding life at Earth's surface. UVA, at 320–400 nm, makes up about 98% of all UV radiation that reaches Earth surface.

The ozone layer is presumed to have been relatively stable over the past several hundred million years (allowing for daily and seasonal fluctuations). Today, however, it is in a state of continuous change. Focus Study 3.1 presents an analysis of the crisis in this critical portion of our atmosphere. Fortunately, international treaties to prevent further ozone losses are working, although the damage continues.

Variable Atmospheric Components

The troposphere contains natural and human-caused variable gases, particles, and other chemicals. In fact, researchers report that the increase in aerosols, particularly

(text continued on page 74)

*Nanometre (nm) = one-millionth of a millimetre; 1 nm = 10^{-9}. For comparison, a micrometre, or micron, (μm) = one-millionth of a metre; 1 μm = 10^{-6} m. A millimetre (mm) = one-thousandth of a metre; 1 mm = 10^{-3}.

Stratospheric Ozone Losses: A Worldwide Health Hazard

Consider these news reports and conditions:

- The stratospheric ozone above Antarctica during the months of Antarctic spring (September to November) achieved its most severe loss in 2006, covering an area three times larger than the United States. Each year, the "ozone hole" (actually a thinning) widens and deepens, even though the rate of accumulation of offending chemicals has leveled off.

- As stratospheric ozone flows into the depleted region from lower latitudes, the protective layer thins over southern South America, southern Africa, Australia, and New Zealand. In Ushuaia, Argentina, surface UVB intensity increased 236% compared to normal levels.

- An international scientific consensus confirmed previous assessments of the anthropogenic, or human-caused, disruption of the ozone layer—chlorine atoms and chlorine monoxide molecules in the stratosphere are of human origin. (See *Scientific Assessment of Ozone Depletion*, by NASA, NOAA, United Nations Environment Programme, and World Meteorological Organization.)

- At Earth's opposite pole, a similar ozone depletion over the Arctic annually exceeds 30%, to a record 45% loss during spring 1997. The Canadian and U.S. governments report an "ultraviolet index" to help the public protect themselves (http://www.ec.gc.ca/ozone/).

- Increased ultraviolet radiation is affecting atmospheric chemistry, biological systems, oceanic phytoplankton (small photosynthetic organisms that form the basis of the ocean's primary food production), fisheries, crop yields, and human skin, eye tissues, and immunity.

More ultraviolet radiation than ever before is breaking through Earth's protective ozone layer. What is going on in the stratosphere everywhere and in the polar regions specifically? Why is this happening, and how are people and their governments responding? What effects does this have on you personally?

Monitoring Earth's Fragile Safety Screen

A sample from the ozone layer's densest part (at 29 km, or 18 mi altitude) contains only 1 part ozone per 4 million parts of air—compressed to surface pressure, the ozone layer would be only 3 mm thick. Yet, this rarefied layer was in steady-state equilibrium for several hundred million years, absorbing intense ultraviolet radiation and permitting life to proceed safely on Earth.

The ozone layer has been monitored since the 1920s. Ground stations with instrumented balloons, aircraft, orbiting satellites, and a 30-station ozone-monitoring network (mostly in North America) observe stratospheric ozone. The total ozone mapping spectrometer (TOMS) began operations in 1978 aboard various satellites. A September 2006 image by the OMI (Ozone Monitoring Instrument) on NASA's *Aura* satellite is in Figure 3.1.1, and shows the all-time record ozone depletion. These measures mean that the ozone column over Antarctica was virtually gone. *Aura* and its OMI package became operational in 2004. (See http://www.nasa.gov/mission_pages/aura/main/index.html.)

Ozone Losses Explained

What is causing the decline in stratospheric ozone? In 1974, two atmospheric chemists, F. Sherwood Rowland and Mario Molina, hypothesized that some synthetic chemicals were releasing chlorine atoms that decompose ozone. These **chlorofluorocarbons**, or **CFCs**, are synthetic molecules of chlorine, fluorine, and carbon. (See Rowland and Molina's report: "Stratospheric sink for chlorofluoromethanes: Chlorine atom catalyzed destruction of ozone," *Nature*, 249 [1974]: 810.)

CFCs are stable, or inert, under conditions at Earth's surface and they possess remarkable heat properties. Both qualities made them valuable as propellants in aerosol sprays and as refrigerants. Also, some 45% of CFCs were solvents in the electronics industry and used as foaming agents. Being inert, CFC molecules do not dissolve in water and do not break down in biological processes. (In contrast, chlorine compounds derived from volcanic eruptions and the ocean are water-soluble and rarely reach the stratosphere.)

Total Ozone (Dobson Units)
110   220   330   440   550

FIGURE 3.1.1 The Antarctic ozone hole.
OMI image for September 24, 2006, shows the largest ozone hole observed, nearly 29.5 million km^2 (11.4 million mi^2). Measurements dropped below 100 Dobson units in the region of blues and purples; greens, yellows, and reds denote more ozone. The ozone "hole" has grown larger since 1979, although the accumulation of damaging chemicals has leveled. [OMI instrument aboard *Aqua* courtesy of GSFC/NASA.]

(continued)

Focus Study 3.1 *(continued)*

Researchers Rowland and Molina hypothesized that stable CFC molecules slowly migrate into the stratosphere, where intense ultraviolet radiation splits them, freeing chlorine (Cl) atoms. This process produces a complex set of reactions that breaks up ozone molecules (O_3) and leaves oxygen gas molecules (O_2) in their place. The effect is severe, for a single chlorine atom decomposes more than 100,000 ozone molecules. The long residence time of chlorine atoms in the ozone layer (40 to 100 years) is likely to produce long-term consequences through this century from the chlorine already in place. More than 22 million metric tons (24 million tons) of CFCs were sold worldwide and subsequently released into the atmosphere.

Of many identified reactions, here are simplified equations that show chlorine monoxide-produced (ClO) and chlorine-produced ozone losses. Note that chlorine monoxide (ClO) reacts with ozone (O_3) to produce a free chlorine atom (Cl) and two oxygen gas molecules (O_2) The free chlorine atom then reacts with an ozone molecule (O_3) to produce more chlorine monoxide (ClO) and oxygen gas (O_2)

Ozone depletion by ClO and by Cl:

$$ClO + O_3 \longrightarrow Cl + 2O_2$$
$$Cl + O_3 \longrightarrow ClO + O_2$$

The chlorine monoxide is then available to go through the cycle all over again. The *net reaction*, with the chlorine catalyst removed, is a loss of ozone (O_3) and its conversion to oxygen gas (O_2) molecules. The problem then is that O_2, unlike O_3, is transparent to ultraviolet radiation. (See **http://www.epa.gov/ozone/index.html**.)

Political Realities—An International Response and the Future

As the science became established, sales and production of CFCs declined until a March 1981 U.S. presidential order permitting the export and sales of banned products. Sales increased and hit a new peak in 1987 at 1.2 million metric tons (1.32 million tons), when an international agreement went into effect halting further sales growth.

Chemical manufacturers once claimed that no hard evidence existed to prove the ozone-depletion model, and they successfully delayed remedial action for 15 years. Today, with extensive scientific evidence and verification of losses, even the CFC manufacturers admit that the problem is serious.

The *Montreal Protocol on Substances That Deplete the Ozone Layer* (1987), as amended five times in 1990, 1992, 1995, 1997, and 1999, aims to reduce and eliminate CFC damage to the ozone layer. With 189 signatory countries the Protocol is regarded as probably the most successful international agreement in history.

CFC sales continue their decline and all production of harmful CFCs will cease by 2010, although there is concern over some of the substitute compounds and a robust black market for banned CFCs, rivaling drug trafficking at some ports. If the protocol is fully enforced, it is estimated that the stratosphere will return to more normal conditions in a century. (See the United Nations Ozone Secretariat at **http://ozone.unep.org/** and Montreal Protocol at **http://www.ec.gc.ca/international/multilat/ozone1_e.htm**.)

The protocol also bans other chemicals, such as bromine, that are damaging to the atmosphere, using different target dates; progress is slow. Bromine sources include halon-charged fire extinguishers and methyl bromide pesticides and soil fumigants. They are about 50 times more effective than chlorine as catalysts causing reactions that destroy ozone, although they have a residence time in the atmosphere of only a couple of years.

The world without this treaty might prove challenging. Imagine possible stratospheric ozone losses of 50% in the midlatitudes, producing 1.5 million more cases of malignant melanoma (a skin cancer). We owe much to doctors Rowland and Molina.

Mario Molina stated, "It was frustrating for many years, but it really paid off with the Protocol, which was a marvelous example of what the international community can do working together. We can see from atmospheric measurements that it is already working" (*Nature* 389, September 18, 1997: 219). For their work, Rowland, Molina, and another colleague, Paul Crutzen, received the 1995 Nobel Prize for Chemistry. In making the award, the Royal Swedish Academy of Sciences said, "By explaining the chemical mechanism that affects the thickness of the ozone layer, the three researchers have contributed to our salvation from a global environmental problem that could have catastrophic consequences."

Ozone Losses over the Poles

How do Northern Hemisphere CFCs become concentrated over the South Pole? Evidently, chlorine freed in the Northern Hemisphere midlatitudes concentrates over Antarctica through the work of atmospheric winds. Persistent cold temperatures over the South Pole and the presence of thin, icy clouds in the stratosphere promote development of the ozone hole. Over the North Pole, conditions are more changeable, so the hole is smaller, although growing each year.

Polar stratospheric clouds (PSCs) are thin clouds that are important catalysts in the release of chlorine for ozone-depleting reactions. During the long, cold winter months, a tight circulation pattern forms over the Antarctic continent—the polar vortex. Chlorine that is freed from droplets in PSCs triggers the breakdown of the otherwise inert molecules and frees the chlorine for catalytic reactions. Figure 3.1.2a graphs the negative correlation between ClO presence and O_3 losses over the Antarctic continent within the polar vortex. Figure 3.1.2b graphs the progressive loss of ozone during the year to its usual September low and Figure 3.1.2c presents satellite data on the areal size of the ozone depleted region during the year.

Atmospheric science is active in Antarctica. The U.S. scientific base, Palmer Station (64° 46' S) on Anvers Island, Antarctic Peninsula, experiences a 285% increase in surface UVB radiation above normal levels in the fall. Nearby at Ukraine's Akademik Vernadsky Station, the former British Faraday Base in the Argentine Islands, one of the original ozone spectrophotometer instruments is actively measuring ultraviolet radiation (Figure 3.1.3). Ukraine scientists are studying UVA (320–400 nm) and UVB (290–320 nm) wavelengths using a variety of instruments, including *biodosimeters* that use biological material to measure radiation impact.

UV Index Helps Save Your Skin

Newspaper and television weather reports regularly include the *UV Index* (UVI) in forecasts, as reported by the National Weather Service (NWS) and the Environmental Protection Agency (EPA) since 1994. A revision in 2004 aligned the UVI with guidelines adopted by the World Health Organization and World Meteorological Organization.

Note the 2004 UVI scale does not rely on "burn times." People were misinterpreting time-to-burn estimates thinking there was some safe level of exposure, or safe tanning time—which was the wrong message. Table 3.1.1 presents the revised UVI. Fair-skinned people (melano-compromised) must exercise more caution than moderate to darker skin types (melano-competent and melano-protected), but all skin types should feel warned, especially for babies and children.

As stratospheric ozone levels continue to thin, surface exposure to cancer-causing radiation climbs. The public now is alerted to take extra precautions in the form of sunscreens, hats, protective clothing, and sunglasses. Remember, damage is cumulative and it may be decades before you experience the ill effects triggered by this summer's sunburn. (For more information, contact the Canadian Cancer Society, 800-227-2345, **http://www.cancer.ca/**; or write the Canadian Association of Dermatology at **http://www.dermatology.ca/english.**)

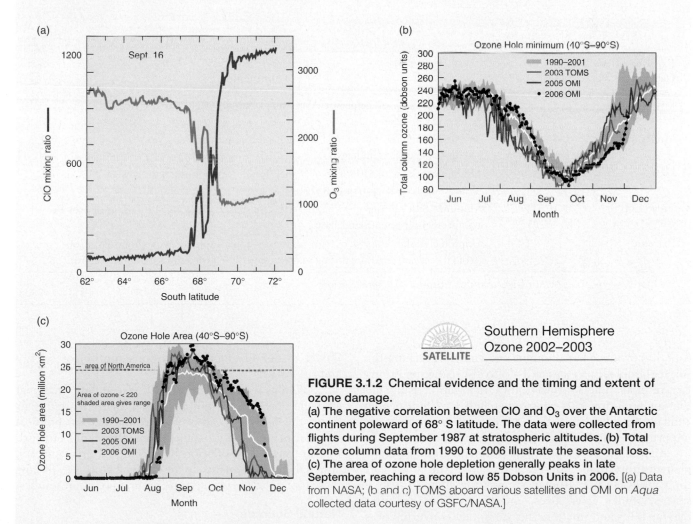

Southern Hemisphere
Ozone 2002–2003

FIGURE 3.1.2 Chemical evidence and the timing and extent of ozone damage.
(a) The negative correlation between ClO and O_3 over the Antarctic continent poleward of 68° S latitude. The data were collected from flights during September 1987 at stratospheric altitudes. (b) Total ozone column data from 1990 to 2006 illustrate the seasonal loss. (c) The area of ozone hole depletion generally peaks in late September, reaching a record low 85 Dobson Units in 2006. [(a) Data from NASA; (b and c) TOMS aboard various satellites and OMI on *Aqua* collected data courtesy of GSFC/NASA.]

(continued)

Focus Study 3.1 *(continued)*

(a)

(b)

FIGURE 3.1.3 Atmospheric science in Antarctica.
(a) Ukraine's Vernadsky Station operates year-round performing valuable scientific research. (b) This ozone spectrophotometer instrument measures the ultraviolet component of insolation arriving through the opening in the science station's roof. [Photos by Bobbé Christopherson.]

Table 3.1.1 UV Index (EPA, NWS, WHO, WMO)

Exposure Risk Category	UVI Range	Comments
Low	less than 2	Low danger for average person. Wear sunglasses on bright days. Watch out for reflection off snow.
Moderate	3–5	Take covering precautions, such as sunglasses, sunscreen, hats, protective clothing, and stay in shade during midday hours.
High	6–7	Use sunscreens with SPF of 15 or higher. Reduce time in the Sun between 11 A.M. and 4 P.M. Use protections mentioned above.
Very High	8–10	Minimize Sun exposure 10 A.M. to 4 P.M. Use sunscreens with SPF ratings of over 15. Use protections mentioned above.
Extreme	11+	Unprotected skin is at risk of burn. Sunscreen application every two hours if out-of-doors. Avoid direct Sun exposure during midday hours. Use protections mentioned above.

See **http://www.epa.gov/sunwise/uvindex.html** for a UVI forecast for your location.

soot, has produced a "dimming" of sunlight reaching the surface—globally, a measured 4% to 8% reduction in surface receipts. The World Health Organization estimated that air pollution kills approximately 4.3 million people annually worldwide. Spatial aspects of these variables are important applied topics in physical geography.

Air pollution is not a new problem. Romans complained more than 2000 years ago about the foul air of their cities. Filling Roman air was the stench of open sewers, smoke from fires, and fumes from ceramic-making kilns and smelters (furnaces) that converted ores into metals. In human experience, cities are always the place where the environment's natural ability to process and recycle waste is stressed. Air pollution is closely

linked to our production and consumption of energy and resources.

Solutions require regional, national, and international strategies, because the pollution sources often are distant from the observed impact—moving across political boundaries and even crossing oceans. Regulations to curb human-caused air pollution have achieved great success, although much remains to be done. Before we discuss these topics, let's examine some natural pollution sources.

Natural Sources

Natural air pollution sources produce a greater quantity of pollutants—nitrogen oxides, carbon monoxide, hydrocarbons from plants and trees, and carbon dioxide—than

Table 3.3 Sources of Natural Variable Gases and Materials

Source	Contribution
Volcanoes	Sulfur oxides, particulates
Forest fires	Carbon monoxide and dioxide, nitrogen oxides, particulates
Plants	Hydrocarbons, pollens
Decaying plants	Methane, hydrogen sulfides
Soil	Dust and viruses
Ocean	Salt spray and particulates

do human-made sources. Table 3.3 lists some of these natural sources and the substances they contribute to the air. However, any attempt to dismiss the impact of human-made air pollution through a comparison with natural sources is irrelevant, for we evolved with and adapted to the natural ingredients in the air. We did not evolve in relation to the comparatively recent concentrations of *anthropogenic* (human-caused) contaminants in our metropolitan regions.

A dramatic natural source of pollution was the 1991 eruption of Mount Pinatubo in the Philippines (15° N 120° E), perhaps the twentieth century's second largest eruption. This event injected nearly 20 million tons of sulfur dioxide (SO_2) into the stratosphere. The spread of these emissions is shown in a sequence of satellite images in Figure 6.1, Chapter 6.

Devastating wildfires on several continents, including widespread fires across the western United States, produce natural air pollution as each year's fire season breaks the previous year's record. Soot, ash, and gases darkened skies and damaged health in affected regions. Wind patterns spread the pollution from the fires to nearby cities, closing airports and forcing evacuations to avoid the health-related dangers. Wildfire smoke contains particulate matter (dust, smoke, soot, ash), nitrogen oxides, carbon monoxide, and volatile organic compounds.

Scientists established the connection between climate change and wildfire occurrence, meaning this source of smoke is on the increase as is the release of enormous quantities of carbon dioxide to the atmosphere. A sample of findings related to climate change impacts and the western United States and Canada as well:

Higher spring and summer temperatures and earlier snowmelt are extending the wildfire season and increasing the intensity of wildfires in the western US. . . . large wildfire activity increased suddenly and markedly in the mid-1980s, with higher large-wildfire frequency . . . longer wildfire durations, and longer wildfire seasons.*

*A.L. Westerling, et. al., "Warming and Earlier Spring Increase Western U.S. Forest Wildfire Activity," *Science*, 18 Aug 2006 (v 313, no. 5789: p. 940).

For example, in drought-plagued southern California, dozens of wildfires across the region burned more than 243,000 ha (600,000 acres) in October 2003 and again in October 2007. Each year since 2002 across the country, wildfire acreage broke the record of the previous year—2006 was triple the acreage lost in 2000 (see **http://www.usgs.gov/hazards/wildfires/**). Similar conditions produced record fires in 2006 with 2.08 million hectares burned (Figure 3.7).

Natural Factors That Affect Air Pollution

The problems resulting from both natural and human-made atmospheric contaminants are made worse by several important natural factors. Among these, wind, local and regional landscape characteristics, and temperature inversions in the troposphere dominate.

Winds Winds gather and move pollutants, sometimes reducing the concentration of pollution in one location while increasing it in another. Wind can produce dramatic episodes of dust movement. (Dust is defined as particles less than 62 μm, microns, or 0.0025 in.). Traveling on prevailing winds, dust from Africa contributes to the soils of South America and Europe, and Texas dust ends up across the Atlantic. Such movement is confirmed by chemical analysis, used by scientists to track dust to its source area (Figure 3.8).

Such air movements make the atmosphere's condition an international issue. For example, prevailing winds transport air pollution from the United States to Canada, causing much complaint and negotiation between the two governments. Pollution from North America adds to European air problems. In Europe, the cross-boundary drift of pollution is a major issue because of the proximity of countries. This issue was a factor in the formation of the 27-country European Union (EU). See "Arctic Haze," High Latitude Connection 3.1, for another aspect of pollution drift, as winds carry pollution into the remote northern polar region.

Local and Regional Landscapes Local and regional landscapes are another important factor in air pollution. Surrounding mountains and hills can form barriers to air movement or can direct pollutants from one area to another. Some of the worst incidents result when local landscapes trap and concentrate air pollution.

Places with volcanic landscapes such as Iceland and Hawai'i have their own natural pollution with which to deal. During periods of sustained volcanic activity at Kīlauea, some 2000 metric tons (2200 tons) of sulfur dioxide are produced a day. Concentrations are sometimes high enough to merit broadcast warnings about health concerns. The resulting acid rain and volcanic smog, called *vog* by Hawaiians (for *vo*lcanic smog), causes losses to agriculture as well as other economic impacts.

Temperature Inversion Vertical temperature and atmospheric density in the troposphere also can worsen pollution conditions. A **temperature inversion** occurs

(a)

FIGURE 3.7 Canadian and American fires in 2003. In 2003, dozens of fires were burning in Canada and the United States. (a) Smoke and wildfires, August 18, 2003, imaged by *Aqua*. Dense smoke flows from the west and sweeps northeastward over Hudson Bay. (b) *Terra* captured fires burning across British Columbia (upper left), Montana (bottom right), and Idaho (bottom centre), creating thick smoke on August 21, 2003. [*Aqua* and *Terra* images courtesy of the MODIS Land Rapid Response Team, NASA/GSFC.]

(b)

when the normal temperature decrease with altitude (normal lapse rate) begins to *increase* at some point. This can happen at any elevation from ground level to several thousand metres. Figure 3.9 compares a normal temperature profile with that of a temperature inversion. The normal profile (Figure 3.9a) permits warmer (less dense) air at the surface to rise, ventilating the valley and

moderating surface pollution. But the warm-air inversion (Figure 3.9b) prevents the rise of cooler (denser) air beneath, halting the vertical mixing of pollutants with other atmospheric gases. Thus, instead of being carried away, pollutants are trapped under the *inversion layer*.

Inversions most often result from certain weather conditions, such as when the air near the ground is

(a) (b) (c)

(d)

FIGURE 3.8 Natural variable dust in the atmosphere.
(a) A dust storm in central Nevada. (b) A *Terra* orbital view of a wind-blown dust plume flowing northward from Africa, across the Mediterranean Sea, toward Turkey. Can you find the Nile Delta? (c) A wall of dust travels many kilometres, blocking the Sun as it moves over Melbourne, Australia. (d) Alkali dust, a serious air pollutant, rises from the exposed shorelines of Mono Lake, California. [(a) Photo by Robert Christopherson; (b) *Terra* image courtesy of the MODIS Land Rapid Response Team NASA/GSFC; (c) photo by Bill Bachman/Photo Researchers, Inc.; and (d) photo by Bobbé Christopherson.]

radiatively cooled on clear nights, or from topographic situations that produce cold-air drainage into valleys. In addition, the air above snow-covered surfaces or beneath

subsiding air in a high-pressure system may cause a temperature inversion. (The concepts of high- and low-pressure systems are in Chapter 6.)

(a)

6.4 C°/1000 m
3.5 F°/1000 ft

Increasing altitude

Decreasing temperature

Mixing in the atmosphere

(b)

Increasing altitude

Warmer air

Inversion layer

Decreasing temperature

Mixing blocked—pollution trapped beneath inversion

(c)

FIGURE 3.9 Normal and inverted temperature profiles.
A comparison of a normal temperature profile in the atmosphere (a) with a temperature inversion in the lower atmosphere (b). Note how the warmer air layer prevents mixing of the denser (cooler) air below the inversion, thereby trapping pollution. (c) An inversion layer is visible in the morning hours over a valley. [Photo by Bobbé Christopherson.]

High Latitude Connection 3.1

Arctic Haze

Arctic haze is a term from the 1950s, when pilots noticed decreased visibility, either horizontally or at a slant angle from their aircraft. Since there is no heavy industry at these latitudes and sparse population, this seasonal haze (concentration of microscopic particles and air pollution that diminishes air clarity) was a mystery at first. When an observer is looking toward the Sun, the haze has a reddish-brown tint, especially when the polar air mass is dominated by stable high-pressure systems and calm weather conditions.

A remarkable attribute of industrialization in the Northern Hemisphere is the haze across the Arctic region, especially from November to April. This winter haze is worse toward Alaska's North Slope. Although the haze can extend up to 8 km (5 mi) in altitude, it sometimes appears layered since sources are at varying distances from the Arctic and the warmer transporting winds are variously lifted over the cold air mass that hugs the surface.

Simply, winds of atmospheric circulation transport pollution to sites far distant from points of origin. There is no comparable haze over the Antarctic continent. Based on this analysis, can you think of why Antarctica lacks such a condition?

Anthropogenic Pollution

Anthropogenic, or human-caused, air pollution remains most prevalent in urbanized regions. Approximately 2% of annual deaths in the United States are attributable to air pollution. Comparable risks are identified in Canada, Europe, Mexico, Asia—especially China and India—and elsewhere.

The human population is moving to cities and is therefore coming in increasing contact with air pollution. By the year 2010, approximately 3.3 billion people (48% of world population) will live in metropolitan regions, some one-third with unhealthful levels of air pollution. This represents a potentially massive public health issue in this century.

Small particles of dust, soot, and pollution suspended in the air comprise **aerosols**. Remote sensing now provides a rough global portrait of aerosols, as described by the atmosphere's *optical depth*, or AOD. Figure 3.10 shows

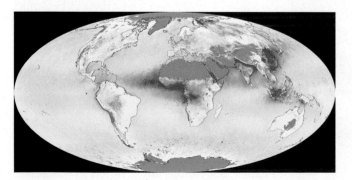

FIGURE 3.10 Portrait of global aerosols, 2006. The MODIS (Moderate Resolution Imaging Spectroradiometer) aboard NASA's *Terra* and *Aqua* satellites captured the average annual AOD for 2006, a composite of daily measurements. Darker tones represent higher AOD—dust, soot, smoke, and pollution suspended in the atmosphere. Areas where data could not be measured are in gray. [Image MODIS aboard *Terra* and *Aqua* satellites compiled by Reto Stockli, Earth Observatory, courtesy of NASA/GSFC.]

a composite MODIS image from NASA's *Terra* and *Aqua* satellites for 2006. Note the high aerosol concentrations in Indonesia (wildfires and burning), northern India and China (urban and industrial pollution), western and central Africa (Saharan dust and agricultural fire smoke), and Russia (drought-plagued Siberian boreal forest wildfires). Bright surfaces reflecting sunlight such as snow and ice, desert, clouds, or sun-glint reflections limit accurate measurements. The limits of MODIS are obvious over the Amazon Basin where cloudiness causes an underestimation of AOD.

Table 3.4 lists the names, chemical symbols, principal sources, and impacts of variable anthropogenic components in the air. The first seven pollutants in the table result from combustion of fossil fuels in transportation (specifically automobiles) and at stationary sources such as power plants and factories. Overall, automobiles contribute more than 60% of United States and 50% of Canadian human-caused air pollution. The apparent manageability of this transportation-pollution problem is obvious to an informed public. Reducing air pollution from the transportation sector involves known technologies and strategies, monetary savings for the consumer, and significant health benefits.

Stationary sources, such as electric power plants and industrial plants that use fossil fuels, contribute the most sulfur oxides and particulates. For this reason, concentrations are focused in the Northern Hemisphere and the industrial, developed countries. The last three gases shown in Table 3.4 are discussed elsewhere in this text: Water vapour is examined with water and weather (Chapters 7 and 8); carbon dioxide and methane are discussed with greenhouse gases and climate (Chapters 4, 5, and 10).

Carbon Monoxide Pollution   Carbon monoxide (CO) is a combination of one atom of carbon and one of oxygen. Incomplete combustion (burning with limited oxygen) of

Table 3.4   Anthropogenic Gases and Materials in the Lower Atmosphere

Name	Symbol	Sources	Description and Effects of Criteria Pollutants (Main sources listed for U.S.)
Carbon monoxide	CO	Incomplete combustion of fuels	Odourless, colourless, tasteless gas Toxicity; affinity for hemoglobin Displaces O_2 in bloodstream; 50 to 100 ppm causes headaches, vision and judgment losses *Source:* 78% transportation
Nitrogen oxides	NO_x (NO, NO_2)	High temperature/pressure combustion	Reddish-brown choking gas Inflames respiratory system, destroys lung tissue Damages plants; 3 to 5 ppm is dangerous *Source:* 55% transportation
Volatile organic compounds	VOC	Incomplete combustion of fossil fuels such as gasoline; cleaning and paint solvents	Prime agents of ozone formation *Sources:* 45% industrial 47% transportation
Ozone	O_3	Photochemical reactions	Highly reactive, unstable gas Irritates eyes, nose, throat Oxidizes surfaces, dries rubber and elastic Damages plants at 0.01 to 0.09 ppm Agricultural losses at 0.1 ppm 0.3 to 1.0 ppm
Peroxyacetyl nitrates	PAN	Photochemical reactions	Produced by NO + VOC photochemistry No human health effects Major damage to plants, forests, crops
Sulfur oxides	SO_x (SO_2, SO_3)	Combustion of sulfur-containing fuels	Colourless; irritating smell 0.1 to 1 ppm; impairs breathing, taste threshold Human asthma, bronchitis, emphysema Leads to acid deposition *Source:* 85% fuel combustion
Particulate matter	PM	Dust, dirt, soot, salt, metals, organics; agriculture, construction, roads	Complex mixture of solid and aerosol particles Dust, smoke, and haze affect visibility Various health effects; bronchitis, pulmonary function PM_{10} negative health effects established by researchers *Sources:* 42 % industrial 33% fuel combustion 25% transportation
Carbon dioxide	CO_2	Complete combustion, mainly from fossil fuel consumption	Principal greenhouse gas Atmospheric concentration increasing; 64% of greenhouse warming effect
Methane	CH_4	Organic processes	Secondary greenhouse gas Atmospheric concentration increasing; 19% of greenhouse warming effect
Water vapour	H_2O vapour	Combustion processes, steam	See Chapter 7 for more on the role of water vapour in the atmosphere.

fuels or other carbon-containing substances produces carbon monoxide. A log decaying in the woods produces carbon monoxide, as does a forest fire or other organic decomposition. Natural sources produce up to 90% of existing carbon monoxide, whereas anthropogenic sources, principally transportation, produce the other 10%. A dangerous point source of carbon monoxide for individuals is from primary and secondary tobacco smoke. Generally, the carbon monoxide from human sources is from the transportation sector and is concentrated in urban areas, where it directly affects human health (see Table 3.4).

In the tropics of south-central Africa, the Amazon region of South America, and Indonesia, a large source of carbon monoxide is the widespread burning of biomass (trees, grasses, brush) from August to October. Figure 3.11a presents carbon monoxide emissions from both

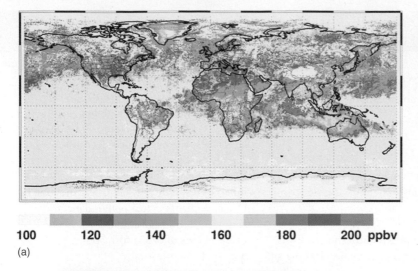

FIGURE 3.11 Forests on fire—a source of global carbon monoxide (CO). (a) Biomass burning and drought-assisted wildfires are imaged by satellite. CO is primarily from the burning of rain forest in Indonesia, Africa, and the Amazon Basin. The soot and ash is lifted high in the atmosphere by strong cloud convection. Higher levels of CO in pink, lower levels in blue. (b) A November 5, 2006, image captures these Indonesian human and natural wildfires. [Images from (a) MOPITT (Measurement of Pollution in the Troposphere) sensor aboard the *Terra* satellite courtesy of MOPITT Science Team NCAR/University of Toronto; (b) MODIS sensor aboard *Aqua* satellite courtesy of NASA/GSFC.]

100   120   140   160   180   200 ppbv

(a)

(b)

human sources and wildfire biomass burning, measured by satellite during November 2006. Note the highest levels from Indonesia, where a prolonged drought caused exceptionally dry conditions and thus wildfire conditions (Figure 3.11b). Carbon monoxide, soot, and dust spread across the Southern Hemisphere. Such conditions coupled with widespread deforestation are introducing more carbon to the atmosphere. The former forests once provided a carbon sink, or removal mechanism; Chapter 20 presents data on forest losses.

Photochemical Smog Pollution Photochemical smog was not generally experienced in the past, but developed with the advent of the automobile. Today, it is the major component of anthropogenic air pollution (Figure 3.12). **Photochemical smog** results from the interaction of sunlight and the combustion products in automobile exhaust (nitrogen oxides and VOCs). Although the term *smog*—a combination of the words *smoke* and *fog*—is misnamed, it is generally used to describe this pollution. Smog is responsible for the hazy sky and reduced sunlight in many of our cities. Figure 3.13 shows such conditions in China and the U.S. Mid-Atlantic states—both regions under an air pollution attack.

The connection between automobile exhaust and smog was not determined until 1953 in Los Angeles, long after society had established its dependence upon individualized transportation. Despite this discovery, widespread mass transit declined, the railroads dwindled, and the polluting, inefficient individual automobile remains America's preferred transportation. Continuing poor gas economy efficiency is principally due to gas-guzzling sport-utility

FIGURE 3.12 Photochemical smog near Denver. Photochemical reactions in the skies over Denver, Colorado, produce the blanket of smog that moves over mountains and forest to the west. What do you notice about air pollution conditions where you live or go to college? [Photo by Bobbé Christopherson.]

(a)

(b)

FIGURE 3.13 Serious air pollution in China and the United States.
(a) Smog and haze blanket most of eastern China. Beijing is about 150 km (93 mi) west of the coast where the heaviest pollution exists. Poor air pollution controls and the burning of coal contribute to the problem. (b) A serious air pollution alert masks most of the Mid-Atlantic region of the United States—from northern Georgia to New York. Prevailing winds were blowing the mass offshore over the **Atlantic Ocean.** [(a) *Terra* MODIS sensor images from courtesy of MODIS Land Rapid Response Team NASA/GSFC; (b) *Terra* MODIS image courtesy of Liam Gumley, Space Science and Engineering Center, University of Wisconsin–Madison and NASA.]

FIGURE 3.14 Photochemical reactions.
The interaction of automobile exhaust (NO₂, VOCs, CO) and ultraviolet radiation in sunlight causes photochemical reactions. To the left, note the formation of nitric acid and acid deposition.

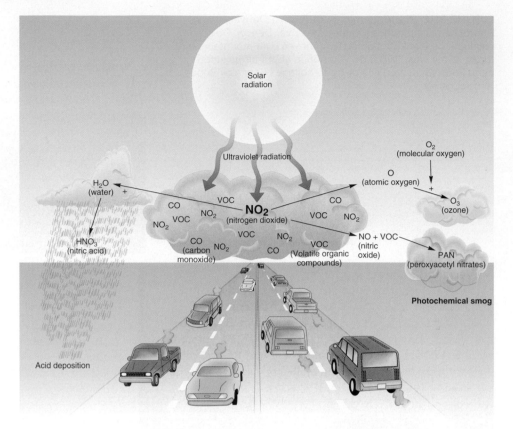

vehicles and pickups that account for more than half of new sales. Efficiency standards for this class of vehicles have not changed since 1975; they are set lower than for cars.

Figure 3.14 summarizes how car exhaust is converted into major air pollutants—PAN, ozone, and nitric acid. The high temperatures in modern automobile engines produce nitrogen dioxide (NO_2). Also, to a lesser extent nitrogen dioxide is emitted from power plants. Worldwide, the problem with **nitrogen dioxide** production is its concentration in metropolitan regions. North American urban areas may have from 10 to 100 times higher nitrogen dioxide concentrations than nonurban areas. Nitrogen dioxide interacts with water vapour to form nitric acid (HNO_3) a contributor to acid deposition by precipitation, the subject of Focus Study 3.2.

In the photochemistry reaction in the illustration, ultraviolet radiation liberates atomic oxygen (O) and a nitric oxide (NO) molecule from the NO_2. The free oxygen atom combines with an oxygen molecule, O_2, to form the oxidant ozone, O_3. In addition, the nitric oxide (NO) molecule reacts with VOCs to produce *peroxyacetyl nitrates* (*PAN*).

Peroxyacetyl nitrates (PAN) produce no known health effect in humans, but they are particularly damaging to plants, including both agricultural crops and forests. Damage in California is estimated to exceed USD$1 billion a year, and it is estimated to be several billion dollars nationwide in the farming and forestry sectors.

Ozone is the primary ingredient in photochemical smog. (This is the same gas that is beneficial to us in the stratosphere in absorbing ultraviolet radiation.) The reactivity of ozone is a health threat, for it damages biological tissues. For several reasons, children are at greatest risk from ozone pollution—one in four children in U.S. cities is at risk of developing health problems from ozone pollution. This ratio is significant; it means that more than 12 million children are vulnerable in those metropolitan regions with the worst polluted air (Los Angeles, Sacramento to Fresno to Bakersfield, Houston, Knoxville, Dallas–Ft Worth, Washington, D.C. and Philadelphia; for more information and city listings of the worst and the best see http://www.lungusa.org). The **volatile organic compounds (VOCs)**, including hydrocarbons from gasoline, surface coatings, and combustion at electric utilities, are important factors in ozone formation. States such as California base their standards for control of ozone pollution on VOC emission controls—a scientifically accurate emphasis.

Industrial Smog and Sulfur Oxides Over the past 300 years, except in some developing countries, coal slowly replaced wood as the basic fuel used by society. The Industrial Revolution required high-grade energy to run machines. The changes involved conversion from *animate* energy (energy from animal sources, such as animal-powered farm equipment) to *inanimate* energy (energy from nonliving sources, such as coal, steam, and water). Air pollution associated with coal-burning industries is known as **industrial smog** (Figure 3.15). The term *smog* was coined by a London physician in A.D. 1900 to describe the combination of fog and smoke containing sulfur gases (sulfur is an impurity in fossil fuels).

FIGURE 3.15 Typical industrial smog.
Pollution generated by industry differs from that produced by transportation. Industrial pollution has high concentrations of sulfur oxides, particulates, and carbon dioxide. [Photo by Robert Christopherson.]

In the United States, coal-burning electric utilities and steel manufacturing are the main sources of sulfur dioxide, principally in the East and Midwest. And, because of the prevailing movement of air masses, they are the main sources of sulfur dioxide in adjacent Canadian regions. A majority of Canadian sulfur dioxide is initiated within the United States.

Particulates Particulate matter (PM) is a diverse mixture of fine particles, both solid and aerosol, that impact human health—refer to Figure 3.11. Haze, smoke, and dust are visible reminders of particulate material in the air we breathe. PM_{10}, particulates smaller than 10 microns (10 μm or less) in diameter, was designated a matter for concern in 1987. $PM_{2.5}$ is currently being debated as an appropriate standard for human health. New studies are implicating even smaller particles, known as *ultrafines*, which are $PM_{0.1}$. These are many times more potent than the larger $PM_{2.5}$ and PM_{10} particles because they can get into smaller channels in lung tissue and cause scarring, abnormal thickening, and damage called *fibrosis*.

Studies in Provo and Orem, Utah (1989), Philadelphia (1992), and other cities and by the American Cancer Society (1995), and more recently the WHO, established links between PM pollution and health. Nationally, a study of major cities disclosed a 26% greater risk of premature death due to respirable particulate pollution as compared with nonpolluted air—further driving up medical costs and related expenses. As science gains more information, the public should take needed action.

We are now contributing significantly to the creation of the **anthropogenic atmosphere**, a tentative label for

Once in the atmosphere, **sulfur dioxide (SO_2)** reacts with oxygen (O) to form sulfur trioxide (SO_3), which is highly reactive and, in the presence of water or water vapour, forms **sulfate aerosols**, tiny particles about 0.1 to 1 μm in diameter. Sulfuric acid (H_2SO_4) can form even in moderately polluted air at normal temperatures. Sulfur dioxide-laden air is dangerous to health, corrodes metals, and deteriorates stone building materials at accelerated rates. Focus Study 3.2 discusses this vital atmospheric issue.

Focus Study 3.2

Acid Deposition: Damaging to Ecosystems

Acid deposition is a major environmental problem in some areas of the United States, Canada, Europe, and Asia. Such deposition is most familiar as "acid rain," but it also occurs as "acid snow" and in dry form as dust or aerosols—tiny liquid droplets or solid particles. In addition, winds can carry the acid-producing chemicals many kilometres from their sources before they settle on the landscape, where they enter streams and lakes as runoff and groundwater flows.

Acid deposition is causally linked to serious problems: declining fish populations and fish kills in the northeastern United States, southeastern Canada, Sweden, and Norway; widespread forest damage in these same places and Germany; widespread

changes in soil chemistry; and damage to buildings, sculptures, and historic artifacts. In New Hampshire's Hubbard Brook Experimental Forest (http://www.hubbardbrook.org/), a study covering 1960 to the present found half the nutrient calcium and magnesium base cations (see Chapter 18) were leached from the soil. Excess acids are the cause of the decline.

Despite scientific agreement about the problem, which the U.S. Government Accountability Office calls a "combination of meteorological, chemical, and biological phenomena," corrective action was delayed by its complexity and politics.

The acidity of precipitation is measured on the pH scale, which expresses

the relative abundance of free hydrogen ions (H^+) in a solution. Free hydrogen ions in a solution are what make an acid corrosive, for they easily combine with other ions. The pH scale is logarithmic: Each whole number represents a 10-fold change. A pH of 7.0 is neutral (neither acidic nor basic). Values less than 7.0 are increasingly *acidic*, and values greater than 7.0 are increasingly *basic*, or *alkaline*. (A pH scale for soil acidity and alkalinity is portrayed graphically in Chapter 18.)

Natural precipitation dissolves carbon dioxide from the atmosphere to form carbonic acid. This process releases hydrogen ions and produces an average pH reading for precipitation of 5.65. The normal range for

(continued)

Focus Study 3.2 (continued)

precipitation is 5.3–6.0. Thus, normal precipitation is always slightly acidic.

Some anthropogenic gases are converted to acids in the atmosphere and then are removed by wet and dry deposition processes. Specifically, nitrogen and sulfur oxides released in the combustion of fossil fuels can produce nitric acid (HNO_3) and sulfuric acid (H_2SO_4) in the atmosphere.

Acid Precipitation Damage

Precipitation as acidic as pH 2.0 has fallen in the eastern United States, Scandinavia, and Europe. By comparison, vinegar and lemon juice register slightly less than 3.0. Aquatic plant and animal life perishes when lakes drop below pH 4.8.

More than 50,000 lakes and some 100,000 km (62,000 mi) of streams in the United States and Canada are at a pH level below normal (that is, below 5.3 pH), with several hundred lakes incapable of supporting any aquatic life. Acid deposition causes the release of aluminum and magnesium from clay minerals in the soil, and both of these are harmful to fish and plant communities.

Also, relatively harmless mercury deposits in lake-bottom sediments convert in acidified lake waters into highly toxic *methylmercury*, which is deadly to aquatic life. Local health advisories in two provinces and 22 U.S. states are regularly issued to warn those who fish of the methylmercury problem. Mercury atoms rapidly bond with carbon and move through biological systems as an *organometallic compound*.

Damage to forests results from the rearrangement of soil nutrients, the death of soil microorganisms, and an aluminum-induced calcium deficiency that is currently under investigation. The most advanced impact is seen in forests in Europe, especially in eastern Europe, principally because of its long history of burning coal and the density of industrial activity. In Germany and Poland, up to 50% of the forests are dead or damaged; in Switzerland, 30% are afflicted (Figure 3.2.1a).

In the United States, regional-scale decline in forest cover is significant, especially red spruce and sugar maples. In some maples, aluminum is collecting around rootlets; in spruce, acid fogs and rains leach calcium from needles directly. Affected trees are susceptible to winter cold, insects, and droughts. In New England, some

stands of spruce are as much as 75% affected, as evidenced through analysis of tree-growth rings, which become narrower in adverse growing years. An indicator of forest damage is the reduction by almost half of the annual production of U.S. and Canadian maple sugar. Acid-laden cloud cover damages trees at higher elevations in the Appalachians (Figure 3.2.1b).

Government estimates of damage in the United States, Canada, and Europe exceed $50 billion annually. Because wind and weather patterns are international, efforts at reducing acidic deposition also must be international in scope. Figure 3.2.2 maps the reduction in sulfate deposition between the 1990–1994 and 1996–2000 periods. However, this progress is only a beginning. According to a study in *BioScience*, power plants and

(a)

FIGURE 3.2.1 The blight of acid deposition.
The harm done to forests and crops by acid deposition is well established, especially in Europe, such as in the Czech Republic (a), and in the forests of the Appalachian Mountains in the United States, such as in the forests on Mount Mitchell (b). [(a) Photo by Simon Fraser/Science Photo Library/Photo Researchers, Inc.; (b) Will and Deni McIntyre/Photo Researchers, Inc.]

(b)

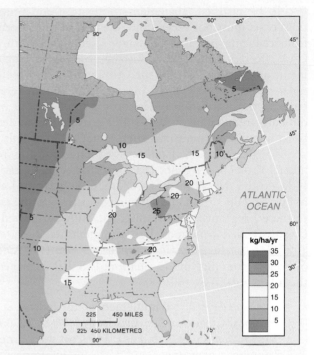

FIGURE 3.2.2 Improvement in sulfate wet deposition rate.
Spatial portrayal of annual sulfate (principally SO_4) wet deposition on the landscape, (a) 1990 to 1994 and (b) 1996 to 2000, in kilograms per hectare per year. The Canadian *Environmental Protection Act*, the Canada–United States Border Air Quality Strategy, and the U.S. *Clean Air Act* regulations lowered levels of emissions that add acid to the environment. [Maps from *Cleaner Air through Cooperation, Canada – United States, Progress under the Air Quality Agreement—2003, Environment Canada, 2003*. Reproduced with the permission of the Minister of Public Works and Government Services Canada.]

other sources must cut sulfur dioxide emissions 80% beyond the Clean Air Act mandate to truly reverse damage trends.

Ten leading acid-deposition researchers reported in an extensive study in *BioScience*:

Model calculations suggest that the greater the reduction in atmospheric sulfur deposition, the greater the magnitude and rate of chemical recovery. Less aggressive proposals for controls of sulfur emissions will result in slower chemical and biological recovery and in delays in regaining the services of a fully functional ecosystem.... North America and Europe are in the midst of a large-scale experiment. Sulfuric and nitric acids have acidified soils, lakes, and streams, thereby stressing or killing terrestrial and aquatic biota.*

Acid deposition is an issue of global spatial significance for which science is providing strong incentives for action. Reductions in troublesome emissions are closely tied to energy conservation and therefore directly related to production of greenhouse gases and global warming concerns—thus, linking these environmental issues.

*C. T. Driscoll *et al.*, "Acidic deposition in the northeastern United States: Sources and Inputs, Ecosystems Effects, and Management Strategies," *BioScience* 51 (March 2001): 195.

Earth's next atmosphere. The urban air we breathe today may be just a preview. What is the air quality like where you live, work, and go to college? Where could you go to find out its status?

Benefits of the Clean Air Act

The concentration of many air pollutants declined over the past several decades because of U.S. Clean Air Act (CAA) legislation (1970, 1977, 1990), resulting in the avoidance of trillions of dollars in health, economic, and environmental losses. Despite this reality, air pollution controls are subject to a continuing political debate, a weakening of some standards, and proposals that will increase pollution emissions.

Since 1970 and the CAA, there were significant reductions in atmospheric concentrations of carbon monoxide (−45%), nitrogen oxides (−22%), volatile organic compounds (−48%), PM_{10} particulates (−75%), sulfur oxides (−52%; see Focus Study 3.2, Figure 3.2.2), and lead (−98%). Prior to the CAA, lead was added to gasoline, emitted in the exhaust, dispersed over great distances, and settled in living tissues, especially in children. These all represent remarkable reductions; a successful linking of science and public policy.

To be justified, abatement (mitigation and prevention) costs must not exceed the financial benefits derived from reducing pollution damage. Compliance with the CAA affected patterns of industrial production, employment, and capital investment. Although these expenditures must be viewed as investments that generated benefits, the dislocation and job loss in some regions were difficult—reductions in high-sulfur coal mining and cutbacks in polluting industries such as steel, for example.

In 1990, the U.S. Congress requested the Environmental Protection Agency (EPA) to answer the question: How do the overall health, welfare, ecological, and economic benefits of CAA programs compare with the costs of these programs? In response, the EPA performed an exhaustive cost–benefit analysis and published a report in 1997. *The Benefits of the Clean Air Act, 1970 to 1990* (Office of Policy, Planning, and Evaluation, U.S. EPA) calculated the following:

- The *total direct cost* to implement all the federal, state, and local Clean Air Act rules from 1970 to 1990 was *$523 billion* (in 1990 dollars). This cost was borne by businesses, consumers, and government entities.
- The estimate of *direct monetized benefits* from the Clean Air Act from 1970 to 1990 falls in a range from $5.6 to $49.4 trillion, with a central mean of *$22.2 trillion*. (The uncertainty of the assessment is indicated by the range of benefit estimates.)

- Therefore, the estimated *net financial benefit* of the Clean Air Act is *$21.7 trillion*! "The finding is overwhelming. The benefits far exceed the costs of the CAA in the first 20 years," said Richard Morgenstern, associate administrator for policy planning and evaluation at the EPA.

The benefits to society, directly and indirectly, were widespread across the entire population, including improved health and environment, less lead to harm children, lowered cancer rates, less acid deposition, and an estimated 206,000 fewer deaths related to air pollution in 1990 alone. These benefits took place during a period in which the U.S. population grew by 22% and the economy expanded by 70%. The benefits continued between 1990 and 2000 as air quality continued to improve. Recent efforts to weaken or rescind CAA regulations seem counterproductive to the progress made. Given a choice, which benefits from the CAA might the public choose to lose?

As you reflect on this chapter and our modern atmosphere, the treaties to protect stratospheric ozone, and the EPA study of benefits from the CAA, you should feel encouraged. Scientists did the research and society knew what to do, took action, and reaped enormous economic and health benefits. An important role for physical geographers is to explain these global impacts through spatial analysis and to guide an informed citizenry toward a better understanding.

Applied Physical Geography

Radiation and Temperature

Radiation laws are the set of rules that summarize the way that matter interacts with the electromagnetic spectrum. We can think of radiation, energy, and temperature—the hotter a body, the more energy it radiates, and the shorter the wavelength of energy it radiates. Two laws are particularly useful in an examination of energy.

First is the Stefan-Boltzmann Law that gives the total amount of energy being emitted at all wavelengths by a body.

$$E = \sigma T^4$$

where E is the energy measured in W/m^2, σ is the Stefan-Boltzmann constant (5.6705×10^{-8} $W/m^2/K^4$), and T is the temperature of the surface measured in the Kelvin scale. Kelvin is a scale of temperature that has an absolute zero: Zero Kelvin means there is no temperature. The measurement units are the same distance apart

as on the Celsius scale—a relative temperature scale. To change from Kelvin to Celsius use the following conversion:

$$K = C + 273$$

Second is the Wien Displacement Law that gives the wavelength of the peak of the radiation distribution.

$$\lambda_{MAX} = c/T$$

where λ_{MAX} is the wavelength in μm that is the maximum radiation at a given temperature, c is a constant (2898 μm), and T is the surface temperature in K. The numerator is a constant measured in angstroms (one ten billionth of a metre).

These laws apply only to something known as a blackbody—a perfectly radiating surface. Most surfaces are not perfect radiators, but the differences in radiation are not significant enough to discount the laws.

To see how these laws are applied, consider normal room temperature of 20°C. Convert this temperature to Kelvin by adding 273 to 20. Room temperature in Kelvin is 293K. How much energy is being emitted by a surface at room temperature?

$$
\begin{aligned}
E &= \sigma T^4 \\
&= (5.6705 \times 10^{-8} \text{ W/m}^2/\text{K}^4) \times (293\text{K})^4 \\
&= (5.6705 \times 10^{-8} \text{ W/m}^2/\text{K}^4) \times 7.37 \times 10^9 \text{K}^4 \\
&= 417.9 \text{ W/m}^2
\end{aligned}
$$

What is the wavelength of the maximum emission?

$$
\begin{aligned}
\lambda_{MAX} &= c/T \\
&= 2898/293\text{K} \\
&= 9.89 \text{ } \mu m
\end{aligned}
$$

At room temperature, a surface emits 417.9 W/m^2 of energy at a wavelength of 9.89 μm.

Summary and Review—Earth's Modern Atmosphere

■ *Construct* **a general model of the atmosphere based on the three criteria, composition, temperature, and function, and** *diagram* **this model in a simple sketch.**

Our modern atmosphere is a gaseous mixture so evenly mixed it behaves as if it were a single gas. The principal substance of this atmosphere is air—the medium of life. **Air** is naturally odourless, colourless, tasteless, and formless.

Above 480 km (300 mi) altitude, the atmosphere is rarefied (nearly a vacuum) and is the **exosphere**, which means "outer sphere." The weight (force over a unit area) of the atmosphere, exerted on all surfaces, is **air pressure**. It decreases rapidly with altitude.

By *composition*, we divide the atmosphere into the **heterosphere**, extending from 480 km (300 mi) to 80 km (50 mi), and the **homosphere**, extending from 80 km to Earth's surface. Within the heterosphere and using *temperature* as a criterion, we identify the **thermosphere**. Its upper limit, called the **thermopause**, is at approximately 480 km altitude. **Kinetic energy**, the energy of motion, is the vibrational energy that we measure and call temperature. The actual amount of heat produced in the thermosphere is very small. The density of the molecules is so low that little actual **heat**, the flow of kinetic energy from one body to another because of a temperature difference between them, is produced. Nearer Earth's surface, the greater number of molecules in the denser atmosphere transmits their kinetic energy as **sensible heat**, meaning that we can feel it.

The homosphere includes the **mesosphere**, **stratosphere**, and **troposphere**, as defined by temperature criteria. Within the mesosphere, cosmic or meteoric dust acts as nuclei around which fine ice crystals form to produce rare and unusual night clouds called **noctilucent clouds**.

The normal temperature profile within the troposphere during the daytime decreases rapidly with increasing altitude at an average of 6.4 C° per kilometre (3.5 F° per 1000 ft), a rate known as the **normal lapse rate**. The top of the troposphere is wherever a temperature of −57°C (−70°F) is recorded, a transition known as the **tropopause**. The actual lapse rate at any particular time and place may deviate considerably because of local weather conditions and is called the **environmental lapse rate**.

We distinguish a region in the heterosphere by its *function*. The **ionosphere** absorbs cosmic rays, gamma rays, X-rays, and shorter wavelengths of ultraviolet radiation and converts them into kinetic energy. A functional region within the stratosphere is the **ozonosphere**, or **ozone layer**, which absorbs life-threatening ultraviolet radiation, subsequently raising the temperature of the stratosphere.

air (p. 64)
exosphere (p. 64)
air pressure (p. 65)
heterosphere (p. 66)
homosphere (p. 67)
thermosphere (p. 69)
thermopause (p. 69)
kinetic energy (p. 69)
heat (p. 69)
sensible heat (p. 69)
mesosphere (p. 69)
noctilucent clouds (p. 69)
stratosphere (p. 69)
troposphere (p. 69)
tropopause (p. 69)
normal lapse rate (p. 70)
environmental lapse rate (p. 70)
ionosphere (p. 70)
ozonosphere, ozone layer (p. 70)

1. What is air? Where did the components in Earth's present atmosphere originate?

2. In view of the cell analogy by Lewis Thomas, characterize the various functions the atmosphere performs that protect the surface environment.

3. What three distinct criteria are employed in dividing the atmosphere for study?

4. Describe the overall temperature profile of the atmosphere, and list the four layers defined by temperature.

5. Describe the two divisions of the atmosphere on the basis of composition.

6. What are the two overall primary functional layers of the atmosphere and what does each do?

■ *List* **the stable components of the modern atmosphere and their relative percentage contributions by volume, and** *describe* **each.**

Even though the atmosphere's density decreases with increasing altitude in the homosphere, the blend (proportion) of gases is nearly uniform. This stable mixture of gases has evolved slowly.

The homosphere is a vast reservoir of relatively inert *nitrogen*, originating principally from volcanic sources and from bacterial action in the soil; *oxygen*, a by-product of photosynthesis; *argon*, constituting about 1% of the homosphere and completely inert; and *carbon dioxide*, a natural by-product of life processes and fuel combustion.

7. Name the four most prevalent stable gases in the homosphere. Where did each originate? Is the prevalence of any of these changing at this time?

■ *Describe* **conditions within the stratosphere; specifically,** *review* **the function and status of the ozonosphere (ozone layer).**

The overall reduction of the stratospheric ozonosphere, or ozone layer, during the past several decades represents a hazard for society and many natural systems and is caused by chemicals introduced into the atmosphere by humans. Since World War II, quantities of human-made **chlorofluorocarbons** (**CFCs**) and bromine-containing compounds have made their way into the stratosphere. The increased ultraviolet light at those altitudes breaks down these stable chemical compounds, thus freeing chlorine and bromine atoms. These atoms act as catalysts in reactions that destroy ozone molecules.

chlorofluorocarbons (CFCs) (p. 71)

8. Why is stratospheric ozone (O_3) so important? Describe the effects created by increases in ultraviolet light reaching the surface.

9. Summarize the ozone predicament, and describe trends and any treaties that intend to protect the ozone layer.

10. Evaluate Crutzen, Rowland, and Molina's use of the scientific method in investigating stratospheric ozone depletion, and public reaction to their findings.

■ *Distinguish* between natural and anthropogenic variable gases and materials in the lower atmosphere.

Within the troposphere, both natural and human-caused variable gases, particles, and other chemicals are part of the atmosphere. We coevolved with natural "pollution" and thus are adapted to it. But we are not adapted to cope with our own anthropogenic pollution. It constitutes a major health threat, particularly where people are concentrated in cities.

Vertical temperature and atmospheric density distribution in the troposphere can worsen pollution conditions. A **temperature inversion** occurs when the normal temperature decrease with altitude (normal lapse rate) reverses. In other words, temperature begins to increase at some altitude.

   temperature inversion (p. 75)

11. Why are anthropogenic gases more significant to human health than those produced from natural sources?

12. In what ways does a temperature inversion worsen an air pollution episode? Why?

■ *Describe* the sources and effects of carbon monoxide, nitrogen dioxide, and sulfur dioxide, and *construct* a simple equation that illustrates photochemical reactions that produce ozone, peroxyacetyl nitrates, nitric acid, and sulfuric acid.

Small particles of dust, soot, and pollution suspended in the air are **aerosols**. Odourless, colourless, and tasteless, **carbon monoxide (CO)** is produced by incomplete combustion (burning with limited oxygen) of fuels or other carbon-containing substances. Transportation is the major human-caused source for carbon monoxide. The toxicity of carbon monoxide is due to its affinity for blood hemoglobin, which is the oxygen-carrying pigment in red blood cells. In the presence of carbon monoxide, the oxygen is displaced and the blood becomes deoxygenated (Table 3.4).

Photochemical smog results from the interaction of sunlight and the products of automobile exhaust, the single largest contributor of pollution that produces smog. Car exhaust, containing *nitrogen dioxide* and *volatile organic compounds (VOCs)*, in the presence of ultraviolet light in sunlight converts into the principal photochemical by-products—*ozone, peroxyacetyl nitrates (PAN)*, and *nitric acid*.

Ozone (O_3) causes negative health effects, oxidizes surfaces, and kills or damages plants. **Peroxyacetyl nitrates (PAN)** produce no known health effects in humans but are particularly damaging to plants, including both agricultural crops and forests. **Nitrogen dioxide (NO_2)** damages and inflames human respiratory systems, destroys lung tissue, and damages plants. Nitric oxides participate in reactions that form nitric acid (HNO_3) in the atmosphere, forming both wet and dry acidic deposition. The **volatile organic compounds (VOCs)**, including hydrocarbons from gasoline, surface coatings, and electric utility combustion, are important factors in ozone formation.

The distribution of human-produced **industrial smog** over North America, Europe, and Asia is related to transportation and electrical production. Such characteristic pollution contains **sulfur dioxide**. Sulfur dioxide in the atmosphere reacts to produce **sulfate aerosols**, which produce sulfuric acid (H_2SO_4) deposition, which can be dangerous to health and affect Earth's energy budget by scattering and reflecting solar energy. **Particulate matter (PM)** consists of dirt, dust, soot, and ash from industrial and natural sources.

Energy conservation and efficiency and reducing emissions are key to reducing air pollution. Earth's next atmosphere most accurately may be described as the **anthropogenic atmosphere** (human-influenced atmosphere).

   aerosols (p. 78)
   carbon monoxide (CO) (p. 78)
   photochemical smog (p. 80)
   nitrogen dioxide (p. 82)
   peroxyacetyl nitrates (PAN) (p. 82)
   volatile organic compounds (VOCs) (p. 82)
   industrial smog (p. 82)
   sulfur dioxide (p. 83)
   sulfate aerosols (p. 83)
   particulate matter (PM) (p. 83)
   anthropogenic atmosphere (p. 83)

13. What is the difference between industrial smog and photochemical smog?

14. Describe the relationship between automobiles and the production of ozone and PAN in city air. What are the principal negative impacts of these gases?

15. How are sulfur impurities in fossil fuels related to the formation of acid in the atmosphere and acid deposition on the land?

16. In summary, what are the results from the first 20 years under Clean Air Act regulations?

17. Summarize the commitments Canada has made to improve air quality.

A. Read the 2003 progress report on "Particulate Matter and Ozone" found at **http://www.ec.gc.ca/CEPARegistry/ documents/agree/PM_resp_03/toc.cfm**. Do you think the Canadian government is making enough progress to improve air quality? What are the economic costs of meeting the tougher standards? How do the costs balance against the benefits to health, the environment, and lower energy costs through efficiency and conservation? The U.S. Environmental Protection Agency Study described in this chapter estimated a benefit-to-cost ratio of 42 to 1. Should this influence a decision as to whether to strengthen the Canadian *Environmental Protection Act*?

B. Relative to item A: In your opinion, why is the public generally unaware of these details? What are the difficulties in informing the public? Why is there such media attention given to antiscience and nonscientific opinions? Take a moment and brainstorm recommendations for action, education, and public awareness on these issues.

C. To determine the total ozone column at your present location, go to **http://toms.gsfc.nasa.gov/teacher/ozone_ overhead.html**, "What was the total ozone column at your house?" Select a point on the map or enter your latitude and longitude and the date you want to check. The ozone column is measured by the Ozone Monitoring Instrument (OMI) sensor aboard the *Aqua* satellite, and is mainly sensitive to stratospheric ozone. (Note also the limitations listed on the extent of data availability.) For several different dates, when do the lowest values occur? The highest values? Briefly explain what your results mean. How do you interpret the values found?

Jet condensation trails stimulate high-cirrus cloud formation. Inset photos and image show thin, newer contrails in contrast to older contrails widening over time as they develop. Note the density of contrails over the Midwest and Great Lakes region in the satellite image. Studies found that such contrails affect daily temperature ranges between daytime maximum and nighttime minimum—another connection between transportation systems and Earth's atmospheric energy budget. [Photos by Bobbé Christopherson; inset image *Terra* satellite courtesy of MODIS Land Rapid Response Team, NASA/GSFC.]

CHAPTER
4

Atmosphere and Surface Energy Balances

■ Key Learning Concepts

After reading the chapter, you should be able to:

- **Identify** the pathways of solar energy through the troposphere to Earth's surface: transmission, scattering, diffuse radiation, refraction, albedo (reflectivity), conduction, convection, and advection.

- **Describe** what happens to insolation when clouds are in the atmosphere, and **analyze** the effect of clouds and air pollution on solar radiation received at ground level.

- **Review** the energy pathways in the Earth–atmosphere system, the greenhouse effect, and the patterns of global net radiation.

- **Plot** the daily radiation curves for Earth's surface, and **label** the key aspects of incoming radiation, air temperature, and the daily temperature lag.

- **Portray** typical urban heat island conditions, and **contrast** the micro-climatology of urban areas with that of surrounding rural environments.

E arth's biosphere pulses with flows of solar energy that sustain our lives and empower natural systems. Changing seasons, daily weather conditions, and Earth's variety of climates remind us of this constant flow of energy cascading through the atmosphere. Earth's shifting seasonal rhythms are described in Chapter 2, and a profile of the atmosphere in Chapter 3. Energy and moisture exchanges between Earth's surface and the atmosphere are essential elements of weather and climate, discussed in later chapters.

91

In this chapter: We follow solar energy through the troposphere to Earth's surface. The *outputs* of reflected light and emitted longwave energy from the atmosphere and surface environment counter the *input* of insolation. Together, this input and output determines the net energy available to perform work. We examine surface energy budgets and analyze how net radiation is spent. The chapter concludes with a look at the unique energy and moisture environment in our cities. The view across a hot parking lot of cars and pavement in summer is all too familiar—the air shimmers as heat energy radiates skyward. The climate of our urban areas differs measurably from that of surrounding rural areas. Focus Study 4.1 discusses solar energy, an applied aspect of surface energy and a renewable energy resource of great potential.

Energy Essentials

When you look at a photograph of Earth taken from space, you clearly see the surface receipts of incoming insolation (see Earth photo on the back cover of this book). Land and water surfaces, clouds, and atmospheric gases and dust intercept solar energy. The flows of energy are manifest in swirling weather patterns, powerful oceanic currents, and the varied vegetation of land cover. Specific energy patterns differ for deserts, oceans, mountaintops, plains, rain forests, and ice-covered landscapes. In addition, the presence or absence of clouds may make a 75% difference in the amount of energy that reaches the surface, because clouds reflect incoming energy.

Energy Pathways and Principles

Solar energy that heats Earth's atmosphere and surface is unevenly distributed by latitude, and fluctuates seasonally. Figure 4.1 is a simplified flow diagram of shortwave and longwave radiation in the Earth–atmosphere system, discussed in the pages that follow. You will find it helpful to refer to this figure, and the more detailed energy balance illustration in Figure 4.12, as you read through the following section. We first look at some important pathways and principles for insolation as it passes through the atmosphere to Earth's surface.

Transmission refers to the passage of shortwave and longwave energy through either the atmosphere or water. Our budget of atmospheric energy comprises shortwave radiation *inputs* (ultraviolet light, visible light, and near-infrared wavelengths) and longwave radiation *outputs* (thermal infrared) that pass through the atmosphere by transmission.

Insolation Input   *Insolation* is the single energy input driving the Earth–atmosphere system. The world map in Figure 4.2 shows the distribution of average annual solar energy received at Earth's surface. It includes all the radiation that arrives at Earth's surface, both direct and diffuse (scattered by the atmosphere).

Several patterns are notable on the map. Insolation decreases poleward from about 25° latitude in both the Northern and Southern hemispheres. Consistent daylength and high Sun altitude produce average annual values of 180–220 W/m² throughout the equatorial and tropical latitudes. In general, greater insolation of 240–280 W/m² occurs in low-latitude deserts worldwide because of frequently cloudless skies. Note this energy pattern in the cloudless subtropical deserts in both hemispheres (for example, the Sonoran, Saharan, Arabian, Gobi, Atacama, Namib, Kalahari, and Australian deserts).

Scattering (Diffuse Radiation)   Insolation encounters an increasing density of atmospheric gases as it travels toward the surface. Atmospheric gases and dust physically

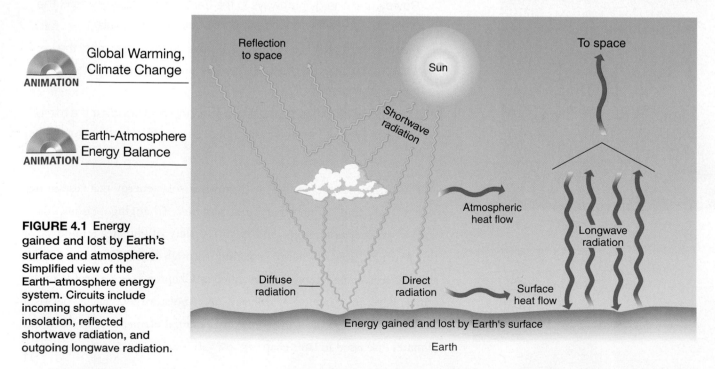

ANIMATION
Global Warming, Climate Change

ANIMATION
Earth-Atmosphere Energy Balance

FIGURE 4.1 Energy gained and lost by Earth's surface and atmosphere. Simplified view of the Earth–atmosphere energy system. Circuits include incoming shortwave insolation, reflected shortwave radiation, and outgoing longwave radiation.

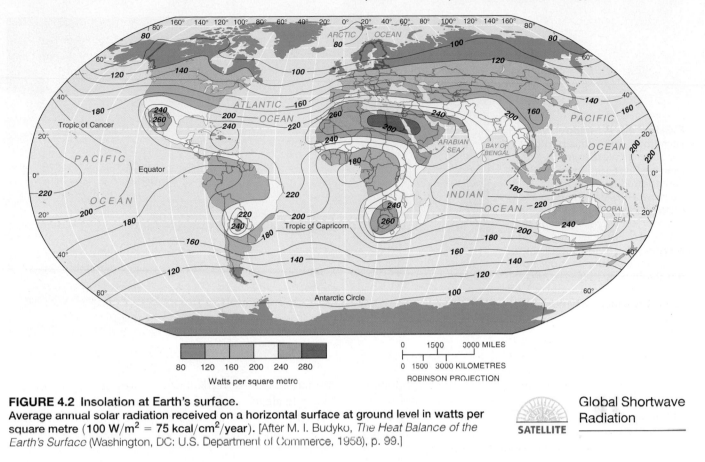

FIGURE 4.2 Insolation at Earth's surface.
Average annual solar radiation received on a horizontal surface at ground level in watts per square metre ($100\ W/m^2 = 75\ kcal/cm^2/year$). [After M. I. Budyko, *The Heat Balance of the Earth's Surface* (Washington, DC: U.S. Department of Commerce, 1958), p. 99.]

SATELLITE

Global Shortwave Radiation

interact with insolation. The gas molecules redirect radiation, changing the direction of the light's movement *without altering its wavelengths*. **Scattering** describes this phenomenon and represents 7% of Earth's reflectivity, or albedo (see Figure 4.12). Dust particles, pollutants, ice, cloud droplets, and water vapour produce further scattering.

Have you wondered why Earth's sky is blue? And why sunsets and sunrises are often red? These simple questions have an interesting explanation, based upon a principle known as Rayleigh scattering (named for English physicist Lord Rayleigh, 1881). This principle relates wavelength to the size of molecules or particles that cause the scattering. The general rule is: *The shorter the wavelength, the greater the scattering; and the longer the wavelength, the lesser the scattering.* Small gas molecules in the air scatter shorter wavelengths of light. Thus, the shorter wavelengths of visible light—the blues and violets—scatter the most and dominate the lower atmosphere. And, because there are more blue than violet wavelengths in sunlight, a blue sky prevails. A sky filled with smog and haze appears almost white because the larger particles associated with air pollution act to scatter all wavelengths of visible light.

The angle of the Sun's rays determines the thickness of atmosphere they must pass through to reach the surface. Therefore, direct rays (from overhead) experience less scattering and absorption than do low, oblique-angle rays that must travel farther through the atmosphere. Insolation from the low-altitude Sun undergoes more scattering of shorter wavelengths, leaving only the residual oranges and reds to reach the observer at sunset or sunrise.

Some incoming insolation is diffused by clouds and atmosphere and transmits to Earth as **diffuse radiation**, the downward component of scattered light (labeled in Figure 4.12). Such diffuse light is multidirectional and thus casts shadowless light on the ground.

Refraction As insolation enters the atmosphere, it passes from one medium to another, from virtually empty space into atmospheric gases, or from air into water. This transition subjects the insolation to a change of speed, which also shifts its direction, a bending action called **refraction**. In the same way, a crystal or prism refracts light passing through it, bending different wavelengths to different angles, separating the light into its component colours to display the spectrum. A rainbow is created when visible light passes through myriad raindrops and is refracted and reflected toward the observer at a precise angle (see Figure 4.3).

Another example of refraction is a **mirage**, an image that appears near the horizon where light waves are refracted by layers of air at different temperatures (and consequently of different densities) on a hot day. The atmospheric distortion of the setting Sun in Figure 4.4 is also a product of refraction—light from the Sun low in the sky must penetrate more air than when the Sun is high; it is refracted through air layers of different densities on its way to the observer.

An interesting function of refraction is that it adds approximately 8 minutes of daylight that we would lack if Earth had no atmosphere. Sunlight refracts in its

FIGURE 4.3 A rainbow. Raindrops, and in this photo moisture droplets from the Niagara River, refract and reflect light to produce a primary rainbow. Note that the colour order in the primary rainbow has the shortest wavelengths on the inside of the bow and the longest wavelengths on the outside of the bow. In the secondary bow, note the colour sequence is reversed because of an extra angle of reflection within each moisture droplet. [Photo by Bobbé Christopherson.]

passage from space through the atmosphere, and so, at sunrise, we see the Sun's image about 4 minutes before the Sun actually peeks over the horizon. Similarly, as the Sun actually sets at sunset its refracted image is visible from over the horizon for about 4 minutes afterward. To this day, science cannot predict the exact time of visible sunrise or sunset given the degree of refraction, which varies with atmospheric temperature, moisture, and pollutants.

Albedo and Reflection   A portion of arriving energy bounces directly back into space without being absorbed or performing any work—this is the **reflection** process. **Albedo** is the reflective quality, or intrinsic brightness, of a surface. It is an important control over the amount of

FIGURE 4.4 Sun refraction.
The distorted appearance of the Sun nearing sunset over the ocean is produced by refraction of the Sun's image in the atmosphere. Have you ever noticed this effect? [Photo by Robert Christopherson.]

insolation that is available for absorption by a surface. We state albedo as the percentage of insolation that is reflected (0% is total absorption; 100% is total reflectance). Examine the different surfaces and their albedo values in Figure 4.5.

In the visible wavelengths, darker colours have lower albedos, and lighter colours have higher albedos. On water surfaces, the angle of the solar rays also affects albedo values; lower angles produce a greater reflection than do higher angles. In addition, smooth surfaces increase albedo, whereas rougher surfaces reduce it.

Specific locations experience highly variable albedo values during the year in response to changes in cloud and ground cover. Earth Radiation Budget (ERB) sensors aboard the *Nimbus*-7 satellite measured average albedos of 19%–38% for all surfaces between the tropics (23.5° N to 23.5° S), whereas albedos for the polar regions measured as high as 80%.

Earth and its atmosphere reflect 31% of all insolation when averaged over a year. Looking ahead to Figure 4.12, you can see that Earth's average albedo is a combination of 21% reflected by clouds, 3% reflected by the ground (combined land and ocean surfaces), and 7% reflected and scattered by the atmosphere. By comparison, a full Moon, which is bright enough to read by under clear skies, has only a 6%–8% albedo value. Thus, with *earthshine* being 4 times brighter than moonlight (4 times the albedo), and with Earth 4 times greater in diameter than the Moon, it is no surprise that astronauts report how startling our planet looks from space. News Report 4.1 presents information on earthshine as a climate status indicator.

Figure 4.6 portrays total albedos for July and January as measured by the Earth Radiation Budget experiments aboard several satellites. These patterns are typical of most years. As compared with July albedos, January

FIGURE 4.5 Various albedo values.
Different surfaces have different albedo values. In general, light surfaces are more reflective than dark surfaces and thus have higher albedo values. [Data from M. I. Budyko, *The Heat Balance of the Earth's Surface* (Washington, DC: U.S. Department of Commerce, 1958), p. 36.]

SATELLITE   Global Albedo Values
Global Shortwave
Radiation

albedos are higher poleward of 40° N, because of the snow and ice that cover the ground. Tropical forests are characteristically low in albedo (15%), whereas generally cloudless deserts have high albedos (35%). The southward-shifting cloud cover over equatorial Africa is quite apparent on the January map. What other seasonal changes do you see on these ERB albedo maps?

Clouds, Aerosols, and the Atmosphere's Albedo An unpredictable factor in the tropospheric energy budget, and therefore in refining climatic models, is the role of clouds. Clouds reflect insolation and thus cool Earth's surface. The term **cloud-albedo forcing** is an *increase in albedo* caused by clouds. Yet clouds act as insulation, trapping longwave radiation from Earth and raising minimum

(a) July   (b) January

FIGURE 4.6 Total albedos for July and January.
Total albedos for a July (a) and a January (b) as measured by the Earth Radiation Budget experiments (ERB) aboard satellites *Nimbus-7, NOAA-9,* and *ERBS (ERB Satellite)*. Each colour represents a 12% interval in albedo values. [Courtesy of Radiation Services Branch, Langley Research Center, NASA.]

News Report

News Report 4.1

Earthshine Studies—Possible Energy Budget Diagnostic

Earth's reflection of light to space might prove to be a useful tool in analyzing energy budgets and climate. Earth's average albedo is 31%—that is, 31% of all incoming insolation returns to space without being absorbed. We have all seen the effect of *earthshine*—Earth's total albedo reflectance to space—as a faint illumination of the dark portion of the Moon, especially in crescent phase, when the dark portion of the lunar disk is barely visible.

In contrast, the Moon reflects only 6% to 8% of the sunlight that hits its surface, producing the "moonlight" familiar to us all. Despite the bright, white appearance of the Moon, the lunar surface albedo is about the same as that of asphalt pavement. Because Earth reflects about 400% as much light as the Moon and is about 400% greater in diameter, Earth is a startling presence in space.

Earthshine, if properly analyzed, is a proxy (substitute, representative) measure of Earth's shortwave reflectance and an important diagnostic tool in climate change studies. The significance of measuring earthshine is this: An approximate 1% change in albedo will produce about a 1 C° (2 F°) change in average atmospheric temperature. Thus, an albedo change can produce a temperature change, which can produce further albedo change and further alter climate. The Sun's average 11-year activity cycle produces about a 0.1% variation in earthshine and is not considered a cause for present global warming.

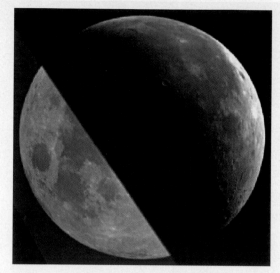

FIGURE 4.1.1 Earthshine illuminates the Moon. Our Moon intercepts some of Earth's shortwave reflectance to space. Earthshine is most visible when the Moon is in a crescent phase. Check this out next time you see the Moon in its crescent to half phase. The combined photos show the moonshine segment (lower-left, dimmed by a filter because it is 10,000 times brighter than earthshine) and the earthshine segment (upper-right). [Composite photos courtesy of Earthshine Project, Big Bear Solar Observatory.]

Cloud cover is the significant factor that drives changes in Earth's shortwave reflectance, although surface changes and atmospheric pollution also are important. Increases in cloud cover are an indicator of increasing atmospheric temperatures. Relative to surface changes, imagine the impact on global albedo values if there were an increase in snow-free landscapes.

Scientists from the New Jersey Institute of Technology and California Institute of Technology now measure earthshine at the Big Bear Solar Observatory during the Moon's crescent phase when Earth's sunlight hemisphere is toward the Moon (see: http://www.bbso.njit.edu/). These data are then compared to the International Satellite Cloud Climatology Project (ISCCP) record. André Danjon of France began earthshine studies in 1925. Current research shows Earth's average albedo was on a steady decline from 1984 to 2000 (less cloudy), whereas 2001–2004 (more clouds) demonstrated a complete reversal with increasing Earth reflectance.

These large variations in reflectance imply climatologically significant cloud-driven changes in Earth's radiation budget, which is consistent with the large tropospheric warming that has occurred over the most recent decades. Moreover, if the observed reversal in Earth's reflectance trend is sustained during the next few years, it might also play a very important role in future climate change.*

A lot remains to be learned about this yardstick for Earth's energy balance. Think about earthshine the next time you take a moonlit walk.

*E. Pallé et al., "Changes in Earth Reflectance over the Past Two Decades," *Science* 304 (May 28, 2004): 1299–1301.

---

temperatures. **Cloud-greenhouse forcing** is an *increase in greenhouse warming* caused by clouds. Figure 4.7 illustrates the general effects of clouds on shortwave radiation and longwave radiation. Chapter 7 details more on clouds.

The eruption of Mount Pinatubo in the Philippines, which began explosively during June 1991, illustrates how Earth's internal processes affect the atmosphere. Approximately 15–20 megatons of sulfur dioxide were injected

into the stratosphere; winds rapidly spread these aerosols (tiny droplets) worldwide (see the images in Figure 6.1). As a result, atmospheric albedo increased worldwide and produced a temporary average cooling of 0.5 C° (0.9 F°).

Other mechanisms affect atmospheric albedo and therefore atmospheric and surface energy budgets. Industrialization is producing a haze of pollution that is increasing the reflectivity of the atmosphere, including sulfate

(a) Shortwave radiation

(b) Longwave radiation

FIGURE 4.7 The effects of clouds on shortwave and longwave radiation.
(a) Clouds reflect and scatter shortwave radiation; a high percentage is returned to space.
(b) Clouds absorb and reradiate longwave radiation emitted by Earth; some longwave energy returns to space and some is radiated toward the surface.

aerosols, soot and fly ash, and black carbon. Emissions of sulfur dioxide and subsequent chemical reactions in the atmosphere form *sulfate aerosols*. These aerosols act as an insolation-reflecting haze in clear-sky conditions.

Scientists are actively analyzing such pollution-dimmed sunlight reductions. The pollution causes both an atmospheric warming through absorption by the pollutants and a surface cooling through reduction in insolation reaching ground and water surfaces. An overall term has emerged that describes this decline in insolation

making it to Earth's surface—**global dimming**. In determining present temperature increases in global warming, this solar dimming is perhaps forcing an underestimation of the actual amount of warming.

Figure 4.8 is from the CERES (Clouds and the Earth Radiant Energy System) sensors aboard satellite *Terra* and shows pollution-haze and soot effects on the atmospheric energy budget in the Indian Ocean region. The increased aerosols (1), containing black carbon, increase reflection off the atmosphere, thus raising atmospheric albedos (2).

FIGURE 4.8 Aerosols impact Earth–atmosphere energy budgets.
Aerosols including black carbon both reflect and absorb incoming insolation as identified in these four images by the CERES sensors aboard satellite *Terra,* made between January and March 2001 over southern Asia and the Indian Ocean. Note the colour scale for each image rating from low to high values.
[CERES images aboard *Terra* courtesy of Goddard Space Flight Center, NASA.]

This causes an increase in atmospheric warming (as aerosols absorb energy), (3) and an increase in surface cooling as less insolation reaches Earth's surface (4). These aerosols reduce surface insolation by 10% and increase energy absorption in the atmosphere by 50%.

Such pollution effects in southern Asia influence the dynamics of the Asian monsoon through alteration of the region's Earth–atmosphere energy budget (see monsoons in Chapter 6). A weakening monsoonal flow will negatively impact regional water resources and agriculture. This research is part of the international, multiagency Indian Ocean Experiment (INDOEX, see **http://www-indoex.ucsd.edu/**).

Absorption **Absorption** is the *assimilation* of radiation by molecules of matter and its conversion from one form of energy to another. Insolation, both direct and diffuse, that is not part of the 31% reflected from Earth's surface and atmosphere is absorbed. It is converted into either longwave radiation or chemical energy by plants in photosynthesis. The temperature of the absorbing surface is raised in the process, and warmer surfaces radiate more total energy at shorter wavelengths—thus, *the hotter the surface, the shorter the wavelengths that are emitted*. Examples are an electric burner beginning to glow as it heats, or molten metal glowing at high temperatures. In addition to absorption by land and water surfaces (about 45% of incoming insolation), absorption also occurs in atmospheric gases, dust, clouds, and stratospheric ozone (about 24% of incoming insolation). Figure 4.12 summarizes the pathways of insolation and the flow of heat in the atmosphere and at the surface.

Conduction, Convection, and Advection There are several means of transferring heat energy in a system. **Conduction** is the molecule-to-molecule transfer of heat energy as it diffuses through a substance. As molecules warm, their vibration increases, causing collisions that produce motion in neighbouring molecules, thus transferring heat from warmer to cooler materials.

Different materials (gases, liquids, and solids) conduct sensible heat directionally from areas of higher temperature to those of lower temperature. This heat flow transfers energy through matter at varying rates, depending on the conductivity of the material—Earth's land surface is a better conductor than air; moist air is a slightly better conductor than dry air.

Gases and liquids also transfer energy by movements called **convection** when the physical mixing involves a strong vertical motion. When horizontal motion dominates, the term **advection** applies. In the atmosphere or in bodies of water, warmer (less dense) masses tend to rise and cooler (denser) masses tend to sink, establishing patterns of convection. Sensible heat transports physically through the medium in this way.

You commonly experience such energy flows in the kitchen: Energy is conducted through the handle of a pan, or boiling water bubbles in the saucepan in convective

FIGURE 4.9 Heat energy transfer processes.
A pan of water on the stove illustrates heat transfer. Infrared energy *radiates* from the burner to the saucepan and the air. Energy *conducts* through the molecules of the pan and the handle. The water physically mixes, carrying heat energy by *convection*. The energy in the water and handle is measurable as *sensible heat*. The vapour leaving the surface of the water contains the *latent heat* absorbed in the change of water to water vapour.

motions (Figure 4.9). Also in the kitchen you may use a convection oven that has a fan to circulate heated air to uniformly cook food.

In physical geography, we find many examples of each physical transfer mechanism:

- *Conduction* examples include surface energy budgets, temperature differences between land and water bodies and between darker and lighter surfaces, the heating of surfaces and overlying air, and soil temperatures;
- *Convection* includes atmospheric and oceanic circulation, air mass movements and weather systems, internal motions deep within Earth that produce a magnetic field, and movements in the crust; and
- *Advection* involves horizontal movement of winds from land to sea and back, fog that forms and moves to another area, and air-mass movements from source regions.

Now with these pathways and principles in mind, we put it all together to describe the energy budgets of the lower atmosphere.

Energy Balance in the Troposphere

The Earth–atmosphere energy system budget naturally balances itself in a steady-state equilibrium. The atmosphere and surface eventually radiate longwave energy back to space, and this energy, together with reflected shortwave energy, equals the initial solar input—think of cash flows into and out of a checking account and the balance when deposits and cash withdrawals are equal.

Greenhouse gases in the atmosphere effectively delay losses to space and act to warm the lower atmosphere. We examine this effect and then develop an overall budget for the troposphere.

The Greenhouse Effect and Atmospheric Warming

Previously, we characterized Earth as a cool-body radiator, emitting energy in longer wavelengths from its surface and atmosphere toward space. (In contrast, the Sun is a hot-body radiator, emitting shorter wavelengths from its surface.) However, some of this longwave radiation is absorbed by carbon dioxide, water vapour, methane, nitrous oxide, chlorofluorocarbons (CFCs), and other gases in the lower atmosphere and then emitted back toward Earth (detailed in Figure 2.7). This absorption and emission delays energy loss to space and is an important factor in warming the troposphere. The rough similarity between this process and the way a greenhouse operates gives the process its name—the **greenhouse effect**.

In a greenhouse, the glass is transparent to shortwave insolation, allowing light to pass through to the soil, plants, and materials inside, where absorption and conduction take place. The absorbed energy is then radiated as longwave radiation back toward the glass, but the glass physically traps both the longer wavelengths and the warmed air inside the greenhouse. Thus, the glass acts as a one-way filter, allowing shortwave energy in but not allowing the longwave energy out, except through conduction. You experience the same process in a car parked in direct sunlight.

Opening the greenhouse roof vent, or the car windows, allows the air inside to mix with the outside environment, thereby removing heat by moving air physically from one place to another—the process of convection. It is surprising how hot the interior of a car gets, even on a day with mild temperatures outside. Many people place a sunscreen across the windshield to prevent shortwave energy from entering the car to begin the greenhouse process. Have you taken steps to reduce the insolation input into your car's interior or through windows at home?

Overall, the atmosphere behaves a bit differently. In the atmosphere, the greenhouse analogy does not fully apply because longwave radiation is not trapped as in a greenhouse. Rather, its passage to space is *delayed* as the longwave radiation is absorbed by certain gases, clouds, and dust in the atmosphere and is emitted to Earth's surface. According to scientific consensus, today's increasing carbon dioxide concentration is forcing more longwave radiation absorption in the lower atmosphere, thus producing a warming trend and changes in the Earth–atmosphere energy system.

Clouds and Earth's "Greenhouse"

Clouds affect the heating of the lower atmosphere in several ways, depending on cloud type. Not only is the percentage of cloud cover important but the cloud type, height, and thickness (water content and density) also have an effect. High-altitude, ice-crystal clouds reflect insolation with albedos of about 50%, whereas thick, lower cloud cover reflects about 90% of incoming insolation.

To understand the actual effects on the atmosphere's energy budget, we must consider both transmission of shortwave and longwave radiation and cloud type. Figure 4.10a portrays the *cloud-greenhouse forcing* caused by high clouds (warming, because their greenhouse effects exceed their albedo effects), and Figure 4.10b portrays the *cloud-albedo forcing* produced by lower, thicker clouds (cooling, because albedo effects exceed greenhouse effects).

Jet contrails (*condensation trails*) produce high cirrus clouds (Figure 4.10c and chapter-opening photo inset)—sometimes called *false cirrus clouds*. The chapter-opening photos and satellite image illustrate how cloud development is stimulated by aircraft exhaust. Scientists were suspicious that these clouds affected atmospheric and surface temperatures. As shown in Figure 4.10a, these high-altitude ice-crystal clouds are efficient at reducing outgoing longwave radiation and therefore contribute to global heating. However, in contrast these contrail-seeded cirrus clouds have a higher density and higher albedo than normal cirrus clouds, thus reducing some surface insolation.

The tragedy that struck the World Trade Center, and humanity, on September 11, 2001, inadvertently provided researchers with a chance to study these effects. Following 9/11, there was a three-day grounding of all commercial airline traffic and therefore no contrails across the United States. Weather data from 4000 stations over 30 years were compared with data during the three-day flight shutdown. *Diurnal temperature range* (DTR)—the difference between daytime maximum and nighttime minimum temperatures—increased during the three days. Specifically, maximum temperatures were more responsive to the missing clouds than minimums.

Later study of synoptic conditions (air pressure, humidity, air mass data—all gathered at a specific time), analysis of Canadian air space, a check on conditions during adjacent three-day periods, and a look at the few military flights that took place during the halt of air travel served to verify the initial findings and strengthen the conclusion.* The elimination of contrail-stimulated clouds produced an increase in DTR—slightly higher afternoon and slightly lower nighttime temperature readings across the United States. The largest effects were in those regions where the greatest number of flights occurred. This ongoing study is helpful in the spatial analysis of possible impacts of future aircraft design and timing of flight schedules on the Earth–atmosphere energy budget.

To better understand the role of natural clouds as well as jet contrails, NASA operates the CERES program, an

---

*See David J. Travis et al., "Contrails reduce daily temperature range," *Nature* 418 (August 8, 2002): 601, from the Department of Geography and Geology, University of Wisconsin–Whitewater; and, D. J. Travis, A. M. Carleton. And R. G. Lauritsen, "Regional variations in U.S. diurnal temperature range for the 9/11–14/2001 aircraft groundings: Evidence of jet contrail influence on climate," *Journal of Climate* 17 (March 1, 2004): 1123–34.

(a) High clouds: net greenhouse forcing and atmospheric warming

(b) Low clouds: net albedo forcing and atmospheric cooling

FIGURE 4.10 Energy effects of two cloud types.
Cloud effects vary depending on cloud type. (a) High, ice-crystal clouds (called *cirrus*) transmit most of the insolation. However, they absorb and delay losses of outgoing longwave radiation, producing a greater greenhouse forcing and a net warming of Earth. (b) Low, thick clouds (*stratus*) reflect most of the incoming insolation and radiate longwave radiation to space, producing a greater albedo forcing and a net cooling of Earth. (c) Jet aircraft exhaust triggers denser cirrus-cloud development. Newer, thinner contrails spread to form cirrus clouds. [(c) Astronaut photo May 15, 2002 courtesy of NASA/JSC.]

(c)

acronym for Clouds and Earth's Radiant Energy System. CERES sensors aboard satellites began operating in 1997 (*TRMM*), in addition to *Terra* and *Aqua* satellites. CERES data are an important part of the study of aerosols and the monsoons in Figure 4.8. (See **http://asd-www.larc.nasa. gov/ceres/**.)

Data collected by CERES sensors cover both reflected and emitted radiation. Figure 4.11 shows the first global monthly images from satellite *Terra* for March 2000 in W/m² flux (meaning energy "flow"). In Figure 4.11a, lighter regions indicate where more sunlight is reflected into space than is absorbed—for example, by lighter-coloured land surfaces such as deserts or by cloud cover such as over tropical lands. Green and blue areas illustrate where less light was reflected.

In Figure 4.11b, orange and red pixels indicate regions where more longwave radiation was absorbed and emitted

(a)

(b)

FIGURE 4.11 Shortwave and longwave images show Earth's radiation budget components.
The CERES sensors aboard *Terra* made these portraits, capturing (a) outgoing shortwave energy flux reflected from clouds, land, and water—Earth's albedo; and, (b) longwave energy flux emitted by these surfaces back to space. The scale beneath each image displays value gradations in watts per square metre. [Images courtesy of CERES Instrument Team, Langley Research Center, NASA]

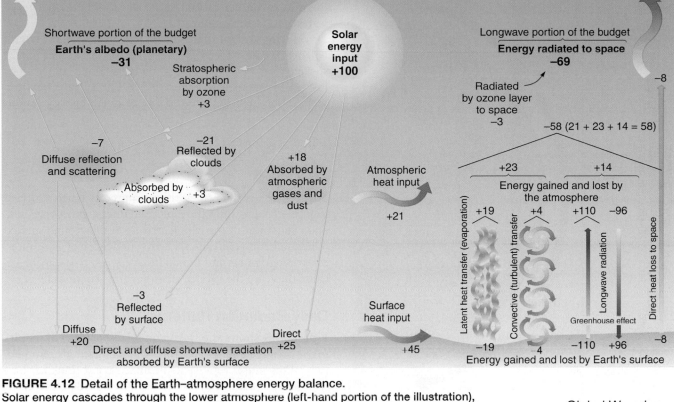

FIGURE 4.12 Detail of the Earth–atmosphere energy balance.
Solar energy cascades through the lower atmosphere (left-hand portion of the illustration), where it is absorbed, reflected, and scattered. Clouds, atmosphere, and the surface reflect 31% of this insolation back to space. Atmospheric gases and dust and Earth's surface absorb energy and radiate longwave radiation (right-hand portion of the illustration). Over time, Earth emits, on average, 69% of incoming energy to space. When added to Earth's average albedo (31%, reflected energy), this equals the total energy input from the Sun (100%).

Global Warming, Climate Change
Earth-Atmosphere Energy Balance

ANIMATION

to space; less longwave energy is escaping in the blue and purple regions. Those blue regions of lower longwave emissions over tropical lands are due to tall, thick clouds along the equatorial region (the Amazon, equatorial Africa, and Indonesia); these clouds also caused higher shortwave reflection. Subtropical desert regions exhibit greater longwave radiation emissions owing to the presence of little cloud cover and greater radiative energy losses from surfaces that absorbed a lot of energy, as we saw in Figure 4.2.

Earth–Atmosphere Energy Balance

If Earth's surface and its atmosphere are considered separately, neither exhibits a balanced radiation budget. The average annual energy distribution is positive (an energy surplus) for Earth's surface and negative (an energy deficit) for the atmosphere as it radiates energy to space. Considered together, these two equal each other, making it possible for us to construct an overall energy balance. However, regionally and seasonally Earth absorbs more energy in the tropics and less in the polar regions, establishing the imbalance that drives global circulation patterns.

Figure 4.12 summarizes the Earth–atmosphere radiation balance. It brings together all the elements discussed to this point in the chapter by following 100% of arriving insolation through the troposphere. The shortwave

portion of the budget is on the left in the illustration; the longwave part of the budget is on the right.

Out of 100% of the solar energy arriving, Earth's average albedo is 31%. Figure 4.11a shows this shortwave radiation reflected from the Earth–atmosphere system. Absorption by atmospheric clouds, dust, and gases involves another 21% and accounts for the atmospheric heat input. Stratospheric ozone absorption and radiation account for another 3% of the atmospheric budget. About 45% of the incoming insolation transmits through to Earth's surface as direct and diffuse shortwave radiation.

The natural energy balance occurs through longwave energy transfers from the surface which are both *nonradiative* (physical motion) and *radiative*. Nonradiative transfers include convection, conduction, and the latent heat of evaporation (energy that is absorbed and dissipated by water as it evaporates and condenses). Radiative transfer is by longwave radiation between the surface, the atmosphere, and space, as illustrated to the right in Figure 4.12's depiction of the greenhouse effect.

To summarize, Earth eventually emits the longwave radiation part of the budget into space: 21% (atmosphere heating) + 45% (surface heating) + 3% (ozone emission) = 69%. This longwave radiation from the Earth–atmosphere system (net outgoing longwave) is shown in Figure 4.11b.

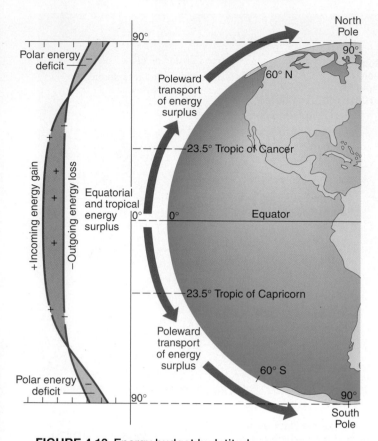

FIGURE 4.13 Energy budget by latitude.
Earth's energy surpluses and deficits by latitude produce poleward transport of energy and mass in each hemisphere—atmospheric circulation and ocean currents. Outside of the tropics, atmospheric winds dominate the transport of energy toward each pole.

Review from Chapter 2, Figure 2.11 showing "Daily Net Radiation" at the top of the atmosphere. The map clearly shows the latitudinal energy imbalance in net radiation—positive values in lower latitudes and negative values toward the poles. Figure 4.13 summarizes the Earth–atmosphere energy balance for all shortwave and longwave energy by latitude:

- Between the tropics, the angle of incoming insolation is high and daylength is consistent, with little seasonal variation, so more energy is gained than lost—*energy surpluses dominate.*
- In the polar regions, the Sun is low in the sky, surfaces are light (ice and snow) and reflective, and for up to 6 months during the year no insolation is received, so more energy is lost than gained—*energy deficits prevail.*
- At around 36° latitude, a balance exists between energy gains and losses for the Earth–atmosphere system.

The imbalance of net radiation from *tropical surpluses* to the *polar deficits* drives a vast global circulation of both energy and mass. The meridional (north–south) transfer agents are winds, ocean currents, dynamic weather systems, and related phenomena. Dramatic examples of such energy and mass transfers are tropical cyclones—hurricanes and typhoons.

Forming in the tropics, these powerful storms mature and migrate to higher latitudes, carrying with them energy, water, and water vapour.

Having established the Earth–atmosphere energy balance, we next focus on energy characteristics at Earth's surface and examine energy budgets along the ground level, as portrayed in Figure 4.12. The surface environment is the final stage in the Sun to Earth energy system.

Energy Balance at Earth's Surface

Solar energy is the principal heat source at Earth's surface. Figure 4.12 illustrates the direct and diffuse shortwave radiation and longwave radiation arriving at the ground surface. These radiation patterns at Earth's surface are of great interest to geographers and should be of interest to everyone because these are the surface environments where we live.

Daily Radiation Patterns

Figure 4.14 shows the fluctuating daily pattern of incoming shortwave energy absorbed and resultant air temperature. This graph represents idealized conditions for bare soil on a cloudless day in the middle latitudes. Incoming energy arrives during daylight, beginning at sunrise, peaking at noon, and ending at sunset.

The shape and height of this insolation curve varies with season and latitude. The highest trend for such a curve occurs at the time of the summer solstice (around June 21 in the Northern Hemisphere and December 21 in the Southern Hemisphere). The air temperature plot also responds to seasons and variations in insolation input. Within a 24-hour day, air temperature generally peaks between 3:00 and 4:00 P.M. and dips to its lowest point right at or slightly after sunrise.

FIGURE 4.14 Daily radiation curves.
Sample radiation plot for a typical day shows the changes in insolation (orange line) and air temperature (dashed line). Comparing the curves demonstrates a lag between local noon (the insolation peak for the day) and the warmest time of day.

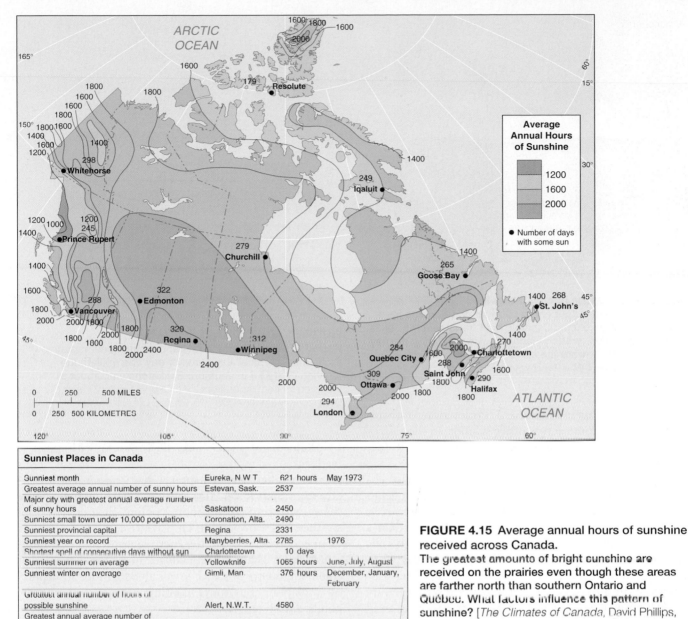

FIGURE 4.15 Average annual hours of sunshine received across Canada.
The greatest amounts of bright sunshine are received on the prairies even though these areas are farther north than southern Ontario and Québec. What factors influence this pattern of sunshine? [*The Climates of Canada*, David Phillips, Senior Climatologist, Environment Canada, 1990. Used by permission, the Minister of Public Works and Government Services Canada.]

Sunniest Places in Canada

Sunniest month	Eureka, N W T	621 hours	May 1973
Greatest average annual number of sunny hours	Estevan, Sask.	2537	
Major city with greatest annual average number of sunny hours	Saskatoon	2450	
Sunniest small town under 10,000 population	Coronation, Alta.	2490	
Sunniest provincial capital	Regina	2331	
Sunniest year on record	Manyberries, Alta.	2785	1976
Shortest spell of consecutive days without sun	Charlottetown	10 days	
Sunniest summer on average	Yellowknife	1065 hours	June, July, August
Sunniest winter on average	Gimli, Man.	376 hours	December, January, February
Greatest annual number of hours of possible sunshine	Alert, N.W.T.	4580	
Greatest average annual number of sunny days	Calgary	329	
Greatest number of sunny days in one year	Medicine Hat	346	1976
Greatest number of sunshine recorder sites	Quebec	84	

The relationship between the insolation curve and the air temperature curve on the graph is interesting—they do not align; there is a *lag*. The warmest time of day occurs not at the moment of maximum insolation, but at the moment when a *maximum of insolation is absorbed* and emitted to the atmosphere from the ground. As long as the incoming energy exceeds the outgoing energy, air temperature continues to increase, not peaking until the incoming energy begins to diminish in the afternoon as the Sun's altitude decreases. In contrast, if you have ever gone camping in the mountains, you no doubt experienced the coldest time of day with a wake-up chill at sunrise!

The annual pattern of insolation and air temperature exhibits a similar lag. For the Northern Hemisphere, January is usually the coldest month, occurring after the December solstice and the shortest days. Similarly, the warmest months of July and August occur after the June solstice and the longest days. Figure 4.15 shows how patterns of bright sunshine vary across the country.

Simplified Surface Energy Balance

Energy and moisture are continually exchanged at the surface, creating worldwide "boundary-layer climates" of great variety. **Microclimatology** is the science of physical conditions at or near Earth's surface. The following discussion is more meaningful if you visualize an actual surface—perhaps a park, a front yard, or a place on campus.

The surface receives visible light and longwave radiation and it reflects light and radiates longwave according to the following simple scheme:

$$\underset{\text{(Insolation)}}{+SW\downarrow} \underset{\text{(Reflection)}}{-SW\uparrow} \underset{\text{(Infrared)}}{+LW\downarrow} \underset{\text{(Infrared)}}{-LW\uparrow} = \underset{\text{(Net Radiation)}}{\text{NET R}}$$

FIGURE 4.16 Surface energy budget.
Idealized input and output energy budget components for a surface and a soil column. Sensible heat transfer in the soil is through conduction, predominantly downward during the day or in summer and toward the surface at night or in winter (SW = shortwave, LW = longwave)

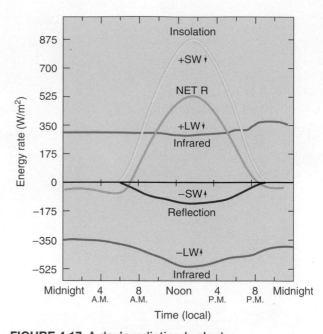

FIGURE 4.17 A day's radiation budget.
Radiation budget components and resulting net radiation (NET R) on a typical July summer day at a midlatitude location (Matador in southern Saskatchewan, about 51° N).
[Adapted by permission from T. R. Oke, *Boundary Layer Climates* (New York: Methuen & Co., 1978), p. 21.]

We use SW for shortwave and LW for longwave for simplicity. You may come across other symbols in the microclimatology literature, such as "Q*" for NET R (net radiation), "K" for shortwave, and "L" for longwave.

Figure 4.16 shows these components of a surface energy balance. The soil column shown continues to a depth at which energy exchange with surrounding materials or with the surface becomes negligible, usually less than a metre. Sensible heat transfer in the soil is through conduction, predominantly downward during the day or in summer and toward the surface at night or in winter. Energy from the atmosphere that is moving toward the surface is a positive (a gain), and energy that is moving away from the surface, through sensible and latent heat transfers, is a negative (a loss) to the surface account.

Adding and subtracting the energy flow at the surface completes the calculation of **net radiation (NET R)**, or the balance of all radiation at Earth's surface. As the components of this simple equation vary with daylength through the seasons, cloudiness, and latitude, NET R varies. Figure 4.17 illustrates the components of a surface energy balance for a typical summer day at a midlatitude location, showing the daily change in the components of net radiation. The items plotted are direct and diffuse insolation (+SW ↓), reflected energy (surface albedo value, −SW ↑), and longwave radiation arriving (+LW ↓) and leaving (−LW ↑) from the surface.

Surface albedo values (−SW ↑) dictate the amount of insolation reflected, and therefore not absorbed, at the surface. As an example, imagine a snow-covered landscape as a surface energy system. Snow has high reflectivity, sending sunlight back to space and reducing the amount of insolation absorbed. Consequently, surfaces and air temperatures are lower, and thus the snow

cover does not melt. This is a system with positive feedback.

Remember from Chapter 1 that *positive feedback* increases response in the system: more cooling–more snow–increasing albedo–more cooling–then colder, drier air–then less snow–and so on. Likewise, in High Latitude Connection 1.1 we see the increasing presence of meltponds on ice as a positive feedback in ice loss—the darker colours of meltponds with lower albedo, more absorption of insolation, thus more melting, forming more meltponds, and so on.

At night, the net radiation value in Figure 4.17 becomes negative because the SW component ceases at sunset and the surface continues to lose longwave radiation to the atmosphere. The surface rarely reaches a zero net radiation value—a perfect balance—at any one moment. However, over time, Earth's surface naturally balances incoming and outgoing energies.

Net Radiation The net radiation (NET R of all wavelengths) available at Earth's surface is the final outcome of the entire energy-balance process discussed in this chapter. Figure 4.18 displays the global mean annual net radiation at ground level. The abrupt change in radiation balance from ocean to land surfaces is evident on the map. Note that all values are positive; negative values probably occur only over ice-covered surfaces poleward of 70° latitude in both hemispheres. The highest net radiation occurs north of the equator in the Arabian Sea at 185 W/m² per year. Aside from the obvious interruption caused by landmasses, the pattern of values appears generally zonal, or parallel, decreasing away from the equator.

FIGURE 4.18 Global net radiation (NET R).
Distribution of global mean annual net radiation (NET R) at surface level in watts per square
metre (**100 W/m² = 75 kcal/cm²/year**). [After M. I. Budyko, *The Heat Balance of the Earth's
Surface* (Washington, DC: U.S. Department of Commerce, 1958), p. 106.]

SATELLITE   Global Net Radiation

Net radiation is expended from a nonvegetated surface through three pathways:

- *LE*, or *latent heat of evaporation*, is the energy that is stored in water vapour as water evaporates. Water absorbs large quantities of this *latent heat* as it changes state to water vapour, thereby removing this heat energy from the surface. Conversely, this heat energy releases to the environment when water vapour changes state back to a liquid (discussed in Chapter 7). Latent heat is the dominant expenditure of Earth's entire NET R, especially over water surfaces.

- *H*, or *sensible heat*, is the back-and-forth transfer between air and surface in turbulent eddies through convection and conduction within materials. This activity depends on surface and boundary-layer temperatures and on the intensity of convective motion in the atmosphere. About one-fifth of Earth's entire NET R is mechanically radiated as sensible heat from the surface, especially over land.

- *G*, or *ground heating and cooling*, is the energy that flows into and out of the ground surface (land or water) by conduction. During a year, the overall *G* value is zero because the stored energy from spring and summer is equaled by losses in fall and winter. Another factor in ground heating is energy absorbed at the surface to melt snow or ice. In snow- or ice-covered landscapes, most available energy is in sensible and latent heat used in the melting and warming process.

On land, the highest annual values for latent heat of evaporation (*LE*) occur in the tropics and decrease toward the poles (Figure 4.19). Over the oceans, the highest *LE* values are over subtropical latitudes, where hot, dry air comes into contact with warm ocean water.

The values for sensible heat (*H*) are distributed differently, being highest in the subtropics (Figure 4.20). Here, vast regions of subtropical deserts feature nearly waterless surfaces, cloudless skies, and almost vegetation-free landscapes. The bulk of NET R is expended as sensible heat in these dry regions. Moist and vegetated surfaces expend less in *H* and more in *LE*, as you can see by comparing the maps in Figures 4.19 and 4.20.

Understanding net radiation is essential to solar energy technologies that concentrate shortwave energy for use. Solar energy offers great potential worldwide and is presently the fastest-growing form of energy conversion by humans, although it is still decades away from its potential. Focus Study 4.1 briefly reviews such direct application of surface energy budgets.

Sample Stations   A couple of real locations help complete our discussion. Variation in the expenditure of NET R among sensible heat (*H*, energy we can feel), latent heat (*LE*, energy for evaporation), and ground heating and cooling (*G*) produces the variety of environments we experience in nature. Let us examine the daily energy balance at two locations, El Mirage in California and Pitt Meadows in British Columbia.

El Mirage, at 35° N, is a hot desert location characterized by bare, dry soil with sparse vegetation

(text continued on page 109)

FIGURE 4.19 Global latent heat of evaporation (*LE*).

Distribution of annual energy expenditure as the latent heat of evaporation (*LE*) at surface level in watts per square metre ($100 \text{ W/m}^2 = 75 \text{ kcal/cm}^2/\text{year}$). Note the high values associated with high sea-surface temperatures in the area of the Gulf Stream and Kuroshio currents. [Adapted by permission from M. I. Budyko, *The Earth's Climate Past and Future* (New York: Academic Press, 1982), p. 56.]

Global Latent Heat Flux

FIGURE 4.20 Global sensible heat (*H*).

Distribution of annual energy expenditure as sensible heat (*H*) at surface level in watts per square metre ($100 \text{ W/m}^2 = 75 \text{ kcal/cm}^2/\text{year}$). [Adapted by permission from M. I. Budyko, *The Earth's Climate Past and Future* (New York: Academic Press, 1982), p. 59.]

Global Sensible Heat

Solar Energy Collection and Concentration

Consider the following:

- The insolation receipt in just 35 minutes at the surface of the United States exceeds the amount of energy derived from the burning of fossil fuels (coal, oil, natural gas) in a year.
- An average building in the United States receives 6 to 10 times more energy from the Sun hitting its exterior than is required to heat the inside.
- Old photographs of homes in southern California and Florida show solar (flat-plate) water heaters on many rooftops. Early twentieth-century newspaper ads and merchandise catalogues featured the Climax solar water heater (1905) and the Day and Night water heater (1909). Low-priced natural gas and oil displaced many of these applied solar energy technologies. In 2005,

installed solar water heating rose to over 125 million m² (1346 ft²) of installed surface area, or 40 million households worldwide.

- Installed photovoltaic capacity increased 45% in 2005, to nearly six times the installed level in 2000. Solar-electric power is the fastest growing energy source in the world, rising to over 6000 MW.
- The U.S. share of total production, which was at 44% in 1996, fell to only 9% in 2005—Japan and Germany lead the world. The U.S. administration continued with budget cuts in its photovoltaic program in 2003, 2004, and 2005. (All statistics from Worldwatch Institute, http://www.worldwatch.org.)

Not only does insolation warm Earth's surface, it also provides an inexhaustible supply of energy far into the future for humanity. Sunlight is

direct and widely available, and solar power installations are decentralized, labor intensive, and renewable. Sunlight has been collected for centuries through various technologies. Yet it is underutilized. The utility energy industry appears to prefer indirect, centralized, power-plant specific, capital intensive, and nonrenewable sources.

Rural villages in developing countries could benefit greatly from the simplest, most cost-effective solar application—the *solar-panel cooker*. For example, people in Kenya walk many kilometres collecting fuel wood for cooking fires (Figure 4.1.1a). Each village and refugee camp is surrounded by impoverished land, stripped of wood. Using solar cookers, villagers are able to cook meals and sanitize their drinking water without scavenging for wood (Figure 4.1.1b). These solar devices in Figure 4.1.1c are simple yet efficient, reaching temperatures

(a)

(b)

FIGURE 4.1.1 The solar-cooking solution.
(a) Five women haul firewood many miles to the Dadaab refugee camp in northeastern Kenya. (b) Kenyan women in training to use their solar panel cookers, which do not require scavenging the countryside for scarce fuel wood. These simple cookers collect direct and diffuse insolation through transparent glass or plastic and trap longwave radiation in an enclosed box or cooking bag (c). This is a small-scale, efficient application of the greenhouse effect. Construction is easy, using cardboard components. Temperatures easily exceed 107°C (225°F) for baking, boiling, purifying water, and sterilizing instruments. [Photos by: (a) and (b) Solar Cookers International, Sacramento, California; (c) Bobbé Christopherson.]

(c)

(continued)

FIGURE 4.21 Radiation budget comparison for two stations.
(a) The graph shows the daily net radiation expenditure for El Mirage, California, east of Los Angeles, at about 35° N, and (b) a typical desert landscape near the hot, dry site. (c) The daily net radiation expenditure for Pitt Meadows in southern British Columbia, at about 49° N, and (d) the irrigated blueberry orchards characteristic of agricultural activity in this moist environment of moderate temperatures. (*H* = turbulent sensible heat transfer; *LE* = latent heat of evaporation; *G* = ground heating and cooling.) [(a) Adapted by permission from William D. Sellers, *Physical Climatology*, Fig. 33, copyright © 1965 by The University of Chicago. All rights reserved. (c) Adapted by permission from T. R. Oke, *Boundary Layer Climates* (New York: Methuen & Co., 1978), p. 23. Photos by Robert Christopherson.]

Figure 4.22 illustrates these traits. Every major city produces its own **dust dome** of airborne pollution, which can be blown from the city in elongated plumes; as noted in the table, such domes affect urban energy budgets.

Table 4.2 compares climatic factors of rural and urban environments. The worldwide trend toward greater urbanization is placing more and more people on urban heat islands. NASA launched its Urban Heat Island Pilot Project (UHIPP) in 1997, through its Global Hydrology and Climate Center, to better understand the role of cities in climate. If ways can be found to make cities cooler, this will reduce energy consumption and fossil fuel use, thus reducing greenhouse gas emissions.

In 1998 as part of UHIPP, NASA's research jet made longwave (thermal infrared) radiation measurements over Atlanta, Georgia; Sacramento, California; Baton Rouge, Louisiana; and Salt Lake City, Utah. Teachers and students on the ground assisted by making temperature measurements at the same time as the flights. Instruments carried by balloons tracked vertical temperature, relative humidity, and air pressure profiles. (See **www.ghcc.msfc.nasa.gov/urban/** for an update.)

Figure 4.23 illustrates a generalized cross section of a typical urban heat island, showing increasing temperatures toward the downtown central business district. Note that temperatures drop over areas of trees and parks.

Table 4.1   Urban Physical Characteristics and Conditions

Urban Characteristics	Results and Conditions
Urban surfaces typically are metal, glass, asphalt, concrete, or stone, and their energy characteristics respond differently from natural surfaces.	Albedos of urban surfaces are lower, leading to higher net radiation values. Urban surfaces expend more energy as sensible heat than do nonurban areas (70% of the net radiation to H). Surfaces conduct up to 3 times more energy than wet, sandy soil and thus are warmer. During the day and evening, temperatures above urban surfaces are higher than those above natural areas.
Irregular geometric shapes in a city affect radiation patterns and winds.	Incoming insolation is caught in mazelike reflection and radiation "canyons." Delayed energy is conducted into surface materials, thus increasing temperatures. Buildings interrupt wind flows, diminishing heat loss through advective (horizontal) movement. Maximum heat island effects occur on calm, clear days and nights.
Human activity alters the heat characteristics of cities.	In summer, urban electricity production and use of fossil fuels release energy equivalent to 25%–50% of insolation. In winter, urban-generated sensible heat averages 250% greater than arriving insolation, reducing winter heating requirements.
Many urban surfaces are sealed (built on and paved), so water cannot reach the soil.	Central business district surfaces average 50% sealed, producing more water runoff than the suburbs that average 20% sealed surfaces. Urban areas respond as a desert landscape: A storm may cause a flash flood over the hard, sparsely vegetated surfaces, to be followed by dry conditions a few hours later.
Air pollution, including gases and aerosols, is greater in urban areas than in comparable natural settings, making increased convection and precipitation possible.	Pollution increases the atmosphere's reflectivity above a city, reducing insolation and absorbing infrared radiation, reradiating infrared downward. Increased particulates in pollution are condensation nuclei for water vapour, increasing cloud formation and precipitation. Urban-stimulated increases in precipitation may occur downwind from cities.

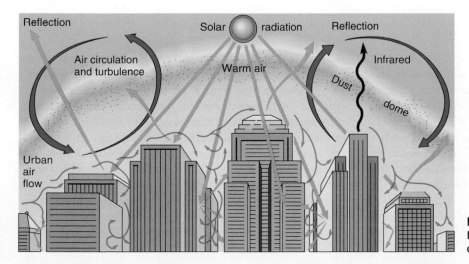

FIGURE 4.22 The urban environment. Insolation, wind movements, and dust dome in city environments.

Table 4.2   Average Differences in Climatic Elements Between Urban and Rural Environments

Element	Urban Compared with Rural Environs	Element	Urban Compared with Rural Environs
Contaminants		**Precipitation (cont.)**	
Condensation nuclei	10 times more	Snowfall, downwind (lee) of city	10% more
Particulates	10 times more		
Gaseous admixtures	5–25 times more	Thunderstorms	10%–15% more
Radiation		**Temperature**	
Total on horizontal surface	0%–20% less	Annual mean	0.5–3 C° (0.9–5.4 F°) more
Ultraviolet, winter	30% less	Winter minima (average)	1.0–2 C° (1.8–3.6 F°) more
Ultraviolet, summer	5% less	Summer maxima	1.0–3 C° (1.8–3.0 F°) more
Sunshine duration	5%–15% less	Heating degree days	10% less
Cloudiness		**Relative Humidity**	
Clouds	5%–10% more	Annual mean	6% less
Fog, winter	100% more	Winter	2% less
Fog, summer	30% more	Summer	8% less
Precipitation		**Wind Speed**	
Amounts	5%–15% more	Annual mean	20%–30% less
Days with <5 mm (0.2 in.)	10% more	Extreme gusts	10%–20% less
Snowfall, inner city	5%–10% less	Calm	5%–20% more

Source: H. E. Landsberg, *The Urban Climate*, International Geophysics Series, vol. 28 (1981), p. 258. Reprinted by permission from Academic Press.

FIGURE 4.23 Typical urban heat island profile.
Cross section of a typical urban heat island. The trend of the temperature gradient from rural to downtown is measurable. Temperatures steeply rise in urban settings, plateau over the suburban built-up area, and peak where temperature is highest at the urban core. Note the cooling over the park area and river.

Sensible heat is lessened because of the latent heat of evaporation and plant effects such as transpiration and shade. Urban forests are important factors in cooling cities. NASA measurements in an outdoor mall parking lot found temperatures of 48°C (118°F), but a small planter with trees in the same lot was significantly cooler at 32°C (90°F)—16 C° (29 F°) lower in temperature! In Central Park in New York City, daytime temperatures average 5–10 C° (9–18 F°) cooler than urban areas outside the park.

Figure 4.24 is a thermal infrared image of a portion of Sacramento, California, taken at midday. The false colours of red and white are relatively hot areas (60°C, 140°F), blues and greens are relatively cool areas (29°–36°C, 85°–96°F); clearly buildings are the hottest objects in the scene. As you look across this landscape, what strategies do you think would reduce the urban heat island effect? Possibilities include lighter-coloured surfaces for buildings, streets, and parking lots; more reflective roofs; and more trees, parks, and open space. (The images from all the test cities are available at **http://science.nasa.gov/newhome/headlines/essd01ju l98%5F1.htm**.)

FIGURE 4.24 Heat island exposed.
Urban Heat Island Pilot Project (UHIPP) thermal-infrared image of Sacramento, California, taken June 29, 1998, at 1 P.M. PDT from a NASA jet at 2000 m (6600 ft). The Sacramento River runs from north to south to the left of centre of the frame, the American River is to the upper right, and the California state capitol building is the red area within the green rectangle right of centre from the river. False colour tags white and red as relatively hot sites; greens and blues are relatively cool. The white rectangles are buildings and the hottest spots. [Image courtesy of UHIPP, Marshall Space Flight Center, Global Hydrology and Climate Center, Huntsville, Alabama.]

Sacramento urban heat island in the distance

Applied Physical Geography

Energy Balance Model

Energy balance models attempt to account for all incoming and outgoing energy of the Earth. In a simple global energy balance, the only variable is the temperature of the Earth, signified T_e. The term "balance" suggests that the system is at equilibrium—no energy is accumulated. See the Shodor Education Foundation Web site for an energy balance computer model (http://www.shodor.org/).

This energy balance model can be described mathematically as follows:

Energy absorbed = energy emitted

$$\pi R_E^2 (1 - \alpha) H_0 = 4\pi R_E^2 \sigma T_e^4$$

where R_e is the radius of the Earth, H_0 is the extraterrestrial solar flux in watt-m^{-2}, α is the albedo or reflectivity of the planet, σ is the Stefan-Boltzmann constant (5.6697×10^{-8} $Wm^{-2}K^{-4}$), and T_e is the effective temperature of

Earth (the temperature of the Earth as it appears from space).

The above model aims to calculate the effective temperature, T_e. We are interested in the temperature at the surface, or T_s. The following calculation is used:

$$T_s = T_e + dT$$

where dT is the greenhouse increment. At this time, the greenhouse

(continued)

Applied Physical Geography *(continued)*

increment is about 33 K, and is a function of the efficiency of the infrared absorption.

This would be fairly simple except that most energy balance models are zonal, not global, models. They focus on the energy balance for a chosen latitude. As such, an equation that accounts for the flow of energy from one latitudinal zone to the next must be used. The model must become:

Radiation energy in = Radiation energy out + transport into another zone.

The incoming energy due to the Sun must be adjusted to account for the spherical shape and orbital variations of the Earth. Because each zone usually has its own albedo, or reflectivity, each zone also has its own zonal surface temperature (including the greenhouse increment). The zonal model calculates total energy received from the Sun per unit time as given by

$$\pi r^2 H_0$$

where r is Earth's radius and H_0 is the solar constant.

Given that the Earth's total area can be calculated by $4r^2$, we can propose the equation:

$$(1 - \alpha)H_0 = \alpha T_e^4$$

The average extraterrestrial solar flux over the entire surface can be calculated by $H_0/4$.

Because all zones do not receive the same amount of incoming radiation (due to the variation of the incident angle of the Sun to a particular zone), a ratio, γ_i, can be used that corrects the average incoming radiation for a given zone. We can then calculate the incoming solar radiation for a given zone as:

incoming radiation = $\gamma_i H_0/4$.

Also, the surface albedo of each zone must be considered. Remember that the albedo depends upon the type of landcover and the varying amounts of land and water on the surface. A critical temperature, T_c, exists below which the land becomes ice covered (typically $-10.0°$ C). If the surface temperature for a zone is below the critical temperature, the albedo for the zone is the albedo of ice, or 0.68. For temperatures above the critical temperature, a typical equation is:

albedo of the zone = (1 − fractional cloud cover for the zone) + (fractional cloud cover × albedo of the clouds).

Cloud albedo is typically specified as 0.5. Fractional cloud cover values are a typical input for a standard energy balance model. The transport of energy between zones is given by:

$$F_i = C(T_i - T_s)$$

where C is a constant equal to 3.80 $W/m^2/C$, T_i is the average temperature of the zone, and T_s is the mean global surface temperature.

More complicated methodologies exist, but this equation represents the fundamental parameters in an energy balance model.

Again, the purpose of the energy balance model is to calculate the temperature of the zone. A final equation for calculating temperatures is as follows:

$$T_i = \frac{(\gamma_i (H_0/4)(1 - \alpha_i) + CT_s - A + 5\varphi_i B}{B + C}$$

where γ_i is the ratio correction of zone to incoming radiation, H_0 is the solar constant, α_i is the surface albedo for the zone, C is the constant 3.8 watt-m$^{-2}C^{-1}$, T_s is the average surface temperature, A is a constant 204 watt-m^{-2}, B is a constant 2.17 watt-m$^{-2}C^{-1}$, φ_i is the fractional cloud cover in each zone.

The equation is repeated for each zone to reach a global energy balance.

Summary and Review—Atmosphere and Surface Energy Balances

■ *Identify* the pathways of solar energy through the troposphere to Earth's surface: transmission, scattering, diffuse radiation, refraction, albedo (reflectivity), conduction, convection, and advection.

Radiant energy from the Sun that cascades through complex circuits to the surface powers Earth's biosphere. Our budget of atmospheric energy comprises shortwave radiation *inputs* (ultraviolet light, visible light, and near-infrared wavelengths) and longwave radiation *outputs* (thermal infrared).

Transmission refers to the passage of shortwave and longwave energy through either the atmosphere or water. The gas molecules redirect radiation, changing the direction of the light's movement *without altering its wavelengths*. This phenomenon is known as **scattering** and represents 7% of Earth's reflectivity, or albedo. Dust particles, pollutants, ice, cloud droplets, and water vapour produce further scattering. Some

incoming insolation is diffused by clouds and atmosphere and is transmitted to Earth as **diffuse radiation**, the downward component of scattered light. The speed of insolation entering the atmosphere changes as it passes from one medium to another; the change of speed causes a bending action called **refraction**. **Mirage** is a refraction effect when an image appears near the horizon where light waves are refracted by layers of air at different temperatures (and consequently of different densities).

A portion of arriving energy bounces directly back into space without being converted into heat or performing any work. **Albedo** is the reflective quality (intrinsic brightness) of a surface; this returned energy is **reflection**. Albedo is an important control over the amount of insolation that is available for absorption by a surface. We state albedo as the percentage of insolation that is reflected. Earth and its atmosphere reflect 31% of all insolation when averaged over a year.

An increase in albedo and reflection of shortwave radiation caused by clouds is **cloud-albedo forcing**. Also, clouds can act as insulation, thus trapping longwave radiation and raising minimum temperatures. An increase in greenhouse warming caused by clouds is **cloud-greenhouse forcing**. **Global dimming** describes the decline in sunlight reaching Earth's surface owing to pollution, aerosols, and clouds, and is perhaps masking the actual degree of global warming occurring.

Absorption is the assimilation of radiation by molecules of a substance and its conversion from one form to another—for example, visible light to infrared radiation. **Conduction** is the molecule-to-molecule transfer of energy as it diffuses through a substance.

Energy also is transferred in gases and liquids by **convection** (when the physical mixing involves a strong vertical motion) or **advection** (when the dominant motion is horizontal). In the atmosphere or bodies of water, warmer portions tend to rise (they are less dense) and cooler portions tend to sink (they are more dense), establishing patterns of convection.

transmission (p. 92)
scattering (p. 93)
diffuse radiation (p. 93)
refraction (p. 93)
mirage (p. 93)
reflection (p. 94)
albedo (p. 94)
cloud-albedo forcing (p. 95)
cloud-greenhouse forcing (p. 96)
global dimming (p. 97)
absorption (p. 98)
conduction (p. 98)
convection (p. 98)
advection (p. 98)

1. Diagram a simple energy balance for the troposphere. Label each shortwave and longwave component and the directional aspects of related flows.

2. What would you expect the sky colour to be at 50 km (30 mi) altitude? Why? What factors explain the lower atmosphere's blue colour?

3. Define refraction. How is it related to daylength? To a rainbow? To the beautiful colours of a sunset?

4. List several types of surfaces and their albedo values. Explain the differences among these surfaces. What determines the reflectivity of a surface?

5. Using Figure 4.6, explain the seasonal differences in albedo values for each hemisphere. Be specific, using the albedo values given in Figure 4.5 where appropriate.

6. Define the concepts transmission, absorption, diffuse radiation, conduction, and convection.

■ *Describe* what happens to insolation when clouds are in the atmosphere, and *analyze* the effect of clouds and air pollution on solar radiation received at ground level.

Clouds reflect *insolation*, thus cooling Earth's surface—*cloud-albedo forcing*. Yet clouds also act as insulation, thus trapping longwave radiation and raising minimum temperatures—*cloud-greenhouse forcing*. Clouds affect the heating of the lower atmosphere, depending on cloud type, height, and thickness (water content and density). High-altitude, ice-crystal clouds reflect insolation with albedos of about 50% and redirect infrared to the surface, producing a net cloud-greenhouse forcing (warming);

thick, lower cloud cover reflects about 90%, producing a net cloud-albedo forcing (cooling). **Jet contrails**, or *condensation trails*, are produced by aircraft exhaust, particulates, and water vapour, and can form high cirrus clouds, sometimes called *false cirrus clouds*.

Emissions of sulfur dioxide and the subsequent chemical reactions in the atmosphere form *sulfate aerosols*, which act either as insolation-reflecting haze in clear-sky conditions or as a stimulus to condensation in clouds that increases reflectivity.

jet contrails (p. 99)

7. What role do clouds play in the Earth–atmosphere radiation balance? Is cloud type important? Compare high, thin cirrus clouds and lower, thick stratus clouds.

8. Jet contrails affect the Earth–atmosphere balance in what ways? Describe the recent scientific findings.

9. In what way does the presence of sulfate aerosols affect solar radiation received at ground level? How does it affect cloud formation?

■ *Review* the energy pathways in the Earth–atmosphere system, the greenhouse effect, and the patterns of global net radiation.

The Earth–atmosphere energy system naturally balances itself in a steady-state equilibrium. It does so through energy transfers that are *nonradiative* (convection, conduction, and the latent heat of evaporation) and *radiative* (by longwave radiation between the surface, the atmosphere, and space).

Carbon dioxide, water vapour, methane, CFCs (chlorofluorocarbons), and other gases in the lower atmosphere absorb longwave radiation that is then emitted to Earth, thus delaying energy loss to space. This process is the **greenhouse effect**. In the atmosphere, longwave radiation is not actually trapped, as it would be in a greenhouse, but its passage to space is delayed (heat energy is detained in the atmosphere) through absorption and counterradiation.

Between the tropics, high insolation angle and consistent daylength cause more energy to be gained than lost (there are energy surpluses). In the polar regions, an extremely low insolation angle, highly reflective surfaces, and up to 6 months of no insolation annually cause more energy to be lost (there are energy deficits). This imbalance of net radiation from tropical surpluses to the polar deficits drives a vast global circulation of both energy and mass.

Surface energy balances are used to summarize the energy expenditure for any location. Surface energy measurements are used as an analytical tool of **microclimatology**. Adding and subtracting the energy flow at the surface lets us calculate **net radiation (NET R)**, or the balance of all radiation at Earth's surface available to do work—shortwave (SW) and longwave (LW).

greenhouse effect (p. 99)
microclimatology (p. 103)
net radiation (NET R) (p. 104)

10. What are the similarities and differences between an actual greenhouse and the gaseous atmospheric greenhouse? Why is Earth's greenhouse effect changing?

11. In terms of energy expenditures for latent heat of evaporation, describe the annual pattern as mapped in Figure 4.19.

12. Generalize the pattern of global net radiation. How might this pattern drive the atmospheric weather machine? (See Figures 4.13 and 4.18.)

13. In terms of surface energy balance, explain the term *net radiation* (NET R).

14. What are the expenditure pathways for surface net radiation? What kind of work is accomplished?

15. What is the role played by latent heat in surface energy budgets?

16. Compare the daily surface energy balances of El Mirage, California, and Pitt Meadows, British Columbia. Explain the differences.

■ *Plot* the daily radiation curves for Earth's surface, and *label* the key aspects of incoming radiation, air temperature, and the daily temperature lag.

The greatest insolation input occurs at the time of the summer solstice in each hemisphere. Air temperature responds to seasons and variations in insolation input. Within a 24-hour day, air temperature peaks between 3:00 and 4:00 P.M. and dips to its lowest point right at or slightly after sunrise.

Air temperature lags behind each day's peak insolation. The warmest time of day occurs not at the moment of maximum insolation, but at that moment when a maximum of insolation is absorbed.

17. Why is there a temperature lag between the highest Sun altitude and the warmest time of day? Relate your answer to the insolation and temperature patterns during the day.

■ *Portray* typical urban heat island conditions, and *contrast* the microclimatology of urban areas with that of surrounding rural environments.

A growing percentage of Earth's people lives in cities and experiences a unique set of altered microclimatic effects: increased conduction, lower albedos, higher NET R values, increased water runoff, complex radiation and reflection patterns, anthropogenic heating, and the gases, dusts, and aerosols of urban pollution. Urban surfaces of metal, glass, asphalt, concrete, and stone conduct up to 3 times more energy than wet, sandy soil and thus are warmed, producing an **urban heat island**. Air pollution, including gases and aerosols, is greater in urban areas than in rural ones. Every major city produces its own **dust dome** of airborne pollution.

urban heat island (p. 109)
dust dome (p. 110)

18. What is the basis for the urban heat island concept? Describe the climatic effects attributable to urban as compared with nonurban environments. What did NASA determine from the UHIPP overflight of Sacramento (Figure 4.24)?

19. Which of the items in Table 4.2 have you yourself experienced? Explain.

20. Assess the potential for solar energy applications in our society. What are some negatives? What are some positives?

Critical Thinking

A. Given what you now know about reflection, albedo, absorption, and net radiation expenditures, assess your wardrobe (fabrics and colours), house or apartment (colours of exterior walls, especially south and west facing; or, in the Southern Hemisphere, north and west facing), and roof (orientation relative to the Sun), automobile (colour, use of sun shades), bicycle seat (colour), and other aspects of your environment to determine a personal "Energy IQ." What grade do you give yourself? Be cool!

B. In Focus Study 4.1, "Solar Energy Collection and Concentration," there are several listings of URLs relating to solar energy applications. Take some time and explore the Internet for a personal assessment of these necessary technologies (solar-thermal, solar-electric, photovoltaic cells, solar-box cookers, and the like). As we near the climatic limitations of the fossil fuel era, and the depletion of the resource itself, these available technologies are destined to become part of the fabric of our lives. Briefly describe your search results. Given these findings, determine if solar technology is available in your area.

C. Examine the photograph below. In Antarctica, on Petermann Island off the Graham Land Coast, we noticed this piece of kelp (a seaweed) dropped by a passing bird. The kelp was resting about 10-cm (4-in.) deep in the snow, in a hole about the shape of the kelp. In your opinion, what energy factors operated to make this scene? Now, expand your conclusion to the issue of mining in Antarctica. There are coal deposits and other minerals in Antarctica. The international Antarctic Treaty (1959, additional measures in 1972, 1982, 1991) blocks mining exploitation, although reconsideration is possible after 2048. Given your energy budget analysis of the kelp in the snow, information on surface energy budgets in this chapter, the dust and particulate output of mining, and the importance of a stable sea level, construct a case opposed to such mining activities based on these factors. [Photo by Bobbé Christopherson]

A November blizzard whistles across the tundra and a frozen pond in northern Canada. Note the downwind accumulation of snow at each rock. At the moment of this photo it didn't seem possible, but increasing temperatures are affecting the Arctic region at more than double the rate of the rest of the globe. The polar regions are acting like a "miners' Canary" early warning system about the state of global temperatures and climate change. [Photo by Bobbé Christopherson.]

Global Temperatures

■ Key Learning Concepts

After reading the chapter, you should be able to:

■ **Define** the concepts of temperature, kinetic energy, and sensible heat, and **distinguish** among Kelvin, Celsius, and Fahrenheit temperature scales and how they are measured.

■ **List** and **review** the principal controls and influences that produce global temperature patterns.

■ **Review** the factors that produce different marine effects and continental effects as they influence temperatures, and **utilize** several pairs of cities to illustrate these differences.

■ **Interpret** the pattern of Earth's temperatures from their portrayal on January and July temperature maps and on a map of annual temperature ranges.

■ **Describe** the human body's response to wind (wind chill) and heat and humidity (Humidex).

What is the temperature now—both indoors and outdoors—as you read these words? How is it measured, and what does the value mean? How is air temperature influencing your plans for the day? Our bodies subjectively sense temperature and judge comfort and react to changing temperature. Air temperature plays a remarkable role in our lives, both at the micro level and at the macro and global levels.

We read of heat waves and cold spells affecting people, crops, events, and energy consumption. For example, in 1995 devastating summer heat and high humidity killed more than 1000 people in the Midwest and East; Europe lost more than 20,000 people in 2003 record heat-index conditions; more than 150 died in a California heat wave in July 2006; and hundreds died in heat waves across southern Europe and the southeastern United States in 2007 (see Focus Study 5.1 on "Air Temperature and the Human Body").

Record warmth is reaching into the Arctic. Ice core data and other proxy measures indicate that present temperatures across the region are higher than at any time during the past 125,000 years. In response, since satellite observations began 3 decades ago, the Arctic Ocean sea-ice extent melted to its lowest area during September 2007. This warming trend in air temperature is the subject of much scientific, geographic, and political action. Temperature of land, air, and water is a key *output* of the energy–atmosphere system.

In this chapter: A variety of temperature regimes affect cultures, decision-making, and resources consumed across the globe. Understanding some temperature concepts helps us begin our study of these Earth systems. We look at the principal temperature controls of latitude, altitude and elevation, cloud cover, and land-water heating differences as they interact to produce Earth's temperature patterns. We end by examining the effect of temperature on the human body and the resultant spatial aspects of hot and cold conditions on human experience.

Temperature Concepts and Measurement

Heat and temperature are not the same. *Heat* is a form of energy that flows from one system or object to another because the two are at different temperatures. **Temperature** is a measure of the average kinetic energy (motion) of individual molecules in matter. We feel the effect of temperature as the *sensible heat* transfer from warmer objects to cooler objects. For instance, when you jump into a cool lake, you can sense the heat transfer from your skin to the water as kinetic energy leaves your body and flows to the water; a chill develops.

Temperature and heat are related because changes in temperature are caused by the absorption or emission (gain or loss) of heat energy. The term *heat energy* is frequently used to describe energy that is added to or removed from a system or substance.

Temperature Scales

The temperature at which atomic and molecular motion in matter completely stops is *absolute zero*, "*0° absolute temperature.*" Its value on the different temperature-measuring scales is −273° Celsius (C), −459.4° Fahrenheit (F), and 0 Kelvin (K). Figure 5.1 compares these three scales. Formulas for converting between Celsius, SI (Système International), and English units are in Appendix C.

FIGURE 5.1 Temperature scales.
Scales for expressing temperature in Kelvin (K) and degrees Celsius (°C) and Fahrenheit (°F), with details of what we experience. Note the distinction between temperature and units of temperature expression, and the placement of the degree symbol.

The Fahrenheit scale places the melting point of ice at 32°F, with 180 subdivisions to the boiling point of water at 212°F. The scale is named for its developer Daniel G. Fahrenheit, a German physicist (1686–1736). He used these odd values based on the coldest temperature he could achieve in his laboratory (which he called 0°F) and on the approximate temperature of the human body, thought to be about 100°F.

About a year after the adoption of the Fahrenheit scale, Swedish astronomer Anders Celsius (1701–1744) developed the Celsius scale (formerly called centigrade). He placed the melting point of ice at 0°C and boiling temperature of water at sea level at 100°C, dividing his scale into 100 degrees using a decimal system.

British physicist Lord Kelvin (born William Thomson, 1824–1907) proposed the Kelvin scale in 1848. Science uses this scale because it starts at absolute zero temperature and thus readings are proportional to the actual kinetic energy in a material. The Kelvin scale's melting point for ice is 273 K, and its boiling point of water is 373 K.

Canada, like most countries, uses the Celsius scale to express temperature. The United States is the only major country still using the Fahrenheit scale. This textbook presents Celsius (with Fahrenheit equivalents in parentheses) throughout.

Measuring Temperature

A *mercury thermometer* or *alcohol thermometer* is a sealed glass tube that measures outdoor temperatures. Fahrenheit invented both the alcohol and mercury thermometers. Cold climates demand alcohol thermometers because alcohol freezes at −112°C (−170°F), whereas mercury freezes at −39°C (−38.2°F). The principle of these thermometers is simple: When fluids are heated, they expand; upon cooling, they contract. A thermometer stores fluid in a small reservoir at one end and is marked with calibrations to measure the expansion or contraction of the fluid, which reflects the temperature of the thermometer's environment.

Figure 5.2 shows a mercury minimum–maximum thermometer. It preserves readings of the day's highest and lowest temperatures until reset (by moving the markers with a magnet). Another type, the recording thermometer, creates an inked record on a turning drum, usually set for one full rotation every 24 hours or every 7 days.

Thermometers for standardized official readings are placed outdoors in small Instrument Shelters (Figure 5.3a)

FIGURE 5.2 A minimum–maximum thermometer.
[Photo by Bobbé Christopherson.]

or Stephenson Screen shelters (Figure 5.3b) that are white (for high albedo) and louvred (for ventilation) to avoid overheating the instruments. They are placed 1.2 m (4 ft) above the ground surface, usually over turf. Official temperature measurements are made in the shade to prevent the effects of direct insolation. If you install a thermometer for outdoor temperature reading, be sure to avoid direct

(a)   (b)

FIGURE 5.3 Instrument shelter. (a) This standard thermistor shelter is white (for high albedo) and louvred (for ventilation). (b) The Stephenson Screen, a louvered wooden box that houses a minimum and maximum thermometer or a wet bulb thermometer apparatus, provides protection from direct insolation.
[Photos by (a) Bobbé Christopherson; (b) Dick Hemingway.]

sunlight on the instrument and place it in an area of good ventilation, and at least 1.2 m off the ground.

The instrument shelter in Figure 5.3a contains a *thermistor* that measures temperature by sensing the electrical resistance of a semiconducting material. Temperature is sensed because resistance changes at 4% per C°, which is reported electronically to the weather station.

Temperature readings are taken daily, sometimes hourly, at more than 16,000 weather stations worldwide. Some stations with recording equipment also report the duration of temperatures, rates of rise or fall, and temperature variation over time throughout the day and night. One of the goals of the Global Climate Observing System (GCOS, **http://www.wmo.ch/pages/prog/gcos/**) is to establish a reference network of one station per 250,000 km² (95,800 mi²). (See the World Meteorological Organization at **http://www.wmo.ch/**.)

The *daily mean temperature* is an average of daily minimum–maximum readings. The *monthly mean temperature* is the total of daily mean temperatures for the month divided by the number of days in the month. An *annual temperature range* expresses the difference between the lowest and highest monthly mean temperatures for a given year.

Principal Temperature Controls

The interaction of complex physical controls produces Earth's temperature patterns. These principal influences upon temperatures include latitude, altitude and elevation, cloud cover, and land–water heating differences.

Latitude

Insolation is the single most important influence on temperature variations. Figure 2.9 shows how insolation intensity decreases as one moves away from the subsolar point—a point that migrates annually between the Tropic of Cancer and Tropic of Capricorn (between 23.5° N and 23.5° S). In addition, daylength and Sun angle change throughout the year, increasing seasonal effect with increasing latitude. The five cities graphed in Figure 5.4 demonstrate the effects of latitudinal position on temperature. From equator to poles, Earth ranges from continually warm, to seasonally variable, to continually cold.

Altitude/Elevation

Within the troposphere, temperatures decrease with increasing altitude above Earth's surface. (Recall that the *normal lapse rate* of temperature change with altitude is 6.4 C°/1000 m, or 3.5 F°/1000 ft; see Figure 3.5). The density of the atmosphere also diminishes with increasing altitude. In fact, the density of the atmosphere at an elevation of 5500 m (18,000 ft) is about half that at sea level. As the atmosphere thins, there is a loss in its ability to absorb and radiate sensible heat. Thus, worldwide, mountainous areas experience lower temperatures than do regions nearer sea level, even at similar latitudes. Note that "altitude" refers to airborne objects above Earth's surface, whereas "elevation" usually refers to the height of a point on Earth's surface above some plane of reference.

The consequences are that, at high elevations, average air temperatures are lower, nighttime cooling is

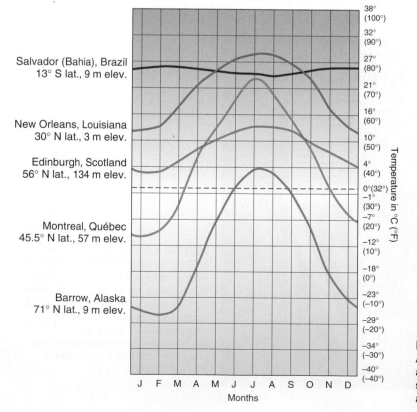

FIGURE 5.4 Latitude affects temperatures. A comparison of five cities from near the equator to above the Arctic Circle demonstrates changing seasonality and increasing differences between average minimum and maximum temperatures.

greater, and the temperature range between day and night is greater than at low elevations. The temperature difference between areas of sunlight and shadow is greater than at sea level. You may have felt temperatures decrease noticeably in the shadows and shortly after sunset when you were in the mountains. Surfaces both gain energy rapidly and lose energy rapidly to the thinner atmosphere.

Also, at higher elevations, the insolation received is more intense because of the reduced mass of atmospheric gases. As a result of this intensity, the ultraviolet energy component makes sunburn a distinct hazard.

The snowline seen in mountain areas indicates where winter snowfall exceeds the amount of snow lost through summer melting and evaporation. The snowline's location is a function both of elevation and latitude, so glaciers can exist even at equatorial latitudes if the elevation is great enough. Permanent ice fields and glaciers exist on equatorial mountain summits in the Andes and East Africa. In equatorial mountains, the snowline occurs at approximately 5000 m (16,400 ft) because of the latitude (more insolation in the tropics produces temperatures that place the snowline at higher elevation). With increasing latitude, snowlines

gradually lower in elevation from 2700 m (8850 ft) in the midlatitudes to lower than 900 m (2950 ft) in southern Greenland.

Two cities in Bolivia illustrate the interaction of the two temperature controls, latitude and elevation. Figure 5.5 displays temperature data for the cities of Concepción and La Paz, which are near the same latitude (about 16°S). Note the elevation, average annual temperature, and precipitation for each location noted on the figure.

The hot, humid climate of Concepción at its much lower elevation stands in marked contrast to the cool, dry climate of highland La Paz. People living around La Paz actually grow wheat, barley, and potatoes—crops characteristic of the cooler midlatitudes—despite the fact that La Paz is 4103 m (13,461 ft) above sea level (Figure 5.6). (For comparison, the summit of Pikes Peak in Colorado is at 4301 m or 14,111 ft, and Mount Rainier, Washington, is at 4392 m or 14,410 ft.)

The combination of elevation and low-latitude location guarantees La Paz nearly constant daylength and moderate temperatures, averaging about 9°C (48°F) every month. Such moderate temperature and moisture

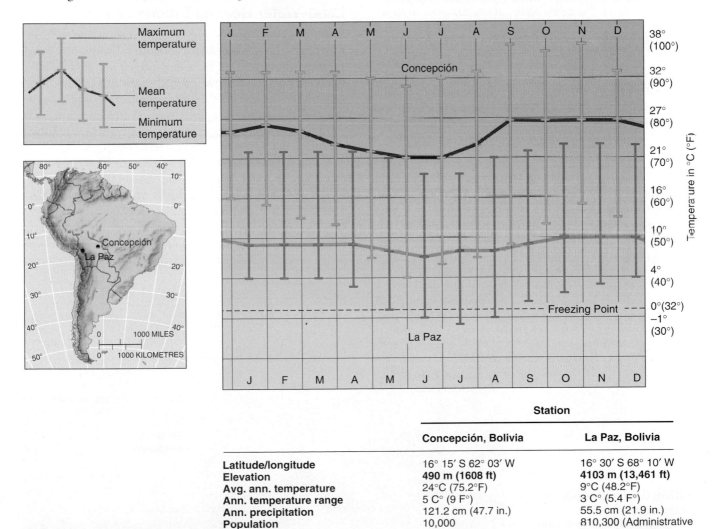

| | Station | |
	Concepción, Bolivia	**La Paz, Bolivia**
Latitude/longitude	16° 15′ S 62° 03′ W	16° 30′ S 68° 10′ W
Elevation	**490 m (1608 ft)**	**4103 m (13,461 ft)**
Avg. ann. temperature	24°C (75.2°F)	9°C (48.2°F)
Ann. temperature range	5 C° (9 F°)	3 C° (5.4 F°)
Ann. precipitation	121.2 cm (47.7 in.)	55.5 cm (21.9 in.)
Population	10,000	810,300 (Administrative division 1.6 million)

FIGURE 5.5 Effects of latitude and elevation.
Comparison of temperature patterns in two Bolivian cities: cooler, drier La Paz (4103 m; 13,461 ft) and warmer, wetter Concepción (490 m; 1608 ft).

FIGURE 5.6 High-elevation farming.
People in these high-elevation villages grow potatoes and wheat in view of the permanent ice-covered peaks of the Andes Mountains. The combination of low latitude and high elevation creates consistent, moderate temperatures throughout the year, averaging about (9°C) (48°F). [Photo by Mireille Vautier/Woodfin Camp & Associates.]

conditions lead to the formation of more fertile soils than those found in the warmer, wetter climate of Concepción, with an annual average temperature of 24°C (75°F).

Cloud Cover

Orbiting satellites reveal that approximately 50% of Earth is cloud covered at any given moment. Clouds moderate temperature, and their effect varies with cloud type, height, and density. Their moisture reflects, absorbs, and liberates large amounts of energy released upon condensation and cloud formation.

At night, clouds act as insulation and radiate longwave energy, preventing rapid energy loss. During the day, clouds reflect insolation as a result of their high albedo values. In general, they lower daily maximum temperatures and raise nighttime minimum temperatures. In the last chapter, Figures 4.7 and 4.10 portrayed cloud-albedo forcing and cloud-greenhouse forcing as they relate to the presence of clouds and cloud types. Clouds also reduce latitudinal and seasonal temperature differences.

Clouds are the most variable factor influencing Earth's radiation budget, making them the subject of much simulation in computer models of atmospheric behavior. The International Satellite Cloud Climatology Project (**http://isccp.giss.nasa.gov/**), part of the World Climate Research Programme (**http://www.wmo.ch/pages/prog/wcrp/**), is presently in the midst of such research. Clouds and the Earth Radiant Energy System (CERES, **http://asd-www.larc.nasa.gov/ceres/**) sensors aboard the *TRMM*, *Terra*, and *Aqua* satellites are assessing cloud effects on longwave, shortwave, and net radiation patterns as never before possible.

Land–Water Heating Differences

Another major control over temperature is the different way in which land and water respond to insolation. Earth presents these two surfaces in an irregular arrangement of continents and oceans. Each absorbs and stores energy differently than the other and therefore contributes to the global pattern of temperature. Water bodies tend to produce moderate temperature patterns, whereas inland in continental interiors more extreme temperatures occur.

The physical nature of land (rock and soil) and water (oceans, seas, and lakes) is the reason for **land–water heating differences**—land heats and cools faster than water. Figure 5.7 visually summarizes the following discussion of the five land–water temperature controls: evaporation, transparency, specific heat, movement and ocean currents, and sea-surface temperatures.

FIGURE 5.7 Land–water heating differences.
The differential heating of land and water produces contrasting marine (more moderate) and continental (more extreme) temperature regimes.

Evaporation Evaporation consumes more of the energy arriving at the ocean's surface than is expended over a comparable area of land, simply because so much water is available. An estimated 84% of all evaporation on Earth is from the oceans. When water evaporates and thus changes to water vapour, *heat energy is absorbed in the process and is stored in the water vapour as latent heat.* We saw this process in the map of energy expended for the latent heat of evaporation in Figure 4.19.

You experience this evaporative heat loss (cooling) by wetting the back of your hand and then blowing on the moist skin. Sensible heat energy is drawn from your skin to supply some of the energy for evaporation, and you feel the cooling. You probably appreciate the water "misters" at an outdoor market or café that lower temperatures. Similarly, as surface water evaporates, it absorbs substantial energy from the immediate environment, resulting in a lowering of temperatures. Temperatures over land, with far less water, are not as moderated by evaporative cooling as are marine locations.

Transparency The transmission of light obviously differs between soil and water: Solid ground is opaque, water is transparent. Consequently, light striking a soil surface does not penetrate but is absorbed, heating the ground surface. That energy is accumulated during times of exposure and is rapidly lost at night or in shadows.

Figure 5.8 shows the profile of diurnal (daily) temperatures for a column of soil and the atmosphere above it at

FIGURE 5.9 Ocean is transparent.
The transparency of the ocean at Taveuni Reef near Fiji permits insolation to penetrate to average depths of 60 m (200 ft), greatly increasing the volume of water that absorbs energy. [Photo by Copr. F. Stuart Westmorland/Photo Researchers, Inc.]

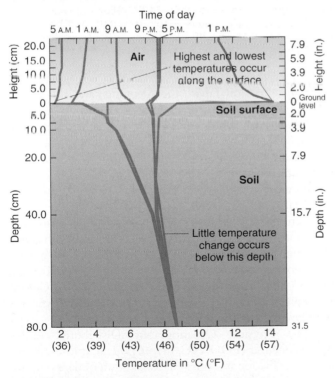

FIGURE 5.8 Land is opaque.
Profile measurements of air and soil temperatures in Seabrook, New Jersey. Note that little temperature change occurs throughout the year at depths beyond a metre, whereas the daily extremes of temperature register along the surface, where insolation is absorbed. [Adapted by permission from John R. Mather, *Climatology: Fundamentals and Applications* (New York: McGraw-Hill, 1974), p. 36.]

a midlatitude location. You can see that maximum and minimum temperatures generally are experienced right at ground level. Below the surface, even at shallow depths, temperatures remain about the same throughout the day. You encounter this at a beach, where surface sand may be painfully hot to your feet, but as you dig in your toes and feel the sand a few centimetres below the surface, it is cooler, offering relief.

In contrast, when light reaches a body of water, it penetrates the surface because of water's **transparency**— water is clear and light transmits through it to an average depth of 60 m (200 ft) in the ocean (Figure 5.9). This illuminated zone is the *photic layer* and has been recorded in some ocean waters to depths of 300 m (1000 ft). This characteristic of water results in the distribution of available heat energy over a much greater depth and volume, forming a larger energy reservoir than that of the surface layers of the land.

Specific Heat When comparing equal volumes of water and land, water requires far more energy to increase its temperature than does land. In other words, *water can* *hold more heat than can soil or rock*, and therefore water is said to have a higher **specific heat**, the heat capacity of a substance. On average, the specific heat of water is about 4 times that of soil. A given volume of water represents a more substantial energy reservoir than an equal volume of soil or rock, so changing the temperature of the oceanic energy reservoir is a slower process than changing the temperature of land.

Likewise, for that oceanic heat reservoir to lose heat energy requires more time than would a similar volume of land. The temperature response of water bodies is "sluggish" in comparison with land surfaces. For this reason, day-to-day temperatures near a substantial body of water tend to be moderated.

Movement   Land is a rigid, solid material, whereas water is a fluid and is capable of movement. Differing temperatures and currents result in a mixing of cooler and warmer waters, and that mixing spreads the available energy over an even greater volume than if the water were still. Surface water and deeper waters mix, redistributing energy. Both ocean and land surfaces radiate longwave radiation at night, but land loses its energy more rapidly than does the greater mass of the moving oceanic energy reservoir.

Ocean Currents and Sea-Surface Temperatures

Warm water adds energy to overlying air through high evaporation rates and transfers of latent heat. Thus, in an air mass, the amount of water vapour that ocean temperature affects forms an interesting *negative feedback* mechanism.

Across the globe, ocean water is rarely found warmer than 31°C (88°F), although Hurricanes Katrina, Rita, and Wilma intensified as they moved over 33.3°C (92°F) sea-surface temperatures in the Gulf of Mexico in 2005. Higher ocean temperatures produce higher evaporation rates and more energy is lost from the ocean as latent heat. As the water vapour content of the overlying air mass increases, the ability of the air to absorb longwave radiation also increases. Therefore, the air mass becomes warmer. The warmer the air and the ocean become, the more evaporation will occur, increasing the amount of water vapour entering the air mass. More water vapour leads to cloud formation, which reflects insolation and produces lower temperatures. Lower temperatures of air and ocean reduce evaporation rates and the ability of the air mass to absorb water vapour.

As a specific example, the **Gulf Stream** moves northward off the east coast of North America, carrying warm water far into the North Atlantic (Figure 5.10). As a result, the southern third of Iceland experiences much milder temperatures than would be expected for a latitude of 65° N, just south of the Arctic Circle (66.5°). In Reykjavík, on the southwestern coast of Iceland, monthly temperatures average above freezing during all months of the year. Similarly, the Gulf Stream moderates temperatures in coastal Scandinavia and northwestern Europe. In the western Pacific Ocean, the Kuroshio, or Japan Current, similar to the Gulf Stream, functions much the same in its

FIGURE 5.10 The Gulf Stream.
Satellite image of the warm Gulf Stream as it flows northward along the North American eastern coast. Instruments sensitive to thermal infrared wavelengths produced this remote-sensing image, which covers approximately 11.4 million km² (4.4 million mi²). Temperature differences are distinguished by computer-enhanced false colouration: reds/oranges = 25°–29°C (76°–84°F), yellows/greens = 17°–24°C (63°–75°F); blues = 10°–16°C (50°–61°F); and purples = 2°–9°C (36°–48°F). [Imagery by Rosenstiel School of Marine and Atmospheric Science, University of Miami.]

warming effect on Japan, the Aleutians, and the northwestern margin of North America.

In contrast, along midlatitude and subtropical west coasts, cool ocean currents flowing toward the equator influence air temperatures. When conditions in these regions are warm and moist, fog frequently forms in the chilled air over the cooler currents. Chapter 6 discusses ocean currents.

Remote sensing from satellites is providing sea-surface temperature (SST) data that are well correlated with actual sea-surface measurements. This correlation permits a thorough global assessment of SSTs in programs such as Tropical Ocean Global Atmosphere (TOGA) and Coupled Ocean-Atmosphere Response Experiment (COARE, **http://lwf.ncdc.noaa.gov/oa/coare/index.html**).

The Physical Oceanography Distributed Active Archive Center (PODAAC, **http://podaac.jpl.nasa.gov/**) is responsible for storage and distribution of data relevant to the physical state of the ocean. Sea-level height, currents, and ocean temperatures are measured as part of the effort to understand oceans and climate interactions.

Figure 5.11 displays SST data for February and July from satellites in the NOAA/NASA Pathfinder AVHRR data set, aboard *NOAA-7, -9, -11,* and *-14*. The Western Pacific Warm Pool is the red and maroon area in the

(a) February

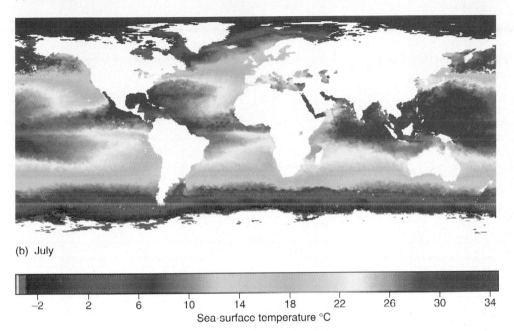

(b) July

Sea-surface temperature °C

FIGURE 5.11 Sea-surface temperatures.
Average annual sea-surface temperatures for February (a) and July (b) 1999 from satellites in the Pathfinder AVHRR data set, aboard *NOAA-7, -9, -11*, and *-14*. The Western Pacific Warm Pool, the warmest area of all oceans, is well defined. These remotely sensed data are closely correlated with actual measurements of the ocean's surface temperature.
[Satellite image data from the NASA PODAAC at the Jet Propulsion Laboratory, California Institute of Technology.]

southwestern Pacific Ocean (north of New Guinea) with temperatures above 30°C (86°F). This region has the highest average ocean temperatures in the world. Note the seasonal change in ocean temperatures; for example, compare the waters around Australia on the two images.

Mean annual SSTs increased steadily from 1982 through 2006 to record-high levels. Increasing warmth is measured at depths to 1000m (3200 ft), and even slight increases were found in the temperature of deep bottom water as reported in 2004. Scientists suggest that the ocean's ability to absorb excess heat energy from the atmosphere may be nearing its capacity.

Summary of Marine Effects vs. Continental Effects

As noted, Figure 5.7 summarizes the operation of the land–water temperature controls presented: evaporation, transparency, specific heat, movement, ocean currents, and sea-surface temperatures. The term **marine effect**, or *maritime*, describes locations that exhibit the moderating influences of the ocean, usually along coastlines or on islands. **Continental effect**, a condition of *continentality*, refers to areas less affected by the sea and therefore having

a greater range between maximum and minimum temperatures on both a daily and yearly basis.

The Canadian cities of Vancouver, British Columbia, and Winnipeg, Manitoba, exemplify marine and continental conditions (Figure 5.12). Both cities are at approximately 49° N latitude. However, Vancouver has a more moderate pattern of average maximum and minimum temperatures. Vancouver's annual range of 16.0 C° (28.8 F°) is far less than Winnipeg's 38.0 C° (68.4 F°) range. In fact, Winnipeg's continental temperature pattern is more extreme in every aspect than that of maritime Vancouver.

Earth's Temperature Patterns

Earth's temperature patterns result from the combined effect of the controlling factors in our discussion. Let us now look at temperatures portrayed on maps that show worldwide mean air temperatures and specific maps for the polar regions for January (Figures 5.13 and 5.14) and July (Figures 5.16 and 5.17). To complete the analysis, Figure 5.18

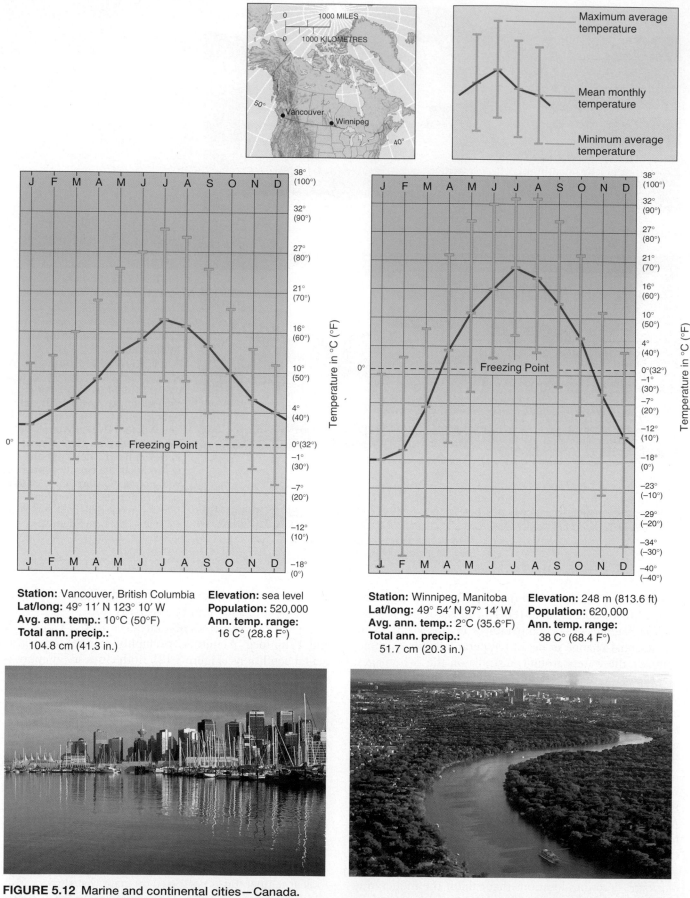

Station: Vancouver, British Columbia **Elevation:** sea level
Lat/long: 49° 11′ N 123° 10′ W **Population:** 520,000
Avg. ann. temp.: 10°C (50°F) **Ann. temp. range:**
Total ann. precip.: 16 C° (28.8 F°)
 104.8 cm (41.3 in.)

Station: Winnipeg, Manitoba **Elevation:** 248 m (813.6 ft)
Lat/long: 49° 54′ N 97° 14′ W **Population:** 620,000
Avg. ann. temp.: 2°C (35.6°F) **Ann. temp. range:**
Total ann. precip.: 38 C° (68.4 F°)
 51.7 cm (20.3 in.)

FIGURE 5.12 Marine and continental cities—Canada.
Comparison of temperatures in coastal Vancouver, British Columbia, and continental Winnipeg, Manitoba. Note that the freezing levels on the two graphs are positioned differently to accommodate the contrasting data. [Vancouver waterfront photo by Robert Christopherson; Winnipeg photo by John Eastcott/Yva Momatiak/The Image Works.]

presents the temperature range differences between the January and July maps, or the difference between averages of the coolest and warmest months.

Maps are for January and July instead of the solstice months of December and June because a lag occurs between insolation received and maximum or minimum temperatures experienced, as explained earlier in Chapter 4. The U.S. National Climate Data Center provided the data for these maps. Some ship reports go back to 1850 and land reports to 1890, although the bulk of the record is representative of conditions since 1950. In using these maps, remember that their small scale permits only generalizations about actual temperatures at specific locations.

The lines on temperature maps are known as *isotherms*. An **isotherm** is an isoline—a line along which there is a constant value—that connects points of equal temperature and portrays the temperature pattern, just as a contour line on a topographic map illustrates points of equal elevation. Isotherms help with the spatial analysis of temperatures.

January Temperature Maps

Figure 5.13 maps January's mean temperatures for the world. In the Southern Hemisphere, the higher Sun altitude causes longer days and summer weather conditions; in the Northern Hemisphere, the lower Sun angle causes the short days of winter. Isotherms generally are zonal, trending east–west, parallel to the equator, and they appear to be interrupted by the presence of landmasses. Isotherms mark the general decrease in insolation and net radiation with distance from the equator.

The **thermal equator** is an isotherm connecting all points of highest mean temperature, roughly 27°C (80°F); it trends southward into the interior of South America and Africa, indicating higher temperatures over landmasses.

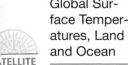

Global Surface Temperatures, Land and Ocean

FIGURE 5.13 Global mean temperatures for January.
Temperatures are in Celsius (convertible to Fahrenheit by means of the scale) as taken from separate air-temperature databases for ocean and land. Note the inset map of North America and the equatorward-trending isotherms in the interior. Compare with **Figure 5.16.** [Adapted and redrawn from National Climatic Data Center, *Monthly Climatic Data for the World*, 47 (January 1994), in cooperation with the WMO and NOAA.]

Isotherms bend equatorward

January

(a)

(b)

FIGURE 5.14 January mean temperatures for Polar Regions.
January temperatures in (a) North Polar region and (b) South Polar region. Use temperature conversions
in Figure 5.13. Note that each map is at a different scale. [Author prepared maps using same sources as
Figures 5.13 and 5.16.]

In the Northern Hemisphere, isotherms shift equatorward as cold air chills the continental interiors. The oceans, in contrast, are more moderate, with warmer conditions extending farther north than over land at comparable latitudes.

As an example in Figure 5.13, follow along 50° north latitude (the 50th parallel) and compare isotherms: 3° to 6°C in the North Pacific and 3° to 9°C in the North Atlantic, as contrasted to −18°C in the interior of North America and −24°C to −30°C in central Asia. Also, note the orientation of isotherms over areas where there are mountain ranges and how they illustrate the cooling effects of elevation. Check the South American Andes as an example of these elevation effects.

The North Polar and South Polar regions (Figure 5.14a and b) are featured on two maps. Remember: the North Polar region is an ocean surrounded by land, in contrast to the South Polar region, which is the Antarctic continent surrounded by ocean. On the northern map (a), the island of Greenland has a summit elevation of 3240 m (10,630 ft) on Earth's second-largest ice sheet, the highest elevation north of the Arctic Circle. Two-thirds of the island is north of the Arctic Circle. Its north shore is only 800 km (500 mi) from the North Pole. This combination of high latitude and interior high elevation on the ice sheet produces cold midwinter temperatures.

In Antarctica (b), "summer" is underway in December. This is Earth's coldest and highest average elevation landmass. January average temperatures for the three scientific bases noted on the map are: McMurdo Station, at the coast on Ross Island, averages −3°C; the Admundsen–Scott Station at the South Pole (elevation 2835 m, 9301 ft)

averages −28°C; and the Russian Vostok Station at its more continental location (elevation 3420 m, 11,220 ft) averages −32°C; respectively, 26.6°F, −18.4°F, and −25.6°F.

For a continental region other than Antarctica, Russia is the coldest area on the map, specifically northeastern Siberia. The intense cold results from winter conditions of consistent clear, dry, calm air; small insolation input; and an inland location far from moderating maritime effects. Verkhoyansk, Russia (located within the −48°C isotherm on the map), actually recorded a minimum temperature of −68°C (−90°F) and experiences a daily average of −50.5°C (−58.9°F) for January. Verkhoyansk (Figure 5.15) has 7 months of temperatures below freezing, including at least 4 months below −34°C (−30°F).

In contrast, Verkhoyansk was hit with a maximum temperature of +37°C (+98°F) in July—an incredible 105°C (189 F°) min–max range! People do live and work in Verkhoyansk, which has a population of 1400; the town has been occupied continuously since 1638 and is today a secondary mining district.

Trondheim, Norway, is near the latitude of Verkhoyansk and at a similar elevation. But Trondheim's coastal location moderates its annual temperature regime (Figure 5.15). January minimum and maximum temperatures range between −17°C and +8°C (+1.4°F and +46°F), and the minimum–maximum range for July is from +5°C to +27°C (+41°F to +81°F). The lowest minimum and highest maximum temperatures ever recorded in Trondheim are −30°C and +35°C (−22°F and +95°F)—quite a difference from the extremes at Verkhoyansk.

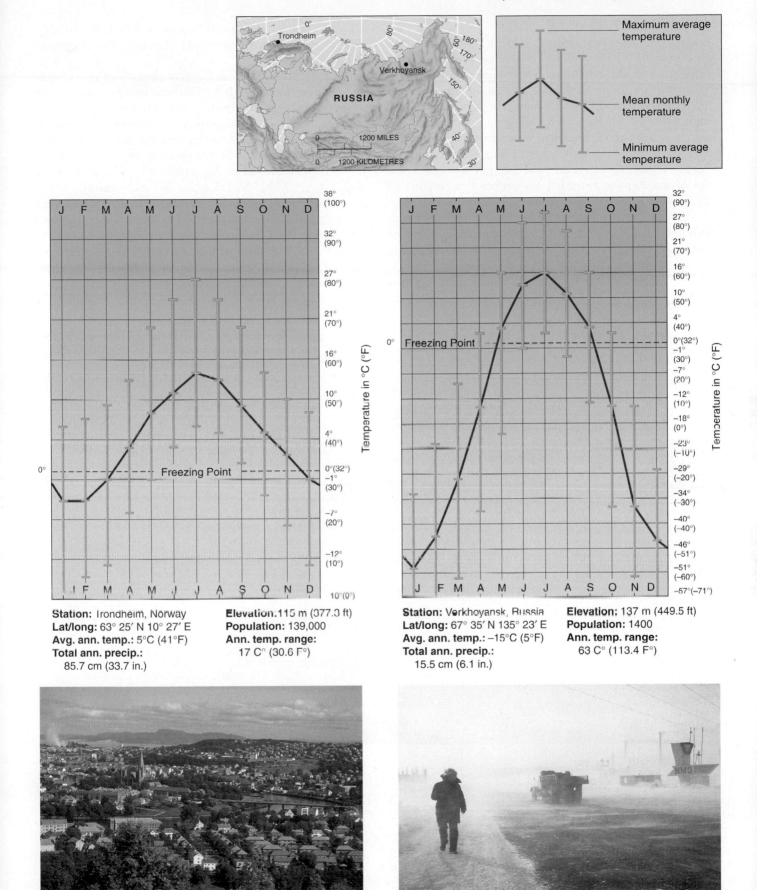

FIGURE 5.15 Marine and continental cities—Eurasia.
Comparison of temperatures in coastal Trondheim, Norway, and continental Siberian Russia. Note that the freezing levels on the two graphs are positioned differently to accommodate the contrasting data. [Trondheim photo by Norman Benton/Peter Arnold, Inc.; Verkhoyansk photo by TASS/Sovfoto/Eastfoto.]

Station: Trondheim, Norway
Lat/long: 63° 25′ N 10° 27′ E
Avg. ann. temp.: 5°C (41°F)
Total ann. precip.:
    85.7 cm (33.7 in.)
Elevation: 115 m (377.3 ft)
Population: 139,000
Ann. temp. range:
    17 C° (30.6 F°)

Station: Verkhoyansk, Russia
Lat/long: 67° 35′ N 135° 23′ E
Avg. ann. temp.: −15°C (5°F)
Total ann. precip.:
    15.5 cm (6.1 in.)
Elevation: 137 m (449.5 ft)
Population: 1400
Ann. temp. range:
    63 C° (113.4 F°)

July Temperature Map

Average July temperatures are presented in Figure 5.16 for the world. The longer days of summer and higher Sun altitude are in the Northern Hemisphere. Winter dominates the Southern Hemisphere, although it is milder than winters north of the equator because continental landmasses are smaller and the dominant oceans and seas store and release more energy. The *thermal equator* shifts northward with the high summer Sun and reaches the Persian Gulf–Pakistan–Iran area. The Persian Gulf is the site of the highest recorded sea-surface temperature of 36°C (96°F), difficult to imagine for a large water body.

During July in the Northern Hemisphere, isotherms shift poleward over land, as higher temperatures dominate continental interiors. July temperatures in Verkhoyansk average more than 13°C (56°F), which represents a 63 C° (113 F°) seasonal range between winter and summer averages. The Verkhoyansk region of Siberia is probably Earth's most dramatic example of continental effects on temperature.

The hottest places on Earth occur in Northern Hemisphere deserts during July. The reasons are simple: clear skies, strong surface heating, virtually no surface water, and few plants. Prime examples are portions of the Sonoran Desert of North America and the Sahara of Africa. Africa recorded a shade temperature higher than 58°C (136°F), a record set on September 13, 1922, at Al 'Azīzīyah, Libya (32° 32′ N, 112 m, or 367 ft elevation).

The highest maximum and annual average temperatures in North America occurred in Death Valley, California, where the Greenland Ranch Station reached 57°C (134°F) in 1913. The station is at 37° N and is −54.3 m, or −178 ft, below sea level. Chapter 15 discusses such hot, arid lands.

Global Surface Temperatures, Land and Ocean

SATELLITE

FIGURE 5.16 Global mean temperatures for July. Temperatures are in Celsius (convertible to Fahrenheit by means of the scale) as taken from separate air-temperature databases for ocean and land. Note the inset map of North America and the poleward-trending isotherms in the interior. Compare with **Figure 5.13.** [Adapted and redrawn from National Climatic Data Center, *Monthly Climatic Data for the World*, 47 (July 1994), in cooperation with the WMO and NOAA.]

FIGURE 5.17 July mean temperatures for Polar Regions.
July temperatures in (a) North Polar region and (b) South Polar region. Use temperature conversions in Figure 5.16. Note that each map is at a different scale. [Author prepared maps using same sources as Figures 5.13 and 5.16.]

The North Polar and South Polar regions (Figure 5.17) are featured on two maps. July is "summer" in the Arctic Ocean (a) and brings a thinning of permanent and seasonal pack ice. See the Midnight Sun photo that opens Chapter 2 to see what continuous daylight is like. Open cracks and leads stretched all the way to the North Pole over the past several years. High Latitude Connection 5.1 presents an overview of temperature trends in the polar regions.

Figure 5.17b is when nights in Antarctica are 24 hours long. This lack of insolation results in the lowest natural temperature reported on Earth, a frigid −89.2°C (−128.6°F) recorded on July 21, 1983, at the Russian Vostok Station, Antarctica (noted on the map). Such a temperature is 11 C° (19.8 F°) colder than the freezing point of dry ice (solid carbon dioxide)! If the concentration of carbon dioxide were large enough, such a cold temperature would theoretically freeze tiny carbon dioxide dry-ice particles out of the sky.

The average July temperature around Vostok is −68°C (−90.4°F). For average temperature comparisons, the Admundsen–Scott Station at the South Pole experiences −60°C (−76°F), and McMurdo Station has a −26°C (−14.8°F) reading. Note that the coldest temperatures in Antarctica are usually in August, not July, just before the equinox sunrise in September at the end of the long polar night.

Annual Temperature Range Map

The temperature range map helps identify areas that experience the greatest annual extremes (continental locations) and the most moderate temperature regimes (marine locations), as demonstrated in Figure 5.18. As you might expect, the largest temperature ranges occur in subpolar locations in North America and Asia, where average ranges of 64 C° (115 F°) are recorded (dark brown area on the map). The Southern Hemisphere, in contrast, has little seasonal variation in mean temperatures, owing to the lack of large landmasses and the vast expanses of water to moderate temperature extremes.

Southern Hemisphere temperature patterns are generally maritime and Northern Hemisphere patterns feature continentality; although interior regions in the Southern Hemisphere experience some continentality effects. For example, in January (Figure 5.13), Australia is dominated by isotherms of 20°–30°C (68°–86°F), whereas in July (Figure 5.16), Australia is crossed by the 12°C (54°F) isotherm. The Northern Hemisphere, with greater land area overall, registers a slightly higher average surface temperature than does the Southern Hemisphere.

Imagine living in some of these regions and the degree to which you would need to adjust your personal wardrobe and make other comfort adaptations. See Focus Study 5.1 for more on air temperature and the human body. The recent summer heat-wave deaths remain a powerful reminder of the role of temperatures in our lives.

FIGURE 5.18 Global annual temperature ranges.
A generalized portrait of the annual range of global temperatures in Celsius degrees, C°, with conversions to Fahrenheit degrees, F°, shown on scale. The mapped data show the difference between January and July temperature means.

F°	5	9	18	27	36	45	54	63	72	81	90	99	108	F°
C°	3	5	10	15	20	25	30	35	40	45	50	55	60	C°

Focus Study 5.1

Air Temperature and the Human Body

We describe our perception of temperature with the term *apparent temperature*, or *sensible temperature*. This perception varies among individuals and cultures. Through complex mechanisms, our bodies maintain an average internal temperature at about 36.8°C (98.2°F), slightly lower in the morning or in cold weather and slightly higher at emotional times or during exercise and work.*

*The traditional value for "normal" body temperature, 37°C (98.6°F), was set in 1868 using old methods of measurement. According to Dr. Philip Mackowiak of the University of Maryland School of Medicine, a more accurate modern assessment places normal at 36.8°C (98.2°F), with a range of 2.7 C° (4.8 F°) for the human population (*Journal of the American Medical Association*, September 23–30, 1992).

Taken together, the water vapour content of air, wind speed, and air temperature affect each individual's sense of comfort. The most discomfort comes with high temperatures, high humidity, and low winds. Modern heating and cooling systems, where available, reduce the impact of extreme temperatures indoors. Deaths still happen, especially among groups of people who can't afford to alter temperatures in their living spaces.

When there are changes in the surrounding air, the human body reacts to maintain its core temperature and to protect the brain at all costs. Table 5.1.1 summarizes the human body's response to stress induced by exposure to *hypothermia* (low temperature) and *hyperthermia* (high temper-

ature). Carefully review these two lists of responses for future reference.

Wind Chill

The wind-chill index is important to people who experience winters with freezing temperatures and was first proposed by Antarctic explorer Paul Siple in 1939. The *wind-chill factor* indicates the enhanced rate at which body heat is lost to the air and at best represents an estimate of heat-energy loss. As wind speeds increase, heat loss from the skin increases. A formula for calculating these relationships was developed in 1945. This older index tended to overestimate heat loss from skin.

The National Weather Service (NWS, http://www.nws.noaa.gov/ om/

windchill/) and the Meteorological Services of Canada (MSC, http:// www.msc.ec.gc.ca/education/windchill/index_e.cfm) revised the wind-chill formula for the 2001–2002 winter season. The new *Wind Chill Temperature Index* (WCT) is an effort to improve the accuracy of heat-loss calculations. Figure 5.1.1 presents the new version that began service in November 2001.

For example, using the new chart, if the air temperature is −7°C (20°F) and the wind is blowing at 32 kmph (20 mph), skin temperatures will be at −16°C (4°F). The lower wind-chill values present a serious freezing hazard to exposed flesh. Imagine the wind chill experienced by a downhill ski racer going 130 kmph (80 mph)—frostbite is a definite possibility during a 2-minute run. The wind chill does omit consideration of sunlight intensity, a person's physical activity, and the use of protective clothing, such as a windbreaker, that prevents the wind access to your skin.

Humidex

Humidex, a Canadian innovation first used in 1965, was devised to describe how hot, humid weather feels to the average person. It represents the heating effect felt as a result of a lack of evaporation from the skin surface, and is only measured in the summer months. Humidex is reported as a temperature—not the recorded temperature, but how hot it "feels" based on humidity. In the United States, the effect of high heat and moisture on the human body is calculated in a similar way (http://www.hpc.ncep.noaa.gov/heat_index.shtml).

Humidex is a calculation based on air temperature and relative humidity (water vapour in the air—see Chapter 7) and, as mentioned, is reported as an equivalent temperature. Water vapour in the air is expressed as relative humidity, a concept presented in Chapter 7. Although it is used widely in Canada, the areas most affected by the Humidex readings are in southern

Ontario and Québec. Here, in summer, the greatest impact of moist tropical air from the Gulf of Mexico is felt.

The following formula is a simplified method used to calculate Humidex:

$$\text{Humidex} = T + 5/9 \, (e - 10)$$

where e = vapour pressure ($6.112 \times 10^{(7.5 \times T/(237.7+T)) \times H/100}$),
T = air temperature (degrees Celsius), and
H = humidity (%).

Table 5.1.2 describes the comfort levels associated with Humidex levels as suggested by the Meteorological Service of Canada.

High Humidex values produce stifling conditions that can be serious, particularly to the sick and elderly. In the summer of 2003, Europe was paralyzed by extreme temperatures that topped 40°C. Official estimates across the continent placed the death count at more than 20,000, triggering controversy as governments were ill-prepared to adequately deal with such a catastrophe.

France was hardest hit, with more than 14,000 deaths, some 11,000 in the first two weeks of August alone. The heat wave began on August 1, the start of a typical summer holiday period when many doctors and nurses leave home for vacation, reducing the number of in-service hospital beds. By August 5, activity increased for paramedics and hospital emergency rooms. As the heat wave continued, government

Table 5.1.1 The Human Body's Response to Temperature Stress

At Low Temperatures (Heat-gaining mechanism)	At High Temperatures (Heat-dissipation mechanism)
Temperature-Regulation Methods	
Constriction of surface blood vessels	Dilation of surface blood vessels
Concentration of blood	Dilution of blood
Flexing to reduce surface exposure	Extending to increase exposure
Increased muscle tone	Decreased muscle tone
Decrease in sweating	Sweating
Inclination to increase activity	Inclination to decrease activity
Shivering	
Increased cell metabolism	
Consequent Disturbances	
Increased urine volume	Decreased urine volume
Danger of inadequate blood supply to exposed parts; frostbite	Reduced blood supply to brain; dizziness, nausea, fainting
Discomfort leading to neuroses	Discomfort leading to neuroses
Increased appetite	Decreased appetite
	Mobilization of tissue fluid
	Thirst and dehydration
	Reduced chloride balance; heat cramps
Failure of Regulation	
Falling body temperature	Rising body temperature
Drowsiness	Impaired heat-regulating centre
Cessation of heartbeat and respiration	Failure of nervous regulation; cessation of breathing

Source: Climatology—Arid Zone Research X. © UNESCO. Reproduced by permission of UNESCO.

(continued)

Focus Study 5.1 (continued)

Actual Air Temperature in °C (°F)

Wind speed, kmph (mph) / Calm	4° (40°)	−1° (30°)	−7° (20°)	−12° (10°)	−18° (0°)	−23° (−10°)	−29° (−20°)	−34° (−30°)	−40° (−40°)
8 (5)	2° (36°)	−4° (25°)	−11° (13°)	−17° (1°)	−24° (−11°)	−30° (−22°)	−37° (−34°)	−43° (−46°)	−49° (−57°)
16 (10)	1° (34°)	−6° (21°)	−13° (9°)	−20° (−4°)	−27° (−16°)	−33° (−28°)	−41° (−41°)	−47° (−53°)	−54° (−66°)
24 (15)	0° (32°)	−7° (19°)	−14° (6°)	−22° (−7°)	−28° (−19°)	−36° (−32°)	−43° (−45°)	−50° (−58°)	−57° (−71°)
32 (20)	−1° (30°)	−8° (17°)	−16° (4°)	−23° (−9°)	−30° (−22°)	−37° (−35°)	−44° (−48°)	−52° (−61°)	−59° (−74°)
40 (25)	−2° (29°)	−9° (16°)	−16° (3°)	−24° (−11°)	−31° (−24°)	−38° (−37°)	−46° (−51°)	−53° (−64°)	−61° (−78°)
48 (30)	−2° (28°)	−9° (15°)	−17° (−1°)	−24° (−12°)	−32° (−26°)	−39° (−39°)	−47° (−53°)	−55° (−67°)	−62° (−80°)
56 (35)	−2° (28°)	−10° (14°)	−18° (0°)	−26° (−14°)	−33° (−27°)	−41° (−41°)	−48° (−55°)	−56° (−69°)	−63° (−82°)
64 (40)	−3° (27°)	−11° (13°)	−18° (−1°)	−26° (−15°)	−34° (−29°)	−42° (−43°)	−49° (−57°)	−57° (−71°)	−64° (−84°)
72 (45)	−3° (26°)	−11° (12°)	−19° (−2°)	−27° (−16°)	−34° (−30°)	−42° (−44°)	−50° (−58°)	−58° (−72°)	−66° (−86°)
80 (50)	−3° (26°)	−11° (12°)	−19° (−3°)	−27° (−17°)	−35° (−31°)	−43° (−45°)	−51° (−60°)	−59° (−74°)	−67° (−88°)

Frostbite times: 30 min. 10 min. 5 min.

FIGURE 5.1.1 Wind Chill Temperature Index.
WCT Index factor for various temperatures and wind speeds. For quick calculations see http://www.srh.noaa.gov/elp/wxcalc/windchill.html (in English units the new formula is: Wind chill $(F°) = 35.74 + 0.6125T − 35.75(V^{0.16}) + 0.4275T(V^{0.16})$, where T = air temperature in °F, V = wind speed in mph. In Canada, heat loss is expressed in watts per square metre.) [Adapted from the National Weather Service and Meteorological Services of Canada, version 11/01/01.]

officials were reluctant to cut their holidays short to deal with the problem. An emergency response was launched August 13—the day temperatures began to fall. This response included calling hospital staff back to work and re-opening wards that were closed for the August vacation season. This action was too late. The impact of the heat wave was felt across Europe: The United Kingdom counted 907 heat-related deaths, Portugal 545, Italy 4127, and Spain 112 official deaths, with estimates as high as 6000.

Table 5.1.2 Comfort Levels and Suggested Activities for Ranges of Humidex

Range of Humidex	Degree of Comfort
Less than 29	No discomfort
30 to 39	Some discomfort; tone down or modify strenuous outdoor activity
40 to 45	Great discomfort; avoid exertion, curtail activity
Above 45	Dangerous
Above 54	Heat stroke is imminent

Source: The Meteorological Service of Canada. Reproduced with the permission of Environment Canada, http://www.qc.ec.gc.ca/meteo/documentation/humidex_e.html.

Record Temperatures and Greenhouse Warming

Future humans will experience greater temperature-related challenges owing to complex changes now under way in the lower atmosphere. Scientists agree that human activities, principally the burning of fossil fuels, are increasing greenhouse gases that absorb longwave radiation, delaying losses of heat energy to space. We are experiencing human-forced climate change, as Earth's natural greenhouse is enhanced.

The Dome C ice core taken from the East Antarctic Plateau shows that present levels of carbon dioxide, methane, and nitrous oxides, and resulting air temperatures, are higher in the present decade than in the entire 800,000-year record! These are remarkable times in which we live. Twelve of the last 13 years, 1995–2007, rank among the warmest years in instrumental records stretching back to 1850.

The Intergovernmental Panel on Climate Change (IPCC), through major reports in 1990, 1992, 1995, 2001, and its *Fourth Assessment Report* (*AR4*) in 2007, confirms that global warming is occurring. The IPCC AR4 reached a consensus, in part stating:

> Warming of the climate system is unequivocal, as is now evident from observations of increases in global average air and ocean temperatures, widespread melting of snow and ice, and rising global average sea level.... Most of the observed increase in globally averaged temperatures since the mid-20th century is *very likely* (>90%) due to the observed increases in anthropogenic greenhouse gas concentrations.... human influences now extend to other aspects of climate, including ocean warming, continental-average temperatures, temperature extremes and wind patterns ... and, *very likely* (<90%) that this is not due to known natural causes alone.*

The Arctic Climate Impact Assessment (ACIA) reported confirmation of conditions in the Arctic in their science report released in late 2004. ACIA stated, "The Arctic is extremely vulnerable to observed and projected climate change and its impacts. The Arctic is now experiencing some of the most rapid and severe climate change on Earth."

*Intergovernmental Panel on Climate Change (IPCC) *Fourth Assessment Report* (2007), Working Group I, *The Physical Science Basis*, "Summary for Policy Makers," (February 5, 2007), IPCC Secretariat, Geneva, Switzerland, pp. 5, 10. See http://www.ipcc.ch/ and download the three Working Group summaries free.

The Association of American Geographers (AAG) at the 2006 Chicago meeting passed the "AAG Resolution Requesting Action on Climate Change." This resolution places the AAG in line with other professional organizations and national academies of sciences that are now on record for action to slow rates of climate change.

An array of sophisticated satellites, remote-sensing capabilities, and powerful computers equip scientists to run global circulation models and decipher the climate trends. Actual field measurements and observations confirm these remotely sensed conclusions and a scientific consensus. With the cause being the exhaust from our fossil fuel consumption and our modern technological society, the political fallout and debate is intense.

Chapter 10 discusses global warming and climate change, and Chapter 17 the vulnerable polar regions and the ice-core record of climate. We address what is known and unknown, how global models work, the radiatively active gases that are forcing the warming, the consequences to natural systems, the uncertainties, and what international action is underway to slow the effects of such change. We should be aware of what scientists are discovering:

> By the end of the 21st century, large portions of Earth's surface may experience climates not found at present, and some 20th-century climates may disappear.... Novel climates are projected to develop primarily in the tropics and subtropics.*

*Jack Williams, *et. al.*, "Projected distributions of novel and disappearing climates by A.D. 2100," *Proceedings of the National Academy of Sciences*, April 3, 2007: p. 5738.

High Latitude Connection 5.1

Overview of Temperature Trends in the Polar Regions

Climate models used by scientists to predict and direct measurements show that the polar regions are experiencing some dramatic global climate change impacts. These changes lead some to say that the high latitudes are providing the global community an early warning signal. The question is, how do we read changing temperature signals, how do they relate to natural circulation cycles, and what are the spatial implications to the rest of the planet?

Arctic Changes

Many proxy and direct measurements confirm that the twentieth century was a time of increasing temperatures at both middle and low latitudes and in the polar regions, especially during the last half century. Daily maximum and minimum temperatures show there is warming in the Arctic at a rate of about 5 C° (9 F°) per century. Since 1978, warming increased to a rate of 1.2 C° (2.2 F°) per decade, which means the last 20 years warmed at nearly 7 times the rate of the last 100 years.

In response to rising air and water temperatures, Arctic sea ice is on a significant decline. The sea ice is melting at a rate of about 9% per decade since 1978, especially in the eastern and central Arctic Ocean. Atmospheric pressure patterns cause sea ice to shift as well.

Record losses have occurred since 2000, as sea ice reached its smallest spatial distribution in the satellite record. Figure 5.1.1 is a composite satellite image for 1979 and 2007 comparing sea-ice coverage in the Arctic. September 14, 2007, marked the lowest sea-ice extent on record during the era of satellite surveillance. The sea ice thins as warmer air melts the surface and warmer waters attack the base of the ice. The summer melt period is increasing as spring arrives earlier and fall is delayed. Since 1970, about 43% of the Arctic sea ice has disappeared. More open water means darker surfaces that absorb more insolation that lead to more warming.

(continued)

High Latitude Connection 5.1 *(continued)*

Chapters 1 and 17 discuss the 400% increase in meltponds on the surface of the Greenland ice sheet, ice shelves, and glaciers. This increase represents a significant positive feedback mechanism. In response to the increased discharge of freshwater in the Arctic, the northern oceans are freshening—actually, lowering in salinity. There is valid concern that these meltwaters riding atop saline water can disrupt important circulation systems in the northern oceans.

In Alaska, temperatures rose over the past 30 years at a 3 C° (5 F°) per decade rate. All 11 mountain ranges experienced glacial ice losses. Glacial thinning reached 1.8 m per year by the late 1990s across Alaska. In response to this unloading of ice mass, Earth's crust is rebounding upward. A News Report in Chapter 17 explains the negative net mass balance of 67 Alaskan glaciers.

All of these changes are affecting living systems as specific high-latitude ecosystems shift across the landscape poleward at 6.1 km (3.8 mi) per decade and spring arrives earlier at a pace of 2.3 days per decade. Changes in tundra soils and the increased depth of active- layer melting in permafrost indicate regional warming, as discussed in Chapter 17. These thawing lands provide less nutrition to caribou and other grazing animals, worsen forest fire conditions, and are an additional source of carbon dioxide to the atmosphere.

By 2080, the Intergovernmental Panel on Climate Change (IPCC) forecasts increasing warmth in the Arctic ranging from 4.0° to 7.5 C° in summer and 2.5° to 14.0 C° in winter over land; and 0.5° to 4.5 C° in summer and 3.0° to 16.0 C° in winter over the Arctic Ocean. With these temperature changes precipitation will increase since warmer air can contain more moisture.

Antarctic Changes

In Antarctica and the Southern Ocean, the temperature records of the permanently occupied research stations over the last 45 years demonstrate an overall warming. This record includes periods of slight cooling within this time

1979

2007

FIGURE 5.1.1 Loss of Arctic sea ice.
A composite of satellite data and surface data from 1979 and 2007 shows remarkable loss of Arctic sea ice. Each composite is a portrait of minimum sea-ice concentrations during summer months. For scale, in just 2 years between the 2005 record low and the new 2007 record, the amount of sea-ice loss exceeded the area of California in size (423,950 km²; 163,700 mi²), or 24% below 2005. Not only did the atmosphere record increased warmth but the Arctic Ocean warmed as well. In addition to sea ice losses, changing pressure patterns cause sea ice to shift. [Images courtesy of Scientific Visualization Studio, GSFC/NASA.]

frame. The present warming rate is less than that of the Arctic, at about a 0.9° to 1.2 C° increase per century.

However, along the Antarctic Peninsula, the location of numerous ice-shelf collapses and disintegrations, the rate of warming is more than twice this rate, as the January 0° isotherm continues to shift southward. The exposed land is open to exotic plants and animals that move into these altered ecosystems. In terms of sea ice, the Antarctic trend is not as pronounced as that of the Arctic, with sea-ice extent reduced by 0.4°–1.8° of latitude over the last century. Continued changes will affect marine life and birds.

By 2080, the IPCC forecasts increasing warmth in the Antarctic ranging from 1.0° to 4.8 C° in summer and 1.0° to 5.0 C° in winter over the continent; and 0.0° to 2.8 C° in summer and 0.5° to 5.0 C° in winter over the Southern Ocean.

For the latest science on both polar regions, please see: "Polar Regions (Arctic and Antarctic)," in *Climate Change 2007: Climate Change Impacts, Adaptation, and Vulnerability*, Working Group II Contribution to the Fourth Assessment Report of the Intergovernmental Panel on Climate—web site is at **http://www.ipcc.ch/**.

Applied Physical Geography

Humidex

Humidex, a calculated parameter that is based on temperature and humidity, can be easily calculated to determine the comfort level of the air at a specific temperature and humidity. It gives a measure of the amount of discomfort felt by the combined effect of the two elements. Humidex is calculated using the following formula:

$$\text{Humidex} = T + 5/9 \times (e - 10)$$

where e = vapour pressure $(6.112 \times 10^{(7.5 \times T/(237.7 + T)) \times H/100})$, T = air temperature (degrees Celsius), and H = humidity (%).

For example, given a temperature of 25°C with relative humidity of 82%, first determine the vapour pressure:

$$e = \text{vapour pressure} \ (6.112 \times 10^{(7.5 \times T/(237.7 + T)) \times H/100})$$
$$= 6.112 \times 10^{(7.5 \times 25/(237.7 + 25)) \times 82/100}$$
$$= 6.112 \times 10^{0.5852683}$$
$$= 23.52078.$$

Then use the vapour pressure value in the Humidex equation:

$$\text{Humidex} = T + 5/9 \times (e - 10)$$
$$= 25 + 5/9 \times (23.52078 - 10)$$
$$= 25 + 7.5115444$$
$$= 25 + 8$$
$$= 33.$$

So, on a day with a fairly moderate temperature, the humidity makes it feel much hotter.

ANIMATION   Global Warming, Climate Change

NOTEBOOK   GISS Surface Temperature Analysis, 1891 to 2006 (Chapter 10)

Summary and Review—Global Temperatures

■ *Define* the concepts of temperature, kinetic energy, and sensible heat, and *distinguish* among Kelvin, Celsius, and Fahrenheit temperature scales and how they are measured.

Temperature is a measure of the average kinetic energy (motion) of individual molecules in matter. We feel the effect of temperature as the sensible heat transfer from warmer objects to cooler objects when these objects are touching. Temperature scales include

- Kelvin scale: 100 units between the melting point of ice (273 K) and the boiling point of water (373 K).
- Celsius scale: 100 degrees between the melting point of ice (0°C) and the boiling point of water (100°C).
- Fahrenheit scale: 180 degrees between melting point of ice (32°F) and the boiling point of water (212°F).

The Kelvin scale is used in scientific research because temperature readings start at absolute zero and thus are proportional to the actual kinetic energy in a material.

temperature (p. 120)

1. Distinguish between sensible heat and sensible temperature.

2. What does air temperature indicate about energy in the atmosphere?

3. Compare the three scales that express temperature. Find "normal" human body temperature on each scale and record the three values in your notes.

4. What is your source of daily temperature information? Describe the highest temperature you have experienced and the lowest temperature. From what we have discussed in this chapter, can you identify the factors that may have contributed to these temperatures?

■ *List* and *review* the principal controls and influences that produce global temperature patterns.

Principal controls and influences upon temperature patterns include *latitude* (the distance north or south of the equator), *altitude* and *elevation*, *cloud cover* (reflection, absorption, and reradiation of energy), and *land–water heating differences* (the nature of evaporation, transparency, specific heat, movement, and ocean currents and sea-surface temperatures).

5. Explain the effect of altitude/elevation on air temperature. Why is air at higher altitude/elevation lower in temperature? Why does it feel cooler standing in shadows at higher elevation than at lower elevation?

6. What noticeable effect does air density have on the absorption and radiation of energy? What role does elevation play in that process?

7. How is it possible to grow moderate-climate-type crops such as wheat, barley, and potatoes at an elevation of 4103 m (13,460 ft) near La Paz, Bolivia, so near the equator?

8. Describe the effect of cloud cover with regard to Earth's temperature patterns. From the last chapter, review the cloud-albedo forcing and cloud-greenhouse forcing of different cloud types and relate the concepts with a simple sketch.

■ *Review* the factors that produce different marine effects and continental effects as they influence temperatures, and *utilize* several pairs of cities to illustrate these differences.

The physical nature of land (rock and soil) and water (oceans, seas, and lakes) is the reason for **land–water heating differences**, the fact that land heats and cools faster than water. Moderate temperature patterns are associated with water bodies, and extreme temperatures occur inland. The controls that cause differences between land and water surfaces are *evaporation, transparency, specific heat, movement,* and *ocean currents and sea-surface temperatures.*

Light penetrates water because of its **transparency**. Water is clear and light transmits to an average depth of 60 m (200 ft) in the ocean. This penetration distributes available heat energy over a much greater volume than could occur on opaque land; thus, a larger energy reservoir is formed. When equal volumes of water and land are compared, water requires far more energy to increase its temperature than does land. In other words, water can hold more energy than can soil or rock, so water has a higher **specific heat**, the heat capacity of a substance, averaging about 4 times that of soil.

Ocean currents affect temperature. An example of the effect of ocean currents is the **Gulf Stream**, which moves northward off the east coast of North America, carrying warm water far into the North Atlantic. As a result, the southern third of Iceland experiences much milder temperatures than would be expected for a latitude of 65° N, just below the Arctic Circle (66.5°).

Marine effect, or maritime, describes locations that exhibit the moderating influences of the ocean, usually along coastlines or on islands. **Continental effect** refers to the condition of areas that are less affected by the sea and therefore have a greater range between maximum and minimum temperatures diurnally and yearly.

land–water heating differences (p. 124)
transparency (p. 125)
specific heat (p. 126)
Gulf Stream (p. 126)
marine effect (p. 127)
continental effect (p. 127)

9. List the physical aspects of land and water that produce their different responses to heating from absorption of insolation. What is the specific effect of transparency in a medium?

10. What is specific heat? Compare the specific heat of water and soil.

11. Describe the pattern of sea-surface temperatures (SSTs) as determined by satellite remote sensing. Where is the warmest ocean region on Earth?

12. What effect does sea-surface temperature have on air temperature? Describe the negative feedback mechanism created by higher sea-surface temperatures and evaporation rates.

13. Differentiate between marine and continental temperatures. Give geographic examples of each from the text: Canada, Norway, and Russia.

■ *Interpret* the pattern of Earth's temperatures from their portrayal on January and July temperature maps and on a map of annual temperature ranges.

Maps for January and July instead of the solstice months of December and June are used for temperature comparison because of the natural lag that occurs between insolation received and maximum or minimum temperatures experienced. Each line on these temperature maps is an **isotherm**, an isoline that connects points of equal temperature. Isotherms portray temperature patterns.

Isotherms generally are zonal, trending east–west, parallel to the equator. They mark the general decrease in insolation and net radiation with distance from the equator. The **thermal equator** (isoline connecting all points of highest mean temperature) trends southward in January and shifts northward with the high summer Sun in July. In January it extends farther south into the interior of South America and Africa, indicating higher temperatures over landmasses.

In the Northern Hemisphere in January, isotherms shift equatorward as cold air chills the continental interiors. The coldest area on the map is in Russia, specifically northeastern Siberia. The intense cold experienced there results from winter conditions of consistent clear, dry, calm air; small insolation input; and an inland location far from any moderating maritime effects.

isotherm (p. 129)
thermal equator (p. 129)

14. What is the thermal equator? Describe its location in January and in July. Explain why it shifts position annually.

15. Observe trends in the pattern of isolines over North America and compare the January average temperature map with the July map. Why do the patterns shift locations?

16. Describe and explain the extreme temperature range experienced in north-central Siberia between January and July.

17. Where are the hottest places on Earth? Are they near the equator or elsewhere? Explain. Where is the coldest place on Earth?

18. From the maps in Figures 5.13 and 5.14, 5.16 and 5.17, and 5.18, determine the average temperature values and annual range of temperatures for your present location.

19. Compare the maps in Figures 5.14 and 5.17: (a) describe what you find in central Greenland between January and July; (b) look at the South polar region and describe seasonal changes between the two maps. Characterize conditions along the Antarctic Peninsula between January and July (around 60° west longitude).

■ *Describe* the human body's response to wind (wind chill) and heat and humidity (Humidex).

The *wind-chill factor* indicates the enhanced rate at which body heat is lost to the air. As wind speeds increase, heat loss from the skin increases. Humidex indicates the human body's reaction to air temperature and water vapour. The level of humidity in the air affects our natural ability to cool through evaporation from skin.

20. What is the wind-chill temperature on a day with an air temperature of −12°C (10°F) and a wind speed of 32 kmph (20 mph)?

21. Explain how the Canadian Humidex measure tells us about sensible temperature and the human body. Give an example based upon your own sense of comfort or discomfort.

Critical Thinking

A. With each temperature map (Figures 5.13, 5.16, and 5.18), begin by finding your own city or town and noting the temperatures indicated by the isotherms for January and July and the annual temperature range. Record the information from these maps in your notebook. The scale of all these maps allows you to make only a rough approximation for your location. As you work through the different maps throughout this text, note atmospheric pressure and winds, annual precipitation, climate type, landforms, soil orders, vegetation, and terrestrial biomes. By the end of the course you will have recorded a complete physical geography profile for your regional environment.

B. Have you ever experienced any of the different responses of the human body to the low-temperature or high-temperature stress noted in Focus Study 5.1, Table 5.1.1? Where were you at the time of each experience? Make copies of the *wind-chill* chart given in the Focus Study for later reference. On an appropriate day, check air temperature and wind speed and determine their combined effect on skin chilling. In contrast, on an appropriate day, check air temperature and relative humidity values and determine their combined effect on the comfort levels in the Humidex chart.

The largest wind turbines in the UK operate at Burger Hill Wind Farm, Birsay Moors, in the Orkney Islands, northeast Scotland. The inset photo shows a maintenance ladder for scale on the *nacelle* that houses the machinery. The towers are 68 m (223 ft) tall with a rotor diameter of 72 m (236 ft); each turbine is rated at 2 MW. [Photo by Bobbé Christopherson.]

Atmospheric and Oceanic Circulations

■ Key Learning Concepts

After reading the chapter, you should be able to:

- ■ **Define** the concept of air pressure, and **describe** instruments used to measure air pressure.

- ■ **Define** wind, and **describe** how wind is measured, how wind direction is determined, and how winds are named.

- ■ **Explain** the four driving forces within the atmosphere—gravity, pressure gradient force, Coriolis force, and friction force—and **describe** the primary high- and low-pressure areas and principal winds.

- ■ **Describe** upper-air circulation and its support role for surface systems, and **define** the jet streams.

- ■ **Overview** several multiyear oscillations of air temperature, air pressure, and circulation in the Arctic, Atlantic, and Pacific oceans.

- ■ **Explain** several types of local winds: land–sea breezes, mountain–valley breezes, katabatic winds, and the regional monsoons.

- ■ **Discern** the basic pattern of Earth's major surface ocean currents and deep thermohaline circulation.

E arly in April 1815, on the island Sumbawa in present-day Indonesia, Tambora erupted violently. The volcano spewed an estimated 150 km² (36 mi²) of material, 25 times the volume produced by the 1980 Mount St. Helens eruption in Washington State. Global atmospheric circulation carried Tambora debris worldwide, creating a stratospheric veil of dust and acid mist. Remarkable optical and meteorological effects lasted in Earth's atmosphere years after the eruption—beautiful sunrises and sunsets and a temporary lowering of temperatures worldwide. Scientists in 1815 lacked remote-sensing satellite capabilities, and had no way of knowing the global impact of Tambora's eruption.

(a)

Luzon Island, Philippines

6/15 – 6/19/91

(b)

7/4 – 7/10/91

(c)

7/25 – 8/1/91

(d)

FIGURE 6.1 Volcanic eruption effects spread worldwide by winds.
Satellite image captures Mount Pinatubo eruption (a). False-colour images (b–e) of aerosols from Mount Pinatubo, smoke from fires, and dust storms, all swept about the globe by the general atmospheric circulation. The dramatic increase in aerosols over the oceans from mid-June 1991 (b) to mid-August (e) is due to the Mount Pinatubo eruption on June 15. The false colour shows aerosol concentration as its aerosol optical thickness (AOT): White is densest, dull yellow indicates medium values, and brown areas have the lowest aerosol concentration. In (b) note the dust moving westward from Africa, smoke from Kuwaiti oil well fires set during the first Persian Gulf War, smoke from forest fires in Siberia, and haze off the east coast of the United States. [(a) *AVHRR* satellite image courtesy of U.S. Geological Survey, EROS Data Center. *AVHRR* satellite AOT images courtesy of Dr. Larry L. Stowe, NESDIS/NOAA. Used by permission.]

8/15 – 8/21/91

Effects cover 42% of globe in just 60 days

(e)

After 635 years of dormancy, Mount Pinatubo in the Philippines erupted in 1991 (Figure 6.1a). This event had tremendous atmospheric impact, lofting 15–20 million tons of ash, dust, and sulfur dioxide (SO_2) into the atmosphere. As the sulfur dioxide rose into the stratosphere, it quickly formed sulfuric acid (H_2SO_4) aerosols, which concentrated at 16–25 km (10–15.5 mi) altitude. This debris increased atmospheric albedo about 1.5%, giving scientists an estimate of the aerosol volume generated by the eruption (see Figure 1.6).

The AVHRR instrument aboard *NOAA-11* monitored the reflected solar radiation from Mount Pinatubo's aerosols as global winds swept them around Earth. Figure 6.1b–e shows images made at three-week intervals that clearly track the spread of the debris worldwide. Some 60 days after the eruption (the last satellite image in the sequence), the aerosol cloud spanned about 42% of the globe, from 20° S to 30° N. Again, for almost two years colourful sunrises and sunsets and a small lowering of average temperatures followed. The eruption provided a unique insight into the dynamics of atmospheric circulation.

Today, technology permits a depth of analysis unknown in the past—satellites now track the atmospheric effects from dust storms, forest fires, industrial haze, warfare, and the dispersal of volcanic explosions, among many others. As an example, millions of tons of dust from African soils cross the Atlantic each year, borne by the winds of atmospheric circulation. This dust sometimes increases the iron content of the waters off Florida, promoting the toxic algal blooms (*Karenia brevis*) known as "Red Tides."

Global winds are certainly an important reason why the United States, the former Soviet Union, and Great Britain signed the 1963 Limited Test Ban Treaty. That treaty banned above-ground testing of nuclear weapons because atmospheric circulation spread radioactive contamination worldwide. Such agreements illustrate how the fluid movement of the atmosphere socializes humanity more than perhaps any other natural or cultural factor. Our atmosphere makes the world a spatially linked society—one person's or country's exhalation is another's inhalation.

In this chapter: We begin with a discussion of wind essentials, consisting of air pressure and its measurement and a description of wind. The driving forces that produce surface winds are pressure gradient, Coriolis, and friction. We examine the circulation of Earth's atmosphere and the patterns of global winds, including principal pressure systems and winds. We consider Earth's wind-driven oceanic currents and explain multiyear oscillations in atmospheric flows, local winds, and the powerful monsoons. The energy driving all this movement comes from one source: the Sun.

Wind Essentials

Earth's atmospheric circulation transfers both energy and mass on a grand scale. In the process, the imbalance between equatorial energy surpluses and polar energy deficits is resolved, Earth's weather patterns formed, and ocean currents produced. Air pollutants, whether natural or human-caused, are spread worldwide by atmospheric circulation, far from their point of origin.

Atmospheric circulation is generally categorized at three levels: *primary circulation* consisting of general worldwide circulation, *secondary circulation* of migratory high-pressure and low-pressure systems, and *tertiary circulation* that includes local winds and temporal weather patterns. Winds that move principally north or south along meridians are known as *meridional flows*. Winds moving east or west along parallels of latitude are called *zonal flows*.

Air Pressure and Its Measurement

Air pressure, its measurement and expression, is key to understanding wind. The molecules that constitute air create **air pressure** through their motion, size, and number—the factors that determine the temperature and density of the air. Air pressure, then, is a product of the temperature and density of a mass of air. Pressure is exerted on all surfaces in contact with the air.

In 1643, Galileo's pupil Evangelista Torricelli was working on a mine-drainage problem. His work led him to discover a method for measuring air pressure (Figure 6.2a). He knew that pumps in the mine were able to "pull" water upward about 10 m (33 ft), but no higher. He did not know why. Careful observation led him to discover that this was caused not by weak pumps but by the atmosphere itself. Torricelli noted that the water level in the vertical pipe fluctuated from day to day. He figured out that air pressure, the weight of the air, varies with weather conditions.

To simulate the problem at the mine, Torricelli devised an instrument at Galileo's suggestion, using a much denser fluid than water—mercury (Hg)—in a glass tube 1 m high. Torricelli sealed the glass tube at one end, filled it with mercury, and inverted it into a dish of mercury (Figure 6.2b). He determined that the average height of the column of mercury in the tube was 760 mm (29.92 in.) and that it did vary day-to-day as the weather changed. He concluded that the mass of surrounding air was exerting pressure on the mercury in the dish that counterbalanced the column of mercury.

Using similar instruments, scientists set a standard of *normal sea-level pressure* at 1013.2 mb (*millibar*, or *mb*, which expresses force per square metre of surface area), or 29.92 in. mercury (Hg). In Canada and other countries, normal air pressure is expressed as 101.32 kPa (*kilopascal*; 1 kPa = 10 mb).

Any instrument that measures air pressure is a *barometer* (from the Greek *baros*, meaning "weight"). Torricelli developed a **mercury barometer**. A more compact barometer design, which works without a metre-long tube of mercury, is the aneroid barometer, shown in Figure 6.2c. *Aneroid* means "using no liquid." The **aneroid barometer** principle is simple: Imagine a small chamber, partially emptied of air, which is sealed and

FIGURE 6.2 Developing the barometer.
(a) Torricelli developed the barometer to measure air pressure while trying to solve a mine-drainage problem. Two types of instruments are used to measure atmospheric pressure: (b) a mercury barometer (idealized sketch), and (c) an aneroid barometer. Have you used a barometer? If so, what type is it? Have you tried to reset it using a local weather information **source?** [(c) Courtesy of Qualimetrics, Inc., Sacramento, California.]

connected to a mechanism attached to a needle on a dial. As air pressure increases, it presses on the chamber; as air pressure decreases, it relieves pressure on the chamber. The chamber responds to these changes in air pressure and moves the needle. An aircraft altimeter is a type of aneroid barometer. It accurately measures altitude because air pressure diminishes with altitude above sea level. For accuracy the altimeter must be adjusted for temperature changes.

Figure 6.3 illustrates comparative scales in millibars and inches used to express air pressure and its relative force. The normal range of Earth's atmospheric pressure from strong high pressure to deep low pressure is about 105.0 to 98.0 kPa (1050 to 980 mb). The figure also indicates the extreme highest and lowest pressures ever recorded in the United States, Canada, and on Earth.

Hurricane Wilma is now the record holder from 2005. For comparison, note hurricanes Gilbert (1988) and Rita and Katrina (2005), and their lowest central pressures.

Wind: Description and Measurement

Simply stated, **wind** is generally the horizontal motion of air across Earth's surface. Turbulence adds wind updrafts and downdrafts and a vertical component to this definition. *Differences in air pressure (density) between one location and another produce wind.* Wind's two principal properties are speed and direction, and instruments measure each. An **anemometer** measures wind speed in kilometres per hour (kmph), miles per hour (mph), metres per second (mps), or knots. (A *knot* is a nautical mile per hour, covering 1 minute of Earth's arc in an hour, equivalent to

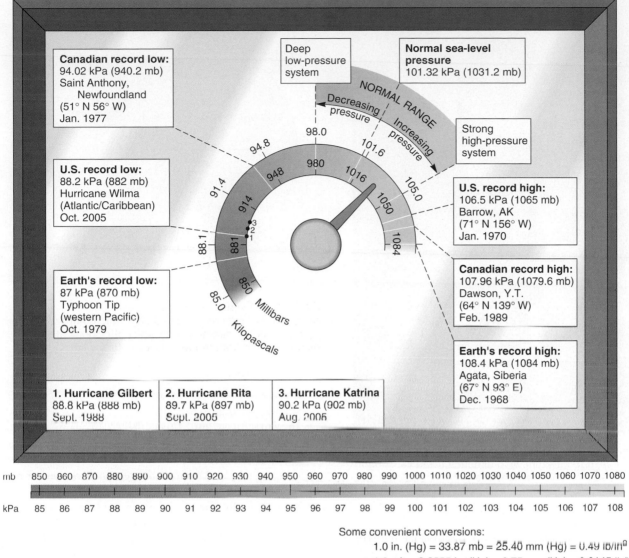

Some convenient conversions:
1.0 in. (Hg) = 33.87 mb = 25.40 mm (Hg) = 0.49 lb/in²
1.0 mb = 0.0295 in. (Hg) = 0.75 mm (Hg) = 0.0145 lb/in²

FIGURE 6.3 Air pressure readings and conversions.
Scales for expressing barometric air pressure in kilopascals and millibars, with average air
pressure values and recorded pressure extremes (10 mb = 1 kPa).

1.85 kmph, or 1.15 mph.) A **wind vane** determines wind direction; the standard measurement is taken 10 m (33 ft) above the ground to reduce the effects of local topography on wind direction (Figure 6.4).

Winds are named for the direction *from which they originate*. For example, a wind from the west is a *westerly* wind (it blows eastward); a wind out of the south is a *southerly* wind (it blows northward). Figure 6.5 illustrates a simple wind compass, naming 16 principal wind directions used by meteorologists.

The traditional *Beaufort wind scale* is a descriptive scale useful in visually estimating wind speed (Table 6.1). Admiral Beaufort of the British Navy introduced his wind scale in 1806. In 1926, G. C. Simpson expanded Beaufort's scale to include wind speeds on land. The National Weather Service (old Weather Bureau) standardized the scale in 1955 (see **http://www.hpc.ncep.noaa.gov/html/ beaufort.shtml**). The scale is still referenced on ocean

charts, enabling estimation of wind speed without instruments. Although most ships use sophisticated equipment to perform such measurements, you find the Beaufort scale posted on the bridge of many ships.

Using no instruments, try the Beaufort scale in Table 6.1 to estimate wind speed as you walk across campus today. Then, moisten your finger, hold it in the air, and sense evaporative cooling on one side of your finger to indicate from which direction the wind is blowing.

Global Winds

The primary circulation of winds across Earth has fascinated travelers, sailors, and scientists for centuries, although only in the modern era is a true picture emerging of global winds. Breakthroughs in space-based observations and Earth-bound computer technology are refining models that simulate total atmospheric and oceanic circulation.

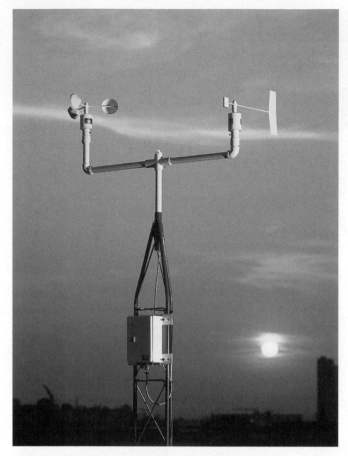

FIGURE 6.4 Wind vane and anemometer.
Instruments used to measure wind direction (wind vane, right) and wind speed (anemometer, left) at a weather station installation. [Photo by Belfort Instruments.]

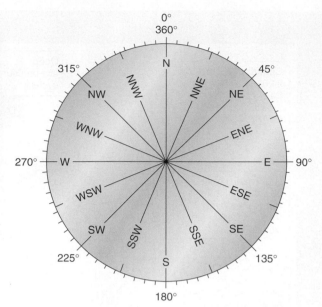

FIGURE 6.5 A wind compass.
Sixteen wind directions identified on a wind compass. Winds are named for the direction from which they originate. For example, a wind from the west is a westerly wind.

Scientists at the Jet Propulsion Laboratory and the University of California, Los Angeles, painstakingly assembled a remarkable portrait of surface winds across the Pacific Ocean (Figure 6.6). The *Seasat* satellite produced the image using radar to measure the motion and direction of ocean waves. Because wind drives waves on the ocean surface, wave patterns indicate winds.

The patterns in the figure are the result of specific forces at work in the atmosphere: *pressure gradient force, Coriolis force, friction force,* and *gravity.* These forces are our next topic. As we progress through this chapter, you may want to refer to this *Seasat* image to identify the winds, eddies, and vortexes it portrays.

Driving Forces Within the Atmosphere

Four forces determine both speed and direction of winds:

- Earth's *gravitational force* on the atmosphere is virtually uniform. Gravity equally compresses the atmosphere worldwide, with the density decreasing as altitude increases. The gravitational force counteracts the outward *centrifugal force* acting on Earth's spinning surface and atmosphere. Without gravity,

there would be no atmospheric pressure—or atmosphere, for that matter.

- **Pressure gradient force** drives air from areas of higher barometric pressure (more dense air) to areas of lower barometric pressure (less dense air), thereby causing winds. Without a pressure gradient force, there would be no wind.

- The **Coriolis force**, a deflective force, makes wind that travels in a straight path appear to be deflected in relation to Earth's rotating surface. The Coriolis force deflects wind to the right in the Northern Hemisphere and to the left in the Southern Hemisphere. Without Coriolis force, winds would move along straight paths between high- and low-pressure areas.

- The **friction force** drags on the wind as it moves across surfaces; it decreases with height above the surface. Without friction, winds would simply move in paths parallel to isobars and at high rates of speed.

All four of these forces operate on moving air and ocean currents at Earth's surface and influence global wind circulation patterns. The following sections describe the actions of the pressure gradient, Coriolis, and friction forces. (The gravitational force operates uniformly worldwide.)

Pressure Gradient Force

High- and low-pressure areas exist in the atmosphere principally because Earth's surface is unequally heated. For example, cold, dense air at the poles exerts greater pressure than warm, less dense air along the equator. These pressure differences establish a *pressure gradient force.*

An **isobar** is an *isoline* (a line along which there is a constant value) plotted on a weather map to connect

Table 6.1 Beaufort Wind Scale

Wind Speed			Beaufort Wind Scale			
kmph	mph	knots	Beaufort Number	Wind Description	Observed Effects at Sea	Observed Effects on Land
< 1	< 1	< 1	**0**	Calm	Glassy calm, like a mirror	Calm, no movement of leaves
1–5	1–3	1–3	**1**	Light Air	Small ripples; wavelet scales; no foam on crests	Slight leaf movement; smoke drifts; wind vanes still
6–11	4–7	4–6	**2**	Light breeze	Small wavelets; glassy look to crests, which do not break	Leaves rustling; wind felt; wind vanes moving
12–19	8–12	7–10	**3**	Gentle breeze	Large wavelets; dispersed whitecaps as crests break	Leaves and twigs in motion; small flags and banners extended
20–29	13–18	11–16	**4**	Moderate breeze	Small, longer waves; numerous whitecaps	Small branches moving; raising dust, paper, litter, and dry leaves
30–38	19–24	17–21	**5**	Fresh breeze	Moderate, pronounced waves; many whitecaps; some spray	Small trees and branches swaying; wavelets forming on inland waterways
39–49	25–31	22–27	**6**	Strong breeze	Large waves, white foam crests everywhere; some spray	Large branches swaying; overhead wires whistling; difficult to control an umbrella
50–61	32–38	28–33	**7**	Moderate (near) gale	Sea mounding up; foam and sea spray blown in streaks in the direction of the wind	Entire trees moving; difficult to walk into wind
62–74	39–46	34–40	**8**	Fresh gale (or gale)	Moderately high waves of greater length; breaking crests forming sea spray; well-marked foam streaks	Small branches breaking; difficult to walk; moving automobiles drifting and veering
75–87	47–54	41–47	**9**	Strong gale	High waves; wave crests tumbling and the sea beginning to roll; visibility reduced by blowing spray	Roof shingles blown away; slight damage to structures; broken branches littering the ground
88–101	55–63	48–55	**10**	Whole gale (or storm)	Very high waves and heavy, rolling seas; white appearance to foam-covered sea; overhanging waves; visibility reduced	Uprooted and broken trees; structural damage; considerable destruction; seldom occurring
102–116	64–73	56–63	**11**	Storm (or violent storm)	White foam covering a breaking sea of exceptionally high waves; small- and medium-sized ships lost from view in wave troughs; wave crests frothy	Widespread damage to structures and trees, a rare occurrence
> 117	> 74	> 64	**12–17**	Hurricane	Driving foam and spray filling the air; white sea; visibility poor to nonexistent	Severe to catastrophic damage; devastation to affected society

points of equal pressure. A pattern of isobars on a weather map provides a portrait of the pressure gradient between an area of higher pressure and one of lower pressure. The spacing between isobars indicates the intensity of the pressure difference, or *pressure gradient*.

Just as closer contour lines on a topographic map indicate a steeper slope on land, so closer isobars denote steepness in the atmosphere pressure gradient. In Figure 6.7a, note the spacing of the isobars (green lines). A steep gradient causes faster air movement from a high-pressure area to a

WIND SPEED, M/S

JPL   0 2 4 6 8 10 12 14 16 18 20   Ucla

(a)

(b)

FIGURE 6.6 Wind portrait of the Pacific Ocean.
(a) Surface wind measured by radar scatterometer aboard the *Seasat* satellite on a September day. Scientists analyzed 150,000 measurements for this image. Colours correlate with wind speeds, and the white arrows denote wind direction. Compare the wind patterns with a visible-light image of the same region (b). Can you identify the pattern of trade winds, westerlies, high-pressure cells, and low-pressure cells from the cloud patterns on the image? [(a) Courtesy of Dr. Peter Woiceshyn, Jet Propulsion Laboratory, Pasadena, California. (b) Satellite image from Laboratory of Planetary Studies, Cornell University. Used by permission.]

low-pressure area. Isobars spaced wider apart from one another mark a more gradual pressure gradient, one that creates a slower airflow. Along a horizontal surface, the pressure gradient force alone acts at right angles to the isobars, so wind blows across isobars at right angles. Note the location of steep ("strong winds") and gradual ("light winds") pressure gradients and their relationship to wind intensity on the map in Figure 6.7b.

Figure 6.8 illustrates the forces that direct winds. Figure 6.8a shows the pressure gradient force acting alone. A field of subsiding, or sinking, air develops in a high-pressure area. Air descends in a high-pressure area and diverges outward at the surface in all directions. In contrast, in a low-pressure area, as air rises, it pulls air from all directions, converging into the area of lower pressure at the surface.

Coriolis Force

You might expect surface winds to move in a straight line from areas of higher pressure to areas of lower pressure. On a nonrotating Earth, they would. But on our rotating planet, the Coriolis force deflects anything that flies or flows across Earth's surface—wind, an airplane, or ocean currents—from a straight path. In simplest terms, this force is an effect of Earth's rotation. Earth's rotational speed varies with latitude, increasing from 0 kmph at the poles (surface is at Earth's axis) to 1675 kmph (1041 mph) at the equator (surface is farthest from Earth's axis). Table 2.2 lists rotational speeds by latitude.

The deflection occurs regardless of the direction in which the object is moving. Because Earth rotates eastward, objects that move in an absolute straight line over a

(a)

(b)

FIGURE 6.7 Pressure gradient determines wind speed.
Pressure gradient (a), portrayed on a weather map (b). The closer spacing of isobars represents a steeper pressure gradient producing stronger winds; wider spacing of isobars denotes a gradual pressure gradient for lighter winds. Here we see surface winds spiraling clockwise out of a high-pressure system and spiraling counterclockwise into a low-pressure system.

distance (such as winds and ocean currents) appear to curve to the right in the Northern Hemisphere and to the left in the Southern Hemisphere (Figure 6.9a). The Coriolis force is zero along the equator, increases to half the maximum deflection at 30° N and 30° S latitudes, and reaches maximum deflection flowing away from the poles. The effect of the Coriolis force increases as the speed of the moving object increases; thus, the faster the wind speed, the greater its apparent deflection. The Coriolis force does not normally affect small-scale motions that cover insignificant distance and time (see News Report 6.1).

We work through a simple explanation here focused on the observed phenomena. If you choose you can use physics and identify the variables that interplay to produce

these observed results. Mathematical formulas explain how the conservation of angular and linear momentum, as our distance to Earth's axis changes with latitudinal location, operates to produce the deflection, as well as the interplay of the opposing gravitational and centrifugal forces.

With this in mind, we observe the Coriolis force from different viewpoints. From the viewpoint of an airplane that is passing over Earth's surface, the surface is seen to rotate slowly below. But, looking from the surface at the airplane, the surface seems stationary, and the airplane appears to curve off course. The airplane does not actually deviate from a straight path, but it *appears* to do so because we are standing on Earth's rotating surface beneath the airplane. Because of this apparent deflection, the airplane

Top view and side view of air movement in an idealized high-pressure area and low-pressure area on a nonrotating Earth.

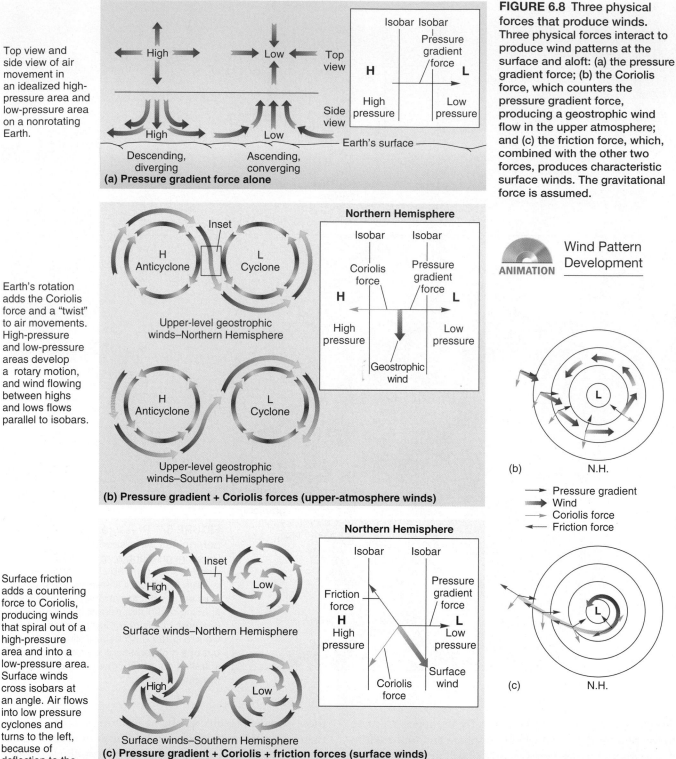

(a) Pressure gradient force alone

Earth's rotation adds the Coriolis force and a "twist" to air movements. High-pressure and low-pressure areas develop a rotary motion, and wind flowing between highs and lows flows parallel to isobars.

(b) Pressure gradient + Coriolis forces (upper-atmosphere winds)

Surface friction adds a countering force to Coriolis, producing winds that spiral out of a high-pressure area and into a low-pressure area. Surface winds cross isobars at an angle. Air flows into low pressure cyclones and turns to the left, because of deflection to the right.

(c) Pressure gradient + Coriolis + friction forces (surface winds)

ANIMATION Wind Pattern Development

FIGURE 6.8 Three physical forces that produce winds. Three physical forces interact to produce wind patterns at the surface and aloft: (a) the pressure gradient force; (b) the Coriolis force, which counters the pressure gradient force, producing a geostrophic wind flow in the upper atmosphere; and (c) the friction force, which, combined with the other two forces, produces characteristic surface winds. The gravitational force is assumed.

must make constant corrections in flight path to maintain its "straight" heading relative to a rotating Earth.

As an example of the effect of this force, see Figure 6.9b. A pilot leaves the North Pole and flies due south toward Quito, Ecuador. If Earth were not rotating, the aircraft would simply travel along a meridian of longitude and arrive at Quito. But Earth is rotating eastward beneath the aircraft's flight path. If the pilot does not allow for this increase in rotational speed, the plane will reach the equator over the ocean along an apparently curved path, far to the west of the intended destination. Likewise flying northward on a return flight, the plane maintains its eastward speed as it makes its way northward over slower rotational speeds of Earth. Without correction, the plane ends up to the east of the pole, in a right-hand deflection. Pilots must correct for this Coriolis deflection in their navigational calculations.

Coriolis Force

FIGURE 6.9 The Coriolis force—an apparent deflection.
Distribution of the Coriolis force on Earth: (a) apparent deflection to the right of a straight line in the Northern Hemisphere and apparent deflection to the left in the Southern Hemisphere; (b) Coriolis deflection of a flight path between the North Pole and Quito, Ecuador, which is on the equator; (c) deflection of a flight path between Vancouver and Gander. Deflection from a straight path occurs regardless of the direction of movement.

News Report 6.1

Coriolis, a Forceful Effect on Drains?

A common misconception about the Coriolis force is that it affects water draining out of a sink, tub, or toilet. Can the Coriolis force cause this twist? When a ship crosses the equator, does the direction of a draining spiral of water in a sink or toilet suddenly reverse?

Moving water or air must cover some distance across space and time before the Coriolis force noticeably deflects it. Long-range artillery shells and guided missiles do exhibit small amounts of deflection that must be corrected for accuracy. But water movements down a drain are too small in spatial extent to be noticeably affected by this force.

Note that we call Coriolis a *force*. This label is appropriate because, as the physicist Sir Isaac Newton (1643–1727) stated, when something is accelerating over a space, a force is in operation (mass times acceleration). This *apparent force* (in classical mechanics, an inertial force) acts as an effect on moving objects. It is named for Gaspard Coriolis (1792–1843), a French mathematician and researcher of applied mechanics, who first described the force in 1831. For deeper insight into the physics of this phenomenon, consider a detailed analysis by Anders Persson, "How do we understand the Coriolis force?" in the *Bulletin of the American Meteorological Society* 79, no. 7 (July 1998): 1373–85.

This effect occurs regardless of the direction of the moving object. A flight from Vancouver to Gander is shown in Figure 6.9c. The Coriolis deflection occurs because, as the airplane flies to Gander, Earth continues to rotate eastward, so the destination moves farther to the east. The pilot must correct for Earth's rotational motion to end up in Gander, and not farther to the south.

Coriolis Force and Winds How does the Coriolis force affect wind? As air rises from the surface through the lowest levels of the atmosphere, it leaves the drag of surface friction behind and increases speed. This increases the Coriolis force, spiraling the winds to the right in the Northern Hemisphere or to the left in the Southern Hemisphere, generally producing upper-air westerly winds from the subtropics to the poles. In the upper troposphere, the Coriolis force just balances the pressure gradient force. Consequently, the winds between higher-pressure and lower-pressure areas in the upper troposphere flow parallel to the isobars.

Figure 6.8b illustrates the combined effect of the pressure gradient force and the Coriolis force on air currents aloft. Together, they produce winds that do not flow directly from high to low, but *around* the pressure areas, remaining parallel to the isobars. Such winds are called **geostrophic winds** and are characteristic of upper tropospheric circulation. (The suffix *-strophic* means "to turn.") Geostrophic winds produce the characteristic pattern shown on the upper-air weather map just ahead in Figure 6.15. Note the inset illustration showing the effects of the pressure gradient and Coriolis forces that produce a geostrophic flow of air.

Friction Force

Figure 6.8c adds the effect of friction to the Coriolis and pressure gradient forces on wind movements; combining all three forces produces the wind patterns we see along Earth's surface. The effect of surface friction extends to a height of about 500 m (around 1600 ft) and varies with surface texture, wind speed, time of day and year, and atmospheric conditions. In general, rougher surfaces produce more friction.

Near the surface, friction disrupts the equilibrium established in geostrophic wind flows between the pressure gradient and Coriolis forces—note the inset illustration in Figure 6.8c. Because surface friction decreases wind speed, it reduces the effect of the Coriolis force and causes winds to move across isobars at an angle. The reason the balance of forces causes the winds to curve to the left into low-pressure cyclones as they are deflected to the right is shown.

In Figure 6.8c, you can see that the Northern Hemisphere winds spiral out from a high-pressure area *clockwise* to form an **anticyclone** and spiral into a low-pressure area *counterclockwise* to form a **cyclone**. (In the Southern Hemisphere these circulation patterns are reversed, flowing out of anticyclonic high-pressure cells counterclockwise and into cyclonic low-pressure cells clockwise.)

Atmospheric Patterns of Motion

With these forces and motions in mind, we are ready to build a general model of total atmospheric circulation. The warmer, less-dense air along the equator rises, creating low pressure at the surface, and the colder, denser air at the poles sinks, creating high pressure. If Earth did not rotate, the result would be a simple wind flow from the poles to the equator, a meridional flow caused solely by pressure gradient.

However, Earth does rotate, creating a more complex flow system. On a rotating Earth the poles-to-equator flow is predominantly zonal (latitudinal), both at the surface and aloft. Winds are westerly (eastward-moving) in the middle and high latitudes and easterly (westward-moving) in the low latitudes toward the equator in both hemispheres. Earth's global circulation system transfers thermal energy, air, and water masses from equatorial energy surpluses to polar energy deficits, using waves, streams, and eddies on a planetary scale.

Primary High-Pressure and Low-Pressure Areas

The following discussion of Earth's pressure and wind patterns refers often to Figure 6.10, isobaric maps showing average surface barometric pressure in January and July. Indirectly, these maps indicate prevailing surface winds, which are suggested by the isobars.

The primary high- and low-pressure areas of Earth's general circulation appear on these maps as cells or uneven belts of similar pressure that stretch across the face of the planet, interrupted by landmasses. Between these areas flow the primary winds, noted in adventure stories and hero myths throughout human history.

Secondary highs and lows, from a few hundred to a few thousand kilometres in diameter and hundreds to thousands of metres high, form within these primary pressure areas. The secondary systems seasonally migrate to produce changing weather patterns in the regions over which they pass.

Four broad pressure areas cover the Northern Hemisphere and a similar set exists in the Southern Hemisphere. In each hemisphere, two of the pressure areas are stimulated by thermal (temperature) factors. These are the **equatorial low-pressure trough** (marked by the ITCZ line on the maps) and the weak **polar high-pressure cells** at the North and South Poles (not shown, as the maps are cut off at 80° N and 80° S). The other two pressure areas are formed by dynamic (mechanical) factors: the **subtropical high-pressure cells** (H) and **subpolar low-pressure cells** (L). Table 6.2 summarizes the characteristics of these pressure areas. We now examine each principal pressure region.

Equatorial Low-Pressure Trough—ITCZ: Clouds and Rain Constant high Sun altitude and consistent daylength (12 hours a day, year-round) make large amounts of energy available in this region throughout the year. The warming creates lighter, less-dense, ascending

(a)

(b)

FIGURE 6.10 Global barometric pressures for January and July.
Maps portray average surface barometric pressure (millibars) for (a) January and (b) July. The dashed line marks the general location of the intertropical convergence zone (ITCZ). Compare specific regions for January and July—for instance, the North Pacific, the North Atlantic, and the central Asian landmass. [Adapted and redrawn from National Climatic Data Center, *Monthly Climatic Data for the World*, vol. 46, no. 1 (1993 January and July issues). Prepared in cooperation with the World Meteorological Organization and NOAA.]

ANIMATION

Global Patterns of Pressure

SATELLITE

Global Sea-Level Pressure

Table 6.2 Four Hemispheric Pressure Areas

Name	Cause	Location	Air Temperature/Moisture
Polar high-pressure cells	Thermal	90° N 90° S	Cold/dry
Subpolar low-pressure cells	Dynamic	60° N 60° S	Cool/wet
Subtropical high-pressure cells	Dynamic	20° to 35° N and S	Hot/dry
Equatorial low-pressure trough	Thermal	10° N to 10° S	Warm/wet

air, with surface winds converging along the entire extent of the low-pressure trough. This converging air is extremely moist and full of latent heat energy. As it rises, the air expands and cools, producing condensation; consequently, rainfall is heavy throughout this zone. Vertical cloud columns frequently reach the tropopause, in thunderous strength and intensity.

The combination of heating and convergence forces air aloft and forms the **intertropical convergence zone (ITCZ)**. The ITCZ is identified by bands of clouds associated with the convergence of winds along the equator and is noted on the January and July pressure maps (see Figure 6.10; the maps show the ITCZ as a dashed line). In January, the zone crosses northern Australia and dips southward in eastern Africa and South America. By July, the zone shifts northward into Pakistan and southern Asia. Note, using precipitation patterns, this ITCZ location on the satellite image in Figure 6.11. You can also easily identify the ITCZ cloudiness on the GOES image in Figure 1.26.

Figure 6.11 shows the equatorial low-pressure trough of the ITCZ and associated precipitation. A broken band of precipitation accumulation (30 days ending 26 July 2007) reveals this low-pressure system and its position slightly north of the equator in July. The equatorial low-pressure trough is an elongated, undulating narrow band of low pressure (converging, ascending airflow), cloudiness, and precipitation, which nearly encircles the planet.

Figure 6.12 shows two views of Earth's general circulation. The winds converging on the equatorial low-pressure

trough are known generally as the **trade winds**, or *trades*. *Northeast trade winds* blow in the Northern Hemisphere, and *southeast trade winds* in the Southern Hemisphere. These are labeled in Figure 6.12a. The trade winds were named during the era of sailing ships that carried trade across the seas.

The trade winds pick up large quantities of moisture as they return through the Hadley circulation cell for another cycle of uplift and condensation (shown in cross section in Figure 6.12b). These *Hadley cells* in each hemisphere, named for the eighteenth-century English scientist who described the trade winds, denote the circuit completed by winds rising along the ITCZ. Air moves northward and southward into the subtropics, descending to the surface and returning to the ITCZ as the trade winds. During the year in each hemisphere, this circulation pattern appears most vertically symmetrical near the equinoxes.

Within the ITCZ, winds are calm or mildly variable because of the even pressure gradient and the vertical ascent of air. These equatorial calms are the *doldrums*, a name formed from an older English word meaning "foolish," because of the difficulty sailing ships encountered when attempting to move through this zone. The rising air from the equatorial low-pressure area spirals upward into a geostrophic flow to the north and south. These upper-air winds turn eastward, flowing from west to east, beginning at about 20° N and 20° S, and form descending masses of air and high-pressure systems in the subtropical latitudes.

26 JUL 2007 Average Rainfall For Last 30 Days (mm/d) 0 5 10 15 20

FIGURE 6.11 July precipitation accumulation portrays equatorial and subtropical circulation patterns.
An interrupted band of average precipitation in millimetres per day for 30 days (June 27–July 26, 2007) along the intertropical convergence zone (ITCZ). Compare the pattern to the location of the ITCZ in Figure 6.10b for July. Note to the north and south of the ITCZ in the subtropics several high-pressure systems and clear skies (lacking colouration). [Image from *TRMM* Microwave Imager on several geosynchronous satellites, courtesy of GSFC/NASA.]

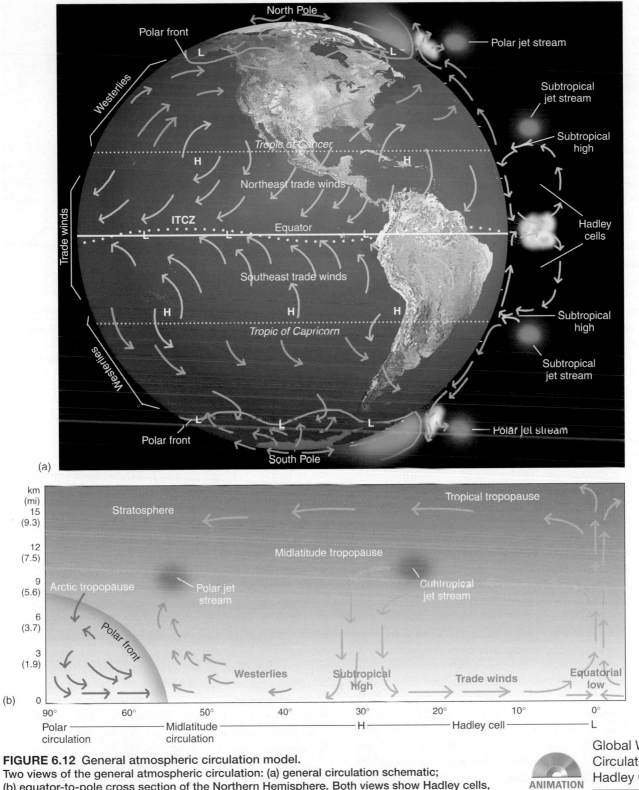

FIGURE 6.12 General atmospheric circulation model.
Two views of the general atmospheric circulation: (a) general circulation schematic; (b) equator-to-pole cross section of the Northern Hemisphere. Both views show Hadley cells, subtropical highs, the polar front, the subpolar low-pressure cells, and approximate locations of the subtropical and polar jet streams.

ANIMATION — Global Wind Circulation, Hadley Cells

SATELLITE — Global Infrared

Subtropical High-Pressure Cells: Hot, Dry, Desert Air   Between 20° and 35° latitude in both hemispheres, a broad high-pressure zone of hot, dry air is evident across the globe (see Figures 6.10 and 6.12). Clear, frequently cloudless skies over the Sahara and the Arabian Desert and portions of the Indian Ocean dominate these regions.

Can you identify these desert regions on the *TRMM* satellite image in Figure 6.11? How about on the photo of Earth on the text's back cover?

The dynamic cause of these subtropical anticyclones is too complex to detail here, but they generally form as air above the subtropics is mechanically pushed downward and heats by compression on its descent to the surface, as Figure 6.12 shows. Warmer air has a greater capacity to absorb evaporation than does cooler air, making this descending warm air relatively dry (large water-vapour capacity, low water-vapour content). The air is also dry because heavy precipitation along the equatorial portion of the circulation removes moisture.

Surface air diverging from the subtropical high-pressure cells generates Earth's principal surface winds: the westerlies and the trade winds. The **westerlies** are the dominant surface winds from the subtropics to high latitudes. They diminish somewhat in summer and are stronger in winter in both hemispheres.

As you examine the global pressure maps in Figure 6.10, you find several high-pressure areas. In the Northern Hemisphere, the Atlantic subtropical high-pressure cell is the **Bermuda high** (in the western Atlantic) or the **Azores high** (when it migrates to the eastern Atlantic in winter). The area in the Atlantic under this subtropical high features clear, warm waters and large quantities of *Sargassum* (a seaweed) that give the area its name—the Sargasso Sea. The **Pacific high**, or *Hawaiian high*, dominates the Pacific in July, retreating southward in January. In the Southern Hemisphere, three large high-pressure centres dominate the Pacific, Atlantic, and Indian oceans, especially in January, and tend to move along parallels of latitude in shifting zonal positions.

The entire high-pressure system migrates with the summer high Sun, fluctuating about 5°–10° in latitude. The *eastern sides* (right-hand side) of these anticyclonic systems are drier and more stable (less convective activity) and feature cooler ocean currents than do the *western sides* (left-hand side). The drier eastern side of these systems and dry-summer conditions influence climate along subtropical and midlatitude west coasts (Figure 6.13). In fact, Earth's major deserts generally occur within the subtropical belt and extend to the west coast of each continent except Antarctica. In Figures 6.13 and 6.21, note the desert regions of Africa come right to the shore in both hemispheres, with the cool, southward-flowing *Canaries Current* offshore in the north, and the cool, northward-flowing *Benguela* current offshore in the south.

Because the subtropical belts are near 25° N and 25° S latitudes, these areas sometimes are known as the *calms of Cancer* and the *calms of Capricorn*. These zones of windless, hot, dry desert air, so deadly in the era of sailing ships, earned the name *horse latitudes*. The origin of this term is popularly attributed to becalmed and stranded sailing crews of past centuries, who destroyed the horses on board, not wanting to share food or water with the livestock. The term's true origin may never be known; the *Oxford English Dictionary* calls it "uncertain."

Subpolar Low-Pressure Cells: Cool and Moist Air
In January, two low-pressure cyclonic cells exist over the oceans around 60° N latitude, near their namesakes: the North Pacific **Aleutian low** and the North Atlantic **Icelandic low** (see Figure 6.10a). Both cells are dominant in winter and weaken or disappear in summer with the

FIGURE 6.13 Subtropical high-pressure system in the Atlantic.
Characteristic circulation and climate conditions related to the Atlantic subtropical high-pressure anticyclone in the Northern Hemisphere. Note deserts extending to the shores of Africa with offshore cool currents, whereas the southeastern United States is moist and humid, with offshore warm currents.

strengthening of high-pressure systems in the subtropics. The area of contrast between cold (from higher latitudes) and warm (from lower latitudes) air forms the **polar front**, where masses of air with different characteristics battle. This front encircles Earth and is focused in these low-pressure areas.

Figure 6.12 illustrates this confrontation between warm, moist air from the westerlies and cold, dry air from the polar and Arctic regions. Cooling and condensation in the lifted air occurs because of upward displacement of the warm air. Low-pressure cyclonic storms migrate out of the Aleutian and Icelandic frontal areas and may produce precipitation in North America and Europe, respectively. Northwestern sections of North America and Europe generally are cool and moist as a result of the passage of these cyclonic systems onshore—consider the weather in British Columbia, Washington, Oregon, Ireland, and the United Kingdom.

In the Southern Hemisphere, a discontinuous belt of subpolar low-pressure systems surrounds Antarctica. The spiraling cloud patterns produced by these cyclonic systems are visible on the spacecraft image in Figure 6.14. Severe cyclonic storms can cross Antarctica, producing strong winds and new snowfall. How many cyclonic systems can you identify around Antarctica on the image?

Polar High-Pressure Cells: Frigid, Dry Deserts
Polar high-pressure cells are weak. The polar atmospheric mass is small, receiving little energy from the Sun to put it into motion. Variable winds, cold and dry, move away

FIGURE 6.14 Clouds portray subpolar and polar circulation patterns.
Centred on Antarctica, this image shows a series of subpolar low-pressure cyclones in the Southern Hemisphere. Antarctica is fully illuminated by a midsummer Sun as the continent approaches the December solstice. The *Galileo* spacecraft made this image during its December 1990 flyby of Earth. [The Solid State Imaging instrument (violet, green, and red filters) image courtesy of Dr. W. Reid Thompson, Laboratory of Planetary Studies, Cornell University. Used by permission.]

from the polar region in an anticyclonic direction. They descend and diverge clockwise in the Northern Hemisphere (counterclockwise in the Southern Hemisphere) and form weak, variable winds named **polar easterlies**.

Of the two polar regions, the **Antarctic high** is stronger and more persistent, forming over the Antarctic landmass. Over the Arctic Ocean, a polar high-pressure cell is less pronounced. When it does form, it tends to locate over the colder northern continental areas in winter (Canadian and Siberian highs) rather than directly over the relatively warmer Arctic Ocean.

Upper Atmospheric Circulation

Circulation in the middle and upper troposphere is an important component of the atmosphere's general circulation. Just as sea level is a reference datum for evaluating air pressure at the surface, we use a pressure level such as 500 mb as a **constant isobaric surface** for a pressure-reference datum in the upper atmosphere.

On upper-air pressure maps, we plot the height above sea level at which an air pressure of 500 mb occurs. The isobaric chart and illustration for an April day in Figures 6.15a and b illustrate such an undulating isobaric surface, upon which all points have the same pressure. In contrast, on surface weather maps we plot different pressures at the fixed elevation of sea level—a *constant height surface.*

We use this 500-mb level to analyze upper-air winds and the possible support they provide for surface weather conditions. Similar to surface maps, closer spacing of the isobars indicates faster winds; wider spacing indicates slower winds. On this constant isobaric pressure surface, altitude variations from the reference datum are called *ridges* for high pressure (with isobars on the map bending poleward) and *troughs* for low pressure (with isobars on the map bending equatorward). Looking at the figure, can you identify such ridges and troughs in the isobaric surface?

The pattern of ridges and troughs in the upper-air wind flow is important in sustaining surface cyclonic (low-pressure) and anticylonic (high-pressure) circulation. Near ridges in the isobaric surface, winds slow and converge (pile up), whereas winds near the area of maximum wind speeds along the troughs in the isobaric surface accelerate and diverge (spread out). Note the wind-speed indicators and labels in Figure 6.15a near the ridge (over Alberta, Saskatchewan, Montana, and Wyoming); now compare these with the wind-speed indicators around the trough (over Kentucky, West Virginia, the New England states, and the Maritimes). Also, note the wind relationships off the Pacific Coast.

Now look at Figure 6.15c. Divergence in the upper-air flow is important to cyclonic circulation at the surface because it creates an outflow of air aloft that stimulates an inflow of air into the low-pressure cyclone (such as what happens when you open a chimney damper to create an upward draft). Convergence aloft, on the other hand, drives descending airflows and divergent winds at the surface, moving out from high-pressure anticyclones.

Rossby Waves   Within the westerly flow of geostrophic winds are great waving undulations called **Rossby waves**, named for meteorologist Carl G. Rossby, who first described them mathematically in 1938. The polar front is the line of conflict between colder air to the north and warmer air to the south (Figure 6.16a). Rossby waves bring tongues of cold air southward, with warmer tropical air moving northward.

The development of Rossby waves in the upper-air circulation is shown in the three-part figure. As these disturbances mature, distinct cyclonic circulation forms, with warmer air and colder air mixing along distinct fronts. These wave-and-eddy formations and upper-air divergence support cyclonic storm systems at the surface. Rossby waves develop along the flow axis of a jet stream.

Jet Streams   The most prominent movement in these upper-level westerly wind flows is the **jet stream**, an irregular, concentrated band of wind occurring at several different locations that influences surface weather systems. (Figure 6.12a shows the location of four jet streams.) Rather flattened in vertical cross section, the jet streams normally are 160–480 km (100–300 mi) wide by 900–2150 m (3000–7000 ft) thick, with core speeds that can exceed 300 kmph (190 mph). Jet streams in each hemisphere tend to weaken during the hemisphere's

Wind Speed Symbol	Miles (statute) per Hour	Knots
◎	Calm	Calm
—	1–2	1–2
	3–8	3–7
	9–14	8–12
	15–20	13–17
	21–25	18–22
	26–31	23–27
	32–37	28–32
	38–43	33–37
	44–49	38–42
	50–54	43–47
	55–60	48–52
	61–66	53–57
	67–71	58–62
	72–77	63–67
	78–83	68–72
	84–89	73–77
	119–123	103–107

Cyclones and Anticyclones

ANIMATION

FIGURE 6.15 Analysis of a constant isobaric surface for an April day.
(a) Contours show elevation (in feet) at which 500-mb pressure occurs—a constant isobaric surface. The pattern of contours reveals a 500-mb isobaric surface and geostrophic wind patterns in the troposphere ranging from 16,500 to 19,100 ft elevation. (b) Note the "ridge" of high pressure over the Intermountain West, at 5760 m altitude, and the "trough" of low pressure over the Great Lakes region and off the Pacific Coast, also at 5460 m altitude, on the map and in the sketch beneath the chart. (c) Note areas of convergence aloft (corresponding to surface divergence) and divergence aloft (corresponding to surface convergence)—upper atmosphere conditions at the 500-mb level support surface cyclones and anticyclones. [Data for map in (a) from the National Weather Service, NOAA.]

(a) Upper-air circulation and jet stream begin to gently undulate.

(b) Longwave patterns begin to form Rossby waves.

(c) Strong development of waves produces cells of cold and warm air—high-pressure ridges and low-pressure troughs.

Warm air   Cool air

ANIMATION   Jet Stream, Rossby Waves

FIGURE 6.16 Rossby upper-atmosphere waves. Development of waves in the upper-air circulation, first described by C. G. Rossby in 1938 and expanded by J. Namias in 1952. Note in (b) undulations in Rossby waves are labeled "L" for troughs and "H" for ridges.

summer and strengthen during winter as the streams shift closer to the equator. The pattern of ridges and troughs causes variation in jet stream speeds (convergence and divergence).

The *polar jet stream* meanders between 30° and 70° N latitude, at the tropopause along the polar front, at altitudes between 7600 and 10,700 m (24,900 and 35,100 ft). The polar jet stream can migrate as far south as Texas, steering colder air masses into North America and influencing surface storm paths travelling eastward. In the summer, the polar jet stream exerts less influence on storms by staying over higher latitudes. Figure 6.17

shows a stylized view of a polar jet stream and two jet streams over North America. An experiment in 1998 inadvertently provided confirming information on the flow of the jet stream see News Report 6.2 for details.

In subtropical latitudes, near the boundary between tropical and midlatitude air, the *subtropical jet stream* flows near the tropopause (see Figure 6.12). The subtropical jet stream meanders from 20°–50° latitude and may occur over North America simultaneously with the polar jet stream—sometimes the two will actually merge for brief episodes.

Focus Study 6.1 (continued)

that this assumes a 65% increase in electricity demand by that date. If realized, this would avoid substantial carbon dioxide emissions. *Wind Force 12* is the name of the EWEA plan.

The Benefits of the Wind Resource

Economic reality should override further delaying actions because of the economic benefits from using wind resources, especially where peak winds are in concert with peak electrical demand for air-cooling, space heating, or agricultural water pumping.

In Europe, smaller turbines produce at 4 cents per kWh. Two Stanford University engineers calculated that the contracted price for wind

power of 3 cents/kWh in the United States is cheaper than coal, when considering all costs. Some coal-cost estimates exclude consideration of the health impacts of coal-mine dust, acid deposition, smog, and global warming. (See M. Z. Jacobsen and G. M. Masters, "Exploiting Wind vs. Coal," *Science* 293 (August 24, 2001): 1438. Also see American Wind Energy Association, "Wind Power Outlook," annual publication.)

Long-term costs favor wind-energy deployment. With *all* costs considered, wind energy is cost competitive and actually cheaper than oil, coal, natural gas, and nuclear power. Relative to concerns about wind turbines hurting birds, a survey studied human-caused

bird mortality and found wind turbines are lowest when compared to communication towers, pesticides, high-tension lines, domestic cats, and hitting buildings and windows.

Whether or not governments and transnational energy corporations support full-scale implementation of renewable resources such as wind, the energy realities of the near future will leave no alternative, and global political realities affirm this urgency. By the middle of this century, wind-generated electricity could be routine, along with other renewable energy sources, conservation, and energy efficiency. Germany, Spain, and the European Union are leading the way for now.

Monsoonal Winds

Some regional wind systems seasonally change direction. Intense, seasonally shifting wind systems occur in the tropics over Southeast Asia, Indonesia, India, northern Australia, and equatorial Africa. A milder version of such monsoonal-type flow affects the extreme southwestern United States. These winds involve an annual cycle of returning precipitation with the summer Sun. The Arabic word for season, *mausim*, or **monsoon**, names them. (Specific monsoonal weather, associated climate types, and vegetation regions are discussed in Chapters 8, 10, and 20.) The location and size of the Asian landmass and its proximity to the Indian Ocean drive the monsoons of southern and eastern Asia (Figure 6.20). Also important to the generation of monsoonal flows are wind and pressure patterns in the upper-air circulation.

The extreme temperature range from summer to winter over the Asian landmass is due to its continentality (isolation from the modifying effects of the ocean). An intense high-pressure anticyclone dominates this continental landmass in winter (see Figures 6.10a and 6.20a), whereas the equatorial low-pressure trough (ITCZ) dominates the central area of the Indian Ocean. This pressure gradient produces cold, dry winds from the Asian interior over the Himalayas and across India. Average temperatures range between 15° and 20°C (60°–68°F) at lower elevations. These winds desiccate, or dry out, the landscape and then give way to hot weather from March through May. The second photo of the GPS unit in News Report 1.4 (Chapter 1) was made 18 m (60 ft) below the summit of Mount Everest on May 20, 1998—the monsoons dictate climbing schedules.

During the June–September wet period, the subsolar point (direct overhead rays of sunlight) shifts northward to the Tropic of Cancer, near the mouths of the Indus and

Ganges rivers. The ITCZ shifts northward over southern Asia, and the Asian continental interior develops a thermal low pressure, associated with high average temperatures (remember the summer warmth in Verkhoyansk, Siberia, from Chapter 5). Meanwhile, subtropical high pressure dominates the Indian Ocean, with a surface temperature of 30°C (86°F). As a result of this reversed pressure gradient, hot subtropical air sweeps over the warm ocean, producing extremely high evaporation rates (Figure 6.20b).

By the time this air mass and the convergence zone reach India, it is laden with moisture in thunderous, dark clouds. When the monsoonal rains arrive from June to September, they are welcome relief from the dust, heat, and parched land of Asia's springtime. Likewise, the annual monsoon is an integral part of Indian music, poetry, and life. World-record rainfalls of the wet monsoon drench India. Cherrapunji, India, received both the second-highest average annual rainfall (1143 cm, or 450 in.) and the highest single-year rainfall (2647 cm, or 1042 in.) on Earth.

The fact that the monsoons of southern Asia involve vast global pressure systems leads us to ask whether future climate change might affect present monsoonal patterns. Researchers are conducting a field experiment in the Indian Ocean, the Indian Ocean Experiment (INDOEX), to examine this question (**http://www-indoex.ucsd.edu/ ProjDescription.html**). Concern increases following events such as July 27, 2005, when a monsoonal deluge drowned Mumbai (Bombay)—in only a few hours, 94.2 cm (37.1 in.) of rain fell, causing widespread flooding. Again in 2007, extensive flooding from an intense monsoon struck across India.

Their model projections forecast higher rainfall if consideration is given to increases in carbon dioxide and

FIGURE 6.20 The Asian monsoons.
Asian monsoon pressure and wind patterns during (a) winter and (b) summer. Note the shifting location of the ITCZ, the changing pressure over the Indian Ocean, and the different conditions over the Asian landmass. The inset climograph for Nagpur shows the severe contrast in seasonal precipitation.
[Adapted from Joseph E. Van Riper, *Man's Physical World*, p. 215. © 1971 by McGraw Hill. Adapted by permission.]

(a) Winter, dry monsoon

(b) Summer, wet monsoon

(c) Precipitation at Nagpur, India

Station: Nagpur, India   **Elevation:** 310 m (1016 ft)
Lat/long: 21° 1′ N 79° 1′ E   **Total ann. precip.:**
124.2 cm (48.9 in.)

its greenhouse warming alone. However, when consideration is given to increases in aerosols—principally sulfur compounds and black carbon—then a drop in precipitation of 7%–14% appears in the model. Air pollution reduces surface heating and therefore decreases the pressure differences at the heart of monsoonal flows. Considering that 70% of the annual precipitation for the entire region comes during the wet monsoon, the actual occurrence of such changes would force difficult societal adjustments to changing water resources. (See the satellite images in Figure 4.8 and review the text discussion.)

Oceanic Currents

The driving force for ocean currents is the frictional drag of the winds, thus linking the atmospheric and oceanic systems. Also important in shaping these currents is the interplay of the Coriolis force, density differences caused by temperature and salinity, the configuration of the continents and ocean floor, and astronomical forces (the tides).

Surface Currents

Figure 6.21 portrays the general patterns of major ocean currents. Because ocean currents flow over distance and through time, the Coriolis force deflects them. However, their pattern of deflection is not as tightly circular as that of the atmosphere. Compare this ocean-current map with the map showing Earth's pressure systems (see Figure 6.10) and you can see that ocean currents are driven by the circulation around subtropical high-pressure cells in both hemispheres. These circulation systems are known as *gyres* and generally appear to be offset toward the western side of each ocean basin. (Remember, in the Northern Hemisphere, winds and ocean currents move *clockwise* about high-pressure cells—note the currents in the North Pacific and North Atlantic on the map—see Figure 6.13. In the Southern Hemisphere, circulation is *counterclockwise* around high-pressure cells, evident on the map.)

In sailing days, the Spanish galleons (the *Manila Galleons*) would leave San Blas and Acapulco, Mexico (16.5° N), and sail southwest, catching the northeast trade winds across the Pacific to the Philippines and Manila (14° N). Goods would be traded and new commodities obtained, and the ships would move northward to catch the westerlies in the midlatitudes to be blown across the ocean to the shores of present-day Alaska or British Columbia and sail along the coast to Northern California. The galleons would sail south, fighting the rain, frequent fog, and the right-hand Coriolis deflection pushing them away from the coast. The journey would end back in Mexico with cargo from the Orient. Thus the

FIGURE 6.21 Major ocean currents. [After the U. S. Navy Hydrographic Office.]

ANIMATION   Ocean Circulation

history of the *Manilla Galleons* is a lesson in oceanic currents around the Pacific gyre. News Report 6.3 dramatically portrays this clockwise circulation around the Pacific Ocean.

Equatorial Currents   In Figure 6.21, you can see that trade winds drive the ocean surface waters westward in a concentrated channel along the equator. These currents, called *equatorial currents*, are kept near the equator by the Coriolis force, which diminishes to zero at the equator. As these surface currents approach the western margins of the oceans, the water actually piles up against the eastern shores of the continents. The average height of this pileup is 15 cm (6 in.). This phenomenon is the **western intensification**.

The piled-up ocean water then goes where it can, spilling northward and southward in strong currents, flowing in tight channels along the eastern shorelines. In the Northern Hemisphere, the *Gulf Stream* and the *Kuroshio* (current east of Japan) move forcefully northward as a result of western intensification. Their speed and depth are increased by the constriction of the area they occupy. The warm, deep, clear water of the ribbon-like Gulf Stream (Figure 5.10) usually is 50–80 km (30–50 mi) wide and 1.5–2.0 km (0.9–1.2 mi) deep, moving at 3–10 kmph (1.8–6.2 mph). In 24 hours, ocean water can move 70–240 km (40–150 mi) in the Gulf Stream.

Upwelling and Downwelling Flows   Where surface water is swept away from a coast, either by surface divergence (induced by the Coriolis force) or by offshore winds, an **upwelling current** occurs. This cool water generally is nutrient-rich and rises from great depths to

replace the vacating water. Such cold upwelling currents exist off the Pacific coasts of North and South America and the subtropical and midlatitude west coast of Africa. These areas are some of Earth's prime fishing regions.

In other regions where there is an accumulation of water—such as the western end of an equatorial current, or the Labrador Sea, or along the margins of Antarctica—the excess water gravitates downward in a **downwelling current**. These are the deep currents that flow vertically and along the ocean floor and travel the full extent of the ocean basins, carrying heat energy and salinity.

Thermohaline Circulation—The Deep Currents

Differences in temperatures and salinity produce density differences important to the flow of deep currents. This is Earth's **thermohaline circulation**, and it is different from wind-driven surface currents. Travelling at slower speeds than surface currents, the thermohaline circulation hauls larger volumes of water. Figure 16.3 illustrates the ocean's physical structure and profiles of temperature, salinity, and dissolved gases; note the temperature and salinity differences with depth on this illustration.

To picture such a deep, salty current, imagine a continuous channel of water beginning with cold-water downwelling in the North Atlantic and along Antarctica, and upwelling in the Indian Ocean and North Pacific (Figure 6.22). Here it warms and then is carried in surface currents back to the North Atlantic. A complete circuit of the current may require 1000 years from downwelling, to deep cold current covering thousands of kilometres, to its reemergence at the surface elsewhere. Even deeper

Labrador Sea   Greenland Sea

→ Warm shallow current
→ Cold and salty deep current
● Cool water subsides to feed deep current

FIGURE 6.22 Deep-ocean thermohaline circulation.
Scientists are deciphering centuries-long deep circulation in the oceans, sluggishly driven by temperature- and salinity-caused density differences. This global circulation is like a vast conveyor belt of water, drawing heat energy from surface warm, shallow currents and transporting it for release in the depths of the ocean basins in deep, cold, salty currents. Four blue areas at high latitudes are where surface water cools, sinks, and feeds the deep circulation.

ANIMATION   Ocean Circulation

Antarctic bottom water flows northward in the Atlantic Basin beneath these currents.

These current systems appear to play a profound role in global climate; in turn, global warming has the potential to disrupt the downwelling in the North Atlantic and the thermohaline circulation. If this sinking of surface waters slowed or stopped, the ocean's ability to redistribute absorbed heat energy would be disrupted and surface accumulation of heat energy would add to the warming already underway. There is a freshening of ocean surface waters in both polar regions, contrasted with large increases in salinity in the surface waters at lower latitudes. Increased rates of glacier, sea-ice, and ice-sheet melting produce these fresh lower-density surface waters that ride on top of the denser saline water. The concern is that such changes in ocean temperature and salinity could dampen the rate of the North Atlantic Deep Water downwelling in the North Atlantic.

This is a vital research frontier because Earth's hydrologic cycle is still little understood. Research groups such as Scripps Institution of Oceanography (http://sio.ucsd.edu/), Woods Hole Oceanographic Institution (http://www.whoi.edu/), Institute for the Study of Earth, Oceans, and Space (http://www.eos.sr.unh.edu/), and Bedford Institute of Oceanography (http://www.bio.gc.ca/ welcome-e.html), to name only a few of many, are places to periodically check for updated information.

News Report 6.3

A Message in a Bottle and Rubber Duckies

To give you an idea of the dynamic circulation of the ocean, consider the following examples. A 9-year-old child at Dana Point, California (33.5° N), a small seaside community south of Los Angeles, placed a letter in a glass juice bottle in July 1992 and tossed it into the waves. Thoughts of distant lands and fabled characters filled the child's imagination as the bottle disappeared. The vast circulation around the Pacific high, clockwise-circulating gyre now took command (Figure 6.3.1).

Three years passed before ocean currents carried the message in a bottle to the coral reefs and white sands of Mogmog, a small island in Micronesia (7° N). A 7-year-old child there had found a pen pal from afar and immediately sent a photo and card to the sender of the message. Imagine the journey of that note from California—travelling through storms and calms, clear moonlit nights and typhoons, as it floated on ancient currents as the galleons once had.

In January 1994, a large container ship from Hong Kong loaded with toys and other goods was ravaged by a powerful storm. One of the containers on board split apart in the wind off the coast of Japan, dumping nearly 30,000 rubber ducks, turtles, and frogs into

FIGURE 6.3.1 Pacific Ocean currents transport human artifacts.
The approximate route of a message in a bottle from Dana Point, California, to Mogmog, Micronesia, assumes a partial circuit around the Pacific gyre. Given the 3-year travel time, we do not know if the message circumnavigated the Pacific Ocean more than once. The rubber duckies voyaged eastward across the Pacific and beyond.

the North Pacific. Westerly winds and the North Pacific current swept this floating cargo at up to 29 km (18 mi) a day across the ocean to the coast of Alaska, Canada, Oregon, and California. Other toys, still adrift, went through the Bering Sea and into the Arctic Ocean (this route is indicated by the dashed line in Figure 6.3.1). Their drifting migration took a decade, but some objects made it around the Arctic Ocean to the Labrador Sea and will end up in the Atlantic Ocean.

The high-floating message bottle and rubber ducks offered a much better opportunity to study winds than did

an earlier spill of 60,000 athletic shoes near Japan. The low-floating shoes tracked across the Pacific Ocean until they landed in the Pacific Northwest. By the way, the shoes that did not make landfall headed (or footed) back around the Pacific gyre into the tropics and westward, back toward Japan! Scientists are using incidents such as the message in a bottle and rubber duckies to learn more about wind systems and ocean currents.

On August 19, 2006, Tropical Storm Ioke formed about 1285 km (800 mi) south of Hawai'i. The storm's track moved across the Pacific

Ocean over Wake Island and Johnston Atoll, becoming the strongest Super Typhoon in recorded history—a category 5, as we discuss in Chapter 8. Turning northward east of Sakhalin Island of Japan and the Kamchatka Peninsula of Russia the storm moved into higher latitudes. Typhoon Ioke eventually swung northeastward and crossed the Aleutian Islands, reaching 55° N as an extratropical depression, dying out September 7. Much coastal erosion resulted in Alaska. The storm roughly followed the path around the Pacific gyre and along the track of the rubber duckies (Figure 6.3.1).

Summary and Review—Atmospheric and Oceanic Circulations

■ *Define* the concept of air pressure, and *describe* instruments used to measure air pressure.

The weight (created by motion, size, and number of molecules) of the atmosphere is **air pressure**, which exerts an average force of approximately 1 kg/cm^2 (14.7 lb/in.^{2}). A **mercury barometer** measures air pressure at the surface (mercury in a tube—closed at one end and open at the other, with the open end placed in a vessel of mercury—that changes level in response to pressure changes) or an **aneroid barometer** (a closed cell, partially evacuated of air, that detects changes in pressure).

air pressure (p. 145)
mercury barometer (p. 145)
aneroid barometer (p. 145)

1. How does air exert pressure? Describe the basic instrument used to measure air pressure. Compare the operation of two different types of instruments discussed.

2. What is normal sea-level pressure in millimetres? Millibars? Inches? Kilopascals?

■ *Define* wind, and *describe* how wind is measured, how wind direction is determined, and how winds are named.

Volcanic eruptions such as those of Tambora in 1815 and Mount Pinatubo in 1991 dramatically demonstrate the power of global winds to disperse aerosols and pollution worldwide in a matter of weeks. Atmospheric circulation facilitates important transfers of energy and mass on Earth, thus maintaining Earth's natural balances. Earth's atmospheric and oceanic circulations represent a vast heat engine powered by the Sun.

Wind is the horizontal movement of air across Earth's surface. Turbulence adds wind updrafts and downdrafts and a vertical component to this definition. Its speed is measured with an **anemometer** (a device with cups that are pushed by the wind) and its direction with a **wind vane** (a flat blade or surface that is directed by the wind). A descriptive scale useful in visually estimating wind speed is the traditional *Beaufort wind scale*.

wind (p. 146)
anemometer (p. 146)
wind vane (p. 147)

3. What is a possible explanation for the beautiful sunrises and sunsets during the summer of 1992 in North America? Relate your answer to global circulation.

4. Explain this statement: "The atmosphere socializes humanity, making all the world a spatially linked society." Illustrate your answer with some examples.

5. Define wind. How is it measured? How is its direction determined?

6. Distinguish among primary, secondary, and tertiary general classifications of global atmospheric circulation.

7. What is the purpose of the Beaufort wind scale? Characterize winds given Beaufort numbers of 4, 8, and 12, and describe specific effects over both water and land.

■ *Explain* the four driving forces within the atmosphere—gravity, pressure gradient force, Coriolis force, and friction force—and *describe* the primary high- and low-pressure areas and principal winds.

Earth's *gravitational force* on the atmosphere operates uniformly worldwide. Winds are driven by the **pressure gradient force** (air moves from areas of high pressure to areas of low pressure), deflected by the **Coriolis force** (an apparent deflection in the path of winds or ocean currents caused by the rotation of Earth and surface distance from Earth's axis as the gravitational force and centrifugal force work in opposition, deflecting objects to the right in the Northern Hemisphere and to the left in the Southern Hemisphere), and dragged by the **friction force** (Earth's varied surfaces exert a drag on wind movements in opposition to the pressure gradient). Maps portray air pressure patterns using the **isobar**—an isoline that connects points of equal pressure. A combination of the pressure gradient and Coriolis forces alone produces **geostrophic winds**, which move parallel to isobars, characteristic of winds above the surface frictional layer.

Winds descend and diverge, spiraling outward to form an **anticyclone** (clockwise in the Northern Hemisphere), and they converge and ascend, spiraling upward to form a **cyclone** (counterclockwise in the Northern Hemisphere). The pattern of high and low pressures on Earth in generalized belts in each hemisphere produces the distribution of specific wind systems. These primary pressure regions are the **equatorial low-pressure trough**, the weak **polar high-pressure cells** (at both the North and South Poles), and the **subtropical high-pressure cells** and **subpolar low-pressure cells**.

All along the equator winds converge into the equatorial low creating the **intertropical convergence zone (ITCZ)**. Air rises along the equator and descends in the subtropics in each hemisphere. The winds returning to the ITCZ from the

northeast in the Northern Hemisphere and from the southeast in the Southern Hemisphere produce the **trade winds**.

Winds flowing out of the subtropics to higher latitudes produce the **westerlies** in either hemisphere. The subtropical high-pressure cells on Earth, generally between 20° and 35° in either hemisphere, are variously named the **Bermuda high**, **Azores high**, and **Pacific high**.

Along the polar front and the series of low-pressure cells, the **Aleutian low** and **Icelandic low** dominate the North Pacific and Atlantic, respectively. This region of contrast between colder air toward the poles and warmer air toward the equator is the **polar front**. The weak and variable **polar easterlies** diverge from the polar high-pressure cells, particularly the **Antarctic high**.

pressure gradient force (p. 148)
Coriolis force (p. 148)
friction force (p. 148)
isobar (p. 148)
geostrophic winds (p. 154)
anticyclone (p. 154)
cyclone (p. 154)
equatorial low-pressure trough (p. 154)
polar high-pressure cells (p. 154)
subtropical high-pressure cells (p. 154)
subpolar low-pressure cells (p. 154)
intertropical convergence zone (ITCZ) (p. 146)
trade winds (p. 146)
westerlies (p. 158)
Bermuda high (p. 158)
Azores high (p. 158)
Pacific high (p. 158)
Aleutian low (p. 158)
Icelandic low (p. 158)
polar front (p. 158)
polar easterlies (p. 159)
Antarctic high (p. 159)

8. What does an isobaric map of surface air pressure portray? Contrast pressures over North America for January and July.

9. Describe the effect of the Coriolis force. Explain how it apparently deflects atmospheric and oceanic circulations.

10. What are geostrophic winds, and where are they encountered in the atmosphere?

11. Describe the horizontal and vertical air motions in a high-pressure anticyclone and in a low-pressure cyclone.

12. Construct a simple diagram of Earth's general circulation; begin by labeling the four principal pressure belts or zones, then add arrows between these pressure systems to denote the three principal wind systems.

13. How is the intertropical convergence zone (ITCZ) related to the equatorial low-pressure trough? How does it appear on a satellite image of accumulated precipitation in Figure 6.11?

14. Characterize the belt of subtropical high pressure on Earth: Name the specific cells. Describe the generation of westerlies and trade winds. Discuss sailing conditions.

15. What is the relation among the Aleutian low, the Icelandic low, and migratory low-pressure cyclonic storms in North America? In Europe?

■ *Describe* upper-air circulation and its support role for surface systems, and *define* the jet streams.

A **constant isobaric surface**, or surface along which the same pressure, such as 500 mb, occurs regardless of altitude, describes air pressure in the middle and upper troposphere. The height of this surface above the ground forms ridges and troughs that support the development of and help sustain surface pressure systems; surface lows are sustained by divergence aloft, and surface highs are sustained by convergence aloft.

Vast, flowing, longwave undulations in these upper-air westerlies form wave motions, the **Rossby waves**. Prominent streams of high-speed westerly winds in the upper-level troposphere are the **jet streams**. Depending on their latitudinal position in either hemisphere, they are termed the *polar jet stream* or the *subtropical jet stream*.

> constant isobaric surface (p. 159)
> Rossby waves (p. 159)
> jet streams (p. 159)

16. What is the relation between wind speed and the spacing of isobars?

17. How is the constant isobaric surface (ridges and troughs) related to surface pressure systems? To divergence aloft and surface lows? To convergence aloft and surface highs?

18. Relate the jet-stream phenomenon to general upper-air circulation. How is the presence of this circulation related to airline schedules from Halifax to Vancouver and the return trip to Halifax?

■ *Overview* several multiyear oscillations of air temperature, air pressure, and circulation in the Arctic, Atlantic, and Pacific oceans.

Several system fluctuations that occur in multiyear or shorter periods are important in the global circulation picture. The most famous of these is the El Niño–Southern Oscillation (ENSO) phenomenon. A north–south fluctuation of atmospheric variability marks the *North Atlantic Oscillation (NAO)* as pressure differences between the Icelandic low and the Azores high in the Atlantic alternate in strength. The *Atlantic Oscillation (AO)* is the variable fluctuation between middle- and high-latitude air mass conditions over the Northern Hemisphere. The AO is associated with the NAO especially in winter, and the two phases of the *AO Index* correlate to the two-phased *NAO Index*.

Across the Pacific Ocean the *Pacific Decadal Oscillation (PDO)* involves variability between two regions of sea-surface temperatures and related air pressure: the northern and tropical western Pacific (region #1) and the area of the eastern tropical Pacific, along the West Coast (region #2). The PDO switches between positive and negative phases in 20- to 30-year cycles.

19. What phases are identified for the AO and NAO indices? What winter weather conditions generally affect the eastern United States during each phase?

20. What is the apparent relation between the PDO and the strength of El Niño events? Between PDO phases and the intensity of drought in the southwestern United States?

■ *Explain* several types of local winds: land and sea breezes, mountain and valley breezes, katabatic winds, and the regional monsoons.

Different heating characteristics of land and water surfaces create **land and sea breezes**. Temperature differences during the day and evening between valleys and mountain summits cause **mountain and valley breezes**. **Katabatic winds**, or gravity drainage winds, are of larger regional scale and are usually stronger than mountain–valley breezes, under certain conditions. An elevated plateau or highland is essential, where layers of air at the surface cool, become denser, and flow downslope.

Intense, seasonally shifting wind systems occur in the tropics over Southeast Asia, Indonesia, India, northern Australia, equatorial Africa, and southern Arizona. These winds involve an annual cycle of returning precipitation with the summer Sun and carry the Arabic word for season, *mausim*, or **monsoon**. The location and size of the Asian landmass and its proximity to the Indian Ocean and the seasonally shifting ITCZ drive the monsoons of southern and eastern Asia.

> Land and sea breezes (p. 164)
> Mountain and valley breezes (p. 165)
> katabatic winds (p. 165)
> monsoon (p. 168)

21. People living along coastlines generally experience variations in winds from day to night. Explain the factors that produce these changing wind patterns.

22. The arrangement of mountains and nearby valleys produces local wind patterns. Explain the day and night winds that might develop.

23. Describe the seasonal pressure patterns that produce the Asian monsoonal wind and precipitation patterns. Contrast January and July conditions.

■ *Discern* the basic pattern of Earth's major surface ocean currents and deep thermohaline circulation.

Ocean currents are primarily caused by the frictional drag of wind and occur worldwide at varying intensities, temperatures, and speeds, both along the surface and at great depths in the oceanic basins. The circulation around subtropical high-pressure cells in both hemispheres is notable on the ocean circulation map—these *gyres* are usually offset toward the western side of each ocean basin.

The trade winds converge along the ITCZ and push enormous quantities of water that pile up along the eastern shore of continents in a process known as the **western intensification**. Where surface water is swept away from a coast, either by surface divergence (induced by the Coriolis force) or by offshore winds, an **upwelling current** occurs. This cool water generally is nutrient-rich and rises from great depths to replace the vacating water. In other portions of the sea where there is an accumulation of water, the excess water gravitates downward in a **downwelling current**. These currents generate important mixing currents that flow along the ocean floor and travel the full extent of the ocean basins, carrying heat energy and salinity.

Differences in temperatures and salinity produce density differences important to the flow of deep, sometimes vertical, currents; this is Earth's **thermohaline circulation**. Travelling at slower speeds than wind-driven surface currents, the thermohaline circulation hauls larger volumes of water. There is scientific concern that increased surface temperatures in the ocean and atmosphere, coupled with climate-related changes in salinity, can alter the rate of thermohaline circulation in the oceans.

> western intensification (p. 170)
> upwelling current (p. 170)
> downwelling current (p. 170)
> thermohaline circulation (p. 170)

24. What is the relationship between global atmospheric circulation and ocean currents? Relate oceanic gyres to patterns of subtropical high pressure.

25. Define the western intensification. How is it related to the Gulf Stream and Kuroshio currents?

26. Where on Earth are upwelling currents experienced? What is the nature of these currents? Where are the four areas of downwelling that feed these dense bottom currents?

27. What is meant by deep-ocean thermohaline circulation? At what rates do these currents flow? How might this circulation be related to the Gulf Stream in the western Atlantic Ocean?

28. Relative to Question 27, what relation do these deep currents have to global warming and possible climate changes?

Critical Thinking

A. Using Table 6.1 and Figure 6.5, on a day with wind, estimate wind speed and wind direction at least twice during the day, and record them in your notebook. If possible, check these against the reports from a local source of weather information. What changes in winds do you notice over several days? How did these changes relate to the weather you experienced?

B. Visit the Canadian Wind Energy Association Web site, http://www.canwea.ca/, and the American Wind Energy Association Web site, http://www.awea.org/. Sample the materials presented as you assess Focus Study 6.1 and the potential for wind-generated electricity. What are your thoughts concerning this resource—its potential, reasons for delays, and the competitive economics presented? What countries are leading the way? Propose a brief action plan for more rapid progress, or for more delays, depending on your point of view.

The Water, Weather, and Climate Systems

CHAPTER 7   Water and Atmospheric Moisture
CHAPTER 8   Weather
CHAPTER 9   Water Resources
CHAPTER 10   Global Climate Systems

PART II

The water, weather, and climate systems stretch to the horizon, across the Arctic Ocean. Distant precipitation makes its way to the surface in grey streaks of moisture. 2007 set a record for the lowest extent of sea ice since the 1970s and the satellite record. The polar regions are the scientific focus of the International Polar Year 2007–2009 that involves topics from throughout *Geosystems*.
[Photo by Bobbé Christopherson.]

Earth is the water planet, a topic at the heart of Part II. Chapter 7 describes the remarkable qualities and properties water possesses, where it occurs, and the way it is distributed. We see the daily dynamics of the atmosphere—the powerful interaction of moisture and energy, the resulting stability and instability, and the variety of cloud forms—as a preamble to understanding weather. Chapter 8 examines weather and its causes. Topics include the interaction of air masses, the daily weather map, and analysis of violent phenomena in thunderstorms, tornadoes, and hurricanes, and the recent trends for each of these.

Chapter 9 explains water circulation on Earth in the hydrologic cycle—an output of the water–weather system. We examine the water-budget concept, which is useful in understanding soil-moisture and water-resource relationships on global, regional, and local scales. Potable (drinking) water is emerging as the critical global political issue in this century. In Chapter 10, we see the spatial implications over time of the energy–atmosphere and water–weather systems and the generation of Earth's climatic patterns. In this way, Chapter 10 interconnects all the system elements from Chapters 2 through 9. Part Two closes with a discussion of global climate change science, a look at present conditions, and a forecast of future climate trends.

177

Cumulonimbus, cumulus, and cirrus clouds perfectly highlight Loch Tay in central Scotland, in the Grampian Mountains of the Highlands. The long loch (or lake) fills a glaciated valley. Annual precipitation averages about 100 cm (39 in.) and is evenly distributed throughout the year. [Photo by Bobbé Christopherson.]

Water and Atmospheric Moisture

■ Key Learning Concepts

After reading the chapter, you should be able to:

- ■ **Describe** the origin of Earth's waters, **define** the quantity of water that exists today, and **list** the locations of Earth's freshwater supply.

- ■ **Describe** the heat properties of water, and **identify** the traits of its three phases: solid, liquid, and gas.

- ■ **Define** humidity and the expressions of the relative humidity concept, and **explain** dew-point temperature and saturated conditions in the atmosphere.

- ■ **Define** atmospheric stability, and **relate** it to a parcel of air that is ascending or descending.

- ■ **Illustrate** three atmospheric conditions—unstable, conditionally unstable, and stable—with a simple graph that relates the environmental lapse rate to the dry adiabatic rate (DAR) and moist adiabatic rate (MAR).

- ■ **Identify** the requirements for cloud formation, and **explain** the major cloud classes and types, including fog.

alden is blue at one time and green at another, even from the same point of view. Lying between the earth and the heavens, it partakes of the color of both.... A lake is the landscape's most beautiful and expressive feature. It is earth's eye; looking into which the beholder measures the depth of his own nature.... Sky water. It needs no fence. Nations come and go without defiling it. It is a mirror which no stone can crack.... Nature continually repairs.... a mirror in which all impurity presented to it sinks, swept and dusted by the sun's hazy brush. A field of *water. . . . is continually receiving new life and motion from above. It is intermediate in its nature between land and sky.* *

Thus did Thoreau speak of the water so dear to him—Walden Pond in Massachusetts, where he lived along the shore.

Water is critical to our daily lives and is an extraordinary compound in nature. Several satellite probes detected ice beneath the poles of the Moon. Three orbiting spacecraft and two robot landers imaged and detected evidence of flowing water early in Martian history. Scientists are finding evidence on Mars of existing subsurface water, polar water ice, and modern erosional features caused by water. Farther from the Sun, icy expanses can be seen on two of Jupiter's moons, Europa and Calisto—exciting discoveries about water in our Solar System. Yet, in the Solar System, water occurs in significant quantities only on our planet—water covers 71% of Earth by area.

Pure water is colourless, odourless, and tasteless; yet, because it is a solvent (dissolves solids), pure water rarely occurs in nature. Water weighs 1 g/cm³ (gram per cubic centimetre), or 1 kg/L (kilogram per litre). In the English system, water weighs 62.3 lb/ft³, or 8.337 lb/gal.

Water constitutes nearly 70% of our bodies by weight and is the major ingredient in plants, animals, and our food. A human can survive 50 to 60 days without food but only 2 or 3 days without water. The water we use must be adequate, both in quantity and quality, for its many tasks—everything from personal hygiene to vast national water projects. Water

*Reprinted by permission of Merrill, an imprint of Macmillan Publishing Company, from *Walden* by Henry David Thoreau, pp. 192, 202, 204. Copyright © 1969 by Merrill Publishing. Originally published in 1854.

indeed occupies that place between land and sky, mediating energy and shaping both the lithosphere and atmosphere, as Thoreau revealed. Water is the medium of life.

In this chapter: We examine water on Earth and the dynamics of atmospheric moisture and stability—the essentials of weather. The key questions answered include: What is the origin of water? How much water is there? And where is water located? An irony exists with this most common compound because it possesses such uncommon physical characteristics. Water's unique heat properties and existence in all three states in nature are critical in powering Earth's weather systems. Condensation of water vapour and atmospheric conditions of stability and instability are key to cloud formation. We end the chapter with clouds, our beautiful indicators of atmospheric conditions.

Water on Earth

Earth's hydrosphere contains about 1.36 billion cubic kilometres of water (specifically, 1,359,208,000 km³, or 326,074,000 mi³). According to scientific evidence, much of Earth's water originated from icy comets and hydrogen- and oxygen-laden debris that were part of the planetesimals that coalesced to form the planet. In 2007, the orbiting Spitzer Space Telescope observed for the first time the presence of water vapour and ice as planets form in a system 1000 light years from Earth. Such discoveries prove water to be abundant throughout the Universe. As a planet forms, water from within migrates to its surface and outgasses.

Outgassing is a continuing process by which water and water vapour emerge from layers deep within and below the crust, 25 km (15.5 mi) or more below Earth's surface. Figure 7.1 presents two such areas, among many sites

(a)

(b)

FIGURE 7.1 Water outgassing from the crust.
Outgassing of water from Earth's crust in geothermal areas: (a) near Wairakei on the North Island of New Zealand; and (b) the Smidur boiling spring in the Geysir area in Haukadalur, Iceland. [Photos by (a) Bill Bachman/Photo Researchers, Inc.; (b) Bobbé Christopherson.]

worldwide, in New Zealand and Iceland. The Haukadalur Geysir geothermal area is in southeast Iceland, about 110 km from its capital, Reykjavik (Figure 7.1b). Written accounts of the Geysir activity date back to A.D. 1294 and it is the namesake of the term *geyser* we use today.

In the early atmosphere, massive quantities of outgassed water vapour condensed and then fell to Earth in torrential rains. For water to remain on Earth's surface, land temperatures had to drop below the boiling point of 100°C (212°F), something that occurred almost 4 billion years ago. The lowest places across the face of Earth then began to fill with water—first ponds, then lakes and seas, and eventually ocean-sized bodies of water. Massive flows of water washed over the landscape, carrying both dissolved and solid materials to these early seas and oceans. Outgassing of water has continued ever since and is visible in volcanic eruptions, geysers, and seepage to the surface.

Worldwide Equilibrium

Today, water is the most common compound on the surface of Earth, having attained the present volume approximately 2 billion years ago. This quantity has remained relatively constant, even though water is continuously being lost from the system. Water is lost when it dissociates into hydrogen and oxygen and the hydrogen escapes Earth's gravity to space, or when it breaks down and forms new compounds with other elements. Pristine water not previously at the surface, which emerges from within Earth's crust, replaces lost water in the system. The net result of these water inputs and outputs is that Earth's hydrosphere is in a steady-state equilibrium in terms of quantity.

Despite this overall net balance in water quantity, worldwide changes in sea level do occur. The concept **eustasy** describes the global sea-level condition. Eustatic changes relate to the water volume in the oceans and not changes in the overall quantity of planetary water. Some of these changes result when the amount of water stored in glaciers and ice sheets vary; these are **glacio-eustatic** factors (see Chapter 17). In cooler times, as more water is bound up in glaciers (on mountains worldwide and in high latitudes) and in ice sheets (Greenland and Antarctica), sea level lowers. In warmer times, less water is stored as ice, so sea level rises.

Some 18,000 years ago, during the most recent ice-age pulse, sea level was more than 100 m (330 ft) lower than it is today; 40,000 years ago it was 150 m (about 500 ft) lower. Over the past 100 years, mean sea level has risen by 20–40 cm (8–16 in.) and is still rising worldwide at an accelerating pace as higher temperatures melt more ice.

Isostasy refers to actual vertical physical movement in landmasses, such as continental uplift or subsidence. Such landscape changes cause apparent changes in sea level relative to coastal environments. Chapter 11 discusses such land elevation changes.

Distribution of Earth's Water Today

From a geographic point of view, ocean and land surfaces are distributed unevenly. If you examine a globe, it is obvious that most of Earth's continental land is in the Northern Hemisphere, whereas water dominates the

FIGURE 7.2 Land and water hemispheres. Two perspectives that roughly illustrate Earth's ocean hemisphere and land hemisphere.

Southern Hemisphere. In fact, when you look at Earth from certain angles, it appears to have an *oceanic hemisphere* and a *land hemisphere* (Figure 7.2).

An illustration of the present location of all of Earth's liquid and frozen water—whether fresh or saline, surface or underground—is in Figure 7.3. The oceans contain 97.22% of all water (Figure 7.3a). A table in the figure lists and details the four oceans—Pacific, Atlantic, Indian, and Arctic. The extreme southern portions of the Pacific, Atlantic, and Indian Oceans that surround the Antarctic continent are collectively the "Southern Ocean." Fourth in size among the five oceans, the Southern Ocean lacks precise definition and boundaries, so we meld it into its three parent oceans in the table.

Only 2.78% of all of Earth's water is freshwater (nonsaline and nonoceanic). The middle pie chart, along with Table 7.1, details this freshwater portion—surface water and subsurface water (Figure 7.3b). Ice sheets and glaciers are the greatest single repository of surface freshwater; they contain 77.14% of all of Earth's freshwater. Adding subsurface groundwater to frozen surface water accounts for 99.36% of all freshwater.

The remaining freshwater, which resides in lakes, rivers, and streams so familiar to us, actually represents less than 1% of all water (Figure 7.3c). All the world's freshwater lakes total only 125,000 km³ (30,000 mi³), with 80% of this volume in just 40 of the largest lakes and about 50% contained in just 7 lakes (listed with Table 7.1).

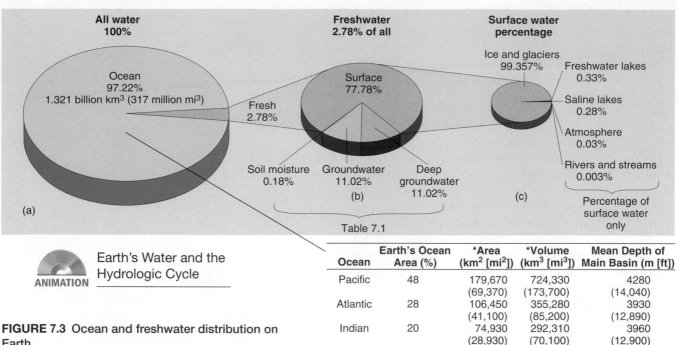

Earth's Water and the
Hydrologic Cycle

Ocean	Earth's Ocean Area (%)	*Area (km² [mi²])	*Volume (km³ [mi³])	Mean Depth of Main Basin (m [ft])
Pacific	48	179,670 (69,370)	724,330 (173,700)	4280 (14,040)
Atlantic	28	106,450 (41,100)	355,280 (85,200)	3930 (12,890)
Indian	20	74,930 (28,930)	292,310 (70,100)	3960 (12,900)
Arctic	4	14,090 (5440)	17,100 (4100)	1205 (3950)

FIGURE 7.3 Ocean and freshwater distribution on Earth.
Pie diagrams show location and percentages of (a) all water, (b) freshwater including subsurface water, and (c) surface water.

*Data in thousands (000): includes all marginal seas.

Table 7.1   Distribution of Freshwater on Earth

Location	Amount [km³ (mi³)]		Percentage of Freshwater	Percentage of Total Water
Surface Water				
Ice sheets and glaciers	29,180,000	(7,000,000)	77.14	2.146
Freshwater lakes*	125,000	(30,000)	0.33	0.009
Saline lakes and inland seas	104,000	(25,000)	0.28	0.008
Atmosphere	13,000	(3,100)	0.03	0.001
Rivers and streams	1,250	(300)	0.003	0.0001
Total surface water	29,423,250	(7,058,400)	77.78	2.164
Subsurface Water				
Groundwater—surface to 762 m (2500 ft) depth	4,170,000	(1,000,000)	11.02	0.306
Groundwater—762 to 3962 m (2500 to 13,000 ft) depth	4,170,000	(1,000,000)	11.02	0.306
Soil moisture storage	67,000	(16,000)	0.18	0.005
Total subsurface water	8,407,000	(2,016,000)	22.22	0.617
Total Freshwater (rounded)	**37,800,000**	**(9,070,000)**	**100.00%**	**2.78%**

*Major Freshwater Lakes	Volume [km³ (mi³)]		Surface Area [km² (mi²)]		Depth (m [ft])	
Baykal (Russia)	22,000	(5280)	31,500	(12,160)	1620	(5315)
Tanganyika (Africa)	18,750	(4500)	39,900	(15,405)	1470	(4923)
Superior (U.S./Canada)	12,500	(3000)	83,290	(32,150)	397	(1301)
Michigan (U.S.)	4,920	(1180)	58,030	(22,400)	281	(922)
Huron (U.S./Canada)	3,545	(850)	60,620	(23,400)	229	(751)
Ontario (U.S./Canada)	1,640	(395)	19,570	(7,550)	237	(777)
Erie (U.S./Canada)	485	(115)	25,670	(9,910)	64	(210)

The greatest single volume of lakewater resides in 25-million-year-old Lake Baykal in Siberian Russia. It contains almost as much water as all five U.S. Great Lakes combined. Africa's Lake Tanganyika contains the next-largest volume, followed by the five Great Lakes. Overall, 70% of lakewater is in North America, Africa, and Asia, with about a fourth of lakewater worldwide in small lakes too numerous to count. More than 3 million lakes exist in Alaska alone, and Canada has almost 32,000 lakes totaling 750,000 km² of surface area.

Not connected to the ocean are saline lakes and salty inland seas. They usually exist in regions of interior river drainage (no outlet to the ocean), which allows salts to become concentrated. They contain 104,000 km³ (25,000 mi³) of water. Examples of such lakes include Utah's Great Salt Lake, California's Mono Lake, Southwest Asia's Caspian and Aral seas, and the Dead Sea between Israel and Jordan.

Think of all the moisture in the atmosphere and Earth's thousands of flowing rivers and streams. Combined, they amount to only 14,250 km³ (3400 mi³), or only 0.033% of freshwater, or 0.0011% of all water! Yet, this small amount is dynamic. A water molecule traveling through atmospheric and surface-water paths moves through the entire hydrologic cycle (ocean–atmosphere–precipitation–runoff) in less than two weeks. Contrast this to a water molecule in deep-ocean circulation, groundwater, or a glacier; moving slowly, it takes thousands of years to move through the system.

Unique Properties of Water

Earth's distance from the Sun places it within a most remarkable temperate zone when compared with the locations of the other planets. This temperate location allows all three states of water—ice, liquid, and vapour—to occur naturally on Earth.

Even though water is the most common compound on Earth's surface, it exhibits most uncommon properties. Two atoms of hydrogen and one of oxygen, which readily bond, comprise each water molecule (suggested in Figure 7.4, upper left). Once hydrogen and oxygen atoms join in a covalent, or double, bond, they are difficult to separate, thereby producing a water molecule that remains stable in Earth's environment. This water molecule is a versatile solvent and possesses extraordinary heat characteristics.

The nature of the hydrogen–oxygen bond gives the hydrogen side of a water molecule a positive charge and the oxygen side a negative charge (see Figure 7.4, upper right). As a result of this *polarity*, water molecules attract each other: The positive (hydrogen) side of a water molecule attracts the negative (oxygen) side of another. This bonding between water molecules is *hydrogen bonding*.

The polarity of water molecules also explains why water "acts wet," sticking to things and dissolving many substances. Because of this solvent ability, pure water is rare in nature because something is usually dissolved in it.

The effects of hydrogen bonding in water are observable in everyday life. Hydrogen bonding creates the *surface tension* that allows you to float a steel needle on the surface of water, even though steel is much denser than water. This *surface tension* allows you to slightly overfill a glass with water; webs of millions of hydrogen bonds hold the water slightly above the rim.

Hydrogen bonding is the cause of *capillarity*, which you observe when you "dry" something with a paper towel. The towel draws water through its fibers because

FIGURE 7.4 Three states of water and water's phase changes.
The three physical states of water: (a) gas, or water vapour, (b) water, and (c) ice. Note the molecular arrangement in each state and the terms that describe the changes from one phase to another. Also note how the polarity of water molecules bonds them to one another, loosely in the liquid state and firmly in the solid state. The plus and minus symbols in the phase changes denote whether heat energy is absorbed (+) or liberated (released) (−).

Table 7.2 Cloud Classes and Types

Class	Altitude/Composition at Midlatitudes	Type	Symbol	Description
Low clouds (C_L)	Up to 2000 m (6500 ft)	Stratus (St)	——	Uniform, featureless, grey, like high fog
	Water	Stratocumulus (Sc)		Soft, grey, globular masses in lines, groups, or waves, heavy rolls, irregular overcast patterns
		Nimbostratus (Ns)		Grey, dark, low, with drizzling rain
Middle clouds (C_M)	2000–6000 m (6500–20,000 ft)	Altostratus (As)		Thin to thick, no halos, Sun's outline just visible, grey day
	Ice and water	Altocumulus (Ac)		Patches of cotton balls, dappled, arranged in lines or groups, rippling waves, the lenticular clouds associated with mountains
High clouds (C_H)	6000–13,000 m (20,000–43,000 ft)	Cirrus (Ci)		Mares'-tails, wispy, feathery, hairlike, delicate fibres, streaks, or plumes
	Ice	Cirrostratus (Cs)		Veil of fused sheets of ice crystals, milky, with Sun and Moon halos
		Cirrocumulus (Cc)		Dappled, "mackerel sky," small white flakes, tufts, in lines or groups, sometimes in ripples
Vertically developed clouds	Near surface to 13,000 m (43,000 ft)	Cumulus (Cu)		Sharply outlined, puffy, billowy, flat-based, swelling tops, fair weather
	Water below, ice above	Cumulonimbus (Cb)		Dense, heavy, massive, dark thunderstorms, hard showers, explosive top, great vertical development, towering, cirrus-topped plume blown into anvil-shaped head

mares' tails. Cirrus clouds look as though an artist took a brush and added delicate feathery strokes high in the sky. Cirrus clouds can indicate an oncoming storm, especially if they thicken and lower in elevation. The prefix *cirro-*, as in *cirrostratus* and *cirrocumulus*, indicates other high clouds that form a thin veil or puffy appearance, respectively.

A cumulus cloud can develop into a towering giant called **cumulonimbus** (again, *-nimbus* in Latin denotes "rain storm" or "thundercloud"; Figure 7.22). Such clouds are *thunderheads* because of their shape and associated lightning and thunder. Note the surface wind gusts, updrafts and downdrafts, heavy rain, and the presence of ice crystals at the top of the rising cloud column. High-altitude winds may then shear the top of the cloud into the characteristic anvil shape of the mature thunderhead.

Fog

By international definition, **fog** is a cloud layer on the ground, with visibility restricted to less than 1 km (3300 ft). The presence of fog tells us that the air temperature and the dew-point temperature at ground level are nearly identical, indicating saturated conditions. A temperature-inversion layer generally caps a fog layer (warmer temperatures above and cooler temperatures below the inversion altitude), with as much as 22 C° (40 F°) difference in air temperature between the cool ground under the fog and the warmer, sunny skies above.

Almost all fog is warm—that is, its moisture droplets are above freezing. Supercooled fog, which occurs when the moisture droplets are below freezing, is special because it can be dispersed by means of artificial seeding with ice crystals or other crystals that mimic ice, following the principles of the ice-crystal formation process described earlier in Figure 7.20b. Let's briefly look at several types of fog.

Advection Fog When air in one place *migrates* to another place where conditions are right for saturation, an **advection fog** forms. For example, when warm, moist air overlays cooler ocean currents, lake surfaces, or snow masses, the layer of migrating air directly above the surface becomes chilled to the dew point, and fog develops. Off all subtropical west coasts in the world, summer fog forms in the manner just described (Figure 7.23). Some coastal desert communities actually extract usable water from such fog formations, as described in News Report 7.2.

Another type of advection fog forms when cold air lies over the warm water of a lake, ocean surface, or even a swimming pool. This wispy **evaporation fog**, or *steam fog*, may form as water molecules evaporate from the water surface into the cold overlying air, effectively humidifying the air to saturation followed by condensation to form fog. When evaporation fog happens at sea, it is a shipping hazard called *sea smoke*.

Advection fog also forms when moist air flows to higher elevations along a hill or mountain. This upslope lifting leads to adiabatic cooling by expansion as the air

(a)

(b)

(c)

(d)

FIGURE 7.22 Cumulonimbus thunderhead.
(a) Structure and form of a cumulonimbus cloud. Violent updrafts and downdrafts mark the circulation within the cloud. Blustery wind gusts occur along the ground. (b) Space Shuttle astronauts capture a dramatic cumulonimbus thunderhead as it moves over Galveston Bay, Texas. (c) Few acts of nature can match the sheer power released by an intense thunderstorm and related turbulence for air travelers. (d) Towering cells over the prairies with cloud tops at the same altitude as the airplane, 9000 m (29,500 ft).
[Photos by (b) Space Shuttle photo from NASA; (c) and (d) by Bobbé Christopherson.]

rises. The resulting **upslope fog** forms a stratus cloud at the condensation level of saturation. Along the Appalachians and the eastern slopes of the Rockies such fog is common in winter and spring. Another advection fog associated with topography is **valley fog**. Because cool air is denser than warm air, it settles in low-lying areas, producing a fog in the chilled, saturated layer near the ground in the valley (Figure 7.24).

Radiation Fog   When radiative cooling of a surface chills the air layer directly above that surface to the dew-point temperature, creating saturated conditions, a **radiation fog**

forms. This fog occurs over moist ground, especially on clear nights; it does not occur over water because water does not cool appreciably overnight. Slight movements of air deliver even more moisture to the cooled area for more fog formation of greater depth (Figure 7.25).

Rime Fog   Similar to radiation fog, **rime fog** consists mostly of tiny supercooled droplets that turn into rime frost on contact with freezing objects. It is very common in cold weather, when the air temperature near the surface is below freezing and the air is fairly moist. Rime fog usually happens when the sky is clear on cold mornings.

Applied Physical Geography (continued)

To use the tables to determine relative humidity (RH, %) and dew point (°C) for a pair of numbers from the sling psychrometer, take the dif- ference between the wet bulb and the dry bulb. Table 2 gives examples of relative humidity and dew-point temperature based on the differences between wet-bulb and dry-bulb read- ings. Fill in the spaces in the last two rows using the tables.

Table 2

Dry Bulb Temperature (°C)	Wet Bulb Temperature (°C)	Difference (°C)	Relative Humidity (%)	Dew Point Temperature (°C)
31	14	17	16	−11
35	25	10	44	21
1	−3	4	31	−15
41	28	13	29	23
17.5	—	—	86	—
−10	−12	—	—	—

Summary and Review—Water and Atmospheric Moisture

■ *Describe* the origin of Earth's waters, *define* the quantity of water that exists today, and *list* the locations of Earth's freshwater supply.

The next time it rains where you live, pause and reflect on the journey each of those water molecules made. Water molecules came from within Earth over a period of billions of years, in the **outgassing** process. Thus began endless cycling of water through the hydrologic system of evaporation–condensation– precipitation. Water covers about 71% of Earth. Approximately 97% of it is salty seawater, and the remaining 3% is freshwater— most of it frozen.

The present volume of water on Earth is estimated at 1.36 billion cubic km³ (326 million mi³), an amount achieved roughly 2 billion years ago. This overall steady-state equilibrium might seem in conflict with the many changes in sea level that have occurred over Earth's history, but is not. **Eustasy** refers to worldwide changes in sea level and relates to the change in vol- ume of water in the oceans. The amount of water stored in glac- iers and ice sheets explains these changes as **glacio-eustatic** factors. At present, sea level is rising because of increases in the temperature of the oceans and the record melting of glacial ice.

outgassing (p. 180)
eustasy (p. 181)
glacio-eustatic (p. 181)

1. Approximately where and when did Earth's water originate?

2. If the quantity of water on Earth has been quite constant in volume for at least 2 billion years, how can sea level have fluctuated? Explain.

3. Describe the locations of Earth's water, both oceanic and fresh. What is the largest repository of freshwater at this time? In what ways is this distribution of water significant to modern society?

4. Why might you describe Earth as the water planet? Explain.

■ *Describe* the heat properties of water, and *identify* the traits of its three phases: solid, liquid, and gas.

Water is the most common compound on the surface of Earth, and it possesses unusual solvent and heat characteristics. Part of Earth's uniqueness is that its water exists naturally in all three states—solid, liquid, and gas—owing to Earth's temperate posi- tion relative to the Sun. A change from one state to another is a **phase change**. The change from solid to vapour is **sublimation**; from liquid to solid, freezing; from solid to liquid, melting; from vapour to liquid, condensation; and from liquid to vapour, va- porization, or evaporation.

The heat energy required for water to change phase is **latent heat**, because, once absorbed, it is hidden within the structure of the water, ice, or water vapour. For 1 g of water to become 1 g of water vapour at boiling requires the addition of 540 cal, or the **latent heat of vaporization**. When this 1 g of water vapour condenses, the same amount of heat energy is liberated, as 540 cal of the **latent heat of condensation**. The **latent heat of sublimation** is the energy exchanged in the phase change from ice to vapour and vapour to ice. Weather is powered by the tremendous amount of latent heat energy involved in the phase changes among the three states of water.

phase change (p. 184)
sublimation (p. 184)
latent heat (p. 185)
latent heat of vaporization (p. 186)
latent heat of condensation (p. 186)
latent heat of sublimation (p. 187)

5. Describe the three states of matter as they apply to ice, water, and water vapour.

6. What happens to the physical structure of water as it cools below 4°C (39°F)? What are some visible indications of these physical changes?

7. What is latent heat? How is it involved in the phase changes of water?

8. Take 1 g of water at 0°C and follow it through to 1 g of water vapour at 100°C, describing what happens along the way. What amounts of energy are involved in the changes that take place?

■ *Define* humidity and the expressions of the relative humidity concept, and *explain* dew-point temperature and saturated conditions in the atmosphere.

The amount of water vapour in the atmosphere is **humidity**. The maximum water vapour possible in air is principally a function of the temperature of the air and of the water vapour (usually these temperatures are the same). Warmer air produces higher net evaporation rates and maximum possible water vapour whereas cooler air can produce net condensation rates and lower possible water vapour.

Relative humidity is a ratio of the amount of water vapour actually in the air to the maximum possible at a given temperature. Relative humidity tells us how near the air is to saturation. Relatively dry air has a lower relative humidity value; relatively moist air a higher relative humidity percentage. Air is said to be at **saturation** when the rate of evaporation and the rate of condensation reach equilibrium, and any further addition of water vapour or temperature lowering will result in active condensation (100% relative humidity). The temperature at which air achieves saturation is the **dew-point temperature**.

Among the various ways to express humidity and relative humidity are vapour pressure and specific humidity. **Vapour pressure** is that portion of the atmospheric pressure produced by the presence of water vapour. A comparison of vapour pressure with the saturation vapour pressure at any moment yields a relative humidity percentage. **Specific humidity** is the mass of water vapour (in grams) per mass of air (in kilograms) at any specified temperature. Because it is measured as a mass, specific humidity does not change as temperature or pressure changes, making it a valuable measurement in weather forecasting. A comparison of specific humidity with the maximum specific humidity at any moment produces a relative humidity percentage.

Two instruments measure relative humidity, and indirectly the actual humidity content of the air; they are the **hair hygrometer** and the **sling psychrometer**.

humidity (p. 187)
relative humidity (p. 187)
saturation (p. 187)
dew-point temperature (p. 187)
vapour pressure (p. 189)
specific humidity (p. 190)
hair hygrometer (p. 191)
sling psychrometer (p. 191)

9. What is humidity? How is it related to the energy present in the atmosphere? To our personal comfort and how we perceive apparent temperatures?

10. Define relative humidity. What does the concept represent? What is meant by the terms *saturation* and *dew-point temperature*?

11. Using different measures of humidity in the air than those used in the chapter, derive relative humidity values (vapour pressure/saturation vapour pressure; specific humidity/maximum specific humidity) in Figures 7.11 and 7.12.

12. How do the two instruments described in this chapter measure relative humidity?

13. How does the daily distribution of relative humidity compare with the daily trend in air temperature?

■ *Define* atmospheric stability, and *relate* it to a parcel of air that is ascending or descending.

Meteorologists use the term *parcel* to describe a body of air that has specific temperature and humidity characteristics. Think of a parcel of air as a volume of air, perhaps 300 m (1000 ft) in diameter. The temperature of the volume of air determines the density of the air parcel. Warm air has a lower density in a given volume of air; cold air has a higher density.

Stability refers to the tendency of an air parcel, with its water-vapour cargo, either to remain in place or to change vertical position by ascending (rising) or descending (falling). An air parcel is *stable* if it resists displacement upward or, when disturbed, it tends to return to its starting place. An air parcel is *unstable* if it continues to rise until it reaches an altitude where the surrounding air has a density (air temperature) similar to its own.

stability (p. 192)

14. Differentiate between stability and instability relative to a parcel of air rising vertically in the atmosphere.

15. What are the forces acting on a vertically moving parcel of air? How are they affected by the density of the air parcel?

■ *Illustrate* three atmospheric conditions—unstable, conditionally unstable, and stable—with a simple graph that relates the environmental lapse rate to the dry adiabatic rate (DAR) and moist adiabatic rate (MAR).

An ascending (rising) parcel of air cools by expansion, responding to the reduced air pressure at higher altitudes. A descending (falling) parcel heats by compression. These temperature changes internal to a moving air parcel are explained by physical laws that govern the behavior of gases. Temperature changes in both ascending and descending air parcels occur without any significant heat exchange between the surrounding environment and the vertically moving parcel of air. The warming and cooling rates for a parcel of expanding or compressing air are termed **adiabatic**.

The **dry adiabatic rate (DAR)** is the rate at which "dry" air cools by expansion (if ascending) or heats by compression (if descending). The term *dry* is used when air is less than saturated (relative humidity less than 100%). The DAR is 10 C°/1000 m (5.5 F°/1000 ft). The **moist adiabatic rate (MAR)** is the average rate at which ascending air that is moist (saturated) cools by expansion, or descending air warms by compression. The average MAR is 6 C°/1000 m (3.3 F°/1000 ft). This is roughly 4 C° (2 F°) less than the dry rate. The MAR, however, varies with moisture content and temperature and can range from 4 to 10 C° per 1000 m (2 to 5.5 F° per 1000 ft).

A simple comparison of the dry adiabatic rate (DAR) and moist adiabatic rate (MAR) in a vertically moving parcel of air with that of the environmental lapse rate in the surrounding air determines the atmosphere's stability—whether it is unstable (lifting of air parcel continues), stable (air parcel resists vertical displacement), or conditionally unstable (air parcel behaves as though unstable if the MAR is in operation, and stable otherwise).

adiabatic (p. 192)
dry adiabatic rate (DAR) (p. 193)
moist adiabatic rate (MAR) (p. 194)

16. How do the adiabatic rates of heating or cooling in a vertically displaced air parcel differ from the normal lapse rate and environmental lapse rate?

17. Why is there a difference between the dry adiabatic rate (DAR) and the moist adiabatic rate (MAR)?

18. What atmospheric temperature and moisture conditions would you expect on a day when the weather is unstable? When it is stable? Relate in your answer what you would experience if you were outside watching.

■ *Identify* the requirements for cloud formation, and *explain* the major cloud classes and types, including fog.

A **cloud** is an aggregation of tiny moisture droplets and ice crystals suspended in the air. Clouds are a constant reminder of the powerful heat-exchange system in the environment. **Moisture droplets** in a cloud form when saturated air and the presence of **cloud-condensation nuclei** lead to *condensation*. Raindrops are formed from moisture droplets through either the *collision-coalescence process* or the *Bergeron ice-crystal process*.

Low clouds, ranging from the surface up to 2000 m (6500 ft) in the middle latitudes, are **stratus** (flat clouds, in layers) or **cumulus** (puffy clouds, in heaps). When stratus clouds yield precipitation, they are **nimbostratus**. Sometimes near the end of the day, lumpy, greyish, low-level clouds called **stratocumulus** may fill the sky in patches. Middle-level clouds are denoted by the prefix *alto-*. **Altocumulus** clouds, in particular, represent a broad category that occurs in many different styles. Clouds at high altitude, principally composed of ice crystals, are called **cirrus**. A cumulus cloud can develop into a towering giant **cumulonimbus** cloud (*-nimbus* in Latin denotes "rain storm" or "thundercloud"). Such clouds are called *thunderheads* because of their shape and their associated lightning, thunder, surface wind gusts, updrafts and downdrafts, heavy rain, and hail.

Fog is a cloud that occurs at ground level. **Advection fog** forms when air in one place migrates to another place where conditions exist that can cause saturation—for example, when warm, moist air moves over cooler ocean currents. Another type of advection fog forms when cold air flows over the warm water of a lake, ocean surface, or swimming pool. This **evaporation fog**, or steam fog, may form as the water molecules evaporate from the water surface into the cold overlying air. **Upslope fog** is produced when moist air is forced to higher elevations along a hill or mountain. Another fog caused by topography is **valley fog**, formed because cool, denser air settles in low-lying areas,

producing fog in the chilled, saturated layer near the ground. Radiative cooling of a surface that chills the air layer directly above the surface to the dew-point temperature creates saturated conditions and a **radiation fog**. **Rime fog**, similar to radiation fog, consists mostly of tiny supercooled droplets that turn into rime frost on contact with freezing objects. It is very common in cold weather, when the air temperature near the surface is below freezing and the air is fairly moist. **Ice-crystal fog** develops at low temperatures, for example in a continental arctic air mass, when the air becomes full of ice crystals that formed by sublimation. Ice-crystal fog seriously limits visibility.

cloud (p. 196)
moisture droplet (p. 196)
cloud-condensation nuclei (p. 196)
stratus (p. 197)
cumulus (p. 197)
nimbostratus (p. 197)
stratocumulus (p. 197)
altocumulus (p. 197)
cirrus (p. 197)
cumulonimbus (p. 200)
fog (p. 200)
advection fog (p. 200)
evaporation fog (p. 200)
upslope fog (p. 201)
valley fog (p. 201)
radiation fog (p. 201)
rime fog (p. 201)
ice-crystal fog (p. 202)

19. Specifically, what is a cloud? Describe the droplets that form a cloud.

20. Explain the condensation process: What are the requirements? What two principal processes are discussed in this chapter?

21. What are the basic forms of clouds? Using Table 7.2, describe how the basic cloud forms vary with altitude.

22. Explain how clouds might be used as indicators of the conditions of the atmosphere and of expected weather.

23. What type of cloud is fog? List and define the principal types of fog.

24. Describe the occurrence of fog in Canada and the United States. Where are the regions of highest incidence?

Critical Thinking

A. Examine the iceberg photographs in Figure 7.5b and 7.5d. These photos show Greenland and Antarctic waters. Determine what caused the "shoreline" thermal notch above the ocean surface around the iceberg in 7.5b. Why do you think the iceberg appears to be riding higher in the water than several weeks earlier? In rough terms, how much ice (in percent) do you think is beneath the surface in comparison to the amount you see above sea level in the iceberg cover photo? Explain why this physical trait can be a hazard to shipping.

B. Using Figure 7.21, begin to observe clouds on a regular basis. See if you can relate the cloud type to particular weather conditions at the time of observation. You may want to keep a log in your notebook during this physical geography course. Seeing clouds in this way will help you to understand weather and make studying Chapter 8 easier.

Such catastrophes as Hurricane Katrina link weather events to the failure of floodplain and levee management discussed in Chapter 14. Damage to houses and cars in the Lakeview neighbourhood of New Orleans (upper-left). New Basin Canal Park, a city park, serves as a temporary dump for life's debris (upper-right). A 91-m (300-ft) break in the London Avenue Canal levee that leads from Lake Pontchartrain partially into New Orleans; inset photo shows the dried, toxic "muck" that covered the region after flood waters retreated (lower-left). Houses missing from their foundations, debris, and broken trees and lives in Long Beach, Mississippi (lower-right). Sadly, after years, the tragedy continues for the region as a result of failure of government institutions.

Weather

■ Key Learning Concepts

After reading the chapter, you should be able to:

■ *Describe* air masses that affect North America, and *relate* their qualities to source regions.

■ *Identify* four types of atmospheric lifting mechanisms, and *describe* four principal examples.

■ *Analyze* the pattern of orographic precipitation, and *describe* the link between this pattern and global topography.

■ *List* the measurable elements that contribute to weather and *describe* the life cycle of a midlatitude cyclonic storm system.

■ *Analyze* various forms of violent weather and the characteristics of each.

Water has a leading role in the vast drama played out daily on Earth's stage. It affects the stability of air masses and their interactions and produces powerful and beautiful special effects in the lower atmosphere. Air masses come into conflict; they move and shift, dominating now one region then another, varying in strength and characteristics. Think of the weather as a play, North America the stage, and the air masses as actors of varying ability.

In this chapter: We follow huge air masses across North America, observe powerful lifting mechanisms in the atmosphere, revisit the concepts of stable and unstable conditions, examine migrating cyclonic systems with attendant cold and warm fronts, and conclude with a portrait of violent and dramatic weather so often in the news in recent years. Water, with its ability to absorb and release vast quantities of heat energy, drives this daily drama in the atmosphere. Also, modern weather forecasting is introduced.

The spatial implications of these weather phenomena and their relationship to human activities strongly link meteorology to physical geography and this chapter. We begin with a look at some weather essentials.

Weather Essentials

Weather is the short-term, day-to-day condition of the atmosphere, contrasted with *climate*, which is the long-term average (over decades) of weather conditions and extremes in a region. Weather is, at the same time, both a "snapshot" of atmospheric conditions and a technical status report of the Earth–atmosphere heat-energy budget. Important elements that contribute to weather are temperature, air pressure, relative humidity, wind speed and direction, and seasonal factors such as insolation receipt related to daylength and Sun angle.

We turn for the weather forecast to the Weather Office of the Canadian Meteorological Centre (**http://www.weatheroffice.ec.gc.ca**), a branch of the Meteorological Service of Canada, Environment Canada, or in the United States to the National Weather Service (**http://www.nws.noaa.gov**), to see current satellite images and to hear weather analysis. Internationally, the World Meteorological Organization coordinates weather information (see **http://www.wmo.ch/pages/index-en.html**). Many sources of weather information and related topics are found in the "Destinations" section for this chapter on the companion website.

Meteorology is the scientific study of the atmosphere. (*Meteor* means "heavenly" or "of the atmosphere.") Meteorologists study the atmosphere's physical characteristics and motions, related chemical, physical, and geologic processes, the complex linkages of atmospheric systems, and weather forecasting. Computers handle volumes of data for accurate forecasting of near-term weather and for studying trends in long-term weather, climatology, and climatic change.

New developments in supercomputing, an Earthbound instrument network in the Automatic Weather Observation System (AWOS; in Canada) and Automated Surface Observing System (ASOS; in the U.S.) arrays, orbiting observation systems, and Doppler radar installations are rapidly advancing the science of the atmosphere. As part of the NEXTRAD (Next Generation Weather Radar) program, 158 WSR-88D (*Weather Surveillance Radar*) Doppler radar systems were operational through the U.S. National Weather Service (125 systems), in conjunction with the U.S. Federal Aviation Administration (12) and the U.S. Department of Defense (21). In Canada, the National Radar Project will have 30 CWSR-98 radars in service (Figure 8.1).

Doppler radar detects the direction of moisture droplets toward or away from the radar, indicating wind direction and speed. This information is critical to weather forecasting and severe storm warnings. An essential part of this modernization in Canada is the deployment of the Weather Workstation, and in the U.S.,

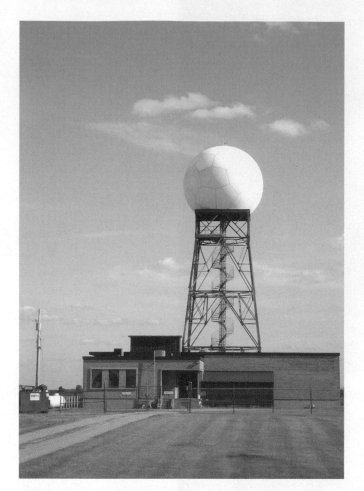

FIGURE 8.1 Weather installation.
Doppler radar installation at Exeter, Ontario, operated by the Meteorological Service of Canada. The radar antenna is sheltered within the dome structure. [Photo by Mary-Louise Byrne.]

the deployment of the Advanced Weather Interactive Processing System (AWIPS). AWIPS will eventually include 148 stations.

The cost of weather-related destruction increased more than 500% between 1975 and 1995, from an average of $2 billion to $10 billion annually. In 1998 alone, weather damage topped $90 billion worldwide, which exceeded the total for all the 1980s, even when adjusted for inflation. Damage costs are rising. Hurricane Katrina alone produced $125 billion in losses. A 2005 U.N. Environment Programme report estimated weather-related damage losses annually (drought, floods, hail, tornadoes, derechos, tropical systems, storm surge, blizzard and ice storms, and wildfires) will exceed $1 trillion by A.D. 2040 (adjusted to current dollars). Scientists recognize that abnormal weather is becoming the new "norm."

Air Masses Affecting North America

Each area of Earth's surface imparts its temperature and moisture characteristics to overlying air. The effect of the surface on the air creates regional air masses with a homogenous mix of temperature, humidity, and stability.

These masses of air interact to produce weather patterns—in essence, air masses are the actors in our weather drama. Such a distinctive body of air is an **air mass**, and it initially reflects the characteristics of its *source region* and sometimes extends through the lower half of the troposphere. For example, weather forecasters speak of a "cold Arctic air mass" and "moist tropical air mass."

The longer an air mass remains stationary over a region, the more definite its physical attributes become. Within each air mass there is a homogeneous mix of temperature and humidity that sometimes extends through the lower half of the troposphere. Such masses of air possess all the physical characteristics of the atmosphere discussed in earlier chapters and thus link the Earth–atmosphere energy budget and water–weather systems.

We classify air masses generally according to the moisture and temperature characteristics of their source regions:

1. *Moisture*—designated **m** for maritime (wet) and **c** for continental (dry).
2. *Temperature* (latitude factor)—designated **A** (arctic), **P** (polar), **T** (tropical), **E** (equatorial), and **AA** (Antarctic).

The principal air masses that affect North America in winter and summer are mapped in Figure 8.2.

Continental arctic (cA) air masses originate in Siberia and northern Canada. These cA air masses dominate the extreme north in winter when they cross over the North Pole and spill into the North American continent. Arctic air, colder than polar air and with a lower dew point, often forms when a high-pressure area becomes nearly stationary over northern Canada, Eastern Alaska, the Yukon, or Siberia. The small amount of winter solar radiation, abundant surface snow/ice cover, and the continuous emission of radiation from Earth's surface cause the air to become increasingly colder. If the jet stream shifts southward the cold air spreads into southern Canada and the United States, where it modifies to continental polar air.

Continental polar (cP) air masses form only in the Northern Hemisphere and are most developed in winter and cold weather conditions. These cP air masses are major players in middle- and high-latitude weather. The cold, dense, cP air displaces moist, warm air in its path, producing lifting, cooling, and condensation. An area covered by cP air in winter experiences cold, stable air, clear skies, high pressure, and anticyclonic wind flow (Figure 8.3). The Southern Hemisphere lacks the necessary continental landmasses at high latitudes to create such a cP air mass.

Maritime polar (mP) air masses in the Northern Hemisphere exist northwest and northeast of the North American continent over the northern oceans. Within them, cool, moist, unstable conditions prevail throughout the year. The Aleutian and Icelandic subpolar low-pressure cells reside within these mP air masses, especially in their well-developed winter pattern (see the January isobar pressure map in Figure 6.10a).

FIGURE 8.2 Principal air masses.
Air masses and their source regions influence North America during winter (a) and summer (b). (*Sea-surface temperature in °C; SH = specific humidity.)

Two maritime tropical (mT) air masses—the *mT Gulf/Atlantic* and the *mT Pacific*—influence North America. The humidity experienced in the East and Midwest is created by the mT Gulf/Atlantic air mass, which is particularly unstable and active from late spring to early fall (Figure 8.4). In contrast, the mT Pacific is stable to conditionally unstable and generally lower in moisture content and available energy. As a result, the western United States, influenced by this weaker Pacific air mass, receives lower average precipitation than the rest of the country.

Please review Figure 6.13 and the discussion of subtropical high-pressure cells.

Air Mass Modification

As air masses migrate from source regions, their temperature and moisture characteristics modify and slowly take on the characteristics of the land over which they pass.

FIGURE 8.3 Winter high-pressure system.
A cP air mass with two high-pressure centres merging north of the Great Lakes Region. These high-pressure systems exceed 1036 mb (103.6 kPa) air pressure. Representative temperatures toward the south are around −9°C, with dew-point temperatures of −18°C. In the northern high-pressure centre temperatures drop to −22°C with dew points as low as −29°C. Associated with these centres are clear, calm stable conditions that dominate a large area. This is a region of extremely dry air.

For example, an mT Gulf/Atlantic air mass may carry humidity to Chicago and on to Winnipeg but gradually loses its initial characteristics of high humidity and warmth with each day's passage northward.

Similarly, below-freezing temperatures eventually reach into southern Texas, as invading winter cold air masses. However, that air mass warms from its source region in central Canada, and it leaves areas covered by dry air.

Modification of cP air as it moves southward produces snowbelts along the Great Lakes. As below-freezing air passes over the Great Lakes, it absorbs moisture from

the lake surfaces and becomes *humidified*. This enhancement produces heavy lake-effect snowfall downwind into Ontario, Québec, Michigan, Pennsylvania, and New York—some areas receiving in excess of 250 cm (100 in.) in average snowfall a year (Figure 8.5). Lake effect snowfall is not limited to the Great Lakes—any large body of open water will produce this effect. Lake effect snowfall continues until lakes completely freeze over. Generally, the greatest accumulations of snow associated with lake effect occur in fall and early winter when storms are most intense.

A couple of such storms in western New York serve as examples. In October 2006, a lake-effect storm dubbed the "surprise storm" dropped 0.6 m (2 ft) of wet snow. This was the earliest date for such a storm in 137 years of records and remarkable because the ratio of snow to water content was 6:1. An "avalanche of a storm" hit February 2007 when 2 m (6.5 ft) of snow fell in 1 day, over 3.7 m (12 ft) over 7 days. Severity correlates to a low-pressure system positioned north of the Great Lakes, with counterclockwise winds pushing air across the lakes. With global warming, regional temperatures are increasing, which leads forecasters to predict enhanced lake-effect snowfall over the next several decades, since warmer air can absorb more water vapour. Later in the century, snowfall will decrease as temperatures rise, although rainfall totals will continue to increase over the leeside region.

Atmospheric Lifting Mechanisms

For air masses to cool adiabatically (by expansion) and to reach the dew-point temperature and saturate, condense, form clouds, and perhaps produce precipitation, they must rise in altitude. Four principal lifting mechanisms operate in the atmosphere:

• Convergent lifting—air flows toward an area of low pressure

• Convectional lifting—stimulated by local surface

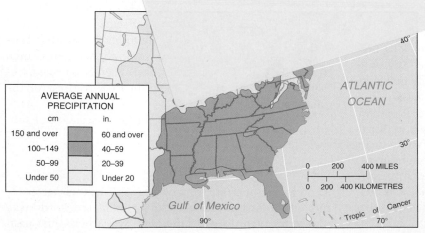

AVERAGE ANNUAL PRECIPITATION

cm	in.
150 and over	60 and over
100–149	40–59
50–99	20–39
Under 50	Under 20

FIGURE 8.4 Influence of mT Gulf/Atlantic air mass.
The pattern of precipitation over the southeastern United States shows the influence of the warm, moist, and generally unstable mT Gulf/Atlantic air mass. Precipitation decreases with distance inland from the source region over the Gulf of Mexico and Atlantic Ocean.

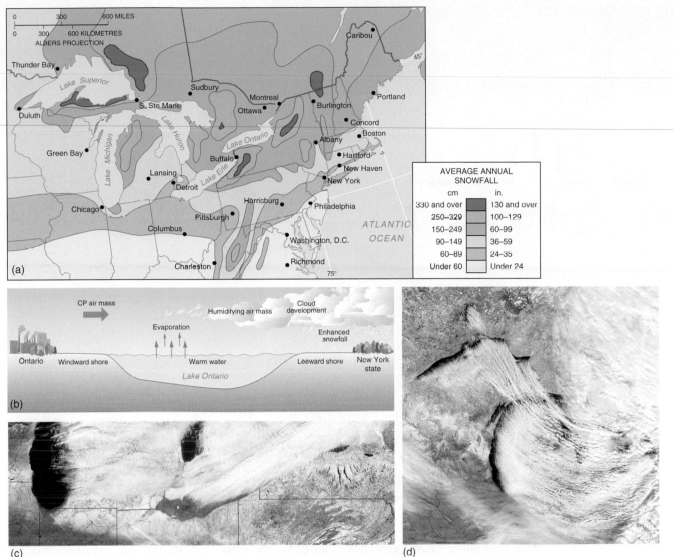

FIGURE 8.5 Lake-effect snowbelts of the Great Lakes.
(a) Locally, heavy areas of snowfall are associated with the lee side of each of the Great Lakes. In winter, cold cP and cA air masses pass from colder land surfaces across the relatively warmer water of these lakes. (b) The air masses are warmed and humidified (water vapour is added) from the lake water. The humid, now unstable air yields heavy snowfall as it moves onshore and becomes chilled. The strongest effect is generally limited to about 50 km (30 mi) inland up to 100 km (60 mi). (c) and (d) Satellite images show the lake-effect weather. [(a) Snowfall data from the *Climatic Atlas of the United States* (Washington, DC: Department of Commerce, NOAA, 1983), p. 53. (c) MODIS *Terra* image, Dec. 7, 2002, courtesy of the Rapid Response Team; and (d) *OrbView-2* image, Dec. 5, 2000, courtesy *SeaWiFS* Project, GeoEye; both NASA/GSFC.]

- Orographic lifting—air is forced over a barrier such as a mountain range
- Frontal lifting—along the leading edges of contrasting air masses

Descriptions of all four mechanisms follow and are in Figure 8.6.

Convergent Lifting

Air flowing from different directions into the same low-pressure area is converging, displacing air upward in **convergent lifting**. All along the equatorial region, the southeast and northeast trade winds converge, forming the intertropical convergence zone (ITCZ) and areas of extensive uplift, towering cumulonimbus cloud development, and high average annual precipitation (see Figures 6.11 and 6.12).

Convectional Lifting

When an air mass passes from a maritime source region to a warmer continental region, heating from the warmer land causes lifting and convection in the air mass. Other sources of surface heating might include an urbanized area heat island, or an area of dark soil in a plowed field—the warmer surfaces produce **convectional lifting**. If conditions are unstable, initial lifting continues and clouds develop. Figure 8.7 illustrates

(a) Convergent

(b) Convectional (local heating)

(c) Orographic (barrier)

(d) Frontal (e.g., cold front)

FIGURE 8.6 Four atmospheric lifting mechanisms.
(a) Convergent lifting; (b) Convectional lifting; (c) Orographic lifting; and (d) Frontal lifting.

ANIMATION Atmospheric Stability

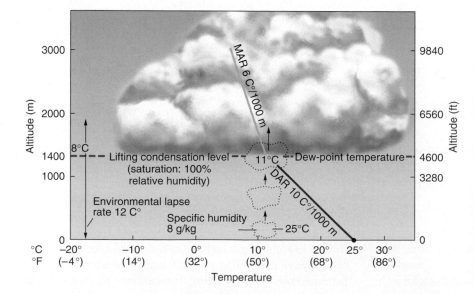

FIGURE 8.7 Convection activity in unstable conditions.
Convection occurs under unstable atmospheric conditions (environmental lapse rate of 12 C°/1000 m). In the air parcel, note that specific humidity is 8 g/kg and beginning temperature is 25°C. If you look back to Figure 7.12, you find that air with a specific humidity of 8 g/kg must be cooled to 11°C to achieve the dew-point temperature. In the example, this dew point is reached after 14 C° of adiabatic cooling at 1400 m (4600 ft). Note that the DAR (dry adiabatic rate) is used when the air parcel is less than saturated, changing to the MAR (moist adiabatic rate) above the lifting-condensation level at 1400 m.

Convectional Heating and Tornado in Florida

SATELLITE

FIGURE 8.8 Convectional activity over the Florida peninsula.
Cumulus clouds cover the land, with several cells developing into cumulonimbus thunderheads, demonstrating convectional lifting. Local heating lifts warm, moist air from the Gulf of Mexico and Atlantic as it passes over the relatively warmer land. [*Terra* image courtesy of the MODIS Rapid Response Team, NASA/GSFC.]

convectional action stimulated by local heating, with unstable conditions present in the atmosphere. The rising parcel of air continues its ascent because it is warmer and therefore less dense than the surrounding environment.

Florida's precipitation generally illustrates both these lifting mechanisms: convergence and convection. Heating of the land produces convergence of onshore winds from the Atlantic and the Gulf of Mexico. As an example of local heating and convectional lifting, Figure 8.8 depicts a day on which the landmass of Florida was warmer than the surrounding Gulf of Mexico and Atlantic Ocean. Because the Sun's radiation gradually heats the land throughout the day and warms the air above it, convectional showers tend to form in the afternoon and early evening, causing the highest frequency of days with thunderstorms in the United States. Florida appears highlighted with clouds.

Orographic Lifting

The physical presence of a mountain acts as a topographic barrier to migrating air masses. **Orographic lifting** (*oro* means "mountain") occurs when air is forcibly lifted upslope as it is pushed against a mountain. The lifting air cools adiabatically. Stable air forced upward in this manner may produce stratiform clouds, whereas unstable or conditionally unstable air usually forms a line of cumulus and cumulonimbus clouds. An orographic barrier enhances convectional activity and causes additional lifting during the passage of weather fronts and cyclonic systems, thereby extracting more moisture from passing air masses.

Figure 8.9a illustrates the operation of orographic lifting under unstable conditions. The wetter intercepting slope is the *windward slope*, as opposed to the drier far-side slope, known as the *leeward slope*. Moisture condenses from the lifting air mass on the windward side of the mountain; on the leeward side, the descending air mass heats by compression, and any remaining water in the air evaporates. Thus, air beginning its ascent up a mountain can be warm and moist, but finishing its descent on the leeward slope it becomes hot and dry.

In North America, **chinook winds** (called *föhn* or *foehn* winds in Europe) are the warm, downslope airflows characteristic of the leeward side of mountains. Such winds can bring a 20 C°(36 F°) jump in temperature and greatly reduced relative humidity on the lee side of the mountains.

The term **rain shadow** is applied to dry regions leeward of mountains. East of the Cascade Range, Sierra Nevada, and Rocky Mountains, such rain-shadow patterns predominate. In fact, the precipitation pattern of windward and leeward slopes persists worldwide, as confirmed by the precipitation maps for North America (Figure 9.5) and the world (Figure 10.2). See News Report 8.1 for more about the role of orographic barriers in setting precipitation records.

The province of British Columbia provides an excellent example of this concept, as shown in Figure 8.10. The Coast Mountains and the Rocky Mountains orographically lift invading mP air masses from the North Pacific Ocean, squeezing precipitation onto the windward sides of the mountains and allowing dry air to descend the leeward sides. The Egg Island Weather Station demonstrates

(a)

(b)

FIGURE 8.9 Orographic precipitation.
(a) Orographic barrier and precipitation patterns—unstable conditions assumed. Prevailing winds force warm, moist air upward against a mountain range, producing adiabatic cooling, eventual saturation and net condensation, cloud formation, and precipitation. On the leeward slope, as the "dried" air descends, compressional heating warms it and net evaporation dominates, creating the hot, relatively dry rain shadow of the mountain. (b) Rain shadow produced by descending, warming air contrasts with the clouds of the windward side. Dust is stirred up by leeward downslope winds. [Photo by Robert Christopherson.]

precipitation on the windward slope of the Coast Mountains, and the Mount Fidelity Station on the edge of Glacier National Park demonstrates the windward slope for the Rockies. The leeward slopes are represented by 100 Mile House in the Caribou (leeward of the Coast Mountains) and Calgary International Airport, both of which show the lesser annual precipitation of the mountain rain-shadow zone.

Frontal Lifting (Cold and Warm Fronts)

The leading edge of an advancing air mass is its *front*. Vilhelm Bjerknes (1862–1951) first applied the term while working with a team of meteorologists in Norway during

World War I. Weather systems seemed to them to be migrating air-mass "armies," doing battle along fronts. A front is a place of atmospheric discontinuity, a narrow zone forming a line of conflict between two air masses of different temperature, pressure, humidity, wind direction and speed, and cloud development. The leading edge of a cold air mass is a **cold front**, whereas the leading edge of a warm air mass is a **warm front**.

Cold Front On weather maps, such as the example in Figures 8.14 and 8.15, a cold front is a line with triangular spikes that point in the direction of frontal movement along an advancing cP or mP air mass. The steep face of the cold air mass suggests its ground-hugging nature,

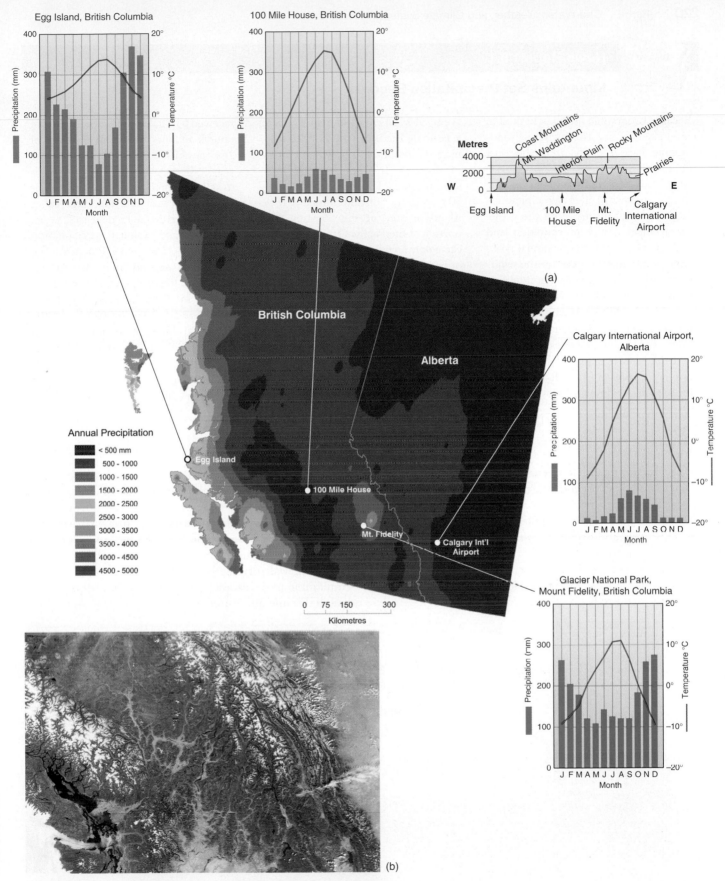

FIGURE 8.10 Orographic patterns in British Columbia and Alberta.
(a) Four stations in British Columbia and Alberta provide examples of orographic effects of windward precipitation and leeward rain shadows. Isohyets (lines connecting points of equal precipitation) that form the boundaries between the colours on the map indicate precipitation (in mm). (b) The windward slopes of the Coast Mountain Range and leeward rain shadow conditions of the Interior Dry Plateau are clearly visible despite the light dusting of snow in this true-colour MODIS image from the *Terra* satellite.
[(a) Data courtesy of Meteorological Service of Canada, and map by Jessica Mueller and Pam Schaus; (b) August 11, 2001, image courtesy of MODIS Rapid Response Team GSFC/NASA.]

News Report 8.1

Mountains Set Precipitation Records

Because orographic lifting is limited in areal extent to locations where a topographic barrier exists, it is the least dominant lifting mechanism worldwide. But mountain ranges are the most consistent of all the precipitation-inducing mechanisms. Both the greatest average annual precipitation and the greatest maximum annual precipitation on Earth occur on the windward slopes of mountains that intercept moist tropical trade winds.

The world's greatest average annual precipitation occurs in the United States on Mount Waialeale, on the island of Kaua'i, Hawai'i. This mountain rises 1569 m (5147 ft) above sea level. On its windward slope, rainfall averaged 1234 cm (486 in., or 40.5 ft) a year for the years 1941–1992 (topping the mountain's previous average of 460 in.). In contrast, the rain-shadow side of Kaua'i receives only 50 cm (20 in.) of rain annually. If no islands existed at this location, this portion of the Pacific Ocean would receive only an average 63.5 cm (25 in.) of precipitation a year.

Another place receiving world-record precipitation is Cherrapunji, India, 1313 m (4309 ft) above sea level at 25°N latitude, in the Assam Hills south of the Himalayas. Because of the summer monsoons that pour in from the Indian Ocean and the Bay of Bengal, Cherrapunji has received 930 cm (366 in., or 30.5 ft) of rainfall in one month and a total of 2647 cm (1042 in., or 86.8 ft) in one year! Not surprisingly, Cherrapunji is the all-time precipitation record holder for a single year and for every other time interval from 15 days to 2 years. The average annual precipitation there is 1143 cm (450 in., 37.5 ft), placing it second only to Mount Waialeale. Record precipitation occurrences in Canada exist for locations along the Pacific Coast, on the windward side of the mountains. Henderson Lake, on Vancouver Island, is the wettest location in Canada with an average annual precipitation of 665.5 cm (262 in.).

caused by its greater density and uniform physical character compared to the warmer air mass it displaces (Figure 8.11).

Warm, moist air in advance of the cold front lifts upward abruptly and experiences the same adiabatic rates of cooling and factors of stability or instability that pertain to all lifting air parcels. A day or two ahead of the cold front's passage, high cirrus clouds appear, telling observers that a lifting mechanism is on the way.

A wind shift, temperature drop, and lowering barometric pressure mark a cold front's advance due to lifting along the front. As the line of most intense lifting passes, usually just ahead of the front itself, air pressure drops to a local low. Clouds may build along the cold front into characteristic cumulonimbus form and may appear as an advancing wall of clouds. Precipitation usually is heavy, containing large droplets, and can be accompanied by hail, lightning, and thunder.

FIGURE 8.11 A typical cold front.
Denser, advancing cold air forces warm, moist air to lift abruptly. As the air is lifted, it cools by expansion at the DAR, cooling to the dew-point temperature as it rises to a level of condensation and cloud formation. Cumulonimbus clouds may produce large raindrops, heavy showers, lightning and thunder, and hail.

ANIMATION
Cold and Warm Fronts

The aftermath of a cold front passage usually brings northerly winds in the Northern Hemisphere and southerly winds in the Southern Hemisphere as anticyclonic high-pressure advances; lower temperatures; increasing air pressure produced by the cooler, more dense air; and broken cloud cover.

The particular shape and size of the North American landmass and its latitudinal position present conditions where cP and mT air masses are best developed and have the most direct access to each other. The resulting contrast can lead to dramatic weather, particularly in late spring, with sizable temperature differences from one side of a cold front to the other.

A fast-advancing cold front can cause violent lifting and create a zone right along or slightly ahead of the front called a **squall line**. Along a squall line, such as the one in the Gulf of Mexico shown in Figure 8.12, wind patterns are turbulent and wildly changing and precipitation is intense. The well-defined frontal clouds in the photograph rise abruptly, with new thunderstorms forming along the front. Tornadoes also may develop along such a squall line.

Warm Front   A line with semicircles facing in the direction of frontal movement denotes a warm front on weather maps (see Figure 8.14 map). The leading edge of an advancing warm air mass is unable to displace cooler, passive air, which is denser along the surface. Instead, the warm air tends to push the cooler, underlying air into a characteristic wedge shape, with the warmer air sliding up over the cooler air. Thus, in the cooler-air region a temperature inversion is present, sometimes causing poor air drainage and stagnation.

Figure 8.13 illustrates a typical warm front in which mT air is gently lifted, leading to stratiform cloud development and characteristic nimbostratus clouds and

FIGURE 8.12 Cold front and squall line.
A sharp line of cumulonimbus clouds near the Texas coast and Gulf of Mexico mark a cold front and squall line. The cloud formation rises to 17,000 m (56,000 ft). The passage of such a frontal system over land often produces strong winds and possibly tornadoes. [Space Shuttle astronaut photo from NASA.]

drizzly precipitation. A warm front presents a progression of cloud development to an observer: High cirrus and cirrostratus clouds announce the advancing frontal system; then clouds lower and thicken to altostratus; and finally the clouds lower and thicken to stratus within several hundred kilometres of the front.

FIGURE 8.13 A typical warm front.
Note the sequence of cloud development as the warm front approaches. Warm air slides upward over a wedge of cooler, passive air near the ground. Gentle lifting of the warm, moist air produces nimbostratus and stratus clouds and drizzly rain showers, in contrast to the more dramatic precipitation associated with the passage of a cold front.

ANIMATION
Cold and Warm Fronts

Midlatitude Cyclonic Systems

The conflict between contrasting air masses can develop a **midlatitude cyclone**, or **wave cyclone**. This migrating low-pressure centre with converging, ascending air spirals inward counterclockwise in the Northern Hemisphere, or inward clockwise in the Southern Hemisphere. Because of the undulating nature of frontal boundaries and the steering flow of the jet streams, the term *wave* is appropriate. The combination of the *pressure gradient force*, *Coriolis force*, and *surface friction* generates this cyclonic motion (see discussion in Chapter 6).

Before World War I, weather maps displayed only pressure and wind patterns. V. Bjerknes added the concept of fronts, and his son Jacob Bjerknes contributed the concept of migrating centres of cyclonic low-pressure systems.

Wave cyclones dominate weather patterns in the middle and higher latitudes of both the Northern and Southern Hemispheres and act as a catalyst for air-mass conflict. Such a midlatitude cyclone can initiate along the polar front, particularly in the region of the Icelandic and Aleutian subpolar low-pressure cells in the Northern Hemisphere. The intense high-speed winds of the jet streams guide cyclonic systems along their tracks (see Figures 6.16 and 6.17).

Life Cycle of a Midlatitude Cyclone

Figure 8.14 shows the birth, maturity, and death of a typical midlatitude cyclone in several stages, along with an idealized weather map. On the average, a midlatitude cyclonic system takes 3–10 days to progress through these stages from the area where it develops to the area where it finally dissolves. However, chaos rules and every day's weather map departs from the ideal in some manner.

Cyclogenesis The atmospheric process in which low-pressure wave cyclones develop and strengthen is **cyclogenesis**. This process usually begins along the polar front, where cold and warm air masses converge and are drawn into conflict.

The polar front is a discontinuity of temperature, moisture, and winds that establishes potentially unstable conditions. For a wave cyclone to form along the polar front, a compensating area of divergence aloft matches a surface point of air convergence. Even a slight disturbance along the polar front, perhaps a small change in the path of the jet stream, can initiate the converging, ascending flow of air and thus a surface low-pressure system (illustrated in Figure 8.14a).

In addition to the polar front, certain other areas are associated with wave cyclone development and intensification: the eastern slope of the Rockies and other north–south mountain barriers, the Gulf Coast, and along the east coasts of North America and Asia.

Open Stage To the east of the developing low-pressure centre, warm air begins to move northward along an advancing front, while cold air advances southward to the west of the centre. See this movement on Figure 8.14b as a trough, or area of beginning convergence. The growing circulation system then vents into upper-level winds. As the midlatitude cyclone matures, the counterclockwise flow draws the cold air mass from the north and west and the warm air mass from the south (here centred over Manitoba). In the cross section, you can see the profiles of both a cold front and a warm front and each air mass segment.

On the map, the cold front has passed over Saskatchewan, affecting wind direction, temperature, and humidity. The wind symbol in Regina clearly shows winds are from the southwest. After the passage of the cold front, winds shift to northwest. To the south of the low-pressure centre, southern Manitoba is experiencing temperatures of −3°C with a dew point of −5°C, while to the west of the centre, the temperature is −10°C with a dew point of −15°C.

Such an open stage of a midlatitude cyclone occurred February 19, 2004, with a low pressure centred over Nova Scotia. Figure 8.15 shows you a portion of a daily weather map for that day and an image from the *GOES-12* weather satellite for eastern North America. Note how the isobars portray the cyclone and the low of 996.2 mb (99.62 kPa) on the map. Also note the cloud pattern stretching along the cold front and swirling around the low. Compare the cold front and warm front and overall patterns with Figure 8.14b. This storm dumped over 1 metre of snow on Halifax in a 24-hour period—the largest one-day snow accumulation recorded in Atlantic Canada.

Occluded Stage Remember the relation between air temperature and the density of an air mass. The colder cP air mass is denser than the warmer mT air mass. This cooler, more unified air mass acts like a bulldozer blade and therefore moves faster than the warm front. Cold fronts can travel at an average 40 kmph (25 mph), whereas warm fronts average roughly half that at 16−24 kmph (10−15 mph). Thus, a cold front often overtakes the cyclonic warm front, wedging beneath it, producing an **occluded front** (*occlude* means "to close") in Figure 8.14c. The cold front is occluding with the warm front just southwest of the low-pressure system. Precipitation may be moderate to heavy initially and then taper off as the warmer air wedge is lifted higher by the advancing cold air mass. On this idealized map, a cold front and a warm front remain active to the south of the occluded area.

When there is a stalemate between cooler and warmer air masses where airflow on either side is almost parallel to the front, although in opposite directions, a **stationary front** results. Such a front is positioned over the Great Lakes in Figure 8.14. Some gentle lifting might produce light to moderate precipitation. Eventually the stationary front will begin to move, as one of the air masses assumes dominance, evolving into a warm or a cold front.

Dissolving Stage The final, dissolving, stage of the midlatitude cyclone occurs when its lifting mechanism is

FIGURE 8.14 Idealized stages of a midlatitude wave cyclone.
(a) Cyclogenesis is noted where surface convergence and lifting begin. (b) The open stage. (c) The occluded stage. (d) The dissolving stage is reached at the end of the storm track as the cyclone spins down, no longer energized by the latent heat from condensing moisture. Standard weather symbols are in the inset box. After studying the text and the map, can you describe conditions in Vancouver, Calgary, Fort McMurray, Saskatoon, Regina, Winnipeg, Churchill, Toronto, Québec, Halifax, and St. John's depicted on this weather map?

Midlatitude Cyclones

completely cut off from the warm air mass, which was its source of energy and moisture. Remnants of the cyclonic system then dissipate in the atmosphere, perhaps after passage across the country (Figure 8.14d).

Storm Tracks   Cyclonic storms—1600 km (1000 mi) wide—and their attendant air masses move across the continent along **storm tracks**, which shift in latitude with the Sun and the seasons. Typical storm tracks that cross

(a)

(b)

FIGURE 8.15 Open stage of a midlatitude cyclone.
(a) *GOES-12* infrared image of a cyclonic system over
Nova Scotia, February 19, 2004. The cloud patterns are
areas of precipitation; clear skies are behind the cold front
as cP air mass covers the landscape. (b) A simplified
weather map for the same day shows a low-pressure
centre of 963 mb (96.30kPa). Winds move up the Atlantic
Coast, converging into the low in a counterclockwise flow.
[(a) Satellite *GOES-12* image courtesy of NOAA. (b) Map data
from Environment Canada.]

North America are farther northward in summer and farther southward in winter (Figure 8.16). Noted on the map are some of the regional names for cyclonic source regions. As the storm tracks begin to shift northward in the spring, cP and mT air masses are in their clearest conflict. This is the time of strongest frontal activity, featuring thunderstorms and tornadoes. Storm tracks follow the path of upper-air winds, which direct storm systems across the continent.

A map of actual storm tracks for March 1991 in Figure 8.16b demonstrates several areas of cyclogenesis: the northwest over the Pacific Ocean, the Gulf of Mexico (Gulf Lows), the eastern seaboard (Nor'easter, Hatteras Low), and the Arctic. Cyclonic circulation also frequently develops on the lee side of mountain ranges, as along the Rockies from Alberta (Alberta Clipper) south to Colorado (Colorado Low). By crossing the mountains, such systems gain access to the moisture-laden, energy-rich mT air masses from the Gulf of Mexico and are strengthened.

The pattern of storm tracks has important implications for Canadian weather. During winter, when storm tracks are shifted south, much of Canada experiences weather associated with the northern half of low-pressure systems. "Northeasters" affect the Maritimes, Québec, and many of the American northeast coastal states. These are storm conditions generated in the northeastern quadrant of the advancing low-pressure system. Northeasters pull in moisture from the Atlantic Ocean and can result in large amounts of precipitation.

The Canadian Prairies experience weather associated with expansion and contraction of continental high-pressure systems. The boundary of a strengthening Arctic high-pressure air mass can expand westward, pushing cold air up mountain slopes and resulting in light precipitation from orographic lifting of the dry, cold air. The weather thus approaches from the East or Northeast, contrary to the usual west to east movement of frontal weather.

On the West Coast, extreme weather develops when arctic outflow conditions develop. Normally, mild, moist air comes inland off the Pacific Ocean and flows from west to east. During an arctic outflow, cold arctic air moves from the north and gets trapped on the western side of the Rockies. Valleys with a west to east orientation, normally filled with mild moist air off the Pacific, are filled with cold, dry arctic air, and drastic temperature changes result.

Analysis of Daily Weather Maps—Forecasting

Synoptic analysis is the evaluation of weather data collected at a specific time. Building a database of wind, pressure, temperature, and moisture conditions is key to *numerical* (computer-based) *weather prediction* and the development of weather-forecasting models. Development of numerical models is a great challenge because the atmosphere operates as a nonlinear system, tending toward chaotic behavior. Slight variations in input data or slight changes in the basic assumptions of the model's behaviour can produce widely varying forecasts. As our knowledge of the interactions that produce weather and as instruments and software improve, so too will the accuracy of our forecasts.

(a) Average storm tracks

(b) Actual storm tracks in March 1991

FIGURE 8.16 Typical and actual storm tracks.
(a) Cyclonic storm tracks over North America vary seasonally. The tracks indicate several locations of cyclogenesis; note regional names. (b) Actual cyclonic tracks during March 1991 over North America. [(b) From *Storm Data* vol. 33, no. 3 (March 1991); Asheville, NC: NOAA/NESDIS, National Climatic Data Center.]

Weather data necessary for the preparation of a synoptic map and forecast include:

- Barometric pressure (sea level and altimeter setting)
- Pressure tendency (steady, rising, falling)
- Surface-air temperature
- Dew-point temperature
- Wind speed, direction, and character (gusts, squalls)
- Type and movement of clouds
- Current weather
- State of the sky (current sky conditions)
- Visibility; vision obstruction (fog, haze)
- Precipitation since last observation

For links to weather maps, current forecasts, satellite images, and the latest radar, please go to the *Geosystems* Student Learning Centre, to Chapter 8, click "Destinations," and you find many related Internet links. With the Internet, there is no need to wait for television or the newspaper to bring you the latest satellite images, for they are at your fingertips.

The Meteorological Service of Canada (MSC; **http://www.msc-smc.ec.gc.ca/msc/contents_e.html**) is responsible for collecting, recording, and reporting accurate and accessible daily weather, water, and ice information. MSC is composed of six directorates, one of which, the Atmospheric Environment Prediction Directorate (AEPD), provides leadership for all prediction activities of the Atmospheric Environment Program.

The Canadian Meteorological Centre (CMC) carries out synoptic analysis. Its three branches—Informatics, Operations, and Development—provide forecast guidance to regional prediction centres. The Informatics Branch provides centralized computing and telecommunications services, and operates and maintains the supercomputer facility in Dorval, Québec, and various telecommunications networks. The Operations Branch is responsible for the meteorological operations of numerous production systems for weather, climate, air quality, and environmental programs at the CMC. The Development Branch is responsible for developing new systems and for technology transfer from research to operations of the Canadian environmental prediction effort.

Typical instrumentation and displays are illustrated in Figure 8.17. Automated stations use the Automatic Weather Observation System (AWOS) developed in partnership between the Atmospheric Environment Service and a private corporation. Canada currently has 31 upper air stations that send two radiosondes up each day at 1200 UTC and 0000 UTC. Additionally, there are six emergency stations and five Department of National Defence stations that occasionally produce upper air soundings. Nationally, there are 31 Doppler weather radar installations and 770 hourly weather observation sites across the country. This includes 261 NAV Canada aviation observation sites, the Department of National Defence sites, and differing types of automated observation sites that have various types of observation equipment. There are 298 Reference Climate Stations (RCS sites) that record maximum and minimum temperatures and precipitation amounts twice a day. Finally, there are 1425 climate stations operated by volunteers. The numbers of hourly observations, reference climate stations, and volunteer climate stations change frequently.

AWOS sensor instrument arrays are a primary surface weather-observing network (Figure 8.17a). An AWOS installation includes: rain gauge (tipping bucket), temperature/dew-point sensor, barometer, present weather identifier, wind speed indicator, direction sensor, cloud height indicator, freezing rain sensor, thunderstorm sensor, and visibility sensor, among other items.

Preparing a weather report and forecast requires analysis of daily weather maps and the use of standard weather symbols, such as those in Figure 8.14. Although the actual pattern of cyclonic passage over North America is widely varied in shape and duration, you can apply this general model, along with your understanding of warm and cold fronts, to reading the daily weather map. A weather map is a useful tool, especially when weather turns dramatic in violent episodes.

(a)

(b)

(c)

(e)

(f)

(d)

FIGURE 8.17 AWOS weather instruments and workstation display.
(a) Automated Weather Observation System (AWOS) weather station—Thunder Bay, Ontario.
(b) Wind towers with anemometers and wind vanes mounted 10 m above the surface.
(c) Meteorologist at Ontario Storm Prediction Centre. Several monitors display information needed to forecast weather. (d) Workstation on which data are analyzed. MetManager is a software package used to display and overlay many different data types. (e) Surface analysis map completed by hand. The computer provides the geography and station plots and the meteorologist adds isobars, fronts, clouds, and precipitation to the map. (f) Unified Radar Processing (URP) at the top is capable of applying a variety of algorithms to detect severe thunderstorms. Storms are identified by red, yellow, green, or white depending on their severity. This software also allows the forecaster to view numerous conventional or Doppler weather radar images to assist in the diagnosis of severe storms in the summer and in the winter. The lower two parts of the figure display MetManager output screens. The middle image displays isobars, lightning data, and Canadian radar data overlayed; the lower image shows isobars overlayed on various station plots. [Photos and surface analysis map courtesy of Geoff Coulson, Canada Climate Centre.]

On the weather map in the Critical Thinking section at the end of this chapter, you can identify the temperatures reported by various stations, the patterns created, and the location of warm and cold fronts. The distribution of air pressure is defined by *isobars*, lines that connect points of equal pressure on the map. Although the low-pressure centre in southereastern Nebraska is not intense, it is well defined, with winds following in a counterclockwise, cyclonic path around the low pressure. This pattern is clear on the satellite image. A high-pressure cP air mass dominates east-central Canada. Note the dryness in the region around Churchill, Manitoba, where the air temperature is –14.4°C (6.0°F) and the dew-point temperature is –16.1°C (3.0°F).

Violent Weather

Weather provides a continuous reminder of the flow of energy across the latitudes that at times can set into motion destructive, violent weather conditions. In dollar value, weather-related damage is increasing each year as population increases in areas prone to violent weather and as climate change intensifies weather anomalies. Environment Canada issues severe weather warnings, watches, and advisories to the public via the media, weather outlets, and Weatheradio Canada (see **http://www.msc-smc.ec. gc.ca/cd/brochures/warning_e.cfm** for a summary of different types of warnings, watches, and advisories).

MSC includes two branches, one for weather and climate research and one for severe weather (**http://www. msc-smc.ec.gc.ca/acsd/mrb/severe_e.html**). In the United States, government research and monitoring of violent weather is centred at NOAA's National Severe Storms Laboratory and Storm Prediction Center in several cities (see **http://www.nssl.noaa.gov**; consult this site for each of the topics that follow). As mentioned earlier, 1998 broke all records for weather-related damage worldwide. We focus on ice storms, thunderstorms, derechos, tornadoes, and hurricanes.

Ice Storms

Ice storms (freezing rain, ice glaze, and ice pellets), snow blizzards, and low temperatures are forms of violent weather. Freezing precipitation occurs when *supercooled* moisture freezes on contact with a surface. The most common types of freezing precipitation are *freezing rain* and *freezing drizzle*, both of which can accumulate on surfaces and cause great damage (Figure 8.18a). Ice storms are a hazard in all parts of Canada except for the far north. They are especially common in the southern and eastern parts of the country, in a swath from southern Ontario to Newfoundland (Figure 8.18b). The thickness of ice accumulation associated with a storm, the storm's duration, and the extent of area affected determine the severity of the event. Typically, an ice storm lasts for 45 to 65 hours and deposits, at most, 30 to 40 mm (1.2 to 1.6 in.) of ice.

The ice storm of 1998 was an exceptional event that knocked out power for several weeks over a wide area—affecting eastern Ontario, southern Québec, the Fundy coast of New Brunswick and Nova Scotia, and the American northeast. During the 1998 storm there were over 80 hours of freezing rain and drizzle, and in some areas near Montréal, over 100 mm (4 in.) of ice accumulated. This particular storm was extraordinary because it hit some of the largest populated and urbanized areas of North America—affecting more people than any previous weather event in Canadian history. Three weeks after the storm, more than 700,000 people were still without electricity!

Eastern Canada suffered widespread effects from the 1998 ice storm. Tragically, hypothermia claimed 25 human lives. Additionally, thousands of dairy cattle died from mastitis and related illnesses after mechanized milking equipment failed due to power outages. The storm sparked the largest peacetime deployment of Canadian troops—nearly 16,000 Canadian Forces assisted with rebuilding the power grid. More than one-third of the cropland in Québec and almost one-quarter of that in Ontario were in the storm zone and many farmers suffered substantial losses. Additionally, more than five million sugar maple taps located in the affected areas had a subsequent decrease in sap output. Recovery could take 30 to 40 years before syrup production returns to normal. In all, economic losses for Montréal and Ottawa and surrounding areas were estimated at $585 million and $114 million, respectively.

Thunderstorms

The condensation of large quantities of water vapour in clouds liberates tremendous amounts of energy. This process locally heats the air, rapidly changing its density and buoyancy and causing violent updrafts. As rising air parcels pull surrounding air into the cumulonimbus cloud system, updrafts become stronger. Raindrops form and descend through the cloud, and their frictional drag pulls air toward the ground, causing violent downdrafts. The resulting giant cumulonimbus clouds signal dramatic weather moments—heavy precipitation, lightning, thunder, hail, blustery winds, and maybe tornadoes.

Such thunderstorms may develop under three conditions: within an air mass (particularly in warm, moist air), in a line along a cold front or other convergent boundary, or where mountain slopes cause orographic lifting. With a slowly rotating updraft, a dangerous convective supercell thunderstorm might develop, featuring strong winds, hail, and persistent tornadoes of great strength.

Thousands of thunderstorms occur on Earth at any given moment. Equatorial regions and the ITCZ experience many of them, exemplified by the city of Kampala in Uganda, East Africa (north of Lake Victoria), which sits virtually on the equator and averages a record 242 days a year of thunderstorms. Figure 8.19 shows the annual distribution of days with thunderstorms across Canada and the United States. You can see that, in North America, most thunderstorms occur in areas dominated by mT air masses.

(a)

FIGURE 8.18 Freezing precipitation and ice storms.
(a) A series of Hydro-Québec high voltage towers near St-Bruno, Québec, south of Montréal, collapsed after a severe ice storm hit southwest Québec in January 1998. The storm left over one million households without electricity for several weeks as crews worked to replace transmission lines.
(b) Average annual hours of freezing precipitation in Canada.
[(a) Jacques Boissinot/CP Photo Archive; (b) Courtesy of Environment Canada. Used by permission of the Minister of Public Works and Government Services Canada.]

(b)

Atmospheric Turbulence Most airplane flights experience at least some turbulence—the encountering of air of different densities or air layers moving at different speeds and directions. This is a natural state of the atmosphere and passengers are asked to keep seat belts fastened when in their seats to avoid injury, even if the seat-belt light is turned off.

Thunderstorms can produce severe turbulence in the form of downbursts, which are exceptionally strong downdrafts. Downbursts are classified by size: a *macroburst* is at least 4.0 km (2.5 mi) wide and in excess of 210 kmph (130 mph); a *microburst* is smaller in size and speed. A microburst causes rapid changes in wind speed and direction and it causes the dreaded *wind shear* that can bring down aircraft. Such turbulence events are short-lived and hard to detect, although the Forecast Systems

Laboratory, among others, is making progress in developing forecasting methods.

Lightning and Thunder An estimated 8 million lightning strikes occur each day on Earth. **Lightning** refers to flashes of light caused by enormous electrical discharges—tens of millions to hundreds of millions of volts—that briefly superheat the air to temperatures of 15,000°–30,000°C (27,000°–54,000°F). A buildup of electrical energy polarity between areas within a cumulonimbus cloud or between the cloud and the ground creates lightning (Figure 8.20a). The violent expansion of this abruptly heated air sends shock waves through the atmosphere as the sonic bang of **thunder**.

NASA's Lightning Imaging Sensor (LIS) aboard the *Tropical Rainfall Measuring Mission* (*TRMM*) satellite

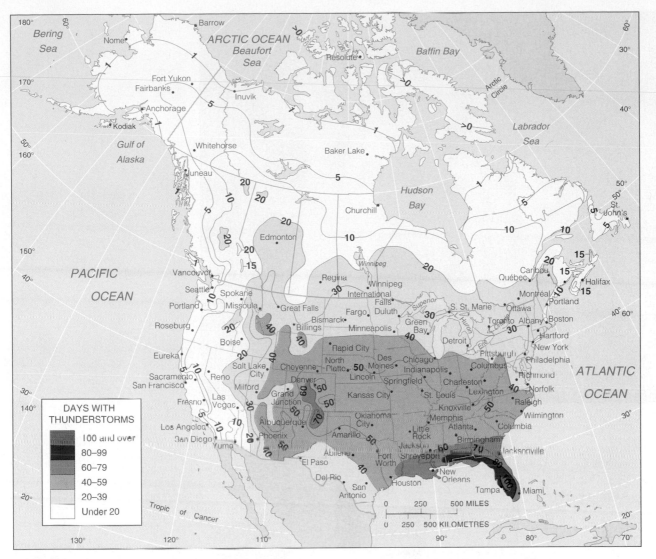

FIGURE 8.19 Thunderstorm occurrence.
Average annual number of days experiencing thunderstorms. [Data courtesy of U.S. National Weather Service; Map Series 3; *Climatic Atlas of Canada*, Atmospheric Environment Service, Canada.]

monitors lightning and other phenomena. The LIS can image lightning strikes day or night, within clouds or between cloud and ground. The sensor's data show that about 90% of all strikes occur over land in response to increased convection over relatively warmer continental surfaces, with expected seasonal shifts with the high Sun, as shown in Figure 8.20b and c (see **http://thunder.msfc.nasa.gov/lis/**).

Lightning poses a hazard to aircraft, people, animals, trees, and structures. The CN Tower, the world's tallest freestanding structure, is particularly susceptible to lightning. It is struck so often that observations and measurements of lightning activity have been conducted at the tower since 1978. The tower was struck 460 times between 1978 and 1994, an average of 75 times per year.

Certain precautions are mandatory when a lightning discharge threatens, because lightning causes nearly 200 deaths and thousands of injuries each year in Canada and the United States. Information about lightning activity in Canada is maintained at the CMC (see **http://www.weatheroffice.ec.gc.ca/lightning/index_e.html** for a real-time lightning strike map and for tips on lightning safety). When lightning is imminent, agencies such as the Meteorological Service of Canada issue *severe thunderstorm warnings* and caution people to remain indoors. If the hair on your head or neck begins to stand on end, get indoors, or if in the open get low to the ground, crouched on both feet and not laying down, in a low spot, if possible. Your hair is telling you that a charge is building in the area. The place *not* to seek shelter is beneath a tree, for trees are good conductors of electricity and often are hit by lightning.

Hail   Ice pellets called **hail** generally form within a cumulonimbus cloud. Raindrops circulate repeatedly above and below the freezing level in the cloud, adding layers of ice until the circulation in the cloud can no longer support

(a)

(b)   Winter (Dec. 1999, Jan. and Feb. 2000)

(c)   Summer (June, July, August 2000)

FIGURE 8.20 Seasonal images show global lightning.
(a) Multiple cloud-to-ground lightning strikes captured in a time-lapse photo. A composite of three
months' data derived from NASA's Lightning Imaging Sensor (LIS) records all lightning strikes between
35° N and 35° S latitudes during (b) winter (December 1999–February 2000) and (c) summer (June, July,
August 2000). The LIS is aboard the *Tropical Rainfall Measuring Mission* satellite launched in 1997.
[(a) Photo from C. Clark, NOAA Photo Library, NOAA Central Library, NSSL; (b) and (c) *TRMM* images courtesy
of NASA's Global Hydrology and Climate Center, Marshall Spaceflight Center, Huntsville, Alabama.]

(b)

(a)

FIGURE 8.21 Hailstones and hailstone damage.
(a) Irregular layers give evidence of numerous convective trips through a cumulonimbus cloud.
(b) Hail can severely damage windows, automobiles, crops, livestock, and people. [(a) © Arthur
C. Smith III/Grant Heilman Photography, Inc.; (b) Photo by *The Denver Post*, 1990.]

their weight (Figure 8.21a). Hail may also grow from the addition of moisture on a snow pellet.

Pea-sized and marble-sized hail is common, although hail the size of golf balls and baseballs happens at least once or twice a year somewhere in North America. For larger hail to form, the frozen pellets must stay aloft for longer periods. The largest authenticated hailstone in the world landed in Kansas in 1970; it measured 14 cm (5.5 in.) in diameter and weighed 758 g (1.67 lb)!

Hail is common in Canada and the United States, although somewhat infrequent at any given place. Hail occurs perhaps every one or two years in the highest-frequency areas. Hail typically occurs in Canada in heavy but localized showers associated with mature thunderstorms. Most hailstorms develop in the continental interior, namely central Alberta's "hailstorm alley," to the lee of the Rockies and the southernmost part of Saskatchewan, east of Cypress Hills. These areas experience four to six major hail events each year. The most frequent hail occurrence is May to July, with nearly three quarters of all hailstorms between noon and 6:00 P.M.

In Canada, hailstorms cause the greatest economic losses of any natural hazard in terms of property and crop damage. This is why, collectively, farmers pay millions of dollars each year for crop insurance. Table 8.1 outlines the twelve hailstorms resulting in the greatest insured losses in Canada. The pattern of hail occurrence across Canada and the United States is similar to that of thunderstorms shown in Figure 8.19.

Derechos

Although tornadoes and hurricanes grab headlines, straight-line winds associated with thunderstorms and bands of showers cause significant damage and crop losses. These strong linear winds in excess of 26 m/s (58 mph) are

Table 8.1	Twelve Largest Recent Canadian Hailstorms	
Date	Location of Storm	Insurance Losses (millions of dollars)
September 1991	Calgary	343
July 1981	Calgary	125
July 1987	Edmonton	148
July 1996	Winnipeg	147
July 1996	Calgary	119
July 1996	Calgary	85
July 1998	Calgary	63
July 1995	Calgary	52
August 1998	Calgary	37
June 1995	Southern Alberta	26
May 1987	Montréal	25
July 1992	Calgary	22

Source: Insurance Bureau of Canada.

known as **derechos**, or in Canada sometimes called "plough winds." Wind outbursts from convective storms can produce groups of downburst clusters from a thunderstorm system. These derechos tend to blast in linear paths fanning out along curved-wind fronts over a wide swath of land.

A derecho in 1998 in eastern Wisconsin exceeded 57 m/s (128 mph). In August 2007, a series of derechos across northern Illinois reached this same intensity. Researchers identified 377 events between 1986 and 2003, an average of about 21 per year. The name, coined by physicist G. Hinrichs in 1888, derives from a Spanish word meaning "direct" or "straight ahead."

ANIMATION Tornado Wind Patterns

FIGURE 8.22 Mesocyclone and tornado formation.
(a) Strong wind aloft establishes spinning along a horizontal axis. (b) Updraft from thunderstorm development tilts the rotating air along a vertical axis. (c) Mesocyclone forms as a rotating updraft within the thunderstorm. If one forms, a tornado will descend from the lower portion of the mesocyclone. (d) A tornado leaves its mark as this *Landsat-7* image captures. The damage path tracks for 39 km (24 mi) where an EF-4 tornado tore through La Plata, Maryland; more than 900 homes and 200 businesses were destroyed. (e) EF-5 tornado damage in May 1999 in Oklahoma. The church visible in the background was used for an emergency shelter. (f) A fully developed tornado swirls dust and debris as it locks onto the ground. (g) A tornado emerges from the base of a wall cloud near Oakfield, Wisconsin. [(d) *Landsat-7* image courtesy of Satellite Systems Branch, USGS EROS Data Center. Photos by (e) Todd Lindlay; (f) C. Lavoie/First Light; (g) Don Lloyd/AP/Wide World Photos.]

Derechos pose distinct hazards to summer outdoor activities by overturning boats, hurling flying objects, and causing broken trees and limbs. Their highest frequency (about 70%) is from May to August in the region stretching from Iowa, across Illinois, and into the Ohio River Valley in the upper Midwest. For more information and a description of numerous derechos, see **http://www.spc.noaa.gov/misc/AbtDerechos/derechofacts.htm**.

Tornadoes

The updrafts associated with a cumulonimbus development appear on satellite images as pulsing bubbles of clouds. Friction with the ground slows surface winds, but higher in the troposphere, winds blow faster. Thus, a body of air moves faster at higher altitude than at the surface, creating a rotation in the air along a horizontal axis parallel to the ground (picture a rolling pin; see Figure 8.22a). When that rotating air encounters the strong updrafts associated with frontal activity, the axis of rotation shifts to a vertical alignment perpendicular to the ground (Figure 8.22b).

According to one hypothesis for *supercell tornadoes*, this spinning, rising column of mid-troposphere-level air forms a mesocyclone. A **mesocyclone** can range up to 10 km (6 mi) in diameter and rotate vertically within a *supercell cloud* (the parent cloud) to a height of thousands of metres (Figure 8.22c). As a mesocyclone extends vertically and contracts horizontally, wind speeds accelerate in an inward vortex (as ice skaters draw their arms in to accelerate while spinning or as water speeds up when it spirals down a sink drain).

As more moisture-laden air draws up into the circulation of a mesocyclone, more energy is liberated and the rotation of air becomes more rapid as a *wall cloud* forms (Figure 8.23). The swirl of the mesocyclone itself is visible, as are dark grey **funnel clouds** that pulse from the bottom side of the parent cloud. The terror of this stage of development is the lowering of such a funnel to Earth. This tightly rotating vortex is the dreaded **tornado**, from the Latin *tornare*, "to make round by turning" (Figures 8.22d and f and 8.23). When tornado circulation occurs over water, a **waterspout** forms, and the sea or lake surface water is drawn up into the funnel.

Tornado Measurement and Science   A tornado's diameter can range from a few metres to a few hundred metres or larger. It can last from a few seconds to tens of minutes. Air pressure inside a tornado funnel usually is about 10% less than in the surrounding air. This disparity is similar to the pressure difference between sea level and an altitude of 1000 m (3300 ft). Such a sharp horizontal-pressure gradient causes an in-rushing convergence and severe wind speeds at the funnel.

The late Theodore Fujita, a noted meteorologist from the University of Chicago, designed the Fujita Scale (1971), which classifies tornadoes according to wind speed as indicated by related property damage. A refinement in the scale, adopted in February 2007, led to the *Enhanced Fujita Scale*, or *EF Scale* (Table 8.2). The revision filled the need to better assess damage, correlate wind speed to damage caused, and

FIGURE 8.23 Supercell tornado.
A supercell tornado descends from the cloud base near Spearman, Texas. Strong hail is falling to the left of the tornado. [Photo by Howard Bluestein, all rights reserved.]

Table 8.2	The Enhanced Fujita Scale
EF-number	**3-Second Gust Wind Speed; Damage Specs**
F0 Gale	105–137 kmph; 65–85 mph: *light damage*: break branches, damage chimneys.
F1 Weak	138–177 kmph; 86–110 mph: *moderate damage*: beginning of hurricane wind-speed designation, roof coverings peel off, mobile homes pushed off foundations.
F2 Strong	178–217 kmph; 111–135 mph: *considerable damage*: roofs torn off frame houses, large trees uprooted or snapped, box cars pushed over, small missiles generated.
F3 Severe	218–266 kmph; 136–165 mph: *severe damage*: roofs torn off well-constructed houses, trains overturned, trees uprooted, cars thrown.
F4 Devastating	267–322 kmph; 166–200 mph: *devastating damage*: well-built houses leveled, cars thrown, large missiles generated.
F5 Incredible	More than 322 kmph; > 200 mph: *incredible damage*: houses lifted and carried distance to disintegration, car-sized missiles fly farther than 100 m, bark removed from trees.

See the EF-Scale pdf file at: **http://www.wind.ttu.edu/EFScale.pdf**

account for construction quality of structures. To assist with wind estimates, the EF-Scale contains 28 Damage Indicators (DI) relating to types of structures and vegetation affected along with Degrees of Damage (DOD) ratings, both of which you can view at the URL listed below the table.

Greensburg, Kansas, was essentially erased from the map by an EF-5 tornado in May 2007. The statistics are unprecedented: winds exceeded 330 kmph (205 mph) in the 2.7-km (1.7-mi) wide funnel that was on the ground along a 35-km (22-mi) track. Canada experienced its first

ever EF–5 tornado near Elie, Manitoba, June 27, 2007. Improved warning systems held the loss of life to 10 people.

North America receives more tornadoes than anywhere on Earth because its latitudinal position, topography, and the nature of the landscape permit contrasting air masses to confront one another. Tornadoes have struck all 50 states and all the Canadian provinces and territories although Fujita-scale ratings are usually lower in Canada than the U.S. May and June are the peak months, as you see in Figure 8.24, based on 54 years of records.

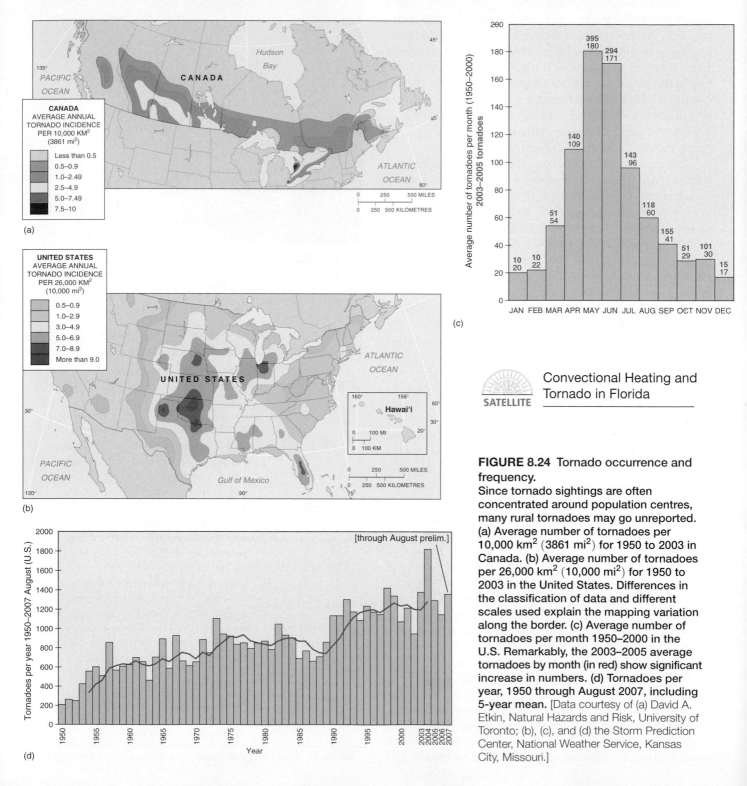

Convectional Heating and Tornado in Florida

FIGURE 8.24 Tornado occurrence and frequency.
Since tornado sightings are often concentrated around population centres, many rural tornadoes may go unreported. (a) Average number of tornadoes per 10,000 km² (3861 mi²) for 1950 to 2003 in Canada. (b) Average number of tornadoes per 26,000 km² (10,000 mi²) for 1950 to 2003 in the United States. Differences in the classification of data and different scales used explain the mapping variation along the border. (c) Average number of tornadoes per month 1950–2000 in the U.S. Remarkably, the 2003–2005 average tornadoes by month (in red) show significant increase in numbers. (d) Tornadoes per year, 1950 through August 2007, including 5-year mean. [Data courtesy of (a) David A. Etkin, Natural Hazards and Risk, University of Toronto; (b), (c), and (d) the Storm Prediction Center, National Weather Service, Kansas City, Missouri.]

Table 8.3 Most Deadly Tornadoes in Canada		
Location	**Date**	**Statistics**
Regina, Saskatchewan	June 30, 1912	28 dead, hundreds injured
Edmonton, Alberta	July 31, 1987	27 dead, hundreds injured
Windsor, Ontario	June 17, 1946	17 dead, hundreds injured
Pine Lake, Alberta	July 14, 2000	12 dead, 140 injured
Valleyfield, Québec	August 16, 1888	9 dead, 14 injured
Windsor, Ontario	April 3, 1974	9 dead, 30 injured
Barrie, Ontario	May 31, 1985	8 dead, 155 injured
Sudbury, Ontario	August 20, 1970	6 dead, 200 injured
Ste-Rose, Québec	June 14, 1892	6 dead, 26 injured
Buctouche, New Brunswick	August 6, 1879	5 dead, 10 injured

Source: The Meteorological Service of Canada. Reproduced with permission of Environment Canada, 2005.

Canada's Worst Tornadoes   Canada places second to the U.S. in the world for tornado occurrences. In Canada, on average, there are 80 tornadoes causing two deaths, 20 injuries, and tens of millions of dollars in property damage each year. The actual number of tornadoes may be higher as tornadoes that strike unpopulated areas remain undetected. Canada's "tornado alleys" are southern Ontario, Alberta, southeastern Québec, and a band stretching from southern Saskatchewan and Manitoba through to Thunder Bay, Ontario. Other tornado zones occur in the interior of British Columbia and in New Brunswick. Annual tornado numbers have been increasing since 1990 in Canada and the United States. Table 8.3 presents the 10 most deadly and damaging tornadoes in Canada.

Recent Tornado Records   In the United States, 48,821 tornadoes were recorded in the 57 years from 1950 through 2006, causing 4793 deaths, or about 84 deaths per year. Of note is the fact that these tornadoes resulted in more than 80,000 injuries and property damage of over $26 billion for this period of record. The yearly average of $500 million in damage is rising each year.

The annual average number of tornadoes before 1990 was 787. Interestingly, since 1990 the average per year has risen to over 1000, with 2004 experiencing 1819 tornadoes, 2005 with 1264, and 2006 with 1105 tornadoes. Importantly, the number of EF-4 and EF-5 tornadoes is on the increase, reaching more than a dozen each season.

Reasons for the annual increase in tornado frequency in North America range from global climate change and more intense thunderstorm activity to better reporting through Doppler Radar and a larger population with videotape recorders. Researchers are pursuing many questions with an enthusiasm for the science and an awe of the subject, as summarized by Howard Bluestein, foremost tornado researcher and meteorologist:

> The source of rotation in some tornadoes appears to be preexisting vortices near the ground above where convective storms are growing; in others, the source seems to be linked to the mesocyclone. Does the mesocyclone itself descend to the ground and intensify to become the tornado, or does it trigger events near the ground that create tornadoes from other sources of rotation? Can it do both? We hope the answers to these questions are soon forthcoming. Our quest for discovery has not taken away from the respect we have for the awesome power the tornado harbors, nor the thrill for viewing the violent motions in the tornado or the beauty of the storm. We eagerly await the next act in the atmospheric play starring the tornado.*

Tropical Cyclones

A powerful manifestation of the Earth–atmosphere energy budget is the **tropical cyclone**, which originates entirely within tropical air masses. The tropics extend from the Tropic of Cancer at 23.5° N to the Tropic of Capricorn at 23.5°S, containing the equatorial zone between 10° N and 10°S. Approximately 80 tropical cyclones occur annually worldwide. Some 45 per year are powerful enough to be classified as hurricanes, typhoons, and cyclones (different regional names for the same type of tropical storm)—30% of these occur in the western North Pacific.

Cyclonic systems forming in the tropics are quite different from midlatitude cyclones because the air of the tropics is essentially homogeneous, with no fronts or conflicting air masses of differing temperatures. In addition, the warm air and warm seas ensure abundant water vapour and thus the necessary latent heat to fuel these storms. Tropical cyclones convert heat energy from the ocean into mechanical energy in the wind—the warmer the ocean and atmosphere, the more intense the conversion and powerful the storm.

What mechanism triggers the start of a tropical cyclone? Meteorologists now think that cyclonic motion begins with slow-moving easterly waves of low pressure in the trade-wind belt of the tropics, such as the Caribbean area (Figure 8.25). For these processes, sea-surface temperatures must exceed approximately 26°C (79°F). Tropical cyclones form along the eastern (leeward) side of these migrating troughs of low pressure, a place of convergence

*H. Bluestein, *Tornado Alley, Monster Storms of the Great Plains* (New York: Oxford University Press, 1999), p. 162.

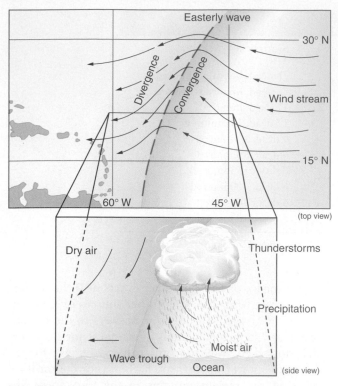

FIGURE 8.25 Easterly wave in the tropics.
A low-pressure centre develops along an easterly (westward-moving) wave. Moist air rises in an area of convergence at the surface to the east of the wave trough. Wind flows bend and converge before the trough and diverge downwind from the trough.

and rainfall. Surface airflow then converges into the low-pressure area, ascends, and flows outward aloft. This important divergence aloft acts as a chimney, pulling more moisture-laden air into the developing system. To maintain and strengthen this vertical convective circulation, there must be little or no wind shear to interrupt or block the airflow.

Hurricanes, Typhoons, and Cyclones Tropical cyclones are potentially the most destructive storms experienced by humans, claiming thousands of lives each year worldwide. This is especially true when they attain wind speeds and low-pressure readings that upgrade their status to a full-fledged **hurricane**, **typhoon**, or *cyclone* (> 65 knots, > 74 mph, > 119 kmph). Across the globe, such storms bear these three different names, among others: *hurricane* around North America, *typhoon* in the western Pacific (Japan, Philippines), and *cyclone* in Indonesia, Bangladesh, and India. By any name they can be destructive killers. Worldwide, about 10% of all tropical disturbances have the right ingredients to become hurricanes or typhoons. For coverage and reporting see the National Hurricane Center at **http://www.nhc.noaa.gov/** or the Joint Typhoon Warning Center at **https://metocph.nmci.navy.mil/jtwc.php**).

The map in Figure 8.26 shows areas in which tropical cyclones form and some of the characteristic storm tracks travelled. The map indicates the range of months during which tropical cyclones are most likely to appear. For example, storms that strike the southeastern United States do so mostly between August and October. Officially, tropical cyclone season for the Atlantic is from June 1 to November 30 each year. (For comparison, the average midlatitude cyclonic storm tracks are in blue on the map.)

Relative to North and Central America, tropical depressions (low-pressure areas) intensify into tropical storms as they cross the Atlantic. A rule of thumb has emerged: If tropical storms mature early along their track, they tend to curve northward toward the North Atlantic and miss the United States. The critical position is approximately 40°W longitude. If a tropical storm matures after it reaches the longitude of the Dominican Republic (70°W), then it has a higher probability of hitting the United States.

In the Southern Hemisphere, no hurricane was ever observed turning from the equator into the south Atlantic (note on the map). However, in March 2004 Hurricane Catarina made landfall in Brazil south of the resorts at Laguna, state of Santa Catarina. NASA's *Terra* satellite in Figure 8.26b clearly shows an organized hurricane, with characteristic central eye and rain bands. Compare the circulation patterns between Hurricane Gilbert (see Figure 8.27a) and Hurricane Catarina (8.26b and 8.27d). What do you see? Note the Coriolis force in action, counterclockwise in the Northern Hemisphere and clockwise in the Southern Hemisphere.

If this Brazilian hurricane wasn't strange enough, in October 2005, the remnants of Tropical Storm Vince became the first-ever Atlantic tropical cyclone to strike Spain (8.26c)! Then in 2006, the first tropical storm to become a category 5 super typhoon developed in the Central Pacific, some 1285 km (800 mi) south of Hawai'i. Super Typhoon Ioke continued for almost three weeks, with final remnants causing large scale erosion along Alaskan shores. And in 2007, Super Cyclone Gonu became the strongest tropical cyclone on record occurring in the Arabian Sea, eventually hitting Oman and the Arabian Peninsula. These four storms apparently are signaling changes underway in tropical meteorology relative to the increased occurrence and intensity of cyclonic systems, as related to higher oceanic and atmospheric temperatures.

Table 8.4 presents the criteria for classification of tropical cyclones on the basis of wind speed and lists features of each designation. When you hear meteorologists speak of a "category 4" hurricane, they are using the *Saffir–Simpson Hurricane Damage Potential Scale* to estimate possible damage from hurricane-force winds. Using wind speeds and central pressure criteria, the scale ranks hurricanes and typhoons in five categories, from smaller, category 1 storms to extremely dangerous category 5. Damage depends on the degree of property development at a storm's landfall site, how prepared citizens are for the blow, the height of storm surge, the presence of embedded tornadoes, and the overall intensity of the storm.

FIGURE 8.26 Worldwide pattern of the most intense tropical cyclones.

(a) Typical tropical storm tracks with principal months of occurrence and regional names. For the North Atlantic region from 1871 to 2000, 1084 tropical cyclones (storms and hurricanes) developed. The peak day in this Atlantic region (assuming a 9-day moving average calculation) is September 10, with 64 cyclones for the 129-year period. Super Typhoon Ioke (2006) and Super Cyclone Gonu (2007) are noted. (b) Hurricane Catarina approaches Brazil's southeastern coast, March 27, 2004—a unique occurrence in recorded history. (c) The remnants of Tropical Storm Vince hit Spain in October 2005, the first-ever storm to take such a track from the tropics. [(b) *Terra* image courtesy MODIS Rapid Response Team, NASA/GSFC; (c) October 11, 2005, *Meteosat–7* image courtesy of University of Ulm.]

Physical Structure Fully organized tropical cyclones have an intriguing physical appearance (Figure 8.27). They range in diameter from a compact 160 km (100 mi), to 1000 km (600 mi), to some western Pacific super typhoons that attain 1300–1600 km (800–1000 mi). Vertically, these storms dominate the full height of the troposphere.

The inward-spiraling clouds form dense rain bands, with a central area designated the *eye*. Around the eye swirls a thunderstorm cloud called the *eyewall*, which is the area of most intense precipitation. The eye remains an enigma, for in the midst of devastating winds and torrential rains the eye is quiet and warm with even a glimpse of blue sky or stars possible. The structure of the rain bands, central eye, and eyewall is clearly visible for Hurricane Gilbert in Figure 8.27a (top view), 8.27b (oblique view from an artist's perspective), and 8.27c (side-radar view). An astronaut photo from the International Space Station (8.27d) shows Hurricane Catarina before it hit Brazil. Note the divergence aloft marked by outward flowing cirrus clouds. And compare the Southern Hemisphere-clockwise winds to those of Gilbert.

Applied Physical Geography (continued)

2000 m (6560 ft), 8°C (46°F). The temperature of the air and the dew-point temperature are the same at 2000 m (6560 ft). Cloud formation begins at this, the lifting condensation level—an elevation at which air temperature is at the dew point. Continued lifting will no longer be at the dry adiabatic rate. Instead, because condensation releases latent heat that warms the atmosphere, the lower, moist adiabatic rate must be used. From 2000 m (6560 ft) upward, the air will cool at an average rate of 6 C° (11 F°) per 1000 m (3280 ft). So, at 3000 m (9840 ft) the air will be at 2°C (36°F) and at 4000 m (13,120 ft), −4°C (25°F) .

Now, imagine the leeward-slope descent. Starting with an air temperature of −4°C (25°F) at an elevation of 4000 m (13,120 ft), what will happen to the cold, dry air on the leeward side of the mountain?

Cold, dry air at the mountaintop will subside and warm adiabatically— its temperature will increase at the dry adiabatic rate and no condensation will occur. At 3000 m (9840 ft), the temperature will be 6°C (43°F); at 2000 m (6560 ft), 16°C (61°F); at 1000 m (3280 ft), 26°C (79°F); and at 500 m (1640 ft), 31°C (88°F). At 500 m (1640 ft), the air is warmer and drier than it was at the same elevation on the windward side of the mountain barrier—thus, a rain shadow.

Summary and Review—Weather

Weather is the short-term condition of the atmosphere; **meteorology** is the scientific study of the atmosphere. The spatial implications of atmospheric phenomena and their relationship to human activities strongly link meteorology to physical geography. Analyzing and understanding patterns of wind, air pressure, temperature, and moisture conditions portrayed on daily weather maps is key to numerical (computer) weather forecasting.

> weather (p. 212)
> meteorology (p. 212)

■ *Describe* air masses that affect North America, and *relate* their qualities to source regions.

Specific conditions of humidity, stability, and cloud coverage occur in a regional, homogenous **air mass**. The longer an air mass remains stationary over a region, the more definite its physical attributes become. The homogeneity of temperature and humidity in an air mass sometimes extends through the lower half of the troposphere. Air masses are categorized by their moisture content—**m** for maritime (wetter) and **c** for continental (drier)—and their temperature, a function of latitude— designated **A** (arctic), **P** (polar), **T** (tropical), **E** (equatorial), and **AA** (Antarctic).

> air mass (p. 213)

1. How does a source region influence the type of air mass that forms over it? Give specific examples of each basic classification.

2. Of all the air masses, which are of greatest significance to Canada and the United States? What happens to them as they migrate to locations different from their source regions? Give an example of air-mass modification.

■ *Identify* four types of atmospheric lifting mechanisms, and *describe* four principal examples.

Air masses can rise through **convergent lifting** (airflows conflict, forcing some of the air to lift); **convectional lifting** (air passing over warm surfaces gains buoyancy); **orographic lifting** (passage over a topographic barrier); and *frontal lifting*. In North America, **chinook winds** (called *föhn* or *foehn* winds in Europe) are the warm, downslope airflows characteristic of the leeward side of mountains. Orographic lifting creates wetter windward slopes and drier leeward slopes situated in the **rain shadow** of the mountain. Conflicting air masses at a front produce a **cold front** (and sometimes a zone of strong wind and rain) or a **warm front**. A zone right along or slightly ahead of the front, called a **squall line**, is characterized by turbulent and wildly changing wind patterns and intense precipitation.

> convergent lifting (p. 215)
> convectional lifting (p. 215)
> orographic lifting (p. 217)
> chinook winds (p. 217)
> rain shadow (p. 217)
> cold front (p. 218)
> warm front (p. 218)
> squall line (p. 221)

3. Explain why it is necessary for an air mass to be lifted if there is to be saturation, condensation, and precipitation.

4. What are the four principal lifting mechanisms that cause air masses to ascend, cool, condense, form clouds, and perhaps produce precipitation? Briefly describe each.

5. Differentiate between the structure of a cold front and a warm front.

■ *Analyze* the pattern of orographic precipitation, and *describe* the link between this pattern and global topography.

The physical presence of a mountain acts as a topographic barrier to migrating air masses. *Orographic lifting* (oro- means "mountain") occurs when air is forcibly lifted upslope as it is pushed against a mountain. It cools adiabatically. An orographic barrier enhances convectional activity and causes additional lifting during the passage of weather fronts and cyclonic systems, thereby extracting more moisture from passing air masses. The precipitation pattern of windward and leeward slopes persists worldwide. The provinces of British Columbia and Alberta are presented in the chapter as excellent examples of this concept.

6. When an air mass passes across a mountain range, many things happen to it. Describe each aspect of a mountain crossing by a moist air mass. What is the pattern of precipitation that results?

7. Explain how the distribution of precipitation in British Columbia is influenced by the principles of orographic lifting.

■ *List* the measurable elements that contribute to weather and *describe* the life cycle of a midlatitude cyclonic storm system.

Synoptic analysis involves the collection of weather data at a specific time. Building a database of wind, pressure, temperature, and moisture conditions is key to numerical (computer-based) weather prediction and the development of weather-forecasting models. Preparing a weather report and forecast requires analysis of a daily weather map and satellite images that depict atmospheric conditions. Weather data from these sources include the following:

- Barometric pressure (sea level and altimeter setting)
- Pressure tendency (steady, rising, falling)
- Surface air temperature
- Dew-point temperature
- Wind speed, direction, and character (gusts, squalls)
- Type and movement of clouds
- Current weather
- State of the sky (current sky conditions)
- Visibility; vision obstruction (fog, haze)
- Precipitation since last observation

A **midlatitude cyclone**, or **wave cyclone**, is a vast low-pressure system that migrates across the continent, pulling air masses into conflict along fronts. **Cyclogenesis**, the birth of the low-pressure circulation, can occur off the west coast of North America, along the polar front, along the lee slopes of the Rockies, in the Gulf of Mexico, and along the East Coast. A midlatitude cyclone can be thought of as having a life cycle of birth, maturity, old age, and dissolution. An **occluded front** is produced when a cold front overtakes a warm front in the maturing cyclone. Sometimes a **stationary front** develops between conflicting air masses, where airflow is parallel to the front on both sides. These systems are guided by the jet streams of the upper troposphere along seasonally shifting **storm tracks**.

midlatitude cyclone (p. 222)
wave cyclone (p. 222)
cyclogenesis (p. 222)
occluded front (p. 222)
stationary front (p. 222)
storm tracks (p. 223)

8. Differentiate between a cold front and a warm front as types of frontal lifting and what you would experience with each one.

9. How does a midlatitude cyclone act as a catalyst for conflict between air masses?

10. What is meant by cyclogenesis? In what areas does it occur and why? What is the role of upper-tropospheric circulation in the formation of a surface low?

11. Diagram a midlatitude cyclonic storm during its open stage. Label each of the components in your illustration, and add arrows to indicate wind patterns in the system.

12. What is your principal source of weather data, information, and forecasts? Where does your source obtain its data? Have you used the Internet and World Wide Web to obtain weather information? In what ways will you personally apply this knowledge in the future? What benefits do you see?

■ *Analyze* various forms of violent weather and the characteristics of each.

The violent power of some weather phenomena poses a hazard to society. Severe **ice storms** involve sleet (freezing precipitation, ice glaze, and ice pellets), snow blizzards, and crippling ice coatings on roads, power lines, and crops. Thunderstorms produce **lightning** (electrical discharges in the atmosphere), **thunder** (sonic bangs produced by the rapid expansion of air after intense heating by lightning), and **hail** (ice pellets formed within cumulonimbus clouds).

Strong linear winds in excess of 26 m/s (58 mph) are known as **derechos**, associated with thunderstorms and bands of showers crossing a region. Straight-line winds can cause significant damage and crop losses. A spinning, cyclonic column rising to mid-troposphere level—a **mesocyclone**—is sometimes visible as the swirling mass of a cumulonimbus cloud. Dark grey **funnel clouds** pulse from the bottom side of the parent cloud. A **tornado** is formed when the funnel connects with Earth's surface. A **waterspout** forms when a tornado circulation occurs over water.

Within tropical air masses, large low-pressure centres can form along easterly wave troughs. Under the right conditions, a tropical cyclone is produced. Depending on wind speeds and central pressure, a **tropical cyclone** can become a **hurricane**, **typhoon**, or cyclone when winds exceed 65 knots (119 kmph, 74 mph). As forecasting and the public's perception of weather-related hazards improve, loss of life decreases, although property damage continues to increase. Great damage occurs to occupied coastal lands when hurricanes make **landfall** and when winds drive ocean water inland in **storm surges**.

ice storms (p. 227)
lightning (p. 228)
thunder (p. 228)
hail (p. 229)
derechos (p. 231)
mesocyclone (p. 233)
funnel clouds (p. 233)
tornado (p. 233)
waterspout (p. 233)
tropical cyclone (p. 235)
hurricane (p. 236)
typhoon (p. 236)
landfall (p. 238)
storm surges (p. 238)

13. What constitutes a thunderstorm? What type of cloud is involved? What type of air mass would you expect in an area of thunderstorms in North America?

14. Lightning and thunder are powerful phenomena in nature. Briefly describe how they develop.

15. Describe the formation process of a mesocyclone. How is this development associated with that of a tornado?

16. Evaluate the pattern of tornado activity in Canada and the United States. Where is Tornado Alley? What generalizations can you make about the distribution and timing of tornadoes?

17. What are the different classifications for tropical cyclones? List the various names used worldwide for hurricanes.

18. What factors contributed to the incredible damage cost of Hurricane Katrina in 2005 and subsequent years? Why have such damage figures increased even though loss of life has decreased over the past 30 years?

19. What have scientists said to explain the intensity of tropical cyclones since 1970? Put in your own words the quotations in this chapter from scientific journals related to changes in storm intensity.

20. Relative to improving weather forecasting, what are some of the technological innovations discussed in this chapter?

Critical Thinking

A. In the following figure you see a weather map of conditions March 31, 2007, 7 A.M. EST, along with a *GOES-12* satellite image of water vapour at the time of the map. Using the legend for weather map symbols in Figure 8.14, briefly analyze the map: Find the centre of low pressure, note the counterclockwise winds, compare temperatures on either side of the cold front, note air temperatures and dew-point temperatures, determine why the fronts are placed where they are on the map, and locate the centre of high pressure.

You can see the air and dew-point temperatures in New Orleans are 68°F and 63°F, respectively; yet, in St. George, Utah (southwest corner of state), you see 27°F and 22°F, respectively. To become saturated, the warm, moist air in New Orleans needs to cool to 63°F, whereas in St. George the dry, cold air needs to cool to 22°F for saturation. In the far north, find Churchill on the western shore of Hudson Bay. The air and dew-point temperatures are 6°F and 3°F, respectively, and the state of the sky is clear. If you were there, what would you experience at this time? Why would you be reaching for the lip balm?

B. Relative to coastal devastation from tropical weather, the following line appears in the text: "This recurrent, yet avoidable cycle—construction, devastation, reconstruction, devastation...." This describes the ever-increasing dollar losses to property from tropical storms and hurricanes, yet at a time when improved forecasts have resulted in a significant reduction in loss of life. (These issues are discussed further in Chapter 16's Focus Study 16.1.) In your opinion, what is the solution to halt these increasing losses, this cycle of destruction? How would you implement your plan?

FIGURE 9.2 The soil-moisture environment. Precipitation supplies the soil-moisture environment. The principal pathways for water include interception by plants; throughfall to the ground; collection on the surface, forming overland flow to streams; transpiration and evaporation from plants; evaporation from land and water; and gravitational water moving to subsurface groundwater. Water moves from the surface into the soil by infiltration and percolation.

to the ground is *stem flow* and can be an important moisture route to the ground. Precipitation that falls directly to the ground, coupled with drips from vegetation (excluding stem flow), constitutes *throughfall*. Water soaks into the subsurface through **infiltration**, or penetration of the soil surface. It further permeates soil or rock through the downward movement of **percolation**. These concepts are shown in Figure 9.2.

The atmospheric advection of water vapour from sea to land and land to sea at the top of Figure 9.1 appears to be unbalanced: 20% (94,000 km³) moving inland but only 12% (57,000 km³) moving out to sea. However, this exchange is balanced by the 8% (37,000 km³) land runoff that flows to the sea. Most of this runoff—about 95%—comes from surface waters that wash across land as overland flow and streamflow. Only 5% of runoff is slow-moving subsurface groundwater. These percentages indicate that the small amount of water in rivers and streams is dynamic, whereas the large quantity of subsurface water in contrast is sluggish and represents only a small portion of total runoff.

The residence time for a water molecule in any part of the hydrologic cycle determines its relative importance in affecting Earth's climates. The short time spent by water in transit through the atmosphere (an average of 10 days) plays a role in temporary fluctuations in regional weather patterns. Long residence times, such as the 3000–10,000 years in deep-ocean circulation, groundwater aquifers, and glacial ice, act to moderate temperature and climatic changes. These slower parts of the cycle work as a "system memory"; the long periods over which heat energy is stored and released can buffer the effects of system changes.

To observe and describe the hydrologic cycle and its related energy budgets, scientists established in 1988 the Global Energy and Water Cycle Experiment (GEWEX). This is part of the World Climate Research Program and represents an important focus in climate-change studies. Canada's contribution to the program is the Mackenzie GEWEX Study (MAGS, **http://www.usask.ca/geography/MAGS/**). The

goal is to improve understanding of water and energy cycles of the Mackenzie River Basin in particular and cold regions in general. A major objective of the study is to develop coupled models of atmospheric and hydrologic processes that can be used to evaluate the impact of both human-induced climate change and natural climate variability on Canada's water resources. Now that you are acquainted with the hydrologic cycle, let's examine the concept of the soil-water budget as a method of assessing water resources.

Soil-Water-Budget Concept

A **soil-water budget** can be established for any area of Earth's surface—a continent, country, region, field, or front yard. Key is measuring the precipitation "supply" input and its distribution to satisfy the "demand" outputs of plants, evaporation, and soil moisture storage in the area considered. Such a budget can examine any time frame, from minutes to years.

Think of a soil-water budget as a money budget: Precipitation income must be balanced against expenditures of evaporation, transpiration, and runoff. Soil-moisture storage acts as a savings account, accepting deposits and withdrawals of water. Sometimes all expenditure demands are met, and any extra water results in a surplus. At other times, precipitation and soil moisture income are inadequate to meet demands, and a deficit, or water shortage, results.

Geographer Charles W. Thornthwaite (1899–1963) pioneered applied water-resource analysis and worked with others to develop a water-balance methodology. They applied water-balance concepts to geographic problems, especially to irrigation, which requires accurate quantity and timing of water application to maximize crop yields.

Thornthwaite also developed methods for estimating evaporation and transpiration. He recognized the important relation between water supply and local water demand as an essential climatic element. In fact, his initial use of these techniques was to develop a climatic classification system.

The Soil-Water-Balance Equation

To understand Thornthwaite's water-balance methodology and "accounting" or "bookkeeping" procedures, we must first understand some terms and concepts. Figure 9.2 illustrates the essential aspects of a soil-water budget. Precipitation (mostly rain and snow) provides the moisture input. The object, as with a money budget, is to account for the ways in which this supply is distributed: actual water taken by evaporation and plant transpiration, extra water that exits in streams and subsurface groundwater, and recharge or utilization of soil-moisture storage.

Figure 9.3 organizes the water-balance components into an equation. As in all equations, the two sides must balance; that is, the precipitation receipt (left side) must be fully accounted for by expenditures (right side). Follow this water-balance equation as you read the following paragraphs. To help you learn these concepts, we use letter abbreviations (such as PRECIP) for the components.

Precipitation (PRECIP) Input   The moisture supply to Earth's surface is **precipitation** (PRECIP, or P). It arrives in several different forms depending upon temperature and moisture supply. Table 9.1 summarizes the different types of precipitation. As you read through this table recall which types of precipitation you have experienced— rain, sleet, snow, and hail being most common.

Precipitation is measured with the **rain gauge**. A rain gauge is essentially a large measuring cup, collecting rainfall and snowfall so the water can be measured by depth, weight, or volume (Figure 9.4). Wind can cause an undercatch because the drops or snowflakes are not falling vertically. For example, a wind of 37 kmph (23 mph) produces an undercatch as great as 40%, meaning that an actual 1-in. rainfall might gauge at only 0.6 in. The *windshield* you see above the gauge's opening reduces this error by catching raindrops that arrive at an angle. According to the World Meteorological Organization (**http://www.wmo.ch/index-en.html**), more than 40,000 weather-monitoring stations are operating worldwide, with more than 100,000 places measuring precipitation.

Figure 9.5 maps precipitation patterns for Canada and the United States. Note the patterns of wetness and dryness, as you remember our discussion of air masses and lifting mechanisms in Chapter 8. (Chapter 10 presents a world precipitation map in Figure 10.2.) PRECIP is the principal input to the water-balance equation (Figure 9.3). All the components discussed next are outputs or expenditures of this water.

Actual Evapotranspiration (ACTET)   Evaporation is the net movement of free water molecules away from a wet surface into air that is less than saturated.

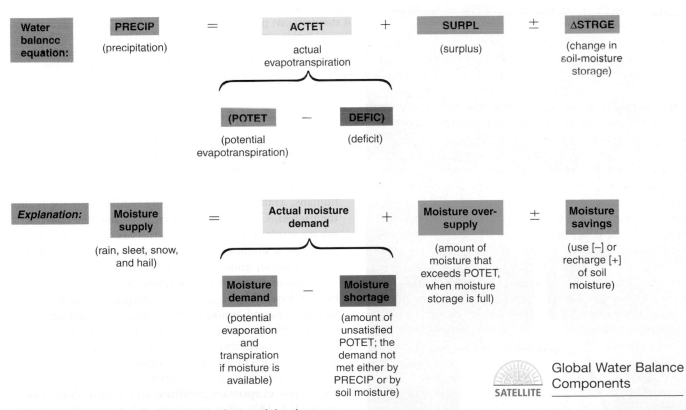

FIGURE 9.3 The water-balance equation explained.
The outputs (components to the right of the equal sign) are an accounting of expenditures from the precipitation moisture-supply input (to the left).

FIGURE 9.6 Lysimeter. A weighing lysimeter for measuring evaporation and transpiration. The various pathways of water are tracked: Some water remains as soil moisture, some is incorporated into plant tissues, some drains from the bottom of the lysimeter, and the remainder is credited to evapotranspiration. Given natural conditions, the lysimeter measures actual evapotranspiration. [Adapted from illustration courtesy of Lloyd Owens, Agricultural Research Service, USDA, Coshocton, Ohio.]

and plant cover, thus allowing measurement of the moisture moving through the sampled area. A weighing lysimeter has this embedded tank resting on a weighing scale (Figure 9.6). A rain gauge next to the lysimeter measures the precipitation input. (See the U.S. Agricultural Research Service at http://www.ars.usda.gov/.)

The number of lysimeters and evaporation pans is somewhat limited across North America, but they still provide a database from which to develop ways of estimating POTET. Several methods of estimating POTET on the basis of meteorological data are widely used and easily implemented for regional applications. Thornthwaite developed one of these methods. He discovered that if you know monthly mean air temperature and daylength, you could approximate POTET. These data are readily available, so calculating POTET is easy and fairly accurate for most midlatitude locations. (Recall that daylength is a function of a station's latitude.) His method can work with data from hourly, daily, or annual time frames or with historical data to re-create water conditions in past environments.

Thornthwaite's method works better in some climates than in others. It ignores warm or cool air movements across a surface, sublimation and surface-water retention at subfreezing temperatures, poor drainage, and frozen soil (*permafrost*, Chapter 17), although there is allowance for snow accumulations. Nevertheless, we use his water-balance method here because of its great utility as a teaching tool and its overall ease of application and acceptable results for geographic studies.

Figure 9.7 presents POTET values derived using Thornthwaite's approach for Canada and the United States. Note that higher values occur in the South, with highest readings in the Southwest where higher average air temperature and lower relative humidity exists. Lower

POTET values are found at higher latitudes and elevations, which have lower average temperatures.

Compare this POTET (demand) map with the PRECIP (supply) map in Figure 9.5. The relation between the two determines the remaining components of the water-balance equation in Figure 9.3. From the two maps, can you identify regions where PRECIP is greater than POTET (for example, eastern Canada)? Or where POTET is greater than PRECIP (for example, the southwestern United States)? Where you live, is the water demand usually met by the precipitation supply? Or does your area experience a natural shortage?

Deficit (DEFIC) The POTET demand can be satisfied in three ways: by PRECIP, by moisture stored in the soil, or through artificial irrigation. If these three sources are inadequate to meet moisture demands, the location experiences a moisture shortage. This unsatisfied POTET is **deficit** (DEFIC, or D).

By subtracting DEFIC from POTET, we determine the **actual evapotranspiration**, or ACTET, that takes place (see Figure 9.3). Under ideal conditions for plants, potential and actual amounts of evapotranspiration are about the same, so plants do not experience a water shortage; droughts result from deficit conditions.

Surplus (SURPL) If POTET is satisfied and the soil is full of moisture, then additional water input becomes **surplus** (SURPL, or S). This excess water might sit on the surface in puddles, ponds, and lakes, or it might flow across the surface toward stream channels or percolate through the soil underground. The **overland flow** combines with precipitation and groundwater flows into river channels to make up the **total runoff**. Because surplus water generates most streamflow, or runoff, the

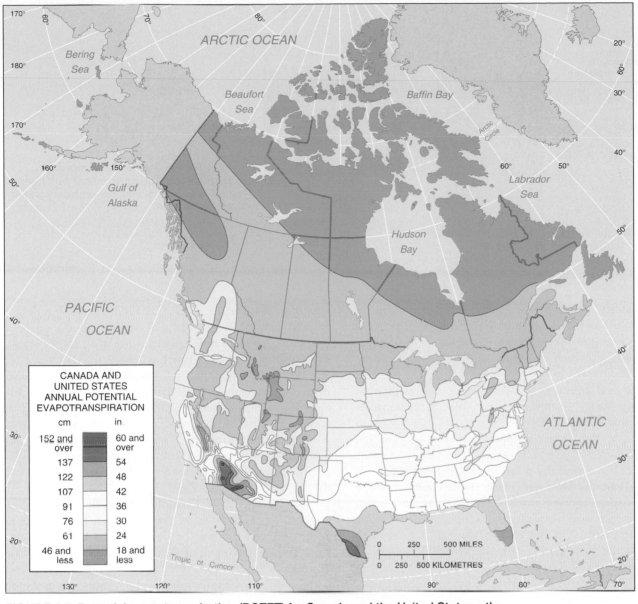

FIGURE 9.7 **Potential evapotranspiration (POTET) for Canada and the United States—the demand.** [From C. W. Thornthwaite, "An approach toward a rational classification of climate," *Geographical Review* 38 (1948): 64. Adapted by permission from the American Geographical Society. Canadian data adapted from M. Sanderson, "The climates of Canada according to the new Thornthwaite classification," *Scientific Agriculture* 28 (1948): 501–17.]

Global Water Balance Components

SATELLITE

water-balance approach is useful for indirectly estimating streamflow.

Soil-Moisture Storage (Δ STRGE) A "savings account" of water that receives recharge "deposits" and provides for utilization "withdrawals" is **soil-moisture storage** (Δ STRGE, or Δ S). This is the volume of water stored in the soil that is accessible to plant roots. The delta symbol, Δ, means that this component includes both *recharge* and *utilization* (use) of soil moisture; the Δ in math means "change." Soil moisture comprises two categories of water—hygroscopic and capillary—but only capillary water is accessible to plants (Figure 9.8).

Hygroscopic water is inaccessible to plants because it is a molecule-thin layer that is tightly bound to each soil particle by the hydrogen bonding of water molecules (Figure 9.8, left). Hygroscopic water exists even in the desert, but it is unavailable to meet POTET demands. Relative to plants, soil is at the **wilting point** when all that remains is this inaccessible water; plants wilt and eventually die after a prolonged period of such moisture stress.

Capillary water is generally accessible to plant roots because it is held against the pull of gravity in the soil by hydrogen bonds between water molecules, which causes surface tension, and by hydrogen bonding between water molecules and the soil. Most capillary water that remains in the soil is **available water** in soil-moisture storage. After some water drains from the larger pore spaces, the amount of available water remaining for plants is termed

Soil particles with forms of soil moisture

Hygroscopic H$_2$O*

Capillary H$_2$O

Gravitational H$_2$O

Soil-moisture availability (increasing ⟶)

H$_2$O unavailable for plants ← → H$_2$O available ← → H$_2$O ⟶

Wilting point   Field capacity   Saturation

Gravitational water

*Note: Some capillary water is bound to hygroscopic water on soil particle and is also unavailable.

FIGURE 9.8 Types of soil moisture. Hygroscopic and gravitational water are unavailable to plants; only capillary water is available. [After D. Steila, *The Geography of Soils*, © 1976, p. 45. Reprinted by permission of Prentice Hall, Inc., Upper Saddle River, NJ.]

field capacity, or storage capacity. It is removable to meet POTET demands through the action of plant roots and surface evaporation (Figure 9.8, centre). Field capacity is specific to each soil type, and the amount can be determined by soil surveys.

When soil becomes saturated after a precipitation event, any water surplus in the soil body becomes **gravitational water**. It percolates from the shallower capillary zone to the deeper groundwater zone (Figure 9.8, right).

Figure 9.9 shows the relation of soil texture to soil-moisture content. Different plant species send roots to different depths and therefore reach different amounts of soil moisture. A soil blend that maximizes available water is best for plants. On the basis of Figure 9.9, can you determine the soil texture with the greatest quantity of available water?

As **soil-moisture utilization** removes soil water, the plants must exert greater effort to extract the amount of moisture they need. As a result, even though a small amount of water may remain in the soil, plants may be unable to exert enough pressure to use it. The resulting

unsatisfied demand is a *deficit* (DEFIC). Avoiding a deficit and reducing plant growth inefficiencies are the goals of irrigation, for the harder plants must work to get water, the less their yield and growth will be.

Whether from natural precipitation or artificial irrigation, water infiltrates the soil and replenishes available water, the process of **soil-moisture recharge**. The texture and the structure of the soil dictate available pore spaces, or **porosity**. The property of the soil that determines the rate of soil-moisture recharge is its **permeability**. Permeability depends on particle sizes and the shape and packing of soil grains.

Water infiltration is rapid in the first minutes of precipitation and slows as the upper soil layers become saturated, even though the deeper soil is still dry. Agricultural practices, such as ploughing and adding sand or manure to loosen soil structure, can improve both soil permeability and the depth to which moisture can efficiently penetrate to recharge soil-moisture storage. You may have found yourself working to improve soil permeability with a houseplant or garden, working the soil to increase the rate of soil-moisture recharge.

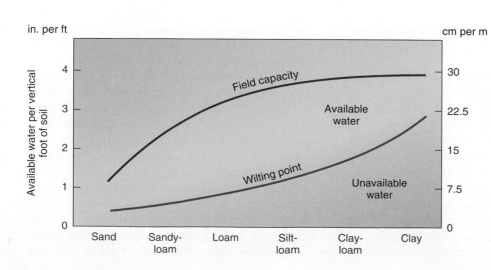

FIGURE 9.9 Soil-moisture availability.
The relation between soil-moisture availability and soil texture determines the distance between the two curves that show field capacity and wilting point. A loam soil (one-third each of sand, silt, and clay) has roughly the most available water per vertical foot of soil exposed to plant roots. [After U.S. Department of Agriculture, *1955 Yearbook of Agriculture—Water*, p. 120.]

Drought

Drought might seem a simple thing to define: less precipitation and higher temperatures make for drier conditions. However, there is no precise definition of **drought**. The key is to know the water-resource demand as it relates to the lack of water. There must be a consideration of not just precipitation, temperature, and soil-moisture content, but whether crops are in the growing season, or if low precipitation is during winter and the season for snow pack accumulation, or the overall relation of precipitation patterns to the climate of a region.

A *meteorological drought* relates to dry conditions of lower precipitation and higher temperatures and losses in soil moisture. An *agricultural drought* occurs when changes in soil moisture and weather elements affect crop yields. Losses can be significant and are running in the tens of billions of dollars each year in the United States, although drought disasters seem to slowly evolve, getting little coverage in the media, and lack the shock of a hurricane or earthquake.

When reservoir levels drop, or mountain snowpack declines, streamflow decreases, and groundwater mining increases, we have a *hydrologic drought*. A more comprehensive measure considers loss of life, water rationing, wildfire events, and other impacts as they become widespread in *socioeconomic drought*.

The National Drought Mitigation Center, University of Nebraska–Lincoln (NDMC, **http://www.drought. unl.edu/**), publishes a weekly "Drought Monitor" map, released each Thursday, and a newsletter *Drought Scape*. In Canada, Agriculture and Agri-Food Canada provide a drought watch map and assessment; see **http://www.agr. gc.ca/pfra/drought/**.

Droughts of various intensities are occurring on every continent through 2007. Australia in 2008 was in the seventh year of its worst drought in 100 years. Regarding the U.S. Southwest drought, underway since late 2000, scientists reported in May 2007 this remarkable situation linked directly to global climate change.

> The projected future climate of intensified aridity in the Southwest is caused by . . . a poleward expansion of the subtropical dry zones. The drying of subtropical land areas . . . imminent or already underway is unlike any climate state we have seen in the instrumental record. It is also distinct from the multi-decadal megadroughts that afflicted the American Southwest during Medieval times . . . The most severe future droughts will still occur during persistent La Niña events, but they will be worse than any since the Medieval period, because the La Niña conditions will be perturbing a base state that is drier than any state experienced recently.[*]

In other words, previous droughts in the region related to sea-surface temperature changes in the distant tropical Pacific Ocean will still occur, but they will be worsened by climate change and the unwanted expansion farther into the region of the hot, dry subtropical high-pressure system and the summertime continental tropical (cT) air mass. The spatial implications of such semi-permanent drought in a region of explosive population growth and urbanization are serious and tie-in directly the need for water resource planning.

Sample Water Budgets

Using all of these concepts, we graph the water-balance components for several representative cities. Let's begin by looking at Hamilton, Ontario, on the western end of Lake Ontario at 43.25° N, 79.85° W, elevation 237 m (777.6 ft).

Figure 9.10 graphs the water-balance components for long-term supply and demand, using monthly averages. The monthly values for PRECIP and POTET smooth the actual daily and hourly variability. On the graph, a comparison of PRECIP and POTET by month determines whether there is a *net supply* or a *net demand* for water. There is a net supply (blue line) from October to May, but the warm days from June to September create a net water demand. If we assume a soil-moisture storage capacity of 100 mm (4.0 in.), typical of shallow-rooted

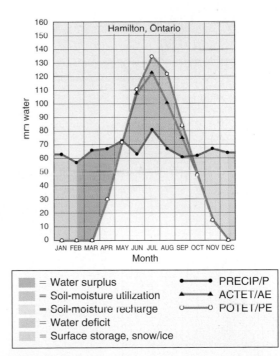

FIGURE 9.10 Sample water budget for Hamilton, Ontario. Compare the average plots for precipitation inputs and potential evapotranspiration outputs to determine the condition of the soil-moisture environment. A typical pattern of spring surplus, summer soil-moisture utilization, a small summer deficit, autumn soil-moisture recharge, and ending surplus highlights the year. Snow accumulation occurs in January and February when average temperatures are below freezing. During this time, snow is stored on top of the ground and does not recharge soil moisture. In March, when temperatures are warm, snow melts, the ground thaws, and soil-moisture storage returns to 300 mm.

---

[*]Richard Seager, *et al.*, "Model Projections of an Imminent Transition to a More Arid Climate in Southwestern North America," *Science* v. 316 no. 5828 (May 25, 2007): p. 1184.

= Water surplus
= Soil-moisture utilization
= Soil-moisture recharge
= Water deficit
= Surface storage, snow/ice

PRECIP/P
ACTET/AE
POTET/PE
*25.4 mm = 1 in.

(a) Vancouver, British Columbia
(b) Seabrook, New Jersey
(c) Saskatoon, Saskatchewan
(d) Ottawa, Ontario
(e) Phoenix, Arizona
(f) San Juan, Puerto Rico

FIGURE 9.11 Sample water budgets for selected stations.
Sample water-balance regimes for selected stations in North America and the Caribbean region.

Table 9.2 Annual, March, and September Water Balances for Hamilton, Ontario

	PRECIP	=	POTET	−	DEFIC	+	SURPL	±	ΔSTRGE
Annual	791.0		617.0		44.0		218.0	+	0
	(31.1)		(24.3)		(1.7)		(8.6)	+	(0)
March	66.0		0*		0		66.0**	+	0
	(2.6)		(0)		(0)		(2.6)	+	(0)
September	61.0		84.0		9.0		0	−	14.0
	(2.4)		(3.3)		(0.4)		(0)	+	(0.5)

Note: All quantities in millimetres (inches).

*When temperatures are at or below freezing in January, February, and early March, the model assumes no POTET, although there are sublimation losses.

**Surplus as snow and ice super storage; leaving taller stubble in fields or using snow fences helps catch snow for melt and soil-moisture recharge.

Source: Average Climatic Water Balance Data of the Continents, Part VI, North America (excluding United States). Publications in Climatology, vol. 17, no. 2, by C.W. Thornthwaite Associates.

plants, the net water-demand months are satisfied through soil-moisture utilization (green area), with a small summer soil-moisture deficit.

Table 9.2 shows the actual data for Hamilton's water-balance equations for the year and for the months of March and September. Here, you can see the interaction of these various components. Check these three equations and perform the functions indicated to see whether we accounted for all the PRECIP received. Compare March and September in the equations with the same months in the graph in Figure 9.10.

Obviously, not all stations experience the surplus moisture patterns of this humid continental region. Different climatic regimes experience different relations among water-balance components. Figure 9.11 presents water-balance graphs for several other cities in North America and the Caribbean Sea region. Among these examples, compare the summer precipitation of Vancouver, British Columbia, with that of Seabrook, New Jersey; the drier prairies of Saskatchewan with the more humid conditions in Ottawa, Ontario; and the precipitation receipts of San Juan, Puerto Rico, with the arid desert of Phoenix, Arizona.

Water Budget and Water Resources

Water distribution is uneven over space and time. Because we require a steady supply, we build large-scale management projects intended to redistribute the water resource either geographically, by moving water from one place to another, or over time, by storing water from time of receipt until it is needed. In this way, deficits are reduced, surpluses are held for later release, and water availability is improved to satisfy evapotranspiration and society's demands. The water balance permits analysis of the contribution streams make to water resources. On the prairies, a farmer augments the water balance with sprinkler irrigation. This counts as more precipitation in the water balance (Figure 9.12).

Streams may be *perennial* (constantly flowing; *perennial* is Latin for "through the year") or *intermittent*. In either case, the total runoff that moves through them

FIGURE 9.12 Irrigated prairie.
Prairie irrigation in the Frenchman River valley south of the Cypress Hills in southwestern Saskatchewan. A field of hay is having its annual water balance augmented by a rolling sprinkler system. [Photo by David Sauchyn.]

comes from surplus surface-water runoff, subsurface throughflow, and groundwater. Figure 9.13 maps annual global river runoff for the world. The highest runoff amounts are along the equator within the tropics, reflecting the continual rainfall along the Intertropical Convergence Zone (ITCZ). Southeast Asia also experiences high runoff, as do northwest coastal mountains in the Northern Hemisphere. In countries having great seasonal fluctuations in runoff, groundwater becomes an important reserve water supply. Regions of lower runoff coincide with Earth's subtropical deserts, rain-shadow areas, and continental interiors, particularly in Asia.

FIGURE 9.16 Groundwater characteristics.
Subsurface groundwater characteristics, processes, water flows, and human interactions. Follow the concepts across the illustration left-to-right as you read along in the text.

Why Is There a Water Table?

Forming a Cone of Depression

of 1909, is an independent binational organization whose purpose is to help prevent and resolve disputes relating to the use and quality of boundary waters and to advise Canada and the United States on related questions. The IJC has more than 20 boards that assist in dispute resolution. Visit the IJC Web site for a complete overview of its mission and a description of the boards (**http://www.ijc.org/en/home/main_accueil.htm**).

An interesting application of the water-balance approach to water resources is analyzing an event, such as the Dust Bowl, an urban flood, or a hurricane. Tropical storms may be devastating along a coastline, but inland they can lessen droughts and fill reservoirs.

Groundwater Resources

Groundwater is an important part of the hydrologic cycle, although it lies beneath the surface, beyond the soil-moisture root zone. It is tied to surface supplies through pores in soil and rock. Groundwater is the largest potential freshwater source in the hydrologic cycle—larger than all surface lakes and streams combined. Between Earth's land surface and a depth of 4 km (13,000 ft) worldwide, some 8,340,000 km^3 (2,000,000 mi^3) of water resides, a volume comparable to 70 times all the freshwater lakes in the world. Despite this volume and its obvious importance, pollution threatens groundwater quality, and overconsumption depletes groundwater volume in quantities beyond natural replenishment rates.

Remember: *Groundwater is not an independent source of water, for it is tied to surface supplies for recharge.* An important consideration in many regions is that groundwater accumulation occurred over millions of years, so care must be

taken not to exceed this long-term buildup with excessive short-term demands.

Globally, groundwater is the raw material extracted most from nature by people, totaling more than 700 km^3/year in volume, and is the basis for agriculture's "green revolution," used for irrigation more widely than surface water in many countries. For many uses, quality groundwater is a better source than surface water. It is available in many parts of the world that lack dependable surface runoff. Whereas surface supplies are affected by short-term drought, groundwater is not (although long-term drought affects both). Except in severely polluted areas, groundwater is generally free of sediment, colour, and disease organisms, although polluted groundwater conditions are considered irreversible.

In Canada, about 6 million people (two-thirds of them in rural areas) rely on groundwater for domestic needs—1.5 billion m^3/year (53 billion ft^3/year). About 50% of the U.S. population derives a portion of its freshwater from groundwater sources. In some states, such as Nebraska, groundwater supplies 85% of water needs and may reach 100% in rural areas. Between 1950 and 2000, annual groundwater withdrawal in the United States and Canada increased more than 150%. Figure 9.15 (on p. 265) shows potential groundwater resources in both countries.

Groundwater Profile and Movement

Figure 9.16 brings together many groundwater elements in a single illustration, and it is the basis for the following discussion. Groundwater begins as surplus water, which percolates downward as gravitational water from the zone of capillary water. This excess surface water moves through the **zone of aeration**, where soil and rock are less than saturated (some pore spaces contain air).

The *porosity* of any rock layer depends on the arrangement, size, and shape of its individual particles, the nature of any cementing elements between them, and their degree of compaction. Subsurface rocks are either *permeable* or *impermeable*. Their permeability depends on whether they conduct water readily (higher permeability) or tend to obstruct its flow (lower permeability).

Eventually, the water reaches an area where subsurface water accumulates, the **zone of saturation**. Here, the pores are completely filled with water. Like a hard sponge made of sand, gravel, and rock, the saturation zone stores water in its countless pores and voids. An **aquifer** is a rock layer that is permeable to groundwater flow adequate for wells and springs. An **aquiclude** is a body of rock that does not conduct water in usable amounts (also called an *aquitard*). The saturated zone may include the saturated portion of the aquifer and a part of the underlying *aquiclude*, even though the latter has such low permeability that its water is inaccessible.

The upper limit of the water that collects in the zone of saturation is the **water table**. It is the contact surface between the zone of saturation, a narrow capillary fringe layer, and the zone of aeration above (all across Figure 9.16). The slope of the water table, which generally follows the contours of the land surface, controls groundwater movement.

Aquifers, Wells, and Springs

For many people, adequate water supply depends on a good aquifer beneath them that is accessible with a well or exposed on a hillside where water emerges as a spring. Is any of the water you consume from a well or spring?

Confined and Unconfined Aquifers Whether an aquifer is confined or unconfined affects its behavior. A **confined aquifer** is bounded above and below by impermeable layers of rock or sediment. An **unconfined aquifer** has a permeable layer on top and an impermeable one beneath (see Figure 9.16).

Confined and unconfined aquifers differ in the size of their recharge area, which is the ground surface where water enters an aquifer to recharge it. For an unconfined aquifer, the **aquifer recharge area** generally extends above the entire aquifer; the water simply percolates down to the water table. But in a confined aquifer, the recharge area is far more restricted, as you can see in the figure. Pollution of this limited recharge area causes groundwater contamination; note in the illustration the improperly located disposal pond on the aquifer recharge area, contaminating wells to the right.

Confined and unconfined aquifers also differ in their water pressure. A well drilled into an unconfined aquifer (see Figure 9.16) must be pumped to make the water level rise above the water table. In contrast, the water in a confined aquifer is under the pressure of its own weight, creating a pressure level to which the water can rise on its own, the **potentiometric surface**.

The potentiometric surface actually can be above ground level (right side in figure). Under this condition, **artesian water**, or groundwater confined under pressure, may rise in a well and even flow at the surface without pumping if the top of the well is lower than the potentiometric surface. (These wells are called *artesian*, for the Artois area in France where they are common.) In other wells, however, pressure may be inadequate, and the artesian water must be pumped the remaining distance to the surface.

Wells, Springs, and Streamflows The slope of the water table, which broadly follows the contour of the land surface, controls groundwater movement (see Figure 9.16). Groundwater tends to move toward areas of lower pressure and elevation.

Water wells can work only if they penetrate the water table. Too shallow a well will be a "dry well"; too deep a well will punch through the aquifer and into the impermeable layer below, also yielding little water. This is why water wells should be drilled in consultation with a *hydrogeologist*.

Where the water table intersects the surface, it creates springs (Figure 9.17). Such an intersection also occurs in lakes and riverbeds. Ultimately, groundwater may enter stream channels to flow as surface water (stream near centre in Figure 9.16). In fact, during dry periods, the water table may sustain river flows.

Figure 9.18 illustrates the relation between the water table and surface streams in two different climatic settings. In humid climates, where the water table generally supplies a continuous base flow to a stream and is higher than the stream channel, the stream is *effluent* because it receives the water flowing out (effluent) from the surrounding ground. The Mississippi River and countless other streams are examples. In drier climates, with lower water tables, water from *influent* streams flows into the adjacent ground, sustaining vegetation along the stream. The Colorado River and the Rio Grande of the American West are examples of influent streams.

Overuse of Groundwater

As water is pumped from a well, the surrounding water table within an unconfined aquifer may experience **drawdown**, or become lowered. Drawdown occurs if the pumping rate exceeds the replenishment flow of water into the aquifer or the horizontal flow around the well. The resultant lowering of the water table around the well is a **cone of depression** (see Figure 9.16, left).

Overpumping Aquifers frequently are pumped beyond their flow and recharge capacities, a condition known as

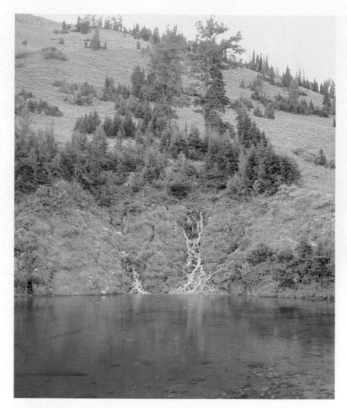

FIGURE 9.17 An active spring.
Springs provide evidence of groundwater emerging at the surface. This spring flows into Crystal Lake, Salt River Range, Wyoming. [Photo by Bobbé Christopherson.]

groundwater mining. The major area of overuse of groundwater in Canada is the Region of Waterloo in Ontario. Here, nearly a half a million people rely on groundwater for municipal supplies. The depletion of groundwater aquifers has led to extensive conservation efforts and exploration of other water sources.

In the United States, chronic groundwater overdrafts occur in large tracts of land in the Midwest, West, lower Mississippi Valley, Florida, and the intensely farmed Palouse region of eastern Washington State. In many places, the water table or artesian water level has declined more than 12 m (40 ft). In the United States, groundwater mining is of special concern in the great High Plains aquifer, which is the topic of Focus Study 9.1.

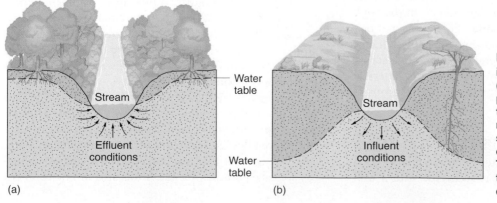

(a)   (b)

FIGURE 9.18 Groundwater interaction with streamflow.
(a) Effluent stream base flow is partially supplied by a high water table, characteristic of humid regions. (b) Influent stream supplies a lower water table, characteristic of drier regions. The water table may drop below the stream channel, effectively drying it out.

High Plains Aquifer Overdraft

North America's largest known aquifer is the High Plains aquifer. It lies beneath the American High Plains, an eight-state, 450,600-km² (174,000-mi²) area from southern South Dakota to Texas (Figure 9.1.1a).

Precipitation over the region varies from 30 cm in the southwest to 60 cm in the northeast (12 to 24 in.).

For several hundred thousand years, the aquifer's sand and gravel were charged with meltwaters from retreating glaciers. However, heavy mining of High Plains groundwater has occurred for the past 100 years, and mining intensified after World War II with the introduction of center-pivot irrigation (Figure 9.1.2). These large

FIGURE 9.1.1 High Plains aquifer.
(a) The High Plains is the largest known aquifer in North America, mapped here showing its average saturated thickness. (b) Water-level changes in the aquifer from 1980 to 2002, given in feet. [Maps: (a) After D. E. Kromm and S. E. White, "Interstate groundwater management preference differences: The High Plains region," *Journal of Geography* 86, no. 1 (January–February 1987): 5; and, (b) adapted from "Water-Level Changes in the High Plains Aquifer, Predevelopment to 2002, 1980 to 2002, and 2001 to 2002," by V.L. McGuire, USGS Fact Sheet 2004–3026, Fig. 2.]

(continued)

Focus Study 9.1 (continued)

FIGURE 9.1.2 Center-pivot irrigation.
Myriad center-pivot irrigation systems water crops in the western Great Plains. A growing season for corn requires from 10 to 20 revolutions of the sprinkler arm, depending on the weather. The arm delivers about 3 cm (1.18 in.) of water per revolution (rainfall equivalent). [Photo by Bobbé Christopherson.]

circular devices provide vital water to wheat, sorghums, cotton, corn, and about 40% of the grain fed to cattle in the United States.

The High Plains aquifer irrigates about one-fifth of all U.S. cropland: 120,000 wells provide water for 5.7 million hectares (14 million acres), or about 30% of all irrigation water for crops in the United States. This is down from the peak of 170,000 wells in 1978. In 1980, water was pumped from the aquifer at the rate of 26 billion cubic metres (21 million acre-feet) a year, an increase of more than 300% since 1950. By the turn of this century, withdrawals had decreased 10% due to declining well yields and increasing pumping costs.

During the past five decades, the water table in the aquifer dropped more than 30 m (100 ft), and throughout the 1980s it averaged a 2-m (6-ft) drop each year. The USGS estimates that recovery of the High Plains aquifer (those portions that have not collapsed) would take at least 1000 years if groundwater mining stopped today!

Figure 9.1.1b maps changes in water levels from 1980 to 2002. Declining water levels are most severe in northern Texas, where the saturated thickness of the aquifer is least, through the Oklahoma panhandle and into western Kansas. Rising water levels are noted in portions of south-central

Nebraska and a portion of Texas owing to recharge from surface irrigation, a period of above-normal precipitation years, and downward percolation from canals and reservoirs.

The USGS began monitoring this groundwater mining from more than 7000 wells in 1988. A six-year High

WATER LEVEL CHANGE IN FEET, Predevelopment to 2002
Declines | Rises

More than 100 | More than 50
50–100 | 25–50
25–50 | 10–25
10–25 | Area of little or no saturated thickness
No significant change

FIGURE 9.1.3 Water-level changes in the High Plains Aquifer, Predevelopment to 2002.
Using 1950 to represent "predevelopment," this map of changes in groundwater levels was derived from sampling some 7000 wells. The colour scale in the legend indicates widespread declines and a few areas of rises in water levels. [Map adapted from "Water-Level Changes in the High Plains Aquifer, Predevelopment to 2002, 1980 to 2002, and 2001 to 2002," by V.L. McGuire, USGS Fact Sheet 2004–3026, Fig. 1.]

Plains Regional Ground Water Study began in 1999 and concluded at the end of 2005. The goal is an overall assessment of the resource, including groundwater quality and contaminant sources. A 2004 USGS map of the water-level changes from predevelopment (about 1950) to 2002 is in Figure 9.1.3. Wells were measured in the winter or early spring when water levels were recovered from the previous irrigation season. (See http://ne.water.usgs.gov/ for links, or http://co.water.usgs.gov/ nawqa/ hpgw/HPGW_home.html.)

Obviously, billions of dollars of agricultural activity cannot be abruptly halted, but neither can profligate water mining continue. This issue raises tough questions: How best to manage cropland? Can extensive irrigation continue? Can the region continue to meet the demand to produce commodities for export? Should we continue high-volume farming of certain crops that are in chronic oversupply? Should we rethink federal policy on crop subsidies and price supports? What changes will biofuels production force? What would be the impact on farmers and rural communities of any changes to the existing system?

Present irrigation practices, if continued, will destroy about half of the High Plains aquifer resource (and two-thirds of the Texas portion) by the year 2020. Add to this the approximate 10% loss of soil moisture due to increased evapotranspiration demand caused by climatic warming for this region by 2050, as forecast by computer models, and we have a portrait of a major regional water problem and a challenge for society.

About half of India's irrigated water and half of industrial and urban water needs are met by the groundwater reserve. In rural areas, groundwater supplies 80% of domestic water from some 3 million hand-pumped bore holes. And, in approximately 20% of India's agricultural districts, groundwater mining through more than 17 million wells (motorized dug wells and tube wells) is beyond recharge rates.

In the Middle East, conditions are even more severe, as detailed in News Report 9.1. The groundwater resource beneath Saudi Arabia accumulated over tens of thousands of years, forming "fossil aquifers," but the increasing withdrawals are not being naturally recharged to any appreciable degree at present due to the desert climate—in essence, it is now a nonrenewable groundwater resource. Some researchers suggest that groundwater in the region will be depleted in a decade, although worsening water-quality problems will no doubt arise before this date.

Like any renewable resource, groundwater can be tapped indefinitely as long as the rate of extraction does not exceed the rate of replenishment. But just like a bank account, a groundwater reserve will dwindle if withdrawals exceed deposits. Few governments have established and enforced rules and regulations to insure that groundwater sources are exploited at a sustainable rate. . . . No government has yet adequately tackled the issue of groundwater depletion, but it is at least getting more attention.*

*L. Brown et al. and the Worldwatch Institute, *Vital Signs, The Environmental Trends That Are Shaping Our Future* (New York: W.W. Norton & Co., 2000), 122, 123.

News Report 9.1

Middle East Water Crisis: Running on Empty

The Persian Gulf states soon may run out of freshwater. Their vast groundwater resource is overpumped to such an extent that salty seawater is encroaching into aquifers tens of kilometres inland. In this decade, groundwater on the Arabian Peninsula may become undrinkable. Imagine having the hottest issue in the Middle East become water, not oil!

Remedies for groundwater overuse are neither easy nor cheap. In the Persian Gulf area, additional freshwater is obtained by desalination of seawater, using desalination plants along the coasts. These processing plants remove salt from seawater by distillation and evaporation processes. In fact, approximately 50% of all desalination plants are in the Middle East. In Saudi Arabia, 30 desalination plants supply 70% of drinking water needs (see Figure 9.21).

One water pipeline proposal brings water overland from Turkey to the Middle East through two branches. The Gulf water line would run southeast through Jordan and Saudi Arabia, with extensions into Kuwait, Abu Dhabi, and Oman. The other branch would run south through Syria, Jordan, and Saudi Arabia to the cities of Makkah (Mecca) and Jeddah. This pipeline would cover some 1500 km (930 mi), the distance from New York City to St. Louis. (See the links listed under Middle East Water Information Network at http://www.columbia.edu/cu/ lweb/indiv/mideast/cuvlm/water. html.)

Other remedies are possible. Traditional agricultural practices could be modernized to use less water. Urban water use could be made more efficient to reduce groundwater demand. Aquifers and rivers could be shared, although at present no negotiated accords exist for this purpose in the Middle East. Conflicts at various scales pose a grave threat to water pipelines and desalination facilities throughout the region.

There are severe water shortages in the Middle East. . . . The resources of the Nile, the Tigris–Euphrates, and the Jordan are overextended owing both to natural causes and to those deriving from human behavior. . . . In addition to a severe shortage in the quantity of water, there is a growing concern over water quality.*

*N. Kliot, *Water Resources and Conflict in the Middle East* (London: Routledge, 1994), p. 1.

Collapsing Aquifers A possible effect of water removal from an aquifer is that the aquifer, which is a layer of rock or sediment, will lose its internal support. Water in the pore spaces between rock grains is not compressible, so it adds structural strength to the rock. If the water is removed through overpumping, air infiltrates the pores. Air is readily compressible, and the tremendous weight of overlying rock may crush the aquifer. On the surface, the visible result may be land subsidence, cracked house foundations, and changes in drainage.

Houston, Texas, provides an example. The removal of groundwater and crude oil caused land within an 80-km (50-mi) radius of Houston to subside more than 3 m (10 ft) over the years. Yet another example is the Fresno area of California's San Joaquin Valley. After years of intensive pumping of groundwater for irrigation, land levels have dropped almost 10 m (33 ft) because of a combination of water removal and soil compaction from agricultural activity.

Surface mining ("strip mining") for coal in eastern Texas, northeastern Louisiana, Wyoming, Arizona, and other locales also destroys aquifers. Aquifer collapse is an increasing problem in West Virginia, Kentucky, and Virginia, where low-sulfur coal is mined to meet current air-pollution requirements for coal-burning electric power plants.

Unfortunately, collapsed aquifers may not be rechargeable, even if surplus gravitational water becomes available, because pore spaces may be permanently collapsed. The water-well fields that serve the Tampa Bay–St. Petersburg, Florida, area are a case in point. Pond and lake levels, swamps, and wetlands in the area are declining and land surfaces subsiding as the groundwater drawdown for export to the cities increases.

Saltwater Encroachment When aquifers are overpumped near the ocean, another problem arises. Along a coastline, fresh groundwater and salty seawater establish a natural interface, or *contact surface*, with the less-dense freshwater flowing on top of the saline groundwater. But excessive withdrawal of freshwater can cause this interface to migrate inland. As a result, wells near the shore may become contaminated with saltwater, and the aquifer may become useless as a freshwater source as local drawdowns allow underlying saltwater to *upcone*, or rise. Figure 9.16 illustrates this seawater intrusion (far-right side). Pumping freshwater back into the aquifer may halt contamination by seawater, but once contaminated, the aquifer is difficult to reclaim.

Pollution of Groundwater

When surface water is polluted, groundwater inevitably becomes contaminated because it is recharged from surface-water supplies. Surface water flows rapidly and flushes pollution downstream, but slow-moving groundwater, once contaminated, remains polluted virtually forever.

Pollution can enter groundwater from many sources: industrial injection wells (wastes pumped into the ground), septic tank outflows, seepage from hazardous-waste disposal sites, industrial toxic waste, agricultural residues (pesticides, herbicides, fertilizers), and urban solid-waste landfills. Groundwater pollution from agricultural practices is the topic of Focus Study 9.2.

Focus Study 9.2

Walkerton, Ontario: Groundwater Contamination, Water System Mismanagement, and Tragedy

In May 2000, the town of Walkerton, Ontario (Figure 9.2.1), was the site of water resources mismanagement that ultimately led to the illnesses of 2300 residents and the deaths of seven people. A period of heavy precipitation in early May resulted in local flooding, which had a tragic impact on the drinking water supply.

The town of Walkerton is among many in a part of Ontario that relies heavily on groundwater. The town has six wells that supply its municipal water needs. During the May 2000 precipitation event, Well 5 became contaminated. Well 5 was an extremely shallow well, directly connected to surface water. Contamination may have entered the well via overland flow but is more likely to have been transported through boreholes (fence posts) and fractures in the bedrock. The groundwater contamination probably occurred after water percolated rapidly through the thin soil that was spread with animal waste from feedlots. Rapid percolation is enhanced by the drawdown around the well when water is pumped.

A secondary source of contamination was from Well 7. This artesian well had an overflow device, allowing excess water to run out when the well was not operating. During periods of heavy precipitation, as in May 2000, the excess water flows out of the wellhead and floods surrounding depression areas. When Well 7 was turned on, the small plastic flap valve was not able to prevent water from flowing down the pipe into the well. In Figure 9.16 you can see how the surface water, seepage from pollution sources, and groundwater wells are interrelated.

On May 19, 2000, several people contacted the regional Medical Health Office (MHO) to relate symptoms including bloody diarrhea, vomiting, cramps, and fever. The MHO began to investigate a possible source of bacterial contamination—beginning with the water system. The Public Utilities Commission (PUC) that managed the water system assured the MHO that the water was fine and that wells were routinely sampled.

As the MHO continued the investigation, more people became ill. Again, the PUC reassured officials that the water was safe. Regardless, the MHO issued a boil water advisory, took its own water sample, and found that the local drinking water was contaminated with *Escherichia coli*, more commonly known as E. coli. The bacteria had been washed into wells and seeped into the groundwater in the area. A judicial inquiry was called to investigate the event.

The results of the inquiry summarized that seven people died and more than 2300 became ill. Of those who became ill, many, especially children, will have lasting effects as a result of the E. coli contamination. The bacteria entered Municipal Well 5 on or about May 12, 2000, when heavy precipitation and local flooding resulted in runoff from fields spread with uncomposted manure. During the precipitation event, the well was not continuously monitored and chlorine levels were not measured. The

FIGURE 9.2.1 Walkerton, Ontario.
Walkerton is typical of the small towns in southern and south-central Ontario that rely on groundwater for freshwater supply.
[Map created by Pam Schaus.]

results of the inquiry determined that the PUC had mismanaged the water system for years. Government budget cutbacks for water monitoring and minimizing water management standards compounded the problem.

Judicial inquiry recommendations included planning and standards for drinking water quality, the management of runoff and other contaminant pathways, increases in monitoring and licensing of water managers, and establishment of electronic access to drinking water information.

For management purposes, about 35% of pollution is *point source* (such as a gasoline tank or septic tank); 65% is *nonpoint source* (from a broad area, such as an agricultural field or urban runoff). Nitrates contaminate nearly all the groundwater that underlies agricultural land in Canada. The levels are below the guidelines for Canadian drinking water quality but, while historical data suggest that nitrate levels have not changed in the last 50 years, the incidence of bacteria in well water has almost doubled in the same time period. The 1996 State of Canada's Environment Report noted that, in some areas, nitrate levels are more than four times greater than the Canadian drinking water guidelines.

Regardless of the spatial nature of the source, pollution can spread over a great distance, as illustrated in Figure 9.16. Since the nature of aquifers makes them inaccessible, the extent of groundwater pollution is underestimated.

Government zoning to prohibit pollution can be effective in the case of confined and unconfined aquifers.

For example, once recharge areas are identified, an informed population should insist on a ban on pollution discharges, septic and sewage-system installations, or hazardous-material dumping.

In the face of government inaction, and even attempts to reverse some protection laws, serious groundwater contamination continues nationwide, adding validity to a quote from more than 20 years ago:

> One characteristic is the practical irreversibility of groundwater pollution, causing the cost of clean-up to be prohibitively high. . . . It is a questionable ethical practice to impose the potential risks associated with groundwater contamination on future generations when steps can be taken today to prevent further contamination.*

*J. Tripp, "Groundwater Protection Strategies," in *Groundwater Pollution, Environmental and Legal Problems* (Washington, DC: American Association for the Advancement of Science, 1984), p. 137. Reprinted by permission.

Our Water Supply

Human thirst for adequate water supplies, both in quantity and quality, will be a major issue in this century. Internationally, increases in per capita water use are double the rate of population growth. Since we are so dependent on water, it seems that humans should cluster where good water is plentiful. But accessible water supplies are not well correlated with population distribution or the regions where population growth is greatest.

Table 9.3 shows estimated world water supplies, world population in 2007, estimated population figures for 2025, a population-change forecast between 2007 and 2050 at present growth rates, and a comparison of population and global runoff percentages for each continent. Also note estimates for urban and rural access to improved sanitation for each region. The table gives an idea of the unevenness of Earth's water supply, which is tied to climatic variability, and water demand, which is tied to level of development, affluence, and per capita consumption.

For example, North America's mean annual discharge is 5960 km³ and Asia's is 13,200 km³. However, North America has only 6.7% of the world's population, whereas Asia has 60.5%, with a population doubling time less than half of North America's. In northern China, 550 million people living in approximately 500 cities lack adequate water supplies. For comparison, note that the 1990 floods cost China $10 billion, whereas water shortages are running at more than $35 billion a year in costs to the Chinese economy. The Yellow River, a water resource for many Chinese, has run dry every year since the early 1970s. In 1997, the river failed to reach the sea for almost 230 days! An analyst for the World Bank stated that China's water shortages pose a more serious threat than floods during this century.

Water is critical for survival. Just to produce our food requires enormous quantities of water for growing, cleaning, processing, and waste disposal. See News Report 9.2 for personal water use and water measurements. We sometimes take for granted the quality and quantity of our water supply because it always seems to be there when we need it.

At present, the world's people are withdrawing 30% of the runoff that is accessible. This idea of "accessibility" is important, because about 20% of global runoff is remote and not readily available to meet water demand. Timing of flows is also important, for approximately 50% of total runoff remains beyond use as uncaptured floodwater. For example, the greatest river in terms of runoff discharge on Earth—the Amazon—is about 95% remote from population centres, that is, not readily available.

Water resources differ from other resources in that there is no alternative for water. The World Water Assessment Program (UNESCO, 2003) summarized that

Table 9.3   Estimate of Available Global Water Supply Compared by Region and Population

Region (2007 population in millions)	Land Area in Thousands of km²	(mi²)	Share of Mean Annual Discharge in km³/yr	(BGD)	Global Stream Runoff (%)	Projected Global Population, 2025 (%)	Projected Population, 2025 (millions)	Projected Population Change (+) 2007–2050 (%)	Population with Access to Improved Sanitation (%) for 2006 Urban / Rural
Africa (944)	30,600	(11,800)	4,220	(3,060)	10.8	17.1	1,359	107	62 / 30
Asia (4010)	44,600	(17,200)	13,200	(9,540)	34.0	59.9	4,768	34	74 / 31
Australia–Oceania (35)	8,420	(3,250)	1,960	(1,420)	5.1	0.53	42	41	98 / 58
Europe (733)	9,770	(3,770)	3,150	(2,280)	8.1	9.0	719	−9	100 / 100
North America (442) (Canada, Mexico, U.S.)	22,100	(8,510)	5,960	(4,310)	15.3	6.4	512	38	100 / 100 Mexico: 90 / 39
Central and South America (463)	17,800	(6,880)	10,400	(7,510)	26.7	7.1	566	41	84 / 43
Global (6625) (excluding Antarctica)	134,000	(51,600)	38,900	(28,100)	—	100.00	7,965	40	More developed: 100 / 92 Less developed: 73 / 31

Note: BGD, billion gallons per day. Population data from *2007 World Population Data Sheet* (Washington, D.C.: Population Reference Bureau, 2007). Numbers are rounded.

News Report 9.2

Personal Water Use in Canada

Canadians are second only to the United States as the highest per capita users of water in the world. Water use for municipal supply stresses surface reservoirs and groundwater aquifers. Treating and distributing water uses energy and has a heavy economic cost. After use, the released water is usually poorer in quality, diminishing the condition of the downstream supply.

An Environment Canada national survey on water use, updated in 1999, emphasizes that more than 8 million Canadians rely solely on groundwater for their water needs. The communities that rely on groundwater (found in interior British Columbia, the southern Prairies, southern Ontario, and Prince Edward Island) have more frequent water shortages, and in 1999, approximately 26% reported water availability problems. Figure 9.2.1a illustrates how the demand per capita in Canada decreased through the 1990s. However, population growth during the same time meant that total water usage increased.

Infrastructure is deteriorating. The leaks in the waterworks create inefficiency in water and wastewater treatment with as much as 30% of municipal water wasted. Estimated costs of rebuilding this infrastructure in the next 10 years are between 40 and 70 billion Canadian dollars.

The direct costs of supplying water are often unnoticed by the average user. In the 1999 national water survey, unmetered households used 433 litres of water per person per day. In metered households where water was paid for by the volume used, the daily residential water use was 288 litres per person per day (Figure 9.2.1b). Water meters are clearly an effective conservation mechanism, saving the consumer money on water bills and future outlays for more waterworks.

A further breakdown of residential water use is shown in Figure 9.2.2. The largest share, about two-thirds, of water used in a household is for personal washing and toilet flushing. Water conservation programs encourage the use of water-saving showerheads and low-flow toilets.

(a)   (b)

FIGURE 9.2.1 Indicators of daily municipal water use.
(a) Per capita daily municipal water use 1983 to 1999. Note the small declining trend in per capita consumption of water. Remember that overall population is rising and that the total demand for water is increasing. (b) The effect of metering water use is dramatic. The metered household uses one-third less water. [Graph data courtesy of Environment Canada's Freshwater Web site (http://www.ec.gc.ca/water). Used by permission of the Minister of Public Works and Government Services.]

FIGURE 9.2.2 Water use in the home, 1999.
The greatest household demand for water is for showers and baths, followed closely by toilet-flushing. [Used by permission of the Minister of Public Works and Government Services.]

more than 2 billion people in over 40 countries are affected by water shortages, 1.1 billion do not have sufficient drinking water, 2.4 billion have no provision for sanitation, and, by 2050, at least one in four people is likely to live in countries affected by chronic or recurring shortages of freshwater. Water shortages increase the probability for international conflict, endanger public health, reduce agricultural productivity, and damage life-supporting ecological systems. New dams and river-management schemes might increase runoff accessibility by 10% over the next 30 years, but population is projected to grow by 32% in the same time period.

Water Supply in Canada

The Canadian water supply derives from surface and groundwater sources. The supply of freshwater and some of the threats to it are outlined on the National Water Research Institute's Web site (**http://www.nwri.ca/threats2full/ perspective-e.html**). Canada has about 9% of Earth's renewable water distributed over 7% of Earth's landmass. Water is accessed through the rivers, lakes, ponds and reservoirs, groundwater aquifers, the snowpack, glaciers, ice fields, and the liquid and solid precipitation that replenishes all other sources. Measurements of precipitation recorded across the country are difficult to aggregate because the hydrology of the landmass varies so greatly.

Figure 9.19 is a map of the streamflow in Canada found on the National Atlas Web site (**http://atlas.gc. ca/site/english/maps/archives/5thedition/environment/ water/mcr4178**). Insets portray the distribution of low flows, peak flows, and runoff. Peak flows occur earlier in the year to the south and are later to the north. Often, this results in spring flooding as the northern mouth of the river is still frozen when the southern headwaters have melted. The map depicts volumes of flow in major streams and the width of the red colouration represents the volume of flow in cubic metres per second (m^3/sec). This surface runoff (runoff plus streamflow), which varies between 75,000 m^3/sec in low flow times to over 134,500 m^3/sec in high flow times, is available for use.

The seeming abundance of water is misleading when you consider that about 60% of Canada's freshwater drains to the north, while about 85% of the population lives within 300 km of our southern border. In other words, much of our water is not available in the heavily-populated areas where it is most needed.

The difference between supply and demand is growing with increasing urbanization. All sources of freshwater are now under pressure from the growing, and often conflicting, demands for domestic water supplies for municipalities, for agriculture and industry, and for maintaining adequate streamflow in rivers that support aquatic ecosystems. There is also the added stress from the uncertain, but predicted, effects of climate change. Despite these growing stresses, many Canadians assume that governments will protect and sustain the freshwater supply.

Instream, Nonconsumptive, and Consumptive Uses

Surface runoff available for use can be classified according to the type of use:

- *Instream* uses are those that use stream water in place: navigation, wildlife and ecosystem preservation, waste dilution and removal, hydroelectric power production, fishing resources, and recreation.
- *Nonconsumptive uses*, sometimes called **withdrawal** or *offstream use*, remove water from the supply, use it, and then return it to the same supply. Nonconsumptive water is used by industry, agriculture, municipalities, and in steam–electric power generation. A portion of water withdrawn is consumed.
- **Consumptive uses** remove water from a stream but do not return it, so it is not available for a second or third use. Some consumptive examples include water that evaporates or is vaporized in steam-electric plants.

When water returns to the system, water quality usually is altered—water is contaminated chemically with pollutants, or waste, or thermally with heat energy. This portion of the budget is returned to runoff and eventually the ocean. This wastewater represents an opportunity to extend the resource through reuse.

Contaminated or not, returned water becomes a part of all water systems downstream. Canada uses only 9% of its withdrawn water for agriculture and 80% for industry. Figure 9.20 compares regions by their use of withdrawn water during 1998, graphically illustrating the differences between more-developed and less-developed parts of the world.

Desalination

Desalination of seawater to augment diminishing groundwater supplies is becoming increasingly important as a freshwater source. Plant construction is expected to increase 140% between 2007 and 2017, some $60 billion in investments; somewhere between 1500 and 2000 plants are now in operation worldwide. Australia has $4.9 billion in construction underway. In the Middle East, desalination is presently in widespread use. Desalination is an alternative to further groundwater mining and saltwater intrusion under Saudi Arabia (Figure 9.21a). Also, along the coast of southern California and in Florida desalination is slowly increasing in use.

The Tampa–St. Petersburg area in Florida took a giant step forward in 2003 with the opening of its own Tampa Bay desalination plant producing 25 million gallons a day (MGD), making it the largest in the United States. The seawater intake is from the Big Bend Power Station's cooling water discharge. The plant produces drinking water through a series of filters to remove algae and particles and a reverse osmosis process where the

FIGURE 9.19 Streamflows in Canada.
The greatest volume of streamflow in Canada exits northward through the Mackenzie River.
This streamflow represents the surface runoff from that drainage basin. Next in volume is the
flow to the Atlantic from the Great Lakes through the St. Lawrence River. The hydrographs
show the effects of seasonality on the timing of the melt. [Map and data used with permission
of Natural Resources Canada.]

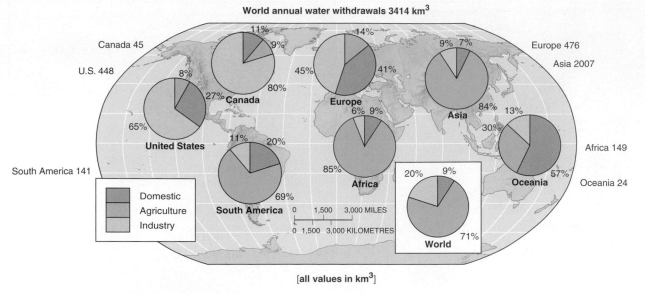

World annual water withdrawals 3414 km³

Canada 45

U.S. 448

Europe 476

Asia 2007

Africa 149

South America 141

Oceania 24

Canada: 11%, 9%, 80%

United States: 8%, 27%, 65%

Europe: 14%, 45%, 41%

Asia: 9%, 7%, 84%

Oceania: 13%, 30%, 57%

South America: 11%, 20%, 69%

Africa: 6%, 9%, 85%

World: 20%, 9%, 71%

Legend:
- Domestic
- Agriculture
- Industry

0   1,500   3,000 MILES
0 1,500 3,000 KILOMETRES

[all values in km³]

FIGURE 9.20 Water withdrawal by sector.
World annual water withdrawal estimated total is 3414 km³ (819.4 mi³). Compare industrial water use among the geographic areas, as well as agricultural and municipal uses.
[After World Resources Institute, *World Resources 2000–2001*, Data Table FW.1, pp. 276–77.]

(a)

(b)

FIGURE 9.21 Water desalination.
(a) Freshwater is supplied to Saudi Arabia from the Jabal water desalination plant along the Red Sea. Saudi Arabia obtains a significant amount of its water from desalination of seawater.
(b) The Tampa Bay desalination plant provides 25 MGD to the region's water resources through filtration and reverse osmosis processes. [Photos by (a) Liaison Agency; (b) Tampa Bay Water.]

water is forced through semipermeable membranes. The plant expands to 35 MGD, or about 10% of the regional water supply, during 2008 (Figure 9.21b).

Future Considerations

When precipitation is budgeted, the limits of the water resource become apparent. How can we satisfy the growing demand for water? Water availability per person declines as population increases, and individual demand increases with economic development, affluence, and technology. Thus, world population growth since 1970 reduced per capita water supplies by a third. Also, pollution limits the water-resource base, so that even before *quantity* constraints are felt, *quality* problems may limit the health and growth of a region.

The international aspect of the water-resource problem is illustrated by the 200 major river drainage basins in the world. One hundred and forty-five countries possess territory within an international river drainage basin—truly a global commons.

Working Group II, *Climate Change Impacts, Adaptation, and Vulnerability*, in their "Summary for Policy Makers," (Intergovernmental Panel on Climate Change *Fourth Assessment Report*, April 2007), concluded that global climate change and greenhouse warming will cause added water problems:

By mid-century, annual river runoff and water availability are projected to increase 10–40% at high latitudes and in some wet tropical areas, and decrease by 10–30% over some dry regions at mid-latitude and in dry tropics, some of which are presently water stressed areas. . . . Drought-affected areas will likely increase in extent. . . . In the course of the century,

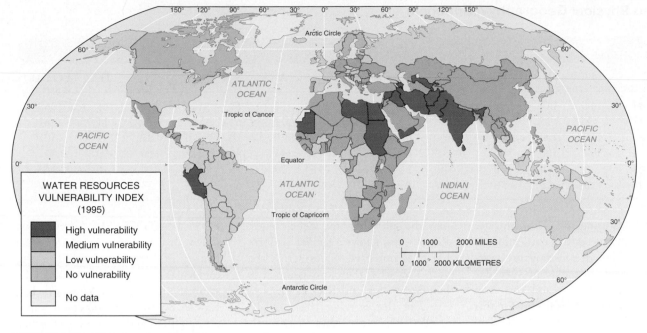

FIGURE 9.22 Global water scarcity.
Water resource vulnerability, a composite index. [Compiled by The World Resources Institute from data gathered by the Stockholm Environment Institute, *Comprehensive Assessment of the Freshwater Resources of the World*, 1997, appearing in *World Resources 1998–1999* (New York: The World Resources Institute, 1998), p. 223.]

water supplies stored in glaciers and snow cover are projected to decline, reducing water availability in regions supplied by meltwater from mountain ranges, where more than one-sixth of the world population currently lives.

The IPCC concluded that given higher temperatures, water demand increases to meet potential evapotranspiration needs and algal blooms arise in the warmer runoff waters. Those areas that experience increased intensity of heavy precipitation events will experience surface and groundwater contamination episodes. Also, where groundwater mining occurs to meet rising demands the drawdown of the water table and salt-water intrusion near coastlines will worsen.

Many ongoing studies of available water resources, withdrawal and consumption patterns, essential water needs of natural systems that should not be available for exploitation, population growth, and national income are revealing regional scarcities and water stress in Africa, the Middle East, Asia, southeastern Australia, Peru, Mexico, the American Southwest and Great Plains. Figure 9.22 portrays regions of water resource vulnerability. An important consideration to remember:

Unlike other important commodities such as oil, copper, or wheat, freshwater has no substitutes for most of its uses. It is also impractical to transport the large quantities of water needed in agriculture and industry more than several hundred kilometers. Freshwater is now scarce in many regions of the world, resulting in severe ecological degradation, limits on agriculture and industrial production, threats to human health, and increased potential for international conflict.*

Clearly, cooperation is needed, yet we continue toward a water crisis without a concept of a *world water economy* as a frame of reference. The geospatial question is: When will more international coordination begin, and which country or group of countries will lead the way to sustain future water resources? The soil-water-budget approach detailed in this chapter is a place to start.

*S. L. Postal et al., "Human appropriation of renewable fresh water," *Science* 271, no. 5250 (February 9, 1996), 785.

Applied Physical Geography

A Thornthwaite Water Balance Problem

Table 1 presents, in random order, data (in mm) for potential evapotranspiration (PE), precipitation (P), soil moisture storage (ST), actual evapotranspiration (AE), water deficit (D), and water surplus (S) for a Northern Hemisphere station. Determine the appropriate label for each of the rows and explain your reasoning. What type of climate is represented?

(continued)

Applied Physical Geography (continued)

Table 1　Weather Station Data

	J	F	M	A	M	J	J	A	S	O	N	D	TOTAL
Row #1	147	117	94	61	48	45	30	37	61	122	141	165	1068
Row #2	8	15	30	48	72	89	85	71	64	45	23	11	561
Row #3	139	102	64	13	0	0	0	0	0	0	35	154	507
Row #4	300	300	300	300	276	232	177	143	140	217	300	300	—
Row #5	0	0	0	0	2	6	24	29	5	0	0	0	66
Row #6	8	15	30	48	74	95	109	100	69	45	23	11	627

We are using the Thornthwaite water balance described earlier in this chapter. Although soil-moisture storage and field capacity can vary depending on soil type and the crop planted, we set it at 300 mm for this example. Therefore, Row #4 is storage because the number 300 does not change from January to April. It decreases from May to September and then increases through October to become recharged in November.

Now consider Row #5, immediately below the row identified as storage. When storage falls below 300 mm, water is being utilized. Water is removed from storage only when there is a shortage of precipitation in meeting demand. Because of the decrease in storage from soil-moisture utilization and the increase in values in Row #5, this row is the moisture deficit—the unmet demand. Note the soil-moisture recharge that begins in October and continues into November when field capacity is restored.

A deficit occurs when the precipitation decreases and there are only two rows that show a decrease in values. Row #1 has values across the year and shows a decrease that begins the month before the deficit appears. This decrease continues across the summer months and then increases

into the fall when the deficit ends. Row #3 also shows a similar pattern, but does not have values across the year. Row #1 is therefore assumed to be precipitation and Row #3 surplus.

This leaves two rows to be labelled. These two rows contain values that are remarkably similar. They represent actual evapotranspiration and potential evapotranspiration. But which one is which? Remember, potential evapotranspiration is the amount of evapotranspiration (evaporation + transpiration) that would occur if the water supply were available. It represents the demand that the atmosphere makes on the available water supply. Remember also that if PRECIP > POTET, then ACTET = POTET, and that water deficit (DEFIC) occurs when PRECIP < POTET, then DEFIC =

POTET–ACTET. An examination shows that the two rows are equal January to April and October to December. When the deficit occurs in the summer months, Row #2 is less than Row #6. So, Row #6 is potential evapotranspiration and Row #2 is actual evapotranspiration.

To determine the type of climate depicted, graph precipitation, potential evapotranspiration, and actual evapotranspiration (Figure 1). Here we see that precipitation is greatest during winter months. Both potential and actual evapotranspiration increase in summer and both decrease in winter. This is typical of the Marine West Coast climate, with all months averaging above freezing, a cool summer, and abundant precipitation.

■ = Water surplus	——	PRECIP/P
■ = Soil-moisture utilization	——	ACTET/AE
■ = Soil-moisture recharge	——	POTET/PE
■ = Water deficit		

FIGURE 1 Sample water balance graph.

Summary and Review—Water Resources

■ *Illustrate* the hydrologic cycle with a simple sketch, and *label* it with definitions for each water pathway.

The flow of water links the atmosphere, ocean, and land through energy and matter exchanges. The **hydrologic cycle** is

a model of Earth's water system, which has operated for billions of years from the lower atmosphere to several kilometres beneath Earth's surface. **Interception** occurs when precipitation strikes vegetation or other ground cover. Water soaks into the subsurface through **infiltration**, or penetration of the soil surface. It further permeates soil or rock through vertical movement called **percolation**.

hydrologic cycle (p. 252)
interception (p. 253)
infiltration (p. 254)
percolation (p. 254)

1. Sketch and explain a simplified model of the complex flows of water on Earth—the hydrologic cycle.

2. What are the possible routes that a raindrop may take on its way to and into the soil surface?

3. Compare precipitation and evaporation volumes from the ocean with those over land. Describe advection flows of moisture and countering surface and subsurface runoff.

■ *Relate* the importance of the water-budget concept to your understanding of the hydrologic cycle, water resources, and soil moisture for a specific location.

A **soil-water budget** can be established for any area of Earth's surface by measuring the precipitation input and the output of various water demands in the area considered. Understanding both the supply of the water resource and the natural demands on the resource is essential to sustainable human interaction with the hydrologic cycle. Water resources represent the ultimate output of Earth's water system.

Groundwater is the largest potential freshwater source in the hydrologic cycle and is tied to surface supplies. Streams represent only a tiny fraction of all water (1250 km³, or 300 mi³), the smallest volume of any of the freshwater categories. Yet streams represent four-fifths of all the water we use.

soil-water budget (p. 254)

4. How might an understanding of the hydrologic cycle in a particular locale or a soil-moisture budget of a site assist you in assessing water resources? Give some specific examples.

■ *Construct* the water-balance equation as a way of accounting for the expenditures of water supply, and *define* each of the components in the equation and their specific operation.

The moisture supply to Earth's surface is **precipitation** (PRECIP, or P), arriving as rain, sleet, snow, and hail. Precipitation is measured with the **rain gauge**. **Evaporation** is the net movement of free water molecules away from a wet surface into air. **Transpiration** is the movement of water through plants and back into the atmosphere; it is a cooling mechanism for plants. Evaporation and transpiration are combined into one term— **evapotranspiration**. The ultimate demand for moisture is **potential evapotranspiration** (POTET, or PE), the amount of water that *would* evaporate and transpire under optimum moisture conditions (adequate precipitation and adequate soil moisture). Evapotranspiration is measured with an **evaporation pan** (*evaporimeter*) or the more elaborate **lysimeter**.

Unsatisfied POTET is **deficit** (DEFIC). By subtracting DEFIC from POTET, we determine **actual evapotranspiration**, or ACTET. Ideally, POTET and ACTET are about the same, so that plants have sufficient water. If POTET is satisfied and the soil is full of moisture, then additional water input becomes **surplus** (SURPL), which may puddle on the surface, flow across the surface toward stream channels, or percolate underground through the soil. The **overland flow** to streams includes

precipitation and groundwater flows into river channels to make up the **total runoff** from the area.

A "savings account" of water that receives deposits and provides withdrawals as water-balance conditions change is the **soil-moisture storage**, ΔSTRGE. This is the volume of water stored in the soil that is accessible to plant roots. In soil, **hygroscopic water** is inaccessible because it is a molecule-thin layer that is tightly bound to each soil particle by hydrogen bonding. As available water is utilized, soil reaches the **wilting point** (all that remains is unextractable water). **Capillary water** is generally accessible to plant roots because it is held in the soil by surface tension and hydrogen bonding between water and soil. Almost all capillary water that remains in the soil is **available water** in soil-moisture storage. After water drains from the larger pore spaces, the available water remaining for plants is termed **field capacity**, or storage capacity. When soil is saturated after a precipitation event, surplus water in the soil becomes **gravitational water** and percolates to groundwater. As **soil-moisture utilization** removes soil water, the plants work harder to extract the same amount of moisture, whereas **soil-moisture recharge** is the rate at which needed moisture enters the soil.

The texture and the structure of the soil dictate available pore spaces, or **porosity**. The soil's **permeability** is the degree to which water can flow through it. Permeability depends on particle sizes and the shape and packing of soil grains.

Drought does not have a simple water-budget definition; rather, it can occur in at least four forms: *meteorological drought*, *agricultural drought*, *hydrologic drought*, and/or a *socioeconomic drought*.

precipitation (p. 255)
rain gauge (p. 255)
evaporation (p. 255)
transpiration (p. 256)
evapotranspiration (p. 256)
potential evapotranspiration (p. 257)
evaporation pan (p. 257)
lysimeter (p. 257)
deficit (p. 258)
actual evapotranspiration (p. 258)
surplus (p. 258)
overland flow (p. 258)
total runoff (p. 258)
soil-moisture storage (p. 259)
hygroscopic water (p. 259)
wilting point (p. 259)
capillary water (p. 259)
available water (p. 259)
field capacity (p. 260)
gravitational water (p. 260)
soil-moisture utilization (p. 260)
soil-moisture recharge (p. 260)
porosity (p. 260)
permeability (p. 260)
drought (p. 261)

5. What does this statement mean? "The soil-water budget is an assessment of the hydrologic cycle at a specific site."

6. What are the components of the water-balance equation? Construct the equation and place each term's definition below its abbreviation in the equation.

7. Using the annual water-balance data for Hamilton, Ontario, in Table 9.2, work the values through the

water-balance "bookkeeping" method. Does the equation balance?

8. Explain how to derive actual evapotranspiration (ACTET) in the water-balance equation.

9. What is potential evapotranspiration (POTET)? How do we go about estimating this potential rate? What factors did Thornthwaite use to determine this value?

10. Explain the operation of soil-moisture storage, soil-moisture utilization, and soil-moisture recharge. Include discussion of field capacity, capillary water, and wilting point concepts.

11. In the case of silt-loam soil from Figure 9.9, roughly what is the available water capacity? How is this value derived?

12. Describe the four types of drought. Why do you think media coverage of drought seems lacking? If wars in the twenty-first century are predicted to be about water availability in quantity and quality, what action could we take to understand the issues and avoid the conflicts?

■ *Describe* the nature of groundwater, and *define* the elements of the groundwater environment.

Groundwater is a part of the hydrologic cycle, but it lies beneath the surface beyond the soil-moisture root zone. Groundwater does not exist independently because its replenishment is tied to surface surpluses. Excess surface water moves through the **zone of aeration**, where soil and rock are less than saturated. Eventually, the water reaches the **zone of saturation**, where the pores are completely filled with water.

The *permeability* of subsurface rocks depends on whether they conduct water readily (higher permeability) or tend to obstruct its flow (lower permeability). They can even be impermeable. An **aquifer** is a rock layer that is permeable to groundwater flow in usable amounts. An **aquiclude** (aquitard) is a body of rock that does not conduct water in usable amounts.

The upper limit of the water that collects in the zone of saturation is the **water table**; it is the contact surface between the zones of saturation and aeration. A **confined aquifer** is bounded above and below by impermeable layers of rock or sediment. An **unconfined aquifer** has a permeable layer on top and an impermeable one beneath. The **aquifer recharge area** extends over an entire unconfined aquifer. Water in a confined aquifer is under the pressure of its own weight, creating a pressure level to which the water can rise on its own, the **potentiometric surface**, which can be above ground level. Groundwater confined under pressure is **artesian water**; it may rise up in wells and even flow out at the surface without pumping, if the head of the well is below the potentiometric surface.

As water is pumped from a well, the surrounding water table within an unconfined aquifer will experience **drawdown**, or become lower, if the rate of pumping exceeds the horizontal flow of water in the aquifer around the well. This excessive pumping causes a **cone of depression**. Aquifers frequently are pumped beyond their flow and recharge capacities, a condition known as **groundwater mining**.

groundwater (p. 266)
zone of aeration (p. 267)
zone of saturation (p. 267)
aquifer (p. 267)
aquiclude (p. 267)
water table (p. 267)
confined aquifer (p. 267)
unconfined aquifer (p. 267)
aquifer recharge area (p. 267)
potentiometric surface (p. 267)
artesian water (p. 267)
drawdown (p. 268)
cone of depression (p. 268)
groundwater mining (p. 268)

13. Are groundwater resources independent of surface supplies, or are the two interrelated? Explain your answer.

14. Make a simple sketch of the subsurface environment, labeling zones of aeration and saturation and the water table in an unconfined aquifer. Then add a confined aquifer to the sketch.

15. At what point does groundwater utilization become groundwater mining? Use the High Plains aquifer example to explain your answer.

16. What is the nature of groundwater pollution? Can contaminated groundwater be cleaned up easily? Explain.

■ *Identify* critical aspects of freshwater supplies for the future, and *cite* specific issues related to sectors of use, regions and countries, and potential remedies for any shortfalls.

Nonconsumptive uses, or water **withdrawal** or *offstream use*, remove water from the supply, use it, and then return it to the stream. **Consumptive uses** remove water from a stream but do not return it, so the water is not available for a second or third use. Regional and global water-resource planning, using water-budget principles, is essential if Earth's societies are to have enough water of adequate quality. **Desalination** as a water resource involves the removal of organics, debris, and salinity from seawater through distillation or reverse osmosis. This processing yields potable water for domestic uses.

withdrawal (p. 276)
consumptive uses (p. 276)
desalination (p. 276)

17. What is the difference between withdrawal and consumptive use of water resources? Compare these with instream uses.

18. Characterize each of the sectors withdrawing water: irrigation, industry, and municipalities. What are the present usage trends in more-developed and less-developed nations?

19. Briefly assess the status of world water resources. What challenges exist in meeting the future needs of an expanding population and growing economies?

Critical Thinking

A. Select your campus, yard, or perhaps a house plant and apply the water-balance concepts. What is the supply of water? Estimate the ultimate water supply and demand for the area you selected. Estimate water needs and how they vary with season as components of the water-budget change.

B. You have no doubt had several glasses of water between the time you awoke this morning and the time you are reading these words. Where did this water originate? Obtain the name of the water company or agency, determine whether it is using surface or groundwater to meet demands, and check how the water is metered and billed. If your province or state requires water-quality reporting, obtain a copy of the analysis of your tap water.

C. What about the water on your campus? If the campus has its own wells, how is the quality tested? Who on campus is in charge of supervising these wells? Lastly, what is your subjective assessment of the water you use: taste, smell, hardness, clarity? Compare these perceptions with others in your class.

Cyclonic storm tracks
(summer convection)

Station: New York, New York
Lat/long: 40°46' N 74°01' W
Avg. Ann. Temp.:
 13°C (55.4°F)
Total Ann. Precip.:
 112.3 cm (44.2 in.)

Elevation: 16 m (52.5 ft)
Population: 8,092,000
Ann. Temp. Range:
 24 C° (43.2 F°)
Ann. Hr of Sunshine:
 2564

(a)

Asian monsoon
effects

Station: Dalian, China
Lat/long: 38°54' N 121°54' E
Avg. Ann. Temp.:
 10°C (50°F)
Total Ann. Precip.:
 57.8 cm (22.8 in.)

Elevation: 96 m (314.9 ft)
Population: 5,550,000
Ann. Temp. Range:
 29 C° (52.2 F°)
Ann. Hr of Sunshine:
 2762

(b)

(c)

(d)

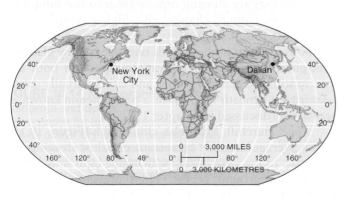

FIGURE 10.15 Humid continental hot-summer climates, New York and China.
Climographs for (a) New York City (*humid continental hot summer* that is moist all year) and (b) Dalian, China (*humid continental hot summer* that is dry in winter). (c) The "Literary Walk" with a canopy of American elms in New York City's Central Park emerging from winter just as spring and the return of leaves and warmth begin. (d) Dalian, China, cityscape and park in summer. [Photos (c) by Bobbé Christopherson; and (d) courtesy of the Paul Louis collection.]

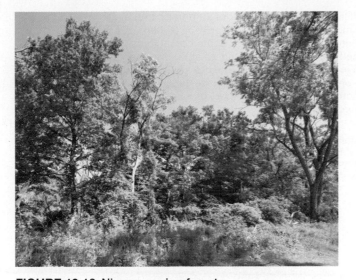

FIGURE 10.16 Niagara region forests.
This forest near Buffalo, NY, and the Ontario border is a characteristic mix of maple–beech–birch, with some elm and ash. It is in transition to an oak–hickory mix as temperatures increase during this century. [Photos by Bobbé Christopherson.]

for the continental polar air mass. Churchill is representative of the *subarctic* climate, with a cool summer: annual temperature range of 40 C° (72 F°) and low precipitation of 44.3 cm (17.4 in.).

The *subarctic* climates that feature a dry and very cold winter occur only within Russia. The intense cold of Siberia and north-central and eastern Asia is difficult to comprehend, for these areas experience an average temperature lower than freezing for 7 months; minimum temperatures of below −68°C (−90°F) were recorded there, as described in Chapter 5. Yet summer maximum temperatures in these same areas can exceed +37°C (+98°F).

An example of this extreme subarctic climate with very cold winters is Verkhoyansk, Siberia (Figure 10.19). For 4 months of the year, average temperatures fall below −34°C (−30°F). Verkhoyansk has probably the world's greatest annual temperature range from winter to summer: a remarkable 63 C° (113.4 F°). Winters feature brittle metals and plastics, triple-thick windowpanes, and temperatures that render straight antifreeze a solid.

(a)

Station: Moscow, Russia
Lat/long: 55°45' N 37°34' E
Avg. Ann. Temp.: 4°C (39.2°F)
Total Ann. Precip.: 57.5 cm (22.6 in.)

Elevation: 156 m (511.9 ft)
Population: 11,460,000
Ann. Temp. Range: 29 C° (52.2 F°)
Ann. Hr of Sunshine: 1597

(b)

(c)

FIGURE 10.17 Humid continental mild-summer climate.
(a) Climograph for Moscow, Russia (*humid continental mild summer*). (b) Fields near Saratov, Russia, during the short summer season. (c) Late-winter scene of Sebago Lake and forests inland from Portland, Maine. [(b) Photo by Wolfgang Kaehler/Liaison Agency, Inc.; (c) photo by Bobbé Christopherson.]

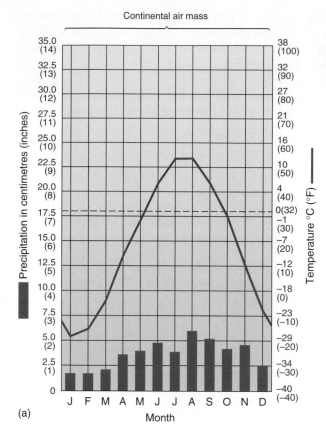

Continental air mass

(a)

FIGURE 10.18 Subarctic cool summer climate.
(a) Climograph for Churchill, Manitoba (*subarctic*, cool summer).
(b) Winter scene on the edge of the boreal forest, young pioneer
spruce trees move into the tundra. (c) Lone polar bear hunkered
down in a protective dugout next to a frozen pond. (d) Mom and two
cubs-of-the-year in the tundra near Hudson Bay, west of Churchill,
characteristic willows in the background. (e) November street scene
in Churchill. [All photos by Bobbé Christopherson.]

Station: Churchill, Manitoba
Lat/long: 58°45' N 94°04' W
Avg. Ann. Temp.: −7°C (19.4°F)
Total Ann. Precip.:
44.3 cm (17.4 in.)

Elevation: 35 m (114.8 ft)
Population: 1400
Ann. Temp. Range:
40 C° (72 F°)
Ann. Hr of Sunshine:
1732

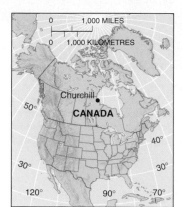

NOTEBOOK

Polar Bear and
High Latitude
Animals Photo
Galleries

(b)

(c)

(d)

(e)

Continental air mass

Station: Verkhoyansk, Russia
Lat/long: 67°35' N 133°27' E
Avg. Ann. Temp.: −15°C (5°F)
Total Ann. Precip.:
   15.5 cm (6.1 in.)

Elevation: 137 m (449.5 ft)
Population: 1500
Ann. Temp. Range:
   63 C° (113.4 F°)

(b)

FIGURE 10.19 Extreme subarctic cold winter climate.
(a) Climograph for Verkhoyansk, Russia (*subarctic*, very cold winter). (b) Scene in the town of
Verkhoyansk during the short summer. [Photo by Dean Conger/National Geographic Society.]

Polar and Highland Climates

The polar climates cover about 19% of Earth's total surface
and about 17% of its land area. These climates have no true
summer like that in lower latitudes. Poleward of the Arctic
and Antarctic circles, daylength in summer becomes continuous, yet average monthly temperatures never rise above
10°C (50°F). These temperature conditions are intolerant to
tree growth. Daylength, which in part determines the amount
of insolation received, and low Sun altitude in the sky are the
principal climatic factors in these frozen and barren regions.
Yet, in winter, the Sun drops below the horizon poleward of
66.5° latitude, producing continuous night.

Principal climatic factors in these frozen and barren regions
are the following:

Tundra
Ice cap and ice sheet
Highland

- Extremes of daylength between winter and summer determine the amount of insolation received.
- Low Sun altitude even during the long summer days is
  the principal climatic factor.
- Extremely low humidity produces low precipitation
  amounts—these regions are Earth's frozen deserts.
- Light-coloured surfaces of ice and snow reflect substantial energy away from the ground surface, thus reducing
  net radiation.

Polar climates have three regimes: *tundra* (high latitude, or elevation); *ice caps* and *ice sheet* (perpetually frozen); and *polar
marine* (oceanic association, slight moderation of extreme cold).

Also in this climate category we include highland climates.
Even at low latitudes the effects of elevation can produce tundra and polar conditions. Glaciers on tropical mountain summits
attest to the cooling effects of elevation. Highland climates on
the map follow the pattern of Earth's mountain ranges.

Tundra Climate

In a *tundra* climate, land is under continuous snow cover for 8–10 months, with the warmest month above 0°C yet never warming above 10°C (50°F). In summer when the snow melts and spring arrives, numerous plants appear—stunted sedges, mosses, flowering plants, and lichens. Some of the little (7.5 cm, 3 in. tall) willows can exceed 300 years in age. The September photo shows the emerging fall colours of these small plants (Figure 10.20a). Much of the area experiences permafrost and ground ice conditions; these are Earth's periglacial regions (see Chapter 17). The *tundra* can be the summer home of mosquitoes of legend and black gnats.

Approximately 410,500 km² (158,475 mi²) of Greenland are ice-free, an area of tundra and rock about the size of California. The rest of Greenland is ice sheet covering 1,756,00 km² (677,900 mi²). Despite the severe climate, a permanent population of 56,500 lives in this province of Denmark. There are only a couple of towns along Greenland's east coast. Ittoqqortoormiit, or Scoresby Sund, has 850 permanent residents (Figure 10.20b). Here is a village on the tundra.

Global warming is bringing dramatic changes to the tundra, its plants, animals, and permafrost ground conditions. In parts of Canada and Alaska, registered temperatures as much as 5 C° above average are a regular occurrence, setting many records. As organic peat deposits in the tundra thaw, vast stores of carbon are released to the atmosphere, further adding to the greenhouse gas problem. Temperatures in the Arctic are warming at a rate twice that of the global average increase.

Tundra climates are strictly in the Northern Hemisphere, except for elevated mountain locations in the Southern Hemisphere and a portion of the Antarctic Peninsula, where plants are now growing for the first time. Because of elevation, the summit of Mount Washington in New Hampshire (1914 m, or 6280 ft) statistically qualifies as a highland *tundra* climate of small scale.

Ice Cap and Ice Sheet Climate

Most of Antarctica and central Greenland fall within the *ice sheet* climate, as does the North Pole, with all months averaging below freezing. Both regions are dominated by dry, frigid air masses, with vast expanses that never warm above freezing. The area of the North Pole is actually a sea covered by ice, whereas Antarctica is a substantial continental landmass covered by Earth's greatest ice sheet. For comparison, winter minimums in central Antarctica (July) frequently drop below the temperature of solid carbon dioxide or "dry ice" (−78°C, or −109°F). Ice caps are smaller in extent than ice sheets, roughly less than 50,000 km² (19,300 mi²), yet they completely bury the landscape like an ice sheet. The Vatnajökull Ice Cap in southeastern Iceland is an example.

Antarctica is constantly snow-covered but receives less than 8 cm (3 in.) of precipitation each year. However, Antarctic ice has accumulated to several kilometres deep and is the largest repository of freshwater on Earth. Earth's two ice sheets cover the Antarctic continent and most of the island of Greenland. Figure 10.21 shows two scenes of these repositories of multiyear ice. The status of this ice is the focus of much attention during the present International Polar Year of scientific research.

This ice contains a vast historical record of Earth's atmosphere. Within it, evidence of thousands of past volcanic eruptions from all over the world and ancient combinations of atmospheric gases lie trapped in frozen bubbles. Chapter 17 presents analysis of ice cores taken from Greenland and

NOTEBOOK East Greenland Photos

FIGURE 10.20 Greenland tundra and a small town.
(a) Tundra is marked by an uneven, hummocky surface of mounds resulting from an active layer that freezes and thaws with the seasons, as it is here in east Greenland. Large trees are absent in the tundra; however, relatively lush vegetation for the harsh conditions includes willow, dwarf birch and shrubs, sedges, moss, lichen, and cotton grass (white tufts). (b) A town in the tundra, Scoresby Sund fjord in the distance. In the foreground, sledge dogs rest to get ready for the winter's work ahead. [Photos by Bobbé Christopherson.]

(a)

(b)

FIGURE 10.21 Earth's ice sheets—Antarctica and Greenland.
These are Earth's frozen freshwater reservoirs. (a) On the Antarctic Peninsula, basaltic mountains and glacial multi-year ice along the Graham Coast and Flandres Bay, Cape Renard in the distance. (b) Three outlet glaciers drain the Greenland ice sheet into the North Atlantic from southeastern Greenland; the glacial front is in retreat. [Photos by Bobbé Christopherson.]

NOTEBOOK

High Latitude
Connection Videos

the latest one from Antarctica, which pushed the climate record to 800,000 years before the present.

Polar Marine Climate

Polar marine stations are more moderate than other polar climates in winter, with no month below −7°C (20°F), yet they are not as warm as *tundra* climates. Because of marine influences, annual temperature ranges are low. This climate exists along the Bering Sea, the southern tip of Greenland, northern Iceland, Norway, and in the Southern Hemisphere, generally over oceans between 50° S and 60° S. Precipitation, which frequently falls as sleet (ice pellets), is greater in these regions than in continental polar climates.

Arid and Semiarid Climates (permanent moisture deficits)

Dry climates are the world's arid deserts and semiarid regions, where we consider moisture efficiency along with temperature for understanding the climate. These regions have unique plants, animals, and physical features. Arid and semiarid regions occupy more than 35% of Earth's land area and clearly are the most extensive climate over land.

The mountains, long vistas, and resilient struggle for life are all magnified by the dryness. Sparse vegetation leaves the landscape exposed; moisture demand exceeds moisture supply throughout, creating permanent water deficits (water balance is discussed in Chapter 9). The extent of this dryness distinguishes desert and steppe climatic regions. (In addition, refer to specific annual and daily desert temperature regimes, including the highest recorded temperatures, discussed in Chapter 5; surface energy budgets covered in Chapter 4; desert landscapes in Chapter 15; and desert environments in Chapter 20.)

Important causal elements in these drylands include

- Dry, subsiding air in subtropical high-pressure systems dominates.
- Midlatitude deserts and steppes form in the rain shadow of mountains, those regions to the lee of precipitation-intercepting mountains.

[Map with labels: Lethbridge, Alberta; Albuquerque, NM; Semey, Kazakstan; Ar Riyad, Saudi Arabia; Walgett, NSW Australia. Legend: Arid deserts; Semiarid steppes]

- Continental interiors, particularly central Asia, are far from moisture-bearing air masses.
- Shifting subtropical high-pressure systems produce semiarid steppe lands around the periphery of arid deserts.

Dry climates are distributed by latitude and the amount of moisture deficits in four distinct regimes: *arid deserts* (tropical, subtropical hot, midlatitude cold) and *semiarid steppes* (tropical, subtropical hot, midlatitude cold).

Midlatitude Cold Desert Climates

Midlatitude cold desert climates cover only a small area: the countries along the southern border of Russia, the Gobi Desert, and Mongolia in Asia; the central third of Nevada and areas of the American Southwest, particularly at high elevations; and Patagonia in Argentina. Because of lower temperatures and lower moisture-demand values, rainfall must be low for a station to qualify as a *midlatitude cold desert* climate; consequently, total annual average rainfall is only about 15 cm (6 in.).

A representative station is Albuquerque, New Mexico, with 20.7 cm (8.1 in.) of precipitation and an annual average temperature of 14°C (57.2°F) (Figure 10.24). Note the summer convectional showers on the climograph. Across central Nevada stretches a characteristic expanse of midlatitude cold desert, greatly modified by a century of livestock grazing (Figure 10.24b). Comparing the *midlatitude cold desert* of Albuquerque and *subtropical hot desert* of Ar Riyāḍ, Saudi Arabia, reveals an interesting similarity in the annual temperature range and a distinct difference in precipitation patterns.

Tropical, Subtropical Hot Steppe Climates

Tropical, subtropical hot steppe climates generally exist around the periphery of hot deserts, where shifting subtropical high-pressure cells create a distinct summer-dry

Station: Albuquerque, New Mexico
Lat/long: 35°03′ N 106°37′ W
Avg. Ann. Temp.: 14°C (57.2°F)
Total Ann. Precip.: 20.7 cm (8.1 in.)

Elevation: 1620 m (5315 ft)
Population: 479,000
Ann. Temp. Range: 24 C° (43.2 F°)
Ann. Hr of Sunshine: 3420

FIGURE 10.24 Midlatitude cold desert climate. (a) Climograph for Albuquerque, New Mexico (*midlatitude cold desert*). (b) Cold, high desert landscape of the Basin and Range Province in Nevada, east of Ely along highway U.S. 50. [Photo by Bobbé Christopherson.]

FIGURE 10.25 Tropical, subtropical hot steppe climate. (a) Climograph for Walgett, New South Wales, Australia (*tropical, subtropical hot steppe*). (b) Vast plains characteristic of north-central New South Wales. [Photo by Otto Rogge/Stock Market.]

and winter-wet pattern. Average annual precipitation in *subtropical hot steppe* areas is usually below 60 cm (23.6 in.). Walgett, in interior New South Wales, Australia, provides a Southern Hemisphere example of this climate (Figure 10.25). This climate is seen around the Sahara's periphery and in the Iran, Afghanistan, Turkmenistan, and Kazakstan region.

Midlatitude Cold Steppe Climates

The *midlatitude cold steppe* climates occur poleward of about 30° latitude and the *midlatitude cold desert* climates. Such midlatitude steppes are not generally found in the Southern Hemisphere. As with other dry climate regions, rainfall in the steppes is widely variable and undependable, ranging from 20 to 40 cm (7.9 to 15.7 in.). Not all rainfall is convectional, for cyclonic storm tracks penetrate the continents; however, most storms produce little precipitation.

Figure 10.26 presents a comparison between Asian and North American *midlatitude cold steppes*. Consider Semey (Semipalatinsk) in Kazakstan (greater temperature range, precipitation evenly distributed) and Lethbridge, Alberta (lesser temperature range, summer maximum conventional precipitation).

Global Climate Change

Significant climatic change has occurred on Earth in the past and most certainly will occur in the future. There is nothing society can do about long-term influences that cycle Earth through swings from ice ages to warmer periods. However, our global society must address short-term changes that are influencing global temperatures within the life span of present generations. This is especially true since these changes are due to human activities—an anthropogenic forcing of climate.

Record-high global temperatures have dominated the past two decades—for both land and ocean and for both day and night. The record year for warmth was 2005 and all the years since 1995 were near this record. Air temperatures are the highest since recordings began in earnest more than 140 years ago and higher than at any time in the last 120,000 years, according to the ice-core record. This warming trend is *very likely**** due to a buildup of

*As standard scientific reference on climate change, the IPCC uses the following to indicate levels of confidence: *Virtually certain* >99% probability of occurrence; *Extremely likely* >95%; *Very likely* >90%; *Likely* >66%; *More likely than not* >50%; *Unlikely* <33%; *Very unlikely* <10%; and *Extremely unlikely* <5%.

FIGURE 10.29 Explaining global temperature changes.
Computer models accurately track observed temperature change (black line) when they factor in human-forced influences on
climate (red shading). Solar activity and volcanoes do not explain the increases (blue shading). [Graphs from *Climate Change
2007: The Physical Science Basis*, Working Group I, IPCC Fourth Assessment Report, February 2007: Fig. SPM-4, p. 11.]

fluctuations (natural) as a key to predicting future climate trends. Figure 10.29 from the IPCC *Fourth Assessment Report* shows a comparison of climate models of forcing from solar output changes and volcanoes (shaded blue area) with anthropogenic (human) forcing (shaded red area) for global, all land, and all ocean regions. The black line on each graph plots observations from 1906–2005. Clearly, only those coupled climate models that include anthropogenic factors accurately simulate increasing temperatures. Solar variability and volcanic output alone do not explain the increase. All the temperature records this decade occurred when the Sun was at an irradiance minimum, lower than the last two minima in its cycle.

Because the enhanced greenhouse gases are anthropogenic in origin, various management strategies are possible to reduce human-forced climatic changes. Let's begin by examining the problem at its roots.

Carbon Dioxide and Global Warming Carbon dioxide and water vapour are the principal radiatively active gases causing Earth's natural greenhouse effect. *Radiatively active* gases include atmospheric gases, such as carbon dioxide (CO_2), methane (CH_4), nitrous oxide (N_2O), chlorofluorocarbons (CFCs), and water vapour, which absorb and radiate longwave energy. Figure 10.30 plots changes in three of these greenhouse gases over the past 10,000 years.

These gases are transparent to light but opaque to the longer wavelengths radiated by Earth. Thus, they transmit light from the Sun to Earth but delay heat-energy loss to space. While detained, this heat energy is absorbed and emitted over and over, warming the lower atmosphere. As concentrations of these greenhouse gases increase, more heat energy remains in the atmosphere and temperatures increase.

The present CO_2 concentration tops anything over the last 800,000 years in the Dome C ice core. In fact, over this ice-core record, changes of as much as 30 ppm in CO_2 took at least 1000 years, yet the concentration has changed 30 ppm in just the last 17 years. With 4.5% of the world's population, the United States continues to produce 24% of global CO_2 emissions. China, with 20% of global population, is responsible for 18% of CO_2

emissions and is increasing its output. Clearly, per capita CO_2 emissions in the United States are far above what an average person in China produces.

Methane and Global Warming Another radiatively active gas contributing to the overall greenhouse effect is methane (CH_4), which, at more than 1% per year, is increasing in concentration even faster than carbon dioxide. In ice cores, methane levels never topped 750 ppb in the past 800,000 years, yet in Figure 10.30 we see present levels at 1780 ppb. We are at an atmospheric concentration of methane that is higher than at any time in the past 800 millennia.

Methane is generated by such organic processes as digestion and rotting in the absence of oxygen (anaerobic processes). About 50% of the excess methane comes from bacterial action in the intestinal tracts of livestock and from organic activity in flooded rice fields. Burning of vegetation causes another 20% of the excess, and bacterial action inside the digestive systems of termite populations also is a significant source. Methane is thought responsible for at least 19% of the total atmospheric warming.

Other Greenhouse Gases Nitrous oxide (N_2O) is the third most important greenhouse gas that is forced by human activity—up 17% in atmospheric concentration since 1750, higher than at any time in the past 10,000 years (Fig. 10.30). Fertilizer use increases the processes in soil that emit nitrous oxide, although more research is needed to fully understand the relationships. Chlorofluorocarbons (CFCs) and other halocarbons also contribute to global warming. CFCs absorb longwave energy missed by carbon dioxide and water vapour in the lower troposphere. As radiatively active gases, CFCs enhance the greenhouse effect in the troposphere and are a cause of ozone depletion and slight cooling in the stratosphere.

Climate Models and Future Temperatures

The scientific challenge in understanding climate change is to sense climatic trends in what is essentially a nonlinear, chaotic natural system. Imagine the tremendous task of

Changes in Greenhouse Gases from Ice-Core and Modern Data

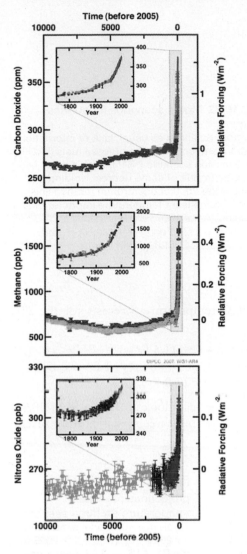

FIGURE 10.30 Greenhouse gas changes over the last 10,000 years.

Ice core and modern data show the trends in carbon dioxide, methane, and nitrous oxide over the last 10,000 years. It is immediately obvious that we are living in unique territory on these graphs. During 2007, CO_2 passed the 387 ppm level, CH_4 was at 1780 ppb, and N_2O approached 330 ppb. [Graphs from *Climate Change 2007: The Physical Science Basis*, Working Group I, IPCC Fourth Assessment Report, February 2007: Fig. SPM-1, p. 3.]

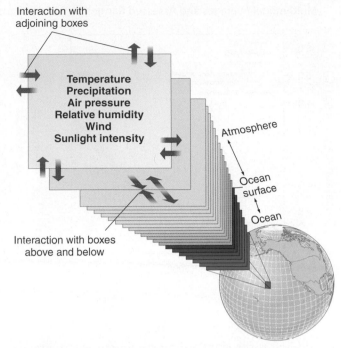

FIGURE 10.31 A general circulation model scheme. Temperature, precipitation, air pressure, relative humidity, wind, and sunlight intensity are sampled in myriad grid boxes. In the ocean, sampling is limited, but temperature, salinity, and ocean current data are considered. The interactions within a grid layer, and between layers on all six sides, are modelled in a general circulation model program.

building a computer model of all climatic components and programming these linkages (shown in Figure 10.1) over different time frames and at various scales.

Using mathematical models originally established for forecasting weather, scientists developed a complex computer climate model known as a **general circulation model (GCM)**. There are at least a dozen established GCMs now operating around the world. Submodel programs for the atmosphere, ocean, land surface, cryosphere, and biosphere operate within the GCM. The most sophisticated models couple atmosphere and ocean submodels and are known as *Atmosphere-Ocean General Circulation Models (AOGCMs)*.

The first step in describing a climate is to define a manageable portion of Earth's climatic system for study. Climatologists create dimensional "grid boxes" that extend from beneath the ocean to the tropopause, in multiple layers (Figure 10.31). Resolution of these boxes in the atmosphere is about 250 km in the horizontal and 1 km (155–0.6 mi) in the vertical; in the ocean the boxes use the same horizontal resolution and a vertical resolution of about 200 to 400 m (650–1300 ft). Analysts deal not only with the climatic components within each grid layer but also with the interaction among the layers on all sides.

A comparative benchmark among the operational GCMs is *climatic sensitivity* to doubling of carbon dioxide levels in the atmosphere. GCMs do not predict specific temperatures, but they do offer various scenarios of global warming. GCM-generated maps correlate well with the observed global warming patterns experienced since 1990.

The 2007 IPCC *Fourth Assessment Report*, using a variety of GCM forecast scenarios, predicted a range of average surface warming for this century. Figure 10.32 illustrates six of these scenarios, each with its own assumptions of economics, population, degree of global cooperation, and greenhouse gas emission levels. The

Multi-model Averages and Assessed Ranges for Surface Warming

FIGURE 10.32 Model scenarios for surface warming.
Ranging from business as usual, lack of international cooperation, and continuation of fossil fuels ("A2Fl") to a low-emission scenario ("B1"), each spells climatic catastrophe of some degree. Holding emissions at the 2000 concentration (orange line plot) results in the least temperature impacts. [Graph from *Climate Change 2007: The Physical Science Basis*, Working Group I, IPCC Fourth Assessment Report, February 2007: Fig. SPM-5, p. 14.]

orange line is the simulation experiment where green-house gas emissions are held at 2000 values with no increases. The grey bars give you the best estimate and likely ranges of outcomes; for example, from a "low forecast" in B1 to a "high forecast" in A1Fl. Even the "B" scenario represents a significant increase in global land and ocean temperatures and will produce consequences. Although regionally variable and subject to

revision, the IPCC temperature forecasts for the 21st century are:

- High forecast: 6.4 C° (11.5 F°),
- Middle forecast: 1.8 C°–4.0 C° (3.1 F°–7.2 F°),
- Low forecast: 1.1 C° (2.0 F°).

Figure 10.33 offers us a look at the world of 2020–2029 and 2090–2099 using three scenarios from several

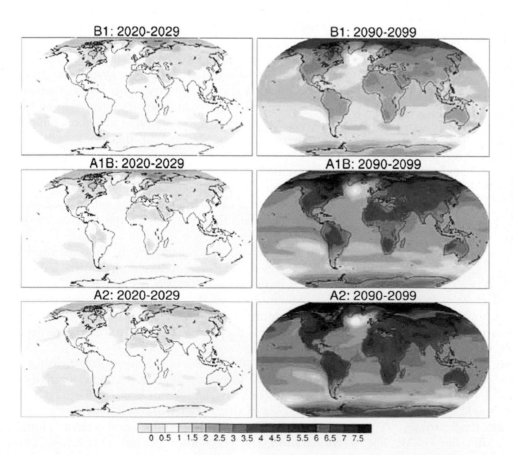

FIGURE 10.33 Model projections of surface temperature for three scenarios. Three pairs of model simulations for 2020–2029 and 2090–2099 for the B1, A1B, and A2 scenarios. The colours are defined in the temperature scale along the bottom. Note the severity of warming in the worst case. Correlate these three cases with the graph in Figure 10.32. [Maps from *Climate Change 2007: The Physical Science Basis*, Working Group I, IPCC Fourth Assessment Report, February 2007: Fig. SPM-6, p. 15.]

different *AOGCMs*. Find the three scenarios used for these three pairs of maps on the graph in Figure 10.32. You can see from these maps why scientists are concerned about temperature trends in the higher latitudes.

Consequences of Global Warming

The consequences of uncontrolled atmospheric warming are complex. Regional climate responses are expected as temperature, precipitation, soil moisture, and air mass characteristics change. Although the ability to accurately forecast such regional changes is still evolving, some consequences of warming have been forecasted and in several regions are already underway. The challenge for science is to analyze such effects on a global scale.

The following list is a brief overview from the IPCC *Fourth Assessment Report* "Summary for Policy Makers" and other sources that summarize global impacts emerging from climate change.

- The observed pattern of tropospheric warming and stratospheric cooling is *very likely* due to greenhouse gas increases and stratospheric ozone depletion.
- Widespread changes in extreme temperatures have been observed over the last 50 years. Cold days, cold nights, and frost are less frequent, while hot days, hot nights, and heat waves are more frequent.
- Observations since 1961 show the average global ocean temperature increased to depths of 3000 m and the ocean absorbed more than 80% of climate system heating. Such warming causes thermal expansion of seawater, contributing to sea level rise.
- There is observational evidence of increased intensity of tropical cyclones correlated with increases of tropical sea-surface temperatures. Total "power dissipation" of these storms has doubled since 1970. Worldwide there are more category 3, 4, and 5 tropical storms than in the previous record.
- Mountain glaciers and snow cover declined on average in both hemispheres, contributing to sea-level rise.
- Mount Kilimanjaro in Africa, portions of the South American Andes, and the Himalayas will very likely lose most of their glacial ice within the next two decades, affecting local water resources. Glacial ice continues its retreat in Alaska.
- The average atmospheric water vapour content has increased over land and ocean as well as in the upper troposphere. The increase is consistent with the fact that warmer air can absorb more water vapour.
- Flow speed accelerated for some Greenland and Antarctic outlet glaciers as they drain ice from the interior of the ice sheets. In Greenland this rate of loss exceeds snowfall accumulation, with losses per year more than doubling between 1996 and 2004 (mass losses of 91 km^3 compared to 224 km^3).

- A JPL/NASA analysis in 2008 found that Antarctic ice loss increased 75% between 1996 and 2006 and is accelerating. Scientists are focusing on loss rates in the West Antarctic Ice Sheet and the Antarctic Peninsula.
- Average Arctic temperatures increased at almost twice the global average rate in the past 100 years. Wintertime lower atmosphere temperatures over Antarctica are warming at nearly three times the global average, first reported in 2006.
- Temperatures in the permafrost active layer increased overall since the 1980s in the Arctic up to 3 C°. The maximum area of seasonally frozen ground decreased 7% in the Northern Hemisphere, with a decrease in spring of up to 15%.
- Since 1978, annual average Arctic sea-ice extent shrunk in summer by 7.4% per decade, according to satellite measurements. September 2007 Arctic sea-ice extent retreated to its lowest area coverage in the record.
- Changes in precipitation and evaporation over the oceans and the melting of ice are freshening mid- and high-latitude oceans and seas, together with increased salinity in low-latitudes. Oceans are acidifying (lower pH) in response to absorption of increasing atmospheric CO_2.
- Mid-latitude westerly winds strengthened in both hemispheres since the 1960s.
- More intense and longer droughts have been observed over wider areas since the 1970s, particularly in the tropics and subtropics. Increased drying linked to higher temperatures and decreased precipitation has been observed in the Sahel, the Mediterranean, southern Africa, parts of southern Asia, Australia, and the American West.
- Higher spring and summer temperatures and earlier snowmelt are extending the wildfire season and increasing the intensity of wildfires in the western United States and elsewhere.
- The frequency of heavy precipitation events increased over most land areas, consistent with warming and observed increases of atmospheric water vapour. Significantly increased precipitation has been observed in eastern parts of North and South America, northern Europe, and northern and central Asia.
- Crop patterns, as well as natural habitats of plants and animals, will shift to maintain preferred temperatures. According to climate models, climatic regions in the midlatitudes could shift poleward by 150 to 550 km (90 to 350 mi) during this century.
- Biosphere models predict that a global average of 30% of the present forest cover (varying regionally from 15% to 65%) will undergo major species redistribution—greatest at high latitudes and least in the tropics.
- Populations previously unaffected by malaria, dengue fever, lymphatic filariasis, and yellow fever

(all mosquito vector), schistosomiasis (water snail vector), and sleeping sickness (tsetse fly vector) will be at greater risk in subtropical and midlatitude areas as temperatures increase the vector ranges.

Changes in Sea Level Sea-level rise must be expressed as a range of values that are under constant reassessment. During the last century, sea level rose 10–20 cm (4–8 in.), a rate 10 times higher than the average rate during the last 3000 years.

The 2007 IPCC forecast scenarios for global mean sea-level rise this century, given regional variations, are:

- Low forecast: 0.18 m (7.1 in.),
- Middle forecast: 0.39 m (15.4 in.),
- High forecast: 0.59 m (23.2 in.).

Unfortunately the new 2006–2008 measurements of Greenland's and Antarctica's ice-loss acceleration are not included in the IPCC report. Scientists are considering at least a 1.2-m (3.94-ft) "high case" for estimates of sea-level rise this century as more realistic given Greenland's present losses coupled with mountain glacial ice losses worldwide. Remember that a 0.3-m rise in sea level would produce a shoreline retreat of 30 m (98 ft) on average. Here is the concern:

> The data now available raise concerns that the climate system, in particular sea level, may be responding more quickly than climate models indicate. . . . The rate of sea-level rise for the past 20 years is 25% faster than the rate of rise in any 20-year period in the preceding 115 years. . . . Since 1990 the observed sea-level has been rising faster than the rise projected by models.*

These increases would continue beyond 2100 even if greenhouse gas concentrations are stabilized. In Chapter 16, News Report Figure 16.1.1, maps present what coastlines will experience in the event of a 1-m rise in sea level.

A quick survey of world coastlines shows that even a moderate rise could bring change of unparalleled proportions. At stake are the river deltas, lowland coastal farming valleys, and low-lying mainland areas, all contending with high water, high tides, and higher storm surges. Particularly tragic social and economic consequences will affect small island states, which are unable to adjust within their present country boundaries—disruption of biological systems, loss of biodiversity, reduction in water resources, and evacuation of residents are among the impacts.

There could be both internal and international migration of affected human populations, spread over decades, as people move away from coastal flooding caused by the sea-level rise—a 1-m rise will displace 130 million people. Presently there is lacking any body of world law that covers "environmental refugees."

*S. Rahmstorf, et al., "Recent Climate Observations Compared to Projections," AAAS *Science* 316 (May 4, 2007): p. 709.

Political Action and "No Regrets"

Reading through all this climate change science must seem pretty "heavy." Instead, think of this information as empowering and motivation to take action, personally, locally, regionally, nationally, and globally.

A product of the 1992 Earth Summit in Rio de Janeiro was the United Nations Framework Convention on Climate Change (FCCC). The leading body of the Convention is the Conference of the Parties (COP) operated by the countries that ratified the FCCC, 186 countries by 2000. Meetings were held in Berlin (*COP-1*, 1995) and Geneva (*COP-2*, 1996). These meetings set the stage for *COP-3* in Kyoto, Japan, in December 1997, where 10,000 participants adopted the *Kyoto Protocol* by consensus. Seventeen national academies of science endorsed the Kyoto Protocol. (For updates on the status of the Kyoto Protocol, see **http://unfccc.int/2860.php**.) The latest 2007 gathering, COP-13, was in Bali, Indonesia.

The Kyoto Protocol binds more-developed countries to a collective 5.2% reduction in greenhouse gas emissions as measured at 1990 levels for the period 2008 to 2012. Within this group goal, various countries promised cuts: Canada is to cut 6%, the European Union 8%, and Australia 8%, among many others. The *Group of 77* countries plus China favor a 15% reduction by 2010. With Russian ratification in November 2004, the Kyoto Protocol is now international law with nearly 140 country signatories; this is without United States participation.

The Intergovernmental Panel on Climate Change (IPCC) declared that "no regrets" opportunities to reduce carbon dioxide emissions are available in most countries. The IPCC Working Group III defines this as follows:

> No regrets options are by definition greenhouse gas emissions reduction options that have negative net costs, because they generate direct and indirect benefits that are large enough to offset the costs of implementing the options.

Benefits that equal or exceed their cost to society include reduced energy cost, improved air quality and health, reduction in tanker spills and oil imports, and deployment of renewable and sustainable energy sources, among others. This holds true without even considering the benefits of slowing the rate of climate change. For Europe, scientists determined that carbon emissions could be reduced to less than half the 1990 level by 2030, at a negative cost. One key to "no regrets" is the untapped energy-efficiency potential.

In the United States, five Department of Energy national laboratories (Oak Ridge, Lawrence Berkeley, Pacific Northwest, National Renewable Energy, and Argonne) reported that the United States can meet the Kyoto carbon emission reduction targets with negative overall costs (cash benefit savings) ranging from −$7 to −$34 billion. (For more, see Working Group III, *Climate Change 2001, Mitigation*, London: Cambridge University Press, 2001, pp. 21, 474–76, and 506–507.)

Summary and Review—Global Climate Systems

■ *Define* climate and climatology, and *explain* the difference between climate and weather.

Climate is dynamic, not static. **Climate** is a synthesis of weather phenomena at many scales, from planetary to local, in contrast to weather, which is the condition of the atmosphere at any given time and place. Earth experiences a wide variety of climatic conditions that can be grouped by general similarities into climatic regions. **Climatology** is the study of climate and attempts to discern similar weather statistics and identify **climatic regions**.

climate (p. 285)
climatology (p. 286)
climatic regions (p. 286)

1. Define climate and compare it with weather. What is climatology?

2. Explain how a climatic region synthesizes climate statistics.

3. How does the El Niño phenomenon produce the largest interannual variability in climate? What are some of the changes and effects that occur worldwide?

■ *Review* the role of temperature, precipitation, air pressure, and air mass patterns used to establish climatic regions.

Climatic inputs include insolation (pattern of solar energy in the Earth–atmosphere environment), temperature (sensible heat energy content of the air), precipitation (rain, sleet, snow, and hail; the supply of moisture), air pressure (varying patterns of atmospheric density), and air masses (regional-sized homogeneous units of air). Climate is the basic element in ecosystems, the natural, self-regulating communities of plants and animals that thrive in specific environments.

4. How do radiation receipts, temperature, air-pressure inputs, and precipitation patterns interact to produce climate types? Give an example from a humid environment and one from an arid environment.

5. Evaluate the relationships among a climatic region, ecosystem, and biome.

■ *Review* the development of climate classification systems, and *compare* genetic and empirical systems as ways of classifying climate.

Classification is the process of ordering or grouping data in related categories. A **genetic classification** is based on causative factors, such as the interaction of air masses. An **empirical classification** is one based on statistical data, such as temperature or precipitation. This text analyzes climate using aspects of both approaches, with a map based on climatological elements.

classification (p. 288)
genetic classification (p. 288)
empirical classification (p. 288)

6. What are the differences between a genetic and an empirical classification system?

7. What are some of the climatological elements used in classifying climates?

■ *Describe* the principal climate classification categories other than deserts, and *locate* these regions on a world map.

Here we focus on temperature and precipitation measures. Keep in mind these are measurable results produced by interacting elements of weather and climate. These data are plotted on a **climograph** to display the characteristics of the climate.

There are six basic climate categories. Temperature and precipitation considerations form the basis of five climate categories and their regional types:

- Tropical (equatorial and tropical latitudes)
  rain forest (rainy all year)
  monsoon (6 to 12 months rainy)
  savanna (less than 6 months rainy)
- Mesothermal (midlatitudes, mild winters)
  humid subtropical (hot summers)
  marine west coast (warm to cool summers)
  Mediterranean (dry summers)
- Microthermal (mid- and high latitudes, cold winters)
  humid continental (hot to warm summers)
  subarctic (cool summers to very cold winters)
- Polar (high latitudes and polar regions)
  tundra (high latitude or high altitude)
  ice caps and ice sheets (perpetually frozen)
  polar marine
- Highland (compared to lowlands at the same latitude, highlands have lower temperatures—recall the normal lapse rate)

Only one climate category is based on moisture efficiency as well as temperature:

- Desert (permanent moisture deficits)
  arid deserts (tropical, subtropical hot, and midlatitude cold)
  semiarid steppes (tropical, subtropical hot, and midlatitude cold)

climograph (p. 293)

8. List and discuss each of the principal climate categories. In which one of these general types do you live? Which category is the only type associated with the annual distribution and amount of precipitation?

9. What is a climograph, and how is it used to display climatic information?

10. Which of the major climate types occupies the most land and ocean area on Earth?

11. Characterize the tropical climates in terms of temperature, moisture, and location.

12. Using Africa's tropical climates as an example, characterize the climates produced by the seasonal shifting of the ITCZ with the high Sun.

13. Mesothermal (subtropical and midlatitude, mild winter) climates occupy the second-largest portion of Earth's entire surface. Describe their temperature, moisture, and precipitation characteristics.

14. Explain the distribution of the *humid subtropical hot-summer* and *Mediterranean dry-summer* climates at similar latitudes

and the difference in precipitation patterns between the two types. Describe the difference in vegetation associated with these two climate types.

15. Which climates are characteristic of the Asian monsoon region?

16. Explain how a *marine west coast* climate type can occur in the Appalachian region of the eastern United States.

17. What role do offshore ocean currents play in the distribution of the *marine west coast* climates? What type of fog is formed in these regions?

18. Discuss the climatic conditions for the coldest places on Earth outside the poles.

■ *Explain* the precipitation and moisture efficiency criteria used to determine the arid and semiarid climates, and *locate* them on a world map.

The dry and semiarid climates are described by precipitation rather than temperature. Dry climates are the world's arid deserts and semiarid regions, with their unique plants, animals, and physical features. The arid and semiarid climates occupy more than 35% of Earth's land area, clearly the most extensive climate over land.

Major subdivisions are *arid deserts* in tropical and midlatitude areas (precipitation—natural water supply—less than one-half of natural water demand) and *semiarid steppes* in tropical and midlatitude areas (precipitation more than one-half of natural water demand).

19. In general terms, what are the differences among the four desert classifications? How are moisture and temperature distributions used to differentiate these subtypes?

20. Relative to the distribution of arid and semiarid climates, describe at least three locations where they occur across the globe and the reasons for their presence in these locations.

■ *Outline* future climate patterns from forecasts presented, and *explain* the causes and potential consequences of climate change.

Various activities of present-day society are producing climatic changes, particularly a global warming trend. The highest average annual temperatures experienced since the advent of instrumental measurements dominated the last 25 years. There is a scientific consensus building that global warming is related to the anthropogenic impacts on the natural greenhouse effect.

The 2007 *Fourth Assessment Report* from the Intergovernmental Panel on Climate Change affirms this consensus. The IPCC predicted surface-temperature response to a doubling of carbon dioxide with a range of increase from 1.1 C° (2.0 F°) to 6.4 C° (11.5 F°) between the present and 2100. Natural climatic variability over the span of Earth's history is the subject of **paleoclimatology**. A **general circulation model (GCM)** forecasts climate patterns and is evolving to greater capability and accuracy than in the past. People and their political institutions can use GCM forecasts to form policies aimed at reducing unwanted climate change.

paleoclimatology (p. 318)
general circulation model (GCM) (p. 321)

21. Explain climate forecasts. How do general circulation models (GCMs) produce such forecasts?

22. Describe the potential climatic effects of global warming on polar and high-latitude regions. What are the implications of these climatic changes for persons living at lower latitudes?

23. How is climatic change affecting agricultural and food production? Natural environments? Forests? The possible spread of disease?

24. What are the present actions being taken to delay the effects of global climate change? What is the Kyoto Protocol? What is the current status of Canadian and U.S. government action on the Protocol?

Critical Thinking

A. The text asked that you find the climate conditions for your campus and your birthplace and locate these two places on Figures 10.3, 10.4, and 10.5. Briefly describe the information sources you used: library, Internet, teacher, and phone calls to state and provincial climatologists. Now, refer to Appendix C to refine your assessment of climate for the two locations. Briefly show how you worked through the Köppen climate criteria given in the appendix that established the climate classification for your two cities.

B. On the *Geosystems* Student Learning Center Web site and in Focus Study 10.1 there are URL references for El Niño and

La Niña. Sample three or four sources and determine the up-to-date status of the phenomena at the present time. How are current conditions different from the record El Niño event in 1997–1998? Or La Niña in 2007? What Internet links were most helpful to you in completing this status report?

C. Many external factors force climate. The chart "Global and annual mean radiative forcing for the year 2000, relative to 1750" is presented here (from IPCC *Climate Change 2001, The Scientific Basis*, Washington: Cambridge University Press, 2001, Figure 3, p. 8, and Figure 6.6, p. 392).

The estimates of radiative forcing in Watts per square metre units are given on the y-axis (vertical axis). The level of scientific understanding is noted along the x-axis (horizontal axis), arranged from "high" to "very low." Those columns above the "0" value (in red) indicate *positive forcing*, such as the greenhouse gases grouped in the far-left column. Columns that fall below the "0" value (in blue) indicate *negative forcing*, such as the haze from sulfate aerosols, fourth column from the left. The vertical line between the markers on each column is an estimate of the uncertainty range. Where no column appears but there is instead a line denoting a range, there is no central estimate given present uncertainties, such as for mineral dust.

Assume you are a policy maker with a goal of reducing the rate of global warming; that is, reducing positive radiative forcing of the climate system. What strategies do you suggest to alter the height of the columns and adjust the mix of elements that cause warming? Assign priorities to each suggested strategy to denote most-to-least effective in moderating climate change. Brainstorm and discuss your strategies with others.

The Global Mean Radiative Forcing of the Climate System for the Year 2000, Relative to 1750

Level of scientific understanding

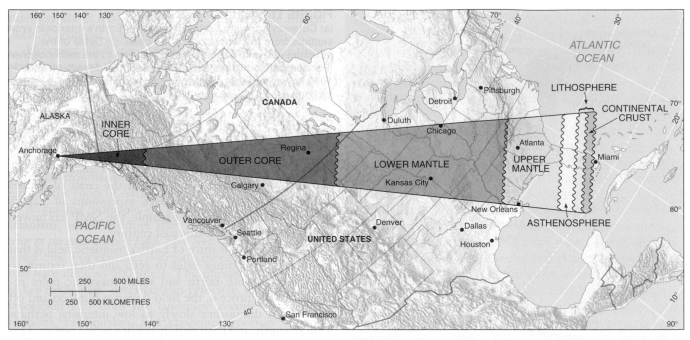

FIGURE 11.3 Distances from core to crust.
The distance from Anchorage, Alaska, across Canada, to Fort Lauderdale, Florida, is the same distance as that from Earth's centre to its outer crust. Earth's cross section overlays the surface map to illustrate Earth's radius. The continental crust thickness only extends an equivalent distance to the outskirts of Fort Lauderdale and its suburbs, some 30 km (18.6 mi) from the coast.

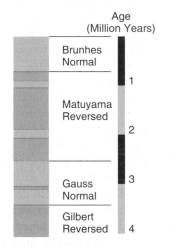

FIGURE 11.4 Geomagnetic reversals.
Periods of normal geomagnetic polarity (shown in blue) alternate with periods of reversed geomagnetic polarity (shown in orange). The radiometric ages of the rocks that preserve this record of paleomagnetism appear at the right of the figure. [Used by permission of the Minister of Public Works and Government Services Canada; Natural Resources Canada, Geological Survey of Canada.]

Earth's Mantle

Figure 11.2b shows a transition zone several hundred kilometres wide, at an average depth of about 2900 km (1800 mi), dividing Earth's outer core from its mantle. Scientists at the California Institute of Technology analyzed more than 25,000 earthquakes and determined that this transition area is uneven, with ragged peak-and-valley-like formations. This is the *Gutenberg discontinuity*.

A *discontinuity* is a place where physical differences occur between adjoining regions in Earth's interior, such as between the outer core and lower mantle.

The **mantle** (lower and upper together) represents about 80% of Earth's total volume. The mantle is rich in oxides of iron and magnesium and silicates (FeO, MgO, and SiO_2). They are dense and tightly packed at depth, grading to lesser densities toward the surface. A broad transition zone of several hundred kilometres, centred between 410 and 660 km (255–410 mi) below the surface, separates the upper mantle from the lower mantle. The entire mantle experiences a gradual temperature increase with depth and a stiffening due to increased pressures. The denser lower mantle is thought to contain a mixture of iron, magnesium, and silicates, with some calcium and aluminum.

The upper mantle divides into three fairly distinct layers: upper mantle, asthenosphere, and *uppermost mantle*, shown in Figure 11.2c. Next to the crust is the uppermost mantle, a high-velocity zone just below the crust, where seismic waves transmit through a rigid, cooler layer. This uppermost mantle, along with the crust, makes up the *lithosphere*, approximately 45–70 km thick.

Below the lithosphere, from about 70 km down to 250 km, is the **asthenosphere**, or plastic layer (from the Greek *asthenos*, meaning "weak"). It contains pockets of increased heat from radioactive decay and is susceptible to slow convective currents in these hotter, and therefore less dense, materials.

Because of its dynamic condition, the asthenosphere is the least rigid region of the mantle, with densities averaging 3.3 g/cm³ (or 3300 kg/m³). About 10% of the asthenosphere is molten in asymmetrical patterns and hot spots. The resulting slow movement in this zone disturbs the overlying crust and creates tectonic activity—the folding, faulting, and general deformation of surface rocks. In return, movement of the crust apparently influences currents throughout the mantle.

The depth affected by convection currents is the subject of much scientific research. One body of evidence states that mixing occurs throughout the entire mantle, upwelling from great depths at the core–mantle boundary, sometimes in small blobs of material; other times "megablobs" of mantle convect toward and away from the crust. Another view states that mixing in the mantle is layered, segregated above and below the 660-km boundary. Presently, evidence indicates some truth in both positions.

As an example, there are hot spots on Earth, such as those under Hawai'i, Easter Island, and Tahiti, that appear to be at the top of tall plumes of rising mantle rock that are anchored deep in the lower mantle, where the upward flow of warmer, less-dense material begins. The plume beneath Iceland appears to begin at the 660-km transition. Yet, there are other surface hot spots that sit atop smaller plumes going down some 200 km (124 mi). In other surface regions, slabs of crust descend and penetrate to the lower mantle. For basics on Earth's interior and plate tectonics, see http://www.solarviews.com/eng/earthint.htm.

Earth's Lithosphere and Crust

The lithosphere includes the **crust** and uppermost mantle to about 70 km (43 mi) in depth (Figure 11.2c). An important internal boundary between the crust and the high-velocity portion of the uppermost mantle is another discontinuity, called the **Mohorovičić discontinuity**, or **Moho** for short. It is named for the Yugoslavian seismologist who determined that seismic waves change at this depth owing to sharp contrasts of materials and densities.

Figure 11.2c illustrates the relation of the crust to the rest of the lithosphere and the asthenosphere below. Crustal areas beneath mountain masses extend deep, perhaps to 50–60 km (31–37 mi), whereas the crust beneath continental interiors averages about 30 km (19 mi) in thickness. Oceanic crust averages only 5 km (3 mi). The crust is only a fraction of Earth's overall mass. Drilling through the crust into the uppermost mantle remains an elusive scientific goal (see News Report 11.2).

The composition and texture of continental and oceanic crusts are quite different, and this difference is a key to the concept of drifting continents. The oceanic crust is denser than continental crust. In collisions, the denser oceanic material plunges beneath the lighter, more buoyant continental crust.

- *Continental crust* is essentially **granite**; it is crystalline and high in silica, aluminum, potassium, calcium, and sodium. (Sometimes continental crust is called *sial*, shorthand for *si*lica and *al*uminum.) Continental crust is relatively low in density, averaging 2.7 g/cm^3 (or 2700 kg/m^3). Compare this with other densities given in Figure 11.2.
- *Oceanic crust* is **basalt**; it is granular and high in silica, magnesium, and iron. (Sometimes oceanic crust is called *sima*, shorthand for *si*lica and *ma*gnesium.) It is denser than continental crust, averaging 3.0 g/cm^3 (or 3000 kg/m^3).

News Report 11.2

Drilling the Crust to Record Depths

Scientists wanting to sample mantle material directly have unsuccessfully tried for decades to penetrate Earth's crust to the Moho discontinuity (the crust–mantle boundary). The longest-lasting deep-drilling attempt is on the northern Kola Peninsula near Zapolyarny, Russia, 250 km north of the Arctic Circle—the *Kola Borehole (KSDB)*. Twenty years of high-technology drilling (1970–1989) produced a hole 12.23 km deep (7.6 mi, or 40,230 ft), purely for exploration and science. Crystalline rock 1.4 billion years old at 180°C (356°F) was reached. The site has other active boreholes, and the fifth is underway. (See an analysis log at http://

www.icdp-online.de/.) A record holder for depth for a gas well is in Oklahoma; it was stopped at 9750m (32,000 ft) when the drill bit ran into molten sulphur.

Oceanic crust is thinner than continental crust and is the object of several drilling attempts. The Integrated Ocean Drilling Program (IODP), a cooperative effort between the governments of Japan and the United States, replaced the former ODP effort directed by Texas A & M University in 2003. However, the university program is still the Science Operator of the research ship *JOIDES Resolution* and lead coordinator (Figure 11.2.1a).

Over the past 40 years, about 1700 bore holes were completed, yielding 160 km of sediment and rock cores and more than 35,000 samples for researchers. Much of this science windfall helped put together the puzzle of geologic time and plate tectonics. See http://www-odp.tamu.edu/ for background or http://www.oceandrilling.org/ for the IODP home page information.

The first expeditions of the largest deep-ocean drilling ship, Japan's *Chikyu*, were in 2006 and 2007. The ship is the first capable of high-latitude drilling in the Arctic. The *Chikyu* is "riserless," where it uses

(continued)

News Report 11.2 *(continued)*

seawater as the primary drilling fluid (Figure 11.2.1b). The new IODP ship will be able to drill to 7 km, more than three times the *JOIDES Resolution* limits. This *JOIDES*, workhorse of the ODP, is being refurbished and converted to upgraded riserless status and reenters active duty in 2008 for the new IODP program.

(a)

(b)

FIGURE 11.2.1 Ocean drilling ship.
(a) A modern ocean-floor drilling ship, the *JOIDES Resolution*. The International Ocean Drilling Program operates the research ship. Since it began operations in 1984, *JOIDES* has spent more than 5000 days at sea through 2003 and recovered hundreds of kilometres of core for analysis.
(b) The new *Chikyu* research ship began drilling core samples from the ocean floor in 2006. [Photos by IODP and Texas A & M University.]

Buoyancy is the principle that something less dense, such as wood, floats in something denser, such as water. The principles of buoyancy and balance were combined in the 1800s into the important principle of **isostasy**, which explains certain vertical movements of Earth's crust.

Think of Earth's crust as floating on the denser layers beneath, much as a boat floats on water. Where the load is greater, owing to glaciers, sediment, or mountains, the crust tends to sink, or ride lower in the asthenosphere. Without that load (for example, when a glacier melts), the crust rides higher, in a recovery uplift known as *isostatic rebound*. Thus, the entire crust is in a constant state of compensating adjustment, or isostasy, slowly rising and sinking in response to its own burdens, as it is pushed, and dragged, and pulled over the asthenosphere (Figure 11.5). An interesting development in Alaska relates this concept of isostatic rebound and climate change, as described in High-Latitude Connection 11.1.

High Latitude Connection 11.1

Isostatic Rebound in Alaska

The retreat of glacial ice following the last ice-age cycle unloaded much weight off the crust in Alaska, among those regions affected. Researchers from the Geophysical Institute at the University of Alaska–Fairbanks, using an array of global positioning system (GPS) receivers, measured isostatic rebound of the crust following glacial ice losses. They expected to find a slowed rate of crustal rebound in southeastern Alaska as compared to the more rapid response in the distant past when the ice first retreated.

Instead, they detected some of the most rapid vertical motion on Earth, averaging about 36 mm (1.42 in.) per year. Scientists attribute this isostatic rebound to the loss of glaciers in the region, especially the areas from Yakutat Bay and the Saint Elias Mountains in the north, through Glacier Bay, Juneau, and on south through the inland passage. Only about 1 mm of this uplift is from post-ice age response. This rapid rebound is attributable to glacial melt and retreat over the past 150 years and correlates with accelerating ice losses and record warmth across Alaska (see News Report 17.1).

For instance, Glacier Bay experienced a retreat of ice of more than 97 km (60 mi) since 1794. The land that was beneath this ice has isostatically rebounded 5.5 m (18 ft). The vertical action appears to be affecting some of the fault systems in the region, although the extent of this and its consequences are unknown at this writing.

FIGURE 11.5 Isostatic adjustment of the crust.
Earth's entire crust is in a constant state of compensating adjustment, as suggested by these three sequential stages. In (a), the mountain mass slowly sinks, displacing mantle material. In (b), because of the loss of mass through erosion and transportation, the crust isostatically adjusts upward and sediments accumulate in the ocean. As the continental crust thins (c), the heavy sediment load offshore begins to deform the lithosphere beneath the ocean. (d) The melting of ice from the last ice age and losses of overlying sediments are thought to produce an ongoing isostatic uplift of portions of the Sierra Nevada batholith. [Photo by Bobbé Christopherson.]

Earth's crust is the outermost shell: an irregular, brittle layer that resides restlessly on a dynamic and diverse interior. Let us examine the processes at work on this crust and the variety of rock types that compose the landscape.

The Geologic Cycle

Earth's crust is in an ongoing state of change, being formed, deformed, moved, and broken down by physical, chemical, and biological processes. While the endogenic (internal) system is at work building landforms, the exogenic (external) system is busily wearing them down. This vast give-and-take at the Earth–atmosphere–ocean interface is the **geologic cycle**. It is fueled from two sources—Earth's internal heat and solar energy from space—influenced by the ever-present leveling force of Earth's gravity.

Figure 11.6 illustrates the geologic cycle, combining many of the elements presented in this text. The geologic cycle is composed of three subsystems:

- The *hydrologic cycle* is the vast system that circulates water, water vapour, ice, and energy throughout the Earth–atmosphere–ocean environment. This cycle rearranges Earth materials through erosion,

(a)

(b)

FIGURE 11.6 The geologic cycle.
(a) The geologic cycle is a model showing the interactive relation among the hydrologic cycle, rock cycle, and tectonic cycle. (b) Earth's surface is where two dynamic systems interact—the endogenic (internal) and exogenic (external).

ANIMATION

Convection in a Lava Lamp

transportation, and deposition, and it circulates water as the critical medium that sustains life. (Chapters 7, 8, and 9 discussed water's properties, weather, and the hydrologic cycle.)

- The *rock cycle*, through processes in the atmosphere, crust, and mantle, produces three basic rock types—igneous, sedimentary, and metamorphic. We examine this next.

- The *tectonic cycle* brings heat energy and new materials to the surface and recycles old materials to mantle depths, creating movement and deformation of the crust. We discuss the tectonic cycle later in this chapter.

Table 11.1 Common Elements in Earth's Crust	
Element	**Percentage of Earth's Crust by Weight**
Oxygen (O)	46.6
Silicon (Si)	27.7
Aluminum (Al)	8.1
Iron (Fe)	5.0
Calcium (Ca)	3.6
Sodium (Na)	2.8
Potassium (K)	2.6
Magnesium (Mg)	2.1
All others	1.5
Total	100.00

Note: A quartz crystal (SiO_2) consists of Earth's two most abundant elements, silicon (Si) and oxygen (O). Inset photo from *Laboratory Manual in Physical Geology*, 3rd ed., R. M. Busch, ed. © 1993 by Macmillan Publishing Co.

The Rock Cycle

To begin our look at the rock cycle, we see that only eight natural elements compose 99% of Earth's crust. Just two of these—oxygen and silicon—account for 74.3% of the crust (Table 11.1). Oxygen, the most reactive gas in the lower atmosphere, readily combines with other elements. For this reason, the percentage of oxygen is greater in the crust (about 47%) than in the atmosphere (about 21%). The internal differentiation process explains the relatively large percentages of lightweight elements such as silicon and aluminum in the crust. These less-dense elements migrate toward the surface, as discussed earlier.

Minerals and Rocks Earth's elements combine to form minerals. A **mineral** is an inorganic, or nonliving, natural compound having a specific chemical formula and possessing a crystalline structure. The combination of elements and the crystal structure give each mineral its characteristic hardness, colour, density, and other properties. For example, the common mineral *quartz* is silicon dioxide, SiO_2, and has a distinctive six-sided crystal (see photo inset in Table 11.1).

Of the more than 4200 minerals, about 30 minerals comprise the *rock-forming minerals* most commonly encountered. *Mineralogy* is the study of the composition, properties, and classification of minerals. (Note that mercury, a liquid metal, is an exception to this definition for it has no crystalline structure. Also, that water is not a mineral but ice does fit the definition of a mineral.) For more on minerals see **http://webmineral.com/**.

One of the most widespread mineral families on Earth is the *silicates*, because silicon and oxygen are so common and because they readily combine with each other and with other elements. Roughly 95% of Earth's crust comprises silicates. This mineral family includes quartz, feldspar, clay minerals, and numerous gemstones. *Oxides* are another group of minerals in which oxygen combines with metallic elements, such as iron, to form hematite, Fe_2O_3. Also, there are the *sulphides* and *sulphates* groups in which sulphur compounds combine with metallic elements to form pyrite (FeS_2) and anhydrite ($CaSO_4$), respectively.

Another important mineral family is the *carbonate* group, which features carbon in combination with oxygen and other elements such as calcium, magnesium, and potassium. An example is the mineral calcite ($CaCO_3$), a form of calcium carbonate.

A **rock** is an assemblage of minerals bound together (such as granite, a rock containing three minerals), or a mass of a single mineral (such as rock salt), or undifferentiated material (such as the noncrystalline glassy obsidian, or volcanic glass), or even solid organic material (such as coal). Thousands of different rocks have been identified. All can be sorted into one of three kinds, depending on the processes that formed them: *igneous* (melted), *sedimentary* (from settling out), and *metamorphic* (altered). Figure 11.7 illustrates these three processes and the interrelations among them that constitute the **rock cycle**. Figure 11.8 maps the distribution of these rock types across Canada. Let us examine each rock-forming process.

Igneous Processes

An **igneous rock** is one that solidifies and crystallizes from a molten state. Familiar examples are granite, basalt, and rhyolite. Igneous rocks form from **magma**, which is molten rock beneath the surface (hence the name *igneous*, which means "fire-formed" in Latin). Magma is fluid, highly gaseous, and under tremendous pressure. It either *intrudes* into crustal rocks, cools, and hardens, or it *extrudes* onto the surface as **lava**.

The cooling history of an igneous rock—how fast it cooled and how steadily its temperature dropped—determines its crystalline physical characteristics, or crystallization. Igneous rocks range from coarse-grained (slower

Sedimentary rock, shale

Mainland Island, Orkneys, Scotland

Metamorphic rocks

Livingstone Island, Antarctica

Kings Canyon, California

Igneous rocks

Magma

From mantle

New material added from depth

Hawaiian lava flows

Active flows, 2002

Sediment

NOTEBOOK The Rock Cycle

FIGURE 11.7 The rock cycle.
A rock-cycle schematic demonstrates the relation among igneous, sedimentary, and metamorphic processes. The arrows indicate that each rock type can enter the cycle at various points and be transformed into other rock types. [Art adapted by permission from R. M. Busch, ed., *Laboratory Manual in Physical Geology*, 3rd ed., © 1993 by Macmillan Publishing Co. Photos by Bobbé Christopherson.]

cooling, with more time for larger crystals to form) to fine-grained or glassy (faster cooling).

Igneous rocks comprise approximately 90% of Earth's crust, although sedimentary rocks (sandstone, shale, limestone), soil, or oceans frequently cover them. Figure 11.9 illustrates the variety of occurrences of igneous rocks, both on and beneath Earth's surface.

Intrusive and Extrusive Igneous Rocks Intrusive igneous rock that cools slowly in the crust forms a **pluton**,

a general term for any intrusive igneous rock body, regardless of size or shape, that invaded layers of crustal rocks. The Roman god of the underworld, Pluto, is the namesake. The largest pluton form is a **batholith**, defined as an irregular-shaped mass with a surface greater than 100 km², or 40 mi² (Figure 11.10a). Batholiths form the mass of many large mountain ranges—for example, the Sierra Nevada batholith in California, the Idaho batholith, and the Coast Range batholith of British Columbia and Washington State.

FIGURE 11.8 Bedrock geology and physiography of Canada.
Distribution of igneous, sedimentary, and metamorphic rocks within the various physiographic regions of Canada. Intrusive igneous rocks, volcanic rocks, and metamorphic rocks dominate the geology of the Canadian Shield. The geology of the Appalachian Orogen and Cordilleran Orogen represents a mixture of intrusive igneous rocks, volcanic rocks, metamorphic rocks, and deformed sedimentary rocks. Deformed sedimentary rocks with minor intrusive igneous and volcanic rocks dominate the geology of the Innuitian Orogen. Clastic and chemical sedimentary rocks dominate the geology of the various sedimentary platforms (Great Lakes–St. Lawrence, Hudson Bay, Arctic, Interior). The geology of the Arctic Coastal Plain consists largely of unlithified clastic sediments. [Map by Keith Bigelow, University of Saskatchewan. Data used by permission of the Minister of Public Works and Government Services Canada; Natural Resources Canada, Geological Survey of Canada.]

Smaller plutons include the magma conduits of ancient volcanoes that have cooled and hardened. Those that form parallel to layers of sedimentary rock are *sills*; those that cross layers of the rock they invade are *dikes*. You see these two forms in Figure 11.9 at Petermann Island, Antarctica. Magma also can bulge between rock strata and produce a lens-shaped body called a *laccolith*, a type of sill. In addition, magma conduits themselves may solidify in roughly cylindrical forms that stand starkly above the landscape when finally exposed by weathering and erosion. Shiprock *volcanic neck* in New Mexico is such a feature, rising 518 m (1700 ft) above the surrounding plain, as suggested by the art in Figure 11.9 and shown in the inset photos; note the radiating dikes in the aerial photo. Weathering action of air, water, and ice can expose all of these intrusive forms.

Volcanic eruptions and flows produce extrusive igneous rock, such as lava that cools and forms basalt (Figure 11.10b). Chapter 12 presents volcanism and treats this in detail.

Classifying Igneous Rocks Mineral composition and texture usually classify igneous rocks (Table 11.2). The two broad categories are:

1. *Felsic* igneous rocks—derived both in composition and name from *fel*dspar and *si*li*c*a. Felsic minerals are generally high in silica, aluminum, potassium, and sodium and have low melting points. Rocks formed from felsic minerals generally are lighter in colour and are less dense than mafic mineral rocks.

2. *Mafic* igneous rocks—derived both in composition and name from *ma*gnesium and *fer*ric (Latin for iron).

Aerial, Shiprock

Volcanic neck
(Shiprock, NM)

Laccolith exposed
by erosion

Radiating dike

Sill

Country
rock

Lava
flows

Volcano

Dike

Rock strata

Dike

Volcanic
conduit

Laccolith

Batholith

Magma

Granite

Dike–Petermann Island, Antarctica

Basalt

FIGURE 11.9 Igneous rock types.
The variety of occurrences of igneous rocks, both intrusive (below the surface) and extrusive (on the surface). Inset photographs show samples of granite (intrusive) and basalt (extrusive) and other igneous forms. [Photos of rock samples and aerial by Bobbé Christopherson; photos of Shiprock volcanic neck by Robert Christopherson.]

ANIMATION

Formation of
Intrusive Igneous
Features

Mafic minerals are low in silica, high in magnesium and iron, and have high melting points. Rocks formed from mafic minerals are darker in colour and of greater density than felsic mineral rocks.

The same magma that produces coarse-grained granite (when it slowly cools beneath the surface) can form fine-grained *rhyolite* (when it cools above the surface—see inset photo in table). If it cools quickly, magma having silica content comparable to granite and rhyolite can form the dark, smoky, glassy-textured rock called *obsidian*, or volcanic glass (see inset photo). Another glassy rock, *pumice*, forms when escaping gases bubble a frothy texture into the

lava. Pumice is full of small holes, is light in weight, and is low enough in density to float in water (see inset photo).

On the mafic side, basalt is the most common fine-grained extrusive igneous rock. It makes up the bulk of the ocean floor, accounting for 71% of Earth's surface. It appears in lava flows such as those on the big island of Hawai'i (Figure 11.10b). An intrusive counterpart to basalt, formed by slow cooling of the parent magma, is *gabbro*.

Sedimentary Processes

Solar energy and gravity drive the process of *sedimentation*, with water as the principal transporting medium. Existing

Table 11.2   Igneous Rock Minerals

	Felsic Minerals (feldspars and silica)			Mafic Minerals (magnesium and iron)		Ultramafic Minerals (low silica)	
General characteristics	Higher ◄———————————— Silica content ————————————► Lower						
	Higher ◄———————————— Resistance to weathering ————————————► Lower						
	◄———— Increased potassium and sodium. Increased calcium, iron, and magnesium ————►						
	Lower ◄———————————— Melting temperatures ————————————► Higher						
	Lighter ◄———————————— Colouration ————————————► Darker						
Mineral families	Quartz	Feldspars		Mica	Amphibole	Pyroxene	Olivine
	Potassium feldspars SiO₂, K, Al, Si (Orthoclase)	Sodium feldspars Na, Al, Si (Plagioclase) (aluminosolicates)	Calcium feldspars Ca, Al, Si	K, Fe, Mg, Al, Si (biotite: black; muscovite: white)	Fe, Mg, Al, Si, Ca, Na (complex) (hornblende: black)	Fe, Mg, Si (dark)	Mg, Fe, SiO₄ (dark green) (no quartz, no feldspars)
Coarse-grained texture (intrusive) slower cooling rate	Granite	Diorite				Gabbro	Peridotite
Fine-grained texture (extrusive) faster cooling rate	Rhyolite	Andesite Dacite (sodic feldspar) (Mount St. Helens)				Basalt	
Other textures	Obsidian (glassy)	Pumice (vesicular)				Scoria (Vesicular)	

Source: Photos from R. M. Busch, ed., *Laboratory Manual in Physical Geology*, 3rd ed., © 1993 by Macmillan Publishing Co.

rock is disintegrated and dissolved by weathering, picked up and moved by erosion and transportation, and deposited along river, beach, and ocean sites, where burial initiates the rock-forming process. The formation of **sedimentary rock** involves **lithification** processes of cementation, compaction, and a hardening of sediments.

Most sedimentary rocks derive from fragments of existing rock or organic materials. Bits and pieces of former rocks—principally quartz, feldspar, and clay minerals—erode and then are mechanically transported by water (lake, stream, ocean, overland flow), ice (glacial action), wind, and gravity.

They are transported from "higher-energy" sites, where the carrying medium has the energy to pick up and move them, to "lower-energy" sites, where the material is dumped.

The common sedimentary rocks are *sandstone* (sand that became cemented together), *shale* (mud that became compacted into rock, as in the part-opening photo), *limestone* (bones and shells that became cemented or calcium carbonate that precipitated in ocean and lake waters), and *coal* (ancient plant remains that became compacted into rock). Some minerals, such as calcium carbonate, dissolve into solution and form sedimentary deposits

FIGURE 11.10 Intrusive and extrusive rocks.
(a) Exposed granite bedrock of the Canadian Shield, Nunavut (67° N 112° W). Glacial erosion has created a hummocky landscape characterized by ice-molded hills and water-filled rock basins. The boulders resting on the surface are erratics deposited by glacial ice that melted thousands of years ago. (b) Basaltic lava flows on Hawai'i. The glowing opening is from a skylight into an active lava tube where molten lava is visible; the shiny surface is where lava recently flowed out of the skylight.
[(a) Photo by Earth Sciences Sector, Natural Resources Canada GSC 2001-235; (b) photos by Bobbé Christopherson.]

by precipitating from those solutions to form rock. This is an important process in both the oceanic and karst (weathered limestone; Chapter 13) environments.

Characteristically, sedimentary rocks are laid down by wind, water, or ice in horizontally layered beds. Different environmental conditions produce a variety of sedimentary forms. Various cements, depending on availability, fuse rock particles together. Lime, or calcium carbonate ($CaCO_3$), is the most common, followed by iron oxides (Fe_2O_3) and silica (SiO_2). Drying (dehydration), heating, or chemical reactions can also unite particles.

The layered strata of sedimentary rocks form an important record of past ages. **Stratigraphy** is the study of the sequence (superposition), thickness, and spatial distribution of strata. These sequences yield clues to the age and origin of the rocks. Figure 11.11a shows a sandstone sedimentary rock in a desert landscape. Note the multiple layers in the formation and how differently they resist weathering processes. The climatic history of this rock's formation environment is disclosed in the stratigraphy—drier periods of former dunes near the top and wetter periods of horizontal deposits in the middle and lower portions. Figure 11.11c shows sedimentary rock strata on Mars that imply water deposition of sediments sometime in the distant Martian past.

The two primary sources of sedimentary rocks are *clastic sediments*, formed from the mechanically transported fragments of older rock, and *chemical sediments* from the dissolved minerals in solution, some having organic origins.

Clastic Sedimentary Rocks Weathered and fragmented rocks that are further worn in transport provide *clastic sediments*. Table 11.3 lists the range of *clast* sizes—everything from boulders to microscopic clay particles—and the form they take as *lithified rock*. Common sedimentary rocks from clastic sediments include siltstone or mudstone (silt-sized particles), shale (clay to silt-sized particles), and sandstone (sand-sized particles ranging from 0.06 to 2 mm in diameter).

Chemical Sedimentary Rocks *Chemical sedimentary* rocks are not formed from physical pieces of broken rock but instead from dissolved minerals, transported in solution and chemically precipitated from solution (they are essentially nonclastic). The most common chemical sedimentary rock is **limestone**, which is lithified calcium carbonate, derived from inorganic and organic sources. A similar form is *dolomite*, which is lithified calcium–magnesium carbonate, $CaMg(CO_3)_2$. Limestone from marine organic origins is most common; it is biochemical—derived from shell and bone produced by biological activity (see inset photo in Figure 11.11). Once formed, these rocks are vulnerable to chemical weathering, which produces unique landforms, as discussed in the weathering section of Chapter 13.

Chemical sediments from inorganic sources are deposited when water evaporates and leaves behind a residue of salts. These *evaporites* may exist as common salts, such as gypsum or sodium chloride (table salt). They often appear as flat, layered deposits across a dry landscape. The pair of photographs in Figure 11.12 dramatically demonstrates this process; one was made in Death Valley National Park one day after a record 2.57-cm (1.01-in.) rainfall, and the other photo was made one month later at the exact same spot.

Chemical deposition also occurs in the water of natural hot springs from chemical reactions between

(a)

(b)

Sandstone

Limestone

Limestone landscape

(c)   Martian sedimentary formations

FIGURE 11.11 Sedimentary rock types.
(a) Hoodoos developed in weakly cemented Cretaceous sandstone, near Drumheller, Alberta. Physical weathering by frost action, associated with the repeated freezing (expansion) and thawing (contraction) of water, acts to break up the rocks to create these landforms. (b) Ball's Falls, Jordan Harbour, Ontario (43° N 79° W), along the length of the Niagara Escarpment in southern Ontario. The exposed cliff face is attacked by the action of running water that erodes the softer shale at the base of the cliff, progressively undermining the Paleozoic limestone until it collapses. Inset photos show whole shells and some clasts (parts) cemented together and a typical limestone landscape. (c) Ancient sediment deposition through repeated cycles of erosion and deposition is evident in the Martian western Arabia Terra (8° N and 7° W).
[(a) Photo by J.A. Kraulis/Masterfile; inset photo by Robert Christopherson; (b) photo by Victor Last/Geographical Visual Aids; inset photo by Bobbé Christopherson; (c) image from Mars Global Surveyor courtesy of NASA/JPL/Malin Space Science Systems.]

minerals and oxygen. This is a sedimentary process related to *hydrothermal activity*. An example is the massive deposit of travertine, a form of calcium carbonate, at Mammoth Hot Springs in Yellowstone National Park (Figure 11.13a).

Hydrothermal activity also occurs on the ocean floor along the rift valleys formed by sea-floor spreading. These "black smokers" belch dark clouds of hydrogen sulphides, minerals, and metals that hot water (in excess of 380°C; 716°F) leached from the basalt. In contact with

seawater, metals and minerals precipitate into deposits (Figure 11.13b). Along the Mid-Atlantic Ridge, one region of hydrothermal activity has 30- to 60-m- (98- to 198-ft-) tall vents of calcium carbonate that are at least 30,000 years old, and still active. Here, the interaction of the mineral-laden spring water reacts with seawater to produce rock. This area is nicknamed "The Lost City" because of the way the towering chimneys look from the observation submersibles.

Table 11.3	Clastic Sediment Sizes and Related Rock Form	
Unconsolidated Sediment	**Grain Size**	**Rock Form**
Boulders, cobbles	>80 mm	Conglomerate (breccia, if pieces are angular)
Pebbles, gravel	>2 mm	
Coarse sand	0.5–2.0 mm	Sandstone
Medium-to-fine sand	0.062–0.5 mm	Sandstone
Silt	0.002–0.062 mm	Siltstone (mudstone)
Clay	<0.002 mm	Shale

Metamorphic Processes

Any rock, either igneous or sedimentary, may be transformed into a **metamorphic rock** by going through profound physical or chemical changes under pressure and increased temperature. (The name *metamorphic* comes from a Greek word meaning "to change form.") Metamorphic rocks generally are more compact than the original rock and therefore are harder and more resistant to weathering and erosion (Figure 11.14).

Several conditions can cause metamorphism. Most common is when subsurface rock is subjected to high temperatures and high compressional stresses occurring over millions of years. Igneous rocks become compressed during collisions between slabs of Earth's crust (see the discussion of plate tectonics later in this chapter). Sometimes rocks simply are crushed under great weight when a crustal area is thrust beneath other crust. In another setting, igneous rocks may be sheared and stressed along earthquake fault zones, causing metamorphism.

Metamorphic rocks comprise the ancient roots of mountains. Exposed at the bottom of the inner gorge of the Grand Canyon in Arizona, a Precambrian (Archean) metamorphic rock, the Vishnu Schist, is a remnant of such an ancient mountain root (Figure 11.14b). Despite the fact that the schist is harder than steel, the Colorado River has cut down into the uplifted Colorado Plateau, exposing and eroding these ancient rocks.

Another metamorphic condition occurs when sediments collect in broad depressions in Earth's crust and, because of their own weight, create enough pressure in the bottommost layers to transform the sediments into metamorphic rock, a process called *regional metamorphism*. Also, molten magma rising within the crust may "cook" adjacent rock, a process called *contact metamorphism*.

Metamorphic rocks may be changed both physically and chemically from the original rocks. Table 11.4 lists some metamorphic rock types, their parent rocks, and resultant textures. If the mineral structure demonstrates a particular alignment after metamorphism, the rock is *foliated*, and some minerals may appear as wavy striations (streaks or lines) in the new rock. The four inset photographs demonstrate foliated and nonfoliated textures. Which form do you see in the far-right inset photo of metamorphic rock from Livingston Island in Figure 11.7 (centre right), foliated or nonfoliated?

Also in the table, note that sedimentary shale rock becomes metamorphic slate, which readily splits into slabs and thin plates. One piece of slate is placed on-edge in the photo to show this physical property. Commercially, slate is made into roofing shingles, monuments, and countertops.

(a)

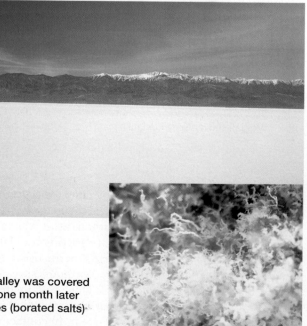
(b)

FIGURE 11.12 Death Valley, wet and dry.
A Death Valley landscape: (a) one day after a record rainfall when the valley was covered by several square kilometres of water only a few centimetres deep; (b) one month later the water had evaporated, and the same valley is coated with evaporites (borated salts) shown in close-up inset photo. [Photos by Robert Christopherson.]

(a)

(b)

FIGURE 11.13 Hydrothermal deposits.
(a) Mammoth Hot Springs, Yellowstone National Park, is an
example of a hydrothermal deposit principally composed of
travertine ($CaCO_3$), deposited as a chemical precipitate from
heated spring water as it evaporated. (b) Hydrothermal vents
with black smokers rise along the Mid-Atlantic ridge. [(a)
Photo by Robert Christopherson; (b) image courtesy of Scripps
Institution of Oceanography.]

(a)

(b)

FIGURE 11.14 Metamorphic rocks.
(a) A metamorphic rock outcrop in Greenland, the Amitsoq
Gneiss, at 3.8 billion years old, one of the oldest rock
formations on Earth. (b) Precambrian Vishnu Schist composes
these rock cliffs in the inner gorge of the Grand Canyon in
northern Arizona. These metamorphic rocks lie beneath many
layers of sedimentary rocks deep in the
continent. [(a) Photo by Kevin Schafer/
Peter Arnold, Inc.; (b) photo by
Robert Christopherson.]

 Foliation
(Metamorphic
ANIMATION Rock)

In this section, you have seen how three rock-forming
processes yield the igneous, sedimentary, and metamorphic materials of Earth's crust. Next we look at how heat
energy and motions originating within Earth move huge
slabs of lithosphere, causing the continents to *drift*. The
fact that the continents migrated thousands of kilometres,
and continue to migrate, is a revolutionary discovery in
the *tectonic cycle* that came to light only in the last century.

Plate Tectonics

Have you ever looked at a world map and noticed that a
few of the continental landmasses—particularly South
America and Africa—appear to have matching shapes, like
pieces of a jigsaw puzzle, as along the African–Arabian
Peninsula coastlines of the Red Sea? The incredible reality
is that the continental pieces indeed once were fitted together! Continental landmasses not only migrated to their
present locations but continue to move at speeds up to
6 cm (2.4 in.) per year.

We say that the continents are *adrift* because the less-
dense lithosphere is migrating around on the denser
upper mantle, the asthenosphere, and the rest of the mantle that is active and in motion. The key point is that the
arrangement of continents and oceans we see today is not
permanent, but is in a continuing state of change.

A continent, such as North America, is actually a col-
lage of crustal pieces that migrated from elsewhere to form

Table 11.4 Metamorphic Rocks

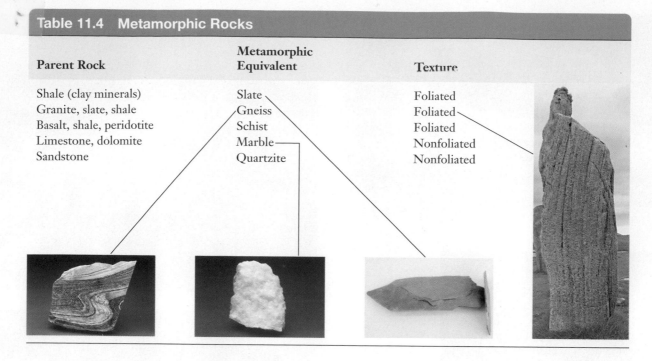

Parent Rock	Metamorphic Equivalent	Texture
Shale (clay minerals)	Slate	Foliated
Granite, slate, shale	Gneiss	Foliated
Basalt, shale, peridotite	Schist	Foliated
Limestone, dolomite	Marble	Nonfoliated
Sandstone	Quartzite	Nonfoliated

the landscape we know. Through a historical chronology, let us trace the discoveries that led to the plate tectonics theory—a major revolution in Earth systems science.

A Brief History

As early mapping gained accuracy, some observers noticed the symmetry among continents, particularly the fit between South America and Africa. Abraham Ortelius (1527–1598), a geographer, noted the apparent fit of some continental coastlines in his *Thesaurus Geographicus* (1596). In 1620, English philosopher Sir Francis Bacon noted gross similarities between the edges of Africa and South America (although he did not suggest that they had drifted apart). Benjamin Franklin wrote in 1780 that the crust must be a shell that can break and shift by movements of fluid below. Others wrote—unscientifically— about such apparent relationships, but it was not until much later that a valid explanation came forward.

In 1912, German geophysicist and meteorologist Alfred Wegener publicly presented in a lecture his idea that Earth's landmasses migrate. His book, *Origin of the Continents and Oceans*, appeared in 1915. Today, Wegener is regarded as the father of this concept, which he first called **continental drift.** Scientists at the time were unreceptive to Wegener's revolutionary proposal. Thus, a great debate began, lasting almost 50 years until a scientific consensus developed that Wegener was right after all.

Wegener thought that all landmasses formed one supercontinent approximately 225 m.y.a., during the Triassic Period. **Pangaea** is the name he gave this one landmass, meaning "all Earth" (see Figure 11.18b). Although his initial model kept the landmasses together too long and his proposal included an incorrect driving mechanism for the moving continents, Wegener's arrangement of Pangaea and its breakup was correct, Pangaea being only the latest of earlier supercontinent arrangements over the span of Earth history.

To come up with his Pangaea fit, he studied the geologic record represented in the rock strata, the fossil record, and the climatic record for the continents. He concluded that South America and Africa correlated in many complex ways. He decided that the large midlatitude coal deposits, which date to the Permian and Carboniferous Periods (251–354 m.y.a.), exist because these regions once were nearer the equator and therefore covered by lush vegetation that became coal.

As modern scientific capabilities built the case for continental drift, the 1950s and 1960s saw a revival of interest in Wegener's concepts and, finally, confirmation. Aided by an avalanche of discoveries, the plate tectonics theory today is universally accepted as an accurate model of the way Earth's surface evolves. *Tectonic*, from the Greek *tektonikùs*, meaning "building" or "construction," refers to changes in the configuration of Earth's crust as a result of internal forces. **Plate tectonic** processes include upwelling of magma; lithospheric plate movements; seafloor spreading and lithospheric subduction; earthquakes; volcanic activity; and lithospheric deformation such as warping, folding, and faulting.

Sea-Floor Spreading and Production of New Crust

The key to establishing the theory of continental drift was a better understanding of the seafloor. The seafloor has a remarkable feature: an interconnected worldwide mountain chain, forming a ridge some 64,000 km (40,000 mi) in extent and averaging more than 1000 km (600 mi) in width. A striking view of this great undersea mountain chain opens Chapter 12. How did this global mountain chain get there?

In the early 1960s, geophysicists Harry H. Hess and Robert S. Dietz proposed **sea-floor spreading** as the mechanism that builds this mountain chain and drives continental movement. Hess said that these submarine mountain ranges were **mid-ocean ridges** and the direct result of upwelling flows of magma from hot areas in the upper mantle and asthenosphere and perhaps from the deeper lower mantle.

When mantle convection brings magma up to the crust, the crust fractures, and the magma extrudes onto the seafloor and cools to form new seafloor. This process builds the mid-ocean ridges and spreads the seafloor laterally, rifting as the two sides move apart. The concept is illustrated in Figure 11.15, which shows how the ocean floor is rifted (moves apart) and scarred along mid-ocean ridges. Figure 11.15b is a remote-sensing image of the mid-ocean ridge and Figure 11.15c is a map of the system in the Atlantic. Figure 11.15d shows a portion of the mid-ocean ridge system that surfaces at Thingvellir, Iceland, forming these rifts—the North American plate along one side and the European plate on the other. Iceland's first Althing (parliament) met here in A.D. 930; leaders used the acoustics of the rift walls to be heard by the gathering.

As new crust generates and the seafloor spreads, magnetic particles in the lava orient with the magnetic field in force at the time the lava cools and hardens. The particles become locked in this alignment as new seafloor forms, which creates a kind of magnetic tape recording in the seafloor. The continually forming oceanic crust records each magnetic reversal and reorientation of Earth's polarity.

Figure 11.16 illustrates just such a recording from the Mid-Atlantic Ridge south of Iceland. The colours denote the alternating magnetic polarization preserved in the minerals of the oceanic crust. Note the mirror images that develop on either side of the sea-floor rift as a result of the nearly symmetrical spreading of the seafloor; the relative ages of the rocks increase with distance from the ridge. These periodic reversals of Earth's magnetic field are a valuable clue to understanding sea-floor spreading, helping scientists fit together pieces of Earth's crust.

These sea-floor recordings of Earth's magnetic-field reversals and other measurements allowed the age of the seafloor to be determined. The complex harmony of the two concepts of plate tectonics and sea-floor spreading thus became clearer. The youngest crust anywhere on Earth is at the spreading centres of the mid-ocean ridges, and, with increasing distance from these centres, the crust gets steadily older (Figure 11.17). The oldest seafloor is in the western Pacific near Japan, dating to the Jurassic Period. Note on the map in the figure the distance between this basin and its spreading centre in the South Pacific west of South America.

Overall, the seafloor is relatively young—nowhere does it exceed 208 m.y.a., (million years ago) remarkable when you remember that Earth's age is 4.6 billion years. The reason is that oceanic crust is short-lived—the oldest sections, farthest from the mid-ocean ridges, are slowly plunging beneath continental crust along Earth's deep oceanic trenches. The discovery that the seafloor is young demolished earlier thinking that the oldest rocks would be found there.

Subduction of the Lithosphere

In contrast to the upwelling zones along the mid-ocean ridges are the areas of descending lithosphere elsewhere. On the left side of Figure 11.15a, note how one plate of the crust is diving, or being dragged beneath another, into the mantle. Recall that the basaltic ocean crust has a density of 3.0 g/cm^3, whereas continental crust averages a lighter 2.7 g/cm^3. As a result, when continental crust and oceanic crust slowly collide, the denser ocean floor will grind beneath the lighter continental crust, thus forming a **subduction zone**, as shown in the figure. The subducting slab of crust exerts a gravitational pull on the rest of the plate—an important driving force in plate motion. This plate motion can trigger through shear traction along the base of the lithosphere a flow in the mantle material beneath. Thus, subduction and plate motion are a complex process.

The world's deep ocean trenches coincide with these subduction zones and are the lowest features on Earth's surface. Deepest is the Mariana Trench near Guam, which descends below sea level to −11,030 m (−36,198 ft); next in depth are the Puerto Rico Trench at −8605m (−28,224 ft) and, in the Indian Ocean, the Java Trench at −7125 m (−23,376 ft) .

The subducted portion of lithosphere travels down into the asthenosphere, where it remelts and eventually is recycled as magma, rising again toward the surface through deep fissures and cracks in crustal rock. Volcanic mountains such as the Andes in South America and the Cascade Range from northern California to the Canadian border form inland of these subduction zones as a result of rising plumes of magma, as suggested in Figure 11.15a. Sometimes the diving plate remains intact for hundreds of kilometres, whereas at other times it can break into large pieces; this is thought to be the case under the Cascade Range with its distribution of volcanoes.

The fact that spreading ridges and subduction zones are areas of earthquake and volcanic activity provides important proof of plate tectonics. Now, using current scientific findings, let us go back and reconstruct the past, and Pangaea. See this in review at **http://geology.er.usgs. gov/eastern/tectonic.html**.

The Formation and Breakup of Pangaea

The supercontinent of Pangaea and its subsequent breakup into today's continents represent only the last 225 million years of Earth's 4.6 billion years, or only the most recent 1/23 of Earth's existence. During the other 22/23 of geologic time, other things were happening. The landmasses as we know them were unrecognizable.

Figure 11.18a begins with the pre-Pangaea arrangement of 465 m.y.a. (during the middle Ordovician Period). Researchers are discovering other, older arrangements of continents. One proposal is for an ancient supercontinent, tentatively called *Rodinia*, that formed approximately a billion years ago, with breakup at about 700 million.

(text continued on page 356)

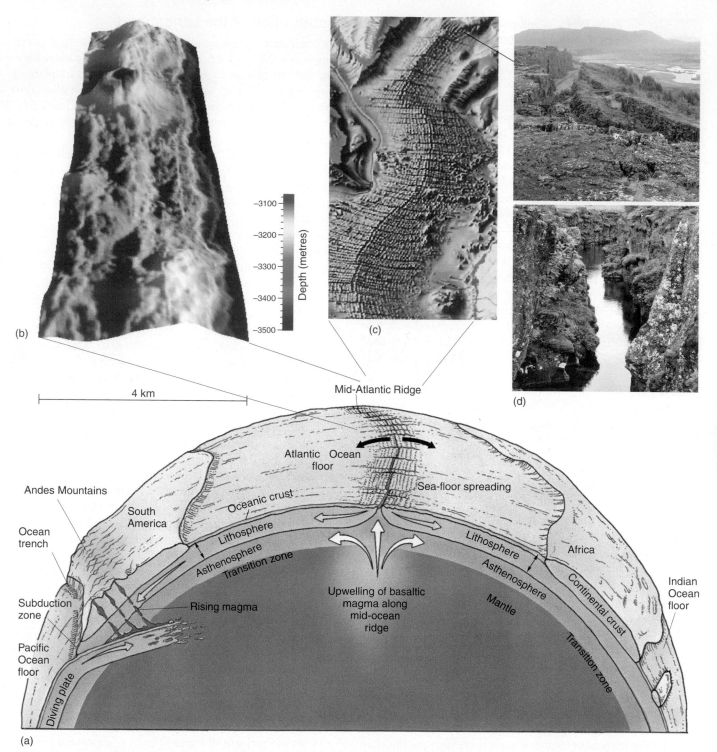

FIGURE 11.15 Crustal movements.
(a) Sea-floor spreading, upwelling currents, subduction, and plate movements, shown in cross section. Arrows indicate the direction of the spreading. (b) A 4-km-wide image of the Mid-Atlantic Ridge showing linear faults, a volcanic crater, a rift valley, and ridges. The image was taken by the TOBI (towed ocean-bottom instrument) at approximately 29° N latitude. (c) Detail from Tharp's ocean-floor map. (d) The mid-Atlantic rift surfaces through Iceland. This scene is at Thingvellir in southeastern Iceland, where the North American and European plates of Earth's crust meet. Only in Iceland does a portion of Earth's 64,000 km (40,000 mi) mid-ocean ridge system surface. [(a) After P. J. Wyllie, *The Way the Earth Works*, © 1976, by John Wiley & Sons, adapted by permission; (b) image courtesy of D. K. Smith, Woods Hole Oceanographic Institute, Woods Hole, Massachusetts. All rights reserved; (c) Bruce C. Heezen and Marie Tharp, courtesy Marie Tharp; (d) photos by Bobbé Christopherson.]

ANIMATION Sea-Floor Spreading, Subduction

FIGURE 11.16 Magnetic reversals recorded in the seafloor.
Magnetic reversals recorded in the seafloor south of Iceland along the Mid-Atlantic Ridge.
Note rocks with similar magnetic orientation are roughly the same distance from the spreading
centre. Colours indicate rocks of similar geologic age, with the rocks getting increasingly older
with distance away from the spreading centre. [Magnetic reversals reprinted from J. R. Heirtzler,
S. Le Pichon, and J. G. Baron, *Deep-Sea Research* 13, © 1966, Pergamon Press, p. 247.]

m.y. = millions of years	
0–2 m.y.	58–66 m.y.
2–5 m.y.	66–84 m.y.
5–24 m.y.	84–117 m.y.
24–37 m.y.	117–144 m.y.
37–58 m.y.	144–208 m.y.

FIGURE 11.17 Relative age of the oceanic crust.
Compare the dark-red colour near the East Pacific rise in the eastern Pacific Ocean
with the same dark-red colour along the Mid-Atlantic Ridge. What does the difference
in width tell you about the rates of plate motion in the two locations? [Adapted with the
permission of W. H. Freeman and Company from *The Bedrock Geology of the World* by
R. L. Larson and others, © 1985.]

FIGURE 11.18 Continents adrift, from 465 m.y.a. to the present.
Observe the formation and breakup of Pangaea and the types of motions occurring at plate boundaries. [(a) From R. K. Bambach, "Before Pangaea: The Geography of the Paleozoic World," *American Scientist* 68 (1980): 26–38, reprinted by permission; (b–e) from R. S. Dietz and J. C. Holden, *Journal of Geophysical Research* 75, no. 26 (September 10, 1970): 4939–4956, © The American Geophysical Union; (f) remote-sensing image courtesy of S. Tighe, University of Rhode Island, and R. Detrick, Woods Hole Oceanographic Institute, Woods Hole, Massachusetts.]

ANIMATION   Plate Motions Through Time

(a) 465 million years ago

Pangaea—all Earth. Panthalassa ("all seas") became the Pacific Ocean, and the Tethys Sea (partly enclosed by the African and the Eurasian plates) became the Mediterranean Sea; trapped portions of former ocean became the present-day Caspian Sea. The Atlantic Ocean did not exist.

Africa shared a common connection with both North and South America. Today, the Appalachian Mountains in the eastern United States and the Atlas Mountains of northwestern Africa reflect this common ancestry; they are, in fact, portions of the same mountain range, torn thousands of kilometres apart.

(b) 225 million years ago

New seafloor that formed since the last map is highlighted (grey tint). An active spreading center rifted North America away from landmasses to the east, shaping the coast of Labrador. India was farther along in its journey, with a spreading center to the south and a subduction zone to the north; the leading edge of the India plate was diving beneath Eurasia.

The outlines of South America, Africa, India, Australia, and southern Europe appear within the continent called *Gondwana* in the Southern Hemisphere. North America, Europe, and Asia comprise *Laurasia*, the northern portion.

(c) 135 million years ago

ANIMATION   Motion at Plate Boundaries

(d) 65 million years ago

Sea-floor spreading along the Mid-Atlantic Ridge grew some 3000 km (almost 1900 mi) in 70 million years. Africa moved northward about 10° in latitude, leaving Madagascar split from the mainland and opening up the Gulf of Aden. The rifting along what would be the Red Sea began. The India plate moved three-fourths of the way to Asia, as Asia continued to rotate clockwise. Of all the major plates, India travelled the farthest—almost 10,000 km.

Convergent plate boundary—plates converge, producing a subduction zone: coastal area features, mountains, volcanoes, and earthquakes

NOTEBOOK   Plate Boundaries

Divergent plate boundary—plates diverge at mid-ocean ridges

(e) Today

Transform fault—plates move laterally past each other between sea-floor spreading centres

Fracture zone
Transform fault

(f) East-Pacific rise, sea-floor spreading ridge (centre of image at 9° N)

From 65 m.y.a. until the present, more than half of the ocean floor was renewed. The northern reaches of the India plate underthrust the southern mass of Asia through subduction, forming the Himalayas in the upheaval created by the collision. Plate motions continue to this day.

Correlating Processes and Plate Boundaries

Forming a Divergent Boundary

Figure 11.18b illustrates an updated version of Wegener's Pangaea, 225–200 m.y.a. (Triassic–Jurassic periods). The movement of plates that occurred by 135 m.y.a. (the beginning of the Cretaceous Period) is in Figure 11.18c. Figure 11.18d presents the arrangement 65 m.y.a. (shortly after the beginning of the Tertiary Period). Finally, the present arrangement in modern geologic time (the late Cenozoic Era) is in Figure 11.18e.

Earth's present crust is divided into at least 14 plates, of which about half are major and half are minor, in terms of area (Figure 11.19). Literally hundreds of smaller pieces and perhaps dozens of microplates that migrated together comprise these broad plates. The arrows in the figure indicate the direction in which each plate is presently moving, and the length of the arrows suggests the rate of movement during the past 20 million years.

Compare Figure 11.19 with the image of the ocean floor in Figure 11.20. In the image, satellite radar-altimeter measurements determined the sea-surface height to a remarkable accuracy of 0.03 m, or 1 in. The sea-surface elevation is far from uniform; it is higher or lower in direct response to the mountains, plains, and trenches of the ocean floor beneath it. This sea-floor topography causes slight differences in Earth's gravity.

For example, a massive mountain on the ocean floor exerts a high gravitational field and attracts water to it, producing higher sea level above the mountain; over a trench there is less gravity, resulting in a drop in sea level. A mountain 2000 m (6500 ft) high that is 20 km (12 mi) across its base creates a 2-m rise in the sea surface. Until Scripps Institution of Oceanography and NOAA developed this use of satellite technology, these tiny changes in height were not detectable. Now we have a comprehensive map of the ocean *floor*, derived from remote sensing of the ocean *surface*!

The illustration of the seafloor that begins Chapter 12 also is helpful in identifying the plate boundaries in the following discussion. It is interesting to correlate the features illustrated in Figures 11.19 and 11.20 and Chapter 12's opening map. For more on the science of plate tectonics, see **http://www.ig.utexas.edu/research/**.

Plate Boundaries

The boundaries where plates meet clearly are dynamic places, although slow-moving within human time frames. The block diagram inserts in Figure 11.18e show the three general types of motion and interaction that occur along the boundary areas:

- *Divergent boundaries* (lower left in figure) are characteristic of sea-floor spreading centres, where upwelling material from the mantle forms new seafloor

FIGURE 11.19 Earth's major lithospheric plates and their movements.
Each arrow represents 20 million years of movement. The longer arrows indicate that the Pacific and Nazca plates are moving more rapidly than the Atlantic plates. Compare the length of these arrows with those same areas on Figure 11.17. [Adapted from U.S. Geodynamics Committee.]

India Collision with Asia

ANIMATION

Plate Boundaries

NOTEBOOK

FIGURE 11.20 The ocean floor revealed.
A global gravity anomaly map derived from *Geosat* and *ERS-1* altimeter data. The radar altimeters measured sea-surface heights. Variation in sea-surface elevation is a direct indication of the topography of the ocean floor. [Global gravity anomaly map image courtesy of D. T. Sandwell, Scripps Institution of Oceanography. All rights reserved, 1995.]

and lithospheric plates spread apart—a constructional process. The spreading makes these zones of tension. An example noted in the figure is the divergent boundary along the East Pacific rise, which gives birth to the Nazca plate (moving eastward) and the Pacific plate (moving northwestward). Whereas most divergent boundaries occur at mid-ocean ridges, there are a few within continents themselves. An example is the Great Rift Valley of East Africa, where crust is rifting apart.

- *Convergent boundaries* (upper left) are characteristic of collision zones, where areas of continental and oceanic lithosphere collide. These are zones of compression and crustal loss—a destructional process. Examples include the subduction zone off the west coast of South and Central America and the area along the Japan and Aleutian Trenches. Along the western edge of South America, the Nazca plate collides with and is subducted beneath the South American plate. This convergence creates the Andes Mountains chain and related volcanoes. The collision of India and Asia is another example of a convergent boundary, shown in Figure 11.19.

- *Transform boundaries* (lower right) occur where plates slide laterally past one another at right angles to a

sea-floor spreading centre, neither diverging nor converging, and usually with no volcanic eruptions. These are the right-angle fractures stretching across the mid-ocean ridge system worldwide.

Related to plate boundaries, another piece of the tectonic puzzle fell into place in 1965 when University of Toronto geophysicist Tuzo Wilson first described the nature of transform boundaries and their relation to earthquake activity (News Report 11.3). All the spreading centres on Earth's crust feature these perpendicular scars (Figure 11.21). Some transform faults are a few hundred kilometres long; others, such as those along the East Pacific rise, stretch out 1000 km or more (over 600 mi). Across the entire ocean floor, spreading-centre mid-ocean ridges are the location of **transform faults**. The faults generally are parallel to the direction in which the plate is moving. How do they occur?

You can see in Figure 11.19 that mid-ocean ridges are not simple straight lines. When a mid-ocean rift begins, it opens at points of weakness in the crust. The fractures you see in the figure began as a series of offset breaks in the crust in each portion of the spreading centre. As new material rises to the surface, building the mid-ocean ridges and spreading the plates, these offset areas slide

Summary and Review—The Dynamic Planet

■ *Distinguish* between the endogenic and exogenic systems, *determine* the driving force for each, and *explain* the pace at which these systems operate.

The Earth–atmosphere interface is where the **endogenic system** (internal), powered by heat energy from within the planet, interacts with the **exogenic system** (external), powered by insolation and influenced by gravity. These systems work together to produce Earth's diverse landscape. The **geologic time scale** is an effective device for organizing the vast span of geologic time. It depicts the sequence of Earth's events (relative time) and the approximate actual dates (absolute time).

The most fundamental principle of Earth science is **uniformitarianism**. Uniformitarianism assumes that the *same physical processes active in the environment today have been operating throughout geologic time*, although dramatic episodes, such as massive landslides or volcanic eruptions, can interrupt the flow of events, leading to a state of *punctuated equilibrium*.

endogenic system (p. 329)
exogenic system (p. 329)
geologic time scale (p. 332)
uniformitarianism (p. 334)

1. To what extent is Earth's crust active at this time in its history?

2. Define the endogenic and the exogenic systems. Describe the driving forces that energize these systems.

3. How is the geologic time scale organized? What is the basis for the time scale in relative and absolute terms? What era, period, and epoch are we living in today?

4. Contrast uniformitarianism science and catastrophism beliefs as models for Earth's development.

■ *Diagram* Earth's interior in cross section, and *describe* each distinct layer.

We have learned about Earth's interior from indirect evidence—the way its various layers transmit **seismic waves**. The **core** is differentiated into an inner core and an outer core, divided by a transition zone. Earth's magnetic field is generated almost entirely within the outer core. Polarity reversals in Earth's magnetism are recorded in cooling magma that contains iron minerals. The patterns of **geomagnetic reversal** frozen in rock help scientists piece together the story of Earth's mobile crust.

Beyond Earth's core lies the **mantle**, differentiated into lower mantle and upper mantle. It experiences a gradual temperature increase with depth and a stiffening due to increased pressures. The upper mantle is divided into three fairly distinct layers. The uppermost mantle, along with the crust, makes up the *lithosphere*. Below the lithosphere is the **asthenosphere**, or *plastic layer*. It contains pockets of increased heat from radioactive decay and is susceptible to slow convective currents in these hotter materials. An important internal boundary between the **crust** and the high-velocity portion of the uppermost mantle is the **Mohorovičić discontinuity**, or **Moho**. *Continental crust* is basically **granite**; it is crystalline and high in silica, aluminum, potassium, calcium, and sodium. *Oceanic crust* is **basalt**; it is granular and high in silica, magnesium, and iron. The principles of buoyancy and balance were combined in the 1800s into the important principle of **isostasy**. Isostasy explains certain vertical movements of Earth's crust, such as isostatic rebound when the weight of ice is removed.

seismic waves (p. 334)
core (p. 334)
geomagnetic reversal (p. 335)
mantle (p. 336)
asthenosphere (p. 336)
crust (p. 337)
Mohorovičić discontinuity (Moho) (p. 337)
granite (p. 337)
basalt (p. 337)
isostasy (p. 338)

5. Make a simple sketch of Earth's interior, label each layer, and list the physical characteristics, temperature, composition, and range of size of each on your drawing.

6. Briefly describe the evidence for changes in the Earth's magnetic field.

7. Describe the asthenosphere. Why is it also known as the plastic layer? What are the consequences of its convection currents?

8. What is a discontinuity? Describe the principal discontinuities within Earth.

9. Define isostasy and isostatic rebound, and explain the crustal equilibrium concept.

10. Diagram the uppermost mantle and crust. Label the density of the layers in grams per cubic centimetre. What two types of crust were described in the text in terms of rock composition?

■ *Illustrate* the geologic cycle, and *relate* the rock cycle and rock types to endogenic and exogenic processes.

The **geologic cycle** is a model of the internal and external interactions that shape the crust. A **mineral** is an inorganic natural compound having a specific chemical formula and possessing a crystalline structure. A **rock** is an assemblage of minerals bound together (such as granite, a rock containing three minerals), or it may be a mass of a single mineral (such as rock salt). Thousands of different rocks have been identified.

The geologic cycle comprises three cycles: the *hydrologic cycle*, the *tectonic cycle*, and the **rock cycle**. The rock cycle describes the three principal rock-forming processes and the rocks they produce. **Igneous rocks** form from **magma**, which is molten rock beneath the surface. Magma is fluid, highly gaseous, and under tremendous pressure. It either *intrudes* into crustal rocks, cools, and hardens, or it *extrudes* onto the surface as **lava**. Intrusive igneous rock that cools slowly in the crust forms a **pluton**. The largest pluton form is a **batholith**.

The cementation, compaction, and hardening of sediments into **sedimentary rocks** is **lithification**. These layered strata form important records of past ages. **Stratigraphy** is the study of the sequence (superposition), thickness, and spatial distribution of strata that yield clues to the age and origin of the rocks.

Clastic sedimentary rocks are derived from the fragments of weathered rocks. Chemical sedimentary rocks are not formed from physical pieces of broken rock, but instead are dissolved minerals, transported in solution, and chemically precipitated out of solution (they are essentially nonclastic). The most common chemical sedimentary rock is **limestone**, which is lithified calcium carbonate, $CaCO_3$.

Any rock, either igneous or sedimentary, may be transformed into a **metamorphic rock** by going through profound physical or chemical changes under pressure and increased temperature.

geologic cycle (p. 339)
mineral (p. 341)
rock (p. 341)
rock cycle (p. 341)
igneous rock (p. 341)
magma (p. 341)
lava (p. 341)
pluton (p. 342)
batholith (p. 342)
sedimentary rock (p. 345)
lithification (p. 345)
stratigraphy (p. 346)
limestone (p. 346)
metamorphic rock (p. 348)

11. Illustrate the geologic cycle, and define each component: rock cycle, tectonic cycle, and hydrologic cycle.

12. What is a mineral? A mineral family? Name the most common minerals on Earth. What is a rock?

13. Describe igneous processes. What is the difference between intrusive and extrusive types of igneous rocks?

14. Characterize felsic and mafic minerals. Give examples of both coarse- and fine-grained textures.

15. Briefly describe sedimentary processes and lithification. Describe the sources and particle sizes of sedimentary rocks.

16. What is metamorphism, and how are metamorphic rocks produced? Name some original parent rocks and their metamorphic equivalents.

■ *Describe* Pangaea and its breakup, and *relate* several physical proofs that crustal drifting is continuing today.

The present configuration of the ocean basins and continents is the result of *tectonic processes* involving Earth's interior dynamics and crust. Alfred Wegener coined the phrase **continental drift** to describe his idea that the crust is moved by vast forces within the planet. **Pangaea** was the name he gave to a single assemblage of continental crust some 225 m.y.a. that subsequently broke apart. Earth's lithosphere is fractured into huge slabs or plates, each moving in response to their own motion of gravitational pull and to flowing currents in the mantle that create frictional drag on the plate. The all-encompassing theory of **plate tectonics** includes **sea-floor spreading** along **mid-ocean ridges** and

denser oceanic crust diving beneath lighter continental crust along **subduction zones**.

continental drift (p. 350)
Pangaea (p. 350)
plate tectonics (p. 350)
sea-floor spreading (p. 351)
mid-ocean ridge (p. 351)
subduction zone (p. 351)

17. Briefly review the history of the theory of continental drift, sea-floor spreading, and the all-inclusive plate tectonics theory. What was Alfred Wegener's role?

18. Define upwelling, and describe related features on the ocean floor. Define subduction, and explain the process.

19. What was Pangaea? What happened to it during the past 225 million years?

20. Characterize the three types of plate boundaries and the actions associated with each type.

■ *Portray* the pattern of Earth's major plates, and *relate* this pattern to the occurrence of earthquakes, volcanic activity, and hot spots.

Occurrences of often-damaging earthquakes and volcanoes are correlated with plate boundaries. Three types of plate boundaries form: divergent, convergent, and transform. Along the offset portions of mid-ocean ridges, horizontal motions produce **transform faults**.

As many as 50 to 100 **hot spots** exist across Earth's surface, where plumes of magma, some anchored in the lower mantle, others originating from shallow sources in the upper mantle, generate a flow upward. **Geothermal energy** literally refers to heat from Earth's interior, whereas *geothermal power* relates to specific applied strategies of geothermal electric or geothermal direct applications.

transform faults (p. 357)
hot spots (p. 361)
geothermal energy (p. 364)

21. What is the relation between plate boundaries and volcanic and earthquake activity? How is this activity manifested along the Pacific Coast of Canada?

22. What is the nature of motion along a transform fault? Name a famous example of such a fault.

Critical Thinking

A. Using the maps in this chapter, determine your present location relative to Earth's crustal plates. Now, using Figure 11.18b, approximately identify where your present location was 225 m.y.a.; express it in a rough estimate using the equator and the longitudes noted on the map.

B. Relative to the motion of the Pacific plate shown in Figure 11.23 (note the map's graphic scale in the lower-left corner), the island of Midway formed 27.7 m.y.a. over the hot spot that is active under the southeast coast of the big island of Hawai'i today. Given the scale of the map, roughly determine the average annual speed of the Pacific plate in centimetres per year for Midway to have travelled this distance.

C. Under the heading "The Pace of Change," the text discusses a possible "Anthropocene" Epoch. The section states, in part,

Holocene is the name given to the youngest epoch in the geologic time scale, characteristic of postglacial conditions since the retreat of the continental glaciers, approximately the last 11,500 years. Because of the impact of human society on planetary systems, discussion is underway about designating a new name for the human epoch. A proposal is to call this time the *Anthropocene*.

Take a moment to explore this concept of naming our human epoch in the geologic time scale. Determine some arguments for such a change, and describe some that argue against such a move to rename the late Holocene. What do you think?

FIGURE 12.9 Folding in the Zagros crush zone, Iran.
The Zagros Mountains are a product of the Zagros crush zone between the Arabian and Eurasian plates. This area was a dispersed terrane (migrating crustal piece) that separated from the Eurasian plate. However, the collision produced by the northward push of the Arabian block is now shoving this terrane back into Eurasia and forming the folded mountains shown. [NASA image.]

In addition to the rumpling of rock strata just discussed, broad warping actions also affect Earth's continental crust. These actions produce similar up-and-down bending of strata, but the bends are far greater in extent than those produced by folding. Warping forces include mantle convection, isostatic adjustment such as that caused by the weight of previous ice loads across northern Canada, or crustal swelling above an underlying hot spot. Warping features can be small, individual, foldlike structures called *basins* and *domes* (Figure 12.10a, b).

In the Queen Elizabeth Islands of Arctic Canada (Figure 12.10e), upwarped domes composed of the evaporite minerals gypsum ($CaSO_4 \cdot 2H_2O$) and anhydrite ($CaSO_4$)—known as *piercement domes*—represent distinctive landforms. The thick evaporite deposits (approximately 400 m) accumulated within a large sedimentary basin during the Carboniferous and Permian periods (approximately 290 m.y.a.). In the middle of the Cenozoic Era, a mountain-building event (Eurekan orogeny) resulted in folding and thrust faulting of the sedimentary rocks. The evaporite rocks were driven upward through the overlying Mesozoic sedimentary rocks (mostly sandstone and shale) to produce the piercement domes. The piercement domes attain heights of several hundreds of metres and diameters up to 10 km.

Faulting

A freshly poured concrete sidewalk is smooth and strong. But stress the sidewalk by driving heavy equipment over it, and the resulting strain might cause a fracture. Pieces on either side of the fracture may move up, down, or horizontally, depending on the direction of stress. Similarly, when rock strata are stressed beyond their ability to remain a solid unit, they express the strain as a fracture. Rocks on either side of the fracture displace relative to the other side in a process known as **faulting**. Thus, *fault zones* are areas where fractures in the rock demonstrate crustal movement. At the moment of fracture, a sharp release of energy occurs, called an **earthquake** or *quake*.

The fracture surface along which the two sides of a fault move is the *fault plane*. The names of the three basic types of faults, illustrated in Figure 12.11, are based on the tilt and orientation of the fault plane. A normal fault forms when rocks are pulled apart by tensional stress. A thrust or reverse fault results when rocks are forced together by compressional stress. A strike-slip fault forms when rocks are torn by lateral-shearing stress.

Normal Fault   When forces pull rocks apart, the tension causes a **normal fault**, or *tension fault*. When the break occurs, rock on one side moves vertically along an inclined fault plane (Figure 12.11a). The downward-shifting side is the *hanging wall*; it drops relative to the *footwall block*. The exposed fault plane sometimes is visible along the base of faulted mountains, where individual ridges are truncated by the movements of the fault and appear as triangular facets at the ends of the ridges. A cliff formed by faulting is commonly called a *fault scarp*, or *escarpment*.

Reverse (Thrust) Fault   Compressional forces associated with converging plates force rocks to move *upward* along the fault plane. This is a **reverse fault**, or *compression*

(a) Dome

(b) Basin

(c) |——— 38 km (24 mi) ———|

(d) 0 ———— 5 KM

(e)

FIGURE 12.10 Domes and basins.
(a) An upwarped dome. (b) A structural basin. Denudation of weak (soft) rock strata has produced valleys and depressions in these landscapes. In contrast, strong (hard) rock strata stand in positive topographic relief forming ridges. (c) The Richat dome structure of Mauritania. (d) Isachsen dome, Ellef Ringnes Island, Nunavut, Canada. This piercement dome consists of Carboniferous evaporite rocks (represented by bright tones in the photograph) flanked by steeply dipping beds of Cretaceous shale (represented by dark tones in the photograph). (e) The distribution of piercement domes within the Queen Elizabeth Islands, Arctic Canada. [(c) Image from *Terra*, October 7, 2000, courtesy NASA/GSFC/MITI, and U.S./Japan ASTER team; (d) ASTER image from NASA and the Earth Remote Sensing Data Analysis Center; (e) "Geology and economic minerals of Canada," *Economic Geology Report No. 1*, Geological Survey of Canada, Ottawa, p. 570, Figure X-8, in Thorsteinsson and Tozer, 1970.]

fault (Figure 12.11b). On the surface, it appears similar to a normal fault, although more collapse and landslides may occur from the hanging wall component. In England, when miners worked along a reverse fault, they would stand on the lower side (footwall) and hang their lanterns on the upper side (hanging wall), giving rise to these terms.

If the fault plane forms a low angle relative to the horizontal, the fault is termed a **thrust fault**, or *overthrust fault*, indicating that the overlying block has shifted far over the underlying block (see Figure 12.8, "thrust fault"). Place your hands palms-down on your desk, with fingertips together, and slide one hand up over the other—this is the motion of a low-angle thrust fault, with one side pushing over the other.

In the Alps, several such overthrusts result from compressional forces of the ongoing collision between the African and Eurasian plates. Beneath the Los Angeles Basin, overthrust faults produce a high risk of earthquakes and caused many quakes in the 20th century, including the $30 billion 1994 Northridge earthquake. These blind (unknown until they rupture) thrust faults beneath the Los Angeles region remain a major earthquake threat.

Strike-Slip Fault   If movement along a fault plane is horizontal, such as produced along a transform fault, it forms a **strike-slip fault** (Figure 12.11c; refer to Figure 11.21 for review). The movement is *right-lateral* or *left-lateral*, depending on the motion perceived when you observe movement on one side of the fault relative to the other side.

Although strike-slip faults do not produce cliffs (scarps), as do the other types of faults, they can create linear rift valleys. This is the case with the San Andreas fault system of California. The rift valley is clearly visible in Figure 12.11c, where the edges of the North American and Pacific plates are grinding past one another as a result of transform-fault movement. The evolution of this fault system is shown in Figure 12.12.

Note in the figure how the East Pacific rise developed as a spreading centre with associated transform faults (1),

(text continued on page 384)

Fault plane

Fault scarp

Footwall side

Hanging-wall side

Tensional stress

(a) Normal fault (tension)

(a)

Hanging-wall side

Footwall side

Compressional stress

(b) Thrust or reverse fault (compression)

(b)

Right-lateral*

Left-lateral**

(c) Strike-slip fault (lateral shearing)

*Viewed from either dot on each road,
movement to opposite side is *to the right*.
**Viewed from either dot on each road,
movement to opposite side is *to the left*.

Pacific plate

North American plate

(d)

(c)

FIGURE 12.11 Types of faults.
(a) A normal fault produced by tension in the crust, visible along the edge in Tashkent, Uzbekistan. (b) A thrust, or reverse fault, produced by compression in the crust, visible in these offset strata in coal seams and volcanic ash in British Columbia. (c) A strike-slip fault produced by lateral shearing, clearly seen looking north along the San Andreas fault rift zone on the eastern edge of the Coast Ranges in California—Pacific plate to the left, North American plate to the right. (d) Can you find the San Andreas fault on the satellite image? Look for a linear rift stretching from southeast to northwest, at the edge of the coastal mountains and San Joaquin Valley. Use the arrows as guides. [(a) Photo by Fred McConnaughey/Photo Researchers, Inc.; (b) photo by Fletcher and Baylis/Photo Researchers, Inc.; (c) Kevin Schafer/Peter Arnold, Inc. (d) *Terra* MISR image courtesy of MISR Team, NASA/GSFC/JPL.]

ANIMATION

Fault Types, Transform Faults, Plate Margins

FIGURE 12.12 San Andreas fault formation.
(a) Formation of the San Andreas fault system as a series of transform faults in three
successive stages. (b) Enlargement shows the portion of southern California where the
1992 Landers, the 1994 Northridge (Reseda), and 1999 Hector Mine earthquakes occurred.
Magnitude ratings are shown for six quakes, including the epicentre location of the January
2001 M 6.8 Nisqually quake, Washington state, related to the subduction zone offshore on map
(a). (c) Trail sign near the epicentre of the 1906 San Francisco earthquake roughly marks the
Pacific–North American plate boundary, Marin County, Point Reyes National Seashore,
California. [(c) Photo by Robert Christopherson.]

FIGURE 12.13 Strike-slip faults in Turkey and California.
Note these two strike-slip, right-lateral faults and the dates of activity along each—the North Anatolian (Turkey) and San Andreas (California). California is oriented with north to the right for comparison purposes. The San Andreas system is a dense network of active faults and is more complex than the North Anatolian. [After USGS map by Ross S. Stein.]

while the North American plate was progressing westward after the breakup of Pangaea. Forces then shifted the transform faults toward a northwest–southeast alignment along a weaving axis (2). Finally, the western margin of North America overrode those shifting transform faults (3). Note the convergence rate is a rapid 4 cm (1.6 in.) per year.

In *relative* terms, the motion along this series of transform faults is right-lateral, whereas in *absolute* terms the North American plate is still moving westward. Consequently, the San Andreas system is a series of faults that are *transform* (associated with a former spreading centre), *strike-slip* (horizontal in motion), and *right-lateral* (one side is moving to the right relative to the other side).

The North Anatolian fault system in Turkey is a strike-slip fault and has a right-lateral motion similar to the San Andreas system (Figure 12.13). A progression of earthquakes have hit along the entire extent of the fault system in Turkey since 1939; the latest devastation occurred in August and November 1999 and again in February 2002.

Faults in Concert   Combinations of faults can produce distinctive landscapes. In the U.S. interior west, the *Basin and Range Province* (featuring a roughly parallel series of faulted mountains and valleys) experienced tensional forces caused by uplifting and thinning of the crust

(illustrated later in Chapter 15, Figure 15.25). This movement cracked the surface to form aligned pairs of normal faults and a distinctive landscape (Figure 12.14a).

The term **horst** applies to upward-faulted blocks; **graben** refers to downward-faulted blocks. One example of a horst and graben landscape is the Great Rift Valley of East Africa (associated with crustal spreading); it extends northward to the Red Sea, which fills the rift formed by parallel normal faults (Figure 12.14b). Another example is the Rhine graben, through which the Rhine River flows in Europe.

Orogenesis (Mountain Building)

The processes that work to produce crust and the tectonic forces that bend, warp, and break crust bring us to orogenesis. Let's now look at specific mountain-building processes.

Orogenesis literally means the birth of mountains (*oros* comes from the Greek for "mountain"). An *orogeny* is a mountain-building episode, occurring over millions of years. It can occur through large-scale deformation and uplift of the crust. An orogeny may include the capture of migrating exotic terranes, adding by accretion to the continental margins, or the intrusion of granitic magmas

FIGURE 12.14 Faulted landscapes.
(a) Pairs of faults produce a horst-and-graben landscape characteristic of the Basin and Range Province in the western United States or the Rhine Graben in Europe. (b) The Red Sea occupies a down-dropped block that is part of the rift system through East Africa. [(b) NASA photo from *Gemini*.]

Horst
(upfaulted block)

Graben
(downfaulted block)

(b)

to form plutons. The net result of this accumulating material is a thickening of the crust. The granite plutons often become exposed by erosion following uplift. Uplift is the final act of an orogenic cycle of mountain building. Earth's major chains of folded and faulted mountains, called *orogens*, are remarkably well correlated with the plate tectonics model.

No orogeny is a simple event; many involve previous developmental stages dating back far into Earth's past, and the processes are ongoing today. Major mountain ranges, and the orogenies that caused them, include:

- Rocky Mountains of North America—*Laramide orogeny*, 40–80 million years ago; third mountain-building episode, beginning 170 m.y.a., including Sevier Orogeny;
- Sierra Nevada and Klamath Mountains of California—*Nevadan orogeny*, with faulting 29–35 million years ago and older batholithic intrusion emplacements dating back 80 to 180 million years;
- Appalachian Mountains and the Ridge and Valley Province (nearly parallel ridges and valleys) of the eastern United States and Canadian Maritime Provinces—*Alleghany orogeny*, 250–300 million years ago, associated with the collision of Africa and North America, preceded by at least two earlier orogenies; in Europe this is contemporary with the *Hercynian orogeny*;
- Alps of Europe—*Alpine orogeny*, 2 to 66 million years ago, principally in the Teriary Period and continuing to the present across southern Europe and the Mediterranean, with many earlier episodes (Figure 12.15);
- Himalayas of Asia—*Himalayan orogeny*, 45–54 million years ago, beginning with the collision of the India plate and Eurasia plate and continuing to the present.

Types of Orogenies

Figure 12.16 illustrates three types of convergent plate collisions that cause orogenesis:

(a) Oceanic plate–continental plate collision orogenesis. This type of convergence is now occurring along the Pacific coast of the Americas and has formed the Andes, the Sierra of Central America, the Rockies, and other western mountains. We see folded sedimentary formations, with intrusions of magma forming granitic plutons at the heart of these mountains. Their buildup has been augmented by capturing displaced terranes, accreted during collision with the continental mass. Also, note the associated volcanic activity inland from the subduction zone, the eruption of plateau (flood) basalts (see Figures 12.29 and 12.37), and the development of composite volcanoes (see Figure 12.38).

(b) Oceanic plate–oceanic plate collision orogenesis. Such collisions can produce either simple volcanic island arcs or more complex arcs, such as Indonesia and Japan, which include deformation and metamorphism of rocks, and granitic intrusions. These processes formed the chains of island arcs and volcanoes that continue from the southwestern Pacific to the western Pacific, the Philippines, the Kurils, and on through portions of the Aleutians.

Both collision types, (a) oceanic–continental and (b) oceanic–oceanic, are active around the Pacific Rim. Both are thermal in nature, because the diving plate melts and migrates back toward the surface as molten rock. Subduction of oceanic lithosphere beneath continental lithosphere is facilitated by the differences in rock density. The lighter continental lithosphere, consisting largely of felsic

FIGURE 12.15 European Alps.
Western (France), Central (Italy), and Eastern (Austria) segments comprise the crescent shape of the Alps. Complex overturned faults and crustal shortening due to compressional forces occur along convergent plates. The Alps are some 1200 km (750 mi) in length, occupying 207,000 km^2 (80,000 mi^2). Note the aerosols and other pollutants concentrated south of the Alps in northern Italy. [*Terra* image courtesy of MODIS Land Rapid Response Team, NASA/GSFC.]

rocks with an average density of 2700 kg/m^3, overrides the heavier oceanic lithosphere that consists largely of mafic rocks with an average density of 3000 kg/m^3. The region of active volcanoes and earthquakes around the Pacific is known as the **circum-Pacific belt** or, more popularly, the **ring of fire**.

(c) Continental plate–continental plate collision orogenesis. Here the orogenesis is mechanical; large masses of continental crust are subjected to intense folding, overthrusting, faulting, and up-lifting. The converging plates crush and deform both marine sediments and basaltic oceanic crust. The formation of the European Alps is a result of such compression forces and includes consider-able crustal shortening, forming great overturned folds, called *nappes* (see Figure 12.15).

As mentioned earlier, the collision of India with the Eurasian landmass produced the Himalayan Mountains. That collision is estimated to have shortened the overall continental crust by as much as 1000 km (about 600 mi) and to have produced telescoping sequences of thrust faults at depths of 40 km (25 mi). The Himalayas feature the tallest above-sea-level mountains on Earth, including Mount Everest at 8850 m elevation (29,035 ft), and all 10 of Earth's highest peaks (measured from sea level).

The disruption created by this plate collision has reached far under China, and frequent earthquakes there signal the continuation of this rapid-paced collision, as India moves northward at about 2 m (6.6 ft) a year. As evidence of this ongoing strain, the January 2001 quake in Gujarat, India, was along a shallow, east–west-tending thrust fault that gave way under the pressure of the northward-pushing India plate. More than one million buildings were destroyed or damaged during this event, along the 2500-m (1553-mi) fault zone that marks this plunging Indian subcontinent. Again, a 40-km (25-mi) segment snapped in October 2005, when a M 7.6 quake hit the Kashmir region of Pakistan, killing more than 83,000 people.

The Appalachian Mountains

The old, eroded, fold-and-thrust belt of the eastern United States and southeastern Canada has origins dating to the formation of Pangaea and the collision of Africa and North America (250–300 million years old). The Appalachians contrast with the higher mountains of western North America (35–80 million years old). As noted, the complexity of the *Alleghany orogeny* derives from at least two earlier orogenic cycles of uplift and the accretion of several captured terranes.

FIGURE 12.16 Three types of plate convergence.
Real-world examples illustrate three types of crustal collisions. (a) Oceanic–continental (example: Nazca plate–South American plate collision and subduction). (b) Oceanic–oceanic (example: New Hebrides Trench near Vanuatu, 16° S, 168° E). (c) Continental–continental (example: India plate and Eurasian landmass collision and resulting Himalayan Mountains). Can you identify more of these plate convergence areas on the chapter-opening map?
[Illustrations on left from *Floor of the Oceans,* 1975, by Bruce C. Heezen and Marie Tharp © 1980. Reproduced by permission of Marie Tharp.]

NOTEBOOK   Plate Boundaries

Each orogenic event was separated by long periods of time during which rock weathering and erosion gradually stripped material from the mountain summits. The end result of these processes was the production of upland plateaux with elevations equal to or greater than 700 m above sea level throughout much of Atlantic Canada, excluding Prince Edward Island.* Fluvial and glacial erosion has created steep-sided valleys that dissect the edge of the upland plateau (Figure 12.17).

Structure and composition link the mountain ranges separated by the Atlantic Ocean and the Pangaea collision

and separation. In fact, the Lesser (or Anti-) Atlas Mountains of Mauritania and northwestern Africa were connected to the Appalachians at some time in the past, but the mountains embedded in the African plate rafted apart from the Appalachians.

The Western Cordillera

The rugged topography that characterizes much of this region developed in response to volcanism and tectonism accompanying the accretion of exotic terranes throughout the Mesozoic and early Tertiary periods (180 to 45 m.y.a.). Mountain peaks commonly exceed elevations of 3000 m above sea level (Figure 12.18). The terrain in this region is composed of a variety of intrusive and extrusive igneous

*A. S. Trenhaile, *Geomorphology: A Canadian Perspective* (Oxford University Press, 2003).

Coulomb stress change (in bars)

Decrease   Increase

-3   0   3

(a)   (b)

ANIMATION   Elastic Rebound

FIGURE 12.24 Buildup and release of stress and strain along a fault system.
The elastic-rebound mechanism illustrated here applies to strike-slip faults such as the North
Anatolian in Turkey and the San Andreas system of faults in California. (a) As two sides of this
right-lateral, strike-slip fault move, they remain locked by friction, creating stress. Such stress
(a force) produces strain (a deformation) in the rock. Note the fence that crosses the fault line.
This stress continues to build to the break point. (b) In an earthquake, such as the M 7.4 shock
that hit Izmit, Turkey, the two sides snap into new positions, strain is released, and the fence
no longer forms a continuous property line. The segments of the fault that remain locked now
have added strain. A Coulomb is a unit of shear-stress failure overcoming friction and
resistance to movement; the colour scale ranges from blue (decreased stress) to red
(increased stress). [Illustrations (a) and (b) courtesy of Serkan Bozkurt, USGS.]

FIGURE 12.25 1995 earthquake in Kobe, Japan.
(a) Catastrophic failure of an elevated freeway; note the failure of the supporting pillars.
(b) Ground failure, mainly liquefaction, tilts this building to near collapse; note the space
between the building and the ground on the right side. [Photos by Haruyoshi Yamaguchi/Sygma.]

The lessons from Kobe are many, especially the occurrence of liquefaction and the failure of filled land. Areas of Osaka Bay reclaimed by landfill taken from the sea liquefied quickly in the shaking. Soil surfaces failed, collapsing the structures they supported (Figure 12.25b). Importantly, these human-made landfills and islands are characteristic of the San Francisco Bay region, where about half the original surface area of the bay is reclaimed with fill and occupied with buildings, since the early 1900s.

Earthquakes and the San Andreas Fault

In 1906, San Francisco was a city of 400,000 people (there are several million in the metropolitan region today). In that year, a M 7.7 (8.25 Richter) tremor rocked the city, felling buildings and initiating a firestorm fed by broken gas pipes. Movement along a fault was evident over 435 km (270 mi), prompting intensive research to discover the nature of such faulting. The elastic-rebound theory developed as a result of research done on this rupture. Realize that this quake occurred 6 years before Wegener proposed his continental drift hypothesis.

The fault system that devastated San Francisco in 1906, and coastal and inland California throughout recorded history, is the San Andreas. The San Andreas fault system provides a good example of a spreading centre overridden by an advancing continental plate (refer to Figure 12.12 for its evolution).

The tectonic history of the San Andreas was brought home to hundreds of millions of television viewers as they watched the 1989 baseball World Series played in Candlestick Park near San Francisco. Less than half an hour before the call to "play ball," a powerful earthquake rocked the region, turning sportscasters into newscasters and sports fans into disaster witnesses. This M 7.0 earthquake involved a portion of the San Andreas fault, near Loma Prieta, approximately 16 km (9.9 mi) east of Santa Cruz and 95 km (59 mi) south of San Francisco (see Figure 12.22). A fault had ruptured at a focus unusually deep for the San Andreas system, more than 18 km (11.5 mi) below the surface.

Unlike previous earthquakes—such as the one in 1906, when the plates shifted a maximum of 6.4 m (21 ft) relative to each other—there was no evidence of a fault plane or rifting at the surface in the Loma Prieta area. Instead, the fault plane suggested in Figure 12.22 shows the two plates moving horizontally approximately 2 m (6 ft) past each other deep below the surface, with the Pacific plate thrusting 1.3 m (4.3 ft) upward. This vertical motion is unusual for the San Andreas fault and indicates that this portion of the San Andreas system is more complex than previously thought. Damage totaled $8 billion, 14,000 people were displaced from their homes, 4000 were injured, and 67 killed.

Los Angeles Region

Since the mid-1980s, an area east of Los Angeles has experienced seven earthquakes greater than M 6.0. After a M 6.1 quake in 1992, a M 7.4 tremor rocked the lightly populated area near Landers, California (see the enlargement map of southern California in Figure 12.12). Although it was the single largest quake in California in 30 years, the remote location kept injuries and damage slight. Involved in this series were four different faults and some unknown segments. The main faulting caused a displacement of 6.1 m (20 ft).

For yet unexplained reasons, related earthquakes over the next few weeks struck in Mammoth Lakes, about 645 km (400 mi) to the north; at Mount Shasta in northern California; in southern Nevada and Utah; and 1810 km (1125 mi) distant in Yellowstone National Park, Wyoming. Evidence is growing that in complex fault systems, such as in the Los Angeles Region, active faults can interact, transferring stress to adjoining systems, with one fault perhaps triggering activity along another fault. This complicates analysis and forecasting.

The 1971 San Fernando, 1987 Whittier, 1988 Pasadena, 1991 Sierra Madre, and 1994 Northridge (Reseda) earthquakes are a few of the many quakes associated with deeply buried thrust faults. Although not directly aligned with the San Andreas, scientists think that southern California will be affected by more of these thrust-fault actions as strain continues to build along the nearby San Andreas system of faults. The fault line that marks the contact between the Pacific and the North American plates is indeed restless.

Earthquake Forecasting and Planning

The map in Figure 12.23 plots the epicentres of twentieth century earthquakes in Canada. These occurrences give some indication of relative risk by region. The challenge is to discover how to predict the *specific time and place* for a quake in the short term. See News Report 12.2 for more on forecasting.

Actual implementation of an action plan to reduce death, injury, and property damage from earthquakes is difficult. The political environment adds complexity since studies show that an accurate earthquake prediction may threaten a region's economy. Research examining the potential socioeconomic impact of earthquake prediction on an urban community shows surprising negative economic impacts in the period before the quake hits. Imagine a chamber of commerce, bank, real estate agent, tax assessor, or politician who would welcome an earthquake prediction and such negative publicity for their city. These factors work against effective planning and preparation.

Long-range planning is a complex subject. After the Loma Prieta earthquake in 1989, the National Research Council concluded in a report:

> One of the most jarring lessons from these quakes may be that earthquake professionals have long known many of the things that could have been done to reduce devastation. . . . The cost-effectiveness of mitigation and the importance of closing the knowledge gap among researchers, building professionals, government officials, and the public are only two of the many lessons from the Loma Prieta that need immediate action.

News Report 12.2

Seismic Gaps, Nervous Animals, Dilitancy, and Radon Gas

How do you forecast an earthquake? One approach is to examine the history of each plate boundary and determine the frequency of past earthquakes, a study called *paleoseismology*. Paleoseismologists construct maps that provide an estimate of expected earthquake activity based on past performance. An area that is quiet and overdue for an earthquake is a *seismic gap*; such an area forms a gap in the earthquake occurrence record and is therefore a place that possesses accumulated strain. The area along the Aleutian Trench subduction zone had three such gaps until the great 1964 Alaskan earthquake filled one of them.

The areas around San Francisco and northeast of Los Angeles represent other such gaps where the fault system appears to be locked by friction and stress is producing accumulating strain. The U.S. Geological Survey in 1988 made a prediction that there was a 30% chance of an earthquake occurring with a magnitude 6.5 within 30 years in the Loma Prieta portion of the fault system. The actual 1989 quake dramatically filled a portion of the seismic gap in that region. The Nojima fault in the area of Kobe occurred in another gap.

One potentially positive discovery from the Loma Prieta disaster was that Stanford University scientists found unusually great changes in Earth's magnetic field—about 30 times more than normal—3 hours before the main shock. These measurements were made 7 km (4.3 mi) from the epicentre, raising hopes that short-term warnings might be possible in the future. A valid research question is whether animals have the ability to detect these minute changes in magnetic fields, an ability that was perhaps lost in humans. If so, strange prequake animal behaviour, often reported, might provide forecasting clues.

Dilitancy refers to the slight increase in volume of rock produced by small cracks that form under stress and accumulated strain. The affected region may tilt and swell in response to strain. Tiltmeters measure these changes in suspect areas. Another indicator of dilitancy is an increase in radon (a naturally occurring, slightly radioactive gas) dissolved in groundwater. At present, earthquake hazard zones have thousands of radon monitors taking samples in test wells.

A seismic network in operation in Mexico City is providing 70-second warnings of arriving seismic-wave energy from distant epicentres. Following the Loma Prieta earthquake, freeway-repair workers were linked to a broadcast system that gave them 20-second alerts of aftershocks from distant epicentres. In southern California, the USGS is coordinating a Southern California Seismographic Network (SCSN at http://www.scsn.org/) to correlate 350 instruments for immediate earthquake location analysis and disaster coordination. Also, for the southern California region, see http://earthquake.usgs.gov/regional/sca/.

Someday, accurate earthquake forecasting may be a reality, but several questions remain. How will humans respond to a forecast? Can a major metropolitan region be evacuated for short periods of time? Can cities relocate after a disaster to areas of lesser risk?

A valid and applicable generalization is that *humans and their institutions are unable or unwilling to perceive hazards in a familiar environment*. In other words, we tend to feel secure in our homes and communities, even if they are sitting on a quiet fault zone. Such an axiom of human behaviour certainly helps explain why large populations continue to live and work in earthquake-prone settings. Similar questions also can be raised about populations in areas vulnerable to floods, droughts, hurricanes and coastal storm surge, and settlements on barrier islands. (See "Coping with Natural Hazards in Canada: Scientific, Government and Insurance Industry Perspectives" at http://www.utoronto.ca/env/nh/toc.htm and Natural Hazards Observer at http://www.colorado.edu/hazards/o/.)

Volcanism

Volcanic eruptions across the globe remind us of Earth's internal energy. Ongoing eruption activity matches plate tectonic activity, as shown on the map in Figure 11.23. A sample of recent eruptions includes: Kīlauea in Hawai'i, Soufriere Hills on Montserrat (Lesser Antilles), Mount Etna (Sicily, Italy), several on the Kamchatka Peninsula (Russia), Rabaul (Papua, New Guinea), Grímsvötn (Iceland), Axial Summit and the Jackson Segment (sea-floor spreading centre off the coast of Oregon), Shishaldin (Unimak Island, Alaska; see Figure 12.38), Lascar (Chile), White Island (New Zealand; see Figure 12.33), Nyiragongo (Congo, Africa), and Mayon (Philippines), among many.

Over 1300 identifiable volcanic cones and mountains exist on Earth, although fewer than 600 are active (have had at least one eruption in recorded history). In an average year, about 50 volcanoes erupt worldwide, varying from modest activity to major explosions. (An index to the world's volcanoes is at http://vulcan.wr.usgs.gov/Volcanoes/framework.html, and the National Museum of Natural History Global Volcanism Program lists information for more than 8500 eruptions at http://www.nmnh.si.edu/gvp/. For more volcanic eruption listings, see http://volcano.und.nodak.edu/, or check http://www.geo.mtu.edu/volcanoes/links/observatories.html for links to volcano observatories across the globe.)

Eruptions in remote locations and at depths on the seafloor go largely unnoticed, but the occasional eruption of great magnitude near a population centre makes headlines. North America has about 70 volcanoes (mostly inactive) along the western margin of the continent. Mount St. Helens in Washington State is a famous active example, and over 1 million visitors a year travel to Mount St. Helens Volcanic National Monument to see volcanism for themselves.

Volcanic Features

A **volcano** forms at the end of a central vent or pipe that rises from the asthenosphere and upper mantle through the crust into a volcanic mountain. A **crater**, or circular surface depression, usually forms at or near the summit. Magma rises and collects in a magma chamber deep below the volcano until conditions are right for an eruption. This subsurface magma emits tremendous heat; in some areas it boils groundwater, producing *geothermal energy*, as seen in the thermal springs and geysers of Yellowstone National Park, and elsewhere in the world where it is harnessed for geothermal power production.

Lava (molten rock), gases, and **pyroclastics**, or *tephra* (pulverized rock and clastic materials of various sizes ejected violently during an eruption), pass through the vent to the surface and build the volcanic landform. There are two principal forms of flowing basaltic lava, both named in Hawaiian terms (Figure 12.26). **Aa** is a basaltic lava that is rough and jagged with sharp edges. This texture happens because the lava loses trapped gases, flows slowly, and develops a thick skin that cracks into the jagged surface. Another principal lava texture that is more fluid than aa is **pahoehoe**. As this lava flows it forms a thin crust that develops folds and appears "ropy," like coiled, twisted rope. Both forms can come from the same eruption, and sometimes pahoehoe will become aa as the flow progresses. Other types of basaltic magma are described later in this section.

A **cinder cone** is a small, cone-shaped hill usually less than 450 m (1500 ft) high, with a truncated top formed from cinders that accumulate during moderately explosive eruptions. Cinder cones are made of pyroclastic material and *scoria* (cindery rock, full of air bubbles).

A **caldera** (Spanish for "kettle") is a large, basin-shaped depression. It forms when summit material on a volcanic mountain collapses inward after an eruption or other loss of magma. A caldera may fill with rainwater, as it did in beautiful Crater Lake in southern Oregon. News Report 12.3 discusses the Long Valley Caldera in California.

In the Cape Verde Islands (15° N 24.5° W), Fogo Island has such a caldera in the midst of a volcanic cone, opening to the sea on the eastern side. The best farmland is in the caldera, so the people choose to live and work there. Unfortunately, eruptions began in 1995, destroying farmland and forcing the evacuation of 5000 people. Previously, eruptions occurred between A.D. 1500 and 1750, followed by six more in the nineteenth century, each destroying houses and crops.

ANIMATION Formation of Crater Lake

Location and Types of Volcanic Activity

The location of volcanic mountains on Earth is a function of plate tectonics and hot-spot activity. Volcanic activity occurs in three settings (with representative examples):

1. Along subduction boundaries at continental plate–oceanic plate convergence (such as Mount St. Helens and Kliuchevskoi, Siberia) or oceanic plate–oceanic plate convergence (Philippines and Japan).
2. Along sea-floor spreading centres on the ocean floor (Iceland on the Mid-Atlantic ridge or off the coast of Oregon and Washington) or areas of rifting on continental plates (the rift zone in east Africa).
3. At hot spots, where individual plumes of magma rise to the crust (such as Hawai'i and Yellowstone National Park).

Figure 12.27 illustrates these three types of volcanic activity, which you can compare with the active volcano sites and plate boundaries shown in Figure 11.22. Figures 12.28 to 12.33 illustrate the various aspects of volcanism presented in Figure 12.27 and in the following discussion.

The variety of forms among volcanoes makes them difficult to classify; most fall in a middle ground between one type and another. Even during a single eruption, a

(text continued on page 402)

ANIMATION Tectonic Settings and Volcanic Activity

(a) Aa   (b) Pahoehoe

FIGURE 12.26 Two types of basaltic lava—Hawaiian examples.
(a) Aa is a rough, sharp-edged lava that is said to get its name from the sounds people make when they take off their shoes and attempt to walk on it. The gold-coloured strands are a clump of natural spun glass formed by the lava as it blew out into the air—called *Pele's hair*. (b) Pahoehoe forms ropy chords in twisted folds. [Photos by Bobbé Christopherson.]

5. What is a migrating terrane, and how does it add to the formation of continental masses?

■ *Explain* compressional processes and folding, and *describe* four principal types of faults and their characteristic landforms.

Folding, broad warping, and faulting deform the crust and produce characteristic landforms. Compression causes rocks to deform in a process known as **folding**, during which rock strata bend and may overturn. Along the *ridge* of a fold, layers *slope downward away from the axis*, which is an **anticline**. In the *trough* of a fold, however, layers *slope downward toward the axis*; this is a **syncline**.

When rock strata are stressed beyond their ability to remain a solid unit, they express the strain as a fracture. Rocks on either side of the fracture are displaced relative to the other side in a process known as **faulting**. Thus, *fault zones* are areas where fractures in the rock demonstrate crustal movement. At the moment of fracture, a sharp release of energy, an **earthquake** or *quake*, occurs.

When forces pull rocks apart, the tension causes a **normal fault**, sometimes visible on the landscape as a scarp, or escarpment. Compressional forces associated with converging plates force rocks to move upward, producing a **reverse fault**. A low-angle fault plane is referred to as a **thrust fault**. Horizontal movement along a fault plane that produces a linear rift valley is a **strike-slip fault**. In the U.S. interior west, the Basin and Range Province is an example of aligned pairs of normal faults and a distinctive horst-and-graben landscape. The term **horst** is applied to upward-faulted blocks; **graben** refers to downward-faulted blocks.

folding (p. 379)
anticline (p. 379)
syncline (p. 379)
faulting (p. 380)
earthquake (p. 380)
normal fault (p. 380)
reverse fault (p. 380)
thrust fault (p. 381)
strike-slip fault (p. 381)
horst (p. 384)
graben (p. 384)

6. Diagram a simple folded landscape in cross section, and identify the features created by the folded strata.

7. Define the four basic types of faults. How are faults related to earthquakes and seismic activity?

■ *Relate* the three types of plate collisions associated with orogenesis, and *identify* specific examples of each.

Orogenesis is the birth of mountains. An orogeny is a mountain-building episode, occurring over millions of years, that thickens continental crust. It can occur through large-scale deformation and uplift of the crust. It also may include the capture of migrating terranes and cementation of them to the continental margins and the intrusion of granitic magmas to form plutons.

Oceanic plate–continental plate collision orogenesis is now occurring along the Pacific coast of the Americas and has formed the Andes, the Sierra of Central America, the Rockies, and other western mountains. *Oceanic plate–oceanic plate* collision orogenesis produces either simple volcanic island arcs or more complex arcs such as Japan, the Philippines, the Kurils, and portions of the Aleutians. The region around the Pacific contains

expressions of each type of collision in the **circum-Pacific belt**, or the **ring of fire**.

Continental plate–continental plate collision orogenesis is quite mechanical; large masses of continental crust, such as the Himalayan Range, are subjected to intense folding, overthrusting, faulting, and uplifting.

orogenesis (p. 384)
circum-Pacific belt (p. 386)
ring of fire (p. 386)

8. Define *orogenesis*. What is meant by the birth of mountain chains?

9. Name some significant orogenies.

10. Identify on a map Earth's two large mountain chains. What processes contributed to their development?

11. How are plate boundaries related to episodes of mountain building? Explain how different types of plate boundaries produce differing orogenic episodes and different landscapes.

12. Relate tectonic processes to the formation of the Western Cordillera.

■ *Explain* the nature of earthquakes, their measurement, and the nature of faulting.

Earthquakes generally occur along plate boundaries; major ones can be disastrous. Earthquakes result from faults, which are under continuing study to learn the nature of faulting, stress and the buildup of strain, irregularities along fault-plane surfaces, the way faults rupture, and the relationship among active faults. Earthquake prediction and improved planning are active concerns of *seismology*, the study of earthquake waves and Earth's interior. Seismic motions are measured with a **seismograph**.

Charles Richter developed the **Richter scale**, a measure of earthquake magnitude. A more precise and quantitative scale that assesses the *seismic moment* is now used, especially for larger quakes; this is the **moment magnitude scale**. The specific mechanics of how a fault breaks are under study, but the **elastic-rebound theory** describes the basic process. In general, two sides along a fault appear to be locked by friction, resisting any movement. This stress continues to build strain along the fault surfaces, storing elastic energy like a wound-up spring. When energy is released abruptly as the rock breaks, both sides of the fault return to a condition of less strain.

seismograph (p. 391)
Richter scale (p. 391)
moment magnitude scale (p. 393)
elastic-rebound theory (p. 393)

13. Describe the differences in human response between the two earthquakes that occurred in China in 1975 and 1976.

14. Differentiate between the Mercalli and moment magnitude and amplitude scales. How are these used to describe an earthquake? Why has the Richter scale been updated and modified?

15. What is the relationship between an epicentre and the focus of an earthquake? Give examples from the Loma Prieta, California, and Kobe, Japan, earthquakes.

16. What local soil and surface conditions in San Francisco severely magnify the energy felt in earthquakes?

17. How do the elastic-rebound theory and asperities help explain the nature of faulting?

18. Describe the San Andreas fault and its relationship to ancient sea-floor spreading movements along transform faults.

19. How is the seismic gap concept related to expected earthquake occurrences as described in News Report 12.3? Are any gaps correlated with earthquake events in the recent past? Explain.

20. What do you see as the biggest barrier to effective earthquake prediction?

■ ***Distinguish*** between an effusive and an explosive volcanic eruption, and *describe* related landforms, using specific examples.

Volcanoes offer direct evidence of the makeup of the asthenosphere and uppermost mantle. A **volcano** forms at the end of a central vent or pipe that rises from the asthenosphere through the crust into a volcanic mountain. A **crater**, or circular surface depression, usually forms at the summit. Areas where magma is near the surface may heat groundwater, producing *geothermal energy*.

Eruptions produce **lava** (molten rock), gases, and **pyroclastics** (pulverized rock and clastic materials ejected violently during an eruption) that pass through the vent to openings and fissures at the surface and build volcanic landforms. Basaltic lava flows occur in two principal textures: **aa**, rough and sharp-edged lava, and **pahoehoe**, smooth, ropy folds of lava. Volcanic activity produces landforms such as a **cinder cone**, a small hill, or a large basin-shaped depression sometimes caused by collapse of a volcano's summit, forming a **caldera**.

Volcanoes are of two general types, based on the chemistry and the viscosity of the magma involved. **Effusive eruption** produces a **shield volcano** (such as Kīlauea in Hawai'i) and extensive deposits of **plateau basalts**, or flood basalts. Magma of higher viscosity leads to an **explosive eruption** (such as Mount Pinatubo in the Philippines), producing a **composite volcano**. Volcanic activity has produced some destructive moments in history but constantly creates new seafloor, land, and soils.

volcano (p. 399)
crater (p. 399)
lava (p. 399)
pyroclastics (p. 399)
aa (p. 399)
pahoehoe (p. 399)
cinder cone (p. 399)
caldera (p. 399)
effusive eruption (p. 402)
shield volcano (p. 404)
plateau basalts (p. 404)
explosive eruption (p. 404)
composite volcano (p. 404)

21. What is a volcano? In general terms, describe some related features.

22. Where do you expect to find volcanic activity in the world? Why?

23. Compare effusive and explosive eruptions. Why are they different? What distinct landforms are produced by each type? Give examples of each.

24. Describe several recent volcanic eruptions.

Critical Thinking

A. Using the topographic regions map in Figure 12.3, assess the region within 100 km (62 mi) and 1000 km (620 mi) of your campus. Describe the topographic character and the variety of relief within these two regional scales. You may want to consult local maps and atlases in your analysis. Do you perceive that this type of topographic region influences lifestyles? Economic activities? Transportation? History of the region?

B. Determine from library, Internet, and local agencies the seismic potential of the region in which your campus is sited. If a hazard exists, does it influence regional planning? Availability of property insurance? If appropriate, are there existing disaster or emergency plans for your campus? For your community, province, or state? Explain any other significant issues you found in working on this critical thinking challenge.

manufacturing and power generation, and form essential transportation networks. Rivers have been important in the geography of human history, influencing where settlements were built, where livelihoods were made, and where borders were drawn. This chapter discusses the dynamics of river systems and their landforms.

Hydrology is the science of water and its global circulation, distribution, and properties, specifically water at and below Earth's surface. For hydrology links on the Web, see: The Water Survey of Canada at **http:// www. wsc.ec.gc.ca/index_e.cfm?cname=main_e.cfm**, The Hydrology Web at **http://hydrologyweb.pnl. gov/index.asp**, or the Global Hydrology and Climate Center at **http:// weather.msfc.nasa.gov/surface_hydrology/**; also see the Amazon River at **http://boto.ocean.washington.edu/eos/ index.html**.

In this chapter: We begin with a look at the largest rivers on Earth. Essential fluvial concepts of base level, drainage basin, and drainage density and patterns follow. With this foundation, we define streamflow discharge, "Q," the essential element in fluvial processes. We discuss factors that affect streamflow characteristics and the work performed by flowing water, including erosion and transport. Stream depositional features such as deltaic forms are illustrated with a detailed look at the Mississippi River Delta. We look at the effects of urbanization on hydrology. Human response to floods and floodplain management are important aspects of river management, with details of the New Orleans levee and floodwall disaster and tragedy concluding the chapter.

Fluvial Processes and Landscapes

At any moment, approximately 1250 km³ (300 mi³) of water is flowing through Earth's waterways. Even though this volume is only 0.003% of all freshwater, the work performed by this energetic flow makes it a dominant agent of landmass denudation. Of the world's rivers, those with the greatest *discharge* (streamflow volume past a point in a given unit of time) are the Amazon of South America (Figure 14.1), the Congo of Africa, the Chàng Jiang (Yangtze) of Asia, and the Orinoco of South America (Table 14.1). In North America, the greatest discharges are from the Missouri–Ohio–Mississippi, Saint Lawrence, and Mackenzie river systems.

Stream-related processes are **fluvial** (from the Latin *fluvius*, meaning "river"). Geographers analyze stream patterns and the fluvial processes that created them. Fluvial systems, like all natural systems, have characteristic processes and produce recognizable landforms. Yet a stream system can behave with randomness and seeming disorder. The term *river* is applied to a trunk, or main stream, or an entire river system. *Stream* is a more general term not necessarily related to size. There is some overlap in usage between river and stream terms.

Insolation and gravity power the hydrologic cycle and are the driving forces of fluvial systems. Individual streams vary greatly from one another, depending on the climate in which they operate, the composition of the surface, topography over which they flow, the nature of vegetation and plant cover, and the length of time they have been operating in a specific setting.

Water dislodges, dissolves, or removes surface material in the **erosion** process. Streams produce *fluvial erosion*, in which weathered sediment is picked up for transport to new locations. Thus, a stream is a mixture of water and solids; the solids are carried in suspension, by mechanical **transport**, and in dissolved solution. Materials are laid down by another process, **deposition**. **Alluvium** is the general term for the clay, silt, sand, gravel, and mineral fragments deposited by running water as sorted or semi-sorted sediment on a floodplain, delta, or streambed.

FIGURE 14.1 Mouth of the Amazon River.
The mouth of the Amazon River discharges a fifth of all the freshwater that enters the world's oceans. The mouth of the Amazon is 160 km (100 mi) wide. Millions of metric tons of sediments are derived from the Amazon's drainage basin, which is as large as the Australian continent. Large islands of sediment are left where the river's discharge leaves the mouth and flows into the Atlantic Ocean. [*Terra* image courtesy of NASA/GSFC/JPL and the MISR Team.]

Table 14.1 Largest Rivers on Earth Ranked by Discharge

Rank by Volume	Average Discharge at Mouth in Thousands of m³/s (cfs)	River (with Tributaries)	Outflow/Location	Length km (mi)	Rank by Length
1	180 (6350)	Amazon (Ucayali, Tambo, Ene, Apurimac)	Atlantic Ocean/ Amapá-Pará, Brazil	6570 (4080)	2
2	41 (1460)	Congo (Lualaba)	Atlantic Ocean/ Angola, Congo	4630 (2880)	10
3	34 (1201)	Yangtze (Chàng Jiang)	East China Sea/Kiangsu, China	6300 (3915)	3
4	30 (1060)	Orinoco	Atlantic Ocean/Venezuela	2737 (1700)	27
5	21.8 (779)	La Plata estuary (Paraná)	Atlantic Ocean/Argentina	3945 (2450)	16
6	19.6 (699)	Ganges (Brahmaputra)	Bay of Bengal/India	2510 (1560)	23
7	19.4 (692)	Yenisey (Angara, Selenga or Selenge, Ider)	Gulf of Kara Sea/Siberia	5870 (3650)	5
8	18.2 (650)	Mississippi (Missouri, Ohio, Tennessee, Jefferson, Beaverhead, Red Rock)	Gulf of Mexico/Louisiana	6020 (3740)	4
9	16.0 (568)	Lena	Laptev Sea/Siberia	4400 (2730)	11
17	9.7 (348)	St. Lawrence	Gulf of St. Lawrence/Canada and United States	3060 (1900)	21
36	2.83 (100)	Nile (Kagera, Ruvuvu, Luvironza)	Mediterranean Sea/Egypt	6690 (4160)	1

Base Level of Streams

Base level is a level below which a stream cannot erode its valley. In general, the *ultimate base level* is sea level, the average level between high and low tides. Imagine base level as a surface extending inland from sea level, inclined gently upward under the continents. Ideally, this is the lowest practical level for all denudation processes (Figure 14.2a).

American geologist and ethnologist John Wesley Powell (1834–1902) put forward the idea of base level in 1875. He was a director of the U.S. Geological Survey, first director of the U.S. Bureau of Ethnology, explorer of the Colorado River, and a pioneer in understanding the western landscape.

Of course, Powell recognized that not every landscape has degraded all the way to sea level; clearly, other intermediate base levels are in operation. A *local base level*, or temporary one, may control the lower limit of local streams for a region. The local base level may be a river, a lake, hard and resistant rock, or a human-made dam (Figure 14.2b). In arid landscapes, with their intermittent precipitation, valleys, plains, or other low points provide local control.

(a)

(b)

FIGURE 14.2 Ultimate and local base levels.
(a) The concepts of ultimate base level (sea level) and local base level (natural, such as a lake, or artificial, such as a dam). Note how base level curves gently upward from the sea as it is traced inland; this is the theoretical limit for stream erosion. (b) A local base level was introduced to the landscape above Glen Canyon Dam when it closed off the canyon. [Photo by Bobbé Christopherson.]

FIGURE 14.3 A drainage basin. A drainage divide separates the drainage basin and its watershed from other basins.

Over time, the work of streams modifies the landscape dramatically. Landforms are produced by two basic processes: (1) erosive action of flowing water, and (2) deposition of stream-transported materials. Before we introduce streamflow characteristics, let us begin by examining a basic fluvial unit—the drainage basin.

Drainage Basins

Figure 14.3 illustrates drainage basin concepts. Every stream has a **drainage basin**, ranging in size from tiny to vast. Every drainage basin is defined by ridges that form *drainage divides;* that is, the ridges are the dividing lines that control into which basin precipitation drains. Drainage divides define a **watershed**, the catchment (water-receiving) area of the drainage basin. In any drainage basin, water initially moves downslope in a thin film called **sheetflow**, or *overland flow*. High ground that separates one valley from another and directs sheetflow is termed an *interfluve*. Surface runoff concentrates in *rills*, or small-scale downhill grooves, which may develop into deeper *gullies* and then on to a stream course in the valley.

The drainage basin acts as a collection system of water comprised of many subsystems from erosion in the headwaters, transportation throughout, to deposition in the lower portions, figure 14.4 illustrates the drainage basin system operation, from the smallest rill and gully, to the main tributaries and stream trunk, to the dispersing lower extremities and mouth, possibly forming a delta or depositing sediments in a water body.

Drainage Divides and Basins Several high drainage divides, called **continental divides**, are situated in Canada and the United States. These are extensive mountain and highland regions separating drainage basins, sending

flows to the Pacific, the Gulf of Mexico, the Atlantic, Hudson Bay, or the Arctic Ocean. The principal drainage divides and drainage basins in Canada and the United States are mapped in Figure 14.5. These divides form

FIGURE 14.4 Drainage basin system. Beginning with intricate drainage patterns, water and sediment are collected and delivered to the stream tributaries. This fluidized mass transports to the main trunk and the dispersing system at the end of the stream where it enters another water body. [Adapted from Hamblin and Christiansen, *Earth's Dynamic System*, 10th ed., Upper Saddle River, NJ: Pearson Prentice Hall, 2004: Figure 12.3, p. 300.]

water-resource regions and provide a spatial framework for water-management planning.

A major drainage basin system is made up of many smaller drainage basins. Each drainage basin gathers and delivers its precipitation and sediment to a larger basin, concentrating the volume into the main stream. A good example from Figure 14.5 is the Peace–Athabasca–Liard–Mackenzie river system.

Precipitation falling in any area collects in streams and travels vast distances. Consider the precipitation that

falls in south-central Alberta. This water collects in hundreds of small streams that join the Athabasca River. At the same time, precipitation in northern Alberta feeds hundreds of streams that flow into the Peace River. The Peace and Athabasca rivers flow into Lake Athabasca, and then into the Slave River, which, in turn, empties into Great Slave Lake. From Great Slave Lake flows into the Mackenzie River. The Liard River collects the outflow of all the streams that gathered precipitation in northeastern British Columbia and then joins the Mackenzie at Fort

FIGURE 14.5 Drainage basins and continental divides.
Continental divides (blue lines) separate the major drainage basins that empty into the Pacific, Atlantic, Gulf of Mexico, and to the north through Canada into Hudson Bay and the Arctic Ocean. Subdividing these large-scale basins are major river basins. The sign in the inset photo would be more accurate if it said "Pacific" and "Arctic". [After U.S. Geological Survey; *The National Atlas of Canada*, 1985, Energy, Mines, and Resources Canada; and Environment Canada, *Currents of Change—Inquiry on Federal Water Policy—Final Report 1986;* photo by Robert Christopherson.]

Simpson, then continues northward past Inuvik and Tuktoyaktuk into the Beaufort Sea and the Arctic Ocean.

Each contributing tributary, large or small, adds its discharge and sediment load to the larger river. When water collects in lakes, the discharge ponds and sediment accumulates. Sediment weathered and eroded in south-central Alberta and northeastern British Columbia is carried by rivers and deposited in the Peace, Athabasca, Slave River, and Mackenzie deltas (see chapter-opening image).

Imagine the complexity of an international drainage basin, such as the Danube River in Europe, that flows 2850 km (1770 mi) from western Germany's Black Forest to the Black Sea. The river crosses or forms the borders between nine countries (Figure 14.6). A total area of 817,000 km^2 (315,000 mi^2) fall within the drainage basin, including some 300 tributaries.

The Danube serves many economic functions: commercial transport, municipal water source, agricultural irrigation, fishing, and hydroelectric-power production. An international struggle is underway to save the river from its burden of industrial and mining wastes, sewage, chemical discharge, agricultural runoff, and drainage from ships. The many shipping canals actually spread pollution and worsen biological conditions in the river. All of this pollution passes through Romania and the deltaic ecosystems in the Black Sea. The river is widely regarded as one of the most polluted on Earth.

Political changes in Europe in 1989 allowed the first scientific analysis of the entire river system. The United Nations Environment Programme (UNEP) and the European Union, along with other organizations, are dedicated to clearing the Danube, saving deltaic ecosystems, and restoring the environment of this valuable resource; see **http://www.icpdr.org/**. The river delta is one of the International Biosphere Reserves, **http://www.unesco.org/mab/** and **http://www.blacksea-environment.org/**.

Drainage Basins as Open Systems Drainage basins are open systems. Inputs include precipitation and the minerals and rocks of the regional geology. Energy and materials are redistributed as the stream constantly adjusts to its landscape. System outputs of water and sediment disperse through the mouth of the river into a lake, another river, or the ocean, as shown in Figure 14.4.

Change that occurs in any portion of a drainage basin can affect the entire system. The stream adjusts to carry the appropriate load of sediment relative to its discharge. If a river system is brought to a threshold where it can no longer maintain its present form, the relations within the drainage basin system are destabilized, initiating a transition period to a more stable condition. A stream drainage system constantly struggles toward equilibrium among the interacting variables of discharge, transported load, channel shape, and channel steepness.

Mackenzie River Basin Let us take a closer look at the Mackenzie River basin within the Arctic Ocean drainage region (Figure 14.7 and chapter-opening image). The main headwaters of the Mackenzie River are in the Peace River and the Athabasca River. The basin encompasses 1.8 million km^2 and is the longest river in Canada. The Mackenzie River's discharge is 9700 m^3/s and is second, in Canada, only to that of the St. Lawrence. Although peak discharge occurs in June, the flow is generally uniform due to the flatness of the land surrounding the river and because the land east of the river contains many large lakes that help sustain its flow. From the head of the Finlay River, a tributary of the Peace, the Mackenzie is 4241 km long, second longest in North America after the Mississippi–Missouri river system.

The Mackenzie Basin includes six sub-basins, three major deltas, three great lakes, and more than 30,000

Danube River delta

FIGURE 14.6 An international drainage basin—the Danube River.
The Danube crosses or forms the border of nine countries as it flows across Europe to the Black Sea. If Kosovo is recognized as an official new country from Serbia, this would increase to ten the number of countries served by the Danube River. The river spews polluted discharge into the Black Sea through its arcuate-form delta. [*Terra* image, June 15, 2002, courtesy of MODIS Land Rapid Response Team, NASA/GSFC.]

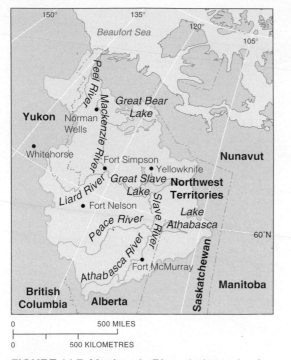

FIGURE 14.7 Mackenzie River drainage basin.
The basin is under study by a group of Earth scientists to assess the potential impact of global warming on a northern river system. [Map courtesy of the Mackenzie River Basin Board and Aurora Research Institute.]

lakes of various sizes. From its headwaters to the Beaufort Sea, it crosses three climatic regions—the boreal, the sub-arctic, and the arctic regions—and four physiographic regions: the Western Cordillera, the Canadian Shield, the Interior Plains, and the Mackenzie Delta. Almost 75% of the basin is affected by permafrost; the average monthly temperature is about −25°C and the mean annual precipitation is 410 mm with mean annual evapotranspiration of 237 mm.

More than 90% of the 360,000 residents of the Mackenzie Basin live in the southern part of the basin. The river system is the source of water, power, and transportation. The management of this resource will be critically important as climate change proceeds.

Internal Drainage   Most streams find their way to progressively larger rivers and eventually into the ocean. In some regions, however, stream drainage does not reach the ocean. Instead, the water leaves the drainage basin by means of evaporation or subsurface gravitational flow. Such streams terminate in areas of **internal drainage**.

Portions of Asia, Africa, Australia, Mexico, and the western United States have regions with such internal drainage patterns. Internal drainage defines the region of the Great Basin of the western United States, as shown on maps in Figures 14.5 and 15.25a. For example, the Humboldt River flows across Nevada to the west, where evaporation and seepage losses to groundwater make it disappear into the Humboldt "sink." Many streams and creeks flow into the Great Salt Lake, but its only outlet is evaporation, so it exemplifies a region of

internal drainage. In the Middle East, the Dead Sea region, and in Asia, the areas around the Aral Sea and Caspian Sea have no outlet to the ocean.

Drainage Density and Patterns

A primary feature of any drainage basin is its drainage density. **Drainage density** is determined by dividing the total length of all stream channels in the basin by the area of the basin. The number and length of channels in a given area reflects the landscape's regional topography and surface appearance. For example, Figure 14.8 reveals a high drainage density in a humid climate. In contrast, the typical desert has a very low drainage density.

The **drainage pattern** is the arrangement of channels in an area. Patterns are quite distinctive, for they are determined by the combination of regional steepness, variable rock resistance, variable climate, variable hydrology, relief of the land, and structural controls imposed by the underlying rocks. Consequently, the drainage pattern of any land area on Earth is a remarkable visual summary of every characteristic—geologic and climatic—of that region.

The *Terra* satellite image and topographic map in Figure 14.8 are of a portion of the province of Québec north of the Ottawa River. The drainage pattern here is *deranged*—the geometry of the drainage is not clear and there are no true stream channels. The drainage pattern developed in this manner because glaciation removed much of the sediment covering the bedrock in the area. The Canadian Shield is close to the surface. Rivers do not have the ability to easily erode downward into the rock and will therefore follow pre-existing, glacially-scoured, low areas in the rock surface. Over a much longer period of time (the glaciers melted about 10,000 years ago), the rivers will be able to erode downward into the rock and create a more organized drainage pattern.

Common Drainage Patterns   The seven most common drainage patterns are shown in Figure 14.9. A most familiar pattern is *dendritic drainage* (Figure 14.9a). This treelike pattern (Greek *dendron*, or "tree") is similar to that of many natural systems, such as capillaries in the human circulatory system, the vein patterns in leaves, and tree roots. Energy expended by this drainage system is efficient because the overall length of the branches is minimized.

The *trellis drainage* pattern (Figure 14.9b) is characteristic of dipping or folded topography. Such drainage exists in the nearly parallel mountain folds of the Ridge and Valley Province in the eastern United States. The inset sketch to Figure 14.9b suggests that a headward-eroding part of one stream (to the lower right of the inset) could break through a drainage divide and *capture* the headwaters of another stream in the next valley, and indeed this does happen. The dotted line is the abandoned former channel. The sharp bends in two of the streams in the illustration are called *elbows of capture* and are evidence that one stream has breached a drainage divide. This type of capture, or *stream piracy*, can also occur in other drainage patterns.

(a)

(b)

FIGURE 14.8 Deranged drainage in Québec.
(a) Deranged drainage on the Canadian Shield in Québec, north of the Ottawa River. The box indicates the area shown in the topographic map.
(b) Topographic map covering a portion of the area in the satellite image. [Image (a) courtesy of NASA/GSFC; (b) map from the Canada Centre for Remote Sensing, Natural Resources Canada. Used by permission of the Minister of Public Works and Government Services.]

The remaining drainage patterns in Figure 14.9 are responses to other specific structural conditions:

- A *radial* drainage pattern (c) results when streams flow off a central peak or dome, such as occurs on a volcanic mountain.
- *Parallel* drainage (d) is associated with steep slopes.
- A *rectangular* pattern (e) is formed by a faulted and jointed landscape, which directs stream courses in patterns of right-angle turns.
- *Annular* patterns (f) are produced by structural domes, with concentric patterns of rock strata guiding stream courses. Figure 12.10c provides an example of annular drainage on a dome structure.
- In areas having disrupted surface patterns, such as the glaciated shield regions of Canada, northern Europe, and some parts of Michigan and other states, a *deranged* pattern (g) is in evidence, with no clear geometry in the drainage and no true stream valley pattern.

The structure and relief of the land dictate these seven drainage patterns. In Figure 14.9h, you see two distinct drainage patterns. Of the seven types illustrated, which two patterns are most like those in the aerial photo, made in central Montana?

Occasionally, drainage patterns occur that are discordant with the landscape through which they flow. For example, a drainage system may flow in apparent conflict with older, buried structures that have been uncovered by erosion, so that the streams appear to be *superimposed*. Where an existing stream flows as rocks are uplifted, the stream keeps its original course, cutting into the rock in a pattern contrary to its structure. Such a stream is a *superposed stream* (the stream cuts across weak and resistant rocks alike). A few examples include Wills Creek, cutting a water gap through Haystack Mountain at Cumberland, Maryland; the Columbia River through the Cascade Mountains of Washington; and the River Arun that cuts across the Himalayas.

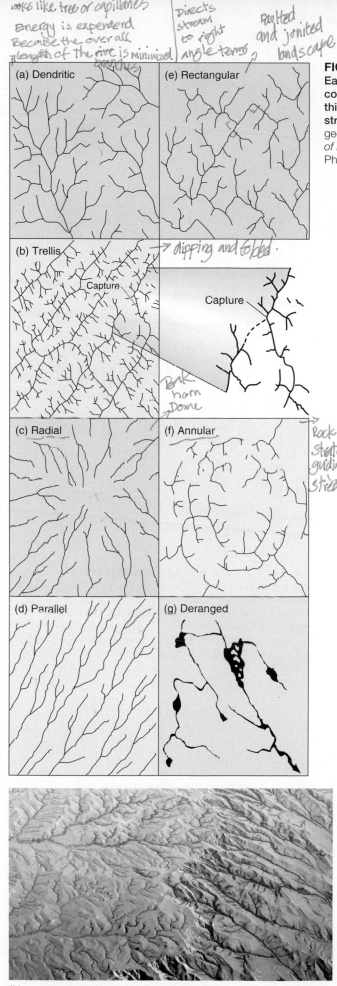

FIGURE 14.9 The seven most common drainage patterns.
Each pattern is a visual summary of all the geologic and climatic conditions of its region. (h) Two of these drainage patterns dominate this scene from central Montana, in response to local relief and rock structure. [(a) through (g) after A. D. Howard, "Drainage analysis in geological interpretation: A summation," *Bulletin of American Association of Petroleum Geologists* 51 (1967): 2248, adapted by permission. (h) Photo by Bobbé Christopherson.]

(handwritten annotations: "looks like tree or capillaries", "Energy is expended Because the overall length of the rive is minimized branches", "Directs stream to right angle terms?", "Faulted and jointed landscape", "dipping and folded.", "Rock horn Dome", "Rock strata guiding streams")

Streamflow Characteristics

A mass of water positioned above base level in a stream has potential energy. As the water flows downslope, or downstream, under the influence of gravity, this energy becomes kinetic energy. The rate of this conversion from potential to kinetic energy depends on the steepness of the stream channel and volume of water involved.

Streams vary in *width* and *depth*. The streams that flow in them vary in *velocity* and in the *sediment load* they carry. All of these factors increase with increasing **discharge**, or the stream's volume of flow per unit of time. Discharge is calculated by multiplying the velocity of the stream by its width and depth for a specific cross section of the channel, as stated in the simple expression:

$$Q = wdv$$

where Q = discharge, w = channel width, d = channel depth, and v = stream velocity. As Q increases, some combination of channel width, depth, and stream velocity increases. Discharge is expressed either in cubic metres per second (m^3/s) or cubic feet per second (cfs).

Figure 14.10 illustrates the relation of discharge to width, depth, and velocity. The graphs show that mean velocity increases with greater discharge, despite the common misperception that downstream flow becomes more sluggish. The increased velocity downstream often is masked by the apparent smooth, quiet flow of the water. Not surprisingly, discharge also increases with width and depth. The Mackenzie River is typical. It starts as many small brooks and grows to a mighty river pouring into the Beaufort Sea.

Given the interplay of channel width and depth and stream velocity with discharge, the cross section of a stream varies over time, especially during heavy floods. Figure 14.11 shows changes in the San Juan River channel in Utah that occurred during a flood. Greater discharge increases the velocity and therefore the capacity of the river to transport sediment as the flood progresses. As a result, the river's ability to scour materials from its bed is enhanced. Such scouring represents a powerful clearing action, especially in the excavation of alluvium. Scouring might provide new recreational beach areas and wildlife habitats, as explored by the Grand Canyon experiment in News Report 14.1.

You can see in Figure 14.11 that the San Juan River's channel was deepest on October 14, when floodwaters were highest (blue line). Then, as the discharge returned to normal, the kinetic energy of the river was reduced, and

(a)

(b)

FIGURE 14.10 Effects of stream discharge.
(a) Relation of stream width, depth, and velocity to stream discharge of the Powder River at Locate, Montana. Discharge is shown in cubic metres per second (m³/s) and cubic feet per second (cfs). (b) The Powder River area near the Wyoming border in southeastern Montana. [(a) After L. Leopold and T. Maddock, Jr., *The Hydraulic Geometry of Stream Channels and Some Physiographic Implications*, USGS Professional Paper 252 (Washington, D.C.: Government Printing Office, 1953), p.7; (b) photo by Joyce Wilson.]

the bed again filled as sediments were redeposited. You can see this process in the progression of the red, green, and purple lines. The flood and scouring process graphed in Figure 14.11 moved a depth of about 3 m (10 ft) of sedi-

(a)

FIGURE 14.11 A flood affects a stream channel.
(a) Stream-channel cross sections showing the progress of a 1941 flood on the San Juan River near Bluff, Utah. (b) Detail of stream-channel profile on September 15, 1941. [After L. Leopold and T. Maddock, Jr., *The Hydraulic Geometry of Stream Channels and Some Physiographic Implications*, USGS Professional Paper 252 (Washington, D.C.: Government Printing Office, 1953), p. 32.]

ment from this cross section of the stream channel. Such adjustments in a stream channel occur as the stream system continuously works toward equilibrium, in an effort to balance discharge, velocity, and sediment load.

Exotic Streams

Most streamflows increase discharge downstream because the area being drained increases. The Mississippi River is typical. It starts as many small brooks and grows to a mighty river pouring into the Gulf of Mexico. In contrast, a stream can originate in a humid region and subsequently flow through an arid region. In that case, the *discharge usually decreases with distance*, because of high potential evapotranspiration rates in the arid area. Such a stream is an **exotic stream** (*exotic* means "of foreign origin").

The Nile River exemplifies exotic streams. This great river, Earth's longest, drains much of northeastern Africa.

News Report 14.1

Scouring the Grand Canyon for New Beaches and Habitats

Glen Canyon Dam sealed the Colorado River gorge north of the Grand Canyon, near Lees Ferry and the Utah-Arizona border (see the map in Focus Study 15.1, Figure 15.1.1). Impoundment of water by the new Lake Powell, and the inundation of many canyons upstream from the dam, began in 1963. The lake began collecting the tremendous sediment load of the Colorado River. Dam operations reduced the volume of water in the river downstream, eliminating the natural seasonal fluctuations in river discharge. The production of hydroelectricity at Glen Canyon further affected the Grand Canyon with highly variable water releases keyed to electrical turbine operations. Water in the canyon rose and fell as much as 4.3 m (14 ft) in a 24-hour period as the distant lights and air-conditioning of Las Vegas and Phoenix went on and off.

All of these changes affected the canyon. Over the years, the beaches were starved for sand, channels filled with sediment, fisheries were disrupted, and backwater channels were depleted of nutrients. In 1996, an unprecedented experiment on the Colorado River took place. The Grand Canyon was artificially flooded with a 1260-m³/s (45,000-cfs) release from Glen Canyon (Figure 14.1.1). The flow lasted for 7 days and then was reduced to 224 m³/s (8000 cfs). Flows were decreased gradually to allow the newly formed beaches to drain, in contrast to the rapid opening of the pipes that initiated the flood. Lake Powell dropped 1 m (3.3 ft), and Lake Mead, downstream behind Hoover Dam, rose 0.8 m (2.6 ft).

The results were initially thought to be positive: 35% more beach area

FIGURE 14.1.1 Glen Canyon Dam floods the Grand Canyon, on purpose. Bypass tubes dramatically discharge water from Lake Powell in a 1996 experiment to correct the damaging effects of the dam on the Grand Canyon. Note for scale the workers on the walkway, who are experiencing a deafening roar and vibration. Another modified experiment took place in 2004 and again in 2008. [Photo by Tom Smart, *Deseret News*.]

was created by the scouring of sand and sediments from the channel. Approximately 80% of the aggradation (building up of beaches) took place in the first 40 hours and was completed by the 100-hour mark. Numerous backwater channels were created, flush with fresh nutrients for the humpback chub and other endangered fish species. However, benefits turned out to be limited, and negatives, in the form of existing ecosystem disruption and immediate losses of some sediment deposits, marred the experiment. Present thinking is that the lack of sediment to supply the floodwaters for downstream deposition and beach building was the problem. Some of the initial beach deposits quickly disappeared. For more on this experiment, see http://water.usgs.gov/pubs/FS/ FS-060-99/.

In November 2004 and again in March 2008, hydrologists conducted

a second and third test. Scientists timed the artificial flood with natural peak runoff that supplies fresh sediment to the system. Tributaries deliver more than 3 million metric tons of sediment to the Colorado River. Also, instead of 7 days, the artificial flood releases from Glen Canyon lasted 60 hours (2.5 days) in each test. The release coincided with local storms that fed tributaries, such as the Paria River, with sediment to accomplish the task of rebuilding beaches downstream. Results of the experiment in sediment redistribution are being monitored. (See Grand Canyon Monitoring and Research Center for progress reports and analysis at http:// www.gcmrc.gov/.) Record low river discharge and low reservoir levels are testing the entire Colorado River basin in this period of sustained drought.

But as it courses through the deserts of Sudan and Egypt, it loses water instead of gaining it, because of evaporation and withdrawal for agriculture. By the time it empties into the Mediterranean Sea, the Nile's flow has dwindled so much that it ranks only 36th in discharge.

In the United States, the Colorado River is notable as an exotic stream. Its flow decreases with distance from its source; in fact, the river no longer produces enough discharge to reach its mouth in the Gulf of California! The exotic Colorado River is depleted not only by passage

(a)

(b)

FIGURE 14.12 Stream velocity and discharge increase together. (a) A low-volume, low-velocity (but turbulent) mountain stream, the Athabasca River in Jasper National Park. (b) High-discharge, high-velocity (but laminar, smooth water flow) portion of the Bow River in Banff National Park. [Photos by Robert Christopherson.]

across dry, desert lands but also by upstream removal of water for agriculture and municipal uses—see Focus Study 15.1 for a satellite image of the river's former mouth.

Stream Erosion

A stream's erosional turbulence and abrasion carve and shape the landscape through which it flows. **Hydraulic action** is the work of flowing water alone. Running water causes hydraulic squeeze-and-release action that loosens and lifts rocks. As this debris moves along, it mechanically erodes the streambed further, through the process of **abrasion**, with rock particles grinding and carving the streambed like liquid sandpaper.

The upstream tributaries in a drainage basin usually have small and irregular discharges, and most of the stream's energy is expended in turbulent eddies. As a result, hydraulic action in these upstream sections is at a maximum, whereas the coarse-textured load of such a stream is small. The downstream portions of a river, however, move much larger volumes of water past a given point and carry larger suspended loads of sediment (Figure 14.12). Stream velocity determines rates of erosion and deposition. Sediment particles are deposited onto the streambed at slower velocities, whereas they are eroded at higher velocities.

Stream Transport

You may have watched a river or creek after a rainfall, the water coloured brown by the high sediment load being transported. The amount of material available to a stream depends on topographic relief, the nature of rock and soil

through which the stream flows, climate, vegetation, and human activity in a drainage basin. *Competence*, which is a stream's ability to move particles of a specific size, is a function of stream velocity and the available energy to suspend materials. *Capacity* is the total possible load that a stream can transport. Four processes transport eroded materials: solution, suspension, saltation, and traction; each is shown in action in Figure 14.13.

Solution refers to the **dissolved load** of a stream. The chemical solution is derived from minerals such as limestone or dolomite or from soluble salts. The main contributor of material in solution is chemical weathering. Sometimes the undesirable salt content that hinders human use of some rivers comes from dissolved rock formations and from springs in the stream channel; as an example, the San Juan and Little Colorado rivers that flow into the Colorado River near the Utah–Arizona border add dissolved salts to the system.

The **suspended load** consists of fine-grained, clastic particles (bits and pieces of rock). They are held aloft in the stream, with the finest particles not deposited until the stream velocity slows nearly to zero. Turbulence in the water, with random upward motion, is an important mechanical factor in holding a load of sediment in suspension.

Bed load refers to coarser materials that are dragged, rolled, or pushed along the streambed by **traction** or by **saltation**, where particles bounce along in short hops and jumps (from the Latin *saltim*, which means "by leaps or jumps"). Particles transported by saltation are too large to remain in suspension but are not limited to the sliding and rolling motion of traction. These processes relate

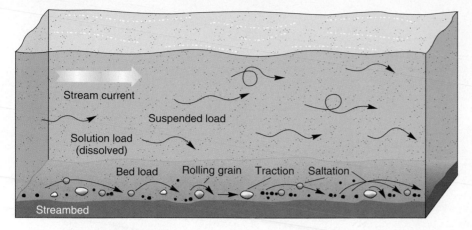

FIGURE 14.13 Fluvial transport. Fluvial transportation of eroded materials through suspension, solution, saltation, and traction.

directly to a stream's velocity and its ability to retain particles in suspension. With increased kinetic energy, parts of the bed load are rafted upward and become suspended load.

The early explorers who visited the Grand Canyon reported in their journals that they were kept awake at night by the thundering sound of the river and rapids. Imagine the tremendous quantity of material being moved along by the natural Colorado River before any dams were built. Dams and reservoirs now trap sediments that formerly contributed to the river's bed load.

If the load (bed and suspended) exceeds a stream's capacity, sediments accumulate as **aggradation** (the opposite of degradation) and the stream channel builds up through deposition. With excess sediment, a stream becomes a maze of interconnected channels that form a **braided stream** pattern (Figure 14.14). Braiding often

occurs when reduced discharge lowers a stream's transporting ability, such as after flooding, or when a landslide occurs upstream, or from increased load where weak banks of sand or gravel exist. Locally, braiding also may result from a new sediment load from glacial meltwaters, as in Alberta's Sunwapta River. Glacial materials also exceed stream capacity in the 15-km (9.3-mi) stretch of the Brahmaputra River about 35 km (22 mi) south of Lhasa, Tibet (Figure 14.14b).

Flow and Channel Characteristics

Flow characteristics of a stream are best seen in a cross-sectional view. The greatest velocities in a stream are near the surface at centre channel (Figure 14.15), corresponding to the deepest part of the stream channel. Velocities decrease closer to the sides and bottom of the

(a)

(b)

FIGURE 14.14 Braided streams.
(a) Sunwapta River, along the Icefields Parkway, southern Jasper National Park, Alberta. (b) A 15-km stretch along the braided Brahmaputra River channel some 35 km (22 mi) south of Lhasa, Tibet, in a narrow valley south of the Tibetan Plateau. These streams reflect excessive sediment load associated with glacial meltwaters filled with fine sediments, or "glacial flour." [Photos by (a) Earth Sciences Sector, Natural Resources Canada GSC 2002-597; (b) October 13, 2001, International Space Station astronaut, courtesy of Earth Science and Image Analysis Lab, JSC/NASA.]

FIGURE 14.15 Meandering stream profile.
Aerial view and cross sections of a meandering stream, showing the location of maximum flow velocity (the *thalweg*), point-bar deposits, and areas of undercut bank erosion.

Stream Processes, Floodplains, Oxbow Lake Formation

ANIMATION

channel because of the frictional drag on the water flow. The portion of the stream flowing at maximum velocity moves diagonally across the stream from bend to bend in a meandering stream, and is termed the *thalweg*.

Flow becomes *turbulent* in shallow streams, or where the channel is rough, as in a section of rapids. Small eddies are caused by friction between streamflows and the channel sides and bed. Complex turbulent flows propel sand, pebbles, and even boulders, increasing the suspension, traction, and saltation.

Three types of stream channels are notable: *braided*, *straight*, and *meandering*. Where slope is gradual, stream channels develop a sinuous (snakelike) form, weaving across the landscape. This action produces a **meandering stream**. The term *meander* comes from the ancient Greek Maiandros River in Asia Minor (the present-day Menderes River in Turkey), which had what came to be known as a meandering channel pattern. The tendency to meander is evidence of a river system's struggle to operate with least effort, between self-organizing order (equilibrium) and chaotic disorder in nature.

The outer portion of each meandering curve is subject to the fastest water velocity and therefore the greatest scouring erosive action; it can be the site of a steep bank, the **undercut bank**, or *cutbank* (Figure 14.16). In contrast, the inner portion of a meander experiences the slowest water velocity and thus receives sediment fill, forming a **point bar** deposit. As meanders develop, these scour-and-fill features gradually work at stream banks.

As a result, the landscape near a meandering river bears meander scars of residual deposits from previous river channels (see Figure 14.22). The photograph of the Itkillik River in Alaska, Figure 14.16a, shows both meanders and meander scars.

Meandering streams create a remarkable looping pattern on the landscape, as shown in the four-part sequence in Figure 14.16b. In (1), the stream erodes its outside bank as the curve migrates downstream, forming a neck. In (2), the narrowing neck of land created by the looping meander eventually erodes through and forms a *cutoff* in (3). A cutoff marks an abrupt change in the stream's lateral movements—the stream becomes straighter.

When the former meander becomes isolated from the rest of the river, the resulting **oxbow lake** (4) may gradually fill with organic debris and silt or may again become part of the river when it floods. Changing patterns of flow affect the river over time. How many of these stream features—meanders, oxbow lakes, cutoffs—can you spot in the aerial photo in Figure 14.17, looking east across northern Argentina? News Report 14.2 looks at the difficulty of using a meandering stream as a political boundary.

Stream Gradient

Every stream runs downhill under the pull of gravity. In the course of this process, each stream develops its own **gradient**, which is the rate of elevation decline from its

(a)

(b)

FIGURE 14.16 Meandering stream development.
(a) Itkillik River in Alaska. (b) Development of a river meander and oxbow lake simplified in four stages.
[(a) U.S. Geological Survey photo.]

headwaters to its mouth. This decline is far from linear; characteristically, the *longitudinal profile* (side view) of a stream features a steeper slope upstream and a gentler slope downstream, forming an uneven concave shape (Figure 14.18). This gradient is concave for complex reasons related to the stream's having just enough energy to transport the sediment load it receives. The longitudinal profile of streams can be expressed mathematically, enabling scientists to categorize and predict stream behaviour.

An important fluvial concept is that of the graded stream, nicely defined by J. H. Mackin, a geomorphologist:

A graded stream is one in which, over a period of years, slope is delicately adjusted to provide, with available discharge and with prevailing channel characteristics, just the velocity required for transportation of the load supplied from the drainage basin.*

*J. H. Mackin, "Concept of the graded river," *Geological Society of America Bulletin* 59 (1948): 463.

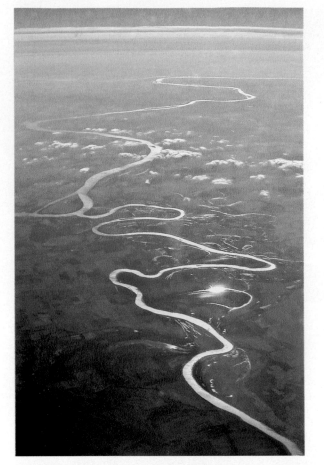

FIGURE 14.17 Meandering stream features.
Meandering streams catch the morning light over northern Argentina. Identify where former meanders were cut off, oxbow lakes, and former stream channels. Several inversion layers are visible in the far distance, as the burning of tropical rain forest to the north fills the air with smoke. [Photo by Bobbé Christopherson.]

In other words, a **graded stream** is one that attains a graded condition; the term does not mean that the stream is at its lowest gradient. Rather, graded represents a present balance, a dynamic equilibrium among erosion, transportation, and deposition over time along a portion of the stream. Both high-gradient and low-gradient streams can achieve a graded condition. The longitudinal profile of a graded stream is its *profile of equilibrium*—a parabolic curve, gently flattening toward the mouth. Stream dynamics can then be compared against this ideal balance.

One problem with applying the graded-stream concept is that an individual stream can have both graded and ungraded portions and may have graded sections without having an overall graded slope. A profile of equilibrium may not be smooth throughout its course and cannot exist for long, for it represents a theoretical perfect balance. With streams, as in all of nature, change is the only constant.

Stream gradient may be affected by tectonic uplift of the landscape, which changes the base level. If tectonic forces slowly lift the landscape, the stream gradient will increase, stimulating renewed erosional activity. A meandering stream flowing through the uplifted landscape becomes *rejuvenated*; that is, the river actively returns to downcutting and can eventually form *entrenched meanders* in the landscape. Figure 14.19 depicts actual rejuvenated landscapes.

Nickpoints When the longitudinal profile of a stream shows an abrupt change in gradient, such as at a waterfall or an area of rapids, the point of interruption is a **nickpoint** (also spelled *knickpoint*). At a nickpoint, the conversion of potential energy in the water at the lip of the falls to concentrated kinetic energy at the base works to eliminate the nickpoint interruption and smooth out the gradient. Figure 14.20a shows a stream with two such interruptions.

Nickpoints can result when a stream flows across a zone of hard, resistant rock or from various tectonic uplift episodes, such as might occur along a fault line. Temporary blockage in a channel, caused by a landslide or a logjam, also could be considered a nickpoint; when the logjam breaks, the stream quickly readjusts its channel to its former grade.

Waterfalls are interesting and beautiful gradient breaks. At the edge of a fall, a stream is free-falling, moving at high velocity under the acceleration of gravity, causing increased abrasion and hydraulic action in the channel below. The increased action generally undercuts the waterfall. Eventually the excavation will cause the rock ledge at the lip of the fall to collapse, and the waterfall will shift a bit farther upstream. The height of the waterfall is gradually reduced as debris accumulates at its base (see Figure 14.21b). Thus, a nickpoint migrates upstream, sometimes for kilometres, until it becomes a series of rapids and is eventually eliminated.

At Niagara Falls on the Ontario–New York border, glaciers advanced over the region and then receded some 13,000 years ago. In doing so, they exposed resistant rock strata that are underlain by less-resistant shales. This tilted

FIGURE 14.18 An ideal longitudinal profile.
Idealized longitudinal profile of a stream, showing its gradient. Upstream segments have a steeper gradient; downstream, the gradient is gentler. The middle and lower portions in the illustration appear graded, or in dynamic equilibrium.

News Report 14.2

Rivers Make Poor Political Boundaries

There are several locations between Canada and the United States where rivers are used as the divide for the international boundary. The International Boundary Commission is responsible for maintaining the boundary between the two countries in a clearly marked fashion. It is also responsible for defining the location of the boundary for any legal situation involving the border. Nowhere is this more difficult than when the boundary is defined as a river. Borders and their demarcations, the boundary, do not change easily. However, rivers are constantly changing their locations and make poor political boundaries. In addition to the idea that the river changes its location through erosion and deposition, the level of the water in the stream affects the determination of the middle of the channel.

An interesting case of river boundaries involves the determination of the St. Croix River as the boundary between Maine in the United States and New Brunswick in Canada (Figure 14.2.1). In 1783 with the Treaty of Paris, the boundaries between the United States and what is now Canada were drawn up. It was agreed that the St. Croix River would be the boundary. However, there were several rivers that could be perceived as this particular stream and another treaty had to be passed to appoint three commissioners to identify the St. Croix River and its source. The boundary was identified in 1798.

The problems of clear identification of the boundary were not yet resolved. Disputes arose over whether the channel margins, channel midline, or some other location was the actual boundary. The St. Croix River was the first to have an identification attached that was based on the function of the

FIGURE 14.2.1 The St. Croix River.
The boundary between New Brunswick and Maine is determined by the function of the St. Croix River.

river. The boundary was determined to be the *thalweg* (zone of maximum flow of the stream) of the river. Recognizing that the thalweg changed over time with erosion and deposition along the riverbank, the commissioners relied on river soundings taken by the United States Coast Guard and the Geodetic Survey to determine the location of the thalweg. The thalweg was then mathematically calculated and plotted on a map. So, although the river was used as the boundary, potential disputes were resolved by measuring the fluvial geomorphology of the time and mapping the location.

The 1909 *Boundary Waters Treaty* established the International Joint Commission (IJC), an independent two-nation organization, to monitor potential border disputes and water issues. Signalling a new era for management of water quality, quantity, and border issues, the IJC adopted a complete watershed model for the St. Croix River in 2000. This ecosystem approach was facilitated by the merger of two important boards—the International St. Croix River Board of Control, established in 1915, and the International Advisory Board on Pollution Control–St. Croix River, in operation since 1962. The two boards had a history of cooperation. This combined effort manages the entire river watershed as a unit with a goal to improve the health of the St. Croix boundary-waters aquatic ecosystem.

formation is a *cuesta*, which is a ridge with a steep slope on one side and beds gently sloping away on the other side (Figure 14.21a). This Niagara escarpment actually stretches across more than 700 km (435 mi) from east of

the falls, northward through Ontario, Canada, the Upper Peninsula of Michigan, curving south through Wisconsin along the western shore of Lake Michigan and the Door Peninsula. As this less-resistant material continues to

(a)

(b)

(c)

FIGURE 14.19 Entrenched meanders.
(a) and (b), the San Juan River near Mexican Hat, Utah, cuts down into the uplifted Colorado Plateau landscape, producing entrenched meanders called the Goosenecks of the San Juan. (c) Entrenched meanders merge in central Montana.
[Photos (a) and (c) by Bobbé Christopherson; (b) by Randall M. Christopherson.]

More resistant strata

Nickpoint

Waterfall

Weaker strata (shale)

Nickpoint slowly migrates upstream

Erosion undercuts more resistant strata

More resistant strata

Weaker strata (shale)

Rapids

Nickpoint

(a)

(b)

FIGURE 14.20 Nickpoints interrupt a stream profile.
(a) Longitudinal stream profile showing nickpoints produced by resistant rock strata. Potential energy is converted into kinetic energy and concentrated at the nickpoint, accelerating erosion, which will eventually eliminate the feature. (b) A nickpoint and dramatic 60 m (197 ft) waterfall interrupts stream gradient on Nigel Creek at Panther Falls, Banff National Park. [Photo by Robert Christopherson.]

FIGURE 14.21 Retreat of Niagara Falls.
(a) Headward retreat of Niagara Falls from the Niagara escarpment. It has taken the falls about 12,000 years to reach this position at a pace of about 1.3 m (4.3 ft) per year. (b) The escarpment seen from below American Falls. (c) Niagara Falls, with the American Falls portion almost completely shut off by upstream controls for engineering inspection. Horseshoe Falls in the background is still flowing over its 57-m (188-ft) plunge. (d) In contrast to (c), American Falls in full discharge. [(a) After W. K. Hamblin, *Earth's Dynamic Systems*, 6th ed. (Upper Saddle River, NJ: Pearson Prentice Hall, Inc. © 1992), Figure 12.15, p. 246. Photos: (c) courtesy of the New York Power Authority; (b) and (d) Bobbé Christopherson.]

NOTEBOOK   Niagara Falls

weather away, the overlying rock strata collapse, allowing Niagara Falls to erode farther upstream toward Lake Erie.

Niagara Falls is a place where natural processes labor to eliminate a nickpoint and reduce this portion of the river to a series of mere rapids. In fact, the falls have retreated more than 11 km (6.8 mi) from the steep face of the Niagara escarpment during the last 12,000 years. A nickpoint is a relatively temporary and mobile feature on the landscape. In the past, engineers have used control facilities upstream to reduce flows over the American Falls at Niagara for inspection of the cliff to assess the progress of natural processes that are working to eliminate the Niagara Falls nickpoint (Figure 14.21c); compare to normal discharge in (d).

Stream Gradient and Landscape Forms   William Morris Davis, a geomorphologist who founded the Association of American Geographers in 1904, introduced evolutionary concepts of erosion that included fluvial processes. Davis incorporated the graded-stream concept into his model, identifying erosion stages in a cyclic model he named *youth*, *maturity*, and *old age*—old age is approached as the floodplain broadens and a low stream gradient produces a wide, meandering flow pattern.

Today, geomorphologists support a *functional model of dynamic equilibrium*. The dynamic equilibrium model emphasizes the effects of individual processes interacting on streams and hillslope systems. Stream form and behaviour result from complex interactions of slope, discharge, and sediment load, all of which are variable within different climates and with different rock types. Landscapes simply do not provide enough clear evidence to support a cyclic model of evolution. Regardless, Davis's work was a breakthrough in understanding landscapes, and many of his terms are still in use.

As suggested by geomorphologists S. A. Schumm and R. W. Lichty, the validity of cyclic or functional landscape models may depend on the *time frame*. Let us consider three time frames: geologic time, graded time, and steady time. Over the long span of *geologic time*, cyclic models of evolutionary development might explain the disappearance of entire mountain ranges through, for example, denudation. At the other extreme of time, *steady time* applies to short-term adjustments ongoing in a drainage basin. *Graded time* is between the two time frames, and within it lies the realm of dynamic equilibrium conditions.

Stream Deposition and Landforms

After weathering, mass movement, erosion, and transportation, deposition is the next logical event in the sequence. In *deposition*, a stream deposits alluvium, or unconsolidated sediments, thereby creating depositional landforms, such as floodplains, terraces, or deltas.

Applied Physical Geography (continued)

Table 1 Peak Discharges 1970–1999

Year	Peak Discharge m³/s	Year	Peak Discharge m³/s	Year	Peak Discharge m³/s
1970	113	1980	227	1990	113
1971	71	1981	2407	1991	241
1972	170	1982	411	1992	113
1973	212	1983	198	1993	311
1974	85	1984	255	1994	184
1975	42	1985	311	1995	198
1976	297	1986	113	1996	991
1977	57	1987	595	1997	71
1978	1770	1988	212	1998	28
1979	57	1989	227	1999	283

Summary and Review—River Systems and Landforms

■ *Define* the term fluvial, and *explain* processes of fluvial erosion, transportation, and deposition.

River systems, fluvial processes and landscapes, floodplains, and river control strategies are important to human populations as demands for limited water resources increase. **Hydrology** is the science of water, its global circulation, distribution, and properties, specifically water at and below Earth's surface. Stream-related processes are **fluvial**. Water dislodges, dissolves, or removes surface material in the **erosion** process. Streams produce *fluvial erosion*, in which weathered sediment is picked up for **transport**, movement to new locations. Sediments are laid down by another process, **deposition**. **Alluvium** is the general term for the clay, silt, sand, gravel, or other unconsolidated rock and mineral fragments deposited by running water as sorted or semisorted sediment on a floodplain, delta, or streambed.

Base level is the lowest elevation limit of stream erosion in a region. A *local base level* occurs when something interrupts the stream's ability to achieve base level, such as is created by a dam or a landslide that blocks a stream channel.

hydrology (p. 448)
fluvial (p. 448)
erosion (p. 448)
transport (p. 448)
deposition (p. 448)
alluvium (p. 448)
base level (p. 449)

1. What role is played by rivers in the hydrologic cycle?

2. What are the five largest rivers on Earth in terms of discharge? Relate these to the weather patterns in each area and to regional potential evapotranspiration (POTET) and precipitation (PRECIP)—concepts in Chapter 9.

3. Define the term *fluvial*. What is a fluvial process?

4. What is the sequence of events that takes place as a stream dislodges material?

5. Explain the base-level concept. What happens to a local base level when a reservoir is constructed?

■ *Construct* a basic drainage basin model, and *identify* different types of drainage patterns and internal drainage, with examples.

The basic fluvial system is a **drainage basin**, which is an open system. *Drainage divides* define the drainage-basin catchment (water-receiving) area of the drainage basin. In any drainage basin, water initially moves downslope in a thin film called **sheetflow**, or *overland flow*. This surface runoff concentrates in *rills*, or small-scale downhill grooves, which may develop into deeper *gullies* and a stream course in a valley. High ground that separates one valley from another and directs sheetflow is an *interfluve*. Extensive mountain and highland regions act as **continental divides** that separate major drainage basins. Some regions, such as the Great Salt Lake Basin, have **internal drainage** that does not reach the ocean, the only outlets being evaporation and subsurface gravitational flow.

Drainage density is determined by the number and length of channels in a given area and is an expression of a landscape's topographic surface appearance. **Drainage pattern** refers to the arrangement of channels in an area as determined by the steepness, variable rock resistance, variable climate, hydrology, relief of the land, and structural controls imposed by the landscape. Seven basic drainage patterns are generally found in nature: dendritic, trellis, radial, parallel, rectangular, annular, and deranged.

drainage basin (p. 450)
watershed (p. 450)
sheetflow (p. 450)
continental divides (p. 450)

internal drainage (p. 453)
drainage density (p. 453)
drainage pattern (p. 453)

6. What is the spatial geomorphic unit of an individual river system? How is it determined on the landscape? Define the several relevant key terms used.

7. In Figure 14.5, follow the Allegheny–Ohio–Mississippi river systems to the Gulf of Mexico. Analyze the pattern of tributaries, and describe the channel. What role do continental divides play in this drainage?

8. Describe drainage patterns. Define the various patterns that commonly appear in nature. What drainage patterns exist in your hometown? Where you attend school?

■ **Describe** the relation among velocity, depth, width, and discharge, and *explain* the various ways that a stream erodes and transports its load.

Stream channels vary in *width* and *depth*. The streams that flow in them vary in velocity and in the *sediment load* they carry. All of these factors may increase with increasing discharge. **Discharge**, a stream's volume of flow per unit of time, is calculated by multiplying the velocity of the stream by its width and depth for a specific cross section of the channel. Most streams increase discharge downstream. But some streams originate in a humid region and flow through an arid region, such that discharge decreases with distance. Such an **exotic stream** is exemplified by the Nile River or the Colorado River.

Hydraulic action is the work of *turbulence* in the water. Running water causes hydraulic squeeze-and-release action to loosen and lift rocks and sediment. As this debris moves along, it mechanically erodes the streambed further, through a process of **abrasion**.

Solution refers to the **dissolved load** of a stream, especially the chemical solution derived from minerals such as limestone or dolomite or from soluble salts. The **suspended load** consists of fine-grained, clastic particles held aloft in the stream, with the finest particles not deposited until the stream velocity slows nearly to zero. **Bed load** refers to coarser materials that are dragged and pushed and rolled along the streambed by **traction** or that bounce and hop along by **saltation**. If the load in a stream exceeds its capacity, sediments accumulate as **aggradation** as the stream channel builds through deposition. With excess sediment, a stream becomes a maze of interconnected channels that form a **braided stream** pattern.

discharge (p. 455)
exotic stream (p. 456)
hydraulic action (p. 458)
abrasion (p. 458)
dissolved load (p. 458)
suspended load (p. 458)
bed load (p. 458)
traction (p. 458)
saltation (p. 458)
aggradation (p. 459)
braided stream (p. 459)

9. What was the impact of flood discharge on the channel of the San Juan River near Bluff, Utah? Why did these changes take place?

10. How does stream discharge do its erosive work? What are the processes at work in the channel?

11. Differentiate between stream competence and stream capacity.

12. How does a stream transport its sediment load? What processes are at work?

■ **Develop** a model of a meandering stream, including point bar, undercut bank, and cutoff, and *explain* the role of stream gradient in these flow characteristics.

Where the slope is gradual, stream channels develop a sinuous form called a **meandering stream**. The outer portion of each meandering curve is subject to the fastest water velocity and can be the site of a steep **undercut bank**. On the other hand, the inner portion of a meander experiences the slowest water velocity and forms a **point-bar** deposit. When a meander neck is cut off as two undercut banks merge, the meander becomes isolated and forms an **oxbow lake**.

Every stream develops its own **gradient** and establishes a longitudinal profile. A portion of the stream is designated a **graded stream** when that stream portion is balanced among available discharge, channel characteristics, its velocity, and the load supplied from the drainage basin. An interruption in a stream's longitudinal profile is called a **nickpoint**. A nickpoint can occur as the stream flows across hard, resistant rock or after tectonic uplift episodes.

meandering stream (p. 460)
undercut bank (p. 460)
point bar (p. 460)
oxbow lake (p. 460)
gradient (p. 460)
graded stream (p. 462)
nickpoint (p. 462)

13. Describe the flow characteristics of a meandering stream. What is the pattern of flow in the channel? What are the erosional and depositional features and the typical landforms created?

14. Explain these statements: (a) All streams have a gradient, but not all streams are graded. (b) Graded streams may have ungraded segments.

15. Why is Niagara Falls an example of a nickpoint? Without human intervention, what do you think will eventually take place at Niagara Falls?

16. What is meant by "the validity of cyclic or equilibrium models depends on which of three time frames is being considered"? Explain and discuss.

■ **Define** a floodplain, and *analyze* the behaviour of a stream channel during a flood.

Floodplains have been an important site of human activity throughout history. Rich soils, bathed in fresh nutrients by floodwaters, attract agricultural activity and urbanization. Despite our historical knowledge of devastation by floods, floodplains are settled, raising issues of human perception of hazard. The flat low-lying area along a stream channel that is subjected to recurrent flooding is a **floodplain**. It is formed when the river overflows its channel during times of high flow. On either bank of some streams, **natural levees** develop as by-products of flooding. On the floodplain, backswamps and yazoo tributaries may develop. The natural levees and elevated channel of the river prevent a **yazoo tributary** from joining the main channel, so it flows parallel to the river and through the **backswamp** area.

Entrenchment of a river into its own floodplain **forms alluvial terraces**.

> floodplain (p. 466)
> natural levees (p. 466)
> yazoo tributary (p. 466)
> backswamp (p. 466)
> alluvial terraces (p. 468)

17. Describe the formation of a floodplain. How are natural levees, oxbow lakes, backswamps, and yazoo tributaries produced?

18. Identify any of the features listed in Question 17 on the Philipp, Mississippi, topographic quadrangle in Figure 14.23d.

19. Describe any floodplains near where you live or where you go to college. Have you seen any of the floodplain features discussed in this chapter? If so, which ones?

■ *Differentiate* the several types of river deltas, and *describe* each.

A depositional plain formed at the mouth of a river is called a **delta**. When the mouth of a river enters the sea and is inundated by seawater in a mix with freshwater, it is called an **estuary**.

> delta (p. 471)
> estuary (p. 471)

20. What is a river delta? What are the various deltaic forms? Give some examples.

21. How might New Orleans change later in this century, especially following Katrina levee breaks and with rising sea level?

22. Describe the Ganges River delta. What factors upstream explain its form and pattern? Assess the consequences of settlement on this delta.

23. What is meant by the statement "the Nile River delta is disappearing"?

■ *Explain* flood probability estimates, and *review* strategies for mitigating flood hazards.

A **flood** occurs when high water overflows the natural riverbank along any portion of a stream. Both floods and the floodplains they occupy are rated statistically for the expected time interval between floods. A 10-year flood is the greatest level of flooding that is likely once every 10 years. A graph of stream discharge over time for a specific place is called a **hydrograph**.

Collective efforts by government agencies undertake to reduce flood probability. Such management attempts include the construction of artificial levees, bypasses, straightened channels, diversions, dams, and reservoirs. Society is still learning how to live in a sustainable way with Earth's dynamic river systems.

> flood (p. 476)
> hydrograph (p. 481)

24. Specifically, what is a flood? How are such flows measured and tracked?

25. How important was the Red River flood of 1997 with respect to the record of flooding on the Canadian prairies? Speculate on what you think are the "lessons learned" by the public from such an event.

26. Differentiate between a hydrograph from a natural terrain and one from an urbanized area.

27. What do you see as the major consideration regarding floodplain management? How would you describe the general attitude of society toward natural hazards and disasters?

28. What do you think the author of the article "Settlement Control Beats Flood Control" meant by the title? Explain your answer, using information presented in the chapter.

Critical Thinking

A. Determine the name of the drainage basin within which your campus is located. Where are its headwaters? Where is the river's mouth? If you are in Canada or the United States, use Figure 14.5 to locate the larger drainage basins and divides for your region. Is there any regulatory organization that oversees planning and coordination for the drainage basin you identified?

B. Relative to the drainage basin you determined in (A), see if there is a topographic map on file in the library, geography department, or at a local outdoor recreation store that covers the portion of the basin near campus. After examining the map, can you discern a prominent drainage pattern for the area (Figure 14.9)?

C. Using your search engine or browser on the Internet, type in "New Orleans flooding, 2005," or "Gulf Coast damage, Katrina," or "New Orleans levee failures." Allow some time to sample through at least 10 of the links. Describe what you found. Did you find photo galleries, engineering reports, news coverage? What is your opinion about this region of the lower Mississippi River, New Orleans, and the Gulf Coast cities and the direction they should take at this point in history: Rebuild things as they were; rethink the hazards and adopt a new strategy of replacing urban with low-density recreation zones; establish possible set-back hazard zoning; walk away except for necessary port functions; continue pumping oil and gas and order corporations to repressurize the fields to raise ground levels; or abandon the region? Are there other options you think arc important? Remember, as you think this through, sea level is still rising at an unprecedented rate.

Ancient sand dunes in the late Jurassic Period (150 m.y.a.) lithified, forming this colourful sandstone. Weathering and some wind processes continue to sculpt these rock surfaces in myriad textures. The sand and rock debris was left by flash flood waters. Earth's arid lands stand in stark contrast on the water planet. [Photo by Bobbé Christopherson.]

CHAPTER 15

Eolian Processes and Arid Landscapes

■ Key Learning Concepts

After reading the chapter, you should be able to:

- ■ **Characterize** the unique work accomplished by wind and eolian processes.

- ■ **Describe** eolian erosion, including deflation, abrasion, and the resultant landforms.

- ■ **Describe** eolian transportation, and **explain** saltation and surface creep.

- ■ **Identify** the major classes of sand dunes, and **present** examples within each class.

- ■ **Define** loess deposits and their origins, locations, and landforms.

- ■ **Portray** desert landscapes, and **locate** these regions on a world map.

W ind is an agent of geomorphic change. Like moving water, moving air causes erosion, transportation, and deposition of materials; moving air is a fluid and it behaves similarly, although it has a lower viscosity (it is less dense) than water. Although lacking the lifting ability of water, wind processes can modify and move quantities of materials in deserts, along coastlines, and elsewhere.

Wind processes modify rocks and move sediment in deserts and along coastlines in a variety of climates. Wind may contribute to soil formation in places far distant from the point of origin by bringing fine material from regions where glaciers deposited it. Elsewhere, fallow fields give up their soil resource to wind erosion. Scientists are only now getting an accurate picture of the amount of windblown dust that fills the atmosphere and crosses the oceans between continents. Chemical fingerprints and satellites are used to trace windblown dust from African soils to North and South America and from Asian landscapes to Europe. Winds even spread living organisms. One study found related mosses, liverworts, and lichens distributed thousands of kilometres between islands in the Southern Ocean.

Earth's dry lands stand out in stark contrast on the water planet. Arid landscapes display unique landforms and life forms: "Instead of finding chaos and disorder the observer never fails to be amazed at a simplicity of form, an exactitude of repetition and a geometric order in the desert."* Although perpetually cold, the polar regions are deserts as well receiving little precipitation, so there should be no surprise that Yuma, Arizona, and weather stations in Antarctica receive the same amount of annual precipitation.

In this chapter: We examine the work of wind, associated erosion, transport, and depositional processes, and resulting landforms. Windblown fine particles form vast loess deposits, the basis for rich agricultural soils. We include the discussion of arid lands in this chapter. Most deserts are rocky and covered with desert pavement, whereas other dry landscapes are covered in sand dunes. In desert environments, landscapes lacking moisture and stabilizing vegetation are set off in sharp, sun-baked relief. Water is the major erosional agent in the desert, yet water is the limiting resource for human development. We examine the causes and distribution of Earth's desert landscapes. The troubled Colorado River and the western drought are the subject of an important focus study.

The Work of Wind

The work of the wind—erosion, transportation, and deposition—is called **eolian** (also spelled *aeolian*). The word comes from Aeolus, ruler of the winds in Greek mythology. British Army major Ralph Bagnold, while stationed in Egypt in 1925, accomplished much eolian research. In the deserts west of the Nile, Bagnold measured, sketched, and developed hypotheses about the wind and desert forms. Imagine the scene in the 1920s: A Model-T Ford chugs across the desert west of Cairo taking Bagnold to his research area. He laid rolls of chicken wire over treacherous stretches of sand to prevent getting stuck. Bagnold's often-cited work, *The Physics of Blown Sand and Desert Dunes*, was published in 1941.

The ability of wind to move materials is actually small compared with that of other transporting agents such as water and ice, because air is so much less dense than those other media. Yet, over time, wind accomplishes enormous work. Bagnold studied the ability of wind to transport sand over the surface of a dune. Figure 15.1 shows that a steady wind of 50 kmph (30 mph) can move approximately one-half ton of sand per day over a metre cross section of dune.

*R. A. Bagnold, *The Physics of Blown Sand and Desert Dunes* (London: Methuen, 1941).

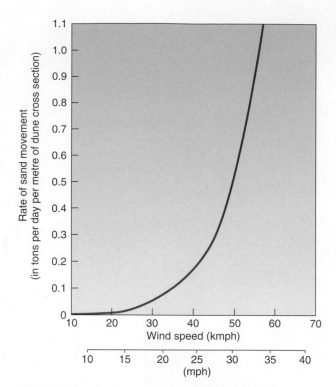

FIGURE 15.1 Sand movement and wind velocity. Sand movement relative to wind velocity, as measured over a square metre cross section of ground surface.
[After R. A. Bagnold, *The Physics of Blown Sand and Desert Dunes* (London: Methuen, 1941). Adapted by permission.]

The graph also demonstrates how rapidly the amount of transported sand increases with wind speed.

Grain size is important in wind erosion. Intermediate-sized grains move most easily—they bounce along. It is the largest and the smallest sand particles that require the strongest winds to move. The large particles are heavier and thus require stronger winds. Small particles are difficult to move because they exhibit a mutual cohesiveness and because they usually present a smooth surface (aerodynamic) to the wind. Yet, the finest dust, once aloft, can be carried from continent to continent (Figure 15.2). In addition, wind can prune and shape vegetation, especially where winds are strong in a consistent direction.

Eolian Erosion

Two principal wind-erosion processes are **deflation**, the removal and lifting of individual loose particles, and **abrasion**, the grinding of rock surfaces with a "sandblasting" action by particles captured in the air. Deflation and abrasion produce a variety of distinctive landforms and landscapes.

Deflation Deflation literally blows away loose or noncohesive sediment and works with rainwater to form a surface resembling a cobblestone street: a **desert pavement** that protects underlying sediment from further deflation and water erosion. Traditionally, deflation was regarded as a key formative process, eroding fine dust, clay, and sand away, leaving behind a concentration of pebbles and gravel as desert pavement (Figure 15.3a).

FIGURE 15.2 The work of the wind.
Streaks of windblown sands cover bedrock south of Atar, in central Mauritania. Note the circular Richat dome structure, just east of the Western Sahara political border corner (refer to Figure 12.10c). [*Terra* image courtesy of NASA Earth Observatory.]

(a) Deflation hypothesis

(b) Sediment-accumulation hypothesis

(c)

FIGURE 15.3 Desert pavement.
(a) Desert pavement may be formed when larger rocks and fragments are left after deflation and sheetwash remove finer dust, silt, and clays. (b) Other desert pavements seem to be formed by wind delivering fine particles that settle and wash downward; through cycles of swelling and shrinking, the gravels gradually migrate upward to form pavement. (c) A typical desert pavement. [Photo by Bobbé Christopherson.]

Another hypothesis that better explains some desert pavement surfaces states that deposition of windblown sediments is the formative agent, not removal. Windblown particles settle between and below coarse rocks and pebbles that are gradually displaced upwards. Rainwater is involved as wetting and drying episodes swell and shrink clay-sized particles. The gravel fragments are gradually lifted to surface positions to form the pavement (Figure 15.3b).

Desert pavements are so common that many provincial names are used for them—for example, *gibber plain* in Australia; *gobi* in China; and in Africa, *lag gravels* or *serir*, or *reg* desert if some fine particles remain. Large depressions in the Sahara Desert are at least partially formed by deflation. The enormous Munkhafad el Qattâra (Qattâra Depression), which covers 18,000 km^2 (6950 mi^2) just inland from the Mediterranean Sea in the Western Desert of Egypt, is now about 130 m (427 ft) below sea level at its lowest point.

Heavy recreational activity damages fragile desert landscapes, especially in the arid lands of the United States, where more than 15 million off-road vehicles (ORVs) are now in use. Such vehicles crush plants and animals; disrupt desert pavement, leading to greater deflation; and create ruts that easily concentrate sheetwash to form gullies.

Military activities can also threaten desert landscapes. A serious environmental impact of both the 1991 Persian Gulf War and ongoing Iraq War is the disruption of desert pavement. Thousands of square kilometres of stable desert pavement were shattered by bombardment of hundreds of thousands of tons of explosives and disrupted by the movement of heavy vehicles. The resulting silt made available for deflation has plagued cities and farms ever since with increased dust and sand accumulations.

Coastal dunes, found along sea and lake shores, are composed of accumulations of sand and are often held in place by dense vegetation. These landscapes are impacted by human activity. Beach goers accessing the waterline disrupt the dunes by trampling vegetation and creating paths that are susceptible to erosion. Shoreline property owners also smooth and flatten the surface of the dunes in order to sculpt a better view of the water. The alteration of the dune profile leads to an erosional instability in the landscape.

Wherever wind encounters loose sediment, deflation may remove enough material to form basins called **blowout depressions**. These depressions range from small indentations less than a metre wide up to areas hundreds of metres wide and many metres deep. Chemical weathering, although slow in the desert owing to the lack of water, is important in the formation of a blowout, for it removes the cementing materials that give particles their cohesiveness. In arid climates chemical weathering is active on the surfaces of particles at the microscopic level, utilizing hygroscopic and capillary water in reactions.

Abrasion   You may have seen work crews sandblasting surfaces on buildings, bridges, or streets to clean them or to remove unwanted markings. Sandblasting uses a stream of compressed air filled with sand grains to quickly abrade a surface. Abrasion by windblown particles is nature's slower version of sandblasting, and it is especially effective at polishing exposed rocks when the abrading particles are hard and angular.

Variables that affect the rate of abrasion include the hardness of surface rocks, wind velocity, and wind constancy. Abrasive action is restricted to the area immediately above the ground, usually no more than a metre or two in height, because sand grains are lifted only a short distance.

Rocks exposed to eolian abrasion appear pitted, fluted (grooved), or polished. They usually are aerodynamically shaped in a specific direction, according to the consistent flow of airborne particles carried by prevailing winds. Rocks that have such evidence of eolian erosion are **ventifacts** (literally, "artifacts of the wind").

On a larger scale, deflation and abrasion are capable of streamlining rock structures that are aligned parallel to the most effective wind direction, leaving behind distinctive, elongated ridges or formations called **yardangs**. These wind-sculpted features can range from metres to kilometres in length and up to many metres in height.

On Earth, some yardangs are large enough to be detected on satellite imagery. The Ica Valley of southern Peru contains yardangs reaching 100 m (330 ft) in height and several kilometres in length, and yardangs in the Lūt Desert of Iran attain 150 m (490 ft) in height. Abrasion is concentrated on the windward end of each yardang, with deflation operating on the leeward portions (Figure 15.4).

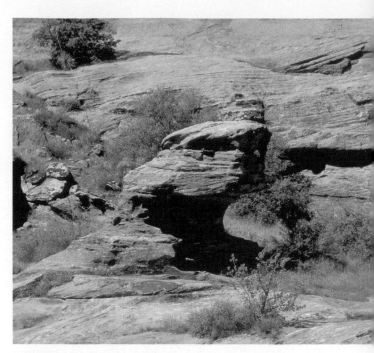

FIGURE 15.4 A yardang.
A small wind-sculpted rock formation located in Snow Canyon outside St. George, Utah. [Photo by Bobbé Christopherson.]

Eolian Transportation

Atmospheric circulation can transport fine material, such as volcanic debris, fire soot and smoke, and dust, worldwide within days. Wind exerts a drag, or frictional pull, on surface particles until they become airborne, just as water in a stream picks up sediment (again, think of air as a fluid). The distance that wind is capable of transporting particles in suspension varies greatly with particle size. Only the finest dust particles travel significant distances, so the finer material suspended in a dust storm is lifted much higher than the coarser particles of a sandstorm.

People living in areas of frequent dust storms are faced with infiltration of very fine particles into their homes and businesses through even the smallest cracks. Figure 3.8 illustrates such dust storms in the Nevada desert, a dust plume from orbit, and alkali dust near Mono Lake, California. People living in desert regions and along sandy beaches, where frequent sandstorms occur, contend with the sandblasting of painted surfaces and etched window glass.

Both human and natural sand erosion and transport from a beach are slowed by conservation measures such as the introduction of stabilizing native plants, the use of fences, and the restriction of pedestrian traffic to walkways (Figure 15.5). As human settlement encroaches on coastal dunes, sand transport becomes problematic. Sediment entrained by wind on the beaches and dunes is carried landward and can bury roads, residential landscaping, and even houses.

The term *saltation* was used in Chapter 14 to describe movement of particles by water. The term also describes the wind transport of grains, usually larger than 0.2 mm (0.008 in.), along the ground. About 80% of wind transport of particles is accomplished by this skipping and bouncing action (Figure 15.6). Compared with fluvial

(a)

(b)

FIGURE 15.5 Preventing sand transport.
(a) Pinery Provincial Park, Ontario. Further erosion and transport of coastal dunes can be controlled by stabilizing strategies, planting native plants, and confining pedestrian traffic to walkways. (b) Tufts of grass are planted to stabilize sand with a fence installed to prevent human foot traffic.
[Photos by (a) Mary-Louise Byrne; (b) Bobbé Christopherson.]

transport, in which saltation is accomplished by hydraulic lift, eolian saltation is executed by aerodynamic lift, elastic bounce, and impact (compare Figure 15.6a with Figure 14.13).

On impact, grains hit other grains and knock them into the air. Saltating particles crash into other particles, knocking them both loose and forward. This type of movement is **surface creep**, which slides and rolls particles too large for saltation and affects about 20% of the material being transported. Once in motion, particles continue to be transported by lower wind velocities. In a desert or along a beach, sometimes you can hear a slight hissing sound, almost like steam escaping, produced by the myriad saltating grains of sand as they bounce along and collide with surface particles.

Through processes of weathering, erosion, and transportation, mineral grains are removed from parent rock and redistributed elsewhere. Wind action is not that sig-

nificant in the weathering process that frees individual grains of sand from the parent rock, but it is active in relocating the weathered grains.

Eolian Depositional Landforms

The smallest features shaped by individual saltating grains are ripples (Figure 15.7). Ripples form in crests and troughs, positioned transversely (at a right angle) to the direction of the wind. Their formation with each windblown bounce is influenced by the length of time saltating particles are airborne. Eolian ripples are similar to fluvial ripples, although the impact of saltating grains is slight in water.

Many people have never been in a desert; they know this arid landscape only from the movies, which leave the impression that most deserts are covered by sand. Instead, desert pavements predominate across most subtropical arid landscapes; only about 10% of desert areas are covered with sand. Sand grains generally are deposited as transient ridges or hills called dunes.

A **dune** is a wind-sculpted accumulation of sand. An extensive area of dunes, such as that found in North Africa, is characteristic of an **erg desert**, or **sand sea**. The Grand Erg Oriental in the central Sahara exceeds 1200 m (4000 ft) in depth and covers 192,000 km^2 (75,000 mi^2), about 2.5 times the size of New Brunswick. This sand sea has been active for more than 1.3 million years and has average dune heights of 120 m (400 ft). The Sahara Marzūq sand sea shown in Figure 15.8a is wider than 300 km (185 mi). On the Martian surface, eolian processes are at work forming similar parallel ridges along the floor of Melas Chasma in Figure 15.8b. Similar sand seas, such as the Grand Ar Rub'al Khālī Erg, are active in Saudi Arabia.

Many types of dunes in arid regions or along coastlines tend to migrate in the direction of strong prevailing winds. Strong seasonal winds or winds from a passing storm may sometimes prove more effective than average prevailing winds. When saltating sand grains encounter small patches of sand, their kinetic energy (motion) is dissipated and they start to accumulate; a dune is born. As height increases above 30 cm (12 in.), a steeply sloping slipface on the lee side of the dune and characteristic dune features form.

By studying the dune model in Figure 15.9 you can see that winds characteristically create a gently sloping *windward side* (stoss side), with a more steeply sloped **slipface** on the *leeward side*. A dune usually is asymmetrical in one or more directions. The angle of a slipface is the steepest angle at which loose material is stable—its *angle of repose*. Thus, the constant flow of new material makes a slipface a type of *avalanche slope*. Sand builds up as it moves over the crest of the dune to the brink; then it avalanches, falling and cascading as the slipface continually adjusts, seeking its angle of repose (usually 30° to 34°). In this way, a dune migrates downwind, as suggested by the successive dune profiles in Figure 15.9.

Dunes have many wind-shaped styles that make classification difficult. We simplify dune forms into three

(text continued on page 494)

(a)

(b)

(c)

(d)

FIGURE 15.6 How the wind moves sand.
(a) Eolian suspension, saltation, and surface creep are mechanisms of sediment transportation. Compare with the saltation and traction that occur in another fluid, water, in Figure 14.13. (b) Sand grains saltating along the surface in the Stovepipe Wells dune field, Death Valley. (c) Sand deposited by eolian processes oversteepens the slope, and failure results in sand flow. (d) Sand deposition buried this abandoned, two-storey life-saving station on Sable Island, Nova Scotia. [Photos by (b) Robert Christopherson; (c) and (d) Mary-Louise Byrne.]

(a)

(b)

FIGURE 15.7 Sand ripples.
(a) Sand ripple patterns later may become lithified into fixed patterns in rock. The area in the photo is about 1 m (3.3 ft) wide. (b) Planed-off ripples reveal the structures created by the migration of ripples on Cavendish Spit, Prince Edward Island. [Photos by (a) Robert Christopherson; (b) Mary-Louise Byrne.]

FIGURE 15.8 A sand sea.
(a) The Sahara Marzūq, an erg desert that dominates southwestern Libya. Effective northwesterly winds shape the pattern and direction of the transverse and barchanoid (series of connected barchans) dunes. This sand sea exceeds 300 km across. (b) A similar pattern of dunes appear on the Martian surface in the southern area of Melas Chasma in Valles Marineris. Note the dust devil in the lower left. The area covered is about 2 km **wide.** [(a) *Terra* image courtesy of MODIS Land Rapid Response Team, NASA/GSFC, November 9, 2001. (b) *Mars Global Surveyor*, Mars Orbiter Camera image courtesy of NASA/JPL/Malin Space Science Systems, July 11, 1999.]

(a)

(b)

Formation of Cross Bedding

ANIMATION

FIGURE 15.9 Dune cross section. Successive slipfaces exhibit a distinctive pattern as the dune migrates in the direction of the effective wind.

Class	Type	Description
Crescentic	Barchan	Crescent-shaped dune with horns pointed downwind. Winds are constant with little directional variability. Limited sand available. Only one slipface. Can be scattered over bare rock or desert pavement or commonly in dune fields.
	Transverse	Asymmetrical ridge, transverse to wind direction (right angle). Only one slipface. Results from relatively ineffective wind and abundant sand supply.
	Parabolic	Role of anchoring vegetation important. Open end faces upwind with U-shaped "blowout" and arms anchored by vegetation. Multiple slipfaces, partially stabilized.
	Barchanoid ridge	A wavy, asymmetrical dune ridge aligned transverse to effective winds. Formed from coalesced barchans; look like connected crescents in rows with open areas between them.

Barchan

Transverse

Parabolic

Barchanoid ridge

FIGURE 15.10 Major dune forms.
Please see table for dune descriptions. Arrows show wind direction. [Adapted from E. D. McKee, *A Study of Global Sand Seas*, USGS Professional Paper 1052 (Washington, DC: U.S. Government Printing Office, 1979).]

classes—*crescentic* (crescent, curved shape), *linear* (straight forms), and massive *star dunes*. Each is summarized in Figure 15.10. The ever-changing form of these eolian deposits is part of their beauty, eloquently described by one author: "I see hills and hollows of sand like rising and falling waves. Now at midmorning, they appear paper white. At dawn they were fog gray. This evening they will be eggshell brown."*

*J. E. Bowers, *Seasons of the Wind* (Flagstaff, AZ: Northland Press, 1985), p. 1.

Star dunes are the mountainous giants of the sandy desert. They form in response to complicated, changing wind patterns and have multiple slipfaces. They are pinwheel-shaped, with several radiating arms rising and joining to form a common central peak. The best examples of star dunes are in the Sahara and the Namib Desert, where they approach 200 m (650 ft) in height (Figure 15.11).

The map in Figure 15.12 shows the correlation of active sand regions with deserts (tropical, continental interior, and coastal). Important is the limited extent of desert

Class	Type	Description
Linear	Longitudinal	Long, slightly sinuous, ridge-shaped dune, aligned parallel with the wind direction; two slipfaces. Average 100 m high and 100 km long, and the "draa" at the extreme in size can reach to 400 m high. Results from strong effective winds varying in one direction.
	Seif	After Arabic word for "sword"; a more sinuous crest and shorter than longitudinal dunes. Rounded toward upwind direction and pointed downwind. (Not illustrated.)
Star dune		The giant of dunes. Pyramidal or star-shaped with three or more sinuous, radiating arms extending outward from a central peak. Slipfaces in multiple directions. Results from effective winds shifting in all directions. Tend to form isolated mounds in high effective winds and connected sinuous arms in low effective winds.
Other	Dome	Circular or elliptical mound with no slipface. Can be modified into barchanoid forms; vegetation can play role in coastal locales.
	Reversing	Asymmetrical ridge form intermediate between star dune and transverse dune. Wind variability can alter shape between forms.

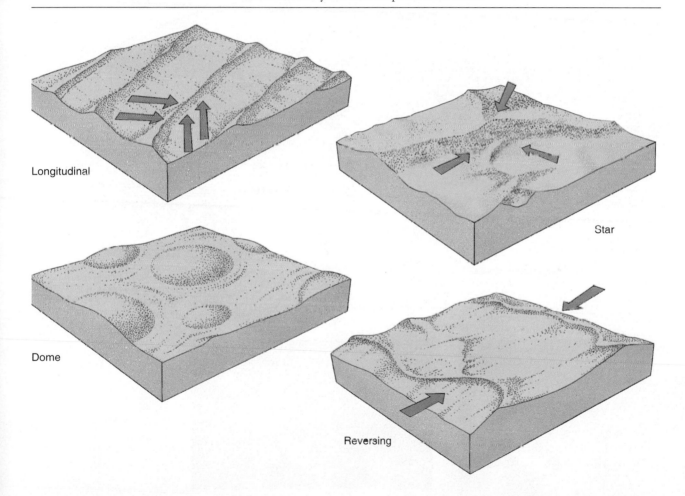

Longitudinal

Star

Dome

Reversing

area covered by active sand dunes—only about 10% of all continental land between 30° N and 30° S. Also noted on the map are dune fields in humid climates outside of this range, such as along coastal Oregon, the shore of Lake Huron (Figure 15.12b), along the Gulf and Atlantic coastlines, in Europe, and elsewhere. The remarkable coastal desert sands of Namibia are pictured in Figure 15.12c.

These same dune-forming principles and terms (for example, *dune* and *slipface*) apply to snow-covered landscapes. *Snow dunes* are formed as wind deposits snow in

drifts. In semiarid farming areas, capturing drifting snow with fences and tall stubble left in fields contributes significantly to soil moisture when the snow melts.

Loess Deposits

Approximately 15,000 years ago, in several episodes, Pleistocene glaciers retreated in many parts of the world, leaving behind large glacial outwash deposits of fine-grained clays and silts. These materials were blown great distances by the wind and redeposited in unstratified,

FIGURE 15.11 Sand mountains of the desert. Star dune in the Namib Desert in southwestern Africa. [Photo by Comstock.]

homogeneous (evenly mixed) deposits. Peasants working along the Rhine River Valley in Germany gave these deposits the name **loess** (pronounced "luss"). No specific landforms were created; instead, loess covered existing landforms with a thick blanket of material that assumed the general topography of the existing landscape.

Because of its own binding strength and its internal coherence, loess weathers and erodes into steep bluffs, or vertical faces. At Xi'an, Shaanxi Province, China, a loess wall was excavated for dwelling space (Figure 15.13a). When a bank is cut into a loess deposit, it generally will stand vertically, although it can fail if saturated (Figure 15.13b).

Significant accumulations throughout the Mississippi and Missouri river valleys form continuous deposits

(a)

MODIFIED GOODE'S HOMOLOSINE EQUAL-AREA PROJECTION

(b)

(c)

FIGURE 15.12 Sandy regions of the world.
(a) Worldwide distribution of active and stable sand regions. (b) Sand dunes along the shore of Lake Huron in Pinery Provincial Park, Ontario. (c) Sandy area in the Namib-Naukluft Park, Namib Desert, Namibia, Africa. (d) Coastal dunes can be large features as exemplified by "The Grand Canyon" at the east lighthouse on Sable Island, Nova Scotia. [(a) After R. E. Snead, *Atlas of World Physical Features*, p. 134, © 1972 by John Wiley & Sons. Adapted by permission of John Wiley & Sons, Inc.; photos by (b) and (d) Mary-Louise Byrne; (c) Nigel J. Dennis/Photo Researchers, Inc.]

(d)

(a)   (b)

FIGURE 15.13 Example of loess deposits.
(a) Loess formation in XI'an, Shaanxi Province, China, has sufficient structural strength to permit excavation for dwelling rooms.
(b) A loess bluff in western Iowa. [Photos by (a) Betty Crowell; (b) Bobbé Christopherson.]

15–30 m (50–100 ft) thick. Loess deposits also occur in eastern Washington State and Idaho. This silt explains the fertility of the soils in these regions, for loess deposits are well drained and deep and have excellent moisture retention. The Loess Hills of western Iowa give evidence of the last ice age, as the finely ground sediments left by the glaciers were windblown to this setting (Figure 15.14). The loess layers in Iowa date from 159,000 to 12,500 years ago.

Loess deposits also cover much of Ukraine, central Europe, China, the Pampas–Patagonia regions of Argentina, and lowland New Zealand. The soils derived from loess help form some of Earth's "breadbasket" farming regions. Figure 15.15 shows the worldwide distribution of loess deposits.

Deflation and wind transport of fine-grained soils produced a catastrophe in the Great Plains of North America

FIGURE 15.14 Loess Hills, western Iowa.
These windblown loess deposits reach heights of about 61 m (200 ft) above the nearby prairie farmlands and Missouri River. The Loess Hills stretch north and south more than 322 km (200 mi).
[Photos by Bobbé Christopherson.]

FIGURE 15.15 Worldwide loess deposits.
Dots represent small, scattered loess formations. [After R. E. Snead, *Atlas of World Physical Features*, p. 138, ©1972 by John Wiley & Sons. Adapted by permission of John Wiley & Sons, Inc.]

in the 1930s, known as the Dust Bowl. Overgrazing and intensive agriculture left soil susceptible to drought and eolian processes. The deflation of many centimetres of soil occurred in the American southwest—southern Nebraska, Kansas, Oklahoma, Texas, and eastern Colorado where there are vast deposits of loess. In the northern Great Plains—Montana and the Dakotas in the United States and the southern prairies of Alberta, Saskatchewan, and southwestern Manitoba—silts and clays were blown out of the disturbed soils.

Fine sediments were lifted by winds to form severe dust storms. The transported sediment darkened the skies of cities and drifted over farmland. The drought that contributed to the Dust Bowl began in 1929, lasted until midsummer in 1937, and affected over 7.3 million hectares of land in Canada alone. In Canada, the Prairie Farm Rehabilitation Administration (PFRA), a branch of Agriculture Canada, was established to combat the out-migration of prairie farmers as the drought caused them to abandon their land. Through soil and water conservation and the development of innovative farming practices, the PFRA assisted farmers through the Dust Bowl of the Dirty Thirties and allowed agriculture to continue in Canada's breadbasket. The PFRA today continues its role in soil and water conservation.

In Europe and North America, loess is thought to be derived mainly from glacial and periglacial sources. The vast deposits of loess in China, covering more than 300,000 km² (116,000 mi²), are derived from windblown desert sediment rather than glacial sources. Accumulations in the Loess Plateau of China exceed 300 m (1000 ft) in thickness, forming complex weathered badlands and some good agricultural land. These windblown deposits are interwoven with much of Chinese history and society.

Overview of Desert Landscapes

Dry climates occupy about 26% of Earth's land surface. If all semiarid climates are considered, perhaps as much as 35% of all land area tends toward dryness, constituting the largest single climatic region on Earth (see Figures 10.4 and 10.5 for the location of these *arid deserts* and *semiarid steppe* climate regions and Figure 20.3 for the distribution of these desert environments).

Deserts occur worldwide as topographic plains, such as the Great Sandy and Simpson Deserts of Australia, the Arabian and Kalahari Deserts of Africa, and portions of the extensive Taklimakan Desert, which covers some 270,000 km² (105,000 mi²) in the central Tarim Basin of China. Deserts also are found in mountainous regions: interior Asia, from Iran to Pakistan, and in China and Mongolia. In South America, the rugged Atacama desert lies between the ocean and the Andes. And Earth's deserts are expanding, as we will discuss shortly. Now, let us look at the link between climate and Earth's deserts.

Desert Climates

The spatial distribution of dry lands is related to three climatological settings:

- subtropical high-pressure cells between 15° and 35°, both N and S latitudes (see Figures 6.10 and 6.12);
- the rain shadow on the lee side of mountain ranges (see Figure 8.9); and,
- areas at great distance from moisture-bearing air masses, such as central Asia.

Figure 15.16 portrays this distribution according to the climate classification used in this text and presents photographs of four major desert regions.

(a) Sonoran

(b) Taklimakan

(c) Atacama

(d) Kalahari

FIGURE 15.16 The world's dry regions.
Worldwide distribution of arid lands (*arid desert* climates) and semiarid lands (*semiarid steppe* climates). (a) Sonoran Desert in the American Southwest. (b) Taklimakan Desert in central Asia. (c) Atacama Desert in subtropical Chile near Baquedano. (d) Kalahari Desert in south-central Africa.
[Photos by (a) Robert Christopherson; (b) Wu Chunzhan/New China Pictures Co./East Photo; (c) Jacques Jangoux/Photo Researchers, Inc.; (d) Nigel J. Dennis/Photo Researchers, Inc.]

Desert areas possess unique landscapes created by the interaction of intermittent precipitation events, weathering processes, and wind. Rugged, hard-edged desert landscapes of cliffs and scarps contrast sharply with the vegetation-covered, rounded, and smoothed slopes characteristic of humid regions.

The daily surface energy balance for El Mirage, California, presented in Figure 4.21a and b, highlights the high sensible heat conditions and intense ground heating in the desert. Such areas receive a high input of insolation through generally clear skies, and they experience high radiative heat losses at night. A typical desert water balance experiences high potential evapotranspiration demand, low precipitation supply, and prolonged summer water deficits (see, for example, Figure 9.11e for Phoenix, Arizona). Fluvial processes in the desert generally are characterized by intermittent running water, with hard, poorly vegetated surfaces of thin, immature soils yielding high runoff during rainstorms (Figure 15.17).

Desert Fluvial Processes

Precipitation events in a desert may be rare indeed, even a year or two apart, but when they do occur, a dry streambed can fill with a torrent called a **flash flood**. These channels may fill in a few minutes and surge briefly during and after a storm. Depending on the region, such a dry streambed is known as a **wash**, an *arroyo* (Spanish), or a *wadi* (Arabic). Signs are usually posted where a desert highway crosses a wash to warn drivers not to proceed if rain is in the vicinity, for a flash flood can suddenly arise and sweep away anything in its path.

When washes fill with surging flash flood waters, a unique set of ecological relationships quickly develops. Crashing rocks and boulders break open seeds that respond to the timely moisture and germinate. Other plants and animals also spring into brief life cycles as the water irrigates their limited habitats.

FIGURE 15.17 Water through a dry land.
The Virgin River is a tributary of the Colorado River, flowing into it at Lake Mead near Mesquite, Nevada. Undependable flows characteristic of an arid-land stream can change from a flash-flood stage or to a sparse trickle. This stream carved the Virgin River Gorge. The riparian vegetation includes willow, cottonwood, and the water-drawing tamarisk, or salt cedar, with mesquite and coyote bush as some of the shrubs visible. [Photo by Bobbé Christopherson.]

At times of intense rainfall, remarkable scenes fill the desert. Figure 15.18 shows two photographs taken just one month apart in a sand dune field in Death Valley, California. A rainfall event produced 2.57 cm (1.01 in.) of precipitation in one day, in a place that receives only 4.6 cm (1.83 in.) in an average year. The stream in the photograph continued to run for hours and then collected in low spots on hard, underlying clay surfaces. The water was quickly consumed by the high evaporation demand so that, in just a month, these short-lived watercourses were dry and covered with accumulations of alluvium.

(a)

(b)

FIGURE 15.18 An improbable river in Death Valley.
The Stovepipe Wells dune field of Death Valley, California, shown (a) the day after a 2.57-cm (1.02-in.) rainfall and (b) one month later (identical location). [Photos by Robert Christopherson.]

The 1985 precipitation event just described was exceeded by one August 15, 2004, when several thunderstorm cells stalled over the mountains along the east side of Death Valley. Rainfall totals reached 6.35 cm (2.5 in.) in little more than an hour. Cars were swept away from the Furnace Creek Inn parking lot, about 4.8 km (3 mi) of Highways 190 and 178 washed out, and there were two fatalities in the Zabriskie Point area. One annex building had a 3-m- (10-ft-) high water mark on it. Again, water is sparse in the deserts, yet it is the major erosional force—sometimes dramatically so. For recent information and maps of Death Valley, see http://www.nps.gov/deva/.

As runoff water evaporates, salt crusts may be left behind on the desert floor in a **playa**. This intermittently wet and dry lowest area of a closed drainage basin is the site of an *ephemeral lake* when water is present. Accompanying our earlier discussion of evaporites, in Chapter 11, Figure 11.12 shows such a playa in Death Valley, covered with salt-crust precipitate over fine clays just one month after the 1985 record rainfall event.

Permanent lakes and continuously flowing rivers are uncommon features in the desert, although the Nile River and the Colorado River are notable exceptions. Both these rivers are *exotic streams*, having their headwaters in a wetter region and the bulk of their course through arid regions. Focus Study 15.1 discusses the Colorado River, the ongoing drought, and the problem of increasing water demands in an arid land.

(text continued on page 505)

Focus Study 15.1

The Colorado River: A System Out of Balance

The headwaters of an exotic stream rise in a region of water surpluses, but the stream flows mostly through arid lands for the rest of its journey to the sea. Exotic streams have few incoming tributaries. Consequently, an exotic stream has a discharge pattern that is different than a typical humid-region stream: Instead of discharge increasing downstream, it decreases (see Chapter 14). The Nile and Colorado rivers are prominent examples.

In the case of the Nile, the East African mountains and plateaux to the south provide a humid source area. The Nile first rises as the remote headwaters of the Kagera River in the eastern portion of the Lake Plateau country of East Africa. On its way to Lake Victoria, it forms the partial boundary of Tanzania, Rwanda, and Uganda. The Nile itself then flows from the lake and continues on its 6650 km (4132 mi) course, with decreasing discharge all the way to its mouth on the Mediterranean Sea near Cairo.

The Colorado River Basin
The river rises in Colorado's Rocky Mountain National Park (Figure 15.1.1a) and flows almost 2317 km (1440 mi) to where a trickle of water disappears in the sand, kilometres short of its former mouth in the Gulf of California.

Orographic precipitation totaling 102 cm (40 in.) per year falls mostly as snow in the Rockies, feeding the Colorado headwaters. But at Yuma, Arizona, near the river's end, annual precipitation is a scant 8.9 cm (3.5 in.), an extremely small amount when compared with the high annual potential evapotranspiration demand in the Yuma region of 140 cm (55 in.).

From its source region, the Colorado River quickly leaves the humid Rockies and spills out into the arid desert of western Colorado and eastern Utah. At Grand Junction, Colorado, near the Utah border, annual precipitation is only 20 cm (8 in.) (Figure 15.1.1b). After carving its way through the intricate labyrinth of canyonlands in Utah, the river enters Lake Powell, behind Glen Canyon Dam (Figure 15.1.1c). The Colorado then flows through the Grand Canyon, formed by the river's own erosive power.

West of the Grand Canyon, the river turns southward, marking its final 644 km (400 mi) as the Arizona–California border. Along this stretch sits Hoover Dam, just east of Las Vegas (Figure 15.1.1d); Davis Dam, built to control the releases from Hoover (Figure 15.1.1e); Parker Dam, for the water needs of Los Angeles; three more dams for irriga-

tion water (Palo Verde, Imperial, and Laguna, Figure 15.1.1f); and finally, Morelos Dam at the Mexican border (Figure 15.1.1g). Mexico owns the end of the river and whatever water is left. Hydrologically exhausted, the river no longer reaches its mouth in the Gulf of California (Figure 15.1.1i).

Figure 15.1.1j shows the annual water discharge and suspended sediment load for the Colorado River at Yuma, Arizona, from 1905 to 1964. The completion of Hoover Dam in the 1930s dramatically reduced suspended sediment. Addition of Glen Canyon Dam upstream from Hoover Dam in 1963 further reduced discharge.

Overall, the drainage basin encompasses 641,025 km² (247,500 km²) of mountain, basin-and-range, plateau, canyon, and desert landscapes in parts of seven states and two countries. A discussion of the Colorado River is included in this chapter because of its crucial part in the history of the Southwest and its role in the future of this drought-plagued arid and semiarid region.

Dividing Up the Colorado's Dammed Water
John Wesley Powell (1834–1902) was the first Euro–American of record to

(continued)

Focus Study 15.1 *(continued)*

(a) Headwaters

(d) Hoover Dam spillways

(e) Davis Dam discharges

(f) Irrigation

(g) Morelos Dam

(b) Near Moab

(c) Glen Canyon Dam

(h) Central Arizona Project

(i)

(j) Sediment interruption

successfully navigate the Colorado River through the Grand Canyon. Powell perceived that the challenge of the West was too great for individual efforts and believed that solutions to problems such as water availability could be met only through private cooperative efforts. His 1878 study (reprinted 1962), *Report of the Lands of the Arid Region of the United States*, is a conservation landmark.

Today, Powell probably would be skeptical of the intervention by government agencies in building large-scale reclamation projects. Lake Powell is named after him. An anecdote in Wallace Stegner's book *Beyond the Hundredth Meridian* tells of an 1893 international irrigation conference held in Los Angeles, where development-minded delegates bragged that the entire West could be conquered and reclaimed from nature and that "rain will certainly follow the plow." Powell spoke against that sentiment: "I tell you, gentlemen, you are piling up a heritage of conflict and litigation over water rights, for there is not sufficient water to supply the land."* He was booed from the hall, but history has shown Powell to be correct.

The Colorado River Compact was signed by six of the seven basin states in 1923. (The seventh, Arizona, signed in 1944, the same year as the Mexican Water Treaty.) With this compact, the Colorado River basin was divided into an upper basin and a lower basin, arbitrarily separated for administrative purposes at Lees Ferry near the Utah–Arizona border (noted on the map in Figure 15.1.1). Congress adopted the Boulder Canyon Act in 1928, authorizing Hoover Dam as the first major reclamation project on

the river. Also authorized was the All-American Canal into the Imperial Valley, which required an additional dam. Los Angeles then began its project to bring Colorado River water 390 km (240 mi) from still another dam and reservoir on the river to the city.

Shortly after Hoover Dam was finished and downstream enterprises were thus offered flood protection, the other projects were quickly completed. There are now eight major dams on the river and many irrigation works. The last effort to redistribute Colorado River water is the Central Arizona Project, which carries water to the Phoenix area (Figure 15.1.1h).

Highly Variable River Flows

The flaw in all this planning and water distribution is that exotic streamflow discharges are highly variable, and the Colorado is no exception. In 1917, the discharge measured at Lees Ferry totalled 24 million acre-feet (maf), whereas in 1934 it was only 5.03 maf, about 80% lower than 1917. In 1977, the discharge dropped again to 5.02 maf, but in 1984 it rose to an all-time high of 24.5 maf. Yet, in contrast, in 2000 to 2006 river discharge fell to exceptionally low levels, with 2002 dropping to a record low of 3.1 maf, and 2003 to 6.4 maf. The 2002 to 2006 water years marked the lowest 5-year average flow in the total record. Please revisit the chapter-opening pair of photos for Chapter 9 showing the comparison of Lake Mead water levels at Hoover Dam in July 1983 and September 2007 as evidence of this variability.

The average flows between 1906 and 1930 were almost 18 maf a year. As a planning basis for the Colorado

River Compact, the government used average river discharges from 1914 up to the Compact signing in 1923, an exceptionally high average of 18.8 maf. That amount was perceived as more than enough for the upper and lower basins, each to receive 7.5 maf, and, later, for Mexico to receive 1.5 maf in the 1944 Mexican Water Treaty.

We might question whether proper long-range planning should rely on the providence of high variability. Tree-ring analyses of past climates have disclosed that the only other time Colorado discharges were at the high 1914–1923 level was between A.D. 1606 and 1625. The dependable flows of the river have been consistently overestimated. This shortfall problem is shown in an estimated budget of 20 million acre-feet for the river (Table 15.1.1): Clearly, the situation is out of balance, for there is not enough discharge to meet budgeted demands.

Presently, the seven states *ideally* want rights that total as high as 25.0 maf. When added to the guarantee for Mexico, this comes up to 26.5 maf of demands. And six states share one common opinion: California's right to the water must be limited to a court-ordered 4.4 maf, which it exceeded every year until California's access to surplus Colorado River water was stopped in 2002. At present, there is no surplus during the ongoing western drought. And U.S. water planners continue to think that Canadian water resources could somehow be brought south.

*W. Stegner, *Beyond the Hundredth Meridian* (Boston: Houghton Mifflin, 1954), 343.

(continued)

FIGURE 15.1.1 The Colorado River drainage basin.
The Colorado River basin, showing division of the upper and lower basins near Lees Ferry in northern Arizona. (a) Headwaters of the Colorado River near Mount Richthofen in the Colorado Rockies. (b) The river near Moab, Utah. (c) Glen Canyon Dam, a regulatory, administrative facility near Lees Ferry, Arizona. (d) Hoover Dam spillways in rare operation during 1983 floods. (e) Davis Dam in full release during flood. (f) Irrigation canal and cropland irrigated with Colorado River water in the Palo Verde district. (g) Morelos Dam at the Mexican border is the final stop as the river dwindles to a mere canal. (h) Central Arizona Project aqueduct west of Phoenix. (i) The Colorado River (far upper left) stops short of its former delta. The bluish-purple water in the former channel is actually an inlet for Gulf of California water; the grey deposits are sediments in mud flats along this inlet. (j) Dam construction affects river discharge and sediment yields. [Photos by (a) Bobbé Christopherson; (b) through (g) Robert Christopherson; (h) Tom Bean/DRK Photo; (i) *Terra* ASTER (thermal emission and reflection) image courtesy of NASA/GSFC/MITI/ERSDAC/JAROS and the U.S./Japan ASTER Science Team, September 8, 2000; and, (j) data from USGS, 1985, *National Water Summary 1984*, Water Supply Paper 2275 (Washington, D.C.: Government Printing Office), p. 55).]

Focus Study 15.1 (continued)

Table 15.1.1 Estimated Colorado River Budget through 2006

Water Demand	Quantity (maf)[a]
Upper Basin (7.5) Lower Basin (7.5)[b]	15.0
Central Arizona Project (rising to 2.8 maf)	1.0
Mexican allotment (1944 Treaty)	1.5
Evaporation from reservoirs	1.5
Bank storage at Lake Powell	0.5
Phreatophytic losses (water-demanding plants)	0.5
Budgeted total demand	**20.0 maf**

Average Flows at Lees Ferry	
1906–1930	17.70 maf
1930–2003 average flow of the river	14.10 maf
1990–2006	11.34 maf
2000	11.06 maf
2001	10.75 maf
2002	3.1 maf
2003	6.4 maf
2004	5.6 maf
2005	8.3 maf
2006	8.4 maf

A water year runs from October 1 to September 30.

[a] 1 million acre-feet = 325,872 gallons; 1.24 million litres; 43,560 ft^3.

[b] In-basin consumptive uses 75% agricultural.

Source: Bureau of Reclamation states and states of Arizona, California, Nevada.

Water Loss at Glen Canyon Dam and Lake Powell

Glen Canyon Dam was completed and began water impoundment, forming Lake Powell, in 1963, 27.4 km (17 mi) north of the upper and lower basin division point at Lees Ferry. The advancing water slowly flooded the deep, fluted, inner gorges of many canyons, including Glen, Navajo, Labyrinth, and Cathedral. Glen Canyon Dam's primary purpose, according to the Bureau of Reclamation, was to regulate flows between the upper and lower basins. An additional benefit is the production of hydroelectric power. Also, there is a recreation and tourism industry around Lake Powell, as previously inaccessible desert scenery now can be reached by boat.

Many thought that Lake Mead, behind Hoover Dam, could have served the primary administrative function of flow regulation, especially considering the serious water-loss problems with the Glen Canyon Dam and the porous rocks that contain its reservoir. Porous Navajo sandstone underlies most of the Lake Powell reservoir. This sandstone absorbs an estimated 0.5 maf of the river's overall annual discharge as bank storage—the higher the lake level, the greater the loss into the sandstone.

Second, Lake Powell is an open body of water in an arid desert, where hot, dry winds accelerate evaporative losses. Another 0.5 maf of the Colorado's overall discharge is lost annually from the reservoir in this manner, equaling about a third of all Colorado River reservoir evaporation losses. Third, now-permanent sand bars and banks have stabilized along the regulated river, allowing water-demanding plants called phreatophytes to establish and extract an additional 0.5 maf of the river flow. Therefore, if Lake Powell ever returns to capacity, some 1.5 maf, or 13.2% of the overall river discharge (1990–2006 average), will be lost from the system budget.

Colorado River Floods–1983

Intense precipitation and heavy snowpack in the Rockies, attributable to the 1982–1983 El Niño (Focus Study 10.1), led to record-high discharge rates on the Colorado, testing the controllability of one of the most regulated rivers in the world. Federal reservoir managers were not prepared for the high discharge, since they had set aside Lake Mead's primary purpose (flood control) in favor of competing water and power interests. What followed was the 1983 human-caused flood on the most engineered river in the world.

The only time the spillways at Hoover Dam ever operated was more than 40 years earlier, when the reservoir capacity was artificially raised for a test; now they were opened to release actual floodwaters (Figure 15.1.1d; Chapter 9 opener). Davis Dam, which regulates releases from Hoover Dam, was within 30 cm (1 ft) of overflow, a real problem for a structure made partially of earth fill (Figure 15.1.1e). In addition, Glen Canyon Dam was over capacity and at risk and was damaged by the volume of discharge tearing through its spillways. The decision to increase releases from Hoover to protect the dam doomed towns and homeowners living on floodplains along the river to the south to floodwaters, especially inundating subdivisions near Needles, California.

The Western Drought and Beyond

The severity of the western drought from 1999 to 2007 surpasses anything in the historical record and is approaching the driest in the record according to tree-ring analyses. Satellites can spot the symptoms of this western drought: reduced snow pack in the Rockies, reduced soil moisture, the drought-stressed conditions of vegetation, the prevalence of wildfires, and lowered reservoir levels.

Since A.D. 1226, nine droughts lasting 10 to 20 years and four lasting more than 20 years occurred. Whether the current drought will be of this duration or be more like the three droughts of the 20th century that ran 4 to 11 years is unknown. However, this is the first drought to occur in the Colorado River system in the presence of a human demand for water that is increasing at such record levels.

Water inflow to Lake Powell is running less than one-third of the 30-year average (1961–1990)—with 2002 at just 25%. System reservoirs are at record lows. The production of hydroelectric power has fallen to a third of capacity from these dams. The system is in an official "drought condition." There is speculation that Glen Canyon Dam might cease operations before the end of the decade because of these low-water conditions, leading some citizen groups to suggest decommissioning, possible removal, and restoration of the canyons to predevelopment status.

The worst appears yet to come. As of 2006, the total system stands at less than 50% of capacity and engineers estimate that it will take 13 normal winters of snowpack in the Rockies and basin-wide precipitation to "reset" the system. This recovery is much slower than previous drought recoveries because of the rapid increase in water demand across the Southwest. Arizona's population doubled between 1990 and 2007, reaching 6.2 million. Las Vegas went from 368,000 in 1985 to 1.8 million by 2007 (490% increase). Present probabilities for the period after 2016 put the chances of surplus discharge occurring in any given year at only 20%. Imagine what the population in the region will be after 2016 if no steps are taken to control growth.

Government stopgap measures include, among others: buying water from farmers to meet contractual obligations for Colorado River water; reopening the desalination plant in Yuma, Arizona, to treat agricultural runoff water for its return to the river to meet international agreements with Mexico; and increasing storage, when possible, in upstream reservoirs in the system where evaporation rates are lower than at Lake Powell.

Conservation (using less water) and efficiency (using water more effectively) are beginning to emerge as ways to reduce the tremendous demand for water. Southern Nevada has launched a campaign to replace lawns with drought-tolerant xeroscaping—desert landscaping. However, limiting or halting further metropolitan construction and population growth in the Colorado River Basin are not part of present strategies to lower demand. Despite the conditions along the river, we still seem to be "supply" focused in our approach and not focusing on "demand." Remember, it is the tremendous increase in the demand for this water that stands in the way of resetting the Colorado River system in the foreseeable future.

We might wonder what John Wesley Powell would think if he were alive today to witness such attempts to control the mighty and variable Colorado. He foretold such a "heritage of conflict and litigation."

In arid climates, a prominent landform is an **alluvial fan**, which occurs at the mouth of a canyon where it exits into a valley. The fan is produced by flowing water that abruptly loses velocity as it leaves the constricted channel of the canyon and therefore drops layer upon layer of sediment along the base of the mountain block. Water then flows over the surface of the fan and produces a braided drainage pattern, sometimes shifting from channel to channel (Figure 15.19). A continuous apron, or *bajada* (Spanish for "slope"), may form if individual alluvial fans coalesce into one sloping surface (see Figure 15.25c). Fan formation of any sort is reduced in humid climates because perennial streams constantly carry away sediment, preventing its deposition.

A logical aspect of an alluvial fan is the natural sorting of materials by size. Near the mouth of the canyon at the apex of the fan, coarse materials are deposited, grading slowly to pebbles and finer gravels with distance out from the mouth. Then sands and silts are deposited, with the finest clays and dissolved salts carried in suspension and solution all the way to the valley floor. Dissolved minerals accumulate as evaporite deposits on the valley floor left after evaporation of the water from the playa, and from salt-laden upward moving groundwater. Figure 15.20 shows the edge of a playa and active dune field, so there is a natural sorting of materials by grain size, with sands dropped in the dunes, silts and clays moving farther toward the playa, and the finest and dissolved materials in the playa.

Well-developed alluvial fans also can be a major source of groundwater. Some cities—San Bernardino, California, for example—are built on alluvial fans and extract their municipal water supplies from them. In other parts of the world, such water-bearing alluvial fans are known as *qanat* (Iran), *karex* (Pakistan), or *foggara* (western Sahara).

Desert Landscapes

Deserts are not wastelands, for they abound in specially adapted plants and animals. Moreover, the limited vegetation, intermittent rainfall, intense insolation, and distant vistas produce starkly beautiful landscapes. And all deserts are not the same: For example, North American deserts have more vegetation cover than do the generally more barren Asian desert expanses, as we saw in Figure 15.16.

The shimmering heat waves and related mirage effects in the desert are products of light refraction through layers of air that have developed a temperature gradient near the hot ground. The desert's enchantment is captured in the book *Desert Solitaire*:

Around noon the heat waves begin flowing upward from the expanses of sand and bare rock. They shimmer

FIGURE 15.19 An alluvial fan.
The photo shows an alluvial fan in a desert landscape. The topographic map shows the Cedar Creek alluvial fan. (Topographic map is the Ennis Quadrangle, 15-minute series, scale 1:62,500, contour interval = 40 ft; latitude/longitude coordinates for mouth of canyon are 45°2′ N 111°35′ W.) [Photo by Bobbé Christopherson; USGS map.]

FIGURE 15.20 Sand and playa—natural sorting of materials.
Playa of dissolved and finer materials (top of photo); sand dunes (middle), and coarser particles on slopes along the mountains (lower area) demonstrate the natural sorting that occurs in desert landscapes. [Photo by Bobbé Christopherson.]

like transparent, filmy veils between my sanctuary in the shade and all the sun-dazzled world beyond. Objects and forms viewed through this tremulous flow appear somewhat displaced or distorted. . . . The great Balanced Rock floats a few inches above its pedestal, supported by a layer of superheated air. The buttes, pinnacles, and fins in the windows area bend and undulate beyond the middle ground like a painted backdrop stirred by a draft of air.*

The buttes, pinnacles, and mesas of arid landscapes are resistant horizontal rock strata that have eroded differentially. Removal of the less-resistant sandstone strata produces unusual desert sculptures—arches, windows, pedestals, and delicately balanced rocks (Figure 15.21). The upper layers of sandstone along the top of an arch or butte are more resistant to weathering and protect the sandstone rock beneath.

*E. Abbey, *Desert Solitaire* (New York: McGraw-Hill, 1968), p. 154. Copyright © 1968 by Edward Abbey.

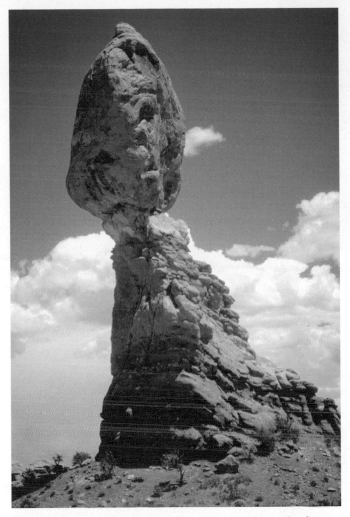

FIGURE 15.21 A balanced rock—differential weathering. Balanced Rock in Arches National Park, Utah, where writer-naturalist Edward Abbey (quoted in text) worked as a ranger years before it became a park. The overall feature is 39 m (128 ft) tall and composed of Entrada sandstone. The balanced-rock portion is 17 m (55 ft) tall and weighs 3255 metric (3577 short) tons. [Photo by Robert Christopherson.]

The removal of surrounding rock through differential weathering leaves enormous buttes as residuals on the landscape. If you imagine a line intersecting the tops of the Mitten Buttes shown in Figure 15.22, you can gain some idea of the quantity of material that has been removed. These buttes exceed 300 m (1000 ft) in height, similar to the Chrysler Building in New York City or First Canadian Place in Toronto.

Desert landscapes are places where stark erosional remnants can stand above the surrounding terrain as knobs or hills. Such a bare, exposed rock is an *inselberg* (island mountain), as exemplified by Uluru (Ayers) Rock in Australia (Figure 15.23).

In a desert area, weak surface material may weather to a complex, rugged topography, usually of relatively low and varied relief. Such a landscape is called a *badland*, probably so named because in the American West it offered little economic value and was difficult to traverse in

nineteenth-century wagons. The Badlands region of the Dakotas and north-central Arizona (the Painted Desert) are so named.

Sand dunes that existed in some ancient deserts have lithified, forming sandstone structures that bear the imprint of *cross-stratification*. When such a dune was accumulating, sand cascaded down its slipface and distinct bedding planes (layers) were established that remained after the dune lithified (Figure 15.24). Ripple marks, animal tracks, and fossils also are found preserved in these sandstones, which originally were eolian-deposited sand dunes.

Basin and Range Province

A physiographic province is a large region that is identified by several geologic or physiographic traits. We find alternating basins (valleys) and mountain ranges that lie in the rain shadow of mountains to the west characterizing the **Basin and Range Province** of the western United States (Figure 15.25). The physiography and geography combine to give the province a dry climate, few permanent streams, and *internal drainage patterns*—drainage basins that lack any outlet to the ocean (see Figure 14.5, "Great Basin" and its internal drainage).

The vast Basin and Range Province—almost 800,000 km² (300,000 mi²)—was a major barrier to early settlers in their migration westward. The combination of desert climate and north–south trending mountain ranges presented harsh challenges. Today, when you follow U.S. Highway 50 across Nevada, you cross five passes of more than 1950 m (6400 ft) and traverse numerous basins. Throughout the drive you are reminded where you are by prideful signs that plainly state: "The Loneliest Road in America." It is difficult to imagine crossing this topography with wagons and oxen (Figure 15.25e).

The Basin and Range formed as a result of tectonic processes. As the North American plate lumbered westward, it overrode former oceanic crust and hot spots at such a rapid pace that slabs of subducted material literally were run over. The crust was uplifted and stretched, creating a tensional landscape fractured by many faults. The present landscape consists of nearly parallel sequences; some are tilted-fault blocks, others have pairs of faults on either side of *horsts* of upward-faulted blocks, which are the "ranges," and *grabens* of downward fault-bounded blocks, which are the "basins." Figure 15.25c shows this pattern of normal faults and tensional stretching.

John McPhee captured the feel of this desert province in his book *Basin and Range*:

Supreme over all is silence. Discounting the cry of the occasional bird, the wailing of a pack of coyotes, silence—a great spatial silence—is pure in the Basin

(text continued on page 510)

(a)

FIGURE 15.22 Monument Valley landscape. (a) Mitten Buttes, Merrick Butte, and rainbow in Monument Valley, Navajo Tribal Park, along the Utah–Arizona border, which have appeared as a backdrop in many movies. (b) A schematic of the tremendous removal of material by weathering, erosion, and transport. (c) Aerial view of Monument Valley. [Photos by (a) Robert Christopherson; (c) Bobbé Christopherson.]

Resistant cap rock   Removed by weathering and erosion

(b)

(c)

FIGURE 15.23 Australian landmark.
Uluru (Ayers) Rock in Northern Territory, Australia, is an isolated mass of weathered rock. The formation is 348 m (1145 ft) high and is 2.5 km long by 1.6 km wide. Uluru Rock is sacred to Aboriginal peoples and has been protected in Uluru National Park since 1950. [Photo by Porterfield/Chickering.]

FIGURE 15.24 Cross-bedding in sedimentary rocks.
The bedding pattern, called cross-stratification, in these sandstone rocks tells us about patterns that were established in the dunes before lithification (hardening into rock). [Photo by Bobbé Christopherson.]

(a)

(b)

(d)

Horst   Playa   Graben
Alluvial   (central salt pan)   Bajada
fans   ├─Bolson─┤

(c)

FIGURE 15.25 Basin and Range Province in the western United States.
(a) Map and (b) *Landsat* image of the area. Recent scientific discoveries demonstrate that this province extends south through northern and central Mexico. (c) A bolson in the mountainous desert landscape of the Basin and Range Province. Parallel normal faults produce a series of ranges and basins. (d) Death Valley features a central playa, parallel mountain ranges, alluvial fans, and *bajada* along the base of the ranges. (e) "The Loneliest Road in America," Highway U.S. 50, slashes westward through the province. [(b) Image from NASA; photos by (d) Robert Christopherson; (e) Bobbé Christopherson.]

(e)

and Range. It is a soundless immensity with mountains in it. You stand . . . and look up at a high mountain front, and turn your head and look fifty miles down the valley, and there is utter silence.*

Basin-and-range relief is abrupt, and rock structures are angular and rugged. As the ranges erode, transported materials accumulate to great depths in the basins, gradually producing extensive desert plains. The basin's elevation averages roughly 1200−1500 m (4000−5000 ft) above sea level, with mountain crests rising higher by another 900−1500 m (3000−5000 ft). Death Valley, California, is the lowest of these basins, with an elevation of −86 m (−282 ft). However, to the west of the valley, the Panamint Range rises to 3368 m (11,050 ft) at Telescope Peak—almost 3.5 vertical kilometres (2.2 mi) of desert mountain relief.

In Figure 15.25c and d, note the **bolson**, a slope-and-basin area between the crests of two adjacent ridges in a dry region of internal drainage. Death Valley provides a dramatic example of these arid-land features. Figure 15.25c also identifies a *playa* (central pan), a *bajada* (coalesced alluvial fans), and a mountain front in retreat from weathering and erosional attack. A *pediment* is an area of bedrock that is layered with a thin veneer, or coating, of alluvium. It is an erosional surface, as opposed to the depositional surface of the bajada.

*J. McPhee, *Basin and Range* (New York: Farrar, Straus, Giroux, 1981), p. 46.

Vast arid and semiarid lands remain an enigma on the water planet. They challenge our technology to access water, our courage, and personal need for water. Yet these lands hold a fascination, perhaps because they are so lacking in the moisture that infuses our lives.

Desertification

We are witnessing an unwanted expansion of Earth's desert lands in a process known as **desertification**, a worldwide phenomenon along the margins of semiarid and arid lands. Desertification is due principally to poor agricultural practices (overgrazing and agricultural activities that abuse soil structure and fertility), improper soil-moisture management, erosion and salinization, deforestation, and ongoing global climatic change, which is shifting temperature and precipitation patterns.

The southward expansion of Saharan conditions through portions of the *Sahel region* has left many African peoples on land that no longer experiences the rainfall of just two decades ago. Other regions at risk of desertification stretch from Asia and central Australia to portions of North and South America. The United Nations estimates that degraded lands have covered some 800 million hectares (2 billion acres) since 1930; many millions of additional hectares are added each year. An immediate need is to improve the database for

FIGURE 15.26 The desertification hazard.
Worldwide desertification estimates by the United Nations. [Data from U.N. Food and Agricultural Organization (FAO), World Meteorological Organization (WMO), United Nations Educational, Scientific, and Cultural Organization (UNESCO), Nairobi, Kenya; as printed in J. M. Rubenstein, *An Introduction to Human Geography*, Figure 14-16, p. 509. ©1999 Prentice Hall, Inc. Used by permission.]

a more accurate accounting of the problem and a better understanding of what is occurring.

Figure 15.26 is drawn from a map prepared for a U.N. Conference on Desertification; although dated, the patterns persist to this day. Desertification areas are ranked: A moderate hazard area has an average 10%–25% drop in agricultural productivity; a high hazard area has a 25%–50% drop; and a very high hazard area has more than a 50% decrease. Because human activities and economies, especially unwise grazing practices, appear to be the major cause of desertification, actions to slow the process are readily available but progress is slow. The severity of this problem is magnified by the poverty in many of the affected regions, for the poor lack the capital to change practices and implement conservation strategies.

One of the successes coming from the 1992 Earth Summit in Rio de Janeiro was an initiative for empowering a Convention to Combat Desertification, which began operations in 1994 and is still underway. International conferences are convened every other year and many programs are underway. For more on these global arid lands, see the U.N. site at **http://www.unccd.int/main.php**; and for the UNDPs Dryland Development Centre work, see **http://www.undp.org/drylands/**.

Climate Change and Increased Aridity in Canada

Greenhouse gas emissions are increasing annually and a doubling of carbon dioxide emissions may take place within the next 50 years. Since 2000, atmospheric carbon dioxide increased at a rate of 3.1% per year, which can lead to a doubling in as little as 20 years. Some climate models predict that changes in precipitation and temperature caused by this doubling will force existent grasslands to shift northward and to grow in regions now covered by boreal plant communities. As the existing grasslands shift northward and to higher elevations, the present day grasslands are predicted to become semi-desert. And in turn, the boreal forest is shifting northward, encroaching on the tundra regions.

When plant communities shift in response to temperature and precipitation changes, the intensity and the nature of geological processes that act in an area are likely to change as well, so increased aridity may influence the distribution and intensity of eolian processes. The change in eolian processes may result in the dramatic reduction of vegetation, exposing soil surfaces. The susceptibility of bare soils to eolian erosion is controlled by surface moisture conditions. Thus, changes in the timing and amount of precipitation and variations in temperature regime may cause changes in eolian erosion.

The Geological Survey of Canada (GSC) modelled the sensitivity of eolian processes to climate change on the basis of predicted shifts of vegetation communities. Climate model results indicate that reactivation and increased movement of sand dunes and the increased erosion of unprotected, bare soils are likely to occur as climate changes. If predicted changes in vegetation cover and moisture conditions increase soil moisture deficits, sensitivity to eolian erosion increases.

A survey of the sensitivity of dune areas in Canada that will be affected by climate change is illustrated in Figure 15.27. The least sensitive regions to potential increased eolian processes either have enough vegetation cover or enough surface soil moisture to suppress wind activity when carbon dioxide is doubled. The arctic, subarctic, boreal, cool temperate forest, and transitional grassland have a low sensitivity to changes in eolian processes.

Moderately sensitive areas include the existing boreal regions that may change to grassland and cool temperate regions that may change to moderate temperate regions. In these moderate regions—central Saskatchewan, some regions of Manitoba, Ontario, Québec, and the Maritimes—some reactivation of sand dunes and some soil erosion are likely. Areas that are currently grassland and moderate temperate regions are likely to become more arid. These regions of increased aridity are therefore predicted to be highly sensitive to climate change, and may experience significant increases in eolian and dune activity. These regions are predicted to change to semi-desert. The Palliser Triangle, including the Great Sand Hills of Saskatchewan and Alberta, has severe sensitivity to eolian activity. Figure 15.27 reflects wind erosion risk as well throughout these low, moderate, and high sensitivity regions.

We now have the first circumarctic scientific analysis of the impact of global warming on the Arctic Region. The Arctic Council empowered the Arctic Monitoring and Assessment Programme (AMAP), Conservation of Arctic Flora and Fauna (CAFF), and the International Arctic Science Committee (IASC) to conduct this study and prepare a comprehensive report. The Arctic Climate Impact Assessment (**http://www.acia.uaf.edu**), released in November 2004 following four years of study by 300 scientists and indigenous peoples, stated in one section of the ACIA report regarding the impact of warming and potential desertification in the high latitudes:

> Because the rate of evaporation increases as temperatures climb, if precipitation does not rise enough to keep up with that increase, land areas would dry out . . . followed by desertification in some areas as warming continues.

Eolian processes and arid lands are dynamic systems.

FIGURE 15.27 Sensitivity to wind erosion with climate change.
Risk for erosion of unprotected soils in areas sensitive to climate change is greatest in the southern and central Prairies and in southernmost Ontario. [Map adapted from *The Atlas of Canada*, with the permission of Natural Resources Canada.]

Applied Physical Geography

Wind Erosion

The ability of wind to move objects is small when compared with other transporting agents (e.g., water, ice, gravity), but over time, the amount of material moved can be large. Figure 15.1 illustrates the exponential increase in the rate of sand movement with an increase in wind velocity. Erosion of surface material, especially soil,

has long been a concern to Prairie farmers. The dry climate, the intensity of farming, and the open spaces of the Canadian Prairies make them especially susceptible to wind erosion.

Wind erosion of the soil occurs in three stages. First, soil must be detached. This is usually accomplished by frost action, mineral expansion and

contraction, alternate wetting and drying, mechanical shear, or abrasion. Once detached, the soil is available for transport. Wind speed is lowest at the ground surface and increases exponentially upward until surface friction is overcome.

The most important factors to consider when calculating wind erosion are air velocity and turbulence; soil structure, density, and moisture content; and surface roughness, cover, obstructions, and topographic features. Mathematical models calculate soil losses by combining these factors. Table 1 shows the calculations of soil loss for a 1992 windstorm in Manitoba.

The loss of soil in metric tons/hectare is a volume measurement. What does this mean for depth of soil lost? If we assume a bulk density of $1 mg/m^3$, then 10 metric tons/hectare of soil loss is equal to 1 mm of soil depth. So, at Site 1, 1.325 mm of soil and, at Site 2, 1.845 mm of soil were lost during a single storm.

Table 1 Soil Loss from 1992 Windstorm and Breakdown of Soil Movement for Two Sites in Manitoba*

	Site 1	Site 2
Total soil loss (metric tons/hectare)	16.25	18.45
% Soil loss from:		
Surface creep	1	1
Saltation	81	69
Suspension	18	30

*The field length was 400 m. Soil loss was calculated in kg on an area of 0.04 hectare (0.1 acre) (1 m wide and 400 m long). Wind speed for this event was 50–75 km/h.
Source: Manitoba Agriculture, Food and Rural Initiatives, **http://www.gov.mb.ca/ agriculture/soilwater/soil/fbd01s01.html**.

Summary and Review—Eolian Processes and Arid Landscapes

■ *Characterize* the unique work accomplished by wind and eolian processes.

The movement of the atmosphere in response to pressure differences produces wind. Wind is a geomorphic agent of erosion, transportation, and deposition. **Eolian** processes modify and move sand accumulations along coastal beaches and deserts. Wind's ability to move materials is small compared with that of water and ice.

eolian (p. 488)

1. Who was Ralph Bagnold? What was his contribution to eolian studies?

2. Explain the term *eolian* and its application in this chapter. How would you characterize the ability of the wind to move material?

■ *Describe* eolian erosion, including deflation, abrasion, and the resultant landforms.

Two principal wind-erosion processes are **deflation**, the removal and lifting of individual loose particles, and **abrasion**, the "sandblasting" of rock surfaces with particles captured in the air. Deflation literally blows away loose or noncohesive sediment and works with rainwater to form a surface resembling a cobblestone street: a **desert pavement** that protects underlying sediment from further deflation and water erosion. Wherever wind encounters loose sediment, deflation may remove enough material to form basins. Called **blowout depressions**, they range from small indentations less than a metre wide up to areas hundreds of metres wide and many metres deep. Rocks that bear evidence of eolian erosion are called **ventifacts**. On a larger scale, deflation and abrasion are capable of streamlining rock structures, leaving behind distinctive rock formations or elongated ridges called **yardangs**.

deflation (p. 488)
abrasion (p. 488)

desert pavement (p. 488)
blowout depressions (p. 490)
ventifacts (p. 490)
yardangs (p. 490)

3. Describe the erosional processes associated with moving air.

4. Explain deflation and overview each hypothesis on the processes that produce desert pavement.

5. How are ventifacts and yardangs formed by the wind?

■ *Describe* eolian transportation, and *explain* saltation and surface creep.

Wind exerts a drag or frictional pull on surface particles until they become airborne. Only the finest dust particles travel significant distances, so the finer material suspended in a dust storm is lifted much higher than the coarser particles of a sandstorm. Saltating particles crash into other particles, knocking them both loose and forward. The motion called **surface creep** slides and rolls particles too large for saltation.

surface creep (p. 491)

6. Differentiate between a dust storm and a sandstorm.

7. What is the difference between eolian saltation and fluvial saltation?

8. Explain the concept of surface creep.

■ *Identify* the major classes of sand dunes, and *present* examples within each class.

In arid and semiarid climates and along some coastlines where sand is available, dunes accumulate. A **dune** is a wind-sculpted accumulation of sand. An extensive area of dunes, such as that found in North Africa, is characteristic of an **erg desert**, or **sand sea**. When saltating sand grains encounter small patches of sand, their kinetic energy (motion) is dissipated and they start to accumulate into a dune. As height increases above 30 cm (12 in.), a steeply sloping **slipface** on the lee side and characteristic dune features are formed. Dune forms are broadly classified as *crescentic*, *linear*, and *star*.

dune (p. 491)
erg desert (p. 491)
sand sea (p. 491)
slipface (p. 491)

9. What is the difference between an erg and a reg desert? Which type is a sand sea? Are all deserts covered by sand? Explain.

10. What are the three classes of dune forms? Describe the basic types of dunes within each class. What do you think is the major shaping force for sand dunes?

11. Which form of dune is the mountain giant of the desert? What are the characteristic wind patterns that produce such dunes?

■ *Define* loess deposits and their origins, locations, and landforms.

Eolian-transported materials contribute to soil formation in distant places. Windblown **loess** deposits occur worldwide and can develop into good agricultural soils. These fine-grained clays and silts are moved by the wind many kilometres, where they are redeposited in unstratified, homogeneous deposits. The binding strength of loess causes it to weather and erode in steep bluffs, or vertical faces.

Significant accumulations throughout the Mississippi and Missouri river valleys form continuous deposits 15–30 m (50–100 ft) thick. Loess deposits also occur in eastern Washington State, Idaho, much of Ukraine, central Europe, China, the Pampas–Patagonia regions of Argentina, and lowland New Zealand.

loess (p. 496)

12. How are loess materials generated? What form do they assume when deposited?

13. Name a few examples of significant loess deposits on Earth.

■ *Portray* desert landscapes, and *locate* these regions on a world map.

Dry and semiarid climates occupy about 35% of Earth's land surface. The spatial distribution of these dry lands is related to subtropical high-pressure cells between 15° and 35° N and S, to rain shadows on the lee side of mountain ranges, or to areas at great distance from moisture-bearing air masses, such as central Asia.

Precipitation events are rare, yet running water is still the major erosional agent in deserts. When precipitation events do occur, a dry streambed fills with a torrent called a **flash flood**. Depending on the region, such a dry streambed is known as a **wash**, an *arroyo* (Spanish), or a *wadi* (Arabic). As runoff water evaporates, salt crusts may be left behind on the desert floor. This intermittently wet and dry low area in a region of closed drainage is called a **playa**, site of an *ephemeral lake* when water is present.

In arid climates, a prominent landform is the **alluvial fan** at the mouth of a canyon where it exits into a valley. The fan is produced by flowing water that abruptly loses velocity as it leaves the constricted channel of the canyon and deposits a layer of sediment along the mountain block. A continuous apron, or **bajada**, may form if individual alluvial fans coalesce. A *province* is a large region that is characterized by several geologic or physiographic traits. The **Basin and Range Province** of the western United States consists of alternating basins and mountain ranges. A slope-and-basin area between the crests of two adjacent ridges in a dry region of internal drainage is a **bolson**. **Desertification** is the ongoing process that leads to an unwanted expansion of the Earth's desert lands.

flash flood (p. 500)
wash (p. 500)
playa (p. 501)
alluvial fan (p. 505)
bajada (p. 505)
Basin and Range Province (p. 507)
bolson (p. 510)
desertification (p. 510)

14. Characterize desert energy and water-balance regimes. What are the significant patterns of occurrence for arid landscapes in the world?

15. How would you describe the water budget of the Colorado River? What was the basis for agreements regarding distribution of the river's water? Why has thinking about the river's discharge been so optimistic? Overview current conditions of the Colorado River system in light of the ongoing drought and increasing water demands.

16. Describe a desert bolson from crest to crest. Draw a simple sketch with the components of the landscape labelled.

17. Where is the Basin and Range Province? Briefly describe its appearance and character.

18. What is meant by desertification? Using the maps in Figures 15.16 and 15.26, and the text description, locate several of the regions affected by desert expansion.

19. With climate change, what changes are predicted for eolian processes in Canada? Which areas are most likely to experience change? Where will sand dunes most likely be active?

Critical Thinking

A. "Water is the major erosion and transport medium in the desert." Respond to this quotation. How is it possible for this to be true when deserts are so dry? What factors have you learned from this chapter that prove this statement true?

B. Where are the nearest eolian features (coastal, lakeshore, or desert dunes, or loess deposits) to your present location? Which causative factors discussed in this chapter explain the features you identified? Are you able to visit the site?

C. Relative to the Colorado River system, define, compare, and contrast what you think is meant by a "supply strategy" or a "demand strategy" in dealing with the present Colorado River water budget (Table 15.1.1, Focus Study 15.1). What political and economic forces do you think are at play in planning for the river? Who are the stakeholders? With your analysis, briefly speculate what strategies you think would be most effective in dealing with this situation.

These deposits provide an extensive frozen record of Earth's climatic history over the past several million years and perhaps some clues to its climatic future. This is Earth's *cryosphere*, the portion of the hydrosphere and groundwater that is perennially frozen, generally at high latitudes and elevations.

Worldwide, glacial ice is in retreat, melting at rates exceeding anything in the ice record. In the European Alps alone some 75% of the glaciers have receded in the past 50 years, losing more than 50% of their ice mass since 1850. At this rate, the European Alps will have only 20% of their preindustrial glacial ice left by 2050. Mount Kilimanjaro in Africa, the South American Andes, and the Himalayas of Asia could lose their glacial ice within the next several decades, affecting local water resources.

Significant to towns and cities is that many mountain cliffs and slopes are held together by permanently frozen conditions (permafrost). With the meltdown underway these slopes are thawing, making rockfalls and landslides an increasing hazard probability.

In this chapter: We focus on Earth's extensive ice deposits—their formation, movement, and the ways in which they produce various erosional and depositional landforms. Glaciers, transient landforms themselves, leave in their wake a variety of landscape features. The fate of glaciers is intricately tied to change in global temperature, which ultimately concerns us all. We discuss the methods used to decipher past climates—the science of *paleoclimatology*—and the clues for understanding future climate patterns. Exciting discoveries are arising from ice cores taken from Earth's two ice sheets, one dating back 800,000 years from the present.

We examine the cold world of permafrost and periglacial geomorphic processes. These periglacial environments may be separated from actual glacial ice across time (glaciers from past ages) and space (physical distance in the present). Approximately 25% of Earth's land area is subject to freezing conditions and frost action characteristic of periglacial regions, including areas that have specific related features of relict, or past, permafrost. These areas near former and existing glaciers contain evidence of the last ice age.

Rivers of Ice

A **glacier** is a large mass of ice resting on land or floating as an ice shelf in the sea adjacent to land. Glaciers are not frozen lakes or groundwater ice. Instead, they form by the continual accumulation of snow that recrystallizes under its own weight into an ice mass. Glaciers are not stationary; they move slowly under the pressure of their own great weight and the pull of gravity. In fact, they move slowly in streamlike patterns, merging as tributaries into large rivers of ice, as you can see in the satellite image and aerial photos in Figure 17.1.

Today, these slowly flowing rivers and sheets of ice dominate about 11% of Earth's land area. As much as 30% of continental land was covered by glacial ice during

(a)

(b)

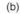

(c)

FIGURE 17.1 Rivers and sheets of ice.
(a) Alpine glaciers merge from adjoining glacial valleys in the northeast region of Ellesmere Island in the Canadian Arctic. (b) Numerous glaciers carve the coast of Greenland. (c) These peaks, known as *nunataks*, rise above the Greenland Ice Sheet. There are no clouds in the photo, for this is all ice at approximately 2500 m (8200 ft) elevation—an accumulation perhaps 100,000 years in the making. [(a) *Terra* image courtesy of University of Alberta, NASA/GSFC/ERSDAC/ JAROS and the U.S./Japan ASTER Science Team, July 31, 2000. (b) and (c) photos by Bobbé Christopherson.]

colder episodes in the past. Through these "ice ages," below-freezing temperatures prevailed at lower latitudes more than they do today, allowing snow to accumulate year after year.

Glaciers form in areas of permanent snow, both at high latitudes and at high elevations at any latitude. A **snowline** is the lowest elevation where snow can survive year-round; specifically, it is the lowest line where winter snow accumulation persists throughout the summer. Glaciers form on some high mountains along the equator, such as in the Andes Mountains of South America and on Mount Kilimanjaro in Tanzania, Africa. On equatorial mountains, the snowline is around 5000 m (16,400 ft); on midlatitude mountains, such as the European Alps, snowlines average 2700 m (8850 ft); and in southern Greenland, snowlines are as low as 600 m (1970 ft).

CRYSYS (CRYosphere SYStem) is a Canadian program in the NASA Earth Observing System Program. The main goal is to monitor and analyze regional and larger-scale variations in sea ice, snow cover, freshwater ice, glaciers and ice caps, and frozen ground/permafrost in the periglacial realm. Also, CRYSYS gathers and maintains historical, operational, and research data sets for climate systems research. The CRYSYS Web site is a good entry point into the cryosphere, at http://www.msc.ec. gc.ca/crysys/overview/crysys_whatis_e.cfm. Additionally, see the Global Land Ice Measurements from Space at http://www.flag.wr.usgs.gov/GLIMS/glimshome.html, or the National Snow and Ice Data Center at http://nsidc.org. *Landsat*-7 images are listed at http://www.emporia.edu/earthsci/gage/glacier7.htm.

Glaciers are as varied as the landscape itself and exist all over the world. Antarctica has most of the world's ice in the form of an ice sheet covering an area of 13.9 million km². This is followed by the Greenland ice sheet with 10.5%, 1.7 million km². Canada's ice, found in alpine glaciers and ice caps, makes up 1.24% of the world's perennial ice in an area totalling about 200,000 km². Canada's glaciers can be classified as Arctic, Coastal, and Rocky Mountain (Figure 17.2). All glaciers fall into two general groups, based on their form, size, and flow characteristics: alpine glaciers and continental glaciers.

Alpine Glaciers

With few exceptions, a glacier in a mountain range is an **alpine glacier**, or *mountain glacier*. The name comes from the Alps of central Europe, where such glaciers abound. Alpine glaciers form in several subtypes. One prominent type is a *valley glacier*, literally a river of ice confined within a valley that originally was formed by stream action. Such glaciers range in length from only 100 m (325 ft) to more than 100 km (60 mi).

In Figure 17.3a, at least a half a dozen valley glaciers are identifiable. These are named on the map and include the Athabasca, Saskatchewan, and Dome glaciers that fill the valleys as they move downslope from the Snow Dome.

As a valley glacier flows slowly downhill, the mountains, canyons, and river valleys beneath its mass are profoundly altered by its erosive passage. Some of the debris created by the glacier's excavation is transported on the ice, visible as dark streaks and bands being transported for deposition elsewhere; other portions of its debris load are carried within or along its base (see Figures 17.1, 17.7f, and 17.14).

Most alpine glaciers originate in a mountain *snowfield* that is confined in a bowl-shaped recess. This scooped-out erosional landform at the head of a valley is a **cirque**. A glacier that forms in a cirque is a *cirque glacier*. Several cirque glaciers may jointly feed a valley glacier, as shown

FIGURE 17.2 Glacial ice in Canada.
Distribution of glacial ice in Canada can be described as Coastal, Arctic, and Rocky Mountain. [Map courtesy of *Canadian Geographic*.]

(a)

FIGURE 17.3 The Columbia Icefield.
(a) This is the accumulation area for several valley glaciers that flow into three different oceans—the Columbia River that flows into the Pacific, the Athabasca River that flows into the Arctic, and the North Saskatchewan and Saskatchewan rivers that flow into Hudson Bay and the Atlantic Ocean. (b) The Athabasca Glacier is a popular tourist destination where the snowcoach takes visitors onto the ice surface along an ice road, visible in the middle ground of the photo. [(a) Map courtesy of *Canadian Geographic*. (b) Photo by Gordon Peterson/firstlight.ca.]

(b)

on the topographic map and photograph in Figure 17.4. The glaciers flowing north from Sugarloaf Mountain in the Battle Range are fed by many cirque glaciers that surround the mountain peak. In the aerial photos in Figure 17.1, how many valley glaciers can you identify?

Wherever several valley glaciers pour out of their confining valleys and coalesce at the base of a mountain range, a *piedmont glacier* is formed and spreads freely over the lowlands. The debris deposits on the surface of the ice form beautiful streaked patterns as the glacier fans out over the coastal plain and into Yakutat Bay. A *tidal glacier*, such as the Columbia Glacier on Prince William Sound in Alaska, ends in the sea, calving (breaking off) to form floating ice called **icebergs** (Figure 17.5). Icebergs usually form wherever glaciers meet the ocean. (See Glaciers of Prince William Sound at **http://www.alaska.net/~sea/glacier.html**.)

(a)

FIGURE 17.4 Topographic map from Glacier National Park.
(a) Numerous cirque glaciers depicted on a topographic map of
Glacier National Park, British Columbia. Blue areas represent active
glaciers. (b) Dramatic landscape of ice and rock in Glacier National
Park. Most glacial ice in the National Park will be melted away by
2030, owing to regional warming trends. [(a) Map used with
permission of Natural Resources Canada; (b) photo by J. A. Kraulis/
Masterfile.]

(b)

(a)

(b)

(c)

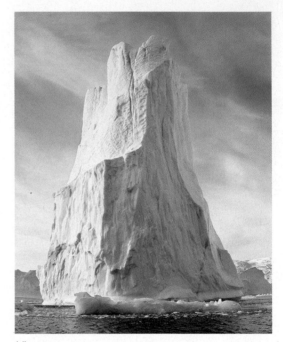
(d)

FIGURE 17.5 Glacial ice ready to calve into the sea and icebergs.
(a) When glaciers reach the sea, large pieces break off, forming icebergs, such as these massive 30-m (98-ft) high blocks ready to fall at Neko Harbour, Antarctica. (b) A tidewater glacier calving numerous icebergs into the ocean in southern Greenland. (c) A weathered iceberg off Antarctica; see the former water line marking where the berg floated lower in the water when it was greater in mass. (d) This iceberg tower in East Greenland is about 60 m (200 ft) tall; imagine its keel extending some 360 m (1180 ft) below the surface. [All photos by Bobbé Christopherson.]

Continental Glaciers

On a much larger scale than individual alpine glaciers, a continuous mass of ice is a **continental glacier**. In its most extensive form, it is an **ice sheet**. Most of Earth's glacial ice exists in the ice sheets that blanket 81% of Greenland, 1,756,000 km^2 (678,000 mi^2) of ice, and 90% of Antarctica, 14.2 million km^2 (5.48 million mi^2) of ice. Antarctica alone has 92% of all the glacial ice on the planet.

The Antarctic and Greenland ice sheets have such enormous mass that large portions of each landmass beneath the ice are isostatically depressed (pressed down by weight) below sea level. Each ice sheet reaches depths of more than 3000 m (10,000 ft), with average depths around 2000 m, burying all but the highest peaks, known as *nunataks* (see Figure 17.1c).

Two additional types of continuous ice cover associated with mountain locations are *ice caps* and *ice fields*. An **ice cap** is roughly circular and, by definition, covers an area of less than 50,000 km^2 (19,300 mi^2). Ice caps are found in polar regions and, like ice sheets, are not constrained by the existing relief. They exert a modifying effect on the climate, cooling the local area. In Canada, there are well-developed ice caps in the high Arctic (Agassiz Ice Cap, Northern Ellesmere Island; Melville Island South Ice Cap; Devon Ice Cap; Meighen Ice Cap, White Glacier on Axel Heiberg Island; Penny and Barnes ice caps on Baffin Island). The Barnes Ice Cap on Baffin Island is the last remnant of the Laurentide Ice Sheet that covered almost all of Canada and a portion of the northern United States at the peak of the Wisconsinan glaciation. The ice in the Barnes Ice Cap is over 100,000 years old, making it Canada's oldest.

The volcanic island of Iceland features several ice caps, such as the Vatnajökull Ice Cap in the *Landsat* image in Figure 17.6a. Volcanoes lie beneath these icy surfaces. Iceland's Grímsvötn Volcano erupted in 1996, and again in 2004, producing large quantities of melted glacial water and floods, a flow Icelanders call a *jökulhlaup*.

An **ice field** is not extensive enough to form the characteristic dome of an ice cap; instead, it extends in a characteristic elongated pattern in a mountainous region. A fine example is the Patagonian ice field of Argentina and Chile, one of Earth's largest. It attains only 90 km (56 mi) width, but stretches 360 km (224 mi), from 46° to 51° S latitude (equivalent in latitude from South Dakota to central Manitoba in the Northern Hemisphere). In an

(a)

(b)

FIGURE 17.6 Ice cap and ice field.
(a) The Vatnajökull ice cap in southeastern Iceland (*jökull* means "ice cap" in Danish). Note the location of the Grímsvötn Volcano on the map and the path of the floods to the sea. (b) The southern Patagonian ice field of Argentina. [(a) *Landsat* image from NASA; (b) photo by cosmonauts G. M. Greshko and Yu V. Romanenko, *Salyut 6*.]

ice field, ridges and peaks form nunataks that are visible above the buried terrain (visible in Figure 17.6b and 17.1c).

In Canada, the Columbia Icefield (see Figure 17.3) straddles the continental divide between Banff and Jasper, Alberta. The highest elevation on the ice field, Snow Dome, reaches 3520 m (11,548 ft) and represents the triple point in the drainage divide system of North America: Arctic, Atlantic, and Pacific. Eight glaciers flow out from the ice field including the Athabasca, Saskatchewan, Dome, Stutfield, Castleguard, and Columbia. Covering an area of about 325 km², the Columbia Icefield is one of the largest in the Rocky Mountains.

Continuous ice sheets or ice caps are drained by rapidly moving, solid *ice streams* that form around their periphery, moving to the sea or to lowlands. Such frozen ice streams flow from the edges of Greenland and Antarctica, through stationary and slower-moving ice. An *outlet glacier* flows out from an ice sheet or ice cap but is constrained by a mountain valley or pass.

An **ice shelf** is a thick sheet of ice with a gently undulating to level surface that extends over the sea and floats on water. It is attached to the land along a coastal *grounding line* and also may be attached where ice flows around islands. On the seaward side, it is bounded by a steep cliff called the *ice front* that can be 2 to 50 m or more above sea level. Ice shelves are important climatic indicators because they respond much more rapidly to changes than glaciers or grounded ice sheets. Ice shelves have formed along polar coasts in Antarctica, in the Canadian Arctic Archipelago, and in Greenland. Ice shelves can be wide, with some extending several hundreds of kilometres from the coastline. Ice shelves increase in mass from annual snow accumulation and from the seaward extension of grounded ice sheets and glaciers. They decrease in size from warming, melting, and calving of icebergs at their seaward margin. (See High Latitude Connection 17.1, page 587.)

Glacial Processes

A glacier is a dynamic body, moving relentlessly downslope at rates that vary within its mass, excavating the landscape through which it flows. The mass is dense ice that is formed from snow and water through a process of compaction, recrystallization, and growth. A glacier's *mass budget* consists of net gains or losses of this glacial ice, which determine whether the glacier expands or retreats. Let us now look at glacial ice formation, mass balance, movement, and erosion before we discuss the fascinating landforms produced by these processes.

Formation of Glacial Ice

Consider for a moment the nature of ice. You may be surprised to learn that ice is both a mineral (an inorganic natural compound of specific chemical makeup and crystalline structure) and a rock (a mass of one or more minerals). Ice is a frozen fluid, a trait that it shares with igneous rocks. The accumulation of snow in layered deposits is similar to sedimentary rock formations. To give birth to a glacier, snow and ice are transformed under pressure, recrystallizing into a type of metamorphic rock. Glacial ice is a remarkable material!

The essential input to a glacier is snow that accumulates in a snowfield, a glacier's accumulation zone (Figure 17.7a and 17.7c). Snowfields typically are at the highest elevation of an ice sheet, ice cap, or head of a valley glacier, usually in a cirque. Avalanches from surrounding mountain slopes can add to the snowfield.

As the snow accumulation deepens in sedimentary-like layers, the increasing thickness results in increased weight and pressure on underlying ice. Rain and summer snowmelt then contribute water, which stimulates further melting, and that meltwater seeps down into the snowfield and refreezes.

Snow surviving the summer and into the following winter begins a slow transformation into glacial ice. Air spaces among ice crystals are pressed as snow packs to a greater density. The ice recrystallizes and consolidates under pressure. In a transition step to glacial ice, snow becomes **firn**, which has a compact, granular texture.

As this process continues, many years pass before dense glacial ice is produced. Formation of **glacial ice** is analogous to metamorphic processes: Sediments (snow and firn) are pressured and recrystallized into a dense metamorphic rock (glacial ice). In Antarctica, glacial ice formation may take 1000 years because of the dryness of the climate (minimal snow input), whereas in wet climates the time is reduced to just a few years because of rapid, constant snow input to the system.

Glacial Mass Balance

A glacier is an open system, with *inputs* of snow and *outputs* of ice, meltwater, and water vapour. Snowfall and other moisture in the *accumulation zone* feed the glacier's upper reaches (Figure 17.7a). This area ends at the **firn line**, indicating where the winter snow and ice accumulation survived the summer melting season. These highways of ice flow from accumulation areas high in the mountains and are marked by trails of transported debris called *moraines*. Toward a glacier's lower end, it is wasted (reduced) through several processes: melting on the surface, internally, and at its base; ice removal by deflation (wind); the calving of ice blocks; and sublimation (recall from Chapter 7 that this is the direct evaporation of ice). Collectively, these losses are **ablation**.

The zone where accumulation gain balances ablation loss is the *equilibrium line* (Figure 17.7b). This area of a glacier generally coincides with the firn line. A glacier achieves *positive net balance* of mass—grows larger—during cold periods with adequate precipitation. In warmer times, the equilibrium line migrates up-glacier, and the glacier retreats—grows smaller—because of its *negative net balance*. Internally, gravity continues to move a glacier

FIGURE 17.7 A retreating alpine glacier and mass balance.
(a) Cross section of a typical retreating alpine glacier. (b) Annual mass balance of a glacial system, showing how the relation between accumulation and ablation controls the location of the equilibrium line. (c) The accumulation zone for a glacier in Antarctica. (d) Four tributary glaciers flow into a compound valley glacier in Greenland. (e) A terminal moraine marks the farthest advance of this glacier on Nordaustlandet Island, Arctic Ocean. (f) Moraine rock and debris form a terminal moraine and lateral moraines left by a retreating glacier. [All photos by Bobbé Christopherson.]

Budget of a
Glacier,
Mass Balance

ANIMATION

Flow of Ice
Within a Glacier

ANIMATION

forward even though its lower terminus might be in retreat owing to ablation. The mass-balance losses from the Peyto Glacier provide a case in point of glacial ice loss (News Report 17.1).

Glacial meltwater loss flows from the glacier in three ways. First, it flows from beneath and is known as *subglacial meltwater*. Often this water flows in streams at the base of the glacier that leave meltwater tunnels

(text continued on page 562)

News Report 17.1

Western Glaciers Lose Mass

Mass balance is a method used to monitor the behaviour of glaciers and can give an indication, if a long enough time series exists, of the regional warming or cooling of climate. A positive balance implies that the glacier accumulation is greater than the ablation in a particular year; a negative balance implies that there is more ablation than accumulation. A zero balance implies that accumulation and ablation are equal. Across the surface of the glacier, there is an elevation where accumulation and ablation are equal—this is marked by the equilibrium line.

Glacial mass budgets are declining along a global trend with significant ice losses in Alaska, the Andes, the European Alps, and the Himalayas. The Columbia Glacier in southern Alaska retreated 12 km (7.5 mi) and reduced its thickness by more than 400 m (1312 ft) between 1982 and 2000. In the same time period, its flow speed increased from 5 to 30 m (16.4 to 98.4 ft) per day. (See R. M. Krimmel, *Photogrammetric Data Set, 1957–2000, and Bathymetric Measurements for Columbia Glacier, Alaska*, USGS Water-Resources Report 01-4089, Tacoma, Washington, 2001.)

The net mass balance of Peyto Glacier, one of the most extensively studied glaciers in North America, demonstrates significant losses between 1966 and 1999. Peyto Glacier, in the Rocky Mountains of Alberta, ranges in elevation from 2140 to 3180 m above sea level and covers an area of about 12 km². The glacier terminus is retreating with the long-term negative mass balance and the surface is lowering along the west side of the glacier.

An analysis of the data for net mass balance reveals that the seasonal balance has been lower than average since 1976 (Figure 17.1.1). The Peyto Glacier mass balance analysis has been coupled with studies in other parts of the Rocky Mountains, the Coast Mountains, and the Cordilleran glaciers in Alaska, and the results

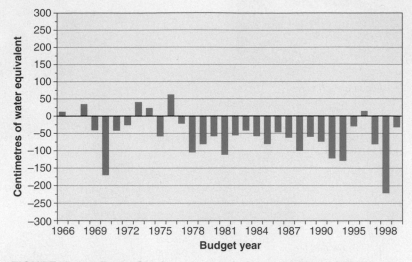

FIGURE 17.1.1 Peyto Glacier net mass balance, 1966 to 1999. A negative net mass balance has dominated this shrinking glacier since 1966. Data are in cm. [Graph by M. N. Demuth and R. Keler, 2004. "An Assessment of the Mass Balance of Peyto Glacier (1966–1995) and Its Relation to Recent and Past Century Climatic Variability." In Chapter 4, *Peyto Glacier: One Century of Science*, M. N. Demuth, D. S. Munro, and G. J. Young (editors). Environment Canada–National Hydrology Research Institute, 83–132.]

show that some of the variability of the winter balance can be related to the El Niño–Southern Oscillation. The pattern of below average winter accumulation ended in the late 1980s, but the 1997 to 1998 budget year resulted in a record mass loss (210 cm/yr of loss). During that time, there was below average accumulation and increased losses through ablation (combined loss from melt, sublimation, and evaporation) that was both intense and prolonged. The balance for the next budget year (1998 to 1999) returned to nearly normal with 31 cm/yr of loss.

The photographs in Figure 17.1.2 portray the magnitude of change in Peyto Glacier over the last half-century. Examination of the glacial deposits allows a determination of the greatest extent of the glacier, noted as the Neoglacial maximum (Figure 17.1.2b). The previous extent of the glacier's terminus in 1966 is drawn on the 2001 photo for comparison.

Research covering almost 50 years of 67 glaciers in Alaska was published in 2002. The study estimated volume

changes in these glaciers. The glaciers were grouped into seven regions, shown in Figure 17.1.3a. The rate of glacier-wide thickness loss for 67 glaciers between the mid-1950s and 1995 and for 28 glaciers between 1995 and 2001 are in Figure 17.1.3b.

A total volume change was estimated to be −52 ± 15 km³ per year (−12.5 ± 3.6 mi³). These losses alone account for a rise in global sea level. Therefore, about 9% of global sea-level rise is coming from the Alaskan meltdown.

The reasons for these losses are complex. Thinning and wastage are not solely a result of climatic warming; however, these changes appear to be initiated by negative mass balances due to the warming. The individual dynamics of each glacier must be considered. Relative to the contribution of the Alaskan meltdown to sea-level rise, the scientists summarized in 2002:

Compared with estimated inputs from the Greenland ice sheet and other sources, Alaskan glaciers

Neoglacial maximum
(around 1840)

(b)

FIGURE 17.1.2 Photographs of Peyto Glacier.
(a) Peyto Glacier in 1966, at the beginning of the mass balance record. (b) In 2001, dashed line represents the extent of glacial ice in 1966 and illustrates the quantity of ice that has retreated since the mass balance was recorded. [Photos by (a) Mike Demuth, National Water Research Institute, Canadian Glacier Information Centre; (b) Mike Demuth.]

FIGURE 17.1.3 Negative mass balances for Alaska's glaciers.
(a) Sixty-seven Alaskan glaciers divided into seven regions: 55 in Alaska, 11 cross the Alaskan–Canadian border, and one is in the Yukon. (b) Rate of change (metres per year) in glacierwide thickness for 67 glaciers in the earlier period (1950s to 1995, solid brown bars) and 28 glaciers in the recent period (1995 to 2001, red bars). Note the grouping of glaciers into seven regions indicated on the map in (a). [Adapted by permission of AAAS, from Anthony A. Arendt et al., Figures 1 and 3, "Rapid wastage of Alaska glaciers and their contribution to rising sea level," *Science 297* (July 19, 2002): 382–86.]

ANIMATION

Budget of a Glacier,
Mass Balance

(continued)

News Report 17.1 (continued)

have, over the past 50 years, made the largest single glaciological contribution to rising sea level yet measured. . . . the different rates of thinning observed in the various Alaskan regions may be important in characterizing patterns of climate change.*

*A. A. Arendt, et al., "Rapid Wastage of Alaska Glaciers and Their Contribution to Rising Sea Level," *Science* 297 (July 19, 2002): 382–86.

(Figure 17.8). Meltwater can also flow englacially, that is, anywhere within the glacial ice. Finally, meltwater can flow supraglacially, in streams across the surface of the glacier (Figure 17.9).

Glacial Movement

Like all minerals, ice has specific properties of hardness, colour, melting point (quite low in the case of ice), and brittleness. We know the properties of ice best from those brittle little cubes in the freezer. But glacial ice has different properties, depending on its location in a glacier. In a glacier's depths, glacial ice behaves in a plastic manner, distorting and flowing in response to weight and pressure

FIGURE 17.9 Supraglacial meltwater channel.
Water flowing on the glacier surface melts a channel with slippery sides and rapid flow. The channel snakes across the glacier surface. [Photo by Brian Milne/firstlight.ca.]

from above and the degree of slope below. In contrast, the glacier's upper portion is more like the everyday ice we know, quite brittle.

A glacier's rate of flow ranges from almost nothing to a kilometre or two per year on a steep slope. The rate of snow accumulation in the formation area is critical to the pace of glacial movement.

Glaciers are not rigid blocks that simply slide downhill. The greatest movement within a valley glacier occurs *internally*, below the rigid surface layer, where the underlying zone moves plastically forward (Figure 17.10a). At the same time, the base creeps and slides along, varying its speed with temperature and the presence of any lubricating water or saturated sediment beneath the ice. This *basal slip* usually is much slower than the internal plastic flow of the glacier, so the upper portion of the glacier flows ahead of the lower portion. The difference in speed stretches the glacier's brittle surface ice.

In addition, the pressure may vary in response to unevenness in the landscape beneath the ice. Basal ice may be melted by compression at one moment, only to refreeze later. This process is *ice regelation*, meaning to refreeze, or re-gel. Regelation is important because it facilitates downslope movement and because the process incorporates rock debris into the glacier. Consequently, a glacier's basal ice layer, which can extend tens of metres above its base, has a much greater debris content than the ice above.

A flowing alpine glacier or ice stream in a continental glacier can develop vertical cracks known as **crevasses**

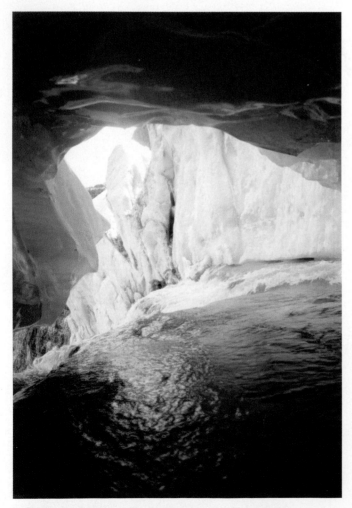

FIGURE 17.8 Meltwater channel beneath a glacier.
Water flowing beneath a glacier can carve channels in the ice that become rapidly flowing meltwater streams. [Photo by Otterburn Geographic.]

(a)

(c)

(b)

(d)

FIGURE 17.10 Glacial movement.
(a) Cross section of a glacier, showing its forward motion and brittle cracking at the surface and flow along its basal layer. (b) Surface crevasses and cracks are evidence of a glacier's forward motion on Yalour Island, Antarctica. (c) Crevasses frame this ice stream flowing off the Greenland Ice Sheet, evidence of great stress forces at work far inland in the ice sheet. (d) Crevasses mark the jumbled surface of this glacier in Hornsund, Spitsbergen, Arctic Ocean. [All photos by Bobbé Christopherson.]

(Figure 17.10b, c, and d). Crevasses result from friction with valley walls, or tension from stretching as the glacier passes over convex slopes, or compression as the glacier passes over concave slopes. Traversing a glacier, whether an alpine glacier or an ice sheet, is dangerous because a thin veneer of snow sometimes masks the presence of a crevasse.

Glacier Surges   Although glaciers flow plastically and predictably most of the time, some will lurch forward with little or no warning in a **glacier surge**. A surge is not quite as abrupt as it sounds; in glacial terms, a surge can be tens of metres per day. The Jakobshavn Glacier on the western Greenland coast, for example, is one of the fastest moving at between 7 and 12 km (4.3 and 7.5 mi) a year.

The doubling of ice-mass loss from Greenland between 1996 and 2005 means that glaciers are surging overall. In southern Greenland in 2007 outlet glaciers were averaging 22.8 m (75 ft) per year. This is significant because in 1999 the average flow rate was 1.8 m (6 ft) per

year. In Greenland, scientists determined that 2006–2007 experienced more days of melting snow at higher elevations than average. The fear is that the meltwater works its way to the basal layer, lubricating underlying *soft beds* of clay.

The exact cause of such a glacier surge is being studied. Some surge events result from a buildup of water pressure under the glacier, sometimes enough to actually float the glacier slightly, detaching it from its bed during the surge. As a surge begins, ice quakes are detectable and ice faults are visible. Surges can occur in dry conditions as well, as the glacier plucks (picks up) rock from its bed and moves forward.

Another cause of glacier surges is the presence of a water-saturated layer of sediment, a so-called *soft bed*, beneath the glacier. This is a deformable layer that cannot resist the tremendous sheer stress produced by the moving ice of the glacier. Scientists examining cores taken from several ice streams now accelerating through the West Antarctic Ice Sheet think they have identified this

FIGURE 17.11 Glacial sandpapering polishes rock. Glacial polish and striations are examples of glacial abrasion and erosion. The polished, marked surface is seen beneath a glacial erratic—a rock left behind by a retreating glacier. [Photo by Bobbé Christopherson.]

cause of glacial surges—although water pressure is still important.

Glacial Erosion The way in which a glacier erodes the land is similar to a large excavation project, with the glacier hauling debris from one site to another for deposition. The passing glacier mechanically plucks rock material and carries it away. Debris is carried on its surface and is also transported internally, or *englacially*, embedded within the glacier itself. There is evidence that rock pieces actually freeze to the basal layers of the glacier in a *glacial plucking*, or a picking up process, and once embedded, enable the glacier to scour and sandpaper the landscape as it moves—a process of **abrasion**. This abrasion and gouging produce a smooth surface on exposed rock, which shines with *glacial polish* when the glacier retreats. Larger rocks in the glacier act much like chisels, gouging the underlying surface and producing glacial striations parallel to the flow direction (Figure 17.11).

Glacial Landforms

Glacial erosion and deposition produce distinctive landforms that differ greatly from the way the land looked before the ice came and went. You might expect all glaciers to create the same landforms, but alpine and continental glaciers each generate their own characteristic landscapes. We look first at erosional landforms created by alpine glaciers, then at their depositional landforms. Finally, we examine the landscape that results from continental glaciation.

Erosional Landforms Created by Alpine Glaciation

Alpine glaciers create spectacular, dramatic landforms that bring to mind the Canadian Rockies, the Swiss Alps, or vaulted Himalayan peaks. Geomorphologist William Morris Davis depicted the stages of a valley glacier in drawings published in 1906 and redrawn here

in Figure 17.12. Study of these figures reveals the handiwork of ice as sculptor:

- In (a), you see typical stream-cut valleys as they exist before glaciation. Note the prominent **V**-shaped valley.
- In (b), you see the same landscape during subsequent glaciation. Glacial erosion and transport actively remove much of the regolith (weathered bedrock) and the soils that covered the stream-valley landscape. As the *cirque* walls erode away, sharp ridges form, dividing adjacent cirque basins. These **arêtes** ("knife-edge" in French) become the *sawtooth*, serrated ridges in glaciated mountains. Two eroding cirques may reduce an arête to a saddlelike depression or pass, called a **col**. A **horn** (pyramidal peak) results when several cirque glaciers gouge an individual mountain summit from all sides. Most famous is the Matterhorn in the Swiss Alps, but many others occur worldwide. A **bergschrund** forms when a crevasse or wide crack opens along the headwall of a glacier, most visible in summer when covering snow is gone.
- In (c), you see the same landscape at a time of warmer climate when the ice has retreated. The glaciated valleys now are **U**-shaped, greatly changed from their previous stream-cut **V** form. You can see the steep sides and the straightened course of the valleys. Physical weathering from the freeze-thaw cycle has loosened rock along the steep cliffs, where it has fallen to form *talus slopes* along the valley sides.

Note in Figure 17.12c that in the cirques where the valley glaciers originated, small mountain lakes called **tarns** have formed. One cirque contains small, circular, stair-stepped lakes called **paternoster** ("our father") **lakes** for their resemblance to rosary (religious) beads. Paternoster lakes may have formed from the differing resistance of rock to glacial processes or from damming by glacial deposits.

The valleys carved by tributary glaciers are left stranded high above the valley floor, because the primary glacier eroded the valley floor so deeply. These *hanging valleys* are the sites of spectacular waterfalls.

Where a glacial trough intersects the ocean, the glacier can continue to erode the landscape, even below sea level. As the glacier retreats, the trough floods and forms a deep **fjord** in which the sea extends inland, filling the lower reaches of the steep-sided valley (Figure 17.13).

FIGURE 17.12 The geomorphic handiwork of alpine glaciers.
(a) A preglacial landscape with V-shaped stream-cut valleys. (b) The same landscape filled with valley glaciers. Note inset photos of a *horn*, a *cirque basin, sawtooth ridge,* and *bergschrund.* (c) When the glaciers retreat, the new landscape is unveiled. Note inset photos of *glacial erratics,* a *hanging valley* and waterfall, *tarn* (lake), and characteristic U-shaped glacial valley, or trough, shown in surface and aerial views. [After W. M. Davis, in Tarbuck, Lutgens, and Pinzke, *Applications and Investigations in Earth Science* (New York: Macmillan, an imprint of Prentice Hall, Inc., 1994), p. 85. Photos: waterfall by Robert W. Christopherson; all other photos by Bobbé Christopherson.]

(a) Preglacial

V-shaped valley

(b) Glacial

Col
Horn
Sawtooth
Arête
Truncated spurs
Cirque
Medial moraine
Main glacier
Bergschrund

Teton Glacier

NOTEBOOK

Glacial erratics

(c) Postglacial

Arête
Col Horn
Paternoster lakes
Cirques
U-shaped glacial trough
Hanging valley
U-shaped valley, aerial
Hanging waterfall
Tarn
U-shaped valley

FIGURE 17.13 Norwegian fjord.
The beautiful Fjoerfjorden, Norway, where an inlet of the sea fills a U-shaped, glacially carved valley. [Photo by Bobbé Christopherson.]

The fjord may be flooded further by rising sea level or by changes in the elevation of the coastal region. All along the glaciated coast of Alaska, glaciers now are in retreat, thus opening many new fjords that previously were blocked by ice. Coastlines with notable fjords include those of Norway, Greenland, Chile, the South Island of New Zealand, Alaska, and British Columbia.

In Figure 17.14 see how many of the erosional forms from Figure 17.12 (arêtes, col, horn, cirque, cirque glacier, sawtooth ridge, **U**-shaped valleys, erratics, tarn, and truncated spurs, among others) you can identify in these two photographs of glaciers at work. In terms of net mass balance, what is your assessment of the status of the merging glaciers in Figure 17.14b?

Depositional Landforms Created by Alpine Glaciation

You have just seen how glaciers excavate tremendous amounts of material and create fascinating landforms in the process. Glaciers produce a different set of distinctive landforms when

(a)

FIGURE 17.14 Erosional features of Alpine glaciation.
(a) Many of the erosional glacial features appear in this scene from southern Greenland. How many of the erosional features illustrated in Figure 17.12 can you find in the photo? (b) These merging glaciers along Beverlysundet, Nordaustlandet Island, Arctic Ocean, form a medial moraine and haul erratic boulders on their surfaces that have cracked off the cliffs through frost action. [Photos by Bobbé Christopherson.]

(b)

they melt and deposit their debris cargo at the glacier's *terminus*. Figures 17.7a, e, and f show that after the glacier melts, debris accumulates in moraines to mark the former margins of the glacier, both its end and sides.

Glacial Drift   The general term for all glacial deposits, both unsorted and sorted, is **glacial drift**. Sediments deposited by glacial meltwater are sorted by size and are **stratified drift**. **Till** describes direct ice deposits left as unstratified and unsorted debris.

As a glacier flows to a lower elevation, a wide assortment of rock fragments becomes *entrained* (carried along) on its surface or embedded within its mass or in its base. As the glacier melts, this unsorted cargo is deposited on the ground surface. Such till is poorly sorted and is difficult to cultivate for farming, but the clays and finer particles can provide a basis for soil development.

Retreating glaciers leave behind large rocks (sometimes house-sized), boulders, and cobbles that are "foreign" in composition and origin from the ground on which they were deposited. These *glacial erratics*, lying in strange locations with no obvious means of transport, were an early clue that blankets of ice once had covered the land (pictured in Figure 17.12c).

Moraines   The deposition of glacial sediments produces a specific landform called a **moraine**. Several types of

moraines are exhibited in Figure 17.15. A **lateral moraine** forms along each side of a glacier. If two glaciers with lateral moraines join, a **medial moraine** may form (see Figures 17.7e and f, and 17.15b). In Figure 17.15c you see tributaries flowing in to form a *compound valley glacier*. The flowing movement of such a valley glacier is different from that of a river with tributaries. Tributary glaciers flow into a compound glacier and merge alongside one another by extending and thinning rather than by blending, as do rivers. Each tributary maintains its own patterns of transported debris (dark streaks, visible on the photo).

A deposition of till that is generally spread across a surface is called a *ground moraine*, or *till plain*, and may hide the former landscape. Such plains are found in portions of the Canadian Prairies and southern Ontario, as well as the upper U.S. Midwest.

Eroded debris that is dropped at the glacier's farthest extent is a **terminal moraine**. However, there also may be *end moraines*, formed at other points where a glacier paused after reaching a new equilibrium between growth and ablation. Lakes may form behind terminal and end moraines after a glacier's retreat, with the moraine acting as a dam.

All of these till types are poorly sorted and unstratified. In contrast, streams of glacial meltwater can carry and deposit sorted and stratified glacial drift beyond a terminal moraine. Meltwater-deposited material downvalley from a glacier is a *valley train deposit*. Peyto Glacier in

(a)

(b)

(d)

(c)

FIGURE 17.15 Depositional features of alpine glaciation.
Medial, lateral, and ground moraine deposits are evident in eastern and southern Greenland. (a) As these tributary glaciers merge, their lateral moraines combine to form a medial moraine. (b) Retreating ice leaves behind these lateral moraines. (c) Note how each lateral moraine remains identifiable as they combine in this valley glacier. How many moraines can you count? Note the medial moraine flowing from the upper-left corner of the photo. (d) A terminal moraine forms this island separated from its ice-cap glacier by more than a kilometre of ocean, at Isispynten Island, Arctic Ocean. [All photos by Bobbé Christopherson.]

FIGURE 17.16 A valley train deposit.
Peyto Glacier in Alberta, Canada, is in extensive retreat. Note valley train, braided stream, and milky-coloured glacial meltwater. [Photo by Robert W. Christopherson.]

watercourse. Commercially valuable deposits of sand and gravel are quarried from some eskers.

Sometimes an isolated block of ice, perhaps more than a kilometre across, remains in a ground moraine, an outwash plain, or valley floor after a glacier has retreated. As much as 20 to 30 years is required for it to melt. In the interim, material continues to accumulate around the melting ice block. When the block finally melts, it leaves behind a steep-sided hole. Such a feature then frequently fills with water. This feature is a **kettle**. Thoreau's famous Walden Pond, mentioned in the quotation in Chapter 7, is such a glacial kettle and is pictured in Figure 17.17c.

Another feature of outwash plains is a **kame**, a small hill, knob, or mound of poorly sorted sand and gravel that is deposited directly by water, by ice in crevasses, or in ice-caused indentations in the surface (Figure 17.17d). Kames also can be found in deltaic forms and in terraces along valley walls.

Alberta, Canada, produces such a valley train that continues into Peyto Lake (Figure 17.16). Distributary stream channels appear braided across its surface. The picture also shows the milky meltwater associated with glaciers, laden with finely ground "rock flour."

Erosional and Depositional Landforms Created by Continental Glaciation

The extent of the most recent continental glaciation in North America and Europe, 18,000 years ago, is portrayed several pages ahead in Figure 17.29. When these huge sheets of ice advanced and retreated, they produced some of the erosional and depositional features characteristic of alpine glaciation. However, because continental glaciers form under different circumstances—not in mountains, but across broad, open landscapes—the intricately carved alpine features, lateral moraines, and medial moraines all are lacking in continental glaciation. Table 17.1 compares the erosional and depositional features of alpine (valley) and continental glaciers.

Figure 17.17 illustrates some of the most common erosional and depositional features associated with the retreat of a continental glacier. A **till plain** forms behind an end moraine; it features *unstratified* coarse till, has low and rolling relief, and has a deranged drainage pattern (see Figure 17.17a and Figure 14.9). Beyond the morainal deposits lies the **outwash plain** of *stratified drift* featuring stream channels that are meltwater-fed, braided, and overloaded with sorted and deposited materials.

Figure 17.17b shows a sinuously curving, narrow ridge of coarse sand and gravel called an **esker**. It forms along the channel of a meltwater stream that flows beneath a glacier, in an ice tunnel, or between ice walls. As a glacier retreats, the steep-sided esker is left behind in a pattern roughly parallel to the path of the glacier. The ridge may not be continuous and in places may even appear to be branched, following the path set by the subglacial

Table 17.1 Features of Valley Glaciation and Continental Glaciation Compared

Features and Landforms	Alpine (Valley) Glacier	Continental Glaciation
Erosional		
Striations, polish, etc.	Common	Common
Cirques	Common	Absent
Horns, arêtes, cols	Common	Absent
U-shaped valleys, truncated spurs, hanging valleys	Common	Rare
Fjords	Common	Absent
Roche moutonnée	Common	Common
Depositional		
Till	Common	Common
Terminal moraines	Common	Common
Recessional moraines	Common	Common
Ground moraines	Common	Common
Lateral moraines	Common	Absent
Medial moraines	Common, easily destroyed	Absent
Drumlins	Rare or absent	Locally common
Erratics	Common	Common
Stratified drift	Common	Common
Kettles	Common	Common
Eskers, crevasse fillings	Rare	Common
Kames	Common	Common
Kame terraces	Common	Present in hilly country

Source: Adapted from L. D. Leet, S. Judson, and M. Kauffman, *Physical Geology*, 5th ed., © 1978, p. 317. Upper Saddle River, NJ.: Prentice Hall, Inc.

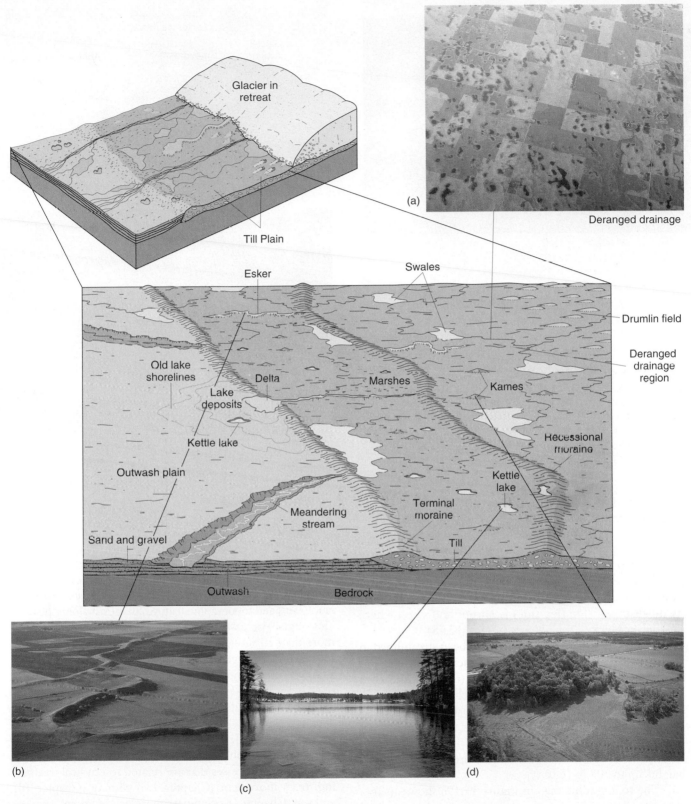

FIGURE 17.17 Continental glacier depositional features.
Common depositional landforms produced by glaciers. (a) Deranged drainage tells us continental glaciers advanced and retreated across the prairies of central Saskatchewan, Canada. (b) An esker through farmland near Dahlen, North Dakota. (c) Walden Pond is a kettle surrounded by mixed forest near Boston, Massachusetts. (d) A kame covered by a woodlot near Campbellsport, Wisconsin.
[Illustration from R. M. Busch, ed., *Laboratory Manual in Physical Geology,* 3rd ed. (New York: Macmillan, an imprint of Prentice Hall, Inc., 1993), p. 188. Photos by (a) and (c) Bobbé Christopherson; (b) and (d) Tom Bean/DRK.]

(a)

(b)

(c)

FIGURE 17.18 Glacial erosion streamlined rock.
Roche moutonnée, as exemplified by (a) this formation on the
Melville Peninsula, Nunavut, and (c) Lembert Dome in the
Tuolumne Meadows area of Yosemite National Park, California.
[Photo (a) courtesy of Earth Sciences Sector, National Resources
Canada; (c) by Robert W. Christopherson.]

Glacial action also forms two types of streamlined hills. One is erosional, called a *roche moutonnée*, and the other is depositional, called a *drumlin*. A **roche moutonnée** ("sheep rock" in French) is an asymmetrical hill of exposed bedrock. Its gently sloping upstream side (stoss side) has been polished smooth by glacial action, whereas its downstream side (lee side) is abrupt and steep where the glacier plucked rock pieces (Figure 17.18).

A **drumlin** is deposited till that has been streamlined in the direction of continental ice movement, blunt end upstream and tapered end downstream (the opposite of a roche moutonnée). Drumlins occur in fields across the landscape in all parts of Canada, with particularly good examples in Nova Scotia and Ontario. Sometimes their shape is that of an elongated teaspoon bowl, lying face down. They attain lengths of 100–5000 m (300 ft to more than 3 mi) and heights up to 200 m (650 ft).

The topographic map in Figure 17.19a shows an area near Peterborough, Ontario, that experienced continental glaciation during the Wisconsinan. The remotely sensed image in Figure 17.19b allows you to see the drumlins as they appear on the surface. From the orientation of the drumlins on the map and in the photo, can you determine the direction of continental ice movement? (Look for gentle, tapered slopes in the downstream direction of each drumlin, left behind as the glacier retreated.)

Periglacial Landscapes

In 1909, Polish geologist W. Lozinski coined the term **periglacial** to describe frost weathering and freeze-thaw rock shattering in the Carpathian Mountains. He expanded the concept in 1910 to include several cold-climate processes, landforms, and topographic features that exist along the margins of glaciers, past and present. Periglacial regions occupy more than 20% of Earth's land surface and include features formed under nonglacial conditions. Under these conditions, a unique combination of frost action and periglacial processes operate, including permafrost, frost action, and ground ice.

Climatologically, these regions are in *subarctic* and *polar* climates, especially *tundra* climate. Such climates occur either at high latitude (tundra and boreal forest environments) or at high elevation in lower-latitude mountains (alpine environments). Processes that are related to physical weathering, mass movement (Chapter 13), climate (Chapter 10), and soil (Chapter 18) dominate periglacial regions.

Geography of Permafrost

When soil or rock temperatures remain below 0°C (32°F) for at least 2 years, **permafrost** ("permanent frost") develops. An area of permafrost that is not covered by glaciers is considered periglacial. Note that this criterion is based solely on *temperature* and has nothing to do with how

(a)

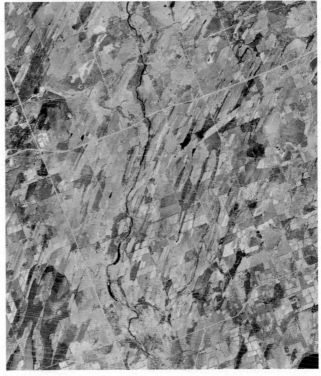

FIGURE 17.19 Glacially deposited streamlined features.
(a) Topographic map of Peterborough, Ontario, featuring
numerous drumlins. (b) aerial photo of Peterborough Drumlin
Field. [From Ontario Ortho Photos, Natural Resources Canada.
Used by permission of the Minister of Public Works and
Government Services.]

(b)

much or how little water is present. Two other factors also
contribute to permafrost: the presence of fossil permafrost
from previous ice-age conditions and the insulating effect
of snow cover or vegetation that inhibits heat loss.

Continuous and Discontinuous Zones   Permafrost
regions are divided into two general categories: continuous
and discontinuous, which merge along a general transition
zone. *Continuous permafrost* is the region of severest cold and
is perennial, roughly poleward of the −7°C (19°F) mean
annual temperature isotherm (purple area in Figure 17.20).
Continuous permafrost affects all surfaces except those
beneath deep lakes or rivers. The depth of continuous
permafrost may exceed 1000 m (3300 ft), averaging approximately 400 m (1300 ft).

Unconnected patches of *discontinuous permafrost* gradually coalesce poleward toward the continuous zone. Permafrost

becomes scattered or sporadic until it gradually disappears
equatorward of the −1°C (30.2°F) mean annual temperature isotherm (dark blue area on map). In the discontinuous
zone, permafrost is absent on sun-exposed south-facing
slopes, areas of warm soil, or areas insulated by snow. In the
Southern Hemisphere, north-facing slopes experience increased warmth.

As much as 50% of Canada and 80% of Alaska are affected by permafrost of either type. In central Eurasia, the effects of continentality and elevation produce discontinuous
permafrost that extends equatorward to the 50th parallel.

Areas of discontinuous permafrost feature a mixture
of *cryotic* (frozen) and *noncryotic* ground. In addition to
these two types of ground, zones of high-altitude *alpine
permafrost* extend to lower latitudes, as shown on the map.
Microclimatic factors such as slope orientation and snow
cover are important in the alpine environment.

FIGURE 17.20 Permafrost distribution.
Distribution of permafrost in the Northern Hemisphere. Alpine permafrost is noted except for small occurrences in Hawai'i, Mexico, Europe, and Japan. Sub-sea permafrost occurs in the ground beneath the Arctic Ocean along the margins of the continents, as shown. Note the towns of Resolute and Coppermine (Kugluktuk) in Nunavut (formerly part of NWT) and Hotchkiss in Alberta. A cross section of the permafrost beneath these towns is shown in Figure 17.21. [Adapted from T. L. Péwé, "Alpine permafrost in the contiguous United States: A review," *Arctic and Alpine Research* 15, no. 2 (May 1983): 146. © University of Colorado. Used by permission.]

Subsea permafrost

Continuous permafrost

Discontinuous permafrost

Alpine permafrost

In the Mackenzie Mountains of Canada (62°N), continuous permafrost extends down to an elevation of 1200 m (4000 ft), and discontinuous permafrost occurs throughout the range. The Colorado Rockies (40°N) experience continuous permafrost down to an elevation of 3400 m (11,150 ft) and discontinuous permafrost to 1700 m (5600 ft).

Behaviour of Permafrost We looked at the spatial distribution of permafrost; now let us examine how permafrost behaves. Figure 17.21 is a stylized cross section from approximately 75° N to 55° N, using the three sites located on the map in Figure 17.20. The **active layer** is the zone of seasonally frozen ground that exists between the subsurface permafrost layer and the ground surface.

The active layer is subjected to consistent daily and seasonal freeze-thaw cycles. This cyclic melting of the active layer affects as little as 10 cm (4 in.) depth in the north (Ellesmere Island, 78° N), up to 2 m (6.6 ft) in the southern margins (55° N) of the periglacial region, and 15m (50 ft) in the alpine permafrost of the Colorado Rockies (40° N).

The depth and thickness of the active layer and permafrost zone change slowly in response to climatic change. Higher temperatures degrade (reduce) permafrost and increase the thickness of the active layer; lower temperatures gradually aggrade (increase) permafrost depth and reduce active-layer thickness. Although somewhat sluggish in response, the active layer is a dynamic open system driven by energy gains and losses in the subsurface environment. As you might expect, most permafrost exists in disequilibrium with environmental conditions and therefore actively adjusts to inconstant climatic conditions.

With the incredibly warm temperatures recorded in the Canadian and Siberian Arctic since 1990, more disruption of surfaces is occurring—leading to highway, railway, and building damage. This warming is causing a large release of carbon from peat-rich thawed ground that in turn influences the global greenhouse—a real-time positive feedback mechanism. In Siberia, many lakes have disappeared in the discontinuous permafrost region as subsurface drainage opens, yet new lakes have formed in the continuous region as thawed soils become waterlogged. In Canada hundreds of lakes have disappeared simply from excessive evaporation into the warm air. These trends are measurable from satellite imagery. The thaw in the active layer in the Alaskan tundra has shortened the number of days that oil exploration equipment can venture out from 200 to only 100 days a year. The weight of the trucks requires a frozen, more solid surface to operate.

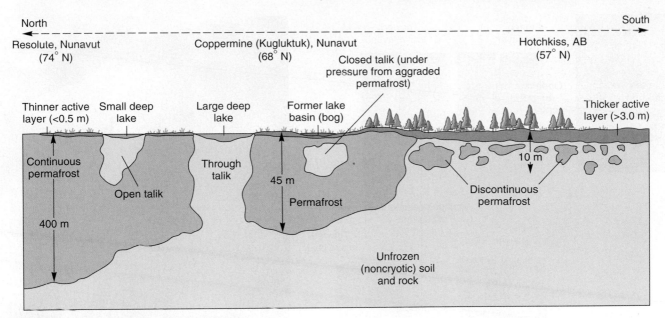

FIGURE 17.21 Periglacial environments.
Cross section of a periglacial region in northern Canada, showing typical forms of permafrost, active layer, talik, and ground ice. The three sites noted are shown on the map in Figure 17.20.

A *talik* is unfrozen ground that may occur above, below, or within a body of discontinuous permafrost or beneath a water body in the continuous region. Taliks occur beneath deep lakes and may extend to bedrock and noncryotic soil beneath large, deep lakes (see Figure 17.21). Taliks form connections between the active layer and groundwater, whereas in continuous permafrost groundwater is essentially cut off from surface water. In this way, permafrost disrupts aquifers and taliks, leading to water-supply problems.

Ground Ice and Frozen Ground Phenomena

In regions of permafrost, frozen subsurface water is termed *ground ice*. The moisture content of areas with ground ice varies from nearly none in drier regions to almost 100% in saturated soils. From the area of maximum energy loss, freezing progresses through the ground along a *freezing front*, or boundary between frozen and unfrozen soil. The presence of frozen water in the soil initiates geomorphic processes associated with *frost action* and the expansion of water as it freezes. Ground ice may occur as:

- Common *pore ice* (subsurface water frozen in the soil's pore spaces)
- *Lenses* (horizontal bodies) and *veins* (channels extending in any direction)
- *Segregated ice* (layers of buried ice that increase in mass by accreting water as the ground freezes, producing layers of relatively pure ice)
- *Intrusive ice* (the freezing of water injected under pressure, as in a pingo, discussed shortly)
- *Wedge ice* (surface water entering a crack and freezing)

Various aspects of frost action as a geomorphic agent are discussed in Chapter 13 ("Physical Weathering Processes" and the section "Classes of Mass Movements," which describes soil creep). Some forms of ground ice may occur at the surface during episodes of *icing*, in which a river or spring forms freezing layers of surface ice. Such icings can occur on slopes as well as level ground. Spring flooding along rivers can result from the presence of icings; it is a particular problem in rivers draining into the Arctic Ocean.

Frost Action Processes   The 9% expansion of water as it freezes produces strong mechanical forces. Such frost action shatters rock, producing angular pieces that form a *block field*, or *felsenmeer*. The felsenmeer accumulates as part of the arctic and alpine periglacial landscape, particularly on mountain summits and slopes (see Figure 13.8a and 13.9).

If sufficient water freezes, the saturated soil and rocks are subjected to *frost-heaving* (vertical movement) and *frost-thrusting* (horizontal movement). Boulders and rock slabs may be thrust to the surface. Soil horizons (layers) may be disrupted by frost action and appear to be stirred or churned, a process termed *cryoturbation*. Frost action also can produce contractions in soil and rock, opening up cracks for ice wedges to form. Also, there is a tremendous increase in pressure in the soil as ice expands, particularly if there are multiple freezing fronts trapping unfrozen soil and water between them.

An *ice wedge* develops when water enters a crack in the permafrost and freezes (Figure 17.22). Thermal contraction in ice-rich soil forms a tapered crack—wider at the top, narrowing toward the bottom. Repeated seasonal freezing

FIGURE 17.22 Evolution of an ice wedge.
(a) Sequential illustration of ice-wedge formation beginning with a crack in the tundra shown in the photo. (b) An ice wedge and ground ice in northern Canada. [(a) Illustration adapted from A. H. Lachenbruch, "Mechanics of thermal contraction and ice-wedge polygons in permafrost," *Geological Society of America Bulletin Special Paper 70* (1962). Photos by (a) Bobbé Christopherson; (b) H. M. French.]

and melting progressively enlarge the wedge, which may widen from a few millimetres to 5–6 m (16–20 ft) and up to 30 m (100 ft) in depth. Widening may be small each year, but after many years the wedge can become significant, like the sample shown in Figure 17.22b.

Thin layers of sediment that form foliations in the wedge mark the annual thickness of ice added. Thus, the age of a wedge can be determined by counting the foliations, like counting annual accumulations recorded in an ice core. In summer, when the active layer thaws, the wedge itself may not be visible. However, the presence of a wedge beneath the surface is noticeable where the ice-expanded sediments form raised, upturned ridges.

Frost-Action Landforms Large areas of frozen ground (soil-covered ice) can develop a heaved-up, circular, ice-cored mound called a *pingo*. It rises above the flat landscape, occasionally exceeding 60 m (200 ft) in height. Pingos rise when freezing water expands, sometimes as a result of pressure developed by artesian water injected into permafrost (Figure 17.23).

A *palsa* (from the Swedish word for "elliptical") is a rounded or elliptical mound of peat that contains thin perennial ice lenses rather than an ice core, as in a pingo. Palsas can be 2–30 m (6–100 ft) wide by 1–10 m (3–30 ft) high and usually are covered by soil or vegetation over a cracked surface.

FIGURE 17.23 A pingo.
An ice-cored pingo resulting from hydraulic pressures that pushed the mound upward above the landscape. Coastal erosion exposed the ice core. This pingo is near Tuktoyaktuk, Mackenzie Delta, NWT, Canada. [Photo by H. M. French.]

Frost-action expansion and contraction results in the transport of stones and boulders. As the water-ice volume changes and an ice wedge deepens, coarser particles are moved toward the surface. An area with a system of ground ice and frost action develops sorted and unsorted accumulations of rock at the surface that take the shape of polygons called **patterned ground**.

Patterned ground may include polygons of sorted rocks that coalesce into stone polygon nets (Figure 17.24). Various terms are in use to describe such ice-wedge and stone polygon forms: nets, circles, vegetation-covered

FIGURE 17.24 Patterned ground phenomena.
(a) Patterned ground in Beacon Valley of the McMurdo Dry Valleys of East Antarctica. (b) Rock nets form polygons and circles (about a metre across) near Duvefjord, Nordaustlandet Island, Arctic Ocean. (c) Patterned ground in stripes, near Sundbukta, Barents Island, Arctic Ocean. (d) Polygons in the Martian northern plains; each coll averages a little more than 100 m across (300 ft). [Photos by (a) writer Joan Myers; (b) and (c) Bobbé Christopherson; and (d) image from the *Mars Global Surveyor,* Mars Orbiter Camera, courtesy of NASA/JPL/Malin Space Science Systems, May 1999.]

(a)

(b)

(c)

(d)

hummocks, and stripes (elongated polygons formed on a hillslope). Ice wedges sometimes are found beneath the perimeter of each cell; however, questions still exist as to how such patterned ground actually develops and the degree to which such ground forms are the vestiges of past eras. Such features may take centuries to form. Such polygon nets in patterned ground provide vivid evidence of frozen subsurface water on Mars (Figure 17.24d). In this 1999 image, the *Mars Global Surveyor* captured a region of these features on the Martian northern plains. To date, some 600 different sites on Mars demonstrate such patterned ground.

Hillslope Processes: Gelifluction and Solifluction

Soil drainage is poor in areas of permafrost and ground ice. The active layer of soil and regolith is saturated with soil moisture during the thaw cycle (summer), and the whole layer commences to flow from higher to lower elevation if the landscape is even slightly inclined. This flow of soil is generally called *solifluction* and may occur in all climate conditions. In the presence of ground ice or permafrost, the more specific term *gelifluction* is applied. In this ice-bound type of soil flow, movement up to 5 cm (2 in.) per year can occur on slopes as gentle as a degree or two.

The cumulative effect of this landflow can be an overall flattening of a rolling landscape, with identifiable sagging surfaces and scalloped and lobed patterns in the downslope soil movements (Figure 17.25). Other types of periglacial mass movement include failure in the active layer, producing translational and rotational slides and rapid flows associated with melting ground ice. Periglacial mass movement processes are related to slope dynamics and processes discussed in Chapter 13, Figure 13.30c.

Thermokarst Landscapes
As ground ice melts, irregular features develop across the landscape, creating *thermokarst* topography. These forms result from thermal subsidence and erosion caused by ice-wedge melting and

FIGURE 17.25 Soil flowage in periglacial environments.
Gelifluction lobes of soil underlain by frozen ground in permafrost conditions, on a hillside on Barents Island, Arctic Ocean. [Photo by Bobbé Christopherson.]

poor drainage. (Note that the term refers only to the topographic style and has nothing to do with the solution processes and chemical weathering that cause limestone karst.)

Thermokarst topography is hummocky, marked by cave-ins, bogs, small depressions, pits, standing water, and small lakes. More thermokarst landforms are found in Siberia and Scandinavia than in North America. In Canada and Alaska, rounded thaw lakes, or cave-in lakes, are thermokarst features. With the incredibly warm temperatures recorded in the Canadian Arctic in the late 1990s, more thermokarst disruption of surfaces is occurring—leading to highway, railway, and building damage.

Humans and Periglacial Landscapes

In areas of permafrost and frozen-ground phenomena, people face several related problems. Because thawed ground above the permafrost zone frequently shifts, highways and rail lines become warped, twisted, and fail and utility lines are disrupted. In addition, any building placed directly on frozen ground will "melt" into the defrosting soil, creating subsidence in structures (Figure 17.26).

Construction in periglacial regions dictates placing structures above the ground to allow air circulation beneath. This airflow allows the ground to cycle through its normal annual temperature pattern. Utilities such as water and sewer lines must be built aboveground in "utilidors" to protect them from freezing and thawing ground (Figure 17.27). Likewise, the Trans-Alaska oil pipeline was constructed aboveground on racks for 675 of its 1285-km (420 of its 800-mi) length to avoid melting the frozen ground, causing shifting that could rupture the line. The pipeline that is underground uses a cooling system to keep the permafrost around the pipeline stable.

The effects of global warming are already showing up in Siberia, where the active layer is now more than twice the depth it was in the past. Buildings constructed with shallow pilings for support will certainly fail if this trend continues. In an era of global change, the regions of permafrost provide further climatic indicators.

The Pleistocene Ice-Age Epoch

Imagine almost a third of Earth's land surface buried beneath ice sheets and glaciers—most of Canada, the northern Midwest, England, and northern Europe, and many mountain ranges, beneath thousands of metres of ice.

FIGURE 17.26 Permafrost thawing and structure collapse.
Building failure due to improper construction and the melting of permafrost, south of Fairbanks, Alaska. [Adapted from U.S. Geological Survey. Photo by Steve McCutcheon, illustration based on U.S. Geological Survey pamphlet "Permafrost" by L. L. Ray.]

Pipeline
1.2 m diameter

Average height
1.5 to 3.0 m

(b)

FIGURE 17.27 Special structures for permafrost.
(a) Proper construction in periglacial environments requires raising of buildings aboveground and running water and sewage lines in elevated "utilidors," here in Barentsburg, a Russian settlement on Spitsbergen Island. (b) Supporting the Trans-Alaska oil pipeline on racks protects the permafrost from heat. [Photos by (a) Bobbé Christopherson; (b) Galen Rowell/Mountain Light Photography, Inc.]

(a)

This is how it was at the height of the Pleistocene Epoch of the late Cenozoic Era. In addition, periglacial regions along the margins of the ice during the last ice age covered about twice their present areal extent.

The Pleistocene is thought to have begun about 1.65 million years ago and is one of the more prolonged cold periods in Earth's history. It featured not just one glacial advance and retreat, but at least 18 expansions of ice over Europe and North America, each obliterating and confusing the evidence from the one before. Apparently, glaciation can take about 90,000 years, whereas deglaciation is rapid, requiring less than about 10,000 years to melt away the accumulation.

The term *ice age*, or *glacial age*, is applied to any extended period of cold (not a single brief cold spell), which may last several million years. An **ice age** is a time of generally cold climate that includes one or more *glacials*, interrupted by brief warm spells known as *interglacials*. Each glacial and interglacial is given a name that is usually based on the location where evidence of the episode is prominent—for example, "Wisconsinan glacial."

Modern research techniques to understand past climates include the examination of ancient ratios of oxygen isotopes, depths of coral growth in the tropics, analysis of ocean and lake sediments worldwide, and analysis of the latest ice cores from Greenland and Antarctica, including the Dome C ice core that plunges the record back 800,000 years. These techniques have opened the way for a new chronology and understanding of past climates and for gaining perspective on the present warming trends. The record is clear and correlates across all proxy methods—present levels of (CO_2) and methane (CH_4) are the highest in 800,000 years, as shown in Chapter 10. Earth systems have no experience in dealing with levels this high during this time span, and these concentrations are increasing.

Glaciologists currently recognize the Illinoian glacial and Wisconsinan glacial interval, with the Sangamon interglacial between them. These events span the 300,000-year interval prior to our present Holocene Epoch (Figure 17.28). The chart shows that the Illinoian glacial actually consisted of two glacials occurring during Marine (oxygen) Isotope Stages (MIS) 6 and 8, as did the Wisconsinan (MIS 2 and 4), which are dated at 10,000 to 35,000 years ago. The oxygen isotope glacial/interglacial stages on the chart are numbered back to MIS 23 at approximately 900,000 years ago. To overcome local bias in core records, investigators correlate oxygen isotope data with other indicators worldwide. Note the label on the chart in the figure at MIS 20.2 for the Dome–C extent of 800,000 years. (For web links on glaciers and the Pleistocene, see **http://userpages.umbc.edu/~miller/geog111/glacierlinks.htm**.)

Changes in the Landscape

The continental ice sheets covered portions of Canada, the United States, Europe, and Asia about 18,000 years ago, as illustrated on the polar map projection in Figure 17.29. Ice sheets ranged in thickness to more than 2 km (1.2 mi). In North America, the Ohio and Missouri river systems mark the southern terminus of continuous ice at its greatest extent during the Pleistocene. The ice sheet disappeared by 7000 years ago.

As both alpine and continental glaciers retreated, they exposed a drastically altered landscape: the rocky soils of New England, the polished and scarred surfaces of Canada's Atlantic Provinces, the sharp crests of the Sawtooth Range and Tetons of Idaho and Wyoming, the scenery of the Canadian Rockies and the Sierra Nevada, the Great Lakes of Canada and the United States, the Matterhorn of Switzerland, and much more. In the Southern Hemisphere, there is evidence of this ice age in the form of fjords and sculpted mountains in New Zealand and Chile.

Age (yr) | Depth (m)

Marine Isotope (Oxygen) Stage (MIS)

122,000
130,000

300,000

5

788,000

900,000
970,000

10

15

1,670,000

1,870,000

20

Colder Warmer

4 Wisconsinan
5 Sangamon
6
7 Illinoian
8
9
10
11 Vostok core — MIS 11
12
13
14
15
16
17
18
19
20 Dome C
21 20.2
22 (2004)
23

Glacial
Interglacial

Pleistocene
Pliocene

FIGURE 17.28 Temperature record of the past 2 million years.
Oxygen isotope fluctuations in fossil planktonic foraminifera (tiny marine organisms having a calcareous shell) from deep-sea cores determine Pleistocene temperatures. Twenty-three Marine (oxygen) Isotope Stages (MIS) cover 900,000 years, with names assigned for the past 300,000 years. [After N. J. Shackelton and N. D. Opdyke, *Oxygen-Isotope and Paleomagnetic Stratigraphy of Pacific Core V28-239, Late Pliocene to Latest Pleistocene.* Geological Society of America Memoir 145. ©1976 by the GSA. Adapted by permission.]

present. During the final retreat, tremendous quantities of glacial meltwater flowed into the isostatically (weight of the ice) depressed basins. Drainage at first was to the Mississippi River via the Illinois River, to the St. Lawrence River via the Ottawa River, and to the Hudson River in the east. In recent times, drainage has shifted through the St. Lawrence system.

Lake Agassiz began to form about 11,700 years ago when water was trapped between the Manitoba Escarpment and the retreating Laurentide ice sheet (Figure 17.30b, c, d, and detailed in e). The ice margin determined the locations of outlet channels. Earth scientists have mapped outlets to the south, east, north, and northwest. About 11,000 years ago, an outlet opened into the basin of present-day Lake Superior and the level of Lake Agassiz fell. As the lake level fell, the rivers that flowed into the lake—the Assiniboine and Saskatchewan rivers—cut downward into their deltas. By 7800 years ago, Lake Agassiz, this largest of all North American lakes, disappeared as the ice sheet disintegrated and water drained into Hudson Bay. All that remains of the former greatest lake are lakes Manitoba, Winnipeg, Dauphin, and Winnipegosis and Lake of the Woods.

Paleolakes

The West was dotted with large lakes 12,000–30,000 years ago. Except for the Great Salt Lake in Utah (remnants of ancient Lake Bonneville) and a few smaller lakes, only dry basins, ancient shorelines, and lake sediments remain today. These ancient lakes are called *paleolakes*.

The term *pluvial* (Latin: "rain") describes any period of wet conditions, such as occurred during the Pleistocene Epoch. During pluvial periods, lake levels increased in arid regions. The drier periods between pluvials are called *interpluvials*. Interpluvials are marked with *lacustrine deposits*, including ancient soils called *paleosols*, which are lake sediments that form terraces along former shorelines.

Are paleolakes of glacial origin like the Great Lakes? Earlier researchers attempted to correlate pluvial and glacial ages, given their coincidence during the Pleistocene. However, few sites actually demonstrate such a simple relation. For example, in the western United States, the estimated volume of melted ice from glaciers is only a small portion of the actual water volume that was in the paleolakes. Also, these lakes tend to predate glacial

Glacial Great Lakes

The continental glaciers came and went several times over the region we know as the Great Lakes (Figure 17.30). The ice enlarged and deepened stream valleys to form the basins of the future lakes. This complex history produced five lakes that today cover 244,000 km² (94,000 mi²) and hold some 18% of all the lake water on Earth.

Figure 17.30 shows the final formation of the Great Lakes, which involved two advancing and two retreating stages—between 13,200 and 10,000 years before the

FIGURE 17.29 Pleistocene glaciation. Extent of Pleistocene glaciation in the Northern Hemisphere 18,000 years ago: North America, a polar perspective, and 9500 years ago (inset map). Earlier episodes produced continental glaciation of slightly greater extent. Note the depth of the continental ice sheets in metres. [From A. McIntyre, *CLIMAP* (Climate: Long-Range Investigation, Mapping, and Prediction) Project, Lamont-Doherty Earth Observatory. © 1981 by the GSA. Adapted by permission.]

18,000 years ago

9500 years ago

FIGURE 17.30 Late stages of Great Lakes formation and glacial Lake Agassiz.

(a)–(d) Four "snapshots" of the Great Lakes' evolving development during the waning of the Wisconsinan glaciation. Note the change in stream drainage between (b) and (d). (e) Note the massive Lake Agassiz at approximately 11,000 B.P. (before the present), when an outlet opened into the Lake Superior basin. The largest of the glacial Great Lakes was trapped between higher ground to the south and the retreating ice sheet. The dashed line delineates the maximum extent of the ancient lake. The lake was never this size; it represents the total area that the lake covered throughout its history, some 4000 years. All that remains of the former greatest lake are lakes Manitoba, Winnipeg, Dauphin, and Winnipegosis in Manitoba and the Lake of the Woods in Ontario. [(a) through (d) After *The Great Lakes—An Environmental Atlas and Resource Book*, Environment Canada, U.S. EPA, Brock University, and Northwestern University (Toronto: Environment Canada, 1987), p. 7; (e) adapted from A. S. Trenhaile, *Geomorphology: A Canadian Perspective*, from Teller, in Karrow and Calkin, 1985.]

times and are correlated instead with periods of wetter climate, or periods thought to have had lower evaporation rates. The term *paleolake* is used in the scientific literature to describe these lakes and to separate their occurrence from specific glacial stages.

Paleolakes existed in North and South America, Africa, Asia, and Australia. Today, the Caspian Sea in Kazakstan and southern Russia has a level of 30 m (100 ft) below mean world sea level, but ancient shorelines are visible about 80 m (265 ft) above the present lake level. In North America, the two largest late Pleistocene paleolakes were in the Basin and Range Province of the West—Lake Bonneville and Lake Lahontan.

New evidence reveals that the occurrence of these lakes in North America was related to specific changes in the polar jet stream that steered storm tracks across the region, creating pluvial conditions. The continental ice sheet evidently influenced changes in jet-stream position.

Study of these glaciated landscapes is important to help us better understand paleoclimatology (past climates) and discover the mechanisms that produce ice ages and climatic change.

Lowered Sea Levels and Lower Temperatures

Sea levels 18,000 years ago were approximately 100 m (330 ft) lower than they are today because so much of Earth's water was frozen and tied up in the glaciers instead of being in the ocean. Imagine the coastline of New York being 100 km farther east, Alaska and Russia connected by land across the Bering Straits, and England and France joined by a land bridge. In fact, sea ice extended southward into the North Atlantic and Pacific and northward in the Southern Hemisphere about 50% farther than it does today.

Sea-surface temperatures 18,000 years ago averaged between 1.4 C° and 1.7 C° (2.5 F° and 3.1 F°) lower than today. During the coldest portion of the Pleistocene ice age, air temperatures were as much as 12 C° (22 F°) colder than today's average, although milder periods ranged to within 5 C° (9 F°) of present air temperatures.

Deciphering Past Climates: Paleoclimatology

Glacials and interglacials occur because Earth's climate has fluctuated in and out of warm and cold ages. Evidence for this fluctuation now is traced in ice cores from Greenland and Antarctica, in layered ocean deposits of silts and clays, in the extensive pollen record from ancient plants, and in the relation of past coral productivity to sea level. This evidence is analyzed with radioactive dating methods and other techniques. One especially interesting fact is emerging from these studies: We humans (*Homo erectus* and *H. sapiens* of the last 1.9 million years) have never experienced Earth's normal (more moderate, less extreme) climate, most characteristic of Earth's entire 4.6 billion-year span.

Apparently, Earth's climates slowly fluctuated until the past 1.2 billion years, when temperature patterns with cycles of 200–300 million years became more pronounced.

The Pleistocene Epoch began in earnest 1.65 million years ago and through which we may still be progressing. The Holocene Epoch began approximately 10,000 years ago, when average temperatures abruptly increased 6 C° (11 F°). The period we live in may represent an end to the Pleistocene, or it may be merely a mild interglacial time. Figure 17.31 details the climatic record of the past 160,000 years.

Medieval Warm Period and Little Ice Age

In A.D. 1001, Leif Eriksson inadvertently ventured onto the North American continent, perhaps the first European to do so. He and his fellow Vikings were favoured by a medieval warming episode as they sailed the less-frozen North Atlantic to settle Iceland and Greenland.

The mild climatic episode that lasted from about A.D. 800 to 1200 is known as the *Medieval Warm Period*. During the warmth, grape vineyards were planted far into England some 500 km north of present-day commercial plantings. Oats and barley were planted in Iceland, and wheat was planted as far north as Trondheim, Norway. The shift to warmer, wetter weather influenced migration and settlement northward in North America, Europe, and Asia.

However, from approximately 1200–1350 through 1800–1900, a *Little Ice Age* took place. Parts of the North

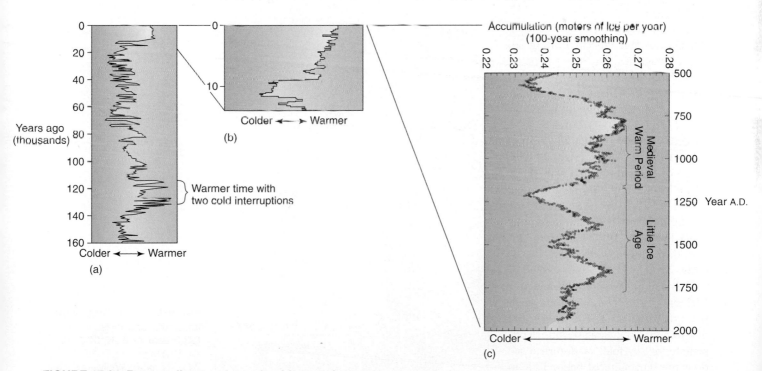

FIGURE 17.31 Recent climates determined from an ice core. (a) Temperature patterns during the past 160,000 years, back to MIS 6. Note the two cold spells that interrupted the earlier interglacial (115,000–135,000 years ago). (b) Higher resolution of the last 12,000 years. The cold period known as the "Younger Dryas" intensified at the beginning of this record. Warming was underway by 11,700 years ago and abruptly began to increase by the Holocene. (c) The accumulation record of snow and ice at the GISP-2 ice-core site is analogous to warmer and colder climatic conditions in Greenland—warmer times yield greater accumulations than colder times because of the moisture capacity of warmer air. Note the Medieval Warm Period and consistent temperatures as compared with the chaotic record of the Little Ice Age. [(a) and (b) Courtesy of the Greenland Ice Core Project (GRIP); (c) from D. A. Meese et. al., "The accumulation record from the GISP-2 core as an indicator of climate change throughout the Holocene," *Science* 266 (December 9, 1994): 1681, © AAAS.]

Atlantic froze, and expanding glaciers blocked many key mountain passes in Europe. Snowlines in Europe lowered about 200 m (650 ft) in the coldest years. The Greenland colonies were deserted. Cropping patterns changed, and northern forests declined, along with human population in those regions. In the winter of 1779–1780, New York's Hudson and East rivers and the entire Upper Bay froze over. People walked and hauled heavy loads across the ice between Staten and Manhattan Islands!

The Little Ice Age was not consistently cold throughout its 700-year reign. Reading the record of the Greenland ice cores, scientists have found many mild years among the harsh. More accurately, this was a time of rapid, short-term climate fluctuations that lasted only decades.

Ice cores drilled in Greenland have revealed a record of annual snow and ice accumulation that, when correlated with other aspects of the core sample, was indicative of air temperature. Figure 17.31c presents this record since A.D. 500. The warmth of the Medieval Warm Period is evident, whereas the Little Ice Age appears mixed with colder conditions around 1200, 1500, and after about 1800.

Mechanisms of Climate Fluctuation

What mechanisms cause short-term fluctuations? And why is Earth pulsing through long-term climatic changes that span several hundred million years? The ice-age concept is being researched and debated with an unprecedented intensity for three principal reasons: (1) Continuous ice cores from Greenland and Antarctica are providing a new, detailed record of weather and climate patterns, volcanic eruptions, and trends in the biosphere (discussed in Focus Study 17.1); (2) to understand present and future climate change and to refine general circulation models, we must understand the natural variability of the atmosphere and climate; (3) anthropogenic global warming, and its relation to ice ages, is a major concern.

Because past occurrences of low temperature appear to have followed a pattern, researchers have looked for causes that also are cyclic in nature. They have identified a complicated mix of interacting variables that appear to influence long-term climatic trends. Let us take a look at several of them.

Focus Study 17.1

GRIP, GISP-2, and Dome-C: Boring Ice for Exciting History

The Greenland Ice Core Project (GRIP) was launched in 1989. A site was selected near the summit of the Greenland Ice Sheet at 3200 m (10,500 ft) so that the maximum thickness of ice history would be accessed (Figure 17.1.1). After 3 years, the drills hit bedrock 3030 m (9940 ft) below the site—or, in terms of time, 250,000 years into the past. The core is 10 cm (4 in.) in diameter.

In 1990, about 32 km (20 mi) west of the summit, the Greenland Ice Sheet Project (GISP-2) began to bore back through time (see Figure 17.1.1). GISP-2 reached bedrock in 1993. This core is slightly larger in diameter, at 13.2 cm (5.2 in.), and collects about twice the data as GRIP. The existence of a second core helped scientists compensate for any folds or disturbed sections they encountered below 2700 m, or about 115,000 years, in the first core. Also clarifying the record are correlations with Antarctic ice cores, core samples of marine sediments from the oceans and Lake Baykal in Siberia, and coral studies that indicate past sea levels.

What is being discovered from a 3030-m ice core? Locked into the core

FIGURE 17.1.1 Greenland ice-core locations.
GRIP is at 72.5° N, 37.5° W. GISP-2 is at 72.6° N, 38.5° W. [Map courtesy of GISP-2 Science Management Office.]

is a record of past precipitation and air bubbles of past atmospheres, which indicate ancient gas concentrations. Of special interest are the greenhouse gases, carbon dioxide and methane.

Chemical and physical properties of the atmosphere and the snow that accumulated each year are frozen in place.

Pollutants are locked into the ice-core record. For example, during cold periods, high concentrations of dust were present, brought by winds from distant dry lands. An invaluable record of past volcanic eruptions is included in the layers, as if on a calendar. Even the exact beginning of the Bronze Age is recorded in the ice core—about 3000 B.C. When the Greeks and later the Romans began smelting copper, they produced ash and smoke that the winds carried to this distant place. The presence of ammonia indicates ancient forest fires at lower latitudes. And, as an important analog of past temperatures on the ice-sheet surface when each snowfall occurred, the ratio between stable forms of oxygen is measured.

Dome–C Ice Core

On the East Antarctic Plateau, 75.1° S, 123.3° E, approximately 900 km (560 mi) from the coast and 1750 km (1087 mi) from the South Pole, sits Dome C. This is the point on the Antarctic continent where the ice sheet is the thickest (see Figure 17.33c for location, and Figure 17.1.2). Here the ice is 3309 m (10,856 ft) deep. The mean annual surface temperature is −54.5°C (−66.1°F); however, the science crews experience temperatures that range from −50°C when they arrive to −25°C by midsummer. Dome C is 560 km (348 mi) from the Vostok base, where the previous coring record of 400,000 years was set. The Dome–C 8-year project is part of a 10-country European Project for Ice Coring in Antarctica (EPICA).

The mechanical drill bit used for coring is 10 cm wide and provides a high-resolution record of ancient atmospheric gases, ash from volcanic eruptions, and materials from other atmospheric events. By December 2004, coring to a 3270.20-m (10,729-ft) depth had brought up 800,000 years of Earth's past climate history (Figure 17.1.3). In Figure 17.28, this is Marine Isotope Stage (MIS) 20.2. This remarkable record contains eight glacial and interglacial cycles. As far as scientists have been able to analyze results, the Dome–C record affirms the Vostok findings and correlates perfectly with the deep-sea core of oxygen isotope

FIGURE 17.1.2 Dome–C station.
An overview of the Dome–C scientific station, with its gathering of tents and semi-permanent structures.
[Photo courtesy of British Antarctic Survey.]

fluctuations in foraminifera shells (microfossils) from the Atlantic Ocean.

Confirmed is the finding that the present concentration of carbon dioxide, methane, and nitrous oxide in the atmosphere is the highest it has been in the past 800,000 years and that these changing levels have marched in step with higher and lower temperatures throughout this time span.

Go, for example, to Figure 17.28 and find MIS 11. This warm spell at MIS 11, from 425,000 to 395,000 years ago, is perfectly recorded in the

Dome–C core and is of interest because CO_2 in the atmosphere during MIS 11 was similar to our preindustrial level of 280 ppm. Earth's orbital alignment was similar to that of today as well. The MIS 11 analogy means that a return to the next glacial period is perhaps 16,000 years in the future. Understanding the past helps decode future trends. The challenge for physical geographers is to put this data through spatial analysis and find the linkages to other Earth systems and to human economies and societies.

(a)

(b)

FIGURE 17.1.3 Dome–C ice-core analysis.
(a) Two members of the British Antarctic Survey carefully inspect one of the ice-core segments. A quarter-section of each ice core is kept at Dome C in case there is an accident in transport back to labs in Europe. (b) Light shining through a thin section from the ice core; Earth's ancient atmosphere is trapped in the ice awaiting analysis. [Both photos courtesy of British Antarctic Survey, http://www.antarctica.ac.uk.]

Climate and Celestial Relations As our Solar System revolves around the distant centre of the Milky Way, it crosses the plane of the galaxy approximately every 32 million years. At that time, Earth's plane of the ecliptic aligns parallel to the galaxy's plane, and we pass through regions in space of increased interstellar dust and gas, which may have some climatic effect.

Milutin Milankovitch (1879–1954), a Yugoslavian astronomer who studied Earth–Sun orbital relations, proposed other possible astronomical factors. Milankovitch wondered whether the development of an ice age relates to seasonal astronomical factors—Earth's revolution around the Sun, rotation, and tilt—extended over a longer time span (Figure 17.32). In summary:

- Earth's elliptical orbit about the Sun is not constant. The shape of the ellipse varies by more than 17.7 million kilometres (11 million miles) during a 100,000-year cycle, from nearly circular to an extreme ellipse (Figure 17.32a).
- Earth's axis "wobbles" through a 26,000-year cycle, in a movement much like that of a spinning top winding down. Earth's wobble is called *precession*. As you can see in Figure 17.32b, precession changes the orientation of hemispheres and landmasses to the Sun.
- Earth's present axial tilt of 23.5° varies from 22° to 24° during a 41,000-year period (Figure 17.32c).

Milankovitch calculated, without the aid of today's computers, that the interaction of these Earth–Sun relations creates a 96,000-year climatic cycle. His glaciation model assumes that changes in astronomical relations affect the amounts of insolation received.

Milankovitch died in 1954, his ideas still not accepted by a skeptical scientific community. Now, in the era of computers, remote-sensing satellites, and worldwide efforts to decipher past climates, Milankovitch's valuable work has stimulated much research to explain climatic cycles and has experienced some confirmation. A roughly 100,000-year climatic cycle is confirmed in such diverse places as ice cores in Greenland and the accumulation of sediment in Lake Baykal, Siberia.

Climate and Solar Variability If the Sun significantly varies its output over the years, as some other stars do, that variation would seem a convenient and plausible cause of ice-age timing. However, lack of evidence that the Sun's radiation output varies significantly over long cycles argues against this hypothesis. Nonetheless, inquiry about the Sun's variability actively continues and research using deep-space satellites us underway. As we saw in Chapter 10, in the IPCC *Fourth Assessment Report* in Figure 10.29, solar variability is not correlated to temperature increases occurring in the atmosphere and oceans.

Climate and Tectonics Major glaciations also can be associated with plate tectonics because some landmasses have migrated to higher, cooler latitudes. Chapters 11 and 12 explain that the shape and orientation of landmasses and ocean basins have changed greatly during Earth's history. Continental plates have drifted from equatorial locations to polar regions, and vice versa, thus exposing the land to a gradual change in climate. Gondwana (the southern half of Pangaea) experienced extensive glaciation that left its mark on the rocks of parts of present-day Africa, South America, India, Antarctica, and Australia. Landforms in the Sahara, for example, bear the markings of even earlier glacial activity. These markings are partly explained by the fact that portions of Africa were centred near the South Pole during the Ordovician Period, 465 million years ago (see Figure 11.18a).

Episodes of mountain building over the past billion years have forced mountain summits above the snowline, where snow remains after the summer melt. Mountain chains influence downwind weather patterns and jet-stream circulation, which in turn guides weather systems. More dust was present during glacial periods, suggesting drier weather and more extensive deserts beyond the frozen regions.

Climate and Atmospheric Factors Some events alter the atmosphere and produce climate change. A volcanic eruption might produce lower temperatures for a year or two. The lower temperatures could initiate a buildup of long-term snow cover at high latitudes. These high-albedo snow surfaces then would reflect more insolation away from Earth to further enhance cooling in a positive feedback system.

The fluctuation of atmospheric greenhouse gases could trigger higher or lower temperatures. Ice cores taken at Vostok, the Russian research station near the geographic centre of Antarctica, Greenland, and Dome–C contained trapped air samples that show carbon dioxide levels varying from more than 290 ppm to a low of nearly 180 ppm. Higher levels of carbon dioxide generally correlate with each interglacial, or warmer, period. In these first few years of a new century, atmospheric carbon dioxide reached 387 ppm in May 2007, higher than at any time in the past

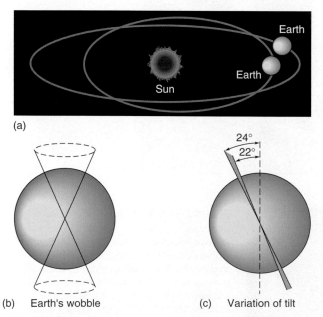

(a)

(b)　Earth's wobble　　　(c)　Variation of tilt

FIGURE 17.32 Astronomical factors that may affect broad climatic cycles.
(a) Earth's elliptical orbit varies widely during a 100,000-year cycle, stretching out to an extreme ellipse. (b) Earth's 26,000-year axial wobble. (c) Variation in Earth's axial tilt every 41,000 years.

800,000 years, principally owing to anthropogenic (human-caused) forcing—refer to Figures 10.30 (10,000-year record) and 10.27 (1000-year record) of carbon dioxide.

Climate and Oceanic Circulation Finally, oceanic circulation patterns have changed. For example, the Isthmus of Panama formed about 3 million years ago and effectively separated the circulation of the Atlantic and Pacific Oceans. Changes in ocean basin configuration, surface temperatures, and salinity and in upwelling and downwelling rates affect air mass formation and air temperature.

Our understanding of Earth's climate—past, present, and future—is unfolding. We are learning that climate is a multicyclic system controlled by an interacting set of cooling and warming processes, all founded on celestial relations, tectonic factors, changes in oceanic circulation, and atmospheric variables and human impacts.

Arctic and Antarctic Regions

Climatologists use environmental criteria to define the Arctic and the Antarctic regions. The *Arctic region* is defined in Figure 17.33 by the green line. This is the 10°C (50°F) isotherm for July, the Northern Hemisphere summer. This line coincides with the visible tree line—the boundary between the northern forests and tundra. The Arctic Ocean is

(a)

(b)

(c)

(d)

FIGURE 17.33 The Arctic and Antarctic regions.
In (a), note the 10°C (50°F) isotherm in midsummer, which designates the Arctic region, dominated by pack ice (b). Do you see any wildlife in the photo, about 965 km (600 mi) from the North Pole? In (c), the Antarctic convergence designates the Antarctic region. Arrows on the ice sheet show the general direction of ice movement on Antarctica. Note the location of the Dome C and Vostok bases. [Photos (b) and (d) by Bobbé Christopherson.]

covered by two kinds of ice: *floating sea ice* (frozen seawater) and *glacier ice* (frozen freshwater), a permanent multi-year ice and seasonal ice. This pack ice thins in the summer months and sometimes breaks up (Figure 17.33b).

As mentioned in Chapter 10, almost half of the Arctic ice pack by volume has disappeared since 1970 due to regional-scale warming. The year 2007 broke the record for lowest sea-ice extent, falling below the previous record low in 2005 by 24% (see Figure 5.1.1 in Chapter 5, High Latitude Connection 5.1). The fabled Northwest Passage across the Arctic from the Atlantic to the Pacific was ice-free in September 2007, as the Arctic ice continues to melt. The Northeast passage, north of Russia, has been ice-free for the past several years.

The *Antarctic region* is defined by the Antarctic convergence, a narrow zone that extends around the continent as a boundary between colder Antarctic water and warmer water at lower latitudes. This boundary follows roughly the 10°C (50°F) isotherm for February, the Southern Hemisphere summer, and is located near 60° S latitude (green line in the figure). The Antarctic region that is covered just with sea ice represents an area greater than North America, Greenland, and Western Europe combined. (For more information on polar-region ice, see the National Ice Center at **http://www.natice.noaa.gov/** and the Canadian Ice Service at **http://ice-glaces.ec.gc. ca/app/WsvPageDsp.cfm**).

Antarctica is a continent-sized landmass surrounded by ocean and is much colder overall than the Arctic, which is an ocean surrounded by land. In simplest terms, Antarctica can be thought of as a continent covered by a single enormous glacier, although it contains distinct regions such as the East Antarctic and West Antarctic ice sheets, which respond differently to slight climatic variations. These ice sheets are in constant motion, as indicated in Figure 17.33c.

Changes Are Underway in the Polar Regions

Review the "Global Climate Change" section in Chapter 10, where a portrait of high-latitude temperatures and ongoing physical changes to pack ice, ice shelves, and glaciers is presented. News Report 17.2 looks at meltpond occurrence as an indicator of changing surface energy budgets. Throughout this text, several High Latitude Connection features described additional dynamics in these polar regions. High Latitude Connection 17.1 covers the Ward Hunt Ice Shelf breakup.

News Report 17.2

Increase in Meltponds Indicates Changing Surface Energy Budgets

An increase in meltponds across the Arctic and Antarctic regions indicates changing surface energy conditions. In Chapter 1, High Latitude Connection 1.1 describes these meltponds as positive feedback mechanisms. The *Landsat*-7 satellite in tandem with aircraft equipped with video cameras spotted this increase in *meltpond* occurrence on glaciers, icebergs, ice shelves, and the Greenland ice sheet.

Figure 17.2.1 compares scenes from west Greenland in June 2001 and June 2003, using the *Terra* satellite. Examine the bare rock along the eastern margin, indicating higher

FIGURE 17.2.1 Meltponds on the increase in Greenland.
Meltponds (blue specks) are on the increase in the Arctic on icebergs, ice shelves, and the Greenland Ice Sheet. (a) Images of west Greenland June 14, 2001, and (b) June 17, 2003, demonstrate these changes. Between the rocky landscape with outlet glaciers and fjords to the west (left) and the ice sheet to the east (right), examine the increased extent of the melt zone— water-saturated surface ice and meltponds (blue specks). [Images by *Terra* courtesy of MODIS Rapid Response Team, NASA/GSFC.]

Meltponds, water-saturated ice

(a) 2001

(b) 2003

Meltponds, water-saturated ice

snow levels. The images show rapidly increasing numbers of meltponds and areas of water-saturated ice in the *melt zone* during this two-year interval. The meltponds look like small blue dots across the ice.

A chance to view these phenomena in September 2004 provided firsthand evidence of these trends. The action of such melting is evident in the potholes mottling this glacier in southern Greenland (Figure 17.2.2a) and the ac-

tual meltponds on the ice sheet (Figure 17.2.2b, c). If you look at the Larsen-B ice shelf breakup in Figure 17.34b, you can identify the presence of meltponds as the ice decayed.

(a)

(b)

(c)

FIGURE 17.2.2 Meltponds close up.
(a) Glacial ice loss is visible in the pockmarked appearance of this Greenland glacier. (b) An aerial photo of meltponds on the ice sheet near the area of the satellite images in Figure 17.2.1. (c) A positive feedback system; the meltponds are darker in colour than surrounding glacial ice and snow, absorbing more sunlight, heating up, melting more ice, forming more meltponds, and so on. [All photos by Bobbe Christopherson.]

High Latitude Connection 17.1

Climate Change Impacts an Arctic Ice Shelf

By late fall 2003, news spread through the climate science community that the Ward Hunt Ice Shelf—largest in the Arctic, on the north coast of Ellesmere Island in Nunavut (noted on the map in Figure 17.33a)—was breaking up. This was shocking news, for the shelf had been stable for at least 4500 years. What scientists observed was that after three decades of mass losses, the ice shelf reached a systems threshold and rapidly broke up between 2000 and 2003 (Figure 17.1.1).

Backed up behind the Ward Hunt Ice Shelf was an *epishelf lake*, an extensive freshwater accumulation some 43 m deep, sitting on about 360 m of salty seawater in the Disraeli Fiord. As the ice-shelf dam failed, the freshwater epishelf lake drained. This was the largest such epishelf lake in the Northern Hemisphere. A unique biological community of freshwater and brackish water plankton was lost and delicate ecosystems disrupted.

Scientists noted that regional temperatures increased between 1967 and

Crack in ice shelf

FIGURE 17.1.1 Ward Hunt Ice Shelf breakup.
The Ward Hunt Ice Shelf is near centre on the north coast, with a large crack down its centre and losses along its seaward front. The northwest coast of Greenland is to the east and Nansen Sound and Greely Fiord are to the west. The centre of the image is at 80° north latitude—noted on the map in 17.33a. [*Terra* image courtesy of MODIS Land Rapid Response Team, NASA/GSFC, September 10, 2003.]

2002 to an average July surface temperature of 1.3°C (34.3°F), which is above the threshold for ice-shelf failure established for Antarctica. Some other factors

that pushed this threshold in Ward Hunt were freeze-thaw cycles, ocean tides and wind strength, sea-surface temperatures, and variations in salinity.

Surrounding the margins of Antarctica, and constituting about 11% of its surface area, are numerous ice shelves, especially where sheltering inlets or bays exist. Covering many thousands of square kilometres, these ice shelves extend over the sea while still attached to continental ice. The loss of these ice shelves does not significantly raise sea level, for they already displace seawater. The concern is for the possible surge of grounded continental ice that the ice shelves hold back from the sea.

Although ice shelves constantly break up to produce icebergs, some large sections have recently broken free. In 1998, an iceberg the size of Delaware broke off the Ronne Ice Shelf, southeast of the Antarctic Peninsula. In March 2000, an iceberg tagged B-15 broke off the Ross Ice Shelf (some 90° longitude west of the Antarctic Peninsula), measuring *twice* the area of Delaware, 300 km by 40 km, or 190 mi by 25 mi. Remotely reporting weather instruments are in place on B-15 as the tabular iceberg breaks into pieces (Figure 17.34a).

Since 1993, six ice shelves have disintegrated in Antarctica. More than 8000 km² (3090mi²) of ice shelf is gone, changing maps, freeing up islands to circumnavigation, and creating thousands of icebergs. The Larsen Ice Shelf, along the east coast of the Antarctic Peninsula, has been retreating slowly for years. Larsen-A suddenly disintegrated in 1995. In only 35 days in early 2002, Larsen-B collapsed into icebergs. Larsen-B was at least 11,000 years old, meaning this collapse was farther south than any

(a)

FIGURE 17.34 Disintegrating ice shelves along the Antarctic coast.
(a) 2003 image of a broken B-15 iceberg which calved off the Ross Ice Shelf, near Roosevelt Island, Antarctica, in 2000; originally twice the size of Delaware. (b) Disintegration and retreat of Larsen-B ice shelf between January 31 and March 7, 2002. Note the meltponds in the January image. [(a) and (b) *Terra* image courtesy Rapid Response Team, NASA.]

(b) January 31, 2002　　　　　　　　March 7, 2002

FIGURE 17.35 Scientific base at the South Pole.
Aerial view of the Amundsen-Scott South Pole Station in 2001. The geodesic dome, completed in 1975, is 50 m wide and 16 m high (165 ft by 52 ft) and shelters buildings from the frigid cold and winds. On the left side you see the new modular buildings, which stand 3 m (10 ft) above the surface to accommodate snow accumulation and protect the ice under the building from melting. Built entirely from materials airlifted to the base, they were completed in 2006. Above this module is the ceremonial South Pole; slightly to the right is the geographic South Pole. This station is at an elevation of 2835 m (9301 ft). [Photo courtesy of Kristan Hutchison, U.S. Antarctic Program.]

previously during the Holocene. Larsen-C, the next segment to the south, is losing mass on its underside since the water temperature is warmer by 0.65 C° (1.17 F°) than the melting point for ice at 300 m depth—warmth is melting the shelf from both the ocean and atmosphere sides. This ice loss is likely a result of the 2.5 C° (4.5 F°) temperature increase in the peninsula region during the last 50 years. In response to the increasing warmth, the Antarctic Peninsula is supporting previously unseen vegetation growth, reduced sea ice, and disruption of penguin feeding, nesting, and fledging activities.

The Pine Island Glacier flows from the West Antarctic Ice Sheet (WAIS) as an outlet glacier to the Amundsen Sea. This glacier accelerated 3.5% in flow rate between April 2001 and April 2003—since the 1970s this brings the increase to more than 25% over previous averages for glacial movement. The Pine Island Glacier is accelerating toward the ocean and calving at a greater rate than

previously recorded along its 40-km-wide ice shelf. Scientists determined that the acceleration is sensed through the ice in the glacier, far back into the WAIS, flows of grounded ice upstream in the glacier that are not yet displacing ocean water are moving toward the sea. In January 2008, JPL/NASA announced that scientists had detected a 75% increase in ice loss between 1996 and 2006, specifically in Pine Island Bay and on the Antarctic Peninsula.

The fact that Antarctica is a place so remote from civilization makes it an excellent laboratory for sampling past and present human and natural variables that are transported by atmospheric and oceanic circulation. High altitude, winter cold and darkness, and distance from pollution sources make the polar region an ideal location for certain astronomical and atmospheric observations (Figure 17.35). Twenty-eight scientists and support people work through the winter (February to October) and 130 personnel, or more, research and work there in the brief summer.

Summary and Review—Glacial and Periglacial Processes and Landforms

■ *Differentiate* between alpine and continental glaciers, and *describe* their principal features.

More than 77% of Earth's freshwater is frozen. Ice covers about 11% of Earth's surface, and periglacial features occupy another 20% of ice-free but cold-dominated landscapes. A **glacier** is a mass of ice sitting on land or floating as an ice shelf in the ocean next to land. Glaciers form in areas of permanent snow. A **snowline** is the lowest elevation where snow occurs year-round and its altitude varies by latitude—higher near the equator, lower poleward.

A glacier in a mountain range is an **alpine glacier**. If confined within a valley, it is termed a *valley glacier*. The area of origin is a snowfield, usually in a bowl-shaped erosional landform called a **cirque**. Where alpine glaciers flow down to the sea, they calve and form **icebergs**. A **continental glacier** is a continuous mass of ice on land. Its most extensive form is an **ice sheet**; a smaller, roughly circular form is an **ice cap**; and the least extensive form, usually in mountains, is an **ice field**.

glacier (p. 552)
snowline (p. 553)
alpine glacier (p. 553)
cirque (p. 553)
iceberg (p. 554)
continental glacier (p. 556)
ice sheet (p. 556)
ice cap (p. 556)
ice field (p. 557)

1. Describe the location of most freshwater on Earth today.

2. What is a glacier? What is implied about existing climate patterns in a glacial region?

3. Differentiate between an alpine glacier and a continental glacier.

4. Name the three types of continental glaciers. What is the basis for dividing continental glaciers into types? Which type covers Antarctica?

■ *Describe* the process of glacial ice formation, and *portray* the mechanics of glacial movement.

Snow becomes glacial ice through accumulation, increasing thickness, pressure on underlying layers, and recrystallization.

Snow progresses through transitional steps from **firn** (compact, granular) to a denser **glacial ice** after many years.

A glacier is an open system with inputs and outputs that can be analyzed through observation of the growth and wasting of the glacier itself. A **firn line** is the lower extent of a fresh snow-covered area. A glacier is fed by snowfall and is wasted by **ablation** (losses from its upper and lower surfaces and along its margins). Accumulation and ablation achieve a mass balance in each glacier.

As a glacier moves downhill, vertical **crevasses** may develop. Sometimes a glacier will move rapidly in a **glacier surge**. The presence of water along the basal layer appears to be important in glacial movements. As a glacier moves, it plucks rock pieces and debris, incorporating them into the ice, and this debris scours and sandpapers underlying rock through **abrasion**.

firn (p. 558)
glacial ice (p. 558)
firn line (p. 558)
ablation (p. 558)
crevasse (p. 562)
glacier surge (p. 563)
abrasion (p. 564)

5. Trace the evolution of glacial ice from fresh fallen snow.

6. What is meant by glacial mass balance? What are the basic inputs and outputs underlying that balance?

7. What is meant by a glacier surge? What do scientists think produces surging episodes?

■ **Describe** characteristic erosional and depositional landforms created by alpine glaciation and continental glaciation.

Extensive valley glaciers have profoundly reshaped mountains worldwide, carving **V**-shaped stream valleys into **U**-shaped glaciated valleys, producing many distinctive erosional and depositional landforms. As cirque walls erode away, sharp **arêtes** (sawtooth, serrated ridges) form, dividing adjacent cirque basins. Two eroding cirques may reduce an arête to a saddlelike **col**. A **horn** results when several cirque glaciers gouge an individual mountain summit from all sides, forming a pyramidal peak. A **bergschrund** forms when a crevasse or wide crack opens along the headwall of a glacier, most visible in summer when covering snow is gone. An ice-carved rock basin left as a glacier retreats may fill with water to form a **tarn**; tarns in a string separated by moraines are called **paternoster lakes**. Where a glacial valley trough joins the ocean, and the glacier retreats, the sea extends inland to form a **fjord**.

All glacial deposits, whether ice-borne or meltwater-borne, constitute **glacial drift**. Glacial meltwater deposits are sorted and are called **stratified drift**. Direct deposits from ice, called **till**, are unstratified and unsorted. Specific landforms produced by the deposition of drift are **moraines**. A **lateral moraine** forms along each side of a glacier; merging glaciers with lateral moraines form a **medial moraine**; and eroded debris dropped at the glacier's terminus is a **terminal moraine**.

Continental glaciation leaves different features than does alpine glaciation. A **till plain** forms behind end moraines, featuring unstratified coarse till, low and rolling relief, and deranged drainage. Beyond the morainal deposits, **outwash plains** of stratified drift feature stream channels that are meltwater-fed, braided, and overloaded with debris that is sorted and deposited across the landscape. An **esker** is a sinuously curving, narrow ridge of coarse sand and gravel that forms along the channel of a

meltwater stream beneath a glacier. An isolated block of ice left by a retreating glacier becomes surrounded with debris; when the block finally melts, it leaves a steep-sided **kettle**. A **kame** is a small hill, knob, or mound of poorly sorted sand and gravel that is deposited directly by water or by ice in crevasses.

Glacial action forms two types of streamlined hills: the erosional **roche moutonnée** is an asymmetrical hill of exposed bedrock, gently sloping upstream and abruptly sloping downstream; the depositional **drumlin** is deposited till, streamlined in the direction of continental ice movement (blunt end upstream and tapered end downstream).

arête (p. 564)
col (p. 564)
horn (p. 564)
bergschrund (p. 564)
tarn (p. 564)
paternoster lakes (p. 564)
fjord (p. 564)
glacial drift (p. 567)
stratified drift (p. 567)
till (p. 567)
moraine (p. 567)
lateral moraine (p. 567)
medial moraine (p. 567)
terminal moraine (p. 567)
till plain (p. 568)
outwash plain (p. 568)
esker (p. 568)
kettle (p. 568)
kame (p. 568)
roche moutonnée (p. 570)
drumlin (p. 570)

8. How does a glacier accomplish erosion?

9. Describe the evolution of a **V**-shaped stream valley to a **U**-shaped glaciated valley. What features are visible after the glacier retreats?

10. How is an arête formed? A col? A horn? Briefly differentiate between them.

11. Differentiate between two forms of glacial drift—till and outwash.

12. What is a morainal deposit? What specific moraines are created by alpine and continental glaciers?

13. What are some common depositional features encountered in a till plain?

14. Contrast a roche moutonnée and a drumlin regarding appearance, orientation, and the way each forms.

■ **Analyze** the spatial distribution of periglacial processes, and *describe* several unique landforms and topographic features related to permafrost and frozen ground phenomena.

The term **periglacial** describes cold-climate processes, landforms, and topographic features that exist along the margins of glaciers, past and present. When soil or rock temperatures remain below 0°C (32°F) for at least 2 years, **permafrost** ("permanent frost") develops. Note that this criterion is based solely on temperature and has nothing to do with how much or how little water is present. The **active layer** is the zone of seasonally frozen ground that exists between the subsurface permafrost layer and the ground surface. **Patterned ground** forms in the periglacial environment where freezing and thawing of the ground create polygonal forms of circles, polygons, stripes, nets, and steps.

periglacial (p. 570)
permafrost (p. 570)
active layer (p. 572)
patterned ground (p. 574)

15. In terms of climatic types, describe the areas on Earth where periglacial landscapes occur. Include both higher latitude and higher altitude climate types.

16. Define two types of permafrost, and differentiate their occurrence on Earth. What are the characteristics of each?

17. Describe the active zone in permafrost regions, and relate the degree of development to specific latitudes.

18. What is a talik? Where might you expect to find taliks, and to what depth do they occur?

19. What is the difference between permafrost and ground ice?

20. Describe the role of frost action in the formation of various landform types in the periglacial region, such as a pingo and patterned ground.

21. Relate some of the specific problems humans encounter in developing periglacial landscapes.

■ *Explain* the Pleistocene ice-age epoch and related glacials and interglacials, and *describe* some of the methods used to study paleoclimatology.

An **ice age** is any extended period of cold. The late Cenozoic Era featured pronounced ice-age conditions in an epoch called the Pleistocene. During this time, alpine and continental glaciers covered about 30% of Earth's land area in at least 18 glacials, punctuated by interglacials of milder weather. Evidence of ice-age conditions is gathered from ice cores drilled in Greenland and Antarctica, from ocean sediments, from coral growth in relation to past sea levels, and from rock. The study of past climates is *paleoclimatology*.

The apparent pattern followed by these low-temperature episodes indicates cyclic causes. A complicated mix of interacting variables appears to influence long-term climatic trends: celestial relations, solar variability, tectonic factors, atmospheric variables, and oceanic circulation. The present anthropogenic forcing of temperatures is not part of a natural cycle.

ice age (p. 577)

22. What is paleoclimatology? Describe Earth's past climatic patterns. Are we experiencing a normal climate pattern in this era, or have scientists noticed any significant trends?

23. Define an ice age. When was the most recent? Explain "glacial" and "interglacial" in your answer.

24. Summarize what science has learned about the causes of ice ages by listing and explaining at least four possible factors in climate change.

25. Describe the role of ice cores in deciphering past climates. What record do they preserve? Where were they drilled?

26. Explain the relationship between the criteria defining the Arctic and Antarctic regions. Is there any coincidence in the Arctic criteria and the distribution of Northern Hemisphere forests on the continents?

Critical Thinking

A. After reading my summary of the *New South Polar Times*, 1993–1998 at the *Geosystems* Student Learning Center, imagine duty there for yourself. Of the 28 people who winter over at the station, some serve as scientists, technicians, and support staff. The station commander and reporter of the 1998 season was Katy McNitt-Jensen, in her third tour at the pole. Remember, the last airplane leaves mid-February and the first airplane lands mid-October—such is the isolation. What do you see as the positives and negatives to such service? How would you combat the elements? The isolation? The cold and dark conditions?

B. Hypothetically, speculate on the relationship between the Alaskan meltdown discussed in this chapter and the occurrence of earthquakes, such as the magnitude 7.9 quake near Denali National Park, Alaska, the largest on Earth during 2002. The rapid melting of glacial ice is causing an isostatic rebound of the landscape (see Figure 11.5). Vertical motion in Alaska is averaging 36 mm (1.42 in.) per year of uplift—the fastest rate anywhere on Earth. Scientists see a tie between the rebounding crust and loss of glacial ice weight over the past 150 years and especially over the past 30 years. How might isostatic rebound, in response to the unloading of glacial ice, produce strain along faults?

Soils, Ecosystems, and Biomes

CHAPTER 18 The Geography of Soils

CHAPTER 19 Ecosystem Essentials

CHAPTER 20 Terrestrial Biomes

CHAPTER 21 Earth and the Human Denominator

PART IV

A pair of Willow Ptarmigans (*Lagopus lagopus*) work the willow branches for seeds in the tundra west of Hudson Bay, Manitoba. Their colouration is a perfect blend against the snow and ice on a November afternoon.
[Photo by Bobbé Christopherson.]

E arth is the home of the only known biosphere in the Solar System—a unique, complex, and interactive system of abiotic (nonliving) and biotic (living) components working together to sustain a tremendous diversity of life. Energy enters the biosphere through conversion of solar energy by photosynthesis in the leaves of plants. Soil is the essential link among the lithosphere, plants, and the rest of Earth's physical systems. Thus, soil helps sustain life and is a bridge between PART III and PART IV of this text.

Life is organized into a feeding hierarchy from producers to consumers, ending with decomposers. Taken together, the soils, plants, animals, and all abiotic components produce aquatic and terrestrial ecosystems, generally grouped together in various biomes. Today we face crucial issues, principally the preservation of the diversity of life in the biosphere and the survival of the biosphere itself. Patterns of land and ocean temperatures, precipitation, weather phenomena, and stratospheric ozone, among many elements, are changing as global climate systems shift. The resilience of the biosphere, as we know it, is being tested in a real-time, one-time experiment. These important issues of biogeography are considered in Part IV.

SOLAR ENERGY

Atmosphere · Hydrosphere · Biosphere · Lithosphere

593

processes. We are using and abusing this legacy at rates much faster than it was formed. Soils do not reproduce, nor can they be re-created.

Soil science is interdisciplinary, involving physics, chemistry, biology, mineralogy, hydrology, taxonomy, climatology, and cartography. Physical geographers are interested in the spatial patterns formed by soil types and the environmental factors that interact to produce them. As an integrative science, physical geography is well suited to the study of soils.

Pedology concerns the origin, classification, distribution, and description of soil (*ped* from the Greek *pedon*, meaning "soil" or "earth"). Pedology is at the centre of learning about soil as a natural body, but it does not dwell on its practical uses. *Edaphology* (from the Greek *edaphos*, meaning "soil" or "ground") focuses on soil as a medium for sustaining higher plants. Edaphology emphasizes plant growth, fertility, and the differences in productivity among soils. Pedology gives us a general understanding of soils and their classification, whereas edaphology reflects society's concern for food and fibre production and the management of soils to increase fertility and reduce soil losses.

In many locales, an *agricultural extension service* can provide specific information and perform a detailed analysis of local soils. Soil surveys and local soil maps are available for most Canadian provinces and for counties in the United States. Agriculture Canada's soil information system is available on the Web (**http://sis.agr.gc.ca/cansis/intro.html**) and the soil landscape of Canada can be viewed online (**http://sis.agr.gc.ca/cansis/nsdb/slc/intro.html**). For the United States, the National Soil Survey Center's site is at **http://soils.usda.gov/** and for links related to world soils, see **http://soils.usda.gov/use/worldsoils/**.

In this chapter: The geography of soils deals spatially with a complex substance, the characteristics of which vary from kilometre to kilometre, and even centimetre to centimetre. We begin with soil characteristics and the basic soil sampling and soil mapping units. The soil profile is a dynamic structure, mixing and exchanging materials and moisture across its horizons. Properties of soil include texture, structure, porosity, moisture, and chemistry—all integrating to form soil types. The chapter discusses both natural and human factors that affect soil formation. A global concern exists over the loss of soils to erosion, mistreatment, and conversion to other uses. The chapter concludes with a brief examination of the Canadian System of Soil Classification (CSSC) and a comparison with other systems that are widely used.

Soil Characteristics

Classifying soils is similar to classifying climates because both involve interacting variables. Before we look at soil classification, let us examine the physical properties that distinguish soils as they develop through time in response to climate, relief, and topography.

Soil Profiles

As a book cannot be judged by its cover, so soils cannot be evaluated at the surface only. Instead, a soil profile should be studied from the surface to the deepest extent of plant roots, or to where regolith or bedrock is encountered. Such a profile is a **pedon**, a hexagonal column measuring 1 to 10 m^2 in top surface area (Figure 18.1). At the sides of

FIGURE 18.1 Soil sampling and mapping units.
A soil pedon (sampling unit) is derived from a polypedon (mapping unit). Shown are typical O, A, Ae, B, C, and R soil horizons within a developed soil pedon. The true soil, or solum, includes the O, A, Ae, and B horizons.

the pedon, the various layers of the soil profile are visible in cross section and are labelled with letters. *A pedon is the basic sampling unit used in soil surveys.*

Many pedons together in one area make up a **polypedon**, which has distinctive characteristics differentiating it from surrounding polypedons. A polypedon is an essential soil individual, comprising an identifiable series of soils in an area. It can have a minimum dimension of about 1 m² and no specified maximum size. *The polypedon is the basic mapping unit used in preparing local soil maps.*

Soil Horizons

Each distinct layer exposed in a pedon is a **soil horizon**. A horizon is roughly parallel to the pedon's surface and has characteristics distinctly different from horizons directly above or below. The boundary between horizons usually is distinguishable when viewed in profile, such as along a road cut, using the properties of colour, texture, structure, consistence (meaning soil consistency or cohesiveness), porosity, the presence or absence of certain minerals, moisture, and chemical processes (Figure 18.2). Soil horizons are the building blocks of soil classification.

At the top of the soil profile is the *O (organic) horizon*, named for its organic composition, derived from plant and animal litter that was deposited on the surface and transformed into humus. **Humus** is not just a single material; it is a mixture of decomposed and synthesized organic materials, usually dark in colour. Microorganisms work busily on this organic debris, performing a portion of the *humification* (humus-making) process. The O horizon is 20%–30% or more organic matter, which is important because of its ability to retain water and nutrients and for the way it acts in a complementary manner to clay minerals.

At the bottom of the soil profile is the *R (rock) horizon*, consisting of either unconsolidated (loose) material or consolidated bedrock. When bedrock physically and chemically weathers into regolith, it may or may not contribute to overlying soil horizons. The A, Ae, B, and C horizons mark differing mineral strata between O and R. These middle layers are composed of sand, silt, clay, and other weathered by-products. (Table 11.3 in Chapter 11 presents a description of grain sizes for these weathered soil particles.)

The *A horizon* is a mineral layer that forms at or near the surface. It exists in the zone of maximum accumulation of organic matter, or in the zone of leaching of materials either in solution or suspension, or both. The accumulation of organic material usually results in a darkening of the surface soil. The A horizon can be enriched in organic matter (Ah) or depleted in mineral matter (Ae). The Ae horizon is lighter in colour, coarser in texture, and is the transition from the A horizon to the B horizon.

The removal of fine particles and minerals by water, leaving behind sand and silt, is termed **eluviation**—thus the "e" notation. Silicate clays and oxides of aluminum and iron are removed by water, or leached, and carried to lower horizons with the water as it percolates through the soil. More soluble material can be fully removed from the soil quickly, while iron and aluminum oxides are residual and may move more slowly.

The accumulation or enrichment of organic matter, oxides, or clay dominates the B horizon. The deposition of these materials is known as **illuviation**. Accumulated organic material (Bh) results in a layer darker in colour relative to the *C horizon*. Finer soil texture or coatings of clay on the peds and in the pores results from clay accumulation (Bt). Soil structure may also develop in the B horizon with prismatic or columnar units and coating or stainings, significant amounts of exchangeable sodium, or other changes of structure from the parent material.

Some materials occurring in the B horizon may have formed in place from weathering processes rather than arriving there by *translocation*, or migration. In the humid tropics, these layers often develop to some depth. Likewise, clay losses in an A horizon may be caused by

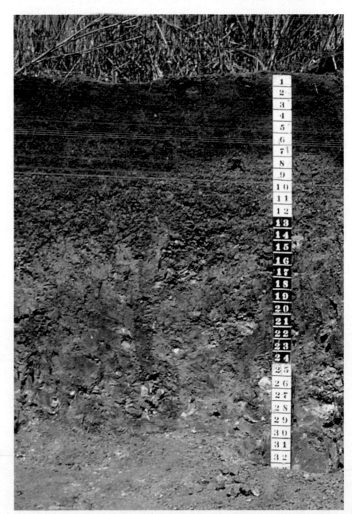

FIGURE 18.2 A typical soil profile.
This is a Gleysol from southern Ontario. The parent material is till and glaciolacustrine sediment and the soil is poorly drained. The dark O and A horizons are above the #7 and transition into the Ae horizon to the #13. Below the #13 is the mottled B horizon.
[Photo courtesy of Agriculture and Agri-Food Canada.]

destructive processes and not eluviation. Research to better understand erosion and deposition of clays between soil horizons is one of the challenges in modern soil science.

The combination of the A and E horizons and the B horizon is designated the **solum**, considered the true definable soil of the pedon. The A, Ae, and B horizons experience active soil processes (labelled in Figure 18.1).

Below the solum is the *C horizon* of weathered bedrock or weathered parent material. This zone is identified as *regolith* (although the term sometimes is used to include the solum as well). The C horizon is not much affected by soil operations in the solum and lies outside the biological influences experienced in the shallower horizons. Plant roots and soil microorganisms are rare in the C horizon. It lacks clay concentrations and generally is made up of carbonates, gypsum, or soluble salts, or of iron and silica, which form cemented soil structures. In dry climates, calcium carbonate commonly forms the cementing material of these hardened layers. In many glaciated parts of North America the C horizon consists of glacial deposits, commonly till.

Soil Properties

Soils are complex and varied, as this section reveals. Observing a real soil profile will help you identify colour, texture, structure, and other soil properties. A good opportunity to observe soil profiles is at a construction site or excavation, perhaps on your campus, or at a road cut along a highway. Manuals for describing, mapping, surveying, and analyzing soils can be found at the Agriculture and Agri-Food Web site (**http://sis.agr.gc.ca/cansis/publications/manuals/**).

Soil Colour

Colour is important, for it sometimes suggests composition and chemical makeup. If you look at exposed soil, colour may be the most obvious trait. Among the many possible hues are the reds and yellows found in soils of New Brunswick and Prince Edward Island and in soils of the southeastern United States (high in iron oxides); the blacks of the prairie soils in parts of southern Alberta and Saskatchewan and portions of the U.S. grain-growing regions and Ukraine (richly organic); and white-to-pale hues found in soils containing silicates and aluminum oxides. However, colour can be deceptive: Soils of high humus content are often dark, yet clays of warm–temperate and tropical regions with less than 3% organic content are some of the world's blackest soils.

To standardize colour descriptions, soil scientists describe a soil's colour by comparing it with a *Munsell Color Chart* (developed by artist and teacher Albert Munsell in 1913). These charts display 175 colours arranged by *hue* (the dominant spectral colour, such as red), *value* (degree of darkness or lightness), and *chroma* (purity and saturation of the colour, which increase with decreasing

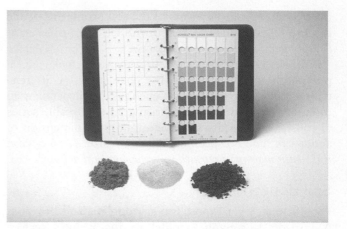

FIGURE 18.3 A Munsell Soil Color Chart page.
A soil sample is viewed through the hole to match it with a colour on the chart. Hue, value, and chroma are the characteristics of colour assessed by this system. [Photo courtesy of Gretag Macbeth, Munsell Color.]

greyness). A Munsell notation identifies each colour by a name, so soil scientists can make worldwide comparisons of soil colour. Soil colour is checked against the chart at various depths within a pedon (Figure 18.3).

Soil Texture

Soil texture, perhaps a soil's most permanent attribute, refers to the mixture of sizes of its particles and the proportion of different sizes. Individual mineral particles are *soil separates*. All particles smaller in diameter than 2 mm (0.08 in.), such as very coarse sand, are considered part of the soil. Larger particles, such as pebbles, gravel, or cobbles, are not part of the soil. (Sands are graded from coarse, to medium, to fine, down to 0.05 mm; silt to 0.002 mm; and clay at less than 0.002 mm.)

Figure 18.4 is a *soil texture triangle* showing the relation of sand, silt, and clay concentrations in soil. Each corner of the triangle represents a soil consisting solely of the particle size noted (although rarely are true soils composed of a single separate). Every soil on Earth is defined somewhere in this triangle.

Figure 18.4 includes the common designation **loam**, which is a balanced mixture of sand, silt, and clay that is beneficial to plant growth. Farmers consider ideal a sandy loam with clay content below 30% (lower left) because of its water-holding characteristics and ease of cultivation. Soil texture is important in determining water-retention and water-transmission traits.

To see how the soil texture triangle works, consider a *Miami silt loam* soil type from Indiana. Samples from this soil type are plotted on the soil texture triangle as points 1, 2, and 3. A sample taken near the surface in the A horizon is recorded at point 1, in the B horizon at point 2, and in the C horizon at point 3. Textural analyses of these samples are summarized in Table 18.1 and in the three pie diagrams to the right of the triangle. Note that silt dominates the surface, clay the B horizon, and sand the C

FIGURE 18.4 Soil texture triangle.
Measures of the ratio of clay, silt, and sand determine soil texture. As an example, points 1 (horizon A), 2 (horizon B), and 3 (horizon C) designate samples taken at three different horizons in the Miami silt loam in Indiana. Note the ratio of sand to silt to clay shown in the three pie diagrams and table. [After USDA–NRCS, *Soil Survey Manual*, Agricultural Handbook No. 18, p. 138 (Washington, DC: U.S. Government Printing Office, 1993).

Table 18.1	Textural Analysis of Miami Silt Loam		
Sample Points	**% Sand**	**% Silt**	**% Clay**
1 = A horizon	21.5	63.5	15.0
2 = B horizon	31.5	25.1	43.4
3 = C horizon	42.4	34.1	23.5

horizon. The *Soil Survey Manual* presents guidelines for estimating soil texture by feel, a relatively accurate method when used by an experienced person. However, laboratory methods using graduated sieves and separation by mechanical analysis in water allow more precise measurements.

Soil Structure

Soil *texture* describes the size of soil particles, but soil *structure* refers to their *arrangement*. Structure can partially modify the effects of soil texture. The smallest natural lump or cluster of particles is a *ped*. The shape of soil peds determines which of the structural types the soil exhibits:

crumb or granular, platy, blocky, prismatic, or columnar (Figure 18.5).

Peds separate from each other along zones of weakness, creating voids, or pores, that are important for moisture storage and drainage. Rounded peds have more pore space between them and greater permeability than other shapes. They are therefore better for plant growth than are blocky, prismatic, or platy peds, despite comparable fertility. Terms used to describe soil structure include fine, medium, or coarse. Adhesion among peds ranges from weak to strong.

Soil Consistence

In soil science, the term *consistence* is used to describe the consistency of a soil or cohesion of its particles. Consistence is a product of texture (particle size) and structure (ped shape). Consistence reflects a soil's resistance to breaking and manipulation under varying moisture conditions:

- A *wet soil* is sticky between the thumb and forefinger, ranging from a little adherence to either finger, to sticking to both fingers, to stretching when the fingers are moved apart. *Plasticity*, the quality of

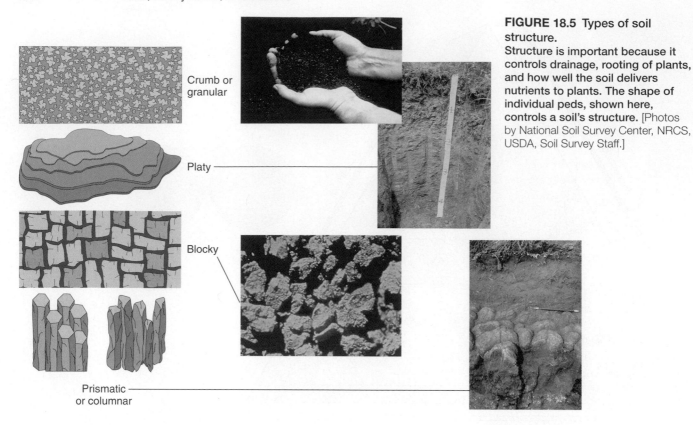

FIGURE 18.5 Types of soil structure.
Structure is important because it controls drainage, rooting of plants, and how well the soil delivers nutrients to plants. The shape of individual peds, shown here, controls a soil's structure. [Photos by National Soil Survey Center, NRCS, USDA, Soil Survey Staff.]

Crumb or granular

Platy

Blocky

Prismatic or columnar

being moldable, is roughly measured by rolling a piece of soil between your fingers and thumb to see whether it rolls into a thin strand.

- A *moist soil* is filled to about half of field capacity (the usable water capacity of soil), and its consistence grades from loose (noncoherent), to *friable* (easily pulverized), to firm (not crushable between thumb and forefinger).
- A *dry soil* is typically brittle and rigid, with consistence ranging from loose, to soft, to hard, to extremely hard.

Soil particles are sometimes cemented together to some degree. Soils are described as weakly cemented, strongly cemented, or *indurated* (hardened). Calcium carbonate, silica, and oxides or salts of iron and aluminum all can serve as cementing agents. The cementation of soil particles that occurs in various horizons is a function of consistence and may be continuous or discontinuous.

Soil Porosity

Soil porosity, permeability, and moisture storage were discussed in Chapter 9. Pores in the soil horizon control the movement of water—its intake, flow, and drainage—and air ventilation. Important porosity factors are pore *size*, pore *continuity* (whether they are interconnected), pore *shape* (whether they are spherical, irregular, or tubular), pore *orientation* (whether pore spaces are vertical, horizontal, or random), and pore *location* (whether they are within or between soil peds).

Porosity is improved by the biotic actions of plant roots, animal activity such as the tunneling of gophers or worms, and human intervention through soil manipulation (ploughing, adding humus or sand, or planting soil-building crops). Much of a farmer's soil preparation work before planting, and for the home gardener as well, is done to improve soil porosity.

Soil Moisture

Reviewing Figures 9.8 and 9.9 in Chapter 9 (soil moisture types and availability) will help you understand this section. Plants operate most efficiently when the soil is at *field capacity*, which is the maximum water availability for plant use after large pore spaces have drained of gravitational water. Soil type determines field capacity. The depth to which a plant sends its roots determines the amount of soil moisture to which the plant has access. If soil moisture is removed below field capacity, plants must exert increased energy to obtain available water. This moisture removal inefficiency worsens until the plant reaches its wilting point. Beyond this point, plants are unable to extract the water they need, and they die. Soil moisture regimes and their associated climate types shape the biotic and abiotic properties of the soil more than any other factor.

Soil Chemistry

Recall that soil pores may be filled with air, water, or a mixture of the two. Consequently, soil chemistry involves both air and water. The atmosphere within soil pores is mostly nitrogen, oxygen, and carbon dioxide. Nitrogen concentrations are about the same as in the atmosphere, but oxygen is less and carbon dioxide is greater because of ongoing respiration processes.

Water present in soil pores is the *soil solution*. It is the medium for chemical reactions in soil. This solution is critical to plants as their source of nutrients, and it is the foundation of *soil fertility*. Carbon dioxide combines with the water to produce carbonic acid, and various organic materials combine with the water to produce organic acids. These acids are then active participants in soil processes, as are dissolved alkalies and salts.

To understand how the soil solution behaves, let us go through a quick chemistry review. An *ion* is an atom, or group of atoms, that carries an electrical charge (examples: Na^+, Cl^-, HCO_3^-). An ion has either a positive charge or a negative charge. For example, when NaCl (sodium chloride) dissolves in solution, it separates into two ions: Na^+, a *cation* (positively charged ion), and Cl^-, an *anion* (negatively charged ion). Some ions in soil carry single charges, whereas others carry double or even triple charges (e.g., sulphate, SO_4^{2-}; and aluminum, Al^{3+}).

Ions in soil are retained by **soil colloids**. These tiny particles of clay and organic material (humus) carry a negative electrical charge and consequently attract any positively charged ions in the soil (Figure 18.6). The positive ions, many metallic, are critical to plant growth. If it were not for the negatively charged soil colloids, the positive ions would be leached away in the soil solution and thus would be unavailable to plant roots.

Individual clay colloids are thin and platelike, with parallel surfaces that are negatively charged. They are more chemically active than silt and sand particles but less active than organic colloids. Metallic cations attach to the surfaces of the colloids by *adsorption* (not *absorption*, which means "to enter"). Colloids can exchange cations between their surfaces and the soil solution, an ability called **cation-exchange capacity (CEC)**, which is the measure of soil fertility. A high CEC means that the soil colloids can store or exchange more cations from the soil solution, an indication of good soil fertility (unless there is a complicating factor, such as a soil that is too acid).

Therefore, **soil fertility** is the ability of soil to sustain plants. Soil is fertile when it contains organic substances and clay minerals that absorb water and adsorb certain

FIGURE 18.6 Soil colloids and cation-exchange capacity (CEC).
This typical soil colloid retains mineral ions by adsorption to its surface (opposite charges attract). This process holds the ions until they are absorbed by root hairs.

Soil Ion Exchange: Soil Particles and Soil Water

ANIMATION

elements needed by plants. Billions of dollars are expended to create fertile soil conditions, yet the future of Earth's most fertile soils is threatened because soil erosion is on the increase worldwide.

Soil Acidity and Alkalinity

A soil solution may contain significant hydrogen ions (H^+), the cations that stimulate acid formation. The result is a soil rich in hydrogen ions, or an *acid soil*. On the other hand, a soil high in base cations (calcium, magnesium, potassium, sodium) is a *basic* or *alkaline soil*. Such acidity or alkalinity is expressed on the pH scale (Figure 18.7).

Pure water is nearly neutral, with a pH of 7.0. Readings below 7.0 represent increasing acidity. Readings above 7.0 indicate increasing alkalinity. Acidity usually is regarded as strong at 5.0 or lower on the pH scale, whereas 10.0 or above is considered strongly alkaline.

The major contributor to soil acidity in this modern era is acid precipitation (rain, snow, fog, or dry deposition). Acid rain actually has been measured below pH 2.0—an incredibly low value for natural precipitation,

FIGURE 18.7 pH scale.
The pH scale measures acidity (lower pH) and alkalinity (higher pH). (The complete pH scale ranges between 0 and 14.)

as acid as lemon juice. Increased acidity in the soil solution accelerates the chemical weathering of mineral nutrients and increases their depletion rates. Because most crops are sensitive to specific pH levels, acid soils below pH 6.0 require treatment to raise the pH. This soil treatment is accomplished by the addition of bases in the form of minerals that are rich in base cations, usually lime (calcium carbonate, $CaCO_3$).

Soil Formation Factors and Management

Soil is an open system involving physical inputs and outputs. Soil-forming factors are both *passive* (parent material, topography and relief, and time) and *dynamic* (climate, biology, and human activities). These factors work together as a system to form soils. The roles of these factors are considered here and in the soil-order discussions that follow.

Natural Factors

Physical and chemical weathering of rocks in the upper lithosphere provides the raw mineral ingredients for soil formation. These rocks supply the parent materials, and their composition, texture, and chemical nature help determine the type of soil that forms. Clay minerals are the principal weathered by-products in soil.

Climate types correlate closely with soil types worldwide. The moisture, evaporation, and temperature regimes of climates determine the chemical reactions, organic activity, and eluviation rates of soils. Not only is the present climate important but many soils exhibit the imprint of past climates, sometimes over thousands of years. Most notable is the effect of glaciations. Among other contributions, glaciation produced the loess soil materials that have been windblown thousands of kilometres to their present locations (discussed in Chapter 15).

Vegetation, animal, and bacterial activity determine the organic content of soil, along with all that is living in soil—algae, fungi, worms, and insects. The chemical makeup of the vegetation contributes to the acidity or alkalinity of the soil solution. For example, broadleaf trees tend to increase alkalinity, whereas needleleaf trees tend to produce higher acidity. Thus, when civilization moves into new areas and alters the natural vegetation by logging or plowing, the affected soils are likewise altered, often permanently.

Topography also affects soil formation. Slopes that are too steep cannot have full soil development because gravity and erosional processes remove materials. Lands that are nearly level inhibit soil drainage and can become waterlogged. The compass orientation of slopes is important because it controls exposure to sunlight. In the Northern Hemisphere, a south-facing slope is warmer overall through the year because it receives direct sunlight. Water-balance relations are affected because north-facing slopes are colder, causing slower snowmelt and lower evaporation rate, providing more moisture for plants than is available on south-facing slopes, which tend to dry faster.

All of the identified natural factors in soil development (parent material, climate, biological activity, landforms and topography) require *time* to operate. Over geologic time plate tectonics has redistributed landscapes and thus subjected soil-forming processes to diverse conditions. Figure 18.8 illustrates how these factors combine to affect soil fertility.

Pedogenic Regimes Soil-forming processes are linked to climatic regions, a connection that serves as the basis for **pedogenic regimes**. Before the present soil classification systems in Canada and the United States, these pedogenic regimes were used to describe soils. Although each pedogenic process may be active in several soil orders and in different climates, not all are present in Canada, like the lateritic processes in the tropics. Such climate-based regimes are convenient for relating climate and soil processes. However, both the Canadian and U.S. soil classification systems *recognize the great uncertainty and inconsistency in basing soil classification on such climatic variables*. Aspects of several pedogenic processes are discussed with appropriate soil orders:

- **Laterization** is a leaching process active in humid and warm climates (in the tropics and subtropics and not in Canada).
- **Salinization** (p. 610) concentrates salts in soils in climates with excessive potential evapotranspiration (POTET) rates, and is discussed with the Solonetzic order.
- **Calcification** (Figure 18.12, p. 610) produces an illuviated accumulation of calcium carbonates in continental climates, and is discussed with the Chernozemic order.
- **Podzolization** (Figure 18.20, p. 618) is a process of soil acidification associated with forest soils in cool climates, and is discussed with the Podzolic order.
- **Gleysation** (p. 610, 614) includes an accumulation of humus and a thick, water-saturated grey layer of clay beneath, and is usually found in cold, wet climates and poor drainage conditions. It is discussed with the Gleysolic order.

The Human Factor

Human intervention has a major impact on soils. Millennia ago, farmers in most cultures learned to plant slopes "on the contour"—to make rows or mounds around a slope at the same elevation, not vertically up and down the slope. Planting on the contour prevents water from flowing straight down the slope and thus reduces soil erosion. It was common to plant and harvest a floodplain but to live on higher ground nearby. Floods were celebrated as blessings that brought water, nutrients, and more soil to the land. Society is drifting away from these commonsense strategies.

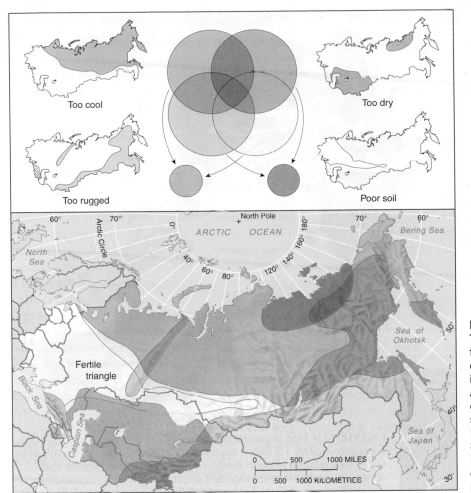

FIGURE 18.8 Soil fertility in Eurasia. Top: Four main factors influence soil fertility. Bottom: The fertile triangle of central Eurasia. The white area is highest in soil fertility (few negative factors). Areas shown with any colour or colour combination are limited for the reasons shown in the top illustration. The least-fertile area in Russia is northeastern Siberia. [After P. W. English and J. A. Miller, *World Regional Geography: A Question of Place*, p. 183, ©1989. Adapted by permission of John Wiley & Sons, Inc.]

A few centimetres' thickness of prime farmland soil may require *500 years* to mature. Yet, this same thickness is being lost annually through soil erosion when the soil-holding vegetation is removed and the land is plowed regardless of topography. Flood control structures block sediments and nutrients from replenishing floodplain soils, leading to additional soil losses. Over the same period, exposed soils may be completely leached of needed cations, thereby losing their fertility. Unlike living species, soils do not reproduce, nor can they be re-created.

Some 35% of farmlands are losing soil faster than it can form—a loss exceeding 23 billion metric tons (25 billion tons) per year. Soil depletion and loss are at record levels from Iowa to China, Peru to Ethiopia, the Middle East to the Americas. The impact on society is potentially disastrous as population and food demands increase (see News Report 18.1).

Soil erosion can be compensated for in the short run by using more fertilizer, increasing irrigation, and planting higher-yielding strains. But the potential yield from prime agricultural land will drop by as much as 20% over the next 20 years if only moderate erosion continues. One study tabulated the market value of lost nutrients and other variables in the most comprehensive soil-erosion study to date. The sum of direct damage (to agricultural land) and indirect damage (to streams, society's infrastructure, and human health) was estimated at more than $25 billion a year in the United States and hundreds of billions of dollars worldwide. (Of course, this is a controversial assessment in the agricultural industry.) The cost to bring erosion under control in the United States is estimated at approximately $8.5 billion, or about 30 cents on every dollar of damage and loss. In Canada as well, erosion prevention is cheaper than the cost of losses from soil erosion. Figure 18.9 maps regions of soil loss.

Our spatial impact on precious soil resources across each agricultural region should be recognized and protective measures taken. There is a need for cooperative international action. Critical to sustaining soil fertility is a long-term assessment of the *cost* of continued behaviour, that is, business as usual, compared to the *benefits* of mitigating damage and preserving the market value of prime soils through conservation actions—a cost–benefit analysis. In sustaining natural systems, the benefits of doing things right far outweigh the continued costs of doing things wrong, over the long term. Focus Study 18.1 (p. 605) examines one case where planning could have avoided huge losses to soil and wildlife.

(text continued on page 606)

A recent article by scientist David Montgomery well summarizes our predicament:

> Recent compilations of data from around the world show that soil erosion under conventional agriculture exceeds both rates of soil production and geological erosion rates by several orders of magnitude. Consequently, modern agriculture—and therefore global society—faces a fundamental question over the upcoming centuries. Can an agricultural system capable of feeding a growing population safeguard both soil fertility and the soil itself?*

Soil Classification

Classification of soils is complicated by the continuing interaction of physical properties and processes just discussed. This interaction creates thousands of distinct soils, with well over 15,000 soil series identified in Canada and the United States alone. Not surprisingly, different classification systems are in use worldwide. Canada, the United States, the United Kingdom, Germany, Australia, Russia, and the United Nations Food and Agricultural Organization each have their own soil classification system. Each system reflects the environment of its country. For example, the National Soil Survey Committee of Canada developed a system suited to its great expanses of boreal forest, tundra, and cool climatic regimes. The remainder of this chapter will outline the Canadian System of Soil Classification (CSSC). Appendix B contains information about the U.S. Soil Taxonomy system for classifying soils. For information on tropical soils not in the CSSC, please refer to the Soil Taxonomy in Appendix B.

The Canadian System of Soil Classification (CSSC)

Canadian efforts at soil classification began in 1914 with the partial mapping of Ontario's soils by A. J. Galbraith. Efforts to develop a taxonomic system spread country-wide, anchored by universities in each province. Regional differences in soil classification emerged, further confused by a lack of specific soil details. By 1936, only 1.7% of Canadian soil had been surveyed (15 million hectares).

Canadian scientists needed a taxonomic system based on observable and measurable properties in soils specific to Canada. This meant a departure from Marbut's 1938 U.S. classification. Canada's first taxonomic system was introduced in 1955, splitting away from the soil classification effort in the United States and the Fourth Approximation stage. Classification work progressed through the Canada Soil Survey Committee after 1970 and was replaced by the Expert Committee on Soil Survey in 1978, all under Agriculture Canada. This committee worked on interpretation, mapping systems, soil degradation, and

soil classification and produced the second edition of the *Canadian System of Soil Classification* in 1987. Work continued with the classification of Vertisols and further development of the CSSC. The third edition of the *Canadian System of Soil Classification* was published in 1998.

The **Canadian System of Soil Classification (CSSC)** provides taxa for all soils presently recognized in Canada and is adapted to Canada's expanses of forest, tundra, prairie, frozen ground, and colder climates. As in the U.S. Soil Taxonomy system, the CSSC classifications are based on observable and measurable properties found in real soils rather than idealized soils that may result from the interactions of genetic processes. The system is flexible in that its framework can accept new findings and information in step with progressive developments in the soil sciences.

Categories of Classification in the CSSC

Categorical levels are at the heart of a taxonomic system. These categories are based on soil profile properties organized at five levels, nested in a hierarchical pattern to permit generalization at several levels of detail. Each level is referred to as a category of classification. The levels in the CSSC are briefly described here, as adapted from *The Canadian Soil Classification System*, Third Edition, Publication 1646 (Ottawa: Research Branch, Agriculture and Agri-Food Canada, 1998), p. 7.

- *Order*: Each of ten soil orders has pedon properties that reflect the soil environment and effects of active soil-forming processes.
- *Great group*: Subdivisions of each order reflect differences in the dominant processes or other major contributing processes. As an example, in Luvic Gleysols (great group name followed by order) the dominant process is gleying—reduction of iron and other minerals—resulting from poor drainage under either grass or forest cover with Aeg and Btg horizons (see Table 18.2).
- *Subgroup*: Subgroups are differentiated by the content and arrangement of horizons that indicate the relation of the soil to a great group or order or the subtle transition toward soils of another order.
- *Family*: This is a subdivision of a subgroup. Parent material characteristics such as texture and mineralogy, soil climatic factors, and soil reactions are important.
- *Series*: Detailed features of the pedon differentiate subdivisions of the family—the essential soil-sampling unit. Pedon horizons fall within a narrow range of colour, texture, structure, consistence, porosity, moisture, chemical reaction, thickness, and composition.

Soil Horizons in the CSSC

Soil horizons are named and standardized as diagnostic in the classification process. Several mineral and organic

---

*D.R. Montgomery, "Is agriculture eroding civilization's foundation?" *GSA Today*, October 2007, p. 4.

Table 18.2 Three Mineral Horizons and Mineral Horizon Suffixes Used in the CSSC

Symbol	Mineral Horizon Description
A	Forms at or near the surface; experiences *eluviation*, or leaching, of finer particles or minerals. Several subdivisions are identified, with the surface usually darker and richer in organic content than lower horizons (*Ah*); or a paler, lighter zone below that reflects removal of organic matter with clays and oxides of aluminum and iron leached (removed) to lower horizons (*Ae*).
B	Experiences *illuviation*, a depositional process, as demonstrated by accumulations of clays (*Bt*), sesquioxides of aluminum or iron, and possibly an enrichment of organic debris (*Bh*), and the development of soil structure. Colouration is important in denoting whether hydrolysis, reduction, or oxidation processes are operational for the assignment of a descriptive suffix.
C	Exhibits little effect from pedogenic processes operating in the *A* and *B* horizons, except the process of gleysation associated with poor drainage and the reduction of iron, denoted (*Cg*), and the accumulation of calcium and magnesium carbonates (*Cca*) and more soluble salts (*Cs*) and (*Csa*).

Symbol	Horizon Suffix Description
b	A buried soil horizon.
c	Irreversible cementation of a pedogenic horizon; e.g., cemented by $CaCO_3$.
ca	Lime accumulation of at least 10 cm thickness that exceeds in concentration that of the unenriched parent material by at least 5%.
cc	Irreversible cemented concretions, typically in pellet form.
e	Used with *A* mineral horizons (*Ae*) to denote eluviation of clay, Fe, Al, or organic matter.
f	Enriched principally with illuvial iron and aluminum combined with organic matter, reddish in upper portions and yellowish at depth, determined through specific criteria. Used with *B* horizons alone.
g	Grey to blue colours, prominent mottling, or both, produced by intense chemical reduction. Various applications to *A*, *B*, and *C* horizons.
h	Enriched with organic matter: accumulation in place or biological mixing (*Ah*) or subsurface enrichment through illuviation (*Bh*).
j	A modifier suffix for *e, f, g, n,* and *t* to denote limited change or failure to meet specified criteria denoted by that letter.
k	Presence of carbonates as indicated by visible effervescence with dilute hydrochloric acid (HCl).
m	Used with *B* horizons slightly altered by hydrolysis, oxidation, or solution, or all three to denote a change in colour or structure.
n	Accumulation of exchangeable calcium (Ca) in ratio to exchangeable sodium (Na) that is 10 or less, with the following characteristics: prismatic or columnar structure, dark coatings on ped surfaces, and hard consistence when dry. Used with *B* horizons alone.
p	*A* or *O* horizons disturbed by cultivation, logging, and habitation. May be used when ploughing intrudes on previous *B* horizons.
s	Presence of salts, including gypsum, visible as crystals or veins or surface crusts of salt crystals, and by lowered crop yields. Usually with *C* but may appear with any horizon and lowercase suffixes.
sa	A secondary enrichment of salts more soluble than Ca or Mg carbonates, exceeding unenriched parent material, in a horizon at least 10 cm thick.
t	Illuvial enrichment of the *B* horizon with silicate clay that must exceed overlying *Ae* horizon by 3% to 20%, depending on the clay content of the *Ae* horizon.
u	Markedly disrupted by physical or faunal processes other than cryoturbation.
x	Fragipan formation—a loamy subsurface horizon of high bulk density and very low organic content. When dry, it has a hard consistence and seems to be cemented.
y	Affected by cryoturbation (frost action) with disrupted and broken horizons and incorporation of materials from other horizons. Application to *A*, *B*, and *C* horizons and in combination with other suffixes.
z	A frozen layer.

horizons and layers are used in the CSSC. Three mineral horizons are recognized by capital letter designation, followed by lowercase suffixes for further description. Principal soil-mineral horizons and suffixes are presented in Table 18.2.

Four organic horizons are identified in the Canadian classification system. O is further defined through subhorizon designations. Note that for organic soils, such layers are identified as *tiers*. These organic horizons are detailed in Table 18.3.

Table 18.3 Four Organic Horizons Used in the CSSC

Symbol	Description
O	Organic materials, mainly mosses, rushes, and woody materials
L	Mainly discernible leaves, twigs, and woody materials
F	Partially decomposed, somewhat recognizable **L** materials
H	Indiscernible organic materials

O is further defined through subhorizon designations:

Of	Readily identifiable fibric materials
Om	Mesic materials of intermediate decomposition
Oh	Humic material at an advanced stage of decomposition—low fibre, high bulk density

The Ten Soil Orders of the CSSC

The ten orders of the CSSC, and related great groups, are summarized below with a general description of properties, related great groups, an estimated percentage of land area for the soil order, a fertility assessment, and any applicable soil taxonomy equivalent. Figure 18.10 is a generalized map of the soil landscapes of Canada. This map illustrates the great variation of soils across the country.

The *Soil Landscapes of Canada* (SLC) site at **http://sis.agr.gc.ca/cansis/** provides a useful assortment of landscape and soil profile photographs, arranged geographically across Canada from east to west. The site also has an interactive GIS online mapping application. Version 2.2 SLC Component Mapping (December 1996) is operational and involves the CSSC and the Canadian Land Resource Network (CLRN). The component mapping involves a GIS model consisting of layers that include the major characteristics of soil and land for all of Canada. You can select a spatial area and a variety of attributes to display on the map (drainage class, soil type, rooting depth, local surface form, slope, and vegetation cover, among others).

FIGURE 18.10 Generalized soils of Canada.
Distribution of the 10 soil orders of Canada. [Map Courtesy of Agriculture and Agri-Food Canada.]

Legend
- Brunisolic
- Chernozemic
- Cryosolic
- Gleysolic
- Luvisolic
- Organic
- Podzolic
- Regosolic
- Solonetzic
- Vertisolic
- ice
- rock

At the heart of the Canadian System of Soil Classification are 10 general orders. These orders were developed specifically for soils in Canada and are presented here with their associated great groups and subgroups. The following descriptions are summarized from the *Canadian System of Soil Classification*.

Brunisolic Order The **Brunisolic** order is the first order alphabetically. These soils are sufficiently developed to exclude them from the Regosolic order, but the degree of development of soil horizons is so low that they are different from other orders (Figure 18.11). These soils form under mixed forest and have brownish Bm horizons,

FIGURE 18.11 Brunisolic order.
(a) Soil profile from southern Ontario. **(b)** Hay and pastureland that is typical of the Melanic Brunisolic landscape in southern Ontario. **(c)** Map of distribution of Brunisolic order in Canada. [Photos by (a) and (b) Agriculture and Agri-Food Canada; (c) map by Pam Schaus, data from Agriculture and Agri-Food Canada, Soil Landscapes of Canada.]

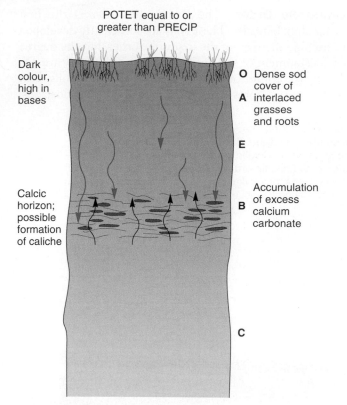

POTET equal to or greater than PRECIP

Dark colour, high in bases

O Dense sod cover of interlaced grasses and roots
A
E

Calcic horizon; possible formation of caliche

B Accumulation of excess calcium carbonate

C

FIGURE 18.12 Calcification in soil.
The calcification process in drier Brunisolic soils (in the U.S. the Aridisol/Mollisol soils) occurs in climatic regimes that have potential evapotranspiration equal to or greater than precipitation.

although various colours are possible. They can also develop under shrubs and grassland. Their B horizon is the most diagnostic feature with Bm, Bfj, thin Bf, or Btj horizons. Brunisols develop under well- to imperfectly drained conditions and lack the Podzolic B horizon of the Podzols, although they are surrounded by them in the St. Lawrence Lowlands. The soils of this order are rated as medium and variable in fertility and account for 14% of the surface area of Canada. The great groups of the Brunisolic order include Melanic Brunisol, Eutric Brunisol, Sombric Brunisol, and Dystric Brunisol. There are 18 subgroups within this order.

Some Brunisolic and Chernozemic soils and other soil orders are highly calcareous. *Calcification* (Figure 18.12) is the accumulation of calcium carbonate or magnesium carbonate in the B and C horizons. Calcification by calcium carbonate ($CaCO_3$), among others, forms a diagnostic subsurface horizon along the boundary between dry and humid climates. These deposits harden or cement to become *caliche*, which can form in the southern prairies.

Chernozemic Order The **Chernozemic** order includes well- to imperfectly drained soils of the steppe–grassland–forest transition in southern Alberta; Saskatchewan; Manitoba; Okanagan Valley, British Columbia, and Palouse Prairie, British Columbia, and accounts for 4% of the solid surface of Canada. The surface horizons are darkened by organic matter accumulation that results from

decomposition of grasses and forbs in the vegetation cover (Figure 18.13). Most soils are frozen in winter and dry in summer with a mean annual soil temperature greater than or equal to 0°C, but usually less than 5.5°C.

Chernozemic soils have high fertility, especially for growing wheat, but can be subject to salinization. Salinization results from excessive potential evapotranspiration rates in deserts and semiarid regions. Salts dissolved in soil water migrate to surface horizons and are deposited there as the water evaporates. These deposits appear as subsurface salty horizons, which will damage or kill plants when the horizons occur near the root zone. This process is especially of concern where soils are irrigated. Focus Study 18.1 outlines the problems associated with salinization and the buildup of toxic materials in the soil. The great groups of the Chernozemic order are Brown Chernozem, Dark Brown Chernozem, Black Chernozem, and Dark Grey Chernozem. There are 38 subgroups within this order. Figure 18.14 shows the transition between great groups within the Chernozem order, principally in response to climate differences.

Cryosolic Order The **Cryosolic** order dominates the northern third of Canada, with permafrost closer to the surface and composed of mineral and organic soil deposits. Generally, it is found north of the treeline, in fine-textured soils in the subarctic forest, or in some organic soils in Boreal forests (Figure 18.15, p. 613). The Ah horizon is lacking or thin. Cryoturbation (frost action) is common and is often denoted by patterned ground circles, polygons, and stripes. Cryosols have a mean annual temperature less than or equal to 0°C. The subgroups of this order are based on the degree of cryoturbation and the nature of the mineral or organic soil material. Fertility ratings are not applicable to these soils that cover 28% of Canada's land area. The great groups are Turbic Cryosol, Static Cryosol, and Organic Cryosol and there are 15 subgroups in this order.

Gleysolic Order *Gleysation* is a soil-forming process in poorly drained conditions where organic matter accumulates in the upper soil layers and mottling occurs in the lower layers resulting from reduction of iron and other elements. The **Gleysolic** order of soils is defined on the basis of colour and mottling that results from chronic reducing conditions inherent in poorly drained mineral soils under wet conditions. A high water table and long periods of water saturation are common to these soils. They are spotty in areal distribution, appearing within other soil orders, occasionally being the dominant soil of an area (Figure 18.16, p. 614), and account for 3% of the land surface. A diagnostic Bg horizon is present in these soils that are rated as high to medium in fertility. The great groups of this order are Luvic Gleysol, Humic Gleysol, and Gleysol. There are 13 subgroups.

Luvisolic Order *Eluviation-illuviation* processes produce a light-coloured Ae horizon and a diagnostic Bt horizon. Soils of this order develop beneath the mixed

(a)

FIGURE 18.13 Chernozemic order.
(a) Soil profile from southern Prairies.
Chernozemic landscape images associated with
dry grasslands can be seen in Figure 18.14.
(b) Map showing distribution of the Chernozemic
order in Canada. [(a) Photo by Agriculture and Agri-
Food Canada; (b) map by Pam Schaus, data from
Agriculture and Agri-Food Canada, Soil Landscapes
of Canada.]

Chernozemic

(b)

deciduous–coniferous forests. There are major occurrences of **Luvisolic** soils in the St. Lawrence Lowlands.
Luvisolic soils occur from the zone of permafrost to the
southern extremity of Ontario and from Newfoundland to
British Columbia. Their greatest areal extent is in the
northern Interior Plains under deciduous, mixed, and
coniferous forest (Figure 18.17, p. 615). The fertility rating
is high for these soils that cover 7% of the land surface.
The great groups of the Luvisolic order are Gray Brown
Luvisol and Gray Luvisol and include 18 subgroups.

Organic Order   Soils of the **Organic** order are composed largely of organic materials. They include peat,
bog, and muck soils and are commonly saturated with
water for prolonged periods of time (Figure 18.18,
p. 616). They are widespread and are associated with
poorly to very poorly drained depressions, but can be
found under upland forest environments (Folisols) and
account for 9% of the land surface. To qualify as organic,
these soils must contain greater than 17% organic
carbon and exceed 30% organic matter by weight

FIGURE 18.14 Soils of the southern Prairies.
(a) Brown Chernozemic soils in the west, Dark Brown Chernozemic in the central portions, and Black Chernozemic in the east—a soil continuum in the southern Canadian Prairies. (b) Brown Chernozemic soil landscape—soils developed in the short grass prairie of the southwestern Prairies in Alberta and Saskatchewan. Photo from south-central Saskatchewan shows typical crops. (c) Black Chernozem landscape—soils are typical of the mixed to tall grass prairie found in eastern Saskatchewan and southern Manitoba. [(a) Illustration adapted from N. C. Brady, *The Nature and Properties of Soils*, 10th ed., © 1990 by Macmillan Publishing Company, adapted by permission; photos (b) and (c) courtesy of Agriculture and Agri-Food Canada.]

overall. Organic soils are rated as high to medium in fertility depending upon drainage and the available nutrients. The great groups contained in this order are Fibrisol, Mesisol, Humisol, and Folisol and include 31 subgroups.

Podzolic Order **Podzolic** soils develop beneath coniferous forests and sometimes heath vegetation and result from leaching of the overlying horizons in moist, cool to cold climates (Figure 18.19, p. 617). They result from *podzolization*, a soil-forming process in which a highly leached soil with

(a)

(b)

Cryosolic

0   500

Kilometres

(c)

(d)

FIGURE 18.15 Cryosolic order.
Cryosols discussed on p. 610. (a) Soil profile of Turbic Cryosolic soil from Northwest Territories. (b) Turbic Cryosolic landscape in Northwest Territories in which patches of soil support vegetation growth. (c) Map of distribution of Cryosolic order in Canada. (d) Turning over the upper organic layer exposes the fibrous organic content and slow decomposition; permafrost is just below this layer that briefly thaws in summer in the Arctic. [Photos (a) and (b) courtesy of Agriculture and Agri-Food Canada; (c) map by Pam Schaus, data from Agriculture and Agri-Food Canada, Soil Landscapes of Canada; (d) photo by Bobbé Christopherson.]

strong surface acidity develops in cool, moist climates (Figure 18.20, p. 618). The Boreal forest that encircles the globe in northern latitudes is largely underlain by Podzolic soils. Iron, aluminum, and organic matter form the L, F, and H horizons and are redeposited in the Podzolic B horizon. A diagnostic Bh, Bhf, or Bf horizon is present depending upon the great group. Podzolic soils dominate in western British Columbia, Ontario, Québec, and Atlantic Canada and account for most of the agricultural surface cover in Canada, 14% of the total land area. The fertility rating for Podzolic soils is low to medium depending on acidity. The great groups in the Podzolic order are Humic, Ferro-humic Podzol, and Humo-ferric Podzol and include 25 subgroups.

(text continued on page 618)

(a) (b)

Gleysolic

0   500
Kilometres

(c)

FIGURE 18.16 Gleysolic order.
Gleysols discussed on p. 610. (a) Soil profile of Gleysol from Atlantic Canada.
(b) Poorly drained soils of the Gleysolic landscape in Atlantic Canada are often used for
forage crops. These soils are highly fertile when drainage is improved. (c) Map of distribution
of Gleysolic order in Canada. [Photos (a) and (b) courtesy of Agriculture and Agri-Food Canada;
(c) map by Pam Schaus, data from Agriculture and Agri-Food Canada, Soil Landscapes of
Canada.]

(a)

(b)

(c)

FIGURE 18.17 Luvisolic order.
Luvisols discussed on pp. 610–611. The southern Ontario vineyards shown in the opening photo of
Chapter 10 are planted in this order. (a) Soil profile of Gray Luvisol from Atlantic Canada. (b) Coniferous
forests are typical of the Gray Luvisol landscape in Atlantic Canada. (c) Map of distribution of Luvisolic
order in Canada. [Photos (a) and (b) courtesy of Agriculture and Agri-Food Canada; (c) map by Pam Schaus,
data from Agriculture and Agri-Food Canada, Soil Landscapes of Canada.]

(a)

(b)

Organic

(c)

FIGURE 18.18 Organic order.
Organic soil order discussed on p. 611. (a) Organic soil profile from Southern Ontario.
(b) Vegetable and market crops are often grown on drained organic soils in southern Ontario.
(c) **Map of distribution of Organic order in Canada.** [Photos (a) and (b) courtesy of Agriculture and
Agri-Food Canada; (c) map by Pam Schaus, data from Agriculture and Agri-Food Canada, Soil
Landscapes of Canada.]

(a)

(b)

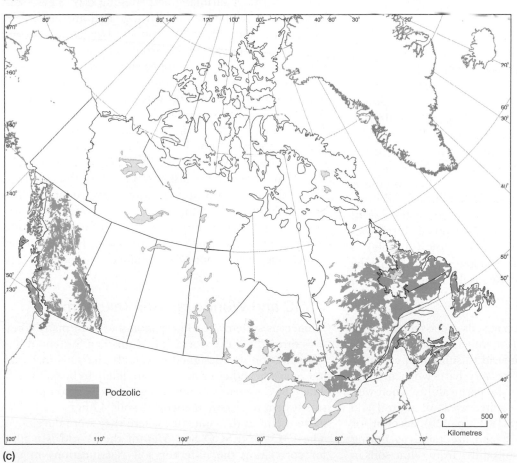

Podzolic

0   500
Kilometres

(c)

FIGURE 18.19 Podzolic order.
(a) Humo-ferric Podzol from coastal forest, British Columbia. (b) Characteristic temperate forest and Podzolic soils in the cool, moist climate of central Vancouver Island. (c) Map of distribution of Podzolic order in Canada. [Photos (a) courtesy of Agriculture and Agri-Food Canada; (b) by Bobbé Christopherson; (c) map by Pam Schaus, data from Agriculture and Agri-Food Canada, Soil Landscapes of Canada.]

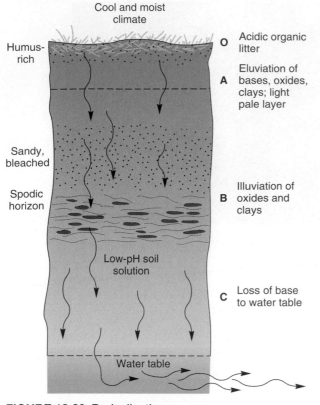

Cool and moist climate

Humus-rich

O Acidic organic litter

A Eluviation of bases, oxides, clays; light pale layer

Sandy, bleached

Spodic horizon

B Illuviation of oxides and clays

Low-pH soil solution

C Loss of base to water table

Water table

FIGURE 18.20 Podzolization.
The podzolization process is typical in cool and moist climatic regimes.

Regosolic Order   Soils of the **Regosolic** order are weakly developed and limited as a result of a number of contributing factors that include young materials, fresh alluvial deposits, material instability, mass-wasted slopes, and dry, cold climatic conditions. Regosolic soils lack Solonetzic, illuvial, or Podzolic B horizons (Figure 18.21), and do not exist where permafrost is within 1 m of the surface or within 2 m of cryoturbated soil. Regosolic soils may have L, F, H, or O horizons or an Ah horizon if it is less than 10 cm thick. It is possible for buried soil horizons to exist. Regosolic soils, which account for 2% of the land surface, dominate in the Northwest Territories and northern Yukon, and are rated as low (variable) in fertility. There are 2 great groups in the Regosolic order—Regosol and Humic Regosol. These contain 8 subgroups.

Solonetzic Order   **Solonetzic** soils are associated with saline or alkaline. These well- to imperfectly drained soils develop under grasses in semiarid to subhumid climates. They have B horizons that are very hard when dry and swell to a sticky mass of very low permeability when wet. Solonetzic soils, existing in limited areas of central and north-central Alberta (Figure 18.22, p. 620), account for only 1% of the surface area and are rated as having variable fertility. Solonetzic soils differ from saline soils in that the bedrock under Solonetzic soils is saline or alkaline and is quite close to the surface. Because of imperfect

drainage, salts are distributed throughout Solonetzic soils and can occur over wide areas. These soils were originally called blowout soils and have a hardened layer close to the surface called a hardpan that prevents the free flow of water in the soil and restricts root growth. The three great groups of the Solonetzic order are Solonetz, Solodized Solonetz, and Solod, and they contain 27 subgroups.

Salinization results from excessive potential evapotranspiration rates in deserts and semiarid regions. Salts dissolved in soil water migrate to surface horizons, which will damage or kill plants when the horizons occur near the root zone. The salt accumulation in Figure 18.22b (p. 620) is an example of this process. Under such semiarid conditions, commercial evaporite mineral deposits can develop (Figure 18.23).

Obviously, salinization complicates farming in these drier lands. The introduction of irrigation water may either waterlog poorly drained soils or lead to salinization. Nonetheless, vegetation does grow where soils are well drained and low in salt content. Focus Study 18.1 discusses the battle between salinization and waterlogging in irrigated lands in California (p. 605).

Vertisolic Order   **Vertisolic** soils occur in heavy-textured material that is high in clay content (≥ 60% clay), especially smectite, a shrinking and swelling clay. These soils have little development of horizons, and are marked by slickensides and severe disruption. The shrinking and swelling of the clays resulting from wetting and drying cycles are strong enough to groove and polish surfaces along internal shear planes in the soil and prevent horizons from fully developing. However, Vertisolic soils may have an A horizon similar to Chernozemic soils, or they may have features similar to Gleysolic soils. Vertisolic soils occur primarily in the cool, subarid to subhumid grassland portion of the Interior Plains of western Canada (Figure 18.24, p. 621) and account for just over 0.28% of the land area. This order may also occur to a more minor extent in valleys of the Cordilleran Region, in parts of the South Boreal Region, and in the cool temperate regions of central Canada. The two great groups of the Vertisolic order are Vertisol and Humic Vertisol, and they contain 6 subgroups.

CSSC and Worldwide Soil Taxonomy

Numerous systems of soil taxonomy exist in many countries throughout the world. The Canadian System of Soil Classification was designed to classify the soils that exist in Canada, whether or not they are likely to be cultivated. The CSSC system was not designed to be a comprehensive system to classify the world's soils. Other systems are more useful in the countries where they were developed. The FAO–UNESCO Soil Map of the World is helpful for correlating the different soil classifications in use. (See **http://www.itc.nl/~rossiter/research/rsrch_ss_class. html#FAO**.)

(a)

(c)

(b)

(d)

(e)

FIGURE 18.21 Regosolic order. (a) Marine Regosol in Atlantic Canada—note the absence of a B horizon. (b) Fertile farm fields on marine Regosol landscape. (c) Alluvial Regosol. (d) Alluvial Regosolic landscape where streams and creeks deposit the sediments that create this fertile soil. (e) Map of the distribution of the Regosolic order in Canada. [Photos (a) to (d) courtesy of Agriculture and Agri-Food Canada; (e) map by Pam Schaus, data from Agriculture and Agri-Food Canada, Soil Landscapes of Canada.]

Regosolic

(a)

(b)

(c)

FIGURE 18.22 Solonetzic order.
Solonetzols discussed on p. 618. (a) Solodized Solonetzic profile in Alberta. (b) Saline
landscape in Alberta. The salt pan in the foreground is an example of extreme salinization of
the soil. (c) Map of distribution of Solonetzic order in Canada. [Photos (a) and (b) courtesy of
Agriculture and Agri-Food Canada; (c) map by Pam Schaus, data from Agriculture and Agri-Food
Canada, Soil Landscapes of Canada.]

FIGURE 18.23 Commercial lake-bed evaporite mineral deposits.

Although a mineral and not a soil, these deposits of sodium sulphate (Na_2SO_4) are mined from a lakebed near Chaplin, in south-central Saskatchewan. Such deposits form in an environment where evaporation exceeds precipitation, thus the evaporites accumulate. This type of water-balance regime can lead to salinization in soils. This semiarid region features some mixed prairie, showing in the foreground. [Photo by Robert Christopherson.]

Perhaps the closest to a comprehensive system is the Soil Taxonomy of the Natural Resources Conservation Service (NRCS) in the United States, a system under development since 1951. The Soil Taxonomy is of major influence on the design and development of the Canadian system and is presented and mapped in Appendix B. Table 18.4 presents the approximate equivalents of the soil orders and great groups in the Canadian system with the FAO-UNESCO system and the U.S. system. This table is adapted from the *Canadian System of Soil Classification*, Third Edition. Both the Soil Taxonomy and CSSC are hierarchical and each defines taxa on the basis of measurable soil properties. However, the Canadian system is designed only to classify soils within Canada, whereas the U.S. system classifies soils of the world. The U.S. system has "suborders," a category that does not exist in the Canadian system. The greatest difference between the two systems is that the Canadian system uses all horizons in diagnosing the soil, whereas the Soil Taxonomy system emphasizes the depth of soil reached through ploughing.

(a)

(b)

FIGURE 18.24 Vertisolic order.

Vertisols discussed on p. 618. **(a) Vertisolic soil profile in Saskatchewan. (b) Map of distribution of Vertisolic order in Canada.** [(a) Photo by Darwin Anderson, University of Saskatchewan; (b) map by Pam Schaus, data from Agriculture and Agri-Food Canada, Soil Landscapes of Canada.]

Table 18.4 Canadian Soil Orders Correlated to World Reference Base for Soil Orders (Food and Agriculture Organization UNESCO) and the U.S. Soil Taxonomy*

Canadian System of Soil Classification	World Reference Base (FAO-UNESCO)	U.S. Soil Taxonomy
Chernozemic	Kastanozem, Chernozem, Greyzem, Phaeozem	Mollisols (Borolls)
Solonetzic	Solonetz	Mollisols, Alfisols (Natric great groups); some Aridisols
Luvisolic	Luvisol	Alfisols (Boralfs and Udalfs)
Podzolic	Podzol	Spodosols, some Inceptisols
Brunisolic	Cambisol	Inceptisols, Aridisols (Psamments)
Regosolic	Fluvisol, Regosol	Entisols
Gleysolic	Gleysol, Planosol	Several orders: "Aqu-" suborders
Organic	Histosol	Histosols
Cryosolic	Cryosol	Gelisols
Vertisolic	Vertisol	Vertisols (six suborders)

*Only generalizations are possible; these are nearest equivalents or orders (or suborders), if applicable.

Source: Canadian System of Soil Classification, 3 ed., Table 18.4 Canadian Soil Orders. Agriculture and Agri-Food Canada © 1998. Reproduced with the permission of the Minister of Public Works and Government Services Canada.

Applied Physical Geography

Soil Density and Porosity

Soil density is a mass per unit volume and can be measured either as bulk density or particle density, which are outlined below.

Calculation of *bulk density* is based on the naturally existing volume of soil (volume of the soil as it would be in the field) after it has been dried. This measure includes the pore spaces that may be filled with either air or water, and organic material. Mineral soils typically range from 1.0 g/cm³ to 1.8 g/cm³, but can exist outside that range. Bulk density of terrestrial soils is used as an indicator of soil compaction.

Particle density is the density of the solid soil particle and excludes pore spaces (air or water). Typically particle density for mineral soil is approximately equal to 2.65g/cm³.

Pores in the soil control the movement of water. Porosity, the measure of the volume of soil that is air or water, can be calculated using the bulk density of the soil.

$$\text{Porosity} = 100 - (\text{BD}/2.65 \times 100)$$

where *BD* is bulk density.

Given two soil samples, calculate the porosity of solid material in each.

Soil Sample	Volume (cm³)	Wet Weight (g)	Dry Weight (g)
Sample A	83.6	115.7	88.8
Sample B	63.6	121.2	101.4

Calculate the porosity of each sample. First, calculate bulk density using the dry weight divided by volume. Bulk density is a mass per unit volume.

A 88.8 g/83.6 cm³ = 1.06 g/cm³

B 101.4 g/63.6 cm³ = 1.59 g/cm³

Then calculate the porosity using:

$$\text{Porosity} = 100 - (\text{BD}/2.65 \times 100)$$

A Porosity = $100 - (\text{BD}/2.65 \times 100)$
= $100 - (1.06 \text{ g/cm}^3/ 2.65 \text{ g/cm}^3 \times 100)$
= $100 - (40)$
= 60

Sample A has a porosity of 60%

B Porosity = $100 - (\text{BD}/2.65 \times 100)$
= $100 - (1.59 \text{ g/cm}^3/ 2.65 \text{ g/cm}^3 \times 100)$
= $100 - (60)$
= 40

Sample B has a porosity of 40%

Each has adequate pore space for the movement of moisture through the soil. The second sample is more compacted than the first.

Summary and Review—The Geography of Soils

■ *Define* soil and soil science, and *describe* a pedon, polypedon, and typical soil profile.

Soil is the portion of the land surface in which plants can grow. It is a dynamic natural body composed of fine materials and contains both mineral and organic matter. **Soil science** is the interdisciplinary study of soils involving physics, chemistry, biology, mineralogy, hydrology, taxonomy, climatology, and cartography. *Pedology* deals with the origin, classification, distribution, and description of soil. *Edaphology* specifically focuses on the study of soil as a medium for sustaining the growth of plants.

The basic sampling unit used in soil surveys is the **pedon**. The **polypedon** is the soil unit used to prepare local soil maps and may contain many pedons. Each discernible layer in an exposed pedon is a **soil horizon**. The horizons are designated O (contains **humus**, a complex mixture of decomposed and synthesized organic materials), A (rich in humus and clay, darker), Ae (zone of **eluviation**, the removal of fine particles and minerals by water), B (zone of **illuviation**, the deposition of clays and minerals translocated from elsewhere), C (*regolith*, weathered bedrock), and R (bedrock). Soil horizons A, Ae, and B experience the most active soil processes and together are designated the **solum**.

    soil (p. 595)
    soil science (p. 596)
    pedon (p. 596)
    polypedon (p. 597)
    soil horizon (p. 597)
    humus (p. 597)
    eluviation (p. 597)
    illuviation (p. 597)
    solum (p. 598)

1. Soils provide the foundation for animal and plant life and therefore are critical to Earth's ecosystems. Why is this true?

2. What are the differences among soil science, pedology, and edaphology?

3. Define polypedon and pedon, the basic units of soil.

4. Characterize the principal aspects of each soil horizon. Where does the main accumulation of organic material occur? Where does humus form? Explain the difference between the eluviated layer and the illuviated layer. Which horizons constitute the solum?

■ *Describe* soil properties of colour, texture, structure, consistence, porosity, and soil moisture.

We use several physical properties to classify soils. Colour suggests composition and chemical makeup. Soil texture refers to the size of individual mineral particles and the proportion of different sizes. For example, **loam** is a balanced mixture of sand, silt, and clay. Soil structure refers to the arrangement of soil peds, which are the smallest natural cluster of particles in a soil. The cohesion of soil particles to each other is called soil consistence. Soil porosity refers to the size, alignment, shape, and location of spaces in the soil. Soil moisture refers to water in the soil pores and its availability to plants.

    loam (p. 598)

5. Soil colour is identified and compared using what technique?

6. Define a soil separate. What are the various sizes of particles in soil? What is loam? Why is loam regarded so highly by agriculturists?

7. What is a quick, hands-on method for determining soil consistence?

8. Summarize the five soil-moisture regimes common in mature soils.

■ *Explain* basic soil chemistry, including cation-exchange capacity, and *relate* these concepts to soil fertility.

Particles of clay and organic material form negatively charged **soil colloids** that attract and retain positively charged mineral ions in the soil. The capacity to exchange ions between colloids and roots is an ability called the **cation-exchange capacity (CEC)**. CEC is a measure of **soil fertility**, the ability of soil to sustain plants. Fertile soil contains organic substances and clay minerals that absorb water and retain certain elements needed by plants.

    soil colloids (p. 601)
    cation-exchange capacity (CEC) (p. 601)
    soil fertility (p. 601)

9. What are soil colloids? How are they related to cations and anions in the soil? Explain cation-exchange capacity.

10. What is meant by the concept of soil fertility?

■ *Evaluate* the principal soil formation factors, including the human element.

Environmental factors that affect soil formation include parent materials, climate, vegetation, topography, and time. Human influence is having a great impact on Earth's prime soils. Essential soils for agriculture and their fertility are threatened by mismanagement, destruction, and conversion to other uses. Much soil loss is preventable through the application of known technologies, improved agricultural practices, and government policies.

Specific soil-forming processes keyed to climatic regions (not a basis for classification) are called **pedogenic regimes**: **laterization** (leaching in warm and humid climates, not present in Canada; see Oxisols is Appendix B), **salinization** (collection of salt residues in surface horizons in hot, dry climates; discussed with Solonetzic soils), **calcification** (accumulation of carbonates in the B and C horizons in drier continental climates; discussed with Chernozemic soils), **podzolization** (soil acidification in forest soils in cool climates; discussed with Podzolic soils), and **gleysation** (humus and clay accumulation in cold, wet climates with poor drainage; discussed with Gleysolic soils).

    pedogenic regimes (p. 602)
    laterization (p. 602)
    salinization (p. 602)
    calcification (p. 602)
    podzolization (p. 602)
    gleysation (p. 602)

11. Briefly describe the contribution of the following factors and their effect on soil formation: parent material, climate, vegetation, landforms, time, and humans.

12. Explain some of the details that support the concern over loss of our most fertile soils. What cost estimates have been placed on soil erosion?

■ *Describe* the 10 soil orders of the Canadian System of Soil Classification and explain their general occurrence.

The **Canadian System of Soil Classification (CSSC)** is built around an identification and analysis of physical properties of the soil that can be observed in the field. The system divides soils into five hierarchical categories: order, great group, subgroup, family, and series.

The 10 soil orders are **Brunisolic** (weakly developed, humid region soils), **Chernozemic** (grassland soils), **Cryosolic** (cold soils underlain by permafrost), **Gleysolic** (saturated, reducing soils), **Luvisolic** (woodland soils), **Organic** (peat, muck, bog, and fen soils), **Podzolic** (northern conifer forest soils), **Regosolic** (soils without B horizons), **Solonetzic** (soils with saline parent materials), and **Vertisolic** (expandable clay soils).

Canadian System of Soil Classification (CSSC) (p. 606)
Brunisolic (p. 609)
Chernozemic (p. 610)
Cryosolic (p. 610)
Gleysolic (p. 610)
Luvisolic (p. 611)
Organic (p. 611)
Podzolic (p. 612)
Regosolic (p. 618)
Solonetzic (p. 618)
Vertisolic (p. 618)

13. Why did Canada adopt its own system of soil classification? Describe a brief history of events that led up to the modern CSSC system.

14. Which soil order is associated with the development of a bog? Account for the use of bog "soil" as a low-grade fuel.

15. Describe the podzolization process occurring in northern coniferous forests. What are the surface horizons like? What management strategies might enhance productivity in these soils? Name the soil order for these areas.

16. Compare and contrast Interior Plains soils with those of the southeastern Canadian Shield.

17. What processes inhibit soil development in the extreme north? Explain.

18. Briefly describe what you found on the *Soil Landscapes of Canada* (SLC) Web site. Please try the SLC Internet Mapping feature for your specific area or region (**http://sis. agr.gc.ca/cansis/nsdb/slc/intro.html**).

19. Which of the 10 soil orders is characteristic of the area where you live or where you attend university? How did you determine the answer?

Critical Thinking

A. Select a small soil sample from your campus or near where you live. Using the sections in this chapter on soil characteristics, properties, and formation, describe as completely as possible this sample, within these limited constraints. Using the general soil map and any other sources available (e.g., local agriculture extension agent, Internet, related department on campus), are you able to roughly place this sample in one of the soil orders?

B. Using the local phone directory or Internet, see if you can locate an agency or extension agent that provides information about local soils and advice for soil management. Is there a place where you can get soil tested?

An ancient forest ecosystem and community of mosses, ferns, heather, grasses, and lush undergrowth cover the forest floor and rock outcrop. The mixed birch forest and marine west coast climate is in central Scotland, near Loch Ness. [Photo by Bobbé Christopherson.]

19

Ecosystem Essentials

■ Key Learning Concepts

After reading the chapter, you should be able to:

■ **Define** ecology, biogeography, and the ecosystem concept.

■ **Describe** communities, habitats, and niches.

■ **Explain** photosynthesis and respiration, and **derive** net photosynthesis and the world pattern of net primary productivity.

■ **List** abiotic ecosystem components, and **relate** those components to ecosystem operations.

■ **Explain** trophic relationships in ecosystems.

■ **Relate** how biological evolution led to the biodiversity of life on Earth.

■ **Define** succession, and **outline** the stages of general ecological succession in both terrestrial and aquatic ecosystems.

Diversity is an impressive feature of the living Earth. The diversity of organisms is a response to the interaction of the atmosphere, hydrosphere, and lithosphere, all powered by solar energy. The evolution of life on Earth, in all its forms, is intertwined with the evolution of Earth's physical and chemical systems. This interaction produces a variety of conditions within which the biosphere exists. The diversity of life also results from the intricate interplay and coevolution of living organisms themselves. We, as part of this vast natural complex, seek to find our place and understand the feelings nature stimulates within us.

The physical beauty of nature is certainly among its most powerful appeals to the human animal. The complexity of the aesthetic response is suggested by its wide-ranging expression from the contours of a mountain landscape to the ambient colors of a setting Sun to the fleeting vitality of a breaching whale. Each exerts a powerful aesthetic impact on most people, often accompanied by feelings of awe at the extraordinary physical appeal and beauty of the natural world.*

The biosphere, the sphere of life and organic activity, extends from the ocean floor to about 8 km (5 mi) altitude into the atmosphere. The biosphere includes myriad ecosystems from simple to complex, each operating within general spatial boundaries. An **ecosystem** is a self-sustaining association of living plants and animals and their nonliving physical environment. Earth's biosphere itself is a collection of ecosystems within the natural boundary of the atmosphere and Earth's crust.

Natural ecosystems are open systems for both solar energy and matter, with almost all ecosystem boundaries functioning as transition zones rather than as sharp demarcations. Distinct ecosystems—for example, forests, seas, mountaintops, deserts, beaches, islands, lakes, and ponds—make up the larger whole.

Ecology is the study of the relationships between organisms and their environment and among the various ecosystems in the biosphere. The word *ecology*, developed by German naturalist Ernst Haeckel in 1869, is derived from the Greek *oikos* ("household," or "place to live") and *logos* ("study of"). **Biogeography** is the study of the distribution of plants and animals, the diverse spatial patterns they create, and the physical and biological processes, past and present, that produce Earth's species richness.

The degree to which modern society understands Earth's biogeography and conserves Earth's living legacy will determine the extent of our success as a species and the long-term survival of a habitable Earth:

> The time is ripe to step up and expand current efforts to understand the great interlocking systems of air, water, and minerals nourishing the Earth. . . . Moreover, without vigorous action toward that goal, nations will be seriously handicapped in trying to cope with proven and suspected threats to ecosystems and to human health and welfare resulting from alterations in the cycles of carbon, nitrogen, phosphorus, sulfur, and related materials. . . . Society depends upon this life-support system of planet Earth.†

Here we are 28 years after this UNEP report and Gilbert White's statement was issued, reading the UNEP assessment *Global Environmental Outlook 4*, published October 25, 2007. In its *Summary for Policy Makers* (p. 12), the UNEP states:

*S. R. Kellert, "The biological basis for human values of nature," in S. R. Kellert and E. O. Wilson, eds., *The Biophilia Hypothesis* (Washington, DC: Island Press, 1993), p. 49.

†G. F. White and M. K. Tolba, *Global Life Support Systems*, United Nations Environment Programme Information, No. 47 (Nairobi, Kenya: United Nations, 1979), p. 1.

Biodiversity decline and loss of ecosystem services continue to be a major threat to future development. The reduction in distribution and functioning of land, fresh water, and marine biodiversity is more rapid than at any time in human history. Ecosystems such as forests, wetlands, and drylands are being transformed and, in some cases, irreversibly degraded. Rates of species extinction are increasing. The great majority of well-studied species, including commercially important fish stocks, are declining in distribution or abundance or both. Genetic diversity of agricultural and other species is widely considered to be in decline.

What was learned in all these years? The essential challenge for us in geographic education is in the last topic sentence, "The degree to which modern society understands Earth's biodiversity. . . ." We must work to better understand and communicate these "Ecosystem Essentials."

Earth's most influential biotic (living) agents are the humans. This is not arrogance; it is fact, because we powerfully influence every ecosystem on Earth. From the time humans first developed agriculture, the raising of animals, and the use of fire, we began a process that has led to our dominance over Earth's physical systems.

Since life arose on the planet, there have been six major extinctions. The fifth one was 65 million years ago, whereas the sixth is happening across the present decades. Of all these extinction episodes, this is the only one of biotic origin, caused for the most part by human activity. We are the greatest evolutionary force as we essentially dominate freshwater quantity and quality, croplands, ocean fishery production, nitrogen and other chemical budgets, the concentration of greenhouse gases, and the present extinction rate.

In this chapter: We explore ecosystems and the community, habitat, and niche concepts. Plants are the essential living component in the biosphere, translating solar energy into usable forms to energize life. The role of nonliving systems, including biogeochemical cycles, is examined. We cover the organization of living ecosystems along complex food chains and webs. The biodiversity of living organisms is seen as a product of biological evolution over the past 3.6+ billion years, approximately. Ecosystem stability and resilience, and how living landscapes change over space and time through the process of succession, are important. Included is coverage of the effects of global change on ecosystems and rates of succession. The chapter ends with a look at the Great Lakes environment and status.

Ecosystem Components and Cycles

An ecosystem is a complex of many variables, all functioning independently yet in concert, with complicated flows of energy and matter (Figure 19.1). The key is to understand the linkages and interconnections within and between

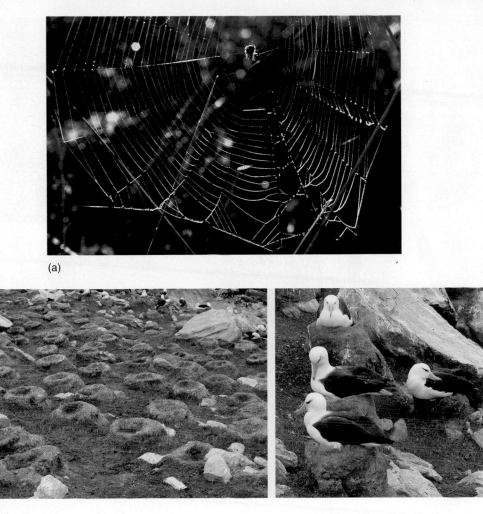

(a)

(b)

FIGURE 19.1 The web of life.

(a) Study the spider web as you read the following quotation:

Life devours itself: everything that eats is itself eaten; everything that can be eaten is eaten; every chemical that is made by life can be broken down by life; all the sunlight that can be used is used. . . . The web of life has so many threads that a few can be broken without making it all unravel, and if this were not so, life could not have survived the normal accidents of weather and time, but still the snapping of each thread makes the whole web shudder, and weakens it. . . . You can never do just one thing: the effects of what you do in the world will always spread out like ripples in a pond.

(b) Abandoned Black-browed Albatross nests indicate a change in government fishing regulations in the surrounding ocean— ". . . snapping each thread makes the whole web shudder. . . ." [(a) Photo by Robert Christopherson; quotation from Friends of the Earth and Amory Lovins, The U.N. Stockholm Conference, *Only One Earth* (London: Earth Island Limited, 1972), p. 20. (b) Photos by Bobbé Christopherson.]

systems. As the quote in the caption says, ". . . The effects of what you do in the world will always spread out like ripples in a pond." The decrease in the Black-browed Albatross (*Diomedea melanophris*) colony evident from the empty nests in Figure 19.1b was the result of changes in regulations in the fishing industry around the Falkland Islands. An increase in quotas for the squid harvest, a primary food source for the albatross, led to the reduction in bird population.

An ecosystem includes both biotic (living) and abiotic (nonliving) components. Nearly all ecosystems depend on a direct input of solar energy; the few limited ones that exist in dark caves, in wells, or on the ocean floor depend on chemical reactions (chemosynthesis).

Ecosystems are divided into subsystems, with the biotic portion composed of producers (plants), consumers (animals), and detritus feeders and decomposers (worms, mites, bacteria, fungi). The abiotic flows in an ecosystem include gaseous, hydrologic, and mineral cycles. Figure 19.2 illustrates these essential elements of an ecosystem.

Communities

A convenient biotic subdivision within an ecosystem is a community. A **community** is formed by interactions among populations of living animals and plants at a particular time. An ecosystem is the interaction of many communities with the abiotic physical components of its environment.

(b)

FIGURE 19.2 Biotic and abiotic components of ecosystems.
(a) Solar energy is the input that drives the biotic and abiotic components. Heat energy and biomass are the outputs from the biosphere. (b) Biotic and abiotic ingredients operate together to form this temperate forest-floor ecosystem in British Columbia, with mosses beginning the process of community development. [Photo by Bobbé Christopherson.]

Some examples help to clarify these concepts. In a forest ecosystem, a specific community may exist on the forest floor, whereas another community functions in the canopy of leaves high above (Figure 19.3). Not all forests appear familiar, as the dwarf willow forest in Greenland demonstrates (Figure 19.3c). Similarly, within a lake ecosystem, the plants and animals that flourish in the bottom sediments form one community, whereas those near the surface form another. A community is identified in several ways—by its physical appearance, the species present and the abundance of each, the complex patterns of their interdependence, and the trophic (feeding) structure of the community.

Within a community, two concepts are important: habitat and niche. **Habitat** is the type of environment where an organism resides or is biologically adapted to live. In terms of physical and natural factors, most species have specific habitat requirements with definite limits and a specific regimen of sustaining nutrients.

Niche (French *nicher*, "to nest") refers to the function, or occupation, of a life form within a given community. It is the way an organism obtains and sustains the physical, chemical, and biological factors it needs to survive. A niche has several facets. Among these are a habitat niche, a trophic (food) niche, and a reproductive niche. For example, the Red-winged Blackbird (*Agelaius phoeniceus*)

occurs throughout the United States and most of Canada in habitats of meadow, pastureland, and marsh. This species nests in blackberry tangles and thick vegetation in freshwater marshes, sloughs, and fields. Its trophic niche is weed seeds and cultivated seed crops throughout the year, and during the nesting season it adds insects to its diet—an aspect of its reproductive niche. These birds disperse seeds of many plants during their travels.

In a stable community, no niche is left unfilled. The *competitive exclusion principle* states that no two species can occupy the same niche (food or space) successfully in a stable community. Thus, closely related species are spatially separated. In other words, each species operates to reduce competition and to maximize its own reproduction rate—literally, species survival depends on successful reproduction. This strategy in turn leads to greater diversity as species shift and adapt to fill each niche. Figure 19.4 shows 11 different community environments and representative life forms.

Some species are *symbiotic*, an arrangement where two or more species exist together in an overlapping relationship. One type of symbiosis, *mutualism*, occurs when each organism benefits and is sustained over an extended period by the relation. For example, lichen (pronounced "liken") is made up of algae and fungi living together. The alga is the producer and food source for the fungus, and

(a)

(b)

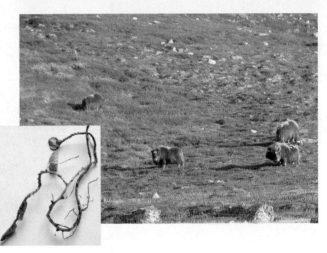

(c)

FIGURE 19.3 Different forest communities.
(a) West coast temperate rain forest, Vancouver Island, British Columbia. Canada's largest trees grow in this region. (b) Turtles bask on a log in a subtropical swamp (low, waterlogged ground) at Juniper Springs Recreation Area, Florida. (c) Fall colours highlight this dwarf willow forest in Greenland. Musk Oxen are foraging for food and drinking meltwater. The inset photo shows a 13-year-old willow, dated by the small annual growth segments below the leaf. Some dwarf willows can range to over 300 years in age. [Photos by Bobbé Christopherson.]

the fungus provides structure and physical support. Their mutualism allows the two to occupy a niche in which neither could survive alone. Lichen developed from an earlier parasitic relationship in which the fungi broke into the algal cells. Today, the two organisms have evolved into a supportive harmony and symbiotic relationship (Figure 19.5). The partnership of corals and algae discussed in Chapter 16 is another example of mutualism in a symbiotic relationship.

By contrast, another form of symbiosis is a *parasitic* relationship, which may eventually kill the host, thus destroying the parasite's own niche and habitat. An example is parasitic mistletoe (*Phoradendron*), which lives on and may kill various kinds of trees. Some scientists are questioning whether our human society and the physical systems of Earth constitute a global-scale symbiotic relationship of mutualism, which is sustainable, or a parasitic one, which is unsustainable.

Plants: The Essential Biotic Component

Plants are the critical biotic link between solar energy and the biosphere. Ultimately, the fate of all members of the biosphere, including humans, rests on the success of plants and their ability to turn sunlight into food.

Land plants (and animals) became common about 430 million years ago, according to fossilized remains. **Vascular plants** developed conductive tissues and true roots for internal transport of fluid and nutrients. (*Vascular* is from a Latin word for "vessel-bearing," referring to the conducting cells.) Presently, about 270,000 species of plants are known to exist, and most are vascular. Many more species have yet to be identified. They represent a great untapped resource base. Only about 20 species of plants provide 90% of the world's food; just three—wheat, maize (corn), and rice—comprise half of the food supply. Plants are a major source of new medicines and chemical compounds that benefit humanity.

(a) Elephant heads

(b) Western yellow-bellied racer

(c) Polar bear and cubs

(d) Svalbard reindeer

(e) Killdeer chicks

(f) Coral mushroom

(g) Desert scene, barrel cactus

(h) Leopard seal

(i) Alligator in swamp

(j) Tricolored Heron

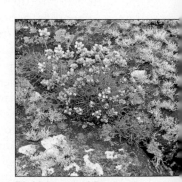

(k) Lichens and flower

FIGURE 19.4 Plants and animals fit specific niches.
(a) Elephant heads (*Pedicularis groenlandica*), a wildflower, above 1800 m (6000 ft) in wet meadows. (b) A western yellow-bellied racer (*Coluber constrictor*) lives in prairies and feeds on insects, lizards, and mice. (c) A female polar bear (*Ursus maritimus*) with two 8-month-old cubs in the Arctic Ocean. (d) A Svalbard reindeer (*Rangifer tarandus platyrhynchus*) on Spitsbergen Island, Arctic Ocean, losing velvet from his antlers. (e) Killdeer chicks (*Charadrius vociferus*) begin life in an exposed rocky nest. (f) Coral mushroom (*Ramaria* sp.), a fungal decomposer, at work on organic matter. (g) A large barrel cactus flourishes in the rocky soils of the desert. (h) A leopard seal (*Hydrurga leptonyx*) resting on a small iceberg near the Antarctic Peninsula; the blood stains are from a recent meal. (i) An alligator (*Alligator mississippiensis*) hides in a mangrove swamp. (j) Tricolored Heron (*Egretta tricolor*) in wetlands. (k) Five kinds of lichen and sea thrift flower in Scotland. [Photos (a, c, d, f, h, i, j, k) by Bobbé Christopherson; (b, e, g) by Robert Christopherson.]

(a)

(b)

FIGURE 19.5 Symbiosis on the rocks.
(a) Lichen, an example of a symbiotic relationship, specifically mutualism, between fungi and algae. (b) Two species of lichen, perhaps more, function under extremely hostile climate conditions in Antarctica. Each small indentation provides some advantage to the darker lichen. [Photos by Bobbé Christopherson.]

Plants also are the core of healthy, functioning ecosystems that sustain all life.

Leaves are solar-powered chemical factories, wherein photochemical reactions take place. Veins in the leaf bring in water and nutrient supplies and carry off the sugars (food) produced by photosynthesis. The veins in each leaf connect to the stems and branches of the plant and to the main circulation system.

Flows of carbon dioxide, water, light, and oxygen enter and exit the surface of each leaf (see Figure 1.4 in

Chapter 1). Gases flow into and out of a leaf through small pores called **stomata** (singular: *stoma*), which usually are most numerous on the lower side of the leaf. Each stoma is surrounded by guard cells that open and close the pore, depending on the plant's changing needs. Water that moves through a plant exits the leaves through the stomata and evaporates from leaf surfaces, thereby assisting the plant's temperature regulation. As water evaporates from the leaves, a pressure deficit is created that allows atmospheric pressure to push water up through the plant all the way from the roots, in the same manner that a soda straw works. We can only imagine the complex operation of a 100-m (330-ft) tree!

Photosynthesis and Respiration

Powered by energy from certain wavelengths of visible light, **photosynthesis** unites carbon dioxide and hydrogen (hydrogen is derived from water in the plant). The term is descriptive: *photo-* refers to sunlight, and *-synthesis* describes the "manufacturing" of starches and sugars through reactions within plant leaves. The process releases oxygen and produces energy-rich food for the plant.

The largest concentration of light-responsive, photosynthetic structures (known as *organelles*) in a leaf rests below the leaf's upper layers. These organelle units within cells are the *chloroplasts*, and within each resides a green, light-sensitive pigment called **chlorophyll**. Within this pigment, light stimulates photochemistry. Consequently, competition for light is a dominant factor in the formation of plant communities. This competition is expressed in the height, orientation, distribution, and structure of plants.

Only about one-quarter of the light energy arriving at the surface of a leaf is useful to the light-sensitive chlorophyll. Chlorophyll absorbs only the orange-red and violet-blue wavelengths for photochemical operations, and it reflects predominantly green hues (and some yellow). That is why trees and other vegetation look green.

Photosynthesis essentially follows this equation:

$$6CO_2 + 6H_2O + Light \rightarrow C_6H_{12}O_6 + 6O_2$$
(carbon dioxide) (water) (solar energy) (glucose, carbohydrate) (oxygen)

From the equation, you can see that photosynthesis removes carbon (in the form of CO_2) from Earth's atmosphere. The quantity is enormous: approximately 91 billion metric tons (100 billion tons) of carbon dioxide per

FIGURE 19.6 How plants live and grow.
The balance between photosynthesis and respiration determines net photosynthesis and plant growth.
[Temperate rain forest photo by Bobbé Christopherson.]

year. Carbohydrates, the organic result of the photosynthetic process, are combinations of carbon, hydrogen, and oxygen. They can form simple sugars, such as *glucose* ($C_6H_{12}O_6$). Plants use glucose to build starches, which are more complex carbohydrates and the principal food stored in plants.

Plants store energy for later use. They consume this energy as needed through respiration by converting the carbohydrates to energy for their other operations. Thus, **respiration** is essentially a reverse of the photosynthetic process:

$$C_6H_{12}O_6 \ + \ 6O_2 \ \rightarrow \ 6CO_2 \ + \ 6H_2O \ + \text{energy}$$
(glucose,   (oxygen)   (carbon   (water)   (heat
carbohydrate)   dioxide)   energy)

In respiration, plants oxidize carbohydrates (stored energy), releasing carbon dioxide, water, and energy as heat. The overall growth of a plant depends on a surplus of carbohydrates beyond those lost through plant respiration. Figure 19.6 presents a simple schematic of this process, which produces plant growth.

The *compensation point* is the break-even point between the production and consumption of organic material. Each leaf must operate on the production side of the compensation point, or else the plant eliminates it—something each of us has no doubt experienced with a houseplant that received inadequate water or light. The difference between photosynthetic production and respiration loss is *net photosynthesis*. The amount varies, depending on controlling environmental factors such as light, water, temperature, soil fertility, and the plant's site, elevation, and competition from other plants and animals.

The rapidly increasing carbon dioxide concentration in the atmosphere stimulates the photosynthetic processes. However, with higher temperatures of global warming

occurring more at night than during the day in many regions, this results in higher respiration rates. One of the key scientific findings is that this unnatural warming is emphasized during the night and during wintertime, whereas a natural warming cycle would be balanced day to night or summer to winter. Plants respire all the time but at night respiration processes are the plant's main operation. Studies of tropical rain forests in Costa Rica determined that increased respiration rates had made the forest a net carbon gain to the atmosphere.

Plant productivity increases as light availability increases—up to a point. When the light level is too high, *light saturation* occurs and most plants actually reduce their output in response. Some plants are adapted to shade, whereas others flourish in full sunlight. Crops such as rice, wheat, and sugarcane do well with high light intensity. Figure 19.7 portrays the general energy budget for green plants, showing energy receipt, energy utilization, and disposition of net primary production—how the energy is spent.

Net Primary Productivity The net photosynthesis for an entire plant community is its **net primary productivity**. This is the amount of stored chemical energy that the community generates for the ecosystem. **Biomass** is the net dry weight of all this organic material and its stored chemical energy.

Net primary productivity is measured as fixed carbon per square metre per year. ("Fixed" means chemically bound into plant tissues.) Study the map and satellite images in Figure 19.8 and you can see that on land, net primary production tends to be highest between the Tropics of Cancer and Capricorn at sea level and decreases toward higher latitudes and elevation. Precipitation also affects productivity, as evidenced by the correlations of abundant precipitation with high productivity adjacent to the

FIGURE 19.7 Energy budget of the biosphere.
Energy receipt, energy utilization, and energy disposition of net primary production by green plants.

(a)

(b)

(c)

FIGURE 19.8 Net primary productivity.
(a) Worldwide net primary productivity in grams of carbon per square metre per year (approximate values). (b) Normalized difference vegetation index. False colouration indicates bare ground in browns, dense vegetation in blues. (c) *SeaWIFS* image of surface chlorophyll concentration for land and sea; intensity of green colour represents higher levels of chlorophyll. This is the first image of a continuous record over a 3-year period for the oceans. [(a) After D. E. Reichle, *Analysis of Temperate Forest Ecosystems* (Heidelberg: Springer, 1970). Adapted by permission. (b) NASA/GSFC. (c) *SeaWIFS* image by NASA/GSFC and GeoEye, Dulles, VA. Used by permission.]

equator and reduced precipitation with low productivity in the subtropical deserts. Even though deserts receive high amounts of solar radiation, other controlling factors limit productivity, namely, water availability and soil conditions.

In the oceans, differing nutrient levels control and limit productivity. Regions with nutrient-rich upwelling currents off western coastlines generally are the most productive. The map in Figure 19.8 shows that the tropical oceans and areas of subtropical high pressure are quite low in productivity.

In temperate and high latitudes, the rate at which carbon is fixed by vegetation varies seasonally. It increases in spring and summer as plants flourish with increasing solar input and, in some areas, with more available (nonfrozen) water, and it decreases in late fall and winter. Productivity rates in the tropics are high throughout the year, and turnover in the photosynthesis–respiration cycle is faster, exceeding by many times the rates experienced in a desert environment or in the far northern limits of the tundra. A lush hectare (2.5 acres) of sugarcane in the tropics might fix 45 metric tons (50 tons) of carbon in a year, whereas desert plants in an equivalent area might achieve only 1% of that amount.

Table 19.1 lists various ecosystems, their net primary productivity, and an estimate of net total biomass worldwide—170 billion metric tons of dry organic matter per year. Compare the various ecosystems, especially cultivated land (in *italics*), with most of the natural communities. Net productivity is generally regarded as the most important aspect of any type of community, and the distribution of productivity over Earth's surface is an important subject of biogeography.

Abiotic Ecosystem Components

Critical in each ecosystem are the flow of energy and the cycling of nutrients and water in life-supporting systems. These abiotic (nonliving) components set the stage for ecosystem operations.

Light, Temperature, Water, and Climate   Solar energy powers ecosystems, so the pattern of solar energy receipt is crucial. Solar energy enters an ecosystem by way of photosynthesis, and heat energy is dissipated from the system at many points. Of the total energy intercepted at Earth's surface and available for work, only about 1.0% is actually fixed by photosynthesis as carbohydrates in plants.

Table 19.1   Net Primary Productivity and Plant Biomass on Earth

| Ecosystem | Area (10^6 km²)[a] | Net Primary Productivity per Unit Area (g/m²/yr)[b] | | World Net Biomass (10^9 tons/yr)[c] |
		Normal Range	Mean	
Tropical rain forest	17.0	1000–3500	2200	37.4
Tropical seasonal forest	7.5	1000–2500	1600	12.0
Temperate evergreen forest	5.0	600–2500	1300	6.5
Temperate deciduous forest	7.0	600–2500	1200	8.4
Boreal forest	12.0	400–2000	800	9.6
Woodland and shrubland	8.5	250–1200	700	6.0
Savanna	15.0	200–2000	900	13.5
Temperate grassland	9.0	200–1500	600	5.4
Tundra and alpine region	8.0	10–400	140	1.1
Desert and semidesert scrub	18.0	10–250	90	1.6
Extreme desert, rock, sand, ice	24.0	0–10	3	0.07
Cultivated land	*14.0*	*100–3500*	*650*	*9.1*
Swamp and marsh	2.0	800–3500	2000	4.0
Lake and stream	2.0	100–1500	250	0.5
Total continental	**149**	—	**773**	**115.17**
Open ocean	332.0	2–400	125	41.5
Upwelling zones	0.4	400–1000	500	0.2
Continental shelf	26.6	200–600	360	9.6
Algal beds and reefs	0.6	500–4000	2500	1.6
Estuaries	1.4	200–3500	1500	2.1
Total marine	**361.0**	—	**152**	**55.0**
Grand total	**510.0**	—	**333**	**170.17**

[a]1 km² = 0.38 mi².

[b]1 g per m² = 8.92 lb per acre.

[c]1 metric ton (10^6 g) = 1.1023 tons.

Source: R. H. Whittaker, Communities and Ecosystems (Heidelberg: Springer, 1975), p. 224. Reprinted by permission.

The duration of Sun exposure is the *photoperiod*. Along the equator, days are essentially 12 hours long year-round; however, with increasing distance from the equator, seasonal effects become pronounced. Plants have adapted their flowering and seed germination to seasonal changes in insolation. Some seeds germinate only when daylength reaches a certain number of hours. A plant that responds in the opposite manner is the poinsettia (*Euphorbia pulcherrima*), which requires at least 2 months of 14-hour nights to start flowering.

Monarch butterflies (*Danaus plexippus*) migrate some 3600 km (2235 mi) from eastern North America to wintering forests in Mexico. The butterflies navigate using an internal time-compensated Sun compass to maintain their southwestward track while they compensate for time-of-day Sun changes. Researchers found receptors in their eyes sensitive to ultraviolet light that play the key role in accurate navigation. For Monarchs, ultraviolet light is an important abiotic component.

Other components are important to ecosystem processes. Air and soil temperatures determine the rates at which chemical reactions proceed. Significant temperature factors are seasonal variation and duration and the pattern of minimum and maximum temperatures.

Operations of the hydrologic cycle and water availability depend on precipitation and evaporation rates and their seasonal distribution. Water quality—its mineral content, salinity, and levels of pollution and toxicity—is important. Also, regional climates affect the pattern of vegetation and ultimately influence soil development. All of these factors work together to form the limits for ecosystems in a given location.

Figure 19.9 illustrates the general relationship among temperature, precipitation, and vegetation. Can you identify the characteristic vegetation type and related temperature and moisture regime that fit areas you know well, such as a place you have lived or an area around the school you now attend?

Life Zones   Alexander von Humboldt (1769–1859), an explorer, geographer, and scientist, observed that plants and animals recur in related groupings wherever similar conditions occur in the abiotic environment. He described the similarities and dissimilarities of vegetation and the associated uneven distribution of various organisms. After several years of study in the Andes Mountains of Peru, he described a distinct relation between elevation and plant communities as his *life zone concept*. As he climbed the mountains, he noticed that the experience was similar to that of travelling away from the equator toward higher latitudes (Figure 19.10a).

This zonation of plants with altitude is noticeable on any trip from lower valleys to higher elevations. Each **life zone** possesses its own temperature, precipitation, and insolation relations and therefore its own biotic communities.

The Grand Canyon in Arizona provides a good example. Plants and animals of the inner gorge at the bottom of the canyon (600 m, or 2000 ft, in elevation) are characteristic of the lower Sonoran Desert of northern Mexico. However, communities similar to those of southern Canadian forests dominate the north rim of the canyon (2100 m, or 7000 ft, in elevation). On the summits of the nearby San Francisco Mountains (3600 m, or 12,000 ft, in elevation), the vegetation is similar to that of the arctic tundra of northern Canada. Needleleaf forest and alpine tundra in the Canadian Rockies at high elevation are pictured in Figure 19.10b and c.

Other Factors   Beyond these general conditions, each ecosystem further produces its own *microclimate*, which is specific to individual sites. For example, in a forest the insolation reaching the ground is reduced and shade from its own trees blankets the forest floor. A pine forest cuts light by 20%–40%, whereas a birch–beech forest reduces it by as much as 50%–75%. Forests also are about 5% more humid than nonforested landscapes, have moderated temperatures (warmer winters and cooler summers), and experience reduced winds.

Slope orientation and Sun exposure are important, too, for they translate into differences in temperature and moisture efficiency, especially in middle and higher latitudes. With all other factors equal, slopes facing away from the Sun's rays tend to be moister and more vegetated than slopes facing toward the Sun. In the Northern Hemisphere, these moister slopes face north. Such highly localized *microecosystems* are evident where changes in exposure and moisture occur related to geographic orientation.

Even Earth's magnetic field, another abiotic component, plays an interesting role in ecosystems. Read about turtle and animal navigation in News Report 19.1.

Elemental Cycles

The most abundant natural elements in living matter are hydrogen (H), oxygen (O), and carbon (C). Together, these elements make up more than 99% of Earth's biomass; in fact, all life (organic molecules) contains hydrogen and carbon. In addition, nitrogen (N), calcium (Ca), potassium (K), magnesium (Mg), sulphur (S), and phosphorus (P) are significant nutrients, elements necessary for the growth of a living organism.

Several key chemical cycles function in nature. Oxygen, carbon, and nitrogen each have *gaseous cycles*, part of which are in the atmosphere. Other elements have *sedimentary cycles*, which principally involve mineral and solid phases; major elements that have these cycles include phosphorus, calcium, potassium, and sulphur. Some elements combine gaseous and sedimentary cycles. The recycling of gases and sedimentary (nutrient) materials forms Earth's **biogeochemical cycles**, so called because they involve chemical reactions necessary for growth and development of living systems. The chemical elements themselves recycle over and over again in life processes.

(text continued on page 640)

FIGURE 19.9 How temperature and precipitation affect ecosystems.
(a) Climate controls (wetness, dryness; warmth, cold) and ecosystem types. (b) Subtropical desert in Namibia. (c) Sonoran desert of Arizona. (d) Cold desert of north-central Nevada. (e) Dry tundra of East Greenland. (f) El Yunque tropical rain forest of Puerto Rico. (g) Deciduous trees in fall colours in Ohio. (h) Needleleaf forest near Independence Pass, Colorado. (i) Moist tundra of Spitsbergen, Arctic Ocean. [Photos by (b) NigelDennis/Photo Researchers, Inc.; (c) and (d) Robert Christopherson; (f) Tom Bean; (e), (g), (h), and (i) Bobbé Christopherson.]

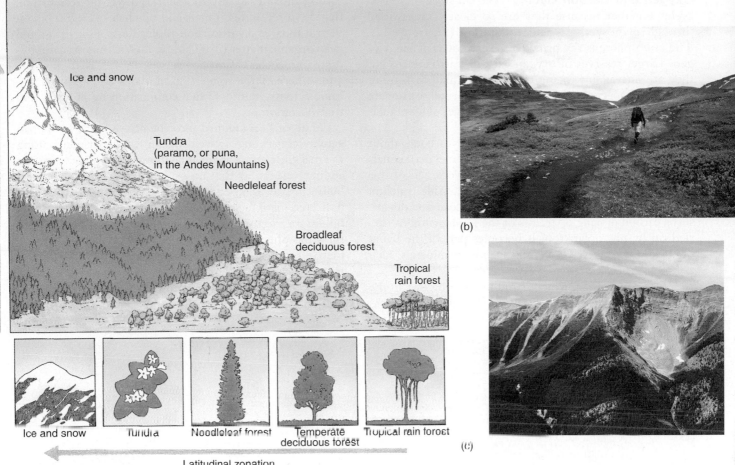

FIGURE 19.10 Vertical and latitudinal zonation of plant communities.
(a) Progression of plant community life zones with changing elevation or latitude. (b) Alpine tundra ecosystem in the Canadian Rockies. (c) The timberline for a needleleaf forest in the Canadian Rockies. The line of trees marks the limit of highest continuous forest, whereas the area above it marks the zone above which no trees grow. [Photos by (b) Darren Alemeida; (c) Robert Christopherson.]

News Report 19.1

Earth's Magnetic Field—An Abiotic Factor

The fact that birds and bees can detect Earth's magnetic field and use it for finding direction is well established. Small amounts of magnetically sensitive particles in the skull of the bird and the abdomen of the bee provide compass directions for bird migration and for alerting the hive to the location of the latest nectar find. For migrating birds, the timing and accuracy of an exact flight path is important, for the birds know the nutritional places they need to visit to build their fat storage for long journeys and where each "pit stop" is located along the way.

A team of biologists from the University of North Carolina, Catherine and Kenneth Lohmann, has found that sea turtles can detect magnetic fields of different strengths and the inclination (angle) of these magnetic fields. This means that the turtles have a built-in navigation system that helps them know where they are on Earth (like our global positioning system, which requires multimillion-dollar satellites). Using magnetic field strengths and inclination, the turtles evidently are aware of their global position—similar to knowing their latitude and longitude. This magnetic

map is evidently imprinted in their brain.

Loggerhead sea turtles hatch in Florida, crawl into the water, and spend the next 70 years travelling thousands of miles between North America and Africa around the subtropical high-pressure gyre in the Atlantic Ocean (see Figure 6.13). The females return to near where they were hatched to lay their eggs! The researchers think that the hatchlings are imprinted with magnetic data unique to the beach where they hatched and then develop a more global sense as they live a life swimming across the ocean.

Oxygen and Carbon Cycles We consider these two cycles together because they are so closely intertwined through photosynthesis and respiration (Figure 19.11). The atmosphere is the principal reserve of available oxygen. Larger reserves of oxygen exist in Earth's crust, but they are unavailable, being chemically bound with other elements, especially the silicate (SiO_2) and carbonate (CO_3) mineral families. Unoxidized reserves of fossil fuels and sediments also contain oxygen.

The oceans are enormous pools of carbon—about 42,900 billion metric tons. (Metric tons times 1.10 equals short tons; or, 47,190 billion tons.) However, all of this carbon is bound chemically in carbon dioxide, calcium carbonate, and other compounds. The ocean initially absorbs carbon dioxide by means of the photosynthesis carried on by phytoplankton; it becomes part of the living organisms and is fixed in certain carbonate minerals, such as limestone ($CaCO_3$).

The atmosphere, which is the integrating link in the cycle, contains only about 700 billion tons of carbon (as carbon dioxide) at any moment. This is far less carbon than is stored in fossil fuels and oil shales (13,200 billion metric tons, as hydrocarbon molecules) or in living and dead organic matter (2500 billion metric tons, as carbohydrate molecules). Carbon dioxide is released into the atmosphere by the respiration of plants and animals, volcanic activity, and fossil fuel combustion by industry and transportation.

The carbon dumped into the atmosphere by human activity constitutes a vast geochemical experiment, using the real-time atmosphere as a laboratory. Annually, we are adding carbon to the atmospheric pool in an amount 400% greater than 1950 levels. Global emissions of carbon from fossil fuels continues to increase, with some 6.88 billion metric tons (7.56 billion tons) of carbon added to the atmosphere in 2005—compare this to the 1.47 billion metric tons (1.61 billion tons) in 1950, or 4.74 billion metric tons (5.21 billion tons) in 1980. About 50% of the carbon emitted since the beginning of the Industrial Revolution and not absorbed by oceans and organisms

FIGURE 19.11 The carbon and oxygen cycles.
Carbon is fixed through photosynthesis and begins its passage through ecosystem operations. Respiration by living organisms, burning of forests and grasslands, and the combustion of fossil fuels release carbon to the atmosphere. These cycles are greatly influenced by human activities.

ANIMATION

The Global Carbon Cycle

remains in the atmosphere, enhancing Earth's natural greenhouse effect, thus global warming.

Nitrogen Cycle   Nitrogen, which accounts for 78.084% of each breath we take, is the major constituent of the atmosphere. Nitrogen also is important in the makeup of organic molecules, especially proteins, and therefore is essential to living processes. A simplified view of the nitrogen cycle is portrayed in Figure 19.12.

This vast atmospheric reservoir of nitrogen is not directly accessible to most organisms. *Nitrogen-fixing bacteria* provide the key link to life. They live principally in the soil and are associated with the roots of certain plants—for example, the *legumes* such as clover, alfalfa, soybeans, peas, beans, and peanuts. Colonies of these bacteria reside in nodules on the legume roots and chemically

combine the nitrogen from the air in the form of nitrates (NO_3) and ammonia (NH_3). Plants use these chemically bound forms of nitrogen to produce their own organic matter. Anyone or anything feeding on the plants thus ingests the nitrogen. Finally, the nitrogen in the organic wastes (sewage, manure) of these consuming organisms is freed by denitrifying bacteria, which recycle nitrogen back to the atmosphere.

To improve agricultural yields, many farmers use synthetic inorganic fertilizers, as opposed to soil-building organic fertilizers (manure and compost). Inorganic fertilizers are chemically produced through artificial nitrogen fixation at factories using the Haber–Bosch process developed in 1913, a process that takes inert nitrogen gas and hydrogen to form ammonia (NH_3) or the ammonium ion NH_4^+, a reactive form of nitrogen that plants can use.

FIGURE 19.12 The nitrogen cycle.
The atmosphere is the essential reservoir of gaseous nitrogen. Atmospheric nitrogen gas is chemically fixed by bacteria to produce ammonia. Lightning and forest fires produce nitrates, and fossil fuel combustion forms nitrogen compounds that are washed from the atmosphere by precipitation. Plants absorb nitrogen compounds and produce organic material. [From T. Audesirk and G. Audesirk, *Biology: Life on Earth*, 4th ed., Figure 45-10, p. 903. © 1996 Prentice Hall Inc. Used by permission.]

ANIMATION   The Nitrogen Cycle

The annual production of inorganic fertilizers far exceeds the ability of natural denitrification systems—and the present production of synthetic fertilizers now is doubling every 8 years; some 1.82 million tons (2 million tons) are produced per week, worldwide. Humans presently fix more nitrogen per year than all terrestrial sources combined. The crossover point when anthropogenic sources of fixed nitrogen exceeded the normal range of naturally fixed nitrogen was 1970.

This surplus of usable nitrogen accumulates in Earth's ecosystems. Some is present as excess nutrients, washed from soil into waterways and eventually to the ocean. This excess nitrogen load begins a water pollution process that feeds an excessive growth of algae and phytoplankton, increases biochemical oxygen demand, diminishes dissolved oxygen reserves, and eventually disrupts the aquatic ecosystem. In addition, excess nitrogen compounds in air pollution are a component in acid deposition, further altering the nitrogen cycle in soils and waterways. For more on this problem, specific to North America, read News Report 19.2.

Limiting Factors

The term **limiting factor** identifies the one physical or chemical abiotic component that most inhibits biotic operations, through either its lack or its excess. Here are a few examples:

- Low temperatures limit plant growth at high elevations.
- Lack of water limits growth in a desert.
- Excess water limits growth in a bog.
- Changes in salinity levels affect aquatic ecosystems.
- Lack of iron in ocean surface environments limits photosynthetic production.
- Low phosphorus content of soils limits plant growth.
- General lack of active chlorophyll above 6100 m (20,000 ft) limits primary productivity.

In most ecosystems, precipitation is the limiting factor. However, temperature, light levels, and soil nutrients certainly affect vegetation patterns.

Each organism possesses a range of tolerance for each limiting factor in its environment. This fact is illustrated in Figure 19.13, which shows the geographic range for two tree species and two bird species. The coast redwood (*Sequoia sempervirens*) is limited to a narrow section of the Coast Ranges in California, covering barely 9500 km² (less than 4000 mi²), concentrated in areas that receive necessary summer advection fog. On the other hand, the red maple (*Acer rubrum*) thrives over a large area under varying conditions of moisture and temperature, thus demonstrating a broader tolerance to environmental variations.

The Mallard Duck (*Anas platyrhynchos*) and the Snail Kite (*Rostrhamus sociabilis*) also demonstrate a variation in tolerance and range (Figure 19.13b). The Mallard, a generalist, feeds from widely diverse sources, is easily

(a)

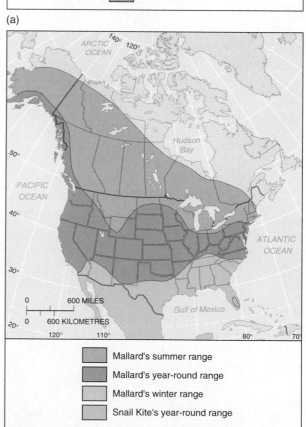

(b)

FIGURE 19.13 Limiting factors affect the distribution of every plant and animal species.
(a) Distributions of coast redwood and red maple demonstrate the effect of limiting factors, (b) as do the distributions of the Mallard Duck and the Snail Kite across North America. The Mallard is a generalist and feeds widely. In contrast, the range of its food, a single type of snail, limits the Snail Kite.

News Report 19.2

The Dead Zone

The flush of agricultural runoff and fertilizers, animal manure, sewage, and other wastes is carried by the Mississippi River to the Gulf, causing huge spring blooms of phytoplankton. By summer, the biological oxygen demand of bacteria feeding on the decay exceeds the dissolved oxygen, and hypoxia develops, killing any fish that ventures into the area. These low-oxygen conditions act as a limiting factor on marine life. Figure 19.2.1 shows the dead zone, a region of oxygen-depleted (hypoxic) water off the coast of Louisiana in the Gulf of Mexico.

The Mississippi drainage system handles the runoff for 41% of the continental United States. When the 1993 Midwest floods hit, the river's nutrient discharge was such that the size of the dead zone doubled to 17,500 km² (6755 mi²). The worst

year was 1999, when it expanded to 20,000 km² (7720 mi²). The agricultural, feedlot, and fertilizer industries dispute the connection between their nutrient input and the dead zone. Following Hurricane Katrina in 2005, the dead zone region was overwhelmed by discharge carrying all the sewage, chemical toxins, oil spills, pesticides, animal wastes and carcasses, and nutrients. Full disclosure of the contents of the "muck" has yet to be made. The approximate temporary plume from this event is plotted on the map.

In other parts of the world, the connection is established. In Sweden and Denmark, a concerted effort to reduce nutrient flows into their rivers reversed hypoxic conditions in the Kattegat Strait (between the Baltic and North Seas). And, with the fall of the U.S.S.R. and state agriculture in 1990,

fertilizer use is down more than 50%, and for the first time in recent decades the Black Sea is getting several months' break from year-around hypoxia off river discharge inlets.

As with most environmental situations, the cost of mitigation is cheaper than the cost of continued damage to marine ecosystems. A cut in nitrogen inflow upstream of 20% to 30% is estimated to increase dissolved oxygen levels by more than 50% in the dead zone region of the Gulf. One government estimate placed the application of excess nitrogen fertilizer at 20% more than needed in Iowa, Illinois, and Indiana. The initial step to resolving this issue might be to mandate applying only the levels of fertilizer needed—a savings in overhead costs for agricultural interests. And, secondly, that action begin to deal with animal wastes in the basin.

(a)

FIGURE 19.2.1 The Gulf Coast dead zone.
(a) Mapped total nitrogen originating in the upstream watershed that feeds the Mississippi River system. (b) The flush of nutrients from the Mississippi River drainage basin enriches the offshore waters in the Gulf of Mexico, causing huge phytoplankton blooms in early spring (red areas). (c) By late summer, oxygen-depleted waters (hypoxic) dominate what is known as the *dead zone*.
[(a) Adapted from R. B. Alexander, et. al., "Effect of stream channel size on the delivery of nitrogen to the Gulf of Mexico," *Nature* (February 17, 2000); 761; (b) *SeaWiFS* image from the NASA/GSFC, courtesy of GeoEye, Dulles, VA.]

(b)

(c)

domesticated, and is found throughout most of North America in at least one season of the year. By contrast, the Snail Kite is a specialist that feeds only on one specific type of snail. This single food source, then, is its limiting factor. Note its small habitat area near Lake Okeechobee in Florida.

Biotic Ecosystem Operations

The abiotic components of energy, atmosphere, water, weather, climate, and minerals make up the life support for the biotic components of each ecosystem. The flow of energy, cycling of nutrients, and trophic (feeding) relations determine the nature of an ecosystem. As energy cascades through this process-flow system, it is constantly replenished by the Sun. But nutrients and minerals cannot be replenished from an external source, so they constantly cycle within each ecosystem and through the biosphere. Let us examine these biotic operations.

Producers, Consumers, and Decomposers

Organisms that are capable of using carbon dioxide as their sole source of carbon are *autotrophs* (self-feeders), or **producers**. These are the plants. They chemically fix carbon through photosynthesis. Organisms that depend on producers as their carbon source are *heterotrophs* (feed on others), or **consumers**. Generally, these are animals (Figure 19.14).

Autotrophs are the essential producers in an ecosystem—capturing light energy and converting it to chemical energy, incorporating carbon, forming new plant tissue and biomass, and freeing oxygen. Solar energy enters each food chain through the producer plant or producer phytoplankton, subsequently flowing through higher and higher levels of consumers.

From the producers, which manufacture their own food, energy flows through the system along a circuit called the **food chain**, reaching consumers and eventually *detritivores*. Organisms that share the same basic foods are said to be at the same *trophic level*. Ecosystems generally are structured in a **food web**, a complex network of interconnected food chains. In a food web, consumers participate in several different food chains, comprising both *strong interactions* and *weak interactions* between species in the food web.

In Figure 19.14b a bearded seal (*Erignathus barbatus*), with body fat exceeding 30%, rests on a bergy bit, or small iceberg, in Arctic waters where they feed on fish and clams. Figure 19.14c shows a male polar bear (*Ursus maritimus*) hauling its bearded seal kill onto the ice. Polar bears are the dominant Arctic predator, a marine mammal. In 19.14d, on the pack ice many kilometres from land we see a mother and her 6-month-old cubs-of-the-year feeding on a seal catch. Even though the cubs still nurse, they share the kill with mom. The polar bear consumes most of the seal except for the bones and intestines, which are quickly eaten by birds scavenging the leftovers. Note the Glaucous Gulls and Ivory Gulls in the photo.

Figure 19.15 illustrates simple terrestrial and oceanic food chains. Primary consumers feed on producers. Because producers are always plants, the primary consumer is an **herbivore**, or plant eater, like the krill. A **carnivore** is a secondary consumer and primarily eats meat, as with the leopard seal and polar bear. A tertiary consumer eats primary and secondary consumers and is referred to as the "top carnivore" in the food chain. A consumer that feeds on both producers (plants) and consumers (meat) is an **omnivore**—a category occupied by humans, among others.

In the Arctic region, the walrus (*Odobenus rosmarus*) has a special diet and adaptation to obtain it. They feed on clams in the shallows near land, brushing aside sand and sediment with their whiskers, pulling the clam into their mouths and, with a powerful sucking action, pulling out the meat. Walrus will occasionally eat squid and fish if needed to sustain their huge calorie requirement.

Detritivores (detritus feeders and decomposers) are the final link in the endless chain. Detritivores renew the entire system by releasing simple inorganic compounds and nutrients with the breaking down of organic materials. Detritus refers to all the dead organic debris, remains, fallen leaves, and wastes that living processes leave. Detritus feeders—worms, mites, termites, centipedes, snails, crabs, and even vultures, among others—work like an army to consume detritus and excrete nutrients that fuel an ecosystem. **Decomposers** are primarily bacteria and fungi that digest organic debris outside their bodies and absorb and release nutrients in the process. This metabolic work of microbial decomposers produces the rotting that breaks down detritus. Detritus feeders and decomposers, although different in operation, have a similar function in an ecosystem.

Examples of Complex Food Webs

An example of a complex community is the oceanic food web that includes krill, a primary consumer (Figure 19.16). Krill (*Euphausia sp.*, at least a dozen species) is a shrimp-like crustacean that is a major food for an interrelated group of organisms, including whales, fish, seabirds, seals, and squid in the Antarctic region. All of these organisms participate in numerous other food chains as well, some consuming and some being consumed.

Phytoplankton began this chain by harvesting solar energy in photosynthesis. *Herbivorous zooplankton* such as krill and other organisms eat phytoplankton. Consumers eat krill at the next trophic level. Because krill are a protein-rich, plentiful food, increasingly factory ships, such as those from Japan and Russia, seek them out. The annual krill harvest currently surpasses a million tons, principally as feed for chickens and livestock and as protein for human consumption. Many of the Antarctic dwelling birds depend on krill and on fish that eat krill.

The impact on the food web of further increases in the krill harvest is uncertain, for little is known about the krill reproduction rate. Their long life span (greater than 8 years) and slow growth rate limit the ultimate extent of

(b)

(c)

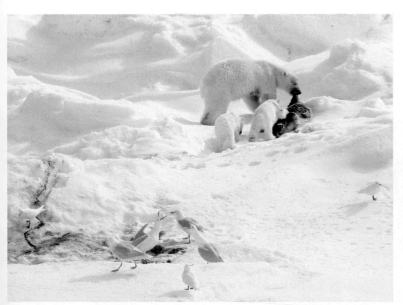

(a)

(d)

ANIMATION   Building a Food Web

FIGURE 19.14 Energy, nutrient, and food pathways in the environment.
(a) The flow of energy, cycling of nutrients, and trophic (feeding) relationships portrayed for a generalized ecosystem. The operation is fueled by radiant energy supplied by sunlight and first captured by the plants.
(b) A bearded seal on a bergy bit in the Arctic Ocean.
(c) A solitary male polar bear drags its seal feast across pack ice. (d) A mother polar bear and cubs eat a meal on an iceberg after mom caught a seal; birds work on the leftovers. [From T. Audesirk and G. Audesirk, *Biology: Life on Earth*, 4th ed., Figure 45-1, p. 892. © 1996 Prentice Hall Inc. Used by permission. Photos (b, c, and d) by Bobbé Christopherson.]

(a)

(b)

FIGURE 19.15 Food chains.
(a) A simplified terrestrial food chain, from leaf to caterpillar to Bobolink to a fast-moving Merlin Hawk. (b) A simplified aquatic food chain from phytoplankton to zooplankton to schooling fish and to a mako shark. [From T. Audesirk and G. Audesirk, *Biology: Life on Earth*, 4th ed., Figure 45-4, p. 895. © 1996 Prentice Hall Inc. Used by permission]

the resource. In addition, the possible effect on krill of increased ultraviolet radiation resulting from the seasonal "hole" in the ozone layer above Antarctica is under investigation.

Another example of a complex food web comes from eastern North America, and a temperate deciduous forest. As with the krill food web, the diagram is simplified from the actual complexity of nature (Figure 19.17). From our discussion find the primary producers and then locate the primary, secondary, and tertiary consumers in this community. Do you find the detritivores (worms are shown) playing a role as well? Bacteria act as decomposers in the system; do you find any other decomposers in the illustration?

Efficiency in a Food Web

Any assessment of world food resources depends on the level of consumer being targeted. Let us use humans as an example. Many people can be fed if wheat is eaten directly. However, if the grain is first fed to cattle (herbivores) and then we eat the beef, the yield of available food energy is cut by 90% (810 kg of grain is reduced to 82 kg of meat); far fewer people can be fed from the same land area (Figure 19.18).

In terms of energy, only about 10% of the kilocalories (food Calories, not heat calories) in plant matter survives from the primary to the secondary trophic level. When humans consume meat instead of grain, there is a further loss of biomass and added inefficiency. More energy is lost to the environment at each progressive step in the food chain. You can see that an omnivorous diet such as with an average North American and European is quite expensive in terms of biomass and energy.

ANIMATION Building a Food Web

ANIMATION Midlatitude Productivity

Krill is a shrimplike crustacean 7.5 cm (3 in.) long overall. "Superswarms" of krill, several kilometres wide, can weigh up to 2 million tons.

FIGURE 19.16 A complex food web.
The food web in Antarctic waters, from phytoplankton producers (bottom) through various consumers. Phytoplankton began this chain using photosynthesis to store solar energy. Krill and other herbivorous zooplankton eat the phytoplankton. Krill in turn are consumed by the next trophic level.

FIGURE 19.17 Temperate forest food webs.
A simplified illustration of food webs in a temperate forest. Examine the art and identify primary producers, and primary, secondary, and tertiary consumers. Featured are strong interactions, but many weak interactions not illustrated hold such natural communities together, affirming the hypothesis that complexity is stabilizing and not weakening the community. [Jay Withgott and Scott Brennan, *Environment, The Science Behind the Stories*, San Francisco: Benjamin Cummings, © 2007, Fig. 6.11, p. 159. Used by permission.]

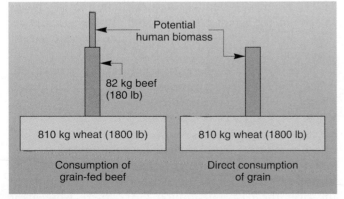

FIGURE 19.18 Efficiency and inefficiency in biomass consumption.
Biomass pyramids illustrate a great difference in efficiency between direct and indirect consumption of grain.

Food web concepts are becoming politicized as world food issues grow more critical. Today, approximately half of the cultivated acreage in Canada and the United States is planted for animal consumption—beef and dairy cattle, hogs, chickens, and turkeys. Livestock feed includes approximately 80% of the annual corn and nonexported soybean harvest. In addition, some lands cleared of rain forest in Central and South America were converted to pasture to produce beef for export to restaurants, stores, and fast-food outlets in developed countries. Thus, lifestyle decisions and dietary patterns in North America and Europe are perpetuating inefficient food webs, not to mention the destruction of valuable resources, both here and overseas. Scientists are studying the impact on world grain supplies from the spread of American meat-based fast-food restaurants across the globe, and the dietary changes these foster.

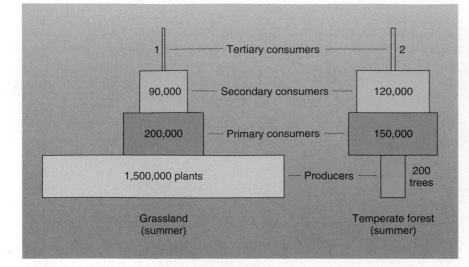

FIGURE 19.19 Population distribution in two ecosystems.
Ecological pyramids for 0.1 hectares (0.25 acres) of land show the difference in producers and consumers between grassland and forest in the summer.
[From E. P. Odum, *Fundamentals of Ecology*, 3rd ed., with permission of Brooks/Cole, an imprint of the Wadsworth Group, Thomson Learning.]

Clearly, some food webs are exceptionally simple, such as eating grains directly, whereas others are more complex. The home gardener's tomatoes may be eaten by a tomato hornworm, which is then plucked off by a passing Robin, which is later eaten by a hawk—and so it goes, in endless cycles.

Ecological Relations

A study of food webs is a study of who eats what and where they do the eating. Figure 19.19 charts the summertime distribution of populations in two ecosystems, grassland and temperate forest. The stepped population pyramid is characteristic of summer conditions in such ecosystems. You can see the decreasing number of organisms supported at successively higher trophic levels. The base of the temperate forest pyramid is narrow, however, because most of the producers are large, highly productive trees and shrubs, which are outnumbered by the consumers they can support.

One approach to ecological study is to analyze a community's metabolism. *Metabolism* is the way in which a community uses energy and produces food for continued operation (the sum of all its chemical processes). In 1957, Howard T. Odum completed one of the best-known studies of this type for Silver Springs, Florida.

Figure 19.20a, an adaptation of his work, shows that the energy source for the community is insolation. The amount of light absorbed by the plants for photosynthesis is 24% of the total amount arriving at the study site. Of the absorbed amount, only 5% is transformed into the community's gross photosynthetic production—and this is only 1.2% of the total insolation input. The net plant production (gross production minus respiration) is 42.4% of the gross production, or 8833 kilocalories per square metre per year. That amount then moves through the food chain of herbivores and carnivores, with the top carnivores receiving only 0.24% of the net plant production of the system.

You can see that, at each trophic level, some of the biomass flows to the decomposers. The largest portion of the biomass is exported from the system in the form of community respiration. In addition, a relatively small portion leaves the system as organic particles by downstream export out of this system. The biomass pyramid shown in Figure 19.20b portrays the same community from the viewpoint of a *standing crop* (all the biomass in a particular environment at one time), which is another way of examining the existing biomass at each trophic level.

Ecosystems, Evolution, and Succession

Far from being static, Earth's ecosystems have been dynamic (vigorous and energetic) and ever changing from the beginning of life on the planet. Over time, communities of plants and animals have adapted, evolved, and in turn shaped their environments to produce great diversity. A constant interplay exists between increasing growth in a community and decreasing growth caused by resistance factors that create limits and disruptions (Figure 19.21). Each ecosystem is constantly adjusting to changing conditions and disturbances in the struggle to survive. The concept of change is key to understanding ecosystem stability.

The nature of change in natural ecosystems can range from gradual transitions from one equilibrium to another, balancing the factors in Figure 19.21, to extreme catastrophes such as an asteroid impact or severe volcanism, among other events. In the evolution of life, or the physical and chemical evolution of Earth's systems, such sudden changes created a punctuated equilibrium. Following each of the five major extinctions of life over the past 450 million years, there were great bursts of diversity and proliferation of new and different species, a process known as *speciation*. Although the extinctions (noted in Chapter 11, Figure 11.1) temporarily

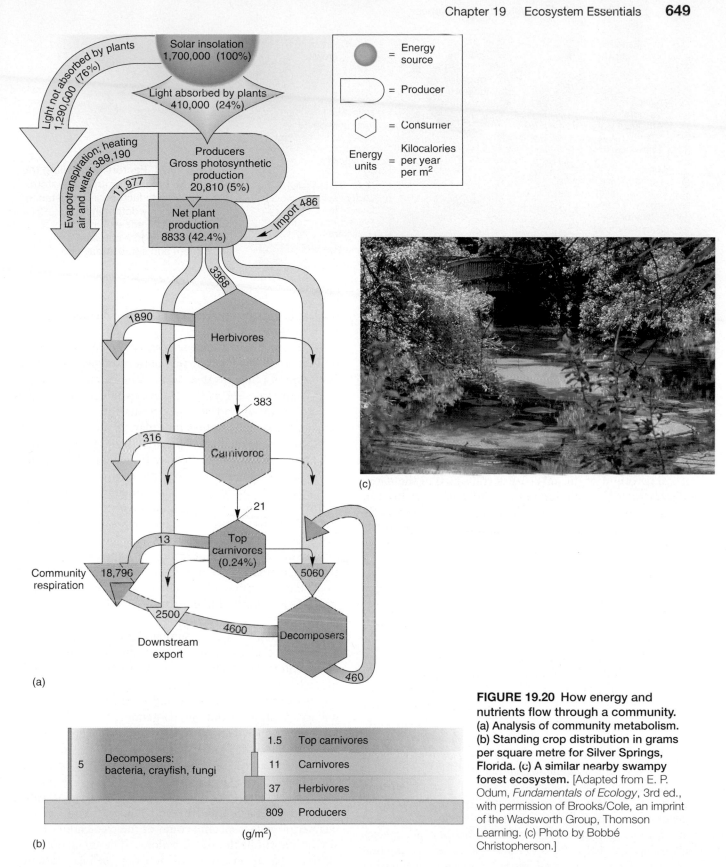

(a)

(b)

(c)

FIGURE 19.20 How energy and nutrients flow through a community. (a) Analysis of community metabolism. (b) Standing crop distribution in grams per square metre for Silver Springs, Florida. (c) A similar nearby swampy forest ecosystem. [Adapted from E. P. Odum, *Fundamentals of Ecology*, 3rd ed., with permission of Brooks/Cole, an imprint of the Wadsworth Group, Thomson Learning. (c) Photo by Bobbé Christopherson.]

limited biodiversity, each created evolutionary opportunities into which life diversified into differentiated populations.

For most of the last century, scientists thought that an undisturbed ecosystem—whether forest, grassland, aquatic, or other—would progress to a stage of equilibrium, a stable point, with maximum chemical storage and biomass. Modern research has determined, however, that ecosystems do not progress to some static conclusion. In other words, there is no "balance of nature"; instead think of a constant interplay of physical, chemical, and living factors in a dynamic equilibrium.

FIGURE 19.21 Factors controlling the population balance of an ecosystem. Potential growth factors and resistance factors ultimately determine the population of an ecosystem—truly a dynamic system in a constant state of adjustment and some imbalance.

Biological Evolution Delivers Biodiversity

A critical aspect of ecosystem stability and vitality is **biodiversity**, or species richness of life (a combination of *bio*logical and *diversity*). Biodiversity includes the number of different species and quantity of each species, the genetic diversity in species (number of genetic characteristics), and ecosystem and habitat diversity. A working estimate places the number of species presently populating Earth at 13.6 million; however, scientists have classified less than 2 million of these.

The origin of this diversity is embodied in the *theory of evolution*. (The definition of a *scientific theory* is given in Focus Study 1.1.) A theory is based on several extensively tested hypotheses and represents a broad general principle and a powerful tool with which to understand nature and the general laws in operation across the planet and the Universe.

Evolution states that single-cell organisms adapted, modified, and passed along inherited changes to multicellular organisms. The genetic makeup of successive generations was shaped by environmental factors, physiological functions, and behaviours that created a greater rate of survival and reproduction, traits that were passed along—literally, "survival of the species that reproduces the most." A species refers to a population that can reproduce sexually and produce viable offspring. By definition, this means reproductive isolation from other species.

Each inherited trait is guided by a *gene* that is a segment of the primary genetic material called *DNA* (deoxyribonucleic acid) that resides in the nest of chromosomes in every cell nucleus. These traits are passed to successive generations, especially those traits that are most successful at maximizing niches different from those of other species or traits that help the species adapt to environmental changes. Such differential reproduction and adaptation passes along successful genes or groups of genes in a process of genetic favouritism called *natural selection*. The process of evolution follows generation after generation and tracks the passage of inherited characteristics that were successful—the failures passed into extinction. Thus, it is not an understatement to say that today's humans are the result of billions of years of positive change and affirmative natural selection.

New mixes in the *gene pool*, or all genes possessed by individuals in a given population, involve *mutations*. Mutation is a process that occurs when a random action, or perhaps an error as the DNA reproduces, forms new genetic material and sets new traits into the inherited stream. Geography comes into play, as spatial effects are important. A species may disperse through migration to different environments, or may be separated by natural *vicariance* (fragmentation of the environment) events that establish natural barriers. Such isolation allows natural selection to evolve new sets of genes. Imagine the migrations across ice bridges or land connections at times of low sea level, or the slowly evolving rise of a mountain range, or the formation of an isthmus such as Panama connecting continents and separating oceans. To restate, the physical and chemical evolution of Earth's systems is closely linked to the biological evolution of life.

The deciphering of complete species *genomes*, or the total genetic identity of an organism, is a scientific triumph and is disclosing a complex history and geography of each species—where species originated, how species are dispersed, what diseases and traumas were of consequence. Analysis of the human genome has indicated our origins and provided a road map of how we got to where we are. Thus, the intricate interplay that led to present biodiversity across myriad ecosystems, both terrestrial and aquatic, is here in Chapters 19 and 20.

All life falls into one of five major groups, called *kingdoms*. Focus Study 20.1 and Table 20.1 in the next chapter provide a specific count of the tremendous diversity of life within the five kingdoms. These kingdoms are classified based on source of nutrition, cellular structure (lacking a nucleus–the *prokaryotes*—or having a membrane-enclosed nucleus–the *eukaryotes*), and numbers of cells. The five kingdoms of life are:

- *Monera Kingdom:* Unicellular prokaryotes, such as bacteria; absorbing food from their environment,

(b)

(a)

FIGURE 19.22 Disruption of stable forest communities.
(a) An example of clear-cut timber harvesting that has devastated a stable forest community and produced drastic changes in microclimatic conditions. Full exposure to sunlight and wind is different from former shade conditions. With few riparian buffer strips of uncut forest along streams, sedimentation will clog streams as soils erode. (b) A logged pine forest and disruptive logging road. About 10% of the West Coast's old-growth forests remain, as identified through orbital satellite images and GIS analysis. [Photos by (a) Bobbé Christopherson; (b) Robert Christopherson.]

some with the capability to photosynthesize (e.g., cyanobacteria).

- *Protista Kingdom:* Usually unicellular eukaryotes, protozoans, such as amoebas; includes slime molds, some with photosynthesizing ability, and some mobile members with simple cilia for propulsion.
- *Fungi Kingdom:* Multicellular eukaryotes, fungi, mushrooms, bread molds, with specialized cells for reproduction and feeding.
- *Plant Kingdom:* Multicellular eukaryotes, dominated by flowering plants including trees, not mobile; photosynthesis for food production, interrelationships with animals for nutrient supplies and pollination; mosses, liverworts, ferns, coniferous trees, food plants, among others.
- *Animal Kingdom:* Multicellular eukaryotes, ingest food, many specialized organs and tissues, specialized cells, sensory ability and mobile; includes vertebrates, worms, mollusks, among other types; largest group of animals are invertebrates such as anemones.

Ecosystem Stability and Diversity

In an ecosystem the tendency of species populations to remain stable (*inertial stability*) does not necessarily foster the ability to recover from change (*resilience*). Think of resilience as an ecosystem's ability to recover from disturbance, its ability to absorb disturbance up to some threshold point before it snaps to a different set of relations, thus altering some logical ecological progression.

Examples of communities with high inertial stability include a redwood forest, a pine forest at a high elevation, and

a tropical rain forest near the equator. But cleared forest tracts recover slowly and therefore have poor resilience. Figure 19.22 shows how clear-cut tracts of former forest have drastically altered microclimatic conditions, making regrowth of the same species difficult. Note the high road density, the inadequate buffers along watercourses to prevent sedimentation of streams, and the drag lines and skid trails to each pickup spot that pockmark the landscape. On nearby U.S. Forest Service land, the rules are clear: a full 95-m (312-ft) tree buffer is left on either side of a stream, road densities are minimized, and harvesting regimes that include partial removals, commercial thinning, and group selection harvests, among others, are all in contrast to the devastation on private lands in the photo. In contrast, a midlatitude grassland is low in stability; yet, when burned, its resilience is high because the community recovers rapidly.

Greater biodiversity in an ecosystem results in greater stability and greater productivity. In other words, the strength of biodiversity is that it spreads risk over the entire community, because several food sources exist at each trophic level. Therefore, biodiversity matters. Consider more than just the diversity of species; rather, think of all the positive interactions of species embodied in the *facilitation concept.* Facilitation describes how a diverse community manages nutrient dynamics among the populations, and pest resistance, and resilience to events such as fire. News Report 19.3 presents an example of biodiversity.

The present loss of biodiversity is irreversible, and yet, here we are in the midst of the biosphere's sixth major extinction episode. Extinction is final no matter how

News Report 19.3

Biodiversity in Alberta and Saskatchewan—Cypress Hills

The highest land elevation between the Rockies and Labrador is a small, erosional plateau that spans the border of Alberta and Saskatchewan and is home to four distinct ecosystems containing a wealth of flora and fauna. This area is preserved in Canada's only interprovincial park (Figure 19.3.1), established in August 1989 by the governments of Alberta and Saskatchewan. This area, Cypress Hills, is made up of three separate blocks, two in Saskatchewan and one in Alberta, that contain freshwater streams and creeks, lakes, forests, rare fescue grasses, marshlands, meadows, and ranchlands.

The hills rise out of the prairie, an elevation difference of 600 m from the plain to the highest elevation, and are composed of sediments that were deposited during the Cretaceous Period in a warm shallow sea. Over time, the sea withdrew and more sediment was laid down, compacting and lithifying to form sedimentary rock. During the last glacial advance, the ice did not completely cover the hills, leaving the top 100 m as an island in the ice. When the ice melted, water carved deeply into the rock and altered the topography.

Today, the area is home to stable ecosystems. Lodgepole pine, aspen, and white spruce woodland compose the montane ecosystem. Lodgepole pine grows at the highest and driest elevations. Aspen woodlands grow below the lodgepole forest, and include trembling aspen and balsam fir.

FIGURE 19.3.1 Cypress Hills Interprovincial Park.
Canada's only interprovincial park, Cypress Hills, preserves a unique habitat with great biodiversity. [Cypress Hills/Canadian Geographic map courtesy of Canadian Geographic.]

The woodlands provide shade and allow a variety of shrubs and herbaceous plants to grow beneath their canopy. The aspen forest extends outward from the hills along creek banks. In the cool, moist areas on north facing slopes of the hills, the white spruce forest grows in three vertical layers. Closest to the ground are low shrubs, orchids, and mosses. About 1 m above this is a niche occupied by red baneberries. Dogwoods, willows, and cranberries occupy the highest layer, up to 2 m above ground level. The woodlands provide shelter for a wide variety of wildlife from small rodents to larger mammals to a wide variety of birds.

The second ecosystem is the fescue grassland ecosystem. Found at the highest elevations of the Cypress Hills, this ecosystem includes a variety of grasses, wildflowers, and birds. The third system, the mixed grass prairie ecosystem, occupies the eastern part of the plateau and the south-facing slopes. Grasses, legumes, rodents, small mammals, and birds make this niche their home. The final of the four ecosystems, the wetland ecosystem, consists of plants growing in or near spring-fed marshes, ponds, creeks, and lakes. The reed grasses and water-loving trees provide habitat for fur-bearing mammals and for birds. Thus, plant biodiversity led to both productivity and better resource utilization among species—the facilitation concept—in Cypress Hills.

---

complex the organism or how long it lived since it evolved. E. O. Wilson, the famed biologist, stated,

> Biological diversity—the full sweep from ecosystems to species within ecosystems, thence to genes within species—is in trouble. Mass extinctions are commonplace, especially in tropical regions where most of the biodiversity occurs. Among the more recent are more than half the exclusively freshwater fishes of peninsular Asia, half of the fourteen birds of the Philippines island of Cebu, and more than ninety plant species growing on a single mountain ridge in Ecuador. In the United

States an estimated 1 percent of all species have been extinguished; another 32 percent are imperiled.[*]

Agricultural Ecosystems Humans simplify communities by eliminating biodiversity, and in this way we place more ecosystems at risk of harmful change and perhaps failure. An artificially produced monoculture community, such as a field of wheat, is singularly vulnerable to failure owing to weather or attack from insects or plant disease.

*E. O. Wilson, *Consilience, The Unity of Knowledge* (New York: Knopf, 1998), p. 292.

In some regions, simply planting multiple crops brings more stability to the ecosystem. This is an important principle of sustainable agriculture, a movement to make farming more ecologically compatible.

A modern agricultural ecosystem not only is vulnerable to failure because of its lack of ecological diversity but also because it creates an enormous demand for energy, chemical pesticides and herbicides, artificial fertilizer, and irrigation water. The practice of harvesting and removing biomass from the land interrupts the cycling of materials into the soil (Figure 19.23). This net loss of nutrients must be artificially replenished. The type of plantation agriculture in Figure 19.23b is depleting of soil nutrients over time; this farming practice requires subsidies of chemical fertilizers and herbicides to eliminate competing vegetation.

Climate Change Obviously, the distribution of plant species is affected by climate change. Many species have survived wide climate swings in the past. Consider the beginning of the Tertiary Period, 75 million years ago. Warm, humid conditions and tropical forests dominated the land as far north as southern Canada, pines grew in the Arctic, and deserts were few. Then, between 15 and 50 million years ago, deserts began developing in the southwestern United States. Mountain-building processes produced higher elevations, creating rain-shadow aridity that affected plant distribution.

Recall, too, that the movement of Earth's tectonic plates created climate changes important in the evolution and distribution of plants and animals (see Figure 11.18a–e). Europe and North America were joined in Pangaea and

(a)

(b)

(c)

(d)

FIGURE 19.23 Agricultural ecosystems.
(a) The Sacramento Valley of California is one of the most intensively farmed regions of the world. Field crops including irrigated rice, an irrigation canal, and the Sacramento River are in the scene. (b) A pine tree plantation (farm) in Ontario, principally for the production of wood pulp—the forest ecosystem is reduced to efficient rows for clear-cutting when mature. Depleting of soil nutrients over time, this farming practice requires subsidies of chemical fertilizers and herbicides to eliminate competing vegetation. (c) Modern mechanized farming and a freshly mowed field of oats near Dokka, Norway. (d) Highly fragmented, fertile agricultural land along the north German plain. [Photos (a), (c), and (d) by Bobbé Christopherson; (b) courtesy of Peaceful Parks.]

positioned near the equator, where vast swamps formed (the site of coal deposits today). The southern mass of Gondwana was extensively glaciated as it drifted at high latitudes in the Southern Hemisphere. Glaciation left matching glacial scars and specific plant and animal distributions across South America, Africa, India, and Australia. The diverse and majestic dinosaurs dispersed with the drifting continents.

The key question for our future is: As temperature patterns change, how fast can plants either adapt to new conditions or migrate through succession (location change) to remain within their shifting specific habitats? Rapid changes in vegetation patterns in northern latitudes since 1980 are indicated from satellite observations. Global warming is reducing spring snow cover, allowing spring greening to occur earlier, up to 3 weeks sooner in some high-latitude locations. Likewise the onset of fall is delayed to a later date than previously experienced.

Nina Leopold Bradley is studying the Wisconsin setting her father, Aldo Leopold, made famous in his book *A Sand County Almanac* (Oxford University Press, 1949). He kept detailed records of all things dealing with nature and seasonal change on his tract of land. Her findings show that more than one-third of animal and plant species start spring activities 4 weeks earlier than they did 50 years ago.

Adaptation to conditions is key to evolution. Through mutation and natural selection, species have either adapted or failed to adapt to changing environmental conditions over millions of years. Current global change is occurring rapidly, at the rate of decades instead of millions of years. Thus, we see die-out and succession of different species along disadvantageous habitat margins. The displaced species may colonize new regions made more hospitable by climate change. Also shifting will be agricultural lands that produced wheat, corn, soybeans, and other commodities. Society will have to adapt to different crops growing in different places.

A study completed by biologist Margaret Davis on North American forests suggests that trees will have to respond quickly as temperatures increase. Changes in the climate inhabited by certain species could shift 100–400 km (60–250 mi) during the next 100 years. Some species, such as the sugar maple, may migrate northward, disappearing from the United States except for Maine, and moving into eastern Ontario and Québec. Davis prepared a map showing the possible impact of increasing temperatures on the distribution of beech and hemlock trees (Figure 19.24).

Changes in the geographical distributions of plant and animal species in response to future greenhouse warming threaten to reduce biotic diversity. . . . The risk posed by CO_2-induced warming depends on the distances that regions of suitable climate are displaced northward [in the Northern Hemisphere] and on the

(a) (b)

FIGURE 19.24 Present and predicted distribution of two tree species.
(a) Beech trees and (b) hemlock trees in North America. The potential future range shown for each reflects expected climate change resulting from a doubling of carbon dioxide. [After M. B. Davis and C. Zabinski, "Changes in the geographical range resulting from greenhouse warming: Effects on biodiversity in forests," in R. L. Peters and T. E. Lovejoy, eds., *Global Warming and Biological Diversity* (New Haven, CT: Yale University Press, 1992), p. 301.]

rate of displacement. . . . If the change occurs too rapidly for colonization of newly available regions, population sizes may fall to critical levels, and extinction will occur.*

Dr. Davis' studies are affirmed by recent research, including the 2007 IPCC *Fourth Assessment Report*.

Ecological Succession

Ecological succession occurs when newer communities (usually more complex) replace older communities of plants and animals (usually simpler)—a change of species composition. Each successive community of species modifies the physical environment in a manner suitable for a later community of species. Changes apparently move toward a more mature condition, although disturbances are common and constantly disrupt the sequence.

Traditionally, it was assumed that plants and animals formed a predictable *climax community*—a stable, self-sustaining, and functioning community with balanced birth, growth, and death—but scientists have abandoned this notion. Contemporary conservation biology, biogeography, and

*M. B. Davis and C. Zabinski, "Changes in the geographical range resulting from greenhouse warming: Effects on biodiversity in forests," in R. L. Peters and T. E. Lovejoy, eds., *Global Warming and Biological Diversity* (New Haven, CT: Yale University Press, 1992), p. 297.

ecology assume nature to be in constant adaptation and nonequilibrium.

Rather than thinking of an ecosystem as a uniform set of communities, think of ecosystems as a patchwork mosaic of habitats—each striving to achieve an optimal range and low environmental stress. This is the study of *patch dynamics*, or disturbed portions of habitats. Within an ecosystem, individual patches may arise only to fail later. The smaller the patch, the faster species loss occurs. Succession is the interaction among patches. Most ecosystems are in actuality made up of patches of former landscapes. Biodiversity in some respects is the result of such patch dynamics.

Given the complexity of natural ecosystems there may be several stages, or a *polyclimax* condition, with adjoining ecosystems, or patches within ecosystems, each at different stages in the same environment. Mature communities are properly thought of as being in dynamic equilibrium. Or at times, these communities may be out of phase and in nonequilibrium with the immediate physical environment because of the usual lag time in their adjustment.

Succession often requires an initiating disturbance. Examples include windstorms, severe flooding, a volcanic eruption, a devastating wildfire, or an agricultural practice such as prolonged overgrazing (Figure 19.25). When existing organisms are disturbed or removed, new communities can emerge. At such times of nonequilibrium

FIGURE 19.25 Disturbances in ecosystems alter succession patterns.
(a) After flooding along Rivière des Ha! Ha!, Québec, extensive aggradation renews the sediment supply to the valley. (b) Community development proceeds in a burned forest, progressing perhaps by chance, as species with an adaptive edge, such as fireweed (*Epilobium* sp.), succeed. (c) Unwise practices cause extensive soil erosion on a hog farm in Iowa; a disrupted prairie landscape. (d) Insect infestation (spruce budworm) weakens trees that turn grey and die off. [Photos by (a) Earth Sciences Sector, Natural Resources Canada; (b) Bobbé Christopherson; (c) USDA Natural Resources Conservation Service; (d) Natural Resources Canada, Canadian Forest Service, Laurentian Forestry Centre.]

(b)

(c)

(d)

transition, the interrelationships among species produce elements of chance, and species having an adaptive edge will succeed in the competitive struggle for light, water, nutrients, space, time, reproduction, and survival.

Land and water experience different forms of succession. We first look at terrestrial succession, which is characterized by competition for sunlight, and then at aquatic succession, characterized by progressive changes in nutrient levels.

Terrestrial Succession

An area of bare rock or a disturbed site with no vestige of a former community can be a place for **primary succession**, the beginning of an ecosystem. Examples include new surfaces created by mass movement of land, areas exposed by a retreating glacier, cooled lava flows and volcanic eruption landscapes, or surface mining and clear-cut logging scars, or an area of sand dunes. Plants taking hold on new lava flows from the Kīlauea volcano, Hawai'i, illustrate primary succession in Figure 19.26. In terrestrial ecosystems, succession begins with early species that form a **pioneer community**. You can see these plants taking hold in the photo. Primary succession often begins with lichens, mosses, and ferns growing on bare rock (see Figure 19.5). These early inhabitants prepare the way for further succession to grasses, shrubs, and trees.

More common in nature is **secondary succession**, which begins if some aspects of a previously functioning community are present. An area where the natural community has been destroyed or disturbed, but where the underlying soil remains intact, may experience secondary succession.

Examples of secondary succession are most of the areas affected by the Mount St. Helens eruption and blast in 1980 (Figure 19.27). Some soils, young trees, and plants were protected under ash and snow, so community development began almost immediately after the event. About 38,450 hectares (95,000 acres) of trees were blown

FIGURE 19.26 Primary succession.
Ferns take hold as primary succession on new lava flows that came from the Kīlauea volcano, Hawai'i. [Photo by Bobbé Christopherson.]

down and burned, however, and as the photos show, the effects of the eruption were devastating and lingering. Of course, the areas completely destroyed near the Mount St. Helens volcano or those buried beneath the massive landslide north of the mountain became candidates for primary succession.

As succession progresses, soil develops and a different set of plants and animals with different niche requirements may adapt. Further niche expansion follows as the community matures. Succession, which is really the developmental process forming new communities, is a dynamic set of interactions with sometimes unpredictable outcomes, steered by sometimes random, unpredictable events that trigger a threshold leap to a new set of relations—the basis of *dynamic ecology*.

Succession Through the Ice Age Glaciation is a large-scale disturbance that well illustrates how succession operates. As Earth cycled through glacial and interglacial ages (Chapter 17), the ecological succession in all ecosystems was affected repeatedly. Imagine the milder midlatitude climate at the beginning of an interglacial warming, with lush herb and shrub vegetation slowly giving way to pioneer trees of birch, aspen, and pine. Winds and animals dispersed seeds, and changing communities readily spread in response to changing conditions. During the warm interglacial, trees increased shade and the organic content of soil increased. Deciduous trees such as oak, elm, and ash spread freely on well-drained soils; willow, cottonwood, and alder grew on poorly drained land.

As climates cooled with the approach of the next glacial, soils became more acidic, so podzolization (cool, moist, forested) processes dominated (see Chapter 18), helped by the acidity of spruce and fir trees. Ecosystems slowly returned to the vegetation community that existed at the beginning of the interglacial. The increased cold produced open regions of disturbed ecosystems. Freezing and the advance of ice disrupted highly acidic soils.

The Holocene (the past 10,000 years) is apparently atypical because of the development of human societies and agriculture. Civilization is creating an artificial and accelerated succession, similar in some ways to the closing centuries of an interglacial. The challenge for biogeographers is to understand such long-term developmental change principles, given the accelerated pace at which change is occurring in the industrial and postindustrial era.

Wildfire and Fire Ecology Fire and its effects are one of Earth's significant ecosystem and economic processes. In Canada, during 2003, more than 1.6 million hectares burned in wildfires, near the average. However, 2004 hectares burned exceeded 3.27 million. 2005 was again near average, but 2006 rose above 2.08 million hectares burned.

Over the past 50 years, the role of fire in ecosystems has been the subject of much scientific research and experimentation. Today, fire is recognized as a natural component of most ecosystems and not the enemy of nature

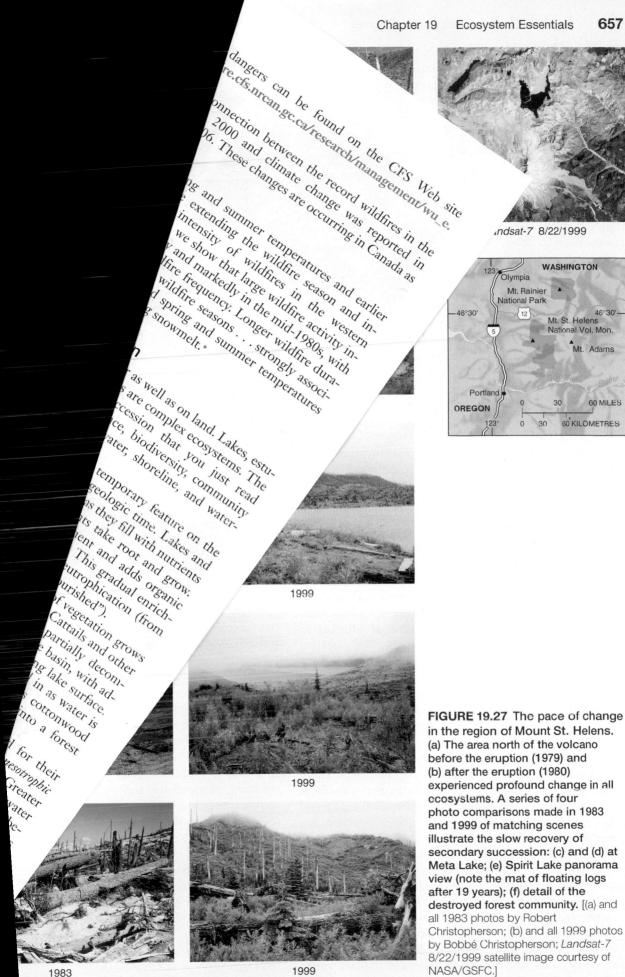

...dsat-7 8/22/1999

1999

1999

1983

1999

FIGURE 19.27 The pace of change in the region of Mount St. Helens. (a) The area north of the volcano before the eruption (1979) and (b) after the eruption (1980) experienced profound change in all ecosystems. A series of four photo comparisons made in 1983 and 1999 of matching scenes illustrate the slow recovery of secondary succession: (c) and (d) at Meta Lake; (e) Spirit Lake panorama view (note the mat of floating logs after 19 years); (f) detail of the destroyed forest community. [(a) and all 1983 photos by Robert Christopherson; (b) and all 1999 photos by Bobbé Christopherson; Landsat-7 8/22/1999 satellite image courtesy of NASA/GSFC.]

dangers can be found on the CFS Web site ...re.cfs.nrcan.gc.ca/research/management/wu_e. ...connection between the record wildfires in the 2000 and climate change was reported in ...06. These changes are occurring in Canada as

...ng and summer temperatures and earlier ... extending the wildfire season and in-
...intensity of wildfires in the western
...we show that large wildfire activity in-
...y and markedly in the mid-1980s, with
...fire frequency. Longer wildfire dura-
...d wildfire seasons . . . strongly associ-
...d spring and summer temperatures
...g snowmelt.*

... as well as on land. Lakes, estu-
...s are complex ecosystems. The
...cession that you just read
...ce, biodiversity, community
...ater, shoreline, and water-

...temporary feature on the
...geologic time. Lakes and
...as they fill with nutrients
...ts take root and grow:
...ent and adds organic
...This gradual enrich-
...utrophication (from
...ourished").
...of vegetation grows
...Cattails and other
...partially decom-
...e basin, with ad-
...ng lake surface.
...in as water is
...s cottonwood
...nto a forest

...d for their
...esotrophic
...Greater
...water
...e-

that was once thought. In fact, in many forests, undergrowth and surface litter is purposely burned in controlled "cool fires" to remove fuel and prevent catastrophic and destructive "hot fires." Forestry experts have learned that, when fire-prevention strategies are rigidly followed, they can lead to the abundant undergrowth accumulation that fuels major fires.

Modern society's demand for fire prevention to protect property goes back to European forestry of the 1800s. Fire prevention became an article of faith for forest managers in North America. But, in studies of the longleaf pine forest that stretches in a wide band from the Atlantic coastal plain to Texas, fire was discovered to be an integral part of regrowth following lumbering. In fact, seed dispersal of some pine species, such as the knobcone pine, does not occur unless assisted by a forest fire. Heat from the fire opens the cones, releasing seeds so they can fall to the ground for germination. Also, these fire-disturbed areas quickly recover with protein-rich woody growth, young plants, and a stimulated seed production that provides abundant food for animals.

The science of **fire ecology** imitates nature by recognizing fire as a dynamic ingredient in community succession. The Canadian Forest Service (CFS, a branch of Natural Resources Canada, **http://www.nofc.cfs.nrcan.gc.ca**), the agency that oversees the management of Canada's forests, recognizes that fire is an important natural disturbance in many of Canada's forest ecosystems. It is especially important in the boreal forest. In the early 1900s, organized forest fire suppression began with the goal of reducing wildfire threat to public safety and to timber resources. The CFS has researched the relationship between forest management and fire management since the 1920s, focusing on the development of an assessment system for evaluating wildfire threats both spatially and temporally; the creation of landscape-level fuel treatments; and the synthesis and distribution of information to mitigate wildfire threat in wildland-urban interface areas. In the United States, the U.S. Department of Agriculture's Forest Service first recognized the principle of fire ecology in the early 1940s and formally implemented the practice in 1972. Controlled ground fires, deliberately set to prevent accumulation of forest undergrowth, now are widely regarded as a wise forest management practice and are used across the country.

Wildland-urban interface areas are the places where urban or agricultural structures are located proximally to trees and other vegetation. These areas in Canada and elsewhere present an increasingly serious problem because wildfires have the potential to burn both buildings and wildland vegetation simultaneously, in what fire managers call *interface fires*. For example, the Canadian Forest Service reports that in Canada during 1998, interface fires forced the evacuation of 18,000 residents, and another 46,000 were placed on evacuation alert. In 2003, interface fires caused massive destruction in Kelowna, British Columbia. Information for living in the interface and suggestions for creating communities that are aware

of fire
(http://f
htm).

The c
West since
Science in 20
well.

Higher spr
snowmelt ar
creasing the
U.S. . . . Here
creased sudden
higher large-wil
tions, and longer
ated with increase
and an earlier sprin

Aquatic Successio

Ecosystems occur in wate
aries, ponds, and shoreline
concepts of terrestrial su
about—stability and resilie
succession—apply to open v
shed systems as well.

A lake or pond is really a
landscape, when viewed across
ponds exhibit successional stages
and sediment and as aquatic pla
This growth captures more sedi
debris to the system (Figure 19.28)
ment in water bodies is known as
the Greek *eutrophos*, meaning "well n

In moist climates, a floating mat
outward from the shore to form a bog.
marsh plants become established, and
posed organic material accumulates in th
ditional vegetation bordering the remaini
Vegetation and soil and a meadow may fil
displaced; willow trees follow, and perhap
trees; and eventually the lake may evolve
community.

The stages in lake succession are name
nutrient levels: *oligotrophic* (low nutrients),
(medium nutrients), and *eutrophic* (high nutrient
primary productivity and resultant decrease
transparency mark each stage, so that photosy
comes concentrated near the surface. Energy
from production to respiration in the eutrophic
oxygen demand exceeding oxygen availability.

Nutrient levels also vary spatially: Oligot
ditions occur in deep water, whereas eutro
tions occur along the shore, in shallow bay

*A. L. Westerling, H. G. Hidalgo, et. al., "Warming an
Increase Western U.S. Forest Wildfire Activity," *Scie
(v 313, no. 5789): pp. 927–27, 940–43.

FIGURE 19.28 Lake–bog–meadow succession.
(a) What begins as a lake gradually fills with organic and inorganic sediments, which successively shrink the area of the pond. A bog forms, then a marshy area, and finally a meadow completes the successional stages. (b) Spring Mill Lake, Indiana. (c) Aquatic succession in a mountain lake. (d) The Richmond Nature Park and its Lulu Island Bog was ocean just 8000 years ago. Frasier River sediment created the mudflats and set the stage for the evolution of this sphagnum bog with acidic soils that "quakes" when you walk on it. Plants in the bog include moss, shore pine, hemlock, blueberry, salal shrubs, and Labrador tea, among others. [Photos by Bobbé Christopherson.]

sewage, fertilizer, or other nutrient inputs occur. Even large bodies of water may have eutrophic areas along the shore. As society dumps sewage, agricultural runoff, and pollution in waterways, the nutrient load is enhanced beyond the cleansing ability of natural biological processes. The result is *cultural eutrophication*, which hastens succession in aquatic systems. As with all ecosystems, we must be aware of the signals that unwanted change is occurring so that mitigating action can be taken. (Refer to the map of the dead zone in the Gulf of Mexico in News Report 19.2.)

The Freshwater Web site (**http://www.ec.gc.ca/water/e_main.html**) outlines the nature of water, water policy and legislation, water management, and water and culture, and provides links to useful resources about water in Canada, including links to aquatic ecosystems. Focus Study 19.1 examines the Great Lakes of North America and their geographically and biologically diverse aquatic ecosystems. These lakes are interrelated with the surrounding terrestrial ecosystems. This is the largest lake system on Earth and is jointly managed by Canada and the United States.

The Great Lakes

The basins of the Great Lakes are gifts of the last ice age to North America (see Figure 17.30 in Chapter 17). The glaciers advanced and retreated over this region, excavating the basins for five large lakes. This international waterway of lakes and connecting rivers has played an important role in the history of Canada and the United States. Today, about 10% of the U.S. population and 25% of Canada's population live in the Great Lakes drainage basin (Figure 19.1.1). Major agricultural regions surround the lakes, as do many centres of industrial activity. Tourism, sport fishing, and maritime commerce are also important.

Society asks much of the Great Lakes: to dilute wastes from cities and industry, to dissipate thermal pollution from power plants, to provide municipal drinking water and irrigation water, and to sustain unique and varied ecosystems—open lake, coastal shore, coastal marsh, lakeplain (former lake bed), inland wetlands, and inland terrestrial (upland areas of forest, prairie, and barrens). Here is a brief profile of this important hydrological and ecological resource. (See Environment Canada's Great Lakes home page at http://www.on.ec.gc.ca/greatlakes/; management policy for the Great Lakes is found on the International Joint Commission Web site (http://www.ijc.org/en/home/main_accueil.htm).

Geography and Physical Characteristics

The Great Lakes—Superior, Michigan, Huron, Erie, and Ontario—contain 18% of the total volume of all freshwater lakes in the world, some 23,000 km^3 (5500 mi^3) of water. Their combined surface area covers 244,000 km^2 (94,000 mi^2), a little less than the state of Wyoming. The entire drainage basin embraces 528,000 km^2 (204,000 mi^2), or an area about the size of Manitoba.

As we tour the lakes, it is useful to follow along in Figure 19.1.1 and to look at their profile in Figure 19.1.2a. Lake Superior is the highest in elevation, highest in latitude, deepest, and largest in the system. It drains through St. Mary's River into Lake Huron. Lake Michigan, the only lake of the five that lies entirely within the United States, is at the same level as Lake Huron because it is joined by the wide connection through the Straits of Mackinac. (This is why, in Figure 19.1.2, we combine these two lakes on one hydrograph.)

The St. Clair River, Lake St. Clair, and the Detroit River carry water on to Lake Erie, the shallowest lake in the system. Compared to an average water retention time of 191 years in Lake Superior, Lake Erie has the shortest retention time of 2.6 years. The Niagara River, plunging dramatically over Niagara Falls, transports water into Lake Ontario. Lake Ontario is drained by the St. Lawrence River, which carries the entire discharge of the Great Lakes system to the Gulf of St. Lawrence and eventually into the North Atlantic Ocean. The entire basin extends over 10° of latitude (41° N to 51° N) and 18° of longitude (75° W to 93° W).

Because of the large size of the overall Great Lakes system, its associated climate, soils, and topography vary widely. Dominating the north are colder microthermal climates, exposed portions of the Canadian Shield bedrock, and vast stands of conifers and acidic soils. To the south, warmer mesothermal climates and fertile, glacially deposited soils provide a vast agricultural base. Farms and urbanization replaced previous stands of mixed forest. Virtually none of the original land cover is undisturbed.

Prevailing winds from the west and seasonal change mix air masses from different source regions, producing variable weather. The presence of the Great Lakes basin strongly influences passing air masses and weather systems, producing lake-effect snowfall to the east (see the dramatic satellite image of this in Figure 8.5). Precipitation over the drainage basin feeds the lake storage as part of the renewable hydrologic cycle. Figure 19.1.2 illustrates Great Lakes water levels from 1918 to 2006. Water levels were above average during 1996 and 1997. During 1998 through 2002, water levels lowered to below-average levels and a 45-year low, reflecting near-drought conditions across the region. Lake levels 2003 to 2006 remained below the 1985 datum, with record lows reached in the fall of 2007.

Short-term lake levels vary from winter to summer; they are higher in summer after snowmelt and the arrival of maximum summer precipitation. Over the long term, highest lake levels occur during years of heavier precipitation and during times of cooler temperatures, which reduce evaporation. Wind also affects lake levels. A wind setup (wind-driven water) occurs along the downwind shoreline, as water is pushed higher onshore.

The Great Lakes Ecosystem

The Great Lakes ecosystem should be thought of as young and a fruitful laboratory for ecological studies. These lakes are not simply large bodies of water with a uniform mixture. A stratification occurs in them related to density and temperature differences. In the summer, the surface and shallow waters are warmed and become less dense so that the lakes develop a sharp stratification. The warm surface water and light penetration in the upper layers support most biotic production and adequate dissolved oxygen. This layering affects water quality because it can prevent mixing of pollution and other effluents with cooler bottom water during the summer months.

(a)

(b)

ELEVATION
ABOVE
SEA LEVEL

metres
Over 500
300–500
200–300
100–200
0–100

DEPTHS
BELOW
LAKE LEVEL

metres
0–100
100–200
Over 200

Metres	Feet
100	328
200	656
300	984
500	1640

(c)

(d)

FIGURE 19.1.1 The Great Lakes Basin.
Elevations above sea level, depths below lake level, and principal urban areas are shown.
The map outline is the limit of the drainage basin for the Great Lakes system. (a) The rocky
shores of Lake Superior, Otter Island lighthouse. (b) Forests along Lake Ontario shores. (c) The
Cuyahoga River enters Lake Erie at Cleveland. (d) Sand dunes along the southern shore of
Lake Michigan. Note the wooden pedestrian walkway to prevent erosion of sand by human
traffic. [(a) Photo by Carl R. Sams, II/Peter Arnold, Inc.; (b) photo by Wayne Lankinen/DRK Photo;
(c) photo by Alex S. MacLean/Peter Arnold, Inc.; (d) photo by Bobbé Christopherson. Map courtesy
of Environment Canada, U.S. EPA, and Brock University cartography.]

(continued)

Focus Study 19.1 *(continued)*

FIGURE 19.1.2 Great Lakes elevation profile and hydrographs.
(a) Average depth and lake surface levels, 1918–1998. (b) Annual hydrographs for each of the Great Lakes, 1918–2006. Both figures were prepared using the International Great Lakes Datum of 1985. [Data courtesy of the Canadian Hydrographic Service, Central Region, and the International Coordinating Committee on the Great Lakes Basin Hydraulic and Hydrographic Data.]

As the fall season matures, surface water cools and sinks, displacing deeper water and creating a turnover of the lake mass. By midwinter, the temperature from the surface to the bottom is uniformly around 4°C (39°F, the point at which water is densest); temperatures at the surface are near freezing. A trend in Lake Superior water temperature is a 2.5 C° (4.5 F°) increase since 1979, higher than the 1.5 C° (2.7 F°) increase in regional air temperatures. It is difficult to imagine Lake Superior surface water at 23.9°C (75°F), which it reached in July 2007. Scientists are analyzing the impact of these temperature increases on lake ecosystems and any relation to climate change.

The lakes support a food chain of producers and consumers, as does any aquatic ecosystem. Native fish populations have been greatly affected by human activities: overfishing, introduced nonnative species, pollution from excess nutrients, toxic contamination of fish, and disruption of spawning habitats.

Peak commercial fishing occurred in the 1880s. The fisheries declined to their lowest levels as water pollution peaked in the 1960s and early 1970s. The Canadian and U.S. governments implemented strong pollution control programs, working in concert with many citizens, industries, and private organizations. These efforts brought the lakes into the present period of recovery. Today, lake trout (in Lake Superior), sturgeon, herring, smelt, alewife, splake, yellow perch, walleye, and white bass are fished. However, health advisories are occasionally issued warning of danger in consuming fish of certain species, sizes, and locales.

Coastline for the five lakes totals 18,000 km (11,000 mi) and is diverse: major dunes and sandy beaches, bedrock shorelines, gravel beaches, and adjoining coastal marsh systems. Marshes can be found at the far western end of Lake Superior in the St. Louis River estuary and at the far eastern end of Lake Ontario and its coastal lagoon. Here, as elsewhere, marshes occupy that key interface between the land and the water, storing and cycling organic material and nutrients into aquatic ecosystems.

Human Activities, Land Use, Loss, and Recovery

Figure 19.1.3 portrays land use in the Great Lakes Basin. Each activity has its own impact on lake systems. Runoff from agricultural areas contains chemicals, nutrients, and eroded soil. The pulp and paper industry was a major polluter but has improved as more was learned about the dangers of pollution; for example, mercury contamination was halted in the 1970s and better disposal methods for wastes were implemented. The forests were not always treated in a sustainable way in terms of reforestation, and today forests may be regarded as a diminished resource in the basin. Recovery efforts are slow to make up for bad past practices, but progress is underway.

Lake Erie was the first of the Great Lakes to show severe effects of *cultural eutrophication*, for it is the shallowest and warmest of the five lakes. About a third of the overall population in the Great Lakes Basin lives in the drainage of Lake Erie, making it the major recipient of sewage effluent from treatment plants. Over the years, dissolved oxygen levels dropped as biochemical oxygen demand increased, caused by sewage-treatment discharges and algal decay. Algae flourished in these eutrophic conditions and coated the beaches, turning the lake a greenish brown.

The most infamous incident in the 1960s was the Cuyahoga River (through Cleveland, Ohio) catching fire because it was so contaminated. In 1972, Canada and the United States signed the Great Lakes Water Quality Agreement and the cleanup was under way. The government, spurred by public opinion, was moved to action, knowing that one of these priceless lakes was actually being lost. One example of the success of these efforts is that the input of phosphorus was reduced by 90% (an element with high biological activity that dramatically stimulates unwanted plant growth in aquatic ecosystems).

Concern for the health of the entire Great Lakes ecosystem remains necessary because of the biological amplification of poisons in the food chain. For example, organic chemicals such as PCBs accumulate to dangerous levels. PCBs (polychlorinated biphenyls) are highly viscous, inert fluids used in electrical transformers and hydraulic systems, and they are

FIGURE 19.1.3 Land use in the Great Lakes Basin. Generalized distribution map of land use, nonagricultural and agricultural, in the Great Lakes Basin. [Map courtesy of Environment Canada, U.S. EPA, and Brock University cartography.]

(continued)

Focus Study 19.1 (continued)

carcinogenic. Samples reported by Environment Canada show PCBs in phytoplankton at 0.0025 ppm, in a rainbow smelt at 1.04 ppm, in a lake trout at 4.83 ppm, and higher in the food chain to a herring gull eggshell at 124 ppm! Later additions to the 1972 agreement reduced toxic levels, organic chemicals, and heavy metals entering the lakes. Since humans are at the end of the amplification process, it is in our own best interest to help the continuing recovery of these lakes.

Biological diversity is at the heart of the integrity of the Great Lakes. Surveys are under way to inventory the entire ecosystem, establish a biodiversity baseline, assess current conditions of imperiled species, and strengthen efforts to conserve the Great Lakes system as a productive environment. Both the Canadian and U.S. governments are involved through an international commission, as is the Nature Conservancy through its Great Lakes Program (http://www.tnc.org). "Conservation Blueprint for the Great Lakes," the first version of the program for Great Lakes biodiversity conservation, is complete.

An ecosystem approach to management of the Great Lakes Basin is the key to recovery. This approach considers the physical, chemical, and biological components that constitute the total system. Thus, a Herring Gull eggshell becomes an indicator of

FIGURE 19.1.4 Orbital view of the Great Lakes.
The Great Lakes region in true colour made March 6, 2000, by sensors aboard *Terra*. [*Terra* image courtesy of NASA/MODIS Land Science Team.]

chemical pollution, blue-green algal blooms denote hastening eutrophication, and a loss of species richness and diversity exposes the destruction of habitat. This is where geographic principles of spatial analysis, an integrative tool such as geographic information systems (GIS), and remote-sensing capabilities come into play (Figure 19.1.4). A holistic, spatial approach to ecological problems is a marked departure from the past, when pollution problems were considered locally and separately.

Progress toward recovery is the goal of the State of the Lakes Ecosystem Conference (SOLEC), which is held biennially to assess the conditions of the Great Lakes ecosystem and progress toward the goals established in the binational Great Lakes Water Quality Agreement (GLWQA). The conference is organized cooperatively between Environment Canada and the United States Environmental Protection Agency (http://www.on.ec.gc.ca/solec/ and http://www.epa.gov/glnpo/solec/).

Applied Physical Geography

Species Diversity and Species Richness

The distribution of species in space is an important property examined by both biogeographers and ecologists. By examining patterns of diversity we gain insight into factors that cause the variation.

Diversity refers to the abundance of taxa that are present in a prescribed area. At its simplest, diversity is measured as species richness: the greater the number of different species in an area, the greater the species richness of that area.

More complex mathematical techniques also are available to measure diversity. These techniques combine information on species richness and the relative abundance of species. Using the expanded definition, an area that has many species (high species richness) and

is not dominated by any one species has high diversity. Under this definition, a forest composed of 20% paper birch, 20% hemlock, 20% white pine, 20% white spruce, and 20% Manitoba maple would have a higher diversity (but the same species richness) than a forest of 95% paper birch, 2% hemlock, 1% white pine, 1% white spruce, and 1% Manitoba maple.

Three areas of eastern Canada were sampled in a study of tree diversity. The data are presented in Table 1.

Using the information in Table 1 we calculate the species richness of each area. This is simply a count of the number of species present. For Site A: Richness = 6, Site B: Richness = 5, and Site C: Richness = 5. By this measure, the sites look relatively similar.

Species diversity can be calculated for each area using Simpson's Index of Diversity:

$$D = 1 - \Sigma(pi^2)$$

where D is the diversity and Pi is the proportion of species i in the study area.

For Site A: $D = 1 - 0.24$
             $= 0.76$

For Site B: $D = 1 - 0.26$
             $= 0.74$

For Site C: $D = 1 - 0.32$
             $= 0.68$

This measure shows that all sites differ in diversity. The diversity of the sites is related to latitude: the most diverse site is the most southerly, the middle in diversity is from the middle region, and the least diverse is from the most northerly region.

Biogeographical Similarity

The biogeographical similarity (also called ecological similarity) of two areas is measured by the similarity of the species found in one area when compared to the other area. Biogeographical similarity is measured mathematically. If two areas (even if far apart in space) have the same species present, they are considered to be similar.

To calculate the biogeographical similarity of the three sites we use the Greig-Smith Index of Similarity:

Table 1   Tree Diversity in Three Sites of Eastern Canada

Site A: Leamington, Ontario (42°03′ N)

Species	Number of Trees	Proportion
White Pine (*Pinus strobus*)	2	0.2
Beech (*Fagus grandifolia*)	4	0.4
Sugar Maple (*Acer saccharum*)	1	0.1
White Oak (*Quercus alba*)	1	0.1
Kentucky Coffee Tree (*Gymnocladus dioicus*)	1	0.1
Eastern Flowering Dogwood (*Cornus florida*)	1	0.1
Total	10	

Site B: Hamilton, Ontario (43°15′ N)

Species	Number of Trees	Proportion
White Pine (*Pinus strobus*)	2	0.2
Sugar Maple (*Acer saccharum*)	4	0.4
Paper Birch (*Betula papyrifera*)	2	0.2
Beech (*Fagus grandifolia*)	1	0.1
Black Cherry (*Prunus serotina*)	1	0.1
Total	10	

Site C: Hull, Québec (45°25′ N)

Species	Number of Trees	Proportion
White Pine (*Pinus strobus*)	10	0.5
White Spruce (*Picea glauca*)	2	0.1
Hemlock (*Tsuga Canadensis*)	2	0.1
Paper Birch (*Betula papyrifera*)	4	0.2
Sugar Maple (*Acer saccharum*)	2	0.1
Total	20	

$$I = 2c/a + b$$

where I is the difference between the two areas (I = 1, no difference; I = 0, completely different), a is the species richness of one site, b is the species richness of the other site, and c is the number of species that occur at both sites.

Compare Site A with Site B
$$I_{(AB)} = 6 + 5/2 \times 8$$
$$= 0.6875$$

Site B with Site C
$$I_{(BC)} = 5 + 5/2 \times 7$$
$$= 0.7134$$

Site C with Site A
$$I_{(AC)} = 6 + 5/2 \times 9$$
$$= 0.6111$$

This comparison shows that sites A and B have a moderate similarity—A is in Carolinian Canada and B is on the edge of the transition zone. The two sites are relatively close to each other (A is closer to B than to C). Sites B and C have the greatest similarity—both are in the transition to Boreal. Sites A and C are the least similar and are the greatest distance apart.

Summary and Review—Ecosystem Essentials

■ *Define* ecology, biogeography, and the ecosystem concept.

Earth's biosphere is unique in the Solar System; its ecosystems are the essence of life. **Ecosystems** are self-sustaining associations of living plants and animals and their nonliving physical environment. **Ecology** is the study of the relationships between organisms and their environment and among the various ecosystems in the biosphere. **Biogeography** is the study of the distribution of plants and animals and the diverse spatial patterns they create.

ecosystem (p. 628)
ecology (p. 628)
biogeography (p. 628)

1. What is the relationship between the biosphere and an ecosystem? Define ecosystem, and give some examples.

2. What does biogeography include? Describe its relationship to ecology.

3. Briefly summarize what ecosystem operations imply about the complexity of life.

■ *Describe* communities, habitats, and niches.

A **community** is formed by the interactions among populations of living animals and plants at a particular time. Within a community, a **habitat** is the specific physical location of an organism—its address. A **niche** is the function or operation of a life form within a given community—its profession.

community (p. 629)
habitat (p. 630)
niche (p. 630)

4. Define a community within an ecosystem.

5. What do the concepts of habitat and niche involve? Relate them to some specific plant and animal communities.

6. Describe symbiotic and parasitic relationships in nature. Draw an analogy between these relationships and human societies on our planet. Explain.

■ *Explain* photosynthesis and respiration, and *derive* net photosynthesis and the world pattern of net primary productivity.

As plants evolved, the **vascular plants** developed conductive tissues. **Stomata** on the underside of leaves are the portals through which the plant participates with the atmosphere and hydrosphere. Plants (primary producers) perform **photosynthesis** as sunlight stimulates a light-sensitive pigment called **chlorophyll**. This process produces food sugars and oxygen to drive biological processes. **Respiration** is essentially the reverse of photosynthesis and is the way the plant derives energy by oxidizing carbohydrates. **Net primary productivity** is the net photosynthesis (photosynthesis minus respiration) of an entire community. This stored chemical energy is the **biomass** that the community generates, or the net dry weight of organic material.

vascular plants (p. 631)
stomata (p. 633)
photosynthesis (p. 633)
chlorophyll (p. 633)
respiration (p. 634)

net primary productivity (p. 634)
biomass (p. 634)

7. Define a vascular plant. How many plant species are there on Earth?

8. How do plants function to link the Sun's energy to living organisms? What is formed within the light-responsive cells of plants?

9. Compare photosynthesis and respiration and the derivation of net photosynthesis. What is the importance of knowing the net primary productivity of an ecosystem and how much biomass an ecosystem has accumulated?

10. Briefly describe the global pattern of net primary productivity.

■ *List* abiotic ecosystem components, and *relate* those components to ecosystem operations.

Light, temperature, water, and the cycling of gases and nutrients constitute the life-supporting abiotic components of ecosystems. Elevation and latitudinal position on Earth create a variety of physical environments. The zonation of plants with altitude is the **life zone concept** and is visible as you travel between different elevations.

Life is sustained by **biogeochemical cycles**, through which circulate the gases and sedimentary materials (nutrients) necessary for growth and development of living organisms. The environment may inhibit biotic operations, either through lack or excess. These **limiting factors** may be physical or chemical in nature.

life zone (p. 637)
biogeochemical cycles (p. 637)
limiting factor (p. 642)

11. What are the principal abiotic components in terrestrial ecosystems?

12. Describe what Alexander von Humboldt found that led him to propose the life zone concept. What are life zones? Explain the interaction among elevation, latitude, and the types of communities that develop.

13. What are biogeochemical cycles? Describe several of the essential cycles.

14. What is a limiting factor? How does it function to control the spatial distribution of plant and animal species?

■ *Explain* trophic relationships in ecosystems.

Trophic refers to the feeding and nutrition relations in an ecosystem. It represents the flow of energy and cycling of nutrients. **Producers**, which fix the carbon they need from carbon dioxide, are the plants, including phytoplankton in aquatic ecosystems. **Consumers**, generally animals including zooplankton in aquatic ecosystems, depend on the producers as their carbon source. Energy flows from the producers through the system along a **food chain** circuit. Within ecosystems, the feeding interrelationships are complex and arranged in a complex network of interconnected food chains in a **food web**.

The primary consumer is an **herbivore**, or plant eater. A **carnivore** (meat eater) is a secondary consumer. A consumer that eats both producers and consumers is an **omnivore**—a role occupied by humans. **Detritivores** are detritus feeders and decomposers that release simple inorganic compounds and nutrients as they break down organic materials. Detritus feeders, including worms, mites, termites, and centipedes, process debris. **Decomposers** are the bacteria and fungi that process organic debris outside their bodies and absorb nutrients in the process—the rotting that breaks down detritus. Biomass and population pyramids characterize the flow of energy and the numbers of producers, consumers, and decomposers operating in an ecosystem.

> producers (p. 644)
> consumers (p. 644)
> food chain (p. 644)
> food web (p. 644)
> herbivore (p. 644)
> carnivore (p. 644)
> omnivore (p. 644)
> detritivores (p. 644)
> decomposer (p. 644)

15. What role is played in an ecosystem by producers and consumers?

16. Describe the relationship among producers, consumers, and detritivores in an ecosystem. What is the trophic nature of an ecosystem? What is the place of humans in a trophic system?

17. What are biomass and population pyramids? Describe how these models help explain the nature of food chains and communities of plants and animals.

18. Follow the flow of energy and biomass through the Silver Springs, Florida, ecosystem. Describe the pathways in Figures 19.14 and 19.20a.

■ *Relate* how biological evolution led to the biodiversity of life on Earth.

Biodiversity (a combination of *biological* and *diversity*) includes the number of different species and quantity of each species, the genetic diversity in species (number of genetic characteristics), and ecosystem and habitat diversity. The greater the biodiversity within an ecosystem, the more stable and resilient it is, and the more productive it will be. Modern agriculture often creates a nondiverse monoculture that is particularly vulnerable to failure.

Evolution states that single-cell organisms adapted, modified, and passed along inherited changes to multicellular organisms. The genetic makeup of successive generations was shaped by environmental factors, physiological functions, and behaviours that created a greater rate of survival and reproduction that were passed along through natural selection.

> biodiversity (p. 650)
> evolution (p. 650)

19. Referring back to Focus Study 1.1, define the scientific method.

20. Construct a simple model to show the progressive stages that lead to the development of a theory, such as the theory of evolution.

■ *Define* succession, and *outline* the stages of general ecological succession in both terrestrial and aquatic ecosystems.

Ecological succession describes the process whereby older communities of plants and animals are replaced by newer communities that are usually more complex. Past glacial and interglacial climatic episodes have created a long-term succession. An area of bare rock and soil with no trace of a former community can be a site for **primary succession**. The initial community that occupies an area of early succession is a **pioneer community**. **Secondary succession** begins in an area that has a vestige of a previously functioning community in place. Rather than progressing smoothly to a definable stable point, ecosystems tend to operate in a dynamic condition, with succeeding communities overlapping in time and space. Wildfire is one external factor that disrupts a successional community. Aquatic ecosystems also experience community succession, as exemplified by the eutrophication of a lake ecosystem.

The science of **fire ecology** has emerged in an effort to understand the natural role of fire in ecosystem maintenance and succession.

> ecological succession (p. 655)
> primary succession (p. 656)
> pioneer community (p. 656)
> secondary succession (p. 656)
> fire ecology (p. 658)

21. What is meant by ecosystem stability?

22. How does ecological succession proceed? What are the relationships between existing communities and new, pioneer communities?

23. Discuss the concept of fire ecology in the context of the British Columbia fires of 1988 and subsequent annual wildfire statistics.

24. Summarize the process of succession in a body of water. What is meant by cultural eutrophication?

Critical Thinking

A. This chapter states, "Some scientists are questioning whether our human society and the physical systems of Earth constitute a global-scale symbiotic relationship of mutualism (sustainable) or a parasitic one (nonsustainable)." Referring to the definition of these terms, what is your response to the statement? How do you equate our planetary economic system with the need to sustain life-supporting natural systems? Mutualism? Parasitism?

B. Over the next several days as you travel between home and campus, a job, or other areas, observe the landscape. What types of ecosystem disturbances do you see? Imagine that several acres in the same area you are viewing had escaped any disruptions for a century or more. Describe what some of these ecosystems and communities might be like.

Today, we see that Earth's natural systems do pose limits to human activity. Scientists are measuring ecosystems carefully, and they are building elaborate computer models to simulate our evolving real-time human-environment experiment—in particular, shifting patterns of environmental factors (temperatures and changing frost periods; precipitation timing and amounts; air, water, and soil chemistry; and a redistribution of nutrients). We know from history that the effect of climate change on ecosystems will be significant. More than 15 years ago, two Harvard researchers assessed the impact of these alterations on ecosystems:

Based on more than a decade of research, it is obvious that the CO_2-rich atmosphere of our future will have direct and dramatic effects on the composition and operation of ecosystems. According to the best scientific evidence, we see no reason to be sanguine [optimistic] about the response of these habitats to our changing environment.*

Compare this to UNEP's 2007 *Global Environmental Outlook–GEO4* quote from their *GEO4 Executive Summary* (p. 4):

Human life and all other species depend on healthy ecosystems. But current biodiversity changes, the fastest in human history, mean losses are restricting future development options. About 60% of the ecosystem services that have been previously assessed are degraded or used unsustainably. Species are becoming extinct at rates which are 100 times faster than the rate shown in the fossil record, because of land-use changes, habitat loss, overexploitation of resources, pollution, and the spread of invasive alien species.

*F. A. Bazzaz and E. D. Fajer, "Plant life in a CO_2-rich world," *Scientific American* 256, no. 1 (January 1992): 74.

What will the quotations about Earth's environment be like 135 years from now, about the same time interval since G. P. Marsh made his assessment? Humans now have become the most powerful biotic agent on Earth, influencing all ecosystems on a planetary scale.

In this chapter: We explore Earth's major terrestrial ecosystems, conveniently grouped into 10 biomes. Each biome is an idealized assemblage because much alteration of the natural environment has occurred. The discussion covers biome appearance, structure, and location; the present conditions of related plants, animals, and environment; and the state of biodiversity. Table 20.1 summarizes most of the information about Earth's physical systems that is presented through the pages of this text. Through biomes, we synthesize the physical geography of place and region.

Biogeographic Realms

Figure 20.1 shows Earth's biogeographic realms. The map illustrates the botanical (plant) realms worldwide, and generally overlaps with the traditional zoological (animal) realms. Each realm contains many distinct ecosystems that distinguish it from other realms.

A **biogeographic realm** is a geographic region where a group of plant and animal species evolved, and traditionally has been used as a basis for establishing terrestrial ecosystem regions. As you can see, these realms correspond generally to continents. The main topographic barrier that separates these realms is the ocean. Every species attempts to migrate worldwide according to its niche requirements, reproductive success, and competition with other species but is constrained by climatic and topographic barriers. Recognition that such distinct regions of flora (plants) and fauna (animals) exist was an early beginning for *biogeography* as a discipline.

The Australian realm is unique, giving rise to 450 species of *Eucalyptus* among its plants and 125 species of marsupials, including four of the six orders (animals such

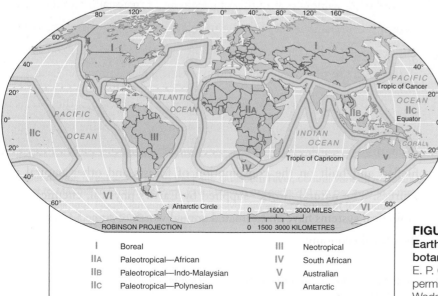

FIGURE 20.1 Biogeographic realms. Earth's biogeographical realms roughly based on botanical realms (after R. D. Good, 1947). [From E. P. Odum, *Fundamentals of Ecology*, 3rd ed., with permission of Brooks/Cole, an imprint of the Wadsworth Group, Thomson Learning.]

I	Boreal	III	Neotropical
IIA	Paleotropical—African	IV	South African
IIB	Paleotropical—Indo-Malaysian	V	Australian
IIC	Paleotropical—Polynesian	VI	Antarctic

FIGURE 20.2 The unique Australian realm.
The flora and fauna of Australia form a special assemblage of communities. [Photo by Mark Newman/Photo Researchers, Inc.]

as kangaroos that carry their young in pouches, where gestation is completed; Figure 20.2). Also, monotremes, egg-laying mammals such as the platypus, add further distinctiveness to this realm. Australia's unique flora and fauna is the result of its early isolation from the other continents. During critical evolutionary times, Australia drifted away from Pangaea (see Chapter 11) and never again was reconnected by a land bridge, even when sea level lowered during repeated glacial ages. New Zealand's isolation from Australia also undoubtedly explains why no native marsupials exist in New Zealand.

Transition Zones

Alfred Wallace (1823–1913), the first scholar of *zoogeography*, used the stark contrast in animal species among islands in present-day Indonesia to delimit a boundary between the Paleotropical and Australian realms (Figure 20.1). He thought that deep water in the straits had completely prevented species crossover. However, he later recognized that a boundary line actually is a wide transition zone, where one region grades into the other. Boundaries between natural systems are "zones of shared traits." Thus, despite distinctions among individual realms and our discussion of biomes, it is best to think of their borders as transition zones of mixed identity and composition, rather than as rigidly defined boundaries.

A boundary transition zone between adjoining ecosystem regions is an **ecotone**. Because ecotones are defined by different physical factors, they vary in width—think of a transition zone instead of a line. Climatic ecotones usually are more gradual than physical ecotones, where differences in soil or topography sometimes form abrupt boundaries. An ecotone between prairies and northern forests may occupy many kilometres of land. The ecotone is an area of tension, as similar species of plants and animals compete for the resource base.

Scientists have identified these boundary and edge areas as generating biodiversity (a species richness) as adaptation and natural selection favour the population with reproductive success. Organisms may compete, yet they may act to facilitate other organisms in a positive interaction in whatever strategies affect rates of ecosystem productivity, such as pollinating insects. A process of *coevolution* is possible where interacting populations in the tension zone can lead to genetic changes in each population (*microevolution*). Edges and ecotones are dynamic areas in the evolution of ecosystems and communities.

Terrestrial Ecosystems

A **terrestrial ecosystem** is a self-sustaining association of land-based plants and animals and their abiotic environment, characterized by specific plant formation classes. Plants are the most visible part of the biotic landscape, and they are key members of Earth's terrestrial ecosystems. In their growth, form, and distribution, plants reflect Earth's physical systems: its energy patterns; atmospheric composition; temperature and winds; air masses; water quantity, quality, and seasonal timing; soils; regional climates; geomorphic processes; and ecosystem dynamics. As discussed in the previous chapter, aquatic ecosystems are likewise important and result from the interaction of physical systems (see News Report 20.1).

A brief review of the ways that living organisms relate to the environment and to each other is helpful at this point. Interacting populations of plants and animals in an area form a *community*. An *ecosystem* involves the interplay between a community of plants and animals and their abiotic physical environment. Each plant and animal occupies an area in which it is biologically suited to live—its *habitat*—and within that habitat it performs a basic operational function—its *niche* (see Chapter 19).

A **biome** is a large, stable terrestrial ecosystem characterized by specific plant and animal communities. Each biome usually is named for its *dominant vegetation*, because that is the single most easily identified feature. We can generalize Earth's wide-ranging plant species into six broad biomes: *forest, savanna, grassland, shrubland, desert,* and *tundra*. Because plant distributions respond to environmental conditions and reflect variations in climate and soil, the world climate map in Figure 10.5 in Chapter 10 is a helpful reference for this chapter. The biome concept can also be applied to aquatic ecosystems: polar seas, temperate seas, tropical seas, seafloor, shoreline, and coral reef.

More specific characteristics are used for the structural classification of plants themselves. *Life-form designations* are based on the outward physical properties of individual plants or the general form and structure of a vegetation cover. These physical life forms include:

- *Trees* (large woody main trunk, perennial; usually exceeds 3 m, or 10 ft, in height)
- *Lianas* (woody climbers and vines)

News Report 20.1

Aquatic Ecosystems and Marine Protected Areas

Oceans, estuaries, and freshwater bodies (streams and lakes) are home to aquatic ecosystems. Poor understanding of aquatic ecosystems has led to the demise of species such as herring in the Georges Bank of the Atlantic Ocean and an overall decline in fisheries worldwide. The conservation and protection of marine life and their habitats is the goal of marine protected areas (MPA). A marine protected area is an area of the sea within Canada's territory that is designated for conservation and protection of one or more of the following: (a) commercial and non-commercial fishery resources, including marine mammals and their habitats; (b) endangered or threatened marine species, and their habitats; (c) unique habitats; (d) marine areas of high biodiversity or biological pro-

ductivity; and (e) any other marine resource or habitat as is necessary to fulfill the mandate of the Minister of the Department of Fisheries and Oceans Canada.

As of 2008, six MPAs have been designated. The first, designated in March 2003, is the Endeavour Hydrothermal Vents, which lies in 2250 m of water, 250 km southwest of Vancouver Island. The vents are part of the active spreading zone where new ocean floor is created. This MPA was designated to protect the vents that enrich seawater in the vicinity (see Figure 11.13b) and the unique ecosystems associated with them.

The second MPA, designated in May 2004, is the Gully, a part of the Eastern Scotian Shelf in the Atlantic

Ocean located about 200 km east of Nova Scotia, near Sable Island. The Gully is a canyon on the edge of the Continental Shelf where bathymetry quickly drops by over 2.5 km. The 65-km long and 15-km wide canyon was designated a marine protected area to safeguard and conserve the biological diversity of the region. Since 2004, four more MPAs have been designated including: Basin Head, Prince Edward Island, Eastport, Newfoundland and Gilbert Bay Labrador in October 2005; and, Musquash Estuary, New Brunswick in March 2007. For more information see the MPA Web site http://www.dfo-mpo.gc.ca/oceans-habitat/oceans/mpa-zpm/designated-designee_e.asp.

- *Shrubs* (smaller woody plants; stems branching at the ground)
- *Herbs* (small plants without woody stems; includes grasses and other nonwoody vascular plants)
- *Bryophytes* (nonflowering, spore-producing plants; includes mosses and liverworts)
- *Epiphytes* (plants growing above the ground on other plants, using them for support)
- *Thallophytes* (lack true leaves, stems, or roots; includes bacteria, fungi, algae, lichens)

These plant assemblages in their general biomes are divided into more-specific vegetation units called **formation classes**, which refer to the structure and appearance of dominant plants in a terrestrial ecosystem. Examples are equatorial rain forest, northern needleleaf forest, Mediterranean shrubland, and arctic tundra. Each formation class includes numerous plant communities, and each community includes innumerable plant habitats. Within those habitats, Earth's diversity is expressed in 270,000 plant species. Despite this intricate complexity, we can generalize Earth's numerous formation classes into 10 global terrestrial biome regions, as portrayed in Figure 20.3 and detailed in Table 20.1.

Now let us go on a tour of Earth's biomes, keeping in mind that they synthesize all we have learned about the atmosphere, hydrosphere, lithosphere, and biosphere in the pages of this text. Here we bring it all together.

Earth's Major Terrestrial Biomes

Few natural communities of plants and animals remain; most biomes have been greatly altered by human intervention. Thus, the "natural vegetation" identified on many biome maps reflects *ideal potential* mature vegetation, given the environmental characteristics in a region. Even though human practices have greatly altered these ideal forms, it is valuable to study the natural (undisturbed) biomes to better understand the environment and to assess the extent of human-caused alteration.

Knowing the ideal in a region guides us to a closer approximation of natural vegetation in the plants we introduce. In Canada and the United States, we humans are perpetuating a type of *transition community*, somewhere between grasslands and a forest—an artificial successional stage, produced by large-scale interruption and disturbance. We plant trees and lawns and then must invest energy, water, and capital to sustain such artificial modifications. Or we graze animals and plant crops that perpetuate this disturbed transitional state.

When these activities cease, natural succession recovers, and we see the land slowly return to its various vegetation-cover potentials. Some irreversible damage might occur when plants, animals, and organisms are knowingly or accidentally brought into an ecosystem or biome in which they are not native. These exotic species pose an increasing concern to scientists and society—a subject of News Report 20.2.

(text continued on page 677)

Table 20.1 Major Terrestrial Biomes and Their Characteristics

Biome and Ecosystems (map symbol)	Vegetation Characteristics	Soil Orders— CSSC and Soil Taxonomy	Climate Type	Annual Precipitation Range	Temperature Patterns	Water Balance
Equatorial and Tropical Rain Forest (ETR) Evergreen broadleaf forest Selva	Leaf canopy thick and continuous; broadleaf evergreen trees, vines (lianas), epiphytes, tree ferns, palms	Oxisols Ultisols (on well-drained uplands)	Tropical	180–400 cm (>6cm/mo)	Always warm (21–30°C; avg. 25°C)	Surpluses all year
Tropical Seasonal Forest and Scrub (TrSF) Tropical monsoon forest Tropical deciduous forest Scrub woodland and thorn forest	Transitional between rain forest and grasslands; broadleaf, some deciduous trees; open parkland to dense undergrowth; acacias and other thorn trees in open growth	Oxisols Ultisols Vertisols (in India) Some Alfisols	Tropical monsoon savanna	130–200 cm (<40 rainy days during 4 driest months)	Variable, always warm (>18°C)	Seasonal surpluses and deficits
Tropical Savanna (TrS) Tropical grassland Thorn tree scrub Thorn woodland	Transitional between seasonal forests, rain forests, and semiarid tropical steppes and desert; trees with flattened crowns, clumped grasses, and bush thickets; fire association	Alfisols (dry: Ultalfs) Ultisols Oxisols	Tropical savanna	9–150 cm, seasonal	No cold-weather limitations	Tends toward deficits, therefore fire- and drought-susceptible
Midlatitude Broadleaf and Mixed Forest (MBME) Temperate broadleaf Midlatitude deciduous Temperate needleleaf	Mixed broadleaf and needleleaf trees; deciduous broadleaf, losing leaves in winter; southern and eastern evergreen pines demonstrate fire association	Podzols, red and yellow Ultisols Some Alfisols	Humid subtropical warm summer Humid continental warm summer	75–150 cm	Temperate with cold season	Seasonal pattern with summer maximum PRECIP and POTET (PET); no irrigation needed
Needleleaf Forest and Montane Forest (NF/MF) Taiga Boreal forest Other montane forests and highlands	Needleleaf conifers, mostly evergreen pine, spruce, fir; Russian larch, a deciduous needleleaf	Gleysols Podzols Spodosols Histosols Inceptisols Alfisols (Boralfs: cold)	Subarctic Humid continental cool summer	30–100 cm	Short summer, cold winter	Low POTET (PET), moderate PRECIP, moist soils, some waterlogged and frozen in winter; no deficits
Temperate Rain Forest (TeR) West-coast forest Coast redwoods (U.S.)	Narrow margin of lush evergreen and deciduous trees on windward slopes; redwoods, tallest trees on Earth	Podzols Spodosols Inceptisols (mountainous environs)	Marine west coast	150–500 cm	Mild summer and mild winter for latitude	Large surpluses and runoff
Mediterranean Shrubland (MSh) Sclerophyllous shrubs Australian eucalyptus forest	Short shrubs, drought adapted, tending to grassy woodlands and chaparral	Luvisols Alfisols (Xeralfs) Mollisols (Xerolls)	Mediterranean dry summer	25–65 cm	Hot, dry summers, cool winters	Summer deficits, winter surpluses
Midlatitude Grasslands (MGr) Temperate grassland Sclerophyllous shrub	Tallgrass prairies and shortgrass steppes, highly modified by human activity; major areas of commercial grain farming; plains, pampas, and veld	Chernozemic Mollisols Aridisols	Humid subtropical Humid continental hot summer	25–75 cm	Temperate continental regimes	Soil moisture utilization and recharge balanced; irrigation and dry farming in drier areas
Warm Desert and Semidesert (DBW) Subtropical desert and scrubland	Bare ground graduating into xerophytic plants including succulents, cacti, and dry shrubs	Aridisols Entisols (sand dunes)	Desert Arid	<2 cm	Average annual temperature, around 18°C, highest temperatures on Earth	Chronic deficits, irregular precipitation events, PRECIP < ½ POTET (PET)
Cold Desert and Semidesert (DBC) Midlatitude desert, scrubland, and steppe	Cold desert vegetation includes short grass and dry shrubs	Aridisols Entisols	Steppe Semiarid	2–25 cm	Average annual temperature around 18°C	PRECIP >½ POTET (PET)
Arctic and Alpine Tundra (AAT)	Treeless; dwarf shrubs, stunted sedges, mosses, lichens, and short grasses; alpine, grass meadows	Organic Cryosols Gelisols Histosols Entisols (permafrost)	Tundra Subarctic very cold	15–180 cm	Warmest months >10°C, only 2 or 3 months above freezing	Not applicable most of the year, poor drainage in summer
Ice			Ice sheet ice cap			

FIGURE 20.3 Major terrestrial biomes.
(a) The 10 major global terrestrial biomes.
(b) Inset contains more detail for Canada.
[(b) Map adapted from *The Atlas of Canada*
http://atlas.gc.ca/site/index.html. © 2004,
used with the permission of Natural
Resources Canada.]

(a)

(b)

REGIONS:

- Taiga plains
- Boreal plains
- Boreal shield
- Boreal cordillera
- Pacific maritime
- Montane cordillera
- Prairies
- Atlantic maritime
- Mixedwood plains

FOREST TYPES:

- Coniferous forest
- Broadleaf forest
- Mixed forest
- Transitional forest
- Tundra and permafrost

News Report 20.2

Alien Invaders of Exotic Species

The title above sounds like that of a cult science fiction movie; instead, it refers to a real problem in the integrity of many ecosystems, both aquatic and terrestrial. Animal and plant species brought or somehow getting into biomes outside their native home is an important subject in biogeography and invasion biology. Niche takeovers by non-native species can prove damaging to otherwise healthy ecosystems. These intruders are known as *exotic species*, or *alien* or *non-native species*.

Environment Canada's Biodiversity Convention Office hosts the Invasive Alien Species Web site at **http://www.cbin.ec.gc.ca/primers/ias.cfm?lang=e**. The site lists some of the most recent invasive species in Canada including purple loosestrife, the zebra mussel, and the brown spruce long-horned beetle. Alien species total 27% of all vascular plants, 181 insects that feed on woody plants, 24 birds, 26 mammals, 2 reptiles, 4 amphibians, and 55 freshwater fish in Canada. Several invasive species that have established in Canada are included on the

World Conservation Union's list of 100 worst invasive alien species including Dutch elm disease, purple loosestrife, leafy spurge, Japanese knotweed, green crab, spiny water flea, gypsy moth, carp, rainbow trout, starling, domestic (feral) cat, and rats.

The Institute for Biological Invasions at the University of Tennessee at **http://invasions.bio.utk.edu/bio_invasions/index.html** is dedicated to studying these invasive plants, animals, and other organisms such as zebra mussels. Some states post warning signs at their borders (Figure 20.2.1a) and others offer Web sites, such as Minnesota's "Prohibited and Noxious Plants by Scientific Name" (**http://www.dnr.state.mn.us/invasives/index. html**).

The African "killer bees" are in the headlines whenever an attack occurs, as are brown tree snakes in Guam, zebra mussels in the Great Lakes, and Eurasian cheatgrass in the Utah desert, to name but a few examples. Brought from Africa to the central coast of Brazil in 1957 to increase honey production, killer bees now

have interbred with native bees and range to southern California, Arizona, New Mexico, Texas, and Puerto Rico. More than 1000 people have died from their attacks. The dangers are in their mass response to disturbances and that some people are allergic to even one bee sting. This is a classic case of geographical diffusion of an exotic species.

Probably 90% of exotic species fail when they try to move into established niches in a community. The 10% that succeed, some 4500 species documented in a 1993 Office of Technology Assessment report, prove damaging to as much as one-fifth of ecosystems they invade. Figures 20.2.1b and c show two such alien invaders: purple loosestrife (*Lythrum salicaria*) and zebra mussels (*Dreissena polymorpha*).

Purple loosestrife (*Lythrum salicaria*) was introduced from Europe in the 1800s as a desired ornamental and had some medicinal applications. The plant's seeds also arrived in ships that used soil for ballast. A hardy perennial, it got loose and invaded wetlands across the eastern portions of Canada

(a)   (b)   (c)

(d)

FIGURE 20.2.1 Exotic species.
(a) A sign in Wallowa County, Washington State, makes a plea for awareness in this agricultural country, listing noxious (non-native, often problematic) weeds at the county line. (b) Invasive purple loosestrife near Lake Michigan and the Indiana Dunes National Lakeshore, Indiana (foreground and left centre). (c) Zebra mussels literally cover most hard surfaces in the Great Lakes. (d) Gorse (yellow-flowering shrub), intended for barriers between pastures, is loose across the landscape in West Point, Falkland Islands. [Photos by (a, b, and d) Bobbé Christopherson; (c) David M. Dennis, Maxximages.com.]

and the United States, through the upper Midwest, and as far west as Vancouver Island, British Columbia, replacing plants on which native wildlife depend (Figure 20.2.1b). The plant is known to infect drier landscapes as well and poses a potential threat to agriculture.

Zebra mussel (*Dreissena polymorpha*) adults are up to 3.8 cm (1.5 in.) long, with shells have alternating brown and black coloured stripes. The females can produce more than 1 million eggs a year. Zebra mussels are native to Europe and Western Russia and were discovered in the Great Lakes in 1988 in ballast water dumped from ocean-going ships. Microscopic larvae travel in the water. Also, they attach to boat hulls, fishing gear and nets, and boat equipment. Zebra mussels foul beaches, disrupt natural food webs, destroy native mussels, clog water systems, and lead to fish and wildlife die-offs (Figure 20.2.1c). They have spread throughout the Great Lakes and most of the Mississippi River, and are now in other rivers and inland lakes.

Gorse (*Ulex*) was introduced into the timber-poor Falkland Islands as a barrier plant, like a substitute fence. Its thorny stickers and dense growth were meant to keep grazing sheep and a few cattle under control. The plant spread beyond this intended use (Figure 20.2.1d).

In learning about biomes, we find out about native plant, animal, and organism locations and the unique place each species occupies. We must avoid knowingly or perhaps unconsciously adding to an escalating problem by bringing exotic species into non-native sites where they do not naturally belong.

The global distribution of Earth's major terrestrial biomes, based on vegetation formation classes, is portrayed in Figure 20.3. Table 20.1 describes each biome on the map and summarizes other pertinent information gathered from throughout *Geosystems*.

Now is a good time to refer to "The Living Earth" composite image that appears inside the front cover of this text and in the Map Reference Library on the *Student Animation* CD-ROM that accompanies this text. A computer artist using hundreds of thousands of satellite images produced this cloudless view of Earth in natural colour typical of a local summer day. Compare the map in Figure 20.3 with this remarkable composite image and see what correlation you can make. Then compare the biomes with population distribution as indicated by the nighttime lighting display that you activate with the slider on the CD.

Equatorial and Tropical Rain Forest

Earth is girdled with a lush biome—the **equatorial and tropical rain forest**. In a climate of consistent year-round daylength (12 hours), high insolation, average annual temperatures around 25°C (77°F), and plentiful moisture, plant and animal populations have responded with the most diverse expressions of life on the planet.

As Figure 20.3 shows, the Amazon region, also called the *selva*, is the largest tract of equatorial and tropical rain forest. In addition, rain forests cover equatorial regions of Africa, Indonesia, the margins of Madagascar and Southeast Asia, the Pacific coast of Ecuador and Colombia, and the east coast of Central America, with small discontinuous patches elsewhere. The cloud forests of western Venezuela are such tracts of rain forest at high elevation, perpetuated by high humidity and cloud cover. Undisturbed tracts of rain forest are rare.

Rain forests represent approximately one-half of Earth's remaining forests, occupying about 7% of the total land area worldwide. This biome is stable in its natural state, resulting from the long-term residence of these continental plates near equatorial latitudes and their escape from glacial activity.

Rain forests feature ecological niches that are distributed vertically rather than horizontally because of the competition for light. Biomass in a rain forest is concentrated high up in the canopy, that dense mass of overhead leaves. The canopy is filled with a rich variety of plants and animals. *Lianas* (vines) stretch from tree to tree, entwining them with cords that can reach 20 cm (8 in.) in diameter. *Epiphytes* flourish there too—plants such as orchids, bromeliads, and ferns live entirely aboveground, supported physically but not nutritionally by the structures of other plants. Calm conditions on the forest floor make wind pollination difficult, so pollination is by insects, other animals, and self-pollination.

The rain forest canopy forms three levels—see Figure 20.4. The upper level is not continuous, but features emergent tall trees whose high crowns rise above the middle canopy. This upper level appears as a broken *overstory* of tall trees breaking through a middle canopy that is nearly continuous (Figure 20.4b). The broad leaves block much of the light and create a darkened *understory* area and forest floor. The lower level is composed of seedlings, ferns, bamboo, and the like, leaving the litter-strewn ground level in deep shade and fairly open.

Aerial photographs of a rain forest, or views along riverbanks covered by dense vegetation, or the false Hollywood-movie imagery of the jungle make it difficult to imagine the shadowy environment of the actual rain-forest floor, which receives only about 1% of the sunlight arriving at the canopy (Figure 20.5a). The constant moisture, rotting fruit and moldy odours, strings of thin roots and vines dropping down from above, windless air, and echoing sounds of life in the trees together create a unique environment.

The smooth, slender trunks of rainforest trees are covered with thin bark and buttressed by large wall-like flanks that grow out from the trees to brace the trunks (Figure 20.5b). These buttresses form angular, open

- 60 m (200 ft) ⎤
  ⎟ High-level
  ⎟ canopy
- 50 m (165 ft) ⎦
- 40 m (130 ft) ⎤
  ⎟ Middle-level
  ⎟ canopy
  ⎟ (heaviest of
  ⎟ the three)
- 20 m (65 ft) ⎦
- 15 m (50 ft) ⎤
  ⎟ Lower-level
  ⎟ canopy
- 5 m (15 ft) ⎦

(a)

(b)

FIGURE 20.4 The three levels of a rainforest canopy.
(a) Lower, middle, and high levels of the rain forest. (b) Undisturbed rain forest on the Peninsula de Osa in Costa Rica. Note a few high-level canopy trees that extend above the dense, continuous cover of the middle canopy. [Photo by Barbara Cushman Rowell/Mountain Light Photography, Inc.]

enclosures, a ready habitat for various animals. There are usually no branches for at least the lower two-thirds of the tree trunks.

The wood of many rainforest trees is extremely hard, heavy, and dense—in fact, some species will not even float in water. Exceptions are balsa and a few others, which are light. Varieties of trees include mahogany, ebony, and rosewood. Logging is difficult because individual species are widely scattered; a species may occur only once or twice per square kilometre. Selective cutting is required for species-specific logging, whereas pulpwood production

takes everything. Conversion of the forest to pasture usually is done by setting destructive fires.

Rainforest soils, principally Oxisols, are essentially infertile, yet they support rich vegetation. The trees have adapted to these soil conditions with root systems able to capture nutrients from litter decay at the soil surface. High precipitation and temperatures work to produce deeply weathered and leached soils, characteristic of the laterization process, with a claylike texture sometimes breaking up into a granular structure. Oxisols lack nutrients and colloidal material. With much investment in

(a)

(b)

FIGURE 20.5 The rain forest.
(a) Equatorial rain forest is thick along the Amazon River where light breaks through to the surface, producing a rich gallery of vegetation. (b) The rainforest floor in Corcovado, Costa Rica, with typical buttressed trees and lianas. [Photos by (a) Wolfgang Kaehler Photography; (b) Frank S. Balthis.]

fertilizers, pesticides, and machinery, these soils can be productive.

The animal and insect life of the rain forest is diverse, ranging from small decomposers (bacteria) working the surface to many animals living exclusively in the upper stories of the trees. These tree dwellers are referred to as *arboreal*, from the Latin for "tree," and include sloths, monkeys, lemurs, parrots, and snakes. Beautiful birds of many colours, tree frogs, lizards, bats, and a rich insect community that includes more than 500 species of butterflies are found in rain forests. Surface animals include pigs (bushpigs and the giant forest hog in Africa, wild boar and bearded pig in Asia, and peccary in South America), species of small antelopes (bovids), and mammalian predators (the tiger in Asia, jaguar in South America, and leopard in Africa and Asia).

The present human assault on Earth's rain forests has put this diverse fauna and the varied flora at risk. It also jeopardizes an important recycling system for atmospheric carbon dioxide and a potential source of valuable pharmaceuticals and many types of new foods— and so much is still unknown and undiscovered.

Deforestation of the Tropics

More than half of Earth's original rain forest is gone, cleared for pasture, timber, fuel wood, and farming. Worldwide, an area nearly the size of Wisconsin is lost each year (169,000 km^2, 65,000 mi^2) and about a third more is disrupted by selective cutting of canopy trees, a damage that occurs along the *edges* of deforested areas.

When orbiting astronauts look down on the rain forests at night, they see thousands of human-set fires. During the day, the lower atmosphere in these regions is choked with the smoke. These fires are used to clear land for agriculture, which is intended to feed the domestic population as well as to produce accelerating cash exports of beef, rubber, coffee, soybeans, and other commodities. Edible fruits are not abundant in an undisturbed rain forest, but cultivated clearings produce bananas (plantains), mangos, jack fruit, guava, and starch-rich roots such as manioc and yams.

Because of the poor soil fertility, the cleared lands are quickly exhausted under intensive farming and are then generally abandoned in favour of newly burned and cleared lands, unless fertility is maintained artificially. The dominant trees require from 100 to 250 years to reestablish themselves after major disturbances. Once cleared, the former forest becomes a mass of low bushes intertwined with vines and ferns, slowing the return of the forests.

Figure 20.6a–c shows satellite false-colour images of a portion of western Brazil called Rondônia, recorded in June 1975 (*Landsat 2*), August 1986 (*Landsat 5*), June 1992 (*Landsat 4*), and in (d) true colour in June 2001 (*Terra*). These images give a sense of the level of rainforest destruction in progress. You can clearly see encroachment along new roads branching from highway BR364. The *edges* of every road and cleared area represent a significant

portion of the species habitat disturbance, population dynamic changes, and carbon losses to the atmosphere—perhaps as much as 1.5 times more impact occurs along these edges than in the tracts of clear-cut logging. The hotter, drier, and windier edge conditions penetrate the forest up to 100 m. Figure 20.6e shows a tract of former rain forest that has just been burned to begin the clearing and road-building process.

In 1998–1999, despite all the efforts to introduce sustainable forestry practices, deforestation was 33,926 km^2 (13,100 mi^2) in 2 years. Since 1972 the losses totaled more than the area of the combined Atlantic Provinces, and portions of Ontario and Quebec, as noted on the map in Figure 20.6f. In 1970 only about 1% of the Brazilian Amazon had been deforested, yet here we see forest area more than that of France lost since 1972.

This is a highly charged issue, as can be seen by the growth of Brazil's cattle industry that use these new pasture lands. Cattle herds increased from 25 million head (1990) to a forecasted 200 million head by 2010. Brazil is a major beef exporter and consumer of its own rainforest resource base.

The United Nations Food and Agricultural Organization (FAO) estimates that if this destruction to rain forests continues unabated, they will be completely removed by 2050. By continent, rainforest losses are estimated at more than 50% in Africa, more than 40% in Asia, and 40% in Central and South America.

To slow this continuing catastrophe of deforestation, in 1985 the FAO, the UN Development Programme, the World Bank, the World Resources Institute, and several nongovernmental organizations initiated the Tropical Forestry Action Plan. This plan, armed with $8 billion in development aid money, instituted an accurate worldwide survey of the rate of deforestation, using satellites to obtain remote measurement of land cover for building more-accurate GIS models. Critics charge that this effort has yet to show progress. Among many references, see the Tropical Rainforest Coalition at **http://www.rainforest. org/**, World Resources Institute publications on forests at **http://www.globalforestwatch.org/english/index.htm**, the Rainforest Information Centre at **http://www. rainforestinfo.org.au/welcome.htm**, or the Rainforest Action Network at **http://www.ran.org/**.

Focus Study 20.1 looks more closely at efforts to curb increasing rates of species extinction and loss of Earth's biodiversity, much of which is directly attributable to the loss of rain forests.

Tropical Seasonal Forest and Scrub

A varied biome on the margins of the rain forest is the **tropical seasonal forest and scrub**, which occupies regions of low and erratic rainfall. The shifting intertropical convergence zone (ITCZ) brings precipitation with the seasonally shifting high Sun of summer and then a season of dryness with the low Sun of winter, producing a seasonal pattern of moisture deficits, some leaf loss, and dry-season flowering. The term *semideciduous* applies to some of the

(text continued on page 684)

(a) 1975

(b) 1986

(c) 1992

(e)

(d) 2001

1972–1999
Clear cut
in Brazil

Hudson Strait

Hudson Bay

Ungava
Bay

Hudson

Bay

Labrador Sea

CANADA

*Gulf of
St. Lawrence*

Amount
added in
2000-2005

**UNITED
STATES**

*ATLANTIC
OCEAN*

0   250   500 MILES

0   250   500 KILOMETRES

(f)

FIGURE 20.6 Amazon rain forest losses.
Satellite images of a portion of western Brazil called Rondônia, recorded in false colour in (a) June 1975 (*Landsat 2*), (b) August 1986 (*Landsat 5*), (c) June 1992 (*Landsat 4*), and in true colour (d) June 1, 2001 (*Terra* MODIS sensor; the area of the other three images is in the upper left). Highway BR364, the main artery in the region, passes through the towns of Jaru and Ji-Paraná near the centre of image (d) at about 62° W 11° S. The branching pattern of feeder roads encroaches on the rain forest. (e) Surface view of burning rain forest. (f) Deforested areas in Brazil compared to the size of areas in North America. Shown are areas cleared from 1972–1999 and 2000–2005. [*Landsat* images courtesy of NASA/USGS EROS Data Center; *Terra* MODIS image courtesy of NASA/MODIS Land Rapid Response Team; (e) photo by George Holton/Photo Researchers, Inc.]

Biodiversity and Biosphere Reserves

When the first European settlers landed on the Hawaiian Islands in the late 1700s, they counted 43 species of birds. Today, 15 of those species are extinct and 19 more are threatened or endangered, with only one-fifth of the original species relatively healthy. Humans have great impact on animals and plants and global biodiversity.

Relatively pristine habitats around the world are being lost at unprecedented rates as an expanding human population converts them to agriculture, forestry, and urban centers. As these habitats are altered, untold numbers of species are disappearing before they have been recognized, much less studied, and the functioning of entire ecosystems is threatened. This loss of biodiversity, at the very time when the value of biotic resources is becoming widely recognized, has made it strikingly clear that current strategies for conservation are failing dismally.*

As more is learned about Earth's ecosystems and their related communities, more is known of their value to civilization and our interdependence with them. Natural ecosystems are a major source of new foods, new chemicals, new medicines, and specialty woods, and of course they are indicators of a healthy, functioning biosphere.

International efforts are under way to study and preserve specific segments of the biosphere, among others: the UN Environment Programme, World Resources Institute, The World Conservation Union, Natural World Heritage Sites, Wetlands of International Importance, and the Nature Conservancy. The International Union for Conservation of Nature and Natural Resources (IUCN) Red List of global endangered species provides an important focus. (See IUCN Red List at http://www.iucnredlist.org/, the IUCN at http://www.iucn.org/, the endangered species home page of the Fish and Wildlife Service at http://www.fws.gov/endangered/, and the World Wildlife Fund at http://www.panda.org/.) The motivation to set aside natural sanctuaries is directly related to concern over the increase in the rate of species extinctions. We are facing a loss of genetic diversity that may be unparalleled in Earth's history, even compared with the major extinctions over the geologic record.

Species Threatened—Examples

The IUCN in 2006 listed the polar bear (*Ursus maritimus*) as *Vulnerable* to extinction, a "Threatened" category on their Endangered Species List—the *Red Book*. In spring 2007, during the 90-day comment period concerning the bears' status, the Fish and Wildlife Service received more than 600,000 letters concerning the inclusion of polar bears under the Endangered Species Act. Research released by the USGS in September 2007, predicted that with the loss of Alaskan, Canadian, and Russian sea-ice habitat, some two-thirds of the world's polar bears will die off by 2050. The remaining 7500 bears will be struggling (Figure 20.1.1). The Fish and Wildlife Service opened a second comment period over these findings but has delayed any decision. Any action society takes now will hopefully result in a slowing of such change and the buying of a little adaptation time.

Black rhinos (*Diceros bicornis*) and white rhinos (*Ceratotherium simum*) in Africa exemplify species in jeopardy. Rhinos once grazed over much of the savanna grasslands and woodlands. Today, they survive only in protected

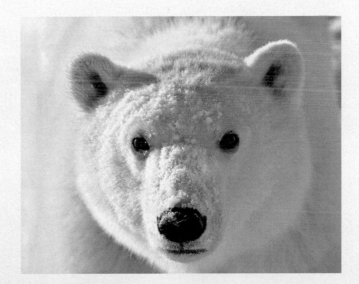

FIGURE 20.1.1 The polar bear.
A male polar bear, snow on his face, seems to be looking directly at us with questions in his eyes, wondering about who we are. Polar bear vision is about the same quality as human sight; however, they have extraordinary sense of smell. One study predicts that 67% of the remaining polar bear population of 23,000 will be gone by 2050 because of climate change and loss of sea ice—that leaves 7590 bears across the Arctic region. [Photo by Bobbé Christopherson.]

*T. D. Sisk, A. E. Launer, K. R. Switky, and P. R. Ehrlich, "Identifying extinction threats," *Bioscience* 44 (October 1994): 592.

(continued)

Focus Study 20.1 *(continued)*

districts in heavily guarded sanctuaries and are threatened even there (Figure 20.1.2). In 1998, 2599 black rhinos remained, 96% less than the 70,000 in 1960. Populations remained statistically stable through the last half of the 1990s; this count is supported by South Africa's guarding about 50% of the remaining population. A slow recovery is underway as numbers of black rhinos rose to 3,600 in 2003 (source: IUCN/SSC/ African Rhino Specialist Group). This is not the case with the western black rhino, a subspecies, which is down to its last few individuals.

There were 11 white rhinos (northern subspecies) in existence in 1984, increasing to an estimated 29 by 1998 (Congo 25, Côte d'Ivoire 4), although the IUCN suggests this number might actually be only 5 to 10 rhinos left in 2005. Political unrest in the Congo and the area of the Garamba National Park has led to the deaths of an unknown number of these few. The southern white rhino population reached 11,000 by 2002. Rhinoceros horn sells for US$29,000 per kilogram for use as an imagined aphrodisiac. These large land mammals

Table 20.1.1   Known and Estimated Species on Earth

| Categories of Living Organisms | Number of Known Species | Estimated Number of Species | | Working Estimate (000) | Accuracy |
		High (000)	Low (000)		
Viruses	4,000	1,000	50	400	Very poor
Bacteria	4,000	3,000	50	1000	Very poor
Fungi	72,000	27,000	200	1500	Moderate
Protozoa	40,000	200	60	200	Very poor
Algae	40,000	1,000	150	400	Very poor
Plants	270,000	500	300	320	Good
Nematodes	25,000	1,000	100	400	Poor
Arthropods					
Crustaceans	40,000	200	75	150	Moderate
Arachnids	75,000	1,000	300	750	Moderate
Insects	950,000	100,000	2,000	8,000	Moderate
Mollusks	70,000	200	100	200	Moderate
Chordates	45,000	55	50	50	Good
Others	115,000	800	200	250	Moderate
Total	**1,750,000**	**111,655**	**3,635**	**13,620**	**Very poor**

Source: United Nations Environment Programme, *Global Biodiversity Assessment* (Cambridge: Cambridge University Press, 1995), Table 3.1–2, p. 118.

are nearing extinction and will survive only as a dwindling zoo population. The limited genetic pool that remains complicates further reproduction.

Table 20.1.1 summarizes the numbers of known and estimated species on Earth (see http://www. wri.org/ecosystems). Scientists have classified only 1.75 million species of plants and animals of an estimated 13.6 million overall; this figure represents an increase in what scientists once thought to be the diversity of life on Earth. And those yet-to-be-discovered species represent a potential future resource for society—the wide range of estimates places the expected species count between a low of 3.6 million and a high of 111.7 million.

Estimates of annual species loss range between 1000 and 30,000, although this range might be conservative. The possibility exists that more than half of Earth's present species could be extinct within the next 100 years. The effects of pollution, climate change, loss of wild habitat, excessive grazing, poaching, and collecting are at the root of such devastation. Approximately 60% of the extinctions are attributable to the clearing and loss of rain forests alone.

FIGURE 20.1.2 The rhinoceros in Africa.
Black rhino and young in Tanzania, escorted by Oxpecker birds. These rhinos are quite nearsighted (they can see clearly only up to 10 m); the birds act as the rhino's early-warning system for disturbances in the distance.
[Photo by Stephen J. Krasemann/DRK Photo.]

The Question of Medicine and Food

Wheat, maize (corn), and rice—just three grains—fulfill about 50% of human planetary food demands. About 7000 plant species have been gathered for food throughout human history, but more than 30,000 plant species have edible parts. Undiscovered potential food resources are in nature waiting to be found and developed. Biodiversity, if preserved, provides us a potential cushion for all future food needs, but only if species are identified, inventoried, and protected. The same is true for pharmaceuticals.

Nature's biodiversity is like a full medicine cabinet. Since 1959, 25% of all prescription drugs were originally derived from higher plants. In preliminary surveys, 3000 plants have been identified as having anticancer properties. The rosy periwinkle (*Catharanthus roseus*) of Madagascar contains two alkaloids that combat two forms of cancer. (Alkaloids are compounds found in certain plants that help the plant defend against insects and are potentially significant as human medicines; examples are atropine, quinine, and morphine.) Yet less than 3% of flowering plants have been examined for alkaloid content. It defies common sense to throw away the medicine cabinet before we even open the door to see what is inside.

Biosphere Reserves

Formal natural reserves are a possible strategy for slowing the loss of biodiversity and protecting this resource base. Setting up a *biosphere reserve* involves principles of *island biogeography*. Island communities are special places for study because of their spatial isolation and the relatively small number of species present. Islands resemble natural experiments, because the impact of individual factors, such as civilization, can be more easily assessed on islands than over larger continental areas.

Studies of islands also can assist in the study of mainland ecosystems,

for in many ways a park or biosphere reserve, surrounded by modified areas and artificial boundaries, is like an island. Indeed, a biosphere reserve is conceived as an ecological island in the midst of change. The intent is to establish a core in which genetic material is protected from outside disturbances, surrounded by a buffer zone that is, in turn, surrounded by a transition zone and experimental research areas. An important variable to consider in setting aside a biosphere reserve is any change that might occur in temperature and precipitation patterns as a result of global change. A carefully considered reserve could end up outside its natural range in several decades as ecotones shift.

Scientists predict that new, undisturbed reserves will not be possible in a decade, because pristine areas will be gone. The biosphere reserve program is coordinated by the Man and the Biosphere (MAB) Programme of UNESCO (http://www.unesco.org/mab/). More than 480 biosphere reserves are now operated voluntarily in 100 countries.

Not all protected areas are ideal bioregional entities. Some are simply imposed on existing park space and some remain in the planning stage, although they are officially designated. In Canada there are 12 biosphere reserve sites (Figure 20.1.3). The Ecological Monitoring and Assessment Network (http://www.eman-rese.ca/eman/) is a network of organizations and individuals in Canada that monitor ecology and ecosystem changes. There are also 40 national parks (see http://www.pc.gc.ca/progs/np-pn/list_alpha_e.asp for an alphabetical list) that exist to protect representative natural areas of Canadian significance. The National Parks Program's stated goal is to promote public understanding, appreciation, and enjoyment of natural areas while maintaining the areas in an unimpaired state for future generations. The United States has 90 biosphere reserves under various jurisdictions. For other MAB links check http://www.mabnet.org/misc/links.html.

Some of the best biosphere reserve examples have been in operation since the late 1970s and range from the struggling Everglades National Park in Florida, to the Changbai Reserve in China, to the Tai Forest on the Côte d'Ivoire (Ivory Coast), to the Charlevoix Biosphere Reserve in Québec, Canada. Added to these efforts is the work of the Nature Conservancy, which acquires land for preservation as a valuable part of the reserve (http://nature.org/).

The ultimate goal, about half achieved, is to establish at least one reserve in each of the 194 distinctive biogeographic communities presently identified. UNESCO and the World Conservation Monitoring Centre compile the United Nations' list of national parks and protected areas. Presently in these biogeographic communities, 6930 areas covering 657 million hectares (1.62 billion acres) are designated in some protective form, representing about 4.8% of national land area on the planet. Even though these are not all set aside to the degree of biosphere reserves, they do demonstrate progress toward preservation of our planet's plant and animal heritage.

The preservation of species diversity is a problem that must today be confronted by one species, *Homo sapiens*. . . . The diversity of species is worth preserving because it represents a wealth of knowledge that cannot be replaced. Moreover, today's extinctions are unlike those in previous eras, in which long periods of recovery could follow extinctions. The present situation is an inexorably irreversible one in which human overpopulation will destroy most species unless we plan for protection immediately. Accepting that the goal is worthwhile requires that more energy be devoted to planning and priorities and less to emotionalism and indignation [on all sides].*

*D. E. Koshland, Jr., "Preserving biodiversity," Science 253 (August 16, 1991): 717.

(continued)

Focus Study 20.1 *(continued)*

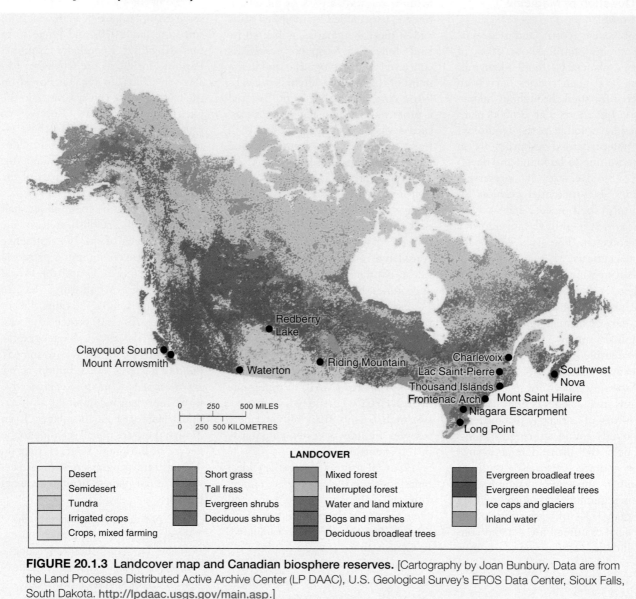

FIGURE 20.1.3 Landcover map and Canadian biosphere reserves. [Cartography by Joan Bunbury. Data are from the Land Processes Distributed Active Archive Center (LP DAAC), U.S. Geological Survey's EROS Data Center, Sioux Falls, South Dakota. http://lpdaac.usgs.gov/main.asp.]

broadleaf trees that lose their leaves during the dry season.

Areas of this biome have fewer than 40 rainy days during their four consecutive driest months, yet heavy monsoon downpours characterize their summers (see Chapter 6, especially Figure 6.20). The climates *tropical monsoon* and *tropical savanna* apply to these transitional communities between rain forests and tropical grasslands.

Portraying such a varied biome is difficult. In many areas humans disturb the natural biome, so that the savanna grassland adjoins the rain forest directly. The biome does include a gradation from wetter to drier areas: monsoonal forests, to open woodlands and scrub woodland, to thorn forests, to drought-resistant scrub species (Figure 20.7). In South America, an area of transitional tropical deciduous forest surrounds an area of savanna in southeastern Brazil and portions of Paraguay.

The monsoonal forests average 15 m (50 ft) high with no continuous canopy of leaves, graduating into orchardlike parkland with grassy openings or into areas choked by dense undergrowth. In more open tracts, a common tree is the acacia, with its flat top and usually thorny stems. These trees have branches that look like an upside-down umbrella (spreading and open skyward), as do trees in the tropical savanna.

Local names are given to these communities: the *caatinga* of the Bahia State of northeastern Brazil, the *chaco* area of Paraguay and northern Argentina, the *brigalow* scrub of Australia, and the *dornveld* of southern Africa. Figure 20.3 shows areas of this biome in Africa, extending from eastern Angola through Zambia to Tanzania and Kenya; in southeast Asia and portions of India, from interior Myanmar through northeastern Thailand; and in parts of Indonesia.

FIGURE 20.7 Kenyan landscapes.
Two views of the open thorn forest and savanna near and in the Samburu Reserve, Kenya, representing a broad ecotone between the two biomes. [Photos by (a) Gael Summer; (b) Stephen J. Krasemann/DRK Photo.]

The trees throughout most of this biome make poor lumber, but some, especially teak, may be valuable for fine cabinetry. In addition, some of the plants with dry-season adaptations produce usable waxes and gums, such as carnauba and palm-hard waxes. Animal life includes the koalas and cockatoos of Australia and the elephants, large cats, rodents, and ground-dwelling birds in other occurrences of this biome.

Tropical Savanna

The **tropical savanna** is large expanses of grassland, interrupted by trees and shrubs. This is a transitional biome between the tropical forests and semiarid tropical steppes and deserts. The savanna biome also includes treeless tracts of grasslands, and in dry savannas, grasses grow discontinuously in clumps, with bare ground between them. The trees of the savanna woodlands are characteristically flat-topped, in response to light and moisture regimes.

Savannas covered more than 40% of Earth's land surface before human intervention but were especially modified by human-caused fire. Fires occur annually throughout the biome. The timing of these fires is important. Early in the dry season they are beneficial and increase tree cover; late in the season they are very hot and kill trees and seeds. Savanna trees are adapted to resist the "cooler" fires.

Forests and elephant grasses averaging 5 m (16 ft) high once penetrated much farther into the dry regions, for they are known to survive there when protected. Savanna grasslands are much richer in humus than the wetter tropics and are better drained, thereby providing a better base for agriculture and grazing. Sorghums, wheat, and groundnuts (peanuts) are common commodities.

Tropical savannas receive their precipitation during less than 6 months of the year, when they are influenced by the shifting ITCZ. The rest of the year they are under the drier influence of shifting subtropical high-pressure cells. Savanna shrubs and trees are frequently *xerophytic*, or drought-resistant, with various adaptations to protect them from the dryness: small, thick leaves; rough bark; or leaf surfaces that are waxy or hairy.

Africa has the largest area of this biome, including the famous Serengeti Plains of Tanzania and Kenya and the Sahel region, south of the Sahara. Sections of Australia, India, and South America also are part of the savanna biome. Some of the local names for these lands include the *Llanos* in Venezuela, stretching along the coast and inland east of Lake Maricaibo and the Andes; the *Campo Cerrado* of Brazil and Guiana; and the *Pantanal* of southwestern Brazil.

Particularly in Africa, savannas are the home of large land mammals (zebra, giraffe, buffalo, gazelle, wildebeest, antelope, rhinoceros, elephant). They graze on savanna grasses (Figure 20.8) or feed upon the grazers themselves (lion, cheetah). Birds include the Ostrich, Martial Eagle (largest of all eagles), and Secretary Bird. Many species of venomous snakes as well as the crocodile are present in this biome.

However, in our lifetime we may see the reduction of these animal herds to zoo stock only, because of poaching and habitat losses, unless preservation efforts succeed. The loss of the rhino is discussed in Focus Study 20.1. Establishment of large tracts of savanna as biosphere reserves is critical for the preservation of this biome and its associated fauna.

Midlatitude Broadleaf and Mixed Forest

Moist continental climates support a mixed forest in areas of warm to hot summers and cool to cold winters. This **midlatitude broadleaf and mixed forest** biome includes several distinct communities in North America, Europe, and Asia. Along the Gulf of Mexico, relatively lush evergreen broadleaf forests occur. Northward are mixed deciduous and evergreen needleleaf stands associated with sandy soils and burning. When areas are given fire protection, broadleaf trees quickly take over. Pines (longleaf,

(a)

(b)

FIGURE 20.8 Animals and plants of the Serengeti Plains.
(a) Savanna landscape of the Serengeti Plains, with wildebeest, zebras, and thorn forest.
(b) Near Samburu, Kenya, Grevy's zebra and reticulated giraffe forage. [Photos by (a) Stephen
F. Cunha; (b) Galen Rowell/Mountain Light Photography, Inc.]

shortleaf, pitch, loblolly) predominate in the southeastern and Atlantic coastal plains. Into New England and westward in a narrow belt to the Great Lakes, white and red pines and eastern hemlock are the principal evergreens, mixed with deciduous oak, beech, hickory, maple, elm, chestnut, and many others (Figure 20.9a). In Canada, part of this forest biome is known as Carolinian forest and occurs in a small area of extreme southwestern Ontario. The region is heavily populated, industrialized, and disturbed by agricultural activity. A non-profit group called Carolinian Canada (**http://www.carolinian.org/site_map. htm**) works to protect and conserve this threatened forest ecosystem.

These mixed stands contain valuable timber, but their distribution has been greatly altered by human activity. Native stands of white pine in Michigan and Minnesota were removed before 1910; only later reforestation sustains their presence today. In northern China these forests have almost disappeared as a result of centuries of harvest. The forest species that once flourished in China are similar to species in eastern North America: oak, ash, walnut, elm, maple, and birch.

This biome is quite consistent in appearance from continent to continent and at one time represented the principal vegetation of the *humid subtropical hot summer* and *marine west coast* (cool summer, winter

(a)

(b)

FIGURE 20.9 The mixed broadleaf forest.
(a) Pioneer Mothers' Memorial Forest near Paoli, Indiana, is 36 hectares (88 acres) of old-growth forest, virtually undisturbed since around 1816, featuring black walnut, white oak, yellow poplar, white ash, and beech trees, among others. (b) A young white-tailed deer grazes in the undergrowth of a mixed forest. [Photos by (a) Bobbé Christopherson; (b) John Shaw/Tom Stack & Associates.]

drought) climatic regions of North America, Europe, and Asia.

A wide assortment of mammals, birds, reptiles, and amphibians is distributed throughout this biome. Representative animals (some migratory) include red fox, white-tail deer, southern flying squirrel, opossum, bear, and a great variety of birds, including Tanager and Cardinal (Figure 20.9b). To the north of this biome, poorer soils and colder climates favour stands of coniferous trees and a gradual transition to the northern needleleaf forests.

Needleleaf Forest and Montane Forest

Stretching from the east coast of Canada and the Atlantic provinces westward to Alaska and continuing from Siberia across the entire extent of Russia to the European Plain is the northern **needleleaf forest** biome, also called the **boreal forest** (Figure 20.10). A more open form of boreal forest, transitional to arctic and subarctic regions, is the **taiga** (Figure 20.3b). The Southern Hemisphere, lacking *humid microthermal* climates except in mountainous locales, has no such biome. But **montane forests** of needleleaf trees exist worldwide at high elevation.

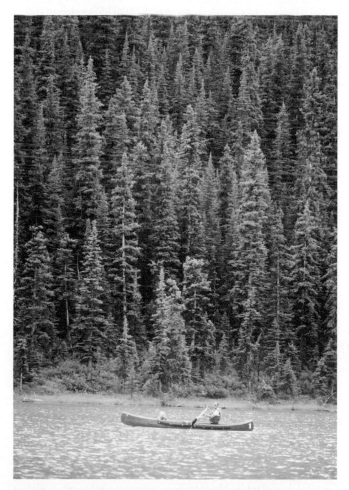

FIGURE 20.10 Boreal forest of Canada (boreal means "northern"). [Photo by Robert Christopherson.]

Boreal forests of pine, spruce, fir, and larch occupy most of the subarctic climates on Earth that are dominated by trees. Although these forests are similar in formation, individual species vary between North America and Eurasia. The larch (*Larix*) is interesting because it is the rare needleleaf tree that loses its needles in the winter months, perhaps as a defence against the extreme cold of its native Siberia (see the Verkhoyansk climograph and photograph in Figure 10.19, Chapter 10). Larches also occur in North America.

Boreal forest is Canada's largest biome and, to balance the demands placed on this forest, the Canadian Forest Service created the Model Forest Network (http://www.modelforest.net/cmfn/en/) in 1992. Of the 11 Model Forests, 5 are boreal, 2 are subalpine/montane/boreal, and 1 is a transition between the boreal and the Great Lakes–St. Lawrence forest type. Table 20.2 summarizes the boreal examples from the Canadian Model Forest Network, and a map of the locations of all Canadian Model Forests is found in Figure 20.11.

The Sierra Nevada, Rocky Mountains, Alps, and Himalayas have similar forest communities occurring at lower latitudes. Douglas fir and white fir grow in the western mountains in Canada and the United States. Economically, these forests are important for lumbering, with trees for lumber occurring in the southern margins of the biome and for pulpwood throughout the middle and northern portions. Present logging practices and the sustainability of these yields are issues of increasing controversy.

In the Sierra Nevada montane forests of California, the giant sequoias naturally occur in 70 isolated groves. These trees are Earth's largest (in terms of biomass) living things, although they began as a small seed (Figure 20.12a). Some of these *Sequoia gigantea* exceed 8 m in diameter (28 ft) and 83 m (270 ft) in height. The largest of these is the General Sherman tree in Sequoia National Park (Figure 20.12c); it is estimated to be 3500 years old. The bark is fibrous, a half-metre thick, and lacks resins, so it effectively resists fire. Imagine the lightning strikes and fires that must have moved past the Sherman tree in 35 centuries! Standing among these giant trees is an overwhelming experience and creates a sense of the majesty of the biosphere.

Certain regions of the northern needleleaf biome experience permafrost conditions, discussed in Chapter 17. When coupled with rocky and poorly developed soils, these conditions generally limit the existence of trees to those with shallow rooting systems. The summer thaw of surface-active layers results in muskeg (moss-covered) bogs and Organic (Histosols) soils of poor drainage and stability. Soils of the taiga are typically Podzolic (Spodosols) subject to podzolization), characteristically acidic and leached of humus and clays. Global warming is altering conditions in the high latitudes, causing increased melting and depth in the permafrost active layer. By the late 1990s, some affected forests were beginning to die in response to waterlogging in soils.

Table 20.2 Canadian Model Forest Network

Model Forest	Forest Region	Size (ha)	Principal Trees	Ecozone* Name	Province	Focus
Western Newfoundland 17 Partners	Boreal	923,000	black spruce, white birch, and balsam fir	Boreal Shield	Newfoundland and Labrador	Pine marten reserve; research; education
Waswanipi Cree 13 Partners	Boreal	209, 600	black spruce, fir, grey pine, white spruce, larch, trembling aspen	Boreal Shield	Québec	Maintain and enhance quality of the area; benefit Aboriginal and white birch other users; assure economic, social and cultural development of Waswanipi First Nation.
Lake Abitibi 27 Partners	Boreal	1,100,000	black spruce, white spruce, jack pine, and larch	Boreal Shield	Ontario	Harvesting and Regeneration Protection system (HARP); education
Manitoba 25+ Partners	Boreal	1,050,000	hybrid aspen, white spruce, ash, chestnut, poplar, black spruce, jack pines	Boreal Shield	Manitoba	Ecosystem-based management; indicators of sustainable management; Aboriginal knowledge
Prince Albert 10 Partners	Boreal	360,000	balsam fir, paper birch, aspen	Boreal Plains	Saskatchewan	Ecosystem health and local level indicators of sustainable forest management; communication and knowledge exchange; integrated resource management
Foothills 40 Partners	Subalpine/ Montane/ Boreal	2,750,000	lodgepole pine, white spruce, aspen poplar, black spruce, balsam poplar	Montane Cordillera	Alberta	Data collection on indigenous fish, plants, and wildlife; natural disturbance studies; grizzly bear habits and habitat
McGregor	Subalpine/ Montane/ Boreal	181,000	hybrid spruce, lodgepole pine	Montane Cordillera	British Columbia	Forest research; modelling; scenario planning; management system development
Bas-Saint-Laurent 40+ Partners	Great Lakes– St. Lawrence/ Boreal	113,100	balsam fir, white spruce, eastern white cedar, black spruce, tamarack, loblolly pine, red pine, sugar maple, white birch, yellow birch, red maple, trembling aspen, balsam poplar	Atlantic Maritime	Québec	Forest management strategy experiments: tenant farming and group management

*An "ecozone" is a large-scale ecosystem, roughly equivalent to a biome.

Source: Summarized from Model Forest Fact Sheets, **http://www.modelforest.net/cmfn/en/forests/**, 2004.

Representative fauna in this biome include wolf, elk, moose (the largest in the deer family), bear, lynx, beaver, wolverine, marten, small rodents, and migratory birds during the brief summer season (Figure 20.13). Birds include hawks and eagles, several species of grouse, Pine Grosbeak, Clark's Nutcracker, and several owls. About 50 species of insects particularly adapted to the presence of coniferous trees inhabit the biome.

FIGURE 20.11 Canadian Model Forest Network.
The Canadian Forestry Service and the Government of Canada cooperated to develop a program to manage the forests of Canada. The program is designed to allow sustainable use of the forest while balancing conservation of natural areas. Model Forests are noted on map.
[Adapted from *The Atlas of Canada* http://atlas.gc.ca/site/index.html. © 2004, used with the permission of Natural Resources Canada.]

(a)

(b)

(c)

FIGURE 20.12 Sequoia: the seed, the seedling, the giant.
(a) A *Sequoia gigantea* seed. About 300 seeds are in each sequoia cone. (b) Seedling at approximately 50 years of age. (c) The General Sherman tree in Sequoia National Park, California. This tree is probably wider than a standard classroom. The first branch is 45 m (150 ft) off the ground and is 2 m (6.5 ft) in diameter! [Photos by Robert Christopherson.]

FIGURE 20.13 Animals of the northern needleleaf forest. An male elk (*Cervus Canadensis*) in a snow storm looking for any available vegetation to eat during winter among needleleaf trees. [Photo by Steven K. Huhtala.]

(a)

(b)

FIGURE 20.14 Temperate rain forest.
(a) The temperate rain forest of Macmillan Provincial Park, central Vancouver Island, British Columbia—an old-growth Douglas fir forest, with western red cedar and hemlock, sword and bracken ferns, and hanging mosses. (b) The Northern Spotted Owl is characteristic of the temperate rain forest. [Photos by (a) Bobbé Christopherson; (b) Greg Vaughn/Tony Stone Images.]

Temperate Rain Forest

Lush forests at middle and high latitudes are in the **temperate rain forest** biome. In North America, it occurs only along narrow margins of the Pacific Northwest (Figure 20.14a). Some similar types of forest exist in southern China, small portions of southern Japan, New Zealand, and a few areas of southern Chile.

This biome contrasts with the diversity of the equatorial and tropical rain forest in that only a few species make up the bulk of the trees. The rain forest of the Olympic Peninsula in Washington State is a mixture of broadleaf and needleleaf trees, huge ferns, and thick undergrowth. Precipitation approaching 400 cm (160 in.) per year on the western slopes, moderate air temperatures, summer fog, and an overall maritime influence produce this moist, lush vegetation community. Animals include bear, badger, deer, wild pig, wolf, bobcat, and fox. The trees are home to numerous bird species, including the famous Spotted Owl (Figure 20.14b).

The tallest trees in the world occur in this biome—the coastal redwoods (*Sequoia sempervirens*). Their distribution is shown on the map in Figure 19.13a in Chapter 19. These trees can exceed 1500 years of age and typically range in height from 60 to 90 m (200 to 300 ft), with some exceeding 100 m (330 ft). Virgin stands of other representative trees, such as Douglas fir, spruce, cedar, and hemlock, have been reduced by timber harvests to a few remaining valleys in Oregon and Washington, less than 10% of the original forest. Replanting and secondary-growth forests are predominant. In similar forests in Chile, large-scale timber harvests and new mills began operations in 2000.

Many studies by the U.S. Forest Service and others noted the failing ecology of these forest ecosystems and suggested that timber management plans should include ecosystem preservation as a priority. The ultimate solution must be one of economic and ecological synthesis rather than continuing conflict and forest losses—the forests can't be all cut down, nor can they be all preserved. The opposing sides in this conflict between logging and society interests should combine their efforts in a sustainable forestry model.

Mediterranean Shrubland

The **Mediterranean shrubland** biome, also referred to as a temperate shrubland, occupies those regions poleward of the shifting subtropical high-pressure cells. As those cells shift poleward with the high summer Sun, they cut off available storm systems and moisture. Their stable high-pressure presence produces the characteristic *Mediterranean dry summer* and establishes conditions conducive to fire.

Plant ecologists think that this biome is well adapted to frequent wildfires, for many of its characteristically deep-rooted plants have the ability to resprout from their roots after a fire. Earlier stands of evergreen woodlands (holm or evergreen oak) no longer dominate.

FIGURE 20.15 Mediterranean chaparral.
Chaparral vegetation associated with the Mediterranean dry-summer climate in southern California. [Photo by Bobbé Christopherson.]

FIGURE 20.16 Grasslands of North America.
Midlatitude grasslands of Alberta, Canada, under cultivation. [Photo by Fotopic/Omni–Photo Communications, Inc.]

The dominant shrub formations that occupy these regions are stunted and able to withstand hot-summer drought. The vegetation is *sclerophyllous* (from *sclero*, for "hard," and *phyllos*, for "leaf"). It averages a metre or two in height and has deep, well-developed roots, leathery leaves, and uneven low branches.

Typically, the vegetation varies between woody shrubs covering more than 50% of the ground and grassy woodlands covering 25%–60% of the ground. In California, the Spanish word *chaparro* for "scrubby evergreen" gives us the word **chaparral** for this vegetation type (Figure 20.15). This scrubland includes species such as manzanita, toyon, red bud, ceanothus, mountain mahogany, blue and live oaks, and the dreaded poison oak.

A counterpart to the California chaparral in the Mediterranean region is the *maquis*, which includes live and cork oak trees (source of cork), as well as pine and olive trees. The overall similar appearance of the California and Spanish oak savannas is demonstrated in Figure 10.14c and d in Chapter 10. In Chile, such a region is the *mattoral*; in southwestern Australia, *mallee scrub*. In Australia, the bulk of the eucalyptus species is sclerophyllous in form and structure in whichever climate it occurs.

As described in Chapter 10, Mediterranean climates are important in commercial agriculture for subtropical fruits, vegetables, and nuts, with many food types produced only in this biome (e.g., artichokes, olives, almonds). Larger animals, such as several types of deer, are grazers and browsers, with coyote, wolf, and bobcat as predators. Many rodents, other small animals, and a variety of birds also proliferate.

Midlatitude Grasslands

Of all the natural biomes, the **midlatitude grasslands** are the most modified by human activity. Here are the world's "breadbaskets"—regions that produce bountiful grain (wheat and corn), soybeans, and livestock (hogs and cattle). Figure 20.16 shows a typical midlatitude grassland under cultivation. In these regions, the only naturally occurring trees were deciduous broadleaf trees along streams and other limited sites. These regions are called grasslands because of the predominance of grasslike plants before human intervention:

> In this study of vegetation, attention has been devoted to grass because grass is the dominant feature of the Plains and is at the same time an index to their history. Grass is the visible feature which distinguishes the Plains from the desert. Grass grows, has its natural habitat, in the transition area between timber and desert. . . . The history of the Plains is the history of the grasslands.*

In North America, tallgrass prairies once rose to heights of 2 m (6.5 ft) and extended westward to about the 98th meridian, with shortgrass prairies in the drier lands farther west. The 98th meridian is roughly the location of the 51-cm (20-in.) isohyet, with wetter conditions to the east and drier conditions to the west.

The deep, tough sod of these grasslands posed problems for the first European settlers, as did the climate. The self-scouring steel plow, introduced in 1837 by John Deere, allowed the interlaced grass sod to be broken apart, freeing the soils for agriculture. Other inventions were critical to opening this region and solving its unique spatial problems: barbed wire (the fencing material for a treeless prairie); well-drilling techniques developed by Pennsylvania oil drillers but used for water wells; windmills for pumping; and railroads to conquer the distances.

*From *The Great Plains*, ©1931 by Walter Prescott Webb, published by Ginn and Company, Needham Heights, MA., p. 32.

Few patches of the original prairies (tall grasslands) or steppes (short grasslands) remain within this biome. For prairies alone, the reduction of natural vegetation went from 100 million hectares (250 million acres) down to a few areas of several hundred hectares each. The Nature Conservancy of Canada is working in conjunction with the Nature Conservancy in the United States to develop a natural corridor that will extend from Canada to the American Midwest. The northern extent of this corridor, the Manitoba Tallgrass Prairie Preserve, strives to preserve the last significant remnants of tallgrass prairie in Canada. More than 5000 hectares (13,000 acres) have been preserved, but another 4000 hectares (10,000 acres) are needed to make this preserve ecologically viable.

In the United States, the Tallgrass Prairie National Preserve is a 4410-hectare (10,894-acre) section of prairie located in the Flint Hills of Kansas. This is the only national park unit preserving this vestige of the former grasslands that covered much of the North American Great Plains. A state-designated 10-hectare (25-acre) remnant of the "prairie" is located 8 km north of Ames, Iowa. This is a patch of original grassland that never has felt the plow. The map in Figure 20.3 shows the natural location of these former prairie and steppe grasslands.

Outside North America, the Pampas of Argentina and Uruguay and the grasslands of Ukraine are characteristic midlatitude grassland biomes. In each region of the world where these grasslands have occurred, human development of them was critical to territorial expansion.

This biome is the home of large grazing animals, including deer, pronghorn, and bison (the almost complete annihilation of the latter is part of American history, Figure 20.17). Grasshoppers and other insects feed on the grasses and crops as well, and gophers, prairie dogs, ground squirrels, Turkey Vultures, grouse, and Prairie Chickens are on the land. Predators include coyote, the nearly extinct black-footed ferret, badger, and birds of prey—hawks, eagles, and owls.

FIGURE 20.17 Bison graze on the grasslands of Montana's National Bison range. [Photo by Lowell Georgia/CORBIS.]

Deserts

Earth's **desert biomes** cover more than one-third of its land area, as is obvious in Figure 20.3. In Chapter 15, we examined desert landscapes and in Chapter 10 desert climates. On a planet with such a rich biosphere, the deserts stand out as unique regions of fascinating adaptations for survival. Much as a group of humans in the desert might behave with short supplies, plant communities also compete for water and site advantage. Some desert plants, called *ephemerals*, wait years for a rainfall event, at which time their seeds quickly germinate and the plants develop, flower, and produce new seeds, which then rest again until the next rainfall event. The seeds of some xerophytic species open only when fractured by the tumbling, churning action of flash floods cascading down a desert arroyo, and, of course, such an event produces the moisture that a germinating seed needs.

Perennial desert plants employ other adaptive features to cope with the desert. Unique xerophytic features include

- Long, deep taproots (example, the mesquite); succulence (thick, fleshy, water-holding tissue, such as that of cacti),
- Spreading root systems to maximize water availability, waxy coatings and fine hairs on leaves to retard water loss, leafless conditions during dry periods (example, palo verde and ocotillo),
- Reflective surfaces to reduce leaf temperatures,
- Tissue that tastes bad to discourage herbivores.

The creosote bush (*Lorrea tridentata*) sends out a wide pattern of roots and contaminates the surrounding soil with toxins that prevent the germination of other creosote seeds, possible competitors for water. When a creosote bush dies, surrounding plants or germinating seeds will occupy the abandoned site, but they must wait for infrequent rains to remove the toxins, according to one hypothesis.

The faunas of both warm and cold deserts are limited by the extreme conditions and include few resident large animals. Exceptions are the desert bighorn sheep (in nearby mountains) and the camel, which can lose up to 30% of its body weight in water without suffering (for humans, a 10%–12% loss is dangerous). Some representative desert animals are the ring-tail cat, kangaroo rat, lizards, scorpions, and snakes. Most of these animals are quite secretive and become active only at night, when temperatures are lower. In addition, various birds have adapted to desert conditions and available food sources—for example, Roadrunners, thrashers, Ravens, wrens, hawks, grouse, and nighthawks.

We are witnessing an unwanted expansion of the desert biome, discussed in Chapter 15 and Figure 15.26. This process, known as *desertification*, is now a worldwide phenomenon along the margins of semiarid and arid lands. Desertification is due principally to poor agricultural practices (overgrazing and agricultural activities that abuse soil structure and fertility), improper soil-moisture management, erosion and salinization, deforestation, and the ongoing climatic change.

Earth's deserts are subdivided into desert and semi-desert associations, to distinguish those with expanses of bare ground from those covered by xerophytic plants of various types. The two broad associations are further separated into warm deserts, principally tropical and subtropical, and cold deserts, principally midlatitude.

Warm Desert and Semidesert Earth's **warm desert and semidesert** biomes are caused by the presence of dry air and low precipitation from subtropical high-pressure cells. These areas are very dry, as evidenced by the Atacama Desert of northern Chile, where only a minute amount of rain has ever been recorded—a 30-year annual average of only 0.05 cm (0.02 in.)! Like the Atacama, the true deserts are under the influence of the descending, drying, and stable air of high-pressure systems from 8 to 12 months of the year.

Remember that these dry regions are defined by low amounts of precipitation that fail to satisfy high amounts of potential evapotranspiration. Deserts receive precipitation that is less than one-half of potential evapotranspiration. *Semiarid steppe* climates receive precipitation that is more than one-half of annual potential evapotranspiration. A few of the subtropical deserts—such as those in Chile, Western Sahara, and Namibia—are right on the seacoast and are influenced by cool offshore ocean currents. As a result, these true deserts experience summer fog that mists the plant and animal populations with needed moisture.

The equatorward margin of the subtropical high-pressure cell is a region of transition to savanna, thorn tree, scrub woodland, and tropical seasonal forest. Poleward of the warm deserts, the subtropical cells shift to produce the Mediterranean dry-summer regime along west coasts and may grade into cool deserts elsewhere.

Vegetation ranges from almost none in the arid deserts to numerous xerophytic shrubs, succulents, and thorn tree forms. The lower Sonoran Desert of southern Arizona is a warm desert (Figure 20.18). This desert landscape features the unique saguaro cactus (*Carnegiea gigantea*), which, if undisturbed, grows to many metres in height and up to 200 years in age. First blooms do not appear until it is 50 to 75 years old!

Cold Desert and Semidesert The **cold desert and semidesert** biomes tend to occur in middle latitudes. Here, seasonal shifting of subtropical high pressure is of some influence less than 6 months of the year. Interior locations are dry because of their distance from moisture sources or their location in rain-shadow areas on the lee side of mountain ranges, such as the Sierra Nevada of the western United States, the Himalayas, and the Andes. The combination of interior location and rain-shadow positioning produces the cold deserts of the Great Basin of western North America.

Winter snows occur in the cold deserts, but generally they are light. Summers are hot, with highs from 30°C to 40°C (86°F to 104°F). Nighttime lows, even in the summer, can cool 10–20 C° (18–36 F°) from the daytime high. The dryness, generally clear skies, and sparse vegeta-

FIGURE 20.18 Sonoran Desert scene.
Characteristic vegetation in the Lower Sonoran Desert west of Tucson, Arizona (32° N; elevation 900 m, or 2950 ft).
[Photo by Robert Christopherson.]

tion lead to high radiative heat loss and cool evenings. Many areas of these cold deserts that are covered by sagebrush and scrub vegetation were actually dry shortgrass regions in the past, before extensive grazing altered their ecology. The deserts in the upper Great Basin today are the result of more than a century of such cultural practices.

Arctic and Alpine Tundra

High Latitude Animals Photo Gallery
Geographic Scenes: East Greenland
Photo Gallery

NOTEBOOK

The **arctic tundra** is found in the extreme northern area of North America, around the coast of Greenland, and in Russia, bordering on the Arctic Ocean and generally north of the 10°C (50°F) isotherm for the warmest month. Daylength varies greatly throughout the year, seasonally changing from almost continuous day to continuous night. Winters in this biome, *tundra* climate

(a)

(b)

FIGURE 20.19 Arctic tundra.
(a) Tundra on the Kamchatka Peninsula, Russia. The Uzon Caldera is in the centre-background mountain range. (b) Lush by tundra standards, flowers, grasses, mosses, and dwarf willow flourish in the cold climate of the Arctic. [Photos by (a) Wolfgang Kaehler Photography; (b) Bobbé Christopherson.]

classification, are long and cold; cool summers are brief. The region, except for a few portions of Alaska and Siberia, was covered by ice during all of the Pleistocene glacial episodes.

Intensely cold continental polar air masses and stable high-pressure anticyclones govern tundra winters. A growing season of sorts lasts only 60–80 days, and even then frosts can occur at any time. Vegetation is fragile in this flat, treeless world; soils are poorly developed periglacial surfaces, which are underlain by permafrost. In the summer months, only the surface horizons thaw, thus producing a mucky surface of poor drainage. Roots can penetrate only to the depth of thawed ground, usually about a metre. The surface is shaped by freeze-thaw cycles that create the frozen-ground phenomena discussed in Chapter 17.

Tundra vegetation consists of low, ground-level herbaceous plant species, such as sedges, mosses, arctic meadow grass, snow lichen, and some woody dwarf willow (Figure 20.19). Owing to the short growing season, some perennials form flower buds one summer and open them for pollination the next. Animals of the tundra include musk ox, caribou, reindeer, rabbit, ptarmigans, lemmings, other small rodents (important food for the larger carnivores), wolf, fox, weasel, Snowy Owls, polar bears (in nearby marine and pack ice environments), and, of course, mosquitoes. The tundra is an important breeding ground for geese, swans, and other waterfowl.

Alpine tundra is similar to arctic tundra, but it can occur at lower latitudes because it is associated with high elevation. This biome usually is described as above the timberline, that elevation above which trees cannot grow. Timberlines increase in elevation equatorward in both hemispheres. Alpine tundra communities occur in the Andes near the equator, the White Mountains and Sierra of California, the American and Canadian Rockies, the

Alps, and Mount Kilimanjaro of equatorial Africa, as well as in mountains from the Middle East to Asia.

Alpine meadows feature grasses, herbaceous annuals (small plants), and stunted shrubs, such as willows and heaths. Because alpine locations are frequently windy sites, many plants appear to have been sculpted by the wind. Alpine tundra can experience permafrost conditions. Characteristic fauna include mountain goats, bighorn sheep, elk, and voles (Figure 20.20).

Because the tundra biome is of such low productivity, it is fragile. Disturbances such as tire tracks, hydroelectric projects, and mineral exploitation leave marks that persist for hundreds of years. As development continues, the region will face even greater challenges from oil spills, contamination, and disruption (News Report 20.3).

FIGURE 20.20 Alpine tundra conditions.
An alpine setting at the edge of the forest and grazing mountain goats in the Canadian Rockies. [Photo by Robert Christopherson.]

News Report 20.3

ANWR Faces Threats

Planning continues for oil exploration and development of the Arctic National Wildlife Refuge (ANWR) on Alaska's North Slope. The May 2001 U.S. *National Energy Policy* recommends oil exploration and development in ANWR, using the latest environmentally sensitive techniques. However, the U.S. Senate defeated the plan in 2002. Political and corporate pressure is fairly constant to exploit these expected reserves of fossil fuels, and the U.S. Congress again began another push for drilling authorization in 2005. In 2008, after delaying a decision on listing the polar bears the U.S. administration went ahead with an ocean floor oil lease auction in the Chukchi Sea off Alaska.

This pristine wilderness is above the Arctic Circle, bordering on the Beaufort Sea and adjoining the Yukon Territory of Canada (Figure 20.3.1). The refuge area sustains almost 200,000 caribou, polar and grizzly bears, musk oxen, and wolves. Some have referred to it as "America's Serengeti," given the annual migration of hundreds of thousands of large animals.

The ANWR remains the only portion of Alaska's Arctic coast that is not open to oil and gas exploration at this time—the other 90% is open. But controversy over this refuge continues, as political and corporate pressures mount to begin oil exploration. In 1995, Congress considered potential ANWR lease revenues in its Budget Resolution, implying a green light for development. A presidential veto stopped this Budget Reconciliation Act. A 1998 USGS assessment disclosed that the oil under the Arctic Refuge coastal plain is likely held in many small reservoirs. Recovering this oil would require extensive alteration of the Arctic National Wildlife Refuge landscape, a point disputed in the National Energy Policy.

Petroleum development could be devastating to arctic wildlife. The Porcupine caribou herd, for example,

FIGURE 20.3.1 Arctic National Wildlife Refuge.
In Alaska's Arctic National Wildlife Refuge, Mount Chamberlin, the second-highest peak of the Brooks Range, overlooks tundra in the foreground. Is this region destined for petroleum exploration and development or for continued preservation as wilderness? [Photo by Scott T. Smith.]

FIGURE 20.3.2 Caribou migration routes and calving grounds in the Arctic National Wildlife Refuge.
[Courtesy of the Alaska Center for the Environment.]

is a population of tundra caribou that inhabit Alaska, Yukon, and Northwest Territories (Figure 20.3.2). Most of the herd migrates to the Alaska coastal plain to calve in early June. The calving area is fairly small and 80–85% of the herd use it year after year. Because the caribou come from areas both within ANWR and from areas in Yukon and Northwest Territories, this is a trans-

boundary issue. In Yukon Territory (Figure 20.3.3), the Canadian and territorial governments and First Nations people established the Ivvavik and Vuntut National Parks to protect the coastal tundra and adjacent mountains. Oil exploration is not permitted in these areas.

In addition to wildlife, oil extraction could be devastating to

(continued)

News Report 20.3 *(continued)*

the fragile tundra, according to a USGS study released in 2002. The cost of development would price the oil at over $30 per barrel. The estimated oil reserve in the ANWR, approximately 3.2 billion barrels (less than a 5-month supply at present U.S. demand levels), could be offset simply by a small increase in U.S. automobile efficiency. However, 2002 and 2003 marked years when mileage efficiency decreased. In 2002, federal funding toward improving automobile mileage efficiency was formally dropped and research monies for hybrid car technology stopped in favour of fuel cell research for the future. Clearly, economic ventures should be weighed against the ecosystem itself, its limitations and its uniqueness, and a total assessment of all costs to the consumer.

FIGURE 20.3.3 Arctic National Wildlife Refuge and Yukon parks and reserves share a boundary.
This map shows the birthplace and nursery grounds of the Porcupine caribou herd. [Courtesy of the Alaska Center for the Environment.]

Summary and Review—Terrestrial Biomes

■ *Define* the concept of biogeographic realms of plants and animals, and *define* ecotone, terrestrial ecosystem, and biome.

Earth is the only planet in the Solar System with a biosphere. An impressive feature of the living Earth is its diversity, which biogeographers categorize into discrete spatial biomes for analysis and study. The interplay among supporting physical factors within Earth's ecosystem determines the distribution of plant and animal communities. A **biogeographic realm** of plants and animals is a geographic region in which a group of species evolved. This recognition was a start at understanding distinct regions of flora and fauna and the broader pattern of terrestrial ecosystems. A boundary transition zone adjoining ecosystems is an **ecotone**.

A **terrestrial ecosystem** is a self-sustaining association of plants and animals and their abiotic environment that is characterized by specific plant formation classes. A **biome** is a large, stable ecosystem characterized by specific plant and animal communities. Biomes carry the name of the dominant vegetation because it is the most easily identified feature: forest, savanna, grassland, shrubland, desert, tundra.

biogeographic realm (p. 670)
ecotone (p. 671)
terrestrial ecosystem (p. 671)
biome (p. 671)

1. Reread the opening quotations and analysis in this chapter. What clues do they give you to the path ahead for Earth's forests and ecosystems? Is our future direction controllable? Sustainable? Explain.

2. What is a biogeographic realm? How is the world subdivided according to botanical (plant) types?

3. Describe a transition zone between two ecosystems. How wide is an ecotone? Explain.

4. Define *biome*. What is the basis of the designation?

■ *Define* six formation classes and the life-form designations, and *explain* their relationship to plant communities.

Biomes are divided into more specific vegetation units called **formation classes**. The structure and appearance of the vegetation is described: rain forest, needleleaf forest, Mediterranean shrubland, arctic tundra, and so forth. Specific life-form designations include trees, lianas, shrubs, herbs, bryophytes, epiphytes (plants growing aboveground on other plants), and thallophytes (lacking true leaves, stems, or roots, including bacteria, fungi, algae, and lichens).

formation classes (p. 672)

5. Distinguish between formation classes and life-form designations as a basis for spatial classification.

■ *Describe* 10 major terrestrial biomes, and *locate* them on a world map.

Biomes are Earth's major terrestrial ecosystems, each named for its dominant plant community. The 10 major biomes are generalized from numerous formation classes that describe vegetation. Ideally, a biome represents a mature community of natural vegetation. In reality, few undisturbed biomes exist in the world, for most have been modified by human activity. Many of Earth's plant and animal communities are experiencing an accelerated rate of change that could produce dramatic alterations within our lifetime.

For an overview of Earth's 10 major terrestrial biomes and their vegetation characteristics, soil orders, climate-type designations, annual precipitation range, temperature patterns, and water balance characteristics, please review Table 20.1.

equatorial and tropical rain forest (p. 677)
tropical seasonal forest and scrub (p. 679)
tropical savanna (p. 685)
midlatitude broadleaf and mixed forest (p. 685)
needleleaf forest (p. 687)
boreal forest (p. 687)
taiga (p. 687)
montane forest (p. 687)
temperate rain forest (p. 690)
Mediterranean shrubland (p. 690)
chaparral (p. 691)
midlatitude grasslands (p. 691)
desert biomes (p. 692)
warm desert and semidesert (p. 693)
cold desert and semidesert (p. 693)
arctic tundra (p. 693)
alpine tundra (p. 694)

6. Using the integrative chart in Table 20.1 and the world map in Figure 20.3, select any two biomes and study the correlation of vegetation characteristics, soil, moisture, and climate with their spatial distribution. Then, contrast the two using each characteristic.

7. Describe the equatorial and tropical rain forests. Why is the rainforest floor somewhat clear of plant growth? Why are logging activities for specific species so difficult there?

8. What issues surround the deforestation of the rain forest? What is the impact of these losses on the rest of the biosphere? What new threat to the rain forest has emerged?

9. What do *caatinga*, *chaco*, *brigalow*, and *dornveld* refer to? Explain.

10. Describe the role of fire or fire ecology in the tropical savanna biome and the midlatitude broadleaf and mixed forest biome.

11. Why does the northern needleleaf forest biome not exist in the Southern Hemisphere, except in mountainous regions? Where is this biome located in the Northern Hemisphere, and what is its relationship to climate type?

12. In which biome do we find Earth's tallest trees? Which biome is dominated by small, stunted plants, lichens, and mosses?

13. What type of vegetation predominates in the Mediterranean dry-summer climates? Describe the adaptations necessary for these plants to survive.

14. What is the significance of the 98th meridian in terms of North American grasslands? What types of inventions enabled humans to cope with the grasslands?

15. Describe some of the unique adaptations found in a desert biome.

16. What is desertification (review from Chapter 15 and this chapter)? Explain its impact.

17. What physical weathering processes are specifically related to the tundra biome? What types of plants and animals are found there?

■ *Relate* human impacts, real and potential, to several of the biomes.

The equatorial and tropical rainforest biome is undergoing rapid deforestation. Because the rain forest is Earth's most diverse biome and is important to the climate system, such losses are creating great concern among citizens, scientists, and nations. Efforts are underway worldwide to set aside and protect remaining representative sites within most of Earth's principal biomes. These biosphere reserves are coordinated by the Man and the Biosphere (MAB) Programme of UNESCO. Nearly 480 such biosphere reserves, covering some 12 million hectares (30 million acres), are now operated voluntarily in 100 countries.

18. What is the relationship between island biogeography and biosphere reserves? Describe a biosphere reserve. What are the goals?

19. Compare the map in Figure 20.3 with the composite satellite image inside the front cover of this text. What correlations can you make between the local summertime portrait of Earth's biosphere and the biomes identified on the map?

Critical Thinking

A. Given the information presented in this chapter about deforestation in the tropics, assess the present situation. What are the main issues? What natural assets are at stake? Natural resources versus sovereign state rights? How are global biodiversity and greenhouse warming related to these issues? What is the perspective of the less-developed countries that possess most of the rain forest? What is the perspective of the more-developed countries and their transnational corporations and millions of environmentally active citizens? What kind of action plan would you develop to accommodate all parties? How would you proceed?

B. Using Figure 20.3 (biomes), Figure 10.5 (climates), Figures 10.2 and 9.5 (precipitation), and Figure 8.2 (air masses), and the printed graphic scales on these maps, consider the following hypothetical. Assume a northward climatic shift in Canada and the United States of 500 km (310 mi) (in other words imagine moving North America 500 km south, to simulate climatic categories shifting north). Describe your analysis of the new conditions in the Prairies of Canada. Describe your analysis of the new conditions from New York through New England and into the Canadian Maritime provinces. What economic dislocations and relocations do you envision as a result of this hypothetical climate shift?

Tourists in raincoats stand under the mist from the Canadian Falls as the Niagara River plunges 57 m (187 ft) over the Niagara Escarpment. Note how the power of the falling water undercuts the cliff, which will eventually produce further collapse. This nickpoint in stream gradient has migrated upstream toward Lake Erie 11 km (7 mi) during the past 12,000 years. [Photo by Bobbé Christopherson.]

Earth and
the Human
Denominator

■ Key Learning Concepts

After reading the chapter, you should be able to:

- **Determine** an answer for Carl Sagan's question, "Who speaks for Earth?"

- **Describe** the growth in human population, and **speculate** on possible future trends.

- **Analyze** "An Oily Bird," and *relate* your analysis to energy consumption patterns in Canada and the United States.

- **List** the subjects of environmental agreements, conventions, and protocols, and **relate** them to physical geography and Earth systems science.

- **List** and **discuss** 12 paradigms for the twenty-first century.

- **Appraise** your place in the biosphere, and **realize** your relation to Earth systems.

During my space flight, I came to appreciate my profound connection to the home planet and the process of life evolving in our special corner of the Universe, and I grasped that I was part of a vast and mysterious dance whose outcome will be determined largely by human values and actions.*

Earth can be observed from profound vantage points, as this astronaut experienced on the 1969 *Apollo IX* mission. Since November 2000, the International Space Station (ISS) has operated at an orbital

*Rusty Sweickart, "Our backs against the bomb, our eyes on the stars," *Discovery*, July 1987, p. 62.

699

FIGURE 21.1 Our orbital perspective—Earth's Space Station.
The International Space Station (ISS) as it looked August 2007. The ISS began scientific operations in November 2000. The station orbits at a speed of 28,000 kmph (17,400 mph), orbiting Earth in 91.6 min., 15.7 times a day. [Photo of ISS courtesy of NASA.]

altitude of about 400 km (250 mi), in the upper reaches of Earth's thermosphere. Just imagine, a 16-nation coalition has built a scientific workstation, in orbit, that is 44.5 m long, 78 m wide, and 27.5 m tall (146 ft by 256 ft by 90 ft), and it is not yet finished (Figure 21.1). The 219-metric ton (482,345-lb) complex has had more than 120 astronauts and scientists aboard in 392 m³ (14,000 ft³) of pressurized work space. Canada is a full partner working on the ISS.

Several hundred scientific investigations and experiments are completed or underway, to help us better understand Earth and life systems through research in the unique space environment. All life-support supplies must be brought from Earth. Water recycling and purification techniques provide the bulk of the water needed. Oxygen is electrolytically derived from water and supplemented by compressed oxygen. Enormous solar-panel arrays generate electricity. Without plants, carbon dioxide must be scrubbed from the air the astronauts breathe.

If completed as planned, the ISS will weigh 455 metric tons (1 million lb) and have the cabin volume of a 747 jumbo jet. This seems like an important fulfillment of our human nature: to question, to explore, to discover, to test the limits of the known, and to push beyond to the unknown. (See http://www.nasa.gov/mission_pages/station/main/index.html for more information and updates.)

Our vantage point in this book is that of physical geography. We examine Earth's many systems: its energy, atmosphere, winds, ocean currents, water, weather, climate, endogenic and exogenic systems, soils, ecosystems, and biomes. We are reminded daily of the power of Earth system operations. However, the inhabitants of the planet who have the greatest impact on these natural systems are human beings. What changes have we made?

We stand in the first decade of the twenty-first century. This century will be an adventure for the global society, historically unparalleled in experimenting with Earth's life-supporting systems. You will spend the majority of your life in this century. What preparations and "future thinking" can you do to understand all that is to occur?

In his 1980 book and public television series *Cosmos*, the late astronomer Carl Sagan asked:

> What account would we give of our stewardship of the planet Earth? We have heard the rationales offered by the nuclear superpowers. We know who speaks for the nations. But who speaks for the human species? Who speaks for Earth?*

Indeed, who does speak for Earth? We might answer: Perhaps we physical geographers, and other scientists who have studied Earth and know the operations of the global ecosystem, should speak for Earth. However, some might say that questions of technology, environmental politics, and future thinking belong outside of science, and that our job is merely to learn how Earth's processes work and to leave the spokesperson's role to others. Biologist-ecologist Marston Bates addressed this line of thought in 1960:

> Then we came to humans and their place in this system of life. We could have left humans out, playing the ecological game of "let's pretend humans don't exist." But this seems as unfair as the corresponding game of the economists, "let's pretend nature doesn't exist." The economy of nature and the ecology of humans are inseparable and attempts to separate them are more than misleading, they are dangerous. Human destiny is tied to nature's destiny and the arrogance of the engineering mind does not change this. Humans may be a very peculiar animal, but they are still a part of the system of nature.†

A fact of life is that Earth's more-developed countries (MDCs), through their economic dominance, speak for the billions who live in less-developed countries (LDCs). The gross state product (GSP) of California's 36.5 million people was $1.4 trillion in 2004, which was about half the gross domestic product (GDP) of China and its 1.325 billion people—that's $38,000 per capita GSP in California, compared to $2100 per capita GDP in

---

*C. Sagan, *Cosmos* (New York: Random House, 1980), p. 329.
†M. Bates, *The Forest and the Sea* (New York: Random House, 1960), p. 247.

FIGURE 21.2 Lands distant from the global centres of power. These lands were depopulated under Stalin when they were part of the former USSR. Only in the last two decades have people returned to this traditional rural landscape in the Pamirs of Tajikistan, beginning life again, so distant from the more-developed countries. [Photo by Stephen F. Cunha.]

China. The scale of disparity on our home planet is difficult to comprehend.

The fate of traditional modes of life may rest in some distant financial capital. But, economics aside, the reality is that the remote lands of Siberia are linked by Earth systems to the Pampas of Argentina, to the Great Plains in North America, and to those harvesting grain by hand in the remote Pamirs of Tajikistan (Figure 21.2).

To understand these linkages among Earth's myriad systems is our quest in *Geosystems* (Figure 21.3). We

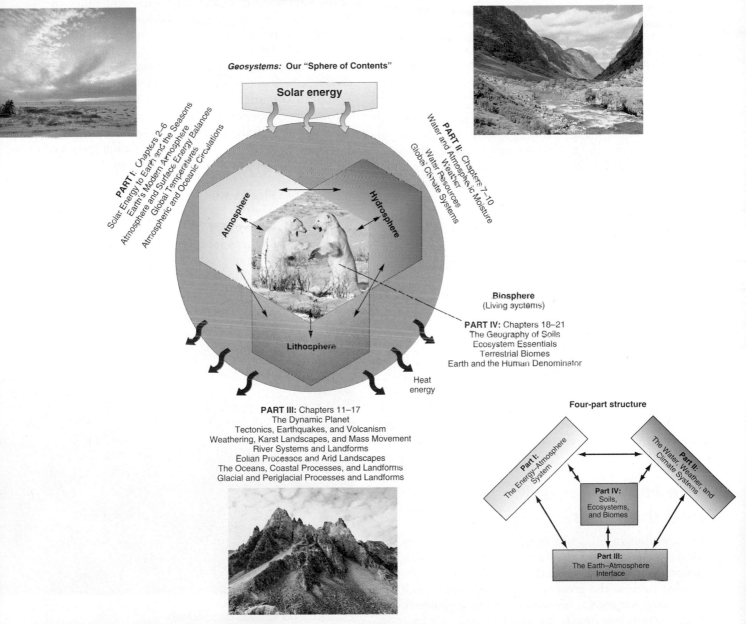

FIGURE 21.3 The spheres within *Geosystems*.
Through this text we covered the atmosphere, hydrosphere, lithosphere, and the synthesizing biosphere—the culmination of life-sustaining interactions. The systems approach shows us the flow of energy and matter and the sequence of events through time and across space. Ultimately, *Geosystems* describes the support systems of life. [All photos by Bobbé Christopherson.]

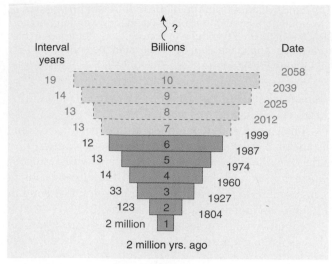

FIGURE 21.4 Human population growth.
The number of years required for the human population to add 1 billion to the count grows shorter and shorter. The twenty-first century should mark a slowing of this history of growth if policy actions are taken. Note the population forecasts for the next half-century.

explored the atmosphere, hydrosphere, lithosphere, and biosphere, synthesizing operating systems into the web of life. We now see global linkages among physical and living systems and how actions in one place can affect change elsewhere. In this sense, Earth can be compared to a spaceship. In the same way the members of a crew aboard the International Space Station are inextricably linked to each other's lives and survival, we too are each connected through the operation of planetary systems. Admittedly, the pace of popular culture makes these connections difficult to perceive.

Growing international environmental awareness in the public sector is gradually prodding governments into action. People, when informed, generally favour environmental protection and public health progress over economic interests. A survey by American polling firm Louis Harris and Associates confirmed these opinion trends. Majorities in 22 nations are willing to "endorse environmental protection at the risk of slowing down economic growth." The public seems to know they are saving money as consumers if things are done right with the environment.

The Human Count and the Future

Because human influence is pervasive, we consider the totality of our impact the *human denominator*. Just as the denominator in a fraction tells how many parts a whole is divided into, so the growing human population and the increasing demand for resources and rising planetary impact suggest how much the whole Earth system must adjust. Yet, Earth's resource base remains relatively fixed.

The human population of Earth passed 6 billion in August 1999, adding another 625 million by mid-2007;

more people are alive today than at any previous point in the planet's long history, unevenly arranged in 192 countries and numerous colonies. In a year about 70 million more people are added—this is 192,000 a day, or a new U.S. population every 4.2 years. Over the span of human history these billion-mark milestones are occurring at closer intervals (Figure 21.4).

Thirty-seven percent of Earth's population live in just two countries (20% in China and 17% in India—2.46 billion people combined). Moreover, we are a young planetary population, with some 28% of those now alive under the age of 15 (2007 data from Population Reference Bureau and U.S. Bureau of Census *POPClock Projection:* **http://www.census.gov/cgi-bin/popclock**).

Virtually all new population growth is in the less-developed countries, which now possess 81.5%, or about 5.4 billion, of the total population; the MDCs have the other 18.5%, or 1.23 billion (Figure 21.5). Table 21.1 illustrates this natural increase principle and the differences found in the MDCs and LDCs.

If you consider only the population count, the MDCs do not have a population growth problem. In fact, some European countries are actually declining in growth or are near replacement levels. However, people in the developed world produce a greater impact on the planet per person and therefore constitute a population impact crisis. An equation expresses this impact concept:

$$\text{Planetary impact } (I) = P \cdot A \cdot T$$

where P is *population*; A is *affluence*, or consumption per person; and T is *technology*, or the level of environmental impact per unit of production. The United States and Canada, with about 5% of the world's population, produce more than 22% ($14.2 trillion in 2004) of the world's gross domestic product and use more than double the

FIGURE 21.5 Dhaka, Bangladesh.
The Bangladesh capital typifies the plight of the less-developed world as millions converge on cities to find work and more modern lifestyles. [Photo by Bruce Bander/Photo Researchers, Inc.]

Table 21.1	Planetary Population Increase Rates			
	Birth Rate	**Death Rate**	**Natural Increase (%)**	**Population Growth 2007–2050 (%)**
World—2007	**21**	**9**	**1.2**	40%
More developed	**11**	**10**	**0.1**	3%
United States	14	8	0.6	39%
Japan	9	9	0.0	−26%
United Kingdom	12	10	0.3	13%
Less developed	**23**	**8**	**1.5**	49%
LDC exclu. China	**27**	**9**	**1.8**	61%
Mexico	21	5	1.7	24%
Nigeria	43	18	2.5	95%
India	24	8	1.6	55%

Source: World Population Data Sheet 2007. Population Reference Bureau, Washington, D.C., http://www.prb.org.

energy per capita of Europeans, more than 7 times that of Latin Americans, 10 times that of Asians, and 20 times that of Africans. Therefore, consideration by people in the MDCs of the state of Earth systems, natural resources, and sustainability of current practices is critical. Earth systems science is here to provide a high level of planetary monitoring and analysis to assist this process.

The concept of an individual's "footprint" has emerged—ecological footprint, carbon footprint, lifestyle footprint. These consider what your affluence and technology, the "A" and the "T" in the equation, cost planetary systems. Footprint assessment is grossly simplified, but it can give you an idea of your impact and even an estimate of how many planets it would take to sustain that lifestyle and economy if everyone lived like you. Your authors have taken action to neutralize the carbon footprint for the production and printing of these textbooks and the publisher used sustainable-forestry green paper for *Geosystems* to lessen ecological impacts. There are many Internet links to try for footprints; here is a sample:

http://www.earthday.net/Footprint/index.asp
http://www.footprintnetwork.org
http://www.ecologicalfootprint.org/
http://www.carbonfootprint.com/calculator.html
https://www.econeutral.com/carboncalculator.html
http://www.ucsusa.org/publications/greentips/whats-
  your-carb.html

The MDCs not only should effect change in their own planetary impact but also provide direction for the LDCs, which have a right to move along the road of progress and improve their living conditions. Let us examine this idea of global impact.

An Oily Bird

At first glance, the chain of events that exposes wildlife to oil contamination seems to stem from a technological problem. An oil tanker splits open at sea and releases its

FIGURE 21.6 An oily bird.
A Western Grebe contaminated with oil from the *Exxon Valdez* tanker accident in Prince William Sound, Alaska. This oily bird is the result of a long chain of events and mistakes. [Photo by Geoffrey Orth/SIPA Press.]

petroleum cargo, which is moved by ocean currents toward shore, where it coats coastal waters, beaches, and animals. In response, concerned citizens mobilize and try to save as much of the spoiled environment as possible (Figure 21.6). But the real problem goes far beyond the physical facts of the spill.

In Prince William Sound off the southern coast of Alaska, in clear weather and calm seas, the *Exxon Valdez*, a single-hulled supertanker operated by Exxon Corporation, struck a reef. The tanker spilled 42 million litres (11 million gallons) of oil. It took only 12 hours for the *Exxon Valdez* to empty its contents, yet a complete cleanup is impossible, and costs and private claims exceeded $15 billion. Scientists are still finding damage and residual oil spill. Eventually, more than 2400 km

FIGURE 21.7 Worldwide oil spills and the 1989 *Exxon Valdez* accident.
(a) Location of visible oil slicks worldwide in the 1990s. **(b)** Track of spreading oil for the first 56 days of the Alaskan spill. [(a) Data from Organization for Economic Cooperation and Development.]

(about 1500 mi) of sensitive coastline was ruined for years to come, affecting three national parks and eight other protected areas (Figure 21.7).

The death toll of animals was massive: At least 5000 sea otters died, or about 30% of resident otters; about 300,000 birds and uncounted fish, shellfish, plants, and aquatic microorganisms also perished. Sublethal effects, namely mutations, now are appearing in fish. The Pacific herring is still in significant decline, as are the harbour seals; other species are in recovery, such as the Bald Eagle and Common Murre. Almost two decades later, oil remains in mudflats and marsh soils beneath rocks.

The immediate problem of cleaning oil off a bird symbolizes a national and international concern with far-reaching spatial significance. And while we search for answers, oil slicks continue their contamination. This is an average of 27 accidents a day, 10,000 a year worldwide, ranging from a few disastrous spills to numerous small ones. There have been 50 spills equal to the *Exxon Valdez* or larger since 1970. In addition to oceanic oil spills, people improperly dispose of crankcase oil from their automobiles in a volume that annually exceeds all of these tanker spills.

The immediate effect of global oil spills on wildlife is contamination and death. But the issues involved are much bigger than dead birds. Let's ask some fundamental questions about the *Exxon Valdez* accident:

- Why was the oil tanker there in the first place?
- Why are only a few of the 28 tankers that traverse the Prince William Sound of the safer double-hulled design?

- Why is petroleum imported from Alaska in such enormous quantities? Is the demand for petroleum products based on real need and the operation of efficient systems?
- The U.S. and Canadian demand for oil is higher per capita than the demand of any other country. Efficiencies and mileage ratings in the transportation sector have not improved for the cars, trucks, and SUVs (light trucks) leading in sales. Why? And what about proven hybrid gas–electric technology?

Yet hypocrisy is apparent in our outrage over energy politics and oil-spill accidents. We continue to consume gasoline at record levels in inefficient vehicles, thus creating the demand for oil imports. The task of physical geography is to analyze all the spatial aspects of these events in the environment and the ironies that are symbolized by an oily bird.

With the shrinking Arctic Ocean permanent and seasonal sea ice, countries and corporations are lining up to exploit the open water and resources (Figure 21.8). Freighters and tankers are being designed wider than the Panama or Suez canals for shipping a decade or two from now through the newly ice-free Northwest and Northeast passages. The exhaust particulates, soot, and smoke, and waste water discharges, will damage the fragile Arctic environment. These pollutants will darken the remaining ice shelves and Greenland's ice sheet, forcing lower albedos, thus increasing insolation absorption, and accelerating the melting of remaining ice inventories. Think of the impact of physical geography's perspective

FIGURE 21.8 Record low Arctic Ocean sea-ice extent, 2007.
Global warming and wind patterns are combining to reduce the Arctic Ocean sea ice. The record low was September 14, 2007 (see Chapter 5). What the image doesn't show is the degraded thickness of the multiyear ice. Not only did the atmosphere record increased warmth but the Arctic Ocean warmed as well. [Image courtesy of Scientific Visualization Studio, GSFC/NASA.]

on this situation using elements from the chapters you have studied. What should be on the planning table for discussion? Commerce or albedo forcing?

The Need for Cooperation

The idea for a global meeting on the environment was put forward at the 1972 U.N. Conference on the Human Environment held in Stockholm. The U.N. General Assembly in 1987 achieved a landmark in global planning by agreeing to hold the Earth Summit. *Our Common Future*, a book written at the time, set the tone for the 1992 Earth Summit:

> The Earth is one but the world is not. We all depend on one biosphere for sustaining our lives. Yet each community, each country, strives for survival and prosperity with little regard for its impact on others. Some consume the Earth's resources at a rate that would leave little for future generations. Others, many more in number, consume far too little and live with the prospect of hunger, squalor, disease, and early death.*

The setting for the 1992 Earth Summit in Rio de Janeiro was ironic, for many of the very problems discussed at the conference were evident on the city's streets, with their abundant air pollution, water pollution, toxics, noise, wealth and poverty, and daily struggle for health and education.

*World Commission on Environment and Development, *Our Common Future* (Oxford, UK: Oxford University Press, 1987), p. 27.

Five agreements were written at the Earth Summit: the Climate Change Framework; the Biological Diversity Treaty; the Management, Conservation, and Sustainable Development of All Types of Forests; the Earth Charter (a nonbinding statement of 27 environmental and economic principles); and Agenda 21 for Sustainable Development. A product of the Earth Summit was the United Nations Framework Convention on Climate Change (FCCC), which led to a series of Conference of the Parties (COP) meetings—COP–13 was in Bali, Indonesia, December 2007; COP–14 is in The Hague, Netherlands, in 2008.

The Kyoto Protocol, agreed to in 1997 to reduce global carbon emissions, was finalized in 2001, in Marrakech, Morocco, at COP–7. Canada ratified the Kyoto Protocol December 17, 2002, promising an emissions reduction of 3.3%. Environment Canada is responsible for recording, monitoring, and verifying the reduction of greenhouse gas emissions. Following Russian ratification, the Kyoto Protocol and Rulebook became international law in March 2005, with the United States alone remaining in noncompliance in its refusal to ratify.

Asking whether the Earth Summit "succeeded" or "failed" is the wrong question. The occurrence of this largest-ever official gathering is a remarkable accomplishment. From the Earth Summit emerged a new organization—the U.N. Commission on Sustainable Development—to oversee the promises made in the five agreements. This momentum lead to a second Earth Summit in 2002 (http://www.earthsummit2002.org/) in Johannesburg, South Africa, that completed an agenda including climate change, freshwater, gender issues, global public goods, HIV/AIDS, sustainable finance, and the five Rio Conventions agreements.

A clear conclusion is that members of society must work to move the solutions for environmental and developmental problems off the bench and into play. We need international cooperation to consider our symbiotic relations with each other and with Earth's resilient, yet fragile, life-support systems (News Report 21.1).

A critical corollary to these international efforts is the linkage of academic disciplines. A positive step in that direction is the Earth systems science approach embodied in physical geography that synthesizes content from across the disciplines to create a holistic perspective. Exciting progress toward an integrated understanding of Earth's physical and biological systems is in progress. Such a multidisciplinary effort began in 2000 at a Ministerial Meeting of the Arctic Council, when the Arctic Climate Impact Assessment (ACIA) was launched. The ACIA final report, *Climate Change in the Arctic*, was released in November 2004 (Figure 21.9). The effort involved 300 scientists, eight countries, and six circumpolar indigenous peoples' organizations. For a look at this international triumph of cooperative science and summary of *Key Findings* see http://www.acia.uaf.edu.

More than a decade ago, *Time* magazine gave Earth an interesting honor and is today a time capsule of

(a)

(b)

FIGURE 21.9 Arctic Climate Impact Assessment Symposium.
(a) Dr. Robert Corell, Chair of the ACIA Integration Team, welcomes nearly 400 scientists, managers, government and non-governmental representatives, student researchers, and indigenous people of the Arctic to a first-ever Arctic climate symposium, held in Reykjavík, Iceland, November 2004. The ACIA released their climate impact assessment to the Arctic Council and to a global audience. (b) The logo of the Arctic Climate Impact Assessment. [Photo (a) by Bobbé Christopherson.]

Earth-systems analysis and activist suggestions (Figure 21.10). As if a victim of short-lived fame, we wonder where Earth awareness fits into the global scheme of things today. Is there a follow-up in pop culture to making the cover of *Time*?

Twelve Paradigms for the 21st Century

As we conclude, a brief list of the dominant themes and patterns of concern for the 21st century seems appropriate. We hope these *paradigms* will provide a useful framework for brainstorming and discussion of the central issues that will affect us in the new century. The paradigms listed in no particular order:

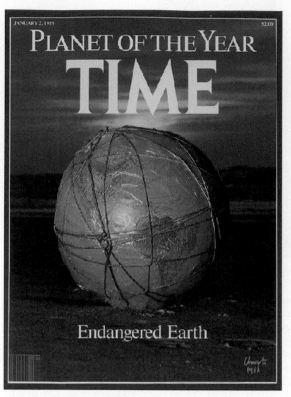

FIGURE 21.10 Earth made the cover of *Time*.
More than a decade ago, global concerns about environmental impacts prompted *Time* magazine to deviate from its 60-year tradition of naming a prominent citizen as its person of the year, instead naming Earth the "Planet of the Year." The magazine devoted 33 pages to Earth's physical and human geography. Importantly, *Time* also offered positive policy strategies for consideration. [January 2, 1989, issue, copyright © 1989 The *Time* Inc. Magazine Company. Reprinted by permission.]

Twelve Paradigms for the 21st Century

1. Population increases in the less-developed countries
2. Planetary impact per person (on the biosphere and resources; $I = P \cdot A \cdot T$), ecological and carbon footprint
3. Feeding the world's population
4. Global and national disparities of wealth and resource allocation
5. Status of women and children (health, welfare, rights)
6. Global climate change (temperatures, sea level, weather and climate patterns, disease, and diversity)
7. Energy supplies and energy demands; renewables and demand management
8. Loss of biodiversity (habitats, genetic wealth, and species richness)
9. Pollution of air, surface water (quality and quantity), groundwater, oceans, and land
10. The persistence of wilderness (biosphere reserves and biodiversity hot spots)
11. Globalization versus cultural diversity
12. Conflict resolution

News Report 21.1

Gaia Hypothesis Triggers Debate

Some scientists and philosophers view Earth as one vast, self-regulating organism. The concept is one of global symbiosis, or mutualism. This controversial concept is the *Gaia hypothesis* (Gaia was the Earth-Mother goddess in ancient mythology). It was proposed in 1979 by James Lovelock, a British astronomer and inventor, and elaborated by American biologist Lynn Margulis.

Gaia is the ultimate synergistic relationship, in which the whole greatly exceeds the sum of the individual interacting components. The hypothesis contends that life processes control and shape Earth's inorganic physical and chemical processes, with the ecosphere so interactive that a very small mass can affect a very large mass. Thus, Lovelock and Margulis think that the material environment and the evolution of species are tightly joined; as species evolve through natural selection, they (including us) in turn affect their environment. The present oxygen-rich composition of the atmosphere is given as proof of this coevolution of living and nonliving systems.

From the perspective of physical geography, the Gaia hypothesis permits a view of all Earth and the spatial interrelations among systems. In fact, such a perspective is necessary for analyzing specific environmental issues. Many variables interact synergistically, producing both wanted and unwanted results.

One disturbing aspect of this unity is that any biotic threat to the operation of an ecosystem tends to move toward extinction itself. This trend preserves the system overall. Earth-systems operation and feedback naturally tend to eliminate offensive members. The degree to which humans represent a planetary threat, then, becomes a topic of great concern, for Earth (Gaia) will prevail, regardless of the outcome of the human experiment.

The maladies of Gaia do not last long in terms of her life span. Anything that makes the world uncomfortable to live in tends to induce the evolution of those species that can achieve a new and more comfortable environment. It follows that, if the world is made unfit by what we do, there is the probability of a change in regime to one that will be better for life but not necessarily better for us.*

The debate is vigorous regarding the true applicability of this hypothesis to nature, or whether it is true science at all. Regardless, it remains philosophically intriguing in its portrayal of the relationship between humans and Earth and stimulates discussion.

*J. Lovelock, *The Ages of Gaia— A Biography of Our Living Earth* (New York: Norton, 1988), p. 178.

Who Speaks for Earth?

Geographic awareness and education is an increasingly positive force on Earth. The Canadian Council for Geographic Education was established in 1993 to serve as the education program of the Royal Canadian Geographical Society. Geographic educators from elementary, secondary, college, or university levels from across the country comprise the Council. Each year, the Council sponsors *The Great Canadian Geography Challenge*, a national competition for students from Grades 4 to 10. There are two levels of competition at provincial and national levels: Level 1, for Grades 4 to 6; Level 2, for Grades 7 to 10. (See the results of the latest competition at **http://geochallenge.ca/geochallenge/en/default.asp?catID=10**). The National Geography World Championship (formerly the International Geography Olympiad) is now an annual event (Figure 21.11). People are learning more about Earth–human relationships.

Yet ideological and ethical differences still remain within society. This dichotomy was addressed by biologist Edward O. Wilson:

> The evidence of swift environmental change calls for an ethic uncoupled from other systems of belief. Those committed by religion to believe that life was put on Earth in one divine stroke will recognize that we are destroying the Creation; and those who perceive biodiversity to be the product of blind evolution will agree. . . . Defenders of both premises seem destined to gravitate toward the same position on conservation. . . . For what, in the final analysis, is morality but the command of conscience seasoned by a rational examination of consequences? . . . An enduring environmental ethic will aim to preserve not only the health and freedom of our species, but access to the world in which the human spirit was born.*

In an ideal sense, we hold all of Earth's systems in common. Now, what about Sagan's question to us? The late Carl Sagan asked, "Who speaks for Earth?" He answered with this perspective:

> We have begun to contemplate our origins: starstuff pondering the stars; organized assemblages of ten billion billion billion atoms considering the evolution

*E. O. Wilson, *The Diversity of Life* (Cambridge, MA: Harvard University Press, 1992), p. 351.

FIGURE 21.11 National Geographic World Championship. Students from across the globe met in Vancouver, British Columbia, August 2001, for the fifth National Geographic World Championship, sponsored by the National Geographic Society, with Canadian Alex Trebek of *Jeopardy!* fame as moderator. Here Alex congratulates the Canadian team on their second-place finish—the United States placed first, the Hungarian team third in the final standings. The 9th National Geographic World Championship will be held in 2009. The championship is an indicator of growing international geographic awareness. [Photo by O. Louis Mazzatenta, 2001 National Geographic Society.]

FIGURE 21.12 View of Earth from Saturn. The Cassini–Huygens spacecraft was on the farside of Saturn so the Sun lit the rings and atmosphere in backlighting. The surprise catch was a glimpse of Earth as a little, pale blue dot, some 1.23 billion km (791 million mi) distant. It was September 19, 2006 on Earth. [Image courtesy of NASA/JPL/Space Science Institute.]

of atoms; tracing the long journey by which, here at least, consciousness arose. Our loyalties are to the species and the planet. We speak for Earth. Our obligation to survive is owed not just to ourselves but also to that Cosmos, ancient and vast, from which we spring.*

*C. Sagan, *Cosmos* (New York: Random House, 1980), p. 345.

The *Cassini–Huygens* spacecraft on its Saturn mission provided us a dramatic perspective of our Home Planet. In September 2006, JPL scientists directed the craft so that Saturn was back-lit by the Sun, a view of the rings that we never see from Earth. The small pale dot to the left of Saturn (see arrow), just inside the bright ring, is us! All that we studied in the text and that we are trying to understand is on that small, blue dot (Figure 21.12).

May we all perceive our spatial importance within Earth's ecosystems and do our part to maintain a life-supporting and sustaining Earth for ourselves and countless generations in the future. "For the polar bears and all the grandchildren who will enjoy them, may there be sea ice."

Critical Thinking and Learning

A. What part do you think technology, politics, and thinking about the future should play in science courses?

B. Assess population growth issues: the count, the impact per person, and future projection. What strategies do you see as important?

C. According to the discussion in the chapter, what worldwide factors led to the *Exxon Valdez* accident? Describe the complexity of that event from a global perspective. In your analysis, examine both supply-side (corporations and utilities) and demand-side (consumers) issues, as well as environmental and strategic factors. And, what about the oily bird?

D. What is meant by the Gaia hypothesis? Describe several concepts from this text that might pertain to this hypothesis.

E. Relate the content of the various chapters in this text to the integrative Earth systems science concept. Which chapters help you to better understand Earth–human relations and human impacts?

F. After examining the list of 12 paradigm issues for the 21st century, suggest items that need to be added to the list, omitted from the list, or expanded in coverage. Rearrange and organize the list as needed to match your concerns.

G. This chapter states that we already know many of the solutions to the problems we face. Why do you think these solutions are not being implemented at a faster pace?

H. Who speaks for Earth?

Appendix A

Maps in This Text and Topographic Maps

Maps Used in This Text

Geosystems uses several map projections: Goode's homolosine, Robinson, and Miller cylindrical, among others. Each was chosen to best present specific types of data. **Goode's homolosine projection** is an interrupted world map designed in 1923 by Dr. J. Paul Goode of the University of Chicago. Rand McNally *Goode's Atlas* first used it in 1925. Goode's homolosine equal-area projection (Figure A.1) is a combination of two oval projections (*homolo*graphic and *sin*usoidal projections).

Two equal-area projections are cut and pasted together to improve the rendering of landmass shapes. A *sinusoidal projection* is used between 40° N and 40° S latitudes. Its central meridian is a straight line; all other meridians are drawn as sinusoidal curves (based on sine-wave curves) and parallels are evenly spaced. A *Mollweide projection*, also called a *homolographic projection*, is used from 40° N to the North Pole and from 40° S to the South Pole. Its central meridian is a straight line; all other meridians are drawn as elliptical arcs, and parallels are unequally spaced—farther apart at the equator, closer together poleward. This technique of combining two projections preserves areal size relationships, making the projection excellent for mapping spatial distributions when interruptions of oceans or continents do not pose a problem.

We use Goode's homolosine projection throughout this book. Examples include the world climate map and smaller climate type maps in Chapter 10, topographic regions and continental shields maps (Figures 12.3 and 12.4), world karst map (Figure 13.17), world sand regions and loess deposits (Figures 15.12 and 15.15), and the terrestrial biomes map in Chapter 20 (Figure 20.3).

Another projection we use is the **Robinson projection**, designed by the late Arthur Robinson in 1963 (Figure A.2). This projection is neither equal area nor true shape, but is a compromise between the two. The North and South poles appear as lines slightly more than half the length of the equator; thus higher latitudes are exaggerated less than on other oval and cylindrical projections. Some of the Robinson maps employed include the latitudinal geographic zones map in Chapter 1 (Figure 1.12), the daily net radiation map (Figure 2.11), the world temperature range map in Chapter 5 (Figure 5.18), the maps of lithospheric plates of crust and volcanoes and earthquakes in Chapter 11 (Figures 11.19 and 11.22), and the global oil spills map in Chapter 21 (Figure 21.7).

Another compromise map, the **Miller cylindrical projection**, is used in this text (Figure A.3). Examples of this projection include the world time zone map (Figure 1.16), global temperature maps in Chapter 5 (Figures 5.13 and 5.16), two global pressure maps in Chapter 6 (Figure 6.10), and degradation map in Chapter 18 (Figure 18.9). This projection is neither true shape nor true area but is a compromise that avoids the severe scale distortion of the Mercator. The Miller projection frequently appears in world atlases. The American Geographical Society presented Osborn Miller's map projection in 1942.

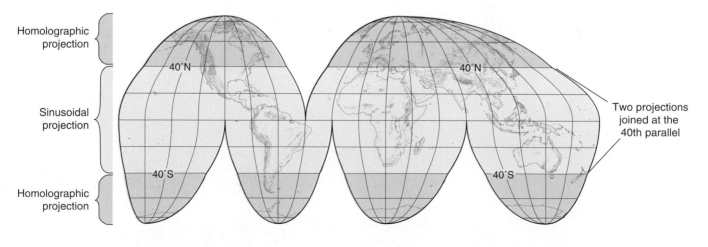

FIGURE A.1 Goode's homolosine projection.
An equal-area map. [Copyright by the University of Chicago. Used by permission of the University of Chicago Press.]

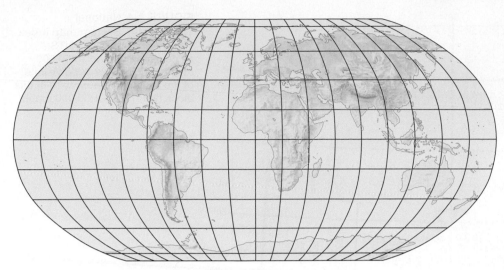

FIGURE A.2 Robinson projection.
A compromise between equal area and true shape. [Developed by Arthur H. Robinson, 1963.]

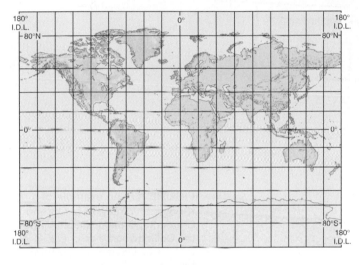

FIGURE A.3 Miller cylindrical projection.
A compromise map projection between equal area and true shape. [Developed by Osborn M. Miller, American Geographical Society, 1942.]

Mapping, Quadrangles, and Topographic Maps

The westward expansion across the vast North American continent demanded a land survey for the creation of accurate maps. Maps were needed to subdivide the land and to guide travel, exploration, settlement, and transportation. In 1785, the Public Lands Survey System began surveying and mapping government land in the United States. In 1836, the Clerk of Surveys in the Land Office of the Department of the Interior directed public-land surveys. The Bureau of Land Management replaced this Land Office in 1946. The actual preparation and recording of survey information fell to the U.S. Geological Survey (USGS), also a branch of the Department of the Interior (see **http://www.usgs.gov/pubprod/maps.html**).

In Canada, Natural Resources Canada conducts the national mapping program. Canadian mapping includes base maps, thematic maps, aeronautical charts, federal topographic maps, and the *National Atlas of Canada*, now in its sixth edition (see **http://atlas.nrcan.gc.ca/**).

The NRC and USGS depict survey information on quadrangle maps, so called because they are rectangular maps with four corner angles. The angles are junctures of parallels of latitude and meridians of longitude rather than political boundaries. These quadrangle maps utilize the Albers equal-area projection, from the conic class of map projections.

Topographic Maps

The most popular and widely used quadrangle maps are **topographic maps**. You will find topographic maps throughout *Geosystems* because they portray landscapes so effectively. As examples, see Figures 13.17 and 13.18, karst landscapes and sinkholes near Orleans, Indiana, and Winter Park, Florida; Figure 14.8, river drainage patterns; Figure 14.22, river meander scars; Figure 15.19, an alluvial fan in Montana; Figure 17.4, glaciers in British Columbia; and Figure 17.19, drumlins in Peterborough, Ontario.

The National Topographic System (NTS) provides general-purpose topographic map coverage of Canada. The maps depict both the physical and human features of the landscape, including ground relief (landforms and terrain), drainage (lakes and rivers), forest cover, administrative areas, populated areas, transportation routes and facilities (including roads and railways), and other human-made features in detail. Natural Resources Canada produces maps that conform to the NTS and are available in two standard scales: 1:50,000 and 1:250,000. The area covered by a single 1:250,000 map is determined by its latitude and longitude and identified by a combination of letters A through P. These maps are then divided into 16 segments and numbered consecutively to form the blocks that make up the 1:50,000 map sheets.

The 1:50,000-scale topographic map is the most commonly used map series because it is an ideal scale for recreational activities (Figure A.5). In this scale, a sheet covers an area approximately

FIGURE A.4 National Topographic System map index. The index displays the NTS system in which the 1:250,000 map is 22F. Further subdivisions of the system are portrayed in this block (22F 13 is a 1:50,000 map).

FIGURE A.5 An example of a topographic map from Ontario. Creemore, Ontario, scanned from the Collingwood map sheet, 41 A8 in the 1:50,000 map series from the National Togographic System. Note the steep slope to the south and west of the Mad River and the flat land to the north and east.

(a)

(b)

FIGURE A.6 Topographic map of a hypothetical landscape.
(a) Perspective view of a hypothetical landscape. (b) Depiction of that landscape on a topographic map. The contour interval on the map is 6 m (19.7 ft). [After the U.S. Geological Survey.]

40 km by 28 km. Hills, valleys, lakes, rivers, streams, rapids, portages, trails and wooded areas; major, secondary, and side roads; and all human-made features such as buildings, power lines, dams, and cut lines are accurately represented on these maps. Maps at this scale are used by all levels of government and industry for flood control, forest-fire control, real-estate planning, development of natural resources, environmental issues, highway planning, and depiction of crop areas.

The 1:250,000-scale topographic map series is the next most common scale. Maps of this scale are commonly used for field reconnaissance. This scale is popular not only as an overview of a large area, but also as a road map for use when travelling. A standard 1:250,000-scale map shows an area approximately the size of Prince Edward Island.

The Centre for Topographic Information Web site (**http://maps.nrcan.gc.ca/index_e.php**) presents an online seminar called MAPS 101 that provides a list of commonly asked questions and explanations for topographic terms, and offers a legend of the many symbols used on Canadian topographic maps.

A **planimetric map** shows the horizontal position (latitude/longitude) of boundaries, land-use aspects, bodies of water, and economic and cultural features. A highway map is a common example of a planimetric map.

A topographic map adds a vertical component to show topography (configuration of the land surface), including slope and relief (the vertical difference in local landscape elevation). These fine details are shown through the use of elevation contour lines (Figure A.6). A *contour line* connects all points at the same

elevation. Elevations are shown above or below a vertical datum, or reference level, which is usually mean sea level. The contour interval is the vertical distance in elevation between two adjacent contour lines (6 m [19.7 ft] in Figure A.6b).

The topographic map in Figure A.6b shows a hypothetical landscape, demonstrating how contour lines and intervals depict slope and relief, which are the three-dimensional aspects of terrain. The pattern of lines and the spacing between them indicates slope. The steeper a slope or cliff, the closer together the contour lines appear—in the figure, note the narrowly spaced contours that represent the cliffs to the left of the highway. A wider spacing of these contour lines portrays a more gradual slope, as you can see from the widely spaced lines on the beach and to the right of the river valley.

The margins of a topographic map contain a wealth of information about its concept and content. In the margins of topographic maps, you find the name, position in the latitude–longitude and other coordinate systems, title, legend, magnetic declination (alignment of magnetic north) and compass information, datum plane, symbols used for roads and trails, the dates and history of the survey of that particular quad, and more.

Topographic maps may be purchased in the U.S. directly from the USGS. In Canada, topographic maps may be purchased through various map dealers recommended by the Centre for Topographic Information, NRC (**http://maps.nrcan.gc.ca/index_e.php**). To find a list of authorized dealers, go to the Canada Map Office (**http://maps.nrcan.gc.ca/distribution_e.php**).

Control data and monuments
Vertical control

Third order or better, with tablet	BM ×16.3
Third order or better, recoverable mark	× 120.0
Bench mark at found section corner	BM 118.6
Spot elevation	× 5.3

Contours
Topographic

Intermediate	
Index	
Supplementary	
Depression	
Cut; fill	

Bathymetric

Intermediate	
Index	
Primary	
Index primary	
Supplementary	

Boundaries

National	
State or territorial	
County or equivalent	
Civil township or equivalent	
Incorporated city or equivalent	
Park, reservation, or monument	

Surface features

Levee	Levee
Sand or mud area, dunes, or shifting sand	Sand
Intricate surface area	Strip mine
Gravel beach or glacial moraine	Gravel
Tailings pond	Tailings pond

Mines and caves

Quarry or open pit mine	
Gravel, sand, clay, or borrow pit	
Mine dump	Mine dump
Tailings	Tailings

Vegetation

Woods	
Scrub	
Orchard	
Vineyard	
Mangrove	Mangrove

Glaciers and permanent snowfields

Contours and limits	
Form lines	

Marine shoreline
Topographic maps

Approximate mean high water	
Indefinite or unsurveyed	

Topographic-bathymetric maps

Mean high water	
Apparent (edge of vegetation)	

Coastal features

Foreshore flat	
Rock or coral reef	
Rock bare or awash	
Group of rocks bare or awash	
Exposed wreck	
Depth curve; sounding	
Breakwater, pier, jetty, or wharf	
Seawall	

Rivers, lakes, and canals

Intermittent stream	
Intermittent river	
Disappearing stream	
Perennial stream	
Perennial river	
Small falls; small rapids	
Large falls; large rapids	
Masonry dam	
Dam with lock	
Dam carrying road	
Perennial lake; intermittent lake or pond	
Dry lake	Dry lake
Narrow wash	
Wide wash	Wide wash
Canal, flume, or aquaduct with lock	
Well or spring; spring or seep	

Submerged areas and bogs

Marsh or swamp	
Submerged marsh or swamp	
Wooded marsh or swamp	
Submerged wooded marsh or swamp	
Rice field	Rice
Land subject to inundation	Max pool 431

Buildings and related features

Building	
School; church	
Built-up area	
Racetrack	
Airport	
Landing strip	
Well (other than water); windmill	
Tanks	
Covered reservoir	
Gaging station	
Landmark object (feature as labeled)	
Campground; picnic area	
Cemetery: small; large	Cem

Roads and related features

Roads on Provisional edition maps are not classified as primary, secondary, or light duty. They are all symbolized as light duty roads.

Primary highway	
Secondary highway	
Light duty road	
Unimproved road	
Trail	
Dual highway	
Dual highway with median strip	

Railroads and related features

Standard gauge single track; station	
Standard gauge multiple track	
Abandoned	

Transmission lines and pipelines

Power transmission line; pole; tower	
Telephone line	Telephone
Aboveground oil or gas pipeline	
Underground oil or gas pipeline	Pipeline

FIGURE A.7 Standardized topographic map symbols used on USGS maps. English units still prevail, although a few USGS maps are in metric. [From USGS, Topographic Maps, 1969.]

Appendix B

The 12 Soil Orders of the U.S. Soil Taxonomy

The U.S. soil classification system, *Soil Taxonomy—A Basic System of Soil Classification for Making and Interpreting Soil Surveys*, was published in 1975 and revised in a new second edition in 1999. Soil scientists refer to it as **Soil Taxonomy**. Over the years, various revisions and clarifications in the system were published in *Keys to the Soil Taxonomy*, now in its ninth edition (2003, **http://soils.usda.gov/technical/classification/tax_keys/**), which includes all the revisions to the 1975 Soil Taxonomy. Major revisions include the addition of two new soil orders: Andisols (volcanic soils) in 1990 and Gelisols (cold and frozen soils) in 1998. Much of the information in this appendix is derived from these two keystone publications.

The classification system divides soils into six categories, creating a hierarchical sorting system (Table B.1). The smallest, most detailed category is the soil series, which ideally includes only one polypedon but may include adjoining polypedons. In sequence from smallest category to the largest, the Soil Taxonomy recognizes *soil series, soil families, soil subgroups, soil great groups, soil suborders*, and *soil orders*.

Diagnostic Soil Horizons

To identify a specific soil series within the Soil Taxonomy, the U.S. Natural Resources Conservation Service describes diagnostic horizons in a pedon. A *diagnostic horizon* reflects a distinctive physical property (colour, texture, structure, consistence, porosity, moisture) or a dominant soil process (discussed with the soil types).

In the solum (A, E, and B horizons), two diagnostic horizons may be identified: the epipedon and the subsurface. The presence or absence of either of these diagnostic horizons usually distinguishes a soil for classification.

- The **epipedon** (literally, "over the soil") is the diagnostic horizon at the surface where most of the rock structure has been destroyed. It may extend downward through the A horizon, even including all or part of an illuviated B horizon. It is visibly darkened by organic matter and sometimes is leached of minerals. Excluded from the epipedon are alluvial deposits, eolian deposits, and cultivated areas, because soil-forming processes have lacked the time to erase these relatively short-lived characteristics.
- The **diagnostic subsurface horizon** originates below the surface at varying depths. It may include part of the A or B horizon or both. Many diagnostic subsurface horizons have been identified.

The 12 Soil Orders of the Soil Taxonomy

At the heart of the Soil Taxonomy are 12 general soil orders, listed in Table B.2. Their worldwide distribution is shown in Figure B.1. Please consult this table and the map as you read the discussion of the Canadian System of Soil Classification (CSSC), where similar soil orders correlate. Because the Soil Taxonomy evaluates each soil order on its own characteristics, there is no priority to the classification. However, you will find a progression in the table and map legend, for the 12 orders are arranged loosely by latitude, beginning with Oxisols along the equator as in Chapters 10 (climates) and 20 (terrestrial biomes).

Table B.1   U.S. Soil Taxonomy

Soil Category	Number of Soils Included
Orders	12
Suborders	47
Great groups	230
Subgroups	1,200
Families	6,000
Series	15,000

**FIGURE B.1 Soil Taxonomy.
Worldwide distribution of the Soil
Taxonomy's 12 soil orders.** [Adapted from
maps prepared by World Soil Resources Staff, Natural
Resources Conservation Service, USDA, 1999.]

Oxisols

Aridisols

Mollisols

Alfisols

Ultisols

Spodosols

Entisols

Inceptisols

Vertisols

Histosols

Andisols

Gelisols

Rock land

Shifting sands

Ice fields

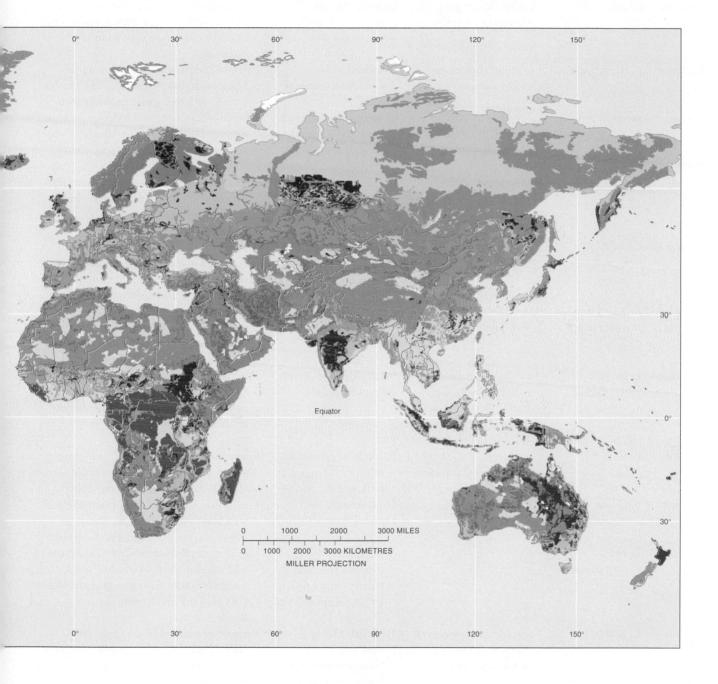

Equator

0	1000	2000	3000 MILES
0	1000	2000	3000 KILOMETRES

MILLER PROJECTION

Table B.2 Soil Taxonomy Soil Orders

Order	Derivation of Term	Marbut, 1938* (Canadian System†)	General Location and Climate	Description
Oxisols	Fr. *oxide*, "oxide" Gr. *oxide*, "acid or sharp"	Latosols, lateritic soils	Tropical soils, hot, humid areas	Maximum weathering of Fe and Al and eluviation, continuous plinthite layer
Aridisols	L. *aridos*, "dry"	Reddish desert, grey desert, sierozems	Desert soils, hot, dry areas	Limited alteration of parent material, low climate activity, light colour, low humus content, subsurface illuviation of carbonates
Mollisols	L. *mollis*, "soft"	Chestnut, chernozem (Chernozemic)	Grassland soils; subhumid, semiarid lands	Noticeably dark with organic material, humus rich, base saturation high, friable surface with well-structured horizons
Alfisols	Invented syllable	Grey-brown podzolic, degraded chernozem (Luvisol)	Moderately weathered forest soils, humid temperate forests	B horizon high in clays, moderate to high degree of base saturation, illuviated clay accum., no pronounced colour change with depth
Ultisols	L. *ultimus*, "last"	Red-yellow podzolic, reddish yellow lateritic	Highly weathered forest soils, subtropical forests	Similar to Alfisols, B horizon high in clays, generally low amount of base saturation, strong weathering in subsurface horizons, redder than Alfisols
Spodosols	Gr. *spodos* or L. *spodus*, "wood ash"	Podzols, brown podzolic (Podzol)	Northern conifer forest soils, cool humid forests	Illuvial B horizon of Fe/Al clays, humus accum.; without structure, partially cemented; highly leached, strongly acid; coarse texture of low bases
Entisols	Invented syllable from *recent*	Azonal soils, tundra (some Regosols)	Recent soils, profile undeveloped, all climates	Limited development; inherited properties from parent material; pale colour, low humus, few specific properties; hard and massive when dry
Inceptisols	L. *inceptum*, "beginning"	Ando, subarctic brown forest lithosols, some humic gleys (Brunisol, Cryosol with permafrost, Gleysol wet)	Weakly developed soils, humid regions	Intermediate development; embryonic soils, but few diagnostic features; further weathering possible in altered or changed subsurface horizons
Vertisols	L. *verto*, "to turn"	Grumusols (1949) tropical black clays (Vertisolic)	Expandable clay soils; subtropics, tropics; sufficient dry period	Forms large cracks on drying, self-mixing action, contains >30% in swelling clays, light colour, low humus content
Histosols	Gr. *histos*, "tissue"	Peat, muck, bog (Organic)	Organic soils, wet places	Peat or bog, >20% organic matter, much with clay >40 cm thick, surface, organic layers, no diagnostic horizons
Andisols	L. *ando*, "volcanic ash"	—	Areas affected by frequent volcanic activity (formerly within Inceptisols and Entisols)	Volcanic parent materials, particularly ash and volcanic glass; weathering and mineral transformation important; high CEC and organic content, generally fertile
Gelisols	L. *gelatio*, "freezing"	Formerly Inceptisols and Entisols (Cryosols, some Brunisols)	High latitudes in Northern Hemisphere, southern limits near tree line	Permafrost within 100 cm of the soil surface; evidence of cryoturbation (frost churning) and/or an active layer; patterned-ground

*C. F. Marbut, USDA soil scientist, developed the first American system of soil classification in the 1930s, first published in the USDA *Yearbook of Agriculture* in 1938.

†For comparison, these are soil orders from the Canadian System of Soil Classification (CSSC), last revised in 1998.

Appendix C

The Köppen Climate Classification System

The Köppen climate classification system was designed by Wladimir Köppen (1846–1940), a German climatologist and botanist, and is widely used for its ease of comprehension. The basis of any empirical classification system is the choice of criteria used to draw lines on a map to designate different climates. Köppen-Geiger climate classification uses average monthly temperatures, average monthly precipitation, and total annual precipitation to devise its spatial categories and boundaries. But we must remember that boundaries really are transition zones of gradual change. The trends and overall patterns of boundary lines are more important than their precise placement, especially with the small scales generally used on world maps.

Take a few minutes to examine the Köppen system, the criteria, and the considerations for each of the principal climate categories. The modified Köppen-Geiger system has its drawbacks, however. It does not consider winds, temperature extremes, precipitation intensity, quantity of sunshine, cloud cover, or net radiation. Yet the system is important because its correlations with the actual world are reasonable and the input data are standardized and readily available.

Köppen's Climatic Designations

Figure 10.4 on page 292 shows the distribution of each of Köppen's six climate classifications on the land. This generalized map shows the spatial pattern of climate. The Köppen system uses capital letters (A, B, C, D, E, H) to designate climatic categories from the equator to the poles. The guidelines for each of these categories are in the margins of Figure C.1.

Five of the climate classifications are based on thermal criteria:

A Tropical (equatorial regions)
C Mesothermal (Mediterranean, humid subtropical, marine west coast regions)
D Microthermal (humid continental, subarctic regions)
E Polar (polar regions)
H Highland (compared to lowlands at the same latitude, highlands have lower temperatures—recall the normal lapse rate—and more efficient precipitation due to lower moisture demand)

Only one climate classification is based on moisture as well:

B Dry (deserts and semiarid steppes)

Within each climate classification additional lowercase letters are used to signify temperature and moisture conditions.

For example, in a tropical rain forest *Af* climate, the *A* tells us that the average coolest month is above 18°C (64.4°F, average for the month), and the *f* indicates that the weather is constantly wet, with the driest month receiving at least 6 cm (2.4 in.) of precipitation. (The designation *f* is from the German *feucht*, for moist.) As you can see on the climate map, the tropical rain forest *Af* climate dominates along the equator and equatorial rain forest.

In a *Dfa* climate, the *D* means that the average warmest month is above 10°C (50°F), with at least one month falling below 0°C (32°F); the *f* says that at least 3 cm (1.2 in.) of precipitation falls during every month; and the *a* indicates a warmest summer month averaging above 22°C (71.6°F). Thus, a *Dfa* climate is a humid-continental, hot-summer climate in the microthermal category.

What's in a Boundary?

Originally, Köppen proposed that the isotherm boundary between mesothermal C and microthermal D climates be a coldest month of −3°C (26.6°F) or lower. That might be an accurate criterion for Europe, but for conditions in North America, the 0°C isotherm is considered more appropriate. The difference between the 0°C and isotherms for January covers an area about the width of the state of Ohio. Remember, these isotherm lines are really transition zones and do not mean abrupt change from one temperature to another.

A line denoting at least one month below freezing extends from New York City roughly along the Ohio River, trending westward until it meets the dry climates in the southeastern corner of Colorado. The line marking −3°C as the coldest month extends farther north along Lake Erie and the southern tip of Lake Michigan. In addition, from year to year, the position of the 0°C isotherm for January can shift back and forth several hundred kilometres as weather conditions vary. The map in Figure C.1 uses the 0°C isotherm for the C–D climate boundary.

Köppen Guidelines

The Köppen guidelines and map portrayal are in Figure C.1. First, check the guidelines for a climate type, then the colour legend for the subdivisions of the type, and then check out the distribution of that climate on the map. You may want to compare this with the climate map in Figure 10.4 that presents causal elements that produce these climates.

FIGURE C.1 World climates and their guidelines according to the Köppen classification system.

Köppen Guidelines
Tropical Climates — A

Consistently warm with all months averaging above 18°C (64.4°F); annual water supply exceeds water demand.

Af — Tropical rain forest:
f = All months receive precipitation in excess of 6 cm (2.4 in.).

Am — Tropical monsoon:
m = A marked short dry season with 1 or more months receiving less than 6 cm (2.4 in.) precipitation; an otherwise excessively wet rainy season. ITCZ 6–12 months dominant.

Aw — Tropical savanna:
w = Summer wet season, winter dry season; ITCZ dominant 6 months or less, winter water-balance deficits.

Mesothermal Climates — C

Warmest month above 10°C (50°F); coldest month above 0°C (32°F) but below 18°C (64.4°F); seasonal climates.

Cfa, Cwa — Humid subtropical:
a = Hot summer; warmest month above 22°C (71.6°F).
f = Year-round precipitation.
w = Winter drought, summer wettest month 10 times more precipitation than driest winter month.

Cfb, Cfc — Marine west coast, mild-to-cool summer:
f = Receives year-round precipitation.
b = Warmest month below 22°C (71.6°F) with 4 months above 10°C.
c = 1–3 months above 10°C.

Csa, Csb — Mediterranean summer dry:
s = Pronounced summer drought with 70% of precipitation in winter.
a = Hot summer with warmest month above 22°C (71.6°F).
b = Mild summer; warmest month below 22°C.

Microthermal Climates — D

Warmest month above 10°C (50°F); coldest month below 0°C (32°F); cool temperature-to-cold conditions; snow climates. In Southern Hemisphere, occurs only in highland climates.

Dfa, Dwa — Humid continental:
a = Hot summer; warmest month above 22°C (71.6°F).
f = Year-round precipitation.
w = Winter drought.

Dfb, Dwb — Humid continental:
b = Mild summer; warmest month below 22°C (71.6°F).
f = Year-round precipitation.
w = Winter drought.

Dfc, Dwc, Dwd — Subarctic:
Cool summers, cold winters.

f = Year-round precipitation.
w = Winter drought.
c = 1–4 months above 10°C
b = Coldest month below –38°C (–36.4°F), in Siberia only.

Dry Arid and Semiarid Climates — B

Potential evapotranspiration* (natural moisture demand) exceeds precipitation (natural moisture supply) in all B climates. Subdivisions based on precipitation timing and amount and mean annual temperature.

Earth's arid climates.

BWh — Hot low-latitude desert

BWk — Cold midlatitude desert
BW = Precipitation less than 1/2 natural moisture demand.
h = Mean annual temperature >18°C (64.4°F).
k = Mean annual temperature <18°C.

Earth's semiarid climates.

BSh — Hot low-latitude steppe

BSk — Cold midlatitude steppe
BS = Precipitation more than 1/2 natural moisture demand but not equal to it.
h = Mean annual temperature >18°C.
k = Mean annual temperature <18°C.

Polar Climates — E

Warmest month below 10°C (50°F); always cold; ice climates.

ET — Tundra:
Warmest month 0–10°C (32–50°F); precipitation exceeds small potential evapotranspiration demand*; snow cover 8–10 months.

EF — Ice cap:
Warmest month below 0°C (32°F); precipitation exceeds a very small potential evapotranspiration demand; the polar regions.

EM — Polar marine:
All months above −7°C (20°F), warmest month above 0°C; annual temperature ra <17 C° (30 F°).

*Potential evapotranspiration = the amount of water that would evaporate or transpire if it were available—the natural moisture dema in an environment; see Chapter 7.

MODIFIED GOODE'S HOMOLOSINE EQUAL-AREA PROJECTION

TROPICAL CLIMATES

Af Tropical rain forest climate
Am Tropical monsoon climate

Aw Tropical savanna climate

MESOTHERMAL CLIMATES

Cfa Humid subtropical, without dry season, hot summers

Cwa
Cwb Humid subtropical, winter-dry

Cfb
Cfc Marine west coast, without dry season, warm to cool summers

Csa
Csb Mediterranean summer-dry

D MICROTHERMAL CLIMATES

Dfa
Dwa Humid continental, hot summers

Dfb
Dwb Humid continental, warm summers

Dfc
Dwc Subarctic, cool summers

Dfd
Dwd Subarctic, very cold winter

w Winter dry
f Without a dry season

B DRY ARID AND SEMIARID CLIMATES

BW Desert climate

BS Steppe climate

h Low-latitude hot **B** climates
k Midlatitude cold **B** climates

E POLAR CLIMATES
H HIGHLAND

ET Tundra climate

EF Ice cap and sheets
H Denotes cold climate due to high elevation

Appendix D

Common Conversions

Metric to English

Metric Measure	Multiply by	English Equivalent
Length		
Centimetres (cm)	0.3937	Inches (in.)
Metres (m)	3.2808	Feet (ft)
Metres (m)	1.0936	Yards (yd)
Kilometres (km)	0.6214	Miles (mi)
Nautical miles	1.15	Statute miles
Area		
Square centimetres (cm^2)	0.155	Square inches ($in.^2$)
Square metres (m^2)	10.7639	Square feet (ft^2)
Square metres (m^2)	1.1960	Square yards (yd^2)
Square kilometres (km^2)	0.3831	Square miles (mi^2)
Hectares (ha) 10,000 (m^2)	2.4710	Acres (a)
Volume		
Cubic centimetres (cm^3)	0.06	Cubic inches ($in.^3$)
Cubic metres (m^3)	35.30	Cubic feet (ft^3)
Cubic metres (m^3)	1.3079	Cubic yards (yd^3)
Cubic kilometres (km^3)	0.24	Cubic miles (mi^3)
Litres (l)	1.0567	Quarts (qt), U.S.
Litres (l)	0.88	Quarts (qt), Imperial
Litres (l)	0.26	Gallons (gal), U.S.
Litres (l)	0.22	Gallons (gal), Imperial
Mass		
Grams (g)	0.03527	Ounces (oz)
Kilograms (kg)	2.2046	Pounds (lb)
Metric tons (tonne) (t)	1.10	Short tons (tn), U.S.
Velocity		
Metres/second (mps)	2.24	Miles/hour (mph)
Kilometres/hour (kmph)	0.62	Miles/hour (mph)
Knots (kn) (nautical mph)	1.15	Miles/hour (mph)
Temperature		
Degrees Celsius (°C)	1.80 (then add 32)	Degrees Fahrenheit (°F)
Celsius degrees (C°)	1.80	Fahrenheit degrees (F°)
Additional water measurements		
Gallons (Imperial)	1.201	Gallons (U.S.)
Gallons (gal)	0.000003	Acre-feet

1 cubic foot per second per day = 86,400 cubic feet = 1.98 acre-feet

Additional energy and power measurements

1 watt (W) = joule/s

1 joule = 0.239 calories

1 calorie = 4.186 joules

$1 \text{ W/m}^2 = 0.001433 \text{ cal/min}$

$697.8 \text{ W/m}^2 = 1 \text{ cal/cm}^2 \text{ min}^{-1}$

$1 \text{ W/m}^2 = 2.064 \text{ cal/cm}^3 \text{ day}^{-1}$

$1 \text{ W/m}^2 = 61.91 \text{ cal/cm}^2 \text{ month}^{-1}$

$1 \text{ W/m}^2 = 753.4 \text{ cal/cm}^2 \text{ year}^{-1}$

$100 \text{ W/m}^2 = 75 \text{ kcal/cm}^2 \text{ year}^{-1}$

Solar constant:

1372 W/m^2

$2 \text{ cal/cm}^2 \text{ min}^{-1}$

English to Metric

English Measure	Multiply by	Metric Equivalent
Length		
Inches (in.)	2.54	Centimetres (cm)
Feet (ft)	0.3048	Metres (m)
Yards (yd)	0.9144	Metres (m)
Miles (mi)	1.6094	Kilometres (km)
Statute miles	0.8684	Nautical miles
Area		
Square inches (in.^{2})	6.45	Square centimetres (cm^2)
Square feet (ft^2)	0.0929	Square metres (m^2)
Square yards (yd^2)	0.8361	Square metres (m^2)
Square miles (mi^2)	2.5900	Square kilometres (km^2)
Acres (a)	0.4047	Hectares (ha)
Volume		
Cubic inches (in.^{3})	16.39	Cubic centimetres (cm^3)
Cubic feet (ft^3)	0.028	Cubic metres (m^3)
Cubic yards (yd^3)	0.765	Cubic metres (m^3)
Cubic miles (mi^3)	4.17	Cubic kilometres (km^3)
Quarts (qt), U.S.	0.9463	Litres (l)
Quarts (qt), Imperial	1.14	Litres (l)
Gallons (gal), U.S.	3.8	Litres (l)
Gallons (gal), Imperial	4.55	Litres (l)
Mass		
Ounces (oz)	28.3495	Grams (g)
Pounds (lb)	0.4536	Kilograms (kg)
Short ton (tn), U.S.	0.91	Metric tons (tonne) (t)
Velocity		
Miles/hour (mph)	0.448	Metres/second (mps)
Miles/hour (mph)	1.6094	Kilometres/hour (kmph)
Miles/hour (mph)	0.8684	Knots (kn) (nautical mph)
Temperature		
Degrees Fahrenheit (°F)	0.556 (after subtracting 32)	Degrees Celsius (°C)
Fahrenheit degrees (F°)	0.556	Celsius degrees (C°)
Additional water measurements		
Gallons (U.S.)	0.833	Gallons (Imperial)
Acre-feet	325,872	Gallons (gal)

Additional Notation

Multiples		Prefixes	
$1,000,000,000 = 10^9$	giga		G
$1,000,000 = 10^6$	mega		M
$1,000 = 10^3$	kilo		k
$100 = 10^2$	hecto		h
$10 = 10^1$	deka		da
$1 = 10^0$			
$0.1 = 10^{-1}$	deci		d
$0.01 = 10^{-2}$	centi		c
$0.001 = 10^{-3}$	milli		m
$0.000001 = 10^{-6}$	micro		μ

Glossary

*The chapter in which each term appears **boldfaced** is in parentheses and is followed by a specific definition relevant to the term's usage in the chapter.*

Aa (12)   Rough, jagged, and clinkery basaltic lava with sharp edges. This texture is caused by the loss of trapped gases, a slow flow, and the development of a thick skin that cracks into the jagged surface.

Abiotic (1)   Nonliving; Earth's nonliving systems of energy and materials.

Ablation (17)   Loss of glacial ice through melting, sublimation, wind removal by deflation, or the calving of blocks of ice (see deflation).

Abrasion (14, 15, 17)   Mechanical wearing and erosion of bedrock accomplished by the rolling and grinding of particles and rocks carried in a stream, removed by wind in a "sandblasting" action, or imbedded in glacial ice.

Absorption (4)   Assimilation and conversion of radiation from one form to another in a medium. In the process, the temperature of the absorbing surface is raised, thereby affecting the rate and wavelength of radiation from that surface.

Active layer (17)   A zone of seasonally frozen ground that exists between the subsurface permafrost layer and the ground surface. The active layer is subject to consistent daily and seasonal freeze-thaw cycles (see permafrost, periglacial).

Actual evapotranspiration (9)   ACTET; the actual amount of evaporation and transpiration that occurs; derived in the water balance by subtracting the deficit (DEFIC) from potential evapotranspiration in the surface.

Adiabatic (7)   Pertaining to the cooling of an ascending parcel of air through expansion or the warming of a descending parcel of air through compression, without any exchange of heat between the parcel and the surrounding environment.

Advection (4)   Horizontal movement of air or water from one place to another (compare with convection).

Advection fog (7)   Active condensation formed when warm, moist air moves laterally over cooler water or land surfaces, causing the lower layers of the air to be chilled to the dew-point temperature.

Aerosols (3)   Small particles of dust, soot, and pollution suspended in the air.

Aggradation (14)   The general building of land surface because of deposition of material; opposite of degradation. When the sediment load of a stream exceeds the stream's capacity to carry it, the stream channel becomes filled through this process.

Air (3)   A simple mixture of gases (N, O, Ar, CO_2, and trace gases) that is naturally odourless, colourless, tasteless, and formless, blended so thoroughly that it behaves as if it were a single gas.

Air mass (8)   A distinctive, homogeneous body of air that has taken on the moisture and temperature characteristics of its source region.

Air pressure (3, 6)   Pressure produced by the motion, size, and number of gas molecules in the air and exerted on surfaces in contact with the air. Normal sea-level pressure, as measured by the height of a column of mercury (Hg), is expressed as 1013.2 millibars, or 760 mm of Hg. Kilopascal equivalents are reported placing normal at 101.32 kPa; 10 mb = 1 kPa. Air pressure can be measured with mercury or aneroid barometers (see listing for both).

Albedo (4)   The reflective quality of a surface, expressed as the percentage of reflected insolation to incoming insolation; a function of surface colour, angle of incidence, and surface texture.

Aleutian low (6)   See subpolar low-pressure cell.

Alfisols (18)   A soil order in the Soil Taxonomy. Moderately weathered forest soils that are moist versions of Mollisols, with productivity dependent on specific patterns of moisture and temperature; rich in organics. Most wide-ranging of the soil orders.

Alluvial fan (15)   Fan-shaped fluvial landform at the mouth of a canyon; generally occurs in arid landscapes where streams are intermittent.

Alluvial terraces (14)   Level areas that appear as topographic steps above a stream, created by the stream as it scours with renewed downcutting into its floodplain; composed of unconsolidated alluvium (see alluvium).

Alluvium (14)   General descriptive term for clay, silt, sand, gravel, or other unconsolidated rock and mineral fragments transported by running water and deposited as sorted or semisorted sediment on a floodplain, delta, or stream bed.

Alpine glacier (17)   A glacier confined in a mountain valley or walled basin, consisting of three subtypes: valley glacier (within a valley), piedmont glacier (coalesced at the base of a mountain, spreading freely over nearby lowlands), and outlet glacier (flowing outward from a continental glacier).

Alpine tundra (20)   Tundra conditions at high elevation (see Arctic tundra).

Altitude (2)   The angular distance between the horizon (a horizontal plane) and the Sun (or any point in the sky).

Altocumulus (7)   Middle-level, puffy clouds that occur in several forms: patchy rows, wave patterns, a "mackerel sky," or lens-shaped "lenticular" clouds.

Andisols (18)   A soil order in the Soil Taxonomy; derived from volcanic parent materials in areas of volcanic activity. A new order, created in 1990, of soils previously considered under Inceptisols and Entisols.

Anemometer (6)   A device that measures wind velocity.

Aneroid barometer (6)   A device that measures air pressure using a partially evacuated, sealed cell (see air pressure).

Angle of repose (13)   The steepness of a slope that results when loose particles come to rest; an angle of balance between driving and resisting forces, ranging between 33° and 37° from a horizontal plane.

Antarctic Circle (2)   This latitude (66.5° S) denotes the northernmost parallel (in the Southern Hemisphere) that experiences a 24-hour period of darkness in winter or daylight in summer.

Antarctic high (6)   A consistent high-pressure region centered over Antarctica; source region for an intense polar air mass that is dry and associated with the lowest temperatures on Earth.

Anthropogenic atmosphere (3)   Earth's future atmosphere, so named because humans appear to be the principal causative agent.

Anticline (12)   Upfolded rock strata, in which layers slope downward from the axis of the fold, or central ridge (compare syncline).

Anticyclone (6)   A dynamically or thermally caused area of high atmospheric pressure with descending and diverging airflows that rotate clockwise in the Northern Hemisphere and counterclockwise in the Southern Hemisphere (compare cyclone).

Aphelion (2)   The point of Earth's greatest distance from the Sun in its elliptical orbit; reached on July 4 at a distance of 152,083,000 km (94.5 million mi); variable over a 100,000-year cycle (compare perihelion).

Aquiclude (9)   A body of rock that does not conduct groundwater in usable amounts; an impermeable rock layer, related to an aquitard that slows but does not block water flow (compare aquifer).

Aquifer (9)   A body of rock that conducts groundwater in usable amounts; a permeable layer of rock (compare aquiclude).

Aquifer recharge area (9)   The surface area where water enters an aquifer to recharge the water-bearing strata in a groundwater system.

Arctic and alpine tundra (20)   A biome in the northernmost portions of North America and northern Europe and Russia, featuring low ground-level herbaceous plants as well as some woody plants.

Arctic Circle (2)   This latitude (66.5° N) denotes the southernmost parallel (in the Northern Hemisphere) that experiences a 24-hour period of darkness in winter or daylight in summer.

Arête (17)   A sharp ridge that divides two cirque basins. Derived from "knife edge" in French, these form sawtooth and serrated ridges in glaciated mountains.

Aridisols (18)   A soil order in the Soil Taxonomy; largest soil order. Typical of dry climates; low in organic matter and dominated by calcification and salinization.

Artesian water (9)   Pressurized groundwater that rises in a well or a rock structure above the local water table; may flow out onto the ground without pumping (see potentiometric surface).

Asthenosphere (11)   Region of the upper mantle just below the lithosphere; the least rigid portion of Earth's interior and known as the plastic layer, flowing very slowly under extreme heat and pressure.

Atmosphere (1)   The thin veil of gases surrounding Earth, which forms a protective boundary between outer space and the biosphere; generally considered to extend out about 480 km (300 mi) from Earth's surface.

Aurora (2)   A spectacular glowing light display in the ionosphere, stimulated by the interaction of the solar wind with oxygen and nitrogen gases and atoms at high latitudes, called aurora borealis in the Northern Hemisphere and aurora australis in the Southern Hemisphere.

Autumnal (September) equinox (2)   The time around September 22–23 when the Sun's declination crosses the equatorial parallel (0° latitude) and all places on Earth experience days and nights of equal length. The Sun rises at the South Pole and sets at the North Pole (compare vernal equinox).

Available water (9)   The portion of capillary water that is accessible to plant roots; usable water held in soil moisture storage (see capillary water).

Axial parallelism (2)   Earth's axis remains aligned the same throughout the year (it "remains parallel to itself"); thus, the axis extended from the North Pole points into space always near Polaris, the North Star.

Axial tilt (2)   Earth's axis tilts 23.5° from a perpendicular to the plane of the ecliptic (plane of Earth's orbit around the Sun).

Axis (2)   An imaginary line, extending through Earth from the geographic North Pole to the geographic South Pole, around which Earth rotates.

Azores high (6)   A subtropical high-pressure cell that forms in the Northern Hemisphere in the eastern Atlantic (see Bermuda high); associated with warm, clear water and large quantities of sargassum, or gulf weed, characteristic of the Sargasso Sea.

Backswamp (14)   A low-lying, swampy area of a floodplain; adjacent to a river, with the river's natural levee on one side and higher topography on the other (see floodplain, yazoo tributary).

Bajada (15)   A continuous apron of coalesced alluvial fans, formed along the base of mountains in arid climates; presents a gently rolling surface from fan to fan (see alluvial fan).

Barrier beach (16)   Narrow, long, depositional feature, generally composed of sand, that forms offshore roughly parallel to the coast; may appear as barrier islands and long chains of barrier beaches (see barrier island).

Barrier island (16)   Generally, a broadened barrier beach (see barrier beach).

Barrier spit (16)   A depositional landform that develops when transported sand or gravel in a barrier beach or island is deposited in long ridges that are attached at one end to the mainland and partially cross the mouth of a bay.

Basalt (11)   A common extrusive igneous rock, fine-grained, comprising the bulk of the ocean-floor crust, lava flows, and volcanic forms; gabbro is its intrusive form.

Base level (14)   A hypothetical level below which a stream cannot erode its valley, and thus the lowest operative level for denudation processes; in an absolute sense, it is represented by sea level, extending under the landscape.

Basin and Range Province (15)   A region of dry climates, few permanent streams, and interior drainage patterns in the western United States; a faulted landscape composed of a sequence of horsts and grabens.

Batholith (11)   The largest plutonic form exposed at the surface; an irregular intrusive mass; it invades crustal rocks, cooling slowly so that large crystals develop (see pluton).

Bay barrier (16)   An extensive barrier spit of sand or gravel that encloses a bay, cutting it off completely from the ocean and forming a lagoon; produced by littoral drift and wave action; sometimes referred to as a baymouth bar (see barrier spit, lagoon).

Beach (16)   The portion of the coastline where an accumulation of sediment is in motion.

Beach drift (16)   Material, such as sand, gravel, and shells, that is moved by the longshore current in the effective direction of the waves.

Beaufort wind scale (6)   A descriptive scale for the visual estimation of wind speeds; originally conceived in 1806 by Admiral Beaufort of the British Navy.

Bed load (14)   Coarse materials that are dragged along the bed of a stream by traction or by the rolling and bouncing motion of saltation; involves particles too large to remain in suspension (see traction, saltation).

Bedrock (13)   The rock of Earth's crust that is below the soil and is basically unweathered; such solid crust sometimes is exposed as an outcrop.

Bergschrund (17)   These form when a crevasse or wide crack opens along the headwall of a glacier; most visible in summer when covering snow is gone.

Bermuda high (6)   A subtropical high-pressure cell that forms in the western North Atlantic (see Azores high).

Biodiversity (19)   A principle of ecology and biogeography: the more diverse the species population in an ecosystem (in number of species, quantity of members in each species, and genetic content), the more risk is spread over the entire community, which results in greater overall stability, greater productivity, and increased use of nutrients, as compared to a monoculture of little or no diversity.

Biogeochemical cycle (19)   One of several circuits of flowing elements and materials (carbon, oxygen, nitrogen, phosphorus, water) that combine Earth's biotic (living) and abiotic (nonliving) systems; the cycling of materials is continuous and renewed through the biosphere and the life processes.

Biogeographic realm (20)   One of eight regions of the biosphere, each representative of evolutionary core areas of related flora (plants) and fauna (animals); a broad geographical classification scheme.

Biogeography (19)   The study of the distribution of plants and animals and related ecosystems; the geographical relationships with their environments over time.

Biomass (19)   The total mass of living organisms on Earth or per unit area of a landscape; also, the weight of the living organisms in an ecosystem.

Biome (20)   A large terrestrial ecosystem characterized by specific plant communities and formations; usually named after the predominant vegetation in the region (see terrestrial ecosystem).

Biosphere (1)   That area where the atmosphere, lithosphere, and hydrosphere function together to form the context within which life exists; an intricate web that connects all organisms with their physical environment.

Biotic (1)   Living; referring to Earth's living system of organisms.

Blowout depression (15)   Eolian (wind) erosion in which deflation forms a basin in areas of loose sediment. Diameter may range up to hundreds of metres (see deflation).

Bolson (15)   The slope and basin area between the crests of two adjacent ridges in a dry region.

Boreal forest (20)   See needleleaf forest.

Brackish (16)   Descriptive of seawater with a salinity of less than 35‰; for example, the Baltic Sea (contrast to brine).

Braided stream (14)   A stream that becomes a maze of interconnected channels laced with excess sediment. Braiding often occurs with a reduction of discharge that reduces a stream's transporting ability or with an increase in sediment load.

Breaker (16)   The point where a wave's height exceeds its vertical stability and the wave breaks as it approaches the shore.

Brine (16)   Seawater with a salinity of more than 35‰; for example, the Persian Gulf (contrast to brackish).

Brunisolic (18)   A CSSC soil order with sufficiently developed horizons to distinguish it from the Regosolic order. Soils under forest cover with brownish horizons, although various colours are possible. Also, can be with mixed forest, shrubs, and grass.

Calcification (18)   The illuviated (deposited) accumulation of calcium carbonate or magnesium carbonate in the B and C soil horizons.

Caldera (12)   An interior sunken portion of a composite volcano's crater; usually steep-sided and circular, sometimes containing a lake; also can be found in conjunction with shield volcanoes.

Canadian System of Soil Classification (CSSC) (18)   A soil classification system based on observable soil properties actually seen in the field; published in 1987 by the Canada Soil Survey Committee. Adapted to Canada's environment, the CSSC consists of 10 soil orders.

Capillary water (9)   Soil moisture, most of which is accessible to plant roots; held in the soil by the water's surface tension and cohesive forces between water and soil (see also available water, field capacity, hygroscopic water, and wilting point).

Carbonation (13)   A chemical weathering process in which weak carbonic acid (water and carbon dioxide) reacts with many minerals that contain calcium, magnesium, potassium, and sodium (especially limestone), transforming them into carbonates.

Carbon monoxide (3)   An odourless, colourless, tasteless combination of carbon and oxygen produced by the incomplete combustion of fossil fuels or other carbon-containing substances; toxicity to humans is due to its affinity for hemoglobin, displacing oxygen in the bloodstream; CO.

Carnivore (19)   A secondary consumer that principally eats meat for sustenance. The top carnivore in a food chain is considered a tertiary consumer (compare herbivore).

Cartography (1)   The making of maps and charts; a specialized science and art that blends aspects of geography, engineering, mathematics, graphics, computer science, and artistic specialties.

Cation-exchange capacity (CEC) (18)   The ability of soil colloids to exchange cations between their surfaces and the soil solution; a measured potential that indicates soil fertility (see soil colloid, soil fertility).

Chaparral (20)   Dominant shrub formations of Mediterranean dry-summer climates; characterized by sclerophyllous scrub and short, stunted, tough forests; derived from the Spanish *chapparo*; specific to California (see Mediterranean shrubland).

Chemical weathering (13)   Decomposition and decay of the constituent minerals in rock through chemical alteration of those minerals. Water is essential, with rates keyed to temperature and precipitation values. Chemical reactions are active at microsites even in dry climates. Processes include hydrolysis, oxidation, carbonation, and solution.

Chernozemic (18)   A CSSC soil order with well to imperfectly drained soils of the steppe–grassland–forest transition in Southern Alberta; Saskatchewan; Manitoba; Okanagan Valley, BC; and Palouse Prairie, BC. Accumulation of organic matter in surface horizon.

Chinook wind (8)   North American term for a warm, dry, downslope airflow; characteristic of the rain-shadow region on the leeward side of mountains; known as föhn, or foehn, winds in Europe (see rain shadow).

Chlorofluorocarbons (CFC) (3)   A manufactured molecule (polymer) made of chlorine, fluorine, and carbon; inert and possessing remarkable heat properties; also known as one of the halogens. After slow transport to the stratospheric ozone layer, CFCs react with ultraviolet radiation, freeing chlorine atoms that act as a catalyst to produce reactions that destroy ozone; manufacture banned by international treaties.

Chlorophyll (19)   A light-sensitive pigment that resides within chloroplasts (organelles) in leaf cells of plants; the basis of photosynthesis.

Cinder cone (12)   A volcanic landform of pyroclastics and scoria, usually small and cone-shaped and generally not more than 450 m (1500 ft) in height, with a truncated top.

Circle of illumination (2)   The division between light and dark on Earth; a day–night great circle.

Circum-Pacific belt (12)   A tectonically and volcanically active region encircling the Pacific Ocean; also known as the "ring of fire."

Cirque (17)   A scooped-out, amphitheatre-shaped basin at the head of an alpine glacier valley; an erosional landform.

Cirrus (7)   Wispy, filamentous ice-crystal clouds that occur above 6000 m (20,000 ft); appear in a variety of forms, from feathery hairlike fibres to veils of fused sheets.

Classification (10)   The process of ordering or grouping data or phenomena in related classes; results in a regular distribution of information; a taxonomy.

Climate (10)   The consistent, long-term behaviour of weather over time, including its variability; in contrast to weather, which is the condition of the atmosphere at any given place and time.

Climatic regions (10)   An area of homogenous climate that features characteristic regional weather and air mass patterns.

Climatology (10)   The scientific study of climate and climatic patterns and the consistent behaviour of weather, including its variability and extremes, over time in one place or region; includes the effects of climate change on human society and culture.

Climograph (10)   A graph that plots daily, monthly, or annual temperature and precipitation values for a selected station; may also include additional weather information.

Closed system (1)   A system that is shut off from the surrounding environment so that it is entirely self-contained in terms of energy and materials; Earth is a closed material system (compare open system).

Cloud (7)   An aggregate of tiny moisture droplets and ice crystals; classified by altitude of occurrence and shape.

Cloud-albedo forcing (4)   An increase in albedo (the reflectivity of a surface) caused by clouds due to their reflection of incoming insolation.

Cloud-condensation nuclei (7)   Microscopic particles necessary as matter on which water vapour condenses to form moisture droplets; can be sea salts, dust, soot, or ash.

Cloud-greenhouse forcing (4)   An increase in greenhouse warming caused by clouds because they can act like insulation, trapping longwave (infrared) radiation.

Col (17)   Formed by two headward-eroding cirques that reduce an arête (ridge crest) to form a high pass or saddlelike narrow depression.

Cold desert and semidesert (20)   A type of desert biome found at higher latitudes than warm deserts. Interior location and rain-shadow locations produce these cold deserts in North America.

Cold front (8)   The leading edge of an advancing cold air mass; identified on a weather map as a line marked with triangular spikes pointing in the direction of frontal movement (compare warm front).

Community (19, 20)   A convenient biotic subdivision within an ecosystem; formed by interacting populations of animals and plants in an area.

Composite volcano (12)   A volcano formed by a sequence of explosive volcanic eruptions; steep-sided, conical in shape; sometimes referred to as a stratovolcano, although composite is the preferred term (compare shield volcano).

Conduction (4)   The slow molecule-to-molecule transfer of heat through a medium, from warmer to cooler portions.

Cone of depression (9)   The depressed shape of the water table around a well after active pumping. The water table adjacent to the well is drawn down by the water removal.

Confined aquifer (9)   An aquifer that is bounded above and below by impermeable layers of rock or sediment (see artesian water, unconfined aquifer).

Constant isobaric surface (6)   An elevated surface in the atmosphere on which all points have the same pressure, usually 500 mb. Along this constant-pressure surface, isobars mark the paths of upper-air winds.

Consumer (19)   Organism in an ecosystem that depends on producers (organisms that use carbon dioxide as their sole source of carbon) for its source of nutrients; also called a heterotroph (compare producer).

Consumptive use (9)   A use that removes water from a water budget at one point and makes it unavailable further downstream (compare withdrawal).

Continental divide (14)   A ridge or elevated area that separates drainage on a continental scale; specifically, that ridge in North America that separates drainage to the Pacific on the west side from drainage to the Atlantic and Gulf on the east side and to Hudson Bay and the Arctic Ocean in the north.

Continental drift (11)   A proposal by Alfred Wegener in 1912 stating that Earth's landmasses have migrated over the past 225 million years from a supercontinent he called Pangaea to the present configuration; the widely accepted plate tectonics theory today (see plate tectonics).

Continental effect (5)   A quality of regions that lack the temperature-moderating effects of the sea and that exhibit a greater range of minimum and maximum temperatures, both daily and annually (see marine, land–water heating differences).

Continental glacier (17)   A continuous mass of unconfined ice, covering at least 50,000 km^2 (19,500 mi^2); most extensive at present as ice sheets covering Greenland and Antarctica (compare alpine glacier).

Continental landmasses (12)   The broadest category of landform, including those masses of crust that reside above or near sea level and the adjoining undersea continental shelves along the coastline; sometimes synonymous with continental platforms.

Continental shield (12)   Generally, old, low-elevation heartland regions of continental crust; various cratons (granitic cores) and ancient mountains exposed at the surface.

Contour lines (Appendix A)   Isolines on a topographic map that connect all points at the same elevation relative to a reference elevation called the vertical datum.

Convection (4) Transfer of heat from one place to another through the physical movement of air; involves a strong vertical motion (compare to advection).

Convectional lifting (8) Air passing over warm surfaces gains buoyancy and lifts, initiating adiabatic processes.

Convergent lifting (8) Airflows in conflict force lifting and displacement of air upward, initiating adiabatic processes.

Coordinated Universal Time (UTC) (1) The official reference time in all countries, formerly known as Greenwich Mean Time; now measured by six primary standard atomic clocks, the time calculations are collected in Paris at the International Bureau of Weights and Measures (BIPM); the legal reference for time in all countries and broadcast worldwide.

Coral (16) A simple, cylindrical marine animal with a saclike body that secretes calcium carbonate to form a hard external skeleton and, cumulatively, landforms called reefs; lives symbiotically with nutrient-producing algae; presently in a worldwide state of decline due to bleaching (loss of algae).

Core (11) The deepest inner portion of Earth, representing one-third of its entire mass; differentiated into two zones—a solid-iron inner core surrounded by a dense, molten, fluid metallic-iron outer core.

Coriolis force (6) The apparent deflection of moving objects (wind, ocean currents, missiles) from traveling in a straight path, in proportion to the speed of Earth's rotation at different latitudes. Deflection is to the right in the Northern Hemisphere and to the left in the Southern Hemisphere; maximum at the poles and zero along the equator.

Crater (12) A circular surface depression formed by volcanism; built by accumulation, collapse, or explosion; usually located at a volcanic vent or pipe; can be at the summit or on the flank of a volcano.

Crevasse (17) A vertical crack that develops in a glacier as a result of friction between valley walls, or tension forces of extension on convex slopes, or compression forces on concave slopes.

Crust (11) Earth's outer shell of crystalline surface rock, ranging from 5 to 60 km (3 to 38 mi) in thickness from oceanic crust to mountain ranges. Average density of continental crust is $2.7 g/cm^2$, whereas oceanic crust is $3.0 g/cm^3$.

Cryosphere (1, 7, 10, 17, 20) The frozen portion of Earth's waters, including ice sheets, ice caps and fields, glaciers, ice shelves, sea ice, and subsurface ground ice and frozen ground (permafrost).

Crysolic (18) A CSSC soil order that dominates the northern third of Canada, with permafrost closer to the surface and composed of mineral and organic soil deposits. Generally found north of the treeline, or in fine-textured soils in subarctic forest, or in some organic soils in boreal forests.

Cumulonimbus (7) A towering, precipitation-producing cumulus cloud that is vertically developed across altitudes associated with other clouds; frequently associated with lightning and thunder and thus sometimes called a thunderhead.

Cumulus (7) Bright and puffy cumuliform clouds up to 2000 m (6500 ft) in altitude.

Cyclogenesis (8) An atmospheric process that describes the birth of a midlatitude wave cyclone, usually along the polar front. Also refers to strengthening and development of a midlatitude cyclone along the eastern slope of the Rockies, other north–south mountain barriers, and along the North American and Asian east coasts (see midlatitude cyclone, polar front).

Cyclone (6) A dynamically or thermally caused area of low atmospheric pressure with converging and ascending airflows. Rotates counterclockwise in the Northern Hemisphere and clockwise in the Southern Hemisphere (compare anticyclone; see midlatitude cyclone, tropical cyclone).

Daylength (2) Duration of exposure to insolation, varying during the year depending on latitude; an important aspect of seasonality.

Daylight saving time (1) Time is set ahead 1 hour in the spring and set back 1 hour in the fall in the Northern Hemisphere. In Canada and the United States, time is set ahead on the second Sunday in March and set back on the first Sunday in November—except in Hawai'i, Arizona, and Saskatchewan, which exempt themselves.

Debris avalanche (13) A mass of falling and tumbling rock, debris, and soil; can be dangerous because of the tremendous velocities achieved by the onrushing materials.

Declination (2) The latitude that receives direct overhead (perpendicular) insolation on a particular day; the subsolar point migrates annually through 47° of latitude between the Tropics of Cancer (23.5° N) and Capricorn (23.5° S).

Decomposer (19) Bacteria and fungi that digest organic debris outside their bodies and absorb and release nutrients in an ecosystem (see detritivores).

Derechos (8) Strong linear winds in excess of 26 m/sec (58 mph), associated with thunderstorms and bands of showers crossing a region.

Deficit (9) DEFIC; in a water balance, the amount of unmet (unsatisfied) potential evapotranspiration; a natural water shortage (refer to POTET, or PE).

Deflation (15) A process of wind erosion that removes and lifts individual particles, literally blowing away unconsolidated, dry, or non-cohesive sediments (see blowout depression).

Delta (14) A depositional plain formed where a river enters a lake or an ocean; named after the triangular shape of the Greek letter delta, Δ.

Denudation (13) A general term that refers to all processes that cause degradation of the landscape: weathering, mass movement, erosion, and transport.

Deposition (14) The process whereby weathered, wasted, and transported sediments are laid down by air, water, and ice.

Desalination (9) In a water resources context, the removal of organics, debris, and salinity from seawater through distillation or reverse osmosis to produce potable water.

Desert biome (20) Arid landscapes of uniquely adapted dry-climate plants and animals.

Desertification (15) The expansion of deserts worldwide, related principally to poor agricultural practices (overgrazing and inappropriate agricultural practices), improper soil-moisture management, erosion and salinization, deforestation, and the ongoing climatic change; an unwanted semipermanent invasion into neighbouring biomes.

Desert pavement (15) On arid landscapes, a surface formed when wind deflation and sheetflow remove smaller particles, leaving residual pebbles and gravels to concentrate at the surface; resembles a cobblestone street (see deflation, sheetflow).

Detritivores (19) Detritus feeders and decomposers that consume, digest, and destroy organic wastes and debris. *Detritus feeders*—worms, mites, termites, centipedes, snails, crabs, and even vultures, among others—consume detritus and excrete nutrients and simple inorganic compounds that fuel an ecosystem. Compare with decomposers (see decomposers).

Dew-point temperature (7) The temperature at which a given mass of air becomes saturated, holding all the water it can hold. Any further cooling or addition of water vapour results in active condensation.

Diagnostic subsurface horizon (18) A soil horizon that originates below the epipedon at varying depths; may be part of the A and B horizons; important in soil description as part of the Soil Taxonomy.

Differential weathering (13) The effect of different resistances in rock, coupled with variations in the intensity of physical and chemical weathering.

Diffuse radiation (4) The downward component of scattered incoming insolation from clouds and the atmosphere.

Discharge (14) The measured volume of flow in a river that passes by a given cross section of a stream in a given unit of time; expressed in cubic metres per second or cubic feet per second.

Dissolved load (14) Materials carried in chemical solution in a stream, derived from minerals such as limestone and dolomite, or from soluble salts.

Downwelling current (6) An area of the sea where a convergence or accumulation of water thrusts excess water downward; occurs, for example, at the western end of the equatorial current or along the margins of Antarctica (compare upwelling currents).

Drainage basin (14) The basic spatial geomorphic unit of a river system; distinguished from a neighbouring basin by ridges and highlands that form divides, marking the limits of the catchment area of the drainage basin or its watershed.

Drainage density (14) A measure of the overall operational efficiency of a drainage basin, determined by the ratio of combined channel lengths to the unit area.

Drainage pattern (14) A distinctive geometric arrangement of streams in a region, determined by slope, differing rock resistance to weathering and erosion, climatic and hydrologic variability, and structural controls of the landscape.

Drawdown (9)   See cone of depression.

Drought (9)   Does not have a simple water-budget definition; rather, it can occur in at least four forms: *meteorological drought, agricultural drought, hydrologic drought,* and/or a *socioeconomic drought.*

Drumlin (17)   A depositional landform related to glaciation that is composed of till (unstratified, unsorted) and is streamlined in the direction of continental ice movement—blunt end upstream and tapered end downstream with a rounded summit.

Dry adiabatic rate (DAR) (7)   The rate at which an unsaturated parcel of air cools (if ascending) or heats (if descending); a rate of 10 C° per 1000 m (5.5 F° per 1000 ft) (see adiabatic; compare moist adiabatic rate).

Dune (15)   A depositional feature of sand grains deposited in transient mounds, ridges, and hills; extensive areas of sand dunes are called sand seas.

Dust dome (4)   A dome of airborne pollution associated with every major city; may be blown by winds into elongated plumes downwind from the city.

Dynamic equilibrium (1)   Increasing or decreasing operations in a system demonstrate a trend over time, a change in average conditions.

Dynamic equilibrium model (13)   The balancing act between tectonic uplift and erosion, between the resistance of crust materials and the work of denudation processes. Landscapes evidence ongoing adaptation to rock structure, climate, local relief, and elevation.

Earthquake (12)   A sharp release of energy that sends waves traveling through Earth's crust at the moment of rupture along a fault or in association with volcanic activity. The moment magnitude scale (formerly the Richter scale) estimates earthquake magnitude; intensity is described by the Mercalli scale.

Earth systems science (1)   An emerging science of Earth as a complete, systematic entity. An interacting set of physical, chemical, and biological systems that produce the processes of a whole Earth system. A study of planetary change resulting from system operations; includes a desire for a more quantitative understanding among components, rather than qualitative description.

Ebb tide (16)   Falling or lowering tide during the daily tidal cycle (compare flood tide).

Ecological succession (19)   The process whereby different and usually more complex assemblages of plants and animals replace older and usually simpler communities; communities are in a constant state of change as each species adapts to conditions. Ecosystems do not exhibit a stable point or successional climax condition as previously thought (refer to primary succession, secondary succession).

Ecology (19)   The science that studies the relations between organisms and their environment and among various ecosystems.

Ecosphere (1)   Another name for the biosphere.

Ecosystem (19, 20)   A self-regulating association of living plants, animals, and their nonliving physical and chemical environments.

Ecotone (20)   A boundary transition zone between adjoining ecosystems that may vary in width and represent areas of tension as similar species of plants and animals compete for the resources (see ecosystem).

Effusive eruption (12)   A volcanic eruption characterized by low-viscosity basaltic magma and low-gas content, which readily escapes. Lava pours forth onto the surface with relatively small explosions and few pyroclastics; tends to form shield volcanoes (see shield volcano, lava, pyroclastics; compare explosive eruption).

Elastic-rebound theory (12)   A concept describing the faulting process in Earth's crust, in which the two sides of a fault appear locked despite the motion of adjoining pieces of crust, but with accumulating strain they rupture suddenly, snapping to new positions relative to each other, generating an earthquake.

Electromagnetic spectrum (2)   All the radiant energy produced by the Sun placed in an ordered range, divided according to wavelengths.

Eluviation (18)   The removal of finer particles and minerals from the upper horizons of soil; an erosional process within a soil body (compare illuviation).

Empirical classification (10)   A climate classification based on weather statistics or other data; used to determine general climate categories (compare genetic classification).

Endogenic system (11)   The system internal to Earth, driven by radioactive heat derived from sources within the planet. In response, the surface

fractures, mountain building occurs, and earthquakes and volcanoes are activated (compare exogenic system).

Entisols (18)   A soil order in the Soil Taxonomy. Specifically lacks vertical development of horizons; usually young or undeveloped. Found in active slopes, alluvial-filled floodplains, poorly drained tundra.

Environmental lapse rate (3)   The actual lapse rate in the lower atmosphere at any particular time under local weather conditions; may deviate above or below the normal lapse rate of 6.4 C° per 1000 m (3.5 F° per 1000 ft). (Compare normal lapse rate.)

Eolian (15)   Caused by wind; refers to the erosion, transportation, and deposition of materials; spelled aeolian in some countries.

Epipedon (18)   The diagnostic soil horizon that forms at the surface; not to be confused with the A horizon; may include all or part of the illuviated B horizon.

Equal area (1, Appendix A)   A trait of a map projection; indicates the equivalence of all areas on the surface of the map, although shape is distorted (see map projections).

Equatorial and tropical rain forest (20)   A lush biome of tall broadleaf evergreen trees and diverse plants and animals, roughly between 23.5° N and 23.5° S. The dense canopy of leaves is usually arranged in three levels.

Equatorial low-pressure trough (6)   A thermally caused low-pressure area that almost girdles Earth, with air converging and ascending all along its extent; also called the intertropical convergence zone (ITCZ).

Erg desert (15)   A sandy desert, or area where sand is so extensive that it constitutes a sand sea.

Erosion (14)   Denudation by wind, water, or ice, which dislodges, dissolves, or removes surface material.

Esker (17)   A sinuously curving, narrow deposit of coarse gravel that forms along a meltwater stream channel, developing in a tunnel beneath a glacier.

Estuary (14)   The point at which the mouth of a river enters the sea, where freshwater and seawater are mixed; a place where tides ebb and flow.

Eustasy (7)   Refers to worldwide changes in sea level that are not related to movements of land but rather to a rise and fall in the volume of water in the oceans.

Evaporation (9)   The movement of free water molecules away from a wet surface into air that is less than saturated; the phase change of water to water vapour.

Evaporation fog (7)   A fog formed when cold air flows over the warm surface of a lake, ocean, or other body of water; forms as the water molecules evaporate from the water surface into the cold, overlying air; also known as steam fog or sea smoke.

Evaporation pan (9)   A weather instrument consisting of a standardized pan from which evaporation occurs, with water automatically replaced and measured; an evaporimeter.

Evapotranspiration (9)   The merging of evaporation and transpiration water loss into one term (see potential and actual evapotranspiration).

Evolution (19)   A theory that single-cell organisms adapted, modified, and passed along inherited changes to multicellular organisms. The genetic makeup of successive generations is shaped by environmental factors, physiological functions, and behaviours that created a greater rate of survival and reproduction and were passed along through natural selection.

Exfoliation dome (13)   A dome-shaped feature of weathering, produced by the response of granite to the overburden removal process, which relieves pressure from the rock. Layers of rock slough ("sluff") off in slabs or shells in a sheeting process.

Exogenic system (11)   Earth's external surface system, powered by insolation, which energizes air, water, and ice and sets them in motion, under the influence of gravity. Includes all processes of landmass denudation (compare endogenic system).

Exosphere (3)   An extremely rarefied outer atmospheric halo beyond the thermopause at an altitude of 480 km (300 mi); probably composed of hydrogen and helium atoms, with some oxygen atoms and nitrogen molecules present near the thermopause.

Exotic stream (14)   A river that rises in a humid region and flows through an arid region, with discharge decreasing toward the mouth; for example, the Nile River and the Colorado River.

Explosive eruption (12)   A violent and unpredictable volcanic eruption, the result of magma that is thicker (more viscous), stickier, and higher in gas and silica content than that of an effusive eruption; tends to form blockages within a volcano; produces composite volcanic landforms (see composite volcano; compare effusive eruption).

Faulting (12) The process whereby displacement and fracturing occur between two portions of Earth's crust; usually associated with earthquake activity.

Feedback loop (1) Created when a portion of system output is returned as an information input, causing changes that guide further system operation (see negative feedback, positive feedback).

Field capacity (9) Water held in the soil by hydrogen bonding against the pull of gravity, remaining after water drains from the larger pore spaces; the available water for plants (see available water, capillary water).

Fire ecology (19) The study of fire as a natural agent and dynamic factor in community succession.

Firn (17) Snow of a granular texture that is transitional in the slow transformation from snow to glacial ice; snow that has persisted through a summer season in the zone of accumulation.

Firn line (17) The snow line that is visible on the surface of a glacier, where winter snows survive the summer ablation season; analogous to a snow line on land (see ablation).

Fjord (17) A drowned glaciated valley, or glacial trough, along a seacoast.

Flash flood (15) A sudden and short-lived torrent of water that exceeds the capacity of a stream channel; associated with desert and semiarid washes.

Flood (14) A high water level that overflows the natural riverbank along any portion of a stream.

Floodplain (14) A flat, low-lying area along a stream channel, created by and subject to recurrent flooding; alluvial deposits generally mask underlying rock.

Flood tide (16) Rising tide during the daily tidal cycle (compare ebb tide).

Fluvial (14) Stream-related processes; from the Latin *fluvius* for "river" or "running water."

Fog (7) A cloud, generally stratiform, in contact with the ground, with visibility usually reduced to less than 1 km (3300 ft).

Folding (12) The bending and deformation of beds of rock strata subjected to compressional forces.

Food chain (19) The circuit along which energy flows from producers (plants), which manufacture their own food, to consumers (animals); a one-directional flow of chemical energy, ending with decomposers.

Food web (19) A complex network of interconnected food chains (see food chain).

Formation class (20) That portion of a biome that concerns the plant communities only, categorized by size, shape, and structure of the dominant vegetation.

Friction force (6) The effect of drag by the wind as it moves across a surface; may be operative through 500 m (1600 ft) of altitude. Surface friction slows the wind and therefore reduces the effectiveness of the Coriolis force.

Frost action (13) A powerful mechanical force produced as water expands up to 9% of its volume as it freezes. Water freezing in a cavity in a rock can break the rock if it exceeds the rock's tensional strength.

Funnel cloud (8) The visible swirl extending from the bottom side of a cloud, which may or may not develop into a tornado. A tornado is a funnel cloud that has extended all the way to the ground (see tornado).

Fusion (2) The process of forcibly joining positively charged hydrogen and helium nuclei under extreme temperature and pressure; occurs naturally in thermonuclear reactions within stars, such as our Sun.

Gelifluction (13, 17) Refers to soil flow in periglacial environments, a progressive, lateral movement; a type of solifluction formed under periglacial conditions of permafrost and frozen ground (see solifluction).

Gelisols (18) A new soil order in the Soil Taxonomy, added in 1998, describing cold and frozen soils at high latitudes or high elevations; characteristic cold tundra vegetation (see Canadian System of Soil Classification for similar types).

General circulation model (GCM) (10) Complex, computer-based climate model that produces generalizations of reality and forecasts of future weather and climate conditions. Complex GCMs (three-dimensional models) are in use in the United States and in other countries.

Genetic classification (10) A climate classification that uses causative factors to determine climatic regions; for example, an analysis of the effect of interacting air masses (compare empirical classification).

Geodesy (1) The science that determines Earth's shape and size through surveys, mathematical means, and remote sensing (see geoid).

Geographic information system (GIS) (1) A computer-based data processing tool or methodology used for gathering, manipulating, and analyzing geographic information to produce a holistic, interactive analysis.

Geography (1) The science that studies the interdependence and interaction among geographic areas, natural systems, processes, society, and cultural activities over space—a spatial science. The five themes of geographic education are location, place, movement, regions, and human–Earth relationships.

Geoid (1) A word that describes Earth's shape; literally, "the shape of Earth is Earth-shaped." A theoretical surface at sea level that extends through the continents; deviates from a perfect sphere.

Geologic cycle (11) A general term characterizing the vast cycling that proceeds in the lithosphere. It encompasses the hydrologic cycle, tectonic cycle, and rock cycle.

Geologic time scale (11) A depiction of eras, periods, and epochs that span Earth's history; shows both the sequence of rock strata and their absolute dates, as determined by methods such as radioactive isotopic dating.

Geomagnetic reversal (11) A polarity change in Earth's magnetic field. With uneven regularity, the magnetic field fades to zero, then returns to full strength but with the magnetic poles reversed. Reversals have been recorded 9 times during the past 4 million years.

Geomorphic threshold (13) The threshold up to which landforms change before lurching to a new set of relationships, with rapid realignments of landscape materials and slopes.

Geomorphology (13) The science that analyzes and describes the origin, evolution, form, classification, and spatial distribution of landforms.

Geostrophic wind (6) A wind moving between areas of different pressure along a path that is parallel to the isobars. It is a product of the pressure gradient force and the Coriolis force (see isobar, pressure gradient force, Coriolis force).

Geothermal energy (11, 12) The energy in steam and hot water heated by subsurface magma near groundwater. Geothermal energy literally refers to heat from Earth's interior, whereas *geothermal power* relates to specific applied strategies of geothermal electric or geothermal direct applications. This energy is used in Iceland, New Zealand, Italy, and northern California, among other locations.

Glacial drift (17) The general term for all glacial deposits, both unsorted (till) and sorted (stratified drift).

Glacial ice (17) A hardened form of ice, very dense in comparison to normal snow or firn.

Glacier (17) A large mass of perennial ice resting on land or floating shelflike in the sea adjacent to the land; formed from the accumulation and recrystallization of snow, which then flows slowly under the pressure of its own weight and the pull of gravity.

Glacier surge (17) The rapid, lurching, unexpected forward movement of a glacier.

Glacio-eustatic (7) Changes in sea level in response to changes in the amount of water stored on Earth as ice; the more water that is bound up in glaciers and ice sheets, the lower the sea level (compare eustasy).

Gleysation (18) A process of humus and clay accumulation in cold, wet climates with poor drainage.

Gleysolic (18) A CSSC soil order defined on the basis of colour and mottling that results from chronic reducing conditions inherent in poorly drained mineral soils under wet conditions. High water table and long periods of water saturation.

Global dimming (4) The decline in sunlight reaching Earth's surface owing to pollution, aerosols, and clouds.

Global positioning system (GPS) (1) Latitude, longitude, and elevation are accurately calibrated using this handheld instrument that calibrates radio signals from satellites.

Goode's homolosine projection (Appendix A) An equal-area projection formed by splicing together a sinusoidal and a homolographic projection.

Graben (12) Pairs or groups of faults that produce downward-faulted blocks; characteristic of the basins of the interior western United States (compare horst; see Basin and Range Province).

Graded stream (14) An idealized condition in which a stream's load and the landscape mutually adjust. This forms a dynamic equilibrium among erosion, transported load, deposition, and the stream's capacity.

Gradient (14)   The drop in elevation from a stream's headwaters to its mouth, ideally forming a concave slope.

Granite (11)   A coarse-grained (slow-cooling) intrusive igneous rock of 25% quartz and more than 50% potassium and sodium feldspars; characteristic of the continental crust.

Gravitational water (9)   That portion of surplus water that percolates downward from the capillary zone, pulled by gravity to the groundwater zone.

Gravity (2)   The mutual force exerted by the masses of objects that are attracted one to another and produced in an amount proportional to each object's mass.

Great circle (1)   Any circle drawn on a globe with its centre coinciding with the centre of the globe. An infinite number of great circles can be drawn, but only one parallel is a great circle—the equator (compare small circle).

Greenhouse effect (4)   The process whereby radiatively active gases (carbon dioxide, water vapour, methane, and CFCs) absorb insolation and emit the energy at longer wavelengths, which are retained longer, delaying the loss of infrared to space. Thus, the lower troposphere is warmed through the radiation and re-radiation of infrared wavelengths. The approximate similarity between this process and that of a greenhouse explains the name.

Greenwich Mean Time (GMT) (1)   Former world standard time, now reported as Coordinated Universal Time (UTC) (see Coordinated Universal Time).

Ground ice (17)   Subsurface water that is frozen in regions of permafrost. The moisture content of areas with ground ice may vary from nearly absent in regions of drier permafrost to almost 100% in saturated soils (compare permafrost).

Groundwater (9)   Water beneath the surface that is beyond the soil-root zone; a major source of potable water.

Groundwater mining (9)   Pumping an aquifer beyond its capacity to flow and recharge; an overuse of the groundwater resource.

Gulf Stream (5)   A strong, northward-moving, warm current off the east coast of North America, which carries its water far into the North Atlantic.

Habitat (19, 20)   A physical location to which an organism is biologically suited. Most species have specific habitat parameters and limits (compare to niche).

Hail (8)   A type of precipitation formed when a raindrop is repeatedly circulated above and below the freezing level in a cloud, with each cycle freezing more moisture onto the hailstone until it becomes too heavy to stay aloft.

Hair hygrometer (7)   An instrument for measuring relative humidity; based on the principle that human hair will change as much as 4% in length between 0% and 100% relative humidity.

Heat (3)   The flow of kinetic energy from one body to another because of a temperature difference between them.

Herbivore (19)   The primary consumer in a food web, which eats plant material formed by a producer (plant) that has photosynthesized organic molecules (compare carnivore).

Heterosphere (3)   A zone of the atmosphere above the mesopause, 80 km (50 mi) in altitude; composed of rarefied layers of oxygen atoms and nitrogen molecules; includes the ionosphere.

Histosols (18)   A soil order in the Soil Taxonomy. Formed from thick accumulations of organic matter, such as beds of former lakes, bogs, and layers of peat.

Homosphere (3)   A zone of the atmosphere from Earth's surface up to 80 km (50 mi), composed of an even mixture of gases, including nitrogen, oxygen, argon, carbon dioxide, and trace gases.

Horn (17)   A pyramidal, sharp-pointed peak that results when several cirque glaciers gouge an individual mountain summit from all sides.

Horst (12)   Upward-faulted blocks produced by pairs or groups of faults; characteristic of the mountain ranges of the interior of the western United States (see graben and Basin and Range Province).

Hot spot (11)   An individual point of upwelling material originating in the asthenosphere, or deeper in the mantle; tends to remain fixed relative to migrating plates; some 100 are identified worldwide, exemplified by Yellowstone National Park, Hawai'i, and Iceland.

Human–Earth relationships (1)   One of the oldest themes of geography (the human-land tradition); includes the spatial analysis of settlement patterns, resource utilization and exploitation, hazard perception and planning, and the impact of environmental modification and artificial landscape creation.

Humidity (7)   Water vapour content of the air. The capacity of the air to hold water vapour is mostly a function of the temperature of the air and the water vapour.

Humus (18)   A mixture of organic debris in the soil worked by consumers and decomposers in the humification process; characteristically formed from plant and animal litter deposited at the surface.

Hurricane (8)   A tropical cyclone that is fully organized and intensified in inward-spiraling rainbands; ranges from 160 to 960 km (100 to 600 mi) in diameter, with wind speeds in excess of 119 kmph (65 knots, or 74 mph); a name used specifically in the Atlantic and eastern Pacific (compare typhoon).

Hydration (13)   A chemical weathering process involving water that is added to a mineral, which initiates swelling and stress within the rock, mechanically forcing grains apart as the constituents expand (contrast to hydrolysis).

Hydraulic action (14)   The erosive work accomplished by the turbulence of water; causes a squeezing and releasing action in joints in bedrock; capable of prying and lifting rocks.

Hydrograph (14)   A graph of stream discharge (in cms or cfs) over a period of time (minutes, hours, days, years) at a specific place on a stream. The relationship between stream discharge and precipitation input is illustrated on the graph.

Hydrologic cycle (9)   A simplified model of the flow of water, ice, and water vapour from place to place. Water flows through the atmosphere, across the land, where it is also stored as ice, and within groundwater. Solar energy empowers the cycle.

Hydrology (14)   The science of water, its global circulation, distribution, and properties, specifically water at and below Earth's surface.

Hydrolysis (13)   A chemical weathering process in which minerals chemically combine with water; a decomposition process that causes silicate minerals in rocks to break down and become altered (contrast with hydration).

Hydrosphere (1)   An abiotic open system that includes all of Earth's water.

Hygroscopic water (9)   That portion of soil moisture that is so tightly bound to each soil particle that it is unavailable to plant roots; the water, along with some bound capillary water, that is left in the soil after the wilting point is reached (see wilting point).

Ice age (17)   A cold episode, with accompanying alpine and continental ice accumulations, that has repeated roughly every 200 to 300 million years since the late Precambrian era (1.25 billion years ago); includes the most recent episode during the Pleistocene Ice Age, which began 1.65 million years ago.

Iceberg (17)   Floating ice created by ice calving (a large piece breaking off) and floating adrift; a hazard to shipping because about nine-tenths of the ice is submerged and can be irregular in form.

Ice cap (17)   A large, dome-shaped glacier, less extensive than an ice sheet ($<50,000$ km^2, $<19,300$ mi^2), although it buries mountain peaks and the local landscape.

Ice-crystal fog (7)   A type of fog that develops at very low temperatures in a continental arctic air mass. Visibility is seriously limited when the air becomes full of ice crystals that have formed by sublimation.

Ice field (17)   The least extensive form of a glacier, with mountain ridges and peaks visible above the ice; less than an ice cap or ice sheet.

Icelandic low (6)   See subpolar low-pressure cell.

Ice sheet (17)   An enormous continuous continental glacier. The bulk of glacial ice on Earth covers Antarctica and Greenland in two ice sheets.

Ice shelf (17)   A very thick sheet of ice with a gently undulating to level surface that extends over the sea and floats on water. It is attached to the land along a coastal grounding line and also may be attached where ice flows around islands. On the seaward side, it is bounded by a steep cliff called the ice front that can be 2 to 50 m or more above sea level.

Ice storm (8)   A major hazard in which supercooled precipitation freezes on contact with surfaces. The severity of the event is determined by the thickness of ice accumulation associated with a storm, the storm's duration, and the extent of area affected. Typically, an ice storm will last for 45 to 65 hours and will deposit, at most, 30 to 40 mm of ice.

Ice wedge (17) Formed when water enters a thermal contraction crack in permafrost and freezes. Repeated seasonal freezing and melting of the water progressively expands the wedge.

Igneous rock (11) One of the basic rock types; it has solidified and crystallized from a hot molten state (either magma or lava). (Compare metamorphic rock, sedimentary rock.)

Illuviation (18) The downward movement and deposition of finer particles and minerals from the upper horizon of the soil; a depositional process. Deposition usually is in the B horizon, where accumulations of clays, aluminum, carbonates, iron, and some humus occur (compare eluviation; see calcification).

Inceptisols (18) A soil order in the Soil Taxonomy. Weakly developed soils that are inherently infertile; usually young soils that are weakly developed, although they are more developed than Entisols.

Industrial smog (3) Air pollution associated with coal-burning industries; it may contain sulphur oxides, particulates, carbon dioxide, and exotics.

Infiltration (9) Water access to subsurface regions of soil moisture storage through penetration of the soil surface.

Insolation (2) Solar radiation that is incoming to Earth systems.

Interception (9) Delays the fall of precipitation toward Earth's surface; caused by vegetation or other ground cover.

Internal drainage (14) In regions where rivers do not flow into the ocean, the outflow is through evaporation or subsurface gravitational flow. Portions of Africa, Asia, Australia, and the western United States have such drainage.

International Date Line (1) The 180° meridian, an important corollary to the prime meridian on the opposite side of the planet; established by the treaty of 1884 to mark the place where each day officially begins.

Intertropical convergence zone (ITCZ) (6) See equatorial low-pressure trough.

Ionosphere (3) A layer in the atmosphere above 80 km (50 mi) where gamma, X-ray, and some ultraviolet radiation is absorbed and converted into infrared and where the solar wind stimulates the auroras.

Isobar (6) An isoline connecting all points of equal atmospheric pressure.

Isostasy (11) A state of equilibrium in Earth's crust formed by the interplay between portions of the lithosphere and the asthenosphere and the principle of buoyancy. The crust depresses under weight and recovers with its removal, for example, the melting of glacial ice. The uplift is known as isostatic rebound.

Isotherm (5) An isoline connecting all points of equal temperature.

Jet contrails (4) *Condensation trails* produced by aircraft exhaust, particulates, and water vapour can form high cirrus clouds, sometimes called *false cirrus clouds*.

Jet stream (6) The most prominent movement in upper-level westerly wind flows; irregular, concentrated, sinuous bands of geostrophic wind, traveling at 300 kmph (190 mph). (See polar jet stream, subtropical jet stream.)

Joint (13) A fracture or separation in rock that occurs without displacement of the sides; increases the surface area of rock exposed to weathering processes.

Kame (17) A depositional feature of glaciation; a small hill of poorly sorted sand and gravel that accumulates in crevasses or in ice-caused indentations in the surface.

Karst topography (13) Distinctive topography formed in a region of chemically weathered limestone with poorly developed surface drainage and solution features that appear pitted and bumpy; originally named after the Krš Plateau in Slovenia.

Katabatic winds (6) Air drainage from elevated regions, flowing as gravity winds. Layers of air at the surface cool, become denser, and flow downslope; known worldwide by many local names.

Kettle (17) Forms when an isolated block of ice persists in a ground moraine, an outwash plain, or valley floor after a glacier retreats; as the block finally melts, it leaves behind a steep-sided hole that frequently fills with water.

Kinetic energy (3) The energy of motion in a body; derived from the vibration of the body's own movement and stated as temperature.

Köppen-Geiger climate classification (10, Appendix C) An empirical classification system that uses average monthly temperatures, average monthly precipitation, and total annual precipitation to establish regional climate designations.

Lagoon (16) An area of coastal seawater that is virtually cut off from the ocean by a bay barrier or barrier beach; also, the water surrounded and enclosed by an atoll.

Landfall (8) The location along a coast where a storm moves onshore.

Land–sea breeze (6) Wind along coastlines and adjoining interior areas created by different heating characteristics of land and water surfaces—onshore (landward) breeze in the afternoon and offshore (seaward) breeze at night.

Landslide (13) A sudden rapid downslope movement of a cohesive mass of regolith and/or bedrock in a variety of mass-movement forms under the influence of gravity; a form of mass movement.

Land–water heating difference (5) Differences in the degree and way that land and water heat, as a result of contrasts in transmission, evaporation, mixing, and specific heat capacities. Land surfaces heat and cool faster than water and have continentality, whereas water provides a marine influence.

Latent heat (7) Heat energy is stored in one of three states—ice, water, or water vapour. The energy is absorbed or released in each phase change from one state to another. Heat energy is absorbed as the latent heat of melting, vapourization, or evaporation. Heat energy is released as the latent heat of condensation and freezing (or fusion).

Latent heat of condensation (7) The heat energy released to the environment in a phase change from water vapour to liquid; under normal sea-level pressure, 540 calories are released from each gram of water vapour that changes phase to water at boiling, and 585 calories are released from each gram of water vapour that condenses at 20°C (68°F).

Latent heat of sublimation (7) The heat energy absorbed or released in the phase change from ice to water vapour or water vapour to ice—no liquid phase. The change from water vapour to ice is also called deposition.

Latent heat of vapourization (7) The heat energy absorbed from the environment in a phase change from liquid to water vapour at the boiling point; under normal sea-level pressure, 540 calories must be added to each gram of boiling water to achieve a phase change to water vapour.

Lateral moraine (17) Debris transported by a glacier that accumulates along the sides of the glacier and is deposited along these margins.

Laterization (18) A pedogenic process operating in well-drained soils that occur in warm and humid regions; typical of Oxisols. Plentiful precipitation leaches soluble minerals and soil constituents. Resulting soils usually are reddish or yellowish.

Latitude (1) The angular distance measured north or south of the equator from a point at the centre of Earth. A line connecting all points of the same latitudinal angle is called a parallel (compare longitude).

Lava (11, 12) Magma that issues from volcanic activity onto the surface; the extrusive rock that results when magma solidifies (see magma).

Life zone (19) A zonation by altitude of plants and animals that form distinctive communities. Each life zone possesses its own temperature and precipitation relations.

Lightning (8) Flashes of light caused by tens of millions of volts of electrical charge heating the air to temperatures of 15,000° to 30,000°C.

Limestone (11) The most common chemical sedimentary rock (nonclastic); it is lithified calcium carbonate; very susceptible to chemical weathering by acids in the environment, including carbonic acid in rainfall.

Limiting factor (19) The physical or chemical factor that most inhibits biotic processes, either through lack or excess.

Lithification (11) The compaction, cementation, and hardening of sediments into sedimentary rock.

Lithosphere (1) Earth's crust and that portion of the uppermost mantle directly below the crust, extending down to about 70 km (45 mi). Some sources use this term to refer to the entire Earth.

Littoral drift (16) Transport of sand, gravel, sediment, and debris along the shore; a more comprehensive term, considers *beach drift* and *longshore drift* combined.

Littoral zone (16) A specific coastal environment; that region between the high-water line during a storm and a depth at which storm waves are unable to move sea-floor sediments.

Loam (18) A soil that is a mixture of sand, silt, and clay in almost equal proportions, with no one texture dominant; an ideal agricultural soil.

Location (1) A basic theme of geography dealing with the absolute and relative position of people, places, and things on Earth's surface.

Loess (15) Large quantities of fine-grained clays and silts left as glacial outwash deposits; subsequently blown by the wind great distances and redeposited as a generally unstratified, homogeneous blanket of material covering existing landscapes; in China, loess originated from desert lands.

Longitude (1) The angular distance measured east or west of a prime meridian from a point at the centre of Earth. A line connecting all points of the same longitude is called a meridian.

Longshore current (16) A current that forms parallel to a beach as waves arrive at an angle to the shore; generated in the surf zone by wave action, transporting large amounts of sand and sediment (see littoral current, beach drift).

Luvisolic (18) A CSSC soil order with eluviation–illuviation processes produce a light-coloured **Ae** horizon and a diagnostic **Bt** horizon. Soils of mixed deciduous–coniferous forests. Major occurrence is the St. Lawrence lowland. Luvisols do not have a solonetzic **B** horizon.

Lysimeter (9) A weather instrument for measuring potential and actual evapotranspiration; isolates a portion of a field so that the moisture moving through the plot is measured.

Magma (11) Molten rock from beneath Earth's surface; fluid, gaseous, under tremendous pressure, and either intruded into existing country rock or extruded onto the surface as lava (see lava).

Magnetosphere (2) Earth's magnetic force field, which is generated by dynamo-like motions within the planet's outer core; deflects the solar wind flow toward the upper atmosphere above each pole.

Mangrove swamp (16) A wetland ecosystem between 30°N or S and the equator; tends to form a distinctive community of mangrove plants (compare salt marsh).

Mantle (11) An area within the planet representing about 80% of Earth's total volume, with densities increasing with depth and averaging $4.5 g/cm^3$; occurs between the core and the crust; is rich in iron and magnesium oxides and silicates.

Map (1, Appendix A) A generalized view of an area, usually some portion of Earth's surface, as seen from above at a greatly reduced size (see scale and map projection).

Map projection (1, Appendix A) The reduction of a spherical globe onto a flat surface in some orderly and systematic realignment of the latitude and longitude grid.

Marine effect (5) A quality of regions that are dominated by the moderating effect of the ocean and that exhibit a smaller range of minimum and maximum temperature than continental stations (see continentality, land–water heating differences).

Mass movement (13) All unit movements of materials propelled by gravity; can range from dry to wet, slow to fast, small to large, and free-falling to gradual or intermittent.

Mass wasting (13) Gravitational movement of nonunified material downslope; a specific form of mass movement.

Meandering stream (14) The sinuous, curving pattern common to graded streams, with the energetic outer portion of each curve subjected to the greatest erosive action and the lower-energy inner portion receiving sediment deposits (see graded stream).

Mean sea level (MSL) (16) The average of tidal levels recorded hourly at a given site over a long period, which must be at least a full lunar tidal cycle.

Medial moraine (17) Debris transported by a glacier that accumulates down the middle of the glacier, resulting from two glaciers merging their lateral moraines; forms a depositional feature following glacial retreat.

Mediterranean shrubland (20) A major biome dominated by Mediterranean dry-summer climates and characterized by sclerophyllous scrub and short, stunted, tough forests (see chapparal).

Mercator projection (1) A true-shape projection, with meridians appearing as equally spaced straight lines and parallels appearing as straight lines that are spaced closer together near the equator. The poles are infinitely stretched, with the 84th north parallel and 84th south parallel fixed at the same length as that of the equator. It presents false notions of the size (area) of midlatitude and poleward landmasses but presents true compass direction (see rhumb line).

Mercury barometer (6) A device that measures air pressure using a column of mercury in a tube, one end of which is sealed, and the other end inserted in an open vessel of mercury (see air pressure).

Meridian (1) See longitude; a line designating an angle of longitude.

Mesocyclone (8) A large, rotating atmospheric circulation, initiated within a parent cumulonimbus cloud at midtroposphere elevation; generally produces heavy rain, large hail, blustery winds, and lightning; may lead to tornado activity.

Mesosphere (3) The upper region of the homosphere from 50 to 80 km (30 to 50 mi) above the ground; designated by temperature criteria; atmosphere extremely rarified.

Metamorphic rock (11) One of three basic rock types, it is existing igneous and sedimentary rock that has undergone profound physical and chemical changes under increased pressure and temperature. Constituent mineral structures may exhibit foliated or nonfoliated textures (compare igneous rock and sedimentary rock).

Meteorology (8) The scientific study of the atmosphere, including its physical characteristics and motions; related chemical, physical, and geological processes; the complex linkages of atmospheric systems; and weather forecasting.

Microclimatology (4) The study of local climates at or near Earth's surface, or that height above the Earth's surface where the effects of the surface are no longer of effect.

Midlatitude broadleaf and mixed forest (20) A biome in moist continental climates in areas of warm-to-hot summers and cool-to-cold winters; relatively lush stands of broadleaf forests trend northward into needleleaf evergreen stands.

Midlatitude cyclone (8) An organized area of low pressure, with converging and ascending airflow producing an interaction of air masses; migrates along storm tracks. Such lows or depressions form the dominant weather pattern in the middle and higher latitudes of both hemispheres.

Midlatitude grassland (20) The major biome most modified by human activity; so named because of the predominance of grasslike plants, although deciduous broadleafs appear along streams and other limited sites; location of the world's breadbaskets of grain and livestock production.

Mid-ocean ridge (11) A submarine mountain range that extends more than 65,000 km (40,000 mi) worldwide and averages more than 1000 km (600 mi) in width; centred along sea-floor spreading centres (see sea-floor spreading).

Milky Way Galaxy (2) A flattened, disk-shaped mass in space estimated to contain up to 400 billion stars; includes our Solar System.

Miller cylindrical projection (Appendix A) A compromise map projection that avoids the severe distortion of the Mercator projection (see map projection).

Mineral (11) An element or combination of elements that forms an inorganic natural compound; described by a specific formula and crystal structure.

Mirage (4) A refraction effect when an image appears near the horizon where light waves are refracted by layers of air at different temperatures (and consequently of different densities).

Model (1) A simplified version of a system, representing an idealized part of the real world.

Mohorovičić discontinuity, or Moho (11) The boundary between the crust and the rest of the lithospheric upper mantle; named for the Yugoslavian seismologist Mohorovičić; a zone of sharp material and density contrasts; also known as the Moho.

Moist adiabatic rate (MAR) (7) The rate at which a saturated parcel of air cools in ascent; a rate of 6 C° per 1000 m (3.3 F° per 1000 ft). This rate may vary, with moisture content and temperature, from 4 C° to 10 C° per 1000 m (2 F° to 6 F° per 1000 ft) (see adiabatic; compare dry adiabatic rate).

Moisture droplet (7) A tiny water particle that constitutes the initial composition of clouds. Each droplet measures approximately 0.002 cm (0.0008 in.) in diameter and is invisible to the unaided eye.

Mollisols (18) A soil order in the Soil Taxonomy. These have a mollic epipedon and a humus-rich organic content high in alkalinity. Some of the world's most significant agricultural soils are Mollisols.

Moment magnitude scale (12) An earthquake magnitude scale. Considers the amount of fault slippage, the size of the area that ruptured, and the nature of the materials that faulted in estimating the magnitude of an earthquake—an assessment of the seismic moment. Replaces the Richter scale (amplitude magnitude); especially valuable in assessing larger-magnitude events.

Monsoon (6) An annual cycle of dryness and wetness, with seasonally shifting winds produced by changing atmospheric pressure systems; affects India, Southeast Asia, Indonesia, northern Australia, and portions of Africa. From the Arabic word *mausim*, meaning "season."

Montane forest (20) Needleleaf forest associated with mountain elevations (see needleleaf forest).

Moraine (17) Marginal glacial deposits (lateral, medial, terminal, ground) of unsorted and unstratified material.

Mountain–valley breeze (6) A light wind produced as cooler mountain air flows downslope at night and as warmer valley air flows upslope during the day.

Movement (1) A major theme in geography involving migration, communication, and the interaction of people and processes across space.

Mudflow (13) Fluid downslope flows of material containing more water than earthflows.

Natural levee (14) A long, low ridge that forms on both sides of a stream in a developed floodplain; they are depositional products (coarse gravels and sand) of river flooding.

Neap tide (16) Unusually low tidal range produced during the first and third quarters of the Moon, with an offsetting pull from the Sun (compare spring tide).

Needleleaf forest (20) Forests of pine, spruce, fir, and larch, stretching from the east coast of Canada westward to Alaska and continuing from Siberia westward across the entire extent of Russia to the European Plain; called the *taiga* (a Russian word) or the *boreal forest*; principally in the microthermal climates. Includes montane forests that may be at lower latitudes at higher elevation.

Negative feedback (1) Feedback that tends to slow or dampen response in a system; promotes self-regulation in a system; far more common than positive feedback in living systems (see feedback loop, compare to positive feedback).

Net primary productivity (19) The net photosynthesis (photosynthesis minus respiration) for a given community; considers all growth and all reduction factors that affect the amount of useful chemical energy (biomass) fixed in an ecosystem.

Net radiation (NET R) (4) The net all-wave radiation available at Earth's surface; the final outcome of the radiation balance process between incoming shortwave insolation and outgoing longwave energy.

Niche (19, 20) The basic function, or occupation, of a life form within a given community; the way an organism obtains its food, air, and water.

Nickpoint (knickpoint) (14) The point at which the longitudinal profile of a stream is abruptly broken by a change in gradient; for example, a waterfall, rapids, or cascade.

Nimbostratus (7) Rain-producing, dark, grayish, stratiform clouds characterized by gentle drizzle.

Nitrogen dioxide (3) A noxious (harmful) reddish-brown gas produced in combustion engines; can be damaging to human respiratory tracts and to plants; participates in photochemical reactions and acid deposition.

Noctilucent cloud (3) A rare, shining band of ice crystals that may glow at high latitudes long after sunset; formed within the mesosphere, where cosmic and meteoric dust act as nuclei for the formation of ice crystals.

Normal fault (12) A type of geologic fault in rocks. Tension produces strain that breaks a rock, with one side moving vertically relative to the other side along an inclined fault plane (compare reverse fault).

Normal lapse rate (3) The average rate of temperature decrease with increasing altitude in the lower atmosphere; an average value of 6.4 C° per km, or 1000 m (3.5 F° per 1000 ft). (Compare environmental lapse rate.)

Occluded front (8) In a cyclonic circulation, the overrunning of a surface warm front by a cold front and the subsequent lifting of the warm air wedge off the ground; initial precipitation is moderate to heavy.

Ocean basin (12) The physical container (a depression in the lithosphere) holding an ocean.

Omnivore (19) A consumer that feeds on both producers (plants) and consumers (meat)—a role occupied by humans, among other animals (compare consumer, producer).

Open system (1) A system with inputs and outputs crossing back and forth between the system and the surrounding environment. Earth is an open system in terms of energy (compare closed system).

Organic (18) A CSSC soil order with peat, bog, and muck soils, largely composed of organic material. Most are water-saturated for prolonged periods. Are widespread in association with poorly to very poorly drained depressions, although Folisols are found under upland forest environments. Exceed 17% organic carbon and 30% organic matter overall.

Orogenesis (12) The process of mountain building that occurs when large-scale compression leads to deformation and uplift of the crust; literally, the birth of mountains.

Orographic lifting (8) The uplift of a migrating air mass as it is forced to move upward over a mountain range—a topographic barrier. The lifted air cools adiabatically as it moves upslope; clouds may form and produce increased precipitation.

Outgassing (7) The release of trapped gases from rocks, forced out through cracks, fissures, and volcanoes from within Earth; the terrestrial source of Earth's water.

Outwash plain (17) Glacial stream deposits of stratified drift of meltwater-fed, braided, and overloaded streams; occurs beyond a glacier's morainal deposits.

Overland flow (9) Surplus water that flows across the land surface toward stream channels. Together with precipitation and subsurface flows, it constitutes the total runoff from an area.

Oxbow lake (14) A lake that was formerly part of the channel of a meandering stream; isolated when a stream eroded its outer bank forming a cutoff through the neck of the looping meander (see meandering stream). In Australia, known as a billabong (Aboriginal for "dead river").

Oxidation (13) A chemical weathering process in which oxygen dissolved in water oxidizes (combines with) certain metallic elements to form oxides; most familiar is the "rusting" of iron in a rock or soil (Ultisols, Oxisols), which produces a reddish-brown stain of iron oxide.

Oxisols (18) A soil order in the Soil Taxonomy. Tropical soils that are old, deeply developed, and lacking in horizons wherever well drained; heavily weathered, low in cation-exchange capacity, and low in fertility.

Ozone layer (3) See ozonosphere.

Ozonosphere (3) A layer of ozone occupying the full extent of the stratosphere (20 to 50 km, or 12 to 30 mi) above the surface; the region of the atmosphere where ultraviolet wavelengths of insolation are extensively absorbed and converted into heat.

Pacific high (6) A high-pressure cell that dominates the Pacific in July, retreating southward in the Northern Hemisphere in January; also known as the Hawaiian high.

Pahoehoe (12) Basaltic lava that is more fluid than aa. Pahoehoe forms a thin crust that forms folds and appears "ropy," like coiled, twisted rope.

Paleoclimatology (10, 17) The science that studies the climates, and the causes of variations in climate, of past ages, throughout historic and geologic time.

Paleolake (17) An ancient lake, such as Lake Bonneville or Lake Lahonton, associated with former wet periods when the lake basins were filled to higher levels than today.

Palsa (17) A rounded or elliptical mound of peat that contains thin perennial ice lenses rather than an ice core, as in a pingo. Palsas can be 2 to 30 m wide by 1 to 10 m high and usually are covered by soil or vegetation over a cracked surface.

PAN (3) See peroxyacetyl nitrate.

Pangaea (11) The supercontinent formed by the collision of all continental masses approximately 225 million years ago; named in the continental drift theory by Wegener in 1912 (see plate tectonics).

Parallel (1) See latitude; a line, parallel to the equator, that designates an angle of latitude.

Parent material (13) The unconsolidated material, from both organic and mineral sources, that is the basis of soil development.

Particulate matter (PM) (3) Dust, dirt, soot, salt, sulphate aerosols, fugitive natural particles, or other material particles suspended in air.

Paternoster lake (17) One of a series of small, circular, stair-stepped lakes formed in individual rock basins aligned down the course of a glaciated valley; named because they look like a string of rosary (religious) beads.

Patterned ground (17) Areas in the periglacial environment where freezing and thawing of the ground create polygonal forms of arranged rocks at the surface; can be circles, polygons, stripes, nets, and steps.

Pedogenic regime (18) A specific soil-forming process keyed to a specific climatic regime: laterization, calcification, salinization, and podzolization, among others; not the basis for soil classification in the Soil Taxonomy.

Pedon (18) A soil profile extending from the surface to the lowest extent of plant roots or to the depth where regolith or bedrock is encountered; imagined as a hexagonal column; the basic soil sampling unit.

Percolation (9) The process by which water permeates the soil or porous rock into the subsurface environment.

Periglacial (17) Cold-climate processes, landforms, and topographic features along the margins of glaciers, past and present; periglacial characteristics exist on more than 20% of Earth's land surface; includes permafrost, frost action, and ground ice.

Perihelion (2) That point of Earth's closest approach to the Sun in its elliptical orbit; occurs on January 3 at $147,255,000$ km ($91,500,000$ mi); variable over a 100,000-year cycle (compare aphelion).

Permafrost (17) Forms when soil or rock temperatures remain below $0°C$ ($32°F$) for at least 2 years in areas considered periglacial; criterion is based on temperature and not on whether water is present (compare frozen ground; see periglacial).

Permeability (9) The ability of water to flow through soil or rock; a function of the texture and structure of the medium.

Peroxyacetyl nitrate (PAN) (3) A pollutant formed from photochemical reactions involving nitric oxide (NO) and volatile organic compounds (VOCs). PAN produces no known human health effect, but it is particularly damaging to plants.

Phase change (7) The change in phase, or state, among ice, water, and water vapour; involves the absorption or release of latent heat (see latent heat).

Photochemical smog (3) Air pollution produced by the interaction of ultraviolet light, nitrogen dioxide, and hydrocarbons; produces ozone and PAN through a series of complex photochemical reactions. Automobiles are the major source of the contributive gases.

Photogrammetry (1) The science of obtaining accurate measurements from aerial photos and remote sensing; used to create and to improve surface maps.

Photosynthesis (19) The process by which plants produce their own food from carbon dioxide and water, powered by solar energy. The joining of carbon dioxide and hydrogen in plants, under the influence of certain wavelengths of visible light; releases oxygen and produces energy-rich organic material, sugars, and starches (compare respiration).

Physical geography (1) The science concerned with the spatial aspects and interactions of the physical elements and processes that make up the environment: energy, air, water, weather, climate, landforms, soils, animals, plants, microorganisms, and Earth.

Physical weathering (13) The breaking and disintegrating of rock without any chemical alteration; sometimes referred to as mechanical or fragmentation weathering.

Pingo (17) Large areas of frozen ground (soil-covered ice) that develop a heaved-up, circular, ice-cored mound, rising above a periglacial landscape as water freezes into ice and expands; sometimes results from pressure developed by freezing artesian water that is injected into permafrost; occasionally exceeds 60 m in height (200 ft).

Pioneer community (19) The initial plant community in an area; usually found on new surfaces or those that have been stripped of life, as in beginning primary succession; including lichens, mosses, and ferns growing on bare rock.

Place (1) A major theme in geography, focused on the tangible and intangible characteristics that make each location unique; no two places on Earth are alike.

Plane of the ecliptic (2) A plane (flat surface) intersecting all the points of Earth's orbit.

Planetesimal hypothesis (2) Proposes a process by which early protoplanets formed from the condensing masses of a nebular cloud of dust, gas, and icy comets; a formation process now being observed in other parts of the galaxy.

Planimetric map (Appendix A) A basic map showing the horizontal position of boundaries, land-use activities, and political, economic, and social outlines.

Plateau basalt (12) An accumulation of horizontal flows formed when lava spreads out from elongated fissures onto the surface in extensive sheets; associated with effusive eruptions; also known as flood basalts (see basalt).

Plate tectonics (11) The conceptual model and theory that encompasses continental drift, sea-floor spreading, and related aspects of crustal movement; accepted as the foundation of crustal tectonic processes (see continental drift).

Playa (15) An area of salt crust left behind by evaporation on a desert floor usually in the middle of a desert or semiarid bolson or valley; intermittently wet and dry.

Pluton (11) A mass of intrusive igneous rock that has cooled slowly in the crust; forms in any size or shape. The largest partially exposed pluton is a batholith (see batholith).

Podzolic (18) A CSSC soil order of the coniferous forests and sometimes heath; leaching of overlying horizons occurs in moist, cool to cold climates.

Podzolization (18) A pedogenic process in cool, moist climates; forms a highly leached soil with strong surface acidity because of humus from acid-rich trees.

Point bar (14) In a stream the inner portion of a meander, where sediment fill is redeposited.

Polar easterlies (6) Variable weak, cold, and dry winds moving away from the polar region; an anticyclonic circulation.

Polar front (6) A significant zone of contrast between cold and warm air masses; roughly situated between 50° and 60° N and S latitude.

Polar high-pressure cells (6) A weak, anticyclonic, thermally produced pressure system positioned roughly over each pole; the region of the lowest temperatures on Earth (see Antarctic high).

Polypedon (18) The identifiable soil in an area, with distinctive characteristics differentiating it from surrounding polypedons that form the basic mapping unit; composed of many pedons (see pedon).

Porosity (9) The total volume of available pore space in soil; a result of the texture and structure of the soil.

Positive feedback (1) Feedback that amplifies or encourages responses in a system (compare to negative feedback, feedback loop).

Potential evapotranspiration (9) POTET, or PE; the amount of moisture that would evaporate and transpire if adequate moisture were available; it is the amount lost under optimum moisture conditions, the moisture demand.

Potentiometric surface (9) A pressure level in a confined aquifer, defined by the level to which water rises in wells; caused by the fact that the water in a confined aquifer is under the pressure of its own weight; also known as a piezometric surface. This surface can extend above the surface of the land, causing water to rise above the water table in wells in confined aquifers (see artesian water).

Precipitation (9) Rain, snow, sleet, and hail—the moisture supply; called PRECIP, or P, in the water balance.

Pressure gradient force (6) Causes air to move from an area of higher barometric pressure to an area of lower barometric pressure due to the pressure difference.

Primary succession (19) Succession that occurs among plant species in an area of new surfaces created by mass movement of land, areas exposed by a retreating glacier, cooled lava flows and volcanic eruption landscapes, surface mining and clear-cut logging scars, or an area of sand dunes, with no trace of a former community.

Prime meridian (1) An arbitrary meridian designated as 0° longitude, the point from which longitudes are measured east or west, at Greenwich, England, selected by international agreement in an 1884 treaty.

Process (1) A set of actions and changes that occur in some special order; analysis of processes is central to modern geographic synthesis.

Producer (19) Organism (plant) in an ecosystem that uses carbon dioxide as its sole source of carbon, which it chemically fixes through photosynthesis to provide its own nourishment; also called an autotroph (compare consumer).

Pyroclastic (12) An explosively ejected rock fragment launched by a volcanic eruption; sometimes described by the more general term tephra.

Radiation fog (7) Formed by radiative cooling of a land surface, especially on clear nights in areas of moist ground; occurs when the air layer directly above the surface is chilled to the dew-point temperature, thereby producing saturated conditions.

Rain gauge (9) A weather instrument; a standardized device that captures and measures rainfall.

Rain shadow (8) The area on the leeward slope of a mountain range, where precipitation receipt is greatly reduced compared to the windward slope on the other side (see orographic lifting).

Reflection (4) The portion of arriving insolation that is returned directly to space without being absorbed and converted into heat and without performing any work (see albedo).

Refraction (4) The bending effect on electromagnetic waves that occurs when insolation enters the atmosphere or another medium; the same process by which a crystal, or prism, disperses the component colours of the light passing through it.

Region (1) A geographic theme that focuses on areas that display unity and internal homogeneity of traits; includes the study of how a region forms, evolves, and interrelates with other regions.

Regolith (13) Partially weathered rock overlying bedrock, whether residual or transported.

Regosolic (18) A CSSC soil order with weakly developed limited soils, the result of any number of factors: young materials; fresh alluvial deposits; material instability; mass-wasted slopes; or dry, cold climatic conditions.

Relative humidity (7) The ratio of water vapour actually in the air (content) compared to the maximum water vapour the air could hold (capacity) at that temperature; expressed as a percentage (compare vapour pressure, specific humidity).

Relief (12) Elevation differences in a local landscape; an expression of local height difference of landforms.

Remote sensing (1) Information acquired from a distance, without physical contact with the subject; for example, photography, orbital imagery, or radar.

Respiration (19) The process by which plants use food to derive energy for their operations; essentially, the reverse of the photosynthetic process; releases carbon dioxide, water, and heat energy into the environment (compare photosynthesis).

Reverse fault (12) Compressional forces produce strain that breaks a rock so that one side moves upward relative to the other side; also called a thrust fault (compare normal fault).

Revolution (2) The annual orbital movement of Earth about the Sun; determines the length of the year and the seasons.

Rhumb line (1) A line of constant compass direction, or constant bearing, which crosses all meridians at the same angle; a portion of a great circle.

Richter scale (12) An open-ended, logarithmic scale that estimates earthquake magnitude; designed by Charles Richter in 1935; now replaced by the moment magnitude scale (see moment magnitude scale).

Rime fog (7) A fog that consists of supercooled water droplets that turn into rime frost on contact with freezing objects.

Ring of fire (12) See circum-Pacific belt.

Robinson projection (Appendix A) A compromise (neither equal area nor true shape) oval projection developed in 1963 by Arthur Robinson.

Roche moutonnée (17) A glacial erosion feature; an asymmetrical hill of exposed bedrock; displays a gently sloping upstream side that has been smoothed and polished by a glacier and an abrupt, steep downstream side.

Rock (11) An assemblage of minerals bound together, or sometimes a mass of a single mineral.

Rock cycle (11) A model representing the interrelationships among the three rock-forming processes: igneous, sedimentary, and metamorphic; shows how each can be transformed into another rock type.

Rockfall (13) Free-falling movement of debris from a cliff or steep slope, generally falling straight or bounding downslope.

Rossby wave (6) An undulating horizontal motion in the upper-air westerly circulation at middle and high latitudes.

Rotation (2) The turning of Earth on its axis, averaging about 24 hours in duration; determines day–night relation; counterclockwise when viewed from above the North Pole and from above the equator, west to east or eastward.

Salinity (16) The concentration of natural elements and compounds dissolved in solution, as solutes; measured by weight in parts per thousand (‰) in seawater.

Salinization (18) A pedogenic process that results from high potential evapotranspiration rates in deserts and semiarid regions. Soil water is drawn to surface horizons, and dissolved salts are deposited as the water evaporates.

Saltation (14, 15) The transport of sand grains (usually larger than 0.2 mm, or 0.008 in.) by stream or wind, bouncing the grains along the ground in asymmetrical paths.

Salt marsh (16) A wetland ecosystem characteristic of latitudes poleward of the 30th parallel (compare to mangrove swamp).

Sand sea (15) An extensive area of sand and dunes; characteristic of Earth's erg deserts (contrast to reg deserts).

Saturation (7) Air that is holding all the water vapour that it can hold at a given temperature, known as the dew-point temperature.

Scale (1) The ratio of the distance on a map to that in the real world; expressed as a representative fraction, graphic scale, or written scale.

Scarification (13) Human-induced mass movements of Earth materials, such as large-scale open-pit mining and strip mining.

Scattering (4) Deflection and redirection of insolation by atmospheric gases, dust, ice, and water vapour; the shorter the wavelength, the greater the scattering, and thus skies in the lower atmosphere are blue.

Scientific method (1) An approach that uses applied common sense in an organized and objective manner; based on observation, generalization, formulation, and testing of a hypothesis, and ultimately the development of a theory.

Sea-floor spreading (11) As proposed by Hess and Dietz, the mechanism driving the movement of the continents; associated with upwelling flows of magma along the worldwide system of mid-ocean ridges (see mid-ocean ridge).

Secondary succession (19) Succession that occurs among plant species in an area where vestiges of a previously functioning community are present; an area where the natural community has been destroyed or disturbed, but where the underlying soil remains intact.

Sediment (13) Fine-grained mineral matter that is transported and deposited by air, water, or ice.

Sedimentary rock (11) One of three basic rock types; formed from the compaction, cementation, and hardening of sediments derived from other rocks (compare igneous rock, metamorphic rock).

Seismic wave (11) The shock wave sent through the planet by an earthquake or underground nuclear test. Transmission varies according to temperature and the density of various layers within the planet; provides indirect diagnostic evidence of Earth's internal structure.

Seismograph (12) A device that measures seismic waves of energy transmitted throughout Earth's interior or along the crust.

Sensible heat (3) Heat that can be measured with a thermometer; a measure of the concentration of kinetic energy from molecular motion.

Sheet flow (14) Surface water that moves downslope in a thin film as overland flow, not concentrated in channels larger than rills.

Sheeting (13) A form of weathering associated with fracturing or fragmentation of rock by pressure release; often related to exfoliation processes (see exfoliation dome).

Shield volcano (12) A symmetrical mountain landform built from effusive eruptions (low-viscosity magma); gently sloped, gradually rising from the surrounding landscape to a summit crater; typical of the Hawaiian Islands (compare to effusive eruption; composite volcano).

Sinkhole (13) Nearly circular depression created by the weathering of karst landscapes with subterranean drainage; also known as a doline in traditional studies; may collapse through the roof of an underground space (see karst topography).

Sleet (8) Freezing rain, ice glaze, or ice pellets.

Sling psychrometer (7) A weather instrument that measures relative humidity using two thermometers—a dry bulb and a wet bulb—mounted side-by-side.

Slipface (15) On a sand dune, formed as dune height increases above 30 cm (12 in.) on the leeward side at an angle at which loose material is stable—its angle of repose (30 to 34°).

Slope (13) A curved, inclined surface that bounds a landform.

Small circle (1) A circle on a globe's surface that does not share Earth's centre; for example, all parallels of latitude other than the equator (compare to great circle).

Snow line (17) A temporary line marking the elevation where winter snowfall persists throughout the summer; seasonally, the lowest elevation covered by snow during the summer.

Soil (18) A dynamic natural body made up of fine materials covering Earth's surface in which plants grow, composed of both mineral and organic matter.

Soil colloid (18) A tiny clay and organic particle in soil; provides chemically active sites for mineral ion adsorption (see cation-exchange capacity).

Soil creep (13) A persistent mass movement of surface soil where individual soil particles are lifted and disturbed by the expansion of soil moisture as it freezes or by grazing livestock or digging animals.

Soil fertility (18) The ability of soil to support plant productivity when it contains organic substances and clay minerals that absorb water and certain elemental ions needed by plants through adsorption (see cation-exchange capacity, CEC).

Soil horizon (18) The various layers exposed in a pedon; roughly parallel to the surface and identified as O, A, Ae, B, C, and R (bedrock).

Soil-moisture recharge (9) Water entering available soil storage spaces.

Soil-moisture storage (9) STRGE, the retention of moisture within soil; it is a savings account that can accept deposits (soil-moisture recharge) or experiences withdrawals (soil-moisture utilization) as conditions change.

Soil-moisture utilization (9) The extraction of soil moisture by plants for their needs; efficiency of withdrawal decreases as the soil storage is reduced.

Soil science (18) Interdisciplinary science of soils. Pedology concerns the origin, classification, distribution, and description of soil. Edaphology focuses on soil as a medium for sustaining higher plants.

Soil Taxonomy (18) A soil classification system based on observable soil properties actually seen in the field; published in 1975 by the U.S. Soil Conservation Service and revised in 1990 and 1998 by the Natural Resources Conservation Service to include 12 soil orders.

Soil-water budget (9) An accounting system for soil moisture using inputs of precipitation and outputs of evapotranspiration and gravitational water.

Solar constant (2) The amount of insolation intercepted by Earth on a surface perpendicular to the Sun's rays when Earth is at its average distance from the Sun; a value of 1370 W/m^2, or 1.968 calories/cm^2, per minute; averaged over the entire globe at the thermopause.

Solar wind (2) Clouds of ionized (charged) gases emitted by the Sun and traveling in all directions from the Sun's surface. Effects on Earth include auroras, disturbance of radio signals, and possible influences on weather.

Solifluction (13, 17) Gentle downslope movement of a saturated surface material (soil and regolith) in various climatic regimes where temperatures are above freezing (compare gelifluction).

Solonetzic (18) A CSSC soil order where solonetz denotes saline or alkaline soils. Well to imperfectly drained mineral soils developed under grasses in semiarid to subhumid climates. Limited areas of central and north-central Alberta.

Solum (18) A true soil profile in the pedon; ideally, a combination of O, A, E, and B horizons (see pedon).

Spatial (1) The nature or character of physical space, as in an area; occupying or operating within a space. Geography is a spatial science; spatial analysis its essential approach.

Spatial analysis (1) The examination of spatial interactions, patterns, and variations over area and/or space; a key integrative approach of geography.

Specific heat (5) The increase of temperature in a material when energy is absorbed; water has a higher specific heat (can store more heat) than a comparable volume of soil or rock.

Specific humidity (7) The mass of water vapour (in grams) per unit mass of air (in kilograms) at any specified temperature. The maximum mass of water vapour that a kilogram of air can hold at any specified temperature is termed its maximum specific humidity (compare vapour pressure, relative humidity).

Speed of light (2) Specifically, 299,792 kilometres per second (186,282 miles per second), or more than 9.4 trillion kilometres per year (5.9 trillion miles per year)—a distance known as a light-year; at light speed Earth is 8 minutes and 20 seconds from the Sun.

Spheroidal weathering (13) A chemical weathering process in which the sharp edges and corners of boulders and rocks are weathered in thin plates that create a rounded, spheroidal form.

Spodosols (18) A soil order in the Soil Taxonomy classification that occurs in northern coniferous forests; best developed in cold, moist, forested climates; lacks humus and clay in the A horizons, with high acidity associated with podzolization processes.

Spring tide (16) The highest tidal range, which occurs when the Moon and the Sun are in conjunction (at new Moon) or in opposition (at full Moon) stages (compare neap tide).

Squall line (8) A zone slightly ahead of a fast-advancing cold front, where wind patterns are rapidly changing and blustery and precipitation is strong.

Stability (7) The condition of a parcel, whether it remains where it is or changes its initial position. The parcel is stable if it resists displacement upward, unstable if it continues to rise.

Stationary front (8) A frontal area of contact between contrasting air masses that shows little horizontal movement; winds in opposite direction on either side of the front flow parallel along the front.

Steady-state equilibrium (1) The condition that occurs in a system when rates of input and output are equal and the amounts of energy and stored matter are nearly constant around a stable average.

Stomata (19) A small opening on the undersides of leaves through which water and gasses pass.

Storm surge (8) A large quantity of seawater pushed inland by the strong winds associated with a tropical cyclone.

Storm tracks (8) Seasonally shifting paths followed by migrating low-pressure systems.

Stratified drift (17) Sediments deposited by glacial meltwater that appear sorted; a specific form of glacial drift (compare till).

Stratigraphy (11) A science that analyzes the sequence, spacing, geophysical and geochemical properties, and spatial distribution of rock strata.

Stratocumulus (7) A lumpy, grayish, low-level cloud, patchy with sky visible, sometimes present at the end of the day.

Stratosphere (3) That portion of the homosphere that ranges from 20 to 50 km (12.5 to 30 mi) above Earth's surface, with temperatures ranging from −57°C (−70°F) at the tropopause to 0°C (32°F) at the stratopause. The functional ozonosphere is within the stratosphere.

Stratus (7) A stratiform (flat, horizontal) cloud generally below 2000 m (6500 ft).

Strike-slip fault (12) Horizontal movement along a faultline, that is, movement in the same direction as the fault; also known as a transcurrent fault. Such movement is described as right lateral or left lateral, depending on the relative motion observed across the fault (see transform fault).

Subduction zone (11) An area where two plates of crust collide and the denser oceanic crust dives beneath the less dense continental plate, forming deep oceanic trenches and seismically active regions.

Sublimation (7) A process in which ice evaporates directly to water vapour or water vapour freezes to ice (deposition).

Subpolar low-pressure cell (6) A region of low pressure centred approximately at 60° latitude in the North Atlantic near Iceland and in the North Pacific near the Aleutians, as well as in the Southern Hemisphere. Airflow is cyclonic; it weakens in summer and strengthens in winter (refer to cyclone).

Subsolar point (2) The only point receiving perpendicular insolation at a given moment—the Sun directly overhead (see declination).

Subtropical high-pressure cell (6) One of several dynamic high-pressure areas covering roughly the region from 20° to 35° N and S latitudes; responsible for the hot, dry areas of Earth's arid and semiarid deserts (refer to anticyclone).

Sulphate aerosols (3) Sulphur compounds in the atmosphere, principally sulphuric acid; principal sources relate to fossil fuel combustion; scatters and reflects insolation.

Sulphur dioxide (3) A colourless gas detected by its pungent odour; produced by the combustion of fossil fuels, especially coal, that contain sulphur as an impurity; can react in the atmosphere to form sulphuric acid, a component of acid deposition.

Summer (June) solstice (2) The time when the Sun's declination is at the Tropic of Cancer, at 23.5° N latitude, June 20–21 each year (compare to winter [December] solstice).

Sunrise (2) That moment when the disk of the Sun first appears above the horizon.

Sunset (2) That moment when the disk of the Sun totally disappears.

Sunspot (2) Magnetic disturbances on the surface of the Sun, occurring in an average 11-year cycle; related flares, prominences, and outbreaks produce surges in solar wind.

Surface creep (15) A form of eolian transport that involves particles too large for saltation; a process whereby individual grains are impacted by moving grains and slide and roll.

Surplus (SURPL) (9)   The amount of moisture that exceeds potential evapotranspiration; moisture oversupply when soil moisture storage is at field capacity; extra or surplus water.

Suspended load (14)   Fine particles held in suspension in a stream. The finest particles are not deposited until the stream velocity nears zero.

Swell (16)   Regular patterns of smooth, rounded waves in open water; can range from small ripples to very large waves.

Syncline (12)   A trough in folded strata, with beds that slope toward the axis of the downfold (compare anticline).

System (1)   Any ordered, interrelated set of materials or items existing separate from the environment or within a boundary; energy transformations and energy and matter storage and retrieval occur within a system.

Taiga (20)   See needleleaf forest.

Talik (17)   An unfrozen portion of the ground that may occur above, below, or within a body of discontinuous permafrost or beneath a body of water in the continuous region, such as a deep lake; may extend to bedrock and noncryotic soil under large deep lakes.

Talus slope (13)   Formed by angular rock fragments that cascade down a slope along the base of a mountain; poorly sorted, cone-shaped deposits.

Tarn (17)   A small mountain lake, especially one that collects in a cirque basin behind risers of rock material or in an ice-gouged depression.

Temperate rain forest (20)   A major biome of lush forests at middle and high latitudes; occurs along narrow margins of the Pacific Northwest in North America, among other locations; includes the tallest trees in the world.

Temperature (5)   A measure of sensible heat energy present in the atmosphere and other media; indicates the average kinetic energy of individual molecules within a substance.

Temperature inversion (3)   A reversal of the normal decrease of temperature with increasing altitude; can occur anywhere from ground level up to several thousand meters; functions to block atmospheric convection and thereby trap pollutants.

Terminal moraine (17)   Eroded debris that is dropped at a glacier's farthest extent.

Terrane (12)   A migrating piece of Earth's crust, dragged about by processes of mantle convection and plate tectonics. Displaced terranes are distinct in their history, composition, and structure from the continents that accept them.

Terrestrial ecosystem (20)   A self-regulating association characterized by specific plant formations; usually named for the predominant vegetation and known as a biome when large and stable (see biome).

Thermal equator (5)   The isoline on an isothermal map that connects all points of highest mean temperature.

Thermohaline circulation (6)   Deep ocean currents produced by differences in temperature and salinity with depth; Earth's deep currents.

Thermokarst (17)   Topography of hummocky, irregular relief marked by cave-ins, bogs, small depressions, and pits formed as ground ice melts; an erosion process caused by ground ice melting; not related to solution processes and chemical weathering associated with limestone (karst).

Thermopause (2, 3)   A zone approximately 480 km (300 mi) in altitude that serves conceptually as the top of the atmosphere; an altitude used for the determination of the solar constant.

Thermosphere (3)   A region of the heterosphere extending from 80 to 480 km (50 to 300 mi) in altitude; contains the functional ionosphere layer.

Threshold (1)   A moment in which a system can no longer maintain its character, so it lurches to a new operational level, which may not be compatible with previous conditions.

Thrust fault (12)   A reverse fault where the fault plane forms a low angle relative to the horizontal; an overlying block moves over an underlying block.

Thunder (8)   The violent expansion of suddenly heated air, created by lightning discharges, which send out shock waves as an audible sonic bang.

Tide (16)   A pattern of daily oscillations in sea level produced by astronomical relations among the Sun, the Moon, and Earth; experienced in varying degrees around the world (see neap and spring tides).

Till (17)   Direct ice deposits that appear unstratified and unsorted; a specific form of glacial drift (compare stratified drift).

Till plain (17)   A large, relatively flat plain composed of unsorted glacial deposits behind a terminal or end moraine. Low-rolling relief and unclear drainage patterns are characteristic.

Tombolo (16)   A landform created when coastal sand deposits connect the shoreline with an offshore island outcrop or sea stack.

Topographic map (Appendix A)   A map that portrays physical relief through the use of elevation contour lines that connect all points at the same elevation above or below a vertical datum, such as mean sea level.

Topography (12)   The undulations and configurations, including its relief, that give Earth's surface its texture, portrayed on topographic maps.

Tornado (8)   An intense, destructive cyclonic rotation, developed in response to extremely low pressure; generally associated with mesocyclone formation.

Total runoff (9)   Surplus water that flows across a surface toward stream channels; formed by sheet flow, combined with precipitation and subsurface flows into those channels.

Traction (14)   A type of sediment transport that drags coarser materials along the bed of a stream (see bed load).

Trade wind (6)   Wind from the northeast and southeast that converges in the equatorial low-pressure trough, forming the intertropical convergence zone.

Transform fault (11)   A type of geologic fault in rocks. An elongated zone along which faulting occurs between mid-ocean ridges; produces a relative horizontal motion with no new crust formed or consumed; strike-slip motion is either left or right lateral (see strike-slip fault).

Transmission (4)   The passage of shortwave and longwave energy through space, the atmosphere, or water.

Transparency (5)   The quality of a medium (air, water) that allows light to easily pass through it.

Transpiration (9)   The movement of water vapour out through the pores in leaves; the water is drawn by the plant roots from soil-moisture storage.

Transport (14)   The actual movement of weathered and eroded materials by air, water, and ice.

Tropical cyclone (8)   A cyclonic circulation originating in the tropics, with winds between 30 and 64 knots (39 and 73 mph); characterized by closed isobars, circular organization, and heavy rains (see hurricane and typhoon).

Tropical savanna (20)   A major biome containing large expanses of grassland interrupted by trees and shrubs; a transitional area between the humid rain forests and tropical seasonal forests and the drier, semiarid tropical steppes and deserts.

Tropical seasonal forest and scrub (20)   A variable biome on the margins of the rain forests, occupying regions of lesser and more erratic rainfall; the site of transitional communities between the rain forests and tropical grasslands.

Tropic of Cancer (2)   The parallel that marks the farthest north the subsolar point migrates during the year; 23.5° north latitude (see Tropic of Capricorn; summer or June solstice).

Tropic of Capricorn (2)   The parallel that marks the farthest south the subsolar point migrates during the year; 23.5° south latitude (see Tropic of Cancer; winter or December solstice).

Tropopause (3)   The top zone of the troposphere defined by temperature; wherever $-57°C$ ($-70°F$) occurs.

Troposphere (3)   The home of the biosphere; the lowest layer of the homosphere, containing approximately 90% of the total mass of the atmosphere; extends up to the tropopause; occurring at an altitude of 18 km (11 mi) at the equator, 13 km (8 mi) in the middle latitudes, and at lower altitudes near the poles.

True shape (1)   A map property showing the correct configuration of coastlines, a useful trait of conformality for navigational and aeronautical maps, although areal relationships are distorted (see map projection; compare equal area).

Tsunami (16)   A seismic sea wave, traveling at high speeds across the ocean, formed by sudden motion in the sea floor, such as a sea-floor earthquake, submarine landslide, or eruption of an undersea volcano.

Typhoon (8)   A tropical cyclone in excess of 65 knots (74 mph) that occurs in the western Pacific; same as a hurricane except for location.

Ultisols (18)   A soil order in the Soil Taxonomy. Features highly weathered forest soils, principally in the humid subtropical climatic classification. Increased weathering and exposure can degenerate an Alfisol into the reddish colour and texture of these more humid to tropical Ultisols. Fertility is quickly exhausted when Ultisols are cultivated.

Unconfined aquifer (9)   An aquifer that is not bounded by impermeable strata. It is simply the zone of saturation in water-bearing rock strata with no impermeable overburden, and recharge is generally accomplished by water percolating down from above.

Undercut bank (14)   In streams, a steep bank formed along the outer portion of a meandering stream; produced by lateral erosive action of a stream; sometimes called a cutbank (compare to point bar).

Uniformitarianism (11)   An assumption that physical processes active in the environment today are operating at the same pace and intensity that has characterized them throughout geologic time; proposed by Hutton and Lyell (compare to catastrophism).

Upslope fog (7)   Forms when moist air is forced to higher elevations along a hill or mountain and is thus cooled (compare valley fog).

Upwelling current (6)   An area of the sea where cool, deep waters, which are generally nutrient rich, rise to replace the vacating water, as occurs along the west coasts of North and South America (compare to downwelling current).

Urban heat island (4)   An urban microclimate that is warmer on average than areas in the surrounding countryside because of the interaction of solar radiation and various surface characteristics.

Valley fog (7)   The settling of cooler, more dense air in low-lying areas; produces saturated conditions and fog.

Vapour pressure (7)   That portion of total air pressure that results from water vapour molecules, expressed in millibars (mb). At a given dew-point temperature, the maximum capacity of the air is termed its saturation vapour pressure.

Vascular plant (19)   A plant having internal fluid and material flows through its tissues; almost 250,000 species exist on Earth.

Ventifact (15)   A piece of rock etched and smoothed by eolian erosion—abrasion by windblown particles.

Vernal (March) equinox (2)   The time around March 20–21 each year when the Sun's declination crosses the equatorial parallel and all places on Earth experience days and nights of equal length. The Sun rises at the North Pole and sets at the South Pole (compare to autumnal equinox).

Vertisolic (18)   A CSSC soil order that occurs in heavy-textured material that is high in clay content ($\geq$ 60% clay), especially smectite, a shrinking and swelling clay. These soils have little development of horizons, and are marked by slickensides and severe disruption.

Vertisols (18)   A soil order in the Soil Taxonomy. Features expandable clay soils; composed of more than 30% swelling clays. Occurs in regions that experience highly variable soil moisture balances through the seasons.

Volatile organic compounds (3)   Compounds, including hydrocarbons, produced by the combustion of gasoline, from surface coatings and from electric utility combustion; participates in the production of PAN through reactions with nitric oxides.

Volcano (12)   A mountainous landform at the end of a magma conduit, which rises from below the crust and vents to the surface. Magma rises and collects in a magma chamber deep below, erupting effusively or explosively and forming composite, shield, or cinder-cone volcanoes.

Warm desert and semidesert (20)   A desert biome caused by the presence of subtropical high-pressure cells; dry air and low precipitation.

Warm front (8)   The leading edge of an advancing warm air mass, which is unable to push cooler, passive air out of the way; tends to push the cooler, underlying air into a wedge shape; identified on a weather map as a line with semicircles pointing in the direction of frontal movement (compare to cold front).

Wash (15)   An intermittently dry streambed that fills with torrents of water after rare precipitation events in arid lands.

Watershed (14)   The catchment area of a drainage basin; delimited by divides (see drainage basin).

Waterspout (8)   An elongated, funnel-shaped circulation formed when a tornado exists over water.

Water table (9)   The upper surface of groundwater; that contact point between the zone of saturation and aeration in an unconfined aquifer (see zone of aeration, zone of saturation).

Wave (16)   An undulation of ocean water produced by the conversion of solar energy to wind energy and then to wave energy; energy produced in a generating region or a stormy area of the sea.

Wave-cut platform (16)   Or shore platform, is a flat or gently sloping tablelike bedrock surface that develops in the tidal zone, where wave action cuts a bench that extends from the cliff base out into the sea.

Wave cyclone (8)   See midlatitude cyclone.

Wavelength (2)   A measurement of a wave; the distance between the crests of successive waves. The number of waves passing a fixed point in 1 second is called the frequency of the wavelength.

Wave refraction (16)   A bending process that concentrates wave energy on headlands and disperses it in coves and bays; the long-term result is coastal straightening.

Weather (8)   The short-term condition of the atmosphere, as compared to climate, which reflects long-term atmospheric conditions and extremes. Temperature, air pressure, relative humidity, wind speed and direction, daylength, and Sun angle are important measurable elements that contribute to the weather.

Weathering (13)   The processes by which surface and subsurface rocks disintegrate, or dissolve, or are broken down. Rocks at or near Earth's surface are exposed to physical and chemical weathering processes.

West Antarctic ice sheet (10)   A vast grounded ice mass held back by the Ross, Ronne, and Filcher ice shelves in Antarctica, drained by several active ice streams, such as the active Pine Island Glacier.

Westerlies (6)   The predominant surface and aloft windflow pattern from the subtropics to high latitudes in both hemispheres.

Western intensification (6)   The piling up of ocean water along the western margin of each ocean basin, to a height of about 15 cm (6 in.); produced by the trade winds that drive the oceans westward in a concentrated channel.

Wetland (16)   A narrow, vegetated strip occupying many coastal areas and estuaries worldwide; highly productive ecosystems with an ability to trap organic matter, nutrients, and sediment.

Wilting point (9)   That point in the soil-moisture balance when only hygroscopic water and some bound capillary water remains. Plants wilt and eventually die after prolonged stress from a lack of available water.

Wind (6)   The horizontal movement of air relative to Earth's surface; produced essentially by air pressure differences from place to place; its direction is influenced by the Coriolis force and surface friction.

Wind vane (6)   A weather instrument used to determine wind direction; winds are named for the direction from which they originate.

Winter (December) solstice (2)   That time when the Sun's declination is at the Tropic of Capricorn, at 23.5° S latitude, December 21–22 each year. The day is 24 hours long south of the Antarctic Circle. The night is 24 hours long north of the Arctic Circle (compare to Summer [June] solstice).

Withdrawal (9)   Sometimes called *offstream use*, the removal of water from the natural supply, after which it is used for various purposes and then is returned to the water supply.

Wrangellia terrane (12)   One of many terranes that became cemented together to form present-day North America and the Wrangell Mountains, arriving from approximately 10,000 km (6200 mi) away; a former volcanic island arc and associated marine sediments.

Yardang (15)   A streamlined rock structure formed by deflation and abrasion; appears elongated and aligned with the most effective wind direction.

Yazoo tributary (14)   A small tributary stream draining alongside a floodplain; blocked from joining the main river by its natural levees and elevated stream channel (see backswamp).

Zone of aeration (9)   A zone above the water table that has air in its pore spaces and may or may not have water.

Zone of saturation (9)   A groundwater zone below the water table in which all pore spaces are filled with water.

Index

Aa, 399
AAAS. *See* American Association for the Advancement of Science
AAG. *See* Association of American Geographers
Abbey, Edward, 505–506
Abiotic ecosystem components, 629–630, 636–637
Abiotic systems, 13
Ablation, of glaciers, 558–560
Abrasion
    by glaciers, 564, 570
    by streams, 458, 462
    by wind, 488, 490
Absolute time scale, 332–333
Absolute zero, 120
Absorption, of radiation, 48, 98–99
ACIA. *See* Arctic Climate Impact Assessment
Acid deposition, 83–85
    soil acidity and, 601–602
    weathering by, 423–427
Acidification, of oceans, 520
Acid rain. *See* Acid deposition; Precipitation
Acid soil, 601–602, 656
Active layer, periglacial, 572–573, 576
Actual Evapotranspiration (ACTET), 255–258
Adaptation
    climate change and, 653–655
    and evolution, 654
Adiabatic processes, 192–194.
Admundsen-Scott Station, 130, 133
Adsorption, to soil colloids, 601
Advanced very high resolution radiometer (AVHRR) sensors, 32–33, 57, 145
Advanced Weather Interactive Processing System (AWIPS), 212
Advection, 98, 254
Advection fog, 200–202
Ae horizon, 597, 610
Aerosols, 78
    albedo and, 96–98
    monsoons and, 169
    sulfate, 83, 96–97, 196
    sunlight and, 70, 74
Aftershock, 391
Agenda 21 for Sustainable Development, 707
Aggradation, 459
Agricultural drought, 261
Agricultural ecosystems, 652–653
Ah horizon, 597
A horizon, 597–598, 618
Air. *See also* Eolian processes
    mining of, 68
    parcels of, 192–196
    saturation of, 187–189
    viscosity of, 487
Air masses, 213
    affecting North America, 212–213
    climate and, 287–288
    lifting mechanisms of, 214–221
    midlatitude cyclones and, 222–227
    modification of, 213–214
Air pollution
    anthropogenic, 78–85
    atmospheric albedo and, 96–98
    automobile emission, 78, 80, 82
    and health risks, 78
    historical problem of, 74
    industrial smog, 82–85
    landscapes and, 75
    monsoons and, 98
    multiyear oscillations and, 163–164
    natural sources of, 74–75, 143–145
    photochemical smog, 80, 82
    regulations for, 74
    temperature inversion and, 75–77
    urban, 109–112
    winds and, 75
Air pressure
    climate and, 287–288
    frontal lifting and, 220–221

global perspective of, 154–155
gravity and, 65–66, 148
measurement of, 145–146
in tornado, 233
vapour pressure and, 189–190
Alaska
    earthquakes, 370, 393
    isostatic rebound in, 338
    temperature changes in, 135
Albedo
    aerosols and, 96–98
    clouds and, 95–99
    definition of, 94
    energy balance and, 101–102
    greenhouse effect and, 101–102
    and reflection, 94–95
    soot and, 96–97, 706
Alcohol thermometer, 121
Aleutian low, 222
Alfisols, 605, A.7–A.9
Algae, 540, 630–631, 663
Alien species, niche takeovers, 676–677
Alkaline soil, 601–602
Alluvial fans, 505–506, 509
Alluvial terraces, 468, 471
Alluvium, 448, 455, 465–466, 468, 471, 510
Alpine glaciers, 552–554, 559
    landforms created by, 564–568
Alpine orogeny, 385–386
Alpine permafrost, 572
Alpine system, 389
Alpine tundra, 674–675, 693–694
Alps, 687
Altitude, of sun, 50–51, 57
Altocumulus clouds, 197–200
Altostratus clouds, 198–200
Aluminum, acid deposition and, 84
Amazon River, 448, 475
American Association for the Advancement of Science (AAAS), 318
Ammonia, formation of, 641
Amplitude magnitude scale. *See* Richter scale
Andesitic magma, 374
Andisols, A.7–A.9
Anemometer, 146–148
Aneroid barometer, 145–146
Angle of equilibrium, 417
Angle of repose, 431, 491
Animal Kingdom, 651
Animals
    aboreal, 679
    biogeographic realms and, 670–671
    kingdoms of, 650–651
    magnetic navigation of, 637, 638
Annan, Kofi, 2
Annapolis Tidal Generating Station, 525
Annual march of the seasons, 54–57
Annual temperature range, 122
    map of, 133–134
Annular drainage, 454
Antarctica, 585–589
    climate change, 588–589
    global warming and, 135, 324
    ice sheet, 553, 556, 558, 563–564, 583, 586
    ice sheet climate of, 310–311
    ozone losses, 71–74
    temperature at, 130, 133, 137
    topographic region, 374
Antarctic Circle, 17, 55
Antarctic Peninsula, 135, 589
Anticline, 379
Anticyclone, 154, 298
ANWR. *See* Arctic National Wildlife Refuge
Aphelion, 42
Appalachian Mountains, formation, 375, 385–388
Apparent temperature, 136
Applied science, scientific method, 8
Aqua satellite, 31, 33, 78, 100, 124
Aquatic ecosystems, 672

Aquatic succession, 658–659, 676–677
Aquiclude, 267
Aquifer, 267–268
    collapsed, 267–268, 272
    recharge of, 267–268
    saltwater encroachment on, 272
    thermal, 364
Aquitard. *See* Aquiclude
Arabian desert, 157
Arabian plate, 379–380
Arabian Sea, tropical cyclones in, 236
Aral Sea, 183
Arboreal animals, 679
Arctic Circle, 17, 55
Arctic Climate Impact Assessment (ACIA), 138, 317–318, 707–708
Arctic Council, 317–318
Arctic Haze, 78
Arctic National Wildlife Refuge (ANWR), 695–696
Arctic Ocean, 159, 177
    ice pack, 585–586
    water in, 181–182
Arctic Oscillation (AO), 162–164
Arctic region, 585–589
    climate change, 587, 707–708
    global warming, 511
    ozone losses, 72–73
    sea ice in, 706–707
    temperatures in, 120, 130, 134–135
Arctic tundra, 674–675, 693–694
Arcuate delta, 471–472
Arêtes, 564
Argon, in homosphere, 68
Arid and semiarid climates, 292, 294–295, 311–315, 498–500. *See also* Deserts
Aridisols, 605, A.7–A.9
Arroyo, 500
Artesian water, 267–268.
Asia
    central desert climates, 498
    monsoon patterns, 168–169
ASOS. *See* Automated Surface Observation System
Asperities, 393
Association of American Geographers (AAG), 3, 138
Asthenosphere, 336–338, 351, 375–376, 399, 402
Aswan High Dam, 472
Atacama Desert, 312, 498–499, 693
Atchafalaya River, 473–474
Athabasca Glacier, 554
Atlantic hurricanes, 2005 season and, 241–245
Atlantic Ocean, 158, 181–182
Atmosphere, 14
    albedo of, 95–98
    ancient history of, 64
    chemical composition of, 66–69
    climate and, 286
    climate change and, 584–585
    energy balance with, 101–102
    free falling through, 67
    functional layers of, 70
    optical depth of, 78
    overview of, 63
    profile of, 64–66
    solar energy pathways in, 92–98
    stability relationships, 192–196
    sunlight filtering by, 39, 63, 70
    temperature zones of, 69–70
    tidal bulges in, 524
    turbulence in, 228
    volcanic eruptions and, 143–145
    water vapour in, 180–181
Atmosphere-Ocean General Circulation Model (AOGCM), 321–323
Atmospheric circulation
    driving forces of, 148–154
    high-pressure and low-pressure areas, 154–159
    multiyear oscillations, 162–164
    upper atmospheric, 159–161
Atolls, 540–541

Atomic clocks, 25
Auroras, 45–46, 70
Australia
    biogeographic realm of, 670–671
    drought in, 261
    tropical, subtropical hot steppe climate of, 315
Automated Surface Observation System (ASOS), 212
Automated Weather Observation System (AWOS),
        212, 225–226
Autumnal equinox, 55–57
Available water, 259–260
Avalanches, 434, 436, 558
Avalanche slope, of dune, 491
AVHRR. *See* Advanced very high resolution
        radiometer sensors
Axial parallelism, of Earth, 53–54
Axial tilt, of Earth, 53, 584
Azores high, 158

Backscatter, 31
Backswamp, 466
Bacteria, chemosynthetic, 433
Badland, 507
Bagnold, Ralph, 488
Bajada, 505, 509–510
Bam earthquake, 370
Bar-and-swale relief, 466
Bare karst, 428
Barometer, 145–147
Barrier beach, 536–537, 542–543
Barrier island, 536–540, 543, 547
Barrier reef, 540–541
Barrier spit, 533, 535, 542, 547
Bar scale, 26–27
Basal slip, 562
Basalt, 337, 341, 344, 346, 426
    in orogenesis, 386
Basaltic magma, 375–376, 399, 401–402
Base level, of streams, 449–450, 471
Basic soil, 601–602
Basin and Range Province, 384–385, 507–510
Basins, 371, 380–381, 507, 509–510
Bates, Marston, 702
Batholith, 342, 374
Bay barrier, 533
Baykal Lake, 182–183
Baymouth bar, 533
Bay of Fundy, 525–527
Bays, 529–530
Beach drift, 530, 536–537
Beaches, 534–537, 543–545
Beach nourishment, 536
Beaufort wind scale, 147, 149
Bed load, 458–459
Bedrock, 418, 596–598
Benguela current, 158
Bergeron ice-crystal process, 196–197
Bergschrund, 564
Berg, Wally, 373
Bermuda high, 158
B horizon, 597–598
Big Bear Solar Observatory, 96
Biodiversity, 627, 650–655, 664–665, 681–684
Biodosimeters, 73
Biogeochemical cycles, 637
Biogeographic realms, 670–672
Biogeography, 628, 670
Biological Diversity Treaty, 707
Biological productivity, 542
Biomass, 634, 636–637
Biomes, 286, 671–696
    arctic and alpine tundra, 674–675, 693–694
    deserts, 674–675, 692–693
    equatorial and tropical rain forest,
        674–675, 677–679
    major terrestrial, 672–674
    Mediterranean shrubland, 674–675, 690–691
    midlatitude broadleaf and mixed forest, 674–675,
        685–687
    midlatitude grasslands, 674–675, 691–692
    needleleaf forest and montane forest, 674–675,
        687–690
    temperate rain forest, 674–675, 690
    tropical savanna, 297–298, 674–675, 684–686
    tropical seasonal forest and scrub, 674–675, 679,
        684–685

Biospeleology, 431
Biosphere, 14–15
    climate and, 286
    overview of, 628
    solar energy in, 91
Biosphere reserves, 681–684
Biotic ecosystems
    components of, 629–630
    operations in, 644–648
Biotic systems, 13
Bird's-foot delta, 473–474
Bjerknes, Jacob, 222
Bjerknes, Vilhelm, 218, 222
Blackbody radiator, 46–47, 86
Black carbon
    albedo and, 96–97
    monsoons and, 169
Black Chernozem, 610, 612
Black rhinos, 681–682
Bleaching, coral, 540–542
Block field, 573
Blowout depression, 490
Blue sky, atmospheric scattering, 93
Bogs, 542
    Organic soils and, 611
    succession of, 658–659
    of thermokarst topography, 576
Bolson, 509–510
Bora, 165
Boreal (needleleaf) forest, ii, 305
    Cryosolic soils and, 610
    fire in, 658
    Podzolic soils and, 612
Brackish water, 520
Bradley, Nina Leopold, 654
Braided delta, 471, 475
Braided stream, 459–460
Brazil
    tropical cyclone, 236–237, 239
    tropical rain forest climate of, 293, 296
Breaker, 528–529
Breakwater, 536–537
Brigalow, 684
Brine, 520
Brown Chernozem, 610, 612
Brunisolic order, 609–610
Bryophytes, 672
Buoyant force
    on air parcel, 192
    on Earth's crust, 338
    loss of glacial ice, 535–536
Bureau de Recherches Géologiques et Miniéres
        (BRGM), 18
Buttes, 506–508
Bypass channels, 476–477

Caatinga, 684
Calcification, 602, 610
Calcium
    acid deposition and, 84
    in biosphere, 637
    in soil, 601
Calcium carbonate, 345–347, 426–427. *See also*
        Lime; Limestone
    cave precipitates, 428–431
    formation of karst, 427–428
    marine organisms and, 540, 640
    in soil, 602, 610
Caldera, 399, 402
California Water Project, 264
Calms of Cancer, 158
Calms of Capricorn, 158
Calving, from glacier, 550, 556, 589
Campo Cerrado, 685
Canada
    biosphere reserve sites, 683–684
    climate change model for, 511–512
    groundwater resources for, 265–266
    hailstorms, 231
    hurricane damage, 238–240
    hydroelectricity in, 264
    ice storms, 227–228
    landslides, 438
    seismic activity, 359–361, 393, 395, 397
    time zones, 24
    tornadoes, 235

volcanoes, 409–410
    water consumption of, 275
    water supply of, 274, 276–277
Canada Geographic Information system (CGIS), 35
Canada Soil Committee, 606
Canadian Council for Geographic Education
        (CCGE), 3, 709
Canadian Environmental Advisory Council, 604
Canadian Forest Service (CFS), 658
Canadian Geomagnetic Reference Field (CGRF), 18
Canadian Land Resource Network (CLRN), 608
Canadian Meteorological Centre (CMC), 212, 225
Canadian Model Forest Network, 687–689
Canadian Rocky Mountains, 388
Canadian Shield, 374–375, 453–454
Canadian System of Soil Classification (CSSC), 596,
        606–622
    Brunisolic order, 609–610
    Chernozemic order, 610–612
    classification categories of, 606
    Cryosolic order, 610, 613
    Gleysolic order, 610, 614
    Luvisolic order, 610–611, 615
    Organic order, 611–612, 616
    Podzolic order, 612–613, 617–618
    Regosilic order, 618–619
    soil horizons in, 606–608
    soil orders of, 608–618
    Solonetzic order, 618, 620–621
    Vertisolic order, 618, 621
Canadian Wind Energy Association, 167
Canaries Current, 158
Capacity, of stream, 458
Cape Hatteras, 536–538
Capillarity, 183–184
Capillary action, of water, 184
Capillary water, 259–260, 420
Carbohydrates, 633–634
Carbonates, 341, 426–427, 640
Carbonation, 426–427
Carbon cycle, 640–641
Carbon dioxide (CO_2)
    in carbon cycle, 640–641
    chemical weathering and, 426–427
    global warming and, 317–321, 584–585
    history of, 138
    in homosphere, 68–69
    in ice cores, 582–583
    longwave absorption by, 99
    monsoons and, 168–169
    natural sources of, 74–75
    in photosynthesis, 633–634
    in seawater, 519–521
    in soil, 601
    from volcanic activity, 402
Carbonic acid, in soil, 601
Carbon, in biosphere, 637
Carbon monoxide, 74–75, 78–80
Carnivore, 644
Carson, Rachel, 518
Cartography, 26
Cascade Mountains, 378, 406
Cascadia subduction zone, 359–361, 378
Caspian Sea, 183
Cassini-Huygens, satellite 710
Cation-exchange capacity (CEC), 601
Caves and caverns, 428–433, 532
Celsius scale, 120–121
Centrifugal force, of Earth, 148
CERES. *See* Clouds and the Earth's Radiant Energy
        System
CFCs. *See* Chlorofluorocarbons
Channel, of streams, 459–460
Chaos theory, 45
Chaotic weather systems, 45
Chaparral, 691
Chemical energy, in landscape dynamics, 416
Chemical sedimentary rocks, 347–348
Chemical weathering, 420, 423–426
    blowout depressions and, 490
    dissolved load and, 458
Chemosynthesis, 629
Chernozemic order, 610–612
Cherrapunji (India), 220
    hydroelectricity in, 264
    population of, 704

Chinook winds, 165–166, 217
Chlorofluorocarbons (CFCs), 8
 climate change and, 320
 longwave absorption by, 99
 ozone depletion and, 71–72
Chlorophyll, 633
C horizon, 597–598
Chrons, geomagnetic polarity, 335
Cinder cone, 399
Circle of illumination, 52–53, 55
Circum-Pacific belt, 386
Cirque, 553, 558, 564
Cirque glacier, 553–555, 564
Cirrocumulus clouds, 198–200
Cirroform clouds, 195, 197–200
Cirrostratus clouds, 198–200
Cirrus clouds, 178, 197–200, 220
Classification, principles of, 288, 291
Clastic sedimentary rocks, 346, 348
Clay deposition
 by glaciers, 495–496, 567
 by streams, 448, 466, 468, 471, 505
Clay in soil, 597–598, 601–602
Clean Air Act (CAA), benefits of, 85–86
Cliffs, 417
 coastal, 532, 543–544
Climate
 components of, 287–288
 definition of, 212, 285
 global-scale linkages and, 286, 289–291
 weathering and, 420–421, 428
 world map of, 294–295
Climate change. See also Global warming
 in Antarctica, 588–589
 in Arctic region, 587, 707–708
 boreal forest, ii
 computers and, 320–323
 desertification, 511–512
 droughts and, 261
 ecosystems and, 670
 and eolian activity, 511–512
 fluctuation, 319–320, 582–585
 forest fires and, 75–76
 frogs and, 11
 greenhouse gases and, 315
 growing seasons and, 284
 models of, 320–323, 511–512
 monsoons and, 168–169
 organizations involved with, 315, 317–318
 paleoclimatology, 581–585
 plant adaptations to, 653–655
 in polar regions, 586–589
 record temperatures and, 136
 tornadoes and, 235
 tropical cyclones and, 244
 water supply and, 276–278
Climate Change Framework, 707
Climate models, 320–323
Climatic regions, 286
 arid and semiarid, 292, 294–295,
  311–315, 498–500
 classification of, 287–289, 291–293
 coastal environments and, 521
 global climate patterns, 292–295
 Köppen-Geiger classification,
  288, 291, 294–295
 mesothermal, 292, 294–295, 298–303, A.10–A.12
 microthermal, 292, 294–295, 303–309, 421, 687,
  A.10–A.12
 polar, 7, 134–135, 292, 309–311, 421, 570,
  586–589, A.10–A.12
 tropical, 292–298, A.10–A.12
Climatic sensitivity, in GCMs, 321
Climatology, 286, 552, 581–585
Climax community, 655
Climograph, 293
Closed systems, 6
Cloud-albedo forcing, 95–96, 99
Cloud-condensation nuclei, 196
Cloud-greenhouse forcing, 96, 99
Clouds. See also Specific cloud types
 albedo and, 95–99
 cold fronts and, 220
 definition of, 196
 formation of, 90, 195–196
 frontal lifting and, 220–221

global atmospheric circulation and, 154–156
 greenhouse effect and, 96, 99–101, 124
 humidity and, 187
 polar stratospheric, 72–73
 solar energy and, 90, 92–93, 95–98, 124
 temperature variations and, 124
 types of, 99–100, 195–200
Clouds and the Earth's Radiant Energy System
  (CERES), 97–100, 124
Coal, 345
Coal mining, aquifers and, 272
Coastal straightening, 529–530
Coastal systems, 521–523
 actions of, 523–532
 coral formations, 540–542
 geomorphology, 546–547
 of Great Lakes, 663
 human development of, 518, 543–546
 inputs to, 521
 landforms of, 532–540
 outputs of, 532–542
 sea level and, 521–524
 shoreline planning and protection, 523, 544–546
 tides and, 521, 524–527
 waves and, 526–532
 wetlands, 542–543
Coast Mountains, 217–219, 378, 388
Cockpit karst, 428, 430
Col, 564
Cold fronts, 218–222
Collapsed aquifers, 267–268, 272
Collapse sinkholes, 428
Collision-coalescence process, 196–197
Colorado Plateau, 348, 374, 464
Colorado River, 250–251, 348, 449, 457–459, 501–505
Colorado Rockies, 572
Columbia Glacier, 560
Columbian Plateau, 404
Columbia River, 475
Columbus, Christopher, 15
Communities, 629–633
 energy and nutrients in, 648–649
 succession in, 655–659, 676–677
 zonation of, 637–639
Compaction, 474
Compensation point, 634
Competence, of stream, 458
Competitive exclusion principle, 630
Composite volcanoes, 400, 404–409
Compound valley glacier, 567
Compression forces, 375, 377, 379–382, 386
Condensation
 of clouds, 196
 latent heat of, 185–186
 relative humidity and, 187–188
 of water, 183–184
Conduction, of heat, 98
Cone of depression, 268
Confined aquifer, 267
Conic projection, 28
Coniferous forests
 Luvisolic soils in, 615
 Podzolic soils in, 612
Constant height surface, 159–160
Constant isobaric surface, 159–160
Consumers, 644
Consumptive uses, of water, 276
Contact metamorphism, 348
Continental arctic (cA) air masses, 213
Continental crust, 336–337, 351
 deformation processes, 375–384, 386
 formation processes, 374–375
 hot spots, 361, 399–400
Continental divides, 450–451
Continental drift, 349–350, 354–356
Continental effect, 127–128, 131
Continental glaciers, 556–558
 landforms created by, 568–570
Continental landmasses, 371
Continental plate-continental plate collision
  orogenesis, 386–387
Continental platforms, 374, 389
Continental polar (cP) air masses, 213–214
 cold fronts, 218–221
 in microthermal climates, 303
Continental shields, 374–375, 389

Continuous permafrost, 571–572
Convectional lifting, 214–217
Convection, of heat, 98
Convergent boundaries, 357, 409
Convergent lifting, 214–216
Convergent plate collisions, 385–387
Cooling, evaporative, 125
Coordinated Universal Time (UTC), 25–26
Coordinate system, for GIS, 34
Coral formation, 540–542
Coral reefs, 540–542
Cordillera, 377–378, 387–388
Cordilleran system, 389
Core, 334–336
Coriolis force, 148, 150–154
 in midlatitude cyclonic systems, 222
 ocean currents and, 169–170
 tropical cyclones and, 236
Coriolis, Gaspard, 153
Coronal mass ejections, 44
Cosmic rays, ionosphere and, 70
Coupled Ocean-Atmosphere Response Experiment
  (COARE), 126
Cousteau, Jean-Michel, 518
Covered karst, 428
Coves, 529–530
Crater, 399, 403
Craton, 374
Creep
 limestone, 437
 soil, 438–439
 surface, in wind, 491–492
Creosote bush, 692
Crescentic dunes, 494
Crevasses, 562–563
Cropland, degradation of, 603–604
Cross-stratification, 507–508
Crust, 334–339, 341
 continental, 336–337, 351, 361,
  374–384, 386
 deformation processes, 375–384, 386
 formation processes, 350–352, 374–376
 oceanic, 337, 351, 353, 356, 368
 orders of relief, 371
 orogenesis, 384–390
 structural regions, 389–390
Crustal swelling, 380
Crutzen, Paul, 72
Cryosolic order, 610, 613
Cryosphere, 14, 552
Cryotic ground, 572
Cryoturbation, 573, 610
Crystallization
 of igneous rock, 421–422
 weathering by, 422–423
CSSC. See Canadian System of Soil Classification
Cultural eutrophication, 659, 663
Cumuliform clouds, 197–200
Cumulonimbus clouds, 178, 200–201,
  217, 227, 233
Cumulus clouds, 178, 197–200
Curtain of fire, 402
Cutbank, 460
Cutoff, 460, 462
Cyclogenesis, 222–225
Cyclones, 154, 159–160
Cyclonic systems, 217
 midlatitude, 222–227, 298
 tropical, 235–241
Cylindrical projection, 28
Cypress Hills Interprovincial Park, 652

Daily mean temperature, 122
Dams, 459, 477–479, 501–505, 547
Danube River, 452, 471
Dark Brown Chernozem, 610, 612
Dark Grey Chernozem, 610
Darwin, Charles, 540
Davis Dam, 501–504
Davis, Margaret, 654–655
Davis, William Morris, 465, 564
Dawn, 57
Daylength
 latitude and, 49, 51
 in polar and highland climates, 309
 seasons and, 54–57

Daylight saving time, 26
Dead Sea, 183
Dead zone, Gulf Coast, 643
Death Valley, 132, 289, 346, 348, 492, 500–501, 509–510
Debris avalanche, 434, 436
Debris slope, 417
Deccan Traps, 404
Declination, of sun, 51
Decomposers, 644
Deep cold zone, 520
Deficit (DEFIC), of water, 255, 258, 260
Deflation, of sediment by wind, 488–490, 497–498
Deforestation, 510
    of tropics, 679–680
Deglaciation, 577
Deltas, 471–475
Dendritic drainage, 453, 471
Denudation, 416–417
    by rivers and streams, 448
    time frame of, 465
Deoxyribonucleic acid (DNA), 650
Depletions, 332
Deposition
    by streams, 448, 450, 452, 456–459, 463, 465–475, 505
    by water, 183–184
    by wind, 487, 491–497
Depositional landforms
    coastal, 532–540
    glaciers and, 566–571
    wind and, 491–495
Depressions, 371–372, 428–430, 490
Depth, streamflow and, 455–456
Deranged drainage pattern, 453–454
Derechos, 231, 233
Desalination, 271, 276, 278
Desertification, 510–512, 692–693
Desert pavement, 488–489, 491
Deserts
    climates, 292, 312–314, 498–500, 693, A.10–A.12
    deflation in, 488–490
    dunes in, 491–496
    energy balance in, 92–93, 101, 105
    environmental degradation, 489–490
    erg, 491, 493
    fluvial processes, 500–501, 505
    fog harvesting in, 200, 203–204
    high-pressure cells and, 157–159, 287
    landscapes, 312, 498–500, 505–508
    precipitation in, 500–501
    rain-shadow, 245
    subtropical high-pressure cells, 287, 693
    temperature, 132
    vegetation, 674–675, 692–693
    water balance in, 500
    weathering in, 420
Detritivores, 644
Dew-point temperature, 187–188, 196
Diagnostic subsurface horizon, A.6
Differential GPS (DGPS), 22–23
Differential weathering, 416, 506–507
Diffuse radiation, 93
Digital elevation models (DEMs), 371
Digital images, 31
Dikes, 343, 468, 474
Dilitancy, 398
Discharge
    of rivers, 448
    of stream, 455–456, 458, 480–481
Discontinuity, 336–337
Discontinuous permafrost, 571–572
Dissolved load, 458
Dissolving stage, of midlatitude cyclone, 222–223
Distances, with latitude and longitude, 20
Distributaries, 471, 474
Diurnal temperature range (DTR)
    jet contrails and, 99–100
    tropical rain forest climate, 293
Divergent plate boundaries, 356–357
DNA. See Deoxyribonucleic acid
Doldrums, 156–157
Dolomite, 346
    karst topography and, 427–428
    weathering of, 426–427

Dome C ice core, 582–583
Domes, 380–381
Doppler radar, 212
Dornveld, 684
Downbursts, 228
Downwelling current, 170
Drainage basins, 450–453, 507
Drainage density, 453–455
Drainage divide, 450, 453
Drainage patterns, 453–455
Drawdown, of groundwater, 268
Drilling, of crust, 337–338
Dripstones, 431–432
Droplet, moisture, 196
Drought, 261, 498
    in Australia, 261
    global warming and, 323
    solar cycle and, 46
    U.S. western, 504–505
    in western United States, 250–251, 261
Drumlin, 570–571
Dry Adiabatic Rate (DAR), 193–196, 217–218
Dry-bulb thermometer, 191–192
Dry soil, 600
Dunes, 488, 490–496
    coastal, 544–545
    lithified, 507–508
Dust
    atmospheric circulation of, 145
    cloud formation and, 196
    insolation scattering by, 92–93
    movement of, 75, 77
    transportation by wind, 488, 490, 498
Dust Bowl, 498
Dust-cloud hypothesis, 42
Dust dome, 110–111
Dynamic ecology, 656
Dynamic equilibrium, 10
Dynamic equilibrium model, of landforms, 416–417, 465
Dystric Brunisol, 610

Earth
    albedo of, 94–95, 101
    axial parallelism of, 53–54
    axial tilt of, 53, 584
    biogeographic realm of, 670
    climate system of, 286–287
    coordinate grid system of, 23–24
    energy budget of, 47–48, 51, 96, 101–114, 186
    geologic time scale, 332–334
    human stewardship of, 709–710
    internal heat energy, 334–339, 364, 374
    location on, 16–23
    magnetism of, 334–335, 351, 353, 637, 639
    orbit of, 42–43, 52, 584
    radiant energy from, 50
    rotation of, 52–53, 153–154
    sphericity of, 13–16, 53
    structure of, 334–339
    surface relief of, 371–374
    temperature and, 122–138
    time on, 23–26
    water distribution on, 180–183
Earth Charter, 707
Earthflows, 436, 438
Earth Observing System (EOS), 33
Earthquakes, 390–398
    analysis of, 34–35
    faulting and, 380–381, 383, 386, 391, 393–397
    forecasting, 391, 397–398
    human impact of, 370
    Los Angeles region, 397
    magnitude and frequency, 391, 393, 410–411
    mass movements and, 433–434
    plate boundaries and, 357, 359–362
    San Andreas fault, 381–384, 397
    tsunami and, 530–532
    volcanism and, 402, 406–407
Earth Radiation Budget Experiment (ERBE), 50
Earth Radiation Budget (ERB) sensors, 51, 94–95
Earthshine, 94, 96
Earth Summit, 707
Ebb tides, 525
Ecological footprint, 704–705

Ecological relations, 648
Ecological similarity, 665
Ecological succession, 655–659
Ecology, 628
    relations in, 648–649
Ecosphere. See Biosphere
Ecosystems, 286
    abiotic components of, 629–630, 636–637
    agricultural, 652–653
    aquatic, 672
    biotic components of, 629–636
    biotic operations in, 644–648
    of caves, 433
    climate change and, 670
    components of, 628–629
    definition of, 628
    elemental cycles in, 637, 640–643
    epishelf lake, 587
    evolution of, 650–651
    of Great Lakes, 660–664
    human impact on, 669–670
    hydrologic cycle and, 637
    limiting factors of, 642, 644
    population balance of, 648–650
    stability of, 651–655
    succession in, 655–659, 676–677
    terrestrial, 671–672
    transition zones between, 670
Ecotone, 671, 685
Edaphology, 596
Effluent stream, 268
Effusive eruptions, 402–404
E horizon, 598
Elastic-rebound theory, 393–394
Elbows of capture, 453
Electromagnetic spectrum, of radiant energy, 46–48
Elemental cycles, 637, 640–642
    nitrogen, 641–643
    oxygen and carbon, 640–641
Elevations, 371–374
    GPS measurement of, 23, 373
    life zones and, 637
    temperature variations with, 122–124, 287
Ellesmerian orogeny, 388
El Mirage, 109–110
El Niño-Southern Oscillation (ENSO), 162, 286, 289–291, 541, 560
Eluviation, 597, 610–611
Emanuel, Kerry, 244
Empirical classification, 288, 291
Endangered species, 681–682
End moraine, 567
Endogenic processes, 329, 339–340, 374, 416
Energy, 5–6
    radiant, 46–48
Energy balance
    of deserts, 92–93, 105
    of Earth, 47–48, 51, 96–97
    global model, 113–114
    in landscape dynamics, 417
    latent heat exchange in, 186–187
    by latitude, 49–50, 101–103
    surface, 102–114
    in troposphere, 98–102
    zonal model, 113–114
Enhanced Fujita Scale, 233–234
ENSO. See El Niño-Southern Oscillation
Entisols, A.7–A.9
Entrenched meanders, 462, 464
Environmental lapse rate, 70, 192, 196
Environmental Policy Act, 605
Environmental Protection Agency, 88
Environment Canada, 275
Envisat satellite, 31
Eolian processes, 487–498
    climate change, 511–512
    defined, 488
    deposition, 487, 491–497
    erosion, 487–490, 511–513
    transportation, 487–488, 490–492, 497–498
Eons, 332
Ephemeral lakes, 501
Ephemeral plants, 692
Epicentre, 391

Epipedon, A.6
Epiphytes, 672, 677
Epishelf lake, 587
Epochs, geologic, 332
Equatorial bulge, 15
Equatorial currents, 170
Equatorial low-pressure trough, 154–156
   climate and, 287
Equatorial parallel, 23
Equatorial rain forest biome, 674–675, 677–679
Equatorial zone, 17, 19
Equilibrium
   in ecosystems, 651–655
   in landscape dynamics, 416–417, 465
   punctuated, 334
   in stream process, 462, 465
   in systems, 9–10
Equilibrium line, of glacier, 558, 560
Eras, geologic, 332
Eratosthenes, 15–16
Erg desert, 491, 493
Eriksson, Lief, 581
Erosion
   of agricultural land, 602–607
   of coastline, 532–534, 543–544, 546–547
   desertification and, 510
   in exogenic system, 329
   by glaciers, 553, 564–566, 568–570
   landforms produced by, 448, 465, 488–490,
     506–507, 532–534
   mass wasting and, 431
   of mountains, 387–388
   of soil, 511–513, 602–606
   by streams, 448, 458–465
   by wind, 487–490, 511–513
Escarpment, 380
Esker, 568–569
Estuaries
   ecosystems of, 672
   human settlement of, 543
   wetlands of, 542–543
Estuarine delta, 471
Eukaryotes, 650–651
Eurasian-Himalayan alpine system, 389
Eurasian plate, 368, 379–381
Eurekan orogeny, 389
European Space Agency (ESA), 31
European Wind Energy Association, 167
Eustasy, 181
Eutric Brunisol, 610
Eutrophication, 658–659, 663–664
Evaporation
   from drainage basin, 453
   from exotic stream, 456–458
   global warming and, 323
   humidity and, 187
   in hydrologic cycle, 253
   latent heat of, 104–106, 109–112, 125–126, 186
   from reservoirs, 478, 504
   soil-water budget and, 254–258
   temperature variations and, 125–126
   of water, 183–184
Evaporation fog, 200–202
Evaporation pan, 258
Evaporimeter, 257
Evaporites, 346, 348, 501
Evapotranspiration
   actual, 255–258
   potential, 255, 257–258, 287
Evolution, 650–651, 654
Excavation, mass movement with, 441
Exfoliation dome, 423–424
Exogenic processes, 329, 339–340, 379,
     415–416
Exosphere, 64
Exotic species, niche takeovers, 676–677
Exotic streams, 456–458, 501, 503
Exotic terranes, 374–378, 384
Expert Committee on Soil Survey, 606
Explosive eruptions, 404–409
Extinctions, 628, 651–652, 681–684
Extrusive igneous rock, 341–344, 346, 401
Exxon Valdez accident, 705–706
Eye, 237
Eyewall, 237

Facilitation concept, 651
Fahrenheit scale, 120
False cirrus clouds, 99
Families, soil, 606
FAO-UNESCO soil classification, 618, 621–622
Fault(s), 352
Faulting, 375, 380–385
   of Basin and Range Province, 507, 509
   earthquakes and, 380–381, 383, 386, 391, 393–397
Fault plane, 380, 390, 392–394, 396–397
Fault scrap, 380
Fault zones, 380
Feedback loops, 7
Feldspar, weathering of, 425–426
Felsenmeer, 421, 573
Felsic igneous rocks, 343, 345, 385–386
Fertilizers, 641–642
Fibrisol, 612
Field capacity, 260, 600
Fire ecology, 656, 658
Firn, 558
Fissures, volcanic, 402
Fjord, 564–565
Flash floods, desert, 500
Fleming, Sandford, 24
Flood(s), 475–481
   Bangladesh, 476
   channel cross section and, 455–456
   on Colorado River, 504
   defined, 476
   desert, 500
   icing and, 573
   lower Mississippi Valley, 474
   New Orleans (2005), 474, 476, 479–480
   North Carolina (1999), 475
   recurrence intervals of, 476, 481–482
   Red River (1997), 466–470
   sea-level rise, 522–523
   urban, 481
   volcanic eruptions and, 410
Flood basalts, 400, 404–405
Flood damage, 668
Floodplains, 465–468, 472, 474–479
   management of, 210
   strategies for, 476–479
   as wetlands, 542
Flood tides, 525
Fluvial erosion, of mountains, 387–388
Fluvial processes, 448–455, 459
   in deserts, 500–501, 505
Fly ash, albedo and, 96–97
Focus of earthquake, 391
Foehn, 166, 217
Fog, 200–203
   definition of, 200
   harvesting of, 200, 203–204
   humidity and, 187–188
   incidence of, 202–203
   marine west coast climates, 300
   types of, 200–202
Folding, 375–380, 379
   in orogenesis, 385, 388
Foliated rock, 348
Folisol, 611–612
Food chain, 644–646
Food web, 644–646
   efficiency in, 646–648
   examples of, 644, 646
Footwall block, 380–381
Forced fluctuation, in climate change, 319–320
Forecasting
   of earthquakes, 391, 397–398
   of volcano eruption, 410
Foreland Belt, 377–378
Foreshocks, 391
Forest
   Brunisolic order and, 609–610
   climate change and, 654–655
   Cryosolic soils and, 610
   different communities, 631
   diversity in, 664–665
   of humid continental hot-summer climates,
     305–306
   midlatitude, 685–687
   needleleaf (boreal), 305, 687–690

   stability of, 651
   of subarctic climates, 305
   temperate rain, 690
   urban, 112
Forest fires
   climate change and, 75–76
   as feedback loop, 7–9
   succession after, 656, 658
Formation classes, 672–673
Fossil fuels
   air pollution and, 80–82
   greenhouse gases and, 136–137, 640–641
Fourth Assessment Report (AR4), IPCC, 137, 317–318,
   320–323
Fractional scale, 26–27
Franklin, Benjamin, 26, 350
Frank (Alberta) slide, 436–438
Fraser River Delta, 474–475
Free face, 417
Freeze-thaw action. *See* Frost action
Freezing
   latent heat of, 185–186
   of water, 183–184
Freezing points, oceanic, 520
Freezing rain, 227–228
Frequency, of radiant energy, 46
Freshening, of northern oceans, 518
Freshwater
   distribution of, 181–183
   ecosystems of, 672
   groundwater source, 266
   supply of, 276
Friction
   in landscape formation, 417, 431
   streams and, 460
   and waves, 526
   wind and, 490
Friction force, 148, 150, 152, 154
   in midlatitude cyclonic systems, 222
Fringing reefs, 540–541
Frogs, at tipping point, 11
Frontal lifting, 215–216, 218–221
Frost, 184
Frost action, 421–422, 438, 573–575
Frost-heaving, 422, 573
Frost-thrusting, 573
Fujita Scale, 233–234
Fujita, Theodore, 233
Fungi Kingdom, 651
Fungus, 630–631
Funnel clouds, 233
Fusion, 42

Gabbro, 344
Gaia hypothesis, 709
Galbraith, A.J., 606
Galileo, 21, 145
Gamma rays, 46–47
   ionosphere and, 70
Ganges-Brahmaputra River, 45, 471, 476
Gaseous cycle, 637
Geiger, Rudolph, 291
Gelifluction, 439, 575–576
Gelisols, A.7–A.9
Gene pool, 650
General circulation model (GCM), 12, 321–323
Genes, 650
Genetic classification, 288
Genomes, 650
Geodesy, 15
Geographic information system (GIS), 34–35
Geography, 2–5. *See also* Physical geography
Geological Survey of Canada (GSC), 511
Geologic cycle, 339–349
Geologic time, 465
   scale, 332–334
Geomagnetic polarity chrons, 335
Geomagnetic reversal, 335–336, 351, 353
Geomorphic threshold, 417, 433
Geomorphology, 416
   of coastal systems, 546–547
Geostationary Operational Environmental Satellites
   (GOES), 33, 188–189
Geostationary orbit, 31
Geostrophic winds, 154, 159–160

Geothermal energy, 361, 364–365, 399
Geysers, 364–365
GIS. *See* Geographic information system
Glacial ages, 577
Glacial drift, 567
Glacial erosion, of mountains, 387–388
Glacial erratics, 567
Glacial plucking, 564
Glacial polish, 564
Glacials, 577, 581
Glacial surge, 563–564
Glaciers, 552–558
   braided stream and, 459
   defined, 552
   at equatorial latitudes, 123
   formation of, 558
   global warming and, 134–135, 323, 552, 560, 589
   ice in, 552–558, 562
   isostatic rebound and, 338
   landforms created by, 564–570, 577
   of Little Ice Age, 582
   loess and, 495–496, 602
   mass balance of, 558–562
   meltwater of, 559, 562–563, 567–568
   movement of, 562–564
   processes of, 558–564
   in soil formation, 495–497, 602
   volcanic activity and, 557
   water quantity in, 181–182
Glacio-eustatic factors, 181
Glen Canyon Dam, 501–505
   scouring experiment, 457, 478
   water losses at, 504
Gleysation, 602, 610
Gleysol, 610
Gleysolic order, 610, 614
Global Climate Observing System (GCOS), 122, 317–318
Global dimming, 97–98
Global Energy and Water Cycle Experiment (GEWEX), 254
Global energy balance, 113–114
Global linkages, 703–704
Global mean temperatures
   for January, 129–130
   for July, 132–133
Global net radiation, 50
Global Positioning System (GPS), 19, 338, 371, 373, 523
   description of, 22–23
   Earth rotation and, 53
   landslides and, 435
   and plate movement, 360–361
Global Warming, 317–321. *See also* Climate change
   in Antarctica, 135, 324
   in arctic region, 511
   carbon dioxide and, 317–321, 584–585
   consequences of, 323–324
   coral bleaching and, 541
   forest effects, 654–655
   glaciers and, 134–135, 323, 552, 560, 589
   greenhouse gases and, 320–321
   ice ages and, 582
   IPCC and, 317–318, 522–523
   permafrost and, 323, 572–573, 576, 687
   political action and, 324
   thermohaline circulation and, 172
   tundra and, 310
Globe, 27
Glucose, 634
Gnomonic projection, 29
Goddard Institute for Space Studies (GISS), 318
Gondwana, 354, 390, 584, 654
Goode's homolosine projection, A.1
Gorse, 676–677
Grabens, 384–385, 507
Graded stream, 461–462, 465
Graded time, 465
Grand Canyon, 348–349, 457, 501, 637
Granite, 337, 341, 344, 346, 377–378
   weathering of, 422–426
Granite magma, 384–385, 388
Granular disintegration, 425–426
Graphic scale, 26–27
Grassland, midlatitude, 691–692

Gravel, 471, 488–489, 505
Gravitational force, 42
   air pressure and, 65–66
   on atmosphere, 192
   defined, 524
   and hydrologic cycle, 448
   landform development and, 417, 441–442
   mass movement and, 431, 433–434, 441–442
   sea-floor topography and, 356
   stream gradient and, 460–462
   tides and, 521, 524–525
   wind and, 148, 150
Gravitational water, 260
Gray Brown Luvisol, 611
Gray Luvisol, 611, 615
Great circle, 19, 21, 23, 29
Great groups, soil, 606
Great Lakes, 182–183, 660–664, 686
   cyclonic system and, 222
   formation of, 578, 580
   geography and physical characteristics of, 660–662
   human activities at, 663–664
   snowbelts and, 214–215
   water pollution in, 660–664
Great Rift Valley, 357, 384–385
Great Salt Lake, 183, 453
Greenhouse effect
   albedo and, 101–102
   and atmospheric warming, 99
   carbon cycle and, 640–641
   clouds and, 96, 99–101, 124
   gases associated with, 99, 318–321, 584
Greenhouse gases
   climate change and, 315
   fossil fuels and, 136, 640–641
   global warming and, 320–321
Greenland
   global warming and, 324
   meltponds in, 586–587
   topographic region, 374
Greenland Ice Core Project (GRIP), 582–583
Greenland ice sheet, 553, 556, 558, 563, 582, 586
Greenland Ice Sheet Project (GISP-2), 582–583
Greenwich Mean Time (GMT), 24
Greenwich prime meridian, 17, 19
GRIP. *See* Greenland Ice Core Project
Ground heating and cooling (G), 105, 109–110
Ground ice, 573–576
Grounding line, 558
Ground moraine, 567
Groundwater, 265–273
   of alluvial fans, 505
   aquifers, wells, and springs, 267–268
   Canada use of, 275
   coastal development and, 543, 545
   contaminated, 272
   global quantity of, 182–183
   in hydrologic cycle, 254
   mining of, 268–271
   overuse of, 268–272
   permanent frost and, 573
   pollution of, 266–268, 272–273
   profile and movement of, 266–267
   radon in, 398
   saltwater encroachment on, 272
   in soil-water balance, 254, 258–259
Growing seasons, climate change and, 284
Groyne, 536–537
Gulf of Mexico, 217, 221, 685
Gulf Stream, 126, 170
Gullies, 450, 486
Gull Island Dam, 264
Gutenberg discontinuity, 336
Gypsum, karst topography and, 428, 431
Gyres, 171

Haber-Bosch process, 641–642
Habitat, 630, 671
Habitat niche, 630
Hadley circulation cell, 156–157
Haeckel, Ernst, 628
Haida Gwaii (Queen Charlotte Islands), 359–360
Hail, 229, 231
Hair hygrometer, 191
Half-life, 332

Halophytic plants, 542
Hanging valleys, 564
Hanging wall, 380–381
Hansen, James, 318
Harlemon, John, 22
Harlequin frog, extinction of, 11
Harmonic tremors, 406–407
Harrison, John, 22
Hawai'i
   tsunami and, 531–532
   volcanism in, 399–404
Hawaiian-Emperor islands chain, 361–362, 368
Hawaiian high. *See* Pacific high
Hazard perception
   earthquakes, 398
   floods, 476
   shoreline planning, 520–521, 544–546
Haze
   in Arctic, 78
   light scattering by, 93
Headlands, 529–530
Heat. *See also* Specific heat
   adiabatic processes and, 192–194
   in atmosphere, 69
   definition of, 120
   in Earth's interior, 334–339, 364, 374
   in landscape dynamics, 416
   transfer of, 98, 101–102, 104–105, 107–108
   water and, 183–187
Heat wave, death toll of, 137–138
Herbivore, 644
Herbivorous zooplankton, 644, 646
Hercynian orogeny, 385
Herodotus, 472
Heterosphere, 65–67
High-elevation farming, 123–124
Highland climates, 292, 309–311, A.10–A.12
High Plains Aquifer, 269–271
High-pressure areas, 150–151, 154
   and atmospheric patterns of motion, 154–159
   desert regions and, 498
   maritime air masses and, 213
   polar high-pressure cells, 154–156, 158–159
   subtropical high-pressure cells, 154–155, 157–158
   winter, 214
High tablelands, 371–372, 374
Hills
   glacial formation of, 570
   topographic definition of, 371–372, 374
Hillslopes. *See* Slopes
Himalayas, 687
   global warming and, 323
   orogeny, 385–386
Histosols, A.7–A.9
Holistic perspective, 709–710
Holocene Epoch, 332, 577, 581, 656
Homosphere, 65, 67–69
Hoover Dam, 250–251, 501–504
Horn, 564
Horse latitudes, 158
Horsts, 384, 507, 509
Hot spots, 337, 359, 361–365, 368, 399–400
Howard, Luke, 196–197
Hue, of soil, 598
Human and cultural geography, 3–5
Human body
   humidity and, 137–138
   temperature variations and, 136–138
   water in, 180
Human–Earth relationships, 3–4
Human-induced mass movement, 439–441
Humic Gleysol, 610
Humic Regosol, 618
Humid continental hot-summer climates, 305–306
Humid continental mild-summer climates, 305, 307
Humidex, 137–139
Humidity, 187–192
   convectional lifting and, 215–217
   expressions of, 188–192
   human body and, 137–138
   instruments for measuring, 191–192
   relative, 187–188, 204–206
   specific, 190–191
   vapour pressure and, 189–190
Humid subtropical hot-summer climates, 299, 686–687

Humid subtropical winter-dry climates, 299–300
Humification, 597
Humisol, 612
Humus, 597
Hurricane(s). *See also* Tropical cyclones
   atlantic, and 2005 season, 241–245
   barrier islands and, 536–538
   loss from, 241–244
   North Carolina floodplain disaster, 475
   prediction and future of, 243–245
Hurricane Bonnie, 238
Hurricane Camille, 238, 245, 536
Hurricane Catarina, 236–237, 239
Hurricane Charley, 241, 536
Hurricane Cindy, 241
Hurricane Dennis, 241, 475, 537–538
Hurricane Floyd, 475
Hurricane Frances, 241, 536
Hurricane Gamma, 241
Hurricane Georges, 538–539
Hurricane Gilbert, 146, 236–237, 239
Hurricane Hugo, 537–538
Hurricane Irene, 475
Hurricane Ivan, 241, 536
Hurricane Jeanne, 241, 536
Hurricane Juan, 238–240
Hurricane Katrina, 126, 146, 186–187, 210, 212,
   238, 241, 245, 476, 479, 538–540
Hurricane Michelle, 188–189
Hurricane Mitch, 238
Hurricane Ophelia, 241
Hurricane Rita, 126, 146, 241
Hurricane Wilma, 126, 146, 241
Hutton, James, 334
Huygens, Christian, 22
Hydration, 424, 433
Hydraulic action, 458, 462
Hydrogen
   in biosphere, 637
   in soil, 601
Hydrogen bonding
   in soil water, 259
   in water, 183
Hydrogen-oxygen bond, 183–184
Hydrogeologist, 268
Hydrograph, 481
Hydrologic cycle, 252–254, 287
   ecosystems and, 637
   fluvial systems and, 448
   geologic cycle and, 339–340
   groundwater, 265–272
   landscape dynamics and, 416
   model of, 253
Hydrologic drought, 261
Hydrologic system, 12
   water in, 183
Hydrology, 448
Hydrolysis, 424–425
Hydrophytic vegetation, 542
Hydrosphere, 14
   climate and, 286
Hydrothermal activity, 347, 349
Hydrothermal reservoir, 364
Hydrothermal vents, deep-sea, 519
Hygrometer, 191
Hygroscopic water, 259, 420
Hyperthermia, 136
Hypothermia, 136, 227
Hypothesis, in scientific method, 8
Hypsometry, 371–372

Ice, 184–185
   changing levels of, 181
   fog and, 200
   glacial, 552–558, 562
   ground, 573–576
   ground heating and, 105
   in hydrologic cycle, 252–254
   sublimation of, 183–184
   weathering and, 421
   world distribution of, 551–553, 556
Ice ages
   defined, 577
   ecological succession and, 656
Icebergs, 185, 554, 556, 588–589

Ice cap, 556–558
   climate, 309–311
Ice cores, 581–584
Ice-crystal fog, 202
Ice-crystal process, 197, 200
Ice field, 556–558
Ice glaze, 227
Iceland, 362, 364, 400, 557
Icelandic low, 222
Ice pellets, 227
Ice regelation, 562
Ice sheets, 309–311, 553, 556, 558, 563–564,
   582–583, 586
   climate, 309–311
   global warming and, 134–135, 323
   of Pleistocene, 576–579
   water quantity in, 181–182
Ice shelves, 552, 558, 587–589
Ice storms, 227–228
Ice streams, 558, 563
Ice wedges, 573–575
Icing, 573
Igneous rocks, 341–344, 401, 426
Illinoian glacial, 577
Illuviation, Luvisolic soils and, 610–611
Inceptisols, A.7–A.9
Indian Ocean, 157–158, 168, 220
   thermohaline circulation, 170–172
   water in, 181–182
Indian Ocean Experiment (INDOEX), 98, 168
India plate, 368
Inductive reasoning, 8
Industrial smog, 82–85
Infiltration, of water, 254
Influent stream, 268
Infrared radiation, 46–47
   greenhouse effect and, 99
   from ozone layer, 70
Infrared sensors, 31
Innuitian Mountains, 388–389
Inselberg, 507
Insolation
   altitude and, 122–124
   climate and, 287–288
   cloud cover and, 124
   daily patterns of, 102–103
   definition of, 47
   at Earth's surface, 92–93
   energy pathways and, 92–98
   and hydrologic cycle, 448
   latitude and, 122–123
   at top of atmosphere, 49
   uneven distribution of, 48–49
Isostacy, 338–339
Isostatic depression by ice sheets, 368
Isostatic rebound, 338, 535–536
Institute for Measurement Standards, 25–26
Instream water uses, 276
Insular Belt, 377–378
Integrated Ocean Drilling Program (IODP), 337–338
Intensity, of earthquake, 391, 393
Interception, of water, 253–254
Interface fires, 658
Interfering waves, 529
Interfluve, 450
Interglacials, 577, 581
Intergovernmental Panel on Climate Change (IPCC),
   135, 138, 278–279, 317–318, 324, 522–523
Intermittent streams, 263
Intermontane Belt, 377–378
Internal differentiation, 334
Internal drainage, 453, 507
International Boundary Commission, 463
International Bureau of Weights and Measures
   (BIPM), 25
International Conference on Fog and Fog
   Collection, 204
International cooperation, need for, 707–708
International Date Line (IDL), 24–25
International Joint Commission (IJC), 264–266
International Polar Year (IPY), 1–2, 177,
   310–311, 319
International Prime Meridian Conference, 24
International Satellite Cloud Climatology Project
   (ISCCP), 96, 124

International Space Station (ISS)
   development of, 701–702
   remote sensing from, 30–31
International Union for Conservation of Nature and
   Natural Resources (IUCN), 681–682
International Year of the Ocean, 518
Interpluvials, 578
Interstellar dust and gas, 584
Intertidal zone, 542
Intertropical convergence zone (ITCZ), 154–156,
   168, 215
   biomes of, 679–680, 685–686
   climates of, 293–298
   storms and, 227
Intrusive ice, 573
Intrusive igneous rock, 341–344, 346
Inversion layer, 76, 200
Ionosphere, 70
Ions, in soil, 601
Iron oxide, 346, 426
Irrigation, 254
   collapsed aquifers, 272
   in High Plains aquifer, 269–270
   in India, 271
   salinization, 605
   in water budget, 263
Islands
   barrier, 536–540, 543, 547
   biogeography of, 683–684
Isobaric maps, 154–155
Isobars, 148–149, 151, 154, 227
   winds parallel to, 154–155
Isostasy, 181, 338–339, 368
Isostatic depression, by ice sheets, 556, 578
Isostatic rebound, 338, 368, 380, 474, 535
Isotherm, 129–130, 132
ITCZ. *See* Intertropical convergence zone

January temperature map, 129–130
Japan Current (Kuroshio), 126
Jet contrails, cloud formation and, 90,
   99–100
Jet Propulsion Laboratory, 118
Jet streams, 157, 159–162
   cyclonic systems and, 222
Jetty, 536–537
Johnston, David, 407
JOIDES Resolution, 337–338
Joint-block separation, 421
Joints, in rocks, 420, 423
Juan de Fuca Plate, 359–360, 400, 406
July temperature map, 132–133

Kalahari Desert, 498–499
Kame, 568–569
Karren, 428
Karst topography, 427–431
Katabatic winds, 165–166
Kelvin scale, 86, 120–121
Kesterson National Wildlife Refuge, selenium
   contamination of, 605
Kettle, 568–569
Kīlauea volcano, 75, 401–403
   primary succession after, 656
Kinetic energy, 5, 69
   in landscape dynamics, 416, 442
   streamflow and, 455, 462, 464
   temperature and, 69
Kingdoms, animals, 650–651
Kittinger, Joseph, Jr., 66–67
Klamath Mountains, 385
Kliuchevskoi Volcano, 32
Kobe earthquake, 394, 396–398
Köppen-Geiger climate classification, 291,
   A.10–A.12
Köppen, Wladimir, 286, 291, A.11
Krill, 644, 646
Kuroshio, 170
Kyoto protocol, 324, 707

Laccolith, 343
Lacustrine deposits, 578
Lagoon, 533, 535
Lahar, 410, 431
Lake Agassiz, 578, 580

Lakes
  in deserts, 501
  ecological succession in, 658–659
  global water distribution in, 181–183
  Pleistocene paleolakes, 578–580
  of thermokarst topography, 576
  tides in, 524
Land-sea breezes, 164–165
Landfall, 238
Landfill sites, and earthquakes, 397
Landforms
  coastal, 532–540
  crustal formation and, 374–375
  denudation of, 416–417, 448, 465
  desert, 498–500, 505–508
  frost action, 574–575
  glacial, 564–570, 577
  models for development of, 416–417, 465
  periglacial, 570–576
  stream processes and, 448, 450, 465–475
  structural regions and, 389–390
  volcanism and, 399–401, 404, 409–410
  wind deposition and, 491–495
  wind formation of, 488–490
Landsat satellites, 32
Landslides, 433–438, 442
  glacial melting and, 552
  submarine, 530–532
Land subsidence, 272
Land–water heating differences, 124–127
La Niña, 286, 291
Lapilli, 404
Latent heat, 185
Latent heat of condensation, 185–186
Latent heat of evaporation (LE), 105, 186
  in different settings, 109–110
  of Earth, 105–106
  land–water heating differences, 125
  sea-surface temperatures and, 126
  transfer of, 104
  in urban environments, 110–112
Latent heat of freezing, 185–186
Latent heat of melting, 185–186
Latent heat of sublimation, 186–187
Latent heat of vaporization, 98, 185–186
Lateral moraine, 567
Laterization, 602
Latitude, 16–17
  air pressure areas by, 154–155
  and Coriolis force, 151–153
  dawn and twilight, 57
  daylength and, 49, 51
  and daylight, 53, 55–56
  determination of, 19–21
  distances with, 20
  energy balance and, 49–50, 101–103
  insolation and, 48–49, 92–93, 122–123
  radiation balance by, 101–102
  temperature variations and, 122–123
Latitudinal geographic zones, 17, 19
Laurasia, 354
Lava, 341, 346, 399–403, 656
Leeward slope, 217–218, 491
Lenses, of ground ice, 573
Leopold, Aldo, 654
Less developed countries (LDCs), 702-705
  solar energy systems for, 108
Levees, 466–467, 473–474, 478–479
  failure of, 474, 476, 479–480
  management of, 210
Lianas, 671, 677
Liaoning earthquake, 391
Lichens, 310, 631–633
Lichty, R.W., 465
Life-form designations, 671–672
Life zones, 637
Lifting condensation level, 195
Light
  interactions with atmosphere, 92–98
  plant productivity and, 636–637
  reflection of, 94–95
  saturation, 634
  speed of, 42
  surface energy balance and, 102–103
  transparency of water, 125

Lightning, 228–230
Lightning image sensor (LIS), 228–230
Light-year, 42
Lime
  in sedimentary processes, 346
  in soil, 602
Limestone, 345–347. See also Calcium carbonate
  caves in, 428–432
  creep, 437
  karst topography and, 427–431
  ocean chemistry, 518
  weathering of, 427–431
Limited Test Ban Treaty, 145
Limiting factors, of ecosystems, 642, 644
Linear dunes, 494
Liquefaction, 475
Lithification, 345, 507–508
Lithosphere, 14–15, 336–339, 356
  climate and, 286
  in cratonic regions, 374
  subduction of, 351–352, 354–357, 385–386
Little Ice Age
  Pleistocene Epoch, 581–582
  theories of causation, 582–585
Littoral cell, 532–533
Littoral current, 530
Littoral drift, 530, 533, 536–537
Littoral zone, 521–522
Loam, 598–599
Local base level, 449
Local winds, 164–166
Location, as spatial theme, 3–4
Loess, 495–496, 600, 602
  deposits, 495–498
Logging, 678, 690
Loma Prieta earthquake, 392, 397–398
Longitude, 17
  determination of, 19–21
  distances with, 20
  GPS and, 22–23
  time and, 19, 21–22
Longitudinal stream profile, 461–464
Longshore current, 530
Longshore drift, 530, 546–547
Long Valley Caldera, 402
Longwave radiation
  absorption and, 98–99
  albedo and, 94
  clouds and, 99–101
  in Earth-atmosphere system, 92–98
  energy balance and, 101–102
  from oceans, 126–127
Lorenz, Edward, 45
Los Angeles Basin, 381
Los Angeles earthquakes, 397
Lovelock, James, 709
Low-pressure areas, 150–151, 154
  and atmospheric patterns of motion, 154–159
  equatorial low-pressure trough, 154–156
  subpolar low-pressure cells, 154–156, 158
Low tablelands, 371–372, 374
Lozinski, W., 570
Luvic Gleysol, 610
Luvisolic order, 610–611, 615
Lyell, Charles, 334
Lysimeter, 257–258

Mackenzie Mountains, 572
Mackenzie River Basin, 254, 452–453
Macroburst, 228
Madison River Canyon landslide, 433–435
Mafic igneous rocks, 343–345, 386
Magellan, Ferdinand, 24
Magma, 341, 343–344
  geothermal energy and, 364
  in sea-floor spreading, 351, 374–376
  in volcanism, 399–408
Magnesium, 336–337
  acid deposition and, 84
  in biosphere, 637
  in soil, 601
Magnetism of Earth, 334–335, 351, 353
  animal navigation and, 637, 638
  earthquakes and, 391, 398
Magnetosphere, 44–45

Magnitude, of earthquake, 391, 393, 410–411
Mallard duck, 642, 644
Mallee scrub, 691
Mammoth Hot Springs, 347, 349
Man and the Biosphere Programme (MBP), 683
Mangrove swamps, 542–543
Manila Galleons, 169–170
Mantle, 336–337, 351
Mantle convection, 380
MANTRA balloon, upper-atmospheric wind
    circulation and, 163
Maps
  cartography, 26
  floodplains, 476
  planimetric, A.4
  projections of, 27–29, A.1–A.2
  scale of, 26–27
  topographic, A.2–A.5
  of weather, 224–227
Margulis, Lynn, 709
Mariana Trench, 351, 371–372
Marine effect, 127–128, 131
Marine Isotope Stage (MIS), 577–578, 583
Marine Protected Areas (MPA), 672
Marine west coast climates, 300–303, 668, 686–687
Maritime polar (mP) air masses, 213
  cold fronts, 218–220
  in marine west coast climates, 300
Maritime tropical (mT) air masses, 213–214, 221
  Gulf/Atlantic, 213–214
  Pacific, 213
  thunderstorms and, 227–229
Mars, 180, 491, 493, 575
Marshes
  of Great Lakes coast, 663
  salt, 542
Marsh, George Perkins, 669–670
Mass budget, glacial, 558–562
Mass movement, 431–442
  classes of, 433–439
    Columbian mudflow, 431
    earthquakes and, 433–434
    human-induced, 439–441
    mechanics of, 431–433
    periglacial, 570–575
Mass wasting, 431, 433, 435, 439
Mattoral, 691
Mauna Kea, 404
Mauna Loa, 404
Mauna Loa Observatory (MLO), 62
Maximum specific humidity, 191
McHarg, Ian, 544, 546
McMurdo Station, 130, 133
McPhee, John, 507, 510
Meandering stream, 460–462, 466, 468, 471
Mean sea level (MSL), 521–524
Mean solar time, 53
Mechanical weathering, 421
Medial moraine, 567
Medieval Warm Period, 581–582
Mediterranean dry-summer climates, 303–304, 690
Mediterranean shrubland biome, 674–675, 690–691
Melanic Brunisol, 610
Melt, 374, 376
Melting, latent heat of, 185–186
Meltponds
  increase in, 134–135
  as positive feedback, 7
  and surface energy budgets, 586–587
Meltwater, glacial, 559, 562–563, 567–568
Meniscus, 184
Mercalli scale, 391
Mercator projection, 29
Mercury barometer, 145–146
Mercury thermometer, 121
Meridians, 17, 19, 23
Meridional flows, 145
Mesa, 506
Mesisol, 612
Mesocyclone, 232–233, 235
Mesopause, 69
Mesosphere, 66, 69
Mesothermal climates, 292, 294–295, 298–303,
    A.10–A.12
Mesotrophic stage, in lake succession, 658–659

Metamorphic rocks, 341–343, 348–350, 377–378
Metastable equilibrium, 10
Meteorological drought, 261
Meteorological Service of Canada (MSC), 136, 225, 227
Meteorology, 212
Methane (CH₃)
    global warming and, 320–321
    history of, 138
    longwave absorption by, 99
Microburst, 228
Microclimate, of ecosystems, 637
Microclimatology, 103–104
Microecosystems, 637
Microthermal climates, 292, 294–295, 303–309, 687, A.10–A.12
    weathering in, 421
Mid-Atlantic Ridge, 347, 349, 351–353, 355, 368, 400
Middle East
    desalination in, 276, 278
    groundwater overuse in, 271
Midlatitude broadleaf and mixed forest, 674–675, 685–687
Midlatitude cold desert climates, 314
Midlatitude cold steppe climates, 315–316
Midlatitude cyclonic systems, 222–227
    forecasting, 224–227
    life cycle of, 222–224
Midlatitude grasslands, 674–675, 691–692
Midnight sun, 40, 55–56
Mid-ocean ridges, 351–352, 357, 362, 368
Midwinter's day, 55
Milankovitch, Milutin, 584
Milky Way Galaxy, 41–43
Miller cylindrical projection, A.1–A.2
Millibar, 189–190
Mineralogy, 341
Minerals, 341
    in soil, 595, 597–598
Mining
    and mass movement, 436–441
    and water pollution, 441
Mirage, 93
MIS. See Marine Isotope Stage
Mississippi River, 466
    delta, 471–474
    fertilizer runoff, 643
Mistral, 165
Mixing zone, 520
Models
    of climate, 320–323
    of landform development, 416–417, 465
    of systems, 12
Moderate-resolution Imaging Spectroradiometer (MODIS), 78
Mohorovičić discontinuity, 337
Moist Adiabatic Rate (MAR), 193–196
Moisture droplet, 196
Molina, Mario, 8, 71–72
Mollisols, A.7–A.9
Moment magnitude scale, 391–393
Monarch butterflies, 637
Monera Kingdom, 650–651
Mono Lake, 183
Monsoons, 168, 220
    air pollution and, 98
    winds of, 168–169
Montane forest, 687–690
Monthly mean temperature, 122
Montreal Protocol on Substances That Deplete the Ozone Layer, 72
Monument Valley, Utah-Arizona, 508
Moon
    albedo of, 96
    distance from Earth, 42
    tides and, 524–525
    water on, 180
Moraines, 558–559, 567–568
More developed countries (MDCs), 702–705
Morelos Dam, 501–503
Mountain-valley breezes, 165
Mountains
    alpine glaciers of, 553–554, 564–568
    of Basin and Range Province, 507–510
    cloud formation and, 196

formation of, 375, 377–380, 384–390
    in monsoon tropical climate, 296–297
    orographic lifting and, 215–220, 312
    precipitation and, 217–220
    rain shadows, 245–246
    systems of, 389–390
    temperatures in, 123–124
    topographic definition, 371–372, 374
Mountaintop removal, 441
Mount Baker, 409
Mount Edziza, 409–410
Mount Etna, 405–409
Mount Everest, 371–373, 386
Mount Garibaldi, 409–410
Mount Kilimanjaro, 293, 323
Mount Logan, 389
Mount Meager, 409–410
Mount Pinatubo, 409–410
    air pollution caused by, 75
    albedo and, 96
    atmospheric effects of, 145, 409
    global system impact of, 10–12
Mount Rainier, 404
Mount St. Helens, 143, 399, 401, 406–408, 656–657
Mount Waialeale, 220
Movement, as spatial theme, 3–4
Mudflows, 431, 435–438
Munsell Colour Chart, 598
Mutations, 650
Mutualism, 630

Namib Desert, 312, 496
Nappes, 386
National Aeronautics and Space Administration (NASA), 31–33
    global climate change and, 318
    UHIPP and, 110–113
National Climate Data Center (NCDC), 318
National Drought Mitigation Center (NDMC), 261
National Environmental Satellite, Data, and Information Service (NESDIS), 318
National Geographic World Championship, 710
National Hurricane Center (NHC), 211
National Institute for Standards and Technology (NIST), 25
National Oceanic and Atmospheric Administration (NOAA), 32–33, 227, 289–291
National Renewable Energy Laboratory (NREL), 108–109
National Research Council of Canada, 25–26
National Topographic System (NTS), 29, A.2–A.3
National Weather Service (NWS), 73, 136, 212
Natural levees, 466–467
Natural Resources Canada (NRC), A.2
Natural Resources Conservation Service (NRCS), 621
Natural selection, 650, 654
NAVSTAR satellites. See Global Positioning System
Neap tide, 525
Needleleaf forest, 305, 674–675, 687–690
Negative feedback, 7, 126
Net photosynthesis, 634
Net primary productivity, 634–636
Net Radiation (Net R), 104–105
    in different settings, 109–110
New Jersey shore, 544–546
New Orleans, flooding of, 474, 476, 479–480
Newton, Sir Isaac, 8, 15, 153
Next Generation Weather Radar (NEXTRAD) program, 212
Niagara Falls, 462–465, 700
Niagara Region, 284
Niche, 630, 671
    succession, 656
    takeovers, 676–677
Nickpoints, 462–465
Nile River, 456–457, 471–472, 501
Nimbostratus clouds, 197–200
Nitrates
    contamination by, 273
    formation of, 641
Nitric acid (HNO₃), 79, 82, 84
Nitrogen, in homosphere, 67–68
Nitrogen cycle, 641–643
Nitrogen dioxide, as air pollution, 79, 82
Nitrogen-fixing bacteria, 641

Nitrogen oxides
    as air pollution, 79–82
    natural sources of, 74–75
Nitrous oxide
    climate change and, 320–321
    history of, 138
    longwave absorption by, 99
Noctilucent clouds, 69
Nojima fault zone, 394, 398
Nonfoliated rock, 348
Non-native species, 676–677
Nonpoint source pollution, 273
Nordicity, 20
"No regrets" options, climate change policy, 324
Normal fault, 377, 380, 382
Normal lapse rate, 70, 122
    atmospheric stability and, 192, 196
North America
    air masses and, 212–213
    groundwater resources for, 265–266
    POTET for, 258–259
    PRECIP in, 257
North American Plate, 359–361, 368, 378, 381–382
North Anatolian fault system, 384, 393–394, 396
North Atlantic Oscillation (NAO), 162
Northeast passage, 706–707
Northeast trade winds, 156–157
North geographic pole, 18
North Geomagnetic Pole, 18
North Magnetic Pole, 18
North polar region
    January mean temperature at, 130
    July mean temperature at, 133
Northridge earthquake, 381, 383, 391, 393–394
Nuée ardente, 407
Numerical weather prediction, 224
Nunatak, 552, 556, 558

Obsidian, 344–345
Occluded stage, of midlatitude cyclone, 222–223
Ocean(s), 518–521
    acidification of, 520
    carbon in, 640
    chemistry, 519
    ecosystems of, 672
    evaporation of, 125
    freshening of, 134–135, 163–164, 518
    in hydrologic cycle, 253
    latent heat and, 105
    multiyear oscillations and, 162–164
    physical structure of, 520–521
    plant productivity in, 635–636
    temperature variation in, 125–127, 289–291
Ocean basins, 371
Ocean currents, 169–172
    climate change and, 585
    coastal environment and, 521
    equatorial, 170
    longshore, 530
    surface, 169–170
    thermohaline, 170–172
Oceanic crust, 337, 351, 353, 356, 368
Oceanic plate-continental plate collision orogenesis, 385, 387, 399
Oceanic plate-oceanic plate collision orogenesis, 385, 387, 399
Ocean trenches, 351, 368
Odum, Howard T., 648
Office of Foreign Disaster Assistance (U.S. AID), 410
O horizon. See Organic horizon
Oil drilling, in Arctic, 695–696
Oil spills, 705–707
Oligotrophic stage, in lake succession, 658–659
Omineca Belt, 377–378
Omineca Mountains, 377
Omnivore, 644
Ontong Java Plateau, 404–405
Open stage, of midlatitude cyclone, 222–224
Open systems, 5–6, 452
Optical depth, of atmosphere, 78
Orbit
    of Earth, 42, 584
    of satellites, 31
Orders of relief, 371
Orders, soil, 606, A.6–A.9.

Oreskes, Naomi, 318
Organic Crysol, 610
Organic (O) horizon, 597
    in CSSC, 607–608
Organic matter, in soil, 595
Organic order, 611–612, 616
Orion Arm, 42
Orogenesis, 384–390
Orogens, 385
Orographic lifting, 215–220
    dry climates and, 312
Ortelius, Abraham, 350
Outgassing, 180–181
Outlet glacier, 558, 563
Outputs, of systems, 12
Outwash plains, 568
Oval projection, 28
Overland flow, 258–259, 450
Overpumping, of groundwater, 268–271
Over-steepened slope, 433
Overthrust faults. *See* Thrust faults
Overturned anticline, 379
Oxbow lake, 460–462, 466–467
Oxidation, 426
Oxisols, 678–679, A.7–A.9
Oxygen
    in biosphere, 637
    in Earth's crust, 341
    in homosphere, 68
    isotope ratios, 577–578, 583
    from photosynthesis, 633–634
    in seawater, 519–521
Oxygen cycle, 640–641
Ozone gas, as air pollution, 79, 82
Ozone layer, 70
    CFCs and, 8
    in homosphere, 67–68
Ozone losses, 71–75
Ozone Monitoring Instrument (OMI), 71
Ozonosphere. *See* Ozone layer

Pacific Coast, of Canada, 359–361
Pacific Decadal Oscillation (PDO), 164
Pacific high, 158
Pacific Ocean, 158
    thermohaline circulation, 170–172
    water in, 181–182
Pacific Plate, 357, 360–361, 368, 381–382
Pacific Rim, 359, 385
Pahoehoe, 399
Paleoclimatology, 318, 552, 581–585
Paleolakes, 578–580
Paleoseismology, 398
Palsa, 574
Pampas, 692
Pangaea, 349–353, 350, 354, 390, 582, 584, 648,
    654, 670–671
    sea-floor spreading, 350–351, 354–355
    subduction zones, 351–352, 354–356
Pantanal, 685
Paradigms, 21st century, 708
Parallel drainage, 454
Parallels of latitude, 17
Parasitic relationship, 631
Parcels, of air, 192–196
Parent rock, 418–420
Particle density, 622
Particulate matter (PM), 83
Passive solar energy system, 108
Patch dynamics, 655
Paternoster lakes, 564
Patterned ground, 574–575
Peat, 572, 594, 611
Ped, 599–600
Pediment, 510
Pedogenic regimes, 602
Pedology, 596
Pedon, 596–597
Percolation, 254, 272–273
Perennial streams, 263
Periglacial landscapes, 570–576
Perihelion, 42
Periods, geologic, 332
Permafrost, 305, 542, 552, 570–573
    Alpine, 694

alpine, 573
    Cryosolic soils and, 610
    defined, 570
    global warming and, 323, 572–573, 576, 687
    human development and, 576–577
    Luvisolic soils and, 611
    soil flows and, 575–576
Permeability, of soil, 260
Peroxyacetyl nitrates (PAN), as air pollution,
    79, 82
Peru Current, 289–290
Petroleum geology, 379
Peyto Glacier, 559–562, 567–568
Phase changes, of water, 183–187
Photic layer, 125
Photochemical smog, 80, 82
Photosynthesis, 633–636
Photovoltaic systems, 107–109
Phreatophytes, 312, 504
pH scale, 601–602
Physical Oceanography Distributed Active Archive
    Center (PODAAC), 126
Physical weathering, 420–424
Phytoplankton, 644, 646
Piedmont glacier, 554
Piercement domes, 380–381
Pine Island Glacier, 589
Pingo, 574
Pinnacles, 506
Pioneer community, 656
Place, spatial theme, 3–4
Plains, 371–372, 374, 692
Planar projection, 28–29
Plane of the ecliptic, 42–43, 53, 584
Planetary impact, 704–705
Planetesimal hypothesis, 42
Planimetric map, A.4
Plant Kingdom, 651
Plants
    biodiversity and, 651–652, 683
    as biotic component, 631–633
    climate change and, 653–655
    in ecological succession, 656
    medicines derived from, 683
    photosynthesis of, 6–7, 633–636
    precipitation and, 634–638
    respiration of, 6–7
    of terrestrial ecosystems, 671–672
    weathering and, 420, 428
Plate(s)
    in orogenesis, 384–390
    of present crust, 356
    terranes of, 374–375
Plateau basalts, 400, 404–405
Plate boundaries, 356–362, 371, 374, 390, 398
Plate tectonics, 349–365
    history of, 350
    hot spots, 361–365, 399–400
    ice ages and, 584
    sea-floor spreading and crust production, 340,
        350–351, 374–375
Platforms
    continental, 374, 389
    wave-cut, 532–533
Playa, 501, 506, 509–510
Pleistocene Ice Age, 576–581
Plough winds. *See* Derechos
Pluton, 342–343, 385, 388, 422
Pluvials, 578
Podzolic order, 612–613, 617–618
Podzolization, 602, 610, 612, 618
POES. *See* Polar Operational Environmental
    Satellites
Point bar, 460, 466
Point source pollution, 273
Polar climates, 292, 309–311, A.10–A.12
    changes in, 586–589
    meltpond trends in, 7, 134–135, 586–587
    periglacial regions in, 570
    temperature trends in, 134–135
    weathering in, 421
Polar easterlies, 159
Polar front, 158
    midlatitude cyclone and, 222
Polar high-pressure cells, 154–156, 158–159

Polaris
    Earth's axis and, 53
    and latitude measurement, 17, 19
Polarity, of water, 183
Polar jet stream, 161
Polar marine climate, 311
Polar oblateness, 15
Polar Operational Environmental Satellites (POES),
    32–33
Polar stratospheric clouds (PSCs), 72–73
Pollution. *See also* Air pollution; Water
        pollution
    of beaches, 543, 545
    excess nitrogen fertilizers, 642–643
    of groundwater, 266–268, 272–273
Polychlorinated biphenyls (PCBs), 663–664
Polypedon, 596–597
Population
    coastal, 518
    growth of, 704–705
    water supply and, 274
Pore ice, 573
Porosity, of soil, 260, 600
Positive feedback, 7
Post-glacial, uplift, 535–536
Potential energy, 5
    landforms and, 416
    streamflow and, 455, 462, 464
Potential evapotranspiration (POTET), 255, 257
    in water budget, 261–263
Potentiometric surface, 267
Powell, John Wesley, 449, 501, 503, 505
Prairies, 691–692
Precession, of Earth's axis, 584
Precipitation (PRECIP)
    acidic, 423–427, 601–602
    climate and, 287–288
    cold fronts and, 220–221
    in desert, 500–501
    desertification and, 510, 693
    drainage basin and, 450–451, 453
    in equatorial low-pressure trough, 154–156
    freezing, 227–228
    global warming and, 323
    humidity and, 187
    in hydrologic cycle, 253–254
    measurement of, 255–256
    in midlatitude cyclonic system, 222
    monsoons and, 168–169
    mountains and, 217–220
    plant production and, 634–638
    soil-water balance, 254–257, 260
    stream discharge and, 481
    tropical climate and, 293, 296–298
    types of, 255–256
    in water-balance equation, 255–257
    in water budget, 261–263
    water supply and, 278
Pressure gradient force, 148–152
    in midlatitude cyclonic systems, 222
Pressure-release jointing, 422–423
Primary atmospheric circulation, 145
Primary dunes, 544–545
Primary succession, 656
Prime meridian, 17, 19
    and standard time, 23–26
Prince William Sound, 705–706
Process, in geographic analysis, 3
Producers, 644
Productivity, of wetlands, 542
Profile of equilibrium, 462
Projections
    map, 27–29, A.1–A.2
    nature and classes of, 28–29
Prokaryotes, 650–651
Protista Kingdom, 651
Protoplanets, 42
Protosun, 42
Province, 507
Psychrometer, sling, 191–192
Pumice, 344–345, 404
Punctuated equilibrium, 334
Purple loosestrife, 676–677
Pyroclastics, 399, 404
Pythagoras, 15

Quartz, 341, 425–426
Quartz clocks, 25
Queen Charlotte Fault, 360

Radar, 31–32
RADARSAT, 31–32
Radial drainage, 454
Radiation. *See also* Shortwave radiation
    absorption of, 48, 98–99
    net, 104–105
Radiation balance
    Earth-atmosphere, 101–102
    at Earth's surface, 102–114
    at surface, 102–114
Radiation fog, 201–202
Radiative cooling, 201
Radiative energy transfer, 101
Radioactive decay, 329
Radiometric dating, 332, 581
Radiosondes, 192
Radon gas, earthquakes and, 398
Rainbow, 93–94
Raindrop formation, 196
Rain forest climates (Af), weathering in, 420
Rain gauge, 255–256
Rain shadows, 217, 498
    adiabatic warming and, 245–246
    deserts and, 312
Ranges, as in horsts, 507, 509–510
Rapids, 462
Rayleigh scattering, 93
Recharge, of aquifer, 267–268
Rectangular drainage, 454
Recurrence intervals, of flooding, 476, 481–482
Red River flood (1997), 466–470
Reefs, coral, 540–542
Reflection, of solar radiation, 94–95
Refraction
    of solar radiation, 93–94
    of water waves, 529–530
Regelation of ice, 562
Regional metamorphism, 348
Region, as spatial theme, 3–4
Regolith, 417–419, 422, 564, 575
Regosolic order, 618–619
Regosol, 618
Rejuvenation, of streams, 462
Relative humidity, 187–188
    measurement of, 204–206
    tables for, 205–206
Relative time scale, 332–333
Relief, 371–374
Remote sensing
    active, 30–31
    of aerosols, 78
    passive, 31–33
Reproductive niche, 630
Reservoirs, 477–478, 504–505
Resilience, 651
Respiration, of plants, 6–7, 635–636, 640
Reverse fault, 377, 380–382
Revolution, of Earth, 52
Rhine River valley, graben, 384
R horizon. *See* Rock horizon
Rhumb lines, 29
Rhyolite, 341, 344–345
Richter scale, 391–393
Ridge and Valley Province, 385, 453
Ridges
    of fold, 379
    on isobaric surface, 159–160
    mid-ocean, 351–352, 357, 362, 368
Rifts, 351, 399–400, 402
Rift valleys, 352, 381, 400
Rills, 450
Rime fog, 201–202
Ring of fire, 359, 386, 531
Rip current, 528–529
Ripples, eolian, 491, 492
River(s)
    defined, 448
    without deltas, 475
    in deserts, 500
    Earth's largest, 448–449
    global volume in, 181–183

importance of, 447–448
    as political boundaries, 463
River deltas, 471–475
River management, 475–481
Robinson projection, A.1–A.2
Roche moutonnée, 570
Rock blisters, 422
Rock cycle, 331–332, 340–341
Rockfalls, 422, 434–435
    glacial melting and, 552
Rock (R) horizon, 597
Rocks, 341
    dating of, 332
    frost action on, 573
    glacial abrasion of, 564, 570
    glacial deposition of, 567
    igneous, 341–344, 401, 426
    metamorphic, 341–343, 348–350, 377–378
    sedimentary, 341–348, 374, 377–378, 389–390
    water percolation through, 254
    weathering of, 602
Rocky Mountains, 217–219, 377, 385, 388, 687
Rondônia (Brazil), 679–680
Rossby waves, 159, 161, 163
Rotational slides, 435–436
Rotation, of Earth, 52–53, 153–154
Rowland, F. Sherwood, 8, 71–72
Runoff
    accessibility of, 274, 278–279
    agricultural, 641–643
    in deserts, 501
    drainage basin and, 450

Saffir–Simpson Hurricane Damage Potential Scale, 236, 238
Sagan, Carl, 702, 709–710
Sagittarius A* (or A Star), 42
Sahara Desert, 132, 157, 312–313, 693
Sahel region, 510
Saline lakes, 183
Salinity, 518–521
Salinization, 602, 605
    of Chernozemic soils, 610
    of Solonetzic soils, 618
Saltation
    in eolian transport, 490–492
    in stream transport, 458–459
Salt-crystal weathering, 422–423
Salt marshes, 542
Saltwater, aquifer encroachment of, 272
San Andreas fault, 358, 360, 381–384, 396–397
Sand, 425. *See also* Dunes; Eolian processes
    of beaches, 543–545
    characteristics, 418–420
    deflation of, 488–490
    deposition by glaciers, 567
    as longshore drift, 530
    transport by wind, 488, 490–492
Sand sea, 491, 493
Sandstone, 345–347
    weathering, 422–424, 506–508
Sandstorms, 490
Sargasso Sea, 158, 520
Satellites, 30–33
    atmospheric effects of volcanic eruptions and, 143–145
    Earth radiation budget and, 50
    for GPS, 22–23
    measurement of rotation of Earth, 53
    orbits of, 31
    for remote sensing, 30–32
    solar winds study, 45
    water vapour imaging, 188–189
    for weather, 33, 212, 225
Saturated air, 187–189
Saturation equilibrium, 187
Saturation vapour pressure, 189–190
Saturation, zone of, 265
Sawtooth ridge, 564
Scale, of maps, 26–27
Scarification, 439–441
Scarp, 417
Scattering, of radiation, 92–93
Scientific method, 8–9
SCISAT satellite, 33

Sclerophyllous vegetation, 691
Scoresby Sund, 310
Scoria, 399, 404
Scouring, by streams, 455–457
Sea(s), 518–520
    inland, 183
Sea arches, 532–534
Sea breezes, 164–165
Sea cliffs, 532–533, 543–544
Sea-floor spreading, 350–358, 368, 374–375–376, 399, 406
Sea-floor topography, 356–357
Sea ice, 134, 585–586
    extent of, 177
    global warming and, 323
    loss of, 134–135, 706–707
Sea level
    changes in, 181, 521–523
    coastal systems and, 521–524
    glaciers and, 560–562
    global warming and, 324
    measurement of, 521–524
    in Pleistocene Ice Age, 580–581
    as ultimate base level, 449
Seamounts, 361–362, 368
Seasat satellite, 31, 148
Sea smoke, 200, 202
Seasons
    annual march of, 54–57
    axial parallelism and, 53–54
    axial tilt of earth and, 53
    humidity and, 188
    insolation and, 49
    reasons for, 52–54
    revolution of earth and, 52
    rotation of earth and, 52–53
    seasonality, 50–52
    sphericity of earth and, 53
Sea stack, 532, 534
Sea-surface elevation, 356–357
Sea-surface temperature (SST)
    data collection, 126–127
    in ENSO, 289–291
    in hurricane forecasting, 241
    in mesothermal climates, 298
    in Pleistocene Ice Age, 581
Seawater
    chemical composition, 518–520
    distribution of, 181–182
Sea waves, 526
Secondary atmospheric circulation, 145
Secondary dunes, 545
Secondary succession, 656
Sediment
    coastal deposition processes, 521, 530, 532–540
    defined, 420
    deflation by wind, 497–498
    deposition by streams, 448, 450, 452, 456–459, 463, 465–475, 505
    paleolakes, 578
    transport by streams, 448, 450, 452, 458–459
    of wetlands, 542
Sedimentary cycles, 637
Sedimentary rocks, 341–348
    of continental platforms, 374, 377–378, 389–390
Sediment budgets, 546–547
Sediment load, 452, 455–461
Segregated ice, 573
Seismic gap, 398
Seismic moment, 392
Seismic sea waves, 530–532
Seismic tomography, 334
Seismic waves, 334, 337, 390–392
Seismograph, 391
Selective cutting, forestry, 678
Selenium, in Western soils, 605
Selva, 677
Semiarid steppes, 693
Sensible heat (H), 69, 105
    definition of, 120
    in different settings, 109–110
    of Earth, 105–106
    evaporative cooling and, 125
    transfer of, 104
    in urban environments, 110–112

Sensible temperature, 136
Sequential landscapes, 416
Sequoia gigantea, 687, 689
Serengeti Plains, 685–686
Series, soil, 606
Severe thunderstorm warnings, 229
Shale, 345–348, 425, 433
Shear, 375, 377, 380–382
Shear strength, 433
Sheetflow, 450
Sheeting, in physical weathering, 423–424
Shields, continental, 374–375, 389
Shield volcano, 404
Shingle beach, 536
Shoreline, 324, 521, 524–525, 535–536
    planning and protection, 523, 544–546
Shore platform. *See* Wave-cut platform
Shortwave radiation, 47-48
    absorption and, 98
    albedo and, 94
    clouds and, 99–101
    daily pattern of, 102–103
    in Earth-atmosphere system, 92–98
    energy balance and, 101–102
Shrubland, Mediterranean, 690–691
Shrubs, 672
Sial, 337
Siberia, 572, 576
Siberian Traps, 404
Sierra Nevadan orogeny, 385
Silica, 425–426
Silicates, 336–337, 341, 425, 640
Silicic magma, 374
Silicon, in Earth's crust, 341
Sills, 343
Silt, deposition of, 448, 466, 468, 472, 495–497,
    505, 578
Siltstone, 346
Sima, 337
Simpson, G.C., 147
Sinkholes, 428–430, 432–433
Siple, Paul, 136
Skin cancer, and ozone losses, 72
Sky, colour of, 93
Slate, 348, 441
Sling psychrometer, 191–192
Slipface, 491, 493, 495
Slopes, 417–419
    geographic orientation of, 420
    human destruction of, 439–441
    mass movement and, 431–433, 441–442
    periglacial, 575
    stream behaviour and, 460–465
Small circles, 21, 23
Smectite, Vertisolic soils and, 618
Smog
    industrial, 82–85
    light scattering by, 93
    photochemical, 80, 82
Snail Kite, 642, 644
Snow
    albedo and, 96
    in glacier formation, 553, 558
    ground heating and, 105
    on mountains, 123
Snowbelts, lake-effect, 214–215
Snow dunes, 495
Snowfield, 553, 558
Snowline, 123, 553
Socioeconomic drought, 261
Sodium, in soil, 601
Soft bed, of glaciers, 563
Soil, 495–498
    characteristics of, 596–602
    definition of, 595
    erosion of, 511–513, 602–606
    FAO–UNESCO classification system, 618,
        621–622
    formation factors of, 602–606
    heat transfer in, 104
    ice in, 573–574
    information resources for, 596, 598
    in microthermal climates, 305
    parent material of, 418–420
    periglacial flows of, 575–576

temperature profile of, 125
    water balance in, 254–266
    water movement through, 254
    weathering and, 418–420, 425–426, 602
    wetland, 542
    worldwide losses of, 603–604
Soil acidity, 601–602, 656
Soil alkalinity, 601–602
Soil chemistry, 600–601
Soil classification, 606, A.6–A.9
Soil colloids, 601
Soil colour, 598
Soil consistence, 599–600
Soil creep, 438–439
Soil density, 622
Soil fertility, 601–603, 610, 613
Soil horizons, 597–598
    in CSSC, 606–608
    diagnostic, A.6–A.9
    mineral, 607
    organic, 597, 607–608
Soil moisture, 600
Soil-moisture availability, 260
Soil-moisture recharge, 260
Soil-moisture storage (Δ STRGE), 255, 259
Soil-moisture utilization, 260
Soil porosity, 260, 600, 622
Soil profiles, 596–597
Soil science, 596
Soil separates, 598
Soil solution, 601
Soil texture, 598–599
Soil-water budget, 254–266
    balance equation, 255–260
Solar cells. *See* Photovoltaic systems
Solar collector, 108–109
Solar constant, 48
Solar energy, 42–50
    in biosphere, 91
    clouds and, 90, 92–93, 95–98, 124
    coastal system and, 521
    collection of, 107–109
    concentration of, 108
    Earth-atmosphere balance of, 101–102
    at Earth surface, 102–114
    ecosystem and, 629–633, 648–649
    electromagnetic spectrum and, 46–47
    future of, 109
    global net radiation, 50
    harmful wavelengths of, 70
    net radiation and, 105
    pathways of, 92–98
    photosynthesis and, 636–637
    reflection of, 94–95
    refraction of, 93–94
Solar maximum, 44
Solar minimum, 44
Solar-panel cooker, 107–108
Solar system
    for energy collection, 108–109
    formation and structure, 42–43
    planets of, 45
Solar wind, 44–46
    effects of, 44–46
    weather effects of, 46
Solifluction, 439, 575
Solod, 618
Solodized Solonetz, 618
Solonetz, 618
Solonetzic order, 618, 620–621
Solum, 598
Solutes, in seawater, 518
Solution, 426–428, 458–459
Solution sinkholes, 428
Sombric Brunisol, 610
Sonoran Desert, 132, 499, 637, 693
Source region, of air masses, 213
Southeast trade winds, 156–157
Southern California Seismographic Network
    (SCSN), 398
Southern Cross, and latitude measurement, 17, 19
Southern Ocean, 181
South polar region
    January mean temperature at, 130
    July mean temperature at, 133

South Pole, 130, 133, 589
Speciation, 648–649
Species, 650–651
    diversity of, 664–665
    extinctions of, 628, 651–652, 681–684
Specific heat, of land v. water, 124–126
Specific humidity, 190–191
Speleology, 433
Sphericity, of earth, 15–16, 53
Spheroidal weathering, 423–425
Spit, barrier, 533, 535, 542, 547
Splay, 437
Spodosols, A.7–A.9
Springs, 267–268
Spring tides, 525
Squall line, 221
Stability
    of atmospheric, 192–196
    geomorphic, 417
Staff gauge, 480
Stalactites, 431
Stalagmites, 431
Standard line or point, 29
Standard parallel or meridian, 29
Standing crop, 648
Starches, 634
Star dunes, 494–496
State of the Lakes Ecosystem Conference
    (SOLEC), 664
Static Crysol, 610
Stationary front, 222–223
St. Boniface landslide, 438
St. Croix River, 463
Steady-state equilibrium, 10
Steady time, 465
Steam fog, 200, 202
Stefan–Boltzmann Law, 86
Stegner, Wallace, 503
Stem flow, 253–254
Stephenson Screen shelters, 121–122
Steppes, 312–315, 693
Stilling well, 480
Stomata, 633
Storm surges, 238
Storm tracks, midlatitude, 223–225
Stoss side, 570
Strain, crustal, 375, 377, 390, 393–394,
    396, 398
Stratified drift, 567–568
Stratiform clouds, 195, 197–200, 217, 221
Stratigraphy, 346
Stratocumulus clouds, 197–200
Stratosphere, 66, 69
Stratus clouds, 99–100, 197–200
Stream(s). *See also* Streamflow
    base level of, 449–450, 471
    channel characteristics, 459–460
    defined, 448
    deposition by, 448, 450, 452, 456–459, 463,
        465–475, 505
    discharge of, 455, 458, 480–481
    drainage basin of, 450–453
    drainage density and, 453–455
    drainage pattern and, 453–455
    erosion by, 448, 458–465
    exotic, 456–458, 501, 503
    flow characteristics, 459–460
    gradient of, 460–465
    transport by, 448, 450, 452, 458–459
    in water budget, 263
Streamflow, 455–475
    in Canada, 276–277
    human use of, 276
    measurement of, 480–481
    urbanization and, 481
    water table and, 268
Stream piracy, 453
Stream terraces, 468, 471
Stress, crustal, 375, 377, 379–380, 390, 393–394,
    396, 398
Strike-slip fault, 377, 381–384, 396
Subarctic climates, 305, 307–309, 570
    weathering in, 421
Subduction zones, 351–352, 354–357, 368, 374, 378,
    385–386

orogenesis and, 385–386
volcanism and, 399–400, 404
Subglacial meltwater, 559
Sublimation, of water, 183–184
Subpolar low-pressure cells, 154–156, 158
Subpolar regions, temperature range at, 133–134
Subsea permafrost, 572
Subsolar point, 48–49, 51, 55
Subtropical high-pressure cells, 154–155, 157–158
    desert regions and, 287, 498
    maritime air masses and, 213
Subtropical jet stream, 161
Succession, ecological, 655–659
Sulfate aerosols
    albedo and, 96–97
    cloud formation and, 196
    formation of, 83
Sulfuric acid (H_2SO_4)
    acid deposition and, 84
    atmospheric circulation of, 145
Sulfur oxides, 82–85
Sulphur dioxide (SO_2)
    albedo and, 96–97
    smog and, 83
    from volcanoes, 75
Sulphur, in biosphere, 637
Sumatra earthquake, 531–532
Summer solstice, 55–57
Sun
    aerosols and, 70, 74
    altitude of, 50–51, 57
    atmospheric filtering of, 39, 63, 70
    calculating energy from, 58
    distance from Earth, 42–43
    energy from in 12-hour period, 58
    refraction of, 93–94
    and seasonality, 50–52
    tides and, 524–525
Sunrise, 54–55, 57, 93–94
Sunset, 54–55, 57, 93–94
Sunspots, 44
    weather and, 46
Supercell tornadoes, 232–233
Supercooled fog, 201
Super Cyclone Gonu, 236
Superposed stream, 454
Superposition, principle of, 332
Super Typhoon Ioke, 236
Surface creep, 491–492
Surface energy balance, 102–114, 586–587
Surface relief, 371–374
Surface tension, of water, 183
Surface water, 181–183
    in hydrologic cycle, 253–254
    pollution of, 272–273
Surge, glacial, 563–564
Surplus (SURPL), water, 255, 258–260
Suspended load, 458–459
Swamps, 654
    of mangroves, 542–543
Swash, 530
Swells, 527–528
Symbiotic relationship, 540
Symbiotic species, 630–631
Synclinal ridge, 379
Syncline, 379
Synoptic analysis, 224–225
Systeme Probatoire d'Observation de la Terre
    (*SPOT*), 33
Systems, theory of, 5–12

Tablelands, 371–372, 374
Taiga, 305, 687
Taklimakan Desert, 498–499
Taku, 165
Taliks, 573
Talus slope, 434–435, 564
Tambora eruption, 143
Tangshan earthquake, 391–392
Tarns, 564
Tectonic activity, 337, 374. *See also* Plate tectonics
Tectonic cycle, 340, 349
Tectonic earthquakes, 391
Tectonic plates, climate change and, 653–654
Temperate rain forest biome, 674–675, 690

Temperature
    atmospheric stability and, 192–196, 215–217
    atmospheric zones and, 69–70
    climate and, 287–288
    daily patterns of, 102–103
    definition of, 120
    Earth's control of, 122–127
    Earth's patterns of, 127–138
    fog and, 200
    global cycle, 522
    global mean, 129–130, 132–133
    global warming and, 323
    history, 578, 582–583
    human body and, 136–138
    in ice ages, 580–582
    jet contrails and diurnal range of, 101–102
    land-water differences, 124–127
    measurement of, 121–122
    ocean, 520–521
    radiation and, 86
    record, 136–137
    scales of, 120–121
    seasonal variations in, 103, 122
    sea-surface, 541
Temperature inversion, air pollution and, 75–77
Tension, 375, 377, 380, 382
Terminal moraine, 567
Terranes, 374–378, 384
Terra satellite, 31, 33, 78, 97, 100, 124, 219, 236
Terrestrial ecosystems, 671–672
Terrestrial succession, 656–658, 676–677
Tertiary atmospheric circulation, 145
Thalweg, 463
Theory of evolution, 650
Theory, scientific, 8
Thermal energy. *See* Heat; Infrared radiation
Thermal equator, 129–130, 132
Thermistors, for temperature measurement, 121–122
Thermocline, El Niño and, 289–290
Thermocline transition zone, 520
Thermokarst landscapes, 575–576
Thermopause, 47–49
Thermosphere, 66, 69
Thomas, Lewis, 64
Thoreau, Henry David, 179–180
Thornthwaite, Charles W., 254–255, 258
Three Gorges Dam, China, 264
Threshold
    geomorphic, 417, 433
    system, 10
Throughfall, 254
Thrust faults, 379, 380–382, 385
Thunder, 228–230
Thunderheads, 200–201
Thunderstorms, 221, 227–231
    derechos and, 231
    tornadoes and, 235
Tidal bulges, 524–525
Tidal glacier, 554, 556
Tidal power generation, 525–526
Tidal range, 525–527
Tides, 521, 524–527
    ocean currents and, 169–170
    salt marshes and, 542
Till, 567–568
Till plain, 567–568
Tiltmeters, 398
Time
    daylight saving time, 26
    International Date Line, 24–25
    longitude and, 19, 21–22
    prime meridian and, 23–26
    UTC, 25–26
Time scale, geologic, 332–334
Time zones, 23–26
Tombolo, 534–536
TOPEX/Poseidon satellite, 523–524
Topographic maps, A.2–A.5
Topography, 371–374
    sea-floor, 356–357
    and soil formation, 602
Tornadoes, 221, 232–235
    formation of, 232–233
    measurement of, 233–234
    occurrence of, 234

records for, 235
    tropical cyclones and, 238
Torricelli, Evangelista, 145–146
Total ozone mapping spectrometer (TOMS), 71
Total runoff, 258–259
Tower karst, 428, 430
Traction, 458–459
Trade winds, 156–157, 169–170
    El Niño and, 289–290
    Hawaiian Islands and, 526
    tropical cyclones and, 235–236
Transform boundaries, 357, 360, 409
Transform faults, 357–359, 368, 381–384, 409
Translational slides, 435
Transmission, of radiation, 92
Transparency, of water, 125
Transpiration, soil-water budget and, 256–258
Transport
    by stream, 448, 450, 452, 458–459
    by wind, 487–488, 490–492, 497–498
Trellis drainage, 453
Tributary glaciers, 564, 567
Trophic niche, 630
Tropical climates, 292–298, A.10–A.12
Tropical cyclones, 235–241
    classification of, 236, 238
    formation of, 235–236
    physical structure of, 237–239
    worldwide pattern of, 236–237
Tropical monsoon climates, 293, 295–297, 684
Tropical Ocean Global Atmosphere (TOGA), 126
Tropical Rainfall Measuring Mission (*TRMM*),
    228–230
Tropical rain forest, 293, 296, 677–679
    deforestation of, 679–680
    map of, 674–675
Tropical savanna, 297–298, 674–675, 684–686
Tropical seasonal forest and scrub, 674–675, 679,
    684–685
Tropical storm Vince, 236
Tropic of Cancer, 17, 51, 55, 122
Tropic of Capricorn, 17, 51, 55, 122
Tropopause, 69
Troposphere, 66, 69–70
    energy balance in, 98–102
    temperature variation, 124
Troughs, on isobaric surface, 159–160
True north, 18
True shape, of maps, 28
Tsunami, 530–532
Tundra, 135, 309–310, 570, 693–694
Turbic Cryosols, 610, 613
Turbulence
    in atmosphere, 228
    in stream, 460
Twilight, 57
Typhoons. *See* Tropical cyclones

Ultimate base level, 449
Ultisols, A.7–A.9
Ultraviolet radiation, 46–47
    altitude and, 123
    ionosphere and, 70
    krill and, 646
    for Monarchs, 637
    ozone layer and, 70–71, 73–74
Uluru (Ayers) Rock (Australia), 508
Unconfined aquifer, 267
Uncovered karst, 428
Undercut bank, 460, 466
Uniformitarianism, 334
United Nations Conference on Desertification, 511
United Nations Educational Scientific and Cultural
    Organization (UNESCO), 203–204, 252, 274,
    276, 683
United Nations Environment Programme (UNEP),
    2, 317–318, 452, 628
United Nations Food and Agricultural Organization
    (FAO), 618, 621–622, 679
Unpaired terraces, 471
Uplift, 374, 384–385, 416–417, 535–536
Upper-air circulation, 159–161
Upper mantle, 336
Upslope fog, 201
Upwelling current, 170

Urban environment, climatic elements of, 109–113
Urban Heat Island Project (UHIPP), 110–113
Urban heat islands, 109–113
U.S. Soil Taxonomy, 606, A.6–A.9
    Oxisols, 678
Utilization, of soil moisture, 255, 259
UV Index, 73–74

Valley breezes, 165
Valley fog, 201–202
Valley, glacial creation of, 564–566
Valley glacier, 553–554, 567–568
Valley train deposit, 567–568
Vaporization. *See* Evaporation
Vapour pressure, 189–190
Vascular plants, 631
Vatnajökull Ice Cap, Iceland, 557
Veins, of ground ice, 573
Velocity, streamflow and, 455–456, 458–460
Ventifacts, 490
Vents, 402
Vernal equinox, 55–57
Vertisol, 618, A.7–A.9
Vertisolic order, 618, 621
Vicariance, 650
Violent weather, 227–246
    derechos, 231, 233
    ice storms, 227–228
    thunderstorms, 227–231
    tornadoes, 221, 232–235
    tropical cyclones, 235–241
Viscosity
    of air, 487
    of magma, 402, 404
Vishnu Schist, 348–349
Vog, 75
Volatile organic compounds (VOC), as air pollution, 79–82
Volcanic debris, winds and, 143–145
Volcanic islands, 361–362, 385, 401
    coral reefs and, 540
    Iceland, 557
Volcanic neck, 343
Volcanism, 398–410
    air pollution caused by, 75
    albedo and, 96
    carbon dioxide and, 640
    climate change and, 584
    crustal formation and, 374–375
    earthquakes and, 402, 406–407
    ecological succession and, 656–657
    eruptions, 370, 398–399, 402–410
    forecasting, 410
    landforms associated with, 399–401, 404, 409–410
    mudflows caused by, 431
    plate boundaries and, 359–362
    settings of, 399–402, 409–410
    Space Shuttle images of, 32
    spatial implications, 409
    structural features of, 399–400
    tsunami and, 530–532
Volcano Disaster Assistance Program (VDAP), 410
von Humboldt, Alexander, 637
Vostok Station, 130, 133

Wadi, 500
Walden Pond, 179–180, 568–569
Walkerton, 266–267, 272–273
Wallace, Alfred, 671
Wall cloud, 233
Waning slope, 417
Ward Hunt Ice Shelf, 587
Warm fronts, 218, 221
Warping forces, 379–380
Wash, 500
Water
    boiling point of, 120–121
    dependence on, 251–252
    desalination of, 271, 276, 278
    Earth distribution of, 180–183
    freezing point of, 120–121, 520
    in hydrologic cycle, 252–254
    hydrosphere, 14, 180–183
    land heating differences with, 124–127

management of, 261–266
measurement of supply, 275
origins of, 180
phases of, 183–187
in soil, 254–266
supply of, 274–279
transparency of, 125
unique properties of, 183–187
use of, 275
weathering by, 420–427
worldwide equilibrium of, 181
Water balance equation, 254–260, 279–280
Water budget
    samples of, 261–263, 279–280
    water resources and, 263–266
Waterfalls, 462–465
Water logging, 605
Water pollution, 452
    by fertilizers, 641–643
    in Great Lakes, 660–664
    groundwater, 266–268, 272–273
    by open-pit mining, 441
Water resources
    assessment of, 254–266
    future considerations for, 278–279
    management of, 252
    problems of, 278–279
    water budget and, 263–266
Watershed, 450
Waterspout, 233
Water supply, 251–252, 274–279
Water table, 267
    Gleysolic soils and, 610
    streamflow and, 268
Water vapour
    global warming and, 323
    human body temperature and, 136
    humidity and, 187–188, 190–191
    in hydrologic cycle, 252–254
    latent heat and, 105, 126
    longwave absorption by, 99
    outgassing of, 180
    phase changes of, 183–187
    satellite imaging of, 188–189
    sea-surface temperatures and, 126
Wave-cut platform, 532–533
Wavelength, of radiant energy, 46
Wave refraction, 529–530
Waves, 526–532
Waves of transition, 527–529
Waves of translation, 528–529
Wave trains, 526, 528–529
Waxing slope, 417
Weather
    chaotic phenomena in, 45, 224
    climate v., 285
    definition of, 212
    ice storms, 227–228
    losses from, 212
    midlatitude cyclone, 222–227
    sunspot cycles and, 46
    violent, 227–246
Weather forecasting, 224–227, 244–245
Weathering
    by acid deposition, 423–427
    chemical, 420, 423–426
    desert landscapes and, 506–508
    differential, 416, 506–507
    in exogenic system, 329–330
    highway and pavement damage, 185
    physical, 420–424
    processes of, 417–431
    slope development and, 417–419
    soil, 418–420, 425–426, 602
Weather instruments, 225–226
Weather maps, 224–227
Weather satellites, 33, 225
Weather stations, 121–122
Weather Workstation, 212
Wedge ice, 573–575
Wedging, frost, 421
Wegener, Alfred, 350
Weirs, 477
Wells, 267–268, 272–273

geothermal, 364–365
West Antarctic Ice Sheet (WAIS), 323, 585, 589
Westerlies, 157–158
    global warming and, 323
Western Cordillera, 377–378, 387–388, 395
Western intensification, 170
Wet-bulb thermometer, 191–192
Wetlands, 542–543
Wet soil, 599–600
White, Gilbert, 628
White rhinos, 681–682
Wien Displacement Law, 86
Wildfires. *See* Forest fires
Willows, on tundra, 310
Wilson, E.O., 651–652, 709
Wilson, J. Tuzo, 359
Wilting point, 259–260
Wind. *See also* Eolian processes
    and air pollution, 75
    circulation by, 145
    cold fronts and, 221
    Coriolis force and, 148, 150–154
    as energy resource, 166–168
    friction force and, 148, 150, 152, 154
    geostrophic, 154, 160
    gravity and, 148, 150
    local, 164–166
    measurement of, 146–147
    monsoonal, 168–169
    pressure gradient force and, 148–152
    rain gauge and, 255–256
    trade, 156–157
    and volcanic debris, 143–145
Wind Chill Temperature Index (WCT), 136–137
Wind power, 166–168
    benefits of, 168
    Burger Hill Wind Farm, 142
    in Canada, 167
    nature of, 166–167
    status of, 167–168
Wind shear, 228
Windshield, of rain gauge, 255–256
Wind speed
    Coriolis effect and, 151
    pressure gradient and, 149–150
    tornado classification scale, 233–234
    tropical cyclone, 236–239
Wind vane, 147–148
Windward slope, 217–218
    of dunes, 491
Winter solstice, 55–57
Wisconsinan glacial, 577, 580
Withdrawal of water, 276
World Climate Research Programme (WCRP), 317–318
World Meteorological Organization (WMO), 317–318
World water economy, 279
World Wildlife Fund, 681
Written scale, 26–27

Xerophytic vegetation, 312, 685, 692–693
X-rays, 46–47
    ionosphere and, 70

Yangtze River, 264
Yardangs, 490
Yazoo tributary, 466
Younger Dryas, 581

Zagros crush zone, 379–380
Zagros Mountains, 379–380
Zebra mussels, 676–677
Zenith, 51
    NET R and, 109
Zirconium silica oxides, 334
Zonal energy balance, 113–114
Zonal flows, 145
Zone of aeration, 265
Zone of saturation, 265

World – Physical

Great Basin	Land features
Caribbean Sea	Water bodies
Aleutian Trench	Underwater features

0   1000   2000 mi
0   1000   2000 km
Scale at the equator
ROBINSON PROJECTION